EVANGELICAL
DICTIONARY
of CHRISTIAN
EDUCATION

Baker Reference Library

Baker Encyclopedia of Christian Apologetics
    Norman L. Geisler
Baker Encyclopedia of Psychology and Counseling, 2d ed.
    Edited by David G. Benner and Peter C. Hill
Evangelical Commentary on the Bible
    Edited by Walter A. Elwell
Evangelical Dictionary of Biblical Theology
    Edited by Walter A. Elwell
Evangelical Dictionary of Christian Education
    Edited by Michael J. Anthony
Evangelical Dictionary of Theology, 2d ed.
    Edited by Walter A. Elwell
Evangelical Dictionary of World Missions
    Edited by A. Scott Moreau
Topical Analysis of the Bible
    Edited by Walter A. Elwell

Michael J. Anthony (Ph.D., Southwestern Baptist Theological Seminary; Ph.D., Claremont) is Professor of Christian Education at Talbot School of Theology at Biola University. He has written and edited several books, including *Introducing Christian Education: Foundations for the Twenty-first Century.*

Warren S. Benson (Ph.D., Loyola University) is Senior Professor of Christian Education and Leadership at Southern Baptist Theological Seminary. He served for many years as Professor of Christian Education, Vice President of Professional Doctoral Programs, and Director of the Doctor of Ministry Program at Trinity Evangelical Divinity School. He is the coauthor of *Christian Education: Its History and Philosophy* and coeditor of *Youth Education in the Church.*

Daryl Eldridge (Ph.D., Southwestern Baptist Theological Seminary) is Dean and Professor of Foundations of Education in the School of Educational Ministries at Southwestern Baptist Theological Seminary. He is the author of several articles as well as *The Teaching Ministry of the Church: Integrating Biblical Truth and Contemporary Application.*

Julie Gorman (D.Min., Fuller Theological Seminary) is Director of the Christian Formation and Discipleship Program and Associate Professor of Christian Formation and Discipleship at Fuller Theological Seminary. Among her many publications is *Community That Is Christian: A Handbook on Small Groups.*

EVANGELICAL DICTIONARY
of CHRISTIAN
EDUCATION

Edited by

Michael J. Anthony

**Associate Editors: Warren S. Benson,
Daryl Eldridge, and Julie Gorman**

Baker Academic

A Division of Baker Book House Co
Grand Rapids, Michigan 49516

Library of Congress Cataloging-in-Publication Data

Evangelical dictionary of Christian education / general editor, Michael J. Anthony ; associate editors, Warren Benson, Daryl Eldridge, and Julie Gorman.
    p.   cm. — (Baker reference library)
    Includes bibliographical references and index.
    ISBN 0-8010-2184-7 (hardcover)
    1. Christian education—Dictionaries. I. Anthony, Michael J. II. Benson, Warren S. III. Eldridge, Daryl, 1951- IV. Gorman, Julie. V. Series.

BV1461.E93 2001
268´.03—dc21
00-050763

Unless otherwise indicated, Scripture quotations are from the HOLY BIBLE, NEW INTERNATIONAL VERSION®. NIV®. Copyright © 1973, 1978, 1984 by International Bible Society. Used by permission of Zondervan Publishing House. All rights reserved.

Scripture quotations identified NASB are taken from the NEW AMERICAN STANDARD BIBLE ®. Copyright © The Lockman Foundation 1960, 1962, 1963, 1968, 1971, 1972, 1973, 1975, 1977, 1995. Used by permission. (www.Lockman.org)

Scripture quotations identified NKJV are taken from the New King James Version. Copyright © 1979, 1980, 1982 by Thomas Nelson, Inc. Used by permission. All rights reserved.

Scripture quotations identified NRSV are taken from the New Revised Standard Version of the Bible, copyright 1989 by the Division of Christian Education of the National Council of the Churches of Christ in the USA. Used by permission.

Scripture quotations identified TLB are taken from The Living Bible © 1971. Used by permission of Tyndale House Publishers, Inc., Wheaton, IL 60189. All rights reserved.

Scripture quotations identified NLT are taken from the Holy Bible, New Living Translation, © 1996. Used by permission of Tyndale House Publishers, Inc., Wheaton, IL 60189. All rights reserved.

For information about academic books, resources for Christian leaders, and all new releases available from Baker Book House, visit our web site:
http://www.bakerbooks.com

Michael Anthony would like to dedicate his work on this volume to several men who have had a significant impact on his life. These include my father Jack Anthony; Ricky Ryan, Senior Pastor of Calvary Chapel, Santa Barbara, Calif., who led me to the Lord; Richard Hall, Senior Pastor of First Evangelical Free Church, Moreno Valley, Calif., who discipled me in the faith; Dr. Paul Magnus, President of Briercrest Family of Schools, whose example led me into Christian education as a career; Dr. Bill Bynum, former Chair of the Christian Education Department at Biola University, for his guidance and support; and Dr. Warren Benson, former Vice President of Professional Doctoral Programs at Trinity Evangelical Divinity School, for his friendship and mentoring.

"As iron sharpens iron, so one man sharpens another."

PROVERBS 27:17

Preface

The field of Christian education is by no means a recent phenomenon. Its origin is found throughout the text of Scripture. Its goal is to bring people to a saving relationship with Jesus Christ (justification), to see that they grow in their newfound faith (sanctification), and to ultimately present them spiritually mature at the throne of God (glorification). From a theological point of view, Christian education stems from a personal knowledge of and passionate relationship with the eternal God. Christians worship God because of who he is and what he has done for them in Christ. The Holy Spirit empowers them to present his Word to a lost and fallen world so that the lost will repent from their sin and undertake a relationship with the true and living God.

The challenge throughout the history of the church has been to present Christ to the world in such a manner that he is seen as relevant. The contemporary world has become increasingly postmodern and biblically illiterate. Norms and values that were once considered foundational for a democratic society have been rejected in favor of a pluralistic worldview. Moral relativity has undermined the social structure of society, and as a result the church is often left bewildered by the events that have ostracized human beings from their Creator. According to Scripture, only two things last for eternity, people and the Word of God (Isa. 40:8). The Christian educator's task is to put these two together. Given the current social environment, however, that task is far more challenging than it might appear.

Dating back to the early church, religious leaders understood the interdependence that existed between their personal relationship with God and their ministry for God. Before they did the work of God they had to become the people of God. Community grew out of fellowship and ministry came as a result of one's relationship with God and others. The indwelling of the Holy Spirit brought a manifestation of the gifts of the Spirit. Men and women were expected to employ their gifts for the benefit of the body of Christ. As this was done, the body grew in maturity, resulting in both numerical and spiritual growth. This process is at the very heart of what Christian education is about, both then and now.

As the church grew it ebbed and flowed in terms of its spiritual priorities. A serious student of church history will concede that God often confounded the wise by using those who, in the eyes of the world, were ill-equipped to do his work. The laity were often used by God to challenge those who had grown dull in their personal walk with Christ because of the demands placed upon them in their professional calling as ministers. Countless times the church's paradigm had to be reset as God moved in new and mysterious ways. This was certainly the case when Robert Raikes brought his new approach to theological instruction to North America in 1780. As an English layman, he understood the importance of dependence upon God for guidance and provision.

Although once synonymous with Sunday school, Christian education has evolved into a complex and multidimensional discipline. It has its roots firmly planted in biblical and theological studies since the infallible Word of God serves as the foundation for all that evangelical Christian educators hold true. However, recognizing the valuable contributions that the social sciences bring to an understanding of how God created humans, Christian educators seek to integrate the truths of Scripture with discoveries made through education, psychology, anthropology, sociology, and philosophy. For example, education helps us understand how people learn, how they develop, and why they act the way they do in a given situation. With this knowledge, Christian educators are able to help men and women discover and learn the eternal truths of Scripture in a way that assists them in their personal spiritual formation. The tension comes in being able to discern the boundaries and limitations of the social sciences. Integration is at the very heart of twenty-first-century Christian education. The articles included in this dictionary represent the salient issues facing Christian educators today. With over 580,000 words, there is something for everyone who is serious about discovering the essence of our field.

When Baker Book House first contacted me regarding my interest in editing this work, I was both honored and overwhelmed. I was honored to be considered for such a task because I knew there were many others in the field far more competent and astute than I to undertake the assignment. I was also overwhelmed as I discussed the project with others and came to a fuller realization of what would be involved. I immediately contacted three of my close friends in the field. Each was selected because of their competence in theological studies and their breadth of understanding in related fields.

My associate editors of this reference work were Warren Benson, Daryl Eldridge, and Julie Gorman. It is no understatement to say that this book would not be possible without their hard work. Together we labored hard to identify approximately fifteen hundred essential entries, reduce that list to a more workable size of 850, and then assign the length of each article. Once done, the associate editors assigned the articles, edited them, and then forwarded them to me for further review. I have profound respect for each of them and count it a privilege to know each as a friend.

I would also like to thank Jim Weaver for envisioning this reference work and for his numerous hours of guidance. Maria denBoer was also a strategic part of the project as the copyeditor in charge of final review. My secretary in the office of the associate provost at Biola University, Judy McGee, was invaluable to me in her dedication and faithful service.

I am especially grateful for the support of my wife Michelle and my children Chantel and Brendon. Many nights they waited for me to come home late from the office because I was immersed in writing and editing, and they are happy to see this work brought to completion. More than anyone else, I am grateful to God for taking a misguided surfer kid off the beaches of Southern California and giving him a bright and glorious future. Grace is truly amazing!

MICHAEL J. ANTHONY
BIOLA UNIVERSITY

Contributors

Allen, Holly. Ph.D. Candidate, Talbot School of Theology, Biola University.

Allison, Richard E. D.Min., Professor of Christian Education (Emeritus), Ashland Theological Seminary.

Andrews, Leslie A. Ph.D., Professor of Christian Education, Asbury Theological Seminary.

Andrews, Steven J. Ph.D., Associate Professor of Old Testament and Hebrew, Southeastern Baptist Theological Seminary.

Anthony, Michael J. Ph.D., Ph.D., Professor of Christian Education, Talbot School of Theology, Biola University.

Anthony, Michelle D. M.A., Children's Pastor, Coast Hills Community Church.

Ashley, Don K. M.A.C.E., Student, Southwestern Baptist Theological Seminary.

Atkinson, Harley. Ph.D., Associate Professor of Christian Education, Toccoa Falls College.

Aukerman, John H. Ed.D., Associate Professor of Christian Education, Anderson University.

Babler, John E. Ph.D., Assistant Professor of Social Work, Southeastern Baptist Theological Seminary.

Ball, Dan K. Ph.D. Candidate, Director of Prior Learning Assessments, Assemblies of God Theological Seminary.

Banks, Robert. Ph.D., Homer L. Goddard Professor of the Ministry, Fuller Theological Seminary; Executive Director, DePree Leadership Center.

Barcalow, Douglas. Ed.D., Professor of Christian Education and Chair of Christian Ministries Department, Taylor University.

Bates, Charlotte K. Ph.D., Assistant to the President/Research and Planning, and Professor of Educational Leadership, Prairie Bible Institute/Prairie Graduate School.

Beck, David. Ph.D., Assistant Professor of New Testament, Southeastern Baptist Theological Seminary.

Becker, Elaine. Ph.D., Education Secretary, USA Central Territory, The Salvation Army.

Beckwith, Ivy. Ph.D., Manager of Curriculum and Christian Education Services, Gospel Light Publications.

Bekker, Gary J. Ph.D., Academic Dean and Professor of Church Education and Missiology, Calvin Theological Seminary.

Benson, Bruce E. Ph.D., Assistant Professor of Philosophy, Wheaton College.

Benson, Scott W. D.Min., Pastor of Small Groups, Mariners Church, Irvine, CA.

Benson, Warren S. Ph.D., Senior Professor of Christian Education and Leadership, Southern Baptist Theological Seminary.

Bergen, Martha S. Ph.D., Chair of Christian Studies Division, Hannibal-LeGrande College.

Black, Wesley. Ph.D., Associate Professor of Youth and Student Ministries, Southwestern Baptist Theological Seminary.

Blackwood, Vernon L. Ed.D., Field Coordinator of Social Research, College of Urban Planning, University of Illinois at Chicago.

Blevins, Dean. Ph.D., Associate Professor of Christian Education, Trevecca Nazarene University.

Blewett, Patrick A. Ph.D., D.Min., Academic Vice President, Grace University.

Bloomer, Thomas A. Ph.D. Candidate, Associate Provost, University of the Nations, Switzerland.

Borchert, Doris. D.Min., Professor of Christian Education and Director of Supervised Ministry, Northern Baptist Theological Seminary.

Botton, Kenneth V. Ph.D. Candidate, Director of Admissions, Trinity Evangelical Divinity School.

Bower, Ray E. Ph.D., Professor of Psychology, Olivet Nazarene Seminary.

Bowling, Jerry. Ph.D., Assistant Professor of Christian Education, Harding University.

Bramer, Paul. Ph.D., Assistant Professor of Christian Education, North Park Theological Seminary.

Breckenridge, Lillian J. Ph.D., Associate Professor of Christian Education, Oral Roberts University, Graduate School of Theology.

Bredfeldt, Gary. Ed.D., Chair of Department of Educational Ministries, Moody Bible Institute.

Brisben, David. Ph.D., Associate Professor of Christian Education and Family Studies, John Brown University.

Buchanan, Edward A. Ed.D., Professor of Christian Education, Southeastern Baptist Theological Seminary.

Budd, Clair Allen. Ph.D., Associate Professor of Christian Ministries, Asbury College.

Contributors

Burgess, Harold W. Ph.D., Professor of Pastoral Ministries and Christian Education, Asbury Theological Seminary.

Bushor, Mark. Ph.D. Candidate, Teaching Fellow, Southwestern Baptist Theological Seminary.

Bustrum, Philip. Ph.D., Associate Professor of Christian Education, Cornerstone University.

Caldwell, William G. Ph.D., Professor of Christian Education, Southwestern Baptist Theological Seminary.

Cannister, Mark W. Ed.D., Associate Professor of Christian Education and Chair of the Division of Humanities, Gordon College.

Carlson, Gregory C. Ph.D., Chair of Christian Education and Dean of Graduate Studies, Grace University.

Chapman, Patricia A. Ed.D., Professor, Theology and World Ministries Division (Retired), Simpson College.

Chechowich, Faye. Ph.D., Assistant Professor of Christian Education and Associate Dean of the Division of Letters, Taylor University.

Choun, Robert J. D.Min., Ph.D., Professor of Christian Education, Dallas Theological Seminary.

Christopher, Steven. Ph.D., Assistant Professor of Christian Education, Concordia University West.

Clement, Dan E. Ph.D., Associate Professor of Psychology and Counseling, Southwestern Baptist Theological Seminary.

Clouse, Bonnidell. Ph.D., Professor of Educational and School Psychology, Indiana State University.

Clymer, Gordon R. M.S., Director of Special Projects, Good News Productions International.

Coley, Kenneth S. Ed.D., Assistant Professor of Christian Education, Southeastern Baptist Theological Seminary.

Coulter, Gordon L. Ph.D. Candidate, Assistant Professor of Christian Education, Azusa Pacific University.

Cunningham, Shelly. Ph.D., Associate Professor of Christian Education, Talbot School of Theology, Biola University.

Currie, David A. Ph.D., Associate Pastor, Northview Community Church, Abbotsford, British Columbia.

Curry, Allen. Ed.D., Vice President for Academic Affairs and Professor of Christian Education, Reformed Theological Seminary.

Dale, Janet L. Ph.D., Assistant Professor of Christian Education and Discipleship, Alliance Theological Seminary.

Daniel, Eleanor A. Ph.D., Dean and Professor of Christian Education, Emmanuel School of Religion.

Davies, James A. Ed.D., Professor of Practical Theology, Simpson College and Graduate School.

Deaton, Barbara Jean. M.A., Professor of Christian Education, Kentucky Mountain Bible College.

DeMott, Nancy L. Ph.D., Adjunct Professor of Christian Education, Northeastern Baptist Theological Seminary.

Desko, Jay. Ph.D., Chair of the Department of Organizational Leadership, Philadelphia College of Bible Graduate School.

Dettoni, John M. Ph.D., President, Chrysalis Ministries.

DeVargas, Robert. Ph.D., Assistant Professor of Christian Education, Southeastern Baptist Theological Seminary.

De Vries, Robert C. D.Min, Ph.D., Professor of Church Education and Director of M.A. Programs, Calvin Theological Seminary.

Dirks, Dennis. Ph.D., Dean and Professor of Christian Education, Talbot School of Theology, Biola University.

Dodrill, Mark A. Ph.D., National Director, Spain, Youth For Christ.

Donahue, Bill. Ph.D., Director of Small Group Ministry, Willow Creek Community Church.

Downs, Perry G. Ph.D., Director of Ph.D. in Educational Studies Program and Professor of Educational Ministries, Trinity Evangelical Divinity School.

Drovdahl, Robert. Ph.D., Professor of Christian Education, Seattle Pacific University.

Dunn, Richard R. Ph.D., Pastor of Pastoral Ministries and Theological Educator in Residence, Fellowship Church, Knoxville, Tennessee.

Eldridge, Daryl. Ph.D., Dean of the School of Educational Ministries and Professor of Foundations of Education, Southwestern Baptist Theological Seminary.

Estep, James Riley. Ph.D., Vice President of Academic Affairs, Great Lakes Christian College.

Falkner, William F. Ed.D., Professor of Religious Education, Canadian Southern Baptist Seminary.

Falls, Douglas. Ed.D., Assistant Professor of Christian Education, Reformed Theological Seminary.

Fawcett, Cheryl L. Ph.D., Associate Professor of Christian Education, Christian Heritage College.

Feinberg, Jeffrey E. Ph.D., Leader of Etz Chaim Congregation, Buffalo Grove, IL.

Fenwick, Tara J. Ph.D., Adjunct Professor of Christian Education, University of Alberta.

Ferris, Robert W. Ph.D., Associate Dean for Doctoral Studies and Professor of Christian Education, Columbia International Seminary.

Freeman, Ronald W. Ed.D., Assistant Professor of Christian Education, Azusa Pacific University.

Friedeman, Matt. Ph.D., Professor of Christian Education and Discipleship, Wesley Biblical Seminary.

Gangel, Kenneth O. Ph.D., Executive Director of Graduate Studies, Toccoa Falls College.

Garland, Ken. Ph.D., Associate Professor of Christian Education, Talbot School of Theology, Biola University.

Geivett, R. Douglas. Ph.D., Associate Professor of Christian Thought, Talbot School of Theology, Biola University.

Gerali, Steven. D.Phil., Chair of the Department of Youth Ministry and Adolescent Studies, Judson College.

Gibbs, Eugene S. Ed.D., Professor of Christian Education, Ashland Theological Seminary.

Glassford, Darwin K. Ph.D., Chair of Christian Education Department, Montreat College.

Gomes, Alan W. Ph.D., Associate Professor of Historical Theology, Talbot School of Theology, Biola University.

Gonlag, Mari. Ed.D., Associate Professor of Religion and Coordinator of Graduate Studies in Religion, Southern Wesleyan University.

Gorman, Julie. D.Min., Director of the Christian Formation and Discipleship Program and Associate Professor of Christian Formation and Discipleship, Fuller Theological Seminary.

Gough, David. M.A., Chair of the Department of Educational Ministries, Washington Bible College.

Gray, C. Samuel. President Emeritus, Christian Service Brigade.

Gray, Rick. Ph.D., Associate Professor of Christian Education, Asbury Theological Seminary.

Griffiths, Ron. M.R.E., Associate Professor of Christian Education, Crown College.

Habermas, Ronald T. Ph.D., McGee Professor of Biblical Studies, John Brown University.

Hammett, John S. Ph.D., Assistant Professor of Theology, Southeastern Baptist Theological Seminary.

Hammonds, Kenneth. Ed.D., Director of Christian Education, West Angeles Church of God in Christ.

Hayes, Edward L. Ph.D., President Emeritus, Denver Seminary.

Headrick, James A. Ed.D., Assistant Professor of Psychology and Counseling, Southwestern Baptist Theological Seminary.

Hedin, Norma S. Ph.D., Associate Professor of Christian Education, Southwestern Baptist Theological Seminary.

Heinemann, Mark H. Ph.D. Candidate, Lecturer in Practical Theology, Freie Theologische Akademie, Giessen, Germany.

Hertig, Young Lee. Ph.D., Adjunct Assistant Professor, Fuller Theological Seminary.

Hobbs, Julia Henkle. Ph.D., Professor Emeritus, George Fox College.

Houglum, Susan L. M.Ed., Director of Christian Education Degree Program, Lutheran Bible Institute of Seattle.

Howard, J. Grant. Th.D., Director of Faculty Development, Phoenix Seminary.

Hutchison, Thomas. Ph.D., Assistant Professor of Christian Education, Cedarville College.

Issler, Klaus. Ph.D., Professor of Christian Education and Theology, Talbot School of Theology, Biola University.

Jessen, Daniel C. Ed.D., Pastor to Missionaries, United World Mission.

Johnson, Lin. M.S., Director, WordPro Communications.

Johnson, Ronnie J. Ph.D., Associate Professor of Christian Education, BMATS.

Johnson-Miller, Beverly. Ph.D. Candidate, Claremont School of Theology.

Jones, Ian F. Ph.D., Associate Professor of Psychology and Counseling, Southwestern Baptist Theological Seminary.

Jones, Karen E. Ph.D., Assistant Professor of Educational Ministries, Huntington College.

Kageler, Leonard. Ph.D., Professor of Christian Education and Christian Education Department Chair, Nyack College.

Kaiser, Walter C., Jr. Ph.D., President and Colman M. Mockler Distinguished Professor of Old Testament, Gordon-Conwell Theological Seminary.

Kane, Michael J. Ph.D., Dean of Educational Services, Moody Bible Institute.

Kennedy, William B. Ph.D., Professor Emeritus of Religious Education, Union Theological Seminary.

Keppeler, Thomas. Ph.D., Country Director, Romania, BEE International.

Kidd, Timothy W. Ph.D., Director of Leadership Challenge Program, Mary Baldwin College.

Kilner, John F. Ph.D., Professor of Bioethics and Contemporary Culture and Director of Bannockburn Institute, Trinity Evangelical Divinity School.

Kim, Heeja. Ph.D., Professor of Christian Education, Chongshin University, Seoul, Korea.

King, Keith R. M.A., Director of Family Ministries, Grace Church, Cyprus, CA.

Kjesbo, Denise Muir. Ed.D., Associate Professor of Christian Education, North American Baptist Theological Seminary.

Klaus, Byron D. D.Min., Chair of the Department of Church Ministries, Southern California College.

Knight, George R. Ed.D., Professor of Church History, Andrews University.

Kuhl, Roland G. Ph.D. Candidate, Associate Dean of Extension and Affiliated Education, Trinity Evangelical Divinity School.

Lamb, Robert L. Ph.D., Professor of Church Administration, School of Divinity, Gardner-Webb University.

Contributors

Lambert, Dan. Ed.D., Assistant Professor of Christian Education, Cincinnati Bible College and Seminary.

Lamport, Mark A. Ph.D., Professor of Educational Ministries, Grand Rapids Baptist Seminary.

Lawson, J. Gregory. J.D., Ed.D., Assistant Professor of Christian Education, Southeastern Baptist Theological Seminary.

Lawson, Kevin E. Ed.D., Director of the Ph.D. Program in Educational Studies and Associate Professor of Christian Education, Talbot School of Theology, Biola University.

Lawson, Michael S. Ph.D., Chair and Professor of Christian Education, Dallas Theological Seminary.

Lay, Robert. Ed.D., Associate Professor of Christian Education, Taylor University.

Leahy, Elizabeth A. M.A., Associate University Librarian, Azusa Pacific University.

Lee, Young Woon. Ph.D., Assistant Professor of Christian Education, Torch Trinity Graduate School of Theology.

LeFever, Marlene. M.A., Director of Church Ministries, Cook Communications Ministries.

Leyda, Richard. Ph.D., Chair and Associate Professor of Christian Education, Talbot School of Theology, Biola University.

Linge, Samuel M. Ph.D. Candidate, Trinity Evangelical Divinity School.

Llovio, Kay M. Ed.D., Professor of Christian Education, San Jose Christian College.

Lockerbie, D. Bruce. M.A., CEO Paideia, Inc., Stony Brook, NY.

Loewen, Eleanor M. Ed.D., Associate Professor of Christian Education, William and Catherine Booth College.

Lynn, Roy F. Ph.D., Christian Education Associate, Church of the Nazarene.

MacGregor, Jerry Chip. Ph.D., Senior Editor, Harvest House Publishers.

MacLeod, Merilyn J. Ph.D., Vice President of Work-Place Influence, Colorado Springs, CO.

MacQuitty, Marcia. Ph.D., Assistant Professor of Childhood Education, Southwestern Baptist Theological Seminary.

Martin, J. E. Harvey. Ph.D., Professor of Christian Education, Northwestern College.

McCracken, Bruce R. Ph.D., Associate Professor or Christian Education, Lancaster Bible College.

McKinney, Larry J. Ed.D., President, Providence College and Theological Seminary, Otterburne, Manitoba, Canada.

McLeod, Philip D. Ph.D., Vice President of Academic Affairs, Valley Forge Christian College.

Mohler, James W. Ph.D., Chair and Assistant Professor of Bible and Christian Ministries, Trinity International University.

Moore, James R. Ph.D., Associate Academic Dean, Trinity Evangelical Divinity School.

Mort, Dale L. Ph.D., Director of Degree Completion Program and Professor of Christian Education, Lancaster Bible College.

Mulholland, D. A. C. Ph.D., Lecturer in Christian Education, New Zealand Assembly Bible School.

Nettles, Tom J. Ph.D., Professor of Historical Theology, Southern Baptist Theological Seminary.

Newton, Gary C. Ph.D., Associate Professor of Christian Education and Associate Dean, Huntington College Graduate School.

Newton, Robert D. Ph.D., Associate Professor of Missions, Concordia Theological Seminary, Fort Wayne, IN.

Nichols, Charles H. Ph.D., Chairman of the Department of Christian Ministries, Providence Theological Seminary.

Norvell, Walter H. Ph.D. Candidate, Southwestern Baptist Theological Seminary.

Parrett, Gary A. Ed.D., Director of Graduate Educational Ministries and Assistant Professor of Christian Education, Gordon-Conwell Theological Seminary.

Patterson, George W. Ed.D., Professor of Christian Education, Southern Christian University.

Patty, Steven. Ph.D., Associate Professor of Youth and Educational Ministry, Multnomah Bible College.

Pazmiño, Robert W. Ed.D., Valeria Stone Professor of Christian Education, Andover Newton Theological School.

Peace, Richard. Ph.D., Robert Boyd Munger Professor of Evangelism and Spiritual Formation, Fuller Theological Seminary.

Penley, David R. M.Div., Instructor of Social Work and Ministry Based Evangelism, Southwestern Baptist Theological Seminary.

Peterson, Gilbert A. Ed.D., President, Lancaster Bible College.

Pettegrew, Hal. Ph.D., Associate Professor of Christian Education and Leadership, Southern Baptist Theological Seminary.

Posterski, Beth. D.Ed., Faculty Coordinator of Early Childhood Studies Program, Ontario Bible College.

Powell, Terry. Ph.D., Associate Professor of Church Ministries, Columbia International University.

Powers, Bruce P. Ph.D., Associate Dean and Professor of Christian Education, Campbell University Divinity School.

Price, Terry. Ed.D., Chairman of Church Ministries Department, Maranatha Baptist Bible College.

Pullman, Ellery G. Ph.D., Professor of Christian Education, Briercrest Family of Schools.

Radcliffe, Robert J. Ph.D., Professor of Educational Ministry, Western Seminary.

Rahn, Dave. Ph.D., Professor of Educational Ministries and Associate Dean for Graduate Studies, Huntington College; Codirector of the Link Institute.

Ratcliff, Donald E. Ph.D., Associate Professor of Psychology and Sociology, Toccoa Falls College.

Redman, Pamela. M.A., Elementary Music Teacher, Saddleback Valley USD.

Reinhart, Larry D. Ph.D., Director of M.A. in Christian Ministries and Professor of Christian Education, Malone College.

Richardson, Brian C. Ph.D., Basil Manly Jr. Professor of Christian Education, Southern Baptist Theological Seminary.

Robbins, Duffy. M.Div., Chair of the Department of Youth Ministry, Eastern College.

Robertson, Sara Anne. Ed.D., Vice President Emeritus, Pioneer Clubs.

Robinson, Edwin. Ph.D., Dean of the Faculty and Professor of Christian Education, Nazarene Theological Seminary.

Root, Jerry. Ph.D., Assistant Professor of Educational Ministries, Wheaton College.

Roth, David L. Ed.D., Headmaster, Wheaton Academy.

Rynd, Ronald H. M.A., Area Director, Christian Service Brigade.

Sabo, Michael F. Ph.D., Adjunct Faculty, Trinity Evangelical Divinity School.

Saffold, Guy S. Ed.D., Vice President and Professor of Administration, Trinity Western University.

Sandvig, Steven K. Ph.D. Candidate, Trinity Evangelical Divinity School.

Schmidt, Stephen A. Ed.D., Professor of Pastoral Studies, Institute of Pastoral Studies, Loyola University.

Sedwick, Jay. Th.M., Assistant Professor of Christian Education, Dallas Theological Seminary.

Seiver, David J. Ph.D., Director of the D.Min./Miss. Program, Trinity Evangelical Divinity School.

Sell, Charles M. Th.D., Professor of Educational Ministries, Trinity Evangelical Divinity School.

Senter, Mark H., III. Ph.D., Associate Professor of Educational Ministries, Trinity Evangelical Divinity School.

Sheridan, Dennis A. Ed.D., Ph.D., Associate Professor and Chair, Department of College Student Affairs and Leadership Studies, Azusa Pacific University.

Shirley, Chris. M.A.C.E., Graduate Student, Southwestern Baptist Theological Seminary.

Siew, Yau-Man. Ph.D., Lecturer in Christian Education and Leadership, Singapore Bible College.

Simpson, Mark E. Ph.D., Associate Dean and Gaines S. Robbins Associate Professor of Christian Religion and Leadership, Southern Baptist Theological Seminary.

Smallbones, Jackie L. Th.D., Assistant Professor of Christian Education and Religion, Northwestern College.

Starr, Eileen. Ph.D., Professor of Christian Education, Alaska Bible College.

Steele, Les. Ph.D., Professor of Religion, Seattle Pacific University.

Stevens, Daniel C. Ph.D., Director of Program Development and Associate Professor of Christian Education, Talbot School of Theology, Biola University.

Stonehouse, Catherine. Ph.D., Professor of Christian Education, Asbury Theological Seminary.

Stubblefield, Jerry M. Ph.D., J. M. Frost Sunday School Board Chair of Christian Education, Golden Gate Baptist Theological Seminary.

Sundene, Jana. M.A., Assistant Professor of Youth Ministry, Trinity Evangelical Divinity School.

Sweeney, Douglas A. Ph.D., Assistant Professor of Church History and History of Christian Thought, Trinity Evangelical Divinity School.

TenElshof, Judy. Ph.D., Assistant Professor of Christian Education, Talbot School of Theology, Biola University.

Thayer, Jerome. Ph.D., Professor of Research and Statistical Methodology, Andrews University.

Thigpen, Jonathan N. Ph.D., President, Evangelical Training Association.

Thornton, Joyce L. Ph.D., Professor of Christian Education, Winebrenner Theological Seminary.

Tiénou, Tite. Ph.D., Professor of Theology of Mission and Evangelism, Trinity Evangelical Divinity School.

Tolbert, LaVerne A. Ph.D., Assistant Professor of Christian Education, Talbot School of Theology, Biola University.

Venugopal, Junias V. Ph.D., Missionary to the Philippines, Help for Christians Inc.

Waller, Anne. M.Ed., Assistant Editor and Publisher of *FAS Times*, FAS Family Resource Institute.

Waller, Gary. Ph.D., Associate Dean and Professor of Administration, Southwestern Baptist Theological Seminary; Professor of Religious Education and Special Ministries, Northwest Nazarene College.

Walter, Jim. Ed.D., Ph.D., Professor of Adult Education, Southwestern Baptist Theological Seminary.

Ward, Ted W. Ed.D., Professor Emeritus of Education and Mission, Trinity Evangelical Divinity School.

Welch, Donald W. Ph.D., Coordinator and Professor of Christian Education, Mid-America Nazarene University.

Contributors

White, Roger. Ed.D., Associate Professor of Christian Education, Azusa Pacific University.

White, Steven. Ph.D. Candidate, Trinity Evangelical Divinity School.

Whiting, Dianne. M.A., Senior Physical Therapist, Casa Colina Hospital for Rehabilitative Medicine.

Whittet, Robert J. M.Div., Assistant Professor of Youth Ministry, Gordon College.

Wilkerson, Barbara. Ed.D., Associate Professor of Christian Education (retired), Alliance Theological Seminary.

Wilkins, Michael J. Ph.D., Dean of Faculty and Professor of New Testament Language and Literature, Talbot School of Theology, Biola University.

Williams, Bud. Ed.D., Associate Professor of Kinesiology, Wheaton College.

Williams, Dennis E. Ph.D., Dean of the School of Christian Education and Leadership and Professor of Christian Education, Southern Baptist Theological Seminary.

Williford, G. Craig. Ph.D., Pastor of Ministries and Staff, Woodmen Valley Chapel, Colorado Springs, CO.

Willis, Wesley R. Ed.D., President, Northwestern College and Radio.

Wilson, Norman G. Ph.D., Director of Program for Accelerating College Education (PACE), Houghton College.

Wine, David. Ph.D., Assistant Professor of Christian Education, Olivet Nazarene University.

Winn, Laverne. M.A.C.E., Leadership Training Consultant.

Wong, Joseph Y. Th.D., Vice President of Educational Development, Multnomah Bible College and Biblical Seminary.

Wyman, Barbara. Ph.D., Professor of Psychology, Canadian Southern Baptist Seminary.

Yarbrough, Robert W. Ph.D., Associate Professor of New Testament Studies, Trinity Evangelical Divinity School.

Yeatts, John R. Ph.D., Professor of Psychology of Religion, Messiah College.

You, Esther. M.A., Student, Talbot School of Theology.

Young, Mark. Ph.D., Associate Professor of World Missions and Intercultural Studies, Dallas Theological Seminary.

Yount, Rick. Ph.D., Ph.D., Professor of Christian Education, Southwestern Baptist Theological Seminary.

Zonnebelt-Smeenge, Susan J. Ed.D., Clinical Psychologist, Pine Crest Mental Health Services.

Zuck, Roy B. Th.D., Senior Professor Emeritus of Bible Exposition, Dallas Theological Seminary; Editor, *Bibliotheca Sacra*.

Aa

Abortion. Abortion is not just an American problem. From a global perspective, it has become the birth control of choice in many countries. It is seen as a reasonable solution to overpopulation. Christians worldwide need to be taught what the Bible says about the sanctity and sacredness of human life.

Key biblical texts teach cardinal truths about the sanctity of the unborn's life. Both Jeremiah and Paul were known and called by God while they were still in the womb (Jer. 1:4–5; Gal. 1:15). God personally fashions each individual in the womb (Job 10:8–12; Ps. 139:13–16). He considers the fetus fully human (Job 3:11; Luke 1:39–44).

The Bible maintains that human life is sacred and unique. Four cornerstones form the foundation for this emphasis: (1) Humankind is different from plant, animal, and celestial life (1 Cor. 15:39–40); (2) Humans are made in the image of God (Gen. 1:26) and have immaterial souls that will live for eternity (Matt. 10:28–29); (3) The unique sacredness of each human life is intensified by the fact that Christ died in order to purchase salvation for all who believe (Rom. 6:6–21); (4) Each believer is then commanded by God to live a life that brings greater glory to our Savior and King (1 Cor. 6:19–20).

Scriptural emphasis on the sanctity and sacredness of all human life causes evangelicals to believe that feticide is murder. Abortion is the willful ending of human life. Some Christians argue that abortions should be allowed only when the fetus presents a danger to the life of the mother, while others maintain that abortions should not be allowed at all.

The church Christian education program should encourage members to think and act Christainly about the abortion issue. Such training may include: upgrading members' passion concerning the fact that God loves every human being, affirming those whom God has called to take an activist position (participating in proper civil disobedience, providing prenatal and legal counseling, foster parenting, supporting homes for unwed mothers, counseling victims of post-abortion stress syndrome, and influencing political leaders), and activating the power of individual and corporate prayer. Action initiatives can be undertaken in at least three broad arenas: familial, congregational and denominational (see Gangel and Wilhoit, 1996).

The number of national groups and ministries is encouraging. Together they provide a network of crisis pregnancy centers; counseling, adoption, and benevolence resources; foster care; educational products; and legislative and political structures that work to protect life from abortion, infanticide, and euthanasia. These groups include: Americans United for Life, Bethany Christian Services, Care Net, Crisis Pregnancy Center Ministry (a division of Focus on the Family), and National Right to Life. Additional groups focus on providing abstinence education and curricula that present the positive reasons to say no to sex outside of marriage: Project Reality, Teen Aid, Why Wait?, and Worth the Wait.

Abortion is an emotional issue. The early church practiced a consistent pro-life ethic but was preoccupied with "conviction and condemnation to the near exclusion of compassion and forgiveness" (Gorman, 1982, 90, 94). Many today are repeating that error. Abortion is not a pleasant topic. When properly educated in the light of Scripture, saints can better decide what their level of involvement should be.

JAMES A. DAVIES

Bibliography. K. Gangel and J. Wilhoit (1996), *The Christian Educator's Handbook on Family Life Education;* M. Gorman (1982), *Abortion and the Early Church.*

Abstinence. The decision to refrain from sexual intercourse. Scripture teaches that sexual relations between a husband and wife are part of God's plan for procreation and mutual fulfillment, but that outside of this covenant relationship sexual relations are immoral. Abstinence is a commitment to refrain from both fornication, sexual intercourse between unmarried persons, and adultery, sex between two persons when at least one of them is married to someone else.

15

The church has continued to teach abstinence as a biblical mandate, though societal trends have changed dramatically throughout the course of history. What once was looked down upon as immoral even by non-Christians has gradually become accepted and even encouraged in popular culture. The conflicting messages given by church and society have resulted in disastrous consequences for the youth population, with sexually transmitted diseases and teenage pregnancies reaching crisis proportions. Especially in the decades of the 1960s, 1970s, and 1980s, teens committed to the biblical concept of abstinence outside of marriage felt alienated from their peers.

In 1993 an abstinence campaign known as True Love Waits was launched in the United States to recognize and affirm youth who are committed to abstinence and to encourage others to make this same pledge of sexual purity. The movement soon became an international campaign involving more than eighty Christian entities. Since it began, hundreds of thousands of students have signed covenants, committing themselves to sexual abstinence until marriage. This high profile campaign for sexual purity, initiated in a time when even non-Christians were looking for answers to the problems associated with teen sexual activity, captured the interest of the media and educational and political leaders. The teenage birthrate dropped in the 1990s for the first time in nearly two decades, and journalists and researchers associated this trend reversal with the abstinence pledges. Prior to the 1990s abstinence was often taught as one option in school-based sex education programs; however, subsequent to the mobilization of the Christian community on this issue, funding was allocated for the first time for programs that teach abstinence exclusively.

KAREN E. JONES

See also TRUE LOVE WAITS

Abstract Thinking. One of the critical capacities by which new knowledge, skills, or attitudes are achieved. All individuals exhibit this proficiency to some degree. Cultural background, the amount of formal education, personal learning style(s), psychological type, the subject area being worked on, and one's chosen profession are variables that help determine the degree to which one uses abstract thinking strategies.

Abstract thinking is typically not dominant in early childhood. According to Piaget, the intensive development of symbolic powers begins between ages 7 and 11, the third stage of cognitive growth. This does not mean there is a total absence of abstract thinking in earlier years. Rather, the child's learning has now developed to the point where it is characterized by activities associated with this type of mental processing.

Piaget called this the stage of Concrete Operations. It is initiated by increased use of mental structures by which the child logically expands classes and relations. The increased structure is like a giant cognitive parking lot whose individual lanes and spaces are alternately occupied and empty. The spaces themselves endure, and form an expanse of potential for future learning. Using the spaces and lanes of the mental parking lot the child can now form concepts and theories. This new style of cognitive processing becomes the basis for all inductive learning. In contrast to the tactile-dominant learning of earlier years, the child now uses this newfound ability to construct mental classes and theories to select and shape her experiences.

"A mind is a terrible thing to waste" could be the motto of abstract thinkers. Their most valued possession may be their thinking ability. Research has documented several general characteristics of abstract thinkers. Such people focus on using logic, ideas, and concepts. They emphasize thinking as opposed to feeling. They evidence concern with building general theories as opposed to intuitively understanding unique, specific areas. An abstract thinker tends to use a scientific, systematic approach to problem-solving rather than following an artistic sense of what to do. People with this modality preference enjoy manipulation of abstract symbols (content data) and orderly analysis. They value precision, the rigor and discipline of analyzing ideas, and the aesthetic quality of a neat conceptual system. They find pleasure in developing general theories and models. For them it is important that a theory be logically sound and precise. Practicality is not a major concern. Abstract thinkers tend to give less attention to people and feelings. They are more centered around ideas and concepts. They thrive on content and information more than emotional sentiment. An orientation toward abstract conceptualization is dominant for almost one-third of the people in western culture (Long, 1987).

Witkin (1975) explains that individuals who favor using learning strategies associated with abstract analytical ability have a cognitive style that is field-independent. Field-independence is associated with cultures that emphasize self-control and encourage individual autonomy. Field-dependent learners feature a cognitive style that is influenced by the environment. They are more "other directed." Cultures stressing obedience, social control, and authority are more likely to produce field-dependent learners. This raises the possibility that many learning difficulties in adults may be a function of the way in which learning is structured.

David Kolb (1984) and Bernice McCarthy (1987) have done much work attempting to integrate abstract conceptualizers with learning styles. Kolb's "Assimilator" and McCarthy's "Analytic Learner" feature characteristics strongly favoring conjectural thinkers. McCarthy has developed an eight-step learning style cycle. She calls this the 4MAT System. It integrates left and right brain hemisphere functions with learning style. For analytic learners her Right Mode task involves Image or beginning to think about the concepts of the lesson. The Left Mode is Define. By this she means differentiating what needs to be known by looking at the parts and expanding the content by learning new material.

Contributions to Christian Education. Abstract thinkers have made treasured contributions to Christian education. The areas of Bible study, teaching, and spiritual formation are highlighted here.

The ancient practice of *Lectio Divina* shows the valuable place abstract thinkers have in Bible study. Developed in the fourth century by John Cassian, the second step (*meditatio*) provides opportunity to think deeply about a particular passage of Scripture. The use of guided questions moves the parishioner to think abstractly about the passage—what it means, its significance in the larger scheme of things, and how this affects his or her understanding of God or of conduct. While all individuals are able to ask and answer these questions, the abstract thinking person does this the best.

The traditional teaching aspects of a Christian education program were made for abstract thinkers. Such learners like sitting in rows of chairs hearing a teacher share from his or her vast amount of information. Being strategic planners, they listen and carefully assess the value of the information presented. They like to consider all sides of an issue before venturing a conclusion. Consequently, they want to have all the data before making a decision. Abstract thinkers are often classified as the best students since they fit the teaching-learning methods traditionally used in Western education. They thrive on facts. They combine a competitive streak with a desire to give the right answers. Consequently they make more than their share of A's in school.

Abstract thinkers have certain preferences for how they learn, which the wise religious instructor will recognize and use in the teaching-learning process. These inclinations include: valuing smart and wise people; being curious about ideas and having a high tolerance for theory; liking teachers who are well prepared and organized, stick to the outline, and are information givers; thinking in terms of correct and incorrect answers; debating to logically prove the correct stance or answer; reading the Bible for concepts and principles; and needing competition (LeFever, 1995). These preferences are a helpful tool for tapping into abstract thinkers' willingness to persist in the learning process of Christian education.

Those who study spiritual formation have also recognized the important place of abstract thinkers. Most significant is the work by Corinne Ware (1995). Her "Spirituality Wheel Selector" identifies four major types of spirituality. Type One is most appropriate in this context. It is centered on an intellectual or thinking religious experience. Content is primary for people in this group. Also important is systematic congruence of thought with belief. Ware calls this "head-type" spirituality. For a person with this style, religious activities center on corporate gathering and the spoken word (via study groups, better sermons, and some sort of theological renewal within the worshiping community). Type One spirituality could be summarized by two key words: "my doctrine."

The contribution of Type One spirituality to the whole is invaluable. This style produces theological reflection and crafts position papers. It supports education and examines the text of our hymns. Head spirituality codifies and preserves the faith story from generation to generation and undertakes to make sense of and to name religious experience (Ware, 1995). However, an abstract thinker's overintellectualizing his spiritual life can lead to sterile orthodoxy and dogmatic dryness. Increased attention to the feeling and experiential side of spirituality is important for proper balance and overall growth.

Abstract thinkers represent a large segment of the population. Their productivity and insights make an important contribution to the church, Christian education, the teaching-learning process, and spiritual development.

JAMES A. DAVIES

Bibliography. D. A. Kolb (1984), *Experiential Learning;* B. McCarthy (1987), *The 4MAT System: Teaching to Learning Styles with Right/Left Mode Techniques;* M. LeFever (1995), *Learning Styles;* H. B. Long (1987), *Adult Learning Research and Practice;* C. Ware (1995), *Discover Your Spiritual Type.*

See also CONCRETE OPERATIONAL THINKING; LEARNING STYLES; MODALITY; PIAGET, JEAN

Abuse. A horrifying number of people are abused—physically, sexually, emotionally, or spiritually. Most stunning is the prevalence of the problem. According to the Center for the Prevention of Sexual and Domestic Violence, one girl in three and one boy in seven is sexually abused by the age of 18. Half of this violence is done by family members. One million children are physically abused by parents every year. Over two million women suffer brutalization every year. More than one million elders are mistreated annually by their adult children. One marriage in four suffers from some form of spousal abuse. In the last quarter century this once-secret plague has become highly visible.

In the early 1980s the problem of abuse within Protestant ecclesiastical institutions was exposed by pioneers like the Rev. Marie Fortune. Her classic study *Is Nothing Sacred?* (1982) is a fine treatment unmasking clergy abuse. It deals primarily with sexual misconduct. More recent efforts, like that of Johnson and VanVonderen (1991), have addressed false spiritual authority and spiritual manipulation. In a religious system where the sheep are there for the "needs" of the shepherd, people's lives are devoured.

The silent plague of abuse is insidious because it exists in our midst invisibly. No institution is immune. A single case, in any form, can rock a congregation.

The role of the sanctuary as a safe place is ancient and holy. The church has a responsibility to protect and serve the visibly and invisibly wounded. Strategies include: (1) Be very sensitive. People who have been chronically abused live with a nightmare of fears. Along with the myriad of fears come guilt and shame. Victims tend to blame themselves, and victimizers often reinforce this twisted judgment. (2) Encourage moving beyond denial. Until truth rules, the abuser and victim will not be helped. (3) Support the healing process. Do not ask victims to take responsibility for changing the behavior of victimizers. Questioning blame is appropriate, expressing anger at the abuser is not. Violation usually crushes self-esteem. Identify the victim's strengths and consider how they might be useful. Explore what the victim wants besides respite. Encourage the survivor to forge his or her own decisions on his or her own timeline. (4) Train leadership to discern abuse. Many victims are hurt, embarrassed, and afraid. They hide the pain. Given the statistics, assume that any large group includes people who are in a long-term cycle of violence. (5) Establish policies and procedures to safeguard participants and workers in church sponsored programs. Protect clergy and volunteer staff with adequate liability insurance. (6) Establish support networks and referral systems. Individuals with a history of abuse should be referred to trained counselors. The church community may provide support recovery groups for general pastoral care and encouragement. The role of the church is to open the door to the possibility of safety and healing. Remember, an important role for clergy is to keep in touch with all parties. Even if we have acted badly in the name of God, his heart is still to gather us to himself. Patience and love are needed as God works to reconcile the abuser to himself.

Many allegations of abuse are true. But false accusation can be equally destructive to the life of a community. Discernment and vigilance are necessary. Complaints should be handled in the context of trust-building, nonviolence, guaranteed due process, and truth-telling.

Congregations will differ in the degree to which they can be an active witness and influence for personal safety in the world. If the worshiping community fails to address the protection of children, battered women and men, or elders in pain, who will stand up for them?

JAMES A. DAVIES

Bibliography. M. Fortune (1982), *Is Nothing Sacred?*; D. Johnson and J. VanVonderen (1991), *The Subtle Power of Spiritual Abuse.*

Academy. The astute reader of educational history will discover that throughout history there have been several academic institutions known as the Academy. There is a reference to such an institution in Asia dating before the time of Christ. In addition, Athens in ancient Greece had its Academy. The Reformation, under the influence of John Calvin, developed a multilevel school known as the Academy, which formed the basis for the structure of education that would later come to America in colonial education. Each reference will be briefly described below.

Asian Reference. The first reference made to such an institution dates back to the Chinese educational system thousands of years before Christ. At that time, the Chinese had no public education for the masses. However, the state did encourage the formation of private schools so that young men could meet state requirements for academic testing. In this approach there were three levels of instruction: elementary, academies, and examinations. After completing a basic mastery of learning, the student progressed to the Academy level of instruction. Here the rigors of learning included systematic memorization, studying the Chinese classics, writing prose, and learning drills that prepared students for the forthcoming state exams (Frost, 1966).

Athenian Reference. During the period of time when Athenian education was prominent (6th century B.C.) wealthy Greeks paid private teachers to come to their communities and provide their children with elementary education. This basic level of instruction covered topics that provided for a well-rounded education and made the child a productive member of society. Beyond this elementary education was a secondary level that catered almost exclusively to the aristocracy. This advanced stage of learning consisted largely of physical conditioning, which therefore required a specialized facility. The government of Athens erected a public gymnasium known as the Academy for the physical conditioning of its youth. Under the direction of a *gymnasiarch*, this institution trained young men and provided a high level of quality instruction (Frost, 1966).

Reformation Reference. During the Middle Ages, there was little consolidated political power in Europe. As a result, the influence of ecclesiastical power (e.g., the Roman Catholic Church) was strong and vast (Sanner and Harper, 1978). The Reformation brought about a shift in power as educational institutions grew in both number and significance. Protestant Reformers such as Luther, Zwingli, and Calvin used education as a means of turning the tide of Catholic influence on the masses. John Calvin's (1509–64) major contribution to reform was his Geneva Academy, which provided two levels of instruction: a private school for children between the ages of 5 and 16, and a public school that served as a university for advanced instruction. The curriculum was humanistic and the students received thorough religious instruction through the church catechism, Scripture memory, meditation, and prayer. This model of instruction was later taken as a basis for founding the University of Leyden in Holland, Emmanuel College at Cambridge in England, and later Harvard in Massachusetts (Reed and Prevost, 1993).

Colonial Reference. In the seventeenth century the first private secondary school in the United States was established in Boston. Known as the Latin grammar school, it specialized in the study of ancient languages and literature (Mayer, 1966). Although the original purpose of the Latin grammar school was the training of ministers (Harvard's goal when it was established in 1636), it was soon decided that this curriculum was far too narrow given the diverse needs of a new country. Consequently, Benjamin Franklin established a new type of school, called the academy, in Philadelphia in 1751. In these new schools the curriculum was broadened to include studies in science, the arts, the classics, and practical subjects such as bookkeeping, reading, writing, mechanics, and merchandising. This expensive private education formed the basis for what would later be known as the public high school. The first public high school was established in Boston in 1821. Though initially only for boys, women would be admitted five years later.

When one reads about schools known as the Academy or academies, it is important to examine the historical context of the reference to determine just which school, era, and historical setting is meant since the term or concept is used rather broadly by many authors.

MICHAEL J. ANTHONY

Bibliography. C. B. Eavy (1964), *History of Christian Education;* E. F. Frost (1966), *Historical and Philosophical Foundations of Western Education;* K. O. Gangel and W. S. Benson (1983), *Christian Education: Its History and Philosophy;* F. Mayer (1966), *A History of Educational Thought;* J. E. Reed and R. Prevost (1993), *A History of Christian Education;* A. E. Sanner and A. F. Harper (1978), *Exploring Christian Education.*

See also ARISTOTLE

Accountability. To be accountable is to be responsible for one's actions. God views accountability seriously: "every careless word that men shall speak, they shall render account for it in the day of judgment" (Matt. 12:36 NASB). Paul, also speaking of the time when all will stand before the judgment seat of God, reinforces Jesus' message, "So then each one of us shall give account of himself to God" (Rom. 14:12 NASB).

Being accountable for one's ministry involves two things: (1) having authority over some area of ministry; and (2) being responsible for the outcomes of that ministry. All authority is ultimately delegated by God. The exercise of authority should be tempered with the recognition that one is wielding authority on God's behalf. Where there is no authority, there can be no accountability.

To "render an account" of one's activity requires a clear job description, feedback mechanisms, and evaluation procedures. A job description should include the title of the position; the name of the person to whom one reports; a broad description of the position; a list of specific tasks of the position; and qualifications needed for the position. Feedback mechanisms might include written progress reports or meetings with one's supervisor to review the status of one's ministry. To evaluate is to ask, "How well did this person do vis-à-vis the specific duties assigned to him or her?" Evaluations should occur at least once a year.

LESLIE A. ANDREWS

See also JOB DESCRIPTION; MANAGEMENT

Accrediting Association of Bible Colleges. North American universities were often founded on explicitly Christian principles, but by the late 1800s most had adopted more secular concepts of education. To meet the need for passionate, biblically faithful training of evangelists and missionaries, A. B. Simpson founded Nyack Missionary College in 1881, and D. L. Moody founded the institute bearing his name in 1886. In Canada, Prairie Bible Institute was organized in 1922 and Briercrest Bible Institute in 1935.

The patterns and principles for liberal arts education had been standardized for nearly a century, but the new biblical education movement was in its formative stages and often led by people of fiercely independent spirit. Bible college and institute programs had a primary focus on Bible learning along with training in techniques for practical ministry, often with some components of general education. However, programs were extremely diverse, commonly accepted standards unknown, and quality sometimes questionable from an educational perspective.

Returning World War II veterans, whose vision for evangelism and missions was expanded by their experiences overseas, swelled enrollments in Bible colleges in the late 1940s and the 1950s. At that time, accreditation was available to Bible colleges only through review by the regional accrediting associations, a process that required adopting the more standard models for liberal arts education. The leaders of Bible colleges viewed this approach as unacceptable, but without accreditation it was difficult for veterans to take advantage of the generous federal programs for furthering their education. Therefore, in October 1947 the Accrediting Association of Bible Institutes and Bible Colleges (AABIBC) was organized at a meeting in Winona Lake, Indiana, under the leadership of Dr. Samuel Sutherland (president at the Bible Institute of Los Angeles). The United States Office of Education quickly recognized AABIBC as the only accrediting agency for undergraduate theological education, and by 1948 the first 12 schools had been accredited. By 1960 membership had grown to 36 and by 1970 to 65.

In 1957 the name was shortened to the Accrediting Association of Bible Colleges (AABC) with a further change in 1973 to the American Association of Bible Colleges (also AABC), a name considered objectionable by many of the association's member colleges in Canada. In 1994 the organization readopted the earlier name, the Accrediting Association of Bible Colleges, addressing the issue of members schools in Canada and reasserting an emphasis on the association's accrediting functions. The association, it was hoped, would serve as an "ark," bearing its member schools safely over the waters of an increasingly hostile secular flood in the field of higher education. Federal endorsement continued through the Commission on Recognition of Postsecondary Accreditation (CORPA) and its successor, the Council for Higher Education Accreditation (CHEA).

In 1998 AABC records listed 86 accredited colleges, 11 candidates and 15 applicants. The association maintains a broader focus as well, providing counsel and assistance to the more than 600 Bible colleges and institutes known to be operating in the United States and Canada. Its goals include "promoting excellence" in Bible college education through accreditation, cooperation and communication among members, and services to stimulate professional competence and achievement by board members, administrators, and students.

GUY S. SAFFOLD

Bibliography. *AABC Directory: 1997–98;* S. A. Witmer (1962), *The Bible College Story: Education with Dimension.*

See also BIBLE COLLEGE MOVEMENT; HIGHER EDUCATION

Acculturation. The process of adapting one's behavior, thinking, customs, and beliefs to those of another culture as the result of firsthand contact of an extended nature; the process of learning another culture. Acculturation may involve adopting the traits of another culture or just blending them with one's primary culture. This adaptation or learning takes place on many levels. For example, it may involve speaking a new language or using cultural idioms; changes in dining habits, such as eating dinner two or three hours later; eating different foods; celebrating new holidays or observing old ones with new traditions; choosing different clothing styles; starting events after most of the group arrives instead of by the clock; or even changing theological positions. In contrast to assimilation, in which a person or group becomes part of another group, acculturation maintains separate identities and distinctions.

A Messianic congregation, composed of both Jews and Gentiles who believe Jesus is the Messiah, is a specific example of acculturation in Christian education. Both groups educate their children in a Jewish context but from a New Testament perspective. As they celebrate holidays like Yom Kippur and Passover, Jewish believers do so with an understanding of Jesus' death as the atonement for their sins. On the other hand, Gentiles adapt their lifestyles to conform to the Jewish calendar of events.

LIN JOHNSON

Acquired Immunodeficiency Syndrome (AIDS). A serious life-threatening disease caused by a viral infection that was first diagnosed in the early 1980s. The most accurate name for this virus is Human Immunodeficiency Virus (HIV). Termed by some as "the leprosy of the modern age," the AIDS epidemic has traumatized our world.

People can become infected through both heterosexual and homosexual contact, shared use of needles and syringes related to illegal drugs, blood transfusions, and contact with bodily fluids such as blood, semen, or vaginal secretions. Babies born to infected mothers may get the virus through the umbilical cord or through breast milk. Approximately one-third of the infants exposed to the virus develop AIDS within four to ten years.

Because the virus is usually not detected until months or even years after the first exposure, an infected person can unknowingly be an agent of the disease and infect many other victims before becoming aware of any serious health problems. It is estimated that up to 80 percent of those infected with the virus in the United States are not aware they have the disease. Eventually the virus attacks a person's natural immune system. Normal infections turn into major problems. Antibiotics usually are of insignificant value in helping an infected person fight off normal illnesses. Simple colds turn into pneumonia. Symptoms such as diarrhea, fatigue, lymph node enlargement, fevers, sores, and weight loss become more and more common. In the later stages of the disease, when a victim's immune system is virtually defenseless against attack, death is inevitable. The most common causes of mortality are pneumonia, tuberculosis, cancer, and bacterial or viral infections. Even with the help of such drugs as AZT, which tend to slow the progression of the disease, death is inevitable.

As grim as this scenario looks in our affluent culture, it doesn't even compare with the devastation of the disease in the Third World. In Uganda in 1994 it was estimated that 15 percent of the population was HIV-positive. Without proper education, medical care, church and family support, and preventive measures there seems to be little reason for hope. Yet the Christian church and community have the opportunity to provide such a hope. Rather than reacting vindictively to this world crisis, the church needs to respond in accordance with biblical principles. Jesus gives us a model of how to respond to persons inflicted with devastating contagious diseases in Mark 1:40–42. He compassionately reaches out in love to touch and heal the leper. Jesus reiterates this principle in an even more biting challenge in which he describes the lifestyle of those who will be invited to heaven:

> Then the King will say to those on his right, "Come, you who are blessed by my Father; take your inheritance, the kingdom prepared for you since the creation of the world. For I was hungry and you gave me something to eat, I was thirsty and you gave me something to drink, I was a stranger and you invited me in, I needed clothes and you clothed me, I was sick and you looked after me, I was in prison and you came to visit me." (Matthew 25:34–36)

Jesus, putting himself in the place of the marginalized in society, reminds us that when we help those who are suffering, we minister to him. Without minimizing the reality of sexual sin, the church must reach out in love to the AIDS victim, regardless of how the virus was contracted. Physicians Wood and Dietrich (1990) challenge the church to follow Jesus' example in our attitude toward AIDS victims, and "not see disease as God's judgment but as an opportunity to show God's glory and mercy (John 9:1–3)" (279).

The church has responded to the AIDS crisis with a variety of effective ministries focused on prevention, education, treatment, and pastoral care. Ministries to homosexuals and AIDS victims are springing up all over the country, especially in urban areas. Wood and Dietrich (1990) suggest five specific ministry areas that we need to focus on: the Christian community, the redeemed sinner, the AIDS patient, the homosexual and drug-using communities, and society at large. Effective ministry must begin with churches becoming more aware of the needs of AIDS victims in their own communities. Preventive measures begin with parents investing quality time and instilling biblical values in their children. In order to minister to redeemed sinners, the church needs to develop warm, redemptive relationships with the former homosexual man, lesbian, drug user, or sexually active heterosexual. Counseling, support groups, informal relationships, and mentoring relationships need to be provided to help the ex-addict to grow toward complete recovery.

The church needs to minister in very practical ways to the specific needs of AIDS patients, including relationships, time, transportation, meals, support groups, and financial support. Although practicing homosexuals and IV drug users may be the most difficult persons to minister to, the church needs to strategize as to how to build relational bridges to them. A key principle behind successful ministries to such individuals is balancing a high personal standard of godliness with a warm, relational style of outreach. Lastly, Wood and Dietrich (1990) suggest that the church develop a wise, thoughtful strategy of ministering to the society as a whole. Suggestions include establishing sex education programs in the public schools that are consistent with biblical moral principles, becoming more politically active on a local level to encourage moral virtue in our communities, and participating in community-based programs of caring for AIDS victims (304–12). The church must respond to the AIDS crisis with the compassion of Christ.

GARY C. NEWTON

Bibliography. A. F. Holmes (1984), *Ethics: Approaching Moral Decisions;* M. Rosenberger, *Issues in Focus: Gaining a Clear Biblical Perspective on the Complex Issues of Our Time;* T. E. Schmidt (1995), *Straight and Narrow? Compassion and Charity in the Homosexual Debate;* R. Shilts (1987), *And the Band Played On: Politics, People, and the AIDS Epidemic;* G. G. Wood and J. E. Dietrich (1990), *The AIDS Epidemic: Balancing Compassion and Justice.*

See also HOMOSEXUALITY; SEX EDUCATION; SUPPORT GROUP

Acting/Playing. *See* Dramatization.

Active Learning. A methodology of teaching and learning that focuses upon the student's participation and control over the learning structure. It is a term usually used in contrast to the worst of traditional teaching (*passive* learning) and especially dull and ineffective approaches.

Active is defined as alive, dynamic, operative, functional, or performing. Students who learn in this style will carry out a set of actions and activities. Habermas and Issler (1992) describe learning as a "change that is facilitated through deliberate or incidental experience, under the supervision of the Holy Spirit, and in which one acquires and regularly integrates age-appropriate knowledge, attitudes, values, emotions, skills, and habits into an increasingly Christ-like lifestyle" (108). Active learning is a particular style or methodology used to accomplish the goals of Christian instruction.

Related theories and methods of teaching and learning are *self-directed learning, experiential learning, generative learning, participative learning, adventure-based education, cooperative learning, on-the-job training*, and *hands-on learning*. While not all the above terms are synonymous, they show the various flavorings of active learning.

Assumptions. Practitioners of active learning operate under three assumptions.

1. Teaching is *active*. "When training is active, the participants do most of the work. They use their brains—studying ideas, solving problems, and applying what they learn" (Silberman, 1995, xi). Active learning assumes we learn best by doing. We cannot know what is happening inside a person unless there is some activity outside. "The wind blows where it wishes and you hear the sound of it, but [you] do not know where it comes from and where it is going; so is everyone who is born of the Spirit" (John 3:8 NASB). The difficulty with teaching is that we sometimes think we are engaging in the teaching-learning process, only to find we have been failing to stimulate the effective application in the life of the learner. In other words, it is "much ado about nothing." Active learning bases its function upon the idea that every learner is active.

2. Learning is *different* for various people according to a number of characteristics. Age is certainly a primary factor. *Andragogy* (the art and science of teaching adults) differs from pedagogy. Age factors exist even within such homogeneous groups as preschoolers or adolescents or middle adults. Level of experience or the ability to translate that experience into meaningful concepts are also factors. Personality traits tint learning. History of success in learning and present attitude toward learning impact a student's response to instruction. Teachers must recognize that learners are different from each other and also from the teacher. Knowles (1975) lists five factors that clarify the differences between learners: "The concept of the learner is self-directed. The role of the learner's experience is a resource. A readiness to learn is viewed as developing from life tasks and problems. The orientation to learning is that of task or curiosity to learn. The motivation of learners is assumed and there are internal incentives" (60–61).

3. Teaching is a *process*. There are three aspects to a learning process: goals, methods, and content (Heimlich and Norland, 1994, 158). Each of these aspects implies active learning. The goal can be evidenced in why adults learn. "Discussions of specific motives for adults' learning are limited to the formal learning activities and the key term for communicating this framework is *participation*" (Long, 1990, 26). The methods chosen for the education of children, youth, and adults are increasingly moving toward more action. Following Houle, K. Patricia Cross (1984) outlines the three types of learners: (1) goal-oriented learners, "using learning to gain specific objectives"; (2) activity-oriented learners, who participate for the sake of activity; and (3) learning-oriented learners, who pursue learning for its own sake (82–83). In other words, even though some learners involve themselves only to obtain something, the vast majority have some active outcome in mind. Finally, some areas of content are applied. In other words, there is no other way to learn them except by doing.

Actions. Active learning involves "providing opportunities for students to meaningfully talk and listen, write, read, and reflect on the content, ideas, issues, and concerns of an academic subject" (Meyers and Jones, 1993, 6). Using these categories, one can see how methods can be utilized to overcome the monotony of lecture and too much teacher-directed methodology. Some of the methods used in active learning are discussion, case studies, forums, panels, simulations, cooperative student projects, informal small groups, and creative games.

Present-Day Usage. There is some criticism regarding active learning. Critics charge that active learning gives learners too much control, diverts attention away from real learning, forces some learners to digress from their dominant cognitive style, and involves more preparation time for the teacher. Even with these limitations, the employment of active learning would seem to be worth the effort. Attitudes, skills, and patterns of lifelong learning seem to be better addressed by the methodology of active learning.

GREGORY C. CARLSON

Bibliography. K. P. Cross (1984), *Adults as Learners;* R. Habermas and K. Issler (1992), *Teaching for Reconciliation;* J. E. Heimlich and E. Norland (1994), *Developing Teaching Styles in Adult Education;* M. S. Knowles (1975), *Self-Directed Learning: A Guide for Learners and Teachers;* H. B. Long (1990), "Understanding Adult Learners," in *Adult Learning Methods;* C. Meyers and T. B. Jones (1993), *Promoting Active Learning: Strategies for the College Classroom;* M. Silberman (1995), *101 Ways to Make Training Active.*

See also ANDRAGOGY; COGNITIVE FIELD THEORY; EXPERIENTIAL LEARNING; TEACHING-LEARNING PROCESS

Adler, Mortimer J. (1902–). Austrian psychiatrist and founder of the school of individual psychology in New York City. In spite of dropping out of high school and taking a position with the *New York Sun* during his teen years, Adler was admitted to Columbia University on the basis of his personal reading habits. Although he completed the academic curriculum in three years and received a Phi Beta Kappa key, he did not receive his B.A. degree due to his refusal to take physical education courses. However, Columbia did ask him to serve as an instructor in psychology, during which time he not only taught but also successfully completed the requirements for a Ph.D., which was awarded to him in 1928.

Adler's early attraction to literature, combined with the influence of a Great Books seminar he took at Columbia under the guidance of John Erskine, led him into a relationship with Robert Hutchins and spawned his best-known work, *How To Read a Book.* When Hutchins became president of the University of Chicago, he invited Adler to join him in developing an academic program based upon the greatest literature of Western civilization. In 1946 they established what became known as the Great Books Program, which eventually developed a fifty-four-volume set of 443 "Great Books."

Strongly influenced by Aristotle and Aquinas, Adler is a proponent of absolute and universal truths and values. As such, he is an outspoken critic of John Dewey and pragmatism, arguing that any view that makes truth relative creates moral and intellectual chaos.

Adler's educational philosophy is summarized in his book *The Paideia Proposal.* Published in 1982, it advocates a reformation of the educational system. For Adler, the best education is one that is general and liberal. He advocates three broad educational objectives: the acquisition of organized knowledge, the development of intellectual skills, and the increased understanding of basic ideas and issues. Furthermore, he argues that "only through reading and discussing books that are over one's head can the skills of critical reading and reflective thought be developed" (*Reforming*, xxxi).

Although he promotes a liberal education, Adler is by no means an elitist or a cognitivist. He argues that there are no unteachable children and that students learn best when they are actively engaged in learning. While rejecting any approach that would sacrifice truth over the individual student, Adler recognizes the main role that the student must have in the process of discovery if learning is to take place. Adler calls readers to stretch, grow, debate, and to clarify those truths and values that govern the universe.

DOUGLAS BARCALOW

Bibliography. M. J. Adler (1982), *The Paideia Proposal: An Educational Manifesto;* idem, (1977) *Reforming Education: The Opening of the American Mind.*

See also AQUINAS, THOMAS, ARISTOTLE; LIBERAL ARTS; *PAIDEA* AND FIRST-CENTURY EDUCATION

Administration. The management of projects, supervision of others, and implementing of policies. Administration is different from leadership in that administration executes policy rather than creating it. The word is actually derived from the Greek word *kubernesis,* the pilot of a ship. Those who administer an organization steer it through trouble, being careful of the currents and dangerous shoals that could sink it.

The Gift of Administration. In 1 Corinthians 12:28, the apostle Paul notes that "in the church God has appointed . . . those with gifts of administration." The Lord has therefore given some people special abilities to guide others. The individual with the gift of administration does not merely have a knack for accomplishing goals, but receives guidance from the Holy Spirit to effectively coordinate the activities of the church. Those who would reject a career in church administration as "too confining" or "too business-like" misunderstand God's eternal purpose: to help the church reach its goal of bringing the world to Christ. The common elements of administration include planning, organizing, staffing, directing, controlling, and evaluating.

Biblical Examples of Administration. When Moses was faced with the administration of the nation of Israel, his father-in-law suggested setting up an administrative structure that would allow decisions and disputes to be dealt with at a lower organizational level (Exod. 18). In doing so, Moses created a workable system that allowed him to attend to the weightier issues of running a country. Nehemiah, needing coordination to complete the building of the Jerusalem wall, went through the process of planning the work, organizing it into achievable units, staffing each section with a family, directing the process, and controlling not only construction but the protection of the workers (Neh. 3–4).

In the New Testament, Jesus also understood the importance of administration, training a handful of committed followers and giving them clear instructions as to how they should carry out their task (Matt. 28:19–20; John 14–17; Acts 1:4–8). The apostle Paul did likewise, establishing new churches in each city he visited, training leaders for each church, and keeping in contact with them to make sure they were following the overall plan. Administration was common in the early church, and administrators took pains to organize, recruit and train leadership, delegate and divide the responsibilities, and ensure the future progress of the gospel.

JERRY CHIP MACGREGOR

See also LEADERSHIP; MANAGEMENT; ORGANIZATION; SPIRITUAL GIFTS

Adolescent Development. Adolescence is a period of time between childhood and adulthood, normally beginning around age 11 or 12 and continuing through the mid-twenties. Often adolescence is divided into three stages: early (ages 11 or 12 through 14), middle (ages 15–18), and late (ages 19–25 or so). Adolescent development occurs in six domains: physical, cognitive, social, affective, moral, and spiritual. Although we can examine each area of development as a separate entity, we must see a person as a whole, not as six identifiable parts. Adolescence begins at the onset of puberty, the age of which has been declining. A few females begin their menstrual period at age 11 or even 10 or younger. Unfortunately, nonphysical areas usually begin to mature a few years later. Consequently, we frequently encounter physically mature adolescents whose cognitive, affective, moral, social, and spiritual development are still at lower stages of development.

The beginning of puberty sets off a host of hormonal changes that affect not only physical development but also the entire developmental process. Relationships, views of life, self-identity, self-acceptance, and a host of other things begin to change, seemingly at the same time. Adolescence has been described as a time of stress and storm. By its very nature, adolescence is a time when the old ways permanently pass away. Entirely new structures of being are developed that are founded on the old but are quite different. The implications of such restructuring are enormous. The internal and external worlds of adolescents are changing, and they do not know what to make of such changes. They have no experience with these changes; they do not know what is happening; they cannot explain their feelings, thoughts, and actions, and often they cannot find anyone else, peers or family, who can explain it all either. Adolescents are too often left to learn through experience. Our key response should be openness and flexibility during this period when they need nurturing, acceptance, encouragement, and approval.

Adolescent development brings about new interests that point to the internal restructuring of the internal and external worlds and result in new processes for dealing with those internal and external worlds. Because these processes are new, adolescents lack the skills to use them effectively, sometimes acting clumsily in all the developmental domains. They are uncoordinated in many aspects of the restructuring of their lives. Their bodies do not develop smoothly but in spurts and they need time to get used to longer arms and legs and other physical changes. In a similar fashion, all their other developmental domains are also changing. Adolescents have a plethora of new tasks in multiple domains. It is difficult at best to keep all of their new structures operating smoothly; in fact, it is nearly impossible. Hence, we have the typical picture of an adolescent who acts like an adult one minute and like a child the next. Who would not want to revert to the relative simplicity of childhood when one's whole being is being reconstructed without the owner's permission! Development proceeds at its own pace; boys' voices change, and little girls become young women, but no one consults them!

Adolescent development occurs in all six developmental domains. Following are some of the major developments, issues, and/or questions that occur during this time.

Physical development affects all areas of adolescents' bodies and continues rapidly, then slowly, then with great spurts, and eventually stops by the end of late adolescence. Primary and secondary sex characteristics develop and mature. Muscle and bone growth are uneven, with bones usually outpacing muscular development. This leads to coordination problems, especially for younger males. Adolescents have high energy spurts but often tire easily, especially in early adolescence. Males especially consume large amounts of food that is not always the most nutritious but is full of calories. They need these calories because their bodies are growing new cells at an enormous rate and because they are expending large amounts of energy daily. Adolescents look for physically challenging experiences that give them emotional thrills. Throughout their development there are wide variations of speed, maturity, and refinements. It is conceivable that one 15-year-old may look physically like a 22-year-old while another 15-year-old may look like a 10-year-old. Neither is abnormal; this is all part of the wide variation of idiosyncratic time tables for physical development.

Physical development raises numerous questions and issues for adolescents. They want to know what is happening to their bodies. They are interested in their own and their peers' physical development. They look at each other, comparing bodies, and feel affirmed if they are ahead of their peers or cheated if they lag behind. Their basic question, couched as both question and plea, is "Am I normal?" They are trying to explain to themselves and their peers why they are different from others in their physical changes. For American youth, and increasingly for youth around the world, there is a great concern about whether they are physically attractive. Adolescents also want to know how to care for their bodies, how to stay in good shape so that they are desirable and can feel accepted. They have many questions about sexual development. Unfortunately they do not find many resources outside of their peers, who are usually equally ignorant, and mass media which is not usually concerned with the moral side of sexual development. Parents and church are not a major source of sex education.

Cognitive Development. Adolescents' minds are restructuring to accomodate both concrete and abstract thinking. They exercise their newfound ability to think abstractly, using that ability as often as possible. They can think about hypothetical situations and even create them for themselves and their peers in order to explore mentally what they could not do physically. They look for mental stimulation, are easily bored with childish teaching, and often act out their boredom in less than socially acceptable ways. They have many questions and seek answers to life's big questions and to social issues and problems. They often ask "Why?" or "Why not?" not to be cantankerous, but because they are able to use their minds in new ways.

Adolescents can develop from a paradoxical stance of listening to the authorities for answers to a pattern of rejecting all authorities to finally realizing that in a world with many possible answers, they must commit themselves to something and move on to maturity. However, even as they move into a state of commitment, they do so with tentativeness. They have had enough experience to know that what has been accepted as true today might not be so tomorrow. So even though commitments are given, they can also be renegotiated. Absolutes are often seen as relative absolutes, not as absolutes for all time.

Adolescents are developing self-identity. They are beginning to make a definitive statement to themselves as to who they are and what they want to be. They need encouragement and comfort to continue the process of self-identification and consolidation. If they cut short this process, they will have a confused self-identity that may only frustrate them in later years.

Adolescents ask deep epistemological questions and they need help in finding the answers, not just being given the answers. Youth look for people who can help them answer every conceivable question about life from the simple to the most complex, from the totally secular to the deeply spiritual. They need helpers who will come alongside them, affirm them, encourage their quest, and be ready to assist when necessary. They need adults who will share their journey, not tell them where to go and how to get there.

Social Development. Adolescents are developing new friendships built on true sharing of self with others. They redefine friendship and kinship. Relationships with adults take on new dimensions that are potentially more adult-like. Adolescents are interested in peer-approved behaviors, acceptance, and feeling comfortable in social situations. They want to talk with whomever will listen seriously. Usually they have a large number of friends, and they tend to change

friends throughout their adolescent years. Early adolescents form small peer groups that "hang around" together. As they mature, adolescents tend to form more permanent friendships that often last lifetimes. Throughout all of the adolescent years, peer groups are often the major support group.

Social development stimulates basic questions about relationships. Youth want to know the meaning of relationships and especially about truthfulness and faithfulness. Adolescents ask who really are their friends. They want to know how to make and keep true friends, and are concerned that friendship be more than a social club. They want their relationships to be a refuge from the world around them. They desire to know to which groups they belong and how to get into those groups. They are concerned with relationships between themselves and members of the opposite sex as well as forming wholesome relationships with those of the same sex. They are concerned with how other people view them and they continue to try out different personalities and dress to see how they feel about these trial identities and how their friends and family respond to them. Finally, adolescents attempt to be independent yet realize that they need others. They wonder how they can be both independent and properly related to others without losing their identity or becoming isolated.

Affective or Emotional Development. Psychologists have observed almost the entire range of human emotions in infants and young children. Thus, the number of emotions that adolescents have in their repertoire is relatively static. How they demonstrate those emotions, the intensity of their demonstrations, and how they control their emotions are what set adolescents apart from children and mature adults. Adolescent emotions are often chaotic, confused, extreme, and contradictory. Adolescents have intense feelings that they often express in rather abrupt ways. They seek emotional stimuli, but lack emotional control in many situations. Adolescents often show worry, anxiety, self-pity, anger, hostility, fear, frustration, loyalty, disloyalty, love, hate, superiority, inferiority—that is, they experience all the emotions of any normal human but lack the controls that adults have learned the hard way. This lack of control is understandable given the enormous changes that are occurring in every aspect of their lives.

Adolescents wonder why they have these inexplicable emotional highs and lows. They wonder how to express emotions that are very real but which are not always acceptable outside their small peer group. They are puzzled about why they have contradictory emotions toward the same person, event, or thing. They sense their fickle emotions but cannot seem to stop them from occurring. They look for controls, but do not find them easily at hand. They wonder if God has some of the same emotional variability as they do. They are looking for an emotionally expressed faith as well as a cognitive one. They seek stable emotional relationships with peers and especially with adults who can help them learn how to control their emotions.

Moral Development. Moral development begins in childhood with an orientation to avoiding punishment and obeying those with the power to reward or punish. They do the right thing, not because it is right in itself but because someone with authority and power can make them conform. From this early stage they move to doing what feels good to them. If something satisfies them and no one else seems to get hurt, then it must be good. The standard phrase is, "If it feels so good, it can't be wrong." In the next stage they begin to make moral judgments and to take action based on what pleases significant others in their lives. Significant others differ according to the time of day and setting. At school, significant others tend to be mostly peers and occasionally teachers. At home, parents or other adults are often significant others whom adolescents respect. Additional significant others can include other relatives, pastors, youth leaders, and other special adult friends. In the fourth stage adolescents perceive society as the significant other, i.e., an abstract society makes rules that all people must obey. If all people disobeyed rules, then there would be chaos. Therefore, adolescents can easily become "law and order" people who obey rules because they have been made by those who are authorities in society. Occasionally older adolescents' moral thinking develops to involve universal principles of justice and righteousness. However, this is a relatively sophisticated stage that even relatively few adults achieve. The final rare stage of agapic love abandons all pretense to external compulsion of doing what is moral and any pretense of philosophically rationalizing moral judgments. Rather, agapic moral development requires a person to make and do the agapic thing regardless of others' circumstances by doing what God does towards us.

Adolescents try to discover what is right and wrong. They want to know who or what is their authority. They struggle with multiple and relativistic moral answers to the problems of life. They look for someone who will stand alongside them during their intense struggles with moral issues and actions. They do not want to be supplied with hackneyed answers but to be helped to think for themselves. They want to have friends, but they do not always want to do what their friends do; yet they seem to lack moral fortitude to resist their friend's temptations. They are interested in experimenting with what is morally acceptable and what is not. They are interested in knowing right and wrong, but they may not always do the morally right thing. They are looking for moral answers in many places and from many different people. They need a sure anchor that will help them weather the storms of moral decay that have been prevalent in societies ever since the beginning of time.

Most adolescents are religious beings. Very few do not believe in some higher power, and most refer to that power as God. In the United States, few youth need to be convinced that there is a God, but many adolescents lack a vital, personal faith. They have an insecure faith, often inherited from parents and handed to them by their church. They find that while their minds, friends, and school environment ask them to think for themselves, their church youth group and church leaders accent acceptance of church dogma without questions. The catechisms and/or membership classes for youth of various denominations are good examples of dogma handed down from elders to youth. Adolescents look for meaning and expressions of their own faith. They look for someone who will help them in their quest for answers to the big philosophical, theological, and social problems of life. They are often tired of being told that if they just believe then God will work it all out. They usually want to follow the will of God for their lives, but are often at a loss to know how to find it. Those who have a strong, vital faith often contagiously share their faith with peers.

During the middle adolescent years young people begin to own their own faith. They have learned some of the basic teachings of the church and are able to begin to articulate a personal faith. This faith often lacks systematization, coherence, and depth, yet it is their faith, and they willingly defend it and speak up for it. In later adolescence and young adulthood, they begin to reflect on their faith and begin to own it more philosophically and to act accordingly. Too often, however, churches cannot help adolescents to this more mature faith development because few if any of those in leadership have developed to this more mature stage. Often older adolescents must turn for help to university Christian organizations that articulate a thoughtful and enriched mature faith.

Adolescents face many basic issues in faith development. They seek to know the Triune God in more intimate ways, going beyond the grand stories of Sunday school and camp to a more intimate relationship that is both warm and friendly and also awe inspiring. They look for a faith that is both cognitive and affective, not sterile or predictable. They often wonder why they have doubts regarding the Bible and God and look for people who can help them through their doubts without disparaging or belittling their questions with facile, shallow answers. They often ask why the organized church functions as it does. They are usually attracted to Christ, but are often repulsed by the organized formality of traditional churches. Adolescents lack an understanding and appreciation of the history of the church, so they have little appreciation for historic hymnody, traditional music, and formal worship with all its liturgical accoutrements. Yet they want both solid meat along with a warm, affective environment that speaks to them holistically. Adolescents struggle with the issue of why they do what they do not want to do, knowing that it is wrong, and not doing what they know they should do. They want help to know how to walk in the Spirit and not fulfill the desires of the flesh. They also want to know why so called "good" Christians are too often hypocritical. They ultimately are looking for a world and life view that integrates their selves into a coherent whole and that is well grounded in a faith that will last and continue to grow with them.

Adolescents are at a crucial crossroads in their lives. They are developing in all of the six areas of human development that will affect them for the remainder of their lives. They are trying to understand the physical changes that they are undergoing. They are learning cognitive material that will either help them to understand and adapt to a rapidly changing world or that will be irrelevant in a few years. They are making friends who will either be great helpers in mutual development or will drag all of the group down. They are looking for ways to control all the emotions that they feel and do not understand, but that they nevertheless want to express in wholesome, acceptable ways. They want to know what is right and wrong, why it is, and how to do what is right and avoid wrong. They want a faith that is theirs, that is worth living for, and ultimately worth dying for.

Adolescence is a time when churches find individuals open to Jesus Christ as Savior and Lord. Youth have a special sensitivity to God and an understanding that goes beyond childhood but is not jaded like that of many adults. Adolescents will respond to those who show them unconditional, agapic love, a love that incarnates the Incarnate One.

JOHN M. DETTONI

Bibliography. R. Gemelli, ed. (1996), *Normal Child and Adolescent Development;* M. L. Jaffe (1998), *Adolescent Psychology;* F. P. Rice (1996), *The Adolescent: Development, Relationships, and Culture;* N. A. Sprinthall and W. A. Collins (1995), *Adolescent Psychology: A Developmental View.*

See also MIDDLE ADOLESCENT, YOUTH MINISTRY TO; YOUTH MINISTRY

Adult Children of Alcoholics. Millions of adult children of alcoholics are discovering that many of their personality problems stem from the experience of growing up in an alcoholic family. In the late 1970s knowledge of the so-called ACoA syndrome became widespread, described by those involved in treating alcoholics (Wegscheider, 1981). Research confirms that not all adult children of alcoholics are severely affected, but many do possess certain traits. They guess what normal behavior is. They judge themselves without mercy and have difficulty having fun and following projects through to the end. Either very irresponsible or very responsible, they are extremely loyal, even in the face of evidence that their loyalty is undeserved. And they are often compulsive, tending to overachieve, overeat, overwork, overexercise, and overspend, exhibiting addictive personalities. The shame many of them feel makes them constantly seek others' approval.

Experts have various explanations for how alcoholic families affect their children. Psychoanalytic theory claims that alcoholic families stifle the development of the child's self, resulting in an immature, damaged "child within" (Whitfield, 1987). Some experts believe many of the ACoA traits can be explained as "post-traumatic disorder."

Family systems theory maintains that the alcoholic family enslaves its members in an enmeshed system that is tied to the self-centered, unpredictable behavior of the addict. The stress prompts children to react with fear, panic, withdrawal, anger, and so on. Under the circumstances, these coping mechanisms and responses are normal. However, when they are woven so deeply into the person's personality, they become stubborn, abnormal behaviors and emotions in adulthood.

Counseling and self-help groups, along with scores of books and articles, have been the major source of ACoAs' treatment. Adult Children of Alcoholics, a national organization built on the twelve-step model of Alcoholics Anonymous, has thousands of groups throughout the world.

Christian churches, too, have provided help by offering their facilities for ACoA meetings or by conducting their own support group based on Christian principles. Several organizations such as Overcomers Outreach, a national Bible-based type of Alcoholics Anonymous, minister to ACoAs.

Recovery for ACoAs includes admitting their problems (denial is common, since most learned it from their parents); trusting God to change them; recalling the past family life (which is sometimes difficult to remember) to discern the source of their personality problems; attempting to accept parents and their substance abuse; overcoming codependency, an unhealthy enmeshment to others; and dealing with emotional and behavioral issues.

ACoAs need the spiritual resources of the church. For them, "Letting go and letting God" means surrendering to God's will and purposes and accepting themselves with their limitations and their struggles. Their striving to overcome shame, sometimes through agonizing efforts to prove themselves, will be eased by the realization that God loves them. Having felt rejected or unloved by their parents, it is sometimes difficult for them to feel God's acceptance. Yet the unconditional care and concern of other Christians can mediate God's favor. This is what ACoAs need most and is what the church has most to offer.

CHARLES M. SELL

Bibliography. S. Wegscheider (1981), *Another Chance: Hope and Health for the Alcoholic Family;* C. L. Whitfield (1987), *Healing the Child Within: Discovery and Recovery for Adult Children of Dysfunctional Families.*

See also ALCOHOLISM; RECOVERY MINISTRY; SUPPORT GROUP

Adult Christian Education. Learning experiences that support and challenge Christians as they move toward spiritual maturity. Christian educators who teach adults participate in a long historical and biblical tradition that draws, in recent years, on research from the social sciences as well. Supplementing biblical and theological foundations with an understanding of adult development, adult learning, and the social and cultural context of adult learners enhances the Christian educator's ability to plan effective educational experiences that foster spiritual growth.

Adult Christian education is done in a variety of settings in the church and community. Church classes and groups, sermons, neighborhood Bible studies, camps and conferences, seminars, workshops, music programs, service and mission projects all contribute to the task of educating Christian adults. Christian colleges, universities, and seminaries offer formal degree and continuing education programs. Adult Christian education also occurs in the context of informal relationships as Christian adults address concerns related to spiritual nurture.

Biblical Traditions of Adult Christian Education. Even though children are mentioned occasionally, biblical references to religious instruction are primarily focused on adults. The Old Testament records countless examples of prophets, priests, poets, and kings instructing adults of the nation of Israel to demonstrate their love and allegiance to Yahweh by keeping his law. Ezra is an outstanding example of a teacher (Ezra 7:10) whom God used to bring about national revival.

In the New Testament, the Gospels portray Jesus as a teacher engaging the religious in the synagogues, teaching crowds in the out-of-doors, confronting individuals, and teaching his disciples in more intimate settings. Even when children were the focus of his teaching, he was teaching adults a lesson. Jesus intended his disciples to continue his pattern of teaching. His last command to them contained an educational mandate. They were to "make disciples, teaching them to obey all his commands" (Matt. 28:19, 20). Paul demonstrated his commitment to teaching adult believers when he visited churches he had founded and when he wrote epistles to instruct growing believers about theology and life practice.

Adult Development and Adult Christian Education. The three broad periods of adulthood—early, middle, and late—must be considered when planning for adult educational ministry. Robert Havinghurst (1970) uses the term "developmental tasks" to describe the distinctive challenges in each phase of development. Understanding these tasks helps educators to connect scriptural and theological content with relevant life situations so that what Havinghurst calls "teachable moments" are more likely to occur. While intergenerational opportunities should be provided, most Christian education experiences are organized around specific life issues, needs, interests, and concerns that are connected to age-related developmental tasks.

In addition to general, age-related developmental characteristics, adult Christian educators also consider the characteristics that mark generations. For example, in the United States those born between 1946 and 1964 are referred to as baby boomers, and are generally characterized by optimism, upward mobility, geographic mobility, growing affluence, focus on self-fulfillment, and diminished institutional loyalty (Roof, 1993). The generation born between 1965 and 1983 is called busters or Generation X. This generation is described as being skeptical and pessimistic about the future, having media savvy, longing for relational connection, and being relativistic in their thinking and moral frame of reference (Barna, 1993). An effective educational ministry reflects sensitivity to these generational characteristics.

Finally, across the adult lifespan there are groups that warrant special consideration by virtue of life experiences that are not necessarily related to age or generational characteristics. Groups with distinctive needs include adults who are new believers or who are new to the community; singles of different age groups; married couples and families at different stages of family life; newly divorced; single parents; parents of troubled adolescents or special needs children; infertile couples; those who are in career transitions; widows, widowers, and others who are grieving; and adults with addictions, eating disorders, or abuse issues.

Adult Learning and Christian Education. Malcolm Knowles (1980) popularized the notion that adults have distinctive ways of learning, and his assumptions and principles of andragogy that prescribe ways of teaching adults are still very widely referenced by adult educators. More recently, Stephen Brookfield (1986) offers six points that summarize findings about how adults learn.

First, learning comes naturally for adults. They continue to learn over the lifespan because each new stage of development presents challenges that precipitate the need for new skills and understandings. This is true into old age. Second, adults exhibit diverse learning styles and are able to use a variety of mental learning strategies depending on the purpose and context of each learning opportunity. Third, adults respond best to learning that feels meaningful because it focuses on current life problems and solutions.

Fourth, adult learning can be enhanced or diminished by past experience and this experience needs to be referenced in the learning environment. Fifth, adults' self-concept comes to bear on how they learn. Those who view themselves as capable learners will be more effective learners. This is particularly important when adults are venturing into a new area of learning. Finally, adults tend to be self-directed learners. The concept of self-directed learning was popularized by Malcolm Knowles and Allan Tough and refers to the capacity for learners to take initiative and responsibility for planning and directing their learning.

Because adult Christian education is almost entirely voluntary, Wlodkowski's work about adult motivation to learn (1993) is particularly relevant. He summarizes the key factors that pique and sustain motivation in adult learners. Understandably, past experiences shape attitudes that affect how willing an adult is to participate. Initial resistance may be the result of a negative experience in a similar setting in the past. Motivation to participate will be high when learning meets current needs and when positive feelings are generated in the learning environment. When learners sense they are gaining competence and confidence, they are motivated to continue learning. Finally, reinforcement enhances adult motivation. Adults can be insecure in class settings and about their ability to contribute. Affirmation and validation of their efforts will enhance their desire to participate. For the more secure adult learner, the internal sense of achievement will be reinforcing.

Teaching Adults. Given the information about the ways adults develop and learn, effective teachers of adults will keep the following principles in mind as they plan learning opportunities.

Cultivate choices by involving adults in decisions about the content of educational experiences. Provide many different content and setting choices at a variety of times during the week. Extend learning options by providing resources for self-directed learners who want further study.

Connect content to life by offering classes that focus on life issues and concerns. In Bible studies and classes train leaders to see the practical connections between the biblical text and the learners' lives. Use interactive teaching methods like problem-solving strategies that allow learners to make connections to their life experience. Give adult learners the opportunity to explore multiple perspectives that reflect what they actually encounter in their life experience. Give them an opportunity to demonstrate or share experiences of growing competence and understanding.

Create community in the learning environment that meets adults' relational needs and provides a safe place for self-disclosure. Plan informal time at the beginning and end of classes. Allow learners to share their life experience. Reinforce participation with appreciation and validation. Diffuse feelings of threat when approaching new topics or using new teaching methods. This sense of community is particularly important for young adults.

Cultivate creative methods that keep adult learners stimulated and that enhance participation. Lecture is an efficient and appropriate method to communicate new information, but with adults it needs to be used in an interactive style. Case studies, dilemmas, examples from the media, effective questions, and debates will draw adult learners into thinking critically about the content. Finally, sensitivity to environmental details like comfort, adequate lighting, and good sound insulation are essential for older adults especially.

Curriculum for Adult Christian Education. The curriculum for adult Christian education in the church extends beyond the options and content for adult classes that are offered each week. The curriculum permeates every dimension of the church's program in which adults participate. Robert Pazmiño (1992) suggests five tasks, or kinds of activities, that are rooted in the patterns established by the early church. These tasks serve as a holistic model for the curriculum of Christian education in the church.

Worship is the first task and the primary focus of the gathered church. Worship will be informed by the second task, the systematic teaching and proclamation of the Word of God. This teaching will be connected to the third task—that of creating opportunities for authentic fellowship and community. This fellowship, centered around the Word of God, will be educative as scriptural principles are brought to bear on life experiences in conversation and in small groups. The fourth task is service, which flows out of the spiritual giftedness of believers. This service happens both within the congregation and in the broader community and creates a need for effective education and training. Finally, the task of advocacy will be a natural extension of service when justice concerns of those who are without power and voice come to light. Participating in these five tasks or activities will provide adults with both the support and challenge that stimulate and nurture their faith.

Because the curriculum of adult Christian education permeates the whole program of congregational life, the professional adult Christian educator will welcome the challenge of equipping other leaders such as pastors, musicians, and even youth and children's staff who work with families and volunteers, to lead and teach adults more effectively.

FAYE CHECHOWICH

Bibliography. G. Barna (1993), *Generation Next;* S. Brookfield (1986), *Understanding and Facilitating Adult Learning;* J. L. Elias (1993), *The Foundations and Practice of Adult Religious Education;* N. T. Folz (1986), *Handbook of Adult Religious Education;* K. Gangel and J. Wilhoit (1993), *The Christian Educator's Handbook on Adult Education;* R. Havinghurst (1970), *Developmental Tasks and Education;* M. Knowles (1980), *The Modern Practice of Adult Education;* R. Osmer (1992), *Teaching for Faith: A Guide for Teachers of Adult Classes;* R. Pazmiño (1992), *Principles and Practices of Christian Education: An Evangelical Perspective;* W. Roof (1993), *A Generation of Seekers;* J. Stubblefield (1986), *A Church Ministering to Adults;* L. Vogel (1991), *Teaching and Learning in Communities of Faith: Empowering Adults Through Religious Education;* R. Wlodowski (1993), *Enhancing Adult Motivation to Learn.*

See also ANDRAGOGY; BABY BOOM GENERATION; BUSTER GENERATION; DEVELOPMENTAL TASKS

Adult Class. A group of adults that meets for a specific purpose. The size of an adult class can vary from five to ten to hundreds. A prime reason adults give for attending an adult Bible class is fellowship. They like being with the people who form the class.

An adult class meets for fellowship, Bible study, discipleship, mission, personal enrichment, skill development, or examination of family or personal issues. Class size varies, depending upon the goals and objectives of the class or material being studied.

Every adult class has a teacher or a facilitator. This may be one person or a team of persons who share responsibility for helping the class to achieve its goals. Other leaders are needed if the class exists for purposes other than study. For instance, an adult Bible study class may have the following tasks or functions: (1) to reach adults for Bible study, (2) to teach adults the Bible, (3) to care for adults, (4) to witness to unsaved adults, (5) to help adults fellowship with other adults, and (6) to lead adults to worship, individually and corporately. To perform these six tasks, the adult Bible study class must have more than a teacher. Someone in the class has the responsibility for outreach and evangelism. Another is the fellowship leader, others are care leaders. An-

other may be the worship leader or prayer leader. Even in a small class these tasks may be done by separate people or by individuals performing more than one task.

Depending upon the focus of the group and the maturity or skills possessed by the members, individuals within the class can provide the leadership and teaching that is needed. An effective adult class provides a place in the church where each adult is known personally and where specific needs can be met by other adults. This is done through the class sessions and personal ministries of class leaders and members.

Adult classes can be grouped in several ways: by gender (male or female), marital status (single, married, separated, divorced), age, the age of members' children, or interest in special study materials.

JERRY M. STUBBLEFIELD

Bibliography. R. Grant (1996), *Adult Class Leader Administration Kit;* F. C. Jordan (1986), *A Church Ministering to Adults;* B. P. Powers (1996), *Christian Education Handbook;* L. Shotwell (1981), *Basic Adult Sunday School Work.*

Adult Committee. A committee charged by the church with planning, coordinating, and evaluating the church's ministry to adults. The committee is composed of people who represent various aspects of the church's adult ministries. It may be a subcommittee of the Christian education committee or another committee or group recognized by the church. Ministries represented are Bible studies, discipleship, missions, family life, men's and women's ministries, recreation, music, singles, single parents, seniors, divorcé(e)s, blended families, and so on.

Membership should include at least one person from each of the church's adult ministries. Committee members may be chosen by the represented groups or by a committee or board of the church. The important issue is that every adult ministry has a representative on the committee so that special needs or interests of that group are shared and met by the church.

An adult committee cannot be effective without a clear and understood purpose statement for adult ministry. The committee must know why it exists and what its mission and ministry are. From the purpose or mission statement, the committee develops three to five objectives (broad areas in which they want to minister), with identified goals issuing in action plans to help meet those goals.

The work of the adult committee includes planning and coordinating the various activities and programs for adults in the church. A key function is to see that the church has a balanced ministry program to all the adults, not just to one group or in one area of ministry. The committee seeks to provide ministry and activities that include evangelism and outreach, worship, fellowship, Bible study, discipleship, missions education, music, and recreation, and it addresses the special needs of such groups as singles, seniors, single parents, and divorcé(e)s. This committee provides and enables at least a twelve-month plan of adult ministry. Someone from the adult committee serves as representative to the church council, church board, or Christian education committee so that the adult program is on the total church calendar.

The adult committee functions as a planning, coordinating, and evaluating committee for all adult activities. It shares with program or activity leaders the responsibility of seeing that the church has a significant ministry for all its adults. It seeks to plan a comprehensive program to meet the various needs of all adults. As plans are made, the committee coordinates these activities and ministries so that balanced needs are met. Each activity should be evaluated by the responsible group and also by the adult committee.

JERRY M. STUBBLEFIELD

Bibliography. K. Gangel (1970), *Leadership for Church Education;* D. E. Williams (1991), *Christian Education: Foundations for the Future.*

See also MANAGEMENT; ORGANIZATIONAL CHART; PLAN, PLANNING

Adult Development. *Definitions.* Adult development is the study of the growth and maturing process of adults. This study may focus on such areas as moral, social, mental, physical, or faith development. Various perspectives of each of these areas of development are listed below.

Experts dispute the point at which adulthood begins. It would appear that a certain age, or taking on adult responsibilities or roles, or acting like an adult would be sufficient to define this stage of life. Cyril Houle (1976) defines an adult in the learning enterprise as "a person (man or woman) who has achieved full physical development and who expects to have the right to participate as a responsible homemaker, worker, and member of society" (229).

Development is defined as the expected growth of a person over time. Tennant and Pogson (1995) assert that development is multidimensional, with various pathways, which have both individual and social dimensions that are constantly changing (193–200). Jesus experienced growth (Luke 2:52). Although this verse shows Jesus at age 12, there is no reason to limit this development to the early years. Development, then, is multifaceted. Whole person development occurs in six major domains: physical, cognitive, social, affective, moral, and faith/spiritual. These domains cover the whole of human personality.

The field of adult development is integrative, drawing on psychology, adult education, teaching-learning theories, faith development theory, moral development theory, and other specific areas of study that involve adult participation and growth.

History. The study of child development has long outdistanced that of adult development. While such theorists as Piaget and Freud have well documented the growth of children, the charting of the adult's progress has not been prolific. Up until the mid-twentieth century, theorists believed that adults stayed rather stable in their growth from the time of reaching maturity until death. This has now been refuted, and a growing number of researchers have given their attention to adult issues.

Three different eras or phases in the study of adult development can be traced. Before 1950 adults were mostly studied in terms of their mental and motor abilities; they were thought to be fairly stable in the areas of intelligence and personality. After 1950 learning theorists began to view adults differently as they began to discover that adults actually *learned differently.* During the third phase, theorists began to develop a mature view of the life span of people, focusing on a number of personality, physical, mental, and other traits to create the field of adult development.

Major Theorists. A number of significant researchers and their viewpoints are summarized below in order to demonstrate the breadth of opinions which comprise the scope of adult development. *Erik Erikson* presented one of the earliest perspectives on adult development. His works from 1963 and 1982 (*Childhood and Society* and *The Life Cycle Completed,* respectively) moved the focus of adult education to viewing adults as having broad-range growth and change similar to that of children. Erickson's eight stages of adult development blend inner maturational plans and societal demands. In the first five stages adults build upon the completion of growth. But it is the last three stages of his model that relate specifically to adult development. Level 6, "Intimacy vs. Isolation" (young adulthood), is a time of establishing a fully intimate relationship with another. "Generativity vs. Stagnation" (adulthood) is a time of struggle between feelings of maintaining and perpetuating society and feelings of self-absorption. "Integrity vs. Despair" (old age) places meaningfulness and accomplishments against the dread of growing old.

Abraham Maslow followed Carl Jung in thinking that all of life exists in a state of polarity. Growth is the reaching toward "self-actualization." Maslow sees this happening through stages which are not necessarily tied to age. He believes that few achieve this high state of self-actualization, and most are preoccupied with the lower levels of his hierarchy. Physiological needs (hunger, thirst, etc.) and safety needs (security and protection) must be attended to before a person can achieve more complex needs such as love and belonging, self-esteem, and self-actualization.

Jane Loevinger focused her work on the idea that ego development has four main streams or channels: physical, psychosexual, intellectual, and ego development are all part of adult development. She outlined eight stages of human development, six of which pertain to the adult. At each stage interpersonal style, character development, conscious preoccupations, and cognitive style converge to form and shape the person's ego. Adults progress from being conformist, to conscientious-conformist, conscientious, individualistic, autonomous, and finally integrated.

Malcolm Knowles became an important figure in adult education by promoting andragogy as the dominant theory of adult education. He believes that adults have a different learning framework than children. Adults are self-directing, value experience, are ready to learn (i.e., set their own goals), are life-and-problem centered, and are internally motivated to learn. These basic theories have impacted adult learning and development with new research and application, a different perspective, and a shift in practice away from traditional models.

Robert Havinghurst pioneered the "developmental task." He outlined in six distinct stages the long series of learning events which bring satisfaction and fulfillment to life. Adult development is divided into three categories: Early Adulthood, Middle Age, and Later Maturity. Generally, most adult life cycle writing follows Havinghurst's scheme.

Lawrence Kohlberg argues that moral reasoning develops throughout the entire life of a person. His theory is defined by a progression of sequenced, invariant, universal growth through discrete levels. Each level has two stages. Level 1 is oriented toward punishment and obedience. The second part of this level deals with the individual and his or her idea of reciprocal exchange. Level 2, stage 3, focuses upon conventional morality and involves conforming to and maintaining the social order. Stage 4 in level 2 maintains this social order by adhering to rules. Level 3 highlights social contract and the individual's rights. Stage 6 of this level is called the *universal ethical principle*.

Daniel Levinson's emphasis on an orderly sequence of events in an adult's life has wide appeal. Gail Sheehy and others have made these views highly visible and accessible, although the samples on which the theory is based are not broad. However, it is an interesting perspective, coming from the social and behavioral areas of life. Occupation, family situation, and changes in view of self add richness to the understanding of adult development.

Roger Gould expands upon the social developmental aspect of an adult's life. Valuable contributions include assessing the nature and character of adult perspective during the developmental process—for example, adults become more tolerant of themselves in relation to the complexities of life's situations. There is more room for self-direction, assuming responsibility, and gaining insight the longer one lives.

Carol Gilligan cautions that most adult research is based on male development. She asserts that women have different perspectives in ego development, and therefore should be considered different in their development of such. "Given the difference in women's conception of self and morality, it is not surprising that women bring to the life cycle a different point of view and that they order human experiences in terms of different priorities" (Gilligan, 1979, 431).

James Fowler has set the contemporary stage for the understanding of faith development. In his view, there are six stages of faith development starting with childhood and moving through to mature adulthood. Stages 1 and 2 normally occur during childhood. In these stages, children receive and respect what the significant others in their lives tell them. Stage 3 becomes a place where many adults find a continual state of equilibrium. In this stage, the adult has an "ideology," which is basically a cluster of values with a consistent framework and corresponding authority structure. Stage 4 is where adults begin to own their faith. Here, the adult takes responsibility for her own commitments. It is a faith that is examined. Tensions between self and community are maintained, and meaning is found in the search and development of service to others and in ratifying one's own judgments. Typical of midlife, stage 5 asserts that there is a deeper self, with all of the inconsistencies and verities, and seeks to balance personal viewpoints with those of others. It is conjunctive faith. Stage 6 is "universalizing faith." Adults rarely achieve this level, but when they do there is a maturity and wholeness in their viewpoint of God and others. They are able to focus inward, find meaning in their world, and become contagious in their impact on others.

Adult Life Cycle. "The adult life cycle refers to the changing patterns of needs, interests, and responses which occur in adulthood from the transition out of adolescence through mid-life and older adulthood to death" (Bruning, 1982, 29). John Dettoni uses Jesus' life as an example, and states that "adult psychology [should be viewed] from a whole person developmental perspective. Whole person development occurs in six major domains: physical, cognitive, social, affective, moral, and faith/spiritual. These domains cover the whole of human personality" (Dettoni, 1993, 77). Although some adult developmentalists divide the adult life cycle into as many as nine stages, we will define three basic adult stages, realizing there could be any number of divisions under each.

Young Adults. Young adults generally have a widening perspective on the world around them. Significant dissonance also occurs within them because of the competing self-interest and world concern that most young adults experience. Idealism, the concept that things will turn out the way they *should*, can often lead to cynicism. However, many young adults express their ideals in active engagement with causes, issues, or a striving for success.

Another developmental task for young adults is the intimacy-independence struggle. It could be called the "dance of the porcupines on a cold day." There is a seemingly natural draw to intimacy. The "wanting to be close" feeling drives young adults together, much like a cold day would cause two porcupines to huddle for warmth. But it is at this point that controversy arises. Young adults also want and need independence from their families in order to develop a sense of self-identity. This structure for life develops in the young adult years, but will be utilized throughout life.

Young adults face many choices as they launch on the vocational voyage. These options are often extended through schooling or delayed decisions. There is a conflict between exploration and settling down, and the young adult's identity needs to be developed or there will be difficulty growing in this area. Experiences, interests, and personality all shape the vocational choices and development of a career. With the resurgent emphasis upon mentoring, career tracks, and apprenticeships, it seems obvious that this vocational area has many developmental tasks for the young adult. Women may experience a particularly pointed conflict during this time. Seeking opportunities to develop in a chosen field of work may be hindered by external expectations of family, church, or community. These conflicts may also be generated from within, where values and desires collide. The need to balance work and family is not unique to the young adult female. Men may also struggle with this, as do older adults of both genders.

Launching a family or stabilizing singleness is a noticeable task among young adults. Marriage and the issues of mate selection surface in the young adult's life. Some find satisfaction in remaining single and in planning to remain so. Still others are frustrated in their development, wanting to be married, yet for any number of reasons finding a union unavailable. Isolation can easily occur, but not just among single persons. Parenthood presents another set of adjustments. Often young adults seem ill-prepared for the challenges and joys of raising children. Divorce is a growing problem among young adults. Starting over

again is difficult, and confidence seems to be lacking. Yet many adults discover wholeness and development even in spite of a divorce.

Moral thinking begins to refine itself during the young adult years. The "owning of one's faith," as opposed to accepting parental or other significant others' opinions, results in growth, or at times, stagnation. Growing in the areas of empathy, risk taking, and exploration, facing life's questions and issues, and gaining a sense of one's own responsibility seem to trace the moral development of young adults.

Middle Adults. Transition is perhaps the best word to describe the developmental tasks of this age group. The midlife crisis is one of the most notable transitions during the years from age 35 or 40 to age 60 or 65. Middle adults feel like the "between" generation, since many of them will take care of their parents for as long as they raise their children. Physical and mental powers usually plateau during this time period. Middle adults begin to count backward as they describe the time they feel they have left and not the time they have already spent.

In the world of vocation, reaching and maintaining satisfactory performance is of crucial concern. Perhaps related is the issue of what to do with one's leisure. Polarities begin to surface and can be seen most readily at work—young-old, creativity-destruction, masculine-feminine, and attachment-separateness. It is at this stage that most adults expect themselves to be most productive, and this can lead to frustration as goals and expectations may have to be adjusted or changed to accommodate events or circumstances of midlife.

Family relationships can prove to be the most challenging. Relating in a meaningful way to one's spouse, launching children into the world, and experiencing the "empty-nest syndrome" all have their joys and struggles. Some middle adults must adjust to changes in sexual expression, and some must deal with the loss of a spouse. Singles have the challenge of building a positive identity and hospitality without a spouse's assistance. It would seem that the storm that occurs in some homes regarding adolescent maturation can be superseded by the weighty decisions of caring for aging parents.

In the area of faith development, evidence supports the idea that middle adulthood can be a rich time of faith expression. However, many middle adults are tempted to back off from their faith or lose zeal. Authenticity and mentoring the next generation may replace the early adult drive, but whole person development is much more in view for the middle adult.

Senior Adults. The graying of America presents unprecedented developmental tasks. The life span of some senior adults will create unique challenges. Social insecurity because of financial struggles may occur. Adjusting to physical decline and health issues is a major concern. Attitudes toward aging and retirement do not help this process. Many people do not picture senior adults as joyful people. This is a gross misconception, as most senior adults succeed in adjusting to retirement, living on reduced income, and discovering different ways of working. For many the completion of life goals is very satisfying and enables them to prepare for whatever declines may be ahead.

Meeting social and civic obligations gives the senior adult many significant roles. Serving as wise leaders in church, home, and community, grandparenting, mentoring, and finding unselfish service to others are admirable opportunities for senior adults. Finding personal worth beyond work or family roles may present a challenge. Dealing with the loss of loved ones is inevitable.

Some seniors seem to disengage themselves from the world. Retirement shields some from the work they have enjoyed. Adjusting to new, perhaps more limited roles is important. Finding suitable living arrangements for the senior years can also be a concern. Health issues and diminishing physical acuity are realities that need to be faced in addition to death and grieving.

Integrity and meaningfulness in old age are related to issues of faith. Establishing affiliation with one's age group is a key area of development. Expressing faith in a biblical way, honoring old age and not despising it, is a very satisfying endeavor of this age group.

Application to Christian Education. Some people argue that one does not need to study adult development in order to practice Christian education. They assert that only faith issues and spiritual dimensions should be the concern of the Christian educator. However, McKenzie (1982) warns that one cannot isolate the various parts of human development from one another; they are parts of a multifaceted system called the adult personality (9–23). However, the Bible seems to encourage a differentiation among adults.

The Bible has much to say regarding both old age and young men. Young adults are encouraged to honor older people (Lev. 19:32). Proverbs 20:29 talks about the differences between the glory of young men (their strength), and that of senior adults (their gray heads). Ecclesiastes warns the young to remember the Lord (Eccles. 12:1). First John 2:12–14 describes three levels of adult believers in their faith development. Some applications may be made:

1. Age should be seen as a stewardship from God (Ps. 90:12).
2. Older men and women should be treated with much respect (1 Tim. 5:1–2).
3. Older adults should teach younger adults how to live in faith and life (Titus 2).

4. Youth especially should be encouraged to walk with the Lord (Eccles. 12:1, 6).
5. Different kinds of ministry for the different age groups is expected (Ps. 78; 1 Cor. 13:11).

GREGORY C. CARLSON

Bibliography. C. Bruning (1982), *Faith Development in the Adult Life Cycle;* J. H. Dettoni (1993), *The Christian Educator's Handbook on Adult Education;* E. Erikson (1963), *Becoming Adult, Becoming Christian;* idem (1950), *Childhood and Society;* idem (1982), *The Life Cycle Completed;* J. Fowler (1981), *Stages of Faith: The Psychology of Human Development and the Quest for Meaning;* C. Gilligan (1979), *Harvard Educational Review* (1979): 431–36; R. Gould (1978), *Transformations: Growth and Change in Adult Life;* R. Havinghurst (1972), *Developmental Tasks and Education;* C. O. Houle (1976), *The Design of Education;* M. Knowles (1973), *The Adult Learner: A Neglected Species;* idem (1970), *The Modern Practice of Adult Education: From Pedagogy to Andragogy;* L. Kohlberg (1974), *Journal of Moral Education* 4 (1974): 5–16; D. J. Levinson (1978), *The Seasons of a Man's Life;* J. Loevinger and R. Wessler (1970), *Measuring Ego Development;* A. H. Maslow (1970), *Motivation and Personality;* L. McKenzie (1982), *The Religious Education of Adults;* C. M. Sell (1985, 1991), *Transitions Through Adult Life;* M. Tennant and P. Pogson (1995), *Learning and Change in the Adult Years: A Developmental Perspective.*

See also ANDRAGOGY; DEVELOPMENTAL TASKS; FAITH DEVELOPMENT; LATE ADULTHOOD; MIDDLE ADULTHOOD; MORAL REASONING, THEORY OF

Adult Division. Group division in the Christian education program. An adult is someone who is 18 years of age or older, has completed high school, or is married. An adult division can be one class or any number of classes and departments and a variety of ministries that target adults.

Within the adult division there is a wide diversity of ages and needs. Many factors must be considered when grouping and grading adults: age, marital status, special needs (e.g., parents of preschoolers), gender, and short-term interests (e.g., grief recovery).

Young adults are designated as being between the ages of 18 and 29 or 34. This span encompasses a great variety of individuals: some are more independent than others; some are continuing in educational pursuits while others are beginning a career; some are married and beginning a family; and others remain single.

Middle adulthood targets ages 30 or 35 to 55 or 59. Middle adults can be married, single (never having married), divorced, widowed, or remarried. Demographically,there are more adults in this age range than in other age spans.

Senior adults are over age 60. Due to improved medical care people are living longer so the number of adults in this group will likely increase. Because of major differences within this target area, many churches will likely consider dividing their senior members into younger and older groups.

The current emphasis on adult learning, fulfillment, and growth (in health, career change, and global involvement) makes this time in history one of increasing opportunity for adults. Creative possibilities are unfolding for adult ministry and Christian education.

JERRY M. STUBBLEFIELD

Bibliography. L. E. Coleman Jr. (1982), *Understanding Today's Adults;* F. C. Jordan (1986), *A Church Ministering to Adults.*

Adultery. Voluntary sexual intercourse between a married person and someone other than his or her spouse. It is a serious offense, and in Leviticus 20:10 the death sentence was pronounced as the penalty. Related to the concept of adultery are fornication and fornication of the mind; that is, voluntary sexual relations between an unmarried person and anyone else and, as Jesus indicated in the Sermon on the Mount, lustful thoughts.

Christian educators need to be cognizant of this cultural dynamic because human depravity, the erotic messages of the media, the progressive loosening of sexual mores across society, and the loss of moral imperatives have all converged to create an explosive growth of sexual liaisons outside of the marriage bond in the Western world. Not only is the conceptual ideal of sexual purity at stake in both the secular and sacred worlds, but cultural stability is at risk as well, as seen in the effects of adultery in this country and across the world over the last several decades: the proliferation of sexual diseases, the statistical demise of the number of women entering first-time marriage, the rise of divorce, and the increase of births to unwed mothers.

There are tremendous challenges ahead for the church. Adultery ought to be considered a sin that the church education program can aim to prevent. From prepubescence through adult education the biblical mandate and obvious desirability of sexual purity should be part of a well-founded program of discipleship. Appropriate and inappropriate physical engagement, control of the thought life, the positive difference a relationship with God can make sexually and relationally, and particularly the purifying activity of the Holy Spirit should be emphasized.

But as pervasive as adultery is in society, the tragic consequences should also be recognized as providing what have been called "trigger events," or crisis points, which indicate a crucial period of vulnerability that, if handled appropriately, may offer an avenue of growth. How these triggers or crises are addressed significantly affects the future life of the person, whether churched or not.

Christian education needs to provide settings of crisis management and teaching that can facilitate the Spirit's working in lives so that God's redemptive purposes might be achieved. Through Bible studies, counseling, friendship, and a community of hope and healing, adultery itself can be prevented and the injurious consequences dealt with appropriately.

MATT FRIEDEMAN

Adult Life Cycle. Process of the passage from the beginning of adulthood to death. This process is viewed to be progressive, sequential, and relatively stable from generation to generation.

The concept of the adult life cycle is a result of our growing understanding of human development. The adult life cycle is generally divided into a scheme that recognizes distinct patterns in developmental growth and behavior during the early, middle, and later years of adulthood. The initial stages of adulthood are characterized by an individual's increasing self-reliance and self-acceptance. As the individual gains independence and moves through the developmental tasks of adulthood, he or she assumes added responsibility for the nurturing of others. The process of progressive maturation culminates ideally in an acceptance of one's life and accomplishments, as well as peace with the approaching end of life.

The adult life cycle is often conceptualized by a journey motif that sees certain developmental tasks as milestones along the way. Some of these milestones include separation from parents and the establishment of independent living, becoming settled in a career, marriage, parenthood, the death of parents, menopause, retirement, and the approach of death. While adult development is strongly influenced by these and other developmental tasks, other factors may also affect the adult life cycle. Baltes, Reese, and Lispitt (1970) point to major historical events (e.g., war, economic depression, the sexual revolution, etc.), as well as to "non-normative influence," such as divorce, illness, and career downturns, as having considerable—though much less predictable— influence.

Some of the more prominent theorists of adult life cycle theory include Carl Jung (*The Stages of Life*), Erik Erikson (*Identity: Youth and Crisis*), and, more recently, Daniel Levinson (*The Seasons of a Man's Life*) and Gail Sheehy (*Passages*).

MARI GONLAG

Bibliography. P. B. Baltes, H. W. Reese, and L. P. Lispitt (1970), *Annual Review of Psychology* 31 (1970): 65–110; E. H. Erikson (1963), *Identity: Youth and Crisis;* F. M. Hudson (1991), *The Adult Years;* C. G. Jung (1933), *The Stages of Life*; D. J. Levinson (1978), *The Seasons of a Man's Life;* G. Sheehy (1976), *Passages;* idem (1995), *New Passages.*

See also ADULT DEVELOPMENT; ANDRAGOGY; ERIKSON, ERIK HOMBURGER; LEVINSON, DANIEL JACOB

Adult Models of Christian Education. Choosing the appropriate model of adult Christian education depends upon the purpose or function of the educational process. Whether one seeks to lead the adult learner in the acquisition of new information or in making a change in attitude or approach to life, the most effective models help the learner discover the truth for oneself.

In choosing a model for adult Christian education, an influencing factor is the fact that the model should focus on living life, not preparing for life, which is what most of us experienced in our elementary and secondary education and into our college and university studies. Any adult model must keep in mind the nature of adulthood and the various developmental tasks the adult faces as he or she progresses through the various stages of adulthood. Models of adult Christian education include the following.

Traditional Model. The traditional adult education model relies heavily on the input of information followed by discussion and integration. The teacher or facilitator has a significant role in this model, seeking primarily to impart knowledge. The leader has the primary responsibility for learning in this model; the learner interacts but usually does not take major responsibility for what happens in the teaching/learning process.

The usual flow of this model begins with a master teacher who presents the heavy content of a lesson, then breaks the larger group into small groups with a facilitator in each small group. The small group seeks to process and apply the truths taught by the master teacher. While this model is designed with a great deal of flexibility in that it can be used in both small and large group settings, an individual component can easily be added to the process.

Andragogical Model. Malcolm Knowles popularized this model for general adult education purposes. His model has been copied and modified by many adult Christian educators. Knowles set out to shift adult education from the model of pedagogy to andragogy. This model is successful because it recognizes some key characteristics of adult learners: (1) the concept of the learner (as persons mature, they move from dependency toward increasing self-directedness); (2) the role of the learner's experience (as people grow and develop they accumulate an increasing reservoir that becomes a rich resource for learning); (3) a readiness to learn (as people experience a need for something they are more ready to learn); and (4) an orientation to learning (adult learners see education as a process for developing increased competence to achieve their full potential in life) (Knowles, 1980, 47).

While Knowles developed andragogy for adult secular education, many adult Christian educators have seen the value of his ideas. The adult learner brings a wealth of experience to the learning situation. The Christian educator seeks to use this experience and to relate it to where the adult is in development both as an adult and as a Christian. This leads to the "teachable moment" when the adult has a deep need and a readiness to learn (Stubblefield, 1986, 239–55).

Intergenerational Model. Most churches have many generations making up their faith community. Few take advantage of the intergenerational approach in their Christian education ministry. Effective use of this model has children and adults working together at times and separately at other times. This model makes the family a group, ideally involving several families in the Christian education activity. This model can be used for either workshops or classes. Some churches use this model for three to six months, then return to age-graded classes.

Study Circle Model. "Study Circles involve formal groups of adults in a democratically directed learning process with the assistance of a facilitator. There is no teacher nor is there a prepackaged program which students are expected to follow" (Wickett, 1991, 128; see 128–37 for a complete description of this model). This model lends itself to social action and community building. The facilitator is not a resource person but is solely a process person. The study circle can help to build group solidarity or help the church to minister in a cause or mission. Using this model, learners begin to develop great respect for themselves and their colearners as they share in the teaching process. Since there is no teacher or authority figure, some find it easier to participate in this approach. This model works best when the membership is between five and twenty. A trained leader should be present for each session to lead the group in following a plan they have determined. An advantage is that this approach treats learners as equals in a democratic process and seeks the promotion of community learning and growth.

Distance Learning Model. Distance learning is now practiced in businesses and industry and in higher education. With the popularity of the personal computer, this is an arena that adult Christian education may find advantageous in the near future. Some elements of distance learning are "separation of teacher and learner through the process, an organization which plans and prepares the materials, use of technical media (print, audio, video, computer) to unite teacher and learner, a two-way communication process" (Wickett, 1991, 152).

Many institutions of higher education offer both required and elective courses, and sometimes even entire degree programs using this new technology. Many adult learners are eager for an opportunity to learn but for various reasons cannot be in a resident program. While lacking face-to-face encounters and nonverbal communication and though limited in expression of feelings, distance learning activities allow adult learners to participate at their own time and pace.

JERRY M. STUBBLEFIELD

Bibliography. D. Keegan (1990), *Foundations of Distance Education;* M. S. Knowles (1980), *The Modern Practice of Adult Education;* L. P. Oliver (1987), *Study Circles: Coming Together for Personal Growth and Social Change;* J. M. Stubblefield (1986), *A Church Ministering to Adults;* J. A. White (1988), *Intergenerational Religious Education: Models, Theory, and Prescription for Interage Life and Learning in the Faith Community;* R. E. Y. Wickett (1991), *Models of Adult Religious Education Practice.*

See also INTERGENERATIONAL LEARNING; KNOWLES, MALCOLM S.

Advanced Organizer. A teaching-learning tool or "scaffolding" that embodies the conceptual outline of a broader knowledge base that the students will encounter. It may take the form of a design, graphic, chart, acrostic, or table giving structure to the ideas and facts of a course of study. Making up the major concepts, propositions, and chief factors of a lesson or sequence, it presents a higher level of abstraction and generality than the learning material itself, thus distinguishing advanced organizers from introductory overviews or previews of the learning material. David Ausubel formulated the advanced organizer to provide students with a cognitive structure for comprehending material presented through lectures, readings, and other media. Since then, it has been one of the most researched concepts in the information-processing family.

Acrostics such as LEARNER (Learner, Expectation, Application, Retention, Need Equipping, and Revival) or TEACHER (Teacher, Education, Activity, Communication, Heart, Encouragement, Readiness), embody "laws" the teacher will cover.

The use of an advanced organizer has numerous values. It provides meaningful intellectual verbal learning as it facilitates logical thinking and strengthens the student's cognitive structures. It also provides an intellectual map with anchors for organizing the material and relating it to the larger curriculum. Its purpose is to explain, integrate, and interrelate the learning material.

GEORGE W. PATTERSON

Bibliography. D. P. Ausubel (1963), *The Psychology of Meaningful Verbal Learning;* idem (1968), *Educational Psychology: A Cognitive View;* B. Joyce and M. Weil (1972), *Models of Teaching.*

See also AUSUBEL, DAVID P.; COGNITIVE FIELD THEORY

Advent. The inaugural point from which the drama of the Christmas story unfolds. The term *advent* is derived from the Latin word *adventus* meaning "coming" or "arrival." It originated in Spain and Gaul during the fifth century, not long after the origin of the Christmas celebration. Advent possesses a mood of expectancy and is used primarily to describe a period of preparation and reflection about the coming of Christ. Originally, it is believed to have begun in mid-November as a time of preparation of candidates for baptism at Epiphany.

Advent has been recognized as the beginning of the church year and over time has varied from four to six weeks. One of the reasons this season was selected for attention was to weaken the gross and sensual festivals that heathens celebrated. The Greek church's observance of Advent was set at a period of forty days, but other churches have generally elected a four week period. By the time of the Middle Ages the four Sundays before Christmas became the accepted period for Advent services.

Advent is a season marked by light and color. A traditional part of the celebration is the lighting of four successive candles in a wreath of evergreens for each of the four weeks in Advent. A fifth candle representing Christ is placed in the middle of the wreath to be lit on Christmas Day and often throughout the eleven days of Christmas time. Violet or blue are the traditional liturgical colors for Advent.

Advent is a word used to refer not only to the birth of Christ but also to his *parousia*, or second coming at the end of time. This second advent does not have a date or time; it will arrive without warning.

DORIS BORCHERT

Advisory Board. *See* Board of Directors.

Affair. *See* Adultery.

Affection. *See* Affective Domain.

Affective Domain. More than 200 years ago Jonathan Edwards wrote that "true religion chiefly consists in holy affections," and more recently James Michael Lee (1985) claimed that "the acquisition of attitudes is one of the most crucial of all product outcomes in religious instruction" (56). Yet Christian educators often struggle with understanding these affections and with how best to assist students in acquiring them. Progress has been made since the time of Edwards's treatise, particularly in the last half century, yet much work remains to be done.

What makes up the affective domain? The *affective domain* is one of three areas or aspects that make up human experience, and for which educators write educational objectives. *Affect* has been variously described as consisting of emotions, feelings, dispositions, attitudes, values, motives, and beliefs. The other two areas are the cognitive domain (intellect/knowledge) and the conative domain (psychomotor/behavioral).

Krathwohl, Bloom, and Masia (1964) developed a *taxonomy* (i.e., classification or orderly arrangement) of objectives for education in the affective domain. The taxonomy consists of five categories as follows:

1.0 Receiving (Attending)
    1.1 Awareness
    1.2 Willingness to receive
    1.3 Controlled or selected attention
2.0 Responding
    2.1 Acquiescence in responding
    2.2 Willingness to respond
    2.3 Satisfaction in response
3.0 Valuing
    3.1 Acceptance of a value
    3.2 Preference for a value
    3.3 Commitment
4.0 Organization
    4.1 Conceptualization of a value
    4.2 Organization of a value system
5.0 Characterization by a value or value
    complex
    5.1 Generalized set
    5.2 Characterization

The developers explain that the organizing principle behind the taxonomy is "internalization"; that is, the student responds almost incidentally and quite passively to an environmental stimulus at the receiving level, but purposefully and with conviction at the characterization level. Educators can use this taxonomy as a helpful tool, but should recognize limitations that critics and the developers themselves have identified.

Compared to their work on the cognitive domain, Krathwohl, Bloom, and Masia (1964) "found the affective domain much more difficult to structure, and we are much less satisfied with the result" (v). Some of this difficulty is due to the complexity of the realities within the affective domain, which may partly explain the diversity of terminology used by different scholars for these realities, and the range of meanings given to the same terms. Wolterstorff (1980), for example, prefers to refer to the affective area as *tendencies*. Though there may be some advantage to his term, the substitution seems to confuse rather than clarify because other educators do not use it in this way.

Of the realities that make up the affective domain, Christian educators often pay least attention to emotions. Roberts (1982) could be right in explaining this avoidance by saying that emotions "may *seem* [italics added] to be intellectu-

ally disreputable" (12). Emotions are spontaneous and temporary responses of an individual to particular occurrences in life; however, the way that a person copes with or expresses emotions through overt action is controllable, and thus, educable. Certainly emotions are powerful forces in human existence and significant in the Christian life, and ought not to be eliminated from educational settings or concerns.

Attitudes share the feeling-tone of emotions but possess the longer-term character of dispositions; that is, they are relatively stable, consistent ways of responding to various stimuli. As in all areas of the affective domain, considerable differences of opinion exist between scholars as to the cognitive component of attitudes, yet most view them as primarily affective. Attitudes are not innate, but learned, and thus educators may facilitate acquisition of attitudes such as trust, love, penitence, compassion, and humility, among others (Jonathan Edwards includes "zeal" in his list of desirable religious affections). Developmental periods that are prime for attitude formation are early childhood, adolescence, and young adulthood. Attitudes toward learning, church, or school have a significant bearing on the level of student participation.

Values are closely related to attitudes, with values being "more deeply internalized" (Ringness, 1975, 23). Values clarification exercises may assist student in identifying what values they hold subjectively, but are inadequate for teaching values that inhere objectively within God and his creation.

Beliefs have a strong cognitive base (i.e., of thought and rationality), but are more than simply a matter of knowing doctrine. At the very least, the holding of a particular belief has an affective quality to it. Little (1983) emphasizes the cognitive aspect of belief, while drawing attention to faith as the religiously important (and affective) category. While a helpful distinction, it seems to strip belief of any affective component. Perhaps a better distinction is the one proposed by Astley (1994) regarding "belief-that" and "belief-in." *Belief-that* includes knowledge about certain things (e.g., God, the church, sin), but does not provide salvific power. In this sense, people may believe that God exists or that God loves them, for "even the demons believe" (James 2:19 NIV). On the other hand, *belief-in* ties such knowledge together with attitudes of trust and worship/adoration.

How is the affective domain to be distinguished from the other domains? The relationship of the three domains is often discussed, particularly the relationship between cognition and affect. A surface understanding of the Bloom (1956) and Krathwohl (1964) taxonomies may make the domains appear to be discrete entities. A careful reading of their work cannot maintain confidence in such a conclusion, however. They recognize the domains as abstractions for the purpose of analysis (and therefore understanding), consistent with the ways in which the Greek philosophers talked about humanity and with the objectives of contemporary educators. Yet they assert that persons respond as whole individuals. Literature supporting the notion that affective learning is inextricably linked with cognitive and psychomotor functioning is growing. No basis exists for treating "heart-learning" and "head-learning" as separate realities, or choosing one as opposed to the other as the goal of real Christian education.

The importance of the affective domain for Christian education is often underestimated. A review of pre-1980 survey texts in Christian education, especially those from evangelical publishers, will find very few references to the affective domain or its various components. With characteristic concern for the authority of Scripture (verbalized religion), most emphasis has been placed on cognitive learning. Church leaders have commonly assumed that a natural and automatic consequence of this learning would be acquisition of appropriate attitudes and values. However, research does not bear this out and even shows learning in the two domains to be independent. For values and attitudes to be acquired, educators must give attention to them in their planning and practice.

There are two ways in which affective issues come into play in Christian education. First is the affective state of students as they enter the learning situation. Motivation for learning is a key issue here, and it has been frequently addressed by writers in educational psychology. Students' self-appraisal also plays an important role in how they enter into learning activities. Considerable research is extant regarding self-concept of students globally and as learners.

Second, some scholars write about "affective content" for Christian education; however, this does not mean that attitudes, values, and beliefs are "taught" in the same way that one might teach the stages of development or Pauline theology. In fact, such things may be said to be nurtured, shaped, or formed in the student rather than taught in the common sense, because affective learning occurs best through nonverbal, nonformal, experiential means. Horace Bushnell (1860) sparked this idea in his well-known book *Christian Nurture*. Long before him, the catechumenate of the early church provided not only an opportunity for new believers to receive doctrinal instruction, but also a probationary period to develop Christian attitudes, values, and behavior.

Catholic religious educator James Michael Lee (1985) strongly asserts that attitudes can be taught intentionally and systematically as the Christian educator gives attention to the four components of the educational enterprise: teacher, learner, subject matter, and environment. However, systematic and intentional teaching does not require direct means. It's one thing to tell a student about love, quite another thing to enable him to become loving. Different learning strategies need to be employed for affective objectives than those used for objectives in the cognitive or psychomotor domains, Lee acknowledges. Strategies such as role-playing and simulations that focus on experiencing rather than verbalizing will best facilitate affective learning.

One objection raised against Lee from an evangelical perspective, however, is that his social scientific approach to religious education leaves little room for the Holy Spirit. In his view attitudes are changed through the instrumentality of human teachers; he does not acknowledge the unmediated work of God's Spirit within the hearts of students. Susanne Johnson (1989), on the other hand, proposes to "view spiritual formation as the key organizing concept for Christian education" (13). In her view, believers are shaped into the character of Christ (her concern for affective learning) through participation in the means of grace (e.g., sacraments, prayer/meditation, study of Scripture). This shaping occurs within the context of the faith community, and is facilitated by pastors and Christian educators, but it is essentially a graceful operation of God's Spirit within the hearts of students.

Christian educators can be instrumental in students' acquisition of "holy affections" as they learn both human affective functioning and the formative work of the Holy Spirit.

CLAIR ALLEN BUDD

Bibliography. J. Astley (1994), *The Philosophy of Christian Religious Education;* B. Bloom, ed. (1956), *Taxonomy of Educational Objectives, Handbook I: Cognitive Domain;* H. Bushnell (1860), *Christian Nurture;* S. Johnson (1989), *Christian Spiritual Formation in the Church and Classroom;* D. R. Krathwohl, B. S. Bloom, and B. B. Masia (1964), *Taxonomy of Educational Objectives: Book 2, Affective Domain;* J. M. Lee (1985), *The Content of Religious Instruction;* S. Little (1983), *To Set One's Heart: Belief and Teaching in the Church;* T. A. Ringness (1975), *The Affective Domain in Education;* R. C. Roberts (1982), *Spirituality and Human Emotion;* N. Wolterstorff (1980), *Educating for Responsible Action.*

See also BELIEF; LEE, JAMES MICHAEL; VALUES CLARIFICATION; VALUES EDUCATION

Afro-American Heritage. *See* Black Theology and Christian Education.

Agape. *See* Love.

Aged/Retired. *See* Elderly.

Agent. *See* Broker.

Age of Accountability. The point in time at which an individual understands the implications of his or her moral judgments. As children move from performing concrete mental operations to formal thinking, they begin to understand that there is a morality outside their immediate circumstances. For example, toddlers may comprehend that disobeying their parents will result in corporal punishment, but cannot yet grasp the eternal significance of sin. However, teenagers understand that their moral choices will lead not merely to reward or punishment because moral behaviors have consequences beyond the immediate.

Scholars believe ancient Jews simply chose a date at which a person was considered accountable; thus the *bar/bat mitzvah*, which occurs on one's thirteenth birthday, signifies the entry into adulthood. Similarly the Roman Catholic Church acknowledges the age of accountability at about age fourteen, when a young person is confirmed. Evangelicals have for the most part believed that the age of accountability occurs when a child begins to comprehend the issue of his or her own sinfulness and the response of repentance demanded by God.

Many Christians believe that a child is innocent in God's eyes until the child can understand the issue of moral choice, and would not be held eternally accountable for his or her sin. In recent years educational psychology has revealed that the age at which one develops an advanced understanding of moral judgment varies widely, and research suggests that cultural pressures are causing people to mature at ever younger ages.

JERRY CHIP MACGREGOR

See also BAR/BAT MITZVAH; JEWISH EDUCATION; ROMAN CATHOLIC EDUCATION

Aging, Ageism. Demographic data that reflect rapidly growing numbers of those over 65, and evidence that the spiritual dimension becomes more salient in old age, make topics related to aging relevant for Christian educators.

Demographic Data. United Nations studies indicate increasing aging populations in Africa, Latin America, and parts of Asia. According to data from the U.S. Bureau of the Census (1992), by the year 2000, it is estimated that almost 35 million Americans, or 13 percent of the population, will be 65 and older. By 2030, 65.5 million or 22 percent people will be over 65. The age group of those over 85 is growing faster than any other. While the total population of the United States increased by 39 percent between 1960 and 1990, the group over 85 increased during those same years by 232 percent.

Social Conditions Related to Aging. Contrary to general perceptions, most elders are quite happy with their lives and experience an adequate support network. There are, however, some difficulties that they face. While many aging persons retire in comfort and ease, 24 percent live below or near the poverty level. African Americans, Hispanics, and women have increased potential for poverty. Seven out of ten elders own their own homes. Most others live in rented apartments, while a very small number, approximately one out of twenty, requires the care of a nursing home. Health care will continue to be an important factor in the lives of elders. Even though over 70 percent report their health as good to excellent, almost half report some kind of chronic condition that requires regular medical care and limits regular activity.

The Religious/Spiritual Domain. There is ample evidence to support the significance of the spiritual domain for the elderly. Religious feelings and beliefs increase with age. Moberg (1990) reports on the Princeton Research for Religion findings from the last fifty years, which demonstrate that people over 65 are more likely than any other age group to attend church, participate in religious groups, and find personal religious practices helpful. While health is the key predictor of morale in the elderly, Koenig (1994) found that once the variance for health is removed, religious behaviors and attitude are the best predictors of positive morale.

Biblical Perspectives on Aging. In keeping with their oriental culture, biblical writers promoted a view of aging that provides a contrast to current Western tradition. A direct command to respect elders is given in Leviticus 19:32—"You shall rise up before the grayheaded, and honor the aged." Long life was hoped for and received as evidence of God's blessing (Job 42:17; Pss. 61:6; 91:16). Long life was a reward for fearing the Lord (Prov. 9:11; 10:27), keeping the commandments (Prov. 3:2), and honoring parents (Exod. 20:12; Eph. 6:1–3). Old age was equated with wisdom and the elders provided leadership in the community (Ruth 4:2; 1 Sam. 16:4; Prov. 31:23). Paul presumed that the older men and women would be teaching younger believers.

Ageism. Ageism is the practice of discriminating against a person or group on the basis of age. Although there are instances in which a young person is the victim of age discrimination, ageism is most often experienced by the elderly. The discrimination may begin in hiring and mandatory retirement policies, but sometimes extends to housing circumstances and can result in poor health care. Ageism is rooted in the value Western culture places on youthfulness. Older people are consistently rated more negatively than younger people on all characteristics. In the church, ageism is experienced when elders are segregated, when the needs of younger members and families are the focus of program development at the expense of attention to the needs of the elderly, or when presumption about ability is based solely on a person's age.

Educational Ministry Strategies. Educational strategies for elders in the church focus on many dimensions of their lives. In some settings where there are limited resources in the community, it is appropriate for the church to consider meeting nutritional, medical, housing, legal, and other support needs of the elderly. There are spiritual needs elders express that can be met in class and small group settings as well as in conversations with individuals. The need to process loss and to reconstruct their lives following loss is key. Being involved in Bible study can give elders the opportunity to ask questions and to explore spiritual issues that concern them. The church can be a place of enrichment and service for elders. Educational strategies need to focus on the whole congregation. Well-designed intergenerational experiences have the potential to provide mutual benefit for young and old while diminishing attitudes of ageism.

FAYE CHECHOWICH

Bibliography. M. Kimble, S. McFadden, J. Ellor, and J. Seeber (1995), *Aging, Spirituality, and Religion;* H. G. Koenig (1994), *Aging and God: Spiritual Pathways to Mental Health in Midlife and Later Years;* H. Koenig, J. Kvale, and C. Ferrel (1988), *The Gerontologist* 28 (1988): 18–28; D. Moberg (1990), *Gerontology: Perspectives and Issues;* J. J. Seeber (1990), *Spiritual Maturity in the Later Years;* L. Vogel (1984), *The Religious Education of Older Adults.*

See also ADULT CHRISTIAN EDUCATION; ELDERLY; LATE ADULTHOOD

Agnostic. *See* Atheism.

Agreement. *See* Contract.

Alcoholism. Without a doubt the number one drug problem in America is alcoholism. The statistics are staggering. Abusers and hard-core alcoholics are estimated to number over 18 million people. Every *day* Americans consume 16.9 million gallons of beer and 1.5 million gallons of hard liquor. Ten percent of people trying their first drink will become alcoholics. Use of alcohol is associated with the leading causes of death and injury among teenagers and young adults (statistics from The Center for Disease Control, 1996).

Alcohol is a drug. Its scientific name is ethyl alcohol and it is classified as a depressant, the drug class that includes barbiturates and tranquilizers. Once absorbed into the bloodstream alcohol acts on the central nervous system. In small doses (one can of beer contains the alcohol equivalent of a shot glass of 80 proof whiskey) it causes eu-

phoria and a mild relaxed feeling. It affects speech, vision, and coordination. Intoxication occurs when higher doses are taken. Responses are varied. Some people feel more outgoing and giddy, while others feel depressed, aggressive, or hostile. An overdose of alcohol can cause unconsciousness, respiratory failure, and death.

Alcoholism is often a familial problem. Research suggests that there may be a genetic predisposition, and that a child of an alcoholic parent runs a much greater risk of becoming an alcoholic. Hence, the benefits of stopping the alcoholic cycle are greatly multiplied when viewed through a generational perspective.

The church's response to the problem of alcohol abuse is varied. Recent efforts include books for alcoholics, their families, and adult children of alcoholics. Recovery groups have proliferated. Many are based on the twelve-step process developed by Sam Shoemaker for Alcoholics Anonymous more than fifty years ago. Youth groups have formed Alateen chapters. Resources are available from Recovery Ministries, Serendipity House, and The National Association of Christians in Recovery. Professional, Christ-centered treatment centers include New Life Treatment Centers, Minirth-Meier Hospitals, Rapha Hospitals, and Lifegate.

Only Christ can bring the alcoholic true healing and deliverance. As he demonstrates with Lazarus in John 11, our Lord chooses others to help unwrap those things that enslave and bind. Through loving support and patience, recovery from alcohol dependency is possible. In Jesus Christ the church can offer hope to a world lost in dependencies and codependencies.

JAMES A. DAVIES

See also ADULT CHILDREN OF ALCOHOLICS; RECOVERY MINISTRIES; SUPPORT GROUP; TWELVE-STEP PROGRAM

Alcuin (735–804). English monk, teacher, administrator, friend of Charlemagne, and prime mover in the pursuit of the king's religious and cultural ambitions for his empire. Of noble birth himself, Alcuin had absorbed the Latin classics under the tutelage of Egbert, archbishop of York and student of the Venerable Bede. In 782, Charlemagne called Alcuin from the cathedral school in York to head his palace school for Frankish nobility in Aachen. The king eventually appointed him abbot of the monastery of St. Martin of Tours in 796 in order that he might establish there a model for cloister schools.

Alcuin's academic writings contain no original theories, but reflect his concern for providing his students a broad education from a Christian point of view. He interpreted Proverbs 9:1—"Wisdom has built her house; she has hewn out its seven pillars"—as referring to the trivium and quadrivium of the seven liberal arts. Consequently, his books are textbooks and summaries of the classic Latin works on grammar, logic, and the like.

It is no accident that the schools of York, Aachen, and Tours flourished under Alcuin's leadership. He had outstanding administrative gifts, and actively used them to further the campaign of Charles to revive learning and culture in his realm. In a series of decrees that historians believe reflect the influence, if not the direct involvement of Alcuin, the king legislated, for example, that every officiating cleric have a certain minimal level of education, that reading schools be established, and that every man should send his son to school and allow him to stay until properly educated.

The most famous document was a circular letter from the king to the leaders of the church. In the only extant copy, addressed to the abbot of Fulda, Charles complains of rumors of uneducated monks. He expresses his concern that this will impede their understanding of and ability to teach the Holy Scriptures, and he demands that immediate steps be taken to teach the clergy to read and speak correctly.

But perhaps Alcuin's greatest contribution is reflected in the lives and writings of his disciples and friends, such as Rabanus Maurus at Fulda, who shared his passion for Christian learning and teaching. The picture we have from the accounts of others and from what remains of Alcuin's own voluminous correspondence is not one of a dull academic. He appears rather as a vibrant and revered master educator, full of poetry and riddles, humor and wisdom. Alcuin corresponded and conversed ceaselessly with men and women of every station, and was deeply concerned for the welfare of the people of his day. Fear did not keep Alcuin from rebuking kings and bishops about their social, educational, and spiritual responsibilities to those under their authority. He admonished them to educate the clergy and to teach people to read the Bible, including the young. Such was his personal influence that it was said that the brethren of the Abbey of St. Martin complained that their new abbot had brought with him a constant swarm of visitors.

MARK H. HEINEMANN

American Sunday School Union. While Robert Raikes is known as the "Father of the Sunday School," there were several efforts that preceded those of Raikes. In England, Hannah Ball, a pious Methodist, brought together a "wild little company" for Bible instruction on Sundays in her home in 1763. John Wesley was known to have taught the Bible to children in 1735 during his missionary work in Georgia (Lynn and Wright, 1980).

Joseph Alleine, a Puritan preacher, taught Scripture to children weekly. He also began a Sunday school for sixty to seventy children in Bath, England, in 1660. C. B. Eavey asserts that there were "many such attempts in England, Ireland, Scotland, Wales, and America." Without question William Fox, founder of the Sunday School Society in England, did more than any other person to spread the methods of ministry employed by the well-known Mr. Raikes (Eavey, 1964, 22).

Raikes was a newspaper publisher of some renown. His father had a profound desire to help the poor and relieve them of their distress. When his father died, Raikes inherited his *Gloucester Journal*, which he used to draw attention to the plight of the unfortunate. This went on for a period of years without much response. In 1780 he began a Sunday school in Mrs. Meredith's kitchen in the area known as Sooty Alley. He deemed it worthless to speak to the parents for they would not respond. They could do nothing with their own children. Raikes was the disciplinarian in his Sunday school who "strapped or caned" the most obstreperous.

In time Raikes started a number of Sunday schools in the poor areas of Gloucester. He first saw his efforts as an experiment. As he passed from the experimental stage, Raikes gained advice from John and Charles Wesley, George Whitfield, his good friend William Fox, and William Wilberforce. Fox and Wilberforce visited the schools and gave encouragement and counsel to Raikes, who finally published some of the children's achievements in his newspaper on November 3, 1783. From then on some pulpits gave him limited approval but most of the preachers neither identified with this tiny movement nor provided financial aid or teachers for this mission.

There was considerable opposition to the Sunday school work from the clergy. Even the Archbishop of Canterbury called the Anglican bishops together to decide how they might stop it. However, the opposition and up-front negativism subsided, and good people, lay and clergy, softened and embraced the Sunday school for their own children. When Raikes died in 1811, Sunday schools were wholeheartedly supported and the total attendance had reached 400,000 children. Following Raikes and Count Zinzendorf, from whom he had learned so much, John Wesley stressed work among the children and eventually founded a Christian academy.

As the Sunday school movement spread to the United States a highly motivated and dedicated group of men and women were ready to attempt great things. Little is known about the First Day Society which was formed in 1790. C. B. Eavey (1964) states: "The remarkable development of the Sunday school was due largely to the zeal, insight, courage, and statesmanship of the leaders of the movement. Chief among these were the manager, officers, and missionaries of the American Sunday School Union, the central agency of Sunday school progress for more than four decades. Though opposed and resisted initially, these devoted laymen successfully planned and carried out a series of enterprises that made the Sunday school an effective agency of Christian education, accepted by churches of every denomination throughout the nation" (22).

One of the strengths of the movement was the powerful thrust of working together theologically in a united stance. The nineteenth century was one in which the gospel of Jesus Christ was preached with clarity and from a singular point of view that was almost thoroughly evangelical until 1875. "By no means perfect, America's oldest independent home mission deserves credit for some remarkable achievements" (Mattocks, 1980, 4).

The ASSU began as the Philadelphia Sunday and Adult School Union in 1817. In 1824 it became the American Sunday School Union. By 1831 it had proposed a mission called the Mississippi Valley Enterprise, and within two years it had established 5,000 Sunday schools reaching 400,000 students. By 1859 the American Tract Society (founded in 1825) joined forces with the ASSU by supplying some of the printed materials for the public libraries it founded. "Three-fifths of all public lending libraries in the United States were the Sunday school libraries planted by the American Sunday School Union" (Mattocks, 1980, 4).

These Sunday school missionaries had a substantive role in ridding the country of ignorance and illiteracy among children on the frontier. Creative and innovative, the ASSU rode on the cutting edge of evangelism being done on America's frontier. In addition, the organization had burgeoning ministries with minorities including Indians, Chinese, and African-Americans. Evangelical theologians Charles Hodge, Philip Schaff, B. B. Warfield, and preacher-teacher F. B. Meyer added strength to the ASSU's efforts.

Historical figures were associated with the Union included Francis Scott Key. The following were vice presidents or managers: Bushrod Washington, nephew of George Washington and Associate Justice of the U.S. Supreme Court; Timothy Dwight, great-grandson of Jonathan Edwards and son of the president of Yale College; the Honorable James Pollock, governor of Pennsylvania and Director of the U.S. Mint, who was responsible for inscribing "In God We Trust" on our coins; and General Oliver O. Howard, who was appointed to head the Freedman's Bureau and after whom Howard University of Washington, D.C., was named.

In 1974 the name of the ASSU was changed to the American Missionary Fellowship. It is now based in Villanova, Pennsylvania. The organization, while no longer in the spotlight on the American scene, continues to serve in inner city ministries and in formerly closed churches in rural areas Many volunteers back the tireless efforts of 125 missionary families who serve Christ and his church.

WARREN S. BENSON

Bibliography. C. B. Eavey (1964), *History of Christian Education;* E. R. W. Lynn and E. Wright (1980), *The Big Little School;* R. Mattocks (1980), *On the Move: A Pictorial History of American Missionary Fellowship,* 1790–1980; *200 Years of Sunday School;* E. W. Rice (1971), *The Sunday School Movement (1780–1917) and the American Sunday School Union (1817–1917);* J. C. Wilhoit (1983), "An Examination of the Educational Principles of an Early Nineteenth Sunday School Curriculum: *The Union Questions,*" unpublished doctoral dissertation; W. R. Willis (1980), *200 Years and Still Counting.*

Analytic Philosophy of Education. Analytic philosophy has only recently been used to delineate a certain kind of philosophical inquiry. There has been widespread concern that this approach to philosophy is not equal to the older, more traditional philosophies. Some would deny that analytical philosophy is a philosophy at all but regard it only as a method of philosophical investigation. Accordingly, the effects of analytical philosophy on education have been ameliorated.

At the heart of this philosophical method is a desire to clarify the language and methods used to communicate ideas. Some claim that analytical philosophy has been derived from realism through the representative writings of G. E. Moore and Bertrand Russell. Others place the beginnings with logical positivism and the writings of Auguste Comte. Later writers in this movement would include A. J. Ayer, Ludwig Wittgenstein, and Gilbert Ryle.

A primary source for analytic philosophy is the writings of Bertrand Russell and Alfred North Whitehead, in *Principia Mathematica.* This "theory of descriptions" seeks precision in the clarifying of meanings, akin to mathematical precision. Ludwig Wittgenstein's *Tractates Logico-Philosophicus* said philosophy should not produce propositions; it merely clarifies the meaning of the propositions. Ayer used the verifiability criterion of meaning, which is a type of inductive approach to philosophy. Generalizations are held tentatively until it can be empirically verified if something is true or false. Gilbert Ryle, a British philosopher, wrote *The Concept of the Mind* and maintained that we have confused "knowing that" and "knowing how."

Though it is agreed that the analytical movement has few beliefs about philosophical concerns such as metaphysics or axiology, its focus on epistemology and logic does not allow it to be assumption-free. When the assumptions of analytic philosophy are explored, the difficulty with this method becomes apparent. For example, repudiating propositions is done by assuming that some propositions are incorrect and that others are correct. When the standard for truth is set aside, no standard exists to determine what is correct and what is not. To claim that the propositions about clarity are correct and other propositions that do not match the clarification propositions are false is illogical. What analytic philosophers appear to have done is to substitute one set of assumptions about truth for another. Instead of clarifying language, there is confusion.

Realizing the difficulty this position reveals should place Christian educators on the alert. The most critical area to watch is change in the interpretation of Scripture. In an effort to clarify meanings, it is possible that words are redefined or used in ways that reduce the ability of persons to communicate. How can a solid theology be built on a shaky foundation of hermeneutics and exegesis? Further, how can a solid base of ministry practice be built on a shifting and unsettled theology?

If great care is used regarding the assumptions involved in analytic philosophy, then it is possible to use the methodology to enrich Christian education. One such use could be the clarification of the values we claim to possess. While analytical philosophy claims no values, the Christian educator can explicate those values that need to be transmitted to the next generation. Another use that analytic philosophy can have for Christian educators is to help us write clear outcome statements. Fuzzy and unclear terms used to state educational outcomes will prove to be worthless. Precision can be very helpful in order to highlight what is intended as well as providing an adequate means to evaluate achievement.

ROBERT J. RADCLIFFE

Bibliography. V. C. Morris and Y. Pai (1976), *Philosophy and the American School;* H. A. Ozman and S. M. Craver (1986), *Philosophical Foundations of Education;* M. L. Peterson (1986), *The Philosophy of Education: Issues and Options;* I. Scheffler (1960), *The Language of Education;* H. H. Titus, M. S. Smith, and R. T. Nolan (1986), *Living Issues in Philosophy.*

Analytic Psychology. *See* Jung, Carl Gustav.

Ancient Foundations. Early cultural influences including Sumerian, Egyptian, Indian, and Chinese. The concept that "people influence thought and make history," and "the assumption that a gradual development and clarification of ideas over the years is essential" (Gangel and Benson, 1983, 13) leads to a study of the educational ideas and philosophies that are among the foundations of today's practice.

Sumerian. The first known center of education and learning is the Sumerian academy, *Edubba* (literally, "house of tablets"), in the third millennium B.C. Archaeological finds of school texts date back to 2,500 B.C. (Kramer, 1961, 253).

The Sumerians inhabited cities in the valley between the Tigris and the Euphrates rivers, and each city was independent, with its own local deity, temples, buildings, and rulers. Sumerians are credited with the invention of writing and the cuneiform script, the earliest recorded stories of the creation and the flood, and laws that were the basis for the famous Code of Hammurabi.

Edubbas, the centers of learning, were attached to Sumerian temples, and students were instructed in the "art" (Woolley, 1928, 108) of cuneiform writing and educated to be scribes.

After learning to write, students learned grammar, followed by mathematics. Memorization, repetitive practice, and problem-solving exercises were some of the teaching methods used. "A teacher was referred to as 'father' and he referred to his pupils as 'sons'" (Morton, 1975, 206).

Graduates worked in the temples making fresh copies of ancient texts and keeping business and legal records of the temple properties. Others worked as administrators in government and business, while some specialized as historians, doctors, and architects. They appear to have kept up their contact with their alma mater (the temple and *Edubba*).

The Sumerians were a methodical people who kept meticulous records of their business transactions, and contracts, so necessary to trade, were carefully written and witnessed. Fraud and carelessness, particularly in business and medicine, were sternly punished (Champdour, 1958, 46).

"Sumerian genius evolved a civilization which persisted for nearly fifteen hundred years after its authors had vanished" (Woolley, 1928, 189).

Egyptian. Egyptian culture was influenced by the Sumerians (and succeeding Mesopotamian cultures) in art, architecture, and "perhaps also in so effective a factor as the idea of writing" (Wilson, 1961, 302). Egypt in turn influenced Palestine in commerce and culture. Like Sumeria, Egypt also had three types of texts: stories and myths, wisdom (proverbial instructions), and biographical texts. Egypt also produced books on "craftsmanship, technology, materials and archeology" (Wilson, 1961, 305).

The education of Egyptian scribes was also conducted at schools attached to temples, called "Houses of Life" (Morton, 1975, 206). In addition to being taught Egyptian thought, students learned the geography and history of the world around them. Later, as the government became more bureaucratic, the scribes who served the temple focused on theology and medicine, while those in the government received an increasingly "secular" (Wilson, 1961, 310) education in language, geography, science, and government duties.

Scholars have noted similarities with Hebrew education in three areas: first, the location of education in religious centers; second, the class of people known as scribes; and third, the references to the teacher as "father" (Morton, 1975).

Chinese. Eastern philosophies, as a systematic development of thought, predate and had a significant historical impact on the Greeks. Some of Plato's ideas are very similar to Indian thinking. While Western thought has favored an empirical approach, Eastern thinking has sought to harmonize an individual's mystical, intuitive, sense experience with that person's outer world of phenomena.

The aim of Eastern education is to bring humanity into harmony with nature, which is considered to be a spiritual task. Hence students are encouraged to develop a right attitude by meditation, fasting, prayer, and almsgiving. The teacher-student relationship is extremely important, and implicit obedience of the teacher is of greater value than the mastery of content.

Confucius (551–479 B.C.) and Lao-tzu (fifth century B.C.) were two prominent Chinese thinkers. Confucius taught that moral teaching was more important than acquiring information or skills. Morality was practical and regulated one's duty toward parents, ancestors, and society. The moral person, *chün-tzu*, was faithful, diligent, and modest and practiced the five constant virtues of right attitude, right procedure, right knowledge, right moral courage, and right persistence. Confucius believed that one's conduct and character were more defining than birth.

While Confucius stressed fulfilling external obligations, Lao-tzu emphasized an inner life of tranquillity (Taoist thought). The famous Taoist dictum of *"wu wei"* (do nothing) actually intends that one's personal desires are not forced into the natural flow of events and that nothing unnatural is done in a particular situation. Taoists believe that nature possesses something greater than logic, and that perfection and harmony result when the natural course of events is allowed to unfold. The Taoist is against competition and does not believe in absolutes.

Chinese education emphasized the rules of proper conduct (Confucianism) and the shaping of an appropriate attitude (Taoism). Students were expected to develop a sense of proportion by arranging their attitudes and actions in accordance with priorities set by family, ancestors, and society.

Indian. Indian philosophy cannot be untangled from Hinduism and is more a way of life than a dogma. It embraces contradictory thinking from idealism to materialism, pluralism to monism, asceticism to hedonism, and it emphasizes the control and regulation of a person's desires. Three Hindu writings are the Vedas, the Upanishads, and the Epics (Ramayana and Mahabharat).

The Vedas teach that natural phenomena like fire and rain are deities who need to be placated when angry and to whom sacrifices are offered when supplications are made for their favors. Human beings are divine in essence and can realize that divinity by a process of purification that may take several lifetimes of reincarnation.

The Upanishads tend toward monism in introducing a supreme deity—Brahma the creator, but they also introduce two other powerful deities of a triumvirate—Vishnu the preserver and Shiva the destroyer. The human soul (*atman*) is liberated, or achieves nirvana, when it is purified and merges with Brahma. The devoted Hindu male passes through three stages of life. First he is a student, trained by a teacher (guru) to discipline mind and body. The guru receives no fee, and there is no prescribed course of study or method, but each student is paced through learning experiences specific to his required development. The next stage (around age 25) is that of being a devoted husband and father. The third stage (around age 50) is the renunciation of family ties, when the man gives over his household to his son and becomes a hermit or sage. The woman also has three stages. In the first she is subject to her father or brothers, in the second to her husband, and in the third to her sons. She never performs a sacrifice or keeps a vow apart from her husband, whom she worships as a god. She is always expected to be cheerful and a clever manager of household affairs.

The epic Mahabharat contains the Bhagavada-Gita, which teaches yoga, pantheism, and other Hindu philosophies.

While the primary (not sole) method of education is yoga, the most important thing is to find the right guru, who can guide the student along the right path.

JUNIAS V. VENUGOPAL

Bibliography. A. Champdour (1958), *Babylon;* K. O. Gangel and W. S. Benson (1983), *Christian Education: Its History and Philosophy;* K. A. Kitchen (1975), *The Zondervan Pictorial Encyclopedia of the Bible;* S. N. Kramer (1961), *The Bible and the Ancient Near East;* A. W. Morton (1975), *The Zondervan Pictorial Encyclopedia of the Bible;* H. A. Ozmon and S. M. Craver (1995), *Philosophical Foundations of Education;* J. Sinha (1952), *A History of Indian Philosophy;* J. A. Wilson (1961), *The Bible and the Ancient Near East;* C. L. Woolley (1928), *The Sumerians.*

Andragogy. The art and science of helping adults learn. This is in contrast to the teaching of children (*pedagogy*). Malcolm Knowles (1913–) is known as the modern-day promulgator of andragogy. He describes it as "simply another model of assumptions about learners to be used alongside the pedagogical model of assumptions, thereby providing two alternative models for testing out the assumptions as to their fit with particular situations" (Knowles, 1980, 43). The term comes from an adaptation of the Greek word *aner*, meaning "man" (as distinguished from boy). It has come to mean adult assumptions about teaching and learning.

It is helpful to compare the assumptions of andragogy with those normally associated with pedagogy (Knowles, 1984, 9–12):

Concept	Andragogy	Pedagogy
1. Concept of the learner	Self-directing	Guided
2. Role of experience	Greater volume, more refinement and discernment	Less volume and sophistication
3. Readiness to learn	Ready because of need or desire to perform more effectively	Not as ready; needs not realized
4. Orientation to learning	Life-centered, task-centered, problem-centered	Subject and relationship-centered
5. Motivation to learn	Internal	External

The assumptions clearly dictate a different approach to education. There are varying degrees of this approach or orientation to education, and these assumptions exist in some formats of all pedagogy. However, the value of andragogy is that it helps to focus and clarify one's assumptions regarding the view of education.

History. Andragogy was practiced before the term was coined. The word *andragogy* was not found in popular usage until Malcolm Knowles used it to describe his philosophy of education in *The Adult Learner: A Neglected Species* (1978). The ideas of lifelong learning were used by such popular movements as Chautauqua and Lyceum, but never was the term *andragogy* used.

The term was first coined by a German grammar school teacher named Alexander Kapp in 1833. Kapp used it to describe the Greek philosopher Plato's educational theory. The concept came into wider usage in Europe, but not until 1924 did American authors Eduard Lindeman and Martha Anderson use it in their book *Education Through Experience*. Indeed, Eduard Lindeman was the "single most influential person in guiding [Knowles's] thinking" (Knowles, 1984, 3). Not until 1968, however, did Knowles use the word *andragogy* to describe the educational philosophy that can be traced back to John Dewey through Eduard Lindeman. Other influences upon Knowles's thinking are possibly Carl

Rogers, Abraham Maslow, and Cyril O. Houle from the University of Chicago.

A number of schools seem to have adopted methodologies similar to andragogy. Significant research occurred during the 1970s and 1980s in relation to this term. The *Adult Education Quarterly* carried tributes to Malcolm Knowles as late as its Winter 1998 volume.

Present Impact. As other assumptions about teaching have emerged, a variety of philosophical distinctions have been made, resulting in what Courtenay and Stevenson called "gogymania" (1983, 10–11). The unfortunate undue separation between teaching children and teaching adults needs to be brought into perspective. The research base for andragogy is not developing as fast as it was, but helpful concepts are still being tested. Yet the distinctives of andragogy seem fertile soil for the planting of Christian education principles and practice.

Knowles has moved andragogy into the field of shaping the way we teach and practice learning. Life histories, reflective practice, and the valuing of experience are recent contributions to the field of adult education.

GREGORY C. CARLSON

Bibliography. *Adult Education Quarterly* 48, no. 2 (1998); B. Courtenay and R. Stevenson (1983), *Lifelong Learning: The Adult Years;* S. D. Brookfield (1995), *Becoming a Critically Reflective Teacher;* K. O. Gangel and J. C. Wilhoit, eds. (1993), *The Christian Educator's Handbook on Adult Education;* M. Knowles (1978), *The Adult Learner: A Neglected Species;* idem (1980), *The Modern Practice of Adult Education: From Pedagogy to Andragogy;* idem (1984), *Andragogy in Action.*

See also ADULT CHRISTIAN EDUCATION; ADULT DEVELOPMENT

Anorexia. *See* Eating Disorders.

Apostolic Teaching. *See* Education of the Twelve.

Aquinas, Thomas (1225–74). Medieval theologian and philosopher born in Roccasecca, a fortress near Naples, Italy. Young Thomas attended the Benedictine School at Monte Casino, where he graduated last in his class. Later he attended the University of Naples. Kidnapped and held prisoner by his family to prevent him from joining the Dominican order, Thomas escaped to Paris to study with Albert the Great, the first of the Scholastics. Thomas followed Albertus Magnus to the University of Cologne and was ordained a Dominican priest in 1250. Soon, Thomas was teaching theology in Paris and several Italian cities. Eventually he was recalled to Naples to lead the Dominican school of theology. At the age of forty-eight, while saying Mass, Thomas believed he had a spiritual vision. He gave up his work, which, in the light of this experience, he considered insignificant. Thomas died soon afterward and was declared a saint by the Roman Catholic Church.

Thomas Aquinas was the greatest of the Scholastics, a group that sat down with a collection of Scriptures, recent translations of Aristotle, and works by the early church fathers, and came up with a system that used philosophy to interpret and support theology. Faith and reason are compatible, Thomas argued, because God is the source of both. Any conflicts between faith and reason had to be the product of faulty logic. Reason cannot completely comprehend God, but it can be used to establish God's existence. Faith, believed Thomas, remains superior to reason, just as the church is superior to the state.

Thomas authored thirty works, including *Summa Theologica, Concerning the Teacher,* and commentaries on the Bible and on the works of Aristotle and Peter Lombard. *Summa Theologica* was a two-million-word work that would replace Lombard's *Sentences* as the definitive text on Roman Catholic doctrine.

Patron saint of Roman Catholic schools, Thomas Aquinas was both theologian and educator. He believed that education should be provided by the state. One of his principles was that students learned not only by instruction, but by the discovery of knowledge through their own senses and powers of reasoning. Teacher and student are like doctor and patient. Teachers can no more instill their own knowledge in students than doctors can transmit their own good health to ailing patients. The teacher's role is to aid the student in the acquisition of knowledge. Thomas trusted the power of human intellect and considered its development a way to glorify its Creator.

Teachers must not only know their material, but also be able to communicate it in simple terms, building a bridge between what students already know and what they need to learn. Curriculum should begin with what is material before advancing to what is abstract. It should start with what can be plainly seen.

Thomas maintained that teachers should be involved in the lives of their students as well as with their own scholarly pursuits. Despite Thomas's urging to lead a life that was both active and scholarly, scholasticism tended to overemphasize intellectualism. Critics declared that debate and discussion had little to do with everyday life. By separating informal schooling that contributed to character formation from more formal training, Thomas managed to drive a wedge between the two.

This emphasis on intellect was later criticized by the fourteenth-century Franciscan, William of Occam. William taught that there is no common ground between faith and reason. The church, in William's view, should focus on faith. William's influence can be seen in the work of Martin Luther and his rejection of Scholasticism.

As the Renaissance flowered in European centers of learning, the glory of man, rather than God, became the center of attention. At best, Thomas and the Scholastics stabilized Christian doctrine, founded schools, and raised the status of the study of theology. At worst, they obscured the simplicity of the gospel.

ROBERT J. CHOUN

Bibliography. T. Aquinas, *Summa Theologia,* ed. A. M. Fairweather; idem, *Selections,* ed. A. C. Pegis; G. K. Chesterton (1933), *Saint Thomas Aquinas;* K. B. Culley, ed. (1963), *The Westminster Dictionary of Christian Education;* C. B. Eavey (1964/1960), *History of Christian Education;* E. Gilson, *Elements of Christian Philosophy;* C. Heston (1990), *St. Thomas Aquinas* (cassettes); R. M. Hutchins and M. J. Adler (1952), *Great Books of the Western World,* vol. 54; J. Pieper (1962/1993), *Guide to Thomas Aquinas;* J. E. Reed and R. Prevost, *A History of Christian Education;* C. Turner (1985), *Chosen Vessels: Portraits of Ten Outstanding Christian Men;* W. Walker (1908), *Great Men of the Christian Church.*

See also IGNATIUS OF LOYOLA; INTELLECTUALISM; LUTHER, MARTIN; RENAISSANCE EDUCATION; ROMAN CATHOLIC EDUCATION

Argument. *See* Discussion.

Aristotle (384–322 B.C.). Aristotle is considered by many to have been the most influential philosopher in the history of Western thought. He was born in Stagira, the son of Nicomachus, court physician to King Amyntas II of Macedon. While Aristotle was still a youth, his father died and he was raised by a guardian, Proxenus. Sent to Athens in 367 B.C., he entered Plato's Academy as a student and remained there as a teacher until Plato's death in 347 B.C. The Academy was an assemblage of learned individuals who taught a wide variety of subjects, ranging from medicine and biology to mathematics and astronomy. Instructors shared no common doctrine, but were united in their systematic effort to organize human knowledge on a firm theoretical base and to expand it in limitless directions. Part of the Academy's purpose was to raise up future political leaders and advisors. Thus, following the death of Plato and after two years in the court of Hermias of Atarneus, Aristotle accepted an invitation in 343 B.C. to become an advisor to Philip II of Macedon. A major responsibility was tutoring Philip's young son, Alexander, who would later achieve renown as the greatest military leader of his day.

In 335 B.C. Aristotle returned to Athens to found his own school, the Lyceum, or Peripatus, as a rival academic center to the Academy. Believing the Academy to have become narrow in its thinking following the death of its founder, the Lyceum taught a wider range of subjects. With the premature death of Alexander the Great in 323 B.C., anti-Macedonian sentiment overtook Athens and the Lyceum fell into disfavor. Aristotle fled the city, taking refuge in Chalcis on the island of Euboea, where he died the following year at the age of sixty-two.

Stories regarding the nature of Aristotle's gradual break with Plato remain vague. He rejected Plato's dichotomy of body and soul, preferring to see "the soul as the form of the body." It is the soul that energizes the body as "rational animal." This basic divergence represented an early delineation of the manner in which man and his world should be viewed. In support of his philosophy, Aristotle insisted on the necessity of empirical observation, in contrast with Plato's introspective procedures, and on the importance of the five senses to the acquisition of knowledge. It was, however, the psyche (or soul) that rendered man capable of receiving knowledge. To Aristotle, therefore, the psyche was the form aspect of existence and life, being the vital principle that distinguished inorganic from organic matter. He further differentiated man from lower life forms, asserting that while some animals can imagine, only man has the capacity to think. But thinking does not imply knowing, which is an active, creative process leading to the recognition of universal truths. He classified living forms into three general categories: vegetative (plants), sensitive (animals), and rational (human beings).

To Aristotle, the chief end of man is not merely to live, but to lead a good life that manifests the rational nature of humanity. The pursuit of happiness is a search for the good life, which is virtuous rather than narcissistic in nature. Virtue lies between two extremes, and thus involves both theoretical and practical wisdom. Not everyone is endowed with such virtue, however, explaining in part Aristotle's eschewal of Athenian democracy.

Only fragments of Aristotle's writings remain, and there is no consensus that they have been pieced together correctly. Nevertheless, many contemporary scientists, educators, philosophers, and theologians lay claim to Aristotle as a forerunner of their own disciplines. Thomas Aquinas (1224–1274), the systematizer of Roman Catholic dogma, largely and presuppositionally based his theology on Aristotelian thought. Aristotle's pedagogical methodology, especially in the areas of logic and rhetoric, remains a major part of the educational classroom. Despite falling into disfavor following the Reformation, many of his concepts have been revived by modern thinkers and have stood the test of time. It is virtually impossible to deny his continuing influence in nearly all of the major academic disciplines, even after more than two millennia.

DAVID GOUGH

Bibliography. D. J. Allan (1952), *The Philosophy of Aristotle;* T. Davidson (1892), *Aristotle and Ancient Educational Ideals;* R. McKeon, ed. (1947), *Introduction to Aristotle.*

See also AQUINAS, THOMAS; AUGUSTINE; GREEK EDUCATION; IDEALISM; PLATO; REALISM

Asian Theology. Broad term that covers attempts to express theological meaning and practical implications of the gospel in the various Asian contexts, from India to Southeast Asia to Korea and Japan. These attempts include the efforts of all the individuals and groups of theologians and church leaders from the evangelical Asia Theological Association (ATA) or the ecumenical Christian Conference of Asia (CCA), from past to present.

Understanding Asian Theology. The development of Asian theology is fairly new because of the short history of Asian Christianity. Asian theology was formed as a reaction to Western theology and was birthed out of the Asian historical and cultural context. Asian theology was formed as follows: (a) mission theology that has been indigenized and contextualized; (b) accommodation theology, and theological pluralism, which is expressed by using their own national terms and concepts to evangelize people; (c) liberation theology which was influenced by a reaction to the colonialism, exploitation, oppression, and poverty caused by Western capitalism and Japanese imperialism; and (d) situational and ethical relativism based on the Asian political and economic situation. The concept of "accommodation theology" in Asia was brought to light in early 1970s by Kosuke Koyama who distinguishes it from syncretistic theology. Theological and religious pluralism is a broader term to cover the concept of religious and cultural accommodation and religious syncretism.

Due to dissatisfaction with Western theology, the quest for a clearer sense of self-identity by Asian Christians, and the Asian cultural and political situation, Asian theologies have adopted contextualized and indigenous forms of Western theologies. Indigenization of theology for Asian churches requires them to be not only "self-governing, self-supporting, and self-propagating," but also "self-theologizing." Kosuke Koyama (1989) lists six characteristics of Asian theology: the relation or relevance of Christ to revolutionary social change, widespread poverty, ethnic and economic minorities, the positive and negative aspects of culture, the plurality of religions, and ecclesiastical divisions. Due to the different emphases of Asian theology and Western theology, the methods and the content of theology are also different. They may be distinguished as follows: (a) exclusive versus syncretistic, to include the cultural and traditional religious mind; (b) doctrinal versus situational and relational, to solve problems (Western theology is formed by intellectual concerns with a relationship between faith and reason); and (c) logical versus pragmatic, to relate their own cultural issues to Christian faith.

Issues in Asian Theology. Modern theologies can be categorized into at least three positions: exclusive (conservative), inclusive or syncretistic (Karl Rahner), and pluralistic or radically liberal (Thick, Samaratha). Exclusive theology contends that salvation comes through Jesus Christ alone, while inclusive theology accepts that there are different ways of finding salvation, including Jesus Christ and the unknown God. Pluralistic theology, however, says that all religion will lead people to salvation; hence, Jesus Christ is not the only way of salvation. These three theological positions exist together in Asian theologies.

Robet Schreiter (1985) defines three models of localized Asian theologies as follows: (a) the translation model, with an unchanging kernel of Christian revelation and an impermanent cultural husk that changes with each different cultural setting in which the gospel finds itself; (b) the adaptation model, which functions as the second stage in the development of a local theology (it takes the local culture much more seriously than the first approach); and (c) the contextual model, which emphasizes the traditions of faith.

After World War II, there have been extensive surveys of the formation of indigenous theologies in Asian Christianity (Anderson, 1976; Elwood, 1976; England, 1981; Honig, 1982). In Asian Christian communities there are two publication groups that represent the three theological positions: the Asia Theological Association (ATA) for the evangelical groups (e.g., Ro and Eshenaur, 1984; Ro and Albrecht, 1988; Ro, 1989), and the Christian Conference of Asia (CCA) and the Association for Theological Education in South-East Asia (ATESEA) for the ecumenical groups (e.g., Kim, 1981; Yap, 1990; Yeow, 1983; *Asia Journal of Theology*).

Inclusive, Pluralistic, Syncretistic, and Liberal Theology. The liberal side has several theologies that are localized with relativistic perspectives of their own cultural situation. (a) Minjung theology of Kim Yong-Bok is a Korean form of liberation theology which was a reaction against political and economic oppression of dictators. (b) Pain of God theology of Kazuo Kitamor is a cultural and situational production of World War II in Japan. (c) Water buffalo theology of Kosuke Koyama is an existential theology in Thailand. (d) Theology of Change/Transposition of Lee Jong-Yong is theology transposed from its Western context to the Asian contexts. It is also known as the "Third-eye theology" of Son Chong-Sen. (e) Christian Karma Marga is a syncretistic theology of "Way of Action" in India with the Hindu way of salvation through meritorious deeds.

Exclusive and Evangelical Theology. Evangelicals have developed contextualized biblical theology. For the evangelical side some prominent Asian theologians are David Kim, Bong Ro, Hojin Jun, John Cho, John Kim, and Byung S. Oh (Korea); Uda Shen (Japan); K. Gnanakan, S. Athyal, K. Ananakan, S. Sunithra, and S. Vinay (India); C. Marantika (Indonesia); Tan K. Say (Malaysia); A Ferando and T. Weersingha (Sri Lanka); S. Chan, W. Chaen, and J. Hsu (Chinese Taipei, Hong Kong, and Singapore); and R. D. Tano (Philippines). However, none of them developed any systematic theology in the sense that Calvin or Luther did; instead, they developed strong evangelical missiology in Asian contexts. Under the Asia Theological Association (ATA), many evangelical scholars have worked cooperatively to develop evangelical Asian theology.

Christian Education and Asian Theology. Historically, Christian education has been fluctuating between two poles: content and context. Based on the emphasis of content or context, Christian education has been related to traditional/orthodox theology, liberal theology, neo-orthodox theology, radical theology, revisionist theology, or new evangelical theology (neo-evangelicalism). At the present time, Asian theology seems to be emphasizing context rather than content. The role of Christian education in Asian theology is to keep balance.

Understanding Asian Culture and Western Culture. Asian theology must be understood within the context of Asian cultural backgrounds. Generally, cultural differences between Western society and Asian society can be identified as individual centered versus community centered. (a) **Relationship:** egalitarianism versus hierarchical relationship. While Westerners primarily see others as equals, Asians see others in hierarchical terms. In Western society, informal interpersonal relationship is important. People practice less complex rules for speech and conduct. Asians, however, think formal interpersonal relationships are more important. Thus, Asians practice very complex rules for speech and conduct. (b) **Values:** individual rights versus community duties and responsibilities. While Westerners focus on the premium attached to an individual's rights, self-reliance, and self-determination, Asians emphasize roles assigned to different hierarchical positions and perform appropriate functions in those positions. (c) **Attitude:** assertiveness and self-expression versus respect for authority. Western attitudes emphasize standing up for personal rights and expression of personal thoughts and feelings, while Asian attitudes emphasize docility and conformity to assigned roles. (d) **Identity:** personal ability and achievement versus individual status in the group. While Western society emphasizes individual competence, achievement, and success, Asian society focuses on individual position in a group such as a family, corporation, or church. For Westerners development of a person's unique qualities and self-initiated activities for personal success are important. However, self-development related to group expectations and ascriptive motivation such as group success is more important for Asians. (e) **Socialization:** active involvement versus observation and emulation. The Western style of socialization is formed by participatory decision-making and frequent exchange of ideas and feelings, whereas Asians watch, listen, and then act in the socialization process. Asians also communicate by commands and demands rather than active involvement. (f) **Thinking style:** abstract, analytical, rational, linear, detailed, specific, and logical versus synthetic, intuitive, concrete, cyclic, global, and impressionistic. Western thinking separates the cognitive from the affective as well as the objective from the subjective with serial exchange among communicants. Teaching-learning situations are relatively loosely structured. However, the Asian thinking style is that the cognitive and the affective, as well as the objective and the subjective, are often combined with spontaneous and/or simultaneous exchanges among communicants. They also have highly structured teaching-learning situations. (g) **Response to mistakes or sin:** law (knowledge), guilt, and transcendence versus honor, shame, and society. In response to any mistake or commitment of sin, Westerners express individual guilt feelings personally for breaking the law, while Asians show their feelings of shame for breaking communal duties and responsibilities.

The Task of Christian Education for Asian Theology. Due to the liberals' inclusive and dangerous syncretism and the position that context takes precedence over content, evangelical Christian education must maintain the authority of Scripture, reject all that is contrabiblical, transform concepts that cohere with Scripture, and keep distinctive Christology.

Christian education has been the means to articulate theology as relational and practical. Christian education is not just the transmission of Christian truth for Asian Christians but the transformation of Christian lives and the manifestation of Christian truth by Asian Christians in Asian contexts. Christian education transforms both individually and socially. Christian education in the Asian context must be communicated in indigenous languages and contexts. Thus, Christian education must be contextualized.

The content of Christian education in Asian contexts needs to include cultural values such as hospitality, strong family relationships, sensitivity to the Holy Spirit's work, and respect for parents and authority. On the negative side, it also needs to include how to deal with ancestor and evil spirit issues, which have little significance for Westerners. Due to the relational, intuitive, cyclic, global, and impressionistic thinking and learning style, the teaching methods need to be different from Western styles. Educators should tell relational stories, using more concrete and strong relationship styles.

From the educational perspective, we may distinguish these particular theologies into three domains of education. Christian educators in Asian countries must learn how to use contextual theology as the cognitive domain (intellectual), the syncretistic method (not syncretistic and inclusive theology) for the affective domain (emotional), and the relational method for the volitional domain (behavioral). Asian theology, therefore, must be biblical as well as missiological, pastoral, and educational.

Young Woon Lee

Bibliography. G. H. Anderson, ed. (1976), *Asian Voices in Christian Theology;* H. Yung (1997), *Mangoes or Bananas?: The Quest for an Authentic Asian Christian Theology;* D. J. Elwood, ed. (1976), *What Asian Christians Are Thinking;* K. Koyama (1989), *An Introduction to Christian Theology in the Twentieth Century,* vol. II; R. Schreiter (1985), *Constructing Local Theologies;* B. Ro and R. Eshenaur, eds. (1989), *An Evangelical Perspective on Asian Theology.*

Assimilation. Assimilation is not a new concept to the church. From the very beginning—house churches (Rom. 16:5; 1 Cor. 16:19; Col. 4:15; Philem. 2) and village communities, as at Lydda and Sharon (Acts 9:35); mixed urban groups, as at Corinth (Acts 18:7–8); migrating groups and individuals, as at Rome (Romans 16); and interracial segments at Roman colonial posts like Philippi (Acts 16)—the Christian body of believers has needed a way in which people may join with and feel a part of the community of believers. This *koinonia*, or fellowship of believers, is a very important function of the church.

Assimilation is the process by which a person feels that he or she is a trusted, respected, and accepted member of the body of believers. It is the process whereby the person feels that his or her contribution to the fellowship will greatly enhance God's great commission as found in Matthew 28.

Although assimilation involves a myriad of issues for the Christian educator, three things are essential. First, discipleship of the individual is critical. Unless a Christian is a growing disciple of Jesus Christ, he or she may only *appear* to be assimilated into the body of believers. Second, the assimilated person will participate in the great commission of evangelism. Although not all Christians are gifted as evangelists, each is mandated to share his or her faith with others. Third, the assimilated Christian expresses his or her spiritual gifting in the local congregation. A person who shows signs of making the church his or her own through the giving and receiving of talents and gifts is on the way toward assimilation.

Assimilation is a very important concept for the Christian. Without a sincere sense of being a part of a community of believers, there may be a feeling of being spectator rather than a participant in God's kingdom work. Being a spectator Christian is contrary to Scripture's mandate that we participate in God's kingdom work.

DONALD W. WELCH

Bibliography. L. E. Schaller (1978), *Assimilating New Members;* W. B. Moore (1983), *New Testament Follow-Up;* W. A. Henrichsen (1977), *Disciples Are Made— Not Born;* D. W. Welch (1989), *The Preacher's Magazine,* 27–29, 60–62.

Assistant Pastor. *See* Associate Pastor.

Associate Pastor. Any local church ministerial staff member who carries out his or her ministry as a supplement or support to that of the senior pastor. The exact titles used are numerous, reflecting at times the breadth or focus of ministry responsibilities these individuals carry (e.g., children's pastor, youth pastor, director of Christian education, minister of evangelism, pastor of family ministries, assistant pastor, associate pastor, executive pastor).

Historically, leadership within a local Jewish synagogue was carried out by a group of elders (e.g., Matt. 21:23). Early Christian congregations also employed this multiple-leadership model, selecting elders to exercise spiritual oversight within the congregation (Acts 14:28). First Peter 5:1–4 describes the functions and character of these elders serving as pastors, and does not limit these functions to one person. In more recent times, associate pastors have been viewed in a variety of ways. In some traditions the associate pastor functions as an assistant to the senior pastor in all aspects of ministry. In other traditions this is a time of on-the-job training, preparing the associate pastor to eventually serve as a senior pastor. In still other traditions, the associate pastor's responsibilities are more focused and specialized, reflecting different ministry callings and spiritual gifts that supplement the work of the senior pastor.

As congregations grow in size,and ministry demands increase, it is common and beneficial for churches to seek ministry associates to work alongside the senior pastor in giving leadership to the ministries of the church.

KEVIN E. LAWSON

See also CLERGY; CLERGY AS EDUCATORS; EXECUTIVE PASTOR; MINISTER; MINISTER OF CHRISTIAN EDUCATION; SENIOR PASTOR; TEAM

Association/Connectionist Theories. Psychology came into its own at the end of the nineteenth century when positivism was at its zenith, and therefore, early psychologists were oriented toward making their field a scientific discipline. Early attempts at formulating psychological theory such as those of William Wundt in Germany and William James in the United States were based on subjects' observations and reports on consciousness. Because such reports were far too subjective to be rigorous science, in 1913 J. B. Watson suggested that the subject matter of psychology be behavior rather than consciousness. The observation of behavior was considered much more objective and therefore more scientific than personal reports on mental consciousness.

This emphasis on behavior led to associationist understandings of learning, which concentrated on animal research under the scientifically based assumption that human organisms are only quantitatively, but not qualitatively, more complex than dogs, rats, and pigeons. In Ivan Pavlov's studies of classical conditioning, for example, he noticed that an unconditioned stimulus like food produced an unconditioned response, salivation, in dogs. Pavlov found that he could teach a dog to associate a conditioned stimulus like a bell with the response of salivation by repeatedly sounding the bell whenever food was presented to the dog. Subsequently, the dog was taught to salivate when the bell was sounded without the presentation of food. The salivation became a conditioned response to the conditioned stimulus of the bell. In this way, salivation was associated with the sounding of a bell. Much simple learning seems to occur in this manner, as in the case of the student who attends Sunday school regularly due to its association with pleasant experiences like candy treats or enjoyable friendships.

Edward L. Thorndike agreed with Pavlov regarding stimulus-response associations, but argued that behavior is not simply a reflex reaction to stimulus as Pavlov thought, but is motivated by expectation of consequences. He believed that learning occurred when the connection between the stimulus and response is stamped in by the effect of positive consequences and that forgetting occurs when this connection is weakened by the absence of such consequences. Thus, in connectionism, as Thorndike's theory has been called, the key to learning is in the consequences of the response to stimuli for future behavior rather than in the simple pairing of stimulus and response. Teachers use the insights of Thorndike's connectionism whenever they reward a student with praise for an intelligent idea or an admirable behavior.

Association/connectionist theories of learning set the stage for the operant behaviorism of B. F. Skinner, who believed with Watson that behavior was the key to understanding humans, with Pavlov that human responses can be conditioned, and with Thorndike that the key to this conditioning is in the expectation of consequences. Skinner went on to speculate that responses could be affected by altering their consequences, either positively or negatively. A particular response could be made more likely by introducing a pleasant stimulus (positive reinforcement) or by removing an unpleasant stimulus (negative reinforcement). For example, the student would be more likely to behave acceptably if the teacher introduced a positive reinforcement like praise or removed a negative reinforcement like nagging. Skinner distinguished between negative reinforcement, which he thought was effective, and punishment, the use of unpleasant stimuli to curtail behavior, which he found to be quite ineffective. Thus, Skinner considered punishing a student for unacceptable behavior to be much less productive than rewarding a student for good behavior.

The major instructional technique that has grown out of association/connectionist theories of learning is programmed instruction, which allows the student, using computer software or books, to progress through an instructional program. Linear programs lead all students through the exact same sequence of experiences while branching programs alter instruction on the basis of responses to previous questions. The former have the advantage of being simple to administer and reliable in terms of covering prescribed material; the latter have the advantage of addressing remedial needs of students and adapting to individual needs. The disadvantage of all programmed instruction, especially for Christian education, is that human interaction is minimal and the student seems to be subordinated to the subject matter to be learned. Moreover, such instruction is more effective in promoting the learning of facts than in the development of higher level cognitive functions or affective or behavioral responses.

Another contribution of association/connectionist theories is in the area of classroom management. Desirable behaviors can be shaped through the discerning use of reinforcement and undesirable ones extinguished by withholding reinforcement. An obvious way of implementing these principles is for the teacher to attend to the student who is behaving admirably and to ignore the misbehaving student. Research seems to indicate that punishing the latter will not be particularly effective in extinguishing obnoxious behavior.

Despite the effectiveness of association/connectionist theories, many Christian educators question their underlying philosophy. The idea that humans are simply organisms that are only quantitatively different from animals is at odds with the traditional Christian understanding of *imago dei*, which holds that humans are unique because of their creation in the image of God. Some of this uniqueness may reside in human rationality and self-awareness. Although animals can be taught through the association of stimulus with response and the connection of response with anticipated consequence, these methods alone seem inadequate to deal with beings created in the image of God. Cultivation of reasoning and personal development are also essential to a complete Christian education program.

JOHN R. YEATTS

Bibliography. I. P. Pavlov (1927), *Conditioned Reflexes;* B. F. Skinner (1968), *The Technology of Teaching;* E. L. Thorndike (1949), *Selected Writings from a Connectionist's Psychology.*

See also BEHAVIORISM, THEORIES OF; JAMES, WILLIAM; SKINNER, BURRHUS FREDERIC; S-R BONDS

Association of Christian Schools International. The mission of the Association of Christian Schools International (ACSI) is to enable Christian educators and schools worldwide to effectively prepare students for life. ACSI has an evangelical statement of faith coming out of the Protestant tradition. Eight regions in the United States, two regions in Canada, and over one hundred non–North American schools combine 3,770 member schools into an aggregate ACSI student enrollment of 796,867.

The stated core values of ACSI are to respond to the needs of Christian schools, to lead its membership to spiritual and academic excellence, and to provide assistance without interference and opportunity without obligation.

Since ACSI was founded in 1978 as a result of the merger of three different associations—the National Christian School Education Association (NCSEA), the Ohio Association of Christian Schools (OACS), and the Western Association of Christian Schools (WACS)—several other regional associations have joined. Additional organizations are the Southeastern Association of Christian Schools, the Association of Teachers of Christian Schools, the Great Plains Association of Christian Schools, and the Texas Association of Christian Schools.

The philosophy of ACSI is to help parents carry out their biblical responsibility to educate their children through the ministries of Christian schools. The organization encourages its member schools to assist students in developing their gifts to the fullest potential in heart, mind, and body. The leadership of ACSI believes that a curriculum based in biblical values and taught by godly, well-trained, and committed faculty allows for the integration of faith and learning.

A concise overview of ACSI's vision is that Christian school students worldwide will acquire wisdom, knowledge, and a biblical worldview as evidenced by a lifestyle of character, leadership, service, stewardship, and worship. Specifically, ACSI envisions that young men and women will mature to loving God with all their heart, mind, and soul (Matt. 22:37); grow in wisdom and stature (Luke 2:52); be willing to stand apart from the world as salt and light (Matt. 5:13–14); and give sacrificially of themselves and their resources, reflecting the essence and love of Christ who lives and dwells within them (Rom. 12:1).

ACSI aids its member schools by providing an array of services and programs through fourteen regional offices inside and outside the United States. At present, ACSI has offices in Lancaster, Pennsylvania; Snellville, Georgia; North Canton, Ohio; Dallas, Texas; Mesa, Arizona; Vancouver, Washington; Sacramento, California; LaHabra, California; Minesing, Ontario, Canada; Three Hills, Alberta, Canada; Washington, D.C.; Budapest, Hungary; Guatemala City, Guatemala; and Kiev, Ukraine. Further assistance to member schools is provided by its eight departments: Academic Affairs, International Ministries, Legal, Legislative Affairs, Preschool Services, School Services, Student Activities, Business and Finance, and Operations.

Through its regional offices and departments, ACSI provides its membership with a variety of benefits. One benefit is the widely circulated periodical, *Christian School Comment*. Regional conventions are held annually and include inspiring general sessions, professional seminars, and exhibits. Regular conferences are held for administrators and board members. ACSI has a limited but growing line of curriculum items. Member schools may seek legal assistance and join insurance programs through ACSI. A national listing of available positions and job applicants is available. Teacher and administrator certification and a comprehensive school accreditation program are overseen by the vice president of academic affairs.

The vision of ACSI founder and president emeritus, Dr. Paul Kienel, was to enable Christian educators and schools worldwide to provide quality Christian education. Current ACSI president, Dr. Ken Smitherman, carries on that theme in schools where students tend to be motivated, focused, and surrounded by like-minded peers, where parents are supportive and involved, and where teachers are well trained, committed, and godly role models. Most ACSI member schools have a well-defined mission and are built on sound biblical principles that guide everything they do.

In 1994, ACSI moved its headquarters from LaHabra, California, to larger facilities in Colorado Springs, Colorado. Over its first two decades of existence the student enrollment of member schools and colleges has grown about 77 percent.

In that same period of time, the number of member schools has grown 72 percent.

DAVID L. ROTH

Association of Professors and Researchers in Religious Education (APRRE). APRRE was organized in 1970 from two groups of the Division of Christian Education of the National Council of the Churches of Christ. The two groups consisted of those who participated in research for denominational bodies, and those who were instructors and professors of religious education at the college and seminary level.

A current brochure indicates that researchers and teachers from thirty-one denominations and eleven countries constitute APRRE's membership. Though the membership is predominantly Protestant, Roman Catholics, Jews, Bahaists, Moslems, and others are members. APRRE schedules its annual meeting at the same time and location as the meetings of the Religious Education Association, the Society of Biblical Literature, and the American Academy of Religion.

At times the disjunctive theological concepts expressed at the APRRE meetings leave evangelicals out of the dialogue. The evangelical has come to a definite theological anchorage that is at serious odds with the widely ranging APRRE commitments to process theology, liberation theology, and the diverse religious groups that are now within its membership. Evangelicals find it difficult to be unable to reach theological conclusions or to seem offensive to adherents of other religions because of their commitment to Scripture and the religious pluralism of APRRE members.

WARREN S. BENSON

Atheism. A term from the Greek word *atheos*, which literally means "without God" or "without a belief in God." Popularly, the term refers to a rejection of the existence of a god. However, many atheists prefer to describe themselves as free from a belief in a god. Atheists are reluctant to deny existence, because this denial involves an acceptance that existence is a rational option. To them it is irrational to believe in theism. Atheists believe that truth is apprehended through the five senses or is limited to that which is built into human experience. Only within this framework can a reasoned analysis of the possibility of a god be determined. The acceptance of this premise is as essential to them as the rejection of it is to theists. Atheists may question, "Which god—the one(s) in the past or the new, relatively violent God of the Bible?" Common arguments such as contradictions in the Bible and questions relating to the source of evil or pain are also used.

On a continuum concerning the existence of God, atheists are at odds with theists. Ideological skeptics (it cannot be known) and agnostics (a profession of ignorance), respectively, are similar to atheists in their beliefs. George Barna's research indicates that 2 percent of Americans believe in atheism, and atheistic sources acknowledge less than 10 percent.

MICHAEL J. KANE

Bibliography. G. Barna (1994), *Virtual America*; M. M. O'Hair and J. G. Murray, *American Atheists*.

See also BELIEF; ENGEL SCALE; EPISTEMOLOGY; EVANGELISM; FAITH

Atonement. Etymologically, the word *atonement* is derived from the archaic middle English *at-one-ment.* So atonement at its heart has the sense of reconciliation. While contemporary theology has recaptured this classic sense (Taylor, 1960), it is less certain whether reconciliation requires the traditional satisfaction of justice and judgment.

Atonement in the Old Testament is reconciliation based on shed blood (*kapar,* see Exod. 29:33; Num. 5:8). Early on, the mercy of reconciliation seems to be implicitly understood as bought by and bathed in blood sacrifice (Job 1; Gen. 15, 22). Ultimately, that requirement was made explicit in Mosaic practice (Lev. 1–7) and explained in the great Levitical dictum: "For the life of the flesh is in the blood, and I have given it to you on the altar to make atonement for your souls; for it is the blood by reason of the life that makes atonement" (Lev. 17:11 NASB).

Later, the New Testament would vividly absolutize that old covenant declaration by insisting, "without shedding of blood there is no forgiveness" (Heb. 9:22 NASB). But in contrast to the past ritualized bloodshed of calves and goats, this text is grounded in the provision of an all-sufficient atonement through the shed blood of Jesus Christ.

The theological use of the term is twofold. Narrowly speaking, *atonement* refers specifically to the ritual reconciliation of people to God. This was effected on the mercy seat cover of the ark, where blood was sprinkled on the Day of Atonement.

But taken broadly, *atonement* has come to stand for everything salvific accomplished by Christ's sacrificial death on Calvary's cross. Atonement's supreme, triumphant achievement was anticipated in Jesus' dying utterance, "It is finished" (John 19:30). To actually accomplish atonement, he died as a substitute (1 Cor. 15:3; 2 Cor. 5:14–15, 21; 1 Peter 2:24; Matt. 20:28). The succeeding resurrection and ascension would establish Jesus' redeeming accomplishments as fully accepted by a holy God and now graciously available (Rom. 4:25; 2 Cor. 5:15–16, 21).

History. In spite of what appears to be clear, consistent, centralist biblical witness, the church's understanding of atonement soon dissipated. After the close of the canon, the straightforward, core New Testament emphasis devolved into a spectrum of speculations known as atonement theories.

Treatments of these theories abound (see Aulen [1961], Driver [1986], McDonald [1985], Warfield [1970]), and the methodology employed might prove enlightening. One common approach treats the views as they emerged, historically. Others consider the possible objects of Christ's salvific work. Is Adam's failed, forfeited obedience in need of revisiting and reliving? Or must Satan's evil bondage be broken and his captives set free? Certainly, God's holy righteousness and governmental credibility are at stake. And how can the stirring motivation of Christ's loving example upon a moral humanity be ignored?

In the broadest sense, redemption must be viewed as the cosmic struggle of good and evil, God and Satan. In the opposite, more narrowly focused view, God is a judge with righteous justice in view, or God is a legislator with his government in view. Another perspective looks at people, and the broadest stirring of their morality, or the specific rekindling of their love for God, or the higher service calling as mirrored in Jesus' servanthood. Or should atonement stay spiritual, limited just to the guilt and sin of humankind?

Assessment of these atonement theories invariably comes down to seeing what is left unspoken as much as what is actually said. Is emphasis placed on the essence or on the extraneous? Sometimes orthodoxy differentiates from heterodoxy by the thinnest distinction of priority or proportion. For atonement, the main thing —the central priority of Christ's substitutionary death—must be kept the main thing (Mark 10:45).

Atonement by christological recapitulation (Rom. 5:19; Phil. 2:8)—the Second Adam reliving the righteous obedient life failed by the first Adam—fails this test. So does a redirected atonement payment (ransom) to Satan—even by Satan—in spite of possible scriptural deductions (Luke 13:16; 2 Cor. 4:4; 1 John 5:19). The classic irony of this view is that a creature—and a fallen one at that—is substituted for the Creator! All exemplary moral influence and motivation-to-love views (1 Peter 2:21) are also totally flawed by their unrealistic view of human depravity. Even a well-intentioned token payment view that tries somehow to justify God's government (purportedly based on Isa. 42:21) needs rectifying.

Other tensions in classic and contemporary theology center around views of self-atonement, substitutionary atonement, or automatic, no-atonement. The former and latter views render the cross superfluous, and have always stood outside of and in opposition to historic biblicism. Self-atonement incurs the wrath of a frightfully damning logic and scriptural condemnation. Any opposite sentimentality repudiating guilt or penalty for sin presumes a personae of God unflattering to his holy self-revelation.

Biblical Theology. Historic Protestant orthodoxy founded on biblical seriousness has always stood for these atonement essentials. It is the shed blood of Jesus Christ, signifying his substitutionary death on Calvary's cross, that fully captures the divinely gracious atonement. This provision alone covers every descendant of Adam's needy, depraved race from "eternity to eternity." Or as satisfaction atonement's able expositor, Saint Anselm of Canterbury, made the case, it is *Cur Deus Homo*, why God became man. Only an infinitely perfect sacrifice would suffice in breadth and depth to atone for all of humanity's sins.

Jesus Christ is God's full, and fully satisfactory, atonement for all sins, for all humanity, for all times (2 Cor. 5:14, 15; 1 Tim. 2:6; Heb. 9:11–28; 10:12–14). As merciful, faithful high priest, "He . . . made propitiation for the sins of the people" (Heb. 2:17 NASB). His position as "a priest forever according to the order of Melchizedek" is not of the "weak and useless" Levitical, Aaronic priesthood (Heb. 7:11–19 NASB). His perfection as "holy, innocent, undefiled, separated from sinners" (Heb. 7:26 NASB) fully meets our needs. And his perpetual priesthood, that "He is able to save forever those who draw near to God through Him, since He always lives to make intercession for them" (Heb. 7:25 NASB), ensures a complete salvation, past, present, and future.

His "finished work on the cross" is atonement's ultimate basis (Matt. 20:28; Rom. 3:23–25; 1 John 2:2; 1 Peter 1:18–19). Jesus' final utterance, "It is finished," indicates that no other means are needed, required, or would suffice.

Specifically, atonement's provision is one of redemption—a sin-focused payment by Christ's death for all guilt, all penalties, for all, forever (2 Peter 2:1; Rev. 5:9). Enslavement to sin is broken (Gal. 3:13; 4:5), and freedom in Christ is made available (Matt. 20:28; 1 Peter 1:18; Titus 2:14). With that freedom comes the obligation to become the Purchaser's possession (Acts 20:28).

Second, this provision is also one of propitiation and satisfaction for a holy God, angered in justice and judgment over the outrage of sin (cf. Rom. 1:18 with 3:25). Twenty different words used over five hundred times convey Scripture's candor about this divine wrath. Jesus Christ personally bore the brunt of God's holy wrath in our place, on our behalf, thereby sparing us to become his children (Heb. 2:17; 1 John 2:2; 4:4).

Third, atonement provides reconciliation—an exchange by payment of enmity for friendship (Matt. 5:24; Rom. 5:10–11; 2 Cor. 5:18–20). The pivotal New Testament passage of reconciliation reminds us that God the initiator, Christ the instigator, and we the informants are all crucial to completing the cycle of reconciliation (2 Cor. 5).

Finally, the underlying character of this finished work is twofold. Picking up the nuance of substitution from the New Testament language, Christ both took our place and secured atonement for our benefit (Mark 10:45; 2 Cor. 5:14, 21).

All of this reality is potential provision, awaiting the personal response of believing and receiving. First Corinthians 5:18–21 reminds us that God's side and God's provision must be matched by human ambassadorship, his proclamation, and even pleading. While the substitutionary potential is unlimited, sadly, those who benefit are few. Christ's atonement is sufficient for all, but efficient for God's chosen as evident in their act of exercising saving faith.

Christian Education. Atonement is the groundwork for true Christian education, with far-reaching implications replete in Scripture:

Response to truth, whether atonement or education, is indispensible for effectiveness and full benefits from God (John 3:16–18).

Atonement, like effective education ministries, produces worshipers like the redeemed creation magnificently pictured, eternally celebrating the Savior's accomplishments (Rev. 1:6; 5:9–10, 12–14).

The atoning Christ and his education carries a commitment for serving one another through dispensed and developed gifts to benefit the whole person, for all of a person's needs, for all of a person's life (Eph. 4:4–16).

Community is what is produced by atonement (Eph. 1:7, 22, 23; Col. 1:13–14, 18–20; Rev. 1:6). Great Christian education promotes and nurtures through community.

Personal wholeness with fully achieved belonging, worth, and competency are the outcomes of atonement and true education (1 Cor. 12:12–14, 27; Gal. 3:28; Phil. 4:13).

JOSEPH Y. WONG

Bibliography. Anselm (1969), *Cur Deus Homo (Why God Became Man)*; G. Aulen (1961), *Christus Victor*; E. Brunner (1947), *The Mediator: A Study of the Central Doctrine of the Christian Faith*; J. Driver (1986), *Understanding the Atonement for the Mission of the Church*; R. Lightner (1991), *Sin, the Savior, and Salvation*; H. McDonald (1985), *The Atonement of the Death of Christ*; L. Morris (1983), *The Atonement: Its Meaning and Significance*; idem (1965), *The Cross in the New Testament*; G. Smeaton (1953), *The Doctrine of the Atonement as Taught by Christ Himself*; V. Taylor (1960), *Forgiveness and Reconciliation*; idem, *The Atonement in New Testament Teaching*; B. B. Warfield (1970), *Person and Work of Christ*.

Attention. The cognitive process of focusing the mind on some object or idea. Rivello (1979) stresses its importance in regard to the sacraments, prayer, and other religious activities. Attention is not the same as intention, which has a focus or a purpose.

In the affective domain taxonomy of educational objectives (Krathwohl, Bloom, and Masia, 1964) the lowest level is receiving. This emphasizes being aware, or more important to teachers, paying attention to the phenomena at hand.

Additional definitions include these: giving an act of courtesy or gallantry; practical consideration of care; and in the military, a prescribed position of readiness to obey orders (*Funk & Wagnalls Standard Dictionary* International Edition, 1963).

Selective attention is the ability to focus on a specific sensory stimulation from among many. It can also be defined as the learner's choice to give effort to learning a particular piece of information. As learners become better at tasks they use fewer cognitive resources to produce selective attention, and they become less aware of it. Learners who engage in a complex learning task may not be able to give attention to all the parts at the same level. Rather, the various parts of the task must be mastered rather individually. In reading, decoding may take most of the learner's attention, with little given to comprehension. A limited vocabulary may result in a demand for selective attention that reduces ability to focus on meanings.

EUGENE S. GIBBS

Bibliography. *Funk & Wagnalls Standard Dictionary of the English Language, International Edition* (1963); D. R. Krathwohl, B. D. Bloom, and B. B. Masia (1964), *Taxonomy of Educational Objectives, Handbook 2: Affective Domain;* R. J. Rivello (1979), *Encyclopedic Dictionary of Religion.*

See also AFFECTIVE DOMAIN; MEMORIZATION; MEMORY

Attention Deficit Disorder (ADD). A common neurobehavioral disorder of childhood. It may affect children from infancy through the school years and even into adulthood. The disorder is often referred to as ADD or ADHD (attention deficit hyperactivity disorder) or as a combination of both terms (ADD/ADHD). ADD may refer to the broad spectrum of the disorder or to attention deficit disorder without hyperactivity.

The definition, nature, and cause of the disorder and its relationship to other learning and behavioral disorders are still under study. It is estimated that 3 to 5 percent of children have the disorder to some extent (Braswell and Bloomquist, 1991).

The causes of ADD/ADHD are still unknown, but research appears to relate the disorder to abnormalities in brain connections. Heredity is a factor in the disorder. About 25 percent of ADD/ADHD children have parents with the disorder. Other possible causes include brain injury, illness, or allergies. The disorder is more common in boys than in girls (Martin, 1992).

The characteristics of the disorder vary along a broad continuum. Generally, ADD/ADHD is characterized by inattention and distractibility, impulsivity (difficulty in controlling behavior), and sometimes hyperactivity or overarousal.

Inattention refers to the person's inability, as compared to their peers, to stay focused and remain on a task until it is completed. Distractibility may be secondary to inattention. When the focus of attention shifts often, the person appears to be easily distracted. Inattention may be manifested in difficulty completing schoolwork or lengthy chores, inability to follow detailed instructions, daydreaming, and lack of focus on the teacher or leader. The person may have difficulty screening out important from unimportant facts and relating to more than one person or stimulus at a time. "Just as surprising, and often frustrating to the parent is the remarkable ability of many ADHD children to pay attention under certain circumstances. An example is watching TV or playing video games" (Martin, 1992, 22). The difficulty is in deciding how much of the attention choosing is conscious and controlled by the child and how much is controlled by the ADD.

Impulsivity refers to a person's inability to think clearly before acting. Due to concentration and attention problems, people with ADD have difficulty relating consequences to actions. Therefore, negative behaviors are often repeated even when they result in negative consequences. Impulsivity in children may result in frequent injuries as a result of leaping before looking, frequent fights with peers, and rule breaking behaviors. These children do not respond to positive or negative reinforcements unless they occur frequently and are very enjoyable. The long-term effects of rewards or punishments are limited.

Hyperactivity or overarousal in children is manifested as difficulty in controlling body movements or difficulty controlling emotions. This may range from fidgetiness to perpetual motion. Children may have trouble sitting still in class and some may have difficulty sleeping. "However, it is important to remember that while hyperactivity used to be the primary descriptive feature of attention disorders, it actually occurs in less than 30 percent of children who have ADHD" (Martin, 1992, 23). Children with attention deficit disorder without hyperactivity will not have as many behavioral problems. They will usually be shy and socially withdrawn and have low self-esteem. The diagnosis of ADD is often missed in these children.

Secondary characteristics that may accompany ADD/ADHD are low self-esteem, poor peer relationships, poor achievement in school, excessive moodiness and strong emotions, disorganization, diminished hopes about future achievements, and family conflicts (Martin, 1992).

Diagnosis of the disorder is not definitive. Diagnosis is difficult because the characteristics vary both in type and intensity in different individuals. The diagnostic process for children involves parent and teacher behavior assessments, parent background information, medical evaluations to rule out medical or neurological causes, and objective clinical testing. The process should involve at least a six-month period of time (Assessment of ADD, Vol. I, No. 6, p. 4, "The Child Therapy News"). ADD/ADHD may be considered a permanent disorder. About 50 to 65 percent of ADD/ADHD children will continue to experience difficulty as adults (Brief Overview of ADD, Vol. I, No. 6 p. 2, "The Child Therapy News"). So far, little research has been done on adult ADD.

Treatment for ADD/ADHD varies widely. The most common medications are central nervous system stimulants such as Ritalin and pemoline. Side effects of the medications have limited their use. Some doctors feel that medication should not be used at all and recommend behavioral modification techniques or nutritional alternatives. Other doctors maintain that the condition and criteria for diagnosis are still not sufficiently defined to promote any particular treatment (*The Wall Street Journal*, 1994).

Parents and Christian educators can help children with ADD/ADHD learn and grow in the church and in the home. Some general guidelines include: give short, clear directions; clarify rules and consequences frequently; set short-term goals with rewards for success; create a positive, organized environment; work one-on-one or in small groups; take breaks and provide time for transitioning and movement; assign many small tasks rather than one large one; give written instructions; and be patient, loving, and kind. The resources listed in the bibliography and Internet sites related to attention deficit disorder will provide further assistance.

EILEEN STARR

Bibliography. L. Braswell and M. L. Bloomquist (1991), *Cognitive Behavioral Therapy With ADHD Children;* G. Martin (1992), *Critical Problems in Children and Youth;* idem (1992), *The Hyperactive Child;* H. C. Parker (1992), *Hyperactivity Handbook for Schools;* P. O. Quinn and J. M. Stern (1991), *Putting on the Brakes: Young People's Guide to Understanding Attention Deficit Hyperactivity Disorder;* S. F. Reif (1993), *How to Reach and Teach ADD/ADHD Children.*

Attention-Deficit/Hyperactivity Disorder (ADHD). The essential feature of attention-deficit/hyperactivity disorder is a persistent pattern of inattention or hyperactivity-impulsivity that is more frequent and severe than is typically observed in individuals at a comparable level of development (*Diagnostic and Statistical Manual of Mental Disorders*, 78). This is just one of the five criteria used in the *Diagnostic and Statistical Manual of Mental Disorders*, 4th ed. (*DSM-IV*).

The *DSM-IV* further states, "Inattention may be manifest in academic, occupational, or social situations. Individuals with this disorder may fail to give close attention to details or may make careless mistakes in schoolwork or other tasks. Work is often messy and performed carelessly and without considered thought. Individuals often have difficulty sustaining attention in tasks or play activities and find it hard to persist with tasks until completion. They often appear as if their minds are elsewhere or as if they are not listening or did not hear what has just been said" (78).

Ritalin, known chemically as methylphenidate, can improve the attention span of affected children. It has been the drug of choice to help maintain normal behavior in children. It is often administered by parents and school nurses to help children function better in the classroom. Ritalin has many side effects and is considered by many to be overused. The concern is that we too quickly diagnose and medicate children. Opponents feel that other methods should be used.

What is of great interest recently is the recognition of several other issues relating to ADHD. One is the recognition of the familial nature of the condition. While only ten years ago there were few studies of the genetics of ADHD, there are now hundreds, and the Human Genome Project is actively pursuing the identification of genes that govern development of this condition. When one carefully looks at cousins, aunts, uncles, and other extended family members of a child with ADHD, the disorder is far more prevalent than in the general population.

Another issue is the widespread recognition that ADHD may be a condition that does not go away at the end of childhood or adolescence. In at least two-thirds of cases significant symptoms continue into adult life and may be as severe at age 45 as they were at age 5 or 10. While it is evident that the classic hyperactivity we see in most ADHD children is less and less prominent as they age, severe impulsivity and inattentiveness may often continue in force and get worse and even more impairing. Most therapists have not been trained to recognize or diagnose this condition in adults. Often these patients have been misdiagnosed with other psychological problems such as bipolar disorder because ADHD has been considered primarily a juvenile condition. Often those suffering with fetal alcohol syndrome are incorrectly diagnosed with ADHD.

GARY WALLER

Bibliography. C. Alexander-Roberts (1994), *The ADHD Parenting Handbook: Practical Advice for Parents from Parents;* G. L. Flick (1998), *ADD/ADHD Behavior Change Resource Kit: Ready To Use Strategies & Activities for Helping Children With Attention Deficit Disorder;*

L. R. Weathers (1998), *ADHD: A Path to Success: A Revolutionary Theory and New Innovation in Drug Free Therapy;* P. Recer (1998), *The Associated Press;* S. F. Rief (1998), *The ADD/ADHD Checklist;* A. Train (1997), *ADHD: How to Deal With Very Difficult Children.*

Augustine (354–430). Bishop of Hippo in Africa from 396 to 430. He is generally recognized as the greatest thinker of the post-Nicene Christian Fathers. Born in Tagaste (now Souk-Aharas, Algeria) of middle-class parents, he undertook the study of rhetoric at an early age. Seeking truth, he probed the writings of Cicero and pursued Manicheism. The preaching of Bishop Ambrose of Milan, combined with his own mystical experience, caused him to convert to Christianity at age thirty-two. In 391 Augustine moved to Hippo (now Bony, Algeria), where he became a priest and later the bishop. As bishop he established a monastery and a school for ministerial training.

Augustine's philosophical and educational writings make significant contributions to Christian education. For the Western church, he was able to successfully fuse Neoplatonic philosophy with Pauline Christianity. He believed that the universe is an ordered structure in which degrees of being are at the same time degrees of value. This universal order requires the subordination of what is lower on the scale of being to what is higher—body is subject to spirit, and spirit to God.

Philosophically he maintained that wherever one may find truth, in the final analysis it has come from God. The individual thinker does not make truth, he finds it; he is able to do so because Christ, the revealing Word of God, is the *magister interior*, the "inward teacher," who enables the thinker to see the truth as he listens to it.

As an educational thinker, Augustine transcended his generation. He combined deep respect for the cultivation of reason with a passionate concern for heart feelings stirred by God. Human beings' ability to reason is what sets them apart from other animals. But sensitivity to "the light within" is necessary for true wisdom.

Equally significant is his recognition that religious truth does not best come from someone outside. One learns in the fullest sense only by internal apprehending. "Our real Teacher is he who is said to dwell in the inner man, namely Christ, that is, the unchangeable power and eternal wisdom of God" (*The Teacher*, 11.38).

For Augustine, education involved considerably more than verbal assent. It meant a change in attitude and behavior. Mere acceptance of truth delivered by another was not sufficient. Genuine learning involved an inner, personal response.

Several characteristics of a Christian teacher are highlighted in the writings of Augustine. Educators should recognize the importance of his work and be genuinely interested in it. They should enjoy the craft of teaching. Augustine saw teaching in terms of encouragement and stimulation rather then coercion and authoritarian control. "We must drive out by gentle encouragement his [the student's] excessive timidity, which hinders him from expressing his opinion." Further, he suggested that teachers temper students' shyness "by introducing the idea of brotherly fellowship" (*The First Catechetical Instruction*, 13.18).

Drawing his example from the life of Christ, Augustine maintained that teachers are to offer themselves for imitation and to display those qualities that their students must develop if they are to become mature persons.

Methodologically he urged teachers to make use of the five senses. "The man who teaches me is one who presents to my eyes or to any bodily sense, or even to the mind itself, something that I wish to know" (*The Teacher*, 11.49).

The physical comfort of the student was another area addressed by the concerned instructor. Teachers ought to offer the tired student a chair. Contrary to popular practice, Augustine suggested that "it is better that the student should listen seated from the first" (*The First Catechetical Instruction*, 13.19).

One of Augustine's best known devotional works is *The City of God*, a masterpiece that draws a symbolic picture of two spiritual powers that contend for allegiance in God's creation—faith and unbelief. His famous *Confessions* were written at age forty-five and are devotional outpourings of penitence and thanksgiving. They tell the story of his spiritual struggles after conversion—feelings of guilt for sin, of inadequacy, and of the frustration of being a recovering sinner. Over the past sixteen centuries many people have found their experiences similar to his. In his encounter with grace, they have found reason to trust God's grace for themselves.

JAMES A. DAVIES

Bibliography. Augustine, *The Teacher;* idem, *The First Catechetical Instruction;* P. R. L. Brown (1967), *Augustine of Hippo;* E. Kevane (1964), *Augustine the Educator;* W. T. Smith (1980), *Augustine: His Life and Thought.*

See also ARISTOTLE; EARLY CHURCH EDUCATION; MODELING; PLATO

Ausubel, David P. (1918–). American educational psychologist. Trained in both medicine and psychiatry at Columbia University, Ausubel studied cognitive psychology, which provides the basis for his educational contributions. He founded the Ph.D. program in educational psychology at the Graduate School of the City University of New York.

Influenced by Piaget's cognitive development theory, Ausubel conducted extensive research on verbal learning and retention in children and adolescents, through which he became concerned with the "meaningful learning of material." Educational methodology must be varied, he contended, because of the complexity of the learning process.

To Ausubel, any learning that is to be meaningful must have relevance for the student. Contending that children learn through reception and listening rather than through self-discovery, he believed that all new learning must be linked with that which the student already knows. According to his subsumption theory, the single most important factor in learning is what the learner already knows. The assimilation of new information into the individual's present body of knowledge, regardless of the level of education, is the core of meaningful learning. Furthermore, Ausubel held that learning is deductive, moving from the general to the specific, or from principle to example. To him, the burden for ensuring learning rests primarily with the teacher, whose task, as he saw it, is to instruct in a deductive manner by establishing patterns of relationships among concepts, with general patterns coming to subsume more specific ones. Therefore, concepts, facts, and principles should be presented in a sequential and organized manner.

Ausubel's pattern of expository teaching begins with the teacher's stating objectives, giving examples, and relating new material to previous learning experiences (advanced organizers), and then presenting the lesson in an organized sequence, carefully moving from the general to the more detailed in a step-by-step manner (progressive differentiation). Integrative reconciliation involves the student giving indication of similarities or dissimilarities of the new material with what he already knows. The final step, mastery, or consolidation, is essential before moving on to the next learning experience.

Ausubel insists that it is imperative for teachers to frequently check the current level of understanding of their students in relation to the material being taught. Thus, the instructor becomes a lesson organizer, clearly presenting the material so that it not only is linked with previous learning, but also serves as a bridge to future learning. The successful teacher, according to Ausubel, is the one who discovers ways to help students subsume new ideas into their cognitive structures. Restatement and application of the material taught are indicators of whether the teacher has successfully fulfilled this task.

DAVID GOUGH

Bibliography. D. P. Ausubel (1963), *The Psychology of Meaningful Verbal Learning: An Introduction to School Learning;* idem (1968), *Educational Psychology: A Cognitive View.*

See also ADVANCED ORGANIZER; ASSIMILATION; COGNITIVE DEVELOPMENT; PIAGET, JEAN; SEQUENCE

Authoritarian Approach. An approach to group organization and leadership that occurs when the leader determines all rules and procedures and does not welcome the ideas of other group participants (Engel and Snellgrove, 1989).

In a classic study, Kurt Lewin et al. (1958) examined the impact of different kinds of leadership on group behavior. Lewin asked eleven-year-old boys to participate in some after-school clubs. Using the authoritarian approach, the leader determined practically all of the club's activities and procedures. The adult assigned a task to each boy, withheld praise and criticism, and stayed aloof from the group. The participants produced more for this type of leader while the leader was present. But, in comparison with other styles, production decreased when the leader left. The boys were less friendly and less team-oriented when under this type of leadership. After experiencing a different style, the boys were much more frustrated and restive when placed under a second authoritarian leader. Conger (1973) found that children raised in authoritarian families lack practice in negotiating for their desires and exercising responsibility. They tend to resent authority and sometimes rebel without apparent cause.

KENNETH S. COLEY

Bibliography. J. J. Conger (1973), *Adolescence and Youth: Psychological Development in a Changing World;* T. L. Engel and L. Snellgrove (1989), *Psychology: Its Principles and Applications;* R. Lippitt and R. K. White (1958), *Reading in Social Psychology,* pp. 446–511.

Authoritative Approach. An approach that occurs when the controlling dynamic of a group's interaction is based on both the exercise of a legitimate position of authority and the acceptance of input from others. An authoritative approach lies somewhere on a continuum between authoritarian, which does not seek the ideas of others, and a democratic approach, which is dependent upon the active participation of others.

Mussen, Conger, and Kagan (1974) state that the authoritative teacher, unlike the authoritarian one, encourages a student's individual initiative, self-esteem, and social responsibility. Also, the authoritative teacher, unlike the permissive teacher, provides guidance and ultimate direction, and sets standards and goals.

Eisenman (1985) discusses the effectiveness of this style in parenting. He describes authoritative parents as providing high support and high control. The authoritative style, when compared with authoritarian, neglectful, and permissive styles, was rated the most effective style for developing a child's self-worth, conformity to authority, and strong religious beliefs.

KENNETH S. COLEY

Bibliography. P. H. Mussen, J. J. Conger, and J. Kagan (1974), *Child Development and Personality;* T. Eisenman (1985), *Big People, Little People.*

Autonomy. The ability to function independently without being under the control of others. Becoming autonomous is an important part of the development of the individual. Jean Piaget, an eminent Swiss biologist whose early work on cognition was instrumental in changing the way educators think about maturation, proposed that developing autonomy is central to an individual's moral reasoning and, therefore, to personal development. Piaget believed that young children live with *heteronomy*—morality derived from the domination of parents. A child thinks that rules are timeless and emanate from God, and that goodness lies in respecting those in authority, obeying their commands, and accepting the rewards and punishments given out by adults. For a youngster, to be moral is to obey the parent's will. But starting around age 7, the child begins to move from an external authority to an internal authority; from being ethnocentric to being egocentric.

Heteronomy is a necessary part of moral development, for it helps train a child to become part of society. Yet at some point individuals must move beyond a morality that is imposed from the outside, and begin to embrace a morality that is guided from within. During the elementary school years, children begin making moral decisions based on fairness and equality. Peer interaction and intellectual growth help autonomy develop as the child learns important things like cooperation, reciprocity, and mutual agreement. Piaget argued that for a time, heteronomy and autonomy coexist, but as the child matures, objective responsibility diminishes while subjective responsibility grows. Rules are still respected, but they are based upon consensus rather than authority, and the rules are subject to change if everyone agrees. As concern for the rights of others begins to grow, children develop a sense of justice and even forgiveness. Eventually they move fully toward autonomy, making their own decisions about right and wrong and even becoming relativists, aware of differing opinions regarding rules.

Behavioral psychologist Lawrence Kohlberg expanded Piaget's process into a six-stage sequence of moral development extending from childhood through adulthood. To Kohlberg, right and wrong is determined by society and is called "convention." A child is preconventional, thinking of right and wrong in terms of rewards and punishments. When children move toward maturity, they become conventional, doing what society thinks is right. A mature adult is postconventional, seeing beyond social norms to make decisions based on principle. While some critics reject the notion of moral stages, many Christian educators have embraced the idea, noting that the initial mark of Christian maturity is spiritual autonomy. A believer who has control of his or her own life is self-directed and can choose to submit to the lordship of Jesus Christ. Without autonomy, a believer has no self-direction and merely follows the dictates of others.

JERRY CHIP MACGREGOR

See also CONTRACT LEARNING; KOHLBERG, LAWRENCE; MORAL EDUCATION; PIAGET, JEAN

Awana Clubs International. Awana is an acronym for *Approved Workmen Are Not Ashamed,* based on 2 Timothy 2:15. Awana Clubs International had its beginnings in the 1920s when Paul Rader, pastor of the Chicago Gospel Tabernacle, was touched with a burden for children. He chose Lance Latham to direct a Sunday afternoon program for young boys. In 1933 Latham assumed the pastorate of the North Side Gospel Center on the northwest side of Chicago. One of his first tasks was to organize clubs for boys and girls. He was assisted in this vision by Art Rorheim, a product of Rader's ministry. Rorheim made use of many volunteers in forming the program, which was organized around three age groups: Pals, Pioneers, and Pilots for the boys; Chums, Junior Guards, and Senior Guards for the girls. Even at this early stage there was a focus on games and competition, which continues to be a thrust of the Awana program. They also inaugurated a camping experience, which has become the Awana Scholarship Camps, still available today for those who earn the privilege of attendance.

Other churches heard about the program and wrote for help in organizing their own clubs. Thus, in 1950, the Awana Youth Association was established, and programming principles evolved that are still utilized. These include the use of handbooks for Bible training, the emphasis on uniforms, and the development of the Awana Game Circle. Ultimately this led to the first Awana Olympics in 1955, an event that also continues today.

In addition to the current handbooks for each age group, Awana also publishes *Awana Signal,* a magazine for leaders, as well as *The Basic Training Manual* to help leaders know how to conduct Awana games.

As the organization grew, staffing needs became apparent. So in 1966 Awana began the Awana missionary program, inviting couples to raise their support and then help local churches start and maintain the program. Today these people conduct Olympic meets, hold leadership training conferences, sponsor Bible quiz meets, and lead Awana Scholarship Camps.

In 1986 the organization officially became Awana Clubs International, in recognition of its International Outreach Ministries program. The current headquarters is located in Streamwood, Illinois. The organization is under the leadership of David Genn, who succeeded Art Rorheim as executive director.

Programs. Age Groups. The program is divided into six clubs and two youth groups.

Cubbies are boys and girls ages 3 and 4.

Sparks are boys and girls in kindergarten, first, and second grades.

Pals are boys in third and fourth grades.

Chums are girls in third and fourth grades.

Pioneers are boys in fifth and sixth grades.

Guards are girls in fifth and sixth grades.

Cross Trainers is an urban program.

Friends is for mentally challenged children.

Jr. Varsity is for youth in seventh and eighth grades.

Varsity is for teenagers in grades 9 to 12.

Program Philosophy. Awana is known for its emphasis on Bible memorization and competition. The Bible used is the King James Bible or the New King James Bible. Awana intends for club members to memorize several hundred verses in the course of their club experience, relying upon the leaders to find opportunities for application.

The focus on competition grows out of the conviction that "Competition is a vital nutrient in the child's physical and mental growth. Everyone desires to be a winner" (*Awana Overview,* 7). Awana includes an emphasis on uniforms. No awards are presented to those who are not in uniform.

Objectives. 1. To get as many young people as possible from the local community into the Awana Club program and under the sound of the gospel of the grace of God so that they have the opportunity to accept Christ as their personal Savior.

2. To prepare young people to accept the responsibility of spreading the gospel through leadership, service, and witness.

Meeting Format. Awana recommends a two-hour period for a club meeting, beginning with a flag ceremony and a forty minute game period. The next forty minutes are devoted to handbook time, when leaders listen to club members recite their memory work, both Scripture and what is called for in the handbooks. This is when handbook awards are earned. The meeting concludes with a group meeting of all club members. This council time contains such programming elements as a song service, testimony time, object lessons, announcements, award presentations, and a Bible lesson.

Church Affiliations. Any churches that agree with the Awana doctrinal statement may use the program and be chartered to conduct Awana Clubs. However, it is Awana's policy not to make the program available to:

1. Churches affiliated with denominations that are members of the National Council of Churches (U.S. only) or the World Council of Churches;
2. Local churches identified with the charismatic movement, although Awana recognizes that there are many true believers involved in the charismatic movement.

Only local churches, missions, or mission agencies may be chartered to use the Awana program. Awana Clubs International is at One East Bode Road, Streamwood, Illinois 60187 (630-213-2000).

SARA ANNE ROBERTSON

Axiology. One of the four branches of the study of classical philosophy, it seeks to answer the question, what is of value? A value is whatever an individual considers important as compared to something else. Persons are valuing beings, born with the desire to decide what is important.

To answer the axiological question, persons concern themselves with three subquestions. First, are values subjective or objective? If values are subjective, they are selected on the basis of personal preference. A person, place, thing, or idea is important because someone believes that it is. If values are objective, they are part of the nature of things. They are based on verifiable facts pertaining to persons, places, things, or ideas without reference to personal preference.

Second, are values changing or constant? If values are changing, they exist independently of any external standard of measurement. What persons hold as important is maintained, altered, or discarded according to personal preference. As personal preferences change so do the values that express them. If values are constant, they are fixed, universal, and timeless. What persons hold as important applies to all people in all places for all time.

Third, are values arranged in order of importance? If values are arranged in order of importance, they are organized as a graduated series of values. Placement of a value within the graduated series is based on the value's perceived degree of importance.

The answers to these three questions will determine a person's system of values. Most evangelical Christians believe that values are both objective and constant. They use biblical principles to guide their decisions about what is of value. Biblical principles are the timeless and universal standards against which Christians evaluate their preferences. Christians' goal is to align what they believe is important with what God says is important.

JOYCE L. THORNTON

Bibliography. I. V. Cully and K. B. Cully, eds. (1990), *Harper's Encyclopedia of Religious Education;* G. R. Knight (1989), *Issues and Alternatives in Educational Philosophy.*

See also EPISTEMOLOGY; PHILOSOPHY OF CHRISTIAN EDUCATION; PHILOSOPHY OF RELIGION

Bb

Baby Boom Generation. Baby boomers are commonly defined by the birth years of 1946 to 1964, when there was a "boom" in the number of births following World War II that continued until the early 1960s. Generational theorists often state that the baby boom occurred initially because of the return of American servicemen from World War II, and then continued because of the relative stability and prosperity of the 1950s. The decline of births in the 1960s may have been because of the turbulence and unrest of that decade, or—perhaps more likely—because of the advent of the birth control pill.

Generational theorists William Strauss and Neil Howe (1991) describe baby boomers as the products of permissive childrearing, conformist parents, and highly competitive schooling fueled by the threat of Russian technological advancement and nuclear war. The result was a generation that rebelled against the values of their parents—by becoming hippies who rejected the materialism of parents, demonstrators who protested the injustice of racism and the Vietnam War, or members of religious cults or radical political groups who rejected traditional values. In early adulthood many baby boomers became "yuppies" (young urban professionals) who were self-absorbed perfectionists, dominating with an influence that significantly outweighed their numbers. Their emphasis on being different from past generations resulted in "culture wars" consisting of antagonism at the popular and political levels.

From a historical framework Strauss and Howe see baby boomers as one part of a four-generation cycle that has occurred repeatedly in history and is even noted in the Bible (they cite Eccles. 3:15 and the Exodus). Boomers are described as "prophets" who are indulged as children, grow up as self-centered crusaders, emphasize moral principles during their middle age years, and are considered visionary and wise in their senior years. This generation is—during each cycle of history—marked by idealism.

Researcher George Barna (1994) notes that boomers were reared in a social context of traditional values, where traditions and rules had meaning and family was cherished. The idealism of boomers means they believe in the basic goodness of people and that improving the world is worth the effort. They view the future with optimism, so that risk-taking makes sense. However, change is balanced with stability and affirmation of what has worked well in the past. Thus boomers affirm the value of education, although they feel personal preferences should be blended with traditional education. Learning in itself is valuable, boomers believe.

Boomers feel they are unique and special, deserving of the best in life, perhaps a reflection of their being prized by parents. Self-indulgence is thus a widespread characteristic, and they enthusiastically exploit the world to achieve their definition of success: prosperity. Yet, Barna continues, boomers often become workaholics whose personal identity is linked to their job performance and status. The relationships boomers cultivate involve continual renegotiation, need not be permanent, and are often utilitarian; boomers "network."

Not all baby boomers are alike; the trends described by researchers can be significant without being universal. It is also important to note that baby boomers, like all generations, tend to change some of their characteristics as they age.

DONALD E. RATCLIFF

Bibliography. G. Barna (1994), *Baby Busters;* G. Collins and T. Clinton (1992), *Baby Boomer Blues;* W. C. Roof (1993), *A Generation of Seekers: The Spiritual Journeys of the Baby Boom Generation;* W. Strauss and N. Howe (1997), *The Fourth Turning: An American Prophecy;* idem (1991), *Generations.*

Balance. *See* Equilibrium.

Bandura, Albert (1925–). Albert Bandura received his Ph.D. in psychology from the University of Iowa in 1952. He is currently a professor of psychology at Stanford University specializing in personality research. Bandura belongs to the behaviorist camp of educational psychology. Though he holds to many of the tenets of classical behaviorism espoused by B. F. Skinner and John Watson, Bandura seeks to broaden understanding of the learning process by including the influence of genetic and biological factors. In addition, Bandura explains learning as a complex process that involves the dynamic interplay between internal and external factors. It is this latter element that led to the development of his social learning theory. His basic premise is that behavior can be explained and understood as a function of experience rather than exclusively by maturation.

Bandura has concentrated much of his career on discovering the basic mechanisms of personal agency through which people exercise control over events that impact their lives. One line of his research is concerned with how people influence their own motivation, thought patterns, affective states, and behavior through beliefs of personal and collective efficacy. A second line of his research is concerned with the role of self-regulatory mechanisms that rely on internal standards and self-influence in human adaptation and change. He has made significant contributions to the establishment of the sociocognitive development field of psychology (LeFrancois, 1994).

As the most prominent spokesman for the social learning theory, Bandura wrote a book detailing his views entitled *Social Foundations of Thoughts and Action* (1986). According to his theory one can learn by observing the behavior of another. Once this observation has occurred, the individual can choose to imitate the conduct and incorporate it into her or his own pattern of behavior. Observing the consequences of the behavior can have a reinforcing effect as well. This phenomena is referred to by Bandura as *vicarious reinforcement*.

Social learning takes place when a protégé makes a rational choice to observe and subsequently imitate the behavior of a mentor. The cognitive thought process that takes place on the part of the protégé differentiates it from a purely behavioristic phenomenon. It combines both a cognitive reasoning approach with a behavioristic approach to learning. Both are at work in the life of the learner.

In the Christian education context of the local church, this approach to learning is seen when a teacher, though in desperate need of improvement, refuses to come to teacher training classes because he or she does not feel in need of help. This conclusion is reached because of imitation of the teaching method. In that process of learning the teacher did not observe any negative consequences impacting either the mentor teacher or his or her students. This negative cycle of teaching continues until something or someone intercedes and helps the teacher come to the conclusion that improvement is indeed needed (Yount, 1996).

It is for this reason that parenting resources should be available for adults in the local church. When a child is reared in a home where both parents are modeling consistent spiritual disciplines of Bible reading, prayer, church involvement, and the like, the child will learn to imitate and incorporate these same elements of godly living into early developmental experience as well. What Bandura refers to as social learning theory is as old as the teachings of Scripture. The Old Testament spoke often of the need to observe the practice of the father and so learn of his ways. It was in such modeling that the Hebrew culture, customs, and religious beliefs were transferred from one generation to the next. In the New Testament Jesus commanded his disciples to imitate his ways and thereby carry on the faith.

MICHAEL J. ANTHONY

Bibliography. D. L. Barlow (1985), *Educational Psychology: The Teaching Learning Process;* G. R. LeFrancois (1994), *Psychology of Teaching;* W. R. Yount (1996), *Created to Learn.*

Baptism. Rite of initiation into the Christian community, indicating commitment of life to Christ and the confession of faith in Christ. It is a testimony of breaking with the old life and the sinful past and of entering into a new life through the work of Christ. It is indicative of one moving from spiritual darkness to spiritual light, from spiritual death to spiritual life. From the very beginning of the Christian church, baptism has been the universal initiatory rite by which new believers were introduced into the fellowship of believers.

The word *baptism* is a transliteration of the Greek word *baptizo* which means to plunge, to dip, or to immerse. It was commonly used by ancient Greeks to signify the dyeing of a garment, the cleaning of vessels, or the dipping of animals. In the Septuagint one reads of Naaman immersing himself in the Jordan River (2 Kings 5:14).

In the New Testament, *baptizo* occurs about seventy-five times with approximately half of the occurrences in relation to the ministry of John the Baptist, who preached a baptism of repentance for the remission of sins (Luke 3:3). John's baptism also entailed a dominant eschatological reference as the nation of Israel was to prepare for the coming of the Messiah and his kingdom. Jesus himself was baptized by John, thereby authenticating John's ministry, identifying himself with sinful humanity, and setting an example for his followers. Also, with the approval of God the Father in heaven, the baptism of Jesus was the public initiation of the Messiah into his ministry of suffering, service, and salvation for humankind.

In addition to the baptism of John, some have pointed to the Jewish proselyte baptism as being a precursor to Christian baptism, indicating as it did a break with the past life and the taking up of a new life. This ceremony, which was reserved for Gentiles who were to be admitted to Judaism, is not mentioned in the Old Testament but primarily in later Jewish literature of the first and second centuries. The few Greek references to it in the Greek literature employ *bapto*, but not *baptizo*, and while there is disagreement among scholars over its influence on the baptism of John and on Christian baptism, the late date of the referent literature is indicative of minimal connections.

It is with the command of Jesus in the Great Commission to make disciples of all nations and to baptize them in the name of the Father, Son, and Holy Spirit that Christian baptism gets its real impetus. The early church immediately began the practice of baptism, as recorded in Acts, where, for example, about three thousand were baptized on the day of Pentecost.

Various writings in the Epistles shed further light on the meaning and significance of baptism, but especially the sixth chapter of Romans. Here Paul says that believers are "buried with him through baptism into death" (v. 4), "indicating the death of the "old self" (v. 6). "But, just as Christ was raised from the dead . . . we too may live a new life" (v. 4). Paul apparently saw in the baptismal act a reenactment of the essential points of the redemptive gospel message of the death, burial, and resurrection of Jesus. And by being baptized one was identifying with the will and purpose of Christ. Consequently, baptism was a declaration of a break with the old life and its power over the person and a commitment to a new life in Christ characterized by "righteousness" (v. 18).

Hence, baptism is in itself an educational event. As suggested above, whenever someone is baptized, the gospel message is dramatically proclaimed and reenacted. The event is a teaching reminder to those who are followers of Christ of what Jesus has done for them and also of the needed concomitant response of the believer to righteous living. It seems especially appropriate that the command to baptize in the Great Commission is preceded by the command to disciple and followed by the command to teach.

In addition to the teaching inherent in baptism, the church has often developed an educational program around the ceremony of baptism, recognizing its significance as the rite of initiation into the church. So, for example, by the third century after Christ, a three year program of Christian instruction was commonly required before a person could be baptized and allowed into the fellowship of the church, and the baptism was often followed by additional teaching on the fundamentals of the faith. Similarly in many churches of the modern era, biblical and theological instruction often precedes or follows the baptismal event.

HAL PETTEGREW

Bibliography. G. Beasley-Murray (1962), *Baptism in the New Testament;* R. L. Browning and R. A. Reed (1995), *Models of Confirmation and Baptismal Affirmations: Liturgical and Educational Issues and Designs;* T. M. Finn (1992), *Early Christian Baptism and the Catechumenate: Italy, North Africa and Egypt;* H. T. Kerr (1944), *The Christian Sacraments: A Sourcebook for Ministers;* A. H. Strong (1907), *Systematic Theology.*

Baptist Young People's Union. The Baptist Young People's Union (BYPU) was a leading youth discipleship movement that was begun in the late nineteenth century and that led to a broad range of Christian education endeavors for all age groups.

A forerunner of the BYPU was Christian Endeavor, established in 1881. This society was founded to lead young people to Christ and into his church as well as to establish them firmly in the faith. During this period, several youth organizations were founded, notably the Epworth League, the Luther League, the Evangelical League, and the Nazarene Young People's League. In May 1890 the Baptist Young People's Union of America was formed in Chicago.

In 1895, Southern Baptists founded the BYPU Auxiliary to the Southern Baptist Convention in Atlanta, Georgia. Though a separate entity, like the Women's Missionary Union of the Southern Baptist convention, the new organization grew closer to the convention, and especially to the Baptist Sunday School Board. Baptist leaders were concerned over the potential separation of their young people from the convention program, as well as the possibility of enlisting their own young people in discipleship. At the time there were those who opposed the organization, principally because they did not like withdrawing from the national organization or they opposed the organization altogether.

Prior to its beginning, Southern Baptist denominational leaders emphasized that the new organization was to be strictly Baptistic and denominational and under the sole authority of the local church. Initially, it emphasized college students, or persons age 17 and above, but it soon expanded to include younger children. The former were called the senior BYPU, the latter were the junior BYPU. The fledgling Baptist Sunday School Board was entrusted to provide literature. This was the first national youth organization in the Southern Baptist Convention. It had theme songs, yells, cheers, and slogans. Leaders sponsored area, state, and national meetings. The BYPU Department of the Sunday School Board was established in 1918.

BYPU continued to grow and by 1921 the program was expanded to other age groups: junior BYPU was for 9- to–12-year olds, intermediates were aged 13–16, and seniors were 17 and above. Shortly thereafter, in 1925, the program took in all age groups. Periodical materials began to be published for adults in 1930. In the following years the organization became fully graded with all age groups represented. The program changed its name to the Baptist Training Union in 1934. The Sword Drill (later called the Bible Drill) and the Speaker's Tournament both emerged as distinctive aspects of the BYPU.

When the BYPU began in 1895, there were 500 unions with approximately 20,000 members. In 1916 the BYPU of the South reported 4,367 unions with a total membership of 153,071. By 1927 that number had grown to nearly half a million.

The BYPU was successful in building a strong Sunday evening program for Southern Baptist churches. With more and more young people, churches added Sunday evening fellowships for youth, laying the groundwork for the development of church recreation programs.

In the first South-wide BYPU conference held from December 31, 1929 to January 2, 1930, in Memphis, Tennessee, I. J. Van Ness set forth the fundamentals for the fledgling organization. The purpose was training in church membership. Van Ness, president of the Baptist Sunday School Board, indicated that the topics pursued were a devotional topic, a Bible study topic, a doctrinal topic, and a missionary topic. At that time this was the regular routine followed in the BYPU. With this agenda, Baptist youth developed a mental structure. The second feature of the organization was the group structure. The union membership was divided into several groups and each group in turn presented the program for the evening. Van Ness felt that this helped to develop future leaders among the young people. Some leaders stressed that this organization was designed only for believers. In fact, unsaved members of BYPU were designated as associate members, and were urged not to participate in the weekly program except for singing.

In 1935 J. E. Lambdin wrote the *B.A.U. Manual*. This was the first book that gave guidance for adult training. At that time some churches began to call the group the adult BYPU. Obviously, the name change to Baptist Adult Union was needed.

The first leader of the Baptist Young People's Union at the Baptist Sunday School Board was Landrum P. Leavell. In 1909 he developed a Systematic Bible Reader's Course with selected daily readings, one of the most important phases of the movement. In 1918 Leavell began publication of the *Intermediate Baptist Young People's Union Quarterly*. More than any other leader, Leavell de-

veloped the fledgling organization from a series of mass meetings to a weekly training meeting. Daily Bible readings became a central feature of the movement.

How would one describe the agenda for the Sunday evening meetings of the BYPU? A succession of manuals or church study course training books written by Arthur Flake, Landrum Leavell, J. E. Landrum, and others carefully explained the agenda, as did the officers who led parts of the meeting. Though there were variations, the weekly meeting contained five parts: an opening period of singing, prayer, and business; a program period with a topic developed by a group of members; and a closing period in which members prayed for the upcoming worship service. From time to time all unions met together.

The curriculum materials, called *quarterlies*, were divided into sections called *parts*. Before the weekly meeting, the group captain assigned each member a part to tell in the next week's program. These were five-minute speeches based on the assigned section of the material. Young people and adults stood up before the group and made their presentations in their own words. Many Baptists attribute their ability to speak in public to these modest speeches in Baptist Young People's Union. This feature helped each person to understand as well as discuss his or her section of the program.

What, then, are the contributions of the Baptist Young People's Union? First, it was a distinct movement for discipleship training for Southern Baptist youth. Second, it provided a new venue for potential leadership training for youth. Third, it emphasized daily Bible reading as a means of developing disciples. Fourth, it laid the groundwork for the development of church recreation. Fifth, it served as a catalyst for youth ministry. Sixth, it led to the development of discipleship training for other groups, including adults and children. Seventh, through its curriculum materials Baptist youth learned Christian doctrine, polity, and church history. Eighth, the development of church study course books or manuals strengthened leaders and provided standards of excellence for the groups.

JIM WALTER

Bibliography. R. A. Baker (1966), *The Story of the Sunday School Board*; P. E. Burroughs (1941), *Fifty Fruitful Years*; J. W. Conley (1913), *History of the Baptist Young People's Union of America*; J. Fletcher (1994), *The Southern Baptist Convention: A Sesquicentennial History*; J. White (1921), *Our B.Y.P.U.: Manual for Baptist Young People on Organization, Programs, and Methods.*

Bar/Bat Mitzvah. The bar mitzvah is one of the most important events in the life of a Jewish man. It is a religious rite practiced by the Jewish people as far back as the thirteenth century. The concept of the bar mitzvah can be traced to the

Talmud. It was there that religious accountability was bestowed when a boy physically became a man.

The word *mitzvah* actually means "a command given by God," though the definition has been expanded to mean anything promoting proper behavior. *Bar* means "son," so at a bar mitzvah service a boy becomes a "son of the commandment." It signifies a change in the boy's standing in the Jewish community. No longer considered an innocent, he must now take on his full religious responsibility. At thirteen years of age he can begin to read from the Holy Scripture, and is no longer a child but a man in the traditions of Judaism.

The Four Privileges. Once the boy has become a son of the commandment, he has four privileges bestowed on him. First, he is counted with the men to make up a *minyan*—a group of ten men needed to conduct a public worship service. This has always been restricted to men only, so the invitation to participate in worship is considered a significant sign of maturity. Second, the bar mitzvah boy is given the privilege of putting on *phylacteries,* two small leather boxes containing slips of paper inscribed with scriptural passages. One is worn on the forehead, the other on the left arm, and he is instructed to wear these each morning while reciting his morning prayers. Third, the boy is told he is now a young man, and has the responsibility to read from the Torah. He can be called on at any time to go up and read Jewish instruction to people. The fourth privilege is that the young man can now be part of the *bet din,* or Jewish court, deliberating disputes.

The Ceremony. The bar mitzvah ceremony, which takes place in a synagogue, involves three parts. The first is the *shepetarni,* or "release." The boy and his father approach the front of the sanctuary, and the boy's father releases him into the world. Quoting from Midrash Genesis 63:10, the father prays, "Blessed be He who has relieved me of this obligation." With that, the sins the young man commits will henceforth fall on himself and not on his father.

The second part of the ceremony is the *aliya,* or "call." The rabbi calls the boy forward to read a section from the Torah (the first five books of Moses) and a section from the *Haftorah* (the prophets). The rabbi and the boy then both recite various blessings and lead the congregation in worship up to the *derashah,* or sermon. In times past this would be the point where the boy revealed his ability to read and speak Hebrew and demonstrated his skill at rightly expounding the Scriptures. In recent years this has evolved into nothing more than a speech in which the boy thanks his parents and others who have helped him arrive at his bar mitzvah.

The third part of the ceremony is the *seudah,* or "festive meal." Originally a time of refreshment and celebration, in the twentieth century it has become simply a party, complete with a band, dance hall, and catered meal. Gifts are given to the young man in recognition of his achievement. The traditional gift was a pen, symbolizing his newfound adulthood, but now it is common for the bar mitzvah boy to receive money.

The Bat Mitzvah. In recent years, more liberal Jewish sects have broadened the bar mitzvah to include girls. Since girls mature faster than boys, the *bat mitzvah* (or "daughter of commandment") is celebrated when a girl turns twelve. This is a similar ceremony, with a release, call, and celebration, though the words are changed and the young lady is not accorded the same privileges as a young man. Bat mitzvahs are celebrated by conservative and reformed Jews, but there are no bat mitzvah services in Israel, where the state religion is orthodox Judaism.

The bar mitzvah is very important to the Jewish people, and it is not uncommon for families to fly to Israel to celebrate the occasion in the Promised Land. Bar mitzvah services take place every Monday and Thursday at the Western Wall in Jerusalem, and on Wednesdays at Masada, the fortress in the Judean desert that symbolizes Jewish freedom. Jews from around the world can be seen celebrating at these services. There is no explicit Old Testament model for such a ritual, though in the first chapter of Numbers all men twenty years and older were counted for service in the army, and that is sometimes offered as the genesis of the bar mitzvah.

JERRY CHIP MACGREGOR

Bibliography. S. Swartz (1985), *Bar Mitzvah;* J. Teleshikin (1991), *Jewish Literacy.*

See also AGE OF ACCOUNTABILITY; CONFIRMATION; JEWISH EDUCATION

Behaviorism, Theories of. Behaviorism is most often associated with B. F. Skinner, who followed John Watson in developing an approach based on a philosophy of what constitutes learning. Outward change, *behavior,* is the definition of learning and the proper realm of study. *Mind* and inner states are not to be considered.

These five basic elements are present in almost all behavioral approaches to education: (1) an emphasis on *present behavior* in relation to educational performance; (2) a focus on precision in *assessment* and *goal setting*; (3) use of *experimental research* in program design; (4) *specificity* in defining procedures and programs; (5) routine *evaluation* of program effectiveness (Maher and Forman, 1987).

Present Behavior. Behaviorists look very carefully at students' present level of academic behavior and conduct. They begin by defining, in a measurable way, students' levels of functioning.

67

This may involve accuracy in school work or the number of times a behavior is repeated in a given time period. The belief is that all learning involves behavior change.

Assessment and Goal Setting. Behavioral objectives, which must be valid (measure what they are supposed to measure) and reliable (consistent over time and setting), describe a student's desired performance following instruction. The behavioral objectives are used both as goals and as standards of performance.

Experimental Research in Program Design. The foundation for educational design is laboratory-based experimental research. Designs must be based on empirically derived principles demonstrated to be effective in controlled basic and applied research.

Specificity. Very careful description is required with any program focused on behavioral change. Curricula can be devised only after goals and objectives have been set and research analyzed. All components of programs, including rewards, time duration, and administration, must be identified with precision.

Evaluation. Behaviorally designed curricula are constantly evaluated. These procedures come directly from the objectives. Results are used for program improvement and to determine degree of success.

Behaviorism in the Classroom. In applying behaviorism to education, the three principal modes of learning are utilized. These are: *classical, or respondent, conditioning; operant conditioning*; and *observational learning* (often called *social learning theory*).

Classical Conditioning. In essence, classical conditioning is a process of influencing one's behavior through reinforcement. It involves the pairing of a neutral stimulus with a stimulus that elicits a particular response (Reese and Lipsitt, 1970). In this case, the *unconditioned stimulus* refers to the stimulus that originally elicited the response. *Unconditioned response* means the response to the unconditioned stimulus. *Conditioned stimulus* is the stimulus that is neutral before conditioning and that will elicit the desired response after being paired with the unconditioned stimulus. The learned response to the conditioned stimulus is the *conditioned response*. The tendency to associate a behavior with a particular stimulus and to show behavior with a similar stimulus is called *stimulus generalization*. When learners apply stimulus/response associations only in specific settings or in limited ways it is called *stimulus discrimination*. When a learned response is weakened or when it disappears it is called *extinction* (Kaplan, 1990).

Operant Conditioning. Teachers are not usually interested in classical conditioning. Behaviors that are more voluntary on the part of the learner are better approached through operant conditioning. Here behavior is followed by some event that increases or decreases the frequency of that behavior. If the event actually increases the desired behavior, then the behavior is said to be reinforced. Operant conditioning results in behavior being controlled by its consequences. If the consequences are pleasing or result in something deemed desirable the behavior will occur more often. If the consequences are displeasing or undesirable the behavior will occur less frequently. However, within a busy classroom it may not be clear what the actual reinforcers are for particular behaviors. Emotional responses of classmates may be more powerful reinforcers than teacher threats or assignments. Generalization and discrimination are also important to operant conditioning.

Reinforcement may be applied in one of three ways. *Continuous reinforcement* is a schedule whereby each case of a desired behavior is reinforced. *Partial reinforcement* is where reinforcement is given after only some instances of the desired behavior. *Fixed ratio reinforcement* is when a predetermined number of desired behaviors must be performed before the reinforcer is administered. *Variable ratio reinforcement* is a partial reinforcement schedule in which the number of required behaviors to gain a reinforcer varies. *Fixed interval reinforcement* is partial reinforcement in which the reinforcer is administered following a fixed period of time. *Variable interval reinforcement* is partial reinforcement in which the time period is varied.

Observational Learning. Sometimes referred to as social learning theory, this approach takes the position that people can learn from watching others. Persons learn by seeing someone else perform a particular behavior. That person being observed is often called a *model*. The learner observes the model, remembers and may imitate the behavior some time later. This is called imitation of the behavior.

Albert Bandura (1986) has added a cognitive element to model-imitation learning. His approach stresses a four-step process. Attention is the first step. This simply means the learner is paying attention to the model. For focused attention the model or the teacher may use a prompt. The next step is retention. This is where the learner remembers the behavior of the model. The third step is motor reproduction. This means the learner selects and reproduces, or imitates, the behavior seen in the model. If a behavior is seen by the learner as negative or morally offensive, inhibitions may intervene and prevent imitation. Step four is motivational processes. After the learner imitates, some reinforcement needs to be administered. This allows the learner to find out what the results of the imitated behavior may be and can serve as a motivator. The learner may remember the consequences of a behavior and then be able to use it for him/herself in the future. Self-efficacy, the belief that one can be successful, and self-regulation are important to these processes (Kaplan, 1990).

EUGENE S. GIBBS

Bibliography. A. Bandura (1986), *Social Foundations of Thought and Action: A Social Cognitive Theory;* P. S. Kaplan (1990), *Educational Psychology for Tomorrow's Teacher;* C. A. Maher and S. G. Forman, eds. (1987), *A Behavioral Approach to Education of Children and Youth;* H. W. Reese and L. Lipsitt (1970), *Experimental Child Psychology.*

See also CLASSICAL CONDITIONING; OBSERVATIONAL LEARNING; SKINNER, BURRHUS FREDERIC; S-R BONDS

Behavior Modification. Some behavior modification programs are very complicated, such as precision teaching and using token reinforcement. Others are relatively simple, such as reinforcement with verbal praise or condemnation. Unless well planned, they are often used with inconsistency.

A typical procedure follows:

1. Target the behavior. Specify what behavior needs to change. The teacher must be able to observe and measure it.
2. Obtain a baseline. Records need to accurately reflect the learner's behavior before the modification program begins. Sometimes charts or graphs are used to keep track of progress toward the desired behavior during the baseline phase and through the completion of the modification program. The baseline work may also reveal the teacher's characteristic behavior.
3. Choose a procedure. The teacher carefully and precisely begins to apply a selected reinforcer to the desired behavior. The criteria for receiving the reinforcer must be clearly understood by the learner. Adjustments to the program may be made as the learner progresses.
4. Analyze and try something else if necessary. The program must be evaluated. Changes may be needed. If behavior is being modified in the desired direction, a maintenance procedure may be called for. If the program is not successful, another, perhaps more intrusive, procedure may be tried (Presbie and Brown, 1987).

An interesting extension of behavior modification as applied to education was developed some time ago by R. M. Gagne (1970). He developed a model of cumulative learning. He felt that higher-level skills are built upon those at lower levels. Movement is upward from the simplest to the most complex.

Eight types of learning are identified in Gagne's model. The first is signal learning. This corresponds directly to classical conditioning. Responding to signals is a common reflexive behavior found in animals and to a lesser extent in humans. The second type is stimulus response (S → R) learning. The main product here is that precise muscle responses to specific stimuli become discriminated from responses to other stimuli. This is a kind of associative learning. The third and fourth types are motor chains and verbal chains. Several separate motor or verbal responses may be combined, or chained, to develop more complex skills. Alphabet learning and vocabulary development are examples of the chained type. The fifth type is discrimination learning. Simple-discrimination learning is much like type two. Multiple-discrimination learning requires that some S → R discrimination has already taken place. The student then learns to discriminate between several chains of items and begins to associate their various properties. Type six is concept learning. This requires the ability to make a common response to stimuli that are dissimilar in various ways. Type seven is rule learning. A rule, for Gagne, is a chain of two or more concepts. It is presumed that when a rule has been learned, it can be applied in solving problems. The final type, and the highest, is problem solving. The learner is able to independently secure new ideas by problem solving. Steps in problem solving include defining the problem, formulating a hypothesis, verifying a final hypothesis, and achieving the solution (Klausmeier, 1975).

EUGENE S. GIBBS

Bibliography. R. M. Gagne (1970), *The Conditions of Learning;* H. J. Klausmeier (1975), *Learning and Human Abilities;* R. J. Presbie and P. L. Brown (1987), *Educational Psychology for Tomorrow's Teachers.*

See also DISCRIMINATION; S-R BONDS

Belief. For some New Testament authors *pistis* (belief or faith) is a comprehensive term describing the appropriate response of humans to God. John wrote his Gospel so readers would "believe that Jesus is the Christ, the Son of God, and that by believing you may have life in his name" (20:31). In Acts the Philippian jailer will be saved if he will "believe in the Lord Jesus" (16:31). Paul explains to the Romans that "it is with your heart that you believe and are justified" (10:10). Yet today one seldom hears *belief* used in such a comprehensive manner or belief and faith used interchangeably. Today *faith* is the more comprehensive term and *belief* typically describes one portion of a faith response to God—the portion that refers to the ideas about Christianity one holds as true. Somewhere between the time of

John, Paul, and Luke and today this more constricted use of *belief* emerged. While its entire path cannot be traced, we can examine the earliest qualifications of belief and the distinctions between faith and belief articulated in the twentieth century.

The earliest qualifications of belief come from within the biblical canon. James argues that *pistis* alone is an insufficient response to God; after all, "Even the demons believe . . . and shudder" (2:19). In James' theology, belief must be accompanied by works to be complete.

In the twentieth century, Wilfred Cantwell Smith's works have both articulated and shaped contemporary thinking about faith and belief. In *Faith and Belief* (1979), Smith outlines three significant shifts in understanding of belief from the early sixteenth century to the twentieth century. First, the object of belief shifted from a person to a proposition. Believing lost its relational dimension and became an intellectually held idea. Second, the object of belief shifted from what could be known as true to what cannot be known. Someone *believes* in aliens but *knows* the capital of Ohio. Third, the condition of the subject shifted from commitment to attestation. Believing once implied the believer was loyally and lovingly engaged with the object of belief; now believing simply describes the holding of certain ideas.

Given today's constricted notion of belief, Christian educators might wisely work with belief as a subset of faith, a necessary but insufficient response to God. A growing number of evangelical scholars treat belief as an important but primarily cognitive response to God described as the content of the Christian story. Christian educators help learners "get the story straight" and, in doing so, help them believe.

ROBERT DROVDAHL

Bibliography. W. C. Smith (1979), *Faith and Belief.*

See also ATHEISM; ENGEL SCALE; FAITH; FAITH DEVELOPMENT

Bellah, Robert N. (1927–). American sociologist, educator, and author. Born in Altus, Oklahoma, in 1927, he was awarded his undergraduate and doctoral degrees from Harvard University in 1950 and 1955, respectively. He served as a research associate with the Institute of Islamic Studies at McGill University in Montreal from 1955 to 1957 before assuming a teaching position at Harvard, where he remained until 1967. From there he moved to the University of California at Berkeley where he taught for thirty years, being appointed the Ford Professor of Sociology and Comparative Studies. Upon his retirement in 1997, he was named the Elliott Professor Emeritus at that institution. His academic contribution has been described as one of evaluating the religious nature of sociological groups, movements, and institutions.

Bellah has authored or coauthored a number of books exploring individualism and cultural dynamics, including *Beyond Belief* (1970), *The Broken Covenant* (1975), and *The New Religious Consciousness* (1976). In *Habits of the Heart: Individualism and Commitment in American Life* (1985), his most highly acclaimed work, Bellah (with others) examines the beliefs and practices that have shaped the character and given form to the American social order. Bellah's argument is that fierce individualism and a self-reliant spirit undermine a society's capacity to commit to one another in roles of active citizenship. Building on the premises of Alexis de Tocqueville, Bellah contends that the citizens of a democracy are able to effectively govern themselves only if they face their common problems in light of how they are defined by their past. Six years after the wide public acceptance of *Habits,* Bellah (with others) argues in *The Good Society* (1991) that shared understanding of the common good, which is fostered within society's economic and political institutions, leads to a vital democracy. In order to achieve and preserve such a goal, the authors plead for renewal and enrichment of public discourse and debate about national and international problems. Such a path, it is held, will result in citizens paying attention to what really matters and increasing rather than depleting the endowment we leave to future generations.

DAVID GOUGH

Bibliography. R. N. Bellah et al. (1991), *The Good Society;* R. N. Bellah et al. (1985), *Habits of the Heart: Individualism and Commitment in American Life.*

Beneficiary. *See* Trustee.

Benson, Clarence Herbert (1879–1954). One of the most influential men in Christian education, Benson didn't begin his career in this field. Born in a pastor's family in 1879, he followed his father's vocation. He studied at the University of Minnesota, Macalester College, and Princeton Seminary, and from 1909 to 1918 he pastored four Presbyterian churches in New York and Pennsylvania. For his fifth pastorate, he served as a missionary in Japan. After Benson came back to the United States in 1922, the president of Moody Bible Institute in Chicago asked him to teach there. He wasn't eager to accept the invitation, but God closed the doors to continued preaching. As a result of being assigned to teach classes on child study, pedagogy, and Sunday school administration, Benson developed an interest in Christian education. Two years later, he began directing the new Christian education department at Moody.

In addition to his teaching responsibilities, Benson founded the Evangelical Teacher Training Association (ETTA) in May 1931. At its beginning, the association used Benson's textbooks, *Introduction to Child Study* and *Sunday School Administration,* for training teachers in Bible colleges and seminaries and incorporated abridged versions into its preliminary training course for lay teachers. Benson also founded the National Sunday School Association while he taught at Moody.

In 1933, with the help of his students, Benson began writing the All Bible graded series of Sunday school lessons. To publish this curriculum he cofounded Scripture Press a year later. He and his students also wrote the Superior Summer School series vacation Bible school curriculum.

Benson authored a number of Christian education books that grew out of the need for textbooks for college classes or for lay level training courses through ETTA. The trademark of Benson's education texts was, in his own words, "to magnify the teaching ministry" (Benson 1950, 7). And that he did. In *The Christian Teacher,* for example, he discussed the task of reaching students on their level, preparing to teach, understanding students and relating to them, and putting together a lesson plan. He also described methods and procedures for teaching, and he provided a look at Christ the master teacher. A *Popular History of Christian Education* provided an overview of education from Bible times through 1943, when it was written. That book became the basis for at least one subsequent history text.

Even after his death in 1954, Benson has continued to impact the discipline of Christian education. In addition to the organizations he founded, he influenced people like Lois E. LeBar, who wrote the textbook *Education That Is Christian,* still used in college and seminary courses. Many of his textbooks for ETTA form the foundation for current revised and updated editions.

LIN JOHNSON

Bible Associations. *See* Bible Societies.

Bible College Movement. The Bible institute (now Bible college) movement began in the late nineteenth century and has had a profound influence on evangelical Protestantism. Its impact has been felt in every part of the world. It has produced a large percentage of North American evangelical missionaries and has served as a primary training center for local church leadership.

From the founding of the Missionary Training Institute (Nyack College) in New York City in 1882, Moody Bible Institute in 1886, and Toronto Bible School (Tyndale College) in 1894, the Bible college movement has proliferated throughout North America over the past century. According to the Accrediting Association of Bible Colleges (AABC), there are now over four hundred Bible schools or colleges in the United States and Canada. Ninety-seven of these are recognized by the AABC, representing over 37,000 students.

The Formative Years: 1882–1920. The Bible college movement came into being when traditional beliefs and customs were challenged within the framework of the church and the academy. First, this was a period of unprecedented change for North American Protestantism that produced a threat and challenge to biblical Christianity. The growing influence of Darwinism, the attacks upon the credibility of the Scriptures through the inroads of higher criticism, and the spread of the social gospel movement as a means of social reform all contributed to the changing state of the Protestant church.

Second, it was a time of unparalleled change for higher education, so significant that educational historian Walter Metzger (1955) refers to it as an "educational revolution."

The first key development in North American higher education, the emergence of the university, was largely affected by the technical needs of agriculture and business. Government legislation was passed favoring public institutions and providing funding and sometimes land. Eventually these public institutions grew in size and influence until they dominated higher education. Concurrent with the emergence of the university was the declining influence of religion in the church-related colleges that had been fundamental to the character of North American higher education from the very beginning. This decline was reflected in the selection of administrators and faculty who did not have an evangelical orientation, and in changes in curriculum, religious programming, and student life. It ultimately affected the types of students attending these religious colleges and also reduced the number of graduates going into clergy-related professions.

Although it appeared that the church and religious colleges were losing ground to the moral and spiritual decline of the late nineteenth century and to the vicious attack against the credibility of the Scriptures, a conservative element in North American Protestantism rose to defend biblical orthodoxy and promote evangelical activities. These individuals, known as revivalists, were pastors and itinerant evangelists who also involved themselves in polemical literature, Bible conferences, foreign mission societies, and Bible schools. Many of these leaders were the founders and key leaders in the early Bible college movement.

The energy produced by the revivalism of the late nineteenth and early twentieth centuries expressed itself in a period of missionary expansion, particularly through the faith mission movement. Concurrent with, and in some respects a result of, the faith mission movement was the development of the Bible institute/college movement. Because many of the new missionary societies were unprepared to provide adequate training for foreign missions, the early Bible schools were able to respond by serving as a link between the need for workers on the foreign fields and the supply of zealous individuals who were volunteering for Christian service.

Between 1882 (the founding date of the first Bible college) and 1920, a total of forty Bible schools were started in North America. Six of them were founded between 1882 and 1890, eight between 1891 and 1900, ten between 1901 and 1910, and sixteen between 1911 and 1920 (Reynhout, 1947, 43–44).

The Fundamentalist-Modernist Movement: 1920–1930. Protestant churches in the United States and Canada experienced major conflict after World War I over theology and purpose. Discontent over these differences ultimately came to a head with the development of a movement known as fundamentalism, a reaction to liberal theological trends within the church. In losing the battle for control of many of the Protestant denominational agencies and institutions, fundamentalists claimed that the denominational colleges and seminaries had sold out to liberal teaching. The result was that they started new colleges and seminaries, among them a large number of Bible schools and colleges. Because of their firm commitment to biblical orthodoxy, these schools perpetuated conservative theological teaching and trained a new generation of church leaders. The Bible schools and colleges actually served as a base of operations for many of the fundamentalist leaders and their various endeavors.

The Growth Years: 1930–1960. The Bible college movement in general, and especially in the United States, experienced moderate but steady growth between 1900 and 1930 and greater development over the next thirty years. There is, however, an unexpected contrast in growth patterns between Canada and the United States. The greatest increase in Canadian schools took place between 1931 and 1950. Sixty-nine percent of the Canadian institutions started by 1960 had been founded in this twenty year time frame, while only 8 percent were started in the decade that followed (Witmer, 1962, 39). The majority of the Canadian institutions were established in the western provinces by specific denominations. Many of these schools, however, were discontinued or merged with other institutions.

Conversely, the greatest increase in American institutions took place between 1941 and 1960, one decade later than in Canada. The founding of American schools hit a high point during the 1940s, when sixty-six schools were started. An-other forty came into being during the decade of the 1950s (Witmer, 1962, 39).

By 1960 the Bible college movement had started to carve out a legitimate place in North American higher education. Approximately 250 schools were classified as Bible institutes or Bible colleges. Major academic progress had been made in upgrading the quality of students, faculty, facilities, and programs. The curricula of many schools had been expanded to include three or four years of study, often resulting in a college degree. A recognized accrediting body, the Accrediting Association of Bible Colleges, had also been started in 1947 to provide standardization, accountability, and higher levels of academic excellence.

The Changing Years: 1960–Present. The period from 1960 to the present is characterized by several significant developments within the Bible college movement, some of which actually began in the 1940s. First, Bible colleges have continued to increase their standards and pursue outside recognition. Second, consistent with these educational advancements, Bible college leaders have attempted to identify their institutions with the larger academic community. This identification is evidenced by baccalaureate degree offerings, expanded general education requirements, and insistence on faculty having graduate degrees (in most cases an earned doctorate) in their particular academic disciplines. Because of these changes, Bible colleges have had to redefine their purpose more clearly in relationship to Christian liberal arts colleges and universities and theological seminaries. Finally, like other colleges and universities, Bible colleges are being forced to reevaluate their traditional roles to determine if changes in mission, programs, and recruitment strategies are necessary to survive current struggles with declining enrollments, rising costs, and financial hardships.

As Bible colleges move into the twenty-first century, there are many changes that will have to be made to respond to the needs of a changing culture. But there must also be a continued commitment to solid biblical instruction and to equipping students for service in the church and society.

Larry J. McKinney

Bibliography. *Accrediting Association of Bible Colleges Directory, 1997;* W. P. Metzger (1955), *Academic Freedom in the Age of the University;* H. Reynhout (1947), *The Bible School on the Mission Field;* S. A. Witmer (1962), *The Bible College Story: Education With Dimension.*

See also Higher Education, Christian

Bible Institutes. *See* Bible College Movement.

Bible Societies. At the height of the missionary movement in the 1800s, Bible societies were formed to produce and distribute Bibles to people all over the world. The Bible societies have their roots solidly planted in the Reformation, and their basic purpose has always been to get the Word of God into as many hands as possible. The societies have worked with dozens of mission organizations to translate the Bible into other languages, produce copies in a suitable form, and make copies available either for free or at a price that is easily affordable.

History of Bible Societies. There have been three great periods of growth for the Bible societies: the early 1800s, the early 1900s, and the period from the close of World War II until the rise of the Vietnam War. The first period saw the formation of the British Foreign Bible Society (BFBS), started in 1804, and the American Bible Society (ABS), founded in 1816. These nonprofit societies were the first Christian organizations outside the church dedicated solely to translating and publishing the Bible in new languages. Begun by mission-minded businessmen in London, the BFBS was instrumental in changing the way people thought about missionary work. Even the average person in the pew could participate in great mission work by helping to publish God's Word and to distribute it to people around the globe. By the mid–1800s, several western European nations had followed England's lead and had created their own national Bible societies. Each worked independently, creating separate but similar operations in various mission lands.

In its first one hundred years, the BFBS issued more than 200 million Bibles, New Testaments, and Gospels. Over the next fifty years it doubled that amount; however, its annual circulation was never able to overtake the annual increase in literate persons around the world. The rise of modernism in the late 1800s slowed Christians' interest in Bible societies.

The second great period of growth occurred in the early 1900s, as communication and travel opened new doors for the gospel around the world. In 1932 the BFBS and the ABS decided to integrate much of their foreign work in order to avoid duplication and to maximize financial resources. Joined by the National Bible Society of Scotland, the societies made a concerted effort to put Bibles into the hands of people in China, Japan, and Singapore. In Indonesia the BFBS and ABS were joined by the Netherlands Bible Society to produce and distribute the Scriptures to tens of thousands. The Japan Bible Society was created in 1938, the Bible Society of Brazil in 1948, and the Korean Bible Society in 1940, and each of these societies worked with the ABS and BFBS to translate and print the Scriptures in its national language. The Bible Society of India, under the auspices of the BFBS, spun off the Bible societies of Ceylon, Pakistan, and, later, Bangladesh. However, much of the work of Bible distribution came to a halt at the outbreak of World War II and the violence caused by the communist civil war in China.

During World War II the ABS worked hard to give away more than one million dollars' worth of Bibles and Testaments to German citizens and prisoners of war. After the war, another million dollars' worth of Bibles was given as aid to the people of Japan. At the close of the war the Bible societies again took a leading role in disseminating the Scriptures, spawning new Bible societies in Austria (1947), Belgium (1946), Czechoslovakia (1947), France (1946), Germany (1948), and Switzerland (1947). Seeking to establish new international cooperation, twenty-four national Bible societies combined into the United Bible Society at a benchmark meeting at Elfinsward, England, in 1948. Headquartered in London, the UBS works in the common interest of all the national societies, assembling data, studying problems, providing services, and making contact with ecclesiastical bodies.

The Ministry Today. New measures of cooperation and integration have taken place over the past fifty years, increasing circulation and effectiveness. The ABS has distributed four billion Bibles in more than five hundred languages, and has worked to produce Bibles in braille, in large print, and on cassette tape. Headquartered in New York, the ABS is staffed by more than sixty thousand volunteers, and receives all of its funding from gifts and endowments. Since the fall of the Berlin Wall, Bible societies are once again growing and receiving interest from local churches as Christians become aware of the possibilities for sharing the gospel in previously closed countries.

The Gideons have become perhaps the most recognizable of the Bible societies, placing Bibles in nearly every motel room in America. Founded in 1898 by two traveling salesmen who met in a Wisconsin hotel lobby and began talking about their faith, the Gideons noted the need for the Scriptures by traveling professionals and came up with a plan to place Bibles in appropriate places for travelers. In the first twenty-eight years of the organization's existence, the Gideons placed one million Bibles. They now place one million Bibles around the world every eight days, including more than half a million a month in Russia. Gideons are at work in 172 countries, printing and distributing the Scriptures in 77 languages, and are the biggest Bible distributors in the world. They have placed Bibles on military bases, in prisons, hospitals, nursing homes, and doctors' offices; on ships, airlines, and school and college campuses; and in missions throughout the world. Headquartered in Nashville, Tennessee, Gideons International has more than

80,000 volunteers working in the United States, and another 137,000 around the globe.

JERRY CHIP MACGREGOR

Bibliography. F. F. Bruce (1978), *History of the Bible in English;* H. Kee, ed. (1993), *The Bible in the 21st Century.*

Bible Study Methods. Bible study is central to growth in the Christian life and is therefore central to Christian education. It is from the Bible that the Christian learns the will of God and receives guidance from the Holy Spirit to live it. Bible study is the basis for preaching and teaching for the Christian, but it is personal Bible study that is essential for a believer to become a self-feeder. Without learning self-feeding skills, the new believer is locked into dependence upon someone else doing the Bible study and providing truth for her or him.

Bible study is done in large and small groups as well as individually. How Bible study is done and the value it has for life depends upon the approach. One approach is *deductive*, looking to Scripture to confirm a previously held conviction, conclusion, or principle. For example, following the deductive approach, a person will search Scripture to find support for a topic or doctrine already believed or accepted. Users of this approach seek to discover verses of Scripture that support their doctrine. Verses that contradict the doctrine are either ignored or explained in a way that removes the contradiction. Concordances and topical Bibles are important to this approach.

Another approach to Bible study is *inductive*. Inductive Bible study allows the specific facts of the text being studied to become the basis for a conclusion, doctrine, or principle of Scripture. An inductive approach to Bible study requires that any doctrines be temporarily set aside or held tentatively. Scripture is examined with fresh eyes, as if it had never been seen before. Those who study inductively learn skills of observation and questioning. No materials other than the Bible, a blank sheet of paper, and a pencil are used. Conclusions are not drawn prematurely but only when they are supported by Scripture.

A third approach to Bible study can be called the *retroductive*. This approach uses the interpretations of the past to guide the interpretations of Scripture in the present. The retroductive approach to Bible study focuses on comments made by those who have previously studied the passage. Commentaries and other Bible study helps such as dictionaries, atlases, handbooks, and the like are central to this approach. Research is pursued and all the expert opinions on a particular text are gathered. A decision is made by the Bible student as to which opinion is correct.

One approach to Bible study is not necessarily better than another, but each should be used when appropriate. The original languages of the Bible (Hebrew and Greek) can be studied in addition to English or any other language into which the Bible has been translated.

Christian education favors equipping believers to become self-feeders in their study of the Bible. The very nature of inductive Bible study seems to encourage self-feeding more than deductive or retroductive study. When dependence of the student is placed on someone else, even an expert, there is less dependence on God's Spirit to teach through his inspired Word, the Bible.

Teachers of the Bible will use one or more of these approaches to study the Bible in preparation to teach. If teachers prepare deductively or retroductively, it is reasonable to assume they will teach their students in these ways. If a teacher prepares inductively, students may or may not be taught in that fashion. The inductively prepared teacher becomes the expert instead of consulting experts in books. Teachers usually teach others the way in which they have been taught.

Bible studies may be focused on specific targets. Some of these include book study, character study, verse study, word study, topical study, and survey. Studies may use lecture, discussion questions, creative expression (drama, art), fill-in-the-blank questions, and almost any methodology available for teaching.

The most important thing about the approach used in Bible study is how it changes lives. The question must be asked, after Bible study, are we more Christlike as a result of the Bible study or are we simply more knowledgeable? Are all three approaches equal as far as their potential to touch the inner person deeply and lead to change? Jesus asked a very penetrating and convicting question of his followers: "Why do you call me, 'Lord, Lord', and do not do what I say?" (Luke 6:46). James said, "But one who looks intently at the perfect law, the law of liberty, and abides by it, not having become a forgetful hearer but an effectual doer, this man will be blessed in what he does" (1:25 NASB). "But prove yourselves doers of the word, and not merely hearers who delude themselves" (1:22). The question that needs to be asked about which approach to Bible study would be better to use is, which is more likely to result in obedience to God's Word?

ROBERT J. RADCLIFFE

Bibliography. L. W. Girard (1978), *Teaching the Bible From the Inside Out: An Inductive Guide;* I. L. Jensen (1963), *Independent Bible Study;* idem (1969), *Enjoy Your Bible;* K. E. Jones (1962), *Let's Study the Bible;* R. W. Leigh (1982), *Direct Bible Discovery;* The Navigators (1975), *The Navigator Bible Studies Handbook;* L. O. Richards (1971), *Creative Bible Study;* H. F. Vos

(1956), *Effective Bible Study;* O. Wald (1975), *The Joy of Discovery in Bible Study;* R. Warren (1980), *Dynamic Bible Study Methods;* A. Wilcox (1985), *Building Bible Study Skills.*

See also INDUCTIVE BIBLE STUDY

Bible Teaching. More than fifty years ago A. W. Tozer (1948) wrote, "Sound Bible exposition is an imperative must in the Church of the Living God. Without it no church can be a New Testament Church in any strict meaning of that term. . . . The Bible is not an end in itself, but a means to bring men to an intimate and satisfying knowledge of God, that they may enter into Him, that they may delight in His Presence, may taste and know the inner sweetness of the very God Himself in the core and center of their hearts" (8).

Such a requirement hardly began in the mid-twentieth century. On a mountain in Galilee after his resurrection, Jesus commanded his disciples to keep making disciples and emphasized a key ingredient, "Teaching them to obey everything I have commanded you" (Matt. 28:20). The original New Testament Bible teachers had learned earlier from their Lord that "everyone who is fully trained will be like his teacher" (Luke 6:40). Enormous modeling responsibilities are attached to the task of teaching.

In some ways, a good teacher performs like a skilled artist. Both create things of beauty through hours of toil and the application of training and dedication to the task. Bible teachers must know how to handle the Scriptures—their first and final textbook—anchoring their instruction with God's Word (2 Tim. 3:14–17).

In Paul's second letter to Timothy he tells the young man that "The Lord's servant must not quarrel; instead he must be kind to everyone, able to teach, not resentful" (2 Tim. 2:24). The concept of a teaching gift forms a significant block of New Testament text, but in this passage the context argues attitude rather than ability. Filling our students' heads with knowledge will not produce kindness. That quality comes about in two ways: the Holy Spirit generates it from inside and we demonstrate it on the outside.

The New Testament emphasis on teaching Scripture flows normally from the Old Testament experience of Israel. Asaph's words in the Psalms emphasize the point.

> O my people, hear my teaching; listen to the words of my mouth. I will open my mouth in parables, I will utter hidden things, things from of old—what we have heard and known, what our fathers have told us. (Psalm 78:1–3)

This Psalm focuses on the centrality of the Bible. Asaph passed on God's truth from earlier generations. Today we have much more revela-

tion, but we still hold Scripture central to all that we teach. Devout Bible teachers avoid the extreme of intellectual idolatry, the concept that knowledge in and of itself brings one closer to God and to holy living. Bible teaching finds its primary role in spiritual maturation, not the accumulation of information.

Human elements in teaching center on teacher, student, process, and environment. Divine results emerge as Scripture comes under the illuminating work of the Holy Spirit. Roy Zuck (1963/1984) reminds us,

> One should not think of the Spirit's work as an excuse for laziness, as a way to avoid hard work in the study of the Scriptures. Discerning the meaning of a Scripture passage may come suddenly, but it is usually the result of (not separate from) intense and even prolonged research and pondering. (65)

Wilhoit and Ryken (1988) claim that effective teaching is "the church's unfinished task." They emphasize both doctrinal and historical issues as well as the practical necessities of the present.

> The Protestant tradition of Bible translation and of commitment to the ideal of the priesthood of all believers has placed effective Bible teaching on the agenda of the church. Good teaching, in turn, requires training and practice. Teachers can learn by doing and by reflecting on what they have done. (39)

The Bible teacher's understanding of students and Scripture forms the essential foundation for effectiveness. Too narrow a view of the text, unwarranted dogmatism, hesitancy to apply truth to life—these and many other errors pollute the river of knowledge and understanding. Wilhoit and Ryken (1988) emphasize the impact of scriptural truth on learners.

> To believe that the Bible speaks to us as whole people has a direct influence on how we teach the Bible. It affects how we approach individual passages in the Bible. If we think only in terms of propositional truth, for example, we will reduce passages to ideas and ignore the other ways in which a passage can speak to us. Our awareness that the Bible takes a multiple approach to truth also affects what passages we choose to teach. In fact, it will open us to the possibility of teaching the whole Bible. (190)

Once we have made satisfactory inroads into the development of the teacher and distinctiveness of the content, we recognize the dynamic involved in applying truth to life. Discovery learning pulls students of all ages into the text, designing interactive experiences which show how Scripture speaks to contemporary questions and problems. Richards (1970) said it well: "This should be one of the major goals of the Bible teacher: not keep the learners dependent on him, but to equip them to study the Word independently, and to study it in such a way that they grow" (122).

Many late twentieth-century churches have been revitalized by Gene Getz's book *Sharpening the Focus of the Church* (1974). Getz emphasizes both the importance and variety of Bible teaching in New Testament congregations: "A church that does not provide good Bible teaching cannot be classified as practicing New Testament principles of church life." He reminds us too, that the New Testament contains "about 100 occurrences of the verb *didasko*, and its uses about evenly distributing each Gospel, the book of Acts, and in the epistles. Interestingly, the word is used about half the time in Acts to describe the teaching-learning process among non-Christians, and about half the time with Christians" (94).

The personal spiritual preparation of the teacher cannot be overemphasized in Bible teaching. Process, atmosphere, structure, media, and a host of other factors, crucial as they certainly are, fade into the background when compared with prayer and Bible study. Lawson stated succinctly: "To be an effective teacher of the Word of God, you first need to be an effective student of the Word. As you are enriched by the wealth of the Bible, you can more effectively help enrich the lives of others" (284).

KENNETH O. GANGEL

Bibliography. F. B. Edge (1995), *Teaching for Results;* K. O. Gangel and H. G. Hendricks, eds. (1988), *The Christian Educator's Handbook on Teaching;* H. G. Hendricks (1987), *Teaching to Change Lives;* L. E. Lebar (1989/1995), *Education That Is Christian;* L. O. Richards (1970), *Creative Bible Teaching;* A. W. Tozer (1948), *The Pursuit of God;* J. Wilhoit and L. Ryken (1988), *Effective Bible Teaching;* R. B. Zuck (1963/1984), *The Holy Spirit in Your Teaching.*

Bible Teaching for Adults. The latter part of the twentieth century has seen a resurgence in Christian education for adults. This trend has mirrored an unparalleled growth in adult education in society at large.

Most Christian educators recognize adults as persons 18 years of age and older. For demographic purposes adults are usually grouped as: emerging adults—18 to 30 years of age; young adults—31 to 50; middle adults—51 to 70; senior adults—71 to 80; and elderly adults—81 and up. Even within these broad ranges there are subgroups (some of which may span one or more age groups) such as singles, sandwiches (adults who are taking care of parents while continuing to raise children), divorced and widowed people, and blended families (second marriages with children from previous marriages). Thus, teaching the Bible to adults is a challenging task.

Malcolm Knowles in his seminal work *The Modern Practice of Adult Education* (first published in 1970), coined the term *andragogy,* which means "the art and science of helping adults learn." Knowles posited four basic assumptions of andragogy. First, adult learning is primarily self-directed. Second, as an adult grows and matures, the adult becomes an important educational resource. Third, adult education is focused on a person's unique needs at a particular moment in time. Fourth, adult learning is focused on problem solving rather than content gathering.

What are the components of andragogy as it relates to teaching the Bible to adults? First, adults cannot be forced to study or learn the Bible. Adults respond positively when given options for studying the Bible. Thus, churches should offer Bible teaching in a variety of contexts instead of simply one opportunity on Sunday morning in an age-graded Sunday school class. Simply put, adults cannot be made to learn the Bible. A successful Bible teaching and learning context for adults is one where the adults have chosen to be participants.

Historically, the role of the teacher has been prominent in the church. Not only was Jesus called teacher more than any other title, but also the New Testament indicates the Holy Spirit has given some people in the church the gift of teaching (Rom. 12:6–8; 1 Cor. 12:28; Eph. 4:11–13).

The second component is the student. As seen above, the adult student is predominantly self-directed. Thus, the teacher must seek to understand adult characteristics and needs in general as well as the specific traits of the adults one is to teach.

The third component is the curriculum. Curriculum encompasses the entire teaching-learning process. It is the game plan developed by the teacher (often with the help of others), and it is concerned with the ultimate objectives of the Bible class as well as with specific short-term objectives for each session. Although the Bible is the focal point of the content of the curriculum, methods must be developed that will not only communicate the meaning of the biblical text but also enable the adult learners in making application of the text.

The fourth component of teaching the Bible to adults is the context. The context includes the backgrounds of the teacher and the students, the physical location of the class meetings, and the social, economic, cultural, and academic context in which the teacher and students live. The context will have a tremendous bearing on the methodology used by the teacher.

JONATHAN N. THIGPEN

Bibliography. W. A. Draves (1997), *How to Teach Adults;* K. O. Gangel and H. G. Hendricks (1988), *The*

Christian Educator's Handbook on Teaching; W. Haston (1993), *Adult Sunday School Ministry;* M. Knowles (1970), *The Modern Practice of Adult Education;* J. Lowman (1995), *Mastering the Techniques of Teaching.*

See also ADULT CHRISTIAN EDUCATION; ANDRAGOGY; METHODOLOGY (TEACHING AND RESEARCH)

Bible Teaching for Children. Children are naturally curious and eager to learn. They will respond to the message of the Bible when scriptural truths are presented at a level they can grasp. Second Timothy 3:14–15 is clear on the mandate to teach the Bible to children: "You, however, continue in the things you have learned and become convinced of, knowing from whom you have learned them; and that from childhood you have known the sacred writings which are able to give you the wisdom that leads to salvation through faith which is in Christ Jesus" (NASB).

General Principles. Although the Holy Spirit is at work in the individual bringing spiritual understanding and insight, God moves in alignment with his creation design. In preparation for teaching the Bible to children, the instructor should study general age-level characteristics of the target group. A child's understanding of Bible content is heavily determined by his or her level of cognitive, social, and moral development.

It is also important that the teacher personally prepare for the high calling of teaching God's Word to children. Prayer should surround the process. The passage to be taught should be studied and the central message identified and applied using appropriate inductive Bible study skills. Children will respond to the life-changing challenges of God's Word as they see evidence of life change in their teacher.

Gilbert Beers (1986) suggests four steps that are necessary for the effective learning of Bible truth. First, the child must be taught what the Bible says. Second, the child must understand clearly what the passage means. Third, the learner needs to be guided in how this truth relates to his or her own life. Finally, children should be led in specific steps of practical application.

The Bible, as the inspired Word of God, is unlike any other book. What makes the Bible unique is that it is "God-breathed" and is able to provide answers to questions about who God is, who we are, and how we should live. Children should be taught in such a way that they realize that God's Word is the final authority. It is instructive for children to own and use their own Bibles. If the children do not have Bibles, provide them and teach children how to use them. When teaching, expose children to passages throughout the Bible using both the Old and New Testament (Gangel, 1986).

Ways to Teach the Bible to Children. Children at all stages learn best through active involvement, interaction, and firsthand experience. All five of their senses are doorways through which truth can be communicated. They relate best to concepts that are presented in concrete terms with specific life application. They are receptive to spiritual truths communicated in an atmosphere of genuine love and acceptance. With this foundation in mind, the following age level guidelines for teaching the Bible to children are provided.

Preschool (ages 1–3). The preschool child is able to grasp that the Bible is a special book when they watch how the teacher handles God's Word. Although long passages or narratives read directly from the Bible are too tedious for the young child to understand, the Bible should be open on the teacher's lap while the story is being told. Children can be helped to "use" their own Bibles in a simple fashion.

Young children enjoy hearing brief Bible stories and will be especially engaged if the story is told with visual aids such as pictures, puppets, flannelgraph, or drama. Even infants and toddlers can be introduced to the Bible with simple Bible words and accompanying visuals. Bible knowledge must then be reinforced through hands-on Bible learning activities and crafts that help the young child to understand how God wants them to live.

Early Childhood (ages 4–6). The narratives of the Old and New Testament are enjoyed by children of this age. They like to hear the stories of Bible people, how they obeyed God and how God responded. Children in kindergarten, first, and second grade can now try their newly acquired reading skills in using and studying the Bible by themselves and in groups. Teachers should emphasize the main truth of the Bible stories and facilitate learning activities that allow the children to reenact the story as well as identify ways to personally apply its message. This can be done through art, drama, music, games, oral communication, and creative writing.

Middle Childhood (ages 6–12). Although children at this stage still enjoy the Bible narratives, they also appreciate the opportunity to discuss Bible topics. Whether studying a Bible story, character, or principle, older children like to be able to ask questions and participate in group discussion. They are able to use their Bibles to solve problems and do research. Teachers can work with the developing cognitive abilities of children at this stage by leading them in making discoveries on their own. This can be accomplished through writing, drama, crafts, music, and interactive games.

SHELLY CUNNINGHAM

Bibliography. M. J. Anthony, ed. (1992), *Foundations of Ministry: An Introduction to Christian Education for a New Generation;* V. G. Beers (1986), *Childhood Edu-*

cation in the Church; R. J. Choun Jr. (1988), *The Christian Educator's Handbook on Teaching;* D. Eldridge, ed. (1995), *The Teaching Ministry of the Church;* E. Gangel (1986), *Childhood Education in the Church;* L. O. Richards (1983), *Children's Ministry;* idem (1970), *Creative Bible Teaching.*

Bible Teaching for Youth. Teachers are responsible to teach youth so that they recognize that Scripture is relevant for them, and so that they are transformed by the vital Word of God. Anything less is extraneous information, something they too often encounter in schools and churches.

In order to teach youth so that Scripture transforms them rather than just informing or boring them, teachers need a high view of Scripture—not merely a theological statement on inspiration, but a commitment to the power of Scripture to transform youth. (See 2 Tim. 3:16; Heb. 4:12; 2 Peter 1:20.) Scripture was given not for memorization but to keep us from sin (Ps. 119:11, 133) and to provide guidance for us in our daily walk (Ps. 119:105, 130). Teachers help youth to see how, through the work of the Holy Spirit (John 14:26; 15:26) and human teachers, Scripture speaks to their individual and corporate lives. Teachers have the dual responsibilities of properly exegeting Scripture and properly understanding youth so that the needs of youth are addressed through the inspired Word.

There are several important principles for teaching youth. First, teachers must know and understand youth. This provides for common ground between the youth, Scripture, and teachers. Unlike Jesus who did not need to ask what was in humans because he made us (John 2:25), human teachers need to inquire about the learners. Teachers need to exegete youth in order to understand them. Exegesis of youth identifies needs, interests, concerns, and problems that youth are facing now.

Second, regardless of approaches to the lesson, whether it is a topical or book study, teachers must eventually consider the scriptural text in light of their exegesis of youth in order to teach God's perspective. Not every verse of the Bible is equally germane to youth. It is the responsibility of teachers to determine which parts of Scripture are most relevant to the needs of youth. Having done this, teachers need to study (exegete) the text to determine God's message for their youth.

Third, using the data from their study of youth and Scripture, teachers must determine what they hope to accomplish in their lessons. Teachers need to state outcomes or goals based on their understanding of the youth whom they will teach. These outcomes or goals answer four basic questions for each lesson. As a teacher: (1) What do I want the youth to know? (2) What do I want them to feel? (3) What do I want them to do once I have taught? (4) What do I want them to be?

Fourth, teachers must plan lessons using the responses to the four outcome questions. The combination of exegesis of youth, exegesis of Scripture, and statements of intended outcomes provides the foundation for a lesson plan. The desired outcomes actually guide teachers in designing their lessons to accomplish these outcomes. A lesson consists of an interactive introduction that catches the attention of youth, interactive study of Scripture so that youth are discovering biblical truth for themselves, and interactive application and closing. Youth learn best when they are involved actively with each other, teachers, and Scripture. The desired outcomes, therefore, guide teachers in choosing various interactive strategies, methods, and materials. Youth will begin to be transformed as they actively engage in the study and understanding of Scripture and in the application of Scripture to their lives.

Effective teaching requires commitment and time from teachers. Teachers use the powerful Word of God to teach eternal truths that are applicable to the world of youth so that the young man or woman of God "may be thoroughly equipped for every good work" (2 Tim. 3:17).

Teachers need to be competent and dedicated to know, both in theory and practice, how to teach, how to interpret Scripture, what their learners are like, and how to structure their lessons.

JOHN M. DETTONI

Bibliography. P. Downs (1994), *Teaching for Spiritual Growth;* M. D. LeFever (1996), *Creative Teaching Methods;* D. Robbins (1990), *The Ministry of Nurture: How to Build Real-Life Faith in Your Kids;* J. W. Wilhoit and J. M. Dettoni, eds. (1995), *Nurture That Is Christian: Developmental Perspectives on Christian Education.*

Bible Translations. Hardly a year goes by which does not see publication of a new translation of the Bible: perhaps a revision of a former work, a children's version, or even one especially prepared for the Internet. Many wonder about the wisdom of vast funds tied up in the translation process; others welcome each new, fresh approach. Among translations currently popular, the New International Version tops the sales list, but the New King James Version follows closely behind. Many still favor the more literal New American Standard Bible and some cling to the original King James Version. The New Living Translation also recently appeared to replace the Living Bible paraphrase.

The identification of the names in the previous paragraph reminds us that the translations come in three types: literal translation (NASB), dynamic equivalence (NIV), and paraphrase (TLB). A literal translation works hard to stay close to the Hebrew or Greek text and therefore occasionally seems to struggle with the English. The NASB, for example, is even more literal than the KJV though it is translated from a different set of texts. The KJV's advocates laud its translation from the widest group of texts, its 350 years of history, and its worshipful language. Children, young people, and new Christians seem to thrive on paraphrased versions, particularly the Living Bible.

But, we might ask, what is the difference between a literal translation and a paraphrase? Don Carson (1979) explains: "In point of fact, there isn't one. . . . To compare examples from either end of the spectrum makes differences stand out; but as we approach the center, there is no rigid pattern, no indisputable step that signals the crossing of the line from 'literal' translation to paraphrase. And even 'literal' I have enclosed in quotation marks because the most literal of translations has to decide what word best suits the original, make decisions about idioms, search out the appropriate syntax in the receptor language. At all of these steps, there are dangers lurking everywhere for the unwary or the unskilled" (87–88).

Of great importance is the original text from which any translation is rendered. Supporters of the King James Version for example, argue strongly for the *majority text*, meaning a translation based on the largest number of ancient manuscripts. Zane Hodges writes, "It is also well known among students of textual criticism that a large majority of this huge mass of manuscripts—somewhere between 80–90%—contain a Greek text which in most respects closely resembles the kind of text which was the basis of our King James Version" (Fuller, 1970, 26). NIV advocates prefer the argument of older texts rather than the majority text. In Carson's words, "The date of the text-type is more important than the date of a particular witness. . . . Manuscripts must therefore be weighed, and not just counted" (Carson, 1979, 29–30). This urges Bible students considering textual evidence to prefer the shorter reading to the longer, the most difficult reading to the easier, and always to "take into account what the original human author was more likely to have written" (Carson, 1979, 30).

Underlying the validity of any text or translation is the crucial doctrine of inspiration. B. B. Warfield (1948) describes Christian understanding of that word when he states, "The Biblical books are called inspired as the Divinely determined products of inspired men; the Biblical writers are called inspired as breathed into by the Holy Spirit, so that the product of their activities transcends human powers and becomes Divinely authoritative. Inspiration is, therefore, usually defined as a supernatural influence exerted on the sacred writers by the Spirit of God, by virtue of which their writings are given divine trustworthiness" (131).

Inspiration is joined by words like *infallible* and *inerrant* to describe the original autographs of both Old and New Testaments. Many agree with Smith (1992) when he claims that "The Bible is not just the record of God's revelations; it is very revelation in and of itself. All that one knows about God and His relationship to Creation is found through Scripture" (23). Pinnock (1971) discusses the many theological delusions that have affected Christian thinking about the Bible as early as the medieval church. "Dissent and attempted evasion of the historic doctrine of inspiration is the saddest chapter in the history of theology. The dissent has been bitter and derogatory, and the evasions incapable of withstanding critical examination. All are desperate to evade the plain teaching of Scripture, thus end in a dream world of untestable religious feelings. The net effect of the modern approaches to Scripture has been, not a liberation of divine truth from bondage to the letter of scripture, but a questioning of any normative significance for the Bible at all" (Smith, 1992, 174).

Few serious evangelicals would hesitate at the word *inspiration*, most feel reasonably comfortable with *infallibility*, but some ponder the issue of *inerrancy*. *Infallibility* simply means "incapable of erring or failing," which is basically the same definition given to *inerrancy*. Are these not interchangeable terms? Why do some late-twentieth-century Bible scholars argue the importance of the word *inerrancy*? Perhaps because the doctrine of Scripture is so important in the cosmos of Christian theology. As used among evangelicals, inerrancy seems to be a tightening specification of infallibility. At the Chicago summit meeting of the International Council on Biblical Inerrancy in October 1978, several hundred key evangelical leaders signed this statement: "Being wholly and verbally God-given scripture is without error or fault in all its teaching, no less in what it states about God's acts in creation, about the events of world history, and about its own literary origins under God, than in its witness to God's saving grace in individual lives" (Boice, 1979, 13).

KENNETH O. GANGEL

Bibliography. D. Beegle (1960), *God's Word into English*; J. M. Boice (1979), *Does Inerrancy Matter?*; D. A. Carson (1979), *The King James Version Debate*; D. O. Fuller (1970), *Which Bible?*; C. H. Pinnock (1971), *Biblical Revelation—The Foundation of Christian Theology*; D. L. Smith (1992), *Handbook of Contemporary Theology*; B. B. Warfield (1948), *The Inspiration and Authority of the Bible*.

See also BIBLE SOCIETIES; EVANGELICALISM

Biblical Doctrine. *See* Biblical Theology.

Biblical Education by Extension. Begun in 1979, Biblical Education by Extension (BEE) is an educational mission whose strategy and curriculum were originally designed to provide theological education from an evangelical perspective to leaders of churches in the countries of Eastern Europe and the former Soviet Union. Due to the restrictions placed on denominations by the communist governments of the region, few church leaders had access to adequate theological training. Further, the establishment of new institutions for theological training was prohibited. In order to address this situation seven mission organizations formed a cooperative educational endeavor that utilized a nonformal extension approach to educating church leaders. Before the dramatic political changes that occurred in the region from 1989 to 1991, BEE training had been established across denominational lines in Romania, Poland, East Germany, Czechoslovakia, Hungary, Bulgaria, and the Soviet Union.

BEE instructional materials were produced in English and translated into seven languages found within the region. The training included self-study guides, textbooks, and periodic seminars, which were generally held covertly due to government opposition. The training emphasized Bible study methods, knowledge of basic doctrine, and essential skills for pastoral leadership. BEE's goal was the establishment of church-based training centers through which trained leaders could reproduce the program throughout their countries. By the late 1980s several thousand students had been involved in BEE courses.

After the communist governments in the region were dismantled, denominational leaders began to establish their own institutions and programs of theological education. In the 1990s BEE adopted new training strategies in order to address the wide range of educational possibilities that emerged. In many settings BEE has taken on more of an educational consulting and resourcing role. BEE programs have been incorporated into indigenous training structures, and its educational materials are now used in a wide variety of educational settings and approaches. BEE training has also been established in other restricted access nations, particularly in Southeast Asia.

Mark Young

Biblical Foundations for a Philosophy of Teaching. Because God desires to be known, he has chosen to reveal himself in ways that are accessible and understandable. Thus, all people may know, love, worship, and serve him in truth. Those who have encountered the truth of God have the privilege of participating in the accomplishment of God's desire to be known, loved, worshiped, and served by all; that participation involves teaching—the communication of God's truth in ways that create genuine understanding

and the desire to change in accordance with God's self-revelation.

Old Testament Foundations. At the center of God's self-revelatory activity in the Old Testament is the Torah, the law. Semantically, *torah* is related to the verb *yarah*, which in the hiphil means "to teach." The law of God teaches people about the nature of God by instructing them how to live as the people of God. The Torah encompasses all of life, giving guidance morally, socially, and religiously; it teaches people how to worship and how to live together in community. According to Deuteronomy 4:5–6 obedience to the teaching of Torah will show those outside the community of God's people a wisdom and understanding that is unique. Thus, the nations will see the greatness of God and his ways.

The Torah is eternally true because its source is the Eternal One; it is true for all people at all times. Therefore, teaching the truth of God is an essential task within the community of God's people in every generation. At the national level teaching was primarily the responsibility of the priestly class (Lev. 10:8–11) and later the prophets and leaders of the nation. Thus, teaching became an institutionalized aspect of life often associated with key moments in Israel's history, for example, when Israel was about to take possession of the land (Deut. 1:5) and when Israel returned to the land after the exile (Neh. 8:1ff.). When the teaching of the priests and prophets was compromised, Israel's destruction was assured (Isa. 9:14–17; Ezek. 13). The sins of Israel's leaders, including those whose task it was to teach the truth of God, are named as a cause of the destruction of the nation (Mic. 3:11–12).

Not only was teaching an institutional aspect of life in the community of God's people, but instruction in the ways of God was also the responsibility of parents. The family is the primary social unit through which the teaching of God is communicated to new generations. Parents are to teach their children to obey the Torah and thus perpetuate the society through which God reveals himself to the nations. The commandments of God are to permeate all of life; they are to be taught every moment of every day (Deut. 6:1–9). Both fathers and mothers are considered a source of wisdom; children must learn discernment from them and make their parents glad (Prov. 23:22–25).

Although human teachers may fail, God himself never fails to instruct his people in the ways they should live. David beseeches the Lord in Psalm 25:4, "Make me know Thy ways, O Lord; teach me Thy paths. Lead me in Thy truth and teach me." Later in the psalm David affirms, "Good and upright is the Lord; Therefore he instructs sinners in the way. He leads the humble in justice and He teaches the humble His way" (vv. 8–9 NASB). Humility is a prerequisite for learning;

pride blinds a person to the need to learn (Prov. 11:2). God promises to teach those who seek to learn from him (Ps. 32:8).

In its verb form *yarah*, coming from a root form that means to "cast" or "shoot," seems to emphasize directive teaching, that is, pointing out the way or directing one in the way. This meaning emerges clearly in Genesis 46:28 where Jacob sends Judah ahead of him to "point out the way" to Egypt. God promises to direct Moses in what to say (Exod. 4:12) and what to do (v. 15). In Psalm 27:11 David beseeches the Lord to direct his way along the straight path, and the same request is repeated in Psalm 119, "Teach me, O Lord, the way of Thy statues" (v. 33).

Several other Hebrew words convey the wide range of meaning associated with the concepts of teaching and learning in the Old Testament. *Lamad* often emphasizes training in particular skills; the word is used to refer to military training (2 Sam. 22:35; 1 Chron. 5:18) and musical training (1 Chron. 25:7). It is also used to describe training an animal for agricultural purposes, as seen in the derived term *malmad*, meaning "oxgoad" or "yoke." In Hosea 10:11 Ephraim is described as a "trained heifer" with a yoke by which the Lord will direct her. Among the other passages where *lamad* is found are Deut. 5:1; 31:13; Isaiah 26:9; and Jeremiah 31:34. One who studies the law of God is called *talmid* (1 Chron. 25:8). For this term the Jewish Talmud is named.

Zahar also signifies teaching in Exodus 18:20. However, the verb is often used in contexts that are better translated "to warn." Teaching includes warning of the consequences of disobedience and foolishness (Ps. 19:11; Ezek. 3:20). Failure to warn those who are on the path of destruction by not speaking the truth will render the one who knows the truth accountable for their destruction (Ezek. 13:7–9).

Of particular importance in understanding the concept of teaching in the Old Testament is Deuteronomy 1:5, where it is written that "Moses began to expound this law." In this passage the term *law* connotes much more than the Ten Commandments and other laws given in Exodus, Leviticus, and Numbers. In Deuteronomy Moses interprets the law, showing how the people of God are to change their thinking, allegiances, and behavior as they prepare to enter the land. In addition, the Book of Deuteronomy itself contains much more than the commands of God. It also calls Israel to remember the mighty acts of God in history and exhorts the people to a life of faithful allegiance to their covenant God.

In summary, the concept of teaching in the Old Testament is intimately related to the renewal of faithfulness to the covenant of God in each generation. Through teaching—directing, training, expounding, exhorting, warning—an understanding of God and his ways that makes his people uniquely blessed among the nations is perpetuated from generation to generation. Although teaching had an institutional identity in the priestly order, the instruction of each new generation was supposed to occur primarily in everyday life, through modeled obedience to social, moral, and Levitical laws.

New Testament Foundations. In the New Testament, God's self-revelation continues to be the foundation for an understanding of teaching. Whereas the law of God was the primary content of revealed truth in the Old Testament, the Son of God, the Lord Jesus Christ, is the focus of God's self-revelation in the New Testament. The Son expands and exceeds the revelation of God given in the Old Testament (Heb. 1:1–3). Indeed, the Son explains God to humankind (John 1:18). Thus, teaching in the New Testament focuses upon the Lord Jesus—his life, teaching, mission, church, and future.

Jesus himself provides the most compelling model for teaching found in the Bible. He based his instruction on the already revealed truth of God in the Old Testament, but did so in a way that challenged the self-serving traditions of conservative Jewish thought in the first century. Jesus moved reflection on the meaning of the law from behavior to attitude (Matt. 5:17–48), from legalism to grace (Matt. 9:9–13). Avoiding the culturally acceptable institutional forms of education, Jesus' teaching developed in the context of meaningful relationships with the disciples (Mark 3:14; John 15:9–15), self-sacrificial obedience to the will of the Father (Luke 9:21–26), and courageous rebuke of those who had corrupted and perverted the privilege of teaching the truth of God (Matt. 23). Jesus interpreted the law, he described the kingdom in word pictures from common experience, he touched those who needed healing, and he welcomed those who needed salvation the most; Jesus knelt before his learners in humble submission in order to serve them. At the end of his time on earth he commissioned his learners to teach all the things they had learned from him (Matt. 28:18–20).

Throughout the New Testament, teaching is seen as a primary responsibility and function of those who have chosen to follow the eternal Son of God. The early church devoted itself to the teaching of the apostles (Acts 2:42), which almost certainly in this context was an explanation of the revelation of God in Christ throughout the Old Testament and an exhortation to respond to that revelation in faith. As the church became more established, the teaching emphasized an explanation of the beliefs about Christ that had been developed by Paul and the apostles, and an exhortation to preserve those beliefs in the face of false teaching (see 2 Thess. 2:15; 2 Tim. 2:2). Such teaching was essential to move the immature in the knowledge of God to spiritual maturity (Col. 1:28; Titus 2:11–13). The Greek terms *didasko* and *paideuo* are primarily used to describe the activity of teaching in these contexts. Accurate teaching of the truth about the Son is so critical to the establishment and growth of the Church that leaders in local congregations are required to be skillful teachers (*didaktikos;* 1 Tim. 3:2; 2 Tim. 2:24), perhaps as a result of a supernaturally endowed ability or office (Rom. 12:6–7; 1 Cor. 12:28).

Teaching formed the centerpiece of the ministry of the church. Not only did people come to a knowledge of God and his Son through an explanation of the gospel that created an understanding of its truth and power (1 Cor. 1:18), but they also continued to grow spiritually through instruction in the truth of God by those in the church who were gifted to teach (Eph. 4:11–16).

MARK YOUNG

Bibliography. B. V. Hill (1985), *The Greening of Christian Education;* R. W. Pazmiño (1988), *Foundational Issues in Christian Education: An Introduction in Evangelical Perspective;* K. Wegenast and D. Furst (1978), *The New International Dictionary of New Testament Theology,* 3:759–81; G. H. Wilson (1997), *The New International Dictionary of Old Testament Theology and Exegesis,* 4:559–64.

Biblical Foundations of Christian Education.

The Bible serves as the cornerstone of theological foundations and as the prolegomenon of the historical foundations of Christian education. As such, Scripture is regarded as the primary lens through which Christian educators perceive and prescribe the character of Christian education.

The main reason for placing such emphasis upon the Scriptures is the claims of revelation and inspiration made by the Bible. It is a special revelation of God, and the Christian educator is compelled to formulate a model of Christian education consistent with it. As Paul contends, Scripture "was written for our *instruction*" (Rom. 15:4 NASB; 1 Cor. 10:5–11; 2 Tim. 3:14–17; Knight, 1996).

The Scriptures are saturated with educational implications and imperatives. The promotion and preservation of the faith are common themes throughout Scripture, but the means employed to fulfill these tasks are distinctive between the Testaments. Within this lies the caution that some models and methods of education in the Scriptures are by nature culturally specific. While the biblical principles are undeniably essential to Christian education, the specific methodology *may* have to be assessed in light of relevance to contemporary culture.

Old Testament. Teaching in the Old Testament was not primarily done to impart a skill or competency, but to help hearers to live a faithful life (Deut. 11:19). While this remained constant

throughout the life of Israel, after the exile education took on the character of restoring the faith of Israel and Judah (2 Chron. 17:7–9; 34:29–31). Education in the Old Testament took place both through socialization and nonformal means, with few formal approaches to education (such as synagogue schools).

Teachers of the Old Testament. Israel's first teacher was God (Job 36:22; Exod. 35:34). Throughout the Old Testament God's revelatory acts, in both deed and word, demonstrate his place as the teacher of the faith community. This explains the centrality of God within the life of the nation (Exod. 20:1–7; Judges 2:10–15). Perhaps his most significant revelatory act was the giving of the Torah, which was used by all the Old Testament prophets and teachers.

Educational responsibility was placed primarily on the Hebrew family (Exod. 12:26–27; 20:4–12; Deut. 4:9–10; 6:6–7; 11:19–21; Ps. 78:2–6; Prov. 6:20). Both parents were to be involved (Prov. 1:8), as well as other family members, making education within the family an intergenerational matter.

The prophets constituted perhaps the most vocal and obvious group of teachers in the Old Testament (Mic. 6:8; Zech. 7:12). Moses served as the paradigm for future prophets (Exod. 18:20; 24:12; Deut. 4:14; 6:1; 31:19). The prophets did indeed make use of the Mosaic law in their instruction (Isa. 8:16; 42:21, 24; Jer. 9:13; 16:11; Zech. 7:12). The "school of the prophets" (2 Kings 2:3–5; 4:38; 6:1; 1 Sam. 10:10; 19:20) should not be misunderstood as a contemporary formal educational institution. The actual phrase is not "school" for prophets, but the "sons [*ben*] of the prophets," indicating a discipling or nonformal approach to instruction rather than an institutional one.

Not only did priests receive formal education, but they also provided instruction to the community (Hag. 2:11; Mal. 2:7). Like the prophets, they made use of the Torah in their instruction. In fact, Deuteronomy 31:9–14 indicates that priests were to read the Mosaic Law to the assembly of Israel for the instruction of the Hebrew nation, including "aliens living in your towns."

Another group of Old Testament teachers are the wisemen or sages (13:14). Not to be confused with the magi of Persia, these were men versed in the Torah and readily able to make application of it.

Similarly, emerging near the close of the Old Testament, but frequently mentioned in the New Testament are the scribes, rabbis, or doctors of Law (Neh. 8; Jer. 8:8). Ezra, who is described as a scribe and teacher, serves as a model for this category of teacher (Ezra 7:10).

The idea of community as a teacher in the Old Testament is often neglected. Israel, being a theocracy, reflected within its very culture a spiritual and religious sense. Community life itself was a teacher. As people came in contact with the culture of Israel they received instruction regarding the very nature of God and his dealings with humankind. For example, the reasons for festivals, memorials, worship sites, and activities of public assemblies all had educational implications (Josh. 8:30–35; 2 Chron. 17:7–11).

Educational Terminology in the Old Testament. *Trh* is used over two hundred times in the Old Testament. It is typically translated "law," but literally means "instructions" or "guidance," placing emphasis on God's role as the teacher of Israel. *Hnk* ("to train or instruct") has a root meaning "to dedicate" or "to consecrate" (Ps. 22:6). *Lmth,* meaning "to teach" or "instruct" (Hos. 10:11), is translated to *ddsk* in the Septuagint. *Musr* is primarily used in the Wisdom literature (especially Proverbs), and is translated "instruction" or "discipline" (Prov. 2:17).

Significant Passages

Passage	Contents	Educational Implications
Deut. 6:1–9	The family is responsible for childhood instruction through teaching and community life.	Both the content and context of Christian instruction are essential. Create teachable moments.
Deut. 30:11–20	The nation of Israel, having been instructed, must choose between faithfulness and rejection of God.	Instruction must lead students toward making a personal decision of faith toward God.
Deut. 31:9–13	Priests are to read the law to the assembly of people (Hebrews and foreigners), including children, so they can know and obey the Law.	Christian education is meant for both those of the community of faith and those outside of it. Both are compelled to acknowledge God and to live in obedience to him.
Ps. 78	The passage recounts the interventions of God on Israel's behalf, noting that these should be taught to the children by their families.	Christian education includes the passing down of traditions, and as such becomes an intergenerational affair.
Neh. 8:1–9	Nehemiah has Ezra read the Mosaic Law to an assembly of the people, and both of them, along	Christian education must be concerned with communicating the contents of the

Passage	Contents	Educational Implications
	with the Levites, provide commentary and further instruction on the meaning of the text.	Bible, and must also provide commentary aiding students in understanding the meaning of the Scriptures.
Ezra 7:10–11	Teachers assume four roles: 1. Devotee 2. Student 3. Disciple 4. Instructor	The teacher's spirituality must be holistic in nature. It must not be merely intellectual, but also developing in the affective and volitional domains.
Wisdom Literature (Proverbs)	Three kinds of teaching: 1. Wisdom (1:20; 8:1–36; 9:1) 2. Instruction (2:17) 3. Correction (13:24; 17:10; 22:15; 29:25–27)	Christian education must seek to maintain the tradition of "wisdom" as not the mere accumulation of knowledge, but the ability to make suitable application of the biblical text to life.
Prophetic Literature	Pazmiño (1997) comments that the prophets were addressing the nation to remind them of their accountability to God, both individually and socially.	Christian education must not only focus on personal needs, but also those of the faith community and the society. God's sovereignty applies to every aspect of life, including the necessity of justice.

New Testament. The cultural developments of the intertestamental period, including those in the field of education, are often reflected in the New Testament. Perhaps the most obvious example of this is the formation of the synagogue. While the beginning of the synagogue has been traced to the time of Ezekiel (possibly based on Jer. 29:7), the synagogue did not reach its full stature within Judaism until the intertestamental period (Josephus, *Ant.* 2.25.632, 4.8.15). Called *Beth hasseper* ("House of the Book"), with the *Beth hamidrash* ("House of Study") typically adjacent to it, the synagogue became the locale for education within Judaism.

Teachers of the New Testament. God is described as teaching the community of faith (Titus 2:11–12). His instruction is primarily conducted through his acts of grace and revelation. As in the Old Testament, he is the primary teacher of his people through deed and word.

Among other titles, Jesus is called "teacher." As Mark 10:1 reminds us, it was Jesus' custom to teach. Hence, the Gospel writers refer to Jesus with a variety of instructional titles: *didaskalos* ("teacher," 35 times), *rabbi* ("teacher," 13 times), *rabboni* ("honored teacher," 2 times), *master* (7 times), and *leader* (once used in educational context) (Zuck, 1995, 25).

The reference to "yoke" in Matthew 2:28–29 reflects metaphoric use of the term describing the relation of teacher to pupil (cf. Sirach, *Ecclesiasticus* 51:25). Similarly, the phrase "come after me" (Mark 1:17) was frequently employed by both Greek philosophers and Hebrew sages to call pupils (Price, 1932, 59). Jesus never opened a school. Discipleship was his instructional context and method. The term "disciple" is used 142 times in Synoptics, adequately demonstrating this fact (Matt. 28:20; Mark 6:30; Luke 12:12).

Jesus' former pupils assumed the task of teaching through instruction, preaching, and writing. Acts depicts the apostles as completing Jesus' mission (Acts 1:1) by making disciples for Christ (Acts 14:21). Doctrine assumes a crucial role in the church through the apostles' instruction (Acts 2:42; 5:28; 13:2; 17:19).

As the church expanded, leaders were selected for newly planted congregations. Elders were indeed far more than teachers; however, among their qualifications the only "ability" listed is that of being "able to teach" (1 Tim. 3:2). The ability to teach is essential for leadership, and hence a qualification for eldership. The pastor-teacher of Ephesians 4:11 would exemplify this task.

The church body introduced and reinforced the formation of faith through exposure to and involvement in the community (Acts 2:42–47). Likewise, the place and function of the teacher is regarded as a gift of God (Rom. 12:3–8; 1 Cor. 12:27–31; Eph. 4:7–13, 5:15–20; 1 Peter 4:10–11).

Educational Terms in the New Testament. Hayes (1991) identifies ten Greek terms used in the New Testament that have educational implications.

didasko ("to teach"; Acts 2:42; 2 Tim. 3:16)

didaskalos ("the teaching"; 1 Tim. 2:7; 2 Cor. 12:28; Eph. 4:11)

paideuo ("to provide guidance or training"; Eph 6:4; 2 Tim. 3:16)

katecheo ("to be informed"; Luke 1:4; Acts 18:25; 21:21; Rom. 2:18; 1 Cor. 14:19; Gal. 6:6)

noutheteo (lit. "to shape the mind"; 1 Cor. 4:14; 10:11; Eph. 6:4; Col. 3:16)

matheteuo ("to disciple" is used predominately in the Gospels)

oikodomeo ("to build up"; 1 Cor. 3:9; 8:1; 1 Thess. 5:11; 1 Peter 2:5)

paratithemi ("to commit"; 1 Tim. 1:18; 2 Tim. 2:2)

ektithemi ("to expound or explain"; Acts 11:4; 18:26; 28:23)

hodegeo ("to guide"; John 16:13; Matt. 15:14; 23:16, 24; Rev. 7:17)

Significant Passages

Passage	Contents	Educational Implications
Matt. 28:18–20	Jesus' commission to his disciples to continue his disciplemaking endeavors, which includes teaching.	Christian education must maintain the focus on making disciples of Christ, a task that does not simply end with conversion, but involves continual instruction.
Luke 24:13–35	Jesus' teaching method: 1. Discussion (v. 14) 2. Inquiry (v. 17) 3. Correction (vv. 25–27) 4. Modeling (vv. 30–31) 5. Response (vv. 33–35)	Pazmiño (1997, 38) comments that Jesus' teaching had three parts: question, listen, and exhort. Teachers must engage their students so they will think and reflect, not merely mimic. Process model of education.
Acts	Acts refers to both the informal teaching (5:42) and the socialization of the Christian community (Acts 2:42).	Christian education is an essential aspect of congregational life. Instruction, both teaching and community encounter, is part of God's design to form the individual Christian and the church.
1 Cor. 2:6–16	The activity of the Spirit in applying the truth of Scripture to a believer's life is emphasized. The spiritually mature are better able to discern spiritual truth.	Teaching must allow for the activity of the Holy Spirit and encourage reflection of the Bible on life. Christian education must encourage the praxis of the Holy Spirit and human spirit.

Passage	Contents	Educational Implications
Eph. 4:7–16	Pastor-teachers are described as being gifts of Christ to the church. Their purpose is the completion and maturity of the church, individually and corporately.	Christian education must not only teach for personal edification, but must include the skills and talents necessary for the maturing of the congregation.
Pastoral Epistles	Hayes (1991, 37–38) notes six aspects of education in 1–2 Timothy: 1. Handling God's Word 2. Soundness of faith 3. Harmony in families 4. Requirements of leaders 5. Spiritual formation 6. Perpetuation of the faith See Titus 2:1–15 for instructional groups within the church.	Christian education has a variety of facets and is not simply given for one reason, one format, or one particular group in the church. Rather, Christian education is multi-dimensional, able to respond to needs ranging from those of the individual to those of the Christian community. Instruction must be tailored to the needs of the specific group or age level.
Heb. 5:11–6:3	Spiritual formation is the result of Christian instruction. Author employs the metaphor of growth from infancy to maturity to illustrate.	Christian education must provide graded levels of instruction for those of different levels of spirituality.

Commonality Between the Testaments. The following educational elements appear in both the Old and New Testaments.

1. *God as Teacher.* Through both word and deed God interacts with his people for the purpose of instructing and forming them into his people. It is for this reason that education in the Bible is God-centered.

2. *Command to Teach.* Family members and members of the faith community are commanded to assume the task of instruction (Deut. 6:6–9; Matt. 28:16–20). Christian education is the fulfillment of a divine imperative; it is not an option.

3. *Community of Faith.* The socialization of the faithful is accomplished through exposure to and involvement in the faith community. Through the church, people, particularly children, become aware of the teachings and traditions of the faith.

4. *The Diversity of Teachers.* In both testaments no single group or individual is *the* instructor. A plurality of teaching contexts, emphases, and styles is maintained because of the heterogeneous nature of God's people.

5. *Variety of Education Formats.* No one format dominates the biblical education landscape. Education is present in all its forms: formal (i.e., schooling), nonformal, and social, with the latter two being the most frequent.

6. *Variety of Instructional Methods.* Instruction in the Bible takes place in many forms. Jesus' teaching style alone demonstrates numerous methods that were commonly employed by many rabbis. Each method employed was obviously geared to the individual situation in which Jesus found himself.

7. *Revelation as Content.* Because of the nature of Scripture, it should dominate the Christian education curriculum. The use of the Torah among teachers in the Old Testament, the Old Testament's use in the New Testament, and the claims of the apostles in the New Testament (cf. 1 Thess. 2:13) emphasize the revelatory content of their instruction.

8. *Faith as Outcome.* Ultimately, the purpose of biblical instruction is the spiritual formation of the individual and the faith community. While it may be expressed in devotion, knowledge, relationship, or obedience, a holistic faith is the primary goal of Christian instruction.

9. *Education for Conversion.* Instruction was also given as a means of leading one to a personal commitment. While this is quite evident in the New Testament (Matt. 28:18–20), even in the Old Testament the resident "alien" was to participate regularly in the community's instruction (Deut. 31:12; 1 Kings 8:41–43). The beginning of spiritual formation is conversion.

JAMES RILEY ESTEP

Bibliography. K. O. Gangel (1991), *Christian Education;* E. L. Hayes (1991), *Christian Education: Foundations for the Future,* pp. 31–42; G. W. Knight, *Journal of the Evangelical Theological Society* 39, no. 1 (1996): 3–13; R. W. Pazmiño (1997), *Foundational Issues in Christian Education;* J. M. Price, ed. (1932), *Introduction to Religious Education;* R. B. Zuck (1995), *Teaching as Jesus Taught;* idem (1997), *Teaching as Paul Taught.*

Biblically Based Counseling. In a very broad sense, biblically based counseling refers to a learning approach in which individuals are helped to deal with personal (emotional, cognitive, and behavioral), relational, and spiritual problems from a biblical perspective. Debate continues over how to define the term; the theories, practices, and resources delimiting the field; and the qualifications necessary to become a biblically based Christian counselor. At one end of the continuum are people who say that counseling is biblically based if the counselor claims to be a Christian. In other words, the field of counseling contains basic skills and techniques common to all practitioners, and the Christian qualifier to the term *counseling* simply identifies the religious orientation of the counselor. At the other end of the continuum are those people who insist that biblically based counseling is a unique approach to caregiving, with a clear biblical and theological foundation that must remain untainted by secular psychological theories and practices.

Biblical Foundations. Helping people who are experiencing difficulties is part of the Judeo-Christian heritage. The Old Testament describes care and nurture within the community of faith in terms of fair and equal treatment (Exod. 20–23), a covenant between God and his people (Exod. 34), equitable justice and appropriate restitution (Exod. 21:12–22:17; Amos 5:15; Micah 6:8), and wise counsel (Prov. 16:21–24). Specific terms capture the language of care and counseling. The Hebrew word *hesed* conveys the idea of expressing goodness or lovingkindness in God's covenant relationship with his people and in our relationship to our neighbor. God shows his lovingkindness to those people who follow him with all their heart (2 Chron. 6:14), and he calls upon us to practice lovingkindness and compassion toward others (Zech. 7:9). *Hakam* means "to be wise." True wisdom comes from respecting and obeying God (Prov. 9:10; 15:33). Wisdom expresses sound judgment, truth, honesty, clear instruction, caution and discretion, righteousness, and justice (Prov. 8:1–21). The words of a wise counselor prod us to seek the will of God (Eccl. 12:11,13). The word *etsah* refers to advice, counsel, and the importance of developing godly plans. First Kings 12:13–14 records the failure of Rehoboam to listen to the counsel and directions of his older advisors; instead, he accepts the unwise advice of his young men, with disastrous consequences. Wisdom and understanding come from God, and the knowledge of God lies at the root of good counseling (Job 38:2, 36; Ps. 1:1–2). *Yaats*, the verb form of *etsah*, conveys the idea of taking counsel together, or deliberating after consultation (1 Kings 1:12; Isa. 45:21). The word *sodh* alludes to holding confidential conversations or the revealing of secrets, whether among family members, friends, or associates, or between God and his people (Ps. 55:14; Jer. 23:18, 22; Job 19:19; 29:4). *Rapha* means to heal physically (Ps. 103:3), spiritually (Jer. 17:14), or in terms of restoration of the soul (Ps. 6:2–3). Wise counseling involves using healing words (Prov. 12:18).

Similar themes of caregiving are found in the New Testament. The Greek word *agape* stresses the importance of loving all people we encounter, even those people who would wish us harm (Matt. 5:43–44). Counseling should reveal the love of God (Mark 12:30–31). Love builds up or edifies (1 Cor. 8:1); it manifests patience, kindness, tenacity, or endurance, and a lack of vanity and arrogance; it desires appropriate behavior and truthfulness (1 Cor. 13:4–8). All counseling must be motivated by godly love, and counselors must speak the truth in love (1 Cor. 16:14; Eph. 4:15). The model of Christian love is the self-sacrificial love of God toward us (1 John 4:9–11). *Boule* (and its verb form *bouleuo*) expresses the idea of planning, advising, and deliberating together to resolve an issue, or rationally assessing a situation (Acts 5:33–34; 27:39; Luke 14:31). Counselors are to seek the will of God underlying all creation and to acknowledge the ultimate and perfect plan or counsel of God (Eph. 1:11; Acts 11:34). *Noutheteo* means to admonish, warn, or correct. Wise teaching should accompany warnings and admonitions in order that we may grow in Christ (Col. 1:28; 3:16). Counselors must be patient with everyone, confronting disorderly people, consoling or encouraging the fainthearted, and supporting or helping the weak (1 Thess. 5:14). *Parakaleo* means to call alongside or call to one's aid. It conveys the notion of appealing for assistance (Matt. 8:5–6), offering encouragement that builds spiritual strength (Acts 15:32), and providing comforting or friendly words that lead to hope (2 Cor. 1:3–7; 7:6; Heb. 6:8). *Therapeuo* is the Greek word for healing, caring for, restoring, or treating. Healing may occur on physical and on nonphysical levels. In the ministry of Jesus, healing is related to teaching (Matt 4:23; 9:35) and faith (Matt. 17:14–20). Faith prepares people for the healing power of God in their lives. Healing and restoration are part of the ministry of counseling.

Historical Expressions. Over the centuries the Christian church has expressed care and provided counseling by building on the importance of repentance, confession, and church discipline. In the tradition of Paul, church leaders sent letters of comfort, correction, exhortation, and preventive care (e.g., Polycarp [d. 156], Gregory of Nyssa [335–395], Chrysostom [347–407], Calvin [1509–64], Baxter [1615–91]). Tertullian (c. 145–220), Wesley (1703–91), and other Christian apologists called for public confession and repentance. Church members and leaders were expected to check, correct, and even rebuke Christians who engaged in inappropriate behavior (e.g., Cyprian [200–258], Gregory the Great [540–604]). Care was expressed through education, visiting people in need, active intervention and nurturance, and referral to competent professionals (e.g., Clement of Alexandria, Lactantius [c. 250–325], Luther [1483–1546], Calvin, Baxter, Herbert [1593–1633], Taylor [1613–67], Zinzendorf [1700–60]). Emotional needs were addressed. Luther, for example, dealt with depression and temptation in his own life by recognizing the relationship between a healthy mind and a healthy body. He counseled people who were sick and depressed to challenge their thinking and to replace negative thoughts with meditation on Christ. The next step was to act on these positive and joyful thoughts; in Luther's case, this meant singing hymns. Contemporary counselors refer to this as *cognitive restructuring* and *rational behavior therapy*.

Contemporary Counseling. Secular models of counseling have dominated the field since Sigmund Freud (1856–1939). Pastoral counseling, as it has developed in the twentieth century, has reflected influence from the theories of Freud, Alfred Adler, Carl Jung, and Carl Rogers more so than its biblical and ecclesiastical roots. Reaction to this loss of biblical identity and the weakness of the secular models arose in the 1960s from both secular (e.g., O. Hobart Mowrer) and Christian sources (e.g., John Drakeford). In 1970, Jay Adams, in *Competent to Counsel*, stridently attacked both Christian and secular theorists in the field. He argued that psychiatric models reject personal responsibility and ignore depravity and sin in human nature, yet Christians rush to embrace these unbiblical approaches. Christian counseling must be based solely on Scripture; it must not be integrated with any psychological theories. In addition to the pastoral counseling and the anti-integration positions, a third movement began a rapid expansion at this time. A number of Christians trained in psychology and psychiatry (e.g., James Dobson, Gary Collins, Larry Crabb, Frank Minirth, Paul Meier) sought to integrate their disciplines and practice with Scripture. Spurred on by critics such as Adams, some integrationists have shifted from baptizing a particular secular counseling model by adding nominal biblical references to more rigorous attempts to develop a solid theological and biblical basis for Christian counseling.

Numerous training programs in biblically based counseling now exist, and the continuing lively debate is evident in the variety of counseling organizations such as the American Association of Pastoral Counselors (AAPC), the Christian Association of Psychological Studies (CAPS), the National Association of Nouthetic Counselors (NANC), and the American Association of Christian Counselors (AACC), along with their respective publications (*Journal of Pastoral Care, Journal of Psychology and Christianity, Journal of Biblical Counseling, Journal of Psychology and Theology,* and *Christian Counseling Today*).

IAN F. JONES

Bibliography. J. E. Adams (1970), *Competent to Counsel;* W. A. Clebsch and C. R. Jaekle (1964), *Pastoral Care in Historical Perspective;* G. Collins (1993), *The Biblical Basis of Christian Counseling for People Helpers;* L. J. Crabb Jr. (1977), *Effective Biblical Counseling;* J. W. Drakeford (1967), *Integrity Therapy;* J. T. McNeill (1951), *A History of the Cure of Souls;* O. H. Mowrer (1961), *The Crisis in Psychiatry and Religion;* D. A. Powlison (1996), "Competent to Counsel? The History of a Conservative Protestant Anti-Psychiatry Movement," Ph.D. dissertation; P. Schaff and H. Wace, eds. (1952), *A Select Library of Nicene and Post-Nicene Fathers of the Christian Church,* vols. 1–14.

See also COUNSELING; NOUTHETIC COUNSELING

Biblical Theology. The term *theology*, sometimes referred to as *theology proper*, indicates disciplined reflection upon the person of God (Greek, *theos*). The term often includes thought concerning God's activity and the truth that he has revealed. In a broader sense, theology customarily denotes a systematic presentation of the beliefs of a religion, denomination, or church.

Theology emerged as a separate field of study in the twelfth century. By the seventeenth century, theology had become the academic study of the concept of God and the philosophical analysis of religious traditions. In opposition to this scholasticism, biblical theology arose as an orderly presentation of the teachings found in the Scriptures. Today, there are at least two major uses of the term.

The first use refers to a biblical theology movement initiated by the publication of Karl Barth's commentary on Romans in the 1920s and Walther Eichrodt's *Theology of the Old Testament* in the 1930s. This "back to the Bible movement" nudged many liberal theologians toward a modern neo-orthodoxy. Significant biblical theology literature was published in the years shortly before, during, and following World War II by Rudolf Bultmann, Oscar Cullmann, Gerhard von Rad, Joachim Jeremias, Martin Buber, John Bright, James Smart, and others. Emphasis was placed on Hebrew (in contrast to Greek) thought, and on the rediscovery of a historical and unified understanding of the Bible and its teaching. Gerhard Kittel's *Theological Dictionary of the Old Testament*, emphasizing word study and contextual interpretation, is an example of the effect of this movement.

The second prominent use of the term *biblical theology* indicates an organized statement of what is taught in the Bible. Two characteristics of biblical theology in this sense are a reflection of the structure of the biblical text and a preference for biblical terminology. There are few examples of biblical theology that set forth the thought of both the Old and New Testaments in one work. Old Testament biblical theology emphasizes the history of Israel, and New Testament biblical theology emphasizes the birth and initial growth of the church. Their relationship is often considered too complex for a unified biblical theology.

Biblical theology is a bridge between two distinct fields of study. Exegesis employs hermeneutic principles to interpret the meaning of biblical texts in their historical and grammatical contexts. Utilizing the truth discovered through exegesis, biblical theology organizes the essential doctrinal content of the entire Bible. From this interpretation-intensive foundation, systematic theology relates biblical truth to contemporary thought in the church or in various world religions and schools of philosophy. Two characteristics of systematic theology are religious or philosophical categories and a preference for contemporary or specialized terminology.

Biblical Theology and Christian Education. The relationship between biblical theology and Christian education is a matter of authority. To the extent that education is the educing, or drawing out (Latin, *educere*), of understanding from a body of knowledge, Christian education is viewed as the guided learning of the Bible and the employment of biblical values in godly living. Systematic theology, as defined above, is helpful in the framing of instruction found within Christian education because it speaks in categories and language that promote student understanding. However, ultimate appeal in the determination of truth must be to the Scriptures. Biblical theology, as defined above, is helpful in this foundational task.

Some schools of religious education rely on historic church creeds or sectarian confessions for authority. Other schools of religious education display a univocal emphasis upon the text of God's Word. Both extremes must be avoided. Christian education is strongest when both its content and methods are guided by the wise counsel of godly individuals who rely upon the truth of the Bible and the contributions of both biblical and systematic theology.

Storytelling is the key to the direct employment of biblical theology in Christian education. Accuracy in storytelling depends upon accuracy in exegesis. In turn, effective telling of the stories found in the Scriptures prevents particular church creeds or dogmatic traditions from replacing the Word of God as the ultimate source of truth in the life of the church.

Bible stories communicate God's values in the context of real-life experiences. As God's children of any age, era, or cultural heritage perceive analogies between the historical context and their life circumstances, ancient truth is applied to modern life with authority and life-changing power.

DANIEL C. STEVENS

Bioethics. A field devoted to ethical reflection on issues of life and health. The term sometimes encompasses environmental concerns. However, the most familiar core of the field addresses ethical issues in health care. *Medical ethics* is an older term for this field, though today medical ethics may refer broadly to issues in health care or more specifically to matters concerning physicians. The standard reference work in the field is the *Encyclopedia of Bioethics*, which provides

overviews and resources on virtually every issue in bioethics. Its theological content, however, is very limited and must be supplemented from other sources, such as bibliographies provided by the Christian centers identified below and indexes such as the *Religion Index*. More attentive to Christian perspectives are the *International Dictionary of Bioethics* (forthcoming from Paternoster Press) and the overview of the field in the *Annual of the Society of Christian Ethics* (1998), which this entry condenses and supplements.

There is certainly no shortage of ethical topics for consideration today. Multiple issues arise at the beginning of life, including abortion, contraception, reproductive technologies, the treatment of neonates, and many other maternal/fetal questions. Other issues may also have special application at the beginning of life, but touch a wider range of people. These include genetics, informed consent, proxy consent, general medical decision making, and experimentation both with adults and children. End of life issues such as withholding and withdrawing treatment, palliative care, assisted suicide, and euthanasia abound as well. Some groups have focused their attention more on public policy and organizational matters, addressing critical issues of access, resource allocation, health care organization, physician and nurse responsibility, managed care, and other institutional financial responsibilities. The issues are constantly in flux as health care itself changes (Kilner et al., 1998).

Debates over such bioethical issues are often vigorous and protracted, even among Christians. When people differ over these questions, it is generally traceable to different understanding of the relevant facts, different guiding beliefs, loyalties to different individuals or constituencies, or differences in ethical reasoning. In bioethics the most influential approaches to ethical reasoning in the broader society are a *utilitarian approach,* in which the right act or policy is that which produces the best consequences; a *principles approach,* in which several guiding principles such as doing good, avoiding harm, pursuing justice, and respecting people's autonomy point the way; and a more postmodern emphasis on *autonomy alone,* in which individuals are to choose what is right for them. Unfortunately, many Christians have adopted such approaches without engaging in biblical-theological analysis first. Human life created in the image of God, death as a conquered enemy, biblical justice and freedom, and above all, love, are among the many Christian convictions with great bioethical significance.

There are signs, however, of a resurgence of explicitly Christian analysis that explains the attraction and shortcomings of various popular approaches and offers constructive Christian alternatives (Rae and Cox, 1999). Bioethics as a field developed in the West over the last fifty years, though similar developments are occurring now in many parts of the world. Particularly in the 1950s and 1960s, much of the bioethical reflection took place in explicitly theological terms. While sustained religious analysis has given way in most settings to more philosophical approaches as people have sought common language for a pluralistic society, the voice of Christian ethics in health care ethics now appears to be strengthening. At the end of the twentieth century there are many places in which the theological dimension of ethical reflection on health care matters is taking place. Centers of higher education continue to play a key role. Health care ethics is addressed in various locations, including seminaries, philosophy and religious studies departments, law programs, nursing schools, and schools for allied health professionals. Some places have developed entire graduate degree programs in bioethics, though only the program at Trinity International University (Deerfield, Ill.) has an explicitly evangelical Christian focus. Syllabi and information on a broader range of religious and secular programs are available from the National Reference Center for Bioethics Literature at Georgetown University in Washington, D.C.

Various other educational organizations and communities are actively involved in bioethics as well. Some major church denominations have convened groups to study particular problems in health care in general or certain ethical problems such as those related to death and dying. Evangelically led organizations include denominational coalitions such as the National Pro-Life Religious Council; professional health care organizations; and bioethically concerned law and public policy organizations such as the Christian Legal Society, Focus on the Family, and Americans United for Life.

Many large health care systems, as they have developed over the last fifteen years, have institutionalized ethics concerns and ethics exploration. Many major systems of religious denominations, and large systems not sponsored by religious bodies, have hired bioethics persons as staff members to support their ethics education, their ethics committees, and their ethics consultation, or to guide boards and senior administrative groups in ethical matters as they relate to clinical and organizational concerns. The voice of Christian ethics in such settings is not usually very audible, but sorely needed nevertheless.

Probably the best source for Christian and other religious audio, video, print, electronic, and live resources for bioethics today are a variety of centers specializing in bioethics. Some have an evangelical Christian focus—for example, the Center for Bioethics and Human Dignity (CBHD) just north of Chicago, which offers several training institutes in bioethics each summer. Others are denominationally oriented, such as the Seventh Day Adventist Center for Christian Bioethics in Loma Linda, Calif. Still others are attached to larger Christian institutions but are not as explicitly Christian in their publications—for example, the Kennedy Institute for Ethics in Washington, D.C. Among the many secular centers—which only occasionally address Christian perspectives—the oldest and most widely known is the Hastings Center in Garrison, N.Y. There are two journals devoted to exploring issues in bioethics from a Christian perspective. One, *Christian Bioethics: Non-Ecumenical Studies in Medical Morality*, is quite diverse theologically. The other, CBHD's journal *Ethics and Medicine: An International Perspective on Bioethics*, is consistently evangelical in perspective. Those seeking more lay-oriented overviews of bioethical issues will find them, both in book form (Meilaender; Orr et al.) and in CBHD's question-and-answer *BioBasics* booklet series.

JOHN F. KILNER

Bibliography. J. F. Kilner et al., eds. (1998), *The Changing Face of Health Care;* Center for Bioethics and Human Dignity, 2065 Half Day Road, Bannockburn, IL 60015 USA. Phone: 847–317–8180; E-mail: cbhd@biccc.org; Web site: www.bioethix.org.

Black Theology and Christian Education.

Black theology is a contextual theology born out of the experiences of blacks in the United States and South Africa. In both cases oppression due to white racism provides the background and the context for the development of the theological movement known as black theology. In a sense, black theology is "a theology in search of new symbols by which to affirm black humanity. *It is a theology of the oppressed, by the oppressed, for the liberation of the oppressed*" (Moore 1973, ix, italics in original). The search for liberation explains why, in the United States and South Africa, we find in black theology the convergence of politics, culture, and theology.

In the United States, the civil rights and the black power movements of the 1960s provide the political and cultural ingredients of black theology, which was articulated by the National Committee of Negro Churchmen (NCNC), founded in 1966. It is not surprising, therefore, that the first book published on black theology should bear the title *Black Theology and Black Power*. It was written by James H. Cone and published in 1969. Cone has, over the years, been one of the chief advocates of black theology. In spite of the precise dating of black theology, it is possible to trace some of its themes back to the spirituals of the pre–Civil War era.

The beginnings of black theology in South Africa are similar to those in the United States. In South Africa civil disobedience, symbolized by the African National Congress (ANC) and the Black Consciousness Movement led by Steve Biko, provided some of the impetus for black theology. The South Africans also learned many lessons from the experiences of blacks in the United States. Manas Buthelezi can be called the father of South African black theology. For him the basic issue is, "If the gospel means anything, it must answer the . . . question 'Why did God create me black?'" (Hopkins 1989, 29).

"Why did God create me black?" is at once an agonizing practical and theological question. It is a question asked by black people, whether they are in Africa or in the diaspora. For black Christians this question takes on special significance. It is a question that links the theological productions of all Africans.

Black theology and African theology are not synonymous. African theology is less concerned with political liberation and white racism. Even though African theology tends to deal more with cultural and religious liberation, it springs from seeking an answer to the basic question of black existence in the world.

Black theology is neither monolithic nor static. From the earliest days of its inception it has had to deal with changing realities as they affect black people in their journey of Christian faith. The changes of the recent decades have shaped the current themes of black theology. For instance, the issues of post-apartheid South Africa have brought theological discussions in that country more in line with those in the rest of the African continent. In this regard, nation building and reconciliation (called the theology of reconstruction by some African theologians) are theological themes that link South Africa to the rest of sub-Saharan Africa.

In the United States multiculturalism and Afrocentrism became the focus of attention in the 1980s and 1990s. This may explain the focus on biblical hermeneutics and the black church as well as investigations of black presence in the Bible. Mention should be made of Cain Hope Felder's *Troubling Biblical Waters: Race, Class and Family* (1988) for the former and Walter A. McCray's *The Black Presence in the Bible: Discovering the Black and African Identity of Biblical Persons and Nations* (1990) for the latter. While scholars discuss black perspectives in biblical hermeneutics, the concerns of ordinary churchgoers are more apparent in debates about blacks in the Bible. Both kinds of discussions point to the relevance of black theology to Christian education.

For McCray, the intention of black Christian theologians is to provide an overview of the subject so that Christian educators, especially black educators, will have a foundation on which to build (McCray 1990, 135). One of the aims of black theologians has been to promote Afrocentric and Christ-centered Christian education. Afrocentric Christian education, however, has generated controversy. Some wonder whether it is possible to be simultaneously that Afrocentric

and Christ-centered (Wright and Birchett 1995, 10). Afrocentric Christian education is nevertheless needed for black Christians provided Afrocentrism does not prevent other ethnic groups and races from seeking ways of relating the Bible to their struggles.

Black theology challenges Christian educators to reexamine aspects of biblical interpretation. One can do so without agreeing with some of the extreme positions taken by specific writers. For example, one need not posit the blackness of any given biblical personality unless there is concrete evidence to the contrary as McCray seems to imply (McCray 1990, 18). It is also a dangerous practice to see race and color in biblical passages where such is not specifically the case. One may, however, challenge translations such as "Dark am I, yet lovely" (Song of Songs 1:5–6) and their traditional interpretations. Race is neither the most important factor in the Bible nor totally absent from it.

In taking the black religious experience seriously, black theology offers theological education a unique and unparalleled opportunity for an interdisciplinary approach to curriculum (Ziengler 1970, 176). Since the black religious experience is doctrine in action, it needs an appropriate curriculum that fosters a theology of action. Theological education for right doctrine as well as right action is also needed for other families of the Christian church worldwide.

Ultimately, black theology attempts to answer black people's questions. It has not always done so to the satisfaction of the ordinary black Christian. Nevertheless, black theology has a pedagogical function that is not limited to black people.

SAMUEL M. LINGE AND TITE TIÉNOU

Bibliography. D. N. Hopkins (1989), *Black Theology USA and South Africa: Politics, Culture and Liberation;* W. A. McCray (1990), *The Black Presence in the Bible: Discovering the Black and African Identity of Biblical Persons and Nations;* B. Moore, ed. (1973), *The Challenge of Black Theology in South Africa;* J. A. Wright and C. Birchett (1995), *Africans Who Shaped Our Faith;* J. H. Ziengler, *Theological Education* 6 (1970):173–231.

See also ACCULTURATION; LIBERATION THEOLOGY; MULTICULTURALISM

Blended Families. Many Christians and churches have adopted the nuclear family—consisting of working husband, homemaker wife, and children—as the normal and biblical model. This is actually a model that had widespread development in the Victorian middle class of the nineteenth century. While it may not be incompatible with biblical values, it does not represent the only biblically acceptable model for family. As early as 1974 only one-third of American families could be described as traditionally nuclear, so the nuclear family can hardly be considered the norm

(Keller, 1974). The church needs to consider the kinds of families to whom it actually ministers.

Blended families, also called binuclear, merged, rebuilt, combined, or reconstituted families, are those in which one or both parents have previously been married (Duvall and Miller, 1985). The blended family is rapidly becoming the experience of the majority of persons in the United States. The product of widespread divorce and remarriage, blended families include the following: (1) those in which children live with their remarried parent and a stepparent; (2) those in which the children from a previous marriage visit with their remarried parent and a stepparent; (3) those in which an unmarried couple livies together and at least one of the partners has children from a previous relationship who live with or visit them; (4) a remarried couple in which each of the spouses brings children into the new marriage from the previous marriage; and (5) a couple who not only bring children from previous marriages but also have a child or children of their own (Knox and Schacht, 1991).

Blended families face, among other things, structural difficulties, women's and men's roles, stresses, solidarity strains, and enhanced conflict. Almost all parties in a blended family experience the loss of a primary relationship. Children may mourn parental loss and so may the adults mourn the loss of a spouse. Power struggles may intensify and are typically harder to resolve. Both children and adults must establish several new relationships at a very intimate level. Stepparent roles are ill-defined and hard to work out. Children may see themselves as part of two families, even when they spend more time with the parent who has custody. A situation with "extra" grandparents may be hard for children to understand and hard for the grandparents to live through.

Often women in blended families are disappointed. They may expect total love and happiness, but they find stress, hostility, and difficulty relating to stepchildren. Stepfathers often experience guilt and confusion in their role with their own children as well as with their "instant," new children. They may try to be a "superdad" with their own children, leaving wives to feel neglected. The stepparent role also reduces the time available for family since it has to be spread across so many people. Working out child-rearing rules with the ex-spouse is also an area for potential stress.

It is very hard for parents in a blended family to create the solidarity expected of families. Most members of the blended family will have lived in at least one other family model, the nuclear family, and many will have lived in a single-parent model, too. In biological families the sense of oneness and a sharing of common goals develops slowly through many experiences. The blended family may unrealistically expect to have the same within a short period of time. Differences in values between the two parts of the blend also interfere with solidarity. It may take two to seven years for a family to really "feel" like a family.

"The significance to the [blended family] of the biological tie between parent and child is the strong emotional bond that accompanies it. The different levels of emotional bonding parents and stepparents have with their children and stepchildren create a context for negative feelings and conflict" (Knox and Schacht, 1991, 543). "A parent's emotional bond with children from a previous marriage may weaken a remarriage from the start" (544). Each spouse may view this bonding differently. Some see the bonding and concern for one's own children as a sign of a nurturing person. Others feel they are being left out of the relationship.

Two systems of living together are brought into the blended family. All families experience conflict, but issues of favoritism, divided loyalty, discipline, and money stress the systems as they accommodate to become one. All of these, as issues of conflict, seem to be intensified in the blended family.

Blended family strengths include improved family functioning, reduced conflict between former spouses, multiple role models for children, more flexibility than in the nuclear family, additional siblings, additional kin, and happily married parents (Strong and DeVault, 1989).

Historically the Christian church has condemned divorce and remarriage as falling below the biblical ideal for believers. However, since blended families are becoming the norm in American society it appears to be in the church's best interest to seek to strengthen rather than stigmatize them. This is especially the case in regard to children. Property, support, custody, and visitation issues are often characterized by bitter conflict and recrimination, resulting in pain for all involved and lowering the quality of coparenting relationships. Divorce mediation and counseling help people come to terms with their situations and resolve feelings of failure and anger. Counseling can help children to avoid a sense of self-blame during the transition to the new family setting.

Assistance for blended family members in regard to stress and related issues can be helpful if the problems are approached before they become uncontrollable. Educational or preventive strategies can explore grief resolution following the end of a marriage. Counselors can create an environment that assists in meeting custodial needs of children and addressing parental rights; teaches problem solving and negotiation skills; discusses alternative roles, rules, and rituals; identifies relationship-enhancing stepparent behaviors; and consolidates adult authority.

EUGENE S. GIBBS

Bibliography. E. M. Duvall and B. C. Miller (1985), *Marriage and Family Development;* S. Keller (1974), *The Family: Its Structure and Functions;* D. Knox and

C. Schacht (1991), *Choices in Relationships: An Introduction to Marriage and the Family;* B. Strong and C. DeVault (1989), *The Marriage and Family Experience.*

Bloom, Allan (1930–92). Author of the best-seller *The Closing of the American Mind: How Higher Education Has Failed Democracy and Impoverished the Souls of Today's Students* (1987). Bloom started what many considered to be a war of ideas within academe and the surrounding intellectual community. He charged that reformers were watering down the classic literary and philosophic works of the Western intellectual tradition. "Bloom's great theme throughout is that ideology has invaded the academy to an absolutely unprecedented degree, *closing* the American mind—at least the academic American mind—to the truth about human nature" (*National Review,* 17).

Born in Indianapolis, Indiana, into an American Jewish home, he grew up being exposed to the ideas of great historians and philosophers, and he studied at universities in Chicago, Paris, and Heidelberg.

Bloom was a professor at the University of Chicago, served on the Committee on Social Thought at Chicago, taught in Chicago's basic program in the 1950s, and served as codirector of Chicago's John M. Olin Center for Inquiry into the Theory and Practice of Democracy. He taught at Cornell University in the 1960s and at the University of Toronto in the 1970s, and he returned to the University of Chicago again from 1979 until his death in 1992. He also taught for shorter periods of time at Yale University and the Universities of Tel Aviv and Paris. Colleagues describe Bloom as a brilliant classicist and political theorist, and as someone who loved teaching. Prior to the publication of *The Closing of the American Mind,* Bloom's writings had grown out of his teaching and were primarily intended for use in the classroom. He is best known for his translations of his favorite classical books, Rousseau's *Emile* and Plato's *Republic.* Besides Rousseau and Plato, Bloom also was heavily influenced by the writings of Shakespeare and Nietzsche.

Bloom's experience on North American campuses in the 1960s and the years following was the catalyst for his cry of alarm in *The Closing of The American Mind.* He began with campus presentations and an essay he published in 1982, and he was later encouraged to expand the essay into a book of cultural criticism and philosophy. Bloom was as surprised as many others when the book sold more than a million copies in the first few months and remained on the New York Times best-seller list for a year.

His success was not without a price. He boldly wrote about the decline of parental authority, the influence of divorce and feminism, the effects of drugs and rock music, and the issues of race, the New Left, and psychobabble. Critics called him an elitist, sexist, and racist. Bloom was one of the first to raise pointed questions about the foundations of modern education. In a tightly argued manner he addressed the intellectual confusion and moral quandary of the American academy. He wanted to challenge the lazy intellectual habits and ideological thinking of college students. Concerned that faculty members were more focused on specialties and personal advancement than on creating learning communities, and more focused on training students for careers than on providing them with the skills necessary for deep thinking and reasoned thought, he charged that serious education was under assault.

Bloom's primary goal, and the lasting result of his work, was to focus piercing attention on the state of the academy. Regarding the condition of liberal education, Bloom observes: "These great universities—which can split the atom, find cures for the most terrible diseases, conduct surveys of whole populations and produce massive dictionaries of lost languages—cannot generate a modest program of general education for undergraduate students. This is a parable for our times." And it remains a top priority for academic reform in the future.

SHELLY CUNNINGHAM

Bibliography. A. Bloom, *National Review* 44 (1992): 16, 17; idem (1987), *The Closing of the American Mind: How Higher Education Has Failed Democracy and Impoverished the Souls of Today's Students; The Chronicle of Higher Education* 43 (1997): A14–A15; C. Orwin, *American Scholar* 62 (1993): 423–30.

See also HIGHER EDUCATION, CHRISTIAN; LIBERAL ARTS; PLATO; ROUSSEAU, JEAN-JACQUES

Board of Directors. An officially chosen group that is charged with defining an organization's philosophy, purposes, and direction; identifying acceptable strategies; setting policies; and holding the chief executive officer accountable. Different organizations have different procedures for officially selecting their board members. In some organizations board members nominate and elect their own successors (self-perpetuating board); in some organizations board members nominate successors, but the entire organization elects; and some organizations have a separate committee to nominate, then the entire organization elects the board. Additional differences include the length of time an individual may serve: some organizations limit the number of consecutive years a person is allowed to be a board member, other organizations have no limit. All of these particulars and more should be defined in the organization's bylaws.

The board of directors is a relatively small group when compared to the size of the organization it serves. For example, a church of a hundred members might have a board consisting of five to ten people, while a church of ten thousand members might have a board of one hundred (in such cases, there is generally an executive committee of the board to handle routine, detailed, or sensitive matters).

Usually a board of directors has officers elected by the board (or by the whole organization) to carry out its responsibilities. Most boards have a president (or chair) who calls a meeting of the board, constructs the agenda, presides at the meeting, and carries out other duties as specified in the bylaws. Most boards have a vice president (or vice chair), who serves in the president's absence and performs other duties as specified in the bylaws. Most boards have a secretary to keep accurate written records of the board's meetings, to produce correspondence on behalf of the board, and to carry out other duties as specified in the bylaws. Depending on the organization's structure, its treasurer may or may not be a member of the board of directors. Other members of the board are responsible for duties assigned to them by the bylaws or by the board itself.

JOHN H. AUKERMAN

See Also ORGANIZATION; TRUSTEE

Body Language. The study of the way we communicate through body language is known as kinesics. Body movement is a form of nonverbal communication and includes facial expressions, posture, body and hand gestures, and total body movement. Small group participants often send messages to other members through their body orientation. For example, a member who is interested in the speaker or the message will often sit up straight in his or her seat and face the message sender. On the other hand, an individual who is disinterested, nonchalant, or bored may slouch and look down. Nonverbal body cues also help control or regulate the flow of discussion in the small group. Speakers often signal that they are finished with what they have to say by relaxing, stopping their hand gestures, or making a noticeable posture shift. Body movements such as shifting around in a chair, swinging a foot, drumming fingers, or twitching an eye may reflect tension, frustration, impatience, or annoyance. Facial expressions are clear communicators of feelings such as anger, joy, disgust, sadness, or surprise.

HARLEY ATKINSON

Bonhoeffer, Dietrich (1906–45). Influential German theologian, pastor, and teacher who served in the leadership of the Confessing Church and began its seminary at Finkenwalde. His writings model the role of community in the life of the church and the "cost of discipleship" to the believer.

At seventeen, Dietrich made the decision to study theology and entered the university at Tübingen and then Berlin. He was influenced by the writings of Adolf von Harnack and Karl Barth. In 1928 he spent a year serving as an assistant pastor of a German-speaking church in Barcelona, then continued in studies, accepting an exchange with Union Theological Seminary in New York. His doctoral thesis, "The Communion of Saints," sought to combine a theological and sociological understanding of the church. He became a lecturer in systematic theology at the University of Berlin in the following year (1931), during which time he also wrote *Act and Being*.

In 1933 the political tide was changing for the German church as it aligned itself with the ideology of the National Socialist movement. Bonhoeffer recognized that this was the end of the true church and this caused him to seriously question whether one could remain in the German church and stay true to the Christian faith. In October Bonhoeffer left for London to assume the pastorate of a German-speaking church, but he stayed in close contact with the struggle in his country.

In 1934 the Barmen Confession was written, establishing the formation of the Confessing Church. The confession was comprised of six articles that delineated the Christian opposition to National Socialist ideology. The leaders of the Confessing Church asked Bonhoeffer to return to Germany to head up the new Preacher's Seminary at Finkenwalde in 1935. The school combined academic studies, prayer and Scripture meditation, group chores, and evening singing. The school was first closed by the Gestapo in 1937 but continued on a makeshift basis until 1940. During these years Bonhoeffer published his books *The Cost of Discipleship* (1937) and *Life Together* (1939).

In 1939, through the help of his brother-in-law, Bonhoeffer became involved with an underground resistance movement dedicated to overthrowing Hitler's regime. He was arrested on April 5, 1943, after engaging in numerous trips to Switzerland and Sweden to work with Allied officials about possible peace terms. During this time he began work on his book *Ethics*, which he was never able to complete.

Bonhoeffer spent most of his imprisonment in the Tegel Military Prison in Berlin. While at Tegel he was able to correspond with family and a few close friends. These letters were later gathered by his dear friend and student Eberhard Bethge, and published posthumously as *Letters and Papers from Prison* (1951). In September 1944 the Gestapo found papers that linked Bonhoeffer to the resistance movement and to a failed attempt on Hitler's life, which led to his execution at Flossenburg, a Gestapo camp, on April 9, 1945, shortly before the camp was liberated by the American army.

ELIZABETH A. LEAHY

Bibliography. E. Bethge (1977), *Dietrich Bonhoeffer;* J. D. Godsey (1965), *Preface to Bonhoeffer: The Man and Two of His Shorter Writings.*

Boomers. *See* Baby Boom Generation.

Boundaries. Things that define limits. For example, one may mark property with a fence, defining where personal property begins and ends. Boundaries also define the identities of individuals, the scope and limitations of one's actions, and the lines of responsibility in one's life as opposed to those in another's. They serve to protect the intellectual, relational, emotional, physical, and spiritual health of an individual. Boundaries can take the form of rules, organizational policies, desires or wishes, personal goals, and disciplines.

Relational boundaries help to define a relationship and keep the relationship growing in a healthy manner. Parents set relational boundaries for their children when they model and establish rules for appropriate language. This defines the level of respect, care, and value in the relationship. *Physical boundaries* may include the appropriateness of touch or may define the setting in which cross-gender counseling can occur. *Intellectual boundaries* require disciplining one's mind. Examples would be setting educational goals or managing self-defeating negative thoughts. *Emotional boundaries* include freedom to own and express one's emotion in an appropriate way as well as not being bound by the manipulative and negative emotions of others. *Spiritual boundaries* are important in the disciplines that generate a healthy relationship with God and his people through an increased knowledge of God and through worship, service, fellowship, and evangelism.

Often ministry hinders an individual from setting healthy boundaries. Many people feel that boundaries may convey that one is not concerned for another. An insatiable "need to be needed" on the part of the minister can make the parishioner more dependent on the minister than on God. Boundaries are needed to define the lines of responsibility in individuals' lives. Christian workers and helpers who take on responsibilities (sometimes in the form of owning another's problems) may often be more of a hindrance than a help. Boundaries help people to trust in God more than in those who do ministry. Ministry boundaries may be as simple as not answering the telephone during certain hours, not making oneself overly accessible by distributing pager and cell phone numbers to congregants, or taking days off; and they may be as complex as limiting the number of times an individual can call in a day or week, limiting the amount of information that one needs to hear, or coming to the realization that you are not the only person that is available during a crisis.

STEVEN GERALI

Bibliography. H. Cloud and J. Townsend (1992), *Boundaries.*

Boys, Mary (1947–). A product of Catholic education, Boys has spent her adult life either preparing for or participating in the fields of teaching and biblical scholarship for which she is well known. Her teaching and scholarship followed a continual and repetitive theme of collaboration and reconciliation. Her first book, *Biblical Interpretation in Religious Education* (1980), established a case for the linking of biblical theology with religious education, for seeing them not as a dichotomy but as interdisciplinary elements vitally intertwined. In an effort to eliminate this dichotomy, Boys offered an alternative definition of religious education, which states, "Religious education is the making accessible of the traditions of religious communities and the making manifest of the intrinsic connection between tradition and transformation" (282). Such redefining of religious education is central to moving from the role of simply handing on religious traditions through various teaching methodologies and strategies to recognizing the collaborative power behind religious education and biblical theology as a society-transforming force.

This theme of collaboration and reconciliation is seen in Boys's other writings as well. She explored the ministry side of religious education in *Ministry and Education in Conversation* (1981). Citizenship and discipleship were her focus in *Education for Citizenship and Discipleship* (1989). The subject of faith encompassed the writing of *Educating in Faith: Maps and Visions* (1989). Scores of journal articles and book chapters have echoed a variety of foci, including feminist issues in religious education, teaching, supervision, fundamentalism, theology, conversion, biblical criticism, and interreligious dialogue, to name a few.

As a renowned biblical scholar and religious educator, Boys enjoys a unique position as mediator and collaborator between these two disciplines. She describes the current gulf between the disciplines:

At present a chasm exists between biblical scholars and religious educators; this divide in many respects is the result of the ever-increasing complexity of biblical studies and the concomitant specialization it demands. But the Bible does not belong to just this guild of scholars. It is imperative that biblical criticism more adequately permeate the life of the church. In order for this to happen, religious educators must collaborate with Scripture scholars. Prerequisite to this collaboration is a threefold, systematic preparation of religious educators in knowledge of the Bible itself, the history of interpretation, and interpretation theory. Moreover, religious educators themselves can contribute to the integration of biblical studies into the life of the church by their expertise in curriculum (the design of educational environments along the lines of material resources, teaching services, and social-political arrangements). (327)

An ongoing interest in biblical and religious education research has produced a number of research projects over Boys's academic career, including Educating for Religious Particularism and Pluralism. This study involves twelve Jewish and Catholic academics and religious educators who are committed to pursuing the question of how religious education in the Catholic and Jewish communities fosters both commitment to one's tradition and the capacity to engage with other traditions. Additionally, Boys is a popular speaker and lecturer among religious educators, biblical scholars, and interfaith groups. She serves as a consultant for several theological seminaries, Catholic orders, and Christian-Jewish committees within academic and ecclesiological circles. Her ability to deal with complex theological constructs with integrity while communicating with and for religious educators has made her contributions to theological and educational scholarship valuable and transforming to the academy and the church.

WILLIAM F. FALKNER

Branching Programming. A form of programmed instruction first suggested by N. A. Crowder in 1961. Unlike linear programming, which requires each learner to move step by step through every unit of information in a specific, predetermined sequence, branching programming allows the learner to create his or her own path through the instructional material. Once an educator identifies a desired learning outcome, he or she divides the instructional material into units, or "frames," which are presented to the learner one at a time. A multiple choice question immediately follows each frame. The learner's response to the question determines which frame is presented next. If, for instance, the learner chooses one of the incorrect answers, the program might branch to a series of remedial frames designed to help the learner better understand the material. If the learner gives a correct response, the program might branch to a series of reinforcement frames that the learner may find entertaining or rewarding. This methodology, which Crowder also called "intrinsic programming," allows the choices of individual learners to influence largely the course and pace of the instructional material.

In its earliest form, a branching program curriculum often existed as a "scrambled textbook." A page of the book contained an instructional frame and a multiple choice question. Instructions at the bottom of the page directed the learner to turn to certain other pages depending upon his or her answer to the question. The other pages might also contain a frame, a question, or a directive to turn to other pages in the book.

Automated teaching machines also utilized branching programming. These electro-mechanical devices often incorporated audio tapes, prints, slides, and motion pictures to present frames to the learner. By the early 1970s, such auto-instruction devices were gradually replaced by the microcomputer, a device that excels in its logical branching abilities. Until the early 1980s, computer-assisted instruction (CAI) almost exclusively used branching programming methodology.

ROBERT DEVARGAS

See also COMPUTER-ASSISTED INSTRUCTION; COMPUTER-ENHANCED LEARNING; INPUT

Brethren of the Common Life. This group with its founder, Geert Groote (1340–84), brought about a far-reaching pre-Reformation movement. It began in the Netherlands, but spread rapidly through northern Europe. Its influence on and its contributions to the field of Christian education are enormous.

As a brilliant young man, Groote was well educated and ambitious, and sought fame and fortune. But during a life-threatening bout with the Black Plague, Groote had a profound and life-changing experience with God, and he saw the emptiness of his life goals. He saturated himself in the Scriptures and gave his life to spreading the gospel. He preached in the streets and on the hillsides. Soon he had a number of followers who helped in his ministry; later, these followers of Groote were called *The Brethren of the Common Life* or the *Devotio Moderna*. These humble Christian servants were not clergy or members of any recognized order, but were joined together in the cause of Christ.

Some of Groote's disciples were schoolteachers: one of these was Johannes Cele. Groote took Cele with him on a walking trip, and began sharing with Cele a vision for reform of the schools that Groote said was given to him by God. The elements of this vision included lofty aims and revolutionary teaching methods. Cele began to put these into practice in his school in Zwolle, Netherlands. Other Brethren teachers did this as well.

Meanwhile, Groote's success in preaching and evangelization caused some consternation among local clergy. Eventually Groote received a communication from the pope forbidding him to preach. This was a serious blow to the movement, because these early reformers believed that the pope was God's spokesman on earth. Shortly after that their leader, Groote, died.

Groote's followers met in a spirit of grief and despair. Should they give up? No. The Brethren decided God had given them a mission in life. During this time of religious persecutions and restrictions, they recognized that their major vehicle for spreading the good news (the *Devotio Moderna*) was that of teaching in the schools of the region. Already, their students were going on to the universities and making their mark. Town councils sent representatives long distances to ask for Brethren teachers to come and reform their city schools, as they had done so remarkably in the Netherlands. Thus, their work spread throughout northern Europe and beyond.

Far more than any of their contemporaries the Brethren taught in the vernacular languages. They continued with the trivium and quadrivium, but at times enhanced their curriculum using the best of ancient Greek, Hebrew, and Latin scholarship. Groote had instructed them in the education plans as part of his vision from God. Among these numerous innovations, they initiated the grade plan and taught in smaller groups according to level of progress. The grade plan and other innovations were put into practice by teachers who had learned from the Brethren of the Common Life. A notable example is Johannes Sturm, who often has been credited with originating the grade plan. But when Sturm initiated these plans in Strasbourg (according to an existing document) he credits the idea to the Brethren in Liege, where he had studied as a boy. Interestingly, while planning to reform the English grammar schools, John Colet learned of the innovations of the Brethren of the Common Life via one of their former students—Erasmus. The concept of promoting a godly life in schools, with new and effective organization and instruction plans, spread throughout Europe into England and was later brought to America by early Puritans.

Finally, the schools of the Brethren produced great leaders in the Protestant Reformation like Martin Luther and Martin Bucer. On the other hand, they also produced great men who labored within the church for counter-Reformation, like Pope Adrian VI, Jean Standonck, and Jean Mombaer. The galaxy of former students and teachers of the Brethren of the Common Life includes more well-known Reformers such as Calvin and Zwingli, renowned teachers like Alexander Hegius at Deventer and Listrius at Zwolle, humble but significant textbook writers like Johannes Murmellius, and developers of libraries such as Gerard Zerbolt.

By 1600, in those fiery days of Reformation, the Brethren of the Common Life had essentially disappeared as an organization. Their desire for humility nearly buried the significance of their work. But their impact on the cause of Christ and on Christian education is immeasurable.

JULIA HENKLE HOBBS

Bibliography. J. S. Henkel-Hobbs, "An Historical Study of the Educational Contributions of the Brethren of the Common Life," unpublished Ph.D. dissertation, University of Pittsburgh; A. Hyma (1950), *The Brethren of the Common Life*; K. A. Strand, ed. (1968), *Essays on the Northern Renaissance*.

See also CALVIN, JOHN; ERASMUS, DESIDERIUS; LUTHER, MARTIN; MEDIEVAL EDUCATION; REFORMATION, THE; RENAISSANCE EDUCATION; ZWINGLI, ULRICH

Broker. Social work term that describes the worker's role in helping a person, family, or group locate the resources required to meet determined needs. The worker and the person in need join together to determine what actual needs exist. The worker as broker then leads the person toward service providers who may be able to help the person meet his needs. A worker must have a good knowledge of other service providers in her area, including what they provide, their eligibility requirements, and their procedures for providing service. Christian social workers can act as brokers within the church setting. They can determine skills of church members, their willingness to use them for those in need, and then help link those members with persons in need as the church becomes aware of them. This allows all of a person's needs to be met—physical, emotional, and spiritual.

DAVID R. PENLEY

Brookfield, Steven (1948–). British educator best known for his contributions to teaching in higher education, particularly within the field of adult education. A product of the United Kingdom's system of higher education, Brookfield received his Ph.D. in adult education from the University of Leicester in 1980. His teaching career, which began in 1970, has included faculty appointments in England, Canada, Australia, and the United States.

He is currently serving as Distinguished Professor at the University of St. Thomas in St. Paul, Minnesota. He also serves as adjunct faculty member in the adult education doctoral program at National-Louis University in Chicago. Prior professional teaching and research experience includes Columbia University Teachers College, New York; University of Technology, Sydney, Australia; University of British Columbia, Vancouver, Canada; Malvern Hills College of Adult Education, United Kingdom; and lectureships at two other United Kingdom institutions.

In his more than twenty-five years of teaching, writing, and research, Brookfield has authored eight books, numerous chapters in edited books, journal articles, papers, and audio and video presentations. He is best known for his works related to the role of teaching in higher education with particular concerns for the adult learner, and he is a popular speaker and consultant for many world-class organizations.

Understanding and utilizing critical thinking when teaching adults is a recurrent theme in Brookfield's writing and pedagogy. He describes the concept of critical reflection in his book *Developing Critical Thinkers* (1987): "Developing critical reflection is probably the idea of the decade for many adult educators who have long been searching for a form and process of learning that could be claimed to be distinctively adult. Evidence that adults are capable of this kind of learning can be found in developmental psychology, where a host of constructs such as embedded logic, dialectical thinking, working intelligence, reflective judgment, post-formal reasoning and epistemic cognition describe how adults come to think contextually and critically" (179). He further explains that the concept of critical reflection centers around three processes: (1) adults question and reframe an assumption that has been heretofore accepted uncritically as common-sense wisdom, (2) adults take an alternative perspective on ideas which had been previously taken for granted, and (3) adults come to the realization that there are forms and processes of learning that could be claimed to be distinctively adult. Brookfield has further identified three trends in the study of adult learning that have emerged during the 1990s and that promise to exercise some influence into the twenty-first century: (1) cross-cultural dimensions of adult learning, (2) adults' engagement in practical theorizing, and (3) the ways in which adults learn within the systems of education (distance education, computer assisted instruction, open learning systems) that are linked to recent technological advances.

WILLIAM F. FALKNER

Bruner, Jerome (1915–). Jerome Bruner was born in New York in 1915. He received his Ph.D. in psychology from Harvard in 1941. He laid the groundwork for an American school of cognitive psychology. His best known books are *The Process of Education* (1962) and *Beyond the Information Given* (1973). Bruner established the Harvard Center for Cognitive Studies in 1960. He was given the Distinguished Scientific Award by the American Psychological Association in 1963 and elected APA president in 1965.

Bruner changed the direction of American psychology, overcoming the dominance of B. F. Skinner and behaviorism with his insights into cognitive processes. Bruner gathered his data from children in classroom settings because he saw little value in studying rats, cats, or pigeons to understand how children learn. Effective Brunerian teachers do not tell students what to know. Rather, they help them develop concepts, build generalizations, and create and understand networks of ideas and how they interrelate. Bruner's model is called *discovery learning* and consists of presenting problems and helping students find appropriate solutions. This can be done individually or in groups. Bruner found that discovery learning develops better problem-solving skills and greater confidence in the ability to learn as students actually learn how to learn.

Structure. Bruner held that any subject can be organized in such a way that it can be taught to almost any student. To determine the structure of a subject is to understand its fundamental ideas and how they relate to one another. These fundamental ideas can be reduced to a diagram, a set of principles, or a formula. Structure is facilitated by modes of representation, economy, and power.

Modes of Representation. Bruner believed that people of all ages possess different modes of understanding. *Enactive understanding* is wordless, based on actions, demonstrations, and hands-on experimentation. One learns to ride a bike, play the piano, or conduct brain surgery by an enactive process of hands-on experience. *Iconic understanding* is based on pictures, images, diagrams, models, and the like. Artists and engineers emphasize iconic understanding. *Symbolic understanding* is based on language and the use of words to express complex ideas. Mathematicians and philosophers emphasize symbolic understanding. Presenting material in the sequence of enactive, iconic, and symbolic helps students develop structural understanding of the subject.

Economy. Excessive information or information presented too quickly confuses listeners. Teachers should present material in small doses and give students time to process the material between doses. They should also provide summaries of facts and concepts periodically to allow students to organize the material.

Power. A powerful presentation is a simple presentation. Reducing large quantities of facts to formulas, models, or diagrams helps students understand the essential relationships in the material.

Motivation. Bruner believed all children have an innate will to learn. Intrinsic, not extrinsic, motivation sustains that will to learn. Intrinsic motivation comes from the students' own curiosity, their drive to achieve competence, and reciprocity—the desire to work cooperatively with others. These are rewarding in themselves, and thus, self-sustaining.

The Teacher. Bruner's initial ideas place great emphasis, following Piaget, on students discovering relationships. Discovery learning emphasizes student activity, student initiative, and student solutions. Bruner acknowledged that students would learn fewer facts through this approach. But they would also gain a deeper understanding of the subject, which could well continue beyond the classroom. It is one thing to be able to answer questions, but it is actually much better for students to learn to ask questions of themselves and then find the answers.

This focus on learner-centered problem-solving has become known as *pure discovery learning*. Teachers must be well versed in the subject so that they can move easily from one interconnected concept to another. They must be a model of thinking competence, weighing student questions before answering, reframing statements to make them more focused, pulling relevant examples into the class discussion, asking probing questions to further student understanding, and the like. Teachers must prepare students for discovery activities by ensuring they understand basic vocabulary and operations required for higher-level thinking. Teachers are group facilitators and presenters of problems more than tellers of facts. Teachers serve as guides for the student-centered learning process, and take care not to short-circuit the discovery process by giving students the answers.

Criticism of Discovery Learning. Pure discovery methods came under attack as being too time-consuming. Teachers began to feel they were wasting precious class time waiting for students to discover for themselves concepts and principles they could more quickly learn with teacher-structured explanations.

Pure discovery methods presented teachers with interpersonal problems. Students became frustrated with those who dominated much of the discussion time and made most of the discoveries. Attitudes of jealousy, resentment, and inferiority were generated. In any educational setting, someone has to do the talking. With pure discovery, this someone was another student. Yet most students would rather hear "the expert" talk about the subject.

Finally, pure discovery methods are simply inappropriate in some settings. If the subject matter is difficult, or if students come from disadvantaged backgrounds, pure discovery is less effective than traditional approaches. Class time is limited and may not allow sufficient time for students to discover all the necessary links among concepts and principles.

RICK YOUNT

See also COGNITIVE DEVELOPMENT; DISCOVERY LEARNING; DISCOVERY TEACHING

Buddhism. *See* Asian Theology.

Budget. A plan that allocates a church's financial resources toward achieving its purpose (mission) and goals. It can be viewed as a snapshot of a church's ministry plan for a fiscal year. A budget incorporates several elements: (1) a plan for revenues and expenditures; (2) a process for building the budget, including feedback mecha-

nisms for accountability; and (3) a stewardship program.

Stewardship. Sound financial planning begins when members of a church acknowledge that they are stewards, not owners, of their resources. God is the source of all things: "Every good thing bestowed and every perfect gift is from above, coming down from the Father of lights" (James 1:17 NASB). A steward is someone who oversees another's property. Jesus spoke of an *oikonomos*, a house manager, who squandered his master's possessions and who, therefore, lost his stewardship (Luke 16). Members of the church are first and foremost "of God's household" (Eph. 2:19).

To be a good steward involves identifying how the owner wants the resources to be used. Since resources may be limited, the church must have a clear picture of what God wants this specific church to accomplish (mission and goals). The financial resources can then be allocated in ways consistent with the church's mission and goals. A budget for a local church or a specific ministry within that church should line up a church's financial priorities with God's purposes for the church. It is for this reason that the goals of the church should be developed prior to the formation of the budget.

Structure of Budget. A sound budget projects anticipated revenues and expenses. Revenues may derive from several sources, including tithes and offerings, special projects, and earnings from endowments. Expenditures normally include two broad areas, operational and capital, as well as occasional special projects. Operational expenditures include fixed categories or line items (e.g., pastoral salaries, mortgage, utilities) over which a congregation has little control. Program areas (ministry action) usually are more flexible. Capital expenditures are those nonrecurring expenses for equipment, buildings, and technology that have value beyond the life of the expense.

The Christian education portion of a church's budget will likely include program areas such as Sunday school, youth ministries, women's ministries, vacation Bible school, and other Christian education programs.

A sound budget will be balanced; that is, its revenues and expenditures will match. It should reflect the purpose, needs, and strategic goals (things to be done within the fiscal year) of the church. Furthermore, a budget should be realistic; that is, it should demonstrate how the congregation anticipates living within its available resources for a year. A realistic budget accounts for vision by clearly identifying at what points the congregation must trust God and stretch to achieve its purpose and goals. Finally, a good budget will be stewardship-based and emphasize tithing versus fund-raising. God has provided the means, through faithful, systematic tithing, whereby his people can accomplish everything he intends for them to do.

Budgeting Process. The budgeting process is fundamentally a decision-making process. It requires the right people, at the right time, committed to the right thing (the mission of the church), working in the right way. Normally the governing body of a congregation appoints qualified individuals to a budget committee. This committee then receives proposals that evaluate programmatic needs and establish functional priorities consistent with the mission of the church. The committee reviews these proposals in light of prior budgets and projected income. It then proposes a balanced budget for presentation to the governing authority of the church. Once the budget is adopted, the budget committee or its appointed representative (e.g., the church treasurer) monitors revenue and expenditures and reports to the appropriate authority on a regular basis. Finally, the budget should be audited annually. Normally, this may be done by competent individuals within the congregation who are outside the normal budgeting and reporting process.

LESLIE A. ANDREWS

Bibliography. B. P. Powers (1981), *Christian Education Handbook: Resources for Church Leaders.*

Builder Generation. Older adults born prior to 1946. The designation "builder" emphasizes the attempt to build a better personal life and a better nation, rather than just maintaining what has been given. Generational theorists Strauss and Howe (1997) refer to this group born between 1925 and 1942 as the "Silent Generation." It should be noted that there is little uniformity in birth year designations; for example, Leith Anderson (1990) cites 1930 to 1945 for builders, while George Barna (1994) marks the generation with birth years of 1927 to 1945.

Strauss and Howe, in their attempt to distill generational trends from historical data, describe builders as marrying early and marked by aversion to risk. As teenagers, builders born in the 1940s tended to become "sensitive" rock and roll fans and advocates of the civil rights movement, yet builders also advocated conformity as the means to success. In middle age they felt torn between the older, impassive G. I. generation and the younger, impassioned baby boomers. As they enter their elder years they are marked by considerable affluence, but also indecisiveness.

Strauss and Howe hold that the builder generation is one generation in a repeating four-generation cycle that has marked most of American history, as well as much of human history. In this cycle, the builder generation functions as an "artist" generation, overprotected in childhood, then sensitive in early adulthood. As middle-aged adults, builders became indecisive, then have developed empathy in their elder years. They are marked by their adaptiveness.

Researcher George Barna describes builders as being more concerned about good health than other generations were, and more likely to believe that close proximity to extended family is important. Builders are also more likely to state that a close relationship with God and being part of a local church are important than are those of successive generations.

Leith Anderson emphasizes that because of the influence of the Great Depression and World War II, the builder generation has come to trust institutions but not the economy, which is just the opposite of their successors, the baby boomers. They are cautious and conserving, and have learned to delay gratification. Builders tend to be cautious, to work hard, and to be self-reliant. Loyalty to organizations and even brand names mark this generation, and their marriages tend to be fairly stable, although that stability is often the result of a sense of duty. Builders are more likely than succeeding generations to turn to the government, family, community, or church in the event of crisis.

In leadership, builders tend to favor top-town organization and a high degree of regulation. Duty to the employer and job security are valued over enjoyment, change, and variety. Tactfulness and manners are encouraged rather than the confrontation and candor that are encouraged by their successors, the baby boomers.

It is important to note that members of the builder generation, like members of all generations, are not all alike—there can be as much variation within a generation as between generations. However, the research in this area is potentially instructive as long as general trends found among builders are not used to stereotype everyone within that generation.

DONALD E. RATCLIFF

Bibliography. L. Anderson (1990), *Dying for Change;* G. Barna (1994), *Baby Busters;* W. Strauss and N. Howe (1997), *The Fourth Turning: An American Prophecy;* idem (1991), *Generations.*

Bulimia. *See* Eating Disorders.

Burnout, Ministerial. Professional burnout is a recent North American phenomenon that is worthy of note, because of its destructive effect upon the church. Congo (1981) reported that three out of four ministers experience a level of personal and professional stress that undermines their ability to perform their duties. Burnout is associated with severe depression, high levels of anxiety, anguish, anger, fear, and alienation. Herbert Freudenberger espoused the first definition of burnout as a result of observations he made in a drug rehabilitation center in East Village, New

York. It is "formally defined and subjectively experienced as a state of physical, emotional, and mental exhaustion caused by long-term involvement in situations that are emotionally demanding" (Pines and Aronson, 1988, 9).

Freudenberger (1980) cites five personality types that seem to be most susceptible to the professional burnout associated with the helping professions. The first type is the *dedicated* worker who commits himself or herself wholeheartedly to the work. Unfortunately, these individuals do not know how to pace themselves and often find their lives controlled by the many assignments they have accepted. The second type is the *consumed* or nonsocial worker. These persons are so enmeshed in their work that they have neglected to establish a life outside of the workplace. They lack contact with friends and family who could serve as a support base for their overextended lifestyle. The third personality is the *dictator,* who is driven to succeed at all costs. This person must be in control of all details and finds it impossible to delegate because no one can do the job as well as he or she can. The fourth personality type is the *overworked administrator* who must assume multiple roles in the organization and always be his or her best in each role and duty. The final personality is the *sympathetic listener* who takes on the emotional pain of coworkers and friends, to his or her detriment. This individual identifies with the personal pain of others to the degree that parishioners' pain actually becomes his or her own.

There is a common misconception among clergy today that strict adherence to the spiritual disciplines of Scripture reading, Bible study, prayer, fasting, and meditation will prevent the ministerial leader from experiencing burnout. However, studies have demonstrated that there is no correlation between such activities and burnout prevention. No matter how faithful to these elements of the Christian faith, any leader can experience burnout at some point in her or his career.

Causes of Ministerial Burnout. Numerous studies have been conducted to determine the causes of professional or career burnout as it applies to careers in education, business, medicine, and religious service. The brevity of this article does not allow an exhaustive list of the causes of ministerial burnout. However, a short list would certainly include the following:

1. Unrealistically high expectations are held by the laity for their pastors.
2. The work of the ministry is never done.
3. Some congregational members are extremely needy and exceed professional capabilities for help—but the minister finds out too late.
4. A common misconception is that the pastor always has life fully under control.
5. Professionals may not take the time to meet physical needs (diet, rest, etc.).

6. Spiritual highs are often succeeded by spiritual lows
7. There may be disappointment about personal progress in one's professional career.
8. Professionals may be relying on human resources to meet spiritual needs.
9. Some professionals are unable to accept personal or professional failure.
10. The increasingly complex nature of clergy responsibilities may cause burnout.

Solutions. Just as there are many causes for ministerial burnout, there are numerous solutions. The following short list is provided to illustrate a variety of measures that may be taken to alleviate this problem:

1. Develop a realistic perspective regarding what you can accomplish given your personal drive, professional training, and church and societal resources. The church already has one Messiah and does not need a second. Simply stated, do your best but do not feel like you have to do it all yourself. Know when to refer difficult counseling situations to other professionals. Sometimes you need to say no to invitations because they do not contribute toward the greater good of your own goals.

2. Seek the support of others. The spiritual gifts were given to the church. God does not expect any one individual to possess them all. Therefore, equip other members of your church to take on added responsibilities and thereby share the load of ministerial leadership. A spouse or trusted friend is an essential element of gaining support as well.

3. Recognize that you have not received your spiritual body yet. You are limited by your need for proper diet, rest, variety from the routines of life, exercise, and recreation. If you lack any of these essential components, you will be traveling on the road toward ministerial burnout. Schedule time for yourself to jog, golf, swim, or do whatever else brings you happiness.

4. Consider making structural changes in your church organization. Perhaps you have too many people depending on you for supervision and advice. Hire or reorganize in order to allow others to share the administrative workload. Train your administrative assistant or secretary to do some of the elementary tasks that can be time consuming to you.

5. Don't be afraid to confront the source of your stress head-on. Identifying what causes stress in your life and then having the courage to confront it will contribute significantly to your long-term well-being. Whether the problem is with an individual or an object, work toward a resolution that will bring about a long-term solution.

Ministerial burnout costs the church a great deal each year. Exhausted pastors avoid visiting members of their church and eventually leave their congregations prematurely. The cost in wasted resources, both human and financial, is monumental. The high turnover rate among members of the clergy is testimony to the extreme demands placed upon them. Careful attention given to the causes and cures of ministerial burnout will contribute a great deal to the long-term success of the pastor and his or her congregation.

MICHAEL J. ANTHONY

Bibliography. D. Congo (1981), "The Role of Interpersonal Relationship Style, Life Change Events, and Personal Data Variables in Ministerial Burnout," Ph.D. dissertation, Rosemead Graduate School of Professional Psychology, Biola University; H. J. Freudenberger (1980), *Burnout: The High Cost of High Achievement;* D. Nuss *Christian Education Journal* 11, no. 2 (1991): 63–73; A. Pines and E. Aronson (1988), *Career Burnout: Causes and Cures.*

Bushnell, Horace (1802–76). American religious writer. Born in Bantam, Connecticut, where he grew up on a farm, he entered Yale College to prepare for ministry but instead turned to teaching. It was at Yale that Bushnell read Samuel Taylor Coleridge's *Aids to Reflection,* a book that influenced him to value human nature and personal experience in spiritual development. Bushnell taught for a while in Norwich before leaving Connecticut for a short-lived career in journalism in New York City. Soon back at Yale, Bushnell studied law and worked as a tutor. It was in 1831 that he was caught up in a religious revival on campus. Bushnell had made an earlier profession of faith to join the Congregational Church as a teenager. This time he focused on a commitment to live a moral life.

Dropping out of law school, Bushnell returned to his earlier ambition to preach. He entered Yale Divinity School and studied with Nathanael Taylor, whose views would rock the Congregational Church. After graduation, Bushnell began a twenty-six-year pastorate at a Congregational church in Hartford. He married and had five children. Two of the children died young. The death of his only son and harsh criticism of his book *Christian Nurture* were struggles that brought a spiritual awakening that Bushnell described as a clearer understanding of God.

In 1856 Bushnell traveled to California while on leave from his church to recover his health, which had been poor throughout his adult life. While in California, he became interested in the progress of the railroad and the development of the West. He also had a hand in the founding of Berkeley College. After his retirement from the pulpit, Bushnell continued to write. He died at the age of seventy-four.

Although he had led revivals at his own Hartford church, Bushnell became discouraged by dwindling numbers of converts and what appeared to be little authentic spiritual growth. He became critical of revivals and their excessive emotional appeals. Insistence on a conversion experience at a mature age as a prerequisite for church membership excluded young children. Bushnell argued that there was no reason to delay religious instruction and force a child to suffer the upheaval of a conversion later. Right from the start, a child could be led to love what is good.

To understand why Bushnell's promotion of early religious training was considered so heretical, it is necessary to review the status of childhood in Bushnell's day. The prevailing thought was that children could not be Christians. Having reached the age of accountability, a child would be pressured to convert. Until then, the role of the parent was to remind the child of his or her sinful nature.

In *Christian Nurture,* Bushnell's best known work, he described conversion not as an event but as a process of growth begun in infancy and nurtured by the home and the church. The church provided infant baptism and welcomed the child into a relationship with God. The all-important work of modeling the Christian life-style belonged to the parents, and especially to the mother. Because a child grows in the likeness of his or her parents, mother and father must be diligent students of parenting skills. They need to prepare for the birth of a child by examining their own spiritual health.

Bushnell stressed that it was better to praise a child and thereby encourage confidence and self-esteem. Parents should teach children to be neat and well-mannered and should pay attention to their physical needs. Children must submit to parental authority, but they must not be disciplined harshly or publicly. Bushnell's promotion of tolerance and gentleness in parenting was as fervent as his criticism of sanctimony and bigotry in Christians. He affirmed family worship as a crucial element in Christian nurture, but cautioned parents to practice what they preached. In *Work and Play* (1864), Bushnell described play as symbolic of Christian freedom. The encouragement of joy in children was cited as an important parental duty.

Christian Nurture was a pivotal work in religious education and earned its author the title "father of modern religious education." Bushnell, who described himself as skeptical in religious matters, opposed the conservative view of instantaneous conversion. As a result, he had many critics. The first edition of *Nurture* was dropped from publication because of the uproar it caused. Bushnell expanded the second edition, and by the time the third edition had been released some of the clamor had died down.

Other works with less impact included *God in Christ* (1849) and *Christ in Theology* (1851), the latter a defense of trinitarianism. In *Nature and the Supernatural,* Bushnell described the effect the fall of man had on the natural world. *The Vicarious Sacrifice* and *Forgiveness and the Law* brought accusations of liberalism because of Bushnell's controversial view of the atonement.

In addition to religious subjects, Bushnell also addressed social and political issues such as slavery and women's suffrage.

Although his theological views are debatable and some of his social and political views need to be considered in the context of his time, Bushnell's contributions are undeniable. He brought a new emphasis to the importance of the family and of the early religious education of children. Many of his ideas about the form of childhood religious training, coming at a time when the Sunday school and public education movements were just beginning, would not be accepted until the 1900s.

ROBERT J. CHOUN

Bibliography. H. Bushnell (1861), *Christian Nurture;* K. B. Cully (1963), *The Westminster Dictionary of Christian Education;* K. O. Gangel and W. S. Benson (1983), *Christian Education: Its History and Philosophy;* W. A. Johnson (1963), *Nature and the Supernatural in the Theology of Horace Bushnell;* J. E. Reed and R. Prevost (1993), *A History of Christian Education;* H. Smith, *Horace Bushnell;* D. Wyckoff (1959), *The Gospel and Christian Education: A Theory of Christian Education for Our Times.*

See also AGE OF ACCOUNTABILITY; CHILDHOOD CHRISTIAN EDUCATION; CHRISTIAN NURTURE; FAMILY LIFE EDUCATION; SELF-CONCEPT

Buster Generation. Baby busters are so named because of the "bust" or sudden decline of births during the early 1960s. The rapid decrease in births coincided with the widespread use of the birth control pill. The buster generation is also termed "Generation X," denoting the unknown, or a supposed lack of commitment. They are sometimes designated the "Thirteenth Generation" because they are—by the reckoning of some writers—the thirteenth generation of Americans. Although writers and researchers disagree, the birth years of busters most commonly cited are 1964 to 1982. They are preceded by the baby boom generation and followed by the millennial generation.

Generation specialists Strauss and Howe (1997), using historical data, describe busters as a "Reactive Generation" that occurs repeatedly in history. A reactive generation is criticized a great deal by prior generations, and is not given the protection in childhood afforded other generations. As a result, they become alienated young adults who readily take risks, yet date and marry cautiously. They mature into pragmatic leaders who prefer freedom over loyalty during middle age. In their older years they are respected and tough, but tend to be reclusive and less influential than other generations. Strauss and Howe describe them as lonely "nomads."

Using telephone interviews, researcher George Barna (1994) found that busters often received unconventional parenting—perhaps because of the increase of divorce, single parenting, and blended families during the 1970s. They are dis-trustful of institutions and people, and thus tend to be pragmatic and skeptical about the future and humankind. They have felt that adaptation is more important than innovation, as they matured in a world constantly marked by change.

Barna concludes that busters value information less than preceding generations, perhaps because of the information explosion during their childhood years. They are the first generation to grow up in a world that is increasingly postmodern, reflected in their suspicion of reason and the scientific method. Education is considered a means to an end, rather than valued for itself as with the builders and baby boomers. Likewise, work is valued for what it leads to; prestige and image from occupational accomplishment are less likely among busters. Long-term commitments to an employer are rare. Busters are also less likely to be workaholics, a problem common in previous generations.

Busters are, at heart, pessimistic. The world rarely offers a chance for advancement, they believe, and thus they tend not to believe in improvements for the future. Barna also discovered deep feelings of inferiority among the busters interviewed, as well as a strong protectiveness of possessions and complaints about what they lacked. Rejecting the impersonal and short-term relationships of their parents, busters accentuate the need for long-term, traditional relationships, although they often have lower expectations regarding such relationships.

Mahedy and Bernardi (1994) underscore the anger, restlessness, and pervasive sense of aloneness sensed by busters. They compare busters with veterans who have suffered trauma in war because of the pervasive neglect and abandonment by parents busy with their own interests and occupations, the trauma of family dissolution, exposure to high levels of violence and sexuality from the media, and widespread abuse by adults. As a result, busters tend to distrust people, often feel life to be pointless and meaningless, and lack a "moral compass." Yet Mahedy and Bernardi see positive signs that busters are less likely to succumb to the narcissism with which they were reared, and that the sense of aloneness can foster a stronger community life and perhaps even moral and religious depth.

Not all busters are alike. There is considerable diversity within any generation—many people do not fit the general pattern—yet this should not obscure discernible trends that exist within the buster generation.

DONALD E. RATCLIFF

Bibliography. G. Barna (1994), *Baby Busters;* idem (1995), *Generation Next;* W. Mahedy and J. Bernardi (1994), *A Generation Alone: Xers Making a Place in the World;* W. Strauss and N. Howe (1997), *The Fourth Turning: An American Prophecy;* idem (1991), *Generations.*

Bylaws. *See* Constitution, Church.

Cc

Calvin, John (1509–64). Born in Noyon, France, he became the primary organizer of Protestant Reformed theology. His early education included training in classical humanism, law, and religion. While studying the principles of the Reformation, he became converted and was forced to flee France to avoid persecution. At Strasbourg in 1538 and later at Geneva, Calvin was a dedicated teaching pastor and educator. He considered a knowledge of Christian doctrine as fundamental to faith and life, and recognized the crucial role of educational ministry in imparting that knowledge.

In 1542 the leaders of Geneva allowed Calvin to revise the city's laws and establish an autocratic government that tightly controlled social and religious life. The school, home, church, and state worked together as one organism to train people in godliness. Rejecting the infallibility of papal instruction, he insisted that much of his doctrine be open for debate.

Calvin recognized the importance of childhood religious education. He twice wrote catechisms for children. The topics of faith, the Commandments, prayer, the Word of God, and the sacraments were emphasized most.

Perhaps his most lasting contribution to education was his Geneva Academy. The purpose of the college was twofold: to provide instruction of the faithful in doctrine, and to train ministers and leaders. It was meant to serve both the children of Geneva and theological students from abroad. There was no cost for attendance; the necessary monies were subsidized by gifts.

The school was patterned after Johann Sturm's *gymnasium*. It had two parts. The *Schola privata* was for children up to about 16 years of age. The curriculum was tightly compressed into 7 years. The lower grades (1–5) included French, Latin, and writing. Cicero and beginning Greek were added at grade 4. History, grammar, classical authors, and dialectic were addressed in the top three grades. In the *Schola publica* pupils worked at their own rate and level under the tutelage of the professors of Hebrew, Greek, the arts, and theology. This dimension later gained renown as the University of Geneva.

All instructors were chosen and supervised by the ministers of the churches; no others were allowed to teach in the city. Teachers were held in honor, as one of the four orders of office in the church. Each educator was considered divinely appointed.

Calvin's educational philosophy was grounded in his theology. He saw no contradiction in being a humanist and believing that a true knowledge of God could be found only in Scripture, not in nature, liberal arts, or science. People were totally depraved, fleshly, and evil. Humankind was incapable of any good act or thought according to the Reformed theology leader. He maintained only the soul was capable of redemption. In the Academy corporal punishment was standard fare among the instructors. The fires of hell were much more severe than their disciplines, they reasoned. Teachers were to instill values which pleased God—sobriety, thrift, hard work, responsibility—into their students. Thus the "Protestant work ethic" was introduced to the populace.

The Institutes of the Christian Religion remains his most widely known work. Calvin wrote as he preached—clearly and directly. The popularity of the *Institutes* tends to obscure his significant role as a Christian educator.

JAMES A. DAVIES

Bibliography. W. J. Bouwsma (1988), *John Calvin: A Sixteenth-Century Portrait;* R. W. Henderson (1962), *The Teaching Office in the Reformation Tradition;* T. B. Van Halsema (1959), *This Was John Calvin.*

See also CATECHISM; CHRISTIAN HUMANISM; CONFIRMATION; LUTHER, MARTIN; REFORMATION, THE

Camping. *See* Christian Camping International (CCI).

Camping Facilities. The possibility of owning, developing, and using camping facilities may seem like a near-perfect solution for the church or parachurch organization interested in outdoor ministries. However, before investing in an undeveloped plot of land or buying a former Boy Scout campground, there are some issues to be addressed.

Site Selection. When considering the selection of a possible site for a camp program, consideration must be given to the two broad areas of programmatic concerns and site concerns. Programmatic issues should be addressed first because one's philosophy and program should determine the site. If this is ignored, the site will determine the program. Questions regarding the type of program to be offered—residential or day camp, primitive or resort, centralized or decentralized—will help determine the suitability of a potential site only if they are given consideration prior to the selection of a site.

After determining the type of program desired, then issues related to the land must be addressed. Areas to be considered would include the number of acres available (a general standard is one acre per camper), the topography of the site, the potential for future development, the availability of local utilities, and the degree of privacy. Another major concern is the accessibility of the site. Not only should the site be accessible to the major constituents (a two- to three-hour drive is ideal); but also, for the sake of potential health problems, it should have emergency care available within a thirty-minute drive.

Site Development. Once a site has been selected or acquired, attention must be given to its development. Any development of a site should be done according to a master plan. This is an underlying principle that can help avoid costly changes in the future. Again, it should be noted that the master plan should reflect not only the buildings, but also the philosophy of the organization.

Along with following a master plan, good management will work to meet all standards and codes. This includes government regulations of state and local authorities, as well as voluntary standards of organizations such as the American Camping Association and Christian Camping International.

Finally, camping facilities should reflect an appreciation for both the Creator and his creation. They should be a means by which those who use them can be drawn into times of reflection which, in turn, lead to worship of the Creator and stewardship of His creation (Ps. 19:1).

DOUGLAS BARCALOW

Bibliography. A. and B. Ball (1995), *Basic Camp Management.*

Campolo, Anthony (1935–). Dr. Anthony Campolo is an internationally known speaker and author. As a sociologist and a Christian, Campolo works to analyze and diagnose the social condition of culture inside and outside the church. He speaks to evangelical and ecumenical gatherings and has also addressed groups in the corporate and business communities. His passion is to see society transformed as Christians go into the world and become agents of reconciliation and challengers of the status quo.

Campolo was born into an immigrant Italian family. He did his undergraduate work at Eastern College in St. Davids, Pennsylvania, and he earned his Ph.D. degree from Temple University. He served on the faculty at the University of Pennsylvania for ten years before returning to Eastern College to teach. At Eastern College, he is professor of sociology and also the director of the Urban Studies Program. In addition to his duties as a professor, Campolo is an associate pastor of the Mount Carmel Baptist Church in West Philadelphia and he serves as an associate for International Ministries of American Baptist Churches.

Campolo has been highly involved in developing church-based urban programs for the poor. He is president of the Evangelical Association for the Promotion of Education, an organization he founded twenty-five years ago to help fulfill his vision for urban ministry. His call for volunteers has targeted college-age young people. Campolo has challenged college students to volunteer their summers and even an entire school year to serve the church and the community in urban areas. While the organization has primarily worked to meet the needs of at-risk young people in urban America, over the years it has expanded to include educational, medical, and economic development programs in a variety of Third World countries such as Haiti and the Dominican Republic.

With his unique appeal to young people to live out a radical Christianity, Campolo is in great demand on college and university campuses. He has been described as dynamic, prophetic, personable, zealous, humorous, and controversial. He believes that Christians have a biblical responsibility to be confronting real issues without regard for politically correct stances. Campolo is not afraid to tackle such issues as abolishing chemical warfare, feeding the starving of Africa, and promoting the full inclusion of women in all aspects and forms of ministry. He believes that making the world a holy place includes being involved in the environmental movement and working intentionally to end racism. For Campolo, there is no such thing as personal holiness without social implications, and he cautions Christians against the seduction of a materialistic culture and the enticement of consumerism.

Campolo urges his reading and listening audiences to seize life and live it passionately. He believes that Christians ought to be celebrating their salvation in the spirit of a party. Over the years, Campolo's orthodoxy has been alternately questioned and exonerated. In his own words,

Campolo identifies himself as an evangelical who holds to a high view of Scripture, who believes in the doctrines as outlined in the Apostles' Creed, and who believes that being a Christian involves a personal relationship with Jesus Christ.

Campolo's provocative views have been expressed in a weekly television program, in numerous articles, and in at least twenty-five published books as a best-selling author. These books include such titles as *Is Jesus a Republican or a Democrat?*, *The Kingdom of God is a Party*, *20 Hot Potatoes Christians Are Afraid to Touch*, *Seven Deadly Sins*, *Who Switched the Price Tags?*, *It's Friday, But Sunday's Comin'*, and *A Reasonable Faith: Responding to Secularism*.

SHELLY CUNNINGHAM

See also MILLENNIAL GENERATION; MISSION; MISSIONS EDUCATION; SHORT-TERM MISSIONS; URBAN CHRISTIAN EDUCATION; YOUTH AND MISSIONS

Campus Crusade for Christ. Founded in 1951 by Bill and Vonette Bright, Campus Crusade for Christ's original singular focus was the communication of the gospel to every student on earth. Commitment to this central evangelistic vision has guided Campus Crusade for Christ from its initial campus ministry to students at the University of California-Los Angeles to diverse ministries in more than 160 countries throughout the world.

Synonymous with Campus Crusade for Christ is the medium that communicates its core message. The message is the gospel of Jesus Christ, and the medium is the *Four Spiritual Laws*. The "four laws," consistent with the vision of Campus Crusade for Christ, are designed to communicate effectively and efficiently the essential elements of the gospel so that multitudes can be approached through personal evangelism. Bright's first version of a four laws booklet appeared in 1954. By the late twentieth century, Campus Crusade for Christ reported to have distributed 1.5 billion copies of this booklet throughout the world, in all major languages. The four laws are:

1. God loves you and offers a wonderful plan for your life.
2. Humans are sinful and separated from God. Thus they cannot know and experience God's love and plan for their lives.
3. Jesus Christ is God's only provision for humanity's sin. Through him you can know and experience God's love and plan for your life.
4. We must individually receive Jesus Christ as Savior and Lord; then we can know and experience God's love and plan for our lives.

While remaining primarily invested in its college campus strategy, Campus Crusade for Christ has also expanded its evangelistic endeavors to include diverse ministry strategies. As Campus Crusade for Christ became a truly global evangelistic ministry, Bright's vision expanded well beyond the focus of reaching student populations only. The mission field of Campus Crusade for Christ now literally includes the entire world. The goal has become to present every human being with an opportunity to respond positively to the gospel.

Bright's comprehensive vision and entrepreneurial spirit has led to expansive global missionary efforts. Campus Crusade for Christ's worldwide distribution of the JESUS film has enjoyed success unparalleled in the history of world evangelization. New Life 2000 is an initiative indicative of the scope of Campus Crusade for Christ's far-reaching ministry. In the late twentieth century Campus Crusade for Christ adopted Bright's vision for communicating the gospel to 6 billion people by the year 2000. Inclusive in this effort were the goals of establishing 5,000 training centers, 1 million churches, and 5 million New Life home Bible discipleship groups. No other evangelical ministry organization has ever attempted the breadth of impact pursued by Campus Crusade for Christ through New Life 2000.

Among the varied initiatives of Campus Crusade for Christ are the development of Worldwide Student Network to coordinate international campus ministries, the birth of Intercultural Resources, which specifically targets the needs of ethnic minorities, and the creation of the World Center for Discipleship and Evangelism in Orlando, Florida. While ministry strategies continue to expand, the founding vision of "using the most strategic, effective means available" (Zoba, 1997, 16) to present the gospel to the unbelieving remains central to the development of each component of the Campus Crusade for Christ organization.

RICHARD R. DUNN

Bibliography. W. M. Zoba, *Christianity Today*, July 14, 1997, 14–27.

Campus Ministry. *See* Campus Crusade for Christ.

Canadian Christian Education. Canada's comparatively small population of over 30 million, spread throughout a large geographic area with the two official languages of English and French, contributes to a nation characterized by diversity and regionalization. These factors also reflect on both the church and Christian education.

The first settlers of Canada were Huguenots from France. These Protestants came primarily to conduct business and to escape persecution. French Roman Catholics followed, and with increasing tension between the two groups a 1628 edict made what is now Quebec exclusively Roman Catholic, with Protestants having no rights. With the virtual disappearance of a Protestant voice, the evangelical church did not reemerge in Quebec until the arrival in 1935 of Swiss missionaries who emphasized youth education.

In the rest of Canada, especially the Maritime provinces and Ontario, Protestantism became the more prominent religious focus. This was particularly true after the British defeated the French in Canada in 1759. While Quebec kept its religious and language emphasis and sought to retain these through the education of youth, English Canada became more Protestant although with a more pluralistic and cooperative approach to the church and education. Canada's roots are distinct from the United States in that even the evangelical church in Canada took a more accommodating approach to diversity. Canadian Christendom has been more deferential in nature with the tendency to emphasize the community good rather than the individual. While religion was a public matter in the earlier days of Canada, it gradually became more privatized with evangelicals not participating as intentionally and actively in public forums related to educational, political, and moral issues. Increasingly, therefore, the evangelical church and consequently Christian education became more marginalized and was seen as inferior to public and university education.

Part of the reality in Canada is also that education is the purview of each province with no national accrediting system at either the kindergarten through high school or on the postsecondary levels; thus regional approaches and issues vary. When it comes to the education of youth, there is full government funding of the public educational system and usually the Roman Catholic school system, but other religious schools are either not funded at all or have limited funding. The province of Newfoundland did have denominational-run schools, but in 1997 all schools were deconfessionalized, and these rights were lost. Parents have grown increasingly concerned about the education of their children, so there has been a significant increase in the number of private Christian schools in Canada. Some of these are connected to the Association for Christian Schools International (ACSI) or with the Christian Schools International (CSI) of the Christian Reformed tradition. Also, more parents are home schooling their children than ever before.

Postsecondary theological education really began in the nineteenth century in Canada. This is also sometimes called the evangelical century with the church growing and new theological educational institutions being founded. By the beginning of the twentieth century, however, the majority of the seminaries established became liberal and not committed to biblical orthodoxy. For instance, Nova Scotia's Acadia University,

which was founded in 1838, clearly contributed to evangelicalism in Canada before taking a liberal turn (Rawlyk, 1996, 269). It was not until the 1960s that Acadia's Divinity College was reclaimed by the evangelicals and today is still providing seminary level ministerial, missionary, and church vocational training to the evangelical church in Canada.

Today the estimates of evangelical educational institutions across Canada place the number of Bible colleges and institutes at around 80, with 12 seminaries and 5 liberal arts institutions (Ryan, 1996, 22). Throughout Canadian history, Christian institutions in Canada have contributed to the learning of many of the current evangelical leaders, but education in Canada has also been the recipient of British and American influence. A number of leaders have taken some of their graduate education in the United States or Britain. In addition there is often a reliance on American materials and influence in the church and in education. Canadian institutions, however, have gained credibility internationally with their ministry impact through education and missions as well as increasing scholarly contributions for the Canadian and global church.

The Bible college/institute movement which began in Canada in the later 1800s has made a significant impact nationally and globally through its emphasis on personal piety, Bible-centered curriculum, mission, and practical ministry. The first Bible college in Canada was Toronto Bible College, now Tyndale College, which was founded in 1894. Some of the notable institutions include Prairie Bible Institute, which is especially known for its contribution to the cause of world mission, and Briercrest Bible College, now the largest in Canada, for its development of people for ministry. The majority of the Bible colleges or institutes are located in western Canada with some in Ontario and Quebec and several in New Brunswick.

The first French language Bible school, Institute Biblique Berée, was started by the Pentecostal Assemblies of Canada in 1941 with a second theological school, College Biblique Québec, begun in the 1970s. With their concern for the education of French leadership and accessibility to French language education, the Fellowship Baptist, Association d'Églises Baptistes, started SEMBEQ in 1973. This was a school of theological education by extension. The Christian Brethren also have a rich history in Quebec and started the first interdenominational Bible school, Institut Biblique Bethel (Smith, 1995, 21). The numbers of students in these schools is small, although growing. Today the French church views these educational approaches as very traditional and as failing to meet the current need for theological education (Smith, 22). One concern is for a higher level of theological education for French leadership, a need the Faculte de Theologie Evangelique (FTE) is seeking to address with their evangelical seminary.

To address common concerns in a diverse context, the Association of Canadian Bible Colleges was founded in 1959. The intention was not to serve as an accrediting body, but to provide fellowship, encouragement, and professional development with an annual conference held in May of each year. There are around fifty institutional members of this association across Canada.

The accrediting body of Bible colleges is called the Accrediting Association of Bible Colleges (AABC) and was originally exclusively for U. S. Bible colleges but has broadened to include Canada. A number of Canadian schools in recent years have pursued AABC recognition in order to improve acceptance with seminaries as well as to establish a basis for recognition with some Canadian universities.

The Bible college movement in Canada is in the midst of a changing landscape. Many schools are vulnerable with limited resources and a keen competition for students. Tuition costs are escalating, and there is an increasing percentage of part-time and older students. The more rural setting of many of the colleges has added to the challenge.

Due to a lack of viability, some Bible colleges have closed. Others have opened, but they tend to be church-based schools in urban settings or associated with a particular denomination. Several Bible schools also exist with a focus on training native or first nations people of Canada for church leadership. A number of Bible colleges are broadening the definition of ministry from pastor and missionary or lay person in the church to include more vocational programs for those who are interested in a marketable skill that is not just ministry oriented. In the midst of the continuing struggle for acceptability in the Canadian milieu, there are encouraging signs. Some universities and governments are exhibiting a new openness to theological education and are beginning to address the marginalization issue. Recognition for some Bible colleges and theological institutions has come through the forging of transfer or affiliation agreements with universities. Others are looking at ways to be more creative and cooperative in their offerings.

Part of the challenge for the Bible college movement involves churches and ministries which are expecting more than a bachelor's degree for many of the ministry positions available. Thus the role of the seminary has taken on increasing importance. A number of the original seminaries in the country were university related, such as Acadia Divinity College, Wycliff College, and McMaster Divinity School, with other universities having faculties of theology. Today seminaries tend to be accredited by the Association of Theological Schools (ATS) in the United States and Canada.

In the past thirty years of the twentieth century more evangelical seminaries have been started. Graduate theological education has also gained a stronger presence through some Bible colleges (including Briercrest Biblical Seminary, Prairie Graduate School, Providence Seminary, and Tyndale Seminary) adding seminary programs institutionally in order to address constituency expectations. Regent College, a graduate school of Christian studies on the campus of the University of British Columbia in western Canada, is well-known for its focus on lay-oriented training, but many ministry people are educated there as well. Regent has assembled some of the most distinguished faculty in North America.

Other expanding approaches to Christian higher education in Canada include Christian universities or liberal arts colleges. Trinity Western University in British Columbia, for instance, is a prominent evangelical institution founded as a two-year college in 1962 but which achieved full university status as a member of the Association of Universities and Colleges of Canada (AUCC) in 1984. Atlantic Baptist University in Moncton, New Brunswick, achieved university status more recently. In 1998 Redeemer College in Ontario was granted a charter to offer programs previously considered only in the purview of the universities.

Christian education in Canada is also reflective of some of the challenges facing the church. The state of Christian education in Canada is in a period of change whether it be the education of youth and adults or through the church, home, and education institution. Along with increasing secularization, Canada has become an expanded multicultural, multiethnic, multilinguistic, and multireligious nation of people that do not have a clear Christian related worldview. In the past decade, for instance, more than 1.6 million people have immigrated to Canada. A majority of these are Asians. Toronto, for example, is known as the most cosmopolitan city in the world with more than 190 ethnic groups making it their home (Thomas, 1997, 1, 4).

In the midst of attempts to silence a religious emphasis and remove a moral Christian center from the public forum, the challenge for evangelicals is how to ensure a legitimate place for Christian education and to promote orthodoxy in the midst of pluralism and a nation driven more by economic factors than by God's truth. Gradually other agendas have crowded out the biblical values on the national scene. The Canadian society's tendency to understate itself and be more accommodating is also reflective of the evangelical church and Christian education to some degree. With the evident secularization of the culture, particularly in the media and politics, the agenda against the exclusivity of truth has to be addressed with faith related to private and public life.

The Evangelical Fellowship of Canada (EFC), which represents many of the denominations, educational institutions, and parachurch organizations in the nation, has become part of the public debate intentionally and sought to intervene in government and the courts in relation to educational, moral, and family issues. EFC has not only become a united voice for the social, political, and educational concerns of evangelicals to the nation, but also a forum to educate evangelicals on how to address the uniqueness that is Canada.

With surveys placing the number of evangelicals in Canada anywhere between 7 percent and 8 percent and up to 15 percent, the challenge before Christian education is mushrooming. A national survey done in early 1993 portrayed about 78 percent of the people identifying themselves as Christians. In other words, while public expressions of faith may be socially unacceptable across the nation, a private faith of some nature is expressed. Fewer than 25 percent of Canadian adults, however, attend religious services weekly. Fifteen percent claim to have had a born-again experience. Evangelicals take a more active role in their church than members of mainline churches, and it is the evangelical churches primarily that are flourishing and growing (*Maclean's*, 1993). In this connection, however, the majority of churches in Canada are small with about two-thirds having 125 people or less in attendance on a Sunday. These often lack the resources to have a strong educational focus.

More recent polls suggest that 11 percent of Canadians fall into the evangelical category with 5 percent of those highly committed (Koop, 1996, 1), while only 20 percent of Canadians attend church regularly (Harvey, 1998, 4). Bible reading and churchgoing are noted as strongest in the Atlantic provinces. The largest evangelical denomination is the Pentecostal Assemblies of Canada, but some of the churches with the most significant growth have different ethnic heritages. The most prominent in Canada are the nearly 300 Chinese churches. An increasing number of Chinese, as well as people of other ethnic origins, are attending seminaries, but the challenge is for the church to educate its lay people, especially when the first language of the people may not be English.

The church has a concern for the education of people involved in lay as well as vocational ministry. While the church often provides basic Bible and life-related knowledge, it is usually dependent on educational institutions for advanced education. In an effort to be more effective in Canadian society, some urban churches in particular have adopted a cell model approach which is based on small groups. These groups may have a variety of formats and purposes, but an educational focus is the orientation for some. Few megachurches exist in Canada, but Northview Community Church in Abbotsford, British Columbia, is an example of a large, growing church with a contemporary approach to church that takes ministry involvement and education seriously. Besides the various programs to nurture learning and growth, there is an intentional focus on providing a context for training as well as opportunities for ministry. Weekly classes are available for educating people in life and ministry. Northview also seeks to serve the rest of the Canadian church by providing seminars to assist church leadership across Canada.

Throughout Canada people are seeking to provide creative alternative opportunities to lifelong learning in Christian education whether through the home, church, or academic institution. Approaches include study centers, seminars, and small focus groups to fill the need for lay education that is not necessarily degree oriented. Some institutions are addressing accessibility issues with more nontraditional approaches such as weekend or modular courses and increasing their distance education and Internet on-line alternatives to the traditional in-class and full-time on-campus expectations. In a global economy some cooperation and partnering with schools and churches from other nations for educational purposes is also occurring.

Although one of the foundation stones of Canada states, "He shall have dominion from sea to sea . . ." (Ps. 72:8), the current mandate for Canadian Christian education whether through the church, home, or institution is for evangelicals to clearly live out their relationship as Christ's followers in the Canadian mosaic in life-changing and nation-impacting ways so that Christ's dominion will be evident.

CHARLOTTE K. BATES

Bibliography. D. G. Hart and R. A. Mohler Jr., eds. (1996), *Theological Education in the Evangelical Tradition*; B. Harvey, *Christian Week*, August 25, 1998, 1, 4; D. Koop, *Christian Week*, November 19, 1996, 1, 10; *Maclean's*, April 12, 1993, 32–50; G. A. Rawlyk (1996), *Canadian Protestant Theological Education*; B. Ryan, *Faith Today*: 20–26; G. Smith, *Ecumenism* 120 (1995): 16–22; T. V. Thomas, *Harvest Partner* (1997): 1, 4.

Case Advocate. Social work term describing the role of the worker as he fights to ensure that individuals, families, or groups receive the services they need. The worker as advocate also works with persons to help them fight for themselves for individual and social betterment. The worker teams with a person to determine her needs and to discover resources to meet that need. Sometimes, those with the resources to meet a need are not interested in helping, or their policies and practices are too rigid. This is when the worker becomes an advocate, as he helps the person collect needed data, helps argue the person's case, and challenges decisions not to help the person.

This is a role God assigns to Christian social workers and the church when he calls them to "open your mouths for the dumb, for the rights of all the unfortunate" (Prov. 31:8).

DAVID R. PENLEY

Case Management. Social work term used to describe the method by which a worker helps individuals, groups, or families. The worker assesses a person's situation, determines needs, works with the person to decide on an intervention strategy to address those needs, and then monitors the person's progress to assure her needs are being met. The worker does not usually provide all the needed services directly, but works with other service providers to make certain the person receives what is needed. Therefore, an awareness of services offered in the area is a necessity. The purpose of case management is to help a person meet her needs, become self-sufficient, and function well in society. Christian social workers include the church in the process as they seek to meet spiritual as well as physical and emotional needs. Church members can be trained to provide counseling, support, and physical necessities.

DAVID R. PENLEY

Case Method. This term is sometimes referred to as "case method," "case work," "case system," or "case history." The case can be a true or hypothetical situation in which an issue or problem is presented which becomes the foundation for the learning experience. Case studies are used as a method of instruction in law, business, medicine, psychology, sociology, and religion, as well as other disciplines.

When a case method of instruction is used in medicine or psychology, the learners may be asked to suggest a diagnosis, prognosis, and ultimate treatment. One common procedure in the education and training of counselors is to have the student write a case description of the counseling session and then to discuss the case with either a supervisor or peer counselor. The case approach in instruction has been most widely used in legal education. Law schools, such as the prestigious Harvard Law School, have effectively utilized the case approach.

Case methods may be presented in written form or orally. They can be acted out with the use of drama or included in any of a wide range of multimedia productions. The case method approach is also found in some forms of computer-assisted instruction. For example, Joseph Lowman developed computer case simulations that allow psychology students to interview counselors via computer keyboard, make a diagnosis, and then write a case evaluation, followed by classroom discussion.

Another area where the case method is being used with great effectiveness is Christian education. Marlene LeFever indicates that when the case method approach is used with adults and teenagers in the context of Christian education, there are some important results: (1) People will be exposed to others who have problems similar to their own and realize the similarities may apply to biblical solutions to their own problems. (2) Students will see that Christian education includes "real-world training." (3) Students will hear opinions other than their own and possibly discover alternative solutions. (4) Scriptures become real to the students, who get involved in the study. (5) In a Christian context, the students will increase their decision-making skills.

Finally, the case method presents an approach to learning that includes the higher levels of learning: analysis, synthesis, and evaluation. Students become actively involved in the learning process. As this method is utilized, education can move from its ivory tower to address the issues and needs of an ever-changing world.

J. GREGORY LAWSON

Bibliography. M. LeFever (1990), *Creative Teaching Methods;* J. Lowman (1995), *Mastering the Techniques of Teaching.*

Case Study. Approach to learning and applying theory to practice through the examination of a specific example. In general, case study is used in two different ways in Christian education: as a research method and as a teaching method.

Case Study as a Research Method. This method is a qualitative research approach that focuses on the intensive study of specific instances, or cases, of a phenomenon (i.e., processes, events, things, persons). Case studies focus on concrete examples of the phenomenon of interest in its natural context, attempting to develop an understanding of the phenomenon from the perspective of the case study participants. Typically, the research is carried out through observation, informal interviews, and the evaluation of artifacts.

The purpose of case study research is generally to produce detailed descriptions or explanations of a complex phenomenon. In descriptive studies, researchers gather data about the phenomenon, develop constructs and themes that characterize it, and relate these to other research findings. In explanatory studies, researchers look for relational or causal patterns in the data that explain the various aspects of the phenomenon.

The development of a case study research project typically follows this pattern: (1) The identification of a problem for study. (2) The development of explicit research questions or objectives. (3) The identification of an accessible setting in which the phenomenon can be studied to yield the desired results. (4) Designing ways of recording what happens in that setting. This may include audio- or videotaping, observation, informal conversations, in-depth interviews, note taking, and diagramming. (5) Designing ways to validate the data collected through different overlapping methods. This attempt to corroborate the evidence through multiple data collection methods or sources is called triangulation. (6) Gaining access to the setting and immersion in it to collect data. Compared to quantitative research approaches, in case studies the researcher is normally the primary data collection instrument, often becoming personally involved in the phenomenon being studied, thereby grasping the meaning of the phenomenon as it is experienced by the people involved. Because of the subjective aspect of this type of study, it is important that researchers systematically examine their reactions to what they see and hear, and carefully audit these reactions for their potential influence on data analysis. Data collection may continue until sources are exhausted and data categories and patterns are clearly established. (7) Analysis of the data collected. This can be interpretational in nature, looking for constructs, themes, and patterns that help in describing or explaining the phenomenon; structural, looking for patterns inherent in the data itself; or reflective, relying on personal judgment and intuition to describe or evaluate the phenomenon.

Although case studies, by their very nature, have limited generalizability, they are beneficial for exploratory study and for developing depth of understanding of complex phenomena. A good case study can be a valuable learning tool.

Case Study as a Teaching Method. Case studies in teaching involve the examination and discussion of a real-life dilemma with no easy or obvious solution. They can be used as an opportunity to explore student attitudes and knowledge and encourage the thoughtful application of principles and theories to life situations. Case studies can be developed from a variety of sources and occur in a variety of formats, including written cases from persons' experiences, movies and home videos, news stories, and Scripture stories. Teaching with case studies challenges established ideas and patterns of behavior, provides the chance for different perspectives to be voiced and heard, forces students to think through the complexities of applying what they have learned to life, and raises learning motivation by making concepts real.

There are a number of elements that make a case study useful for teaching and learning. First, a good case study allows for several viable courses of action, making it clear that there are different options and no one clear solution. Second, it grows out of actual situations, reflecting the complexity of real-life dilemmas. Third, it focuses on problems that learners can identify with and find interesting. Fourth, it provides enough clues to allow the identification and discussion of significant issues that relate to learning goals of the group. Fifth, it helps if the case is written from one person's point of view, allowing learners to see it develop from one perspective. Finally, in Christian education, a good case study encourages students to apply God's truth to unclear or problematic situations.

Developing a written case for teaching can be facilitated by the following four steps. First, choose an event or situation that poses a question or requires a decision fraught with difficulty and ambiguity. Make sure it will be of interest to your learners. Second, gather information to describe the background, individuals involved, the situation or dilemma, and the possible courses of action. Third, where appropriate, be sure to secure permission from the people involved or disguise the case well. Fourth, in writing the case, begin with an overview of the dilemma, provide background to the case, explain the flow of events, and bring the case to the point of decision.

Teaching a case study can be done in a variety of ways, but most involve group discussion. The teacher then acts as a catalyst by probing, recording, and facilitating the discussion process. It is important to be clear about your goals for the teaching session, determine how you will introduce the case and get the learners involved, and how you will help the group explore the relevant characters and issues the case presents and the options and implications of various responses to the dilemma. Finally, learners can be encouraged to reflect on what they have learned from examining the case, and how it may affect their thoughts, attitudes, and actions in the future.

Teaching with case studies can be an excellent way to motivate and involve students in the learning process. A case study can provide a setting to explore relevant issues without the risks of actually experiencing them. It can help bridge classroom instruction to life situations, encouraging higher order cognitive processes and the development of discernment and wisdom in the use of knowledge.

KEVIN E. LAWSON

Bibliography. M. D. Gall, W. R. Borg, and J. P. Gall (1971), *Educational Research: An Introduction*, 6th ed.; J. E. Layman (1977), *Using Case Studies in Church Education*; R. E. Stake (1995), *The Art of Case Study Research*; S. Wassermann (1994), *Introduction to Case Method Teaching: A Guide to the Galaxy*.

See also CASE METHOD

Catechetical School of Alexandria. The exact details surrounding the foundation and development of this school, also referred to as "The Christian school in Alexandria" or the *Didaskaleion* by Eusebius, are difficult to reconstruct. According to tradition, Saint Mark opened the first catechetical school in Alexandria to instruct converts from paganism to Christianity, including basic teaching in preparation for baptism, but the certainty of this is dubious. The general consensus indicates a recognized catechetical school was commenced around A.D. 185.

The establishment of this school in Alexandria is significant. The city, founded by Alexander the Great over three hundred years before Christ, was a great center of commerce, the focus of Jewish and Greek learning, the intellectual center for Christians, and the location of possibly the greatest library in the ancient world. Its influence, for example, is reflected in the fact that the Old Testament was translated into Greek in Alexandria. The school was established, and became notable, in this academic context.

The first known leader or superintendent of the school was Pantaenus. This man was possibly a native of Sicily and a convert to Christianity from Stoic philosophy. Very little is known of him, and there are no sizable extant writings, but it seems certain that one of his pupils was Clement of Alexandria (not to be confused with Clement of Rome), who later became head of the school sometime between A.D. 190 and 202. It was under the leadership of Clement and later Origen, who had been a pupil of Clement, that the school reached its zenith. Subsequent leaders included Heraclas, Dionysius, and, in the fourth century, the blind Didymus.

Although teaching new converts was the original purpose of the school and remained a significant reason for its existence, in time it also became recognized as a school of higher theological understanding. This was due, in part, to the stand that it took against perversions of Christianity, in particular Gnostic heresies promoted by Valentinus, and Neoplatonic philosophers such as Celsius. In this role the school sought to use the arguments of the prevailing philosophies to uphold and vindicate the truths of Scripture. Additional distinguishing features of the school included an emphasis on Christ (with consideration of him both before and after his incarnation) as the epitome of all reason and truth, and the use of the allegorical method to interpret Scripture.

Current Western notions of schools should not be imposed on this school at Alexandria. The practice of the time was for philosophers to accept and tutor students who wished to acquaint themselves with the philosopher's particular branch of philosophy, with reputation, learning, and skill in teaching determining the popularity of the teacher. While some instruction was to groups, most was usually undertaken on an individual basis and in the private rooms of the philosopher rather than in a designated building or institution. This pattern, a group of students gathered about a master, was followed by Pantaenus and the successive leaders. In the Alexan-drian sense the term *school* referred primarily to a style of pedagogy and a set of theological understandings.

Gregory Thaumaturgus, a student of Origen, in an address of appreciation at the time he left the school, emphasized the holistic nature of his training. Origen was committed not only to the ideal of training in the cognitive domain but also in the areas of moral and spiritual formation. He expected his students to adopt a new way of life, as his goal was to mold the lives of his students to conform to the ideal set forth in the Scriptures and as demonstrated by Christ. To this end, the teacher sought to have a personal and deep relationship with each student. This was a pedagogy based on friendship rather than rules or prescribed course of studies. Thus to enter the school was to submit to a system of spiritual direction.

The influence of the school diminished toward the end of the fourth century; this was attributed in part to the demise of Alexandria as a significant city and to the rise of other similar schools around the Mediterranean basin. In time, the school's unduly idealistic and spiritualistic emphasis along with its excessive use of allegorical interpretations further aided its lessening influence and eventual demise. Despite this, the school had a profound influence on the Christian world in general and should be commended for its strong apologetic and christological emphases.

D. A. C. MULHOLLAND

Bibliography. Eusebius (1965), *The History of the Church from Christ to Constantine;* J. L. Gonzalez (1987), *A History of Christian Theology;* P. H. Henry (1984), *Schools of Thought in the Christian Tradition;* K. S. Latourette (1964), *A History of Christianity;* P. Schaff (1910), *History of the Christian Church.*

Catechism. Protestant, Roman Catholic, and the Orthodox faiths each have catechism as part of their religious instruction. Derived from the original Greek word *katechê,* meaning "to make hear" or "to instruct," the term *catechism* evolved throughout the first fifteen centuries of church history to describe three entities: the actual content of religious instruction; the pedagogical process; and, eventually, the literature itself, in the form of small tracts and books. It was the latter meaning that prevailed, once the Reformation began.

Some authorities traced this concept of Christian education back to the New Testament Scriptures, citing passages like 1 Thessalonians 4:1–5:11 and Colossians 3:5–15 as implicit, if not direct, expressions of the earliest catechetical curriculum. Noncanonical instructional materials surfaced in the Didache and in Justin Martyr's works, especially in his doctrinal and moral teachings. Portions of Irenaeus's *Proof of the Apostolic Preaching* at the end of the second century also appeared to offer guided training for new Christian converts. Specifically, Irenaeus's writings featured God's work in history, from creation to judgment, as filtered through the person and work of Christ. Furthermore, the message of the Old Testament prophets was framed by this church father to complement the Christian gospel.

The end of the second century brought a more formalized structure together, in terms of education, through the founding of the Catechetical School at Alexandria. Alongside the "profane sciences," Christian faith was taught. Clement (c. 190–202) and Origen (c. 202–231) served as this school's most distinguished faculty.

The early third century provided the initial evidence of a fully organized plan of catechism. In particular, Hippolytus' *Apostolic Tradition* called for a rigorous three-year training period before a believer could be baptized (perhaps the major reason why catechisms were first initiated in the early church), yet that author clarifies that it was not so much the length of time that mattered but the testing required for godly conduct. During the fourth through sixth centuries, as infant baptism gradually overshadowed adult baptism, the historical purposes and forms of catechism shifted.

With such new forms of catechism, a broad—even contradictory—range of opinions swept across the church's pedagogical philosophies: on the one hand, Tertullian (c. 160–215) contrasted sacred and secular knowledge with his famous rhetorical inquiry that pitted "Jerusalem" against "Athens." On the other hand, some later church leaders valued a broad-based, general education, advocating that the most comprehensive education provided a great advantage to Christians. These leaders included: Basil the Great (c. 329–379), Gregory of Nazianzus (330–389), and Augustine of Hippo (359–430), who is generally credited with the now-popular motto: "All truth is God's truth."

A standardized curriculum soon emerged from these early centuries, a core of resources that would make their mark on the Reformation era of catechetical instruction. Specifically, an analysis of most early church education revealed the consistent pattern of the Lord's Prayer and the Apostles' Creed. By the thirteenth century, the Ten Commandments were added to this list, even though spokespersons like Augustine had lobbied for the Decalogue's inclusion almost one thousand years before.

By the advent of the Reformation, catechism was shaped by several brands of critique—even from within the Roman Catholic Church. Luther's earliest training materials held parents accountable for teaching Christian truths to the next generation. His focus was quickly diverted away from the home, however, in favor of government-run catechetical schools. Best known for his Large

Catechism (April, 1529) and his Small Catechism (released just one month later), Luther did not neglect to challenge the church, since these two works primarily addressed the pastoral leadership. Beyond the content that Luther provided, his three-part structure was noteworthy, as he took the basic organizational components of traditional instruction and reshaped their sequence into what he deemed most accurate. First, Luther introduced the "Code" of Christian belief (based on his understanding of God's laws), which this reformer contended would show people their sinfulness and their need for a Redeemer. Second, Luther provided the "Creed," whereby the central message of faith in Christ was developed. Third, the former Catholic priest offered the "Cult" portion of instruction, which referred to the appropriation of Christ's redemption through prayers and sacraments.

Anabaptist tradition refocused on the church's historic prebaptismal format. Balthasar Hubmaier's 1527 publication, *A Christian Catechism That Every Person Should Know Before He is Baptized in Water* (English equivalent), scrapped Luther's three-part division for a completely different, two-part design: the believer's vertical responsibility to God, by faith, represented in the act of baptism; and the believer's horizontal duty to love one's neighbor, portrayed in the ordinance of the Lord's Supper.

John Calvin's *Instruction* guide of 1537 advanced the Reformed cause. His *Catechism of the Church at Geneva* (English) in 1542 adopted a question-and-answer approach, intended to be used as a dialogue between pastor and child. In 1563 two commissioned Reformed theologians penned the Heidelberg Catechism, which incorporated 129 questions and answers. Its three parts included the depraved nature of humans ("Human Misery"); the Christian solution to this predicament ("Human Redemption"); and necessary human response to divine redemption through gratitude.

The first Anglican catechism surfaced in 1549 via *The Book of Common Prayer*. Thomas Cranmer is believed to have played a significant part in its preparation. Ten years later a new version appeared, containing a unique contribution on "Confirmation" for children. Adopted as the official catechism of the Church of England, this curriculum brought a new level of literacy and expectancy to the home and church.

Roman Catholic reform, in large measure, ignited in the light of Desiderius Erasmus's fiery calls for educational reform in 1514. Eight years later, he submitted a plan to recapture the church's traditional stance of instructing youth who were baptismal candidates. Jesuit Peter Canisius fashioned three popular catechisms between 1554 and 1558. Following the now popular question-and-answer format, Canisius reaffirmed

Augustine's instructional order by designing materials that incorporated five features: the Christian's faith (citing the Apostles' Creed); hope (the Lord's Prayer and the Hail Mary); charity (the Commandments and other church laws); the sacraments; and righteousness (expressed through diverse vices and virtues). Furthermore, a commissioning from the Council of Trent produced a lengthy catechism in 1566. Its quick acceptance transferred this document into the primary doctrinal manual for parish priests. Known as the Roman Catechism, popes from Pius V on regarded this publication as authoritative.

The Orthodox Church, from the ninth century, extended a lengthy dispute with the Western Church, eventually ending in the Great Schism of 1054, largely over issues of papal authority, interpretations of the common Creed, and perceptions of icons. Orthodox churches recognized the authoritative witnesses of the Christian tradition as found in the instructive designs of the first seven ecumenical councils, from Nicea (325) to Nicea II (787). Specifically these councils provided the core of Orthodox education pertaining to the doctrines of the Trinity; the two natures and wills of Christ; and the validation of icon creation and veneration, which reverence the God-man. For the Orthodox, these historic connections provide the unbroken religious educational continuity between the early church and contemporary believers, established by Christ and his apostles.

Historically, monasticism expressed much of the Orthodox's contribution to education. This was especially true since monaticism comprehensively included three types: those who lived in solitary settings; those in communal life, under common monastic rule; and those from a more loosely knit group of believers who lived in a community under the direction of a spiritual director (known as starets in Russian Orthodoxy). Based on these traditions, contemporary Orthodox education is seen to center itself within the context of the church; to offer a comprehensive approach to curriculum (going beyond cognition to life experiences); and to appeal to transformative personal growth though interpersonal commitments of faith.

RONALD T. HABERMAS

Bibliography. E. Ferguson (1990), *Encyclopedia of Early Christianity;* D. R. Janz (1996), *The Oxford Encyclopedia of the Reformation;* D. B. Lockerbie (1991), *New 20th-Century Encyclopedia of Religious Knowledge;* C. J. Tarasar (1995), *Theologies of Religious Education.*

Catechumenate. The modern discipline of Christian education has its roots in the early church's practice of baptism. At the birth of the church, adult converts were baptized with little formal instruction as seen in Acts 2:38–41; 8:12–13; 8:35–39; 9:17–19; 10:44–48; and 16:14–15. But as the number of baptized converts began to increase, seven reasons made it necessary to subject these individuals to a probationary course of instruction and discipline preparatory to baptism and admission into the church. First, non-Jewish people were being converted out of paganism and needed to be instructed in the Hebrew Scriptures. Second, it was necessary to determine the reasons why people were joining the church. Third, a biblical lifestyle was a process and not a product, so time and opportunity to change a convert's personal lifestyle were needed. Fourth, care had to be taken for those who professed conversion to Christianity because of the possibility that the stress of persecution might cause them to recant their faith. Fifth, few converts could read. Writing materials were difficult to obtain, which made oral instruction imperative. Sixth, the oral method of question and answer aided in the memorization of the content because of the opportunity for repetition and the personal relationship between the one who asked the questions and the one who answered the questions. Seventh, the Christian community became concerned about the doctrinal purity and survival of the content that was being transmitted to the new converts.

This lifestyle journey to baptism became known as the catechumenate, deriving from the Greek word *kataxeo,* which is formed from the word *kata* meaning down and *aexo* meaning sound or reverberate. The word *kataxeo* can refer to sound in the ears, the action of poets or actors who speak down from a stage, and the act of giving instruction concerning the content of faith. The word *kataxeo* is used seven times in the New Testament: Luke 1:4; Acts 18:25; 21:21; 21:24; Romans 2:18; 1 Corinthians 14:19; and Galatians 6:6. A study by Beyer (1965, 638–640) reveals that this rare Greek word was used as a technical term for the Christian instruction given to one preparing for baptism. The following words find their root in the Greek word *kataxeo.* The people who were preparing for baptism were called the catechumens [they appear as a distinct class in Tertullian (c. 160–220)]; the teacher who did the instruction was called the catechist; the catechumenate was the period of preparation before baptism; catechesis was the act of teaching or oral instruction; and the catechism was the content being taught. An historical development of the catechumenate can be seen in the work by Michel Dujarier (1979).

The catechumenate, or period of preparation for baptism, covered a period of two to three years. The catechumens were divided into three basic groups, according to C. B. Eavey (1964, 85). The "hearers" were permitted to listen to the reading of Scriptures and sermons, received elementary instruction in doctrines, and had to display proper conduct to be promoted. The "kneelers" were permitted to listen to the readings and remain for prayers, received more advanced instruction, and had to show by their lifestyle that they were ready to be promoted. The "chosen" were given intensive doctrinal, liturgical, and ascetical training to complete the last stage of their probationary period in preparation for baptism.

Three descriptions of baptism during the first two centuries of the church's life help us understand the development of the catechumenate (Bridge and Phypers, 1977, 75–80). First, the *Didache* or *Teaching of the Twelve Apostles* (c. 140) displays the character of the early Christian community. Second, the *First Apology* of Justin Martyr (c. 114–165) showed that preparation was necessary before baptism. Third, the *Apostolic Tradition of Hippolytus* (c. 170—c. 235) provides a description of the practice of the church in Rome.

By the end of the second century, the catechumens experienced: instruction in what they must give up; instruction in what they must believe; a series of exorcisms by which the evil spirits were to be driven out of the candidates; anointing and the laying-on-of-hands; and the actual baptism. The bishop's presence was essential for the final ceremony, which usually took place on Easter. It eventually became physically impossible for the bishop to preside over all baptisms. Also, the acceptance of infant baptism became widespread in the sixth century because of the belief that baptism removed the taint of original sin derived through Adam. Therefore, the catechumenal teaching deteriorated and the systematic instruction shifted from before to after baptism.

To deal with this problem, it became necessary to develop more clergy and to equip them so that they were on an intellectual level with the learning of the day. Thus there evolved out of catechumenal schools a new type of Christian school known as the catechetical school. As the major increase in the church shifted to a focus on the birth and baptism of children rather than the conversion of pagans, the idea of instruction passed from being that of a preparation for baptism to that of being a culture of baptized children.

The Reformation brought about a great revival in the religious training of children and adults through works like Luther's Larger and Smaller Catechisms of 1529. The term *catechism* can be dated to the Reformation period where it was presented as a document or manual of instruction using the responsive method (Buchanan, 1978, 199–201). Several catechisms appear in this period of time. First, Luther's Catechism in 1529 was based upon the Ten Commandments, the Creed, the Lord's Prayer, and the Sacraments; second, Calvin's Instruction and Confession of Faith for the use of the Church of Geneva in 1541; third, the Book of Common Prayer in 1549 used by the Anglican Church; fourth, the Heidelberg Catechism in 1563 for the Reformed churches;

fifth, the Roman Catholic Catechism in 1566; sixth, the Eastern Orthodox Catechism compiled by Peter Moghlia in 1640; seventh, the Westminster Confession of Faith and Shorter Catechism in 1647; eighth, the Baltimore Catechism in 1885.

J. E. HARVEY MARTIN

Bibliography. W. B. Hermann (1965), *Theological Dictionary of the New Testament*, 3:638–40; M. Dujarier (1979), *A History of the Catechumenate: The First Six Centuries;* C. B. Eavey (1964), *History of Christian Education;* D. Bridge and D. Phypers (1977), *The Water That Divides: The Baptism Debate;* C. Buchanan (1978), *New International Dictionary of the Christian Church*, pp. 199–201.

Categorization. *See* Classification.

Cell Church. Pattern of church organization and philosophy characterized by small groups or "cells" meeting in homes with a common commitment to grow through the intentional multiplication of cells while fulfilling the priority functions of evangelism, discipleship, and leadership development within each cell.

While the cell church has been described as merely an "off-campus" version of the traditional Sunday school (Rainer, 1993), its proponents argue that the cell church is a different paradigm of church growth. Carl F. George, director of the Charles E. Fuller Institute of Evangelism and Church Growth, stated in his book, *Prepare Your Church for the Future* (1991), "I believe that the smaller group within the whole—called by dozens of terms, including the small group or the cell group—is a crucial but underdeveloped resource in most churches. It is, I contend, the most strategically significant foundation for spiritual formation and assimilation, for evangelism and leadership development, for the most essential functions that God has called for in the church. . . . It's so important that everything else is to be considered secondary to its promotion and preservation" (41).

Ralph Neighbour believes the only church model that mirrors the New Testament pattern of the church is based upon small groups or cells. He draws a strong dichotomy between the cell church and the traditional Program Based Design Church, which relies upon its programs and structure for growth as opposed to the relational dynamic of the cell group. In describing the cell, Neighbour (1990) says, "The cell is the 'Basic Christian Community.' The Church is formed from them and is the sum of them. Cells never grow larger than 15 people and multiply as they reach this figure. There are no other activities, which exist in competition with the cells. Everything in the church is an extension of them and flows from their combined strength" (194).

The cell church model has experienced dramatic growth in highly populated urban cities across Asia, Europe, Australia, and, to a lesser degree, North America. The premiere example is Yoido Full Gospel Church in Seoul, Korea, under the leadership of senior pastor Paul Yonggi Cho, a church of more than six hundred thousand members meeting exclusively in cell groups except for periodic larger "celebration" gatherings for worship. The typical cell church is tightly organized within a hierarchical progression of single cells led by a lay pastor or shepherd. Another unpaid worker called a zone servant guides five shepherd groups. Twenty-five shepherd groups then become a congregation. The congregations meet periodically for celebration services, and there is no limit to the number of congregations a particular church can have (Neighbour, 1990).

According to Neighbour, the pure cell church places little or no emphasis upon a building or permanent structure that geographically identifies the church. The use of a building is simply to facilitate the occasional celebration gatherings of one or more congregations within the cell church. However, the cell church concept is often questioned as to its inclusion of children and youth in its ministry scope. The primary thrust of most cells is toward adults, thereby requiring the cell church to consider the ministry needs of these age groups.

A recognized strength of cell churches is their ability to reach lost or unconverted persons. Cell church advocates explain that the emphasis upon a servant model of leadership, where each cell member is expected to reach others, is a key to evangelism success. Lay members have more daily contact with lost persons through secular work and community relations than pastors and clergy. Therefore, the cell church utilizes the natural relationships of the cell members to evangelize the lost.

The cell church also seems particularly effective in terms of numerical growth in the large, world population center cities of Asia, Africa, and other parts of the world. Neighbour feels that the cell church is the answer to touching the unreached millions in the world's urban centers more effectively than ever achieved by traditional churches. The cold, impersonal nature of most cities creates a natural climate from which to reach lonely people by emphasizing a personal relationship with Christ as modeled by cell members in their world.

WILLIAM F. FALKNER

Bibliography. C. F. George (1991), *Prepare Your Church for the Future;* R. W. Neighbour Jr. (1990), *Where Do We Go from Here?;* T. S. Rainer (1993), *The Book of Church Growth.*

Cell Groups. *See* Climate, Small Group.

Centering. Way of learning that is inherent in a child's mental processing of facts. It refers to the way children typically focus on one aspect of truth while ignoring others. Piaget found that children primarily in the preoperational stage had the capacity to operate on the basis of one variable at a time. They could find the red objects in a group, or the round objects in a group, or the big objects—but not the red, round, big objects, until they developed the ability to hold all three variables in their minds at the same time. This limiting factor plays a part in the child's concept of conserving—the tallest glass has the most water even though the short, wide beaker held the same amount of water before being poured into the glass. Tallness is the factor centered on. The car that gets to the finish line first is the fastest, irregardless that it started midway on the track. Speed is the only variable considered. In viewing a picture of Moses "standing on holy ground" the child centered on Moses being shoeless rather than on the burning bush—barefootedness being much more within a child's scope than burning trees. This inability to deal with more than one concept at a time affects teachers of children when they give instructions (one step at a time) and when they teach (one conceptual truth must be processed before trying to teach another). More important, the gradual decentering that takes place in the developing child plays a part in the child's moral reasoning as he or she reasons the complexities of establishing right from wrong.

JULIE GORMAN

Chaplain. *See* Ordination.

Character Education in the Early Church. In order to understand how the early church of the first three centuries approached character education, it is important to note that when talking of "character," reference is being made to the moral and ethical life that Christians in the first three centuries pursued and were expected to live out in society. Such an exemplary moral life assumes that even beginning in the New Testament period, there was an identifiable "Christian" ethic of which the church and community of believers were conscious. Thus, the question at hand is, what were the forces and dynamics in the church of the first three centuries that stimulated, challenged, and were educationally significant in spurring Christians on to an exemplary life of Christian moral virtue and holiness?

Christian Ethics and Morality in the Early Church. Unlike much of Greek philosophy, early Christians of the first century looked upon ethics as part of one's personal relationship to God rather than an independent discipline or philosophical subject (Womer, 1987, 3). The ethic of the early church, which was to shape the Christian's character, can be summarized in at least three major points. First, in New Testament times, the belief in the presence and power of the Holy Spirit was a vital part of the Christian ethic. Therefore, followers of Christ were those who under the power and influence of the Holy Spirit sought to follow Christ in what was then a hostile and pagan sociopolitical climate. A second aspect of the early church's conception of morality and ethics was the widespread conviction among Christians or followers of "The Way" that the world in which one lived was very much an alien place and that if a person indeed was a follower of Christ, his or her life must stand apart from that world in anticipation of Christ's imminent return. Martyrdom was a common phenomenon and at times embraced as the noblest and highest expression of Christian commitment and valor. Third, the Christian ethic embraced Christ himself as the supreme example of loving, humble, selfless submission that his true followers were to emulate. Grassi (1982) suggests that the Christian ethic in the first-century church was rooted deeply in the form of teaching imparted to candidates for baptism. He notes that the baptismal admonitions in Paul's letters to the Ephesians and Colossians contain an important dimensional emphasis on acting and speaking "in the Lord" (127–28). These admonitions, and the phrase "in the Lord," suggest that Christians were to act and speak in such a way as to transform ordinary actions and speech of the day and be radiant vessels of God's presence in the world.

The Kinds of Christian "Teaching" Prevalent in the First-Century Church.

The teaching ministry of the early church in its early stages utilized preaching as a principal means of spreading the gospel. However, along with the preaching ministry that was common, there did exist a distinct form of teaching and a corresponding *didaskalos*, or teacher, in the early church. Sherrill notes that itinerant men with charismatic gifts kept appearing even after the middle of the second century and some of these men exercised the teaching function (Sherill, 1944, 144). During the lifetime of the apostles and in the first-century church, five general kinds of teaching seemed to prevail: The Christian interpretation of the Hebrew Scriptures, the teaching of the gospel or "traditions" spoken of in the New Testament, the Christian's confession of faith, teachings concerning the sayings of Jesus, and teaching concerning the "Two Ways" of living (Sherrill, 1944, 144–49). In Paul's writings and through the first three centuries of the early church, reference and teaching regarding "The Way" suggests an early but clear understanding of Christian moral virtue and conduct. The early church manual, *The Didache*, written somewhere between A.D. 120 and 180, contrasts "Two Ways," the way of life and

the way of death, and was probably used as a manual for ethical instruction for converts to Christianity (Sparks, 1978, 307–19).

The Influence of the Religious and Philosophical Context on "Character" Education.

As the followers of the "The Way" grew in number and a recognizable movement of Christian communities developed, it is important to note that aspects of the surrounding philosophical and religious context played an important role in shaping how moral and ethical education took place in the first-century church. Eavey notes that Jewish forms of training and education were an important starting point in shaping both church organization and educational approaches (Eavey, 1964, 84). Jewish models of moral education in the first century began in the home through the imitation of the parents; thus a living model was necessary so that the "way of life" was to be learned by children. The scribes' and Pharisees' approach to teaching the Torah also assumed a certain way of life and pupils learned from their teachers in close association, imitating their actions and life. In classical Greece, the view of the teacher-pupil relationship also had an influence on the early church. The relationship of the teacher and male student was seen in classical Greek culture as one of the highest and closest bonds of love. This relationship inculcated in the pupil the desire to imitate an ideal of excellence that he found in his teacher (Grassi, 1982, 10–23).

The Role of the Family in Character Education.

As the early church grew and blossomed, its Jewish heritage no doubt influenced in a positive way the role of parents in nurturing the spiritual development of children. Indeed, various passages in the apostle Paul's writings allude to the importance of parents raising their children in the fear and knowledge of the Lord. Paul's admonition to parents and children in Colossians (3:20, 21) and Ephesians (6:4) reflect the strong notion in Jewish tradition of the importance of the family as the locus for training and passing on the faith of the parents to the children—a faith which embraces a clearly defined way of life and ethic rooted in a relationship with God. Sherrill notes that Paul's use of the word *paideia* ("but nurture them in the *paideia* and admonition of the Lord") in Ephesians 6:4 carries a strong educational imperative, which in Greek thought implied training, instruction, and education in the arts. This notion of *paideia* implies that the ideals of a whole culture were to be taught to children through education. Sherrill (1944) suggests that Paul's frequent use of the term *paideia* conveys the importance of emphasizing both moral conduct and instruction—two dynamics that were to have taken place in the context of the Christian home (158–59). Laistner notes that apart from general exhortations to parents to bring up their children in the Christian way of life, there is little written in the first three centuries by the early fathers that directly addresses the moral and religious training of children (Laistner, 1951, 35). In the late fourth century, John Chrysostom wrote a treatise entitled *An Address on Vainglory and the Right Way for Parents to Bring Up Their Children*. This lesser-known work of Chrysostom is one of the few treatises of the first four centuries that deals directly with exhorting parents on their role they are to play in the Christian moral education of the children (for a fuller discussion, see Laistner, 1951, 85–122).

Organized Approach to "Character Training" in the Early Church. One of the most important and significant dynamics in the early church's approach to character education was the catechumenal "schools" or *catechumenate* of the first three centuries. The *catechumenate* was designed to train adult converts for church membership and at the same time provide a context to instill devotion and discipline to the Christian faith and way of life. *Catechumens* were those individuals being instructed before baptism and *catechesis* refers to the content being taught. Eavey notes that the verb form of the word "catechumen" means "to instruct" or to "din into the ear." The method of teaching in the catechumenal schools was catechetical, that is, by question and answer with the focus on the candidate or learner being "caused" to know the truth, not just hear it.

In the first two centuries, the details and procedures of the catechumenal schools are not clear and only in the third century are the features and details more ample. Even though it is difficult to demonstrate a given, fixed pattern of instruction for catechumens in the first-century church, two general patterns of instruction can be ascertained—one for Jewish converts and one for Gentile converts. Since Jewish converts were already acquainted with the Hebrew Scriptures, a further study of the Scriptures was required with attention mainly given to the messianic elements. In addition, the "curriculum" consisted of the Christian gospel, the passion and resurrection of Christ, and instruction in the sayings of Jesus. Sherrill (1944) notes that moral instruction such as that in "The Ways" was not given to Jewish converts because they were already familiar with such teaching from their Jewish background. The pattern for Gentile converts was moral instruction such as "The Ways" referred to in *The Didache* and instruction in the Hebrew Scriptures, as well as the other previously mentioned elements of the "curriculum" that Jewish converts received (152).

The development of the early church's worship and meeting practices of the first two centuries were intimately related to the approach taken in the catechumenate for the instruction and teaching of men and women. In the first century,

Christians gathered in different kinds of meetings: meeting for the Word and meeting for the common meal and Lord's Supper. By the second century, these two meetings were combined into one, and eventually the common meal was discontinued. Thus, as the service of worship expanded and developed in the early church, two main divisions were maintained: the didactic element, or *missa calechumenorum*, and the sacramental, element, or *missafidelium*, which was the celebration of the Eucharist where only the baptized faithful were allowed to partake. The catechumens were allowed to be present during the *missa catechumenorum* and this served an instructional purpose as they heard discourses and homilies based on scriptural texts.

In the second century, there appears to have existed at least three kinds of identifiable teaching in the catechumenate: elementary teaching took place, which was assisted by such early church manuals as *The Didache*, Irenaeus's *The Demonstration of the Apostolic Preaching*, and *Shepherd of Hermas*. The second kind of teaching is that didactic element mentioned above which took place in the first part of the service of worship, the *inissa catechumenorum*. A third kind of teaching was more thorough and entailed seeking out competent teachers or reading the works of contemporary authors and theologians.

By the third century, the methods and approach of the catechumenal schools are much more distinct and clear. Origen alludes to three distinct stages which comprised the catechumenate in the third century. As individuals passed through the various grades or stages, the degree of intimacy and participation with the Christian community increased, culminating in the baptism of the new convert. The first stage was a preliminary inquiry into the person's character and occupation and also included some private instruction. Candidates entered the second stage when they were given the status of *hearer*. The *hearers* were permitted to listen to the reading of Scripture and sermons in the church and also received elementary teaching in the basic doctrines and practices of the church. During this period, the *hearers* were also encouraged to readjust their lifestyle to be in line with the Christian ethic. The period of time that someone remained a *hearer* was usually two to three years and toward the end of that period, an inquiry or *scrutiny* took place which was in essence a moral examination of the candidate to see if he or she was worthy for baptism.

The *competens* were the catechumens who had passed the scrutiny and were in the final preparations for baptism. This marked the third and final stage in preparation for baptism. These candidates began an intensive period of preparation, which included daily instruction and various liturgical acts. The *competens* were baptized only after they understood the way of Christian living to which they were committing themselves and their life proved worthy from a moral and ethical standpoint. An excerpt from *The Apostolic Tradition* of Hippolytus, usually dated about 215, proves a helpful picture of the early church's catechumenal approach and underscores the importance of the scrutiny of the candidate's moral life before he or she is baptized: "Have they lived good lives when they were catechumens? Have they honored the widows? Have they visited the sick? Have they done every kind of good work?" (Mitchel, 1981, 51).

During the third century, catechumenal instruction took place in two main contexts. First, instruction continued to take place during the service of worship and the *missa catechunienoruni* continued to play an important didactic role in the initiation and instruction of interested seekers. The second kind of instruction took place apart from the worship service and included private instruction on an individual basis and in groups. The materials used for this instruction included many of the works of the early fathers used in the first two centuries and included such works as Tertullian's *On Repentance* and *On Baptism* which were apparently written specifically for *hearers* as was his treatise *On Prayer*. Cyprian's *Three Books of Testimonies* was also used for teaching adult converts and served as a condensed compendium of Christian teaching. Origen's *First Principles* was also purportedly used in the instruction of catechumens and presents a brief statement of the church's tradition (Sherrill, 1944, 190).

Sherrill (1944) points out that until the fourth century the catechumenate embraced a very militant tone and its purpose was to gradually integrate men and women into the Christian community who were strongly committed to pledge themselves to live a life of dedication, holiness, and loyalty to Christ in a hostile society (187). In a real sense, the catechumenate was a proving ground where men and women were instructed in the traditions and teachings of the Christian faith and where the development of their Christian character and moral purity was encouraged and scrutinized. The culmination of the catechumenate was the administration of the sacrament of baptism, which was also viewed as the spiritual equivalent of a military oath, and where the new adult "converts" were fully initiated and enlisted as fellow "soldiers" in Christ's church. By the middle of the fifth century, the catechumenate began to decline. As the church was now allied with the state, she no longer existed in a hostile environment and many turned to Christianity for reasons other than personal conviction and faith in Christ. Thus the strong ethical and militant tone that the catechumenate emphasized so well in the first three to four centuries was much

more difficult to maintain. As well, infant baptism began to become the norm and the doctrinal understanding of baptism emphasized the priestly nature of the act effectively eliminating the need for education prior to baptism since it was believed that the essential spiritual realities signified by baptism had taken place through the rite itself (Sherrill, 1944, 196–97).

Character education in the church of the first three centuries was a process that was taken seriously by a vibrant Christian movement which expanded and grew among difficult and hostile circumstances. Adult converts came from both Jewish and pagan backgrounds, and the cost of following Christ was often high. The catechumenal system of the early church sought to ensure a high level of commitment, dedication, and moral virtue among those who would eventually be baptized and enter fully into the church. As well, the ongoing role of the family in bringing up future generations dedicated to Christ was an important legacy that the early church carried over from its Jewish roots. These two factors alone represent provocative dynamics that should neither be lost nor overlooked by today's contemporary church which bears the responsibility and challenge of making disciples of all *ethne*, teaching obedience to Christ, the one who is the supreme example of holy virtue, purity, and character.

THOMAS KEPPELER

Bibliography. J. Chrysostom (1951), *Christianity and Pagan Culture;* C. B. Eavey (1964), *History of Christian Education;* J. A. Grassi (1982), *Teaching the Way: Jesus, the Early Church and Today;* M. L. Laistner (1951), *Christianity and Pagan Culture in the Later Roman Empire;* L. L. Mitchell (1981), *A Faithful Church: Issues in the History of Catechsis;* L. J. Sherrill (1944), *The Rise of Christian Education: The Teaching of the Lord to the Gentiles by the Twelve Apostles* (The Didache) in *The Apostolic Fathers,* J. Sparks, ed. (1978); J. L. Womer, ed. (1987), *Morality and Ethics in Early Christianity.*

See also CATECHISM; CATECHUMENATE

Charisma. The leadership quality of charisma is one of the least understood yet desperately needed qualities of our present age. Understanding the factors of effective leadership has long been the emphasis of study by the military, business community, politicians, and social scientists. All have agreed that the most effective leader is one who possesses the illusive quality of charisma. However, when asked to define charisma or the factors which contribute to its development, most researchers fail to provide comprehensive explanations even though they all agree that it is essential to effective performance. There has long been a debate in church growth circles regarding the influence of this character quality as it relates to church growth. In essence, do charismatic leaders produce faster growing churches?

Toward an Understanding of Charisma. Defining charisma can be a significant challenge for those who look for textbook definitions or concise explanations. It is most easily understood when seen in the lives of those who possess this elusive quality. In the realm of politics John F. Kennedy, Margaret Thatcher, Adolph Hitler, Martin Luther King, Jr., and Ronald Reagan are seen as charismatic leaders. In the business world there is Chrysler's Lee Iacocca, Apple Computer's Steven Jobs, and AT&T's Archie McGill. In sports the personalities of former baseball Commissioner Peter Ueberroth, Chicago Bears Coach Mike Ditka, and former heavyweight champ Muhammad Ali are prime examples. Movie stars also have their charismatic personalities such as Robert Redford, Bob Hope, and Johnny Carson. In religious channels there are the personalities of Billy Graham, Jim Bakker, Jim Jones, and E. V. Hill.

In a biblical sense the word charisma comes from the well-known Greek noun *char*. It is from this stem that several popular Greek words originate, such as: "grace" (*charis*), "rejoicing" (*chairo*), "gift" (*charis*), and "thanks" (*eucharistia*). According to Koening (1978), the frequently encountered word "charismatic," which today refers to either a gift or a gifted person, does not even occur in the Bible (14). However, due to its word stem this popular term is clearly understood as having strong biblical origins.

In a sociological sense German sociologist Max Weber (1968) first developed the concept of charismatic leadership. By far, most research on charisma follows Weber's thinking. Weber (1947) stated that the charismatic leader possesses extraordinary qualities that make him attractive to potential followers: "the term charisma will be applied to a certain quality of the individual personality by virtue of which he is set apart by ordinary men and treated as endowed with supernatural, superhuman, or at least exceptional powers and qualities" (358–59).

Theoretical Constructs of Charismatic Leadership. The first theory regarding the development of leadership charisma is the Social Skills Model espoused by Dr. Ronald E. Riggio, a professor at California State University of Fullerton, California. Riggio, in his book entitled *The Charisma Quotient* holds to the view that charisma is primarily a composite of complex social traits greatly influenced and controlled by one's communications skills. This multifaceted view of charisma has two essential components: first, nonverbal communication skills, and second, verbal communication skills.

Nonverbal Communication Skills. Using a variety of nonverbal communication techniques, the charismatic individual is able to express his/her feelings in such a manner as to get others to follow his/her lead. This is done in three

ways: (1) emotional expressivity, / sensitivity, and (3) emotional cont..

Verbal Communication Skills. While sku .. verbal communication is important to charisma, charismatic persons are also identified as individuals who possess superior verbal communication skills. They are able to carry on conversations with almost anyone and to adjust to a wide spectrum of social situations. A charismatic leader is one who possesses three additional basic communication skills. These are: (1) social expressivity, (2) social sensitivity, and (3) social control.

Concluding his theory of charismatic leadership, Riggio (1987) states that "charisma is not a single characteristic, but rather a composite of six basic social skills. The basic social skills are added together to determine charisma potential. But the skills must also be in balance. If any one of the skill levels is disproportionately high or low in relation to the other basic skills, it may lead to problems and an actual reduction of charisma potential" (49).

The second theoretical construct of charisma is the Trait Composite Model developed by Dr. Jay Conger, assistant professor of organizational behavior at McGill University. As an expert in the field of study related to organizational development Conger says that "leaders from the traditional molds are temperamentally disposed toward lower levels of risk, preferring to administer rather than truly lead, and more inclined toward the pragmatic rather than the visionary. Management, in the traditional sense, runs counter to these (charismatic) qualities with its emphasis on the rational, the status quo, certainty, and consensus" (Conger, 1989, 17). The emphasis of his construct is observable behavior.

A list of characteristics presented by Conger that describe charismatic leaders would include descriptors such as visionary, skilled verbal communicator, change agent, creative, risk-taker, unconventionality, and inspirational. Says Conger, "These charismatic leaders are potential sources of enormous transformation for organizations. If managed well, charismatics can be of great help to organizations seeking to adapt to changing environments, for they challenge the forces that blunt expressions of strategic vision and an inspired work force" (18).

Stages in Charismatic Leadership. Conger's model is based upon a stage theory to explain the origination and development of charismatic leadership. These stages are sequential and qualitatively distinct. The stages in Conger's charismatic leadership model are as follows.

Stage One: Sensing Opportunity and Formulating a Vision. Research conducted by Bass (1985), Conger and Kanungo (1988), and House, Woycke, and Fodor (1988) indicates that charismatic leaders possess two skills that characterize this stage. When combined, these skills work together to set this leader apart from his/her peers in the organization. The first skill is a sensitivity to their constituents' needs.

Stage Two: Articulating the Vision. In stage two the charismatic leader articulates the vision that he/she has for a better state of existence through the use of profound oratorical skills. They are first characterized by a strategic sense of vision. They communicate this vision by first describing the present condition and explaining why this current condition is unacceptable. In so doing, the speaker will express his/her thoughts using highly animated gestures seasoned with various modes of expression, enthusiasm, and genuine determination.

Stage Three: Building Trust in the Vision. It is essential that the followers of a charismatic leader desire the goals the leader proposes. They must be viewed as co-owned and shared. Anything less marks progress toward the goal as unlikely. Charismatic leaders build this cooperative spirit by instilling trust in their message. This, in turn, is done by demonstrating concern for followers' needs rather than for their own self-interest. As Conger points out, "The greater the personal risks taken to achieve the vision, the greater the trustworthiness that is likely to be developed" (Conger, 1989, 33).

Stage Four: Achieving the Vision. In this final stage the charismatic leader differs from others by extensive use of personal example and role modeling, their reliance on unconventional tactics, and their use of empowerment strategies to demonstrate how their vision can be achieved (Conger, 1989, 35).

This second theoretical construct of charismatic leadership is based upon a realization that no one behavior trait is responsible for the origination of charisma. It is seen rather as a constellation of behavior since several behavior traits combined create the perception of charisma. It is this composite of behavioral traits that distinguishes a charismatic leader from other leaders.

Developing Leadership Charisma. Charismatic leaders present an interesting paradox to the church. In a very real sense we cannot live without them for they provide the church with vision, motivation, and enthusiasm. Yet, at the same time, it is a significant challenge to live with them. Managing a charismatic leader must be done using a delicate balance of freedom and restraint.

If one does not hold to the theoretical construct that charisma is an endowed trait then it should be possible to develop this dimension in one's leadership. In addition, if one is aware of the dangers associated with the misuse of charisma and is willing to seek positive benefits from its development, then there are several ways one can foster and develop personal leadership charisma.

Vision. It may not be possible to train a person to develop vision per se, but it is possible to train him/her to think in ways that contribute to the development of vision. Since vision is linked to a person's experience and certain cognitive abilities, organizations should look for ways to expand an employee's range of experiences and encourage more creative approaches to leadership such as the use of creativity in problem solving, brainstorming, and goal setting.

Communication Skills. There are a number of ways to improve one's skills in communication. The answer does not lie in adding more stories, metaphors, and paralanguage but rather developing techniques of persuasive language. Kruger (1970) suggests several steps to improve one's communication skills: improvement of vocal expressiveness (i.e. develop skills in rate, pitch, and loudness of one's voice); learn to articulate clearly—to eliminate poor speaking habits and to enhance the way one articulates; improve one's body language—to regulate the body's expressions to the message one is delivering so that the eyes, hands, and face are all coordinated while speaking; learn to develop, organize, and support ideas—to present one's ideas and facts clearly and persuasively without a lot of clutter (4–5).

Trust Building Skills. Though much of the trust a person receives is built upon intangible qualities difficult to reproduce in a training seminar, some aspects of trust building can be taught. For example, Conger (1989) states a person can be taught to demonstrate self-confidence and shared values with subordinates. Leaders can also be trained in sensitivity skills to enable them to understand the needs and values of their subordinates. Lastly, leaders can be taught ways in which they can be more expressive of the commitment to a particular project (170).

Empowerment Skills. Bestowing rewards and expressing confidence in a leader on the part of an executive can produce feelings of confidence and security. When subordinates know their leader is respected and affirmed by the powers over them they feel more secure in their leadership. This, in turn, contributes to their empowerment. Installing reward systems that foster innovative performance is one method. Structuring jobs that provide more autonomy and self-direction is another. These practices encourage the development of empowerment managers and organizational leaders.

Conclusion. Effective leadership is one of the most powerful resources that any organization can possess. It is unfortunate that it is so seldom identified and developed by corporate America. The church, too, has underutilized its leadership potential. It can be discouraging to realize that it can take years for a truly charismatic leader to rise to the surface and be properly trained in the use of his/her leadership skills. It is when these skills are not shaped and nurtured in a healthy manner that they are allowed to penetrate the dark side of leadership. The end result is a loss of leadership potential and a setback for the kingdom of God.

Charismatic leadership can be one of the greatest strengths or weaknesses available to the church today. A charismatic leader can instill a vision among people who are without direction. He is also able to raise people's hopes and emotions, in essence to give them motivation and enthusiasm. The challenge comes in keeping the charismatic leader in control of his/her unique gifts and channeling his/her energies in a direction that benefits the entire body of Christ. One must not, however, rely too heavily upon his/her charismatic personality as a primary means for building the church. This study reveals that more than persuasive speech, expressive animation, and empathy are needed to build up the body of Christ.

MICHAEL J. ANTHONY

Bibliography. D. Abodaher (1982), *Iacocca;* B. Armstrong (1979), *The Electric Church;* B. J. Avolio and B. M. Bass (1985), *Transformational Leadership, Charisma and Beyond;* idem (1985), *Leadership and Performance Beyond Expectations;* C. Camic, *Sociological Inquiry,* 50 (1990): 5–23; J. A. Conger (1985), *Charismatic Leadership in Business: An Exploratory Study;* idem (1988), *Charismatic Leadership;* J. A. Conger and R. A. Kanungo, *Academy of Management Review,* 12, no. 4 (1987): 637–47; idem (1988), *Charismatic Leadership;* J. A. Conger, R. Kanungo, and Associates, eds. (1988), *Charismatic Leadership: The Elusive Factors in Organization Effectiveness;* J. A. Conger and R. N. Kanungo (1988), *Charismatic Leadership in Organizations: Test of a Behavioral Model;* idem *Academy of Management Review* 13, no. 3, (1988): 471–82; idem (1988), *Charismatic Leadership;* T. E. Dow Jr., *Sociological Quarterly,* 10 (1969): 306–18; G. F. Freemesser and H. B. Kaplan, *Journal of Youth and Adolescence* 5, no. 12 (1976): 1–9; M. Galanter, *American Journal of Psychiatry* 139, no. 2 (1982): 1539–48; R. J. House (1977), *Leadership: The Cutting Edge;* R. J. House, J. Woycke, and E. M. Fodor (1988), *Charismatic Leadership;* M. F. R. Kets de Vries (1988), *Charismatic Leadership;* C. King (1969), *My Life with Martin Luther King,* Jr.; R. Riggio, *Journal of Personality and Social Psychology* (1986).

Child Care. *See* Day Care.

Child Care Centers. *See* Day Care Centers.

Child Development. *Introduction.* Child development is a specialized field of study within the developmental branch of psychology. It has been only in the past few centuries that childhood has come to be viewed as more than a bump on the road to adulthood. Prior to the 1800s, children were expected to assume adult responsibilities early in their lives and were more often considered a burden than a gift from God.

Today childhood is still at risk. Longitudinal studies are showing the effects of divorce on children. Abuse and mistreatment plague children now as in the past. Confused messages about sexuality and the pressure to grow up fast make it difficult for children to be children. The physical and emotional signs of stress-related problems are showing up at early ages.

In this environment, and throughout history, Christianity has been a steady voice in the child advocacy movement. Jesus was unique in his day in his recognition and valuing of children. A renewed commitment to the study and nurture of children and the protection of childhood is essential to building strong societies and strong churches.

In the following sections, a summary of general developmental characteristics for each stage of childhood is provided. It is important to remember that in childhood there are wide differences in individual growth patterns. Because development is influenced by both heredity and environment, the developmental characteristics of one child will often vary greatly from another's.

Infant and Toddler. Physical Development. During the first twelve to eighteen months of life, changes in physical growth and motor development are rapid. The infant's birthweight doubles by the fourth or fifth month and length will increase ten to twelve inches by age one. Development proceeds from the head downward and from the center of the body outward. Large muscle development precedes the development of fine motor skills.

During this period, infants are developing the motor skill of prehension—the ability to grasp and hold an object, and the skill of locomotion—the ability to move about and get from one place to another. The increasing efficiency of motor activity is influenced by the rapid development of the brain. The child's brain grows faster during the first two years of life than it will at any other time.

Freud described this early stage of life as the oral period of development in which children are learning about their world primarily through the mouth. As a result, provision needs to be made for regular sanitation of cribs, changing tables, and toys.

Cognitive/Perceptual Development. Piaget, a developmental psychologist, labeled the cognitive characteristics evident in this first stage of life from birth to age two as the sensorimotor stage. Children are responding to the variety of stimuli in their environment with motor activity. They are learning about object permanence, how to manage their body's actions, and the principle of cause and effect. Their active sensory systems allow them to learn through processing visual stimuli, taste, hearing, and touch.

During the second year of life, children are beginning to imitate adult facial gestures and sounds and will develop a vocabulary of up to ten words. They can understand simple commands and enjoy repetition of sounds, words, and movement. Although their attention spans are brief, they are naturally curious and will attend to environmental stimuli that are novel and surprising.

Early in life children appear to learn best in a context that facilitates discovery and guided play. Using large story visuals to teach a single Bible truth reinforced with simple songs and physical movement will engage the child at an appropriate level of cognitive stimulation.

Social/Emotional. In infancy, one of the key developmental indicators of emotional security is the nature of the attachment bonds formed between child and primary caregivers. According to Erik Erikson's psychosocial theory, from birth to age one, children are learning about trust through these significant interactions. Children need adults who are present, responsive, attentive, and affectionate. They also need caregivers and teachers who are patient as they are prone to display a wide and unstable range of emotions.

In preparation for future separation and independence, the infant is beginning to distinguish between "you" and "me." Although this is experienced first at a physical level, it progresses to the cognitive and social/emotional levels during the latter part of the first year and into the second year.

Spiritual. The infant's first lessons about God are learned through interactions with parents and other caregivers. Ronald Goldman referred to this stage as one of undifferentiated faith. James Fowler refers to the first stage of faith in his faith development theory as primal faith and notes that it is shaped through relatedness with others. By implication, one of the primary emphases for ministry in infancy is selecting, training, and developing volunteers who are living models of God's love for children.

Preschool (Ages 3–6). *Physical.* Growth appears to level off during this next stage and rates of increase in height and weight remain fairly constant from ages two to six. Neuromuscular development is becoming more coordinated and, when not sleeping, preschoolers are constantly running, climbing, and jumping. Although fine motor skills are developing and they are beginning to gain control over small muscle movement, it is not until about four or five years of age that a child is able to use crayons, pencils, or scissors, or do puzzles with some success.

According to Freud's psychosexual theory, early preschoolers (ages two and three), find their primary source of gratification through anal activity. This is also the time that the anal sphincter muscles are developing and activities related to toilet training are of interest. At age four or five children move into Freud's genital stage, charac-

terized by a focus on genital interest and sexual desire.

Cognitive. The time-space world of the child is expanding as the ability to mentally represent people, objects, and events develops toward the end of Piaget's sensorimotor stage and into the preoperational stage. With the appearance of this symbolic functioning comes the ability to put thoughts and ideas into words, although their vocabulary exceeds their comprehension. Their thinking is concrete and illogical. They fixate on particulars and are unable to generalize. When speaking to a preschooler, symbolism and figures of speech should be avoided. They enjoy using their imaginations and engaging in imitative play. For many children, attention spans are brief and the length of participation in any one activity is limited. The predominant learning channel for this age group is personal exploration and hands-on interaction.

Social/Emotional. Moving into Erikson's second stage of autonomy and separation versus shame and doubt (1 to 2 years) and into the third stage of initiative versus guilt (3 to 5 years), preschoolers prefer to do things without the help of others and look for ways to be assertive in initiating activities on their own. While growing in self-confidence, they crave personal attention and praise. They test limits and require the security of consistent discipline.

Early preschoolers, ages two and three, engage in parallel play—playing alongside of others while not directly interacting with them. Later preschoolers, ages four, five, and six, are beginning to play in groups with other children. As a result of these interactions and the reinforcement of primary caregivers, gender role socialization is taking place. They are sensitive to adult feelings and attitudes and pick up cues related to the appropriateness of their own behavior and that of others around them.

Most preschoolers are loving and expressive and eager to please their parents and teachers. It is more helpful to reinforce and praise evidence of desirable behavior than to punish less desirable actions. Clear behavior guidelines with simple and immediate natural consequences bring a sense of constancy to the preschooler's fast-changing world. In this period of new discovery and aggressive exploration, fears are more pronounced and the preschool child needs an accepting environment in which to express such feelings.

Spiritual. The preschool child's understanding of religious concepts is literal and concrete. God is perceived to have human characteristics along with human limitations, although these perceptions can vary greatly among individual preschoolers. In line with their more egocentric orientation to the world, God is often understood as a deity dedicated to attending to their personal welfare.

According to Fowler, faith for the preschool child is primarily imitative. They will imitate the faith and religious behaviors of adults in their lives and stories.

Children are able to grasp simple religious concepts when presented through Bible stories that are concrete, engaging, and action-oriented. They can understand that God loves them and made them, that the Bible is a special book with stories about God and Jesus, and that prayer is talking to God. They need opportunities and encouragement to practice concrete responses to what they are learning and enjoy participating in simple worship experiences. Preschoolers are beginning to distinguish between right and wrong and can grasp that God cares and wants to help them do right things.

Primary/Middler (Ages 6–9). Physical. In psychosexual terms, Freud calls the next period of childhood the latency stage. At this time the focus for the child is on physical and social activities. Growth is slow and steady until the next spurt between the ages of 10 and 12. As the shape of the body changes to assume a more adultlike contour, girls tend to be almost two years ahead of boys in height and weight. Children are increasing in strength and in the coordination of fine motor skills. They enjoy athletics and team sports and are learning how to play together.

Cognitive. In contrast to the concrete but illogical stage of preschool, children are shifting to think in more logical and reasonable terms. According to Piaget, by the age of seven, children have moved into the stage of concrete operations. Their thinking is still limited to what they have observed and personally experienced; however, they are beginning to engage in a number of mental operations such as classification, conservation of volume, and mentally retracing actions or thoughts.

Although still somewhat limited in time-space concepts, their world is expanding beyond the here and now. They are eager to learn and ask a lot of questions, especially related to the "why" of events. While six- and seven-year-olds may focus on only one or two details of an experience, by the ages of eight or nine the child is able to grasp a sense of the "whole."

Children in this stage are highly creative, inventive, and curious. Academic achievement becomes prominent as reading, writing, and language skills are developed and strengthened. Although memorization comes easily to this stage child, understanding needs to be tested. Symbolism should be avoided and active, hands-on learning activities should be employed.

Social/Emotional. Children in this stage are moving away from the egocentric position of preschool and are growing in their ability to appreciate that others may have a different viewpoint. This is closely related to the cognitive abil-ity of reversibility in thinking. Growing understanding about reciprocity and interrelatedness in human relationships is foundational to the development of appropriate social behavior and moral reasoning.

As children become more aware of the differences between themselves and others, social comparisons are used to shape their self-concept. While generally positive, self-confident, and outgoing, they are alert to the evaluations of adults and friends and are especially sensitive to critical judgments and peer ridicule.

Group influence is strong, and companionship with friends is becoming more important. Through these friendships and attentiveness to adult actions and behaviors, they are developing ideas about gender-specific and sex-appropriate behaviors. Their primary involvement at this time is with same-sex friends. While growing closer to friends and beginning to separate from family, competitive attitudes and behaviors are evident. Beginning first with siblings and extending to friends, children are competing for attention and praise and personal power.

Children are concerned about matters of justice and fair play. They are looking for adult models of acceptable and Christlike behavior. Children are not looking for perfection, but genuine transparency. During this time of fluctuating emotions and periods of moodiness, they need to see caregivers and teachers who experience the normal range of human feelings and know how to appropriately express such emotions as fear, guilt, excitement, and anger.

Spiritual. Coinciding with their expanding cognitive capabilities and accompanying limitations, children are continuing to develop their understanding of God. God is still perceived in primarily physical terms, but he is also understood to have magical powers. Many children at this stage are beginning to relate to God at an increasingly personal level. They can understand that although God is all-wise and all-powerful, he also hears and answers their prayers. They can sense a need for God's help on a daily basis and may now express a desire for personal salvation.

In Fowler's faith stage model, children in this second stage of faith are growing in their ability to distinguish between fantasy and reality. Their perspective of Bible stories and concepts is predominantly literal. The narratives of the Old and New Testaments are especially helpful in communicating biblical truths in a concrete manner.

Junior/Preteen (Ages 10–12). Physical. Depending on the onset of puberty, this stage of development could exhibit almost no growth or rapid growth in the extreme. Puberty brings growth spurts for girls sometime between 10 and 12 years of age. For boys, puberty growth spurts are delayed until 12 to 14 years of age. Although girls tend to remain ahead of boys in height and weight until adolescence, boys are now moving ahead in muscle strength and endurance. This can be a time of stress for the child who is uncomfortable with his or her appearance and the preadolescent needs sensitive adults during the transition and adjustment.

As preteens are becoming well adapted to their bodies and gaining mastery over both large and small muscles, they exhibit tremendous energy and engage in seemingly constant activity. With their growing coordination of fine motor ability, they are able to attempt a wider range of learning activities, hobbies, and skills. Along with their younger counterparts, preteens also need learning environments which are interactive and provide opportunity for movement.

As the physical shape of their body is changing, their curiosity about sex is increasing. Although this age group falls into Freud's latency period, many of them are concerned about puberty and are intrigued with details concerning sexual development and sexual behaviors.

Cognitive. Preteens are further refining the new cognitive skills achieved during the first few years of Piaget's concrete operations stage. Even though their verbal responses may indicate a higher level of mental reasoning, they are still concrete in their approach to life experiences, and rote memory needs to be checked for comprehension. In addition to more rational patterns of thought development throughout middle childhood, preadolescents enjoy fantasizing about the future and "trying on" various career choices. They are curious and questioning and like to "stump" adults with challenging questions and tough situational dilemmas.

Children in this stage need opportunities to think through their own possible responses to challenging problems. They need to be guided in applying biblical principles to these real-life situations. This is the time to lay the foundation and cover the basics of their faith with topics like the evidence for biblical creationism and simple apologetics. Preteens can be taught how to search the Scriptures and how to make use of a variety of Bible study aids such as concordances and dictionaries. Any task presented to them must be appropriate to their cognitive level of functioning. It must not be overly challenging—they fear failure and appearing stupid in front of peers; nor must the task appear overly simplistic and too childish.

Social/Emotional. Overall, the preadolescent is emotionally stable, although outbursts can appear and tempers may flare. As puberty approaches, emotions become more erratic. Preteens like to tease and have a sharp sense of humor.

Children in this stage are working on taking steps toward independence. They want to make their own choices. This may be evidenced in their conflicts with parents and challenges to authority. As preteens begin to separate from the influence of parents and adult caregivers, the peer group grows in power. Children in this stage enjoy group activities and respond to organized clubs and teams. Adult guidance is still needed, but a low profile is preferred.

Preteens are eager to get involved. Leadership skills are waiting to be developed. They are looking for opportunities to participate in creative service projects and challenges beyond their neighborhood. Children at this stage are concerned with issues of moral justice and will begin to wrestle with current topics at a level they can deal with.

Spiritual. A child in this stage of development is capable of expressing deep feelings of love for God and will seek his guidance when faced with making choices in life. They are asking more questions about Christianity, but are able to explore many of the answers on their own.

One outgrowth of the increased peer group interaction is that preteens will often share naturally about God and their faith with friends and invite them to join them in group activities at church. Their sense of ownership as a member of a local church can be strengthened if given opportunities to get involved.

During this time of hero worship, the heroes of the Bible need to be featured. Further, preteens need to see how matters of faith work out practically in real life. Small discipleship groups and times of interpersonal sharing have a great impact at this time. The lives of volunteers and teachers will be watched closely. Children are critical of discrepancies they see between walk and talk.

Conclusion. Children are more than miniature adults, and childhood is more than a roadside rest stop on the way to adulthood. They are more impressionable during these formative years than at any other time in their development. Jesus invited the children to come to Him. We should do no less.

SHELLY CUNNINGHAM

Bibliography. M. J. Anthony (1992), *Foundations of Ministry: An Introduction to Christian Education for a New Generation;* R. E. Clark, J. Brubaker, and R. B. Zuck, eds. (1986), *Childhood Education in the Church;* D. A. Elkind (1974), *A Sympathetic Understanding of the Child, Birth to Sixteen;* S. K. Fitch and D. Ratcliff (1991), *Insights into Child Development;* R. Goldman (1964), *Religious Thinking from Childhood to Adolescence;* A. V. Gormly and D. M. Brodzinsky, eds. (1993), *Lifespan Human Development;* D. Ratcliff (1988), *Handbook of Preschool Religious Education;* F. P. Rice (1992), *Human Development: A Life-span Approach;* L. O. Richards (1983), *Children's Ministry;* B. J. Wadsworth (1977), *Piaget's Theory of Cognitive Development.*

See also FOWLER, JAMES W., III; PIAGET, JEAN; PRESCHOOL EDUCATION; SENSORY REGISTERS

Child Evangelism Fellowship. According to its own purpose statement, Child Evangelism Fellowship is a Bible-centered, worldwide organization dedicated to winning boys and girls to Christ, establishing them in the Word of God, and involving them in a local church. CEF has local chapters in every state of the United States, every province in Canada, and over 130 countries. Though serving as a resource agency for local churches, Bible schools, and other parachurch groups, Child Evangelism Fellowship is an independent ministry independent from any denomination or association of churches.

This outreach to children began in 1923 when Irvin Overholtzer launched Bible classes for children. In 1934, his burden was formalized with the incorporation of CEF in Chicago, Illinois. Currently the home office is in Warrenton, Missouri.

CEF accomplishes its purpose through home Bible classes (called Good News Clubs), summer Bible classes (five-day clubs), open-air evangelism, camps, school-related release-time classes, state fair outreach, and mass communication ministries. Educational programs include a Children's Ministries Institute (required of all staff and board members), continuing education conferences, and teacher training seminars offered for volunteers in local churches. CEF Press produces and disseminates an extensive amount of literature, including Bible lessons, Children's Church Kits, Vacation Bible School materials, tracts, and the bimonthly *Evangelizing Today's Child* magazine.

The Children's Ministry Institute is a twelve-week program offered annually at the international headquarters, as well as at extension sites throughout the United States and Canada. The curriculum includes "Teaching Children Effectively," "Understanding Today's Child," "Progressive Methods of Child Evangelism," "Dynamics of Teacher Training," "Instructor of Teachers Course," "Ministry Strategy and Development," and "Dynamics of Christian Leadership." In addition to CEF missionary candidates, participants include Christian college students who desire to supplement their training or specialize in children's ministries. The institute also welcomes parents and church volunteers with a burden for children's ministry.

CEF is a *faith* ministry, relying on God to supply needs through churches and individuals. Their fund-raising policy is to "ask God and tell His people." Though Good News Clubs and five-Day Clubs are taught primarily by local volunteers, the organization seeks career missionaries with a vision for reaching children and training lay adults in evangelistic outreach. Qualifications for a full-time missionary include a college degree, the equivalent of one year of Bible training, plus a track record of faithful ministry in a church. All CEF missionaries obtain their own financial and prayer support.

According to CEF, ministering to young people is the key to a growing, healthy local church. Staff members on the state and local levels implement a *Christian Youth in Action* program in which teens receive training in child evangelism that equips them for neighborhood outreach efforts, Vacation Bible School leadership, as well as church-sponsored short-term mission ventures.

CEF staff members are motivated by the conviction that kids represent the highest potential for conversion. They cite research suggesting that two out of every three adults who are Christians made their decision to accept Christ as Savior before the age of eighteen.

To obtain a resource catalog, or informative brochures introducing this children's ministry, write CEF, P.O. Box 348, Warrenton, MO 63383. Or call 1–800–300–4033.

TERRY POWELL

Childhood Christian Education. *Biblical and Historical Background.* Moses instructed the Israelites to teach their children about God (Deut. 6:6–7). Daily ritual, annual celebrations, and monuments all provided opportunities for parents to teach children the nature and history of their people's relationship with the Creator. As time passed, home instruction was supplemented by teaching in schools and synagogues. Biblically, the responsibility for a child's religious training rested, and still remains, with the child's parents. In the beginning of the Christian era, Hellenistic culture made education widely available but encroached on biblical content. Many Jewish and Christian parents opted for private instruction. For example, the home-based nature of Timothy's early education was the work of his mother and grandmother (2 Tim. 3:15). When Rome fell, all responsibility for education was left to the church. Privileged children of noble families and children destined for a religious life were educated in monasteries across Europe. Cathedral schools had opened their doors by the ninth century, but most people remained illiterate. What children learned about God was drawn mostly from stained glass windows, sculpture, and church drama.

Education rose in importance during the Renaissance, but once again it was at the cost of biblical content. The Reformers put the Bible back into the curriculum and brought improvements in methodology. Literacy and Bible knowledge grew with the invention of the printing press and the widespread distribution of reading material, including God's Word in everyday languages. Educators and philosophers called attention to the nature of the child and the process of learning. Researchers began to focus on the important years of early childhood. As the public school became more secular, churches recognized the need for new agencies to provide Christian education for children.

Sunday school had been created as an educational opportunity for eighteenth-century children who worked six days a week. Now it began to gain popularity as an avenue of religious instruction for public school children. During widespread religious revival in nineteenth-century America, various denominations founded Sunday schools, secondary schools, colleges, and seminaries. As the number of Sunday schools increased, so did the need for their organization. Conferences and conventions were set up to provide standards, curriculum, and teacher training.

The religious instruction of children changed radically in the years that followed. Children had been believed to be incapable of conversion before the age of accountability. Until that time, children were repeatedly lectured on their sinful, hopeless condition. Some parents even refused to allow their children to read the Bible. A new, more benevolent view arose. It took advantage of the teachability of young children to form positive attitudes toward God in young hearts and minds.

Today, Christian education is an international ministry designed to serve the whole child. Both church and parachurch organizations combine efforts and resources to meet needs that are not only spiritual, but also intellectual, physical, social, and emotional. The ministry's goal is to teach children the Word of God so that they will come to a saving knowledge of Jesus Christ and become not only disciples, but disciple-makers (2 Tim. 2:2).

There are many additional biblical directives for children's religious instruction. In the Great Commission, the command is given to make disciples of *all* people (Matt. 28:19–20). Proverbs 22:6 urges parents and teachers to "train up" impressionable young children so that they will continue to follow that training in later years. In Deuteronomy, Moses' instructions are to teach children by integrating Bible truths with everyday activities.

Goals and Objectives. In the United States and many other nations, the goals of children's ministry are shared by church and parachurch organizations such as publishers, Christian schools, camps, and club programs. Within the local church, the children's educational program is usually staffed by volunteers who may be led by a trained Christian education specialist. The local church program typically features a Sunday school, a club, and additional events such as camps and retreats. Some churches provide children with a worship time geared to their age level. Others may have a children's music program and a choir. A multifaceted program should provide children with opportunities for worship, instruction, fellowship, and evangelism (Acts 2:42–47).

Programs. The most popular program for instruction is traditionally the Sunday school. Although a wide variety of approaches can be found in churches today, the organization of a typical Sunday school is modeled after the public school. Administrative structure also varies, but usually the teachers of individual classes are supported and supervised by a director or committee. A representative of the educational ministry is usually part of the governing body of the church, such as the church board. Although the traditional time slot for Sunday school is just prior to morning worship, creatively scheduled programs serve children throughout the week. Some public school systems have used the "release time" system to allow part of the school day to be set aside for religious instruction. Most instruction takes place within the church facility, but special needs create responsive programs in playgrounds, housing projects, and wherever children gather.

The designation "children's ministry" also includes first grade through sixth grade. Within that span, many churches divide children into the primary (1st–2nd grades), middler (3rd–4th grades), and junior (5th–6th grades) divisions. The more closely graded the classes, the more age-appropriate the methods and materials can be. Teachers are trained in age-appropriate practice and are normally supplied with professionally prepared lesson materials. Classrooms are designed to facilitate learning with age-appropriate furnishings, activity centers, and educational resources. Opportunities afforded by breaks in the school schedule are often filled with vacation Bible schools. Although there are large churches that boast of a children's Sunday school in the thousands, the average American church will have a program of fewer than one hundred children.

The Contemporary Challenge. Children's Christian education today faces a wide variety of needs. The decline of the nuclear family in America has given rise to family-centered ministries for teaching parenting skills. Working parents are served by church-sponsored child care. Humanism in some public schools has prompted the founding of Christian day schools. Children living in poverty require programs to meet more than their educational needs. Teachers must be prepared to minister to increasing numbers of learning-disabled and physically impaired children who are now mainstreamed. The children of new Americans must be welcomed into God's family with multicultural sensitivity.

In contemporary Christian education, teachers can take advantage of what science has discovered about how children learn. Research bears out the scriptural directives. To impact behavior, teaching must reach beyond simple head knowledge to touch the heart. These cognitive and affective levels of learning are doorways to a changed life. Researchers agree with Moses that lessons in morality must be applied to real-life situations so that children will understand their relevance. An active learner will retain more than a passive listener. Discoveries in the function of the brain remind parents to "train up" a child in the early formative years when attitudes are being formed to last a lifetime. Lessons and methods must be appropriate to the interests and abilities of the learner's age level, something Paul knew when he offered only spiritual "milk" to immature believers. Although only God's Holy Spirit knows the depth of a child's spiritual maturity and readiness for salvation, the age-level indicators of emotional, social, intellectual, and physical development have been standardized. These standards are valuable guidelines for teachers. Studies on different learning styles have pointed out the need for a variety of teaching methods. A wide scope of learning activities now include music, drama, games, research, creative writing, and different forms of discussion.

Even before the Renaissance, those concerned with children's religious instruction recognized the special needs of young learners and had written simplified texts of Bible stories and church doctrine for use with young believers. Published, age-graded curriculum was not widely available until Sunday schools were firmly established in America. Contemporary curriculum has replaced the traditional teacher-centered model with a learner-centered process.

Understanding the Child. Standards for age group characteristics and needs allow teachers to make informed choices when designing schedules, furnishing rooms, and selecting teaching methods. Instead of treating children like miniature adults, teachers can tailor their lessons to meet specific needs of each level of development. Although standards are only assessments of the average child of an age group, they can identify a child who lags so far behind the norm that he or she would benefit from professional intervention.

First- and second-graders are very physical and need plenty of room and opportunity for large muscle activity. Informed teachers of these primaries will plan periods of activity alternating with times of sitting and listening. A child whose physical needs are not being met is not prepared to learn. Activities should be planned to last no more than ten minutes, because a primary's attention span is about one minute per year of his or her age. A first- or second-grader's mood changes rapidly. A child of this age needs a teacher who understands feelings and helps label emotions. This child thinks in literal terms, so teachers should avoid the use of symbolism. The child at this age is still struggling with the concepts of fantasy and reality. Teachers must help primaries fit into the group, because children of this age are sensitive about being "left out." At

every age, but especially with younger learners, teachers must be aware that their own example speaks louder than all their lectures.

Third- and fourth-graders have achieved mastery of the basic skills and are now ready to enjoy learning. Lessons can include reading and writing tasks such as independent research using age-level resources like maps and dictionaries. Art and music activities can utilize their more dexterous small muscle control. Because these middlers tend to live in the present, Bible lessons must have immediate application to their lives. This is the prime age for club programs, because middlers want to be part of a group. Group activities are more manageable because third- and fourth-graders can understand the need for rules. They have improved memories and reasoning skills and will learn from a teacher who uses carefully planned questions that lead to self-discovery.

Juniors in the fifth and sixth grades are moving toward independence. They are more interested in peer approval than in adult praise. Because of peer pressure and increased exposure to the world, juniors need teachers who will help them make discerning choices. Juniors enjoy competition, but adults must be careful that competition is kept to reasonable limits and does not become both the means and end of an activity intended to be education. Because juniors have increased historical and geographical background on which to draw, lessons can include more Bible chronology. Because juniors need to practice social skills, teachers can plan group cooperative projects. To hold their interest, teachers of juniors should provide them with choices of activities.

The teacher must be less of an authoritarian and more of an enabler and facilitator. Even though lessons are now learner-centered, the teacher/learner relationship remains a vital factor in Christian education. Bible truth is best learned in the context of a caring relationship. To make this relationship easier to develop and maintain, classes should be kept to a reasonable teacher/student ratio.

Although often regarded as less important than adult educational ministries, children's programs reach individuals at the stage in their lives where most will make their decisions for Christ. It is as children that people form lifelong attitudes toward God and his church.

ROBERT J. CHOUN

Bibliography. J. Capehart (1992), *Becoming a Treasured Teacher;* R. J. Choun and M. S. Lawson (1998), *The Christian Educator's Handbook on Children's Ministry;* idem (1998), *The Complete Handbook of Children's Ministry;* R. E. Clark, J. Brubaker, and R. Zuck (1986), *Childhood Education in the Church;* R. E. Clark, L. Johnson, and A. K. Sloat, eds. (1991), *Christian Education: Foundations for the Future;* K. O. Gangel and H. G. Hendricks (1988), *The Christian Educator's Handbook on Teaching;* R. Habermas and K. Issler (1992),

Teaching for Reconciliation: Foundations and Practice for Christian Educational Ministry; M. S. Lawson and R. J. Choun (1998), *Christian Education for the 21st Century;* idem (1992), *Directing Christian Education;* J. C. Wilhoit and J. M. Dettoni, eds. (1995), *Nurture That Is Christian;* R. B. Zuck (1996), *Precious in His Sight: Childhood and Children in the Bible.*

Children's Church. In the early part of the twentieth century, "junior church" was established to evangelize and to meet the worship needs of elementary through high school aged youth. This was an antecedent to present-day "children's church." Congregations began to look at specific developmental needs of children in relationship to worship practices. Programs have been established that invite children to a separate space for worship and education. These are geared toward preschool through elementary ages. Older children and youth are expected to participate in regular worship.

There are three models for children's church. The first model is a combination of worship and education time that emphasizes Bible learning activities, Bible stories, and children's Christian music. In the second model children begin worship with families and then move to a different location for child-centered learning, worship, and music. This movement usually occurs before the adult sermon. A third model is that of a second Sunday school hour that continues the lesson from the previous hour. All three models are found in churches today.

Some controversy surrounds the practice of children's church. Those who advocate a separate space emphasize the developmental needs of children, the often conceptual nature of some adult worship, and the need to excite children about God. They believe this can best be achieved in a separate program where active learning through storytelling, puppet shows, or object lessons can provide a valid worship service that is understandable to children. Several religious publishing houses offer specialized curriculum for children's church. Children's church is often requested by adults who are distracted by active children in regular worship. Pastors, too, sometimes prefer to preach to a mostly adult congregation.

Others prefer to include children in regular "family" worship. They believe that the presence of children in worship is necessary for becoming the whole people of God. Children, observing and participating with their parents in worship, learn about trust, discipleship, stewardship, and the gospel of Christ. Those who prefer that children be a part of worship contend that our culture has already divided families far too often. To separate the body of Christ is bowing to cultural norms. The church ought to be a place of joining together in worship and fellowship. To meet the worship needs of whole families, many churches

have included more contemporary music with repetitive lyrics, simplified prayers, and sermons that include more illustrations and stories.

Children's church is an option for worship that should be studied carefully. Denominational theology often informs individual churches about the role of children in their church and the responsibility churches hold for nurturing the faith. Specific congregational demographics must be weighed. The needs of the entire body of Christ must be taken into consideration when making decisions concerning children's church.

SUSAN L. HOUGLUM

Children's Ministry Models. The basic needs and characteristics of childhood are unchanging. Preschoolers will crave adult attention. Juniors will value peer approval over adult praise. Toddlers will play by themselves. Middlers want to join clubs.

Biblical principles for childhood education are also unchanging. Learning must begin in early childhood. Timothy's exposure to the Scriptures began in infancy. Lessons must relate to everyday life. Moses' directives to the Israelites ordered them to teach their children about God in the context of common experiences. The advice to train up a child while he is young referred to the lifelong retention of lessons learned in childhood. Since there is no description of formal religious instruction for children in the early church, these God-ordained childhood characteristics and teaching methods are the only absolutes on which to build a biblical philosophy of ministry.

As scientific research reveals additional information on the learning process, we are better equipped to understand the biblical directives and design our educational programs to better serve the child.

The basic needs of children do not change as society changes, but special circumstances can bring different needs to the forefront at different times. Because of these changing factors, the church must strike a balance in its ministry to children. The church must take a stand on God's design for childhood growth and the process of learning, but the church must also be willing to respond to societal change by changing the format of its institutions. Preserve the message, but let the medium remain flexible.

In response to cultural change and enlightened educational practices, many local churches have developed new models for Christian education of children. No single model is the best choice for all churches, for each local body must respond to unique needs.

For many churches, the standard children's ministry format works well. The program is anchored by the Sunday school in its traditional premorning worship time slot. Children's classes usually cover age levels from three-year-olds through sixth grade. Younger children are cared for in a nursery and older teens generally attend youth classes. Midweek clubs usually supplement the Sunday morning session. Vacation Bible schools, camps, and retreats complete the package and fulfill children's needs for worship, instruction, fellowship, and expression. In the traditional Sunday school facility, small rooms accommodate age-graded classes. An adjacent large room provides space for group assemblies for worship and sharing. Sunday school generally lasts forty-five to sixty minutes.

As churches grow and Sunday school classes begin to exceed ideal teacher/student ratios, classes are further divided into closely graded groups for age-appropriate learning. Churches large enough to need a second worship hour on Sunday morning are faced with the choice of back-to-back identical Sunday schools for children or Sunday school followed by a children's church. Because there are mixed views on children in adult worship, there are a variety of alternatives. Churches large enough to provide staff and facilities for a children's church have the option of offering young worshipers an experience on their own level. Some churches prefer that children accompany their families to adult worship services. Others take a middle road, welcoming children to the opening of the adult service and dismissing them before the sermon. Another common practice is the distribution of crayons and activity papers to children in adult worship.

Churches that emphasize family learning will use curriculum that features the same theme across all age levels on any given week. Parents are encouraged to develop the theme during the week in family devotional times. A step in the same direction is the model of the intergenerational Sunday school. A variety of ages study the same theme in age-graded classes and then come together to discuss the theme, share insights, and worship as a group. Intergenerational education often includes midweek meetings in family clusters.

Churches whose emphasis is outreach have a variety of options. Many use buses to bring children to the church facility, where they are divided into age groups. Often a meal will be provided. Other churches, especially those with already cramped facilities, reach out by holding Bible studies for children wherever children can be found. Playgrounds, empty apartments, and storefronts are utilized to minister to children and their families who might be alienated by the church facility. These Bible studies can often link children with social services they need.

In an effort to encourage Sunday school attendance by making it more convenient, churches are rescheduling classes to meet on Sunday night, Saturday morning, or any other time of the week that will boost participation. Renamed "Bible studies" instead of the traditional "Sunday school," the classes still serve the original purpose.

Realizing they do not have the staff or other resources to meet all the needs of all the children, most churches join forces with one or more parachurch organizations. Clubs like AWANA or Pioneer Ministries, camps, and curriculum publishers are all examples of parachurch groups. Christian schools provide academics integrated with Bible study, but even some public school systems have a "release time" option for a weekly session of religious instruction.

Curriculum designers are responding to improved educational methodology by moving away from the lecture format to learner-centered lessons. Classrooms are equipped with theme-related interest centers and teachers serve more as guides than as authoritarian figures. Large rooms encourage movement from center to center and permit easy transitions from small-to-large group activities. Class size is kept small in order to guarantee the teacher/student ratio required by this approach. Small group projects and Bible studies culminate in a large group worship and sharing time. The traditional interage group opening assembly is replaced with activities that involve learners in the lesson theme as soon as they arrive.

Some publishers offer curriculum that spans several ages with a single lesson. These programs answer the need of small churches who must group children together in classes with wide age differences. Larger churches that choose to build large classes of various ages instead of small age-graded groups will also use this kind of material.

Another approach that is not a model as much as a theory is the church that pays minimal attention to its children's ministry and focuses instead on the education of its adults. The adults are expected to follow the biblical directive and instruct their own sons and daughters.

The best model for children's ministry is one founded on biblical principles, sound educational practice, and a realistic evaluation of the needs of the children. Religious instruction is not limited to a specific time and place, but to the purity of the message and the dedication of those who teach it.

ROBERT J. CHOUN

Bibliography. R. J. Choun and M. L. Lawson (1998), *A Christian Educator's Handbook on Children's Ministry;* I. V. and K. B. Culley, eds., *Harper's Encyclopedia of Religious Education;* R. Habermas and K. Issler (1992), *Teaching for Reconciliation: Foundations and Practice for Christian Educational Ministers;* W. Haystead (1995), *The Twenty-First Century Sunday School;* M. L. Lawson and R. J. Choun (1998), *Christian Education for the 21st Century;* D. Ratcliff, ed. (1988), *Handbook of Preschool Religious Education;* E. L. Towns (1993), *Sunday Schools That Dared to Change.*

Children's Sermon. *See* Storytelling, Children's.

Choices. *See* Decision Making.

Christian Camping International (CCI). Most historians consider the establishment of organized camping in the latter half of the nineteenth century as a North American innovation while giving recognition to the contribution of camping concepts from the camp meetings of the Second Great Awakening at the beginning of that century. Many of these early camp leaders were devout Christians whose zeal not only led them to create their own camping ministries but to help others do likewise.

The American Camping Association (ACA) emerged from a camp directors' meeting in New York in 1910 to address the promotional and professional needs of these early camping pioneers and eventually formed an affinity group of religiously affiliated camps within ACA. As more of the camps in this religiously affiliated group strayed from their Christian doctrinal roots, evangelicals in camping were left without a solid kindred group that could speak for them and address their special concerns.

The need for mutual encouragement, fellowship, and sharing of ideas and resources drew evangelical camp leaders together simultaneously on both coasts in 1950 and in the Midwest and Canada shortly thereafter. The 1950 meeting of thirteen camp/conference center directors at Mount Hermon Conference Center in California precipitated the formation of the Western Conference and Camp Association (WCCA). This organization coexisted with the Association of Bible Conferences and Camps founded in New England in the same year and with other similar regional camping associations for nearly a decade.

In 1960 the Evangelical Camping Association of the Midwest and the Fellowship of Christian Camps in Canada merged with the WCCA. At that point WCCA's journal, *Camp Life*, had a circulation of five thousand and the WCCA had created an insurance program for its members. Annual conferences and a yearbook highlighting innovative ideas in camping plus a full-time executive director, Graham Tinning, allowed WCCA to serve its members well.

To reflect its more extensive geographic constituency, WCCA voted to change its name to Christian Camp and Conference Association (CCA) in 1961. The following year, the Association of Bible Conferences and Camps disbanded and joined CCA to consolidate efforts.

In 1963, CCA officially incorporated as a nonprofit organization as Christian Camp and Conference Association (CCCA) and added the word "international" because its members existed in over a dozen nations. Later, in 1968, CCCA International's name was shortened to Christian Camping International (CCI).

The Japan Christian Camping Association began with an all-Japan Christian camping conference in 1964. In 1966, the officers were formally installed in the newly formed Central American Region of CCCA International. In 1973, the regions were renamed divisions and consisted of Central America-Colombia, Canada, United States, and Japan-Orient. In 1974, the Australian Division was formed at a meeting at Mill Valley Ranch in Victoria. New Zealand had its organizational beginnings in 1976 at Kiwi Ranch in Rotorua.

A turning point in the development of CCI came in 1976 when the International Board of Directors voted to allow the divisions to become autonomous associations operating through an international coordinating committee. However, it was not until the divisional leaders met in Taiwan at the First Asia Pacific Conference of CCI in 1985 that a solid proposal was put forth to fully implement a truly autonomous association model in the form of an alliance. This proposal was approved by the International Board that fall and adopted by the divisional leaders in Vancouver, Canada, in 1986.

Meanwhile, Southern Africa, Japan, and Taiwan were recognized as official divisions in 1979 and Korea in 1982. Brazil was officially declared a division of CCI in 1985. In 1988, both the United Kingdom and the Philippines became official association members of CCI, and in 1997 Russia and Romania both became members.

CCI is now an alliance of national and regional associations organized similarly to the World Evangelical Fellowship of which it is an associate member. Its purpose is to assist Christian camping associations develop effective Christ-centered camps, conferences, and retreat ministries; to help new evangelical Christian camping associations come into existence; and to promote the values of evangelical Christian camping through appropriate channels. Each member association of CCI commits to a common statement of faith and mission statement and agrees to follow the Operations Manual of CCI.

Member, associate member, and emerging national and regional associations meet biennially in different host countries for mutual sharing, training, and fellowship and to develop strategies for meeting its objectives. An elected executive committee is commissioned to coordinate the work of CCI between these biennial meetings. CCI publishes *NetWork*, the journal of national and regional associations of CCI, and has an active partnership program whereby associations are encouraged to work with another association for mutual strengthening.

Currently, thirty-five countries are organized into CCI associations in Japan, Korea, the Philippines, the United States, the United Kingdom, Australia, New Zealand, Southern Africa (region), Brazil, Latin America (region), Romania, Russia, and the Netherlands (associate member). Camps exist in at least thirty other countries and many are members of CCI associations in other neighboring countries.

BUD WILLIAMS

Bibliography. E. Eells (1986), *Eleanor Eells' History of Organized Camping: The First 100 Years;* B. Williams (1997), *Organizational History of Christian Camping International.*

Christian Counseling. Counseling consists of a myriad of issues related to assisting people in successful communication with God and to others. Both the Old and New Testament describe the importance of good counsel.

Counseling is at its basic root the act of assisting another person to work with and through issues that may impair his or her healthy relating to God and others. Although the scientific field of counseling is only a little older than one hundred years, counseling was a part of the early church and its adherents. The Bible is not a book on counseling methods; it does, however, reveal God's truth in how we are to manage our life and relationships. Therefore, Christian counseling is not an option for the Christian educator; it is mandatory. Obviously, there are differences of opinion regarding the integration of theology and psychology. For the purposes of this article, it is assumed such integration is possible and with mutual benefit.

The ability to relate to God and subsequently to his or her fellow human beings in a healthy way is vital for the growing disciple. As Christian educators, we are called upon to encourage others to relate well to God first (as articulated in the Shema passage in Deuteronomy 6:4–9 and by Jesus in the New Testament, Matthew 22:37–39) and then to others. Often in counseling one finds the discouraged person is feeling alienated from God and others; he or she may be struggling to become better connected with others without first relating to God. Often, an individual expresses feelings of alienation from human relationships when the first and greatest need may be a right relationship between him or her and God. Therefore, it is the Christian counselor's first responsibility to encourage the person to be in right relationship to God.

Christian counseling may include pastoral care, pastoral counseling, pastoral psychotherapy, pastoral ministry to couples, singles, and more. Certainly the Christian educator is uniquely placed to provide therapeutic assistance to people. He or she is often given the opportunity to engage in the stressful arena of families, couples, or an individual's dilemma when no other person in the helping fields is permitted to enter. Since the Christian educator is overtly concerned for the spiritual and psychological health of the individual(s) involved in cases, the educator is often invited and expected to explore both arenas: spiritual and psychological.

Although it is important to give advice and to instruct the person as to the steps necessary for getting centered, typical Christian counseling resembles more the art of being attentive and focused than giving advice. Jesus often asked questions of those alienated from God. The person's thoughtful response to Jesus' presence and question(s) led the person into a healing process that a Christian educator would define as the core of counseling.

Jesus was the master counselor: he knew himself. We read in the Bible about how Jesus intentionally assisted the person being challenged to introspectively understand his or her presenting issue(s) before advice or counsel was offered. Once the person attempted to resolve the presenting issue in Jesus' presence, Jesus would freely offer his significant and life-changing insights and advice. Essentially, advice was the outcome of God's gift to the person(s) being able to sort out the difficulty. Consequently, and since Jesus is the only true example of Christian counseling, the more fully one is able to understand himself or herself in a healthy relationship to God, the more healing and wholeness the counseled will experience while working through an effective Christian counselor.

Before being able to be truly focused on another individual, couple, or family, the counselor must understand his or her reactivity towards the client's presenting issues. For example: How does the counselee's issue cause the counselor to remember and re-experience situations and issues from the past? Is the counselor able to be fully attentive and a careful listener with the person seeking counsel? Or, is the counselor reacting and responding to his or her own issues rather than being meticulously focused on the counselee and his or her issues?

Early on, it is vital that a Christian educator learn the referral skills needed in order to adequately care for those individuals God has placed in his or her care. Knowing when to refer is perhaps the greatest skill development in this area. Since a Christian educator may not have acquired training as a therapist, he or she is not prepared to diagnose a person encountering serious mental illnesses. Without meticulous care in this area, many persons may be cared for incorrectly by the best-intended Christian counselor. Learning to refer to those more qualified to handle situations beyond your skill level is a gift of love to the person in need.

Christian counseling is practiced in many areas and by many different people, including chaplains, pastors, and the laity. Christian counseling is greatly needed in our society because of the complexity of today's family and an individual's need for acceptance from God and others. Although there are many definitions of counseling, one thing is certain: the Bible encourages one to seek good counsel and there are those who will be gifted to counsel.

Christian counseling provides an atmosphere in which a person may become "rightly" related to God and others. Acceptance, nonjudgmentalism, and careful listening are just a few of the qualities needed for successful counseling. Along with God's guidance, these are a few of the keys needed for bringing about wholeness into an individual's life. Careful application of the Word of God is an essential component of the Christian counselor's approach. It requires significant knowledge of the Scriptures, a conservative hermeneutic, and an attitude of grace. The Holy Spirit guides the counselor to the appropriate passage of Scripture and helps bring about the application of that passage to the individual's circumstance. A skilled Christian counselor does far more than simply quote a passage of Scripture like a spiritual bandage. Christian counseling involves careful study, artful listening, and companionship with the Great Counselor himself.

DONALD W. WELCH

Bibliography. G. R. Collins (1988), *Christian Counseling;* H. Clinebell (1983), *Basic Types of Pastoral Counseling;* E. H. Friedman (1985), *Generation to Generation;* M. Worden (1994), *Family Therapy Basics.*

See also BIBLICALLY BASED COUNSELING; COUNSELING; NOUTHETIC COUNSELING

Christian Education. To define Christian education is indeed a significant task because of the many different views, opinions, and questions involved. Indeed it has changed substantially over the years of its existence as well. Its definition must therefore take into consideration the historical period involved, for clearly how one would define it at the turn of the century is vastly different from its meaning and purpose today.

Is there a difference between religious education and Christian education? Is Christian education only for Christians? How is Christian education different from "secular" education? What makes Christian education Christian? What is the purpose of Christian education? How are goals and values determined? What is the setting for Christian education? What specifically is Christian education? These questions must be addressed as a definition for Christian education is developed.

Religious Education or Christian Education? For years the term "religious" education was used because it was broad and covered many different perspectives. It was not limited to Protestants or evangelicals, but included Roman Catholics and Jews, as well as other faiths. This grouping is best seen through the Religious Education Association, which counts in its membership people of many different theological persuasions. Evangelical educators, however, were not comfortable with this inclusiveness and wanted to make a definite statement that they were not open to just anything religious, but to that which is taught in the Word of God. This became a theological and biblical distinction. Seminaries had for years offered the Master of Religious Education (MRE) degree, but many evangelical schools changed this to the Master of Arts in Christian Education (MACE). Though some in evangelical churches may refer to religious education as a term when describing the educational ministry, the understanding is that they are referring to a Bible-based ministry of education, and not something that is so inclusive that every kind of religious group is accepted.

At one time there was a distinction between religious education and Christian education that was not tied to the inclusive problem. Christian education was defined as anything that dealt with schools, such as Christian day schools and schools on the mission field. Religious education was anything that involved the local church ministry such as Sunday school, leadership development, and family life education. Though some may still use this distinction, it is no longer universally accepted.

The Scope of Christian Education. For whom is Christian education designed? Taken literally, it means education for Christians, but in reality it is far more than this in scope. It includes preconversion, conversion, and postconversion learning experiences. People come to faith in Christ through the faithful teaching of God's Word and the convicting power of the Holy Spirit. After conversion, the learner moves into the discipleship stage and is to develop and grow as a believer. This is Christian education in action. It is not a one-time learning experience, but a lifetime dedicated to learning more about God and his Word. It includes the application of this truth in the life of the learner so that it can be passed on to others in service and ministry. Christian education is designed to bring people to faith, to develop people in their faith, and to lead people to minister to others through the ministry of the church.

There has been much discussion on the difference between secular education and Christian education. Some state that there is no difference because the same learning theories, methodologies, and approaches to learning prevail. It is true that content is shared in both. It is true that both want to see change, which many will call learning. It is also true that Christian education is more than just teaching about the Bible and that secular subjects can be taught from a Christian perspective. There is a difference, however, because of the role of the Holy Spirit in Christian education. Through the illumination of the Holy Spirit, believers are shown the truth of God's Word, and this is not present in secular education. Both secular and Christian educators may use similar methodologies, but this does not make them the same. Christian education is indeed unique because of the ministry of the Holy Spirit.

Christian education is Christian when teachers and learners are dependent on the work of the Holy Spirit in the learning environment. It is Christian when the purpose and goals are honoring to the Lord and to his kingdom. It is Christian when the curriculum is developed from the teachings of the Word of God and from an understanding of biblical theology. It is Christian when there is an overall understanding and perspective that God is in control and that teachers and learners are sincerely seeking to fulfill God's will and purpose in all things.

The Purpose of Christian Education. The purpose of Christian education is to bring people to a saving faith in Jesus Christ, to train them in a life of discipleship, and to equip them for Christian service in the world today. It is to develop in believers a biblical worldview that will assist them in making significant decisions from a Christian perspective. It is helping believers to "think Christianly" about all areas of life so that they can impact society with the message of the gospel. In essence, it is the development of a Christian worldview.

The purpose, goals, and values of Christian education are derived from a theological foundation that is biblically based. This is quite different from the more inclusive "religious" education approach. Worship, evangelism, discipleship, fellowship, and service are all drawn from the Scriptures and are included in any purpose and value statement for Christian education. Goals are developed from these key functions of the church, and effective Christian education can be measured based upon the accomplishment of these important functions.

The Context of Christian Education. The primary setting for Christian education is the church. Actually, the educational ministry of the church is probably the largest educational endeavor in the world. Considering the youngest child through the oldest adult, the numbers involved in some kind of Christian education ministry through the church are significant. Christian education also takes place outside the walls of the church through Christian schools, Bible studies, camps, parachurch organizations, and other kinds of varied ministries. It is important to note that Christian education is not limited to just one kind of organization or ministry and is found outside the church in many different venues.

We come now to those definitions of Christian education which have come before this one. A helpful beginning is found in *Introduction to Biblical Christian Education* edited by Werner G. Graendorf (1981), which states that Christian education is a Bible-based, Holy Spirit-empowered (Christ-centered), teaching-learning process that seeks to guide individuals at all levels of growth through contemporary teaching means toward knowing and experiencing God's purpose and plan through Christ in every aspect of living, and to equip them for effective ministry, with the overall focus on Christ the Master Educator's example and command to make mature disciples (16). This definition includes the role of the Holy Spirit, the teaching/learning function, God's purpose and plan, the equipping for service, along with the focus on Christ and his command to make disciples. Though assumed, it does not specifically state the role of the church in this process, nor does it make intentional reference to the heritage of our faith.

Robert W. Pazmiño (1997) states his definition in *Foundational Issues in Christian Education* when he asserts that Christian education is the deliberate, systematic, and sustained divine and human effort to share or appropriate the knowledge, values, attitudes, skills, sensitivities, and behaviors that comprise or are consistent with the Christian faith. It fosters the change, renewal, and reformation of persons, groups, and structures by the power of the Holy Spirit to conform to the revealed will of God as expressed in the Scriptures and preeminently in the person of Jesus Christ, as well as any outcomes of that effort. This definition includes a cooperative relationship between the learner and God, a clear description of the cognitive, affective and psychomotor dimensions of learning, change and renewal, the work of the Holy Spirit, and the model of Christ. No specific reference to the church is given, nor is there a strong statement on evangelism, though both could be implied (87).

Beth E. Brown presents the following definition: Christian education is the interaction with truth and its implications for life under the guidance and power of the Holy Spirit, so as to affect change in the life of the learner—this change being conformity to the image of Christ. Included here, we find the elements of the interaction of truth with application to life working with the Holy Spirit. Change is the goal and the change is defined as conformity to the image of Christ. The church, the heritage of our faith, and evangelism are implied, but not specifically stated.

All of these definitions include the significant basics that evangelicals will consider important such as: Bible-based, theologically sound, Holy Spirit-empowered, the elements of teaching/learning/growth/equipping, change, the church, evangelism, and service. Christian education, then, is more than merely teaching Christians. It is all of the above and much more.

DENNIS E. WILLIAMS

Bibliography. W. G. Graendorf (1981), *Introduction to Biblical Christian Education;* R. W. Pazmiño (1997), *Foundational Issues in Christian Education.*

Christian Educator. *See* Clergy as Educators.

Christian Endeavor International. Christian Endeavor International can trace its roots to the nineteenth century. On February 2, 1881, Reverend Francis Clark, pastor of Williston Congregational Church in Portland, Maine, proposed the idea of a Christian Endeavor society. He wanted to challenge young people who had recently made commitments to Christ to develop a Christian lifestyle that included daily Bible reading and prayer, as well as Christian service.

Clark's magazine article describing the program for their denominational magazine was reprinted by other publications and brought many requests for information. Thus the Christian Endeavor movement was launched.

Conventions, which brought together society members, became an important aspect of the ministry. At the convention in 1887, Clark was elected president of the United Society. During this convention, at his suggestion, *For Christ and the Church* was adopted as the Christian Endeavor motto.

Biannual conventions are still a part of the ministry, now known as Christian Endeavor International in light of its worldwide impact.

Program and Principles. While the program in each individual church is very flexible, the basic principles remain the same as those articulated by Clark in 1900. They are: (1) Confession of Christ, (2) Service for Christ, (3) Fellowship with Christ's People, and (4) Loyalty to Christ's Church.

The Christian Endeavor program operates within the local church according to the church's own regulations. Groups select their own officers and committee chairs, under the guidance of the adult sponsors. Officers have standard job descriptions, and committees operate within the framework of the committee system established by Clark.

The five basic committees are:

Devotional: Responsible for the preparation, direction, and presentation of the society's regular devotional or discussion meeting, usually held on Sunday evenings.

Lookout: On the lookout for new members and for the faithfulness of those already in the society. They keep attendance and follow up absentees.

Missionary: Arranges for regular missionary meetings, interests members in missionaries and their work, aids the cause of home and foreign missions.

Recreation: Promotes friendliness, fun, and fellowship at the social functions of the society.

Church Activity: Works in cooperation with the pastor and church leaders to find and complete projects which benefit the church.

Christian Endeavor offers graded materials as well as programming assistance. It is open to any church that desires to use the program. Christian Endeavor International, 1221 East Broad Street, P.O. Box 2106, Columbus, OH 43216–2106, (614) 258–3947.

SARA ANNE ROBERTSON

Christian Formation. Process and product of motivating, nurturing, and internalizing values, priorities, perspectives, and responses that are from God. It asks the question, "How are Christians formed?"

Components include teaching and preaching the Word of God, stimulating, and guiding to understanding and integration of truth into life. Formation involves motivation—becoming actively involved in desiring growth, wanting to become what God has designed us to be. It includes information—knowing who God is and what God wants, knowing who I am and how I grow. It involves will—deliberate commitment to respond to truth in life once known. Under the guidance of the Spirit, learning that integrates all three of the above leads to a transformation of the person into increased likeness to Christ.

Scripture gives evidence that Jesus and the biblical writers expected that persons would live differently as a result of knowing God and internalizing his truth. Both being and doing were to be transformed. While potentially this transformation is already a reality to the one who is "in Christ," the Scriptures also indicate that there is a process of putting off and putting on, of increasing in intensity of likeness toward fulfilling a predetermined design. The Spirit is the Instrument of this change. "We, who with unveiled faces all reflect the Lord's glory, are being transformed into his likeness with ever-increasing glory, which comes from the Lord, who is the Spirit" (2 Cor. 3:18).

There is also indication that the person, upon encountering God, has responsibility in this wondrous formational journey. "Do not conform any longer to the pattern of this world, but be transformed by the renewing of your mind" (Rom. 12:2). And important especially for Christian educators is the fact that the human instrument plays a formational role in this creating of another in

Christ. "My dear children, for whom I am again in the pains of childbirth until Christ is formed in you . . ." (Gal. 4:19). The apostle Paul was co-laborer with the Spirit of God in helping to bring about formation in the lives of the Galatians.

As Christian educators we support this process which moves a person beyond information and beyond desire into the realm of life-changing transformation.

Research makes us aware that such formation occurs in a spontaneous way in life. God utilizes our experiences to move us in the direction of fulfilling his design. Often these formational "classrooms" are disruptive crises, moments we cannot control. Out of them come new perspectives, new priorities, new persons. At other times, the unavoidable processes of life (getting older), become formation-linked experiences. A third formational instrument is moments of grace in our lives, the goodness we cannot explain. The Spirit often utilizes these occasions to create our Christian formation.

Is there also a deliberate fostering of formation? Can Christian educators learn to provide a setting, work with the Spirit to cultivate a learning situation that may be conducive to the Spirit's moving persons toward fulfillment of God's plan for their participation in the likeness of his Son? Christian formation answers yes. Just as the practice of the disciplines places us in a position for God to work in us, so Christian formation focuses on God and in doing whatever will foster his positioning learners' movement into formative moments of life change. Such servant posturing in teaching requires continual attentiveness to what God wants, allows learners to become actively involved in processing with God, and leads toward inevitable response to God on the part of the learner. The teacher becomes a forerunner, a preparer of the way, a spiritual connector assisting learners to recognize God in their lives and experiences, an explainer of truth while helping students experience it, a shadow who fosters increasing awareness of God's major role in any learning encounter.

Christian formation is characterized by these factors:

a. There is constant awareness of moving toward the goal of maturing and maturity. Information is evaluated by "How does this enable the learner to move toward maturity in Christ?" Learner situations are assessed by "What is needed to experience God's truth in this situation?" Methodology is chosen on the basis of "What process will best enable this person to move toward maturity?" Experiences are part of the maturity process through such queries as, "What does this experience contribute toward maturing in godliness? How can this learning experience be best structured to lead to a step of maturation?" "Christ being formed in them" is the filter by which all teaching, nurturing, and information processing is examined.

b. The whole person is included. Since persons are integrated wholes and since formation requires a holistic response, Christian formation takes into consideration the total person and seeks to tap into all parts of the whole. It is never enough just to stimulate the mind. The heart and will must be challenged also. A conceptual response is never sufficient—tests, projects, and evaluations must call for life responses that integrate them all.

c. Formation always involves openness to God and his Word. That Word is never seen as just knowledge to be acquired but as reality to be lived. It is always framed in "believing this, how then shall we live?" Knowing God is personal, relational, and priority. He is the Source and End of all learning for formation. Everything is evaluated or enhanced by him. There is no source of learning where he is not found.

d. Formation is developmental, building on previous concepts and moving toward a goal—that of maturity in Christ. The formational stages of human development may affect the process of spiritual formation and should be factored in by the Christian educator. However, the Creator is greater than those delineated stages and is not limited by them.

e. Formational learning requires the learner to be actively involved in interacting with the truth on a personal basis. The teacher's role is conditioned by this factor, giving away responsibility for learning and opportunity for personal processing whenever possible. This will mean diminishing of the teacher role as the learner grasps and begins to apply truth. It will affect the choice of methodology to gain maximum learner involvement. Formation empowers the learner to learn.

f. Christian formation is always related to life. This means it will begin and end in life perceptions and experiences as shaped by God for knowing him and for a person's growth in him. This factor ensures that truth and life will always be teamed together in a formational learning experience.

g. Christian community plays a powerful role in formation. It is in community that the learner discovers needed arenas of growth and in community that the learner receives insight, support, and opportunity to express his or her uniqueness as a facet of the person of Christ to the group.

h. The Spirit of God is the primary force in moving persons toward maturity and in forming Christ in them. Christian formation follows his lead. The human teacher serves as "teaching assistant," always acknowledging the supremacy of the master Teacher in bringing about God's plan.

JULIE GORMAN

Bibliography. P. Downs (1994), *Teaching for Spiritual Growth;* L. LeBar (1998), *Education That Is Christian;* R. Mulholland (1985), *Shaped by the Word;* P. Palmer (1993), *To Know as We Are Known;* L. O. Richards (1975), *A Theology of Christian Education.*

Christian Humanism. Humanism is a term often used by evangelical Christians, almost always in a pejorative mood—even more so when refined as secular humanism. From a biblical perspective, the origins of secular humanism go back to the garden of Eden and the creature's rebellion against the Creator. In the history of education, by the fifth century B.C. , a brand of philosophy had arisen in Greece to oppose belief in the gods. Its motto was the straightforward assertion by Protagoras, "Man is the measure of all things."

As commonly understood, therefore, modern secular humanism refers to a human-centered and pervasive contempt for any notion of a supernatural, transcendent deity to whom the human race, as created beings, must be accountable. Secular humanism offers instead a material world, limited by time and space, in which only the here-and-now matters and in which human beings are the final arbiters of whatever is just and good.

Given such assumptions regarding humanism and, in particular, secular humanism, some evangelicals will be surprised to find in this dictionary an entry for *Christian humanism.* Surely it is an oxymoron! Yet far from being a contradiction in terms, Christian humanism is a historic designation dating at least to the period of the Renaissance and the Reformation that followed. In fact, enlightened students of history will recognize that, from the time of Paul of Tarsus and his protégé Timothy, educated church fathers and their successors throughout the centuries exemplified the best qualities of Christian humanism.

But what are those qualities that comprise Christian humanism? And what does Christian humanism represent today? Many believers will be surprised to discover that much of what we have come to value in modern discipleship training and Sunday school programs has its roots in the early tenets of Christian humanism. In essence, it is placing a high value on the individual (human) created by God in his image with worth and value.

Accepting that Jesus Christ is Truth, Christians believe that discerning truth from error is an essential consequence of faith. To do so requires a reasoning mind. Within the early church, educated persons had been taught the Greco-Roman curriculum known as the "studia humanitatis" or study of the humanities: languages, literature, the fine arts, history, philosophy, and theology, with very little emphasis on science or mathematics. In time, this course of study became known as

"the liberal arts" because of its liberating of the mind from the shackles of ignorance.

Church fathers recognized "the unity of all truth under God" (Gaebelein 1954). In the middle of the second century, Justin Martyr told the Roman senate that "whatever has been uttered aright by any man in any place belongs to us Christians." Two and a half centuries later, Augustine of Hippo said, "Every good and true Christian must recognize that wherever he may find truth, it is his Lord's."

Throughout the Dark Ages and Middle Ages, Christian scholars maintained the hope of spiritual and intellectual freedom to think, to reason, to ask difficult questions, to argue, to disagree. But as the Roman Church assumed absolute political power across Europe, some aspects of intellectual freedom were stifled; opportunities for formal schooling were restricted. Furthermore, the privations of life in medieval Europe were so austere that the only hope seemed to be "the life everlasting." This world, this life, had almost nothing to commend it.

But by the beginning of the 1300s, artists had taken up the cause of freedom to express themselves in new forms and styles. Painters began depicting religious scenes using peasant figures familiar in their own villages; poets found their themes among the common nuances of life; musicians wrote and sang their songs about human aspirations. The church's stranglehold on daily existence could be broken, if only by the power of human imagination to project a meaning enhanced by faith.

The arrival of the Renaissance, marked by rediscovery of classical languages and literature, Gutenberg's invention of movable type, and a new focus on the Scriptures impelled theologians like Martin Luther and John Calvin toward Reformation. They and others like them brought to their ecclesiastical reform the ideas of the Renaissance, including the radical notion that the incarnation meant God's special participation in and ratifying of the human experience. If Jesus of Nazareth—the Christ of God—lived and loved and suffered and died like an ordinary human being, then what better proof could God offer to affirm the special nature of human life?

This axiom became known again as humanism and was affirmed by all the Reformers, as well as by Erasmus who remained a Roman Catholic. But in recognition of the commitment of these godly persons, historians have come to speak of them as Christian humanists; we might even prefer to call them biblical humanists. Among their greatest contributions was the emphasis upon schooling for literacy among the masses.

Today's biblical humanists will be marked by a similar commitment to the authority of Scripture and to the historic creeds; but they will also demonstrate a reasonable faith, a profound appreciation for all that can be learned and known about nature and human nature; an earnest desire to respect and enhance the uniqueness and distinctives of every human culture, understanding that God is no respecter of persons and that, as the poet Gerard Manley Hopkins wrote, "Christ plays in ten thousand places, / Lovely in limbs, and lovely in eyes not his / To the Father through the features of men's faces."

D. BRUCE LOCKERBIE

Bibliography. M. J. Anthony, *Christian Education Journal*, 12, no. 1 (1991): 79–88; J. Baillie (1945), *What Is Christian Civilization?*; F. E. Gaebelein (1954), *The Pattern of God's Truth*; H. E. Harbison (1956), *The Christian Scholar in the Age of the Reformation*; W. A. Hoffecker (1986), *Building a Christian World View*; D. B. Lockerbie (1989), *Thinking and Acting Like a Christian*; idem (1994), *A Passion for Learning: A History of Christian Thought on Education*; R. Schwoebel, ed. (1971), *Renaissance Men and Ideas*; J. M. Shaw et al. (1982), *Readings in Christian Humanism*.

Christianity. We so commonly use the word "Christian" that it will come as a surprise to most people that the term itself only appears three times in the New Testament: Acts 11:26, where Luke tells us that the disciples were first called Christians in Antioch; Acts 26:28; and 1 Peter 4:16. The word "Christianity" does not occur in the Bible but was first used by Ignatius in *Ad Magnes* 10. Emmet Russell says about the term, "The name was made by Christians to designate all that which Jesus Christ brought to them of faith, life, and salvation. Its character is summed up in the words of Jesus, 'I am the way, the truth, and the life: no man cometh unto the Father but by me' (John 14:6) . . . OT and NT together form the authoritative revelation of what Christianity is" (Tenney, 1963, 162).

Although the name may have first been applied to believers in Antioch about A.D. 40, the roots of Christianity remain deeply buried in the soil of the incarnation. The Roman Empire was barely two generations old at Jesus' birth (ca. 4 B.C.). The new faith inherited its strong monotheism as well as its emphasis on moral and ethical standards from Old Testament Judaism, the soil around its roots. Its uniqueness however, is described even by secular historians.

"But, although rooted in Judaism, Christianity was original, not only in the belief that Christ was the long-awaited Messiah, the savior of mankind through whose redeeming sacrifice the faithful might obtain eternal salvation, but also in the quality of its ethical teaching, a quality perhaps best represented by Christ's Sermon on the Mount" (Ferguson, 1969, 84).

We find ample evidence in the Book of Acts that the early Christians understood themselves as a part of Judaism and were so accepted by Roman authorities on several occasions. At first,

Christianity spread most rapidly among underprivileged peoples, including slaves (Col. 3). When persecution by the empire began in earnest, Christians held their meetings in secrecy. Ferguson and Bruun (1969) show an amazing grasp of foundational Christian theology. "This faith in a personal Savior, whom his first disciples had known in the flesh and whose words they reported, carried with it a definiteness of conviction in the reality of salvation, the expiation of sin, and of the immortality of the soul (all questions that obsessed the mind of the ancient world) far greater than was possible for the mythological pagan or mystery cults. At the same time, Christianity gave men hope for the future, not only for themselves as individuals, but for the world" (85).

The term "Christian," coined in Antioch, gained popularity among the people to whom it was applied and became familiar throughout the empire during the time of Nero (ca. A.D. 64). Hardman (1974) says, "As the church adopted the name, deeper meanings began to be seen in it. The Greek word *christos* (anointed) suggested the more familiar term *chrestos* (gracious, good). Such terms witnessed to the dignity of the church's Founder and Lord, 'the Anointed One,' and Peter (1 Peter 2:3) may be making a play on the word 'Christ' when he writes, 'Now that you have tasted that the Lord is good'" (220).

Martin Marty (1959) frequently describes Christianity as an historical religion. Nevertheless, some question whether Christianity's truth claims are based on historical events such as the death of Jesus, his resurrection, and the founding of the early church. Not all essentials of Christian faith are subject to verification through historical inquiry and one can always make a sharp line of demarcation between secular history *(Weltgeschichte)* and salvation history *(Heilsgeschichte)*. Marsden (1975) emphasizes the cruciality of historical perspective. He writes, "The historical documents collected in the Bible provide the record of God's acting in history, and it is in the context of those acts, centering in the death and resurrection of Christ, that we must view ourselves and our world. The prominence of historical events as the basis of our faith suggests that in the Christian world view, the past has profound significance. Christians who accept biblical revelation as an authoritative record of what God has done definitely to care for man's condition cannot absolutize either the prevailing standards of the present (as tends to be done in modern Western thought) or abstract absolutes (as was the tendency in Greek thought). One of the motifs in the philosophy of our civilization (among both moderns and Greeks) has been to regard the past as either relative or of little meaning. The Christian, on the other hand, must view himself as participating in an on-going active relationship between God and man in which the revelation of God's acts and will in the past provides continuing norms for creative responses to the present" (33).

By A.D. 500, 22 percent of the world's people were believers in Jesus Christ, but by A.D. 1500 the figure had fallen to 19 percent. In the first four-fifths of this century, the number of Christians in the world increased from 558 million to 1.433 billion—and those statistics were written before the fall of the Berlin Wall and the end of the Cold War. *The World Christian Encyclopedia* tells us, "Christianity has surged ahead in the world's less-developed countries from 83 million in 1900 to 643 million by 1980. During the twentieth century, in fact, Christianity has become the most extensive and universal religion in history. There are today Christians and organized Christian churches in every inhabited country on earth. The church is therefore now, for the first time in history, ecumenical in the literal meaning of the word: Its boundaries are co-extensive with the oikumene, the whole inhabited world" (Barrett, 1982, 3).

Above all historical, sociological, and literary applications, Christianity focuses primarily on a personal relationship with Jesus Christ. In the words of Justin Martyr, "Our teacher of these things is Jesus Christ, who also was born for this purpose, was crucified under Pontius Pilate, procurator of Judea, in the times of Tiberius Caesar; and that we reasonably worship Him, having learned that He is the Son of the true God, Himself" (Lockerbie, 1994, 66).

KENNETH O. GANGEL

Bibliography. D. B. Barrett, ed. (1982), *The World Christian Encyclopedia*; J. D. Douglas, ed. (1974), *The New International Dictionary of the Christian Church*; W. K. Ferguson and G. Bruun (1969), *A Survey of European Civilization*; D. B. Lockerbie (1994), *A Passion for Learning*; G. Marsden and F. Roberts (1975), *A Christian View of History*; M. E. Marty (1959), *A Short History of Christianity*; M. C. Tenney, ed. (1963), *Zondervan Pictorial Bible Dictionary*.

See also EARLY CHURCH EDUCATION

Christian Nurture. Interpersonal sharing among Christians characterized by love, spiritual nourishment, and spiritual direction that results in the edification of the Christian church. Nurture, by its very nature, requires a vital relationship and interaction among persons. Christian nurture is an expression of pastoral care that is a responsibility of all followers of Jesus Christ who seek to make disciples of other persons, thus fulfilling the commission of Matthew 28:18–20. The making of disciples often begins in one's family (Deut. 6:4–9, 20–25; Prov. 22:6; Eph. 6:4).

Biblical use of the term is related to the Greek concept of *paideia* that in its verb form refers to the act of nursing, suckling, and nourishing persons from the very beginning of life. Nurture as a noun refers to the training, upbringing, instruction, and discipline of persons for a righteous life that fulfills God's purposes and the deepest longings of the human heart for a relationship with the Holy. Christian nurture is reflective of God's providential care for persons which begins at procreation (Ps. 139:13–16), but also extends across the life span and even to life after death. A perennial spiritual concern for persons in the New Testament is how to foster the formation and growth of their faith as disciples of Jesus the Christ. Persons have worth and dignity as God's creatures, created in God's image, who are therefore deserving of care and nurture at every age and stage of life (John 21:15–17).

The description of Jesus' growth as a person in Luke 2:52 provides a pattern for Christian nurture: "Jesus kept increasing in wisdom and stature, and in favor with God and men." Jesus was nurtured in a Jewish family with parents who honored God and God's will for their lives. He grew up in the town of Nazareth that included a synagogue and likely a school where he learned the Scriptures, the First or Old Testament. His relationship with his community and with his peers and siblings influenced his formation as a person. The formal, nonformal, and informal educational experiences of Jesus nurtured his life and faith so that he grew in wisdom and stature. His growth in favor with God and other persons required nurture in the spiritual and social dimensions of life. A pattern for nurture emerges that suggests the need to foster relationships with family members, teachers, peers, community acquaintances, religious leaders, strangers who may venture into one's town, and above all, God as Abba (Mark 14:36; Rom. 8:15; Gal. 4:4–7).

The commitment to the nurture of persons follows from a Christian understanding of persons, from a theological anthropology that affirms the worth and dignity of individual persons and their value to God and humanity. Persons are viewed as having bodies, minds, and spirits or souls that are considered essential in their nurture and care. The nurture of persons therefore attends to the various physical, intellectual, emotional, psychological, ethical, and spiritual dimensions of persons. Persons as created are also historical, cultural, political, and social beings. Therefore the nurture of persons involves seeing them in relation to wider networks of corporate life. Christian nurture attends to the corporate responsibilities of persons and aspects of life they hold in common with others and the entire creation. Persons struggle with the realities of sin and being sinned against, and nurture includes the ministries of forgiveness, reconciliation, healing, and transformation as the Holy Spirit works with persons. Persons have intuition and aspects of character, personality, imagination, and values that transcend any analytical categories that have been used to describe them. Christian nurture therefore attends to the individuality and uniqueness of persons.

Christians in the twentieth century have drawn upon the discipline of psychology in formulating strategies for the nurture of persons. Various theorists have tapped into the distinct dimensions of the development of persons in proposing what should be emphasized in nurture. These dimensions have included cognitive, affective, psychosocial, moral, sociocontextual, cultural, and faith development. The challenge in drawing upon such sources is to discern the possible integration or interface with a Christian life view of persons. For example, if cognitive development is a priority, then persons primarily need intellectual nourishment and challenge to grow in their faith understanding. In a similar fashion, if affective development is a priority, then persons primarily need emotional support and care to mature in their spiritual life.

For the contemporary field of Christian education, one key historical work that considered the place of nurture was Horace Bushnell's book *Christian Nurture*, which was originally written in 1847 and published in its final form in 1861. Bushnell's proposition in this work was that "the child is to grow up a Christian, and never know himself as being otherwise" (Bushnell, 1979, 10). Bushnell grappled with the scriptural injunction of Ephesians 6:4, where parents are commanded to bring up children in the nurture or "discipline and instruction of the Lord." He was reacting against extreme forms of Calvinist theology in which revivalists taught that a young child could not possibly be a Christian given the need for a radical conversion later in life. Bushnell saw conversion more as a process with parents playing a crucial role in the formation of Christian character and virtue from the time of birth and even prior to birth through their own spiritual preparation. Bushnell's challenge was for the church to support parents in their calling to nurture faith so that faith and obedience to God was a natural outcome of their training. Theological understandings of the nature of conversion and human cooperation with the work of the Holy Spirit in faith development are issues posed by Bushnell's work. His work also raises the matter of who is nurturing the nurturers in a faith community. An additional question with contemporary application is: How do Christians nurture in a societal situation that does not emphasize the care of children and youth?

Christians need to ask themselves what is Christian about Christian nurture. At its basic level Christian nurture strives to foster in persons a faith in Jesus Christ as Lord and Savior and a lifelong following of him as a disciple. Such a commitment includes a vital relationship with the Christian church and a willingness to live in accordance with the teachings of Jesus as revealed in the Scriptures. A variety of educational structures can become vehicles for this nurture and include the family, the church, the Sunday school, parachurch ministries such as camps and voluntary associations, the Christian or parochial school, and religious media, among others. In the effort to nurture persons within these structures, the modeling of a Christian lifestyle is crucial, as well as the affirmation of persons as they strive to live in ways that are faithful and true to the gospel.

Nurture assumes a growth metaphor for the Christian faith, with persons being in the nursery of faith formation throughout their lives. A concern for their spiritual growth and maturation recognizes the place of discipline and freedom if persons are eventually to assume their own responsibilities for the processes of sanctification and edification as God works within them (Phil. 2:12–13). The Christian nurture of persons assumes a source of nourishment which is found in God. To sustain the Christian life and spiritual growth, persons need to daily abide in Jesus Christ (John 15:4) and to be filled with the Holy Spirit (Eph. 5:18).

A question related to nurture is the readiness of persons to digest the nourishment that is offered and shared with them. Hebrews 5:11–6:3 points up the need for discernment in the nurture that is offered depending upon the maturity of the recipients. Other passages of Scripture describe various levels of maturity (1 Cor. 2:6–3:4; 9:19–23; Titus 2:1–15; 1 Peter 5:1–7) that need to be assessed and considered in any effort to nurture others. Christian nurturers are called to have discernment in adjusting their efforts to the spiritual, social, cultural, economic, and political characteristics of persons with whom they are ministering. Nurture requires the effort to relate to persons at appropriate levels of their understanding and readiness.

ROBERT W. PAZMIÑO

Bibliography. J. L. Adams (1976), *On Being Human Religiously*; H. Bushnell (1979), *Christian Nurture*; M. E. Drushal (1991), *On Tablets of Human Hearts: Christian Education with Children*; A. J. Heschel (1959), *Between God and Man: An Interpretation of Judaism*; C. E. Nelson (1971), *Where Faith Begins*; idem (1989), *How Faith Matures*; L. O. Richards (1975), *A Theology of Christian Education*; L. L. Steele (1990), *On the Way: A Practical Theology of Christian Formation*; J. H. Westerhoff III (1980), *Bringing Up Children in the Christian Faith*; J. C. Wilhoit and J. M. Dettoni, eds. (1995), *Nurture That Is Christian: Developmental Perspectives on Christian Education*.

Christian Service Brigade. An energetic and visionary Wheaton College sophomore began a weekly club meeting for his restless Sunday school class of sixth-grade boys which featured games, Bible study, crafts, and a story. Thus in Glen Ellyn, Illinois, in 1937 Joseph W. Coughlin formed the Christian Service Squad, which launched the interchurch movement officially established as Christian Service Brigade in 1940. A parallel girls' program, eventually to be called Pioneer Girls, took root among Wheaton College women and became a partner in Coughlin's mission. By 1987 CSB recognized fifty years of "winning and training boys for Christ" in churches throughout the United States and Canada, with overtones stretching around the world.

As readily as he attracted boys, Coughlin drew adults around him who shared his vision for evangelism and discipleship. Businessman Herbert Taylor helped underwrite expenses through his Christian Workers Foundation in the early 1940s. He was influential in establishing a board of directors that included V. Raymond Edman, P. Kenneth Gieser, and Robert C. Van Kampen. Robert A. Walker, the first general secretary, promptly recruited Kenneth N. Hansen as his successor (1943–47). Werner C. Graendorf provided leadership until 1955 when Joseph B. Bubar was appointed general director, beginning a period of major expansion which extended into the mid 1970s. The post–World War II expansion was fueled by the return of servicemen, the subsequent growth of families, and the increasing number of suburban churches.

The CSB program curriculum began with an eight-page handbook for boys in 1939. It developed through eleven editions by 1998, with five separate age levels serving youth from four to eighteen years of age. The first adult leaders' handbook issued in 1942 reached its fifth edition by 1987 (7th printing, 1998). Supplementary program resources for leaders have been issued annually since 1945. The Brigade motto, "Bright and Keen for Christ," was an early program feature represented by a shield emblem which still identifies CSB after sixty years.

C. Samuel Gray became executive director in 1970 and remained as president until 1991. A member of Coughlin's teenage Frontiersmen team in the mid–1940s, Gray joined the CSB staff in 1954 and prepared popular editions of the boys' achievement manuals in the late 1950s. He inherited a serious financial deficit and a staff that was divided over the organization's priorities for the future.

As the era of rapid growth slowed, the Brigade movement encountered a series of internal and external challenges. During the late 1960s the ferment of a changing youth culture and Vietnam War unrest created dissatisfaction with traditional programs. The increase of professional youth staff in evangelical churches brought an emphasis on coeducational activities that dampened interest in same-gender programs for teens. The youth population itself was shrinking by the late 1970s as the baby boom generation passed into adulthood, and competition increased among youth-serving organizations as each vied for a larger share of the market.

Despite these obstacles, CSB proved as resilient as it was in its earliest years. The addition of a father-son program for primary-age boys set the stage for a Christian fathering thrust in the 1980s. The staff also experimented with a wide range of new program ideas based on Brigade's in-depth discipleship approach. Regional summer camping activity, with roots in the pioneering work of Joseph Coughlin in the mid–1940s, continues to flourish fifty years later.

Anticipating retirement in the 1990s, Gray initiated a leadership transition and Kenneth F. Keeler became president in 1991. David E. Hall succeeded him in 1996. Under Hall's leadership CSB broadened its appeal to churches with a gender-specific format for girls to fill a gap created when Pioneer Girls reorganized as Pioneer Clubs in the 1980s and emphasized coed programs for children.

The pattern of CSB in Canada paralleled that in the United States after the first groups were formed in the early 1940s. By 1972 CSB in Canada realized autonomy under a license agreement with the U.S. organization. CSB of Canada was reorganized in 1997 and continues to have close ties with its parent in the United States.

The impact of Christian Service Brigade can be measured by the thousands of boys who professed faith in Christ around a campfire or in a church basement. Beyond them are thousands of Christian men active in the church today who are better husbands and fathers because of the influence of a concerned Christian man when they were boys.

The organization itself is known as an outstanding form of evangelical boys' work that achieved a remarkable balance of spiritual depth, leadership growth, and physical challenge. It has always had progressive ideas and unique personalities. It should be remembered as a testimony to the diversity of God's people who, in spite of great differences, have been able to work together to advance Christ's kingdom.

C. SAMUEL GRAY

Bibliography. P. H. Heidebrecht (1987), *The Brigade Trail: Fifty Years of Building Men to Serve Christ.* P. H. Heidebrecht, ed. (1987), *Building Men: Serving Christ among Boys.*

Christian Worldview. Worldview refers to foundational beliefs concerning the nature and purpose of reality, often shared by persons within a culture, that either constitute or determine the way that human experience is interpreted. Occasionally, the German term *Weltanschauung* is used in place of its English equivalent.

A Christian worldview includes the following:

God exists, and he is the Creator and Sustainer of the physical universe,

God has revealed himself and objective truth in the Scriptures,

God is the origin of life, creating man and woman with personality likeness to himself,

God's purposes have been and are being fulfilled in history, even through suffering and in the presence of evil, and

God will judge every person with the result that, by his grace and through faith in him, some will inherit eternal life.

Agnosticism, a prevalent non-Christian worldview, claims that modern people cannot know if God exists. In this personal perspective, truth is relative, the origins of the universe and life are impersonal, history and the suffering it contains has no purpose, and the future is uncertain. Rather than an eternal, personal, and moral God, agnosticism offers a temporal, materialistic, and secular existence.

The concept of worldview is often indistinguishable from metaphysics, the branch of philosophy dealing with the nature of reality (ontology), the origin and structure of the universe (cosmology), and the purpose or ultimate causes of existence (teleology). A worldview emerges from an epistemological commitment to a body of truth. A worldview then constitutes a frame of reference out of which flows axiology—ethical judgment about what ought to be done.

When considering worldviews, as with the concept of personality, there is temptation to artificially separate what is actually one thing. Just as intellect, emotion, and will are aspects of unified human personalities, epistemology, metaphysics, and axiology are aspects of personal worldviews—cohesive contexts in which conscious or unconscious beliefs induce emotional states and ordain behavior.

Consequently, in order to promote the development of the "whole person," educators must utilize cognitive, affective, and behavioral objectives through instruction, motivation, and training. What students know, feel, and do should be integrated in a holistic process that permits God's truth to inform personal values and establish moral behavior.

Unified worldviews prepare learners to judge truth claims, to assign proper significance to both God's creation and the experiences of life, and to do what is right. Worldviews based upon the revelation of God and his truth promote godly living and strong personal relationships with God, his people, and all humankind.

Crucial elements of a Christian worldview are found in the Old and New Testaments. Moses commanded Israel to not only listen to the Law, but to do it (Deut. 6:1–3). The reason for attending to the Law was its source in a personal God (v. 5) who acted in history (vv. 12, 20–23) and who promises blessing for the obedient (vv. 6–9, 24–25).

Jesus repeated these words, declaring that loving God with all of one's heart and soul and mind is the great and foremost commandment (Matt. 22:37–38). He indicated that this metaphysical perspective, combined with love, its relational equivalent, are the two commandments on which the whole Law and the Prophets depend (vv. 39–40).

In a similar way, after rehearsing the historical basis for the Christian faith (1 Cor. 15:1–8), Paul interpreted his existence and the purpose of life in accord with a God-centered worldview (vv. 10–11). Finally, encouraging growth from childish things to maturity, Paul focused singular attention upon the theological virtues of faith, hope, and love—the cognitive, affective, and conative components of a thoroughly Christian worldview.

DANIEL C. STEVENS

Bibliography. R. H. Nash (1992), *Worldviews in Conflict;* J. W. Sire (1997), *The Universe Next Door: A Basic Worldview Catalog.*

Christian Youth Education. *See* Bible Teaching for Youth.

Chunking. Information processing theory identifies learning as an interaction between environmental stimuli and the learner. In teaching the Bible, the learner registers some aspect of biblical truth through at least one of the five senses and proceeds to move that sensory input from the barely conscious, sensory register stage of memory through short-term memory and finally into long-term storage. Chunking is a memory-enhancing process that operates at the short-term stage of the information processing cycle.

Short-term or working memory acts as the clearinghouse or gatekeeper for material moving from our sensory awareness into more permanent storage locations. It consists of information a person is currently conscious about, lasts approximately twenty seconds, and can hold about seven unrelated items of information at any given point in time. Although the goal of Bible teaching is to move information into the permanent storage cell of long-term memory, material must first be organized and retained through rehearsal in the short-term memory bank. The limited storage capacity of short-term memory can be enhanced by "chunking" material into meaningful units of smaller and easier to manage pieces of information.

Chunking is the process of grouping related items of information together. Instead of memorizing the books of the Bible as 66 independent titles, chunk like books together while learning the names: the books of the Law, major prophets, minor prophets, the Gospels, etc. Although short-term memory capacity attends only to about seven discrete items of information, when like concepts are grouped together, each grouping or chunk becomes one item thus expanding the individual capacity to incorporate multiple pieces of information.

The chunking principle encourages teachers to organize their material into related units of information. Teachers should look for similarities and themes running through topical studies and Bible passages. It is especially important to present difficult material in more manageable, yet related, chunks which learners can identify, rehearse, and encode for easier transfer into long-term memory.

SHELLY CUNNINGHAM

Bibliography. K. Issler and R. Habermas (1994), *How We Learn: A Christian Teacher's Guide to Educational Psychology;* W. R. Yount (1996), *Created to Learn.*

Church. When an individual gives his or her life to Christ, a new relationship is born as that person is enfolded spiritually into the family of God. The bond is described by Jesus as that of being like a bride coming into relationship with her husband. An understanding of love and shared intimacy is gained that had been unknown before the bonding of that relationship, one to another. The church of Christ is not an organization, but rather a description of the living relationship between the risen and ascended Christ and those who have turned their hearts over to him. It has often been said that the church is not so much an organization as it is an organism.

That special relationship is intimately linked to the new birth found in Christ, which results in a person's becoming a part of the church. In our society, the church is often confused with the facility in which members of the church gather to worship. Rather when a person becomes a Christian, he or she is engrafted into a relationship with other believers as brothers and sisters in Christ. Individually, they are members of the church, and corporately they form the church universal. The word *church* means "those called out."

In the Book of Exodus, God called on Moses, the adopted son of Pharaoh's daughter, to travel back into Egypt to call his people, the nation of Israel, out of the bondage of slavery. In the Gospels, God sent his own son, Jesus Christ, to call his people out of the bondage of sin. The price was paid with Jesus' death on the cross. It was out of this act of love that the church was born. Empowered by the Holy Spirit, the church is the people of God living out the work of and teachings of Jesus Christ on a daily basis (Acts 2:42–47).

An understanding of the church universal is best gained when traveling and visiting a worship service. The bond of welcome and belonging that often greets the visitor is an experiential acknowledgment of the commonality which we have as believers in our relationship with Christ. This is clearly understood when visiting foreign countries where the bond of fellowship between believers, in life and in worship, can bridge even differences in language. The church, crossing international boundaries and including believers from all corners of the earth, is catholic, or universal.

Hence, the church is people in relationship with Christ, seeking to be the very presence of Christ in the lives of others and within society. It is the coming together of these individuals which forms the church, or as Paul describes it in 1 Corinthians 12, the body of Christ. In drawing this analogy, Paul is noting that as individual members of the body, we each bring our gifts and abilities to contribute to the body as a whole. Paul writes, "If the ear should say, 'Because I am not an eye, I do not belong to the body,' it would not for that reason cease to be part of the body" (1 Cor. 12:16). In the same way, each member of the church, as the body of Christ brings his or her contribution, none more or less important than any other. The head of the body is Jesus Christ.

The church, begun as a result of God's investment of his Son, ministers today through the work and power of the Holy Spirit. It shall be made complete at the second coming of Jesus Christ.

ROBERT J. WHITTET

Bibliography. L. and B. Hybels (1986), *Rediscovering Church;* S. A. Macchia (1999), *Becoming a Healthy Church;* R. C. Sproul (1992), *Essential Truths of the Christian Faith;* R. Warren (1995), *The Purpose Driven Church.*

Church Expansion. *See* Church Growth.

Church Growth. The church growth movement of the late 1900s helped transform worship patterns for tens of thousands of Americans. It had its genesis in the Jesus movement of the early 1970s, which brought many people into the faith who had traditionally been outside normal church circles. Charismatic churches in particular began seeing remarkable attendance growth as they focused on evangelism and new styles of worship. Breaking from the staid traditional patterns of most churches, which had remained largely the same since the 1930s, the church growth movement transformed mainstream churches across North America.

The Hallmarks of the Church Growth Movement. While it is not hard to find evidence of the church growth movement in Western culture, it can be quite difficult to specify the exact changes the movement wrought. Research into church growth literature reveals ten principles that stand as the hallmarks of the movement.

1. *Set specific goals.* Churches were encouraged to take an organizational approach to management, setting goals, and planning strategies to meet them.
2. *Create dynamic worship.* Those raised in an entertainment culture need an uplifting, emotional experience in their worship.
3. *Develop significant relational groups.* Churches were reminded that people's greatest desire is to draw close to others; therefore small groups, often age-specific, were encouraged.
4. *Institute participatory decision making.* Most of the congregations involved in the church growth movement tried to create a streamlined organizational structure, empowering the laity in ministry and involving everyone in the decision-making process.
5. *Design plenty of quality programs and activities.* No longer the place only for Sunday worship, churches became activity centers, around which the lives of the members revolved.
6. *Develop leaders.* One of the common goals of the movement was not simply evangelism but discipleship—moving believers toward maturity in Christ and thereby increasing the leadership base of the church.
7. *Spend significant time in prayer.* Every major revival has been bathed in prayer, and the church growth movement of the 1970s and 1980s was no different.
8. *Create a sense of excitement.* People respond to excitement, so the writers and spokesmen for the church growth movement, particularly Win Arn, Donald McGavran, and Gary MacIntosh, urged churches to develop the feeling that something new and exciting was happening.
9. *Make it visible.* Churches in the movement spent considerable time talking about marketing, trying to move the church beyond its traditional borders and into new areas of society.
10. *Focus on quality.* The books on church growth all talked about the importance of quality, whether it be in child care, landscaping, the financial footings, or the parking lot.

A New Perspective on Church. Congregations involved in the church growth movement were largely led by and ministering to baby boomers—the generation born after the close of World War II. This generation took an entirely different approach to the structures of the church. The result was a new "wineskin" that altered nearly every aspect of church life. The times of services changed as many congregations questioned the utility of eleven o'clock services. In many cases even the day of worship changed, as weeknight services sprung up as an alternative for those who found Sunday mornings inconvenient. The order of service changed radically, as the stiff formality of many congregations gave way to warmer, more personal expressions of faith. Modern music displaced ancient hymns, and the focus of many songs shifted from singing *about* God to singing *toward* God. As congregations spent considerable time singing, there was also a renewed emphasis on prayer and a newfound faith in the work of the Holy Spirit.

Perhaps because baby boomers had been raised on television entertainment, new expectations were raised for churches. Those involved in the church growth movement strove to make worship services more exciting and vibrant, and they demanded quality in all aspects of church life, be it children's programs or church bulletins. Even the reason for selecting a church changed. With the growth of new congregations that had no ties to older denominations, believers began "shopping" for churches much as they might shop for a house or a car. Whereas Christians used to choose churches based primarily on doctrine or denomination, largely due to the church growth movement most people now select a church based on the Sunday morning worship style and the quality of the various programs offered. Rather than "becoming members," people spoke of "joining a fellowship" or "establishing a relationship" with a body of believers.

The view of the pastor also changed considerably. Those born before World War II generally viewed the pastor as a chaplain, whose primary responsibility was to care for those in need. In contrast, the new generation preferred to view the pastor as the equipper of the saints and leader of the ministry team, and the changed expectations often caused discord among members. A renewed interest in evangelism also marked this movement, as people began sharing the gospel with a new energy.

Church Growth Models. There is no single model that can serve as the pattern for the church growth movement. Mainline congregations as well as start-up fellowships have followed the principles espoused by those in the movement, with varying degrees of success. However, seven common models have emerged. First, there is *the seeker church*, which tries to reach out to the unchurched by making its central worship service comfortable and entertaining, offering avenues for spiritual growth outside the central service. The second model is *the healing church*, which places an emphasis on counseling, recovery, and meeting the specific needs of those experiencing difficult times. A third model is *the preaching church,* which builds the organization around the unique preaching ability of a high-profile senior pastor. Fourth is *the worshiping church,* which makes music, drama, and alternative arts the focus of its efforts, drawing people into a unique worship experience. The fifth model is *the cell church,* which places everyone in small groups for ministry and growth, often dividing the groups based on geography rather than age. A sixth model, *the body-life church,* emphasizes the believer's commitment to the body and encourages openness and ministry to one another. The final model, *the program-centered church,* attracts people not so much through worship or relationship but through a full slate of activities for all age levels and stations in life.

The impact of the church growth movement has been varied. It revitalized evangelism and renewed interest in the work of the Holy Spirit in many churches. It also helped spawn a new generation of churches with few denominational ties, has caused the growth of many church staffs and ministry specializations, and was the main impetus to the development of the mega church. The vast majority of North American churches over 1,500 people are the result of the church growth movement. However, overall church attendance has not increased considerably over the past twenty-five years. Some critics have charged that the most lasting results of the church growth movement has been bringing new music into worship services and simply shifting crowds of people from smaller churches into larger churches.

JERRY CHIP MACGREGOR

Bibliography. W. Easum (1990), *Church Growth Handbook;* K. Hadaway (1991), *Church Growth Principles: Separating Fact from Fiction;* D. McGavran and G. Hunter III (1990), *Church Growth: Strategies That Work.*

See also BABY BOOM GENERATION; SEEKER SERVICES; WORSHIP SERVICE

Church Library. Libraries located in and established for the use of the local congregation are a recent development within Christian education. While many church libraries may resemble a collection of books from the attics of church members, the potential for ministry, both personal and cooperate, is as notable today as it was when they were first established.

History of the Church Library Movement. Though the Reformers consistently promoted the establishment of libraries for Christian and public education, it was not until the nineteenth century that libraries in congregations became popular. The development of church libraries paralleled the formation of the Sunday school

and public libraries in the United States. "The library was the true mark of a *bona fide* Sunday school" (Lynn and Wright, 1980, 57). Two initial efforts at establishing church libraries were (1) the Sunday school movement, in both England (1786) and America (1789), and (2) the Methodist Book Concern, established in 1789.

Originally, church libraries were not much more than stored curricula. However, the New York Union Society "was foremost in the introduction of Sunday-school circulating libraries" (Rice, 1917, 59). By 1830 the American Sunday School Union, now American Missionary Fellowship, had circulated over six million pieces of printed texts for the establishment and expansion of church libraries. So successful were these efforts that by 1859 three-fifths of the libraries in the United States were started by the Sunday school (Lynn and Wright, 1980, 57). In fact, by the turn of the twentieth century, the establishment of libraries on the church's mission fields became a standard missiological practice (Rice, 1917, 221, 233–34; Lynn and Wright, 1980, 57). Likewise, denominational entities became interested in the formation of church libraries. For example, in 1927 the Southern Baptist Convention was the first to establish a denominational library service.

George Scofield (1810–87) devised a plan to further stimulate the establishment of church libraries. It was called the "Ten Dollar Library," which allowed congregations to purchase a collection consisting of one hundred books, varying from seventy-two to two-hundred-and-fifty pages each, for the sum of ten dollars. Within the first ten years of the program's existence over ten million volumes were marketed (Lynn and Wright, 1980, 57). Programs such as these aided in the formation and expansion of the church library movement.

The current status of the church library is somewhat less than ideal. The once solid presence of the church library in Christian education has been in a steady state of decline throughout the latter half of this century. Numerous factors can be cited as the cause of the decline: (1) the general decline of the Sunday school; (2) changes in the form of Christian education, to which the library did not readily adapt itself; (3) the decline of education in general, both within the church and culture; and (4) the independent nature and underestimated value of the library by Christian educators.

The Church Library and Contemporary Christian Education. The library's educational emphasis should be coordinated with the tasks of other church educational programs. The church library can readily accomplish this in two ways: (1) provide supplemental information and materials used in educational programs, and (2) support the training and equipping of teachers and other leaders in the congregation's education ministry.

Educational programs in the congregation can make significant use of the church library. The use of homework, reading assignments, and audiovisual materials in the teaching process are beneficial to the student. Likewise, many of the more innovative and substantial teaching methods being used in the congregation's teaching program require the availability of materials such as those contained in a church library; for example, debates, discussions, case studies, or panel presentations.

Keith Mee (1976) recommends six improvements that permit the church library to reach more of its potential: (1) "Superavailability," requiring the library to be open not only on Sunday, but whenever the congregation has an event or program. (2) "Selected resources," emphasizing *quality* of the collection over *quantity*. (3) "Serviceable systems," suggesting that the library needs to be more concerned with maintaining a readily accessible system of information distribution for its patrons rather than simply being concerned with the Dewey Decimal system. (4) "Study facilities" or opportunities, suggesting that the library allocate space or times for reading or sponsor book clubs. (5) "Staff assistance," which requires that the library workers be trained and knowledgeable not only about the library's collection and procedures, but the educational programs in general so as to provide the correct resources and materials. Finally, (6) "Be open longer," suggesting that libraries open prior to and after *all* services, and even during the week periodically.

JAMES RILEY ESTEP

Bibliography. J. Anderson (1994), *Church Media Library Administration;* C. Businaro (1994), *Church Media Library: Church and Synagogue Library Association, Standards for Church and Synagogue Libraries;* D. Conniff, *The Church Media Library Ministry;* M. J. Dotts (1988), *You Can Have a Church Library;* R. W. Lynn and E. Wright (1980), *The Big Little School;* K. Mee (1976), *The Learning Team;* E. W. Rice (1917), *The Sunday-School Movement (1780–1917) and the American Sunday-School Union (1817–1917).*

Church Ministry Convention Network. With the demise of the National Sunday School Association in the 1970s the nearly two hundred Sunday school and Christian ministry conventions held throughout the United States had no national organization or leadership. Informally, leaders of these conventions would contact each other for ideas, problem solving, and planning. Over the years conversations were held regarding the need to create an organization that could function as a clearinghouse for ideas and resources for the existing conventions.

The first official meeting of Church Ministry Conventions Network was held in Denver, Colorado, February 10, 1993, in conjunction with the Denver Christian Ministries Convention. Twelve associations had representatives present, along with several publishing house personnel. A mission statement was adopted along with the identification of six major functions for the group.

"The mission of CMCN is to encourage the growth of Church Ministry Conventions through networking." Note that this is a somewhat different emphasis from that of the former National Sunday School Association, which clearly had as its mission the revitalization of the Sunday school. Of course, if the conventions succeeded, the Sunday schools would be strengthened so, though not as clearly articulated, the CMCN did share somewhat the same mission of the earlier National Sunday School Association. One difference between the NSSA and the CMCN is that CMCN is an independent organization crossing denominational lines while the NSSA was fully aligned with the National Association of Evangelicals.

Six major functions were outlined in the organizational meeting of CMCN. The first was to build a national convention calendar. Some earlier groups made efforts at this, primarily the evangelical publishing houses, but much of the time the information was either out of date or inaccurate. No national organization kept up on this information, and the convention leadership set their dates for conferences with no knowledge of what other groups were doing. It was not unusual to find five or six major conventions scheduled on the same weekend. When this happened publishing houses found it difficult to participate in all of the conferences. CMCN now publishes a convention calendar each year.

The second function was to work on the standardization of forms for all of the conventions. This included contracts for speakers, exhibitors, musicians, sound systems, and practically any other need where written communication was necessary. Individual conventions may use any of the forms or modify them for their own use.

A national file or profile of speakers, both workshop and keynote, was the third major function. This resource was especially helpful to smaller conventions who did not have the contacts with major speakers. The resource provides names, addresses, speaking topics, and an indication of expense. If individuals are sponsored by publishers, this is also indicated. While the National Convention Calendar is so important to the resource providers and exhibitors, this speakers' file is an essential document for any convention planner. Updated each year, this is the only volume available with this important information.

The fourth major function was the sharing of information. Though done informally in the past, CMCN provides a platform where conventions report their statistics, personnel, events, and programs. This provides a view on the state of conventions in a given year. It also, through networking with other conventions, provides ideas and information that can be used to improve the quality of conventions across the country. The major way this is done is through the annual membership meeting held in conjunction with one of the regional conventions. Moving across the country to allow a broader participation, this membership meeting shares information and opportunities such as: successes of other conventions, opportunity to visit other conventions, exchange creative ideas, a forum for problem solving, workshops to address convention and resource provider issues, hear experts on marketing and planning, and network with convention directors to develop a strong partnership in church ministry conventions. A list of resource providers or exhibitors is also available for convention planners. A quarterly newsletter is sent to all CMCN members, and this includes reports and updates, articles of interest to directors and resource providers, new membership listings, and convention stories.

To spawn new conventions was the fifth major function. The Executive Group of CMCN is committed to beginning new conventions as well as assisting those who are struggling. Some assistance has been given in this area, but with a totally volunteer board, it cannot be as extensive as perhaps it should be.

The final major function as outlined in the organizational meeting was to support each other with help, love, and prayer. Some convention directors work with a small handful of volunteers and they give their time as well. Very few conventions have full-time directors, and finances are always a problem. These people need love and encouragement and the prayers of God's people. Though the last of the major functions to be listed, this, no doubt, is the most significant.

The strength of CMCN today is that it is in the hands of good leadership. Marian Morris, who serves as chair, is the key contact person and working with her is a board of directors who have accepted the challenge, the vision, and the functions of CMCN. The phone number for CMCN is 800–304–0649.

A major concern for CMCN is that it does not have the financial support necessary to maintain a solid foundation for the future. Income comes from membership dues and special gifts of evangelical publishers and individuals.

If the financial issue can be solved and if the leadership commitment is maintained and expanded, the organization will continue to make a significant impact on ministry conferences throughout the country.

DENNIS E. WILLIAMS

Church Officer. *See* Deacon.

Church Resources. *See* Church Library.

Civilization. *See* Culture.

Classical Conditioning. Classical conditioning, sometimes called respondent or Pavlovian conditioning, is a learning procedure that was first thoroughly investigated by the Russian physiologist Ivan P. Pavlov. Pavlov presented his findings in a book entitled *Conditioned Reflexes* published in 1927.

In the basic paradigm, a neutral stimulus (NS) acquires the power to elicit a reflexive response that it would not initially elicit. However, after being paired with an unconditioned stimulus (US) that is innately capable of eliciting a given reflexive response (called the unconditioned response or UR), the NS becomes a conditioned stimulus (CS) capable of eliciting that same reflexive response (now called a conditioned response or CR).

For example, as applied in one of Pavlov's experiments, food in the mouth of a dog was found to elicit salivation. The food is all US and the salivation UR, since no learning or conditioning is necessary for salivary flow to occur in response to food in the dog's mouth. Pavlov showed that if a NS (perhaps the sound of a bell) is paired properly with the food, then it could acquire the power to elicit salivation. Thus, if one sounds a bell (NS) immediately prior to placing food (US) in the dog's mouth several times, the bell gradually becomes a CS that will elicit the CR of salivation, even when presented without the food. Of course, if one then sounds the bell repeatedly, without the food, the CR will eventually extinguish.

The impact of classical conditioning upon behavior is magnified considerably when one considers higher order conditioning. Pavlov demonstrated that once a NS had become a CS via the basic paradigm, that CS could then function like a US to classically condition a new NS. For example, if one had conditioned the dog in the above example to salivate (CR) in response to the sound of a bell (CS), the bell could then be used to condition salivary flow in response to a light bulb being switched on. Since humans, as well as animals, can be classically conditioned, and since virtually any type of reflexive response is capable of being conditioned (e.g. involuntary muscular responses, glandular secretions, and emotional response), this learning procedure has enormous significance for human behavior. For example, a child may come to fear the family physician (CS) who has been paired with a painful injection (US). Or, a spouse may begin to have negative feelings toward his or her partner because of financial pressures and other stressors (US) continually experienced in the presence of that partner (CS). Finally, the positive emotional response one experiences when he or she hears the word "mother" (CS) probably is determined by the loving relationship one has with the person who bears that label. Such knowledge has been used to enforce behavior as well as break destructive habits.

RAY E. BOWER

Bibliography. P. Chance (1999), *Learning and Behavior;* J. P. Houston (1991), *Fundamentals of Learning and Memory;* J. E. Ormrod (1999), *Human Learning;* I. P. Pavlov (1927), *Conditioned Reflexes.*

See also ASSOCIATION/CONNECTIONIST THEORIES; BEHAVIORISM, THEORIES OF; COGNITIVE FIELD THEORY; LEARNING THEORIES; SR BONDS

Classification. Ability to divide things or ideas into sets or subsets and to consider their interrelationship. The concept is foundational to Piaget's work on cognitive development. The ability to classify usually begins to emerge in the early years of the concrete operational stage, which is approximately ages 7–11, and is generally well developed by the end of the stage. The ability to classify permits children to move up and down a hierarchy and allows them to handle complex logical ideas. The simplest classification deals with simple hierarchies: (1) composition in which a combination of two elements are combined to produce a third element (e.g., the twelve apostles plus other followers of Jesus equals disciples), (2) associativity by which two elements can be combined in a different order with the same results (e.g., 2+2+2 is the same as 2+(2+2), and (3) reversibility by which the child can understand dual relationships and moving in inverse order (e.g., Johnny's brother also has a brother). All of these elements are especially valuable for mathematical thinking, but they also provide the basis for any kind of logical thinking. The idea of classification is expanded to include not only classes, but also relations.

ELEANOR A. DANIEL

Classroom Setting. Arrangement of physical features in the learning environment. A well-prepared and well-executed lesson plan is easily thwarted if attention is not given to the practical reality that humans are influenced and impacted by the spaces they occupy. Christian educators give great care to both minimize aspects of the learning environment that may hinder spiritual growth and maximize those features that enhance spiritual impact.

Among the most important basic considerations for excellent classroom management are the following:

1. Adequate space: Educators recommend 35 square feet per learner for early childhood; 30 square feet per learner for grades 1–6; 25 square feet for youth; and 15 square feet for adults.

2. Ventilation and temperature: There is nothing like a hot, stuffy room to make children cranky, youth restless, and adults sleepy. Adrenaline keeps the teacher awake in these situations but especially adult learners will find a hot/stuffy room to be sleep-inducing.

3. Lighting and appropriate decor: Children, youth, and adults are accustomed to well-lit malls, restaurants, and other public spaces. A poorly lit room with colors popular in the 1970s will give the message of "outdated" and "unworthy," despite good material in the actual lesson. The wise Christian educator will also make sure furniture and wall decor is age-appropriate. Especially teenagers find it offensive to be in a room with childish furniture or decoration. Similarly, adults will be distracted by the "visual feasts" characterized by the typical teenage-decorated room.

Beyond the basics the astute Christian educator will give careful thought as well to the following:

1. Philosophy of ministry and room arrangement congruence: If the purpose of one's ministry is to promote relationships, straight rows of metal chairs will not advance one toward that goal. Chairs arranged in a circle, or chairs arranged around tables are more conducive to getting people to speak with each other. Similarly, a "living room feel" with carpet, padded chairs, and Hazelnut coffee available will foster sharing among adults.

2. Accessibility and use of technology: Flannelgraphs can be great, but children, youth, and adults live in a technologically rich and media-enhanced world. The use of video, computer-generated overheads, and other technological updates can never replace the message of the gospel, but technology in the classroom can facilitate learning.

3. Use the allotted space creatively and with variety: A change in the room arrangement may be unsettling at first glance, but it can also set the stage for openness to new teaching and methodologies.

LEONARD KAGELER

Bibliography. W. Haystead (1995), *The 21st Century Sunday School.*

Clergy. Term from the Greek *kleros* meaning "lot, portion, or heir." In the biblical story, this idea traces its historical roots to the special allotment granted by God to the Levites in the allocation of the land among the Israelites. Levites received "all the tithes in Israel as their inheritance in return for the work they do" (Num. 18:21). Some argue that based on this historical perspective the priestly class with their special allotment among God's people was abandoned with the advent of the New Testament church since all believers are now considered to be priests.

By A.D. 95 Clement of Rome reconstituted the priestly class by differentiating clergy from laity and limiting the role of laity in the liturgy. By 313, the division was complete. In a letter to a provincial leader in that year, Emperor Constantine decrees that those "who proffer their services to this holy religion, who are usually called clerics, be completely exempt from public duties" (Bettenson, 1963, 17).

Although the services clerics rendered were primarily in the context of worship, clerics were also Christian educators, involved in establishing and leading catechumenal, catechetical, and cathedral schools in the early and medieval church. The contributions of four representative cleric educators demonstrate the importance of clergy involvement in both the theory and practice of Christian education.

John Comenius and Richard Baxter are significant seventeenth-century clergy educators. Comenius developed a theory of education that emphasized learning as a natural, pleasurable activity. He set forth his teachings in *The Great Didactic* and is often credited with founding modern education. Richard Baxter wrote *The Reformed Pastor* in 1646, outlining his pastoral work among his English congregation. Baxter advocated and practiced individualized instruction of his congregation and clearly saw teaching as central to the pastoral office. He advises the laity to "obey your faithful teachers. Take heed that you refuse not to learn what they would teach you" (Baxter, 1982, 9).

Both Comenius and Baxter assumed that teaching inhered to the pastoral office. In contrast, Bushnell and Smart wrote in reaction to eras in which the clergy were distanced from the church's teaching ministry. The historical basis for the hiatus was the rise of the Sunday school as the dominant form of Christian education in Protestant churches.

The Sunday school movement was a lay movement from its beginning. It was started by laypersons and its audience (poor, illiterate children) and format (crossing denominational lines in staffing and meeting locations) kept the schools independent from denominational control. Both Bushnell and Smart write in an effort to recapture the pastor's role in Christian education. Bushnell seeks to correct the miseducation he believed resulted from Sunday schools dominated by evangelistic and revivalistic goals. In *Christian Nurture* Bushnell asks, "What is the true idea of Christian or divine nurture . . . ? What is its aim? What its method of working?" (Bushnell, 1979, 9).

Smart (1960) addresses the abdication of teaching by pastors. In *The Rebirth of Ministry* he laments, "Many pastors do not regard teaching as an essential part of their ministry. Jesus was a teacher. Paul was a teacher. But these pastors are not teachers!"(60). Smart hoped to reinterest pastors in the teaching ministry by understanding themselves as teachers and by assuming a greater level of responsibility and involvement in the church's educational programs.

Smart's challenge remains today. If we can legitimately grant some people a "special allotment" for rendering service to the church and thus create a clergy class, the teaching ministry must be included in the clergy's portfolio.

ROBERT DROVDAHL

Bibliography. H. Bettenson (1963), *Documents of the Christian Church,* 2nd ed.; J. Smart (1960), *The Rebirth of Ministry.*

See also ASSOCIATE PASTOR; BUSHNELL, HORACE; CLERGY AS EDUCATORS; COMENIUS, JOHANN AMOS; DIAKONIA; MINISTER; MINISTER OF CHRISTIAN EDUCATION; SENIOR PASTOR; SUNDAY SCHOOL MOVEMENT

Clergy as Educators. When Jesus Christ was about to leave the earth, he left one last command with those who were his followers: "Go . . . make disciples . . . teaching them to observe all that I commanded you" (Matt. 28:19–20). This command to be about the business of teaching his disciples is the foundation of the educational ministry of the church.

The apostle Paul outlines the general responsibilities of ministry leadership with a broad brushstroke in Ephesians 4:11–13. God's call to the clergy is that they be about the task of equipping God's people for "works of service." The immediate goal is the "building up" of the body of Christ, moving toward the ultimate goal of full maturity in Christ. So important is this teaching ministry that Paul later identifies the ability to teach as a prerequisite for church leadership (1 Tim. 3:2).

The clergy, then, bear significant responsibility for the teaching ministry of the church. This responsibility defines itself in at least five distinct areas.

To fulfill this teaching responsibility, the minister must first be a diligent student of the Word. Second Timothy 2:15 proclaims the fact that correctly handling the "word of truth" requires study. The pastor who values the Word and demonstrates that value through personal study teaches by example as well as by precept.

Perhaps most obviously, the minister must be a proclaimer of the Truth. Proclaiming Christ (Col. 1:28), teaching sound doctrine (Titus 2:1), commanding, urging, admonishing, instructing—these tasks are all the responsibility of the faithful pastor/teacher. It is in the word of truth that salvation is found (Eph. 1:13), and the knowledge of truth leads to godliness (Titus 1:1).

Clergy educators are also called to be disciplers—not only ones who instruct in the truth, but who walk together with their followers, demonstrating, guiding, and nurturing life transformation. The power of example was a dynamic tool of the Master Teacher Jesus Christ (see John 13:1–17). Paul instructs the Corinthians to follow him as he follows Christ (1 Cor. 11:1). The process of disciple-making requires more than instruction. Paul describes the ministry of the Spirit as a process of walking together with God's people in order that we may all be "transformed into his likeness" (2 Cor. 3:18).

Another task of the clergy educator is the equipping of God's people for service. Helping God's people identify and use their spiritual gifts and teaching them to be communicators of God's truth are critical responsibilities of the pastor/teacher (Eph. 4:11–13).

Finally, the clergy must be the motivators and cheerleaders of the educational ministry of the church. The task is too great for the clergy alone. The teachings of the Word and the teaching ministry of the church must be entrusted to "reliable" teachers who will in turn teach others (2 Tim. 2:2). Having equipped others to serve, the clergy must delegate, motivate, and supervise the ministry of the laity in the fulfillment of the Great Commission.

MARI GONLAG

Bibliography. D. M. Geiger (1991), *Christian Education: Foundations for the Future*, pp. 411–25; R. Yount (1995), *The Teaching Ministry of the Church: Integrating Biblical Truth with Contemporary Application*, pp. 121–39.

Climate, Classroom. To nurture the process of learning in a classroom, a climate must be created that envelopes the teacher and the students in a trusting, nurturing, open atmosphere. Even among the class members themselves a trusting, open environment needs to prevail. To develop such a climate involves knowing one another as persons with needs, concerns, and interests; participating together; sharing insights and questions; acknowledging one another's contributions, and correcting one another's errors without belittling each other. Providing an opportunity for sharing honestly one's feelings, sharing from one's own life experiences, working from a place of equality with one another, and having common learning experiences all provide a climate of mutuality.

Numerous activities make possible the opportunity for encouraging a healthy classroom climate. These activities include student participation in agenda building; identifying common areas of interest and need related to the subject; discovering one another's backgrounds, life experiences, and concerns; enjoying informal and relaxed times together; and reflecting upon one's own behavior, attitudes, and motivations through self-descriptions, autobiography, or telling one's story. To the extent that children can participate, they, too, need to be involved in creating such an atmosphere.

In order to build a learning climate, the whole group should set learning goals together; share present knowledge and information; express their beliefs and values as related to the subject at hand; determine the most important issues to be handled or those in which they are least informed; and share questions about the topics that need to be addressed.

The responsibility for creating a healthy classroom climate begins with the teacher and needs to be embraced by the students through the modeling and encouragement of the one responsible for the class.

DORIS BORCHERT

Climate, Small Group. Climate refers to the environmental atmosphere or conditions prevailing in the small group setting. The climate or environment of a small group consists of two dimensions: the physical and the emotional.

Small group experts and learning theorists argue that a room's environment significantly influences interaction and the extent of learning that takes place in small group discussions (Lee, 1973, 71; Tubbs, 1995, 96). A number of variables contribute to the physical climate of a group setting.

The effect of group size on member satisfaction, group effectiveness, and discussion patterns has been well documented. As groups grow beyond five members, participants often complain that the group is too large and that they are not able to participate as effectively as they would like to (Tubbs, 1995, 102).

Seating arrangement also has a major impact on group interaction. The preference for small group members is a U-shaped or circular seating arrangement whereby good eye contact is made with each of the group members and participants can easily address one another. Motivation to interact with other individuals is greater when one can see them clearly (Gorman, 1993, 132).

Finally, the immediate physical environment in which the small group operates exerts a powerful influence on the climate of a group. Temperature, lighting, size of room, aesthetic quality of a room, and noise distractions affect the nature and quality of interaction that takes place.

For maximum effectiveness in the small group tasks of self-disclosure, sharing, learning, and discussion, the emotional or psychological climate should be warm, accepting, and nonthreatening. There are many psychological components of a healthy group climate, the most significant of which are trust, intimacy, and supportiveness.

Clearly the most important ingredient for a healthy emotional climate is *trust,* the general sense that group members can rely on one another. Group trustworthiness is demonstrated when members do not take advantage of the vulnerability of those who self-disclose and when there are expressions of warmth toward one another. When group members express warmth toward one another, a high level of group trust is built because there is assurance that disclosure will be responded to with acceptance and support.

Intimacy or cohesiveness refers to the attachment or closeness group members feel toward each other. In a highly intimate group, members share a strong sense of belonging, speak favorably about the group and other group members, and conform to group norms. In intimate or highly cohesive groups, members feel freer to disclose risky thoughts or feelings (Galanes and Brilhart, 1997, 142–43).

Finally, in a *supportive climate,* small group members respect each other, care about one another, and encourage each other. Consequently, in a supportive climate, participants are more willing to self-disclose, feel freer to express personal thoughts, tend to trust one another more, and sense a greater closeness to each other (Galanes and Brilhart, 1997, 144).

HARLEY ATKINSON

Bibliography. G. Galanes and J. Brilhart (1997), *Communication in Groups: Applications and Skills;* J. Gorman (1993), *Community That Is Christian;* J. Lee (1993), *The Flow of Religious Instruction;* S. Tubbs (1995), *A Systems Approach to Small Group Interaction.*

Codependency. The concept of codependency is a new insight into the old problem of loving appropriately. It has become a buzzword in the self-help and professional counseling fields. The term codependency has been used to describe a one-way relationship.

The concept of codependency was born of extensive work with alcoholics and their spouses. The alcoholics were dependent because of their addiction to alcohol. The spouses of alcoholics came to be called the codependents, because they were also trapped by the dependence of the addicts. Those around the dependent person often feel responsible for his/her behavior and try to gain their self-worth by helping them gain freedom.

Theorists have described codependence as compulsive caretaking behavior, a personal character defect, personality disorder, and pattern of painful dependency. Codependency is a word often used to describe persons who have been affected by difficult life circumstances. They feel as though they are responsible for the thoughts and actions of others, are susceptible to control by others and are controlling of others, and feel

guilty for things about which they have no control. As a result they may experience a life of loneliness, guilt, and isolation as they try to cope with the painful realities of life.

Codependency is the tendency to love, care, or give for the wrong reasons. It is also the professional term for the desperate need to love in order to be loved, to give in order to be cared for, to please in order to be accepted, to pamper and placate in order to avoid consequences.

JAMES A. HEADRICK

Bibliography. A. H. Ells and P. B. Moore (1992), *One-Way Relationships Workbook: The 12-Week, Step-by-Step, Interactive Plan for Recovery from Codependent Relationships;* D. and J. Ryan (1990), *Recovery from Codependency;* P. Springle (1994), *Conquering Codependency;* idem (1995), *Untangling Relationships: A Christian Perspective on Codependency.*

Coe, George A. (1862–1951). American psychologist of religion. He was educated at the University of Rochester, the Boston University School of Theology, and the University of Berlin. His teaching career, which spanned more than forty years, included faculty appointments at four academic institutions: the University of Southern California, Northwestern University, Union Theological Seminary, and the Teachers College of Columbia University, from which he retired in 1927.

Coe authored eleven books and hundreds of articles and reviews. He remained active throughout his latter years; two of his most noteworthy volumes, *What Is Religion Doing to Our Consciences?* and *What Is Christian Education?* (1929), were published after his retirement. The founder of the Religious Education Association (REA) in 1903, he expounded a theory of Christian education based on two primary theological assumptions: the existence of God and the infinite value of the individual. Certainty of the former, according to Coe, is what gives meaning to the latter. Recognizing, however, that religious experience varied from person to person, Coe encouraged dialogue and constructive debate among differing theological positions. His moderating stance allowed him to retain a leadership role in the REA throughout his life; he served as its honorary president until his death in 1951.

In *The Psychology of Religion,* he sought to establish a copacetic relationship between the disciplines of theology and psychology. His most influential work, *The Spiritual Life: Studies in the Science of Religion* (1901), was among the first to use actual case studies to investigate that link. In it Coe examined the conversion experiences of twenty-seven individuals and attempted to discuss them in terms of prevailing psychological theories. On the basis of his observations, he found that individuals who were emotionally passive and highly prone to suggestibility (what he called the "subliminal self") were the most likely candidates for sudden and dramatic conversion experiences. Time has substantiated many of Coe's theories, often leaving contemporary theologians and religious educators with a moral dilemma in discerning the fine line between motivation and manipulation in compelling others toward their religious conversion.

DAVID GOUGH

Bibliography. G. A. Coe (1901), *The Spiritual Life: Studies in the Science of Religion;* idem (1929), *What Is Christian Education?*

See also EVANGELISM; PSYCHOLOGY OF RELIGION; RELIGIOUS EDUCATION ASSOCIATION

Cognitive Development. Human beings have been created in the image of God (Gen. 1:27). Rationality is an important aspect of being an image-bearer (Col. 3:10). Paul prays that believers will grow in knowledge and wisdom (Eph. 1:18), and Luke reports that even Jesus grew in wisdom (Luke 2:52).

How does the mind function? Infants obviously do not "think" or process environmental stimuli in ways similar to adults. How does one's cognitive capacity grow or develop? Are there predictable patterns applicable to all human beings?

In order to answer these questions, one must turn to the social sciences. While Scripture can provide theological insights into the human mind and wisdom, Scripture was not intended to provide an exhaustive theory of cognitive development. Yet any theory of cognitive development must be evaluated in the light of scriptural teaching. The theory ought not violate the unique, created nature of humankind. The theory must be consistent with the scriptural assertion that human rationality is unique from the rest of created beings, that objective (absolute) truth is established independent of the human mind, and that as God's creatures we are to constantly search and study God and his creation as part of our created mandate.

Modern theories of cognitive development have their origin in the writing of Jean Piaget, whose work has dominated the field of genetic epistemology since the 1950s. Piaget's fundamental premise was that the function of the mind remained constant while the structures of the mind changed systematically and predictably as the child developed. The function of the mind was to link, store, and retrieve the multitude of sensory data being processed. Structures changed when data could no longer be assimilated into existing patterns of thinking.

Basic to his theory is the premise that the mind seeks a state of equilibrium, or balance, relative to the environment. When new sensory data appear, the mind seeks to assimilate the data into existing structures or, if that is not possible, to accommodate the data by revising the cognitive structure. On a macro-level, this process of accommodation leads, according to Piaget, to at least four formal stages or forms of cognitive processing which are age specific. From birth to around the age of two, the infant primarily functions in a "sensorimotor" frame in which the physical sensations trigger an appropriate response. Around the age of two the child begins to process cognitions in a more deliberate manner, primarily discovering the capacity to recognize symbols as representations of reality. Known as the preoperational stage, Piaget sees this level as essential for acquisition of language. The child learns to speak and begins to develop basic concepts such as categorizing animals as "dogs" or "cows." Around the age of seven the child moves into the concrete operational stage in which the child engages in an exchange of ideas, projects or anticipates results, and begins to engage in moral reasoning. Much of this thought pattern, however, is still conditioned by reference to specific objects. By the age of fourteen the child begins to develop the capacity (in what he calls the formal operational stage) to engage in abstract conceptual thought. Concepts such as love, truth, and justice are increasingly considered abstractly, without reference to a specific object or incident.

Other theories have amended Piaget's work. Lev Vygotsky balanced Piaget's nearly exclusive consideration of internal, personal factors associated with development by giving greater place to environmental influences. His theory of "development-in-context" recognizes that contextual matters have a powerful influence on cognitive development in addition to internal and/or genetic influences.

Piaget's theories have also been applied to other specific settings, most notably to moral development through the work of Lawrence Kohlberg and faith development as articulated by James Fowler. While each of these writers amend Piaget's theories, they use Piaget as the foundation for theorizing how one cognitively processes issues of morality and faith.

In the 1990s a new wave of theories has emerged, led in part by Howard Gardner and his associates in which they contend that Piaget's theory of intelligence, while valid, is too limited. Gardner posited a theory of multiple intelligences which asserts that in addition to the linguistic and logical/mathematical intelligences measured by Piaget, other intelligences exist such as musical, bodily kinesthetic, spatial, interpersonal, intrapersonal, and naturalist.

Other theorists study the physiology of the brain in search for the answer to the question "how does the mind function?" Various areas of the brain, so the theory goes, control different cognitive functions. The left hemisphere controls analysis, the right hemisphere synthesis. The frontal lobe is associated with critical thinking and problem solving; the prefrontal cortex is associated with planning and rehearsal; the temporal lobe with hearing and speech. The parietal lobe is associated with touch and the occipital lobe with vision.

Theories abound. The Christian educator can be served by critically reviewing many of these theories. Foremost, however, the educator must work toward developing a theologically sound theory which is consistent with his or her view of sanctification, the role of the Holy Spirit, and the appropriate goal (or telos) of a developmental theory.

ROBERT C. DE VRIES

Bibliography. H. Gardner (1983), *Frames of Mind: The Theory of Multiple Intelligences;* H. Ginsburg and S. Opper (1969), *Piaget's Theory of Intellectual Development;* R. A. Sylwester (1995), *A Celebration of Neurons: An Educator's Guide to the Human Brain.*

See also COGNITIVE LEARNING, THEORIES OF; FOWLER, JAMES W., III; KOHLBERG, LAWRENCE; LEARNING THEORIES; PIAGET, JEAN

Cognitive Dissonance. The theory of cognitive dissonance suggests that the human mind seeks a steady state of harmony with its environment. This theory can rest theologically on the doctrine of creation where all creation, humankind, and God dwell in perfect harmony. The picture of our final glory is also that of shalom.

This theological principle finds a parallel in the theory of cognitive dissonance. Jean Piaget referred to this phenomenon as equilibrium—the mind seeking a state of balance or harmony between two poles previously in conflict with one another. Piaget saw a state of disequilibrium as the primary motivation for learning. The mind seeks to either assimilate the new concept into the existing schema of cognition or adjust the schema in order to accommodate the new insight.

Other theorists also promote a cognitive dissonance theory of learning, most notably Leon Festinger. Festinger (1957) contended that any two elements of knowledge could be related in one of three ways: consonant with each other, dissonant with each other, or irrelevant to each other. The theory revolves around the middle of these three terms, and two basic corollaries have been developed for his theory.

The first corollary is that the magnitude of the dissonance increases as the value of the respective elements increase. A person will experience only minor dissonance if the items in conflict have little value or importance. On the other hand, items which are highly valued will, when in opposition, create a much higher level of dissonance.

The second corollary is that the dissonance gives rise to pressures to reduce or eliminate that dissonance. The strength of the pressure to re-

duce the dissonance is directly related to the magnitude of that dissonance.

Cognitive dissonance is an ally to the teacher who knows how to uncover the naturally occurring cognitive dissonance within the learner and then guide the learner toward a healthy and appropriate way to reduce or eliminate the dissonance. The Christian educator must, of course, insure that the reduction or elimination of dissonance is done in reference to the true knowledge revealed through God's Word and his world.

ROBERT DEVRIES

Bibliography. L. Festinger (1957), *A Theory of Cognitive Dissonance;* J. M. Snapper (1984), *Christian Approaches to Learning Theory: A Symposium.*

See also COGNITIVE DEVELOPMENT; DISEQUILIBRIUM; PIAGET, JEAN

Cognitive Field Theory. Cognitive field theory investigated the process through which structures of the human mind organize material being learned. In reaction to the associationist/connectionist theories of behaviorism, which understood humans to be organisms like rats and pigeons, cognitive theorists investigated the unique ability of humans to process information received by categorizing and structuring it mentally. Thus, cognitive field theory turned from observing the external behavior of humans to speculation regarding the ways their minds internally processed information. One model for processing information was borrowed from computer science. If behaviorism relied on the parallelism between animal and human learning, information processing theory explored the analogy between the human mind and the computer. The assumption was, not that the mind was a computer, but that computer programs could be used to develop models of how human minds processed certain input, transforming it into observed output.

This model for explaining humans has generated volumes of research regarding how humans learn which have enormous influence on Christian education. Cognitive field theory allowed psychologists to move beyond understanding the learning of involuntary behavior through association and simple skills through trial-and-error connections to comprehending how persons acquired concepts, principles, and problem-solving skills. Cognitivists defined concepts as abstractions that categorize objects or events with similar qualities and principles as relationships between two or more concepts. They were concerned with how students discriminated among phenomena with different attributes so that categorization could accurately be made among them and they could be coded into systems that facilitated learning and retention. For example, being able to discriminate between a fig as a fruit and corn as a vegetable or Josiah as a king and Ezekiel as a prophet allows students to structure the subject matter to make learning much more efficient than learning isolated, unrelated facts.

Various mental processes have been categorized, each with its optimal method for promoting learning. Facts are best learned by organizing and coding them; concepts by the presentation of prerequisite knowledge, definitions, and examples; and principles by understanding the embedded concepts and allowing the student to paraphrase the principles. Cognitive field theorists have made it evident that simple association-connectionist theories are totally inadequate for understanding the complex ways humans learn especially concepts and principles, which are essential in the Christian education setting.

Two general ways of teaching have grown out of cognitive field theory—expository teaching and discovery learning. David Ausubel advocated expository teaching, which occurs when well-organized and meaningful material is presented to the learner in a lecture format, including a brief organized overview of the lesson followed by discussion of the concepts and principles involved and accompanied by appropriate, specific examples. The technique is an efficient way of communicating cognitive content to a large audience in a short period of time, but the learners remain quite passive. Another technique with roots in cognitivism is discovery learning. Championed by Jerome Bruner, it involves the teacher structuring the environment with a variety of examples from which the students are expected to induce principles on their own. This method is more time-consuming, but what is lost in efficiency is hopefully gained in increased understanding due to active personal involvement in the information processing.

A major corollary of the cognitive field theorists' understanding of learning was that all humans do not process information in a similar way, as the associationist/connectionist theorists before them had assumed. Instead, cognitive developmentalists showed how humans, in the course of their development, process input in progressively complex ways. Piaget demonstrated that students proceed from processing direct input of the senses (Sensorimotor) to employing symbols to stand for sensory input (Preoperational) to categorizing symbols in concrete form (Concrete Operational) to manipulating abstract concepts based on several symbols (Formal Operational). Piaget also gave educators language to speak about how students process information at the successive stages. At each stage, the person deals with new input either by assimilating it directly without significant alteration to mental structures or by altering the mental structures, thus accommodating the new input. In either case the mental structures reach equilibration at a new level of cognitive functioning. The Russian psychologist Lev S. Vygotsky built on Piaget's cognitive theory by speculating that at the students' "zones of proximal development" they can be aided by adults to process material at a higher level than they could without such aid. In addition, Lawrence Kohlberg applied Piaget's stages to moral reasoning and James Fowler to faith, an area particularly relevant to Christian education.

Although cognitive field theory brings a clear advance on association-connectionist theories of learning by more adequately dealing with human rationality, especially by incorporating the learning of concepts and principles, the cognitivists did not address sufficiently other areas like self-understanding and human interaction and the effects of these on learning. Because these areas are of particular concern to Christian educators, it is quite fortunate that his shortcoming was later addressed by humanistic theory.

JOHN R. YEATTS

Bibliography. D. P. Ausubel (1963), *The Theory of Meaningful Verbal Learning;* J. S. Bruner (1966), *Toward a Theory of Instruction;* E. R. Hilgard and G. H. Bower (1975), *Theories of Learning;* B. Inhelder and J. Piaget (1958), *The Growth of Logical Thinking from Childhood to Adolescence;* L. S. Vygotsky (1962), *Thought and Language.*

See also AUSUBEL, DAVID P.; BRUNER, JEROME; DISCOVERY LEARNING; PIAGET, JEAN

Cognitive Learning, Theories of. The concept of cognitive learning is not foreign to the Scriptures. God is deeply concerned with the intellectual growth of his people. When Paul wrote to the church at Corinth he declared, "When I was a child, I used to speak as a child, think as a child, reason as a child; when I became a man, I did away with childish things" (1 Cor. 13:11). Paul was pointing to the undeniable reality that children and adults talk, think, and reason differently. Not only did Paul recognize that there were developmental differences, but he also commented on the progressive nature of development when he said; "I gave you milk to drink, not solid food; for you were not yet able to receive it. Indeed, even now you are not yet able" (1 Cor. 3:2).

In the letter to the Hebrews, the writer paints a similar picture of the required stages of development by contrasting babes in Christ who need milk with mature Christians who require solid food (Heb. 5:12–14). Jesus developed that maturity in his youth according to the Gospel of Luke: "And Jesus kept increasing in wisdom and stature, and in favor with God and men" (Luke 2:52). While Scripture only reveals two stages of development, in moving from childhood to adulthood, the concept is clear. In order to mature one must move from the milk stage of life to the solid food stage of life.

Developmental psychology has revealed several more stages of cognitive development, but the theory of growth and maturity is revealed throughout Scripture. An individual is primarily responsible for his or her intellectual development, and that development occurs in stages through the first two decades of a person's life.

Swiss researcher Jean Piaget is the person most closely associated with cognitive developmental theory. As a genetic epistemologist Piaget sought to understand how a person's thinking matures over time. His primary concepts involve assimilation and accommodation as the two ways in which the mind adapts to knowledge and experience. Assimilation occurs when a person takes in new knowledge and changes it to fit what is already understood. When a child is introduced to a playmate's father, she assimilates the friend's father into a previously constructed concept of father and family.

Accommodation occurs when a person moves beyond changing the new information to fit present understanding and changes the very thought structures to accommodate the new knowledge or experience. This is often seen in the "a-ha" moment when a student declares, "I never thought of it that way before." Suppose the friend's parents are divorced and the child comes to understand that her playmate only sees Daddy once a week and Daddy does not live in the same house. In order to include the friend's father into her own understanding of what a father is, she must change her concept of father and does so by declaring, "I never met a father who didn't live with his children before!"

Through assimilation and accommodation people develop thought structures as ways of viewing life that are constantly changing. As people mature these thought structures develop into stages with each stage involving more complex structures. Through his research Piaget developed four stages of qualitative reasoning that a person logically and systematically progresses through from birth to young adulthood. The first stage is known as the Sensorimotor Period, which ranges from birth to 2 years of age. Infants are very self-centered and rely mostly on reflexes to explore their world through sensory perceptions and motor activities. Piaget terms this "practical intelligence." As infants become less self-centered, they become aware of objects and people. Interaction with the objects and people in their environment begin to develop concepts such as: cause and effect, space and time, and abilities such as intentional behavior, symbolic representation of physical actions, and basic communications skills.

The second stage of cognitive development is known as the Preoperational Period, often referred to as incomplete thinking, which ranges from 2 to 7 years of age. Children at this stage begin to encounter life on a symbolic level. Dreams, mental images, make-believe friends, and language all contribute to the symbolic nature of the preoperational period. Preschoolers learn to adjust to the norms of the world by imitating the activities of adults.

In the first half of this stage, often known as preconceptual, children are unable to differentiate identical items from the same class. In the latter part of this stage, often known as intuitive, a child's thinking becomes more semilogical even though concepts are still intuitive and somewhat confused. Not only do children in this stage believe that everything has a reason or purpose, they also believe that everything is caused by the actions of the adults around them, even natural events. This grouping of unrelated events or thoughts also leads children to spin yarns composed of a variety of unrelated ideas, stories, or activities. Finally, these students believe that their thoughts and feelings are shared by everyone in their environment.

Stage three is known as the Concrete Operational Period, which ranges from 7 to 11 years of age. At this point a child's thinking becomes more flexible, complex, and decentered. At this point a child is able to think about a variety of issues at the same time. Children are able to apply this logical thought to concrete situations which include real objects and classify them mentally. Mathematics (addition, subtraction, multiplication, and division) are now possible by using objects to organize the child's thinking process.

As children develop the characteristic of reversibility in this stage, they are able to perform a concrete operation (such as addition) and then reverse the process (subtraction) to check the accuracy of their conclusion. This characteristic also allows children to predict the consequences of their actions by considering the logical outcome of an action or the lack thereof.

Stage four is known as the Formal Operational Period, which ranges from 11 to 15 years of age and beyond. Previously limited to that which could be observed concretely, an adolescent is able to think about thoughts and ideas. Multiple combinations of ideas allow adolescents to approach new situations with an array of possibilities. Cognitive reasoning now includes abstract thinking, hypothetical concepts, inductive and deductive logic, and the ability to test hypotheses. Symbols may now be substituted for real objects and parabolic analogies are possible to understand.

While Piaget's insights are helpful in understanding the cognitive structures of human development, he does not address the moral absolutes upon which Christians base their personhood. This objective interpersonal relationship with

God, which exists apart and above cultural constructs of reality, provides a standard for cognitive reasoning. Piaget was merely concerned about the intellectual process, whereas Christians must also be concerned with the content that is being processed.

Jerome Bruner based much of his theory of cognitive learning on Piaget as he identified three characteristics of the ways in which people attain knowledge. His first concept is simply that to know is to do. He does not mean to imply that there is a logical correlation between knowing and doing, but that knowledge is always affected by a person's behaviors. Knowledge is constantly being formed and reformed as it is explored in a variety of environments, tested against experience, and reshaped in accordance with an individual's particular worldview.

Second, Bruner asserts that a person must do something with the knowledge attained if that knowledge is to become purposeful. Knowledge in a vacuum is meaningless. Only when knowledge is applied does it become cogent and lead to wisdom. Finally, Bruner claimed that acquiring knowledge necessitates a social context. Knowledge is formed and reformed in community as people interact with one another.

Within the cognitive domain of learning, Benjamin Bloom developed a taxonomy of educational objectives which includes six degrees of cognitive performance. The first level of Bloom's taxonomy is Knowledge. This level of knowledge is simply the ability to match a mental picture with a concrete object.

The second level is Comprehension. At this level a person understands an idea well enough to be able to communicate the mental concept to another person based on his or her own understanding. The communication of the concept may be accomplished in a variety of ways: conversation, illustration, demonstration, and so on. This level is distinguished from the first level by the learner's ability to express the concept from within.

The third level is Application. This occurs when a person applies existing knowledge to a new situation. By transferring known principles into an unknown situation, a problem becomes solvable. Often people may not know the solution to a problem, but they are able to "figure it out" through the transference of common principles.

The fourth level is Analysis. At this level a person must know the operational components of a concept and the relationship of the components to each other and to the whole. This level is essential for the development of problem-solving abilities. In order to solve complex problems, a person must know the functions of each component and the contribution that each component makes to the concept.

The fifth level is Synthesis. This is the level where true creativity is expressed. Synthesis involves using the known components of a concept and creating a new or variant concept. This is also the challenge of integrating two different concepts in such a way as to develop an alternative concept.

Evaluation is the final level. This is the task of making a judgment based on a set of criteria. Evaluation void of criteria cannot be considered valid, though evaluation can be either objective or subjective in approach.

While theories of cognitive learning lay a foundation for understanding the process of learning, it is important for Christian educators to remember the Hebrew concept of knowledge. The Hebrew word for "know" is *yada* which means "to experience or encounter." To say that Adam knew Eve is to say that Adam experienced or encountered Eve. God calls his people to encounter him wholly.

As Bruner's theory suggests, knowing must be accompanied with doing. Attaining a certain amount of information falls short of God's concept of knowledge; there must be a response from the practical facet of life. More than a mere intellectual activity, cognitive learning must affect the whole human personality, including its behaviors and morality.

MARK W. CANNISTER

Bibliography. B. Bloom (1985), *Developing Talent in Young People;* J. Bruner (1966), *Studies in Cognitive Growth;* H. Ginsburg and S. Opper (1988), *Piaget's Theory of Intellectual Development;* D. Elkind (1981), *The Hurried Child: Growing Up Too Soon;* idem (1984), *All Grown Up and No Place to Go;* K. Issler and R. Habermas (1994), *How We Learn: A Christian Teacher's Guide to Educational Psychology;* J. Piaget (1975), *The Development of Thought: Equilibration of Cognitive Structures;* R. Pazmiño (1997), *Foundational Issues in Christian Education: An Introduction in Evangelical Perspective.*

See also BRUNER, JEROME; INFORMATION PROCESSING; PIAGET, JEAN

Cognitive Processing. *See* Information Processing.

Cohabitation. Two individuals who are living together without being married. In the broadest sense of the word, two people of the same sex who share a dorm room, apartment, or other similar housing arrangement technically qualify as "cohabitants." However, in most cases, when the term cohabitation is used, it is referring to a man and woman who share the same housing arrangement but are not married.

Cohabitation is a popular alternative for many people before they rush into a marriage which statistics show has only a fifty-fifty chance of survival. According to demographers Sweet and

Bumpass (1988), in half of all marriages at least one of the individuals had lived with another partner before getting married. Most revealing is the realization that only 60 percent of those who cohabitated before marriage with the intent of eventually getting married ever followed through with the ceremony.

Cohabitation: Living Together before Marriage. When moral absolutes, and the values which are based upon them, no longer remain constant and society's moral ethics become clouded by a lack of consistent standards of conduct, decision making becomes more difficult and complex. In this light many Americans have chosen to reject the traditional bonds of marriage for more flexible living arrangements.

During the Colonial period of American history, it was rare for a couple to cohabitate. Such a lifestyle would have been met with social scorn and isolation. Today, however, such alternative lifestyles are becoming more commonly accepted.

Between 1970 and 1980, the number of live-in couples in the United States had more than tripled to 1.6 million. According to the 1987 United States Bureau of Census, approximately 2.3 million unmarried American couples are currently cohabitating (Koon, 1991). No doubt, this number continued to climb in the 1990s, although an exact figure will not be known until after the year 2000 census is taken.

But according to Brothers (1988), many single adults, especially women, are discovering that living together has some major drawbacks. They reported a number of reasons why such an alternative living arrangement does *not* work out. These include:

1. Divorce can be more likely. According to a recent study conducted by the National Bureau of Economic Research, couples who live together before getting married have nearly an 80 percent higher divorce rate than couples who do not.

2. Lower level of marital satisfaction. A 1983 study by the National Council of Family Relations of 309 recently married couples finds that couples who live together before marriage are less happy in their marriages. The report indicates that women are less happy in terms of the quality of communication with their spouse after the wedding.

3. Men move in primarily for sex. A 1973 study of Northeastern University students found that the number one reason women lived with a lover was because they wanted to get married. However, the number one reason for men was "sex—when you want it, where you want it."

This motivation for living together has not changed much over the years as indicated by a 1988 article in the Gazette Telegraph. Their study reveals that many men lie about their sexual past or their drug use in order to make a positive impression on a potential sexual partner. In their study, 35 percent of the men admitted that they had lied to a woman in order to have sex with her, a rate the researchers consider a low estimate. Sixty percent of the women surveyed said they thought a man had lied to them. The most common lies included telling a potential partner that he cared more for her than he really did, and that he had had fewer sex partners than was actually the case.

4. Few marriages actually result from cohabitation. The real truth about cohabitation relationships is that they do not last. In the heat of tension and turmoil, one of the partners has no binding reason to stay and walks out. According to a 1985 Columbia University study, only 26 percent of the women surveyed—a scant 19 percent of the men—ended up marrying the person with whom they were cohabitating.

5. Higher risk for communicable diseases. A 1973 study cited in the Journal of Marriage and the Family reported that live-in males sleep around more than married men do. If that trend continues, and there is no reason to believe it has not, live-in males can potentially put their partners in serious health risk from AIDS, herpes, and other sexually transmitted diseases.

6. Greater sexual hostility. In the 1986 *New Woman* sex survey, a whopping 40 percent of cohabitating women said they had endured a kind of sex they didn't want or enjoy. This compares with 35 percent for divorced and separated women. "The main problem," according to California sociologist Dr. Jack Balswick, "is . . . there is no commitment in a live-in relationship. It's all for immediate pay off, immediate gratification. So the man figures, 'If I don't get what I want now, then I'll just get out of the relationship.' A falsehood many people who buy into temporary relationships believe is the notion that they can build a meaningful relationship without full commitment."

7. Cohabitating women felt less secure. Single women who share their living arrangements with a partner feel more insecure about the future of their love relationship than do other women.

8. Breaking up is just as painful. The misconception that says they are "free to leave any time they want" is simply not true. There is a great deal of emotional bonding that takes place during the period of cohabitation and the pain of a partner's departure is every bit as painful and real.

Who Are Most Likely to Cohabitate before Marriage? The stereotypical image of single adults who cohabitate portrayed by the media today are college students and young urban professionals. But according to a recent study conducted at the University of Wisconsin, these stereotypical images are simply not accurate. They discovered that financial problems seem to be the significant factor that caused people to live together before marriage. They believed the old adage that "two could live as cheaply as one" and were willing to see if it was true. Here is some of what they discovered in their study:

1. People who have not completed high school have a 30 percent higher rate of cohabitation than those who go on to college. Those with lower incomes and less education are considerably more likely to live together without getting married.

2. Those with more money are more likely to be married or live alone. Money allows people the "luxury" of living alone or the ability to afford marriage.

3. Between half and two-thirds of the decline in marriage among young people can be accounted for by the rise in cohabitation.

4. For those under the age of 20, the percent of those married declined from 27 percent in 1970 to 14 percent in 1985. But the percent of those involved in some type of "union" (marriage or cohabitation) dropped only 20 percent to 23 percent.

5. Of all couples who married between 1970 and 1985, 40 percent had lived together first (Koons, 1991, 140).

MICHAEL J. ANTHONY

Bibliography. J. Brother (1988), *New Woman,* pp. 54–57; C. Koons and M. J. Anthony (1991), *Single Adult Passages: Uncharted Territories;* J. A. Sweet and L. Bumpass (1988), *American Families and Households.*

Cohesion in Groups. One of the most important measures of a group's health is a somewhat slippery attribute known as cohesiveness. It is defined as "the desire of members to remain as members of a group" (Zander, 1979, 433). Research consistently points to the following three variables being present in the best groups: (1) sharing a common purpose; (2) members' understanding of their particular role in the group; and (3) experiencing the invisible glue leading to group cohesion. When these are present, group members are likely to report high degrees of satisfaction with their group experience (Griffin, 1982). These factors are not wholly independent of one another.

Group cohesion is a social science cousin to the important biblical value of unity. There is an evangelistically strategic benefit to a visible display of loving unity: the world will be able to observe that believers belong to Jesus Christ and be drawn to closer inspection by this attractive witness.

What are the key factors contributing to a group's cohesiveness? Two have been consistently identified. First, in groups that see themselves as called to accomplish a particular task, the success of the group's efforts is a source of group cohesion. Second, in groups that perceive their role as socially supportive, the quality of interpersonal attraction is attributed to the similarity between members.

The desirable quality of group cohesiveness in ministry can be positively facilitated when groups are engaged in interdependent tasks where there is a high likelihood that they will experience success. As these ministry experiences become a part of their common heritage, similar values will be forged that further enhance group cohesion.

DAVE RAHN

Bibliography. J. A. Gorman (1993), *Community That Is Christian;* E. Griffin (1982), *Getting Together: A Guide to Good Groups;* D. Rydberg (1985), *Building Community in Youth Groups;* A. Zander (1979), *Annual Review of Psychology* 30.

Coles, Robert Martin (1929–). Child psychiatrist. Born in Boston the son of an engineer, he grew up and was educated in the Boston area, including his undergraduate studies at Harvard. It was as a student at Harvard that Coles came under the influence of William Carlos Williams, a physician with a strong interest in the humanities. The impact Williams had on Coles was significant, and he decided to follow in the footsteps of Williams and study medicine. Coles enrolled in medical school at Columbia University, where he specialized in child psychiatry and received his M.D. in 1954.

Following a one-year internship at University of Chicago clinics, Coles returned to the Boston area for a series of residencies in the mid–1950s. The late 1950s found Coles in the deep South. A two-year stint as an air force physician in Mississippi was followed by a study of school desegregation in New Orleans. The importance of the surrounding events was noted by Coles: "Had I not been right there, driving by the mobs that heckled six-year-old Ruby Bridges, a black first-grader, as she tried to attend the Frantz School, I might have pursued a different life" (1990, xi).

Coles was trained as a child psychiatrist, but it was during this time in his life that the influence of Williams blossomed. One lesson Coles learned from his mentor was to listen to his patients and to see them as individuals rather than subjects.

Coles's interest in the integration movement led him to begin a field study of the children affected by the events around them. His interviews and observations resulted in his first book, *Children of Crisis: A Study of Courage and Fear* in 1964. This was the first of what was to become a five-volume series, and through it Coles became a recognized voice in the study of children. Various awards and grants came Coles's way as a result of his work, including the Pulitzer Prize in 1973 for volumes 2 and 3 in the series.

In choosing to study children, Coles acknowledged his indebtedness to Anna Freud and Erik Erikson. Coles brought to his work the scholarship of a trained academician, yet wrote in a warm, unassuming style. By listening to the children he interviewed and allowing them to tell their own stories, Coles avoided the coldness of most clinical studies. Instead of analyzing, Coles collected and shared the observations, dreams, and fears of the children themselves.

The success of the *Children of Crisis* series and his continued work in child psychiatry earned Coles a five-year MacArthur fellowship in 1981. This provided the resources necessary to expand his studies of children to those from other countries. Coles drew on interviews he had with children from South Africa and Brazil, and added ones from Northern Ireland, Poland, Southeast Asia, Nicaragua, and French-speaking Canada. During the same period, at the suggestion of Anna Freud, he reviewed his interviews of American children. The result was his trilogy: *The Inner Lives of Children: The Moral Life of Children* (1986), *The Political Life of Children* (1986), and *The Spiritual Life of Children* (1990). In all three books, Coles continued to provide insight into the way in which children think, form opinions, and reach conclusions.

In addition to his writings on children, Coles also teaches at Harvard. Again demonstrating the influence of Williams, Coles' classes include a strong component of literature. His emphasis on the study of the humanities is characteristic of Coles' belief that professional studies need to be well-rounded and should help students connect with humanity.

As an author, Coles has much to offer. His observations and insights into child psychiatry have already been acknowledged. Additionally, his methods of doing research provide an excellent example of the value of field-based research. His skill as a listener and as a storyteller is noteworthy.

Another major contribution is Coles's identification and acknowledgment of the moral and spiritual dimensions of life. In addition to addressing the economic, racial, and political issues of the day, Coles makes it clear that man has a moral and spiritual dimension as well, and it is in these areas that individuals find the strength to face the more obvious crises.

DOUGLAS BARCALOW

Bibliography. R. M. Coles (1964), *Children of Crisis: A Study of Courage and Fear;* idem (1997), *The Moral Intelligence of Children;* idem (1986), *The Moral Life of Children;* idem (1986), *The Political Life of Children;* idem (1990), *The Spiritual Life of Children.*

See also ERIKSON, ERIK HOMBURGER; PSYCHOLOGY OF RELIGION

Collaborative Learning. Learning that occurs when persons of like experience, training, or education work together to achieve a common goal. The most likely biblical example of "collaborative" learning is the Upper Room after Jesus' ascension into heaven. The disciples all had similar experience (only twelve of them had more extensive experience with Jesus than the others) and the same focus. They were going to obey Jesus' last command to wait "for what the Father had promised" (Acts 1:4). They went to the Upper Room and "waited." They "devoted themselves to prayer" (Acts 1:14). They collaborated. The end result of their collaboration (working together for a common purpose) was that the Holy Spirit came on each of them.

Perhaps the most evident life example of collaborative learning is given by birds. When they fly to warmer or cooler climates they do so through collaboration. They pool their similar experience and instincts to achieve a common goal. The end result is they make the trip in a shorter time, and they all make it together. If these trips were done separately, many would not be physically able to complete the trip, and it would certainly take the capable ones much longer. This is the best part of collaborative learning. Those who participate take turns leading, and the rest take turns urging the leader on. The result is that all who participate learn more and they learn it quicker than they would otherwise.

The biblical verse that best exemplifies collaborative learning is Proverbs 27:17, "Iron sharpens iron, So one man sharpens another." The idea is that as one piece of iron helps rough parts of another piece of iron be smoothed out, both become sharper because of the mutual action. So it is with collaborative learning. When two or more persons with similar experience or training help each other, both more clearly develop toward Christlikeness. The goal could be less lofty, such as helping each other better understand the original intent of an author being considered.

Collaborative learning is least helpful when those involved are intimidated by each other or are suffering from a sense of inferiority. It is most helpful when those involved give help from a position of strength to others who are in a position of strength. The strengths in this case need not be identical. One may be a medical doctor and another a lawyer, and the subject may be medical ethics.

ROY F. LYNN

College. *See* University.

Colonial Education. Education in the American colonies is best understood by studying the demographics of three geographical sectors: the New England colonies, the Middle States, and the southern colonies. Each region was populated by the immigrant influx from Europe—men, women, and children seeking religious freedom and the opportunity to live according to the dictates of their faith. Although these immigrants were from a wide diversity of cultures and religious practices, they were primarily Protestant in faith.

In the New England colonies, education was influenced by the heavy Calvinistic beliefs of the Puritan colonists who immigrated to that region. Most notable was the influence of the 1642 General Court Act in Massachusetts that required parents to teach their children to read so that they could understand on their own the practices of their religious faith and the laws of the land. By 1647 the Old Deluder Act was enacted, requiring the establishment of state schools to educate children. The Puritans believed that Satan desired to keep the minds of children ignorant so that they could not come to know Christ. The Old Deluder Act was the Puritans' attempt to ensure that the devil's efforts met with failure. Arising from this concern for literacy to combat the schemes of the devil was the development of the New England primer. First published around 1690, the primer taught the alphabet using biblical analogies for each letter, as well as the Lord's Prayer, the Ten Commandments, and other lessons intended to strengthen the religious values of youth. In addition to the formation of the common schools for the training of children, Harvard College was founded as the first institution of higher education to educate ministers in the doctrines of Calvinism for service in the new world.

In the Middle States colonies, educational practice was extremely diverse, largely due to the pluralism of cultures and religious beliefs of the immigrants who settled in that region. A limited number of denominational schools were planted in Pennsylvania, New York, and New Jersey, but education remained primarily a private endeavor. Several religious groups formed private and parochial schools to preserve their respective religious heritages. In these schools, educational curriculums were created that combined religious training with the basics of reading, writing, and arithmetic. Notable religious groups in the Middle States colonies who created their own schools were the Calvinists, Quakers, Anglicans, Lutherans, Moravians, Dunkers, Anabaptists, Presbyterians, Roman Catholics, and Jews. The Pietist movement also arose in the midst of this pluralism of beliefs and practices. The Pietists believed that the faith of the heart was being distorted by the faith of the mind so prominent in many religious schools. Pietist agricultural communities were formed to separate the faithful from the fallen, and to inhibit the faithful from being led astray by intellectualism.

In the southern colonies, the influence of the Anglican Church was keenly evident in the educational practices of the colonists. The formation of plantations resulted in the stratification of social classes that prevented the formation of state schools like those in New England. As in the Mid-

dle States colonies, education became a private matter, but primarily only the wealthy went to school. Distances between plantations made the placement of schools problematic, so tutors were commonly employed by the rich to train their children at home. Poor whites could not afford to attend the public schools or hire tutors, and the black slave population was prohibited from being educated. Unlike the New England colonies with their strong Calvinistic heritage, the dominance of the Anglican Church did not result in a strong religious orientation in the schools that were formed in the south.

Across the three colonial sectors, two types of schools developed. The common or vernacular school at the elementary or primary level and the Latin grammar school of the upper education track. The vernacular schools provided training for children in the essential religious doctrines of the parent church, as well as providing skills in reading, writing, spelling, and arithmetic. Children usually did not progress beyond the vernacular schools to the Latin grammar schools unless they were privileged or destined for leadership in the church. In the Latin grammar schools, the curriculum was heavily influenced by the classical studies of the Renaissance, with a heavy emphasis on languages and religious instruction.

Beyond the Latin grammar schools were the first American colleges. Several of the prominent and highly respected universities of contemporary society were founded during the colonial era as religious colleges for the training of leadership for the church. Although the religious heritage of many of these schools would be hard to identify today, in the colonial era they served as the primary training centers in orthodoxy for ministers for the New World. Among the several American colleges founded at this time were Harvard (Puritan), William and Mary and King's College (Anglican), Yale and Dartmouth (Congregationalist), Princeton (Presbyterian), Brown (Baptist), and Rutgers (Dutch Reformed).

MARK E. SIMPSON

Bibliography. K. O. Gangel and W. S. Benson (1983), *Christian Education: Its History and Philosophy;* G. L. Gutek (1991), *Education in the United States: An Historical Perspective;* M. J. Taylor, ed. (1960), *Religious Education: A Comprehensive Survey.*

Comenius, Johann Amos (1592–1671). Educator and theologian. Born in Moravia (part of what is now the Czech Republic) and educated at Herborn and Heidelberg, Comenius was a parish minister and the last bishop of the Church of the Bohemian Brethren. The hostilities of the Thirty Years' War and attendant religious persecution necessitated that he and other religionists flee from Bohemia to Lissa, Poland, in 1621. While living in Lissa, he was rector of the gymnasium and wrote his major educational work, *The Great Didactic,* which was published in 1632. Continued religio-political unrest forced him to travel from place to place. His travels also provided a forum for innovative educational ideas as well as his clerical commitments.

Comenius, though known for his contributions as a parish pastor and bishop, is most remembered for his development of a system of pedagogy that was revolutionary to teaching practices of the day. Troubled by the horrible human and societal costs of a bloody war, he saw education as the medium to bring peace. His book, *The Great Didactic,* introduced teaching methodologies, which are basic to modern instructional approaches. Utilizing picture books for small children, the conversational method of learning languages, and the introduction of singing, art, politics, geography, science, and crafts in children's school curriculum were Comenius's innovations. Although these were significant additions to an methodologically impoverished educational system, of greatest benefit was the new philosophical basis that Comenius brought to learning. A forerunner of modern liberal arts education, he opposed coerced education and was committed to educating the whole person for life. That education necessitated the inclusion of the disciplines of science, history, and biblical studies. The subtitle of *The Great Didactic* seems to describe this educational pioneer's passion: "the whole art of teaching all things to all men . . . that the entire youth of both sexes, none being excepted, shall quickly, pleasantly, and thoroughly become learned in the sciences, pure in morals, trained in piety, and in this manner trained in all things necessary for the present and for the future of life."

The language of the *The Great Didactic* was Latin, the general written form for European culture of the time. It was also an important feature of Comenius's plan to demonstrate how Latin could be mastered in the schools he envisioned. Comenius was opposed to the restrictive methods of the day, which included memorization and drill over untranslated words from an ancient, largely undecipherable text without the help of a nonexistent dictionary. He created his own primer, *Janua Linguarum Reserata,* or "An Introduction to Language," to fill the void. *Janua Linguarum Reserata* and its easier successor, *Vestibulum,* were soon established as the best books of their times and underwent numerous translations and reprintings as accepted texts well into the late 1800s.

The educational reforms of Comenius, however, were met with far less acceptance. His beliefs in millennialism (he said the world would end in 1672) and the blatant discrimination against the Brethren sect left his name discredited and suspect at his death. Because of this, his educational contributions went virtually unnoticed until the nineteenth century, and *The Great Didactic* itself was not translated into English until 1921. At that time Comenius was recognized as having proposed details of the schoolhouse environment such as a separate classroom for each class, a desk for the teacher and chairs for the pupils, and designating an area for dramatic presentations and speeches. His *Orbis Sensualium Pictus* (The Visible World in Pictures) was the precedent for elementary school textbooks that combine words and pictures. Many of the ideas of Rousseau and Pestalozzi are found in his writings in fully developed form.

Comenius traveled extensively throughout Europe and was sought after to represent his pedagogical views. He was called to Sweden to examine and reform their whole educational departments. Though ahead of his educational times, Comenius saw education as a way to mold students into the image of Christ. He was committed to making the development of Christian character more important than the mere absorption of facts. Comenius was the author of *Pansophiae Prodromus, Janua Linguarum Reserata, Orbis Sensualium Pictus,* and *Didactica Magna.*

WILLIAM F. FALKNER

Commission. *See* Mission.

Common Morality. *See* Heteronomous Morality.

Communication, Styles of. Term used most frequently in human communication dynamics to signify the way that a communicator gives ideas meaning through verbal and nonverbal delivery of a message. Style deals with choice of words, tone, sentence structure, and mode of transmission.

Communicators develop a personal style, a manner of conveying a message that is specific to them. This is inevitably true, since all speakers have a unique range of vocabulary, varying cultural backgrounds that have influenced language usage, assumptions based on values and beliefs, diverse cognitive strengths that impact communication, and personality characteristics that affect how messages are both sent and received.

As unique as a personal style may be to communicators, different situations also have a bearing on rhetoric, conversation, and other presentation forms. Formal or informal, debate or panel discussion, small or large group—these and other situational expectations in a communication encounter will substantially affect verbiage, tone, and body language.

The ability to adapt one's style to maximize influence is very crucial, and flexibility serves to enhance the strength of stylistic aptitude. One personal style might work best with adults, another with children, yet another with youth. But it is generally accepted that a communicator can adapt personal communication style to effectively teach a biblical *pericope* to all age groups if there is a willingness to adapt.

The New Testament illustrates personal style and its adaptation in the ministries of both Jesus and Paul. Jesus had a communication style, it is assumed, unique to him and that enabled him to be recognized as the teacher par excellence in human history. But his style is adapted to various situations. A survey of Scripture reveals that he talked to the authorities with a different tone and intensity than he did with his disciples and different with his disciples than with the larger crowds. Even within the group of disciples, Jesus' style is adapted to their various educational levels, that is, a different and more intensive tack was used the longer Jesus had taught them and the closer he was to the cross.

Paul, known as the first great Christian missionary, used his style with adaptations to communicate differently with those in the synagogue than with Greeks. His written style changed according to situation, as can be seen by comparing his missive to the problematic church in Corinth to his letter to the beloved church at Philippi. And, as with Jesus, his tone and message evolved over time as his demise grew imminent.

Another interesting study looks at God's communication style throughout Scripture. At times he reveals himself in a voice, through prophets, as the Son of God in the incarnation, as a rushing wind in the upper room of Acts, as well as a bright light on a road leading to Damascus, and eventually through the entire sixty-six books of canonical Scripture, culminating in a revelatory vision.

Matt Friedeman

Communication Theory. Communication is the transmission of signals to a receptor by a sender in hopes of relating a message. Communication theory deals with the academic pursuit of knowledge in the field through the scientific gathering of data and its systematic compilation and usage.

Communication theory equips the student to organize conceptual tools designed to better understand the process of communication and improve skills in various vocational endeavors. Since communication has increasingly been recognized for its central role in culture, job markets, and ministry, the study of related theory has gained popularity in recent years. The maturity of the field of communication is evidenced by the number of journals now produced, the departments of communication at public and private institutions of higher learning, and the utilization of communication research and theory in a wide variety of fields.

Four perspectives are frequently considered in communication theory: (1) the behavioristic perspective, which focuses on stimulus-response and how receptors are influenced by messages; (2) the transmissional perspective, which stresses linear sending and receiving of messages via communication media; (3) the interactional perspective, which takes into consideration the reciprocal nature of communicators; and (4) the transactional perspective which views communication as a dynamic process given to fulfilling individual and corporate functions and which examines shared meaning.

Some issues that communication theory must continue to address in an attempt to be relevant to Christian ministry are: how language is acquired and the definition of meaning; symbols and meanings as the foundation for communication in general which includes, but is not limited to, language; how such symbols and meanings reach consensus in society; ways in which individual and social communication reflect, assimilate, adapt to, and accommodate economic, spiritual, and cultural values; providing an understanding of why communication changes contextually from one setting to another; the role of communication in constructing social interaction and interdependence; the nature of persuasion and the vital elements of communication that changes thought and behavior; the nature of conflict and the type of communication that escalates or reduces dissension; and the optimal balance of relational and task-related communication to achieve group objectives.

Matt Friedeman

Bibliography. S. W. Littlejohn (1983), *Theories of Human Communication.*

Communion. Worship practice of partaking in bread and wine or juice in order to remember the sacrificial atonement of Jesus Christ on the cross. Some Christian traditions refer to the practice as the Lord's Supper as a way of pointing to its beginning with Jesus' Last Supper with the disciples. Others, typically those with a more formal worship style, refer to the practice as the Eucharist. *Eucharist* is an English transliteration of the Greek word meaning "thankful praise."

Beginnings. The practice of communion originated in the early church as recorded in 1 Corinthians 11:23–25. Here we have what are called the words of institution, which are stated at communion services and seem to reflect the practice of the early church. All four Gospels record the initiating event where Jesus shares the Passover meal with his disciples prior to his Passion. The story of the disciples on the road to Emmaus is a powerful illustration of the importance of communion. Christ is revealed to the disciples in the breaking of the bread. This illustrates the significance of communion as a memorial. From early Christian documents such as the First Apology of Justin Martyr and the Didache, we know that communion was practiced regularly in the early church. Christians would meet and the first part of worship would be the sharing of Scripture with a sermon, then prayers. Following this, the catechumens would be dismissed and the communion service would begin.

Forms. The frequency and form in which communion is practiced varies. Some churches practice communion every Sunday as a central act of worship, some once a month, and others less frequently. The form varies from formal to informal. Typical of the more formal services would be the Roman Catholic, Lutheran, and Episcopal traditions, where the liturgy of the service is prescribed and those partaking in communion come forward to receive the elements. In less formal services the minister has considerable flexibility in the service, and the elements are typically distributed to the partakers in their seats.

Meaning. The meaning of communion is related to the Passover meal, which was the setting of Jesus' meal with the disciples. The Jewish tradition and roots of the Christian faith are rich with celebratory and ritual meals. Passover is the meal that celebrates the liberation of the children of Israel from slavery in Egypt. It is a celebration of deliverance. As such, communion is a celebratory meal in which Christians give thanks for their deliverance from the captivity of sin.

For many Christian traditions communion is understood as a sacrament. A sacrament is defined as a symbol of grace or a means of grace; we partake in communion as a tangible way of partaking in God's grace. It is understood that Christ is present in the practice, and we sense his grace through the practice. Many refer to communion as a mystery of grace which reflects the significance of the sacred being present in the mundane elements of bread and wine.

In other traditions the practice of communion is not as central. These traditions tend to refer to communion as an ordinance, not a sacrament. They practice communion less often and do not place emphasis on communion as an event where grace is offered. These traditions tend to emphasize it as a memorial act. In communion we remember what God has done for us through Christ.

In summary, communion means remembrance, Christ's presence and grace, fellowship with Christ and fellow Christians, and a sending out to serve the world in the name of Christ.

Education: Participation and Preparation. In the early church, unbaptized catechumens were excluded from communion until moral and creedal instruction was completed. Currently, most traditions allow all baptized Christians to participate no matter what the age or preparation. This is problematic in that both children and adults have little formal education to help them understand the significance of communion. The educational question thus becomes one of preparing Christians for meaningful participation in communion. Following a developmental rationale, education for communion could be described in three phases; manners, meaning, and mystery.

Young children need to learn how to participate in the service, that is, manners. This includes what type of attitude is most acceptable as well as how to partake in the service. Education in the theological significance of the service would not be helpful to young children; the emphasis should be on fellowship and remembrance. In school-age children through young adolescents, the emphasis could shift to being educated in the theological meaning of communion. Here the theology of atonement and the meaning of Christ's sacrifice can be explained. Finally, education can focus on the mystery of Christ's presence in communion. Here the power of symbol and the deeper mystery of God's love revealed in Christ can become central. For adult converts, all three need to be a part of their preparation.

LES STEELE

Bibliography. Y. Birlioth (1961), *Eucharistic Faith and Practice: Evangelical and Catholic;* K. Stevenson (1989), *The First Rites: Worship in the Early Church.*

Community, Christian. Community is a word commonly used but uniquely framed in the context of being Christian. Related concepts include mutuality, equality, interconnectedness, commonality, interdependence, relatedness. We speak of living in a community—a civic model of persons gathered together to enjoy mutual benefits, share common resources, and resolve mutual concerns. Writing about the Benedictine community, Joan Chittister declares,

> Simply living with people does not by itself create community. People live together in armies and prisons and college dormitories and hospitals, but they are not communities unless they live out of the same reservoir of values and the same center of love—the truth about Christian community is that we have to be committed to the same eternal things together. What we want to live for and how we intend to live out those values are the central questions of community. (Chittister, 1991, 44)

Community is easier described than defined. It is hard for us as humans to understand because it is God-created and finds its complete essence and definition only deep in the nature of God. Scripture calls this mode of being "oneness." Each of us as created in the image of God reflects this longing that comes from the very being of

God imprinted in us. Bilezikian describes it as a "mourning for the closeness that was ours" (Bilezikian, 1997, 15).

Jesus prayed for the experiencing of this oneness to be present in his corporate body—"I in them and you in me" (John 17:22–23). Such community is an interrelatedness characterized by mutuality and equality as experienced by the plurality of persons in the Godhead. This resulted in their oneness of being while still being separate persons, who were intimately connected to each other. This interdependence of the Godhead is reflected in Jesus' carrying out the will of the Father, in his speaking only what he heard from the father (John 8:26, 28; 14:24); in the Father's glorifying the Son that the Son might glorify the Father (John 17:1); in the Spirit's glorifying Jesus by taking what was of Jesus and making it understood (John 16:14). Each drew from or enhanced the person and work of the other enforcing "oneness" amid three.

Thus our human copies of small group community, classroom community building, and corporate community experiences in the body of Christ are mere reflections of what is perfectly depicted in the Godhead. Nevertheless, the desire for such in our earthly settings reveals our divine imprint. True community, while imperfect in our present framework, does enhance learning, impact, security, healing, growth, esteem development, and output.

A mark that always colors true community (in the human framework) is that of being dependent upon communion with God, of all being in submission to his being Authority and to responding to one another in obedience to him. This is living out of a common "center of love" and "reservoir of values" as previously described by Chittister.

Such "community" development is not an optional choice for Christians. It is a divine mandate, "a compelling and irrevocable necessity" (Bilezikian, 1997, 25). It is part of our corporate reflection of who God is. However, community is also impossible for us to create. God has created community. As believers (teachers, congregations, group members) we are called to practice the disciplines that provide fertile ground for God to create among us the community he has designed for us to reflect. The Scriptures do not exhort us to—"build community" that is God's work. The Spirit brings about this oneness imaging God in his people. We are exhorted

to practice intentional loving responses to one another,

to place ourselves in a submissive posture before one another,

to give ourselves away to one another in sacrificial ways,

to magnify and lift up one another,

—all out of mutual valuing and in deference to our mutually shared God. These are the disciplines that pave the way for God's incendiary igniting of community in our midst.

Thus those items listed as barriers to community in forms of human togetherness are simply the opposites of these "disciplines" that require our wills to come under his. Such barriers to community as listed by sociologists, psychologists, and educators are:

fears that prompt us to take steps of aggression or protection and inhibit trust;

limitations in perspective;

rigidities that come from a self-centered focus;

the need to control and manipulate;

expressions of anger, prejudice, devaluing.

A group stage known as pseudocommunity is often substituted for the real thing, particularly at the beginning of a group, although some groups remain in this stage their whole existence. This phase gives the impression of closeness and communal response through the façade of formality and politeness, avoiding all evidence of disagreement and difference. Strict rule compliance, safe subjects, good manners, pretending to agree, surface talk, and always complying with the leader's requests without question give the impression of mutuality but without the reality that comes from a blending of differences and freedom to be who you are.

Community building takes time, requires commitment, and often comes about through great sacrifice or crisis. It is forged out of disagreements that issue in the realization of commitment to a higher value that esteems oneness over getting one's own way. It is in community that individuality is valued as a component that enhances the whole. In community we enjoy interdependence, acceptance, and freedom to be who we are, a strong awareness of belonging, and a sense of accomplishing more through shared efforts than alone—all these play a part in the fulfillment of a personal need to belong, to be cared for, and to make a difference.

The benefits of community are life-giving. "In community we work out our connectedness to God, to one another, and to ourselves. It is in community where we find out who we really are" (Chittister, 1991, 48).

JULIE GORMAN

Bibliography. G. Bilezikian (1997), *Community 101;* J. Chittister (1991), *Wisdom Distilled from the Daily;* J. Gorman (1993), *Community That Is Christian.*

Compassion. *See* Empathy.

Competency-Based Education. Although competency-based educational programs are varied, they share some common characteristics. First, competency-based education focuses on students acquiring specific competencies that are composite skills, behaviors, or knowledge. Second, learning objectives are stated so their accomplishment can be observed through the individual student's performance. Third, minimum levels of achievement of these objectives serve as criteria of success. Fourth, learning activities assist each student in acquiring these levels of competence. Each student is aware of the objectives and levels of mastery and accountability. Finally, demonstrated competence precedes professional certification or licensing.

Competency-based education programs may take many forms. For instruction, these programs may be formatted as a module that is a learning unit focused on a single competence. They include objectives, a pretest, learning activities to help students acquire competencies the pretest indicates are lacking, and an evaluation to measure the success of the learning. A student works through a module individually at his or her own speed or with a small group. For support, a learning resource center provides written and media materials and other instructional resources for student use. For capitalization on individual strengths and interests, faculty may work in interdisciplinary teams to help students develop competencies. For an emphasis on field experiences, students work with in-service professionals with opportunities for faculty to be included in the experiences. For attention to the needs of the whole person, a counseling psychologist may be available to students. For communication, several kinds of channels are established among self-paced students, faculty teams, and professionals involved in field experiences with students.

The role of the teacher in the process of competency-based education is clear. Teachers are accountable for aiding students by arranging external conditions until the students learn. Students are not declared competent in a specific area until they have demonstrated competence. When a student's performance indicates learning, teaching has taken place. Thus, in competency-based education, the focus is on the learner, and teaching is dependent on learning.

Assessment takes place throughout the competency-based education process and as a culminating experience because accountability is foundational. Performance is a clear emphasis in assessment; what a professional can do is as important as what information that professional knows. Rather than comparing what one student does with other students, achievement is measured by comparing what the student does against predetermined behavioral objectives, often through standardized testing. It is necessary that these tests be congruent with the actual curriculum and instruction, and thus the accountability of teachers is rightly assessed and the assessment of students is fair. The judgment of a student's competence may be shared by several people, such as the teacher, administrators, and field experience professionals.

Historically, the main thrust for competency-based education in the 1960s likely came from four factors: There was (1) a surplus of teachers, (2) a shift in expectations about college education by both society and students, (3) a public demand for accountability in professional training, and (4) research and development efforts concerning instruction and learning. Competency-based education focused on teacher education in its inception, before spreading to other professions.

Three assumptions undergird competency-based education: (1) important knowledge is measurable and objective; (2) it is intelligent to state preestablished or arbitrary levels of mastery; and (3) evaluation is essential. These assumptions reflect the scientific management theory with its use of input-output control for efficiency and its conviction that given time and effort, humans can know precisely. Education is organized around clearly specified tasks that are achieved through standardization of methods and assessment. Competency-based education emphasizes the utilitarian and focuses on fixed norms and measurement of the student's performance during and at the end of the program.

JANET L. DALE

Bibliography. L. H. Bradley (1987), *Complete Guide to Competency-based Education: Practical Techniques for Planning, Developing, Implementing, and Evaluating Your Program;* G. E. Hall and H. L. Jones, *Competency-based Education: A Process for the Improvement of Education;* H. Sullivan and N. Higgins (1983), *Teaching for Competence;* M. E. Wirsing, *Educational Forum* 47, no. 1 (1982): 9–23.

See also CONTRACT; CONTRACT LEARNING

Computer-Assisted Instruction (CAI). General use of computer technology for the presentation of instructional materials to the learner and evaluation by the learner. The earliest forms of CAI programs, circa late 1950s, were computerized versions of branching programs where the computer functioned as little more than an electronic page turner. By the late 1970s, CAI applications advanced to become a more robust means of programmed instruction utilizing sound and graphics in a drill-and-practice format. The wide availability of powerful microcomputers by the mid-1980s allowed CAI programs to evolve into other more complex forms such as real-time simulation programs, educational games, problem-solving applications, and dialogue systems incorporating various levels of artificial intelligence.

A significant shift in the approach of CAI applications has come with the introduction of multimedia technologies and the graphical user interface (GUI) now common in today's personal computers. Although earlier CAI applications allowed user interaction and complex branching scenarios, learners still had very limited control of program content, structure, and presentation style. Multimedia and the object-oriented approach of software development have now given the learner almost complete control of educational applications. This new style of software, referred to as unstructured or open-ended, allows the learner to interact with and communicate through a wide range of media. He/she can make decisions about what material will be presented and how it will be presented. The learner also has the freedom to define his or her own problem definitions and analytical procedures, and engage in creative problem solving.

ROBERT DEVARGAS

Bibliography. E. L. Dejnozka and D. E. Kapel (1982), *American Educator's Encyclopedia;* D. M. Rhodes and J. W. Azbell (1985), *Training and Development Journal.*

See also BRANCHING PROGRAMMING; COMPUTER-ENHANCED LEARNING

Computer-Enhanced Learning (CEL). Educational experiences that are enriched through the exposure to and use of computer technology. Whereas, computer assisted instruction (CAI) refers to the specific use of computer technology for the presentation and testing of instructional materials, the CEL environment focuses more broadly upon the general uses of computer technology in learning. In step with the increasingly ubiquitous nature of computer technology in the home, school, and workplace, CEL seeks to support and integrate traditional learning methods with the most up-to-date computer and information technologies. Such a CEL environment, which will take the student beyond the walls of the classroom, may utilize applications such as: (1) word processors, spreadsheets, presentation software, and other productivity-oriented applications; (2) multimedia and "edutainment" programs that help to develop creativity, interactivity, and multiple intelligences; (3) programming languages and mathematics applications; (4) diagnostic, problem-solving, logic and simulation programs; (5) content-specific educational programs including CAI applications; (6) industrial applications; and (7) Internet, telecomputing, and communications applications.

Beyond the primary goal of enriching the learning experience through computer technology, the CEL approach also functions to equip the learner with the skills necessary to interact effectively in a technological society. These skills include: (1) basic computer literacy and etiquette; (2) research skills on the Internet and other on-line resources; (3) written language skills; (4) logic and mathematics skills; and (5) enhanced collaborative and task-based learning.

As classrooms adopt CEL methodology, students become more autonomous as active learners. The role of the teacher also shifts to include the jobs of facilitating students to find and use information and of mediating or interpreting the experiences of the cyberworld in terms of real life.

ROBERT DEVARGAS

Concentration. *See* Attention.

Concrete. *See* Abstract Thinking.

Concrete Operational Thinking. Based on his direct and systematic observation of children, Jean Piaget (1896–1980), a Swiss psychologist, postulated a revolutionary theory of intellectual growth that consists of four stages. *Concrete operational thinking* refers to the Concrete Operational Stage, the third of these four stages, which has an associated age range of 7 to 11 years.

The term *operation* refers to actions a person carries out by thinking them through rather than literally performing them. Operational thinking is rational rather than physical (as in Stage One: Sensorimotor) and logical rather than magical or fantastic (as in Stage Two: Preoperational). Operational thought overcomes egocentrism (things are as I see them), centration (the inability to focus on more than one aspect of a situation at a time), and the inability to conserve (properties remain the same despite changes in appearance or position). The term *concrete* refers to the actual presence of the objects or events to which logical thought is applied. Therefore, children in this stage can think logically and systematically (operationally) about specific problems which can be solved by weighing, measuring, and calculating (concrete). Although children in this stage can distinguish between fantasy (Preoperational, ages 2–7) and fact (Concrete Operational, ages 7–11), they cannot distinguish between fact and hypothesis (Formal Operational, ages 11 and above). Once facts have been established, new, conflicting information will not easily change their minds.

Elkind conducted research in which he listed many facts purporting to show that Stonehenge was an ancient fort (size of stones, circular placement, inner and outer "trenches"). He then presented just a few facts (open field, heel and altar stones that line up at summer solstice) that suggest it was a religious temple. Although the second conclusion is essentially more logical, few children changed their minds. Elkind found that the number of specific facts carried more weight than the better logic of an explanation based on fewer facts. He concluded that complex scientific and logical thinking is not yet available to elementary-age children (Sprinthall, 1994, 11).

We can improve the quality of learning for elementary-aged children by using visual aids and concrete props to illustrate concepts; by allowing students to manipulate objects; by making presentations brief and well-organized; by using familiar examples to explain more complex ideas; and by presenting problems that require analytical, logical thinking (Woolfolk, 1993, 36).

Research in the 1980s reinforced Piaget's contention that his age ranges are merely descriptive, not prescriptive, and should not be rigidly applied to individual children or classes (Eggen and Kauchak, 1992, 55).

RICK YOUNT

Bibliography. G. D. Borish and M. L. Tombari (1995), *Educational Psychology: A Contemporary Approach;* P. D. Eggen and D. Kauchak (1992), *Educational Psychology: Classroom Connections;* N. A. Sprinthall, R. C. Sprinthall, and S. N. Oja (1994), *Educational Psychology: A Developmental Approach;* A. E. Woolfolk (1993), *Educational Psychology;* W. R. Yount (1996), *Created to Learn: A Christian Teacher's Introduction to Educational Psychology.*

Concrete Thinking versus Abstract Thinking. The concepts of concrete and abstract thinking are important to developmentalists. They maintain that when young children think they use intuitive logic (they internalize mental pictures and do not make connections between the pieces). By middle childhood (ages 7 and 8) the mental process practiced is called *concrete* operations. Children of this age group think logically about actual events, objects, or commands. The ability to think abstractly (i.e., to process concepts represented only in words) is called *formal* operations. It is typically developed at age 11 and beyond as the older child moves into adolescence.

Many developmental researchers suggest that growth may be predicated upon one's stage of cognitive development. Piaget (1972), provides seminal research in this area. His four stages represents a structural logic, a sequentially different way of thinking and reasoning. He believed that all persons go through these stages in the same order, although the rate of development may vary from person to person.

Characteristics of Concrete Thinking. Concrete thinking (or the Concrete Operational Stage) is the third phase of Piaget's schemata. He maintains that several new thinking aptitudes move a child to this different level of cognitive operation. These abilities include: (1) *Reversibility*—a child can now carry thought backward as well as forward. When faced with a liquid-conservation task, a child can now recognize that water poured into a shorter, fatter container would once again look the same if it were poured back into its original container. This is thought to be the most important operation differentiating elementary students from preschoolers. (2) *Class Inclusion*—a child can now classify objects using multiple factors and discover relationships between classes and subclasses such as shape and size or shape and color. (3) *Decentration*—older children find it easier than younger ones to think about distances, directions, time, and action sequences such as drawing a detailed map to grandmother's house. (4) *Relational Logic*—concrete operators are now able to arrange things mentally. They are capable of *sedation*—ability to mentally arrange items by quantifiable dimensions such as height or weight—and *transitivity*—describing elements in serial order.

Characteristics of Abstract Thinking. By age 11 or 12 children begin abstract cognitive processing. This is Piaget's last stage and is called Formal Operational. The abstract thinking phase is contrasted from concrete thinking by several mental shifts: (1) *Propositional Thinking*—individuals can perform mental actions on ideas and propositions. This is in contrast to concrete thinking students' use of actual events and objective reality. (2) *Experimental Reason*—students become capable of forming hypotheses and deducing possible consequences. (3) *Conceptualizing Combinations*—the abstract thinker's approach to problem solving becomes increasingly systematic and abstract. The use of hypothetical-deductive reasoning is seen, in which the possible solutions to a problem are generated and then systematically evaluated to determine the answer. (4) *Understanding Historical Time*—students develop the ability to comprehend historical (future) time, the distant past and other cultures. (5) *Idealistic Egocentricism*—abstract thinking may also be related to some of the more painful aspects of the adolescent experience. Adolescents can actually become so centered on themselves and their thinking that they exhibit two unique forms of egocentrism: the "imaginary audience" phenomenon and the "personal fable" indestructibility belief (Elkind, 1967, 1981a).

It is important to note, however, that although the potential for abstract reasoning is realized in many teenagers, some people go through life never becoming comfortable thinking abstractly (Stonehouse, 1998).

In addition, Piaget was aware of inconsistencies in his research findings. For example, one form of conservation (mass) is understood much sooner than others (area or volume). Piaget called such inconsistency "horizontal decalage." He saw this as a child's inability to solve all problems requiring the same mental operations. Thus the line between concrete thinking and abstract thinking is often blurred and partial.

In Christian Education. The work of Ronald Goldman in England and John Peatling in the United States awakened religious educators' interest in Piaget's stages of cognitive development in the 1960s and 1970s. Many sought to apply the insights found therein to classroom teaching and curricula. This gave rise, in part, to concerns for "age-appropriate" activities and materials. Other Christian educators maintained it was not sufficient to just think religiously. They chose to focus either on more holistic growth or educational implications from Kohlberg's moral development theory.

Recent Criticism and Value. Piaget's strict, stage-level structure has come under recent attack. Methodologically, many researchers believe he underestimated the abilities of preschool children because his problems were too complex to allow them to demonstrate what they actually knew. Later studies consistently indicate that similarly aged subjects have had a reasonably good understanding of many ideas that they could not articulate (Bullock, 1985; Gelman and Kremer, 1991). Structurally, Kohlberg and Armon (1984) argue that the rational thought of such a "hard structural" model may prove inadequate to address the wisdom and experience of adulthood. In spite of these difficulties, current pondering recognizes that the differences between concrete and abstract thinking provides valuable insights into the general pattern of cognition, and that these are of important, though limited, help in the total Christian education experience.

JAMES A. DAVIES

Bibliography. D. Alkanet (1984), *All Grown Up and No Place to Go;* K. Issler and R. Habermas (1994), *How We Learn;* J. Piaget and B. Inhaler (1969), *The Psychology of the Child;* D. E. Ratcliff, ed. (1992), *Handbook of Children's Religious Education;* C. Smokehouse (1998), *Joining Children on the Spiritual Journey;* R. Strom and H. Bernard (1982), *Educational Psychology.*

Conference. For an educational event to legitimately bear the name "conference," two features must be present: (1) an exchange of ideas, opinions, and information; and (2) a common text, subject, or problem that centers the exchange. Large-scale, location-specific gatherings continue to characterize Christian education conferences for most people: Bible and missionary conferences, professional conferences, or annual denominational conferences. While these brief, intensive events have traditionally defined the conference format (and Christian education has used this format extensively), the term also describes two newer formats.

First, conference describes one-to-one meetings between teachers and students/parents where the *text* is a student's portfolio: a paper, project or other work. Effective conferencing involves a two-way exchange of ideas around the text. These conferences provide individualized feedback and mutual evaluation of the text. Though not used extensively in Christian education, this format might provide a useful lens for improving several important one-on-one ministry interactions. For example, many youth ministries emphasize discipleship training. Imagining a meeting between the youth pastor and a student as a *conference* and the student's week as the text might affect how they use their time together.

Changing technologies have made a second, newer format for conferencing possible. Teleconferencing and videoconferencing have eliminated the location-specific character of traditional conferences. Computer conference participants meet in cyberspace, unbounded by either time or space. Along with space/time flexibility, computer conferences may also increase participation by providing more psychological freedom for people reluctant to speak in group settings.

Christian education makes extensive use of the traditional conference format. Time will tell what role these newer conference formats will play in educational ministry. Christian educators should monitor research on these formats to learn effective practices and consider where they might fit into the church's teaching ministry.

ROBERT DROVDAHL

Bibliography. L. and Z. Nadler (1987), *Successful Conferences and Meetings.*

Confession. The Hebrew word *yada* and the Greek word *homologeo*, along with their derivatives and related concepts, are the words used in Scripture to refer to confession. *Praise, promise, declare,* and *confess* are other English words used to translate these words. Confession has a wide range of use with a central concept of agreement.

The secular usage of confession was primarily in legal settings. One agreed with the pronouncement of guilt before a court or judge, along with the resulting judgment. The term was also used in contractual and treaty contexts in that one promised to keep the terms. Examples of this legal sense can be seen in the public oath by Herod to his stepdaughter (Matt. 14:7) and God to Abraham as a promise (Acts 7:17).

The legal use is behind the act of public or private confession of sins, either personally (Ps. 32:5; 1 John 1:9) or corporately (Lev. 16:21). In this context confession of sins and repentance are often tied together (Dan. 9:3–19).

In the Old Testament the word is used over a hundred times to mean praise and the concept of thanks. Confession as praise is also in the New Testament (Matt. 11:25; Rom. 15:9). Praise focuses on an attribute or past deed of God. It is a declarative act of who God is and what he has done.

Confession has a close linkage to the concepts of praise and thanks with that of acknowledgment of sin. In Joshua 7:19–21 Achan was instructed to give glory to God, to praise him, and to tell what he had done. Achan then acknowledged that he had sinned against the Lord and gives the exact details of his sin. God is praised and receives glory, because Achan admits he is not in agreement with God—that he has broken the covenant he had agreed to with God.

A declaration of truth is another meaning of confession. In John 1:20, John the Baptist makes a public oath or declaration that he is not the Christ. True believers do not deny that Jesus is the Christ (1 John 2:2) but acknowledge that Jesus is the Son of God who came in the flesh (1 John 4:2, 15). This declaration of truth or a creed is linked to the concept of praise. It is a formal, public act of confession, which serves ultimately as a praise to God for who he is and what he has done.

MICHAEL J. KANE

Bibliography. D. Furst, *The New International Dictionary of New Testament Theology;* W. H. Mare, *Evangelical Dictionary of Theology,* p. 262.

Confession of Faith. *See* Catechism.

Confidence. *See* Belief.

Confirmation. Throughout the history of the church, to confirm one's faith has, at various times, been linked to the gifting of the Holy Spirit, to one's receiving first communion, to becoming a member in the congregation, or to the fulfillment of baptismal vows taken by the parents.

The term "confirmation" was used as early as A.D. 439. It referred to a rite that followed baptism. This rite consisted of laying on of hands and anointing, and was administered by the bishop soon after baptism. This practice spread gradually during the Middle Ages; the time period between baptism and confirmation began to lengthen by several years. By A.D. 1000, the confirmation rite had become independent of baptism, taking on the status of a sacrament itself. It also became quite controversial. Throughout its history, confirmation has been called into question, from scholastic theologians in the Middle Ages to local pastors struggling with it today. Biblically, we are commanded to baptize, but there is no such command to confirm. While it is now generally understood to be an opportunity to grow in grace and to be strengthened in faith, it continues to be theologically related to baptism and to be grounded in the Holy Spirit.

Confirmation has undergone recent changes in many Protestant denominations. By the 1970s, its name, and thus its focus, had become "affirmation of baptism" in the Evangelical Lutheran Church in America, the United Methodist Church, the Presbyterian Church, the United Church of Christ, the Episcopal Church, and the United Church of Canada (Browning and Reed, 1995, 20). This designation supports the theological and historical idea of the connection between the sacrament of baptism and the rite of Confirmation.

In the 1990s, many denominations have reexamined their confirmation practices in light of the number of students leaving the church shortly after the rite. The methods of teaching and the content of confirmation instruction are shifting away from a time of indoctrination into the church to a period of growth and understanding of Christian behavior and Christian lifestyle. Confirmation is now often viewed as a step in a lifelong relationship with Christ. It is a part of one's faith journey, an opportunity for spiritual growth. The role of the family is resurfacing. In biblical times, and during the Reformation era, parents were admonished to teach their children. In more recent Christian education practice, the Church has assumed the primary role of teacher. Effective confirmation ministry views the family as vital to the transmission of faith. Laity, too, through the concept of mentors, have become involved in the faith journeys of confirmands. Many congregations are integrating confirmation into their entire educational and worship life. Confirmation will continue to lead young people on a journey of faith and a commitment to the church of Christ.

SUSAN L. HOUGLUM

Bibliography. R. Browning and R. A. Reed (1995), *Models of Confirmation and Baptismal Affirmation.*

See also CATECHISM; FAMILY LIFE EDUCATION; MEDIEVAL EDUCATION

Confraternity of Christian Doctrine. The Confraternity of Christian Doctrine, popularly known as the CCD, is the Roman Catholic organization entrusted with the religious instruction of its parishioners. The CCD began in 1536 in Milan, when Italian priest Castellino da Castelli created the first religious education center for the training of children in Christian doctrine.

Similar to the catechumenate of the early church, the Confraternity was created to provide children and adults with the rudiments of Christian doctrine essential to the fulfillment of the baptismal commitment. Castellino trained select laity to serve as instructors. In time, the Confraternity grew from one to several parishes, assisted by the introduction of catechisms written by the Dutch Jesuit, Peter Canisius. Local bishops, however, were reluctant to support the Confraternity until St. Charles Borromeo, archbishop of Milan, endorsed the endeavor. Thereafter, the practice of Confraternity of Christian Doctrine spread more easily to other dioceses throughout Italy.

In 1905, Pope Pius X prescribed the establishment of the CCD in every parish worldwide in an attempt to overcome the ignorance in Christian doctrine observed in the laity. Clergy were called to mobilize and utilize devout laity in the religious instruction of parishioners. As a lay organization, the goal of the CCD was to provide for the religious instruction of men and women for purposes of increased knowledge in the faith and application of spiritual works of mercy. Unlike the Protestant Sunday school, which is not mandated but common to almost every congregation, the CCD is a mandated educational organization in the Roman Catholic Church. Like the Protestant Sunday school, the Confraternity is built upon lay leadership. Pope Pius XI stressed the value of the participation of the new apostolate of the laity in the CCD as an historic identification with the work of the first apostles in the redemption of the world.

While religious formation is seen as a cradle-to-grave process, the Confraternity has evolved into focused religious training during the highly formative adolescent years. The CCD does not seek to take away the responsibility of parents to train up their children in the faith. Instead, the Confraternity seeks to provide a concomitant means of instruction in the Good News to supplement and support the teaching of parents. In addition, the CCD also seeks to provide opportunities for adolescents to have guided experiences in the life of the church and participation in the sacraments, particularly the Eucharist and Mass. Seven broad areas of adolescent religious development are addressed in the Confraternity:

1. Academic religious instruction. Formal academic training is seen as a primary function of the CCD. Patterned after the emphasis on the acquisition and dissemination of knowledge in formal schooling, the CCD utilizes weekly formal instructional settings to train youth in essential faith concepts and religious practices. This formal instruction is intended to prevent the shallow emotionalism and superstition that shadows uninformed faith practice. Confraternity classes typically are held weekdays after regular school hours.

2. Liturgical experience. Participation in the sacraments, especially Mass, is an essential expression of religious instruction. Without this experience, religious instruction is considered to be intellectual abstraction.

3. Apostolic witness and experience. Accompanying religious instruction is an emphasis on the sharing of faith-in-action. In the CCD, this sharing is done in joint ventures with adults in order to enhance the faith experience of the young people.

4. Guidance. The assimilation of Christian values is the goal of religious instruction in the Confraternity. Guidance is provided each student so that he or she applies correctly in his or her own life what has happened (the Bible), what is happening (liturgy), and what it means (doctrine). Thus the student is not left to make connections between training and experience, but rather is guided in making those connections and helped to respond appropriately.

5. Spiritual renewal. In addition to weekly academic religious instruction, special spiritual retreats are held through the Confraternity, culminating in celebration of the Eucharist. Similar to spiritual life retreats in Protestant churches, spiritual renewal in the CCD is seen as an opportunity for intensive reflection and meditation through song, dialogue, and recreation in places besides the parish.

6. Parental cooperation. The success of the CCD is as much a function of the home as it is the church. Parents are visited in the home to keep them informed of the needs and progress of the student, as well as the teaching and resources needs of the CCD. Without parental support, the formal training of the CCD has been observed to be less effectual.

7. Student council. Much like the student councils in public schools, the CCD utilizes a student council to allow students to have a voice in the development of their religious instruction. This council also encourages student participation in the planning of other parish activities in preparation for full leadership in these activities as adults.

Just as the Protestant Sunday school has struggled to remain relevant to the needs of believers in the midst of a rapidly changing society, so also the CCD has struggled to remain an effectual organization in the instructional ministry of the Roman Catholic Church. The term CCD, like the term Sunday school, has been seen by some to be a stumbling block for the advancement of religious instruction through the laity. James Michael Lee noted that the name "Confraternity of Christian Doctrine" conjures up in the minds of American Catholics the cognitive training of children and youth because CCD fails to communicate that religious education is provided for adults and that the learning taking place is broader than the training of the mind. Lee suggests that the more holistic and easily understood term "religious education program" replace the CCD nomenclature as a first step in the reformation of this vital lay ministry. Many parishes did drop the term CCD for other nomenclatures for their parish religious education classes, yet they have continued to build upon the rich heritage and spirit of the CCD. Although the Confraternity is mandated for each parish, the Roman Catholic Church has not established a central publishing house to produce curriculum for the CCD. As a result, parishes have been left to find appropriate curriculum resources for themselves. The available resources often have been the result of private publishing endeavors, resulting in a quality of curriculum that has at times been problematic for both the lay instructor and the student.

MARK E. SIMPSON

Bibliography. E. C. Burkhardt (1968), *Guidelines for High School CCD Teachers;* J. B. Collins (1961), *Religious Education through CCD*, pp. 3–27; J. M. Lee (1986), *Renewing the Sunday School and the CCD*, pp. 211–44; A. D. Thompson (1986), *Renewing the Sunday School and the CCD*, pp. 65–87.

Confucianism. *See* Asian Theology.

Congregation. *See* Church.

Congruent. *See* Convergent/Divergent Thinking.

Conjunctive Faith. *See* Fowler, James W., III.

Conscience. Innermost thoughts of an individual surrounding moral and ethical judgments. It is an internal recognition, knowledge, feeling, or sense of right and wrong. The apostle Paul states that this is God's moral code written on people's hearts and that their conscience bears witness of this (Rom. 2:15). The word *conscience* comes from the same Greek root word that is used in the word *consciousness*, referring to moral awareness. The conscience governs feelings of guilt, disdain, and remorse over sinful behavior and thinking as well as feelings of satisfaction, fulfillment, and peace over right or moral behavior.

While Scripture teaches that the conscience is internalized in people by God, it also alludes to the fact that the conscience can be manipulated, taught, and changed (1 Tim. 4:2; Heb. 9:14; 10:22; 1 Peter 3:16). The Holy Spirit also prompts the conscience (Rom. 9:1). Social scientists, theologians, and educators have formulated views on the development of morality in individuals. Erik Erikson theorized that right and wrong is learned as the individual experiences the tension created by a series of bipolar developmental stages in the process of becoming a mature adult. Jean Piaget proposed a two-stage theory of moral development in children. Piaget called these stages *morality of constraint* in which egocentric children accept an adult value system before they understand it; and *morality of cooperation* in which the child learns morality through social interaction and reward. Lawrence Kohlberg's theory of moral development involved three levels, each containing two stages. Kohlberg's basic premise was that moral development was somewhat linked to cognitive development. As individuals increased in their ability

to reason, they became more morally aware. James Fowler synthesizes and builds on the theories of Erikson, Piaget, and Kohlberg. Fowler proposes a developmental theory of "faith formation" that includes six stages over the life span.

STEVEN GERALI

Bibliography. E. Evans, ed. (1970), *Adolescents: Readings in Behavior and Development;* R. Hunter, ed. (1990), *Dictionary of Pastoral Care and Counseling;* L. Kohlberg (1964), *Review of Child Development Research;* T. Lidz (1983), *The Person: His and Her Development Throughout the Life Cycle;* J. Piaget (1948), *The Moral Judgment of a Child.*

See also FAITH DEVELOPMENT; KOHLBERG, LAWRENCE; MORAL DEVELOPMENT

Conservation. Cognitive ability to understand that properties remain the same when they go through a change in appearance, position, or shape. Conservation deals with the concepts of reason and perception in areas of length, numbers, right/left, and combinations.

According to Piaget, children develop cognitively in a predictable manner, going through various stages. Conservation, as explained by Piaget, can be best understood by looking at experiments he used to illustrate the processes children use when answering questions regarding changes in mass, liquid, and relationships. The most famous experiment involved two equal amounts of liquid in two identical glasses.

The children were asked to watch as the two glasses of liquid were placed on a table. Then one glass of liquid was poured into a tall, thin glass. The question was then asked, "Which glass now has more liquid?" The children younger than 6 said that the tall, thin glass had more liquid. The children 6 and older said that both glasses still had the same amount of liquid. The younger children were relying on perception and the older children were relying on logic.

A second experiment with children involved modeling clay of equal amounts rolled into two equal balls. One ball of clay is then divided into several smaller balls, or rolled into a long sausage-like object or flattened to look like a pancake. Children of different ages were then asked, "Which contains more clay, the one ball or the smaller balls, sausage, or pancake?" Children who have not progressed in their ability to reason must rely on perception and will say that the one ball is smaller than the other smaller balls/shapes.

Piaget believed that as children mature they learn cognitive concepts related to conservation through various experiences. These concepts may also be taught, and children with greater intellectual abilities may learn them earlier and more easily.

MARCIA MACQUITTY

Constitution, Church. In most states in the United States, a church is defined as a nonprofit corporation. A constitution and bylaws document must be filed with the appropriate state authority in order for a church to be incorporated. An effectively written constitution must provide several important elements. Each is important to the overall value of the document.

The church constitution is a document that states the legal name of the church, specifies what offices will exist, and outlines the procedures for operating the church. In most churches the final section specifies such things as requirements for membership in the church, church business sessions, qualifications for holding an office, procedures for election of officers, the calling of a pastor or pastors, the formation of committees, the process for amending the constitution and bylaws, and other procedural items.

Whether a church constitution is a help or a hindrance to the efficient function of the church is dependent on its wording to a great extent. A constitution in which the procedures are worded so specifically that they hinder making of policy becomes a hindrance to effective church leadership. On the other hand, a document that is not specific enough, often gives rise to dissension and conflict over interpretation. A good rule to follow to avoid either extreme is to put wording into the constitution that establishes how policy is to be made, but make sure the constitution does not establish ministry policy within itself.

With regard to Christian education, a good church constitution will identify the persons charged with administering the Christian education ministry of the church as well as specify where these individuals fit in the organizational scheme of the church government. It is desirable for each person involved in the Christian education ministry of the church to know and be comfortable with that management flow and its implications for his or her ministry.

KEN GARLAND

Bibliography. J. Anthony, *Foundations of Ministry;* R. K. Bower, *Administering Christian Education.*

See also ADMINISTRATION; BOARD OF DIRECTORS; CHURCH; MANAGEMENT; NONPROFIT ORGANIZATIONS; TRUSTEE

Constructive Activities. Learning processes that engage persons in actions with formative or positive results. Activities may be planned by teachers with particular objectives in mind, or an unplanned interaction between persons may help them construct new understandings. Teachers enhance the formation of their students by involving them in constructive activities out in the real world of nature or social interaction. Whatever the setting, constructive activities involve active participation on the part of the learner and positive outcomes, the construction of new understandings, or formation. A constructive activity often results in the integration or synthesis of concepts, knowing, feeling, and doing.

From his extensive study of cognitive development, Jean Piaget (1896–1980) identified direct experience as one of the four factors essential for development (the other three are heredity and maturation, social interaction, and the process of equilibration). Teachers who desire to see qualitative growth in the understandings of their students will give them opportunities for direct experience with what is to be learned. The religious educator James Michael Lee believes that people do not automatically transfer what they know into their living. He challenges teachers to operationalize truth, by which he means they should ask what that truth or concept looks like when it is lived out, and then design activities that allow the students to experience the concept. Learning that comes to children, adolescents, or adults through such constructive activities will probably lead to deeper understanding and is more likely to be lived out than learning that comes through students simply listening to teachers talk.

Persons have a variety of learning style preferences. Some like to actively experiment with concepts or concrete experiences and learn best when actively experimenting. Others prefer to learn through reflective observation. Many formal learning settings cater to the reflective learners and do not offer much for the active experimenters. Some persons are kinesthetic learners, that is, they learn best when their bodies are moving, when they can be doing something with their hands. Constructive activities enhance the learning of both the kinesthetic learners and those who want to actively experiment.

Learning games give children fun, active ways of mastering biblical facts. Role play and drama help students comprehend the feelings of others and grow in understanding the other person's perspective as well as their own. Creative expressions such as drawing, making something, or writing are constructive activities. In the creative process learners often discover what they think and feel. Through all these activities, teachers receive glimpses of where their students are in their learning and with that knowledge are better equipped to guide them toward deeper understandings and growth in their spiritual formation.

CATHERINE STONEHOUSE

Constructivism. Approach to learning that describes how humans acquire concepts of time, space, and causality. It postulates that knowledge is a process rather than a state, and it defines the relationship between the knower and the known. It characterizes theories of learning that assume the learner is active in the learning process. Constructivists, such as Jean Piaget with his theory of stages of cognitive development and those identified as information-processing investigators who study the flow of information through the cognitive system, believe that persons "learn" by acting on the environment. Learners are active, themselves shaping the form of knowledge.

Learners' knowledge of the world changes as their cognitive systems develop. As learners change, so does the known as they actively select and interpret information in their environment and link it to memory. On this basis, they devise inferences which in turn form the foundation for future learning. Researchers in memory, attention, learning, and language are all sensitive to learners' strategies of receiving and processing information. The notions of constructivism have also influenced the work of moral learning theorists, such as Kohlberg, and faith development theory, such as that of Fowler.

Constructivists have significantly influenced the shape of learning strategies in educational settings. Learners are identified as active, not passive. Therefore, learning strategies are carefully devised to actively involve the learner in the learning process in order to aid connections between the known and the unknown, to enhance memory, and to facilitate transfer of learning from mere repetition to use in other situations. The notion of "active learning" strategies is critical to a constructivist educator. Teachers become facilitators of learning rather than dispensers of information. Learners become doers, rather than merely passive recipients of information. Learning centers and other active teaching methods are chosen to guide the learning process.

ELEANOR A. DANIEL

Contemplation. Practice of looking intently to God; it is the quiet, simple practice of paying attention to God. The contemplator says little and listens attentively and expectantly, seeking to be quiet and open to hearing God speak. In some Christian traditions a few words may be repeated in order to focus one's attention on God. In the Eastern Orthodox tradition, the "Jesus Prayer" is used in this way. The contemplator repeats continually, "Lord Jesus Christ, Son of God, have mercy on me, a sinner," until the phrase moves to the background and attention is turned undividedly to God.

Contemplation and meditation are often and appropriately used synonymously, helping to bring a more complete definition to both. Within the Christian tradition, however, there is a subtle difference between the two. Meditation is often understood as a more cognitive process than contemplation; it is an exercise of the mind, seeking increased knowledge through serious reflection.

Meditation often utilizes the study of Scripture and other devotional material in an orderly and prayerful manner. Contemplation is understood to be more affective than cognitive—more an exercise of the heart than of the mind. However, care must be taken not to separate the head from the heart. Contemplation seeks an increased openness, awareness, and love for God. It is the soul at rest with God. It does not require texts to study, and it does not seek to think in an orderly fashion.

For some in the Christian tradition, the discipline of meditation may lead to contemplation. As one knows more about God through meditation, he or she desires more time to bask in God's love and to hear God's voice through contemplation. Others, such as St. John of the Cross or Teresa of Avila, understood the relationship between meditation and contemplation as one of the stages of the spiritual life. Those who progressed to the "upper" stages of spiritual life were contemplatives.

Cautions must be raised concerning the practices of contemplation and meditation. First, these must not be understood as a means of escape from reality and the pains of life. It is through these disciplines that God most fully reveals himself and reveals our true selves, which can often be painful. They are the avenues to authentic self-knowledge before God. Second, the practice of contemplation may lead to syncretism, or moving away from explicitly Christian views. If one meditates on Scripture, this will help to keep the focus of contemplation on Christ.

Christian growth can be assisted greatly by contemplation. Christian education needs to teach the rich tradition of contemplation and encourage Christians to utilize this practice for the development of faith.

LES STEELE

Content. A critical area of concern for the Christian educator is determining the content of instruction. In its simplest form, content addresses the question of what will be taught. This is an essential corollary question to, Why are we teaching? Who is teaching? How are we teaching? and so on.

Evangelicals, especially since the rise of the Sunday school movement as a dominant player in Christian education, often answer the question of content in very simple terms—"We teach the Bible, of course." But what does this actually mean for the curriculum of the church? We know that there are many good and profitable things that we can teach in our homes, classes, and small groups, and from the pulpit. But are there any things that we must teach? While uncertainty may exist around this question today, for most of Christian history there was widespread agreement, as a survey of the development of catechesis reveals.

From the earliest centuries of the church, it is evident that certain things were regarded as essential content in Christian instruction. Of first importance was the gospel itself—the message of the good news of Jesus' sacrificial suffering and death on behalf of sinners and his triumphant resurrection from the dead (1 Cor. 15:1–11). A second fundamental area of instruction was the larger story of the biblical drama, from the creation to the consummation of human history. This teaching could be included in framing the gospel message for unbelievers, as in Stephen's message in Acts 7. But it also meant instructing new believers in the basics of the Bible, introducing the various biblical books, presenting an outline of their contents and an overview of their interrelationship. Jesus himself models such instruction in his conversation with disciples in the days after his resurrection (see Luke 24:27, 44–45).

Building upon the truths of the gospel message and the overall biblical story, Christian educators for most of the church's history generally taught children and new believers in three additional areas. First, there was instruction in "the faith which was once for all delivered to the saints" (Jude 3). That is, believers were taught the basics of Christian theology, or what Christians "believe." Such training equips believers with both a greater appreciation of their own faith and a greater ability to articulate that faith to unbelievers.

Second, Christians were instructed in the Christian Way, or in how believers are to "behave." This was a training in lifestyle that is pleasing and acceptable to God. Such an emphasis is evident in the early Christian teaching document, *The Didache*, which begins with discussion of the contrast between the way of life and the way of death. Catechumens in the first centuries of the church were generally required to demonstrate growing obedience to this Way before they were admitted to baptism. Training in this area equips believers both for genuine fellowship and for lives of service both inside and outside the church.

Third, Christians were taught how to properly approach God in prayer and worship. This would ensure that there was no mere intellectual assent to God's truth, nor an essentially externalized obedience to his commands. Instead, the believer was to nurture a living and vital relationship with the Lord. Such teaching enhances both the congregational experience of the life that is ours in Christ and the determination to offer that life to others.

Augustine, in his early fifth-century work, *The Enchiridion*, dealt with these three issues under the headings of three theological virtues, "faith, hope and love," offering these to an enquirer as the essential components of Christian teaching. By the time of the Reformation, as catechisms began to be published and distributed, the same three emphases were normally introduced through the teaching of the Apostles' Creed, the Ten Commandments, and the Lord's Prayer. Luther was convinced that these three things represented the core of Christian teaching from the earliest times and asserted that any who refused to receive this instruction, ". . . deny Christ and are no Christians. They should not be admitted to the sacrament, be accepted as sponsors in Baptism, or be allowed to participate in any Christian privileges" (from the preface to the Small Catechism in Tappert, 1959, The Book of Concord, 339.)

In recent decades, evangelical Christians have largely moved away from teaching an established core such as outlined above. Often, instruction centers around a certain Bible book or what is considered to be a timely topic. Such studies are important and should be provided for, but it is clearly incumbent upon the church to provide, on an ongoing basis, some form of systematic training in the biblical and historic essentials of the faith.

In any case, evangelical Christian educators must continue to ask the question, What content must we teach in order to see believers increasingly conformed to the image of Jesus Christ?

GARY A. PARRETT

Bibliography. Augustine (1961), *The Enchiridion on Faith, Hope and Love;* H. Burgess (1966), *Models of Religious Education;* J. M. Lee (1985), *The Content of Religious Instruction;* M. Luther (1529, 1959), *The Book of Concord.*

Content, Elements of. A term used in curriculum design that refers to what is dealt with in the curriculum. Content is an expression of what is studied in the lesson. In the church's curriculum, content is viewed as the subject, Scripture passage, biblical commentary, or the lesson plan in the teacher's curriculum materials. However, content is more than the printed matter in the student's or teacher's materials. Content involves everything that is in fact studied in the lesson (Colson and Rigdon, 1981, 46). Content involves the discussion of the students, questions which are asked, illustrations, and personal faith stories which are told by teachers and students. Even the rabbits that are chased in a lesson become part of the content. The curriculum materials provide the target for the subject to be taught. However, the content is what is actually studied in the lesson.

DARYL ELDRIDGE

Bibliography. H. P. Colson and R. M. Rigdon (1981), *Understanding Your Church's Curriculum;* L. Ford (1991), *A Curriculum Design Manual for Theological Education.*

See also SCOPE

Context in Teaching and Ministry. With its primary roots in linguistics, the term *context* in its current usage also has origins in anthropology, theology, and cognitive psychology. Grammatically, the context is what immediately surrounds a specific word or passage. The Latin *contexere* means "to weave together," "to join together," or "to compose," thus, an interconnected whole that lends meaning to a particular part.

Sociocultural Context. The physical, social, and cultural context provides a setting in which learning and behavior are both shaped and interpreted. Different cultural contexts may give contrasting meanings to identical behaviors, and the learner's locus in a culture may affect the context as well—a marginal member of a social group, for example, has a different context than a mainstream member of the same group. The concept of "sociocultural tightness" distinguishes between high-and low-context cultures. In high-context cultures people tend to be more sensitive to their physical and social surroundings than people in low-context cultures. High- and low-context cultures have contrasting orientations to time, social relationships, reasoning processes, and communication. High-context cultures typically function with loose time schedules and varied concurrent activities; intuitive reasoning processes tend to dominate. Low-context cultures more often employ tight schedules and linear events; analytic reasoning generally dominates. These cultural differences affect the teaching-learning process. High-context people may prefer a personal and authoritative teaching style in order to maintain group harmony. Low-context people, tending to focus on verbal and conceptual cues, are more likely to prefer independent and autonomous learning tasks.

Teaching and Context. Studies of the teaching process have shifted from a concern with teaching behaviors to a focus on the teaching context. Reforms are needed to respond to the realities of economic conditions and the social, cultural, and political forces in which teachers and learners are immersed. Proponents offer a dual agenda for creating a new context for teaching: learner-centered schools and teacher involvement in decision making and program development.

Churches need to ask how the context of teaching is different in present-day churches than in earlier years when Sunday schools were established and run by the teachers themselves. Might the context of ownership result in a higher sense of calling and more enduring commitments? In making curriculum decisions, churches should identify and elaborate aspects of the multiple contexts—cultural, social, economic, and religious—in which the curriculum will be taught and learned.

Learning and Context. Research on context, learning, and cognition has explored the link between contextual factors and the acquisition of knowledge. Some cognitive psychologists find thinking itself to be "situated" in the context—physical, social, and cultural. These theorists are particularly concerned with learners' success or failure in transferring new learning from one context to another. They note that learners perform identical cognitive tasks better in one context than in another. Informal, everyday settings evoke better responses than formal settings (as, for example, homemakers who easily calculate bargains in the supermarket but do poorly on paper-and-pencil tests of the same calculations). They theorize that learners create a meaningful mental context for an activity, and that effective teachers create a contextual framework that supports further learning. The learning does not exist independently of the way the learner contextualizes it. Teachers should strive to bring experiences in and outside of the classroom into active relationship, grounding knowledge in real-world contexts.

Christian educators and ministers may be ready to accept the educational significance of context because of the salience of contextualization for biblical/theological and missiological endeavors. Church teachers have the two-pronged task—first, understanding the meaning of Scripture in its original context in order to interpret it in the present context, and second, constructing with the learners a new context for biblical knowledge transferable to their everyday lives.

BARBARA WILKERSON

Bibliography. E. T. Hall, *The Educational Forum* 54 (1989): 21–34; A. Lieberman, ed. (1992), *The Changing Contexts of Teaching;* P. Light and G. Butterworth, eds. (1993), *Context and Cognition: Ways of Learning and Knowing;* J. E. Plueddemann (1991), *Internationalizing Missionary Training: A Global Perspective,* pp. 217–30.

Contiguity. One of five types of learning emerging from the learning theory of behaviorism. Learning, as described by behaviorism, is based on the idea of the relationship between learning and response. The most basic behavioristic explanation states that a stimulus occurs followed by a response, which may then be reinforced. Learning comes from experience: learners acquire new behaviors and modify old ones as they encounter the stimuli in the social and physical world.

However, some learning occurs not in a direct stimulus-response sequence, but because two stimuli occur close together in time. This kind of learning is contiguity—learning that occurs as a result of external events paired together. A child may "learn" that honking a horn makes a traffic light turn green because once the light turned green just as a driver tooted the horn. It is in this way that stereotyping easily occurs; for example, African-Americans are depicted in negative terms in most or all movies seen by an individual, or all Southerners have drawls, or all women carry out certain tasks to the exclusion of men. Learning strategies that emphasize drill, rote learning, and repetition, all important for simple factual learning, are based on this understanding.

ELEANOR A. DANIEL

See also BEHAVIORISM; S-R BONDS

Continental Philosophy of Education. The major thread of what might be thought of as the Continental philosophy of education runs through the contributions of a series of reforming educational theorists who sought to humanize education. The adversary of these theorists was the controlling educational practices of their day that emphasized deduction, mindless memory, and a curriculum that centered on a degenerate form of humanistic education that too often focused on the linguistics and grammar of the classical literature of Greece and Rome.

An early theorist to challenge the prevailing philosophy and practice of education was John Amos Comenius (1592–1670). A Moravian bishop, Comenius viewed lifelong learning as the avenue to universal peace. One aspect of his philosophy focused on the organizing of the totality of human knowledge into an encyclopedic form, which he called "pansophism." This would allow individuals to proceed in an orderly way from the known to the unknown until they had covered the whole of knowledge in its logical order. The secret to world peace would be to teach every person everything.

If that ambitious task was to be accomplished, Comenius suggested, three things were essential: good methods, good textbooks, and good teachers. His methodology rejected the reigning deduction of the day in favor of Baconian induction. "As far as possible," Comenius claimed, children must "be taught to become wise by studying the heavens, the earth, . . . but not by studying books; . . . they must learn to know and investigate things for themselves." Education in the use of the senses must precede learning from words.

That methodology was carried over into Comenius's ideal textbook. His *Orbis Pictus* (The World in Pictures) was history's first illustrated textbook for children. It keyed Latin vocabulary to objects in pictures. Comenius summed up his educational philosophy in his *Great Didactic*. In many ways he was a forerunner of modern educators.

Another educational theorist in the line of Comenius was Jean Jacques Rousseau (1712–78), one of history's most influential educational philosophers. Rousseau can be thought of as the Copernicus of education. Whereas education had traditionally centered on adult interests and adult social life, Rousseau argued that the needs and activities of the child must be at the center of the educational process.

Rousseau was a firm opponent of the formal education that had been in vogue for centuries on the Continent. He advocated a natural education that gave the instincts, impulses, and feelings of the child unrestricted opportunity of expression.

He held that experience rather than instruction forms the foundation of a healthy education. Thus his approach to education was negative in terms of teacher intrusion and imposition. Natural curiosity is an inbuilt motivator. As might be expected, according to Rousseau every age had its own learning tasks, and these needed to be respected as a child developed. His best and most influential treatment of his educational philosophy was set forth in his *Emile*.

The disciples of Rousseau were many, but none was more prominent in the struggle against the established educational ideas than Johann Heinrich Pestalozzi (1746–1827). Pestalozzi attempted to apply the principles set forth by Rousseau to his own child but found them to be impractical. That led him to a study of child nature and the educational process. He agreed with Rousseau that education should seek to develop a child's native powers and capacities naturally and freely and that education should include the hands and the heart as well as the mind, but he based his educational practices on an investigation of child nature that brought him to the frontier of modern educational psychology.

Like other reformers in the Continental tradition, he disdained the universal stress on memory and sought to appeal to the senses of his students. Along that line, he took a giant step beyond Comenius with his appeal to pictures by developing a methodology that utilized things in the form of object lessons. He also moved beyond the negative education of Rousseau to a positive view of a teacher's contribution that eventually led to teacher education and the study of education as a science. His work also led to the grading of subject matter in harmony with the laws of student development. Thus his work laid the foundation for modern elementary education.

Two of Pestalozzi's disciples would also make major contributions to the Continental philosophy of education in its struggle with the deductive, bookish educational establishment. The first was Johann Friedrich Herbart (1776–1841), who did much to rationalize the teaching-learning process through his exposition of the "formal steps" that take place in the acquisition of knowledge. As with Rousseau and Pestalozzi, Herbart held that learning should be based upon a child's natural and spontaneous interest.

A second Pestalozzian of note was Friedrich Froebel (1782–1852). Froebel uplifted such educational concepts as free self-activity, creativeness, social participation, and motor expression. The modern kindergarten is one of the outgrowths of his work.

These five educational theorists did much to defeat the bookish, deductive, subject-matter orientation of traditional education and to prepare the way for the modern approaches of both education and educational psychology.

GEORGE R. KNIGHT

Bibliography. J. A. Comenius (1967), *John Amos Comenius on Education;* G. L. Gutek (1968), *Pestalozzi and Education;* A. E. Meyer (1975), *Grandmasters of Educational Thought;* J.-J. Rousseau (1979), *Emile,* or *On Education.*

Continuing Education. Directed learning opportunities that extend beyond traditional points of educational termination, such as graduation from college. Continuing education refers to an adult's intentional, ongoing effort toward personal enrichment or vocational improvement through participation in courses or specialized training opportunities.

Once primarily the domain of higher educational institutions, now the crowded field of providers includes employers, professional associations, social service agencies, and nonprofit organizations. According to Queeney, reasons for escalating demand include demographic factors; the rising educational level of the populace; the burgeoning number of women in the workplace; early retirement; the growing number of adults who change careers; and technological advances and the knowledge explosion (1995, 8–12). The primary factors for participating in learning projects are to meet expectations of employers and to enhance the possibility of professional advancement. To keep up-to-date, it is estimated that each person in the workforce needs to accumulate every seven years learning that is equivalent to 30 credit hours of instruction (Dolence and Norris, 1995, 7).

In the twenty-first century, continuing education will be learner-driven rather than provider-driven. The burgeoning use of the Internet and other national and international networks is creating environments where intellectual capacity, information and knowledge bases, methodologies, and other valuables are made available to adults anywhere, anytime. Successful providers will create "education on demand" delivery models that are responsive, convenient, and accessible to learners. Educators must realign continuing education opportunities to the information age and redesign delivery processes in order to remain connected with adult learners.

TERRY POWELL

Bibliography. M. Dolence and D. Norris (1995), *Transforming Higher Education: A Vision for Learning in the 21st Century;* D. Queeney (1995), *Assessing Needs in Continuing Education.*

Continuous Reinforcement. A schedule of reinforcement of responses to stimuli as defined by the theory of behaviorism. Behaviorism is based on the notion that learning is the result of accumulated responses to specific stimuli introduced into the environment of the learner as those responses are made permanent. However, for a behavior to become permanent, it must be reinforced in some way.

Reinforcement schedules are either intermittent or continuous. Intermittent reinforcements may be presented on an interval schedule, either fixed or variable, or on a ratio schedule, again either fixed or variable. Continuous reinforcement, however, occurs following *every* response to the stimulus. It is especially useful when teaching a new behavior because it quickly strengthens the response. But the use of continuous reinforcers does not result in much perseverance by the learner, either in the laboratory or the classroom. Extinction occurs rather rapidly when the reinforcement schedule is interrupted.

Reinforcers need not be material to be effective for human learners. Affirmation and praise serve as powerfully as reinforcers as do various tangible rewards.

Though the original research in behaviorism was done primarily in a laboratory setting using animals, extensive research has also been done among human learners. These observers criticize continuous reinforcement as a means of shaping human learning. They have observed that it fosters low frustration tolerance, lack of perseverance, impulsiveness, impatience, and low ego strength. Many criticize Western culture and parents for providing immediate gratification to the desires of children and adults. The result, they believe, is a population with the inability to delay gratification. They advise parents and educators to use intermittent schedules of praise and reward for children and other learners because this schedule produces more permanent learning as well as desirable character qualities such as perseverance, ability to withstand frustration, patience, and ego strength.

ELEANOR A. DANIEL

Contract. Social work term that describes the part of the helping process in which the worker comes to a written or verbal agreement with the individual, family, or group he or she is helping. The worker and the person requiring assistance determine the needs of the person. Next, they design the contract, which includes the goals the person has determined are necessary to achieve the desired results to deal with the needs identified. It will also include steps needed to reach the goals and dates by which the goals should be achieved. Finally, it will include the role of both the worker and the person in need in the process.

The contract gives clear direction for the worker and person in need, and can be used for assessment of progress in the process. Contracts can be altered during the course of the helping process as new goals are developed.

DAVID R. PENLEY

Contracting in Groups. Contracting is closely related to the concept of group goal setting. Goals are the ends that individuals pursue individually and as a group. Through the dynamic processes of finding common ground and working toward consensus, a group agrees upon its goal(s). This then becomes a standard by which group progress can be measured. In a relationally oriented group the term *covenant* is frequently substituted for *contract*.

In volunteer groups such as those frequently experienced in church life, the contracting process typically involves a number of elements: the goals the group will pursue; the procedures that will structure their work together; their respective roles; and the working arrangements of time, cost, and place. Issues of attendance, confidentiality, honesty, sensitivity to others, accountability, and prayer may also be addressed. Difficulties may result during future meetings when covenant elements are too hastily addressed.

Effective boundary drawing in a group can produce a "container effect" and will make experiences much more potent than if the boundaries were drawn more loosely. The cost of noncompliance needs to be carefully thought through, especially if one of the group goals is to promote "fellowship."

Participation in the contracting process is important, even when choices are constricted because of institutional concerns or designated types of group experience. In its most concrete form, a group works best when members know each other's strengths and weaknesses, abilities and disabilities, and when the group's tasks and ambitions are well matched to those of its members. Since group contracting often takes place at the early or forming stage of group life, members are, during this time period, laying a foundation for the degree of disclosure, trust, and intimacy they desire of one another. Wise leadership will help the group develop ways of attending to their mission while placing priority on the nurturing, self-caretaking activities.

The issues of membership, emotional bonding, degree of involvement with a group, and corporate behavioral expectations (boundaries) are associated with contract discussions. During this time prospective members evaluate how closely their needs and desires match with those of other prospective members. If an individual does not like the norms of the group, conflict or absenteeism will result. Frequently groups will spend one to three weeks discussing elements of contract, and conclude with a ceremonial signing of a covenant by which members commit themselves to the agreed-upon goals.

By engaging the members as fully as possible in contract negotiations, leadership affirms their rights to self-determination and provides an opportunity for them to become full partners in the group.

Individual performance in a group is enhanced if each member has an opportunity to participate in setting the group goal(s), if all members have the same information, and if adequate time is allowed for the completion of the goals.

In groups lasting six months or less, contracting may be addressed initially and may not need to occur again. In groups of longer duration, a periodic review of contract—with resultant adjustments, if any—is recommended every six months.

JAMES A. DAVIES

Bibliography. A. Hare, H. Blumberg, M. Davies, and M. Kent (1995), *Small Group Research: A Handbook;* J. Mallison (1980), *Building Small Groups in the Christian Community;* K. Smith and D. Berg (1987), *Paradoxes of Group Life.*

Contract Learning. One of the learning approaches recommended by Malcolm Knowles as an alternative to existing traditional models. Students, usually in later adolescence and on into adulthood, enter into a written contractual form of agreement with a facilitator. According to Brookfield, learning contracts have emerged as the major approach to self-directed learning in numerous content areas (Brookfield, 1986, 81, 82).

Clearly contract learning follows the principles of andragogy and enhances the decision-making role of the learner. Effective learning contracts are based on learner experience and felt needs. In fact, Knowles identifies "pre-conditions" for the effective utilization of contracts:

1. A felt need.
2. A supportive physical and psychological environment for the contract.
3. Learner identification with the goals of the learning contract.
4. Learner-shared responsibility for planning and conducting the learning.
5. Active involvement by the learner in all parts of the learning process.
6. A connection between the learner's life experience and the learning process.
7. A feeling of some degree of success in progress toward the goals of the learning (Knowles, 1986, 7, 8).

Student choice is crucial in learning contracts through goals and objectives drawn up by the student and subject variability as the study progresses. Of this learning model, Wickett says, "It satisfies the requirement of the clear and precise plan or curriculum for learning while enabling the learner to participate in the plan's formulation. Its greatest advantage may be found in the commitment of the learner which has been in evidence in so many situations where the model has been used" (Wickett, 1991, 110).

KENNETH O. GANGEL

Bibliography. S. Brookfield (1986), *Understanding and Facilitating Adult Learning;* K. O. Gangel and H. G. Hendricks (1988), *The Christian Educator's Handbook on Teaching;* M. S. Knowles (1986), *Using Learning Contracts: Practical Approaches to Individualizing and Structuring Learning;* J. M. Peter et al., (1991), *Adult Education;* R. E. Y. Wickett (1991), *Models of Adult Religious Education Practice.*

Control. In the area of management, to control is to implement an ongoing process for evaluating organizational accomplishment against established criteria. These relevant standards are usually the domain of a systems approach to ensuring objective accomplishment. Control is to formally communicate procedures and information routines so that a pattern of organizational functioning and activity is followed.

To control means to exercise authority or influence over a group of people or an organization. It means to command, decide, rule, or judge. However, in Christian management circles, there is a servant dimension, which means that controllers function according to biblical standards and that performance is measured according to those standards. It also implies humility, allowing room for God to direct and guide attitudes, actions, or circumstances. Controlling means that leaders are establishing performance standards, measuring performance, evaluating performance, and correcting performance (Lawson and Choun, 1992).

To control is the fifth of the five functions of the typical management cycle (e.g., planning, organizing, staffing, directing, and controlling). The usual behaviors that are included in the function of controlling are the establishment of a reporting system, the development of performance standards, the measurement of results, taking corrective action, and rewarding. In summary, to control is to ensure progress toward objectives according to the agreed-upon plan.

To establish a reporting system involves determining exactly how, when, and what activities and functions are to take place. Biehl (1989) suggests that a supervisor should answer questions regarding decisions, problems, plans, progress, and personal issues. A regular reporting system facilitates communication, and minimizes misunderstandings and problems.

The development of performance standards should include as wide a participation in instituting conditions that will exist when key duties are well done. To measure results means to ascertain the extent of departure from these norms. Adjusting plans to enable the attainment of the performance standards is the definition of corrective action. The controlling process would view reward as praise, remuneration, or perhaps even discipline.

The major goals accomplished by effective control are the correction of divergences from your intended direction, protection of legitimate interests, the rewarding of achievement, and the continued development of your organization. Several positive corollary outcomes are the strengthening of lines of communication, the defining of acceptable levels of achievement and behavior, and the proper writing of job descriptions. The dangers of controlling are an unthinking following of the guidelines, a tension between supervisors and subordinates, an excess of information, and a temptation to conceal inappropriate activity. However, the results of a properly managed control system far outweigh the dangers.

GREGORY C. CARLSON

Bibliography. B. Biehl (1989), *Increasing Your Leadership Confidence;* M. Lawson and R. Choun (1992), *Directing Christian Education.*

See also ADMINISTRATION; LINE-STAFF RELATIONSHIPS; MANAGEMENT

Controversy. *See* Debate.

Convention/Seminar. *See* Conference.

Convergent/Divergent Thinking. Convergent and divergent thinking are related factors of intelligence and creativity. Convergent thinking is the process of forming a singular answer to a particular problem or question. Inversely, divergent thinking is the intellectual operation used to generate a variety of responses to questions or problem situations (Dembo, 1994, 344–45).

These concepts are associated with the work of J. P. Guilford. His "Structure of Intellect" model is an extensive explanation of the factors of intelligence. Guilford concluded that intellect can be divided into three categories (Sprinthall, 1994, 637). The first is *content,* or the information to be processed. The second category, *operation,* includes the procedures through which the information is processed. The final division, *product,* is the outcome of the processed content. Convergent and divergent thinking are included in the operation category of Guilford's model (Dembo, 1994, 344–45).

The structure of questions or problems determines the intellectual process one would use.

Problems that have wide parameters and few restrictions, or those that call for a diversity of interpretations encourage divergent thinking. In contrast, questions that are highly organized, sharply focused, or that demand a specific or unique answer promote convergent responses (Guilford, 1967).

Gifted students can be adept at convergent thinking, divergent thinking, or both. Yet, divergent thinking is most identified with giftedness (Biehler and Snowman, 1993, 224–25) because of these students' ability to think creatively. Guilford identifies four characteristics of creative thinking demonstrated by divergent thinkers. The first, *fluency*, is the ability to produce an increased quantity or "flow" of ideas. *Flexibility*, the second characteristic, is the ability to adapt and modify ideas, or move thinking in new directions. The third factor, *originality*, is the capacity to use the imagination and think in unique, uncommon ways. The fourth characteristic, *elaboration*, is an ability to respond with expanded detail, to "fill out" the answers with specifics (Guilford, 1967).

CHRIS SHIRLEY

Bibliography. R. Biehler and J. Snowman (1993), *Psychology Applied to Teaching;* M. H. Dembo (1994), *Applying Educational Psychology;* J. P. Guilford (1967), *The Nature of Intelligence;* N. A. Sprinthall, R. C. Sprinthall, and S. N. Oja (1994), *Educational Psychology: A Developmental Approach.*

Conversation. Talking together, which involves an exchange of information, ideas, and opinions and requires two-way communication consisting of listening and oral expression. Conversation is a natural part of human interaction, but it may also be intentionally used to enhance teaching and learning. With young children discussions take the form of conversation.

To effectively use conversation, teachers and parents must develop their listening and communication skills. When persons talk together they often do not listen with a desire to understand. Real listening is an intentional act motivated by the belief that the other person has something to say that is worth hearing, and that it is important to truly understand what is being said. Good listeners assume that they may not fully understand what has been said or why the other person made the comment. They will therefore check their interpretations and probe for deeper understandings.

Listening communicates that one values the person who is speaking and builds trust into relationships. When teachers listen to their students, they discover what the learners understand and what misconceptions they hold. As students gather before class, the teacher who listens to their conversations can learn about the activities of the class members and their values.

Such knowledge sets the stage for more effective teaching focused on issues important to the learners.

Carol Gilligan (1990) in her study of moral development discovered that listening is a moral issue for women. Not listening to another is an injustice, an expression of lack of care. Women believe that most problems can be solved if people invest time in conversation, sincerely trying to understand one another and find the best solution for all.

The other side of conversation is the expression or communication of thoughts and ideas. Clear communication calls for vocabulary that is appropriate to the listener's mental development and experience. It is also important to remember that words can never transplant an idea from the mind of one person into the mind of another. As we listen to words, we construct our own understanding of what those words mean. Therefore, effective communication involves checking to see what the other person thought we said and clarifying the communication if need be.

Jean Piaget believed that social interaction, which occurs in conversation, stimulates development. When talking together we clarify our own thinking on a subject. Also, as we begin to understand another person's perspective, our own beliefs may be brought into question, and this causes inner conflict or what Piaget called disequilibration. In times of disequilibration, conversation may allow a teacher, parent, or friend to become aware of the inner struggle. And conversation is often the means by which we offer support, raise additional questions, or point to resources and ideas that may lead to new understandings and development.

CATHERINE STONEHOUSE

Bibliography. C. Gilligan, N. P. Lyons, and T. J. Hanmer, eds. (1990), *Making Connections: The Relational Worlds of Adolescent Girls at Emma Willard School.*

Conviction. *See* Belief.

Cooperative Learning. A well-kept secret among teachers of small children and among doctoral seminar faculty is that when learners relate well to each other, they make learning a very active process. In general, the educational procedures used in much formal education seem more to deny than to affirm this key to effective teaching and learning.

Instead, learners are made more "self-reliant" by isolating them during the central parts of learning experience. "Everyone, do your own work now! . . . Don't look on anyone's paper! Come on, Charlie, you can do better than that! . . ." The underlying assumption is that competition motivates and motivation is fed by the desire to surpass someone else. One's grade on a test, a project paper, even a piece of art, becomes the essence of learning; the grade is more important than the experience, the effort, and the personal identity of the one who produces, the one who thinks, believes, and invests. The grade shows how well the performance or product was accepted by the small but overpowering audience—the teacher. What one person (on his or her own, mind you) says about the worthiness of the private project ultimately determines what the learner is worth. Small wonder that schools—as well as other forms of education built on the schooling model—have become mechanistic, remote, threatening, and often boring. Why should Christian education be copied from such practices that so seriously degrade the worth of God's special creation?

At its heart, cooperative learning is the investment of trust in the worth of each person in that learning group (often called the learning community). This trust leads the teacher to become a sharer and a peer more than a commander. Talking down is replaced by talking at eye-level, symbolically and actually. The worth of each learner is affirmed. But beyond this, the valuing of interaction and shared responsibility is developed as surely as is the concern for individuals. In such a learning environment, competition is less important than cooperation. People learn to derive their satisfactions from each other and from the collaboration process itself, not merely from their own privatized activity and output. Learning exercises are more apt to be group projects; investment in time is in longer but fewer blocks; evaluation is part of the learning experience, and the learners become more accomplished in assessment, playing a significant role in discriminating judgments and setting subsequent goals.

In public schools and higher education, cooperative learning has become more widely used within the past twenty-five years. Arising partly from insights into teaching derived from the "mainstreaming" movement (accommodating a wider range of skills and competencies within one learning group), the necessity for cooperative learning has become recognized as a desirable way for teachers and learners to help each other, not just a necessity.

TED W. WARD

Bibliography. M. Greene (1995), *Releasing the Imagination;* T. R. Hawkins (1997), *The Learning Congregation—A New Vision of Leadership;* W. F. Hill with J. Rabow, M. A. Charness, J. Kipperman, and S. Radcliffe-Vasile (1994), *Learning Through Discussion;* D. W. Johnson, R. T. Johnson, and E. J. Holubec (1988), *Cooperation in the Classroom;* D. W. Johnson and R. T. Johnson (1987), *Learning Together and Alone;* S. Kagan (1989), *Cooperative Learning Resources for Teachers;* C. Meyers (1986), *Teaching Students to Think Critically;* F. M. Newman and J. Thompson (1987), *Effects of Cooperative Learning on Achievement in Secondary Schools: A Summary of the Research;* S. Papert (1980), *Mindstorms: Children, Computers and Powerful Ideas;* S. Sharanm and C. Shachar (1988), *Language and Learning in the Cooperative Classroom;* R. E. Slavin, *Education Leadership,* 45, 3:7–13; idem (1978), *Using Student Team Learning;* G. H. Wood (1992), *Schools That Work.*

Correspondence Course. *See* Distance Education.

Counseling. Counseling, or "pastoral care," as it was called for most of Christian history, has been a central part of the pastor's work from the patristic period to the present. Up until the twentieth century, pastors gleaned understanding of this task primarily from Gregory the Great's sixth-century work, *Pastoral Care,* supplemented by works of Thomas Aquinas, Hugh of St. Victor, Luther, Zwingli, Richard Baxter, Jonathan Edwards, John Wesley, and others. This classical view included praying for the sick of body and soul, hearing confessions, applying Scripture for absolution, providing admonition and consolation, as well as applying scriptural teaching to life situations. However, in this century Christian theorists began to move away from this classical view of pastoral care and to reinterpret pastoral care in light of the new psychotherapies that emerged after Freud.

In the 1950s mainline Protestant pastoral theologians began to distinguish "pastoral *care*" from "pastoral *counseling.*" The first term refers to the spectrum of activities designed to sustain and nurture a congregation; the second term refers to the narrowly defined relationship between a pastor and a troubled person. This postwar pastoral counseling movement produced a flood of books and new journals. Particularly noteworthy were the writings of Seward Hiltner, Howard Clinebell, Wayne Oates, Carroll Wise, and Paul Johnson. These leading theorists were heavily influenced by the neo-Freudians like Eric Fromm and by Carl Rogers's client-centered therapy. Central themes in this literature are self-realization and acceptance. There was growing stress upon the pastoral counselor as one who offers "acceptance" and who helps the counselee achieve "self-acceptance" in the face of oppressive social institutions. Carl Rogers's approach, particularly, offered counseling techniques simple enough that they could fit nicely into the seminary curriculum.

Therapeutic language increasingly supplanted theological language. The human potential movement, with its profoundly humanistic outlook, began to take center stage. Leaders of the pastoral counseling movement, observing some of the maturing fruits of humanistic psychology, began to qualify their early enthusiasm. The gulf between self-realization and spiritual growth appeared to be wider than many had first thought.

Conservative or evangelical Protestants tended to be sharply critical of the pastoral counseling movement. Evangelical leaders initially castigated mainline Protestants for their easy embrace of the therapeutic spirit of the age and the undermining of biblical authority that seemed to accompany it. But by the 1970s, as James Hunter has shown in his extensive research, evangelicals were following in the footsteps of the mainline and liberal Protestants they had once criticized. With great enthusiasm—and sometimes little theological critique—they embraced therapeutic values and language, becoming preoccupied with self-realization, acceptance, and psychological balance.

Counseling, in the general shape given it in the earlier pastoral counseling movement, assumed a much larger place in the work of many evangelical pastors. Training programs and parachurch counseling centers proliferated; indeed, Christian counseling by the 1980s had assumed a life of its own in a realm largely separate and apart from congregational life. Professional standards, organizations, certification, and fees established Christian counseling as a profession. In the process much of the traditional burden of pastoral care was shifted from churches to counseling clinics.

While evangelical theorists all sought to uphold a high view of the Bible's inspiration and authority, they faced tensions over the nature and purpose of "biblical counseling." At least three different approaches emerged: (1) "nouthetic counseling" set forth by Jay Adams adopted a directive and confrontational style and rejected psychotherapeutic theory; (2) "discipleship counseling" adumbrated by Gary Collins was open to dialogue with psychotherapeutic approaches; and (3) an integrational approach represented by Lawrence Crabb.

In the 1980s and especially the 1990s the Christian counseling movement, whether in its older mainline or more recent evangelical streams, recognized the need to deepen its theological roots and to draw more upon the classical resources of the Christian tradition. Focus began to turn more to the challenge of equipping lay caregivers in the context of congregational life.

In the mid–1990s Lawrence Crabb, one of the influential shapers of counseling theory and practice among evangelicals, issued a controversial call for Christian counseling to be returned to the congregation of believers as its primary locus. Sharply questioning the isolated clinical setting of much Christian counseling, Crabb called for the renewal of "eldering" within the Christian community.

As the twenty-first century opens, Christian counseling is returning to its "pastoral care" roots, adjusting its therapeutic, psychological bases in order to readmit those ancient practices of classical pastoral care, that is, praying, confessing, and teaching from Scripture.

HOLLY ALLEN

Bibliography. J. Adams (1979), *More Than Redemption: A Theology of Christian Counseling;* H. Clinebell (1984), *Basic Types of Pastoral Care and Counseling: Resources for the Ministry of Healing and Growth;* G. Collins, ed. (1980), *Helping People Grow: Practical Approaches to Christian Counseling;* L. J. Crabb, Jr. (1997), *Connecting: Healing Ourselves and Our Relationships—A Radical New Vision;* H. E. Fosdick (1960), *The Ministry and Psychotherapy: Pastoral Psychology;* E. B. Holifield (1983), *A History of Pastoral Care in America: From Salvation to Self-Realization;* J. D. Hunter (1983), *American Evangelicalism: Conservative Religion and the Quandary of Modernity;* T. C. Oden (1984), *Care of Souls in the Classic Tradition;* A. Outler (1954), *Psychotherapy and the Christian Message;* P. Vitz (1994), *Psychology as Religion: The Cult of Self-worship.*

Counselor. *See* Case Advocate.

Course. In this article *course* refers to a single unit of instruction. A teacher's course construction includes *writing objectives* for the topic to be examined; selecting content elements to cover during class sessions; mapping out a logical sequence of the material (course outline); choosing teaching methods and materials; and determining evaluative criteria and procedure.

Newble and Cannon (1989) give helpful criteria against which to measure the propriety of new and existing course content. *Philosophical criteria* are the ultimate values one seeks for those participating. *Professional criteria* consist of explicit legal and professional requirements that must be met before a student is ready to practice a profession. *Psychological criteria* seek content that develops higher-level intellectual skills, such as reasoning, problem solving, critical thinking, and creativity. The feasibility of teaching something in light of existing resources relates to *practical criteria*. Are the necessary library materials and classroom equipment available? *Student criteria* relates to student characteristics, course content matched to the intellectual and maturity level of learners.

As a result of course participation students should know more than they knew before; understand something they did not previously grasp; develop a new skill; feel differently about a subject than they did previously; or develop an appreciation for something where there was none (Mager, 1968).

When planning or implementing a course, teachers define their understanding of what constitutes "Christian" education. What makes education "Christian" is not just the faith of participants, the doctrinal statement of the sponsoring institution, behavioral standards, or even the coverage of Scripture. Rather, a course is "Christian" when the teaching-learning *process* is as biblical as the content.

TERRY POWELL

Bibliography. R. Mager (1968), *Developing Attitude Toward Learning;* D. Newble and R. Cannon (1989), *A Handbook for Teachers in Universities and Colleges: A Guide to Improving Teaching Methods.*

Course of Study. *See* Curriculum.

Crafts. Manual skill activities usually designed to be completed in one to five learning sessions. Carefully chosen, they serve the function of being an aid in the teaching process rather than an activity apart from that process. Some fundamental questions need to be asked. These relate to the age-appropriateness of the craft; the opportunity for creativity allowed by the craft; the ability of the child to work without excessive adult help; the amount of teaching time to be consumed; and the sense of accomplishment and self-worth derived.

Crafts can provide opportunities for using one's imagination. They can uncover new interests and talents and teach new skills. They allow for learning to work alone and with others and for expression of one's emotions. They serve as a constructive use of leisure time and help develop patience and discipline.

Children should have a choice of craft activities that reinforce the teaching. Preschoolers may have an art activity which involves making a collage of pictures of friends to reinforce the teaching about "God gave us friends." They may color a leaf placed between waxed paper to reinforce the teaching of "God made the world." Children may construct Old Testament villages. They may make greeting cards using a variety of colors and textures of paper plus ribbon and flowers and send those greetings to a sick classmate or residents of a nursing home. Those crafts which involve the use of as many of the five senses as possible are best.

Extended time in vacation Bible school, after-school day care, or day camps are examples of events in which crafts are creative, with their primary purpose not necessarily reinforcing a particular teaching. Even then it is appropriate for the leader to connect a Bible thought or verse as the children work.

Crafts may also be a part of ministry to adults. Women enjoy the fellowship of other women who share common interests. Seniors enjoy the opportunity to try something new while spending time with Christian friends.

Craft ideas should have clear instructions with diagrams; a suggested skill and age-appropriate level; a list of supplies and equipment; the time needed to complete the craft; an indication of what the pupil might learn, accomplish, or un-

derstand; and suggestions for a tie-in to biblical teaching or outreach activities.

BARBARA WYMAN

Bibliography. S. Roberts, comp. (1993), *VBS Craft Ideas.*

Creativity, Biblical Foundations of. God is the ultimate source of creativity since he is the Creator of the universe. To create is to bring into existence. To be able to create everything, one must be sovereign, omnipresent, omniscient, and omnipotent. Only God qualifies for this. He alone reigns supreme, is everywhere, knows everything, and can do anything. He is the one and only Creator. Genesis 1–2 speaks eloquently to this fact. Therein we are informed that he created the world of nature and the world of human beings.

To be creative is to take the things that have been created and to use them in new and different ways. In this sense, God is also the Creative One. He created water, soil, and time. Then he used them creatively to fashion a Grand Canyon. He created color, air, clouds, and sun. He combines these creatively into spectacular sunsets. God's creativity will always be in harmony with his character. He cannot creatively reorganize the Trinity, nor disband it. He cannot redefine holiness, so that unsaved sinners might slip into heaven. But the self-imposed restrictions within the Godhead do not hamper his creativity. There are an infinite number of ways God can glorify himself. He is not only the author of creativity; he is the epitome of it. His commentary on all that he created was that it was "very good" (Gen. 1:31). He could say that not only because of the quality of his creation, but also because of the potentially unlimited quantity of ways it provided for him to creatively express himself.

Creativity and Humankind. Humanity, being made in the image of God, is likewise creative but to a more limited degree. To create is to bring into existence. Humans cannot do that. Only God can. At the end of the sixth day, he completed his work of creation, certified its intrinsic and supreme goodness, and rested. Creation, for this life and in this world, is finished. However, God is not an absentee God. He continues to be involved; as Sustainer rather than Creator; as creative rather than creating (Acts 17:24–28; Col. 1:15–17). But when God moved into his creative and sustaining mode, humanity moved into its ruling and subduing mode.

Humans, though not creators per se, are still creative. The most creative couple in history was Adam and Eve. That was because they were doing everything for the first time. Everything was in a "start-up" phase. They had no prior experience. They undoubtedly consulted God, but he did not tell them all they wanted to know (Deut. 29:29). Adam started his creative stewardship by naming all the beasts and the birds. So many sizes, shapes, colors, and sounds! The couple no doubt discussed when to prune, what to eat, where to sleep, tools needed, and so on.

Creativity and the Fall. Adam and Eve went their way, creatively enjoying Eden and each other, keeping the rules set by their Creator. Then it happened. Challenged to think and act incorrectly, they chose to pit their human wills against the sovereign will of their Creator. The fall profoundly affected our minds. We can still think, but we cannot always think correctly. Adam thought he could hide from God. He thought he could blame Eve. His sons inherited this flawed thinking. Cain came to the conclusion that the best way to solve a sibling squabble was to commit murder. Within a few generations the human mind had deteriorated to the point that "every intent of the thoughts of his heart was only evil continually" (Gen. 6:5). The natural man cannot always think correctly.

But can humans think creatively? Does satanic blindness mean cerebral blankness? Not at all. Just because the natural person has problems thinking correctly does not mean he or she is unable to think creatively. Look at Ephesians 4:17–19. Fallen folk are classified as ignorant and calloused, but that does not silence them. They have committed themselves to "practice every kind of impurity." They are not satisfied to be dull, traditional deviates. They sin creatively; even using their depraved minds to become inventors of evil (Rom. 1:28–30).

This does not mean that non-Christians do nothing but immoral acts. They may do good deeds, seeking creative ways to sidestep conviction while searching for innovative substitutes for sin, righteousness, and judgment (John 16:7–11).

Creativity and the Christian. The unsaved person has the propensity to think incorrectly and the potential to think creatively. We must not let this lead us to the erroneous conclusion that because the saved person now has the potential to think correctly, there is no reason to worry about thinking creatively. Correct thinking neither rules out nor replaces creative thinking. Both are mandatory.

Scripture weaves correctness and creativity together. For example, in Romans 12:1–2 the renewing of the mind is essential. It enables us to live correctly with regard to the world and God's will. Where is creativity? It is in the exhortation to "be transformed." This conveys the idea of changing, becoming new and different. This happens as we allow the Spirit of God to blend his pervasive truth into our unique personalities. The result: a custom-made Christian. Creativity at its highest!

Paul's philosophy of evangelism combined correctness and creativity. Five times in 1 Corinthians 9:19–23 he reiterates his goal—to win others to Christ. That is a correct goal. It never changes. Paul's methods, however, frequently changed, for he creatively adapted his approach to the nature and needs of his audience. He summarized his innovative ministry by saying, "I have become all things to all men, that I may by all means save some." While there is one reason to do evangelism, there are many ways to do it. The apostle was committed to creative outreach.

First Corinthians 10:31 says, "So whether you eat or drink or whatever you do, do all to the glory of God." This is a call to cautious living, wherein every believer carefully strives to do what is right. But even more so, it is a call to creative living, wherein all Christians are challenged to discover new and different ways to glorify God.

J. GRANT HOWARD

Bibliography. E. de Bono (1992), *Serious Creativity;* J. G. Howard (1987), *Creativity in Preaching;* L. Ryken (1989), *The Liberated Imagination;* R. Von Oech (1990), *A Wack on the Side of the Head.*

Criteria. *See* Criterion-Referenced Tests.

Criterion-Referenced Tests. Tests are used to evaluate both the current condition of individuals or groups and the degree of change in those individuals or groups. To evaluate the relative condition or degree of change of individuals or groups compared to other individuals or groups, norm-referenced tests are used; to evaluate the absolute condition or degree of change compared to a clearly defined standard, criterion-referenced tests are used. If the purpose of the test is for general description or research purposes, either criterion or norm-referenced tests may be appropriate, but if the purpose is to provide specific information which will form the basis for specific action or to determine the precise change resulting from an action, criterion-referenced tests are more approriate.

Criterion-referenced tests measure a relatively narrow and clearly defined domain, whereas tests are based on a more limited sampling of items from a broader domain. Criterion-referenced tests report scores that provide absolute information such as percentages that indicate the extent of the individual's status with respect to the domain being measured (e.g., the student answered 95 percent of the items correctly) while norm-referenced tests give scores that provide relative information such as percentiles that compare the student to the norm group (e.g., the student scored at the 50th percentile—above 50 percent of students in the norm group).

A criterion-referenced score on an achievement test evaluates the performance of the student in terms of how much there is to know, while a norm-referenced score compares the student's achievement to other students. For criterion-referenced scores to be valuable, both the domain that is being measured and the meaning of a score of 100 percent need to be clearly defined. For norm-referenced tests both the domain and the norm group need to be clearly defined, but a score of 100 percent typically has little or no meaning.

While most criterion-referenced measurements have been tests of achievement in the cognitive domain, criterion-referenced measures of behavior or affective objectives are appropriate if constructed around a narrow and clearly defined behavioral or affective domain and if they provide scores that indicate an individual's status with respect to that domain. For example, criterion-referenced scales to measure devotional practices or belief about God using either frequency or agreement response options (e.g., never—frequently or strongly agree—or strongly disagree) would have scores that indicate specifically what the person's devotional practices are or that describe the person's belief about God rather than providing scores for research purposes or to indicate whether a person was above or below average in devotional practices or belief about God.

JEROME THAYER

Critical Reflection. Employment of a set of cognitive skills to sort through available information, evaluate it, and use it to reach conclusions or make decisions. It is an area of interest for philosophers, psychologists, and educators. In philosophy the focus is on the development of skills in questioning assumptions and the use of logic to draw legitimate inferences and conclusions. In psychology the emphasis is on cognitive structures, the activities of the mind, and the ways human cognition is used in solving problems and making judgments and decisions. In education the emphasis is on moving beyond the rote recall and restatement of facts and ideas presented by a teacher or a text to encourage the students' evaluation and active use of this information. While there is some disagreement over exactly which processes are involved in critical reflection, Dressler and Mayhew (1954, 179–80), describe five basic skills: (1) the ability to define a problem, (2) the ability to select pertinent information for the solution of the problem, (3) the ability to recognize stated and unstated assumptions, (4) the ability to formulate and select relevant and promising hypotheses, and (5) the ability to draw conclusions validly and to judge the validity of inferences.

Within the field of Christian education, concern for critical reflection has focused on moving beyond a knowledge of what Scripture says and what Christians believe to an understanding of their meaning, implications, and application to life. In short, reflection helps people think about and decide what to believe and what to do in their life situation in light of these beliefs. This kind of concern is evident in the works of a wide range of writers, from Paulo Freire's (1974) call for the development of "critical consciousness," to Larry Richards's (1970) "guided self-application" Bible teaching approach, to Donald Joy's (1969) "inductive-deductive" Bible study method, and Thomas Groome's (1980) "shared praxis" approach to Christian religious education. If we are to encourage people toward spiritual maturity and faithful living, a passive or rote acquisition of Bible knowledge and Christian doctrine is not enough. Overreliance on religious experts (whether pastors, teachers, or parents) for knowing what to believe and what to do can result in an immature faith and limit the learner's ability to work through the validity, implications, and applications of the facts and principles learned. This can result in a dependence of the learner on the teacher, or a nominal faith that has no impact on the learner's life. In its worst form, it can lead to a kind of indoctrination that does not equip learners to evaluate what they are taught or how to apply it to new situations.

While a certain amount of learner dependence is normal in teaching children, as the learner grows and matures, the need for developing critical reflection skills and using them to examine and apply what is believed becomes more and more important. In John Westerhoff's (1976) model of faith development, youth move from an "affiliative faith" to an "owned faith" through a period of testing and questioning what they have been raised to believe ("searching faith"). For this positive growth to occur, youth and adults need to develop the skills of critical reflection, and be encouraged and supported as they employ them in examining both the content of their faith and the ways it needs to impact their lives.

The development and use of critical reflection skills can be encouraged through the use of learning methods that promote evaluation, problem solving, and raising and discussing student questions and concerns. Working through case studies, discussing student questions about the content of study or its implications, the use of "devil's advocate" presentations, student debates, and writing assignments that encourage personal reflection, are examples of methods that can promote the kind of critical reflection that will stimulate a growing and vital faith.

KEVIN E. LAWSON

Bibliography. P. L. Dressel and L. B. Mayhew (1954), *General Education: Explorations in Evaluation;* P. Freire (1974), *Education for Critical Consciousness;* T. H. Groome (1980), *Christian Religious Education: Sharing Our Story and Vision;* D. Joy (1969), *Meaningful Learning in the Church;* L. O. Richards (1970), *Creative Bible*

Teaching; J. H. Westerhoff III (1976), *Will Our Children Have Faith?*

Critique. *See* Critical Reflection.

Cues. One of the goals of biblical instruction for the Christian teacher is to see the lives of learners conformed to the image of Christ. While teachers are committed to the right handling of Scripture, they are also concerned with what kinds of conditions and teaching techniques are likely to facilitate and encourage Christlike changes in behavior. Using cues is a technique, suggested by the educational psychology branch of behaviorism, to aid in positively influencing behavioral change.

Behaviorism focuses on how behavior is shaped or determined by its consequences. According to behaviorism, actions that are followed by rewards are "reinforced" and will tend to be repeated. Behaviors followed by punishment or disapproval tend to be extinguished. Because teachers have the opportunity to control many of the elements in the environment which may serve as rewarding or inhibiting consequences, it is important to study how this influence can be used in a positive manner. The use of cues is one such method.

In the learning sequence of behaviorism, learners emit behaviors, or "responses" to their environment. If this results in the learners receiving a reinforcing stimulus, it is likely that the behavior will be repeated. To help the learners make particular behavioral responses that will be reinforced, teachers may provide an antecedent stimulus, or cue, just before the desired behavior. These cues aid learners in making correct and appropriate responses.

Cueing is an intentional way for teachers to guide learners toward desired behavioral goals. It indicates to the learner what is needed to experience satisfying consequences. A cue could be written or verbal as when a teacher provides information or prompts to help learners answer questions or complete an exercise correctly. It may also take the form of a nonverbal prompt such as body language, pointing, demonstrating, or even modeling. Whether verbal or nonverbal, the goal of using cues is to point learners in the right direction.

SHELLY CUNNINGHAM

Bibliography. K. Issler and R. Habermas (1994), *How We Learn: A Christian Teacher's Guide to Educational Psychology;* W. R. Yount (1996), *Created to Learn.*

Cult. The word "cult" comes from the Latin verb *colere,* which means "to worship or give reverence to a deity" (Lewis and Short, 1984, 370). In Latin texts this verb was used in the general sense of worshiping a deity, regardless of the god(s) in question. Since this was the common

word for "worship" in the Latin language, the early Christian writers who wrote in Latin naturally used this same word, whether speaking of the worship of the one true God or of the worship of false, pagan deities. The Vulgate, a Latin translation of the Bible, uses *colere* to speak of worship, both of pagan deities (Acts 17:23) and of the true, biblical God (Acts 17:25).

In modern English usage, the word "cult" has a much more specific emphasis. Rather than referring generally to any sort of worshipping community, the word "cult" is reserved for religious groups that are deemed aberrant or deviant in some respect. Some modern definitions place the primary or exclusive emphasis on the group's *behavior and practices,* while other definitions place the predominant or sole emphasis on the group's *belief system.* In other words, cults have been defined either in terms of psychology and sociology, or in terms of theology.

Behavioral Definitions. In recent years, academic sociologists have abandoned the word "cult" as too judgmental, pejorative, and prejudicial. They now favor more value-neutral terms such as "new religious movements," "alternative religions," "emergent religions," and the like. A few sociologists, such as Ronald Enroth of Westmont College, retain the word. According to Enroth's (1977) definition, "Cults are defined as religious organizations that tend to be outside the mainstream of the dominant religious forms of any given society" (168). Other behaviorally oriented definitions commonly cite certain alleged cultic "hallmarks." These may include the presence of a "prophet-founder," who is a "charismatic" and "authoritarian" leader; an "exclusivistic" and "legalistic" outlook; a "persecution mentality"; etc. (Tucker, 1989, 16, 24).

While it is not unreasonable to examine the behaviors and practices of a religious group, behaviorally oriented definitions of the word "cult" suffer from relativism, subjectivity, and imprecision by the nature of the case. For example, if cults are groups that are "outside the religious mainstream," then when a society's religious standards change, the frame of reference shifts accordingly; what was once a cult may no longer be so and vice versa. The early Christians certainly were "aberrant" when compared to Roman society at large; by such definitions the early Christians would be "cultic." Also, one might reasonably ask just how far "outside" of the "mainstream" a group has to be before it can be labeled a cult. Even determining what constitutes the "mainstream" religiously is fraught with difficulties, especially in our increasingly pluralistic climate. Definitions that employ certain "hallmarks" are similarly problematic. For example, if cults are "exclusivistic," then what of the belief that Jesus Christ is the only way to salvation, which most evangelical Christians hold? Many of the commonly cited hallmarks apply to Jesus himself, who claimed that he alone was the way to the Father (John 14:6) and made what can easily be interpreted as "authoritarian" demands on his followers (e.g., Matt. 16:24; Matt. 8:22).

Furthermore, behavioral definitions provide no basis for properly classifying groups that are doctrinally deviant but sociologically and behaviorally "normal," such as the Mormon Church. Though sociologically and behaviorally mainstream, Christians have rightly classified Mormonism as a cult due to its aberrant theology (e.g., God is a man who lives on another planet; Jesus is the spirit brother of Satan; etc.).

Doctrinal Definitions. Theological or doctrinal definitions of cults focus on the group's departure from the standard of orthodox, biblical teaching. Here the emphasis is on the group's *truth claims* and how those claims comport with the essentials of the Christian faith. Cults are measured against the absolute, unchanging, objective standard of God's inerrant Word. Gomes (1995) has suggested the following theological definition: "A cult of Christianity is a group of people claiming to be Christian, which embraces a particular doctrinal system taught by an individual leader, group of leaders, or organization, which (system) denies (either explicitly or implicitly) one or more of the central doctrines of the Christian faith as taught in the sixty-six books of the Bible" (7).

According to this definition, cults of Christianity are groups that claim to be Christians, in contradistinction to other world religions—such as Judaism, Islam, and Hinduism—which distinguish themselves from the Christian faith. (Note that these groups also may have "cults" that arise from within them. For example, the Nation of Islam may be considered to be a "cult of Islam.") Despite their claim to be Christian, cults fail the test because they deny at least one central—that is, constitutive or defining—doctrine of the faith. Included in Christianity's inventory of central doctrines are the Trinity, the deity of Christ, his bodily resurrection, his atonement for our sins through his death on the cross, and salvation by God's grace. These doctrines are "central" in the sense that their removal would change the fundamental character of the belief system from Christian into something else. Central doctrines must be distinguished from peripheral (i.e., nonessential) teachings, such as the method of baptism or the timing of the tribulation (Gomes, 1995, 10–11).

Reaching the Cultist. *Know Why People Join*— In dealing with those involved in cults, it is important to understand why people join such groups in the first place. Typically, people join cults because of needs in their lives that are not being met. These may include the need to form close, loving interpersonal attachments; the need

to commit oneself to a significant cause; and the desire for intellectual and spiritual fulfillment. While such aspirations per se are natural and healthy, the cults offer a spiritually counterfeit source of fulfillment; cultic involvement will leave the adherent ultimately unsatisfied. Christians must reach out to cultists in love and show how their deepest needs can truly be met by Jesus Christ, the true "bread from heaven" that satisfies (John 6:48, 50–51).

Confront the False Doctrinal Teaching—It is also important to confront lovingly the cultist's false belief system. Christians should focus on the central issues (mentioned above) rather than on peripheral matters. Particular emphasis should be given to the person and work of Christ and to the nature of God, since cults are almost invariably askew on these crucial matters. As the late Dr. Walter Martin would often say, Christians need to know "what they believe and why they believe it" and should "contend earnestly for the faith," as Jude 3 commands. To fulfill the biblical mandate, we are to reason with them from the Scriptures (Acts 17:17; 18:4; 19:8–9) in order to show the falsity and ultimate bankruptcy of the cultic beliefs.

Though some argue that cultists are "brainwashed" or "mind controlled," (Hassan, 1990) and therefore impervious to reasoned scriptural and apologetical appeals, this is not true. There is a considerable body of literature—psychological, sociological, and legal—that has debunked the mind-control thesis (Passantino, 1997, 49–78). Christians should evangelize cultists as they would any other unbeliever, keeping in mind that the cultist has committed himself or herself to a system of belief that needs to be refuted in a compelling and yet compassionate way (1 Peter 3:15).

ALAN W. GOMES

Bibliography. R. Abanes (1998), *Cults, New Religious Movements, and Your Family;* A. W. Gomes (1995), *Unmasking the Cults;* idem (1998), *Truth and Error;* idem (1995), *The Zondervan Guide to Cults and Religious Movements;* J. McDowell and D. Stewart (1992), *The Deceivers: What Cults Believe: How They Lure Followers;* R. and G. Passantino (1981), *Answers to the Cultist at Your Door;* idem (1997), *Kingdom of the Cults;* R. Rhodes (1994), *The Culting of America;* R. Tucker (1989), *Another Gospel.*

Cults and Youth. The late 1960s and early 1970s saw the rise of Eastern religious movements and religious cults in the United States and Canada. Groups such as the Children of God, the "Moonies," the Krishna Consciousness Society, and other groups began to draw thousands of teenagers and young adults into their ranks. To parents, the conversion of their youth to cultish beliefs and practices was generally seen as a crisis. The crisis continued as many of these young people did not soon disavow their newfound religious beliefs and lifestyle. The "Anticult Movement" grew in response to these twin crises.

Almost immediately the rise of cults drew the attention of social science researchers. What were the factors that were associated with cult joiners? What is the appeal of cults to youth? Social science has tried to answer these questions from a variety of viewpoints.

One locus of study has to do with youth themselves, and their "experience of emptiness" in modern society. It was early noted that many cult joiners were sons and daughters of financially affluent parents, not impoverished ones. Youth were not finding their deepest needs met by material wealth, and were seeking something deeper and more "real." A certain amount of rebellion among teenagers in reaction to parental mores and values is the experience of many youth, and some express this rebellion as a complete rejection of the parents' religion in favor of a new religion or cult.

Another focus of research has centered on family factors related to relationships and dynamics within the home. Youth who were highly bonded with communicative, affiliative, and loving parents have been shown to be far less likely to be drawn to the cultish group. Conversely, those youth whose home experience was anything but warm and loving are much more at risk to fall to the influence of cults.

Sociologists use the vocabulary of "rational choice" theory to account for the decision to join a cult. Though the costs in joining a cult are high (commitment of time, lifestyle, and even physical appearance), the rewards are also perceived as high. Among the perceived gains are close relationships, a feeling of family, constant affirmation on this earth, and magnified rewards in the next.

Christian educators seek to help Christian families be places of loving acceptance and warmth. This help can be in the form of programs, resources, and personal assistance to parents in understanding the needs of their children and how to communicate with them. Similarly, there are programs and resources to help teenagers get along with and even appreciate their parents, as well as how to grow in their understanding that true self-worth and love are only found in a relationship with God through Jesus Christ.

LEONARD KAGELER

Bibliography. D. Bromely and A. Shupe, *Social Compass* 45 (1955): 2; S. Wright and E. Piper, *Journal of Marriage and the Family* 48 (1986): 1.

Culture. Beliefs and behaviors transmitted by symbols such as language, rites, and artifacts. The word *culture* has its roots in the concept of worship (from cult) and tilling the soil (from cul-

tivation). Culture, then, comprises ideas and concepts as well as actions and behaviors. Culture is transforming and transmissive. That is, it is constantly changing and is passed on from one generation to the next by means of formal and nonformal education. Stated succinctly, culture is how one views reality.

Richard Niebuhr in his classic study of *Christ and Culture* (1952) identified from church history five Christian approaches toward culture: Christ against culture, the Christ of culture, Christ above culture, Christ and culture in paradox, and Christ the transformer of culture.

The *Christ against culture* motif sees loyalty to Christ standing in opposition to human culture. A Christian rejects the world along with its institutions because culture reflects a way of life contrary to the spirit of Christ. The duty of the Christian, according to this view, is to withdraw from earthly desires and contact with the outside world in order to develop a community with divine standards of loyalty to God. Based on their writings, Niebuhr cited Tertullian and Tolstoy as proponents of this view.

The second motif, *Christ of culture,* moves to the other end of the spectrum and assimilates culture and obedience to Christ. Culture and Christ are not separated by a gulf as in Christ above culture, but are part of the same thing. When culture reflects the goodness of Christ, culture reaches its highest form. There is no tension between the world and Christianity. Instead, the Christian finds those things in culture that exemplify Christ and his teaching and uses them in creating a better world. This viewpoint is exemplified by the Gnostics, Abelard, and liberal Protestantism.

Niebuhr's third motif is *Christ above culture.* Adherents of this motif fit between the first two. They do not reject culture as Tertullian or accommodate culture as do liberal Protestants, but attempt to synthesize both positions. They value both the divinity of Christ, which the Christ against culture motif emphasizes, and the humanity of Christ, which is emphasized by Christ in culture. The Christ above culture position tries to reconcile the lordship of Christ and the value of culture, particularly natural laws. The majority of Christendom falls into this category, including the Roman Catholic Church, Thomas Aquinas, Clement of Alexandria, and Bishop Butler.

The fourth attitude is *Christ and culture in paradox.* More than the other attitudes this view attempts to deal with the active tension between Christ and culture. They see Christ and culture as a both/and issue. They recognize the reality of Christ and culture, although they hold that culture is infected with the disease of godlessness and cannot help our sinful condition. Nevertheless, we must live in the world and are inescapably involved in culture. Despite the disease, God does use culture to bring about right-eousness. The tension of life is to bring Christ and culture together, to affirm the kingdom of God and the kingdom of the world by our allegiance to God. Although the Christ-culture issue, according to this position, will only be resolved in eternity, the Christian continues to work out his or her salvation here on earth. The works of the apostle Paul, Luther, and Kierkegaard represent this motif.

The final attitude or motif is *Christ the transformer of culture*. This view emphasizes that although originally created good, the fall has left culture corrupt and defiled. Culture stands in opposition to Christ. But as Christ came to redeem us, so culture has the possibility of redemption or conversion by radical transformation. Our work is to transform culture to the glory of God into a new Christendom. Representatives of this view are Augustine, Calvin, and F. D. Maurice.

Niebuhr gives a good starting point for a discussion of Christianity and culture. Yoder (1996) points out, however, that it is wrong to assume that the types he suggests are closed systems or that people espouse one particular motif consistently. In his definition of Christ, Niebuhr also seems to dismiss that Christ as the God-man depicts the eternal along with the humanness of culture.

Of the five views Christians have toward culture—separation, accommodation, synthesis, paradox, and transformation—evangelical Christianity has followed the first, fourth, and fifth motifs. Missionary educators Kraft (1981) and Mayers (1987) have taken the Christ and culture in paradox position and have attempted to show that culture can be used to communicate the gospel message. Others, such as Lingenfelter (1994) have called for a transformation of culture.

Culture is a dominant force in Christian education. It is the backdrop for communicating the gospel, and it is the world in which the gospel message takes form. The Christian message cannot be isolated from culture, nor can it be infused with cultural relativity or diluted with syncretism. The historic dangers of these approaches are well known. The task of the Christian educator is to take the eternal truths of Scripture, dress them appropriately with culture, and make them applicable in the culture in which we live.

PHILIP BUSTRUM

Bibliography. C. H. Kraft (1981), *Christianity in Culture;* S. G. Lingenfelter (1994), *Transforming Culture: A Challenge for Christian Mission;* M. K. Mayers (1987), *Christianity Confronts Culture;* H. R. Niebuhr (1952), *Christ and Culture;* J. H. Yoder (1996), *Authentic Transformation: A New Vision of Christ and Culture,* pp. 31–90.

See also ACCULTURATION; ENCULTURATION; ETHNIC IMPLICATIONS FOR CHRISTIAN EDUCATION; ETHNOCENTRICITY; MISSION, MISSIONS EDUCATION

Curriculum. The term *curriculum* comes from the Latin word *currere*, which means to run a race. Students use the term to refer to their program of studies or their degree plans. The curriculum can represent all the courses and experiences at an institution. In essence, educational transcripts reflect the educational race students have run—it's their curriculum.

When church members use the word "curriculum," they usually mean the materials, resources, or teaching guides. They are, in fact, referring to a curriculum plan. A curriculum plan is "an orderly arrangement of subject matter and activities designed to facilitate specified learning experiences" (Colson and Rigdon, 1981, 150). The term curriculum involves more than the curriculum materials. Curriculum is "the sum total of all learning experiences resulting from a curriculum plan used under church guidance and directed toward a church's mission" (Colson and Rigdon, 1981, 149). Curriculum involves the subject matter and the methods used in the study. It is both content and process.

This broader definition of curriculum means that a publishing house does not provide the curriculum. The curriculum is what occurs in the teaching/learning situation (Colson and Rigdon, 1981, 40). The publisher only provides a curriculum plan and curriculum materials. The teacher is responsible for ensuring that curriculum (the sum total of learning) takes place. This is an important distinction. Curriculum plans and materials are resources for the teacher. They are designed to help a teacher in planning and preparation. Curriculum plans are static. On the other hand, curriculum is dynamic and spontaneous. A teacher can never anticipate all of the questions students might ask, or the interaction that might occur between students. A teacher cannot forsee the experiences each student brings to the learning environment. The dynamics of the classroom situation makes each learning experience an adventure. This is why teaching is an art, and not a science. A curriculum plan provides a guide to learning, but the curriculum is the responsibility of the teacher.

DARYL ELDRIDGE

Bibliography. H. P. Colson and R. M. Rigdon (1981), *Understanding Your Church's Curriculum;* L. Ford (1991), *A Curriculum Design Manual for Theological Education.*

Curriculum, Hidden. Covert, implicit, unintentional messages communicated throughout the entire educational process. Two examples are the exclusive use of "he" rather than "he or she," and the underlying individualism that permeates writings of many North American authors, implying validation of that perspective and subtly teaching it. The hidden curriculum may be distinguished from the graded course of study or written, formal curriculum. Philip Jackson (1968) originally used the term to reveal how schools latently transmitted and reinforced attitudes and behaviors which went beyond traditional concerns. John Dewey (1938) stated,

> Perhaps the greatest of all pedagogical fallacies is the notion that a person learns only the particular thing he is studying at the time. Collateral learning in the way of formation of enduring attitudes, or likes and dislikes, may be and often is much more important. (18)

More recently, Gail McCutcheon (1988) explains that this unintended curriculum "is transmitted through the everyday, normal goings-on in schools" (191). The written curriculum is evident, but this disguised force is often hidden even from educators.

There are several sources of hidden curriculum. One source is books. The bias of the writer, translator, and publisher is reflected in the chosen content, while the perspectives of ethnic groups, female students, and working-class people may be ignored.

A second source of hidden curriculum is teachers who choose emphases, procedures, teaching strategies, and model attitudes reflecting only their own viewpoint and expectations. They may not encourage students' self-esteem and abilities.

Teachers convey values and behaviors in subtle ways.

A third source of hidden curriculum is the atmosphere and structure of the local context. Examples include the emotional climate of a church or denomination (e.g., critical versus affirming), group norms, rituals and routines (e.g., liturgical versus informal), work ethic (e.g., mediocrity versus excellence), levels of conformity (e.g., uniformity versus individualistic), and socialization processes. Students learn attitudes, interests, and habits from a hidden curriculum transmitted through activity patterns, use of time, physical arrangements, and atmosphere. Critical theorists, such as Paulo Freire (1973), point to the instilling of passivity and the using of social control and oppression to impose middle-class values, as opposed to offering resources and opportunities to liberate minority and disadvantaged people. Education is not only for conserving culture but also for the bettering and liberating of people.

There always have been and will be hidden effects in curriculum. Hidden curriculum has a powerful impact on learning values and norms.

JANET L. DALE

Bibliography. J. Dewey (1938), *Experience and Education;* P. Freire (1973), *Education for Critical Consciousness;* P. Jackson (1968), *Life in Classrooms;* G. McCutcheon (1988), *The Curriculum: Problems, Politics, and Possibilities,* pp. 191–203.

Dd

Day Care. Day care for young children remains a topic of debate and emotional involvement. Day care may range from one hour per week to full-time (more than thirty hours) and from center-based to home-based. Some researchers have hypothesized that more than twenty hours per week of child care in the first year puts at risk the mother-child bond, which may stunt personal security and emotional and social development. Other studies, however, found "negligible differences" between the attachment to their mothers of day care and home-reared children.

A summary of research concludes that programs rated high quality are associated with children who have greater social competency, higher levels of language development, higher levels of play, better ability to regulate their own behavior, greater compliance with adults, and fewer behavioral problems in elementary school.

Quality of day care is the important consideration. High-quality centers have low adult/child ratios, trained staff with low turnover, age-appropriate activities, and nurturing, responsive caregivers. The quality of caregiver interaction is a strong predictor of cognitive and emotional well-being.

Day care centers are subject to governmental regulations. Regulation of day care in the home varies from area to area. Parents must become informed of the kind of care the child will receive. Issues such as cleanliness, nutrition, adequate supervision, and the provision of learning opportunities may be complicated when the caregiver is a friend or relative.

Parents should tour facilities and observe caregiver-child interactions. The caregiver must be experienced and know about nutrition, child development and learning characteristics and disabilities, hygiene, first aid, and childhood diseases. She should call the child by name and use normal voice tone. Intervention in conflict must be done calmly with no shouting or physical discipline. The center or home should be bright, preferably with natural light, colorful, and spacious.

Churches have seen the provision of day care as a ministry opportunity. They should, however, do careful long-range planning which takes into consideration how the provision of day care will enhance the goals of the church. Church members may feel that the center will become a part of the ministry of their church, but the day care may operate quite separately from the church. Government regulations involving sanitary procedures, room size, equipment usage, and so on may make it difficult for rooms used for the day care to be utilized by the church for their regular teaching ministry. When religious instruction is a part of the curriculum, parents must be informed of the nature of that instruction.

BARBARA WYMAN

Day Care Centers. The term *day care* generally refers to physical-nurturing care, while *preschool* has been used more specifically to refer to educationally oriented care. However, the distinctions have become blurred and both types are often referred to collectively as child care. Day care usually refers to care for children prior to kindergarten, although many such centers now provide after-school care for older children as well.

Mothers in the workplace is an accepted part of modern life. More than a hundred countries around the world have recognized this fact by providing maternity/paternity policies which include paid, job-protected leaves. However, America has not shown a similar concern through policies designed to provide such leave without losing income and, indirectly, employment. Consequently, the issue of child care, almost from the birth of a child, becomes a major concern for parents.

More children are in day care today than at any other time in history. It is estimated that approximately two million children are in formal, licensed day care with millions more being cared for by unlicensed baby-sitters. This trend means the majority of children will spend some time being cared for by someone other than a parent at home.

Child care can be categorized into three general classifications: care in the child's home, care in another's home, and day care centers. The day care center is the type of child care most often meant by the term *day care*. Such centers may be for profit or for nonprofit and vary in size from fewer than 15 to more than 300 children.

There are six common types of day care centers. Private day care centers are operated for profit and are usually open to anyone. Commercial centers are a business that is also for profit and is often part of a national or regional chain. An example is KinderCare which has more than 900 centers. Community church centers may be run for profit but are often developed with the purpose of providing a service for the community or church family. Company centers are established by corporations, often as a fringe benefit for employees. Public service centers are government sponsored and may be limited in availability. They are usually designed to serve children of low-income families. The final type of day care is the research center, which models what research recommends for a quality day care center. These are often affiliated with universities and provide the setting for research studies.

Historical Background. The historical roots of the day care movement go back farther than most realize. In 1816, a cotton mill manager in Scotland, Robert Owen, opened the New Lanark School because he was concerned about the young children parents were forced to leave behind at home when they went to work in his mill. Similar provisions called nursery schools and day nurseries were started in America between 1815 and 1860. In 1838, Mrs. Joseph Hale opened the first day nursery in Boston for children of seamen.

In the early 1930s, universities developed nursery schools for the purpose of research. These were primarily attended by children from middle-and upper-class homes. Children from working-class families were more likely to be found in Work Projects Administration schools developed during the depression years to provide jobs for unemployed teachers and nurses.

During World War II, the needs of working parents influenced the development of day cares as the Lanham Act provided federal funds for mothers working in factories. The Kaiser Child Service Centers developed for the children of workers in the Kaiser shipyards is possibly one of the best examples of such institutions. They were located at the entrance to the shipyard and were open 364 days a year, twenty-four hours a day. The Kaiser Centers are often cited as models for work-based child care centers today. Following the war, interest in day cares decreased as women were discouraged from working outside the home. Many of the centers closed as women were no longer employed in the shipyards and factories.

This picture changed again in the 1970s when large numbers of women began moving into the workforce. Currently 61 percent of mothers with preschool children and 75 percent of mothers of school-age children are working outside the home (Goodman, 1997). Over one-half of the mothers with children under age one are in the labor force. In fact, the single largest category is working mothers who have children under age three (Zigler, 1991). With the increase of women in the workforce, there has been a corresponding need for day care centers. Two-thirds of the children less than five years of age in America are in some form of child care today (Kaplan, 1998).

Developmental Consequences. Of upmost importance is the long-term developmental consequence of day care. Only limited conclusions have been reached, however, due to the lack of research and inconsistency in results. Authorities in this area give conclusions in a tentative tone, well aware that further research may present a different perspective.

A summary of the findings does provide some conclusions which have general acceptance:

(1) The most significant factor is the quality of day care. Negative outcomes were the result of inferior day cares. This was especially true for full-time care of infants one year of age or less (Santrock, 1997). Results were positive when the quality of the day care was good. Recent federal research shows that children receiving high-quality day care are not different from children raised at home (Kaplan, 1998). No evidence exists that children in high-quality day cares are at risk as a result of their day care experiences.

(2) The effects of day care were most positive for disadvantaged children. They evidenced more rapid height and weight gain and advancement in motor skills as a result of their day care experience.

(3) Children with day care experiences may show an increase in social competence but they also may display more aggression.

(4) The effect of the day care experience depends on the child's total environment and the personal characteristics of the child (Clarke-Stewart, 1993).

Quality Day Care. What constitutes a high-quality day care program? The National Association for the Education of Young Children (NAEYC) has provided an authoritative voice in its recommendations (1986) for a quality day care. These can be summarized as follows:

Adult Caregivers. The National Day Care Study launched by the federal government in the mid–1970s concluded that one of the most important ingredients of quality was the ongoing relevant training of the teacher-caregiver. There is general agreement that the best day care centers employ teachers who specialize in day care services, but this represents only about 25 percent of all day care personnel (Galinsky, 1988). A controlled ratio of staff to children insures that individual needs are met. NAEYC recommends an adult caregiver/child ratio of 4 to 1 for infants, 8 to 1 for 2- to 3-year-old children, and 10 to 1 for 4- to 5-year-old children.

Program Activities and Equipment. The environment and equipment should foster the development of young children playing together. Activities should be organized around the needs and interests of the child. Trained staff will be aware of the expected development of children within an age span so that activities are developmentally appropriate. Young children should be helped to increase their language skills and their understanding of the world.

Relations with Parents and the Community. A good day care program will consider the needs of the entire family and encourage parents to be actively involved with the center. The center should be aware of community resources and share this information with families.

Ability to Meet the Demands of All Involved. The health and safety of all—children, staff, and parents—should be a primary concern. To have adequate space, NAEYC recommends 35 square feet of space indoors per child and 75 square feet of outdoors play space per child.

LILLIAN J. BRECKENRIDGE

Bibliography. National Academy of Early Childhood Programs (1984), *Accreditation Criteria and Procedures*; S. Bredekamp and T. Rosegrant, eds. (1992), *Reaching Potentials: Appropriate Curriculum and Assessment for Young Children*, vol. I; Dorthy M. Steele et al., eds. (1992), *Congregations and Child Care*; A. Clarke-Stewart (1993), *Daycare*; B. Couch (1990), *Church Weekday Early Education Administrative Guide*; M. Freeman (1991), *Partners in Family Child Care, Opportunities for Outreach: A Guide for Religious Congregations*; E. Galinsky and J. David (1988), *The Preschool Years: Family Strategies That Work from Experts and Parents*; E. Goodman (1997, April 11), *Dallas Morning News*, p. A31; M. Kaplan (1998, March 20), *Tulsa World*, A19; J. Santrock (1997), *Life-Span Development*; idem (1987), *Helping Churches Mind the Children: A Guide for Church-Housed Child Care Programs*; idem (1986), *How to Choose a Good Early Childhood Program*; D. Townsend-Butterworth (1992), *Your Child's First School*; E. Zigler and M. Lang (1991), *Child Care Choices: Balancing the Needs of Children, Family, and Society*.

Deacon. The word group *diakonia, diakoneo, diakonos* undergirds the contemporary English word *deacon*. First used by Herodotus, *diakonia* meant personal service, usually in the household such as waiting at table. The work of a *diakonos* was laborious, undignified, and menial.

In the New Testament the prototype and wellspring of *diakonia* is the birth, life, and death of Jesus Christ. The way of Jesus is the way of serving others in love. Jesus incarnated a whole new way of being in the world that is contrary to the predominant system of power and dominance. Jesus came not to be served, but to serve (Mark 10:45). He inaugurated a kingdom or spiritual commonwealth in which humble, self-giving love replaces self-centered, hierarchical social patterns. In his person and work Jesus exemplifies the love of God by eschewing privilege and prestige and instead serving the disciples and also the hurting and marginalized in the first-century Palestinian world. In the ultimate self-sacrifice, Jesus laid down his life for others. Following the death and resurrection of Jesus, the church imitates the suffering servant Jesus by embodying the countercultural servant way of Jesus. This new redeemed society of servants expresses *diakonia* both within the body of Christ in a diverse array of ministries characterized by servanthood and outside the body through giving aid and seeking justice for the poor and the oppressed.

First, the local congregation enacts the servant way of Jesus as the Holy Spirit establishes a whole panoply of spiritual gifts referred to as *diakoniai* (1 Cor. 12:5). Through the Holy Spirit all are gifted, all are ministers of the manifold grace of God. Moreover, the way of doing ministry centers not on the status or position of the giftbearer, but on the edification of the entire body. Thus in the New Testament the church becomes a genuine community, a social organism dedicated to living together not in the way of power and rank and titles, but in the way of other-centered, self-giving love. The Spirit aims to foster unity and maturity of the whole by orchestrating the contributions of each participant. *Diakonia* as the fundamental principle of church dynamics creates a community of equality, mutuality, freedom, and responsibility for one another in every way. As such, the model of the church is a radically new form of human society, unlike the relations of power universally operative in social groups of all kinds.

Within the context of the servant community, the social function of *diakonia* emerges in some local bodies into an organized diaconate. The social function of servanthood applies to apostles, evangelists, prophets, and servants of all sorts. In the church in Rome Phoebe is designated as a *diakona* (Rom. 16:1). In Philippi an organized group of servants are also called deacons. When writing to Timothy Paul outlines the qualities that deacons should possess (1 Tim. 3:8–13). Deacons are viewed by some as a loose designation of persons who excel in the gift of *diakonia* (Rom. 12:7); for others it has the ring of a formal office. While the specific structures in the house churches of the New Testament vary according to context and era, the nature of the church as a family of servants building up one another in love prohibits the community from degenerating into a pattern of lording it over one another (Matt. 20:25–27). Among the people of God deacons and all member-ministers serve one another as coequals. Hierarchy and authoritarianism are antithetical to the servant way of Jesus. Ranks and titles and rigid structures have no place. Rather, the creation of a diaconal function within the local congregation is intended to underscore the humble, self-giving, other-centered quality of servanthood as the seminal principle for all body relations. It keeps alive for all the example of Jesus as the paradigm of the compassionate servant who enters into the suffering of the lowly and disinherited in society. Thus it is that specialized servant roles grounded in spiritual gifts do not undermine the new community of equals loving one another in mutuality.

Second, parallel to the congregational expression of humble servanthood, the radical new way of Jesus overflows in care to the poor and needy. In Acts 6:1–6 the Jerusalem church spontaneously responds to the material needs of the Greek-speaking widows by recognizing and organizing workers to distribute food equally rather than partially. This episode highlights the general meaning of *diakonia* in classical Greek as serving at table. In the body of Christ, however, this subservient role becomes transformed. Here the servant of Jesus takes the form of compassion, of emptying oneself of rights and position (Phil. 2:2–11) and voluntarily entering into the suffering and struggle of social outcasts—the poor, the diseased and disabled, women, racial and ethnic minorities, the elderly. This is not a top-down, superior-to-inferior posture, but a coming alongside in solidarity, becoming a partner in the struggle for wholeness and justice, a walking with the disenfranchised, an empowering.

The practice of *diakonia* is transformative in three ways: (1) it transforms the socially powerful and privileged into humble, self-giving fellow-suffering servants in partnership with the poor and the oppressed; (2) it transforms those on the margins of society through empowering, liberating, and re-creating their hearts and lives; and (3) it transforms the social world by dismantling the structures and barriers that divide rich and poor, persons of color and whites, male and female, able-bodied and disabled, young and old, educated and uneducated, and so on. The servant way of Jesus is a way of engagement with evil in all its forms: personal, social, economic, political, and environmental. Followers of the suffering servant Jesus will imitate his radical way of life that renounces and denounces power as the general modus operandi in human affairs and embraces the weak and powerless through self-giving solidarity and partnership.

VERNON L. BLACKWOOD

Bibliography. C. Ceccon and K. Paludan, *My Neighbor—Myself: Visions of Diakonia*; J. Collins, *Diakonia: Re-interpreting the Ancient Sources*; T. Halton and J. Williman, eds., *Diakonia: Studies in Honor of Robert T. Meyer*; J. I. McCord and T. H. L. Parker, eds., *Service in Christ*; J. Van Klinken, *Diakonia: Mutual Helping with Justice and Compassion*.

Deaconess. Feminine derivation of the word *deacon*, from the Greek *diakonos*, typically translated servant or minister. In the early church, deacons fulfilled an ecclesial office concerned with works of charity and assisting the clergy.

The New Testament does not contain the feminine form of the word, but does apply the word *deacon* to Phoebe in Romans 16:1. Paul commends Phoebe, a deacon in the church at Cenchreae. Although the nature of the office that Phoebe fulfilled is under discussion by scholars, her designation as a deacon may infer there was little or no distinction between the role of male and female deacons in the early church.

First Timothy 3:8–13 details the qualifications for deacons in the early church. Verse 11 refers to women and has been the subject of great discussion. The question is whether the women referred to in this verse are female deacons, or the wives of male deacons, since the Greek word, *gyne*, can be translated either "women" or "wives." However, the word lacks a possessive pronoun ("their women") which would infer wives, so it is best translated "women." In addition, the use of the term "likewise" seems to introduce a group of women who corresponded to the men. Therefore, the reference is most likely to a female order of ministry which parallels the order of male deacons.

While there is great discussion among exegetes and theologians regarding these Scripture passages, historians state that without question there were female deacons functioning in the early church.

The term *deaconess* can be traced to the fourth century. Two fourth-century texts, the *Didascalia* and *The Apostolic Constitutions*, detail the duties of deaconesses. They were to assist the clergy in baptizing women, ministering to the poor and sick, and teaching the new women converts. They were ordained by the bishop through the laying on of hands and a prayer of consecration. Changes in the baptismal customs (fewer adult baptisms) and concern about usurping the priestly function contributed to the decline of deaconesses between the fifth and eleventh centuries.

The modern deaconess movement began in 1836 with Lutheran pastor T. Fliedner in Kaiserswerth, Germany. The primary purpose of the modern deaconess was to give pastoral care to congregations and to assist clergy in works of charity, often connected with nursing. Deaconesses were single women (either never married or widowed).

The deaconess movement spread from Germany throughout Europe. In 1871 the Church of England approved the order, followed by the Church of Scotland and the Methodist Church in 1888. In 1849 four deaconesses came from Kaiserswerth to Pennsylvania and established the Passavant Hospital in Pittsburgh. The "American motherhouse" of deaconesses was established in 1890 in Philadelphia.

By the middle of the twentieth century, the order of deaconesses had virtually disappeared. As new doors opened for women to be vocationally involved within the church, the deaconess movement waned. The modern-day deaconess movement was more closely parallel to the Catholic sisters of charity in their works of community service than the early female deacons who ministered primarily within the context of the church.

Various denominations continue to elect, appoint, or ordain female deacons or deaconesses as an office of the local church. Their roles vary depending upon the denominational setting. Some have specific duties related to the women of the congregation, while other settings do not differentiate between the responsibility of male and female deacons.

DENISE MUIR KJESBO

Bibliography. R. Tucker and W. Liefeld (1987), *Daughters of the Church;* S. Grenz and D. Muir Kjesbo (1995), *Women in the Church.*

See also ADMINISTRATION; DEACON; DIAKONIA; FEMINISM; MINISTER; TRUSTEE; WOMEN IN MINISTRY

Debate. Procedure in which two or more people compete in trying to persuade others to accept or reject a proposition as a foundation for belief or behavior. Classroom debates offer a dialogical or participative approach to learning. Speakers who represent opposing views on a controversial subject receive equal time to present reasons for their conviction, and to rebut their opponent's position.

In formal debate, the issue is structured into a positive proposition. The person or group answering affirmatively begins, followed by a briefer rebuttal. After presentation of the negative position, the affirmative side offers a rebuttal. Each constructive speech and rebuttal fits into a prescribed time limit.

Participants prepare in advance and bring written notes to the debate. Their preparation includes anticipation of opposing arguments. The teacher steers both sides to equally valuable resources.

During informal debate, the instructor may intervene in order to keep the speakers on track or cut off repetitive and irrelevant arguments. To avoid intrusive verbal comments and help non-participating students follow a speaker's line of reasoning, a teacher summarizes arguments on the board as the debate proceeds.

An assessment of the debate maximizes learning. A wise instructor involves the whole class with the following questions: How convincing and valid were the arguments? Did arguments reflect research on the issue or just personal opinion? How directly did the rebuttal address the previous argument? What possible arguments for either position were omitted? How did the debate affect or change your thinking about the topic? If you were starting the debate over again, what would you do differently? Why?

TERRY POWELL

Bibliography. J. Tomsen, S. Albright, N. Braun, and K. Martin (1997), *The Teaching Professor.*

Decentration. From a young age, we are told to focus on what we are doing so that we might become proficient at whatever that particular task might be. Yet, at a higher level of learning, the ability to focus on multiple aspects of the same situation are developed. In his book, *Created to Learn,* William Yount defines decentration as the ability to focus on more than one aspect of a situation at a time. In a society in which terms like "tunnel-vision" are used to describe our ability to be singularly focused, the concept of decentration becomes all the more a challenge.

Look at Jesus' encounter with the Samaritan woman (John 4:1–26) as an example. The woman came to the well seeking water to drink. Jesus, while requesting a drink of water from her, begins to look at a much larger concept of thirst and quenching than the woman expected or initially understood. Jesus had expanded the conversation to include her spiritual thirst and need, while she remained focused on relieving physical thirst. When Jesus first mentions the living water (vv. 13–14) that will cause her thirst (spiritually) to be quenched, the woman's response (v. 15) demonstrates her inability to understand that Jesus was no longer simply discussing physical needs.

Jean Piaget has stated the belief that as a child becomes less self-centered and begins to understand the larger picture in various situations, the moral development of that child is affected and enhanced. Piaget believes that decentration can help motivate our behavior.

If decentration is the ability to focus on a number of aspects of the same situation simultaneously, at what age does the ability to think in this manner become possible, if not expected? This is the essence of the debate that has raged for years concerning this aspect of developmental theory. Jean Piaget stated that decentration and reversibility develop when a child is approximately six or seven years old, while other developmental theorists would argue that decentration takes place later in one's development.

Robert J. Whittet

Bibliography. R. F. Kitchner (1986), *Piaget's Theory of Knowledge;* W. M. Kurtines and J. L. Gewirtz (1995), *Moral Development: An Introduction;* W. R. Yount (1996), *Created to Learn.*

Decision Making. Process of choosing between options, on both individual and corporate levels. The process includes identifying possible choices, evaluating potential results, and choosing the alternative that best reflects personal values and commitments.

While decisions are made almost every moment of the day, the most critical ones are those having moral and spiritual significance. Individual Christians face decision-making challenges such as what to do with expendable financial resources in a world filled with hunger, whether to get involved when a coworker is being mistreated by management, or how to invest personal gifts and talents to serve the work of God's kingdom most effectively. Groups of persons must likewise engage in weighty decision making. A local church's pastoral staff or elder board, for instance, may have to determine how to respond in discipline when a leader's immoral behavior has been discovered, or they may have to discern the best strategies for reaching the unchurched in their local community.

Christian education can assist persons and groups at several points in their decision-making processes. First, Christian education teaches the biblical/theological content that sets the standard by which morality and spirituality are critiqued. Second, Christian education provides a context to explore the implications of decisions. Learners may examine issues through the lens of a case study discussion or a role play among group members. Third, Christian education creates opportunities for building genuine Christian community. Meaningful, interdependent relationships offer feedback from multiple perspectives, encouragement, prayer support, and accountability for learners as their decisions are made and executed. Fourth, Christian education contributes to the development of decision-making skills and maturity. By confronting learners with biblical values and guiding them through the process of choosing according to those values, educational experiences not only enable good decisions but also promote the development of higher levels of moral reasoning.

Nurturing decision-making skills and promoting the development of moral reasoning are particularly important in the Christian education of children and youth. Knowing what is right is not always synonymous with choosing what is right. Teaching biblical truths to young believers without also assisting them in the process of how to make decisions consistent with their convictions can lead to frustration and spiritual impotency in the lives of the learners as they mature. Christian education, therefore, engages learners in the process of knowing, choosing, and doing that which is according to God's righteousness.

Richard R. Dunn

Bibliography. B. Clouse (1993), *Teaching for Moral Growth;* S. Garber (1996), *The Fabric of Faithfulness;* L. Kuhmerker (1994), *The Kohlberg Legacy for the Helping Professions;* C. Shelton (1983), *Adolescent Spirituality: Pastoral Ministry for High School and College Youth.*

Decoding/Encoding. *See* Memory.

Deductive Learning. Deductive learning, or the process of deduction, has its conceptual history rooted in the study of formal logic. The science of logic was established by Aristotle and refined by such scholars as Frege, Peirce, Descartes, Russell, Whitehead, and Hull. It was Descartes who emphasized that knowledge could be created deductively by the use of rational intuition. Deduction has played an important role in the development of such disciplines as mathematics, theoretical science, philosophy, and theology.

Generally, the process of deductive learning involves the movement from the general concept to the more specific facts that support and contribute to that general concept. This movement from a hypothesized general conclusion or premise to the particular instances that validate the hypothesis or premise forms the basis for any educational process employing deduction.

Deductive learning is often associated with the use of syllogistic logic. A syllogism is a three-part argument with two propositions that imply a third:

> All humans are sinners.
> I am a human.
> Therefore, I am a sinner.

The use of deductive learning in Christian education can be found in any examination of biblical texts done to identify particular instances that support and illustrate a general truth. For example, beginning with the premise that one of God's characteristics is his desire to forgive persons for their sins, learners may search the Bible for evidence of this characteristic of God. They might also examine their own lives and the lives of others in search of evidence to support this premise. By finding instances of God's forgiveness in the scriptural text or in contemporary life, learners then deductively come to understand the forgiving nature of God. In essence, deductive teaching would involve the presentation of a conclusion or rule followed by exercises in which learners would attempt to discover examples that verify the premise.

Critics of deductive learning challenge the premises or assumptions that are the starting point of deductive logic and assert that deduction is not useful in creating new knowledge. They argue that the original hypothesis or premise at the beginning of the deductive process must have itself been established by some process other than deduction. Critics would further argue that there is a temptation to begin the deductive process with assumptions that have no basis in fact.

Supporters of deductive learning insist that the epitome of human learning is insight and that insight is essentially the result of the deductive process. Those of the Gestalt school associate insight with deductive learning and argue that facts and details only become meaningful when placed against a contextual background. For this reason, they would argue that beginning with a premise, or a general truth, provides that necessary context to make specific facts and information relevant.

Deductive learning is most frequently contrasted with inductive learning, the process of moving from the specific facts to the general truth. Most Christian educators would agree that effective teaching and learning strategies employ a blend of both deductive and inductive learning processes.

DENNIS A. SHERIDAN

See also INDUCTIVE LEARNING.

Deferred Gratification. Deferred gratification concerns "the ability to postpone immediate gratification for the sake of future consequences, to impose delay of reward on oneself, and to tolerate such self-initiated frustration" (Mischel, 1974, 249). Unwillingness or inability to delay gratification, usually associated with immaturity, is often seen as a contributing cause in antisocial behaviors.

In the related construct of self-control, Freud provided early theorizing with postulation of "ego strength" and developing "superego" through which internalized parental values guide moral behavior. In recent decades, delay of gratification has been looked at largely from the behavioristic viewpoint of social learning theory, with its proposed mechanisms for changing individual behavior. Social learning theory posits both situational and personal determinants of behavior; change in reward-deferring behavior may therefore be attributed to multiple causes.

Maslow (1970) takes the perspective, in discussing his hierarchy of "basic needs," that satiation "helps to determine character formation" and "tends toward the improvement, strengthening, and healthy development of the individual" (61–62). It should be noted that Maslow (1970)

was addressing "basic needs" and was not advocating indulgence—"some experience with firmness, toughness, frustration, discipline, and limits is also needed by the child" (70). He also recognized that some healthy individuals do voluntarily defer gratification of basic needs for altruistic purposes.

In studies conducted with children (e.g., Mischel et al., 1989), a number of variables appear as determinants in a child's ability and willingness to forego immediate rewards; among these are age, length of waiting time for reward, prior success or failure, and the child's faith that the reward will actually be received. For example, evidence shows that children are increasingly able to delay gratification with age. Observation of behavioral models have been found to aid in teaching deferred gratification. Models whose moral behavior and example were consistent with what they taught verbally appeared to have the greatest positive effect on deferral behaviors of the children observing them. Children who were better able to defer immediate gratification also experienced more success in areas calling for resourcefulness and self-control, such as academic performance.

Funder, Block, and Block (1983) reported many positive correlates for children who delayed gratification. In general, correlates for girls were tied to ego resiliency (i.e., responsiveness to the environment), while for boys they were tied more strongly to ego control. The researchers explain this as due to differential socialization for boys and girls. Interestingly, children who delayed gratification came from homes that were calm and peaceful, focused on practicality, and where relatives were significant in providing socialization.

Much of the teaching of the New Testament regarding rewards seems to emphasize the deferral of present pleasure and comfort in light of the future, eternal blessing. These truths are intertwined with teaching concerning persistent faith, hope, and self-control. Jesus teaches deferred gratification when he instructs the disciples to "lay up treasures in heaven" (Matt. 6:19–20) as opposed to accumulating earthly treasures. Moses is an example of one who, by faith, gave up the pleasures of this world because he was looking for future eternal reward (Heb. 11:25–26). The basis of expectation of such rewards is the trustworthiness of God and the belief that he rewards those who seek Him (Heb. 11:6).

Learning to defer immediate gratification in light of future reward is a vital content for growth in Christian character and maturity. Social learning theory, particularly in the area of observation of models, has potential for the teaching of delay of gratification behaviors. Christian educators should be concerned that children's basic needs are met in order to provide for psychological health. Older students need to learn to deal with frustration deferral and come to value self-denial for purposes of personal spiritual growth and service to others.

RICHARD LEYDA AND CLAIR ALLEN BUDD

Bibliography. W. Mischel (1974), *Advances in Experimental Social Psychology*, pp. 249–92; W. Mischel, Y. Shoda, and M. L. Rodriguez (1989), *Delay of Gratification in Children*, pp. 933–38; A. Bandura and W. Mischel, *Journal of Personality and Social Psychology* 2 (1965): 698–705; R. W. Fairchild (1971), *Research on Religious Development*, pp. 156–210; D. C. Funder, J. H. Block, and J. Block, *Journal of Personality and Social Psychology* 44 (1983): 1198–1213; A. H. Maslow (1970), *Motivation and Personality*.

See also MASLOW, ABRAHAM HAROLD; SOCIAL COGNITIVE THEORY

Delayed Rewards/Benefits. *See* Deferred Gratification.

Democratic Approach to Groups. Approach to group organization and leadership that occurs when the leader works within the group and accepts contributions made by other group members. Many church groups follow the democratic approach in their polity as each member has a vote on important matters.

In democratic families, children participate in decision making. Parents discuss and negotiate with their children and make an effort to explain their rules and expectations. Studies suggest that adolescents who have grown up in democratic families are more autonomous and independent (Conger, 1973).

Dreikurs (1968), a psychiatrist well known for his work in student discipline, argues that firmness combined with caring is one characteristic of a democratic teacher. Firmness indicates that teachers respect themselves, and caring shows respect for others. In addition, the classroom is orderly with limits and rules into which the students had input. The teacher maintains order and guides learning while promoting a sense of ownership and belonging among students.

In a classic study, Kurt Lewin et al. (1958) examined the impact of different kinds of leadership on group behavior. Lewin asked 11-year old boys to participate in some after-school clubs. The leader using the democratic approach allowed the group to set its own policies whenever possible, with active encouragement and assistance by the adult leader. Each boy was allowed to work with whomever he chose, and the divisions of responsibility were left up to the group. The boys were most productive in this type of group compared with other styles over the long run, and they were also more friendly and more team-oriented in this type of group.

KENNETH S. COLEY

Bibliography. R. Dreikurs (1968), *Psychology in the Classroom;* J. J. Conger (1973), *Adolescence and Youth: A Psychological Development in a Changing World;* R. Lippitt and R. K. White (1958), *Readings in Social Psychology*, pp. 446–511.

Demons. Literature from earliest religions have attested to the existence of demons. Neoorthodox teachings deny the reality of demons and angelic beings, but these beliefs appear to no longer have popular acceptance. The anecdotal evidence for spirit beings can be very powerful, and biblical revelation, though far less comprehensive than most would like, is clearly supportive. Angels are spoken about over 265 times, appearing widely in both Testaments. Jesus refers to angels and demons as real beings (Matt. 18:10; 25:41).

Theories about the origin of demons are abundant. One theory, based on conjecture, is that they are spirits of a pre-Adamic race who have reentered this world. It assumes a time gap in Genesis 1:2 and conjectures that Satan's rebellion resulted in a re-creation process. Some postulate that demons are the spirits of wicked, deceased people, but this runs contrary to evidence that neither people nor demons can return to earth once they are confined (Ps. 9:17; Luke 16:26; Heb. 9:27). Others have suggested that they are the offspring of the sons of God (Gen. 6:1–4). Even if the fathers were demons, there is no evidence that the progeny were demons. In fact, the text implies they had real bodies.

Demons are most likely fallen angels. This can be seen in the eternal punishment to be given to both Satan and "his angels" (Matt. 25:41). Demons, like angels, are created beings (Ezek. 28:15; Col. 1:16). They are spirit beings without bodies (Luke 8:2; Eph. 2:2; Heb. 1:14), though when confronting humans they can appear in human form (Gen. 6:2). The head of the demons is Satan (Matt. 12:22–28) and they are organized into at least two ranks, rulers and authorities (Eph. 3:10; 6:12).

Scripture presents demons as persons, not a force (Matt. 8:29; Luke 8:28, 27–30, 32). While they were created holy (Jude 6), they apparently had one chance to rebel with Satan and took it (2 Peter 2:4). At this time some were permanently confined (Luke 8:31) and others remain temporarily loose (Eph. 6:11–12). Demons and angels are superior to men in terms of power (Mark 5:3; Rev. 16:14) and intellect (2 Peter 2:11). As spirit beings, they are not restricted by material limitations of speed, space, or physical closures (Luke 8:30).

The most controversial element relating to demons is the extent of their power over humans, particularly Christians. While Luke makes it clear that not all disease and harm that befall people comes from demons (Luke 7:21; 9:1; Acts 5:16), demons have the power to inflict physical diseases (Matt. 9:33; 12:22; 17:15–18), mental disorders (Mark 5:4–5), and even death (Rev. 9:14–19). Christ and the apostles miraculously cast demons out of people who had lost control over their lives (Mark 5:15–18; Acts 5:16; 8:7; 16:16–18; 19:12). In one case there appears to be Christians who were demonized (Acts 5:3). Anecdotal evidence collaborates this. It is unclear what demonization exactly means for Christians, but the same word "to fill" is used in Acts and Ephesians (5:18). This control does not extend into eternity, since some have been delivered to Satan and still had their spirit saved (1 Cor. 5:5). The condition is very rare in the Bible and in most churches. The keys to victory over this control are the same keys given for Christian growth: faith in God's power and prayer (Mark 9:23–29). In addition, Christians should avoid the possibilities of evil as well as evil itself, and must be prepared for Satan's attacks (1 Cor. 7:5; 2 Cor. 2:11; Eph. 6:10ff.).

C. S. Lewis in *The Screwtape Letters* offers sage advice in dealing with devils, "There are two equal and opposite errors into which our race can fall about the devils. One is to disbelieve in their existence, the other is to believe and to feel an unhealthy interest in them!"

MICHAEL J. KANE

Bibliography. C. F. Dickason (1975), *Angels, Elect and Evil;* S. H. T. Page (1995), *Powers of Evil;* C. C. Ryrie (1986), *Basic Theology.*

See also SPIRITUAL WARFARE

Demonstration. A demonstration illustrates by example a task, project, method, or experiment that the knowledgeable party wishes to communicate. Often the demonstration is a model performance the teacher desires the learner to replicate or an example of a principle to grasp. The demonstrator exercises particular skill in the presentation and answers questions that clarify the process and illustration. The learner observes in detail the objects, tools, and actions demonstrated. Demonstration involves art on the part of the demonstrator who facilitates the connection between the objective illustrated and the process enacted.

Demonstrations possess: (1) carefully defined learning objectives; (2) clearly organized illustrative processes; (3) details accentuated so as to be easily comprehended; (4) explanation of the step-by-step process; and (5) identifiable correlation between the illustration and stated objective.

A demonstration is frequently followed by a supervised practice session where the learner repeats the demonstration under the guidance of the teacher. Then the learner repeats the activity a second time independently. Thus the model: "I will demonstrate. You do the activity with me. Then you do the activity on your own."

Learning to tie a shoe might be learned by demonstration. The teacher places a shoe on the

table and proceeds in a step-by-step procedure to show how it might be tied. The objective is carefully stated—to tie a shoe. The process is clearly illustrated in step-by-step fashion. Attention is given to the demonstration details to ensure all participants can see clearly what is happening in the interaction of the strings. The correlation is easily seen in that the action results in the stated objective of shoe tying.

Demonstration historically relates to apprenticeship practiced in the medieval guilds where a craft was passed by example from a master to the apprentice. Audiovisual tools allow for demonstrations that previously have been limited to outside the classroom now to be incorporated into the classroom setting.

JAMES R. MOORE

Denomination. *See* Confraternity of Christian Doctrine.

Depression. Depression is the most common emotional condition treated by psychiatrists, and some estimate that over half of all Americans will suffer from clinical depression at some point in their lives (Minirth and Meier, 1978). Though some identify depression with feeling a little "down," clinical or major depression describes a dramatically different condition than being a little blue.

Signs of clinical depression include:

1. A despondent or empty feeling which lasts at least two weeks and may last months or years without relief
2. Loss of interest in normal activities such as work, relationships, children, sex, food, etc.
3. Sleep irregularities (normally insomnia but can be excessive sleep)
4. Complaints of low energy or fatigue
5. Thoughts of worthlessness, hopelessness, or guilt which consistently resist efforts at change
6. Lack of concentration and memory problems which may bring more discouragement as the person realizes how drastic these changes are
7. Thoughts about the futility of life and possibility of suicide

In children depression may look quite different as parents or teachers see bed-wetting, crying, isolation, fighting or school problems, though some children may even make suicidal statements. Adolescents may also show depression in behaviors such as delinquency, irritability, isolation, grooming/clothing changes, drug or alcohol abuse, and school problems. Such behaviors can be the cry for help of someone who cannot put his or her feelings into words. Literally the depressed person will wonder, "What's happening to me?"

Depressed young people and adults may strongly resist offers of help, and a strong yet loving approach may be necessary to get the help they need. Suicide is a significant problem among the depressed, and ministers or friends should feel no reluctance to share private information about the person's thoughts if suicide is mentioned or hinted at. Persons who try to honor wishes for secrecy may become increasingly uneasy and find themselves absorbing anxiety which could do much more good somewhere else. A simple question may be helpful in escaping this anxiety—"Who, if they knew what I know, could do something to help?" The answer often leads to sharing information with a parent, spouse, counselor, physician, or the police and has helped save many lives. With appropriate medical and psychological treatment clinical depression is highly treatable with the majority of people finding significant relief once treatment is started.

The church's role can be critical as ministers and friends take pains to convey God's acceptance and support. Though depression certainly has a spiritual element (Hart, 1987), confronting the clinically depressed person about his or her sin or lack of spiritual maturity may oversimplify the need to think on pleasant things (Phil. 4:8) while failing to convey love by your patience and kindness (1 Cor. 13:4). Viewing depression solely as a sin issue may stigmatize the depressed person, possibly increasing guilt or hopelessness. Concerned Christians will do well to resist the temptation to confront the depressed person's faulty thinking directly and to wait until the emotional tidal wave has subsided before sharing heavier spiritual truths. Understanding the multiple factors which are a part of clinical depression may be helpful to those who live with or regularly relate to the depressed person.

Heredity is a likely factor in some depression and in its "roller coaster cousin" manic-depression. In manic-depression, or bipolar disorder, people may cycle between unusually high energy/emotional excitement (the manic state) and very low energy/depression. If these mood disorders are present in blood relatives, the possibility of finding similar problems in the patient is increased. Numerous physiological factors may contribute to depression, so a medical exam to consider low blood sugar, hormonal imbalances, brain trauma, and medication interactions, etc. is usually the first step in treatment.

Traumatic early childhood experiences, painful memories of wartime or catastrophic events, or a pattern of repressed anger can contribute to depression, though their influence may not be fully recognized by the patient. As stress accumulates through family and marital problems, job loss, health or legal problems, single factors in the depression are normally easily identified, but the cumulative impact may be overlooked as each new loss reawakens a history of grief and loss.

In the spiritual dimension sinful thoughts and behaviors must be considered in depression that revolves around preoccupation with guilt. The discerning helper will recognize the need to separate conviction from the Holy Spirit from false guilt and what Paul calls the sorrow which produces death (2 Cor. 7:5–10). Helping the individual sort through a confusing mixture of genuine conviction and destructive guilt from family or society is a difficult but rewarding task.

DAN E. CLEMENT

Bibliography. A. T. Beck (1967), *Depression: Causes and Treatment;* G. R. Collins (1980), *Christian Counseling: A Comprehensive Guide;* A. D. Hart (1987), *Counseling the Depressed;* F. B. Minirth and P. D. Meier (1978), *Happiness Is a Choice.*

Descriptive Anthropology. *See* Ethnography.

Developmental Stage. *See* Adolescent Development.

Developmental Tasks. In the normal course of life span development, a number of skills and competencies (or, in some cases, life events) must be mastered in order to pave the way for subsequent development and maturation. These tasks are often the result of societal prescription, obligation, or responsibility. When accomplished, they become milestones or rites of passage that mark the progressive stages of maturation and development. The tasks may involve physical, intellectual, social, or emotional skills.

The definition of these tasks ranges from the abstract and theoretical (Erikson, 1963) to what Havighurst (1953) described as the "bio-social-psychological." They are seen as progressive and sequential tasks, most often requiring that the less complex tasks be successfully completed in order to lay the groundwork for the more complex tasks which follow.

Havighurst's tasks tend to be somewhat biologically and culturally determined. Referring to adult development, he recognized tasks generally related to three developmental periods. In early adulthood, the tasks include selecting a mate (or adjusting to singleness), starting a family, managing a home, and becoming settled in a career. During the middle adult years, tasks focus on nurturing children, achieving civic and social responsibility, and adjusting to aging parents. The later adult years are characterized by adjusting to declining physical strength and health, retirement, and adjusting to the death of a spouse.

Erik Erikson's stages of psychosocial development outline eight stages of human ego development, with each stage characterized by a psychosocial crisis requiring resolution prior to advancement to the next stage. Though somewhat abstract, Erikson's tasks, including the development of trust, autonomy, initiative, industry, ego identity, intimacy, generativity, and integrity, are helpful keys to the process of psychosocial development.

While the terminology of developmental tasks is most often used in reference to psychosocial development, it is sometimes used to refer to tasks related to cognitive development (Piaget), moral development (Kohlberg), or other spheres where the process of human development is evident.

MARI GONLAG

Bibliography. E. Erikson (1963), *Childhood and Society;* R. J. Havighurst (1953), *Human Development and Education;* J. M. Stubblefield (1986), *A Church Ministering to Adults.*

Developmental Teaching. Communication that attends to the maturation process of the learner. Though the focus is often on cognitive development, other vital aspects include psychosocial, moral, and religious. An interdisciplinary approach to developmental teaching considers all these various aspects of development within the changing stages of life.

Developmentalism is thought to be a gradual, step-by-step process that arises from one's own being (rather than socialization) with sequential stages through which one passes. Often developmental stages are hierarchical and move from simple to complex. Developmental theories are sometimes tied to chronological age and physical maturation—using broad categories such as infancy, childhood, adolescence, adulthood, and aging—but age may not always correlate with developmental processes.

Developmental teaching considers the way the world is viewed by the learner at different stages of life. Developmental theories are descriptive, attempting to delineate general patterns present in particular life periods within the population at large. Developmental teaching is based on these general descriptions seeking to intersect learners at their developmental stage and thus facilitate educational goals. A significant limitation of developmental teaching is consideration of the individual person in light of his or her particular capabilities.

Developmental theories may be traced back as early as the work of Jean-Jacques Rousseau (1712–78). Rousseau's early theory of child development centered in children growing "according to Nature's plan, which urges them to develop different capacities and modalities at different stages" (Crain, 1992, 8). This self-oriented development birthed what has become developmental psychology.

Rousseau describes four stages of child development. *Infancy* (birth to 2 years) is when the child learns primarily through the senses. *Childhood* (2 to 12 years) is when a child begins to develop independence in eating, walking, and talking, and begins to reason intuitively based on body movements and senses. During *late childhood* (about age 12 to 15) a child gains in physical strength and in cognitive understanding through concrete tasks. *Adolescence* ushers in abstract reasoning, puberty, and strong influence by social beings.

Developmental theory was stimulated by ethology (the study of animal and human behavior in an evolutionary context) in the work of Charles Darwin (1809–82). Darwin's 1859 *The Origin of Species* provided a scientific construct in which development became the driving paradigm for the twentieth century. Darwin proposed the common origin of all species who had adapted to meet the changes of their environment.

Twentieth-century psychologists further described development in a broad range of human life experiences. Arnold Gesell (1880–1961) forwarded maturation theory, articulating that child development is primarily related to the action of the genes. Gene-initiated development was mechanistic, thus "maturational mechanism" describes Gesell's theory. Robert Havighurst suggested that there are identifiable physical, social, and psychological developmental patterns throughout the entire life cycle. Erik Erikson (1902–94) described in detail eight stages of psychosocial development. Daniel Levinson studied the role of development specifically in adult males. Carol Gilligan and Anita Spencer examined the development of adult women. Gail Sheehy's journalistic volume *Passages* (1974) popularized the idea of adult development.

Jean Piaget's (1896–1980) research on cognitive development is the most comprehensive theory to date. Piaget spent hundreds of hours observing his own children, wrote a number of books, and provided a framework for future developmentalists. Piaget's cognitive stages may be summarized as follows. The first stage (birth to 2 years) is the *sensorimotor period* concerned with the abilities necessary to construct and reconstruct objects. The second stage (2 to 7 years) is the *preoperational stage*, which concerns itself with symbolic functions and the representation of things. During this stage the acquisition of language skills, symbolic play, and early attempts at drawing and graphic illustration begin. The third stage (7 to 11 years) is the *concrete operations stage*, when a child begins to internalize the actions previously accomplished through real actions. The last stage (12–15 years) is the *formal operations stage*, when adolescents begin to think about their thoughts, construct ideals, and reason realistically about the future. Piaget's monumental research in cognitive thinking has influenced subsequent studies of development in many areas.

Lawrence Kohlberg (1927–87) built on Piaget's theory to describe stages of moral development, focusing on the determination of right and wrong. His six stages fall into preconventional, conventional, and postconventional levels, ranging from external powerful authorities in society who dictate moral obedience, to universal moral principles in which justice prevails for all.

David Elkind was the first to publish research applying Piaget's stages of development to religious identity in children. He concluded that there are developmental stages in the identification of religious thinking, similar to those described by Piaget in intelligence.

James W. Fowler, basing his research on Piaget, Erickson, and Kohlberg, produced descriptive studies investigating the connection between cognitive and affective stages with the meanings and construction of faith throughout the life cycle. Fowler defines faith as the ability to make meaning and construct an ultimate environment. His concern is primarily psychological and focuses on *how* faith develops in terms of form throughout the life cycle, rather than on the *content* of faith. Thus his theory is primarily a psychological theory and not a theological construct.

Research in both specific and in age grouping developmental theories abounds. Merton P. Strommen was the first to synthesize research in religious development (1971). Kenneth E. Hyde published a comprehensive review of child and adolescent religious development (1990).

Developmental theory has primarily influenced psychology rather than education; however, educators study the descriptive dimensions of developmental theories and use that data in the construction of curricula objectives, educational tasks, and the learning environment. Care should be given to avoid using developmental stages as broad sweeps tied to chronological age, failing to devote attention to the individual, who may be incapable of functioning or reasoning at that level, or who is operating at a different level. Christian educators must also avoid utilizing developmental theory as a series of hierarchical categories by which the learner can be evaluated. Consideration should also be given to the role of the Holy Spirit in the educational experience at varying developmental stages, creating results that are often impossible to categorize.

JAMES R. MOORE

Bibliography. B. Clouse (1993), *Teaching for Moral Growth: A Guide for the Christian Community Teachers, Parents, Pastors;* R. Coles (1990), *The Spiritual Life of Children;* W. Crain (1992), *Theories of Development: Concepts and Applications;* K. P. Cross (1981), *Adults as Learners: Increasing Participation and Facilitating Learning;* C. Dykstra and S. Parks, eds. (1986), *Faith Development and Fowler;* D. Elkind (1988), *The Hurried Child: Growing Up Too Fast Too Soon;* J. W. Fowler, K. E. Nipkow, and F. Schweitzer (1991), *Stages of Faith and Religious Development: Implications for Church, Education, and Society;* K. E. Hyde (1990), *Religion in Childhood and Adolescence: A Comprehensive Review of the Research;* D. E. Ratcliff, ed. (1992), *Handbook of Children's Religious Education;* idem (1988), *Handbook of Preschool Religious Education;* M. P. Strommen, ed. (1971), *Research on Religious Development: A Comprehensive Handbook.*

Devotion. *See* Meditation.

Devotional Literature. *See* Journal Writing.

Dewey, John (1859–1952). Philosopher and educator. Probably no individual has influenced the course of education in America as has John Dewey, often called the "father of the progressive education movement." As a primary developer of the philosophy of pragmatism, Dewey was chiefly concerned with ideas that work in the experienced world. As a naturalist, he rejected God and supernatural influences, yet his ideas about learning through experience, student-centered methods, and the educational process have profoundly affected contemporary religious education.

He was born in Burlington, Vermont. His deeply religious mother brought him up in the church and Sunday school. Viewing ideas of a supreme being as too confining for the creative intellect, he later renounced these early Christian roots. He taught high school for a short time after graduating from the University of Vermont. Pursuing his Ph.D. from Johns Hopkins University, he was mentored by the noted pragmatist Charles Peirce. Graduating in 1884, he taught philosophy and psychology, primarily at the University of Michigan, for the next ten years. Studying with G. H. Mead, the social psychologist, Dewey there focused on psychology as his primary area of writing. He next accepted the University of Chicago's chair of philosophy, psychology, and pedagogy, where he and his wife founded the University Laboratory School, later informally called the "Dewey School." The children's learning processes at this famous institution focused on use of the senses and solving problems. Out of this endeavor emerged many of his important writings on education, such as *The Child and the Curriculum* (1963) and *The School and Society* (1963). Dewey moved to Columbia University in 1904 to continue his teaching, writing, and involvement in academic and public affairs. In spite of retirement in 1930, he continued his speaking and writing activities until his death. His literary production totaled at least forty-six volumes and over seven hundred articles.

Two key concepts in Dewey's thinking can be drawn from the title of one of his most important works, *Experience and Nature* (1925). The central concept in his philosophy is experience. For Dewey the essential and irreducible quality of human experience is its felt immediacy. Such experience involves not only the reflective cognitive processes, but also the noncognitive aspects of emotion and action. Rather than all experience being a form of knowing, as the idealists contended, Dewey viewed knowing as only one subset of experience. Thinking is a mediating process from one experience to another leading to a more comprehensive, integrated experience. In accord with this, he saw each individual experience as a unit having an integrity of its own. Life is composed of many such experiences and situations that overlap and interpenetrate each other. Consistent with this conception of experience, Dewey believed that nature and natural knowledge comprehend the whole of what could be understood; it is ultimate reality. He believed intelligent human action to be the only resource available to people in every field of study. As an avowed humanist and atheist, he contended that man had only himself to look to for answers. He rejected any transcendent conception of eternal truth and moral absolutes as well as many other tenets of conservative religion, including the existence of a continuing human soul. In his thinking, these were beyond the realm of human experience and the natural world and thus not testable by the experimental method of inquiry and therefore unknowable. On this basis, some have categorized Dewey's philosophy as a type of naturalistic empiricism.

As a pragmatist, he emphasized the utility of ideas. He called his philosophy "instrumentalism" since he viewed concepts simply as useful instruments for solving problems. Carrying on in the tradition of earlier pragmatists, Charles Peirce and William James, Dewey believed that all inquiry should take place in a disciplined, experimental manner. Following Peirce, he rejected appeals to traditional belief, external sources of authority, or reason alone as final means of settling beliefs, viewing each as inferior to the experimental method. Only this type of inquiry, he maintained, included its own ongoing self-corrective. Detailed in the volume *How We Think* (1910), his experimental method was a five-step approach which he believed could be applied universally to gaining knowledge in any field. The first step for the inquirer is the experience of a "felt difficulty" or a confusion which demands resolution. Second, an intellectual response is made in an attempt to formulate and articulate the nature of the problem. Third, a testable hypothesis is presented, which, if proven true, will resolve the problem. Fourth, the hypothesis is tested through what Dewey called "thought experiments," reflective thought processes and reasoning as well as possible quantification. The final stage of inquiry is a testing which involves overt action in the "real world" to determine if the problem that precipitated the original inquiry is resolved.

For Dewey, ethics and values were to be determined in new and unique situations by the disciplined use of human intelligence to make choices between competing options and to take decisive action. This process is conducted in the context of society's norms and values and should result in concrete reformations to improve the human condition.

Dewey strongly affirmed that an adequate and comprehensive philosophy of education is foundational for the process of teaching. He developed his philosophy of education in two important works, *Democracy and Education* (1916)—called by some the most influential book on American education ever written—and *Experience and Education* (1958)—containing his impressions of progressive education. He viewed education more as the process of learning to think than as the acquisition of a static body of knowledge; more as actually living than as a preparation for living. For example, he contended that no better way to learn democracy exists than to have students actively participate in a decision-making process within an educational setting. Rather than primarily an individualistic pursuit, education according to Dewey is a social process meant to benefit society. Educational institutions are to be the primary agents of social progress and reform in society. Social studies and social activities are the appropriate concerns of education and an experiential, problem-solving approach is the correct method. Problems emerging out of the interests and experience of the students are the stimuli that challenge them to grow and to mature in their thinking and behavior. Knowledge of the past is important only as it informs present action. Dewey was early attracted to Hegel's idealism with its emphasis on societal progress through reconstructive synthesis. In opposition to Hegel, however, he believed that societies do not change on a grand scale, but only as individuals and groups, aided by education, intentionally work for progress in their own situations. He was also heavily influenced by Darwin's theory of evolution. Education is evolutionary in the sense of a continuous experiment in which the teacher encourages students to actively adapt to an ever-varying set of circumstances.

Balanced pedagogy for Dewey is to avoid either of two extremes. Those who are preoccupied solely with the subject matter of the curriculum and passive absorbing of factual materials neglect the experience of the student and an active experimentation process leading to discovery. On the other extreme are those who focus on the independent self-expression of the child as the chief aim of education. Later in life, Dewey criticized those in the progressive education movement, many his former pupils, who rejected the disciplined use of intelligence and the active role of the teacher in guiding the student. Dewey held that neither the subject matter nor the child's interests should be emphasized at the expense of the other.

An analysis of Dewey's beliefs and philosophy reveals a number of weaknesses. One of Dewey's basic presuppositions is that everything is in a state of change or flux—nothing is absolute, eternal, or stable. One criticism is that Dewey apparently contradicts himself, having established at least one absolute and ultimate principle—that of continuous change. In addition, by contending that principles of logic could possibly change, he attempts to make logic dependent on science and the scientific method. Yet science by its very nature depends on logic and is not possible without it. If foundational principles of logic are not consistent and unchangeable, no rational thinking or arguments can stand. In its opposition to such timeless logical absolutes, Dewey's instrumentalism appears to be irrational at its foundation. One other criticism of Dewey concerns his attempt to justify certain ends or values as inherent within the scientific method itself. Science by its very nature, however, is instrumental and simply the means to achieve certain ends. Dewey makes inseparable and therefore confuses method and content, and means and ends, within his system. He contends against eternal and universal values, but the values he espouses appear to be imported from his own biases since they cannot emerge from his methodology. Science is used in the service of values and morals, good and bad, which are extrinsic to it. For this and other reasons religious educators have criticized as woefully inadequate Dewey's humanistic foundation for societal morality and values apart from belief in absolute truth and religious faith.

The influence of Dewey and the progressive education movement can be clearly seen in the practice of contemporary Christian education. A teaching approach taking into account the needs and experience of the student as well as a problem-solving orientation regarding church and societal problems can be attributed to him. An emphasis on practical applications of knowledge, on the activity of the student, and measurable results from ministry show the influence of Dewey as well. Curriculum planning has reflected his practical approach to teaching. Virtually all religious education curriculum published today has lesson content grouped into units supported by a variety of activities and projects. Incorporating these ideas wholesale into religious education, however, has been seen by some to have created a dangerous imbalance. For example, following his approach to education, a focus on process and the student's experience may result in a neglect of in-depth study of the content of the faith, particularly of Scripture, and a lack of spiritual maturity.

While Christians today cannot accept Dewey's opposition to religious teaching and faith or the naturalistic and humanistic presuppositions of his philosophy, his concept of the role of experience in the growth of the person and his insights about learning and problem-solving methods contribute toward a more comprehensive understanding and practice of Christian education.

RICHARD LEYDA

Bibliography. G. H. Clark (1960), *Dewey;* K. O. Gangel and W. S. Benson (1983), *Christian Education: Its History and Philosophy.*

Diakonia. Greek word, generally rendered in English as "service" or "ministry." In secular Greek, the verb *diakoneo* generally refers to waiting on tables or caring for household needs, and the New Testament uses the word this way in a number of passages. Generally, however, Christians use the term to speak of the office and ministry of a deacon or deaconess, or to refer to Christian service in general. Regarding the former usage, we may think of the choosing of the seven servants in Acts 6:1–17 and of the instructions from Paul to Timothy regarding the selection and duties of the deacons (1 Tim. 3:8–13). The latter usage reminds Christian educators of an important element of the Christian lifestyle to be taught and modeled for all believers.

Christians are called to a life characterized by love of God and neighbor (Mark 12: 29–31). Service is a critical part of this. Jesus demonstrated such humility and service to his disciples and commanded them to follow his example (see, for example, Mark 10:42–45; John 13:1–17). While the Old Testament did command God's covenant people to love their neighbors (Lev. 19:18) and to care for the poor, it is interesting that the verb *diakoneo* does not appear in the Septuagint, the Greek translation of the Hebrew Scriptures. Perhaps it is in this sense of loving as a servant that Jesus' commandment to "love one another, *even as I have loved you*" is a "new commandment" (John 13:33–34). Christians are called to take the servant's role in one another's lives, as Jesus took that role with his disciples. The apostle Peter did not understand how Jesus could humble Himself in love to the point of washing his feet (John 13:6–8), but he later came to heed his message and to enjoin it upon those that he taught (1 Peter 5:1–6). Paul, likewise, used the example of Jesus as the ultimate model for the Christian life of service (Phil. 2:1–11).

A lifestyle of *diakonia* is to be expressed in every relationship of the Christian, whether with fellow believers or with unbelievers (Gal. 6:10). In the church, servanthood takes many forms, from providing financial resources for the ministry and for brothers and sisters in need, to discerning and exercising one's gifts for the building up the body of Christ; from humbly seeking to exalt others above oneself, to treating each member and newcomer with hospitality and graciousness; from speaking the truth in love, to weeping with those who weep and rejoicing with those who rejoice. Outside the community of faith, our service takes the expression of doing justly and loving mercy (Mic. 6:8). We engage in the ministries Jesus outlined in Matthew 25:31–46 and, in doing so, we find ourselves imitating the kind of life he lived during his earthly sojourn. We follow the example of the Good Samaritan, treating all persons as our neighbors.

Diakonia ought, then, to be both a central feature of the *content* of Christian education and of the *character* of those engaged in the educational ministry of the church. In an age that seems increasingly characterized by cynicism, incivility, and selfishness, *diakonia* must be reasserted as an essential component of our teaching. Believers need to be trained in this vital aspect of the biblical emphasis on walking in *the Way* of the Lord.

For those who seek to train others as servants, it is most critical that we teach by our example. This is precisely how Jesus taught and led (John 13:14–15, 34). It is the style of leadership that Paul exercised (1 Cor. 11:1; Phil. 4:9) and that Peter commanded church elders to employ (1 Peter 5:3). Indeed, the ministry of teaching itself is to be done in an attitude of servanthood, whether we are instructing believers, or answering unbelievers (2 Tim. 2:22–26; 1 Peter 3:15–16).

GARY A. PARRETT

Bibliography. H. J. M. Nouwen, *In the Name of Jesus;* P. J. Palmer (1993), *To Know as We Are Known;* J. O. Sanders (1994), *Spiritual Leadership.*

See also DEACON; DEACONESS; ELDER

Dialogue. *See* Conversation.

Dialogue Approach to Teaching. Approach to teaching that assumes that the exchange of ideas between teacher and learner is a valuable educational mode of instruction. Some practitioners of the method deem it more than merely a tool; there is an educational paradigm that regards dialogue as necessary to a truly humane pursuit of instructional objectives.

Perhaps the best-known practitioner of the dialogue approach was the famous Greek master Socrates, who asked his students to take a position on an issue—thereby making a value judgment—and then he challenged the student's position and attempted to expose its perhaps faulty philosophical underpinnings. Often forgotten is the fact that Jesus was also a practitioner of the question approach and used inquiry over 150 times to direct his disciples to the lessons at hand. Critics of this assertion observe that Scripture contains scant dialogue of a sophisticated cognitive level between Jesus and his followers. In answer it is noted that the primary intent of the Gospel writers was to record the life and teachings of Jesus rather than the comments of others. Nonetheless, the rabbi Jesus probably extensively exercised a common rabbinic model of education by using questions and student answers to generate significant learning opportunities.

The notion of an inhumane pursuit of educational objectives was provocatively addressed by Paulo Freire in *The Pedagogy of the Oppressed.* In this volume, education is described as suffering from "narration sickness." The teacher, who sees his job to "fill" the student, is condemned because in monological methodology the teacher is the subject, the students are objects, instruction becomes lifeless and petrified, contents are detached from reality, and words emptied of their concreteness.

Practitioners of dialogue see the inquiry paradigm, which culminates in the sharing of ideas, as a process whereby participants are encouraged to pool their "fulness" as opposed to merely correcting their ignorance using the instructor's educated response. Learning is a process of active and ongoing inquiry, not merely passive acceptance of content that has been vocalized by the teacher.

Dialogue, while useful as an independent educational mode (or, when used alone), also works well in conjunction with a variety of other educational methods, including lecture, case study, and role playing. While dialogue has utility when used with children, historically it has been most evident in the education of adults and today is perceived as absolutely essential to andragogical approaches to learning.

MATT FRIEDEMAN

Bibliography. P. Freire (1970), *The Pedagogy of the Oppressed;* M. Knowles (1973), *The Adult Learner: A Neglected Species.*

Dictatorial. *See* Authoritarian Approach to Groups.

Didache. "The Teaching of the Apostles" is the title of the early Christian discipline also known by the Greek word *didache,* which means "teaching." The manuscript was discovered in 1873 by P. Bryennios. Scholars have debated the date of origin, with some suggestions being as early as A.D. 70 and other dates falling within the next hundred years. It may be a composite document that served many Christian communities over a period of time. The place of origin has also been debated, with two locations given preference. It was used extensively in Egypt, but the content may suggest Syria.

The Didache may be regarded as an early church manual used for teaching catechumens. Beginning with a contrast between the way of life and the way of death, the first six chapters could be based on early Jewish sources, including Jeremiah 21:8, plus the teaching of Jesus especially as found in the Sermon on the Mount. Directions for worship are found in chapters 7–10. Instructions for baptism include a triune blessing and a preference for cold running water. The Lord's Prayer similar to Matthew's version is given with the doxology. It is to be prayed three times each day. Only the baptized may drink the Eucharist thanksgiving.

Testing and receiving itinerant teachers and prophets are the subject of chapters 11–15. Itinerant teachers may stay only three days. The appointment of bishops and deacons is described in chapters 11–15. The final chapter is focused on eschatology. The return of the Lord is expected at an unknown hour, and Christians are instructed to be watching and ready.

The instructions advance from the contrast of two ways, baptism, Eucharist, worship, authority in leadership, and finally the return of Christ. It is also interesting to note how this order is similar to the outline followed in the arrangement of the books of the New Testament.

LARRY D. REINHART

See also CATECHUMENATE; LITURGY

Direct. To guide the course of an activity, program, group, or series of events. In Christian education, it would seem to relate most to the function described in 1 Peter 5:2a: "Shepherd the flock of God among you, exercising oversight not under compulsion but voluntarily."

Directing means that leaders are managing, operating, steering, supervising, or showing the way to a group of people in order to fulfill the responsibility of oversight they have. In secular circles it means to govern, rule, give orders, or exercise authority over those who are in the leader's charge. However, this view is inconsistent with the scriptural view of a servant leader as described in Mark 10:42–45.

To direct is the fourth of the five functions of the typical management cycle (planning, organizing, staffing, directing, and controlling). The usual behaviors that are included in the directing function are delegation, motivation, coordination, managing differences, and managing change. Delegation is the assigning of tasks to responsible people and the establishment of accountability structures. Motivation is the inspiring and persuasion of people to take a desired action or path. Coordination is communication with other agencies and people so that a maximum combination

for effectiveness occurs. When direction manages differences, participants are given sufficient power to think independently and resolve conflict. Managing change stimulates creativity and innovation in pursuing new goals and tasks. In summary, to direct is to cause purposeful action toward desired goals, which in turn, contribute to the accomplishment of institutional mission.

It is difficult for many Christian leaders to perform this managerial function since it often requires the ability to confront a person's poor work performance. Most leaders prefer a less directive approach. Miller distinguishes between supportive and directive behavior in management. Directive behavior enables people to know what to do, when, where, and how to do it, and then supervises their behavior and accomplishments. Supportive behavior listens, encourages, facilitates, and builds the confidence of the people involved.

In thinking of staff positions within the church, there is a role known as the director of Christian education (DCE) or minister of Christian education. Cionca (1986) says that the DCE will "work with the Christian Education Committee in developing educational aims and policies, coordinating the educational program, promoting the educational program, staffing and training those who will serve in the program, and evaluating each program's effectiveness" (63). Lawson and Choun (1992) interpret the roles of a Christian education specialist (CES) as "supervision, administration, control, leadership, and management" (43). Whatever the designation or job description of this staff person, it would seem that she or he is responsible for the organization and conduct of the comprehensive programming of the church in the areas of training and nurture.

GREGORY C. CARLSON

Bibliography. J. Cionca (1986), *The Trouble-shooting Guide to Christian Education;* M. Lawson and R. Choun (1992), *Directing Christian Education;* C. Miller (1995), *The Empowered Leader;* O. Tead (1959), *Administration.*

See also ADMINISTRATION; EXECUTIVE PASTOR; LEADERSHIP; LINE-STAFF RELATIONSHIPS; MANAGEMENT; MINISTER OF CHRISTIAN EDUCATION; SPAN OF CONTROL; STAFF, STAFFING; TRUSTEE

Director of Christian Education (DCE). Professional member of a church staff. The exact title depends on the denomination and on the congregation; some examples of variant titles are minister of Christian education, director of religious education, and associate pastor. Usually any of these titles refer to a ministry position quite similar to the one being described here as DCE.

In different denominations and congregations, the DCE can be any combination of the following: employed full-time or part-time, layperson or ordained pastor, generalist or specialist, nurtured within the congregation or called to the congregation from elsewhere, holding any level of educational preparation, young adult or senior adult.

The DCE may be employed by the congregation either full-time or part-time. Generally speaking, it is usually larger churches with greater financial resources that can offer a full-time professional salary and benefits package, while smaller churches cannot. It is these smaller congregations that employ a DCE on a part-time basis.

The DCE may be a layperson or an ordained pastor. In some denominations, by definition the DCE is a layperson without pastoral privileges and responsibilities (e.g., preaching, serving Holy Communion, performing baptisms, weddings, and funerals). In other denominations, the DCE may in fact be an ordained pastor who performs the full range of pastoral ministry along with the specifically educational ministry.

The DCE may be a generalist or a specialist. The generalist has oversight and responsibility for the entire educational program of a congregation. The specialist is concerned only with one area of educational ministry, usually a particular age group. For example, a DCE might specialize in children's ministry, youth ministry, adult ministry, or family ministry (in these instances, the DCE usually carries a specialist title, reflecting that segment of ministry, e.g., director of children's ministry, youth director, etc.).

The DCE may be nurtured within the congregation or called to the congregation from elsewhere. Many DCEs are products of a congregation's educational ministry; they have been members of a particular church for a number of years (some were born and raised in that congregation). They have become active in educational leadership, the congregation has recognized their gifts for ministry, and they have been employed by the congregation to direct some segment of the educational ministry. There are many other DCEs who have heard God calling them into this ministry and have prepared themselves for it vocationally. They may serve one congregation for a number of years, then move to another congregation.

There is no standard educational preparation for a DCE. Some denominations (and congregations) have minimal educational requirements; some do not. The result is that some DCEs serve without any formal educational preparation, while others have completed a bachelor's degree, master's degree, or doctorate. Regardless of the specific educational route into this profession, it is generally agreed that a DCE needs to have knowledge and skills in certain areas. It is important that a DCE understands education, learning theories, human development, teaching methods, and administration. Knowledge of the Bible and Christian theology is essential. A DCE also needs

skills in working with people and in dealing redemptively with conflict.

The responsibilities of a DCE include developing educational programs, administering programs, knowing materials and methods, and enlisting and training lay people in educational ministry.

The DCE develops educational programs. In order for this to be effective, it must be done systematically. Program development includes a philosophy of Christian education, needs assessment, knowledge of the local context, goal setting, objective writing, curriculum selection, leadership development, and evaluation. The evaluation serves as the needs assessment for the next round of program development; evaluation of programs is based on the objectives, identifying the extent to which each objective was fulfilled.

The DCE administers programs. No one person can deliver all of the educational ministry needed in a congregation; therefore the DCE develops programs that involve lay people directly in ministry. The programs then need competent administration. The administrator does not do the ministry; the administrator enables the people of the congregation to do the ministry.

The DCE knows materials and methods. An effective DCE keeps current with materials supplied by publishers, both Christian and secular. An effective DCE also keeps abreast of new teaching-learning methods. This is not to say that every new material and method is good and therefore ought to be used in the church. Indeed, much new material is not necessarily good: it may not be based in sound philosophy, or it may not be biblical, or it may be faddish. The effective DCE evaluates all new materials and methods and determines which are useful in the ministry.

The DCE enlists and trains lay people. Since effective biblical teaching and Christian education practice requires laypeople to be involved in ministry, the effective DCE does not attempt to do everything solo. The DCE searches for laypeople with gifts for ministry, and calls them to serve God in the context of this congregation. Once those whom God has gifted are called to minister, they need to learn certain knowledge and skills. Therefore, the DCE arranges for the necessary leadership training.

JOHN H. AUKERMAN

See also ADMINISTRATION; CLERGY; MINISTER; MINISTER OF CHRISTIAN EDUCATION; STAFF, STAFFING

Discernment. *See* Discrimination.

Disciple. The term *disciple*, or follower, is the standard English translation of the Greek *mathetes/mathetria* and its verb form *matheteuo*. Related forms are *mathema* (something that is learned, knowledge, teaching) and *matheteia* (lesson, instruction). The noun form appears at least 230 times in the four Gospels, 28 times in Acts, but nowhere else in the New Testament. The verb form for the action of being or making a disciple appears four times in the New Testament: Matthew 13:53; 27:57; 28:19; Acts 14:21. The word *disciple* derives from the late Latin word *discipulus* (pupil).

Old Testament Background. Old Testament writers speak much of knowing, teaching, and learning. However, except for indirect references in 1 Chronicles 25:8 and Isaiah 8:16 the Old Testament does not speak of disciples or pupils. Rengstorf (1967) asserts that this lack of discussion of a relationship between teachers and their disciples stems from the nature of the Old Testament view of a godly life: "In the sphere of revelation there is no place for the establishment of a master-disciple relation, nor is there the possibility of setting up a human word alongside the Word of God which is proclaimed, nor of trying to ensure the force of the divine address by basing it on the authority of a great personality. For here God's Word alone is justified, no matter whether we be dealing with Moses or the Prophets. . . . If in the Old Testament there is no place whatever for the veneration of the religious leader as master, or for the cultivation of his memory as an almost religious duty, the final reason for this is that in the Old Testament the disclosure of God is regarded as continuous and dynamic" (Rengstorf, 431).

Greek Background. In Greek usage *disciple* denotes an indissoluble personal relationship between disciple and teacher (*didaskalos*) in which the disciple imitates or emulates the teacher. This relationship obtains whether the learning and teaching involves technical or academic learning, or the learning of a skill. The word is also used to denote an inner fellowship between disciple and teacher as well as the practical effects of that fellowship. As Rengstorf observes, this latter usage has considerable significance in relation to the development of the Christian use of *disciple*.

New Testament. In the New Testament the word *disciple* usually refers to those who followed Jesus, either the twelve (Matt. 10:1–4; see also Mark 3:13–19) or a large group from whom the twelve were chosen (Luke 6:12–16). The New Testament writers also speak of disciples of Moses (John 9:28), of the Pharisees (Matt. 22:16; Mark 22:18); and of John the Baptist (Mark 2:18; Luke 11:1). Acts 9:25 refers to those who enabled Paul to escape from those who sought to kill him in Damascus as "his disciples."

Disciples of Jesus are those who follow Him. As Dietrich Bonhoeffer indicated in his *Nachfolge* (1937; *The Cost of Discipleship*, 1948), those who follow after Jesus can expect to pay a cost. Such disciples must be prepared to deny themselves, take up their crosses, and follow Jesus (Luke 14:27; see also Matt. 10:38; 16:24; Mark 8:34; Luke 9:23).

The task of making disciples was assigned by Jesus to his 11 disciples shortly before his ascension (Matt. 28:19). The scope of disciple making extends to all nations or social groups. The process for making disciples consists of baptizing people in the name of Father, Son, and Holy Spirit (v. 19); and of teaching them to observe all that Jesus has commanded (v. 20). The authority for assigning this task rests on the cosmic authority granted by the Father to Jesus the Son (v. 19). Those called to make disciples do so knowing that Jesus remains with them always (v. 20). Although the specific language of disciple making is little used in the remainder of the New Testament, Acts 14:20 does use *disciple* to refer to those who know Christ. The next verse (Acts 14:21) uses the verb form of *disciple* for the process of making them so. Acts 6:1–7 9:36 11:26 and 19:1–7 all refer to members of the post-Pentecost community of faith as *disciples*. See Michael Wilkins (1992), *Following the Master*.

Modern Usage. In modern usage *disciple, discipleship,* and *disciple making* have become standard words for referring to Christians, to the process of growing in Christ and to the key task of the church. A comprehensive example is provided by O'Connell (1998), who sees the making of disciples as the whole purpose of the church. He identifies disciples in five categories. First, Jesus' disciples define themselves by their relationship to him. He leads. They follow. Second, they understand him in the sense that they know him as the object of their devotion. Third, they are committed to him such that maintaining their relationship with him is a personal, ongoing priority. Fourth, they behave in ways that fit their commitment. Fifth, because humans are social beings, "discipleship involves affiliation with others similarly committed, such that support is given and received, wisdom offered and accepted" (142).

GARY J. BEKKER

Bibliography. D. Bonhoeffer (1937), *The Cost of Discipleship;* R. P. Meye (1968), *Jesus and the Twelve: Discipleship and Revelation in Mark's Gospel;* T. E. O'Connell (1998), *Making Disciples: A Handbook of Christian Moral Formation;* J. C. Ortiz (1975), *Disciple;* K. H. Rengstorf (1967), *Theological Dictionary of the New Testament;* F. T. Segovia (1985), *Discipleship in the New Testament;* M. Wilkins (1992), *Following the Master: Discipleship in the Steps of Jesus.*

Disciple Training. *See* Navigators.

Discipline, Family. Active measure parents take in guiding and nurturing the human spirit within their children to live according to biblical standards and, consequently, meet societal standards. It is important to understand that in purpose, focus, attitude, and results, discipline is very different from punishment. When punishing a child, a parent out of hostility and frustration inflicts a penalty for a past misdeed which results in the child feeling fear and guilt. Discipline, on the other hand, is done out of love and concern for the correction, training, and maturity of the child with a focus on future correct deeds that will ultimately make the child feel secure in the parent's love.

Discipline can be accomplished if parents know their own frustration level and share together the responsibility of discipline. They together need to set limits ahead of time or as soon as the child commits an infraction. When actual discipline is necessary, the feelings of the child need to be acknowledged, the limit needs to be communicated, and acceptable alternatives need to be targeted.

Discipline, from the root word *disciple,* indicates the child is a disciple who follows the parent as a master teacher. Consequently, in disciplining, rather than using an unassertive or aggressive style of communication, parents need to be assertive. An assertive style of communication reveals the parents' feelings and makes requests of the child in a firm, clear, concise way. Parents need to accept conflict as inevitable but refuse to be treated in an unfair manner by the child. Anger is not only controlled, but need not take a position. The child is expected to comply, but not necessarily agree with requests (Osborne, 1989).

This kind of discipline complies with the discipline all Christians should be receiving according to Hebrews 12. In this passage, love is the basis of discipline which proves our sonship or acceptance into God's family so we share in his holiness. It helps us to respect all authority and yields fruits of righteousness. Discipline is not joyful at the moment it is given but builds inner strength and produces peace in the home.

JUDY TENELSHOF

Bibliography. D. B. Guernsey (1982), *A New Design for Family Ministry;* P. Osborne (1989), *Parenting for the 90's.*

Discipline in the Classroom. The goal of Christian discipline is to assist the child to grow like Christ in wisdom and in favor (relating effectively) with God and with other people (Luke 2:52). Paul enumerates in Galatians 5:22–23 the values that will help the child grow toward Christian maturity. Christian discipline is not merely seeking to assist the child in controlling his or her own behavior but also helping to shape the child's character. The root word from which *discipline* arises is *disciple,* meaning "to learn." Discipline seeks to instruct and nurture the child in order that the child might respond in a positive

fashion. Christian discipline emerges out of love—as Hebrews 12:6 says, "The Lord disciplines those he loves."

Social and moral philosophies regarding children tend to influence strongly contemporary beliefs regarding what constitutes proper discipline. As philosophies change so do views of discipline. The range of responses, from highly permissive methods of discipline to severe, harsh, or even abusive conduct, often create antisocial behavior and a breakdown in the disciplinary process. Rather than the child developing initiative and responsibility, poor disciplinary methods seem to lead to low self-esteem and the development of fear of and hatred for the person administering the discipline.

A number of theories can assist people in determining the appropriate approaches to discipline. One view is Freudian psychoanalysis and its understanding of personality development. This theory is grounded in the understanding that gratification of needs is the basis for personal happiness and mental health. Writers such as Selma Fraiberg and Anna Freud have applied the psychoanalytic theory to discipline, showing that the child responds to external demands either out of love or fear or anger and gradually begins to take on desired behaviors as his or her own while building internal controls. Rather than using punishment, deprivation, or force, explaining reasons in a loving manner is a much stronger way of enhancing moral development.

Another rich reservoir of information concerning various aspects of discipline comes from developmentalists. One such person is Piaget. His research on cognitive and moral development points to a discipline that seems to emphasize that knowing the good will lead to choosing the good. Children, however, transform what is given to them like social customs in such a way that it is consistent with their present level of cognitive development. Consequently, the way in which children think about moral issues changes dramatically as they move from one cognitive stage to the next. Other developmentalists such as Kohlberg have taken these changing structures and created moral-development stages. Discipline for those who base their understanding on developmental patterns will follow the child's moral and cognitive developmental level in order to be effective and understood by the child.

Rational-emotive discipline is based on Albert Ellis's theory, which stresses the interdependence of thinking, feeling, and behaving. He taught clients rational thinking skills in order to promote appropriate emotions. Discipline for children, therefore, is aimed at helping the child achieve inner control, self-direction, tolerance, acceptance of uncertainty, and flexibility. Adults must make rules simple and concrete so that both acceptable and unacceptable behavior is understood by the child and an explanation given which the child understands. The important issues for children to know are: what is the rule, why was it made, and what is the consequence if it is broken. They must realize that the rule will be enforced. In this way the child learns self-discipline.

These and other theories are explained in full in the book entitled *The Psychology of Discipline.* Other models of discipline include assertive discipline, developed by Lee Canter. As a former elementary school teacher and specialist in child guidance, Canter's model is simple: if children obey the rules and do not disrupt the process of learning, they are rewarded. If the opposite is true, they are punished. In other words, the teacher is the authority and has all the power. The teacher makes the rules, explains them, enforces them, and administers rewards or punishments. Punishments can involve having one's name written on the board. Each time the child misbehaves a check is placed next to the name. Each check adds fifteen minutes to the time spent after school. Rewards for the class may include accumulating enough "marbles" to have a party. Some obvious weaknesses may be the lack of involvement by the children or expecting certain types of behavior from all children. This methodology may only be effective with elementary children.

William Glasser, creator of the reality therapy approach, is a psychiatrist and writer. His goal is to bring about self-understanding, self-discipline, knowing the power of choice, and not making excuses or blaming the past for present behavior. Glasser's model helps children to understand that there is hope, to determine what their behavior is doing to keep them from achieving hope, and to control their behavior by making a plan and keeping it. The important and difficult aspect of Glasser's model is helping students believe a change is possible and in their best interest.

In teacher effectiveness training by clinical psychologist Thomas Gordon, the teacher and students work together to find satisfactory solutions to problems in the classroom. One of the major emphases is the use of "I" messages ("I feel angry") rather than "you" messages ("You make me feel angry").

Alfred Alschuler's model of social literacy training searches for causes of discipline problems, first at the system level rather than at the personal level of the teacher or student. It sees classroom management as a joint enterprise of the students and teacher through the discussion of rules, roles, and goals of the system rather than blaming one another.

Another popular disciplinary model is "dare to discipline" by James Dobson. He believes that authority is needed to enforce clearly defined rules and limits. Dobson emphasizes teaching politeness, manners, morals, citizenship, and respect for authority. He does not withhold physical punishment.

Austrian-born Rudolf Dreikurs based his theory on the ideas of Alfred Adler. In Dreikurs's model he outlines his beliefs and explains natural and logical consequences. He also presents reasons children misbehave. This model and the models presented immediately above are discussed at length in the book by Robert L. Major.

DORIS BORCHERT

Bibliography. D. Dorr, M. Zax, and J. W. Bonner III, eds. (1983), *The Psychology of Discipline;* R. L. Major (1990), *Discipline: The Most Important Subject We Teach;* K. Walsh (1991), *Discipline for Character Development: A Guide for Teachers and Parents.*

Discipling. Investment of concentrated time, energy, and attention in a relatively small number of students by a spiritual formation leader to facilitate Christlike qualities. Disciple making as a New Testament notion is at the heart of the Great Commission of Jesus, expressed in his final words from the Gospel of Matthew: "Go, therefore, and make disciples." This command certainly implies conversion. But based on the ministry of Jesus, it was intended to move beyond initial salvation and produce holy character, vital service in the world, and involvement in Christian community.

Jesus, in his brief ministry, attracted to himself concentric circles of followers: (1) the masses, those present at itinerant preaching/teaching events and the large public feedings of the five thousand and four thousand; (2) the seventy disciples and friends, who were impacted by Jesus' teachings and healings and were committed to following him; (3) the Twelve, whom Jesus chose over a year into his ministry to spend concentrated time in a rabbinic mode of intensive instruction; and (4) Peter, James, and John, three of the Twelve with whom Jesus spent several intimate moments and, it is assumed, had an especially close relationship.

Discipling recognizes that while all these concentric emphases are important and various aspects of discipleship are reflected in each, the most effective instruction for kingdom purposes occurs with the few. Contemporary small group advocates therefore rely on the smaller of Jesus' educational entities and suggest that three to twelve people is the optimal number for a small Bible study or support group; discipling experts maintain that somewhere between one and six is more appropriate for the kind of intense instruction common in "discipleship" groups.

While methodologies vary substantially, discipleship groups are frequently characterized by mutually agreed-upon disciplines for which group members hold each other accountable (e.g., daily prayer and Bible study, Scripture memorization, weekly fasting, corporate worship, etc.) and a curriculum that establishes the disciples in fundamental doctrine.

Perhaps even more critical is the recognition and practice of "life-to-life transference" inherent in close relationships and extended time teacher and students spend with each other. This "transference" includes modeling certain behaviors; frequently, such modeling is spontaneous. Jesus' actions and reactions as he moved among the people of Palestine provided his disciples with a curriculum possible only in a life context. This pattern was established early in Israel's history, as recorded in Deuteronomy 6, where God's people were instructed in one of the most famous passages of Hebrew Scripture, the *Shema*. Here, the family is intimated as the primary educational context and parents are told to speak of the commandments of God "when you sit in the house, when you walk in the way, when you lie down and when you rise up. And you shall bind them as a sign on your hands, and they shall be as frontals on your forehead." The Law was entrusted to the modeled life of small group leaders.

The most ardent and high-profile proponents of discipling in the past several decades have been campus ministries such as Campus Crusade for Christ and the Navigators. As a consequence of the disciple making emphases of these groups, many local churches have recognized the effectiveness of the approach and devised programs of pastor- and lay-led groups to emulate what these parachurch groups have done on college and university campuses.

The Master Plan of Evangelism by Robert Coleman addresses the discipleship ministry of Jesus and suggests that his plan was nothing less than worldwide conquest with a method that is worthy of acceptance and contemporary adaptation.

MATT FRIEDEMAN

Bibliography. R. Coleman (1974), *The Master Plan of Evangelism.*

Discovery Learning. Jerome Bruner (1960) observed that the acquisition, transformation, and evaluation of knowledge is significantly enhanced when learners "figure out" or "discern" knowledge for themselves. The active nature of this discovery learning allows learners to rearrange knowledge for themselves in such a way that new content is assimilated and/or existing knowledge is transformed into additional insights.

Discovery learning has been observed to have significant effects upon memory processing and learning transfer, learning motivation, and socialization. When a person learns by discovery, there is a gain in the ability to organize or transform the information acquired, as well as a gain

in the ability to retrieve and transfer the information to new problem-solving situations. Discovered concepts are more meaningful to the learner and thus are remembered longer and made more readily available for future thinking and critical reflection.

The process of discovery is highly self-rewarding, eliminating the need for external rewards to instill a motivation to learn. While external reinforcement may be necessary to get learning started, it is usually insufficient for maintaining that motivation. Discovery learning, in contrast, increases the active involvement and participation of the learner in the learning process, resulting in an increased and sustained intrinsic motivation to learn.

Discovery learning, by nature, is a cooperative process and places a great deal of emphasis on social interaction. Whereas education has tended to encourage competition between learners through the awarding of grades and academic awards, discovery learning fosters cooperation between learners, putting the competition between the student and the task. Learners have the opportunity to develop positive social skills as they engage in dialogue during the discovery process. Such opportunities are typically neglected or negated in lecture-type methodologies.

Like didactic instruction, discovery learning has its limitations. The process of discovery is an inefficient system for covering large amounts of material. Because it is a process of learning, students take longer to reach original learning criterion. In some instances, the discovery method is ineffective when it is abruptly introduced in a learning environment built extensively upon didactic instruction, especially when the content is of a complex nature. The relatively novel nature of learning by discovery can be frustrating for both student and teacher, as there is no constant feedback to show learning progress.

Discovery learning is favorable for the acquisition of inquiry and problem-solving skills, whereas didactic instruction is favorable for factual-conceptual achievement. Self-confidence in the learner is increased through the discovery process, encouraging critical reflection. The resulting assimilation and transformation of knowledge by the learner increases the likelihood that learning will transfer to new situations.

MARK E. SIMPSON

Bibliography. J. S. Bruner, *Harvard Educational Review* 31, no. 1 (1960): 21–32; K. T. Henson, *Contemporary Education* 51, no. 2 (1980): 101–3; G. Hermann, *Journal of Experimental Education* 38, no. 1 (1969): 58–72; R. N. Singer and D. Pease, *Research Quarterly* 47, no. 4 (1976): 788–96; B. Thomas and B. Snider, *Journal of Research in Science Teaching* 6, no. 4 (1969): 377–86; D. C. Vidler and J. Levine, *College Student Journal* 13, no. 4 (1979): 387–90; C. Wisner, *Journal of Educational Research* 64, no. 5 (1971): 217–19.

See also COGNITIVE FIELD THEORY; BRUNER, JEROME; TRANSFER

Discovery Teaching. This learner-centered teaching method is based on the principle that people learn best when they can be actively involved in the process. Research has shown that the rate of comprehension and retention improves with every physical sense added to the information-processing effort. The learner who sits passively listening to a lecture is unlikely to remember most of its content or apply it to his life. A learner who has been tactfully guided to his own discoveries and provided with strategic resources will remember and apply what he has learned.

Discovery teaching does not advocate a complete abandonment of curriculum or classroom control. It is by nature, however, more flexible and noisy than a traditional lecture-based lesson. In its most literal application, discovery teaching allows the learner to pursue his own subject of interest, learning interdisciplinary skills such as research techniques as they are needed. The teacher asks the right questions and provides the best resources, but does not function as the source of information. In this way, the student relearns how to learn. Most classrooms use a modified version of this approach. The teacher selects an appropriate learning aim and plans discovery activities that will lead the learner in the predetermined direction.

Discovery learning begins not with a statement of fact, but with a provocative question. This is similar to the method used by Jesus, who often began a lesson with a question to engage his listeners. "Whose portrait is this?" (Matt 22:20), "Who do you say I am?" (Luke 9:20), "Which of the three do you think was a neighbor?" (Luke 10:36). Jesus spoke with authority, but he also used visual aids, discussion, and thought-provoking questions to lead listeners to the truth.

A sample discovery-style lesson on God's mastery of nature could feature the following learning centers:

1. Learners use a tree identification book to match leaves with seeds and answer the question, "How does God provide future trees?"

2. Learners examine photos of snowflakes and cut their own from folded paper. After comparing their work with their classmates', they discuss, "God makes each snowflake different. What does that fact tells us about God?"

3. Learners examine calendar photos of seasonal change, looking for examples of the changes in plants and animals throughout the year. After reading Psalm 147:8, 16–18, they answer, "What are God's reasons for some of the changes you observed? Would they 'just happen' without his direction?"

After a time of discovery in small groups, the learners would come together to share what they had found. A time of praise and worship would be the natural expression of the attitude created by their discoveries.

ROBERT J. CHOUN

Bibliography. B. Bolton (1982), *How to Do Bible Learning Activities* (grades 1–6); I. V. Cully and K. B. Cully, eds. (1990), *Harper's Encyclopedia of Religious Education*; K. Klein (1982), *How to Do Bible Learning Activities* (ages 2–5); E. Stewart and N. McBride (1982), *How to Do Bible Learning Activities* (grades 7–12); idem (1982), *How to Do Bible Learning Activities* (adult).

Discrimination. Term used in behaviorism to describe the ability of an organism to differentiate between two similar stimuli by giving different responses to each stimulus.

This kind of discrimination was first noted by Ivan Pavlov in his experiments with the physiological, or involuntary, responses of dogs. Dogs were presented with a musical tone paired with a reinforcement such as food. This process was repeated until a conditioned response (salivation rate) was well established. A similar musical tone was then repeatedly presented but never paired with reinforcement. The response of the dogs to the new tone was initially weak. With further repetition it progressed to the level of the reinforced tone. Giving the same response to similar stimuli is called generalization. After further unreinforced repetition, the similar musical tone elicited no response from the dogs, thus they had learned to discriminate between the reinforced and unreinforced stimuli. Pavlov's conception of discrimination has limited application in the classroom.

B. F. Skinner expanded on the work of Pavlov proposing that discrimination between two stimuli could be associated with voluntary responses. He further proposed that a response can be followed by a reinforcing stimulus. Skinner thought reinforcement contingencies could be designed to help children develop greater discrimination in subjects such as music and geometry.

Skinner has been criticized for focusing too much on reinforcement contingencies to explain learning, including the ability to discriminate. While discrimination takes into account that a learner succeeds in differentiating between two similar stimuli, it only gives a superficial explanation of the internal processes that accomplished it.

Despite these criticisms, discrimination is a necessity in learning how to respond in different situations. In order for discrimination to be learned in a classroom environment, the instructor must give immediate feedback to the learner that is based on performance and contains corrective information.

DON K. ASHLEY

Bibliography. P. Eggen and D. Kauchak (1994), *Educational Psychology: Classroom Connections;* S. Harnad (1988), *The Selection of Behavior: The Operant Behaviorism of B. F. Skinner, Comments and Consequences;* I. P. Pavlov (1927), *Conditioned Reflexes: An Investigation of the Physiological Activity of the Cerebral Cortex;* B. F. Skinner (1968), *The Technology of Teaching;* idem (1969), *Contingencies of Reinforcement: A Theoretical Analysis;* A. Woolfolk (1993), *Educational Psychology;* W. R. Yount (1996), *Created to Learn: A Christian Teacher's Introduction to Educational Psychology.*

See also ASSOCIATION/CONNECTIONIST THEORIES; BEHAVIORISM, THEORIES OF; REINFORCEMENT; S-R BONDS

Discussion. The verb *discuss* stems from the Latin word that means "to shake apart." When two or more persons discuss an issue or concept, they mentally take it apart and examine it in piecemeal fashion. In an educational setting, discussion refers to guided oral interaction that strives to enhance understanding of a topic, arrive at some conclusion, or identify practical implications for participants.

In a Bible study group, discussion is a cooperative search for God's timeless truth and the bearing it has on participants' lives. Successful Bible discussions have at least six components:

- A teacher or facilitator who originates and directs the conversation
- One or more questions to incite thought
- A meaningful, specific goal for the oral interaction
- Two or more interested participants
- An authoritative source: God's Word
- A supportive learning environment

Values of Discussion. Lefever (1985) identifies the following benefits: stimulates student interest; promotes critical thinking and analysis; helps learners crystallize and review content they have previously absorbed; provides opportunities to learn from the insights and experiences of other group members; and encourages application of content to everyday life situations. Discussion allows teachers to become students of their learners: ascertaining how well students are grasping concepts, discovering student attitudes toward the subject matter, and determining whether a different pace is needed. Involving learners through discussion also raises retention of content (McKeachie, 1986).

Questions that send learners to God's Word for answers or spur thinking about application strengthen learners' study skills. Discussion methods also foster fellowship among God's people as group members identify with others' comments and personal needs. Verbal exchanges enable teachers/facilitators to spot budding leaders.

Preparation for a Discussion. Some teachers erroneously believe that the more they plan to involve students, the less they need to prepare. Good lesson preparation requires formulating at least three kinds of questions: (1) *observation,* to spot important facts or patterns in the text; (2) *interpretation,* to mull over the meaning suggested by passage information; and (3) *application,* to ponder how God's truth should affect priorities, decisions, relationships, and attitudes.

Good discussion leaders design questions for *clarity, accuracy, sensitivity,* and *ability to incite thought.* For clarity, avoid beginning with "what about"; flinging consecutive questions without waiting for a reply; and wordiness.

For accuracy, seek only information disclosed in the text; ask *relevant* questions that consider the larger context and connect with the governing theme. Steer clear of questions that encourage participants to look within themselves, rather than in the text, for answers (e.g., *"What does this verse mean to you?"*).

A question is insensitive when it insists on an individual's intimate self-disclosure, or seeks background information not readily available in the passage. Avoid questions that can be answered with merely "yes" or "no" or call for *obvious answers.*

Responding to Group Members. A leader's behavior, after posing a question, is a hinge on which the direction of successful discussions turn. Good leaders reward participation by expressing excitement over quality discoveries, praising specific aspects of learner contributions. (*"I like the way you supported your conclusion with facts from the Bible passage."*) Helpful leaders give learners time to formulate responses before answering or rephrasing, and are aware of the nonverbal messages sent in listening to a response, maintaining eye contact and posturing that convey interest. They ask follow-up questions that spur learners to modify, expand, or illustrate their answers.

Discussion can take numerous forms: question-answer, buzz groups, debates, panels, interviews, word associations, and brainstorming. Whereas lecture is the primary means of dispensing information, discussion methodologies solidify that information in the mind, enable students to transfer it to new situations, and use it to solve problems.

TERRY POWELL

Bibliography. M. Lefever (1985), *Creative Teaching Methods;* W. McKeachie (1986), *Teaching Tips;* T. Powell (1996), *You Can Lead a Bible Discussion Group;* M. Weimer (1993), *Improving Your Classroom Teaching.*

Discussion Method. The most likely biblical illustration of the discussion method is when Jesus was at the Temple for three days at age twelve

(Luke 2:46–47). The sense of his activities, though they are described as asking and answering questions, is that He was involved in a discussion with the teachers.

Discussion means more than one person is speaking to persuade others of his or her perspective. Discussion helps all involved to better understand the subject being considered because all are actively involved. Discussion is often referred to as "debate" though it lacks the organization of a formal debate. True discussion elicits ideas and feelings from many persons as each speaks, in turn.

The sense of a "teacher" or "leader" and "pupils" or "learners" is lost in a discussion. The "teacher" or "leader" usually takes on the role of "facilitator" whose function is to keep the discussion within certain parameters. The leader's function is to (a) introduce the topic, (b) remind everyone of the purpose of the discussion when it begins to stray from the original purpose, (c) give a summary of progress when the discussion lags, and (d) suggest further courses of action based on what has been said by the participants. Nothing here implies the leader provides all the "right" answers or that the leader is to approve or disapprove of what is said. These are matters to be considered with different methods than discussion. In the discussion method the ratio of teacher talk to student talk may be 1:10 or even less (1:20 or 1:30) depending on the quality of discussion.

The discussion method should be used when the group leader wants to (a) explore an issue from several different perspectives at the same time, (b) expose participants to information and resources which will help them solve their own problems, based on the way others in the group have solved theirs, and (c) get a more accurate reading about what particular participants think and feel about the subject being discussed.

The secret to using the discussion method is to never ask a factual question (Who was John's . . . ?), or one that can be answered with "yes" or "no" (Do you think . . . ?). The best discussion topics are those limited to the experience of those involved. Otherwise there may be just a pooling of inadequate knowledge.

There are some definite advantages to using the discussion method. (1) Participants are usually more physically relaxed because they know they do not "have" to participate and draw attention to themselves unless they decide to. (2) Group rapport is fostered, providing a sense of emotional security for members of the group. (3) An expression of "self" in a free discussion atmosphere builds social confidence and allows the participants to learn "give and take" as they help each other learn. (4) Those who participate (whether actively or not) receive a sense of self-respect as their ideas are used by others. This

often translates into mutual respect as participants learn the courtesy of allowing another to talk even when they really have something "important" to say. (5) Participants have an opportunity to explore "new" ideas and have others respond to those ideas with an accepting attitude. This gives all participants an opportunity to have a sense of achievement. (6) Participants have an opportunity to grow spiritually since they can have their spiritual development authenticated by others and they "see" how others are developing. (7) The teacher/leader learns how different persons think or feel about the subject and is thus better able to determine future interactions.

The discussion method can be used in either a large or small group setting. Participation by a limited number of participants is one liability of this method in a large group setting. The asset in this setting is that it helps stimulate thinking. When used in a small group setting, the discussion method is a liability if one or two persons dominate or must speak more than once or twice while the others have a limited opportunity to express themselves. The advantage in this setting is that all present have an opportunity to express themselves, whether or not they take advantage of it.

The discussion method can be used in connection with many other methods, e.g., agree-disagree, brainstorming, circle response, debate reaction, listening to team reports, and panel discussion response. Care should be taken, however, not to use the discussion method all the time. As good as this method is, it is not a panacea. This method should be used, as should all others, based on the specific goal of the group in this session.

ROY F. LYNN

Disequilibrium. Often associated with Jean Piaget and his theory of equilibrium, the theory of disequilibrium is more correctly attributed to Claude Bernard. In its simplest form, disequilibrium upsets the cognitive balance of understanding that people have about a given subject, ideally resulting in a reconstructing of knowledge that helps them know more about themselves or the world around them. In Piaget's theory of equilibrium, individuals either assimilate new stimuli into their current ways of knowing or somehow change to accommodate the stimuli. When these two processes are appropriately balanced, the result is cognitive equilibrium. The result of introducing new information or experiences is called *disequilibrium*.

Disequilibrium can be a helpful educational tool. A skillful teacher might present a problem, ask a question, or create a situation that forces the students to reconsider what they know. Students who are motivated to deal with this dilemma can be challenged to peak performance in that area. Part of the maturing process in nearly every area of human development involves struggling with problems posed by new, unexpected, and/or difficult situations. An astute educator can use simulations, real-life experiences, hostile environments, problem posing, and many other strategies to create a sense of disequilibrium and then guide learners back into a healthy sense of balance. One of the most important keys in using this, however, is that the learners must have total trust in the facilitator of the exercise due to the inherent emotional and mental risk involved in the process.

Jesus often created a sense of disequilibrium in those around him. From the time the Lord asked John to baptize him (Matt. 3:1–17), and from his handling of those trying to trick him (e.g., Mark 14:13–17) to his resurrection appearances (e.g., Luke 24:36–49), Jesus frequently made comments or asked questions that caused his listeners to rethink much of what they had been taught about God.

The theory of disequilibrium is important to understand both as a cognitive development issue and as a teaching strategy. Forming and reforming knowledge is a task all people are engaged in most of their lives. The ability to do this effectively can prove beneficial in a variety of educational and ministry settings.

DAN LAMBERT

Bibliography. V. B. Gillespie (1988), *The Experience of Faith;* J. W. VanderZanden (1997), *Human Development;* J. C. Wilhoit and J. M. Dettoni, eds. (1995), *Nurture That Is Christian: Developmental Perspectives on Christian Education.*

See also ACCOMMODATION; ASSIMILATION; EQUILIBRIUM

Distance Education. Education involving a teacher and a student separated by physical location, culture, language, or time. Consequently, issues of quality instruction over a distance are complex. The history of distance education includes instances of simply replacing lecture content with reading, research, and writing. In these instances, successful learning is correlated with quality of prior learning, individual student motivation, and richness of the instructional context. Superior academic achievement is attainable when program designs incorporate expert personal mentoring, strong developmental activities, and well-defined learning outcomes.

Contemporary distance education evolved from European correspondence study. It became established in the United States in the late nineteenth century when William Raney Harper in 1892 implemented correspondence study at the University of Chicago. A revival of collegiate independent study occurred after World War II, eventually becoming established through organizations such as the National University Continuing Education Association. The two most prevalent forms of Christian distance education have been correspondence study and theological education by extension (TEE), which frequently includes a mixture of instruction, mentoring, and correspondence study. Noncredit correspondence study has enabled effective evangelism and Christian nurture in conjunction with radio broadcasting in regions of the world closed to direct missionary efforts.

Necessary elements of excellent distance education are educational planning, instructional design, mediated delivery, and learning assessment. Transformations of classroom courses into distance learning are less effective than dedicated designs. The former tend to modify academic delivery while the latter intend to deliver educational modification. The former change methods while the latter employ methods to change behavior.

Traditional classroom instruction normally employs synchronous interaction. Teachers and students communicate locally and immediately. Distance education interaction is customarily asynchronous. International distance education participants regularly experience communication gaps of days and weeks. Technology has reduced dialogue delay, but time zones, technology lag, and life circumstances require asynchronous learning networks (ALNs). On-campus asynchronous "distributed learning" strategies blur distinctions between classroom instruction and distance learning.

Education across linguistic and cultural boundaries has received less attention. Communication difficulties in distance learning mirror translation challenges in Bible translation. Answers lie in the theory and practice of dynamic equivalence in concept transmission. Differences in reasoning patterns, learning preferences, and contextual dynamics must be accommodated. In many cases, on-site instructional facilitators can maximize cross-cultural understanding. However, significant media and method adjustments are necessary for many target populations. The most effective approaches employ partnerships among curriculum designers, content experts, and regional practitioners in demonstration of Christian community.

DANIEL C. STEVENS

Bibliography. M. G. Moore and G. Kearsley, *Distance Education: A Systems View;* B. L. Watkins and S. J. Wright, *The Foundations of American Distance Education.*

See also BIBLICAL EDUCATION BY EXTENSION; THEOLOGICAL EDUCATION BY EXTENSION

Distortion. Psychological concept, emerges from the psychoanalytic theory of Sigmund Freud. It is the modification of unconscious impulses into forms acceptable by the conscious.

Freud believed that personality is composed of three structures. The first is the *id*, the seat of innate desires which provides the primary source of psychic energy. It operates on the pleasure principle, seeking immediate gratification. The second structure is the *ego*, operating on the *reality principle*, the rational, the link to the external world. The third structure is *the superego*, composed of the conscience and the ego ideal, which opposes both the pleasure principle and the reality principle. The conscience is primarily negative, made up of prohibitions, while the ego ideal provides ideals toward which the person strives. The ego serves three masters: the id, the superego, and the external world. When possible, the ego makes the mediation in a realistic way, using problem-solving skills. But it is in this mediation that distortion may occur, that is, usual problem-solving skills are inadequate so that unconscious impulses are made acceptable to the external world and the superego through defense mechanisms.

Defense mechanisms occur when the anxiety of the ego cannot be resolved in a realistic way. Five main defense mechanisms are described in Freudian literature. *Repression* prevents a threatening thought from emerging into the conscious. *Reaction formation* masks an unacceptable emotion by focusing on its opposite. *Projection* attributes anxiety-producing thoughts to people and objects in the external world. *Regression* allows a person to revert to an earlier level of development. *Fixation* halts a component of personality development. These mechanisms serve a useful purpose in times of high anxiety by allowing a person to deal with high anxiety, but they may prevent personality from developing appropriately because reality becomes distorted to the extent that normal adjustment is deterred.

ELEANOR A. DANIEL

Divorce. Marriage was viewed among the Hebrews as a binding contract between families that covered a lifetime. Occasionally, as in most other societies, there was in some marriages a perceived need for dissolution of that contract. Divorce, in these instances, was the judicial term which indicated, etymologically, a cutting off.

In the Old Testament era it would seem that the power of divorce lay with the husband. It could be exercised when he found "something indecent about her" (Deut. 24:1–4), which Jesus later seems to describe as marital unfaithfulness, or adultery. "But I tell you," said the Lord, "that anyone who divorces his wife, except for marital unfaithfulness, causes her to become an adulteress, and anyone who marries the divorced woman commits adultery" (Matt. 5:32). And, "Anyone

who divorces his wife and marries another woman commits adultery, and the man who marries a divorced woman commits adultery" (Luke 16:18). It is instructive that in Matthew, when talking about divorce, Jesus speaks first about God's marital ideal and then interprets the "indecency" of the Deuteronomy pericope as "marital unfaithfulness" (Matt. 19:3–12).

A question that naturally arises in a culture where divorce has proliferated significantly in the last half of the twentieth century is: Should divorced persons remarry? It would appear that remarriage was allowed in the Bible, even encouraged in some circumstances (Ruth; Rom. 7:3; 1 Tim. 5:14). But in the case of divorce, the answer is less clear, particularly in light of the words of Jesus. Debate has ensued as to the legitimacy of remarriage after divorce, and when and why it is appropriate. Varying denominations and their respective disciplines approach the subject with a wide range of biblically informed conclusions although increased leniency seems to be a common propensity.

The dilemma for Christian educators is developing an appropriate response in light of a nation, world, and church with far too many families torn asunder by divorce. This response may well define the efficacy of discipleship training and retraining in the local church for years to come.

The first line of defense against widespread marital dissolution is a proper introduction to the concepts of love, sexual purity, the family, marital commitment, and related topics at the early ages of Christian maturity and continuing through adulthood. Not only should these emphases be taught in the classrooms of the church but within nuclear families as well. One of the challenges of the church, therefore, is how to enable families to become self-educating entities that, through lessons modeled and verbally proclaimed, teach future participants in the marriage covenant how to maximize future wedded relationships.

Premarital counseling has long been viewed as a facilitator of the marriage bond. But much of what happens in this "counseling" should, in fact, be educational in nature, including the introduction of biblical principles and the instruction of practical, biblically based guidelines. Seminars and multimedia resources have been found helpful at these points, but mentorships with older and successfully married couples are among the best ways to teach necessary concepts. One of the demonstrated effects of such counseling and education is the reduction of divorce; in communities where pastors have covenanted together to provide counseling to all who choose to have church weddings, the divorce rate has been significantly impacted.

After marriage, Christian educators can continue to disseminate concepts vital to the spiritual and emotional growth of a marriage through discipleship groups tailored to the married couple and through seminars. While crisis intervention will undoubtedly still be necessary in some marriages, Christian education can have a fortifying effect for those experiencing marriage and all its potential opportunities and challenges: financial difficulties, job changes, children, marital disagreements, etc.

There is also a need for education and counseling at the point of re-entry into marriage after death or divorce. The various issues that surround second and subsequent unions are obviously different than those of the first marriage and should be treated with renewed educational intensity. Part of the educational function of the church should include lending aid at these points, especially given the fact that second and subsequent marriages have a diminishing success rate as compared to initial unions.

In sum, the educational ministry of the church entails the entire array of issues involving Christian discipleship. From Genesis forward the family has been the strategic primary focus of the instruction of God's people. When divorce threatens the healthy survival of the nuclear family of those in and beyond the church, Christian educators must be willing to rise to meet the challenge.

MATT FRIEDEMAN

Divorce, Children of. *Current Situation.* Divorce affects millions of children in the United States. The numbers change on a yearly basis, but annually one divorce is awarded for every two marriages in America.

One-quarter of Americans who are married have also experienced one divorce. Two out of every three marriages that occur at the present time will not survive as long as both spouses live (Sell, 1995, 42). Half of first-time marriages and two-thirds of second marriages end in divorce (Dycus and Dycus, 1987, 19).

The Family Research Council has estimated that as many as one-third of today's children will experience their parents' divorce and close to half will spend some time in a single-parent family before the age of 18 (Sell, 1995, 28). Seventy percent of all couples who divorce have children under the age of 18 (Dycus and Dycus, 1995, 19). While mothers head 90 percent of single-parent homes, single-parent homes headed by fathers are becoming more common (10 percent). The percentage of families with two parents and children under age 18 has declined from half of all families in 1970 to 36 percent of families in 1995. Single-parent homes have become more common, comprising approximately 12 percent of families in the United States (Olson and Leonard, 1996, 38).

Children's Responses to Their Parents' Divorce. Children may respond positively and negatively to their parents' divorce. On the negative side a child may learn to hate, to be fearful, and to distrust others. On the positive side a child may learn to be more compassionate and kind, to be forgiving, to be strong and persevere in difficult circumstances.

Reactions of children to divorce relate to the age when the divorce occurs. In early childhood through preschool, the child often shows fear and regressive behaviors (bed-wetting, thumb sucking), desires physical contact, may struggle in peer relationships, feels a loss of security, retreats into fantasy, is confused, angry, or guilty.

Schoolage children may express behavior changes at school with a drop in grades, experience trouble concentrating, or may give up easily. They may become irritable, moody, aggressive, or possessive. Depression and aimlessness may also become problems for schoolage children. Children report self-blame, feelings of being different than their peers, and a heightened sensitivity to interpersonal incompatibility.

Teenagers may respond to the divorce by becoming angry, intolerant, or depressed. They may withdraw, become isolated from others, run away from their problems (literally or figuratively), and act out sexually at an early age. As they move into young adulthood and begin to contemplate their own marriage, they may express fear of commitment and worry about stability in marriage.

Physical responses to divorce which may be present in children of any age include headaches, stomachaches, nervousness, sleeplessness or excessive sleeping, overeating, or loss of appetite (Dycus and Dycus, 1987, 68).

Custody arrangements directly affect a child's experience of divorce. Some researchers advocate the development of a "binuclear family system," or a family system with two nuclei. This assumes joint custody and may not be possible in some situations. Research indicates that the child's sense of loss is diminished if contact with both parents is maintained (Olson and Leonard, 1990, 42–43).

A Biblical Response to Children of Divorce. Biblical themes of care for widows and orphans, care for the poor, and justice are especially appropriate when discussing children of divorce.

> James 1:27 states, 'Religion that is pure and undefiled before God . . . is this: to visit orphans and widows in their affliction.' Would it be too farfetched to suspect that not only widows but all attempting to rear children without a spouse's partnership might be included in this verse? (Olson and Leonard, 54)

In both Old and New Testaments, special care is advocated for widows and orphans. The prophets, psalmists, and Jesus spoke of care for the poor. Children of divorce are often among the poor in our country with half of all single-parent families living below the poverty level. Jesus was tender and compassionate with children. Jesus spoke of the church as the "family of God" and emphasized that the church was to function as a family that supports, loves, nurtures, and empowers its members.

The Church's Response to Children of Divorce. There are three types of support the church can offer to children of divorce: (1) emotional support that communicates care and appreciation; (2) esteem support, helping persons know they are valued and valuable; (3) network support, providing a group of people with mutual care for one another, information, and other aid for solving problems. This can come through formal channels (professionally facilitated support or therapy groups) and informal channels (sharing with other children of divorce in the school, neighborhood, and church).

The following are specific suggestions for how the church can help children of divorce:

- Do a church or community assessment to discover how many families are in need of support and ministry. An assessment can also uncover community and church resources that are available to help in the process.

- Offer specialized ministries for children of divorce: offer a support group for children of various ages, provide resources for parents to read together with their children, develop a mentor program that links adults in the congregation with the children of divorce, provide prayer partners for children of divorce and their parents, provide family support by connecting newly divorced families with families who have successfully navigated the troubled waters of divorce and emerged healthy and whole on the other side.

- Adapt current church ministry programming to be more friendly to children of divorce. Encourage teachers to use illustrations of single-parent families in their teaching. Encourage teachers to visit in the homes of children of divorce so that they have a better understanding of the students' home situation. Make sure that children of divorce are not excluded from church activities due to visitation schedules. Things such as perfect attendance awards or projects that carry over from week to week may be difficult for a child who only attends every other week. Providing transportation and funding for events may be helpful. Be sensitive about parent/child functions such as a father/son outing or a mother/daughter banquet, when the child may have only one

parent who is regularly involved in his or her life. Provide "surrogate" parents from the church for events such as these if they are held.

- Confront attitudes that assume that children of divorce come from "broken" homes. Their single-parent homes may have more potential for "wholeness" than if their parents had remained married (especially if there was domestic violence, or drug and alcohol abuse). Offer unconditional love and acceptance to children regardless of the type of home from which they come. Act upon the belief that God can heal the pain of divorce and bring wholeness to all members of the family, regardless of the family structure (Dycus and Dycus, 1987, 83).

- Affirm the church as the family of God. Create relationships within the church which provide family-like connections for children of divorce.

DENISE MUIR KJESBO

Bibliography. J. Conway (1990), *Adult Children of Legal or Emotional Divorce: Healing Your Long-Term Hurt;* J. and B. Dycus (1987), *Children of Divorce;* K. Gangel and J. Wilhoit (1996), *The Christian Educator's Handbook on Family Life Education;* R. Olson and J. Leonard (1996), *A New Day for Family Ministry;* idem (1990), *Ministry with Families in Flux: The Church and Changing Patterns of Life;* C. Sell (1995), *Family Ministry;* J. Smoke (1984), *Living Beyond Divorce: The Possibilities of Remarriage.*

Dobbins, Gaines Stanley (1886–1978). A pioneer in religious education who greatly influenced the Southern Baptist Convention. Born in Mississippi, he was the son and grandson of farmers. In spite of growing up in Sunday school and church, he was a self-proclaimed agnostic and a rebellious teenager. After finishing high school, he worked as a journalist, then entered Mississippi College, a Baptist school, in 1905 with enough advanced-standing credits to skip a year. A year later, he became a Christian. After graduation, he taught English at South Mississippi College for a year. Still searching for God's will, Dobbins enrolled in Southern Baptist Theological Seminary in Louisville, Kentucky, and graduated in 1913 with a Th.M. and a Th.D. a year later.

During seminary and for a year afterward, Dobbins pastored churches. In the fall of 1916, he accepted an invitation to work as an editor at the Sunday School Board of the Southern Baptist Convention and served there with different publications. In 1920, he reluctantly started a thirty-six-year teaching career at Southern Baptist Theological Seminary, beginning as professor of Sunday school pedagogy (Christian education) and church efficiency (administration), while continuing to edit. He inaugurated a new department, now called the School of Christian Education. Because textbooks in these areas were inadequate, Dobbins began writing his own. To broaden his knowledge and improve his teaching, he studied education at five other schools, earning an M.A. at Columbia and almost completing a Ph.D. from the University of Chicago. (He refused to rewrite his dissertation to criticize the educational methods of Southern Baptists. Later his alma mater gave him two honorary doctorates.) This background helped him teach seminary students how to be administrators in their churches as well as preachers.

After his retirement from classroom teaching, he served as seminary treasurer and interim president. Then he became dean of the School of Religious Education from 1953 to 1956. After retiring from the Seminary, he moved to Golden Gate Baptist Theological Seminary as professor of church administration where he stayed for ten years. But he continued to teach as a visiting lecturer, preach, and write until he died.

Dobbins's long list of books focus primarily on Christian education but also include volumes on evangelism, the church, and the spiritual life. *A Ministering Church* became a standard textbook for church administration classes in Bible colleges and seminaries. In his classic book, *Learning to Lead*, Dobbins addressed the need for "consecrated, competent, conscientious leadership" (7). He focused on principles more than methods with a view to motivate, enlist, develop, and guide potential leaders. A number of books trained Sunday school teachers and enlarged Dobbins's influence beyond the seminary level.

LIN JOHNSON

Doctrine of the Church. The word *church* has come to be used in a variety of ways. Context and intent alone must be understood to determine which meaning is being implied. The scope of the meaning is broad. *Church* could refer to the physical building, the programmatic activities of a congregation, the worship service specifically, the actual adherents of a local congregation themselves, or, in the universal sense, all those who are genuine in faith worldwide.

Definition. The current English word *church*, which comes from the Greek adjective *kyriakos*, was first used to mean "the house of the Lord," the focus being on the structure itself. The New Testament use of church is derived from the Greek word *ekklesia*, which referred to a public gathering or assembly of people for any purpose, but with time came to mean an assembly of those of Christian faith. Other related Hebrew words are *edah*, which is simply translated as "assembly," *synagoge*, meaning "to push together" and thus became the sacred gathering of the cho-

sen ones of Israel; and *qahal*, which is best translated as "the assembly of God's people."

Usage. The word church (*ekklesia*) in the New Testament refers primarily to the community of God's people (109 times). Its usage is well dispersed within the New Testament, including the two passages in the Gospels (Matt. 16:18; 18:17), 23 times used in Acts, 46 times in Paul's writings, 20 times in Revelation, with the remaining few instances in Hebrews and James. In most cases church refers to the local assembly of believers with a few referring to the universal church (Acts 8:3, 9:31; 1 Cor. 12:8, 15:9; 2 Cor. 1:1; Eph. 1:22–23; Col. 1:18).

Metaphors. To capture fully the rich meaning of church in Scripture, a variety of metaphors need to be understood. The church is referred to as the people of God (Heb. 4:9, 11:25; 1 Peter 2:10), the kingdom of God (Matt. 6:33, 12:28), the temple of God (1 Cor. 3:16, 17), the bride of Christ (Eph. 5:22–32; Rev. 21:9), the body of Christ (Eph. 1:22, 23; 1 Cor. 12:27), God's building (1 Cor. 3:9), God's vineyard (Matt. 12:31), God's household (Eph. 2:19), the flock of God (1 Peter 5:2; John 10:16), the family in heaven and earth (Eph. 3:15), the salt of the earth (Matt. 5:13), the light of the world (Matt. 5:14), a letter from Christ (2 Cor. 3:2–3), the branches of the vine (John 15:5), the chosen lady (2 John 1), Christ's ambassadors (2 Cor. 5:20), the children of God (1 John 3:1–2), and members of Christ (1 Cor. 6:15), a chosen people, a royal priesthood, a holy nation, a people belonging to God (1 Peter 2:9).

Purpose. The church, as designed by God, determined by Jesus Christ, and delineated by the writers of Scripture, has become the central agency through which God is accomplishing His work in the world. Jesus said, "Upon this rock I will build my church and the gates of Hades will not overcome it" (Matt. 16:18).

The purpose of the church is to build God's kingdom, his rule in the hearts and lives of people. This purpose is achieved through five avenues:

1. Evangelism: sharing the Good News of Jesus Christ throughout the world.
2. Teaching and preaching: clearly and publicly declaring God's Word and will for mankind.
3. Training and discipling: assisting new believers to become grounded in their faith.
4. Developing community: enjoying both fellowship and accountability with brothers and sisters.
5. Exercising spiritual gifts: encouraging the development of individual service within the body of Christ.

The church is further identified by the Christ-ordained sacraments of baptism and the Lord's supper (Matt. 3:13–17, 26:26–29).

DAVID A. CURRIE

Bibliography. R. Banks and R. P. Stevens, eds. (1997), *The Complete Book of Everyday Christianity;* C. Brown, ed. (1975), *The New International Dictionary of New Testament Theology;* W. A. Elwell, ed. (1984), *Evangelical Dictionary of Theology;* W. A. Elwell, ed. (1996), *Evangelical Dictionary of Biblical Theology;* E. F. Harrison, ed. (1960), *Baker's Dictionary of Theology;* X. Léon-Dufour (1980), *Dictionary of the New Testament.*

Dogmatic Approach. *See* Authoritative Approach.

Drama as a Teaching Method. The Old Testament provides ample precedent for dramatic teaching, notably in the work of the prophets, and more specifically, Elijah and Ezekiel. Drama, not to be confused with role playing as a teaching method, may require long rehearsals, costuming, stage layout, and other preparations. Consequently, most teachers use it rarely. But when used effectively, it becomes a powerful teaching approach. Drama can enhance worship experiences as well as stimulate thought on significant issues. Often it serves as a good introduction to group discussion. In such situations, the problems of costuming and rehearsal can be bypassed.

In addition to full-length plays, one must consider in this category improvisations, short scenes, and one-act plays. Drama becomes most effective as a learning experience when teachers exercise patience and great care in the choice of the play. The role of the director is important as well.

Knowles recommends heavy involvement by the "audience" in dramatic presentations aimed at learning. He suggests, "Bring representatives from the audience on to the platform to serve as reaction or watchdog teams. . . . to the extent that the people selected to serve on the panel are truly representative of the main characteristics of the audience (age, occupation, special interests, sex, geography), to that extent will the audience be psychologically identified with the interaction on the platform" (Knowles, 1970, 153).

KENNETH O. GANGEL

Bibliography. J. L. Elias (1982), *The Foundation and Practice of Religious Education;* K. O. Gangel (1974), *24 Ways to Improve Your Teaching;* M. S. Knowles (1970), *Modern Practice of Adult Education;* J. M. Peters et al. (1991), *Adult Education;* R. E. Y. Wickett (1991), *Models of Adult Religious Education Practice.*

Dramatization. It was Edgar Dale who reminded educators of the greater impact of a truth that is experienced over the truth that is simply heard. As the old Chinese proverb puts it, "Tell me, I forget; show me, I remember; involve me, I understand." Thus, the use of drama in the classroom becomes a very effective tool for making Christian truth vivid, memorable, and real. Like the greater drama of redemption played out on the stage of time, drama in the classroom helps an educator make "the word become flesh."

The use of drama can take many forms in the classroom of the Christian educator. But, essentially, at its heart is the simple idea of using our bodies to learn more effectively. Drama may be used in the classroom to help students more vividly experience a biblical narrative, or more personally understand and wrestle with issues raised by a particular biblical truth. Drama can be used to give students the opportunity to articulate their own thoughts and ideas through the mouth of an imaginary character when they might not feel free enough to articulate them as their own thoughts and ideas. And drama can be a wonderful way of building community and enhancing the learning atmosphere by just allowing people to have fun together.

Although most of us think of drama simply in terms of a "skit" or a "role-play," the various uses and forms of drama in a classroom are limited only by our imagination. Here is a sampling of some of the varied formats in which people have made use of drama in the classroom:

Scripture Role-Play: Students act out a biblical narrative based on the actual words of the text in Scripture.

Imaginative Role-Play: Students act out a conversation that *might* have happened, drawing from a biblical episode that *did* happen. For example, a husband and wife walking home together, talking about the amazing miracle they had been a part of that afternoon when "that man Jesus fed that huge crowd of us, with only the loaves and fish of that small boy."

Spontaneous Melodrama: A narrator reads through a script, based on anything from a biblical passage to a comic episode or a children's fairy tale. As the narrator reads the script, the students act out the parts spontaneously. If there is a spoken line, they speak it; if there is an action taken, they act it out.

Mime: This common dramatic technique of portraying a scene without use of dialogue can be a way to make biblical narratives, ideas, and applications more vivid. For example, a group of students read the story of Jesus' encounter with Zacchaeus (Luke 19) and are told that they may choose only one line from the narrative that can be spoken. The rest of the story must be told without use of words. Or, small groups of students are given the assignment of brainstorming and acting out what Jesus means when he says, "Love your neighbor."

Tag Team Dialogue: Two teams of participants act out an ongoing dialogue between two characters, with a new person from each team taking on the role at the prompting of the teacher. For example, the role play is between two husbands talking about the difficulties of balancing the sometimes competing responsibilities of father-hood, husband-hood, and livelihood. There are three people actually assigned to play *each* of the two characters. The dialogue begins with the two characters talking to each other, and at the prompting of the teacher, two new people play the same characters picking up the dialogue right where it had been left by the two previous people. This is a technique that involves more people than a normal two-person dialogue and a fun way to get new ideas into a dialogue.

DUFFY ROBBINS

Bibliography. C. Bolte and P. McCusker (1987), *Youth Ministry: Drama and Comedy;* P. Burbridge and M. Watts (1979), *Time to Act;* M. LeFever (1996), *Creative Teaching Methods.*

Dramatize. *See* Play, Role in Childhood Education.

Dream. *See* Vision.

Drugs. The use and abuse of chemical substances is one of the most critical societal problems impacting today's church. The international narcotics industry is the *largest* growth industry in the world. Its annual revenues exceed *half a trillion* dollars (Mills, 1987). Cocaine, heroin (opium), alcohol, and marijuana have all been cultivated and used for centuries. They are now such a severe problem, in part, because we live in an age that has lost its spiritual compass. In small towns and large, drugs are being used to fill the vacuum in human hearts that only God can truly satisfy.

The majority of people with drug dependency began their cycle of addiction by experimenting with a gateway drug. Alcohol, cigarettes, and marijuana are the three gateway drugs. While not everyone who tries them becomes addicted, most addicts began their habits with one member of this triad.

Addiction develops from an unhealthy choice of using drugs as a coping mechanism for dealing with the pain of living. Pain is a normal and necessary part of life. It promotes us to change, to grow, and to stay out of trouble. How we learn to deal with pain is most important. Many today maintain that having any kind of pain is unacceptable. But the reality is that "the sin of drug addiction is the *loss* of what we have been created to be" (Cleave, 1987, 47).

Experts believe that the problem of drug abuse is just as great in the church as it is for society. However, it is frequently covered up and its existence is denied. There is often additional guilt-stigma attached to drug abuse—"This couldn't happen to my family because we're Christians."

It is helpful to distinguish four common types of drug users. *The Experimenter* uses up to four or five times to gain acceptance and "be in the know." The use is short-term and low in frequency. *The Recreationist* takes drugs to share pleasurable experiences with friends. *The Seeker* seeks to achieve altered mood or mental state and uses drugs regularly to achieve a sedative or intoxicant effect. *The Drug Head* has moved to regular use of hard drugs. Often addicted to cocaine or heroin, this person shows serious deficiencies in interpersonal relationships (Parrott, 1993). Different coping and counseling strategies may be employed with each type of user.

Religious organizations have historically sent clear messages against substance abuse. To promote this they can: (1) Make substance abuse education a regular part of youth groups. Focus on the Family's video *Masquerade* is a fine tool for this. (2) Educate clergy, volunteers, and parents about substance abuse and addiction. (3) Reach out to teens who are experimenting with addictive substances. (4) Openly discuss the feelings and emotions which might cause individuals to use drugs. (5) Provide case studies to develop decision-making skills and value clarification. (6) Support families coping with addicted abusers. (7) Establish recover groups. *The Eleventh Step* of La Canada Presbyterian Church and *T O U C H—* Transforming Others Under Christ's Hand—offer church-based recovery materials. *Overcomers Outreach Inc.* is a Christian twelve-step program with support groups in forty-six states. (8) Develop inpatient and outpatient referral systems. One-year residential programs are available from *His Mansion* and *Teen Challenge.*

JAMES A. DAVIES

Bibliography. S. V. Cleave (1987), *Counseling for Substance Abuse and Addiction,* vol. 12, *Resources for Christian Counseling;* J. Mills (1987), *The Underground Empire;* L. Parrott, III (1993), *Helping the Struggling Adolescent. His Mansion,* Box 210, Hillsboro, NH 03244–0040. TOUCH, 1226 S. Presa, San Antonio, TX 78210. Teen Challenge, Box 198, Rehrersburg, PA 19550. La Canada Presbyterian Church, 626 Foothill Blvd., La Canada, CA 91011.

Drunkenness. *See* Alcoholism.

Dysfunctional. One of the basic theories of sociology is "functionalism," which emphasizes the importance of each segment of society accomplishing the purpose for which it exists. Thus schools are functional when they educate and prepare people for living in society. Likewise, churches and families can be considered functional when they accomplish their respective purposes. Functionalism has much in common with some of the central doctrines of evangelical Christianity (Ratcliff, 1988).

To be *dysfunctional,* an organization or segment of society acts in a manner that directly undercuts the original purpose for which it is intended. For example, if an excellent teacher is promoted to an administrative position and a poorer teacher takes her place, the educational function of the school is less likely to be accomplished. Similarly, if a church exists for the purpose of teaching the Bible and providing fellowship for believers yet spends most of its time in fundraising and committee work, the net result may be that the church is not accomplishing the intended goals. Dysfunctional behavior is not just something added to the purposes for which the group was created (such as fundraising added to Bible teaching); rather, dysfunctions make the original purposes of the group less likely to occur (fundraising begins to replace Bible teaching).

Dysfunctions are particularly likely to occur in the more advanced stages of an organization's development. Moberg (1984) diagrams the development of religious organizations in five stages, with dysfunctions being most likely to occur in the final stages. Similarly, Ratcliff (1994) found parallel stages in a home Bible study group, with dysfunctions surfacing in the latter stages of the group's development. While Moberg emphasizes the long-term development of church organizations, Ratcliff found the stages and dysfunctions emerging during the first few months of the group's existence.

Families can also be dysfunctional. Charles Sell (1995) and Jon Harris (1995) describe the potential role of Christian educators providing family ministry to help counteract family dysfunctions. Harris describes three common dysfunctional characteristics that undermine healthy family life: extreme rigidity, maintaining silence about problems, and isolation from those outside the family. He also states that dysfunction can be the product of "generational sin," the unhealthy influence passed from parents to children, grandchildren, and other descendants (Exod. 20:4–6). Family ministry at its best encourages the vibrant practice of faith as a means of replacing dysfunctional family life with healthy interpersonal relationships.

DONALD E. RATCLIFF

Bibliography. J. R. Harris (1995), *Handbook of Family Religious Education;* D. O. Moberg (1984), *The Church as a Social Institution,* 2nd ed.; D. Ratcliff, *Creation, Social Science, and Humanities Quarterly* 10, no. 4 (1988); idem (1994), *Christian Views of Sociology,* pp. 143–48; C. M. Sell (1995), *Family Ministry,* 2nd ed.

Ee

Early Adolescence. The early adolescent experience is marked by overwhelming transitions. The onset of puberty affects students physically, socially, emotionally, mentally, and spiritually. Guiding students through this life-changing metamorphosis that occurs between ages eleven and fourteen can be a challenge for parents, teachers, and ministers alike.

A young adolescent can exhibit a wide range of behaviors within a very short time frame. Without warning she can erupt with a case of the giggles or burst into tears. His flash of high energy can crash into lethargy at a moment's notice. Seemingly mature adult behavior can nosedive into a childish tantrum in an instant. Deciding to do something one moment and then doing the exact opposite the next moment is not uncommon. When ministering to early adolescents it is important to remember that most often abnormal *is* normal for this age group.

Some students weather this transition with little if any difficulties, but the majority of students struggle during these years and many find it nearly impossible to cope with the pressures and demands of the middle school years. In his classic work *Identity, Youth and Crisis*, Erik Erikson (1968) suggests that it is during this time in life that individuals begin to see themselves as having a past and a future that are exclusively theirs. This is a pivotal time of both review and anticipation. Students are searching for their personal uniqueness, a continuity of experience, and a solidarity with group ideals as they strive to form a distinct identity.

These early years of adolescence are filled with failed attempts to leave childhood behind in the search for a unique identity. This is the first time that young people try to sever ties with their families or other established authority figures in an attempt to gain some independence. With parents often misunderstanding this transition time and reluctant to grant the independence their children seek, all too often early teens see the only avenue to search for identity and independence as all-out rebellion. Juvenile crime, running away, drug use, pregnancy, and suicide are not uncommon among this age group. There is overwhelming evidence to demonstrate that early adolescence is a uniquely troubling time that requires the full and undivided attention of the church.

Anyone ministering to or teaching early adolescents should fully understand the unique opportunity that has been granted to them. Middle school students are remarkably inquisitive and unashamedly open. As their minds are rapidly developing they often call into question much of what they have been taught. Childhood fables crumble as they discover new ways of perceiving reality. Truth is no longer blindly accepted, without question, when dispensed by teachers and parents. Students want to understand truth for themselves.

Questioning their childhood faith is normal during this time of transition. Middle schoolers often question or reject the values and beliefs that they acquired during childhood. It is often not until they can confirm that their childhood values and beliefs are relevant to their newly formed identity that they accept the faith which has been imparted to them as their own. Understanding that this is a time of important questioning, the church must be prepared to offer middle schoolers thoughtful and honest answers to the questions and issues that dominate their emerging faith. When the church has attempted to retrieve their high school dropouts, more than one student has responded: "Where were you when I was asking those questions a few years ago?"

In the midst of a very confusing time of life, early adolescents are extremely open to new ideas and opportunities. Because the search for identity is a complex process of trial and error, students may take on a behavior which they feel coincides with their idea of who they want to be and how they want to be perceived by others. But if they become dissatisfied with the feedback they receive, they will dismiss the behavior and seek out an alternative. This is why middle school is such an adventure, accepting a behavior, a concept, a faith one week and then rejecting it the next.

Middle school ministry expert Wayne Rice (1997) suggests that the great danger of such openness is when it takes the form of gullibility. The middle schooler is an easy target for Madison Avenue, the music industry, TV advertising, drug dealers, or anyone selling anything. They are all after the soul of the early adolescent and there could not be a more appropriate time for the evangelical church to offer a Christian alternative.

If children grow up in the church, they will have amassed a significant amount of knowledge about God by the time they reach early adolescence. But it is the use of Bible knowledge, not the mere possession of it, which produces growth and maturity in Christ. Middle school students will make numerous decisions and commitments, only a few of which will last a lifetime. If the decisions of students are to be meaningful, they will have to be made as a result of their own reasoning, understanding, and process of elimination. To that end, one of the most important roles that the teacher or pastor can play in the life of an early adolescent is that of a role model.

Modeling the Christian life for middle school students should be both planned and spontaneous. As teachers plan their lessons for Sunday school, Bible study, or youth group they should ask themselves: "How will I be modeling the Christian life before my students as I teach this lesson?" This provides students with a Christlike standard to imitate. As unexpected situations arise, teachers and ministers should be prepared to offer a Christlike response. Through positive Christian modeling students will be influenced in their understanding and assimilating of the attributes of Christ and perhaps make lasting faith decisions.

These are critical years in which the evangelical church has a unique opportunity. At no other time in a person's life are so many options considered, changes made, and lives shaped. Youthful minds and open hearts have numerous questions that require honest responses as they try to establish an identity that might include Christ.

MARK W. CANNISTER

Bibliography. E. Erikson (1968), *Identity, Youth and Crisis;* R. Habermas and K. Issler (1992), *Teaching for Reconciliation: Foundations and Practice of Christian Educational Ministry;* K. Issler and R. Habermas (1994), *How We Learn: A Christian Teacher's Guide to Educational Psychology;* W. Rice (1997), *Junior High Ministry;* J. Wilhoit and L. Ryken (1988), *Effective Bible Teaching.*

Early Childhood. Early childhood is often used as a synonym for the preschool child, although educators sometimes use the designation to include the early elementary years as well. Infancy and middle childhood can be contrasted with early childhood.

Young children were generally equated with infancy prior to the modern era. Child abuse was common in earlier eras, and sometimes adults wrongly justified abuse by a theology of inbred sin that must be expunged by adults. In stark contrast, Rousseau emphasized an inherently positive view of the child's basic nature, which is distorted by society's influences. A third position, held by Locke and others, underscores the amoral "blank slate" nature of a child, who is shaped by parents and society. The Bible describes the self-centered and sinful nature of the child (Prov. 22:15), yet also underscores the beauty of this creation of God (Ps. 139:14) and the importance of parents and others training the child in basic values of religious faith (Deut. 6:7).

The number of youngsters in this age range is expected to increase well into the next century, as the number of births each year from 1989 to 1993 equaled the highest birth rates during peak years of the baby boom generation. The rate of births was nearly as high in the years subsequent to 1993. Yet parents commonly report an inadequate amount of Christian education in the home because they have little idea how this can be accomplished (Fay, 1993). This underscores the need for Christian educators teaching parents how to instruct their children, as well as the increased need for Christian education of young children in the church.

Early childhood is considered a relatively unimportant time for Christian education efforts by some churches. Goldman's (1964) research is sometimes cited to substantiate this position, although that is a serious misreading of his position. Goldman discouraged the use of theological content in teaching younger children because of its abstract nature, yet encouraged active experiential learning that would help prepare children for later theological instruction.

Piaget portrayed young children as using intuitive thought, then developing new conceptual abilities at about six or seven years in which they could use logic with concrete objects. While there are important changes during these years for many children, including significant shifts in reading and mathematical abilities, a broad survey of research (Ratcliff, 1988) indicates that changes in most areas of thinking are incremental during early childhood rather than marked by abrupt change as implied by most stage theories. This seems to be implicitly acknowledged by Piaget himself in the phenomenon of *decalage*, in which children develop concrete operational abilities in various areas at different ages.

The intuitive thinking characteristic of young children may indicate that they may profit from Christian education efforts that appeal to intuitive thought rather than logic and abstractions.

Jerome Berryman (1991), for example, encourages experiential physical involvement with parables in which children are told these biblical stories, using movable figures and other props. Children are encouraged to use the story materials and experience the story in their own retelling and movement of the figures.

A very different approach is advocated by Barber (1981), who emphasizes the learning of attitudes through behavioral influence, particularly reinforcement. She outlines an approach that encourages positive attitudes and understandings of the Bible, prayer, worship, and other aspects of faith. A more behavioral approach in teaching young children is also congruent with the moral development characteristics of preschool and early elementary children (Ward, 1979).

Torrance and Torrance (1988) encourage Christian educators to teach young children more abstract concepts such as God being infinite and God as a spirit. Like Berryman, they encourage the use of concrete objects in such learning, although they do not emphasize the intuitive experiencing of religious language as does Berryman.

Play and stories are important Christian education resources with young children (Ratcliff, 1988). The enactment of stories is a vivid means of helping children physically participate as part of their learning, an aspect of many strategies recommended in the Christian education of young children.

An important issue that is sometimes raised in the Christian education of young children is the possibility of salvation. Can they be genuinely converted and should Christian educators make strong appeals for personal commitment? Many Christians report early commitments to Christ, yet the intuitive thinking—characteristic of young children—makes the abstract understanding of salvation unlikely. It may be that youngsters can experience God and the Bible, as Berryman concludes, yet their conceptual reference may be limited. This being the case, it seems likely that a fuller commitment of a more conceptual nature becomes more likely at a later point in life. Assuming this is the case, young children can be encouraged to make decisions to become Christians without requiring them to possess a great deal of theological understanding. In addition, youth ministers can consider the possibility that the common "recommitment to Christ" may reaffirm an earlier intuitive decision, yet broadens that earlier experience to encompass theological concepts and applications that were impossible in early childhood.

The general environment, including the physical surroundings and teachers who relate positively with children, are important components of Christian education. Youngsters probably learn as much from the general context of instruction as they do from the substantive content intended.

This includes the nonverbal components of instruction, peer interactions, and contacts with people in the broader church context. The affective, feeling-centered aspects of Christian education may impact the child as significantly as the prescribed lesson.

Churches have become increasingly aware of the need to prevent physical and sexual abuse of young children, encouraged in this respect by potential and actual litigation. As a result, many Christian education programs now require a careful screening of volunteers (Ratcliff and Neff, 1993), strict abuse prevention guidelines in churches (for example, see *Recruiting Volunteers*), and participation in child abuse seminars.

While there are many programs and curricular designs for young children, and a great deal of research conducted at major universities on general characteristics of preschoolers, there has been very little research of the religious experience and understanding of these youngsters. How do young children conceptualize what they are taught in Christian education contexts, and to what extent do their religious experiences impact their long-term spiritual development? What events occur in Christian education efforts that are not intended, and how do these unplanned experiences influence young children's experiences and conceptualizations? What methods, curricula, and styles of teaching maximize the influence of Christian education with young children? These are important questions that should be addressed by future researchers.

DONALD E. RATCLIFF

Bibliography. L. W. Barber (1981), *The Religious Education of Preschool Children*; J. W. Berryman (1991), *Godly Play: A Way of Religious Education*; M. Fay (1993), *Do Children Need Religion?*; D. Ratcliff (1988), *Handbook of Preschool Religious Education*; D. Ratcliff and B. J. Neff (1993), *The Complete Guide to Religious Education Volunteers*; *Recruiting Volunteers*; E. P. and J. P. Torrance (1988), *Handbook of Preschool Religious Education*; T. Ward (1979), *Values Begin at Home*.

Early Church Education. Christian education in the early church consisted largely of the meeting of believers in local gatherings and the training of children in the context of daily family life. The early church modeled its training paradigm extensively on the Jewish religious education model where the home was the absolute center of education. Churches often met in homes, but also frequently utilized the local synagogue, place of prayer, or marketplace as a forum for teaching and training as well.

Socialization was a powerful method of instruction for the early church, as evident in the emphasis on koinonia in the frequent gatherings of believers (Acts 2:37–47; 4:32–37). These gatherings often followed the pattern of holding a shared meal, followed by instruction in the teachings of Jesus Christ. In the earliest days of the church following Christ's ascension, believers were taught by the apostles themselves. What was taught by the apostles in the local gathering of believers was to be modeled and communicated by the parents to the children through the context of family life. The educational objective was the communication of sound doctrine reflected in a lifestyle of obedience to the gospel message.

Every believer was considered a missionary in the early church and was encouraged to witness to unbelievers; the radical change in lifestyle of Gentile converts often served as the natural opening for sharing the message of the gospel. Persecution of the church did not hinder the expansion of the faith or the education of believers as was intended, for in many circumstances persecution only strengthened the church. As believers gathered together for mutual support and instruction in the midst of persecution, they departed encouraged and empowered to continue boldly in the faith, which had the result of furthering the expansion of the church.

Participation in the Lord's Supper and the observance of baptism of new converts were primary instructional aids of the day, since both practices taught in word and deed the death, burial, and resurrection of Jesus Christ, the heart of the Good News of the Christian faith. As the missionary activity of the church took the apostles across the Roman Empire, teaching and preaching shifted from the apostles to elders trained at the feet of the apostles. The primary text was what is now called the Old Testament, supplemented with the letters from the itinerant apostles, some of which became part of the New Testament canon.

The radical separation of teaching and preaching predominant in Christian education today was not evident in the practices of the early church. The terms *teaching* and *preaching* were used interchangeably in describing the missionary activity of believers. Greek terms in the New Testament such as *paideuo* (training), *noutheteo* (shape the mind), and *hodegeo* (showing the way) suggest that the emphasis on instruction was not just through exhortations on the faith as so often is the focus of contemporary preaching, but through the modeling of that faith in such a way that the thoughts, attitudes, values, and behaviors of believers were shaped to imitate the thoughts, attitudes, values, and behaviors exemplified in the life of Christ.

In addition to the teaching/preaching ministry of the apostles, over time additional teachings of significant leaders in the early church became part of the educational curriculum. These significant leaders are often referred to as the early church fathers. The more famous of these men include: Clement, Bishop of Rome; Ignatius,

Bishop of Antioch; Justin; Irenaeus; Tertullian; Clement of Alexandria; Origen; Cyprian; Athanasius; and Augustine. The common mission of these early church fathers was the defense of sound doctrine in the faith in opposition to the growing number of doctrinal heresies that were infiltrating the teachings of the church. Many of the heresies addressed by the early church fathers were the result of pagan influences brought into the church by Gentile converts. Catechumenate training schools thus arose to educate the growing number of Gentile converts who did not know or respect the Jewish faith heritage of family education so central in the Old Testament era, and who brought with them deep-seated pagan values and behaviors that influenced lifestyle practices. These catechumenate were the first formal education institutions of the early church. The focus of training was on the systematic instruction of sound doctrine and the moral development of those preparing for Christian baptism. Curriculum included the Didache, the Shepherd of Hermas, and other writings by the early church fathers.

As Christianity spread throughout the Roman Empire, the early church found itself at odds with the existing private and public educational systems available for the training of children. Parents were reluctant to keep their children from this training that would give their offspring an advantage in the marketplace, but they worried that the pagan influences in these educational institutions would lead their children astray from the Christian faith. Reluctantly, Christian parents sent their children to these schools that Tertullian described as a necessary evil because of the great need for the training they provided. However, by the time of Julian, the concern over pagan influence lessened as the church essentially annexed the Roman educational system and baptized pagan educational practices for use in the service of the church.

MARK E. SIMPSON

Bibliography. C. V. Anderson (1981), *Introduction to Biblical Christian Education*, pp. 36–52; W. Barclay (1959), *Educational Ideals in the Ancient World;*. K. O. Gangel and W. S. Benson (1983), *Christian Education: Its History and Philosophy*; E. L. Hayes (1981), *Introduction to Biblical Christian Education*, pp. 25–36; M. J. Taylor, ed. (1960), *Religious Education: A Comprehensive Survey.*

Eating Disorders. We live in a nation obsessed with thinness. Scrawny models smile at us from magazines and the television. Their message is clear: "If you want to be happy, popular, and beautiful, you cannot be too thin." Most people are not overly convinced by the "thin-is-in" idea.

However, this message attracts two deeply disturbed groups of people: young preadolescent females and female collegiates. For them, thinness takes priority over everything else. It is patholog-ical. It is compulsive and self-destructive. Bodies cannot go on forever when they lack proper nutrients. The two groups are anorexics (those who starve themselves) and bulimics (those who binge-eat and purge).

Eating disorders are a disease that must be treated with care and competence. Unless handled properly by a person who looks at the underlying attitudes and behaviors from which the destructive behaviors come, the outcome will often be further deterioration and even death. This is particularly true with anorexics, who are frequently rather brittle (Vath, 1986).

Anorexia nervosa is "a life-threatening, self-induced starvation syndrome characterized by the relentless pursuit of thinness and a morbid, near-phobic fear of being fat" (Parrott, 1993, 103). Studies show as many as 4 percent of the young adolescent population (ages 14–18) suffer from it. The death rate for anorexia nervosa can be up to 22 percent. Anorexics are predominately from middle to upper-middle-class white families. Ninety percent of the victims are female. They suffer from severe distoration of body image. Even when obviously emaciated the victims claim to "feel fat."

Bulimia nervosa is characterized by repeated cycles of binge eating with compensaton for food intake by self-induced vomiting, laxative abuse, diuretic abuse, and/or fasting, and excessive exercise. Often depression, discouragement, and conflict tend to cause a rapid and sudden increase in bingeing. Unlike anorexia, the bulimic adolescent is aware her eating pattern is abnormal. Binge eating typically begins around age 18. The average duration is about five years. Half to two-thirds of the victims are on college campuses.

Muscle dismorphia is an obsession with body bulk and is marked by an imbalance of saratonin. The condition occurs predominately among males. Individuals see themselves as small and believe they need to work out for hours every day.

Church educational programming may include: (1) Training parents and church volunteers to recognize the signs of and the difference between anorexia and bulimia. (2) Encouraging Christian parents to raise children who are wise and self confident, not merely submissive and obedient. This involves teaching offspring decision-making and problem-solving skills from data rather than obedience only. (3) Providing solid biblical teaching and preaching on what it means to love self and how to love being a woman. A strong sexual identity and positiveness about being female are critical factors in the development of adolescent Christian young women. (4) Developing pastoral care networks for prayer, acceptance, and encouragement. These diseases are often long-term in nature. It may take months and years of support for the victim and

her family. (5) Establishing a referral system of competent, trained professionals. Rapha and the Minirth Meier New Life Clinics offer fine Christian based inpatient and residential treatment programs.

Eating disorders are a staggering problem among adolescents today. With support groups, counseling, and God's empowerment the person can make a successful, healthy recovery.

JAMES A. DAVIES

Bibliography. L. Parrott III (1993), *Helping the Struggling Adolescent;* R. E. Vath (1986), *Counseling Those with Eating Disorders.*

Echoic Memory. The term *echoic memory* comes from information processing theory (IPT), a cognitive learning theory. IPT uses the analogy of computer processing to explain the storing of meaningful information in humans. When information from the environment (sound, sight) first stimulates a sense organ (ear, eye), it is held for a brief time in sensory memories. These memories, also called registers, are called iconic memory for visual items and echoic memory for auditory items. From sensory registers, information passes to short-term memory where it is encoded into long-term storage in a form which can be recalled and decoded at a later time.

A visual item stored in iconic memory is called an icon because of its pictorial quality. An auditory item stored in echoic memory is called an echo because of its sound quality. Information is stored as electrochemical changes in neurons, called neutron traces, in nerves leading to the brain. Sensory memory holds information from the environment long enough for further processing to take place. Echoic memory endures long enough to piece together sounds in music or syllables in speech, whereas iconic memory endures for only a few milliseconds. This initial stage is where pattern recognition begins. Since information held in sensory registers is raw, unprocessed information, it is seen as an intermediary stage between the environment and internal memory, consisting of short-term and long-term memories.

RICK YOUNT

Bibliography. G. D. Borich and M. L. Tombari (1995), *Educational Psychology: A Contemporary Approach,* pp. 194–95; P. D. Eggen and D. Kauchak (1992), *Educational Psychology: Classroom Connections,* pp. 308–10; N. A. Sprinthall, R. C. Sprinthall, and S. N. Oja (1994), *Educational Psychology: A Development Approach,* pp. 286–88; W. R. Yount (1996), *Created to Learn: A Christian Teacher's Introduction to Educational Psychology,* p. 212.

Ecumenical Education. Founded in 1903 the Religious Education Association (REA) is the oldest ecumenical professional organization for religious educators. It has a current membership of 3,300 composed of Protestant, Catholic, Jewish, and other faiths employed in church and synagogue organizations or in colleges, universities, and seminaries. REA seeks to stimulate research in religious and character education and the development of faith in adults. It publishes *Religious Education Quarterly* and is the primary journal of its kind.

REA holds consultations on religion and higher education, and advises leaders of national boards of education and agencies concerned with the role of religion in public education. They conduct studies on legal problems dealing with religion and higher education. REA confers the William Rainey Harper Award to leading religious educators.

Their publications include the quarterly *Reach: Religious Education Association Clearing House*—a newsletter giving information about developments in religious education and a calendar of upcoming events and obituaries. Another publication is *Religious Education*—a journal of essays, research reports, and book reviews. REA meets annually in various parts of the United States (Gordon, 1993, 2038).

The North American Professors of Christian Education (NAPCE) was founded in 1947 and has a current membership of 250. Their membership includes teachers, former teachers, and professors concerned with Christian education and related subjects in Christian higher education institutions.

NAPCE serves as a professional organization for professors of Christian education in colleges, universities, and seminaries to stimulate professional growth and development through fellowship. They give direction to the formulation and clarification of a policy of evangelical Christian education. They promote research and also give a student scholastic award.

Currently, *Christian Education Journal* is published by Trinity Evangelical Divinity School. It was formerly produced by Scripture Press Publications. NAPCE publishes three times a year *NAPCE Newsletter* containing association news, brief articles, book reviews, and announcements of Christian education meetings. NAPCE was formerly known as the Research Commission of National Sunday School Association (Gordon, 1993, 1684).

The Association of Professors and Researchers in Religious Education (APRRE) is an interfaith organization founded in 1970 and now has 350 members. APRRE is an organization of professors and researchers in religious education in institutions of higher learning and denominational and ecumenical organizations.

APRRE fosters scholarly research and professional development in religious education and provides a forum for the exchange of research and experience. They sponsor presentations and discussions for critical response and diverse viewpoints among members. APRRE bestows an annual recognition award to a doctoral student who submits an outstanding dissertation in religious education.

APRRE publishes annually *Association of Professors and Researchers in Religious Education—Membership Directory*, semiannually *Association of Professors and Researchers in Religious Education—Newsletter*. APRRE publishes *Religious Education* with the REA. They hold their annual meeting in conjunction with the annual meeting of REA. APRRE formerly was known as the Professors and Researchers Section of the Division of Christian Education of the National Council of Churches (Gordon, 1993, 240).

JERRY M. STUBBLEFIELD

Bibliography. J. G. Melton (1993), *Directory of Religious Organizations in the United States.*

Edge, Findley (1916–). Born in Albany, Georgia, he earned his A.B. degree from Stetson University, his Th.M. and Th.D. degrees from Southern, and an M.A. degree from Yale University. Prior to joining the Southern Baptist Theological Seminary faculty, Edge served as pastor in churches in Florida and Kentucky and then as minister of education, Louisville, Kentucky. Edge served as professor of religious education at Southern Baptist Theological Seminary from 1945 until his retirement.

Edge once wrote, "One of the reasons we have not been able to achieve desired results [in Christian living through Sunday school] is that our aims, and therefore our teaching, have not been sufficiently specific. Teachers have been guided by aims that were general and often vague" (1965, 8). The same can be said of much of the Bible teaching that occurs today in our Sunday school classes and cell groups.

Edge's particular interest throughout his ministry was helping Sunday school teachers improve the practical quality of their teaching through training. *Teaching for Results* is perhaps his most popular book, in which he detailed the essential elements of quality teaching in Sunday school: emphasizing results, securing purposeful Bible study, testing our teaching, and securing church-home cooperation, among others.

Edge was "one that recognized the place and importance of personal experience in both theology and education. An experiential philosophy of education places primary emphasis on the conversion experience; holds to the principle of a regenerate church membership; seeks to give adequate consideration to the present, ongoing experience of individuals as well as the incarnation of God in Christ and the Bible; utilizes the test indicated by Jesus, 'By their fruits ye shall know them,' and is based upon individual responsibility before God and free access to Him" (Southern Seminary bio sheet).

Edge deeply influenced the quality of Bible study across the Southern Baptist Convention and beyond through the books he wrote and the students he taught. Edge retired from Southern Seminary in 1982.

RICK YOUNT

Bibliography. F. Edge (1956), *Teaching for Results;* T. T. Sparkman (1985), *Findley B. Edge: Teacher, Theorist, Prophet;* D. Williams (1986), *Newman Findley Bartow Edge: A Search for Authenticity.*

Education in the Epistles. The New Testament Epistles burst with educational directives and implications. Every page rearranges the priorities of natural thinking. In these letters, the reeducation of humanity begins with the gospel. Christian education means more than a simple acceptance of new ideas and facts. Knowledge must mix with faith, love, and obedience.

Paul, Peter, John, Jude, James, and the writer of Hebrews discuss a broad range of educational ideas. The following modern educational categories provide one way to isolate and study their thoughts.

1. Goals of education
2. Content and curriculum
3. Student development
4. Teacher's responsibilities
5. Knowledge
6. Thought processes
7. Methods
8. Testing and evaluation

Goals of Christian Education. Christian education is central to the mission of the church in this age. Without it, worship is without content, fellowship is without boundaries, and service is without mandate. If the goal of Christian education were only the acquisition of correct content, then Christians should spend a great deal of time making sure they have the right answers. In the New Testament, instruction in content serves the higher goal of love. While instruction provides the direction, the Holy Spirit provides the power to love God, love family, love brothers and sisters in Christ, and even love enemies. New Testament love is measured by concrete behavior of patience and kindness (1 Tim. 1:5; Gal. 5:22; 1 Cor. 13:1–8).

The end product of Christian education is a mature life. Mature Christians evidence love and sound judgment by living within the principles and commands laid out by God through the apostles. Over time, each Christian should move toward maturity. Maturity evidences itself in stable theology, sound moral judgment, healthy relationships, and sacrificial service. The New Tes-

tament writers continually invite Christians to begin and remain on the journey to maturity (1 Cor. 2:6; 14:20; Heb. 5:12, 14; Eph. 4:13).

Content and Curriculum of Christian Education. Christian education depends on a truth-based system. Unlike postmodern thinking, the New Testament Epistles make a clear distinction between truth and error. Peter predicts some teachers will deliberately teach "destructive heresy." Throughout the Epistles, New Testament authors urge their readers to resist and correct error (2 Peter 2:1).

Unlike philosophical truth, New Testament truth always evidences itself in changed lives. In New Testament terms, truth must meet the standard of correct answers in words, attitudes, and behavior. Mere verbal assent falls short of the New Testament standard. The New Testament writers constantly measure truth by Christians' attitudes and behavior. No ancient or modern standard for truth reaches so high (Gal. 2:14; James 3:14).

Not everything written on the pages of the New Testament Epistles makes sense to the casual observer. Even as the authors read each other, they acknowledge the complex nature of their writings. The content at times requires effort, deep thinking, and even research into Old Testament backgrounds (2 Peter 3:16).

The curriculum contemplated by the New Testament authors moves from elementary to sophisticated or in its own metaphor, from milk for babes to strong meat for mature Christians. The beginning teachings always anchor the foundation for future development. Believers retain the elementary foundations and expands on them as they grow (Heb. 5:12).

Student Development in Christian Education. Candidates for Christian education include everyone. This broad target frustrates most educators, who prefer to deal exclusively with exceptionally bright and motivated students. However, the audience anticipated by the New Testament documents includes a wide range of innate capacities, motivations, and life circumstances. While several categories of students exist among adults, the traditional categories of rich and poor, male and female, slave and free disappear. New Testament categories measure the individual's movement toward maturity and evidence of the Holy Spirit's work. Each category requires an adjustment in curriculum and approach. For example, Christian teachers must cope with the natural man's inability to accept spiritual things until the Holy Spirit enlightens that person's mind. On the other hand, mature Christians require more substantive teaching. The Jewish background of the early converts in Acts 2 provided a different starting place than the early Greek believers in Acts 11 (1 Cor. 2:14; Col. 1:28; 1 Cor. 4:17).

While Christian education began among adults, the concern of the New Testament authors turns quickly to children. Paul recognizes that children think and reason differently than adults. Nevertheless, he commends an education in the Scriptures that begins as an infant. Other New Testament writers charge both mothers and fathers with this responsibility. Even grandmothers receive commendation for their role in the strategic education of children. These injunctions presuppose that parents have acquired substantial teaching in the Christian faith. All the warnings and injunctions to teachers come to bear on parents as they represent the truth to their children not just through their words but through their actions and attitudes (Eph. 6:4; 2 Tim. 1:5; 1 Cor. 13:11; 2 Tim. 3:14–15).

Teachers' Responsibilities. Leaders within the Christian community were expected to teach. That ability commended them along with other qualifying factors to their office. In Christian education, teachers' attitudes and behaviors validate the truth of their teaching. Teaching was so crucial to the Christian community that the Holy Spirit gave that gift as one of the four foundational gifts. Although many may be called upon to teach, some have particular gifting which broadens the horizon of their ministry. The New Testament authors expect both men and women to teach. This presupposes that both genders have been fully educated in the Christian faith. At the time, teachers were the most respected people in the community. Therefore, warnings about more severe judgment must have caught everyone's attention (1 Tim. 3:2; 2 Tim. 2:2; Titus 2:3; Eph. 4:11–12; James 3:1).

Knowledge. While acquisition of knowledge lies at the center of public education, true Christian knowledge remains a lowly servant to obedience. Paul's note in 2 Corinthians suggests that a passing grade cannot be gained without complete obedience in everything taught and known by the learner. In other words, if someone does not obey what he knows, he really does not know it in the Christian sense. In one way, coming to an understanding of Christian knowledge is passive because the Holy Spirit must work upon the disciple. In another way, remaining in ignorance becomes the responsibility of the learners if their hearts remain hard instead of tender toward God (2 Cor. 2:9; Eph. 1:18; 4:18).

Knowledge from a Christian perspective provides only the means to the end. When knowledge remains unmixed with faith, love, and obedience, it ensnares the unwary. Left alone, knowledge breeds an unhealthy personal attitude of superiority. True Christian education most assuredly must change the attitudes of the follower of Christ (1 Cor. 8:1).

Thought Process. No more amazing feature of New Testament education in the Epistles exists than the call for mental renewal. If done correctly, the believer manifests in an external fashion the internal reality of an indwelling Christ. Unlike the event of salvation, renewal occurs as an ongoing daily process. Furthermore, the Holy Spirit facilitates this daily renewal.

The New Testament expects the renewed mind to bring a different quality of life when compared to the unregenerate or unrenewed person. Ideally, a believer carries around no unwanted thoughts. Instead, each thought reflects the teachings of the New Testament and bears fruit in correct attitudes and behavior. In the midst of life's chaos, the believer chooses to think differently. When tragedy strikes, the believer wraps it in the blanket of a sovereign God and a secure destiny. In reality, the follower of Christ appears out of step with the rest of the world and gives onlookers cause to reflect on the invisible source of strength demonstrated by his or her calm even joyful resolve. The new information about a separation from immorality and other forms of godlessness fuels a new way of thinking about oneself while the world around swims in sin. Reflection on truth keys the process of mental renewal (Rom. 12:2; 2 Cor. 4:16; Eph. 4:23; Rom. 8:6; Rom. 8:7; 2 Cor. 10:5; Phil. 4:8; Col. 3:5; 2 Tim. 2:7).

Methods. The New Testament Epistles reveal many methods of education. Among the more obvious are reading, teaching, thinking, reflecting, suffering, enduring, practicing, listening, exhorting, preaching, reminding, disciplining, instructing, reproving, and correcting. These occur in formal, informal, and nonformal contexts and presuppose more than affirming new information. Both active and passive methods appear on the pages of the New Testament Epistles, but the expected results are always the same. The authors expect change in attitude and behavior based on the true information.

At times the educational method takes a remedial form. Some Christians must go back through the basics. Their regression calls for a repentant change of mind. At times, a simple reminder of truth somehow forgotten refreshes the believers and refocuses their attention on a proper set of priorities (a concordance check of the above words will render dozens of examples).

Testing and Evaluation. The results of Christian education in the New Testament are impressive. The believer can cope with suffering in a positive way or even rejoice knowing that suffering produces the character of Christ so desired by Christians. The follower of Christ looks only forward and presses on toward the goal. Past sins are forgiven. Worry about the future is needless. So, the believer can freely focus on the present, exhibiting the fruit of the Spirit each day. Moreover, good judgment comes while the believer practices making good decisions over time. As believers submit to one another their decisions are evaluated and reaffirmed by the community of faith.

No education program can really achieve excellence without true evaluation. Checking out the believer's life comes from internal and external sources. Much of the believer's evaluation rests in his or her own judgment. They must test themselves to be sure they are actually in the faith and not false pretenders. The New Testament warns about the possibility of self-deception in these matters. On the other hand, others need to see the fruit of the Spirit. More importantly, those closest must see the fruit of the Spirit! Having passed those tests, the believer looks to see if he or she is obedient in all things . . . a comprehensive exam if you please. As an external check, the community of faith excludes from fellowship any that do not abide in the teaching or exhibit proper moral behavior. Last, and certainly not least, the resurrected and glorified Christ himself wrote seven letters calling churches, leaders, and individuals to challenge false teaching and pursue holy living. Thus we end where we began . . . with truth dispelling error (2 Tim. 2:25; Rev. 2:5; Rev. 2:16; 1 Peter 3:3; Rev. 3:19; Rev. 14:6; Rev. 21:5; Rom. 15:15; 1 Cor. 4:17; 2 Tim. 2:14; Titus 3:1; 2 Peter 1:12; Rom. 8:18; Heb. 12:11; James 1:2; Col. 3:5; Heb. 5:12).

MICHAEL S. LAWSON

Education in the Gospels and Acts. "On the surface Jesus seems to have no predetermined method of instruction and no stated plan of teaching. Nevertheless, like Socrates, he always looked for the right teaching occasion" (Nakesteen, 1965). This quotation seems to retrieve the essence of education in the Gospels and Acts. As one searches these five books, finding an educational model comparable to what is done today is difficult. However, one can discern a clear educational approach, as one analyzes Jesus' and his disciples' teaching. Before this analysis can be done two Greek words, *didasko* and *mathetes*, must be understood.

Mathetes (disciple) or *matheteuo* (to be or make a disciple) denotes a pupil who is in a close relationship with a teacher. Used some 250 times in the Gospels and Acts, it emphasizes attachment to a person. The process started with a call by Jesus (Mark 1:17), which differed from the rabbinic practice of the student seeking out the teacher. The call required a commitment, especially to the person of Christ, followed by obedience and involvement (Mark 1:18). Also, unique to Jesus' discipleship was the selection process. It was open to all, if the disciple showed true readiness to follow (Luke 9:56, 61). The reason for this stringent requirement was that the disciple learned by hearing, observing, and doing. Thus,

the New Testament usage of this word, whether in the Gospels or Acts, called for a partnership between the teacher and disciple (Luke 5:1ff.), and a partnership between the disciples (Acts 6:1ff.; 11:19).

Didasko means to teach or give instruction. It is the most common word for teaching and learning in the New Testament and emphasizes both a fixed body of content to be mastered and application of that mastery. Almost two-thirds of its usages are found in the Gospels and Acts. *Didasko* was the main word for the teaching of Jesus and his disciples.

However, their stress was different from the common usage of the Greek word, where emphasis was placed on the intellectual process. Jesus did not seek to impart information solely but to awaken commitment (Mark 1:21). The same held true for the disciples in Acts (Acts 20:20). This would clearly come from Jewish tradition, which stressed doing rather than theorizing. K. H. Rengstorf stated: "A novel feature in the Gospels is the absence of the intellectual emphasis which is common everywhere else among Greek writers. . . . In this respect Jesus with his total claim represents what is perhaps a truer fulfillment of the OT concept" (Kittel, 1985).

The force of these two words is demonstrated in Matthew 28:18–20. Jesus called his disciples to make disciples (*matheteuo*) by teaching (*didasko*). Their responsibility was to emulate his teaching, in content and practice, by making disciples. The modifying phrase after teaching, ("to observe all that I commanded you") catches the practical aspect of Jesus' teaching. As one studies the Book of Acts, this is exactly what occurred.

Jesus had a clear purpose in mind for his teaching. He aspired to glorify the Father, to do the Father's work and develop disciples who could lead the work after he was gone (John 17; Acts 1:1–4). To accomplish this purpose he taught at levels of readiness (John 3–5), starting at where people were and leading them to higher levels. He took people through the process by starting at their entry point, drawing out their knowledge, arousing their curiosity (John 3–4), allowing for inner struggles (Mark 5:21ff.; John 9), and involving them in the lesson (John 6). He used a variety of methods and venues to teach. His most familiar method was the parable (a metaphor or simile drawn from nature or everyday life), which was commonly used in an agrarian society. However, he could present a long discourse (Matt. 5–7) or gnomic (short, pithy) statements. He could do these anywhere, because four walls did not bind Jesus. Most important, he taught by example (Luke 11; John 13).

To accomplish these tasks Jesus relied totally on the Holy Spirit (Luke 4:14–15), who is the essential figure in the educational process of the Gospels and Acts. Jesus told his disciples that the

Holy Spirit would be their teacher and assist them in teaching (John 14:26; 16:13–15). It was this reliance which enabled his disciples to teach with authority (Matt. 7:28–29; Acts 4:31).

Thus the educational philosophy Jesus used included:

1. Total reliance on the Holy Spirit: he was the only perfectly Spirit-filled person.
2. A balancing of procedures: association, instruction, demonstration, operation, and testing were all part of his strategy.
3. Modeling by the teacher in all situations: he fleshed out his content.
4. Integration of learning and doing: he was not satisfied with just cognitive development.
5. Allowances for individual differences: he based his methods on the student's ability and developmental level.
6. Variety in methodology: he selected his methods according to his purpose, content and student attitude.
7. Variety in venue: he was not bound by four walls.

The purposes of education in the Book of Acts were to continue the work of "all that Jesus began to do and teach" (Acts 1:1), to present a historical, resurrected Jesus (Acts 2:14–36), to develop a dynamic church life (Acts 2:41–47), and to develop purity and practicality of doctrine (Acts 15). These were the elements of the apostles' teaching (Acts 2:42), which was the curriculum of the church. Acts 5:42 relates well the purpose of education in the Acts, "and every day, in the temple and from house to house they kept right on teaching (*didasko*) and preaching (*euangelizo*) Jesus as the Christ."

Three words (*kerusso*, to proclaim; *euangelizo*, to evangelize; *didasko*, to teach) are primarily used to relate the activity (instruction) used to accomplish these purposes. All three words were used in connection to unbelievers (Acts 4:2; 8:4–5) but *didasko*, to teach, was directed at believers. Preaching as practiced today was not the norm in Acts. The idea of discipleship was still common (Acts 14:21), but seems to carry a community connotation rather than the one-on-one style prevalent today. Modeling, especially by leadership, was still dominant (Acts 20:18–19), as was witnessing by life and death. While the venue for education was anywhere (Acts 20:20), homes became the major place for carrying out the process. It seems that *oikos* (family) was a literal and figurative concept in Acts.

The Holy Spirit was the major teacher (Acts 1:1), but teaching was done by both the apostles (the leadership: Acts 4) and laity (Acts 18:24–28). The church in Acts, like Jesus in the Gospels, seemed to follow the Jewish pattern of education rather than adopting the Greco-Roman model.

Emphasis was on practical living, community life and recognition of Christ as the Head of the church. C. B. Eavey (1964) summarizes these thoughts well: "The truth taught by apostolic teachers was not the same as the truth they learned under Judaism, but the method of teaching seems to have been essentially the same. As people were converted, groups were formed for the purpose of instruction, fellowship, and worship. All centered in Christ, and it was of Him the teachers taught" (82).

Thus the educational pattern in Acts included:

1. Reliance on the Holy Spirit: everyone was to be Spirit-filled.
2. Christ as the core of the content: everything taught related to him and his church.
3. The didache as the main curriculum: they continued in the apostles' teaching.
4. A process demanding involvement: learning involved action.
5. A variety in methodology: there were a variety of words for teaching/learning.
6. A variety in venue: teaching took place anywhere.
7. Homes becoming the major institution for education: parents were important teachers.

CHARLES H. NICHOLS

Bibliography. G. Kittel, ed. (1985), *Theological Dictionary of the New Testament;* C. B. Eavey (1964), *History of Christian Education;* M. Nakosteen (1965), *The History and Philosophy of Education.*

Education in the Monarchy and the Prophets. When Israel established the monarchy with Saul as its first king, the nation was still suffering from several centuries of spiritual decline. One judge after another rescued Israel from her downward slide into sin and defeat. Many priests and parents had become inept as teachers. The paramount example is Eli, who bungled his role as both a priest and a father. Therefore in the monarchy God raised up two other categories of teachers: wise men and prophets.

Jeremiah 18:18 highlights the three leadership strands of priest, sage, and prophet. The priests were to teach the Law (Deut. 17:10–11; 33:10), the prophets were to communicate the word (i.e., messages from God), and the sages were to give counsel. Wise men in the monarchy (not to be confused with the magicians in Egypt or the astrologers and sorcerers in Babylon) were older men, who were revered for insights gained by experience, and these were viewed as teachers.

Ezekiel referred to the same three classes of leaders. When Babylon would come against Jerusalem, the Jews, he said, would "seek a vision from a prophet, but the law will be lost from the priest and counsel from the elders" (Ezek. 7:26). Clearly, elders were synonymous with sages.

Priests in the monarchy ministered at the tabernacle, as in Moses' day, and then the temple. However, for some time after the nation was divided into the northern kingdom of Israel and the southern kingdom of Judah, the priests failed to carry out their teaching responsibilities ("For many days Israel was without . . . a teaching priest," 2 Chron. 15:3). But in 870 B.C., the third year of Jehoshaphat's reign, he sent out five officials, nine Levites, and two priests to teach the people God's Law "throughout all the cities of Judah" (17:7–9). Judah's king Jehoash (835–796 B.C.) was taught by the priest Jehoiada (2 Kings 12:2). In the reigns of Jotham, Ahaz, and Hezekiah, eighth-century kings of Judah, the priests were teaching but they were so corrupt that they did so "for a price" (Mic. 3:11). Priests were expected to provide instruction (Mal. 2:7). Also in the reign of Josiah (640–609) Levites were engaged in teaching (2 Chron. 35:3).

A key example of a teaching priest is Ezra, who after the exile taught God's "statutes and ordinances in Israel" (Ezra 7:10; cf. v. 25). Teaching Levites are mentioned in Ezra 8:15–16. After Nehemiah rebuilt Jerusalem's wall, Ezra and other Levites read and explained the Law (Neh. 8:8). Priests will also teach, Ezekiel prophesied, in the millennium (Ezek. 44:23).

God raised up a number of prophets in the days of Israel's kings. Because of the nation's spiritual decadence, the prophets denounced personal sins and social wrongs, reminded the people of the serious consequences of disobedience to God, proclaimed the need for personal and national righteousness, urged the people to repent and return to the Lord, extolled God's holy character, and prophesied of God's plans for the future. These national educators fearlessly taught and preached their messages, often to hostile audiences. The first prophet (and the last judge) was Samuel, who told the nation, "I will instruct you in the good and right way" (1 Sam. 12:23).

Some groups of prophets, called "sons of the prophets," were associated with Samuel (1 Sam. 19:20) and Elisha (2 Kings 2:3, 5; 4:38; 6:1). Perhaps these associates assisted Samuel and Elisha in their various ministries, including teaching.

The prophets' teaching methods included oral instruction; written messages; proverbs (Jer. 31:29; Ezek. 12:22–23; 16:44; 18:2–3); parables (Ezek. 17:1–24; 24:1–14); symbolic acts (1 Kings 11:29–39; Isa. 20:1–6; Jer. 19:10–13; 51:63–64; Ezek. 4:1–5:17; 12:1–28; 24:15–27); and allegories (Isa. 5:1–7; Ezek. 16:1–17:24; 23:1–49).

Kings, too, were engaged in teaching. David taught the people a lament he wrote after Saul and Jonathan died (2 Sam. 1:17–18), and he taught sinners (Ps. 51:13). In the Book of Ecclesiastes, the "Preacher," who may well have been Solomon, "taught the people knowledge" (Eccles. 12:9). David's interest in music education shows up in his ability to play the harp (1 Sam. 16:17–20, 23) and other instruments (2 Sam. 6:5), the many psalms he wrote (73 of the 150 psalms), his appointing musicians to serve in the tabernacle (1 Chron. 6:31–32) and the temple (15:16–22; 16:4–6, 42; 25:1–8; cf. 2 Chron. 5:11–14), and his crafting of musical instruments (1 Chron. 23:5; 2 Chron. 7:6).

While some parents in the days of the prophets taught their children to lead godly lives (e.g., Hannah, mother of Samuel; Jesse, David's father; Isaiah, father of two boys; the parents of Daniel, Shadrach, Meshach, and Abednego), others failed as parents. Some fathers, unfortunately, even taught their children to worship false gods (Jer. 9:14; cf. 12:16). However, a good father, as Hezekiah said, "tells his son about Thy faithfulness" (Isa. 38:19).

God himself teaches his people, presumably through human means (1 Kings 8:36; Isa. 1:10; 28:26; 30:9, 20; 48:17; Jer. 32:33). This will be especially true in the millennium (Isa. 2:3; 54:13; Mic. 4:2).

ROY B. ZUCK

Bibliography. K. O. Gangel and W. S. Benson (1983), *Christian Education: Its History and Philosophy;* J. A. Motyer (1980), *The Illustrated Bible Dictionary,* 3:1276–84; H. W. Perkin (1988), *Baker Encyclopedia of the Bible,* 1:657–62.

Education in the Pentateuch.

Religious instruction—teaching directed toward the spiritual development of the learners—was carried on in Pentateuchal times through three channels: God himself, national leaders, and parents. In the early years of human history individuals learned of God as he revealed his nature, his plans, and his standards to them directly. These early recipients of God's oral teaching included, among others, Adam, Eve, Enoch, Noah, Abraham, Jacob, Job (assuming he lived in patriarchal times), and Moses.

Three times Elihu reminded Job that God is a Teacher (Job 33:16; 35:11; 36:22). God taught Moses, Israel's leader, what to say and do in opposing Pharaoh (Exod. 4:12, 15). God the Holy Spirit used the Israelites' desert wanderings as a means of learning (Neh. 9:20).

Moses, Aaron, and the priests served as national educators, teaching the Israelites the Law. (Even the Hebrew word "Law" means teaching or instruction.) Jethro, Moses' father-in-law, urged Moses to delegate all but the most serious disputes to capable, God-fearing men, and for Moses to teach the people God's statutes (Exod. 18:19–22). Later, as Moses looked back on the wilderness wanderings, he reported to the people that he had indeed taught them "statutes and judgments just as the Lord my God commanded me" (Deut. 4:5; cf. v. 1). This great forty-year educational experience helped prepare the nation to be obedient to the Lord in the land of Canaan (4:14; cf. 5:31; 6:1).

Knowing God's commands was not an end in itself; his words were to be learned so that the Israelites would fear God (Deut. 4:10; 5:29), that is, recognize who he is and respond in awe and obedience. This was also to be true of Israel's future kings; they were to learn to fear the Lord by observing his words (17:19).

Every seven years, when the people assembled at the annual Feast of Tabernacles, the entire Mosaic Law was to be read aloud so that the people would "learn and fear the Lord your God, and be careful to observe all the words of this law" (Deut. 31:12). The Israelites also learned music. Moses, their music teacher, taught them his "Song of Moses" (31:19, 21–22; 32:1–43), which recounted God's miraculous deliverance of his people from Egypt and his punishment of their sins. Bezalel and Oholiab, skilled tabernacle craftsmen (Exod. 35:30–32; 36:1–2; 38:23), were gifted by God to teach others (35:34).

The priests constituted another strand of national leadership, responsible to teach the people God's ways. The priests were to instruct the people verbally to follow the details of the Law (Deut. 17:10–11; 33:10; cf. 24:8). While the priesthood was limited to the descendants of Aaron, the Levites, who assisted the priests, were a larger group since they descended from Jacob's son Levi. Levites, too, were teachers. (When the temple was rebuilt in 516 B.C., Levites explained the Law, read it, and taught the people [Neh. 8:7–9].)

Parents comprised another channel of God's teaching in Pentateuchal days. Education was primarily a family concern. The home was the school, and the parents were the teachers. They were to "teach their children" (Deut. 4:10; 11:19). An early example of this "home schooling" is related in Genesis 18:19. Abraham, God said, was to "direct his children . . . to keep the way of the Lord by doing what is right and just" (NIV). By giving specific direction and commands to his children, Abraham was the spiritual teacher and leader of his family. Moses used the same word when he encouraged the Israelites to "command your sons to observe . . . this law" (Deut. 32:46).

Methods of parental instruction included example (Deut. 6:5–8; 31:12): oral communication ("talk," Deut. 6:6–7; 11:18–19); informal discussion in various "teachable moments" (when you sit, walk, lie down, rise up, 6:7; 11:19); answering questions ("What does this rite [Passover] mean?" Exod. 12:26; or "What is this [redeeming of the firstborn]?" 13:14; or "What do the . . . statutes . . . mean?" Deut. 6:20–21); visuals (e.g. *Write them on the doorposts of your house and on your gates,* Deut. 6:9; 11:20); observation (of priests and Levites serving at the tabernacle, of individuals bringing sacrifices to the tabernacle,

of the pillar of cloud that guided the nation, of sinners being punished for disobeying the Law); memorization of the Law; and participation in Sabbath observance, religious festivals, and pilgrimages (Deut. 16:16). Attending the seven annual feasts as family members would make indelible impressions on children, teaching them important truths about themselves, their national history, and God's grace.

When Moses told parents to "teach" God's words "diligently" to their children (Deut. 6:7), he used the word "impress," which means "to sharpen a tool." In its intensive form it conveys the idea of teaching incisively or inculcating. The goal of parental institution to sons and grandsons (Exod. 10:2; Deut. 4:9) and children (Exod. 12:26; Deut. 4:10) was that they come to fear the Lord (Deut. 31:12–13) by seeing who God is and what he has done.

ROY B. ZUCK

Bibliography. W. Barclay (1959), *Educational Ideals in the Ancient World;* C. B. Eavey (1964), *History of Christian Education;* K. O. Gangel and W. S. Benson (1983), *Christian Education: Its History and Philosophy;* A. Lemaire (1992), *Anchor Bible Dictionary,* 2:305–12; R. B. Zuck, *Bibliotheca Sacra* 121 (1964): 228–35.

Education in the Psalms and Proverbs. Known as Israel's hymnal, the Book of Psalms also stands as a powerful educational tool. Several factors demonstrate its remarkable pedagogical value. First is its doctrinal content. If Christians today had only the Book of Psalms and no other portion of the Bible, they would learn an imposing amount of content about God and themselves. The psalms reveal God's names (Adon, Adonai, El, Elohim, Eloah, Elyon, Shaddai, Yah, Yahweh); his attributes (eternality, holiness, majesty, sovereignty, omnipotence, omnipresence, omniscience, love, mercy, grace, faithfulness, longsuffering, justice, righteousness, wrath); and his actions (as Creator, Ruler, Protector, Controller of nature, Lord of history, King, Messiah, Teacher). Also much is written in the psalms about humankind's sin, finiteness, worship, problems, and emotions (including fear, doubt, worry, discouragement, defeat, guilt, shame, loneliness, sorrow, awe, trust, joy, victory, peace, confidence, relief, strength). Thus as individuals read, sing, or meditate on the psalms, they are directed to learn about God and are encouraged to express their needs to him. No wonder Athanasius (c. A.D. 293–373) wrote that the psalms are "a kind of mirror for everyone" and that John Calvin referred to the psalms as "an anatomy of all parts of the soul."

Second, the Book of Psalms holds educational worth because of its frequent reminders that God teaches. The following verses demonstrate God's involvement in teaching believers about himself:

"He teaches the humble His way" (Ps. 25:9); "I will instruct you and teach you" (32:8); "Thou hast taught me from my youth" (71:17); "He . . . teaches man knowledge" (94:10); he teaches "out of Thy Law" (94:12); "Thou Thyself hast taught me" (119:102); and "Thou dost teach me Thy statutes" (119:171).

The psalmists asked that God teach them his paths (25:4), his truth (25:5), his way (27:11; 86:11), awesome things (45:4), to number their days (90:12), his statutes (119:12, 26, 33, 64, 68, 124, 135), discernment and knowledge (119:66), his ordinances (119:108), how they should conduct themselves (143:8), and how to do his will (143:10).

Third, the psalms have instructional merit by demonstrating how learning can be encouraged. Acrostics (Pss. 9–10; 25; 34; 37; 111; 112; 119; 145), alliteration, word plays, chiasms, synonymous and antithetical statements, numerical sayings, evocative language, figures of speech, repetition, and musical notations occur frequently in the psalms, no doubt to add literary beauty and to enable readers to memorize the statements.

Fourth, the variety in the kinds of psalms points up their pedagogical worth. Petitions, praises, exhortations, complaints or laments, questions, reflections, accusations, confessions, narrations, vows—all those modes of expression teach believers ways to commune with God.

Fifth, educational goals shine forth in the psalms. Believers are to learn God's commands (119:7, 71, 73) and to fear God (72:5; 86:11), and parents are to teach their children to fear and obey him (34:11; 78:5–7).

Proverbs portrays the preeminent role parents are to have in educating their children in God's ways and in moral conduct. Both fathers (Prov. 1:8; 4:1–4; 6:20; 23:22) and mothers (1:8; 6:20; 31:1) taught their young at home, though the father is the one who addressed his son(s) in Proverbs (1:8, 10, 15; 2:1; 3:1, 11, 21; 4:1, 10, 20; 5:1, 7, 20; 6:1, 3, 20; 7:1, 24; 8:32; 19:27; 23:15, 19, 26; 24:13, 21; 27:11).

Means of instruction in Proverbs entail admonitions, numerical sayings, better-than sayings, beatitudes, an acrostic (31:10–13), terse observations, repetition, and parallelisms.

The goal of teaching children is to make them wise (1:2–6; 8:33; 9:9; 13:14; 15:33; 19:20), the essence of which is fearing the Lord (1:7; 2:5; 9:10; 15:33). By fearing God, children and youth acquire insight (2:5), turn from evil (8:13; 16:6); lead longer lives (10:27; 14:27; 22:4) and richer lives (19:23). Biblical wisdom (*hokmah*) does not mean having a high IQ; it means being skillful or experienced in godly living.

To acquire this wisdom, children and youth are to listen to parental instruction (1:8; 3:1; 4:1, 10, 20; 5:1, 7; 7:24; 22:17; 23:19, 22, 26), and to pursue wisdom vigorously (2:1–5; 4:5–9; 23:23). This involves heeding parental discipline (3:12; 12:1; 13:1; 15:5; 19:20, 27; 23:12; 29:15, 17) and verbal reproof (12:1; 13:1; 15:10, 32). The Hebrew word for discipline means moral discipline or teaching, whether given physically (13:1) or verbally (it is often translated "instruction," e.g., 1:2–3; 4:1).

Proverbs 22:6 sums up parental responsibilities: "Train up a child in the way he should go." The four other Old Testament occurrences of *hanak* ("train") refer to dedicating a house (Deut. 20:5), Solomon's temple (1 Kings 8:63; 2 Chron. 7:5), and Nebuchadnezzar's gold image (Dan. 3:2). Since the verb in these occurrences conveys the idea of "narrowing" or specifying the use of the house, temple, and image, the command in Proverbs 22:6 means to limit, narrow, focus, or "hedge in" the child's conduct in godly directions. "In the way he should go" does not mean the training should accord with the child's personality or level of understanding at a given stage of development. Instead it refers to the wise, godly path in contrast to the foolish, wicked path.

Children and young people also are encouraged to learn by observation, noting, for example, the consequences of foolhardy living (e.g., 10:1b, 4a, 9b, 10, 17b; 24:30–34) and the results of wise conduct (e.g., 10:1a, 4b, 9a). In addition many admonitions include reasons or motives, a point parents and educators are wise to heed.

Proverbs is unparalleled as an educational guide to a meaningful, fulfilling life (16:22)—a teaching manual with instructions on relationships in the home, business, and society.

ROY B. ZUCK

Bibliography. T. A. Hildebrandt (1995), *Cracking Old Testament Codes*, pp. 233–54; T. Longman, III (1988), *How to Read the Psalms;* R. B. Zuck (1991), *A Biblical Theology of the Old Testament;* idem (1996), *Precious in His Sight: Childhood and Children in the Bible.*

Education of the Twelve. A definitive objective of Jesus' form of discipleship was that his disciples would obey his teachings. While Jesus bore some similarity to other Jewish masters of the first century, his distinctive teachings marked him off from the religious authorities of Israel (cf. Matt. 7:28–29) and established the distinctive boundaries of Christian discipleship. But knowing these teachings was not enough. Jesus' disciples were to "obey" all that Jesus commanded (Matt. 28:19–20). Jesus' disciples will live different kinds of lives than other kinds of disciples, because they will be obeying the most distinctive teacher and teachings of history. This is one reason why we should be hesitant to refer to Jesus' "disciples" simply as "learners." Jesus' disciples will know the content of his teachings, but the real difference in their lives will be manifested because they *obey* his teachings. Jesus' teachings are the foundation of the discipleship life of the new community.

On the practical level, then, disciples of Jesus must know Jesus' teachings and they must live them out in their daily world. This is where the community of disciples is crucial. The gifts of the Spirit must be exercised for the Word to be properly dispensed to other disciples. This includes those who have been gifted as teachers, who have the responsibility for delivering and making relevant Jesus' teachings. The community of disciples is also crucial for encouraging and stimulating one another to obey Jesus' teachings, to live them out, in everyday life.

The four Gospels are unanimous in witnessing to a core of twelve disciples who were called by Jesus into a special relationship with him. These twelve disciples became so prominent in the ministry of Jesus that at many points in the Gospel record to speak of the disciples was to speak of the Twelve. The distinction between the Twelve and the rest of the disciples resided primarily in the fact that the Twelve received an additional call which designated them as "apostles." At a fairly early point in Jesus' ministry he chose the Twelve out from among the larger number of disciples and named them as apostles (cf. Luke 6:13, 17). The Twelve were first called to follow Jesus, by which they became disciples ("believers"). Then they were chosen and named as apostles (commissioned representatives/leaders) (cf. Matt. 4:18–22; Mark 1:16–20 with Matt. 10:1–2 and Mark 2:13). As "disciples" the Twelve are examples of what Jesus accomplishes in all believers; as "apostles" the Twelve are specified as the leaders within the new movement to come, the church. Therefore, when we look at the education of the Twelve we will need to distinguish teachings designed for their varied roles. What follows is a description of these categories.

Teachings for Jesus' Earthly Ministry. First, *certain teachings were addressed to the Twelve primarily with reference to their life with Jesus in his earthly ministry.* On occasion the Twelve were given teaching which was intended to equip them for the specific circumstances of Jesus' earthly ministry, not for the circumstances of the church.

An illustration of this category of teachings is found in the discourse Jesus gave to the disciples prior to their short missionary outreach in Israel (cf. Matt. 10). We find there injunctions which have special reference *only to that trip.* For example, the command, "Do not go in the way of the Gentiles, and do not enter any city of the Samaritans; but rather go to the lost sheep of the house of Israel" (Matt. 10:5 NASB) had special salvation-historical significance only for the time of Jesus' earthly ministry. That command was not carried over to the church. Jesus, in Acts 1:8, specifically countermanded that injunction by sending the disciples to Jerusalem, Judea, Samaria, and the uttermost parts of the earth, including the Gentiles. Other injunctions given in the first part of the discourse in Matthew 10:5–16, such as not taking bag or tunic or sandals (Matt. 10:10), should be seen as relevant only for the time of the disciples' short missionary journey in Israel during Jesus' earthly ministry.

However, careful examination of the missionary discourse reveals that Jesus not only gave directives to govern the mission in Israel (Matt. 10:5–15), but he also gave directives *in the future tense* to govern their future worldwide missionary travels after Pentecost (Matt. 10:16–22). Jesus clearly envisages a far more extensive ministry—now even to Gentiles! Finally, Jesus gave general discipleship teaching that is relevant for both ages, pre- and post-Pentecost (Matt. 10:24–42). In this one discourse Jesus gave explicit teaching that educated them for a short-term itinerary and also gave them a paradigm of the longer mission stretching into the years ahead.

Another more general example includes the occasions when Jesus admonished the Twelve not to reveal his messianic identity (e.g., Matt. 16:20; Mark 9:9). This silence was necessary because of the misconceptions that could be raised in the minds of the Jewish populace. Jesus understood that the expectations of what the people wanted in a Messiah and what he came to accomplish were often quite different, so he wanted to reveal his identity in his own way, without risking misunderstanding. Therefore, he warned the disciples on several occasions not to reveal certain phenomena about himself. But that silence is not the same in the latter part of his ministry as in the first, and we do not find the admonition to silence repeated in Acts.

We must be careful to distinguish those discipleship teachings that are intended for instruction about the circumstances of Jesus' earthly ministry. However, *principles* of discipleship may be derived from these teachings, even though the specifics may be transcended.

Teachings for the Twelve as "Apostles." The second category of disciple teachings include *instructions or statements which were directed toward the Twelve with special reference to their foundational leadership role in the church.* The Twelve had a special salvation-historical role in founding the church, and part of their training by Jesus was directed toward that specific role. Some of these discipleship teachings may be used *in principle* as examples for leaders in the church today, but we must be careful to heed the salvation-historical distinctiveness of some teaching directed toward the Twelve.

An example of this category of discipleship teaching is the famous interplay between Peter and Jesus near Caesarea Philippi. After Peter makes his confession of Jesus' messianic identity, Jesus states of Peter,

"Blessed are you, Simon son on Jonah, for this was not revealed to you by man, but by my Father in heaven. And I tell you that you are Peter, and on this rock I will build my church, and the gates of Hades will not overcome it. I will give you the keys of the kingdom of heaven; whatever you bind on earth will be bound in heaven, and whatever you loose on earth will be loosed in heaven" (Matt. 16:17–20).

Many misunderstandings of this passage could be avoided if interpreters would recognize that Jesus is here declaring Peter's unique role in salvation-history in the establishment of the church. This is seen clearly by the use of personal pronouns and verbs in the second person singular throughout the passage (e.g., "I will give *you*," v. 19, *soi* . . ." whatever *you bind*," *deses*). That which is said to Peter personally here is unfolded in his unique role in opening the door to the kingdom to Jews (Acts 2), Samaritans (Acts 8), and Gentiles (Acts 10). Once Peter utilized the "keys" to open the door to these people-groups, he fulfills his unique role and he increasingly passes from the scene of Acts. This saying emphasizes the unique role of Peter and the Twelve salvation-historically, but it does not imply ongoing significance in apostolic succession.

Teachings for the Twelve as "Disciples." The third category are those *discipleship teachings which are directed toward all disciples, both pre- and post-Pentecost*. This category includes the majority of Jesus' discipleship teachings. We can say generally that those teachings that are not excluded by the first and second categories are included in the third. But even here, it is vitally important to observe the guiding hermeneutical principle that recognizes the first-century historical setting of all teachings. Even general discipleship teachings directed toward all disciples will naturally be conditioned by the social/historical circumstances of the first century. Nonetheless, disciples of the church should feel confident to apply this third category of Jesus' discipleship teachings to ourselves today.

This matter becomes extremely important, because these teachings are designed to guide the lives of all believers in the church today. Those who have become disciples are to be taught to observe all that Jesus commanded in his earthly ministry (Matt. 28:18–20). This is clearly what the apostles did from the earliest days, as the fledgling church continually "devoted themselves to the apostles' teaching" (Acts 2:42). The apostles were committing all that which they knew of Jesus and his teachings to these new disciples. Jesus had focused his ministry on making disciples, and his goal was for the Twelve to make what he had made of them.

An Educational Manual on Discipleship. Matthew's Gospel is a critical place for us to understand the significance of the education of the Twelve. It was the favorite Gospel of the church for much of church history because it was intended, at least in part, as a resource tool to help Jesus' disciples in their task of making and developing future disciples. Some refer to it as a "manual on discipleship," because in it we find the most extensive and most intentionally organized collection of Jesus' teaching. Matthew points to Jesus as the supreme Lord and Teacher of the disciples.

Although the Twelve were still susceptible to incomprehension and misunderstanding in his earthly ministry, Matthew emphasizes that Jesus' teaching brought them understanding and obedience. That same understanding and obedience will continue to be the hallmark of disciples in the ongoing age, because Matthew has constructed a gospel that will equip the disciples in the making of disciples. Through the "Great Commission" (Matt. 28:16–20) Jesus focuses his followers on the ongoing importance of discipleship through the ages. Everything Jesus taught the Twelve they were now to pass on to new disciples.

The Great Commission implies more than securing salvation as Jesus' disciple. Implied in the use of the imperative "make disciples" is both the call to and the process of becoming a disciple. Even as one is "called" from among the nations to start life as a disciple, one must in turn "follow" the Lord through baptism and through obedience to Jesus' teaching. The process will not be exactly the same as what Jesus did with them, because the circumstances after Pentecost will change the process. However, the process will be similar in many ways.

Matthew's Gospel is readily usable for this purpose. First, there are five major blocs of Jesus' teaching materials or "discourses" in Matthew (ch. 5–7, 10, 13, 18, 24–25), which are directed at least in part to the Twelve, making them instructions in Christian discipleship. These discourses are intended as instruction in, and clarification of, what it meant to be Jesus' unique kind of disciple, as opposed to, or distinct from, other kinds of disciples (see Wilkins, 1992, 174–93).

Second, a progression of teaching in the discourses addresses the fullness of the disciple's life—i.e., discipleship. The ultimate goal of discipleship is transformation into the image of the Master, Jesus Christ (cf. Luke 6:40; Rom. 8:29; 2 Cor. 3:18). The discourses are the teachings that Jesus gave the Twelve that facilitated that process while he was with them, and which would carry them forward in that process once he ascended to the Father. Matthew's Gospel, therefore, is a natural catechetical tool designed to develop wholistic disciples. The basic thrust of each discourse points to that kind of intentional well-roundedness, as we can see briefly:

Kingdom life. The Sermon on the Mount (Matt. 5–7) addresses all aspects of what life lived in the presence and power of the kingdom would be like in this age, emphasizing transformation that begins with the heart, but which includes all aspects of life, including ethical, religious, marital, emotional, economic, and so on.

Missionary responsibility. The missionary discourse (Matt. 10) gives principles for all disciples, both in the original missionary outreach of the Twelve and the ongoing missionary endeavor throughout the ages. It explains life as a *mission-driven disciple* in an alien and often hostile world until the coming of the Son of man.

Presence of the kingdom. The parabolic discourse (Matt. 13) explains that the kingdom would not manifest itself in the political, militaristic, dominant cultural kingdom that much of Israel expected to arrive with Messiah. Jesus explained for the disciples then, and now, that the mysteries of the kingdom of heaven will result in a very different kind of expectation regarding how the kingdom will grow, what is its value, and how we are to live in the kingdom while still in this world.

Community life. In the community discourse (Matt. 18) Jesus declared how the community life of the kingdom is expressed through the church, with an emphasis upon purity, accountability, forgiveness, and restoration.

Expectation of Jesus' return. The Olivet discourse (Matt. 24–25) explains how Jesus' disciples are to live with an appropriate kind of expectation of Jesus' return, the end of the age, and the establishment of Messiah's throne.

The education of the Twelve, therefore, provides an example for us today of the education of all Christians. Some final implications: (1) A clear articulation of Jesus' form of discipleship, which includes conversion and transformation, evangelism and follow-up, enables us to be more precise in our use of biblical terminology and the establishment of objective goals. (2) The intentional, wholistic development of disciples is at least partly the intended purpose for the writing of Matthew's Gospel. The five discourses can be used as a ready-made catechetical tool for teaching disciples today. (3) Develop outcomes that achieve the objective of each discourse, and then maintain a regular schedule that rotates through these discourses as a teaching base, especially for new disciples. (4) The objective of the Great Commission must be achieved in *community,* because it is not enough simply to impart data; disciples must be taught how to obey through *modeling.* They must be held accountable to obey through *mutuality.* (5) Develop a strategy whereby everything Jesus taught the Twelve becomes the guiding force in the transformation process of disciples into the image of Christ (Wilkins, 1997; Willard, 1998).

MICHAEL J. WILKINS

Bibliography. A. B. Bruce (1871, 1894), *The Training of the Twelve;* J. L. Crenshaw (1998), *Education in Ancient Israel: Across the Deadening Silence;* J. D. G. Dunn (1992), *Jesus' Call to Discipleship;* M. Hengel (1968), *The Charismatic Leader and His Followers;* R. L. Longenecker (1996), *Patterns of Discipleship in the New Testament;* R. H. Stein (1995), *The Method and Message of Jesus' Teachings;* M. J. Wilkins (1992), *Following the Master: A Biblical Theology of Discipleship;* idem (1997), *In His Image: Reflecting Christ in Everyday Life;* idem (1988), *The Concept of Disciple in Matthew's Gospel: As Reflected in the Use of the Term;* D. Willard (1998), *The Divine Conspiracy: Rediscovering Our Hidden Life in God.*

Educator as Theologian. Miller (1950) asserted that the guiding premise of Christian education is that one's theological perspective should serve as the premise for the church's educational role. Christian educators have the responsibility to contribute to the church's continuing theological dialogue. In essence, Christian educators are theologians in the service of the church.

Little (1976) indicated that the relationship between Christian education and theology is expressed in primarily one of four ways. First, theology provides the content of what is to be taught to the community of faith. Christian education's role is the transmission of interpreted truth to the people of God. Second, theology is normative in that a community of faith's theology acts as a grid to influence both content and the educational methods that are employed. Third, education fosters the "doing" of theology. This calls for educators to be engaged in the theologizing task, as well as leading learners to reflect critically upon their lives and actions in light of God's presence and activity in human history. In this process educators join together with theologians, clergy, and laity to contribute to the theological formulations of the church. Fourth, education is viewed as being in dialogue with theology. In church ministry educational and theological disciplines are dependent upon one another and influence and inform each other. Decisions about education emerge out of an understanding of the nature of God (theology) and the nature of man (anthropology). Together, they form an awareness of God's mission in the world now (soteriology) and in the future (eschatology) and how he desires to empower his church with the Holy Spirit (pneumatology) to impact the world for Christ.

The particular relationship between theology and education that Christian educators adopt for themselves determines the extent to which they will be engaged in the theologizing task. Educators need not be deeply immersed in theology if they regard their primary role as being transmitters of theological content. Though more theological awareness is necessitated by dialoguing with theology or by regarding theology as normative for educational content and practice, clearly, an educator most deeply embraces the role of theologian through participation in the "doing" of theology.

As educators embark on their role as theologians, Nelson (1984) notes that their first concern needs to be the development of an adequate theology, and the second concern involves assessing how they function as theologians (15, 16). Functioning as theologians involves at least three qualities: (1) dealing with the biblical text with integrity in order to develop an adequate theology; (2) developing the discipline of thinking about faith which involves reading, learning, dialoguing with theologians, and being open to the Spirit of God; and (3) formulating a theology with enough certainty to offer one's beliefs to others.

First, dealing with the biblical text with integrity calls for the use of theological methods that give authority to the scriptural text. Carson (1992) feels that the theologian must consider the biblical canon in its entirety and regard it as truthful and trustworthy. The theologian, in understanding that the biblical writers themselves matured in their understanding of God, or that different writers presented differing perspectives and concerns, must recognize that this diversity does not make Scripture self-contradictory. Rather, it is vital for the theologian to seek out the inherent unity of Scripture holding different understandings in tension because they are a part of the same biblical tapestry. Further, the theologian must repeatedly judge formulations in light of exegesis of the biblical text, biblical theology, and historical theology, with the final authority resting with the Scriptures alone. Finally, theologians need to be cautious in applying truth. Truths in Scripture are to be understood in their context and not applied context-free to any situation; rather, the understanding of truth is to be applied to similar contexts and to similar functions in the theologizing process.

Second, the educator as theologian must develop the discipline of thinking about faith theologically with the help of the Spirit of God. Theological reflection involves focusing upon one's theological heritage and one's experience in light of Scripture in order to discover the meaning of God's present activity in the world and what is required for faithful living to God's demands. Through prayerful theological reflection which involves reading, meditation, study, and conversing with others, the theologian is brought to decision regarding the tension between present action and God's vision. This results in the development of new insights for a renewed and deeper faith leading to repentance, the transformation of one's character, and a commitment to act in accordance with God's desire.

Third, the theologian needs to develop a certainty regarding the faith she or he is formulat-

ing. It is in wrestling with the faith that convictions are derived and made one's own. It is in founding one's faith in the Scriptures that ensures orthodoxy. It is in reliance upon the Spirit of God that assurance or certainty comes. This faith, then, needs to be expressed with confidence, though not with arrogance, in order to contribute to the theological dialogue which the church seeks in order to live faithfully to Christ Jesus in this world.

The question arises as to how the educator is specifically to engage in theologizing. First, the educator must begin with the biblical material. Rather than starting with educational philosophies, and adapting them in accordance with gospel, educators need to bring their educational questions and concerns into dialogue with Scripture. Second, in adhering to the above guidelines, Christian educators must recognize their role as theologians, not only as ones who dialogue with theologians, but as ones who contribute to the ongoing theological development of the church. Further, the educator as theologian, both by example and through teaching the process of theological inquiry, leads learners into theological inquiry for themselves, so that each individual person is equipped to think and live theologically in order to engage culture as followers of Christ Jesus.

ROLAND G. KUHL

Bibliography. D. A. Carson (1996), *The Gagging of God: Christianity Confronts Pluralism;* idem (1992), *Scripture and Truth;* S. Little (1976), *Foundations for Christian Education in an Era of Change,* pp. 30–40; R. C. Miller (1950), *The Clue to Christian Education;* R. C. Miller, ed., (1995), *Theologies of Religious Education;* C. E. Nelson (1984), *Changing Patterns of Religious Education,* pp. 10–22; R. W. Pazmiño (1994), *Latin American Journey: Insights for Christian Education in North America;* idem (1997), *Foundational Issues in Christian Education;* J. L. Seymour and D. E. Miller, eds., (1990), *Theological Approaches to Christian Education.*

Edwards, Jonathan (1703–58). One of early America's most renowned preachers, Edwards had a profound effect on the nation through his sermons and prolific writings. Raised under the influence of New England's Puritan values, Edwards sought to counter the declining moral values of his day by proclaiming the holy nature of God and man's need for repentance and salvation. Edwards championed the theological tenet of the depravity of man.

Schooled at Yale College, he was ordained to the ministry in the Congregational church in Northampton, Massachusetts, in 1727. Together with other notable preachers of his day, Theodore Frelinghuysen (1691–1747), Gilbert Tennent (1703–58), and George Whitefield (1714–70), Edwards was instrumental in the beginning of the first Great Awakening in America (1730–70). It was during this span of time that Edwards traveled extensively throughout Europe and the American colonies preaching the Calvinist message of a mandatory new birth experience. His famous sermon, "Sinners in the Hands of an Angry God," demonstrated his passion for the salvation of lost souls. Though his preaching style was less than exuberant, he was well esteemed for his brilliant biblical reasoning and skilled intellect. In his book *Treatise Concerning Religious Affections* (1746) he espoused his views regarding the role of both one's personal will and intellect in shaping their religious life. Each had a unique part to play in spiritual formation.

Edwards was an ardent opponent of Arminianism; he fought long and hard to herald the theological position of Calvinist theology. As an early evangelical, he credited the movement of God's Holy Spirit for the revivals that took place through the land during his lifetime. As these revivals began to subside later in his life, he preached with relentless vigor in an effort to sustain the effects that these revivals had had in the shaping of societal norms and values.

Shortly before his death he was dismissed as pastor of his congregation because of strict adherence to qualifications for communion. After leaving his church he set out to serve Christ as a missionary to the Indians in Stockbridge, Massachusetts. It was during this season of ministry that he wrote *Freedom of the Will* (1754) which presented his perspective on man's free will and the election of God. In 1757 he became president of the College of New Jersey (which was later renamed Princeton). However, his life was cut short when he contracted smallpox and died.

In hindsight, Edwards is viewed as one of early America's greatest theologians and philosophers. Fortunately for those who would follow after him, he left a legacy of numerous writings, books, sermons, and lectures. The Great Awakenings which were to follow in the history of the American experience would owe a great deal to the theological foundations that laid under the spiritual leadership of Jonathan Edwards.

MICHAEL J. ANTHONY

Bibliography. F. L. Cross and E. A. Livingstone (1997), *The Oxford Dictionary of the Christian Church;* C. B. Eavey (1964), *History of Christian Education;* K. O. Gangel and W. S. Benson (1983), *Christian Education: Its History and Philosophy;* J. E. Reed and R. Prevost (1993), *A History of Christian Education.*

Effective. Effectiveness is doing the right thing in contrast to efficiency, which is the ability to do things right. According to Drucker, mastery of five practices will lead to effectiveness: (1) knowing where one's time goes; (2) focusing on results rather than work; (3) building on strengths; (4) concentrating on the few major areas where superior performance will produce outstanding results; and (5) making sound decisions.

Maxwell (1993) describes effectiveness in terms of self-discipline as "achieving what you really want by doing things you don't really want to do. After successfully doing this for some time, discipline becomes the choice of achieving what you really want by doing things you now want to do!" (161).

In addition to understanding effectiveness as self-mastery, it can also be understood as achieving results through other people. The "effective cycle" as described by Hersey and Blanchard (1982) suggests that high expectations coupled with genuine confidence in subordinates results in high performance. Effective styles of leading other people integrates relationship behavior with task behavior adjusted to the maturity level of followers.

LESLIE A. ANDREWS

Bibliography. P. F. Drucker (1996), *The Effective Executive;* P. Hersey and K. Blanchard (1982), *Management of Organizational Behavior: Utilizing Human Resources;* J. C. Maxwell (1993), *Developing the Leader Within You.*

Efficient. Efficiency is doing something the right way, in contrast to effectiveness, which is doing the right thing. Once the right thing has been identified, a leader focuses on producing results with a minimum of wasted effort.

The leader develops a *plan* to accomplish a goal ("right thing"), which includes needed personnel, training, resources (e.g., curriculum), budget, timeline, ongoing support, and feedback mechanisms. Planning entails an up-front commitment of one's time and energy in order to minimize costly mistakes committed due to limited or no planning and haste to get the job done.

It is possible to be efficient and still not be effective; efficiency and effectiveness should go hand in hand. Knowing what God wants a church to do (the right thing) coupled with wise stewardship of all resources, human and material, maximizes the potential of a church and its ministry areas. The dictum "When we fail to plan, we plan to fail" holds true in achieving the desired goal and maximizing all our God-given resources (efficiency).

LESLIE A. ANDREWS

Egalitarian. Word used to describe a particular body of beliefs held about appropriate gender roles for men and women in church, home, and society. It is generally presented as a contrasting view to the hierarchical or traditionalist position on the roles of men and women in ministry and in the family.

Groups of scholars representing both sides have produced position statements summarizing their views. Although these statements cannot be said to speak in their entirety for all who hold to the represented position, they do provide a basis for understanding the general distinctives. The egalitarian position is articulated in the following excerpt from a statement published by a group of evangelicals who banded together and formed an organization called Christians for Biblical Equality.

> The Bible teaches that woman and man were created for full and equal partnership. . . . in the New Testament economy, women as well as men exercise the prophetic, priestly and royal functions. . . . In the church, spiritual gifts of women and men are to be recognized, developed and used in serving and teaching ministries at all levels of involvement. . . . In the Christian home, spouses are to learn to share the responsibilities of leadership on the basis of gifts, expertise, and availability.

A brief summary of the egalitarian support for their position based on their interpretation of related Bible passages is provided here. For a more complete account of their biblical exegesis, see the reference list at the end of the entry.

Genesis 1–2. Male and female are unified and similar because they are created in God's image. It is their mutual responsibility to rule and exercise dominion over the rest of creation. Woman is to be Adam's helpmate in the sense of being his equal partner and coregent.

Genesis 3. The account of the fall is not prescriptive in outlining a new order God is establishing; rather, it is descriptive and is simply recording the consequences of the fall. Male dominance and female submission are the result of sin and are not God's intended design for male-female relationships.

Galatians 3:28. Women are coheirs with men of salvation. In redemption it is God's intent to restore human relationships to their original state of equality without role distinctives based on gender.

Ephesians 5:23. The understanding of headship is based on an ancient Greek translation of *kephal* as "source of life" as in the head of a river. This translation emphasizes the unity and interdependence between men and women.

Ephesians 5:21–33. The principle of mutual submission is applied to marriage in verse 21 and is further developed in verses 22–33. The focus of this passage is on marriage, not on church order. Paul is using the church as a model for marriage and not the other way around. Submission in marriage is best understood as the sacrificial self-giving of the husband in partnership with the voluntary submission of the wife.

Passages on Women Teaching (1 Cor. 11, 14; 1 Tim. 2:8–15). These passages contain instructions to a local body of believers and are not to be interpreted as permanent injunctions against all women. Any limitations that Paul placed on

women were a cultural and historical necessity to address specific confusions in the church and were only intended to be temporary restraints.

Disciples and Apostles. Many women followed Jesus and ministered to him alongside the twelve disciples. In Romans 16:7, the reference to Junias could be translated as Junia, a feminine form of the name, thus supporting the position that women indeed served as apostles.

Deacons and Elders. In translating 1 Timothy 3:11, the most probable interpretation indicates that women held the office of deacon. Since there are no gender distinctions in the assigning of spiritual gifts by the Holy Spirit, women should be given freedom to use their gifts in any direction God leads, including pastoring or teaching.

SHELLY CUNNINGHAM

Bibliography. M. J. Anthony, ed. (1990), *Foundations of Ministry;* Christians for Biblical Equality, *Christianity Today* 37; C. S. Cowles, *A Woman's Place?: Leadership in the Church;* R. Hestenes, *Christianity Today* (October 3, 1986): 4-I–10-I; A. Mickelsen, *Women, Authority and the Bible;* A. Spencer, *Beyond the Curse: Women Called to Ministry.*

See also DEACONESS; EGALITARIAN RELATIONSHIPS; FEMINISM; WOMEN IN MINISTRY

Egalitarian Relationships. An egalitarian is one who views all people as equal. In the broadest sense, it refers to the relationship between husband and wife. In Christian education, the term generally refers to the roles of men and women in the church, particularly teaching and leadership roles. An egalitarian relationship is one in which two persons of opposite gender teach or mentor others alongside one another in equally supportive roles.

The role of women in the church is one of the most controversial within the evangelical community, mostly because of three passages of Scripture: In 1 Corinthians 11:2–16, Paul follows the creation order recorded in Genesis 1–3, expressing that "the man is the head of the woman," following as apparent chain of command order beginning with God, followed by Christ, man, and then woman; later, Paul challenges the Corinthian churches in 1 Corinthians 14:34–37, stating that the women were to "keep silent in the churches, for they are not permitted to speak . . ." (v. 34); and in 1 Timothy 2:12 Paul writes to Timothy, "I do not allow a woman to teach or exercise authority over a man, but to remain quiet."

Those who support the egalitarian position suggest that these passages must be examined in light of significant cultural influences. In Paul's day, women were deprived of the opportunity for a religious education, thus they may have had more questions about their new faith. In the church or Sabbath service, women may have been seated in the balcony, at some distance from the men. This was done to avoid distractions. The women were said to have asked their husbands questions during the service, thus disrupting the flow of the worship service. If such a scenario is true, then Paul provided these instructions to avoid such disruptions. In essence, he wanted the women to ask their questions at home where such discussions would not distract from the service itself. Therefore, Paul's rules for women were given to assist with the consistent flow of worship. This interpretive view finds consistency within each of these passages.

In addition, egalitarians use other passages of Scripture to support their view. They point out examples of women in leadership positions, even teaching positions, in both the Old and New Testaments. The story of the priest Hilkiah seeking out the prophetess Huldah, even though the more famous Jeremiah, Habakkuk, and Zephaniah were available to him, is a striking example of a woman in a teaching, prophetic role in the male dominated Jewish culture (2 Kings 22:15–19).

Another argument egalitarians raise is the lack of gender distinctions in Paul's teachings concerning spiritual gifts. Spiritual gifts are distributed to each believer, as the Holy Spirit desires, and are not subject to race, economic class, or gender (1 Cor. 12:11–14, 18; Eph. 4:7). This is a critical point for those who hold the egalitarian position. Because the egalitarian relationship involves people who strive to support one another regardless of gender, strong emphasis is placed on empowering each Christian with the ability to use one's spiritual gifts. If a person is gifted to teach and has demonstrated that through effective teaching, affirmation by students, and by an attitude of humility, then that person should be allowed to use his or her gift. If the individual has demonstrated leadership gifts, then that person should be allowed to lead (Rom. 12:6–8). One of the primary responsibilities of the Christian educator is to equip people to discover and use their spiritual gifts in building up the body of Christ, the church (Eph. 4:11, 12).

The difficulty comes when one applies these principles to the role of the senior pastor since there seems to be evidence within the text of scripture for a male dominated headship of the church. Generally speaking, as applied to other leadership positions within the church (e.g. Children's Ministry Director, Youth Pastor, Counselor, etc.) the tension does not seem to be as great. Some church leaders have navigated this mine field by changing or rewording the title from "Minister" or "Pastor" to "Director" or "Leader."

In the egalitarian relationship, sometimes both persons share leadership responsibilities. This approach can benefit the field of Christian education by modeling supportive roles, the uniqueness each gender brings to life, demonstrating effective use of spiritual giftedness. Those that choose to minister within an egalitarian relationship may find teaching to be more sensitive, and therefore more effective, to people of both genders.

JAMES W. MOHLER

Bibliography. B. Clouse and R. G. Clouse, eds. (1989), *Women in Ministry: Four Views;* D. Elliot and G. Olson, eds. (1995), *Breaking the Gender Barrier in Youth Ministry;* S. J. Grenz (1995), *Women in the Church: A Biblical Theology of Ministry;* H. W. House (1995), *The Role of Women in Ministry Today;* L. E. Maxwell (1995), *Women in Ministry: An Historical & Biblical Look at the Role of Women in Christian Leadership;* R. A. Tucker (1992), *Women in the Maze.*

Egocentrism. Inability to see another person's point of view. Egocentric children believe that they are the center of the world or universe. They may believe that human beings created the sun, moon, stars, and are generally responsible for making the flowers grow.

Egocentrism is most often seen in preschoolers (babies through five year olds) who find it difficult to recognize the needs and feelings of others when they are different from their own. When a preschooler cries because he cannot have a certain toy in the hands of another child, adults may say that the child is misbehaving, when in reality the preschooler is behaving normally. The child believes that because he or she wants the toy it should be given to him or her immediately.

Two and three year olds often talk *at* one another rather than *to* one another. Such a conversation would be:

"My mommy bought me a new dress!"
"I want the big block for my house."
"I have new shoes, too!"

As the young preschoolers grow mentally and socially, they begin to see themselves as being a part of a group, part of a world in which they must live and work. Egocentrism can be seen as part of the growth process which allows preschoolers to process information, events, and experiences from their own perspective. In terms of language development and play, egocentrism may be perceived as positive.

In the broader sense, egocentrism may be seen as a way of thinking at all levels and ages. Young teenagers experience egocentrism in regards to preoccupation with physical appearances. Their thinking about how they look in regards to others, dwelling on physical aspects, often causes them much anxiety. Teenagers may feel that they are constantly being watched and judged by other people. They live with the idea that their feelings are uniquely their own, and no one has ever or will ever feel exactly the same way. In some situations, adolescents may express their troubled feelings in outward behaviors which are inappropriate. This self-absorption can become an obstacle to learning to see yourself as a part of the world.

Teenagers need to see that they are part of God's family, not an isolated human being. They need to see that they are God's unique creation with a purpose to fulfill on the earth. If teenagers continue to harbor thoughts of egocentrism as they move towards adulthood, they may have difficulty in forming relationships in marriage and functioning in the workplace. While egocentrism is seen as a normal part of development in the preschool years and teenage years, it is not a desirable quality in adulthood.

MARCIA MACQUITTY

Eisner, Elliott (1933–). Professor of education and art. He maintains that teaching is more art than science. His current research focuses on the use of critical methods from the arts for improving educational practice. Most recently he has published on the practical uses of critical qualitative methods from the arts for the description, interpretation, and evaluation of schools, classrooms, and instructional process.

A champion in identifying some of the problems and issues that pervade educational planning and evaluation, he contends that many of the assumptions currently used in education are inappropriate for the problems with which teachers must deal.

Eisner's ideas aim at stretching the perceptions that now dominate contemporary thinking about education and evaluation. He maintains that the process of acculturation and professional socialization have caused instructors to unwittingly internalize subtle, powerful concepts about schooling. These concepts include the image of school as a factory assembly line, reducing rationality to scientific verification (i.e., knowing) rather than scientific discovery, an overemphasis on the behavioral sciences determining what is important and what should be studied, emphasis on technology rather than the artistry of teaching, and favoring operationalism and measurement over the quality of the student's experience.

A prolific author with fifteen books and over three hundred articles and chapters, Eisner suggests that "the ultimate test of a set of educational ideas is the degree to which it illuminates and positively influences the educational experience of those who live and work in our schools" (1991, 11).

He considers the practice of education to be dynamic, continually changing over time. There are no fixed solutions, no "right way" of doing things. He maintains that "no single educational program is appropriate for all children, everywhere, forever. Which educational values are appropriate for children and adolescents depends on the characteristics of those the program is designed to serve, the features of the context in which they live, and the values that they and the

community embrace." These values are continually in flux. Consequently, "educators cannot rest with fixed solutions to educational problems or with 'breakthroughs' that once and for all define or prescribe how and what should be done" (1994, v).

Eisner's articulate writing addresses shortcomings in the premises of prevailing educational policies and curricular approaches. These propositions deserve careful scrutiny by Christian educators. His responsible thinking on assessment can be integrated into a local church or higher Christian education plan.

JAMES A. DAVIES

Bibliography. E. W. Eisner (1982), *Cognition and Curriculum;* idem (1994), *The Educational Imagination: On the Design and Evaluation of School Programs,* 3rd ed.; idem (1991), *The Enlightened Eye: Qualitative Inquiry and the Enhancement of Educational Practice.*

Elder. Term derived from the Old English term *eald* ("old") and used synonymously with presbyter (from the Greek *presbyteros*).

The Old and New Testaments provide examples of elders serving in leadership within the community of faith. Under the leadership of Moses, the "elders of Israel" are introduced as a representative group (Exod. 3:16; 17:5; 18:12; 24:1) and later demonstrate administrative functions (Josh. 20:4; Ruth 4:2; 1 Sam. 8:4).

This practice carried over into the church, where elders/presbyters were present in Jerusalem (Acts 11:30; 15:2) and later appointed in the newer churches (Acts 14:23). The teachings of Paul (Acts 20:17–35; Titus 1:5–9) and Peter (1 Peter 5:1–5) indicate that the elders were to be not only administrators but pastors and shepherds. During the Reformation, Calvin distinguished between teaching elders and ruling elders, based on 1 Timothy 5:17. This distinction provided greater opportunity for lay leadership within the Reformed Church.

DOUGLAS BARCALOW

See also ADMINISTRATION; CLERGY; DEACON; MINISTER; TRUSTEE

Elderly. Scripture is replete with instances of care and concern for the elderly. It is quite likely that many of the biblical writers were elderly themselves. Though age is not equated with wisdom or goodness, it is readily associated with these qualities. Psalm 71 is the testimony of God's provision to an older man. Paul did not limit spiritual maturity to the aged, but thought age was properly on the side of maturity. He spoke of the themes of respect for the elderly in the pastoral Epistles. Paul was an old man himself when he wrote Philemon. It appears that the Bible endorses several perspectives on old age. In general, age was more favored than youth. Biblical principles stand against agism, the practice of denying any person her/his God-given rights on the basis of age.

However all biblical references to elders do not refer to older persons. In the Jewish context elders referred to those whose opinion counted more than others possibly because of their age, or because their family had held offices. In ancient civilizations respect for elders has been typical, but, under the guise of modernization and urbanization, this tradition has eroded. It is doubtful whether a case can be made for older persons ascending to church leadership (the elders of the church). In the ancient world leadership naturally fell to the older men.

At present, the focus of many writers in the field of religion and aging is upon spirituality, a term which is not only ecumenical, but often inclusive of non-Christian positions, such as humanism, and new age spirituality. Evangelical believers have yet to respond to this theological challenge, preferring instead to describe church activities for the elderly. A distinct Christian spirituality begins with conversion, and one grows toward Christlikeness.

Demographic realities in the twenty-first century mandate that churches plan and provide excellent ministries with elders. For example, less than 4 percent of elders, those beyond 65, are in institutions, such as nursing facilities. Most elders, then, live in their own homes, or with relatives. In the United States, we are becoming a nation of Floridas, as the number of seniors increase in the proportion of the population. The first cohort of baby boomers, that large birth cohort born since 1945, will arrive at sixty-five in 2010. Churches cannot ignore these population changes. While maintaining a traditional evangelistic thrust with children and youth, church leaders must see the elder population swell as a choice period for reaping a spiritual harvest. While it is thought that elders grow more religious as they age, such is not the case. Elders tend to continue their patterns of church involvement established in earlier years.

Typically, church ministry with elders is fivefold: worship, pastoral care, social activities, ministry by the elders themselves, and Christian education. While the first two functions traditionally have been carried out by the clergy, churches are moving toward a more diverse and creative approach to meeting their spiritual and personal needs. An increasing number of churches are employing full- and part-time ministers to senior adults to direct these ministries. At times these church staff responsibilities are combined, such as minister of music and senior adults.

Effective ministries with older persons need to be grounded upon the realities, rather than myths and stereotypes of aging. Unfortunately, individual believers, including clergy, are prone to offer ministry based on erroneous and misleading attitudes and knowledge about aging persons. Ministry to the elderly must be based upon biblical as well as factual truth. In fact, the church can perform a meaningful ministry by focusing on prevailing myths which impede evangelism and spiritual growth.

What are some spiritual/agist traps that ministers may believe? First, ministers may believe that elderly believers are unlikely to change their religious lives very much, since they are "set in their ways." This myth suggests that change and growth in Christian living is only appropriate during earlier years. Accordingly, ministry toward growth is replaced by ministry maintenance. According to this view, ministry is offered perfunctorily with little enthusiasm, as if going through the motions. If clergy are uncomfortable talking with elders, they may resort to "god-talk" instead of conducting a genuine discussion of spiritual concerns.

Agism in the church may appear as an attitude of splitting the "good" and the "bad" about aging and creates the assumption that elders live at one extreme or the other. Either they are actively involved in the church and need no special attention, or they are isolated at home or in an institution and must be ministered to. Most elders are in between these two extremes, calling the church to offer creativity in ministry models.

Also, there is the common misconception that working with the elderly requires no special training. One pastor said, "if we just love them, they will be OK." Love is a positive force with seniors, but ignorance and misunderstanding of their needs may lead to disappointment and ineffective ministry.

Practitioners and researchers in this field find common interests in the American Society on Aging's special interest group, the Forum on Aging and Spirituality, as well as *The Journal of Religion and Aging*.

JIM WALTER

Bibliography. A. Becker (1986), *Ministry With Older Persons;* W. M. Clemons, ed. (1981), *Ministry With the Aging;* W. L. Hendricks (1986), *A Theology of Aging;* J. J. Seeber, ed. (1980), *Spiritual Maturity in the Later Years;* F. Stagg (1981), *The Bible Speaks on Aging.*

Elementary School. *See* Middle Childhood.

Emotionally Disturbed Child. The emotionally disturbed child is one who has serious difficulty in relationships with other people. Ill-equipped to deal with everyday life, disturbed children are often unable to apply themselves in order to use their abilities and interests. Such an inability may cause them to have expectations of failure regardless of their intelligence. It is essential to establish the kind of environment in which a regulated set of experiences enables the child to learn and grow and to return to a more satisfactory social and emotional state of being. The home, school, and church school must work together to bring about growth in the child's sense of achievement and well-being.

Religious education should seek to provide instruction and nurture that is developmentally appropriate and meaningful to every child. Because of the behavior problems of emotionally disturbed children, providing such an environment is difficult to plan for and to guide.

Larry Richards' emphasis on involving parents in the educational ministry of their child, both in the home and in religious settings, is very important, especially with the emotionally disturbed child. Experiencing normal peer models in small group settings means integrating the child as much as possible into the normal routine of religious education. Here educational ministries can offer one more opportunity to bring a positive environment into the child's world.

Providing every child with religious nurture and instruction that is developmentally sound and provides a meaningful context in which to grow is the responsibility of the church. To this responsibility, when dealing with the disturbed child, one must add acceptance of those who are both different and difficult. Herein lies another reason for the involvement of the parents who are able to explain the child's needs and the best way in which to manage behavior irregularities.

DORIS BORCHERT

Empathy. Placing yourself in another person's position where you experience the feelings, thoughts, and acts of that person. Identification is the key word in empathy, and the empathizer uses imagination to associate closely to the situation. Empathy differs from sympathy. Empathy is an intellectual identification with another where you place yourself in his or her position. Sympathy is just feeling sorry for someone because you cannot do anything to help change his or her situation, and you feel as if you are that person. Christ had empathy with the lost world, and He came to reconcile the sinner to God the Father (Rom. 8:1–14). Jesus modeled an unreserved empathetic style during His earthly life. He identified completely with those whom he had been sent to serve by becoming flesh (John 1:14). So fully did He identify with the needs and hurts of all people that He took the sins of a lost world upon Himself in His death on the cross, (Acts 5:30; 1 Cor. 15:5; Gal. 1:4).

People who are submissive, trusting, self-accepting, and self-sufficing tend to be more empathic toward others. Submissive attitudes result from interpersonal relationships. Empathy contributes to an experience of community. An empathic disposition involves the capacity to think

intuitively about people and to understand their feelings and attitudes (Matt. 25:34b–36). Emotions are distinguished through body language as well as with words. Empathetic people are listeners and observers; therefore, they tend to respond with both care and objectivity. The empathic person faces the same vulnerability as the subject when he responds to the needs of the other person. He will take some type of action to remedy the situation, and he is often inconvenienced. He serves and cares for others (2 Cor. 3:4–6) and nothing is expected in return for services rendered. The empathic person assists rather that suppresses the other's self-initiation and freedom. He builds up and encourages others (1 Thess. 5:11a).

LAVERNE WINN

Bibliography. R. J. Corsini, ed. (1984), *Encyclopedia of Psychology*, pp. 479–80; E. Farley (1996), *Divine Empathy*; G. G. Roper (1992), *Who Cares? Cultivating the Fine Art of Loving One Another*; G. L. Sapp (1993), *Compassionate Ministry*; R. L. Underwood (1985), *Empathy and Confrontation in Pastoral Care*; N. G. Wilson (1995), *Christian Education Journal*, pp. 53–69.

Empirical Theology and Christian Education. Empirical theology is deeply intertwined with the American scene. Its energy and shape are deeply indebted to the seminal writings of such thinkers as William James, Henry Nelson Wieman, and Alfred North Whitehead. As suggested by the term "empirical," its methodology is rooted in observation, empirical testing, reason, and experience. "Experience" is perceived as broader than mere sense experience in that it includes relationships, a sense of the whole, and what Meland has termed "appreciative consciousness." Following Whitehead, experience is so defined that it incorporates an affective dimension that is closely linked with the prevailing culture. Miller (1995) suggests that out of this perspective come theological presuppositions within a historical and metaphysical perspective which can be significantly influenced by modern assumptions. This, in turn, may lead one to a naturalistic theism.

Evidence employed in the construction of a theology is sought, evaluated, and interpreted in a scientific spirit. Religion and science, then, are effectively brought into the same arena and made subject to essentially the same evidential criteria. This seemingly hard, scientific evaluative process is softened by the insertion of what Meland has termed the "appreciative consciousness." This concept enlarges the scope of and adds a certain sensitivity to the character of the awareness by which religious judgments are made. It is still empirical in nature, but with a distinctive difference. Revelation does play a role in empirical theology, but it is not considered as having its source in the supernatural realm. Its role, accordingly, is as a source of empirical data (a revealing event) that can be grasped and interpreted by an appreciative mind. It follows that there are no revealed truths, as such, but there are empirically based truths of revelation (data requiring interpretation).

Empirical theology does not allow a separation of values from facts. Values are linked to appreciative experiences that one both feels and grasps with the mind. Indeed, values arise through the creativity found in events. This, in turn, gives support to the concept of God. In sum, empirical theology may be understood as a realistic theology framed within a naturalistic perspective.

Taken from this point of view, it is quite understandable why empirical theology has a tendency to interpret the force of Jesus' life in terms of the creative event, especially in relation to the concept of reconciliation. Rooted in the worship experiences of early Christians and the inheritor of historical events, the church exists wherever people gather in the name of Jesus Christ.

As it relates to Christian education, empirical theology understands learners as human beings who have emerged from the evolutionary process with a unique genetic and cultural inheritance. Dynamically, they are engaged in the process of forging a new culture through application of, and interaction with, their genetic inheritance and their fund of cultural information. A key assumption for Christian education is that the learner is capable of growth. Miller regards this assumption as lending support to the traditionally stated purpose of religious education, which is to place God at the center of the universe and to bring the learner into a proper relationship with his Creator.

From the perspective of empirical theology, Christian education will be effective only in so far as it enlightens, strengthens, and undergirds the actions of individuals in the face of real-life situations.

HAROLD W. BURGESS

Bibliography. R. C. Miller (1995), *Theologies of Religious Education*, pp. 148–71.

Empowering. In Luke 9:1 Jesus empowered his disciples when he gave them power and authority to drive out demons and cure diseases. They were further empowered by the Holy Spirit in Acts 2:2. Ford (1991) emphasizes the empowering influence of Jesus in demonstrated servanthood, such as washing the disciples' feet.

Empowering is unleashing the Holy Spirit within the believer, and it is a role for believers to pass to others (Eph. 4:12–13). Every saved person receives authority or power at the moment of salvation and is indwelt by the Holy Spirit. New believers are spiritual novices that need cognitive input as well as character formation. Empowering gives the believer tools and skills to make informed decisions for the authority that one possesses. Christian educators are responsible for mentoring others with discernment during disciplining, fellowshipping, identifying, and developing spiritual gifts; equipping with Bible study skills; aiding others to recognize their calling and potential through practice and training, and cultivating leadership skills. Paul admonishes Timothy to pass on what he had learned to faithful men who would be able to teach others (2 Tim. 2:2).

Leaders who give their followers power, authority, or influence are said to empower them. When someone is authorized to make decisions, that person is empowered by his superior. Leaders practice empowering by giving others the ability to act. When a teacher trains a student in a special field or skill, that student is empowered by this new knowledge or ability.

Blanchard (1996) explains that there are three keys to empowering others. First, the leader begins by sharing information with everyone so that the followers will understand the organization and trust will be developed. Next, the leader creates autonomy by establishing boundaries through clarifying goals of the group and individuals' roles. At this point, people receive whatever training they need and are held accountable for results. The third key for empowering calls for replacing traditional hierarchies with self-directed teams. The leader gradually turns over control to the teams, while providing support and encouragement.

Robinson (1997) discusses two words in Scripture which are closely related to empowering, the terms *equipping* and *edifying*. The word equipping is used in the New Testament for mending nets in preparation for fishing and in a more general sense for outfitting, getting ready, or preparing. Edifying is used to refer to a carpenter building a house and to describe how ministers build up the body of Christ. Gifted leaders can be understood to empower their followers as the leaders equip and edify them (see Eph. 4:11–13).

There are three stages of empowering. (1) One has authority (indwelling Holy Spirit) and no preparation (tools and skills). (2) One has preparation and no authority. (3) One has both authority and preparation. Educators teach the "why" of what Christians do through empowering. The Holy Spirit gives educators tools to nurture babes in Christ who can evangelize and teach others to replicate the Christian cycle. Zuck (1998) states about empowering that "we should call for action and response; we should encourage our students to put into practice what they have learned, and to apply the truth to their own lives each week" (151). Educators must trust their students to do ministry. Jesus states, "All power has been given to Me in heaven and earth." His disciples are to go and "make disciples of all nations, baptizing them in the name of the Father and the Son and the Holy Spirit, teaching them to observe all that I commanded you" (Matt. 28:18–20). He said they will have power (Acts 1:8), and they will be able to do greater works than him (John 16:7).

KENNETH S. COLEY AND LAVERNE WINN

Bibliography. K. Blanchard, J. P. Carlos, and A. Randolph (1996), *Empowerment Takes More Than a Minute;* L. Ford (1991), *Transforming Leadership;* W. C. Graendorf (1981), *Introduction to Biblical Christian Education;* R. W. Pazmiño (1994), *By What Authority Do We Teach?;* D. W. Robinson (1997), *Total Church Life;* D. E. Schroeder (1993), *Christian Education Journal,* pp. 28–39; D. P. Smith (1996), *Empowering Ministry;* F. R. Tillapaugh (1982), *Unleashing the Church;* J. Westerhoff (1994), *Spiritual Life: The Foundation for Preaching and Teaching;* R. B. Zuck (1998), *Teaching as Paul Taught.*

Empowerment. *See* Collaborative Learning.

Empty Nest. State of a family when all the children have grown and left the home of their parents. Parents are usually between the ages of 45 and 55 when this occurs. An empty nest is a characteristically sensitive period in a marriage. If, for example, the children were the focus of the parents' attention, when the last of the kids moves out, there is often a void left behind. Some parents find they have little in common without the children present. Why are so many parents shocked and dismayed when children actually move out? The preparation of the child may have been accomplished, but was the preparation of the parent achieved?

Adults who are experiencing the empty nest may have another kind of stress. Having just finished supporting their children, they may find their parents need support. Parents of the empty nesters may need support as they age and require assistance. If both the children and the parents simultaneously need support, the middle adults can find themselves "sandwiched" between the two generations. Empty nesters can find themselves shifting support from children to parents and possibly to both. When children divorce or have other problems and need some help, parents are an easy refuge. Children who return home are sometimes called "boomerang" progeny. A major survey by ICR Survey Research Group found in 1996 that three out of four caregivers for older parents are women and that there is stress due to time constraints and increased financial obligations (*AARP Bulletin,* 4).

Empty nesters need support from others who have successfully transitioned through this period in their life. The church can address this need through special small groups or age appropriate Sunday school classes. Some curriculum materials or references may also provide additional insights.

ROBERT J. RADCLIFFE

Bibliography. AARP Bulletin 38, no. 5 (1997); J. Conway (1978), *Men in Mid-Life Crisis;* S. Coontz, (1997), *The Way We Really Are;* D. J. Levinson (1978), *The Seasons of a Man's Life;* D. J. Levinson and J. D. Levinson (1996), *Seasons of a Woman's Life;* M. E. McGill (1980), *The 40- to 60-Year Old Male;* N. Meyer (1978), *The Mid-Life Crisis;* L. Rubin (1979), *Women of a Certain Age: The Mid-Life Search for Self.*

Encoding. Ability of the individual to take various forms of incoming stimuli (e.g., verbal, musical, visual, etc.) and process that information for storage and subsequent retrieval (Gage and Berliner, 1988, 280). Learning is a dynamic and complex process. It involves the learner being involved with numerous forms of outside stimuli. The learner must listen, observe, and take in information. The learner learns best if he or she has a desire to learn the new material.

Outside stimuli can work as a positive or negative reinforcement for the learner. Stimuli must get the attention of the learner and hold it long enough to be recorded in his or her brain. Each learner must comprehend and understand the ideas which the stimuli are representing. He or she then takes the ideas and stores them in his or her brain as verbal or picture symbols.

The learner must see a need to organize the new information in a way that he or she can retrieve it when needed. New information must reinforce old information and be familiar to the learner in order to be useful. The learner must construct meaning out of this new information by associating it with concepts already learned. This is put in short-term or long-term memory. An example of learning for short-term memory would be for learning a zip code to use on a letter. An example of long-term memory would be memorizing for a Christmas play.

Reinforcement of ideas aids the retention of what is learned. The ability to rephrase in the learner's own words shows a greater understanding of the ideas he is learning. The learner must organize the new information that he has learned and be able to take it and transfer it to an appropriate situation in life. This constitutes the goal of learning which is change in the learner's attitudes and actions.

BARBARA JEAN DEATON

Bibliography. N. L. Gage and David C. Berliner (1988), *Educational Psychology;* D. L. Barlow (1985), *Educational Psychology and the Teaching-Learning Process;* W. R. Yount (1996), *Created to Learn.*

See also CHUNKING; INFORMATION PROCESSING; MEMORY

Encounter Groups. Encounter groups are also known as T-groups (training groups) or sensitivity groups. A group leader guides each member of a group, usually made up of ten to fifteen members, to explore his or her own feelings and motives, as well as those of the other group members. In an atmosphere of love and understanding, members are asked to be aware of feelings they usually do not express in public because of guilt or fear of punishment. Through this experience, they learn to express their true feelings and to develop better social relationships (Engle and Snellgrove, 1989).

Different techniques, some of which are controversial, are used in groups to assist members in overcoming restrictions they feel in everyday life and to teach them about interpersonal relations. One exercise requires each person to say something to every other person while touching him or her in some way. Such techniques are designed to increase honesty, openness, and sensitivity.

Role playing is another common encounter group technique. The goal in this form of theater is to help people expose hidden feelings and understand themselves better. One group member may try portraying a character in one of his dreams. Another person may pretend to be herself as a child talking to her father, played by another member. By switching roles and placing themselves in each other's situation, group members are better able to see themselves as others see them. A person's hidden and true feelings are often brought out by acting out a past experience or playing the role of another person.

KENNETH S. COLEY

Bibliography. K. W. Back (1972), *Beyond Words: The Story of Sensitivity Training and the Encounter Movement;* T. L. Engel and L. Snellgrove (1989), *Psychology: Its Principles and Applications.*

Enculturation. Process of learning the correct cultural patterns in order to survive in a culture. Enculturation is the method by which children, during their formative years, unconsciously learn cultural patterns and cultural competence from other members of society. Families and schools are the main teachers of these cultural patterns.

According to Segall, Dasen, Berry, and Poortinga (1990), enculturation is the link between the group's influences from historical, ecological, and sociopolitical contexts and the observable behaviors and inferred characteristics of a person. It includes voluntary awareness, or socialization, and unconscious influences. Since culture is constantly changing enculturation is adaptive and never static. From a developmentalist view, the factors that influence enculturation are the physical and social contexts, which would include child rearing and education.

Luke in his Gospel gives us a model of enculturation when he says of Jesus—he grew "in wisdom, and stature, and in favor with God and men" (Luke 2:52). Jesus learned and developed intellectually, physically, spiritually, and culturally. From his environment of family, friends, and probably synagogue schooling, he learned and practiced the cultural patterns of his day. In other words, he became enculturated.

To understand enculturation it is helpful to compare and contrast it with acculturation. Acculturation involves two or more cultures and occurs in adulthood, while enculturation is learning one's own culture and happens in childhood. Both involve the process that produces acceptable cultural practices.

Finding acceptable cultural practices for the outworking of the gospel message is the task of Christian education. Christian educators need to understand the importance of the relationship between the gospel and enculturation and in doing so answer the question, "How does a Christian enculturate the gospel message into her or his world?" The answer lies in recognizing the two cultures in which every Christian educator works: the culture of Scripture and the culture of this world. In creating the world God created a cultural environment. He used these cultural forms to reveal himself and his plan. When God discussed the obligation of worship and obedience with Adam and Eve, He clothed his statements with the cultural guidelines "from the tree of the knowledge of good and evil you shall not eat" (Gen. 2:17). The children of Israel were also given specific cultural guidelines for worship and practice, including those for building an earthly dwelling place for God. God sent his Son to be a Jew in the Jewish culture. In order to properly understand Scripture, then, one must understand the culture in which the Bible was written. In this process the Christian educator will distinguish the fundamental issues and eternal principles of faith. After peeling back the cultural layers in Scripture and finding the eternal or core truths, the Christian educator takes these principles of Scripture and incorporates them into her own culture. The second culture, then, that the Christian educator needs to understand is his or her own.

An illustration of this is found in the New Testament. In the early church new and different cultural patterns of worship were used. The enculturation of the message of Scripture with specific rules and practices, which had been the practice in the Old Testament, was not stressed. Believers within the body of the church were given greater freedom to enculturate the gospel in their own way, as long as the principles of godly living were adhered to. The conclusions of the Council of Jerusalem (Acts 15) clearly brought this home. Jewish believers led by the apostle Peter were attempting to require Gentile believers to adopt Jewish cultural practices in worship and lifestyle. The Council refused to allow the gospel to be enculturated with Jewish practices. The Gentiles with their lifestyle were allowed to worship God without adapting the cultural patterns of the Jews. The task of the Christian educator is not made easy by this shift from rigid cultural forms of worship. The task today is to separate the biblical truth from the cultural environment of Scripture and transfer these eternal principles into an appropriate cultural practice in today's world.

Another task of the Christian educator is to critique cultural practices and worldviews based on the timeless truths of Scripture. The product of this critique will sometimes be a changed and different cultural set of practices and beliefs for the church.

The enculturation of the gospel and critiquing the culture is the ongoing and never ending task of the Christian educator. The transcendent truth of the Word of God remains immutable. But the culture changes constantly, creating opportunities for new and different cultural forms of the timeless truth of Scripture.

PHILIP BUSTRUM

Bibliography. M. H. Segall, P. R. Dasen, J. W. Berry, and Y. H. Poortinga (1990), *Human Behavior in Global Perspective: An Introduction to Cross-Cultural Psychology;* W. S. F. Pickering (1992), *The Contours of Christian Education,* pp. 87–97.

See also ACCULTURATION; CULTURE; ETHNIC IMPLICATIONS FOR CHRISTIAN EDUCATION; ETHNOCENTRICITY

Engel Scale. According to James Engel, this model of the spiritual decision process was first suggested to him by Viggo Sogaard, a student at Wheaton Graduate School where Engel served as director of the Billy Graham Graduate Program in Communications. It was revised by Engel and published in the *Church Growth Bulletin* in 1973. A further modified form appeared with an explanation in *What's Gone Wrong with the Harvest?* by Engel and H. Wilbert Norton (1975). This article is based on the form which appeared in that book.

The scale describes the steps involved in moving from unbelief to a growing relationship with Christ as his disciple. It begins by distinguishing among God's role, the communicator's role, and the human response in the spiritual decision process. God's role is viewed under the categories of general revelation, conviction, regeneration, and sanctification. The communicator's role is proclamation, persuasion, and follow-up/cultivation. But the most important aspect of the scale is the more detailed list of steps involved in the human response, and how the roles of God and the communicator change as one moves through those steps.

Engel delineates eight steps leading from unbelief to conversion. He begins with level –8, in which general revelation gives awareness of a Supreme Being but no knowledge of the gospel. Levels –7, –6, and –5 signify an increasing awareness of the gospel and its implication for one's life. In these steps, the role of the communicator is proclamation. Levels –4 and –3 are more attitudinal and volitional than cognitive, including a positive attitude toward the gospel and the perception that the gospel offers the solution to a problem recognized by the nonbeliever. Level –2 is the point of decision, at which the individual comes to faith and repentance or rejects the gospel and regresses to level –5, in need of further persuasion from the communicator and further communication from God.

Engel adds five postconversion steps, reflecting the fact that the mandate of the Great Commission is not to make converts, but disciples. These steps include postdecision evaluation, incorporation into the church, growth in both understanding and behavior, communion with God, and stewardship of all one's resources and ministry both inside and outside the body. In all these stages, the role of the communicator is that of follow-up and cultivation, and the role of God is sanctification.

There are a number of caveats that may be issued with regards to this scale. Some may want to add or rearrange some of the steps. Others may feel uneasy about any attempt to lock God into any set number of steps in bringing anyone to faith in Christ. Yet, despite these possible reservations, this model can offer help to Christian communicators in a number of areas.

First, the recognition that there are a number of steps involved in becoming a disciple of Christ, and that the role of a communicator changes depending on where a person is in the process, can help believers more effectively communicate the gospel. For example, Engel states that many gospel presentations will be ineffective for persons who have not yet reached level –3 in their understanding of the gospel. Their need is for more in-depth proclamation of the gospel prior to being asked to make a decision. Conversely, those who have reached level –5, or possibly –4, may not need more cognitive information about the gospel, but ministry that will help them come to a positive attitude toward the gospel or to personal problem recognition.

Also, seeing the process of becoming a disciple as involving a number of steps allows one to see the immediate goal of an evangelistic encounter in a different way. The ultimate goal is always to bring one to faith in Christ and eventually discipleship, but the immediate goal may be seen as moving the individual one step closer to the ultimate goal.

A third helpful aspect of the scale is the guidance it gives when one encounters rejection of the gospel. The scale allows one to examine a variety of possibilities: Has the individual fully understood the gospel? Does she have a positive attitude toward the gospel? Is there a recognition that the gospel is the solution to a perceived problem in her life? The answer to questions like these can give guidance in how to continue to reach out to those who reject the gospel.

This Engel scale has been available for more than twenty years and deserves wide recognition and dissemination. It can and should serve as a helpful supplement for many evangelism training programs.

JOHN S. HAMMETT

Bibliography. W. Arn and C. Arn (1982), *The Master's Plan for Making Disciples*; J. F. Engel, D. T. Kollat, and R. D. Blackwell (1973), *Consumer Behavior*; J. F. Engel and H. W. Norton (1975), *What's Gone Wrong with the Harvest?*; M. Green (1970), *Evangelism in the Early Church*; J. Petersen (1980), *Evangelism as a Lifestyle*.

Enlightenment. The eighteenth century was known as the age of reason. It is also known as the Enlightenment because of its humanistic influence upon intellectual development. This period of human history had as its emphasis the study of reason, science, and naturalism. The Enlightenment impacted most areas of human life and played a large part in contributing to the American and French Revolutions (Reed & Prevost 1993). A number of educators had a major influence on the study of science, philosophy, theology, and education. Prominent educators of the Enlightenment period include John Amos Comenius, Friedrich Wihelm Froebel, Johann Friedrich Herbart, David Hume, John Locke, Johann Heinrich Pestalozzi, and Jean-Jacques Rousseau.

Up until this point in history, it was believed that there were three sources from which it was possible to acquire knowledge (epistemology). These three sources included the senses, reason, and faith. During the Enlightenment period, the latter source was found to be insufficient while the former two were to be highly esteemed. This trend would have far-reaching implications for the separation of church and state, and the removal of religious and moral influence from public school curriculum (Eavey 1964). Humanistic thought, which once had strong ties to biblical theology and Christian education, was now losing that relationship and becoming increasingly secular. The result was an exaltation of humankind and a marginalization of the world from God.

The Enlightenment placed such a high emphasis upon knowledge through the senses and reason at the expense of faith that the exploration of the natural world via the scientific method took on an atmosphere of rediscovery. What had been discovered regarding the nature of humankind up to this point was now subject to reexamination. As a result, new theories regarding human nature were put forth by educators in the fields of law, political science, sociology, education, religion, and human relations. Serious academicians rejected tenets of theological revelation and ridiculed Christianity. Those who held to anything other than a naturalistic view of the universe were seen as plebian or naive (Eavey 1964).

The study of comparative ideas was a major emphasis during the period of the Enlightenment. Voltaire felt that Western Europe had much to gain from interacting with Confucianism (Mayer 1966). This sharing of ideas often resulted in the loss of universal truth and values. Such an educational philosophy prepared the way for the amoral and agnostic teachings of Charles Darwin, T. H. Huxley, and John Dewey. With this foundation of evolutionary thought it was felt that science had a more credible explanation for the formation and existence of the universe than theology. Humankind had now become "enlightened" to the real meaning and purpose of life—self-indulgence.

For those who had their philosophical and educational roots in secular humanism the period of the Enlightenment brought about a great educational emancipation. No longer forced to view the cosmos through the restrictive lens of a conservative church-based educational system, people were now free to explore the fields of social science through the lenses of reason and naturalism. The educational implications of the Enlightenment period have been far reaching and profound. Some of the greatest educators of its day espoused theories of knowledge and meaning that shaped the foundation of the twentieth-century school system.

Enlightenment and Christian Education. From the standpoint of Christian education, the philosophy and education of the Enlightenment era brought about a divorce from all supernatural foundations. The church, which had once been the champion of education for the masses, was now ostracized and seen as antithetical to informed thought. This is not to say that the Enlightenment produced no positive effect for the church. Indeed, God used what would appear to be a loss of spiritual influence to produce a major victory for Christian education. The theological and moral vacuum that developed across Europe over the eighteenth century prepared the way for a new spiritual and political revolution that would take place across the Atlantic Ocean in colonial America. America would be the place where those who would reject the amoral and antibiblical values perpetuated by the secular humanists of the Enlightenment period could escape. There in the safety of a new world these explorers would be free to develop a society based upon universal laws integrated with their Christian worldview.

MICHAEL J. ANTHONY

Bibliography. C. B. Eavey (1964), *History of Christian Education;* E. F. Frost (1966), *Historical and Philosophical Foundations of Western Education;* K. O. Gangel and W. S. Benson (1983), *Christian Education: Its History and Philosophy;* F. Mayer (1966), *A History of Educational Thought;* J. E. Reed and R. Prevost (1993), *A History of Christian Education;* A. E. Sanner and A. F. Harper (1978), *Exploring Christian Education.*

See also CHRISTIAN HUMANISM; COMENIUS, JOHANN AMOS; HERBART, JOHANN FRIEDRICH; HUMANISM, CLASSICAL; HUME, DAVID; LOCKE, JOHN; PESTALOZZI, JOHANN HEINRICH; ROUSSEAU, JEAN-JACQUES

Environment. Although educational research leaves no doubt as to the effect of environmental factors on learning, Christian educators have a mixed record in employing these factors. Burgess (1966) finds that four twentieth-century models of religious education give contrasting degrees of attention to the learning environment.

Proponents of the *classical liberal* religious education movement recognize the influence of the total social environment, but ignore any deliberate structuring of environmental factors. For the *mainline* model, the life and fellowship of the church is the essential environment in which Christian nurture takes place. The Christian community (including the home) is responsible for providing an atmosphere in which God's Spirit can work. In the *evangelical/kerygmatic* model, representative of Roman Catholic and most Protestant evangelical Christian education, behavior is generally ascribed to inner intellectual or spiritual factors, so the environment is largely ignored as a useful construct for teaching practice. The *social science* model presents the environment as a major and multifaceted element of the instructional act. The religious educator shapes the learning environment so that an encounter between the learner and Jesus Christ is facilitated.

Most Christian educators would agree that the success or failure of a learning event often hinges on the teacher's attention to and use of key environmental factors.

The Cultural Environment. Learners absorb from their culture not only language and social behaviors, but attitudes toward government and authority, religion, race, and class. In a multicultural environment like that in much of North America, learners may be members of more than one culture, requiring Christian educators to inform themselves continually concerning the particular cultural environments that daily impact learners.

The Home Environment. The effects of cultural, economic, and social factors in the larger environment tend to be mediated by the family. Until they leave high school, children spend only about 13 percent of their waking hours at school. What parents *do* in the home matters, not their socioeconomic status (Kelleghan et. al., 1993, 145.) The values taught in the home are impacted by the family environment, which in turn affects how the learner views content and the process of learning about God.

The Church Environment. The relative warmth, health, and perceived effectiveness of a church's total ministry creates a climate in which disciples wither or thrive. A healthy church conveys caring, trust, and respect through clear communication and openness concerning policies. The church's regard for a nurturing environment is evident when curriculum, equipment, staff, and facilities are well provided for and maintained. Personal regard is conveyed when names and faces are recognized, personalities are engaged, and emotional needs are met. Beyond what may be taught in the classroom or youth group, the church climate provides learners with an image of themselves as Christian persons. A servant-leadership structure teaches believers that they are members of a gifted "holy priesthood"; an authoritarian structure teaches them to be subservient, passive followers in the chain of command.

The Group Environment. The nature and size of the learning group determines participants' involvement. A warm emotional climate conveyed through the teacher's body language, interactions with group members, and careful deployment of all environmental factors elicits positive attitudes toward the group and the subject matter. Successful cooperative activities have been shown to strengthen relationships within the group. The size of the group affects the quality and quantity of interactions: the larger the group, the more active members dominate and others remain passive. For children, class size is crucial. In large groups preschoolers show more aggressive behavior and higher levels of frustration. Careful attention to group size and dynamics helps leaders create the sense of coherence, community, and solidarity essential to Christian nurture.

The Physical Environment. The immediate environment in which learning takes place powerfully impacts that learning. Aesthetics, physical comfort, and richness of stimuli influence participants' attitudes and behavior. Color and light affect responses: people move faster through dark-painted rooms than through light-painted ones. People emerge from ugly rooms in measurably more negative mental sets, from beautiful rooms feeling more positive. Comfort factors involving temperature, sound, and space affect participation. Low temperatures inhibit students' learning performance; too-comfortable seating or depletion of oxygen may cause them to "drop out."

Conflicting voices distract adults more than children, but annoying, high-pitched sounds may be heard by children but not by adults. Spatial distance is related to verbal communication: the greater the distance between teacher and learners, the more teachers talk and learners remain passive. Interaction increases as learners are placed in small circles, or seated opposite or at right angles to each other. Stimulus factors like furnishings, equipment, and media enrich the environment and heighten the learning experience. A "Home Corner" encourages preschoolers to act out their learning; posters, maps, models, and other media help older students visualize Bible events; field trips deepen and concretize concepts and values.

Structuring the environment for a hillside crowd, Jesus once stepped in a boat to distance himself and augment his voice. For a last evening with his disciples, he arranged an intimate dinner in an upper room. Later, when he wished to heal and strengthen relationships with them, he arrived at their workplace and cooked breakfast on the beach. On that occasion, Jesus did little direct teaching; the environment he so carefully designed taught more than words.

BARBARA WILKERSON

Bibliography. C. A. Bowers and D. J. Flinders (1990), *Responsive Teaching: An Ecological Approach to Classroom Patterns of Language, Culture, and Thought;* H. W. Burgess (1996), *Models of Religious Education: Theory and Practice in Historical and Contemporary Perspective;* J. Elias (1982), *The Foundations and Practice of Adult Religious Education;* T. Kellaghan, K. Sloane, B. Alvarez, and B. S. Bloom (1993), *The Home Environment and School Learning;* J. M. Lee (1973), *The Flow of Religious Instruction.*

Episodic Memory. The term *episodic memory* comes from information processing theory, a cognitive learning theory. IPT uses the analogy of computer processing to explain the storing of meaningful information in humans. Information which is received by sensory receptors, transmitted by electrochemical changes in neurons, and processed by short-term memory is encoded in three types of long-term memory. These types are procedural, semantic, and episodic memories. Episodic memory stores events as images from personal experiences. These images are organized on the basis of when and where they occurred. Episodic memory is our internal autobiography, which we might consider like a movie reel or videotape of our life. Our ability to recall what we did yesterday, last week, or years ago, is based on the retrieval of episodic memory. Can you remember your first grade classroom? The playground where you spent recess? Your childhood home? The way your room was decorated? These images are related by space and time.

Information from episodic memory is often hard to retrieve because later events interfere with earlier ones unless a particular episode has special significance. The author was a high school sophomore in his geometry class when the assassination of President John Kennedy was announced. That event was indelibly encoded into the author's memory and has remained there ever since. Semantic memory stores facts, concepts, and thinking processes such as mathematical formulas. Procedural memory stores specific psychomotor skills, such as tying shoes or skiing.

RICK YOUNT

Bibliography. P. D. Eggen and D. Kauchak (1992), *Educational Psychology: Classroom Connections;* N. A. Sprinthall, R. C. Sprinthall, and S. N. Oja (1994), *Educational Psychology: A Developmental Approach,* 6th ed.; W. R. Yount (1996), *Created to Learn: A Christian Teacher's Introduction to Educational Psychology.*

Epistemology. Study of knowledge and how one knows, the kinds and sources of knowledge, and the means for understanding and verifying truth. The essential elements relate to the source of knowledge and to the process for attaining knowledge.

The source of knowledge and the process by which one learns have two polar positions, each with a continuum of interpretation. Is the source of knowledge in the subjective, transcendent dimension of creation, or is it in the objective, experienced dimension of human life? Ultimate truth for the Christian is from God, but there are often differing perceptions whether the sensing and trusting (subjective) or the experiencing and proving (objective) are more biblical. Consequently, many Christians rely on interpreters—preachers, teachers, evangelists, and authors—to explain truth. This results in varying interpretations that have divided believers.

How does one learn? Does a person acquire knowledge by learning facts and developing understanding, or does one learn by discovering meaning and developing values? Although personality traits influence a learner's response, most people learn both ways. At first, awareness, recall, and understanding are required. Unless one develops conviction about that which has been learned, however, no action is taken and knowledge dissipates. Conversely, if one discovers meaning and becomes convicted, he or she acts on and reinforces patterns of behavior based on that knowledge.

Most evangelicals seek to tie truth to God through use of the Bible and basic doctrines. While these objective sources are basic and fundamental, many evangelicals also rely on guidance from the Holy Spirit—often a sensory experience.

In regard to how one learns, pastors and teachers historically have focused largely on cognitive means and ignored the power of affective experiences. It was not until the Great Awakening, especially under the preaching of Jonathan Edwards, that the power of blending head and heart, cognitive and affective, began to find a place in American Christianity.

The conviction level of learning likely is the most ignored phase of Christian education. The primary cause is that teachers use methods designed primarily to transmit information, such as lectures and readings. Conviction and values always emerge as learners get into dialogue, discussing meanings and implications. From the crucible of searching and questioning, Christians listen to each other, check their interpretations against Scripture and views of mentors, and then decide what level of commitment they will make. If conviction is strong, they will act on it. If little or no commitment is made, the information presented or material studied does not affect life.

The ultimate issue is how one knows the Lord and trusts in salvation, whether by grace and trust (through faith) or by doctrine and practice (through works). Evangelicals support Paul's view of being saved by grace through faith (Eph. 2:8), but also recognize James's position, that believers should be doers of the word (James 1:22).

BRUCE P. POWERS

Epworth League. Primary Methodist youth organization from its founding in 1889 until about 1930. Named after the small English town of Epworth, birthplace of Methodism's founder, John Wesley, the League arose because of a perceived need to bridge the gap between the Sunday school and the church. In the 1870s and 1880s John H. Vincent, who popularized the Chautauqua, applied his energies to developing a youth education program that would emphasize the importance of church loyalty, give appropriate attention to spiritual and social development, and encourage personal involvement in Methodist missions. Drawing upon Vincent's work, Jessie L. Hurlbut and C. A. Littlefield offered a complete organizational plan for the Epworth League that was adopted in Cleveland, Ohio, in 1889. The Hurlbut and Littlefield plan soon gained the sanction of a number of Methodist Conferences and membership expanded rapidly during the years just before the turn of the century. As early as 1894, only five years after its founding, the League's official organ, the *Epworth Herald*, had reached a circulation of more than one hundred thousand. By the turn of the century, the *Herald* was among the largest denominational publications in the world.

Perhaps the most characteristic feature of the Epworth League was its creation and adoption of Sunday afternoon (or evening) devotional meetings. Because League meetings were commonly held apart from the Sunday evening church serv-

ices, Methodist pastors often complained that the local chapters exercised too much autonomy. Indeed, it was not uncommon for youth to attend League meetings rather than the traditional church services of the period. Even though the League was eventually placed under the leadership of Methodist pastors, a chain of events had been set in motion that resulted in the dissolution of the Epworth League's charter (1930). The League's work was reassigned to the Youth Division, which functioned more directly within the defined educational structure of the church. In due time, the Methodist Youth Fellowship was created. This organization included youth between the ages of 12 and 21 and was charged with carrying on exactly the same sort of work that had earlier been within the province of the Epworth League.

The question of whether the Epworth League was ultimately a success or a failure has been rather fully debated in a number of Methodist journals. The evidence suggests that, on balance, the League contributed positively to the shape of the church. Perhaps most important, it provided a forum for youth to gain experience in public settings and so functioned as a training school for several generations of church leaders.

HAROLD W. BURGESS

Bibliography. D. B. Brummitt (1992), *The Efficient Epworthian: Being Epworth League Methods;* W. W. Sweet (1953), *Methodism in American History.*

Equilibrium. Commonly associated with Jean Piaget's theories of adaptation, assimilation, and accommodation, equilibrium is the result of the process (which Piaget called "equilibration") of bringing stability and balance to an organism biologically and cognitively. As a person grows and matures, new information and new experiences cause a type of crisis for the individual. The crisis occurs because a person's current knowledge is interrupted by the new stimuli. The person then either absorbs the new information into the current knowledge base (assimilation) or somehow changes to accept the new information (accommodation). This process results in a balancing of old and new knowledge. The resulting equilibrium is often referred to as an "ah-ah" experience.

Equilibration helps keep one from becoming overwhelmed by new thoughts, ideas, experiences, and information. This process takes place both within a person and between individuals and their environment. When equilibrium is not achieved, the result is some type of cognitive dysfunction.

Piaget saw this as true and essential for all living beings. He believed equilibration to be a dynamic, intrinsic process involving both specific needs or circumstances and a person's entire body of knowledge. Piaget also tied this concept together with the developmental factors of heredity, environment, and social education. While these three aspects of development overlap very little, equilibration takes place as they interact with each other to help give each person the unique attributes and traits that sets him or her apart from everyone else.

For a good illustration of the process of equilibration, consider how a child learns about dogs. At a very young age, a child learns that a small furry animal that barks is a dog. Not being able to differentiate more specific characteristics, that child may also say that cats, horses, and even hamsters are "doggies." If a parent says, "That's not a dog, that's a cat," then there is a momentary crisis in the mind of that child. In order to make sense of this new information, if the child is at the appropriate stage of development, she might choose to keep calling everything with four legs a dog, or figure out what makes a dog different from a cat. When she determines that a dog barks and a cat meows, she can refer to the respective animal by its appropriate label based on her new knowledge. The child has successfully adapted information about one difference between dogs and cats by assimilating what she was told into what she already knew and accommodating her understanding of dogs to include a new understanding of cats. This process is called equilibration, while the result is known as equilibrium.

DAN LAMBERT

Bibliography. J. C. Bringuire (B. Miller Gulati, trans.) (1980), *Conversations with Jean Piaget;* P. G. Downs (1994), *Teaching for Spiritual Growth: An Introduction to Christian Education;* H. E. Gruber and J. J. Voneche, eds. (1977), *The Essential Piaget;* J. W. Vander Zanden (1997), *Human Development.*

See also ACCOMMODATION; ASSIMILATION; DISEQUILIBRIUM

Equipment. *See* Facility.

Erasmus, Desiderius (1469–1536). Dutch humanist and scholar. He was born out of wedlock in Rotterdam, Holland, October 27, 1469 (although he maintained it was 1466). His parents never married, and he was orphaned as a teenager. A student all his life and a noted scholar, he attended Brethren of the Common Life schools in the Netherlands, was forced into a monastery by his guardians, was ordained a priest in 1492, and then studied languages and literature of ancient times at universities in Paris, Oxford, and Italy, earning a doctor of divinity degree in 1506 from the University of Turin, Italy. During and after his formal education, he studied and taught at a variety of centers of learning throughout Europe. He died in Basel, Switzerland.

Erasmus taught and wrote to combat ignorance and its results. Some of his most influential books were translations of the Greek New Testament and works of the church fathers. Through such writings, he contributed to religious revival. Although he criticized Roman Catholic theology and the Latin Vulgate Bible and sided with Martin Luther on many doctrines, he stayed in the Catholic Church.

Erasmus's educational philosophy was humanistic, putting fundamentally good man at the center of all things. He believed the purpose of education was "to promote study of a wide selection of the works of classical authors, the church fathers, and the Scriptures in the original and in their uncorrupted form that the spirit of these writings may be thoroughly imbibed" (Eavey, 1964, 138). According to Erasmus, these works provided all the guidance people needed and were the antidote for the religious abuses of his day. He firmly believed theology must be lived out in everyday life.

Erasmus emphasized studying the nature of children, the importance of games in education, praise and rewards instead of discipline, helping students, and providing more education for women. Moreover, he was one of the first people to champion systematic teacher training.

LIN JOHNSON

Bibliography. C. Augustijn (1991), *Erasmus: His Life, Works, and Influence;* C. Eavey (1964), *History of Christian Education;* J. Olin, ed. (1987), *Christian Humanism and the Reformation: Selected Writings of Erasmus.*

Erikson, Erik Homburger (1902–94). German-American psychoanalyst, best known for his psychosocial theory of emotional development. He studied at the Vienna Psychoanalytic Institute, where he was trained and analyzed by Sigmund Freud's daughter, Anna. In 1933 Erikson emigrated to the United States, where he was affiliated with Harvard University (1934–35, 1960–70), Yale University (1936–39), and the University of California (1939–51).

The life-span theory of Erikson builds on the psychosexual development theory of Sigmund Freud and emphasizes the synthesis of the inner, private emotional experience (psyche) and the external influences of culture, environment, and society (social). The interplay between these two forces contributes, to a large degree, to the development of an individual's personality. Although a student of Freud, Erikson believed the Freudian focus was too confined. While Freud believed personality traits were fixed at about age 6, Erikson preferred a framework of development that spanned the entire life cycle. Furthermore, Freud focused on the sexual dimension of personality dimension, while Erikson emphasized interaction between the psyche and the ethos.

Intrinsic to Erikson's personality theory is the notion of *epigenesis,* a biological term that refers to a predetermined growth pattern inherent in the embryo. According to Erikson "this principle states that anything that grows has a ground plan, and that out of this ground plan the parts arise, each part having its time of special ascendancy, until all parts have arisen to form a functioning whole" (1968, 92).

Erikson described eight stages of growth, each stage developing in increasing complexity, emerging directly from the previous stage, and building on earlier stages in a cumulative manner. His stages are bipolar in nature and each stage can emerge in either a healthy or unhealthy direction, depending on whether influences are enriching or abusive. These bipolar *crises* must be confronted and negotiated before an individual can successfully resolve subsequent phases. In addition, each stage contributes a quality or virtue to the developing personality.

1. Infancy: trust versus mistrust. During the first year or two of life, a child's development is characterized by learning to trust or mistrust an environment. If children's needs are met by warm, loving parents, they will learn to trust; if met by cold, unsupportive parents, they will develop personalities characterized by feelings of fear, insecurity, and suspicion. The virtue of hope is associated with this stage. According to Iris Cully (1984, 125–26), James Fowler, and Erikson himself (Fowler, 1981, 109), trust is the first step and primary ingredient in the development of faith and the spiritual life.

2. Early childhood: autonomy versus shame and doubt. At this stage (ages 2 and 3) children begin to emerge from total dependence on their parents. They begin to do things on their own, such as feeding themselves and crawling or walking. The positive resolution, which comes from adequate parental support and encouragement, is the ability to carry out certain age-appropriate tasks alone. The negative resolution, the result of either overly punitive or restrictive parents, is a sense of shame at their failures or doubting of their capabilities. The emerging strength is the will to do what is expected.

3. Play age: initiative versus guilt. At ages 4 and 5 children begin to explore their environment and expand their world of experience. If they are encouraged and supported in their endeavors to discover and learn new things, they will likely develop self-confidence. If they are discouraged from or punished for their self-initiated activities, guilt and fear of trying new things will be produced. The quality that comes forth at this point is purpose.

4. School age: industry versus inferiority. Children from ages 6 to 11 expand their social environment from home and family to the neighborhood and school. Successfully learning to relate to peers, performing academic tasks, and playing by the rules leads to industry. Inability to func-

tion in this expanded environment may result in a sense of inferiority throughout life. The basic strength that arises at this stage of life is competence.

5. Adolescence: identity versus identity confusion. Erikson is best known for his contribution to adolescent development (ages 12 to 18) and the understanding of identity achievement. During this pivotal transition stage from dependence to independence, adolescents endeavor to answer critical questions such as "Who am I?" and "Where am I going?" They seriously question the values, beliefs, and attitudes they received from their parents and other significant people. Identity is achieved when the adolescent has a clearly defined definition of self, a self-definition comprised of beliefs, values, attitudes, and goals to which he or she is personally committed. The negative resolution is identity diffusion, reflected in a sense of confusion and uncertainty about who one is. The virtue that emerges during adolescence is fidelity, the ability to maintain commitment in a social environment of contradicting value systems.

6. Young adulthood: intimacy versus isolation. In the years beginning around the age of 18 and extending to age 30, adults are faced with the task of nurturing and developing intimate relationships with others. The negative resolution for this stage is isolation, characterized by an inability to relate to others, self disclose, or give of oneself to others. The basic strength or virtue that is associated with this stage is love.

7. Middle adulthood: generativity versus stagnation. The positive resolution for those between 30 and 65 is generativity, the giving of oneself to the guiding and establishing of the next generation. The nongenerative individual is self-absorbed in his or her own needs, and possesses relatively little interest in helping others. The emerging quality is care.

8. Old age: integrity versus despair. The final stage of life focuses on the fulfillment or lack of fulfillment one feels about life. The integrated person experiences a sense of satisfaction or well-being about his or her life; the despairing individual reflects on life with a certain amount of regret for what has not been accomplished. The final virtue to come forth is wisdom.

Erikson's theory has had a significant impact on the understanding of faith development and spiritual formation. Developmental theory such as Erikson's is especially helpful to Christian educators in determining personality issues that emerge at various stages of the life cycle. For example, if hope and trust are critical issues in infancy and early childhood, Christian educators must be careful to nurture hope and trust in both children and parents. Teachers will be more effective if they apply these insights to their efforts of nurturing spiritual formation at various phases of life (Cully, 1979, 1984; Steele, 1990). Erikson is especially helpful to Christian educators and youth workers for his contribution to the understanding of identity formation in adolescence and early adulthood (Atkinson, 1997, 18–65).

Erikson is one of the leading figures in the field of human development and psychoanalysis. In addition to his teaching and clinical practice, he was a productive writer. His major books include *Childhood and Society* (1950), *Young Man Luther* (1958), *Identity and the Life Cycle* (1959), and *The Life Cycle Completed* (1982).

HARLEY ATKINSON

Bibliography. H. Atkinson (1997), *Ministry with Youth in Crisis;* I. V. Cully (1979), *Christian Child Development;* idem (1984), *Education for Spiritual Growth;* E. H. Erikson (1968), *Identity: Youth and Crisis;* L. L. Steele (1990), *On the Way;* W. R. Yount (1996), *Created to Learn.*

Eros. One of the Greek words for love which first had its meaning in reference to a Grecian god of love named Cupid. This god of love was the personification of the common Greek noun *eros,* meaning desire, especially of a sexual nature. Eros has been defined as an appetite, a yearning desire, which is aroused by the attractive qualities of its object. The root word *eros* is found in the word *erotica* and has been connected to a selfish oriented love. Although the eros form of the word *love* is not used in the New Testament, it has been said that in the eros form of love man seeks God in order to satisfy his own personal needs and desires. In contrast, Agape excluded all egocentric expression and is concerned primarily with the needs of others.

Nygren (1953) saw *eros* as being based on desire; an acquisitive, possessive form of love. He viewed it as a yearning, a striving to have the object that one regards as having value. He described eros as egocentric. It is primarily humanity's love, and its movement is generally horizontal.

Thielicke (1964), who equated eros with sex, realized that past theological guidance on sexuality, which stressed the procreational function of married sex, was inadequate for addressing the situation. He maintained that moral guidelines were needed that did not ostracize eros completely, yet did not leave eros totally unchecked. Thielicke saw eros as the form of love that measured a person's worth in terms of function and of how one's interests could best be served by the other. One of the finest discussions about the eros form of love by an evangelical author was produced by John White in his book entitled *Eros Defiled* (1977). In this book, he discusses the societal forces which have caused mankind to devalue sexuality and defile its original intent by God. His subsequent book, *Eros Redeemed* (1993)

further redeems the use of eros as a God-ordained (within limits) expression of love between a husband and wife.

JAMES A. HEADRICK

Bibliography. M. Gallagher (1989), *Enemies of Eros;* A. B. Gilson (1995), *Eros Breaking Free: Interpreting Sexual Theo-Ethics;* A. Nygren (1953), *Agape and Eros: Part 1—A Study of the Christian Idea of Love, Part 2—The History of the Christian Idea of Love;* L. Paul (1969), *Eros Rediscovered: Restoring Sex to Humanity;* A. Soble, ed. (1989), *Eros, Agape, and Philia: Readings in the Philosophy of Love;* H. Thielicke (1964), *The Ethics of Sex;* J. White (1977), *Eros Defiled: The Christian and Sexual Sin;* idem (1993), *Eros Redeemed: Breaking the Stranglehold of Sexual Sin.*

Eschatology. Doctrine or study of "last things," coming from the Greek word *eschatos,* meaning "last." Traditionally the study has been divided into two main divisions: individual or personal eschatology (comprising the topics of death, the intermediate estate, resurrection, judgment, second death, and eternal life), and collective or world eschatology. Accordingly, eschatology deals with the second coming of Christ, the end of this age, and the introduction of the eternal state with God forever.

Immediately these topics call for some assessment on the biblical concept of time. Contrary to what is popularly thought, this study is not restricted to the absolute end of the world, nor does it build its concepts on a cyclical or a purely linear view of time. Rather than being limited to the end of the world the Hebrew expressions "In the latter days," or "In that day," can denote with equal ease either the end of the present order or the eternal state that flows from that climactic work of God. While the Greeks thought that time went in cycles, doomed to double back on itself repeatedly, the Bible saw time beginning in eternity past and continuing toward a goal which merged into eternity future.

Thirty times in the New Testament "time" was viewed as being involved in either "this age," or "the age to come" when Jesus, by the power of God, began casting out demons and signaling that the kingdom of God had begun to come upon the world (Matt. 12:28; Luke 11:20). "This age" will endure up until "the end," when the kingdom of this world and all its powers are handed over to God the Father and everything has been put under his feet (1 Cor. 15:24–27). "The age to come," then, merges on into the eternal state of eternity and lasts forever.

Now and Not Yet. It is important to note that there is a deliberate tension between the "already" and the "not yet" of the Christian hope. For example, 1 John 3:2 says, "Now are we children of God, and what we will be has not yet been made known. But we know that when he appears, we shall be like him." Similarly, 1 John

255

2:18 says, "The antichrist is coming, [but] even now many antichrists have come." Thus, the kingdom of God with many of its powers have already come upon us, but the full manifestation awaits the conclusion to history that Jesus will introduce.

Individual Eschatology. Ancient mortals reflected more on immortality than moderns do. One need only think of the ancient Egyptians who focused the whole economy of the state on providing for the Pharaoh's pyramid and his life after death.

Resurrection. But even prior to that Enoch, the seventh from Adam (the Bible does not say whether it was the seventh individual or the seventh significant person), was "taken" immediately into the presence of God (Gen. 5:24) "so that he did not experience death" (Heb. 11:5). Thus, even before the argument got started, it was possible for mortals to inhabit immortality: Enoch's translation to glory demonstrated it prior to any commentary that existed in the Word of God on the subject.

An inferential argument making the same point occurs in Luke 20:37–38 from the burning bush of Moses' day. There Moses called the Lord "The God of Abraham, and the God of Isaac, and the God of Jacob" (Exod. 3:6). The point Jesus found in that form of address was this: "He is not the God of the dead, but of the living, for to him all are alive" (Luke 20:38). Abraham, Isaac, and Jacob had not evaporated, but were as alive as the God who declared he too was alive and therefore the God of these ancient worthies. Likewise Job declared that even after he had died he would one day look on his Redeemer with his own eyes and from his own flesh (Job 14:10–12; 19:25–27).

The primary teaching passage on the resurrection of individuals is 1 Corinthians 15. Paul's argument is that Christ himself blazed the way for all other resurrections when he came back from the grave on Easter Sunday. He was seen by more than five hundred people after his triumph over death. Thus, if Christ was raised from the dead, so would all of those be who placed their faith in him.

Three Separate Resurrections. Will all participate in this event? No. Each must be raised in his or her own group. There are three major resurrections: (1) Christ's on the first Easter Sunday morning, (2) all who belong to Christ will rise when he comes again a second time, and (3) at the end all others will be raised to face the judgment at the Great White Throne of God (1 Cor. 15:21–27; Rev. 20:11–15).

The Nature and Mechanisms of the Resurrected Body. This raises the question, "How are the dead raised? With what kind of body will they come?" (1 Cor. 15:35). The answer is observable from life about us: things do not grow until they first die. And it is always by the power of God.

The body they are given is one that has continuity with their mortal bodies (notice the emphasis on the repeated "it" in 1 Cor. 15:42–44), but it is also an improved body (15:50–57).

The Intermediate State. The key passage on what happens between death and the second coming of Christ if one has already died is 2 Corinthians 5:1–10. Paul taught there that to be absent from the body was to be at home with the Lord. Therefore, when the present mortal body, there called "an earthly tent," had its pegs pulled and collapsed as a result, there was every assurance that there was a "building from God, an eternal house in heaven." Whether that body is given immediately upon one's death, prior to the second coming, is still debated, for most scholars argue for an immediate, personal, conscious presence with God, but without the advantage of one's new body until the second coming.

The Second Death. Scripture also mentions the "second death" (Rev. 20:6, 14). That death is reserved for those who fail to believe in the Lord Jesus Christ. When they are judged out of the Book of Life at the Great White Judgment throne, after being given a body to appear before the Judge of the whole earth, they will be forever cast from the presence of God in what is called a "second death."

Collective or National Eschatology. God's program for the future deals with large groups as well as individuals. It begins on the Day of the Lord.

The Day of Yaweh. The "Day of the Lord" is one of the themes frequently found in the prophets. It is that group of events occurring in connection with the second coming of Jesus where God will publicly and powerfully vindicate himself and his people. Specifically, he would come to "judge the world in righteousness" (Pss. 96:13; 98:9). All too many, in the time of the prophet Amos, looked upon this "Day of the Lord" as one only of hope and deliverance for Israel, but Amos rebuked his people for hoping for that day when they were not prepared for it. Instead for them it would be a time of darkness, judgment, and gloom (Amos 5:18–20). The very righteousness of God must involve his judgment on unrighteousness wherever it appeared. The nations would be judged for their sins just as surely as individuals would be judged.

The Nation Israel. At the center of the nations stood Israel, God's ancient covenantal people. Even though they had deserted and abandoned their God, by and large, yet the promise that God would restore them to their land even after they had returned from the Babylonian captivity stands as one of the hallmarks of God's grace and a witness to his faithfulness to his unconditional covenant that he made as far back as the time of the patriarchs (Zech. 10:6–12; Jer. 32:37–41). The promise of restoration to their land was as much part of the eternal covenantal promise of God as was the promise of the Seed (Messiah) or the promise of the gospel ("In your seed shall all the nations of the earth be blessed" Gen. 12:3b).

Romans 9–11 looked forward to a final day when Israel would once again turn, only now in massive numbers, back to their Messiah. The natural branches (Israelites) that had been cut off from the trunk that had secured the promises of God, would be regrafted back to the trunk. This event would occur when the "full number" of the Gentiles were saved and Israel had been made jealous by the power of the gospel she observed working in the church.

The Church. The church was never meant to be a replacement for Israel. While all who believed were in the Messiah were a part of "Abraham's seed," or "the people of God," this did not mean that they were to be equated as the same entities. They were two separate aspects of the One People of God, just as there were other nonessential aspects such as male, female, slave, and free in the one "people of God."

Nor were there two separate programs, as if Israel championed God's earthly program and the church championed his heavenly program. The One Program of God was the kingdom of God. This was the rule and reign of God over everything. It too had many aspects, but that in no way divided the program.

The Coming of Christ. The final day that was coming was called in the New Testament the *parousia* of Christ (1 Cor. 15:23; 1 Thess. 4:15). The word means the "arrival" or "presence" of Christ. It is known also as the "second coming" of Jesus (Heb. 9:28) and is the event where he comes back to earth to finish the whole redemptive story that he began when he was here in his first advent.

Judgment, Heaven, and Hell. Believers will possess eternal life forever while the unredeemed will suffer eternal torment. The significant thing about hell is not the temperature or the geography, despite Virgil, Milton, and others, but the fact that it is eternal separation from God (2 Thess. 1:9–10; Matt. 7:23; 10:32f.).

Hell, the final destiny of those who have rejected Jesus comes from the Hebrew *Ge Hinnon,* "Valley of Hinnon," hence the Greek *Gehenna.* This was the valley outside Jerusalem where child sacrifices to the god Molech were performed (2 Chron. 28:3; 33:6). So revolting and despicable were the thoughts about what had taken place here that when Israel came to her senses, she in turn made it the city dump. Thus the picture in the Gospels of the reality of this place of real suffering with its symbols of smoldering fire, outer darkness, and a place where the worm never perishes (Matt. 8:12; Mark 9:43) pictured eternal torment as the final separation from God.

Heaven, on the other hand, is a place where God has prepared a place for the believer to go (John 14:1–2).

The Millennium. The thousand-year rule and reign of Christ on the earth is mentioned only in one passage in the Bible, Revelation 20:1–10. This rule of Christ is bounded on either side of the thousand years by the resurrection of the unbelievers at its end. Satan is released briefly at the end of the thousand years to try one more assault on the kingdom of God, but he will fail.

This view, called the premillennial view of the earthly reign of Christ, was the prevailing view for the first four centuries of the Christian era, but when Christianity became a legal religion under Emperor Constantine, the fortunes of the state and the church became confused and the amillennial and postmillennial views gained ascendancy. The former denied that there was any millennium at all while the latter viewed this present age as one that optimistically enjoyed the millennium here and now.

Interpretation of Eschatological Events. The history of the church has had a sad story of attempts to set the date for the coming of the Lord and to be overly specific in identifying particular happenings with predictions in Scripture. But students of the Scripture should take note of the fact that history is the final interpreter of prophecy. Furthermore, we are told about the future not that we should be able to scope the local newspapers for headlines, but that we should realize that Jesus is the One who knows the end from the beginning. These two principles are taught in John 13:19—"I am telling you now before it happens, so that when it does happen you will believe that I am he" (cf. John 14:29; 16:4).

WALTER C. KAISER JR.

Bibliography. G. C. Berkouwer (1972), *The Return of Christ;* O. Cullmann (1967), *Salvation in History;* D. E. Gowan (1986), *Eschatology in the Old Testament;* M. J. Harris (1983), *Raised Immortal;* A. A. Hoekema (1979), *The Bible and the Future;* G. E. Ladd (1974), *The Presence of the Future.*

Essentialism. One of the five traditional education philosophies, the others being idealism, realism, Thomism, and perennialism. The things about which they agree are: subject matter/curriculum, knowledge arranged in a hierarchy, authority of the teacher, the school as an intellectual agency, and content over method.

Pragmatic philosophies of education are experimentalism, progressivism, and reconstructionism. The ideas that can bring them together are: emphasis on change, an activity or problem-solving curriculum, a focus on learner-centered instruction, the use of experience and scientific method, and relative "truth" or value.

Existentialism and philosophical analysis are seen as emergent educational philosophies which do not trust philosophical systems and categories.

In effect then, essentialism in its very essence goes back to Plato, Aristotle, and Thomas Aquinas. It requires an emphasis on the fundamental or basic subjects that retain their value across time. There is an essential body of knowledge that a public school should be expected to teach. Teaching students to read and write and do mathematics would be seen as essential skills or content for a person to grasp at elementary school level.

The same primary body of knowledge that is generated down from idealism, realism, and Thomism should be taught in a Christian day school. However, in that it is Christian, the crucial biblical concepts that bear on each idea or proposition should be interfaced and integrated from a biblical life view. In the Sunday school or church school a Christian philosophy of education should find full expression as well.

Central Components of Essentialism. Essentialism is comprised of the following tenets:

1. Learning, by its very nature, demands the discipline and diligence of the student.
2. The major initiative in the teaching/learning process is with the teacher.
3. The focus of the teaching/learning act is the acquiring of the stated curriculum by the student.
4. The teacher is to identify and employ the finest teaching methods which call for mental response and discipline of the child. The school must support the teacher in the endeavor.

In discussing essentialism and religious education Wayne Rood utilizes the approach of Maria Montessori. He presents her work with the child in this manner:

> Freed to respond to a supporting environment in their own ways, the children demonstrated "the interior laws of the formation of man." They are love of the environment (exhibited in the desire for natural order), a love of work (not playing, but an intense kind of task-accomplishment), spontaneous concentration (the needs of species acting through the individual), love of silence (though many children are working near each other), sublimation of the possessive attitude (not "to have" but "to use"), power to act from choice (not mere curiosity), obedience (a sense of mutual aid rather than competition), self-discipline (always the fruit of liberty), and joy (a sheer satisfaction produced by obedience to the laws of one's own nature). (Rood, 1970, 181)

While Montessori remains idealistic, her ideas of the instructor being the "dynamic link" between the young student and what she described as the prepared environment, are crucial. A staunch Roman Catholic, she "often used biblical language to describe relationships between children and their world, and regularly suggested that teachers see their children as Jesus saw them" (Gangel, 1983, 311).

The elementary school child possesses some intrinsic motivation to learn. Yet he or she must be quite dependent on the adult teacher to erect the goals and to provide an environment where the child learns best.

A Brief History. As previously stated Plato, Aristotle, and Thomas Aquinas held to the view that certain content, skills, and tools should have an enduring role in the education of all people. In the Middle Ages the monastics kept the educational light aglow by their copying of the Scriptures and monographs and the instruction of the young and not incidentally, the students who would become priests. The monastic schools, both cathedral and episcopal schools, dominated the educational scene in Europe from the sixth to the tenth or eleventh centuries.

If one were to determine the educational philosophy of the monastic schools, one would find it difficult to choose any other than essentialism. They held the fundamentals high during that somewhat dismal period of history.

In terms of classical education of people who ascribed to the basics of essentialism, John Amos Comenius (1592–1670) made an interesting contribution in his elaborate dream for a pansophistic, universal education approach that he proposed might unite Europe and out of which possibly a "Christian republic" might be created (Rood, 1970, 311).

Another leading educator in Europe was Johann Friedrich Herbart (1776–1841) who was in fact an essentialist. He contributed significantly to the German cultural renaissance. He was convinced that the presentation of the correct ideas would captivate the interest of the student and produce the right response and behavior.

Herbart impacted American education through advocating the circular additions of literature and history in the elementary and secondary schools. He was of the opinion that such content would assist in the development of character.

In this century some of the secular essentialists were Henry Clinton Morrison and Arthur E. Bestor, Jr. Morrison developed the unit plan which gave rise for the organizing and teaching of subject matter in secondary schools. Contracting with students with the agreement that certain subjects be mastered to a particular level has a continuing influence to the present. Bestor, a noted historian, called for a stress on the development of the concept of intellectual discipline in the educational enterprise.

The evangelical Christian advocates that the center of religion and all of life is Jesus Christ. Teaching the Scriptures is of monumental importance because of Christ being the central person of the Bible and the unifying figure of all of space, time, and experience. Therefore, Scripture must be taught, and taught with surpassing focus and prowess. There is no place for inferior education. The essential knowledge and one's basic attitudes should emerge from the Book that must be taught with consummate joy and superlative methodology.

WARREN S. BENSON

Bibliography. K. O. Gangel and W. S. Benson (1983), *Christian Education: Its History and Philosophy;* W. R. Rood (1970), *Understanding Christian Education.*

Ethics. Ethics is the discipline dealing with what is morally right and wrong. It is a moral value system as expressed in a person's actions and attitudes. Thus ethics may be described as religious, Christian, work, or professional. Our intention in this citation is to limit our discussion to Christian ethics.

Major Ethical Systems. According to Geisler, there are only six major ethical systems or ways of determining what is right and wrong (Geisler, 1989, 25–27).

1. Antinomianism asserts that there are no moral or general laws. Therefore, stealing is not wrong or right. Since there are no objective moral laws in this system, deciding right and wrong is subjective and personal.
2. Situationism maintains that there is one absolute law: love. Therefore, stealing may be right if a person does it as an act of love to keep someone from starving to death. Everything except love is relative.
3. Generalism teaches that there are no absolute laws, only some general ones. Therefore, stealing is generally wrong; but there may be times when it is permissible. In this system, the end justifies the means. If the end is good, stealing is not wrong.
4. Unqualified absolutism declares that there are many absolute laws, but they don't conflict. Therefore, stealing is always wrong. In fact, no absolute law, such as truth or love or the sanctity of life, may be broken without consequences. The end never justifies the means. This is the biblical view.
5. Conflicting absolutism says there are many absolute laws that do conflict, and we should choose the lesser evil. Therefore, stealing is forgivable. When we face moral dilemmas, we must decide which absolute laws to keep and then ask for forgiveness for the one we break.
6. Graded absolutism states that there are many absolute laws that do conflict, and we should obey the higher one. Therefore, stealing is sometimes right. When we face moral dilemmas, we must decide which absolute law is more important than the others and follow it, making it permissible to break the others.

Characteristics of Christian Ethics. In contrast to other ethical systems, Christian ethics seeks to formulate an epistomology based upon the infallible Scriptures. In essence, we view what is right and wrong through the lens of general and special revelation. Such a perspective provides us with the following insight:

1. It is based on biblical teaching. God has revealed himself and given us his Word with specific commands and principles to follow in order to determine what is right or wrong in different situations. Not knowing or acknowledging God and the Bible as resources for moral decision making does not excuse a person: "For when Gentiles who do not have the Law do instinctively the things of the Law, these, not having the Law, are a law to themselves, in that they show the work of the Law written in their hearts, their conscience bearing witness; and their thoughts alternately accusing or defending them" (Rom. 2:14–15). People do know what is right even if they don't want to do it.
2. It is absolute, not relative. Whatever God commanded that is based on his unchanging moral character is always right or wrong and does not change from situation to situation. It is true for everyone regardless of race, creed, gender, or ethnic origin. For example, murder is always wrong (Gen. 9:6; Exod. 20:13; Rom. 13:9) because God created man in his image and every person is valuable to him (Gen. 1:27). Other moral absolutes include love, mercy, faithfulness in marriage, truth, and holiness.
3. It is based on God's will, not human opinions. God's will is never contrary to his moral character or attributes so right and wrong are determined by what he wills. For example, God said, "Be holy for I am holy" (Lev. 11:45). And Jesus said to "Love your neighbor as yourself" (Matt. 22:39) because "God is love" (1 John 4:16).
4. It is prescriptive, not descriptive. God prescribed, or ordained, what is right. Consequently, we don't determine rightness by someone's description of it or by comparing our behavior with what everyone else is doing. Morality deals with how we ought to behave, not with how we do behave.

Teaching Ethics. Christian education needs to include teaching on what is right and wrong. This should be a vital component of childhood education since value formation is strongly correlated with age development. Some ways of helping people develop a biblical moral system are:

1. With preschoolers, often repeat to them what is right and wrong. Say, for instance, "It is

wrong to take Jason's crayons." "God is pleased when you do right by being kind to Caitlin."

2. Consistently model what is right and wrong. Your life is the most influential teaching method you can use. When you sin, confess it to the group, if it's appropriate, so they learn how to handle wrong decisions.

3. Teach children, youth, and adults God's character and nature and how moral absolutes spring from his nature.

4. Teach that there are moral absolutes that God expects us to obey. So many children, adolescents, and adults do not know this basic fact. They've been immersed in a culture and educational system that teaches just the opposite.

5. Teach God's commands and the principles behind them, applying them to contemporary situations. For example, by the time teens enter high school, they should have studied the Ten Commandments (Exod. 20) and the Sermon on the Mount (Matt. 5–7) in depth.

6. With teens and adults, discuss moral dilemmas to help them think through their values and wrestle with ethical decisions. Insist that they support their decisions with specific teachings from God's Word.

7. Don't tell older elementary children through adults how to act; instead, lead them into Bible study to discover for themselves. They will have greater ownership of God's moral absolutes.

8. Teach a course in ethics to teens and adults so they recognize false ethical systems and formulate their own values in relation to contemporary ethical problems like abortion and euthanasia.

9. Teach children through adults the consequences of doing right and wrong.

10. Don't forget to pray for students by name that they will develop a biblical moral system and live by it, no matter what.

LIN JOHNSON

Bibliography. N. Geisler (1989), *Christian Ethics: Options and Issues;* S. Grenz (1997), *The Moral Quest: Foundations of Christian Ethics;* A. Holmes (1984), *Ethics: Approaching Moral Decisions;* R. McQuilkin (1995), *An Introduction to Biblical Ethics;* S. Rae (1995), *Moral Choices: An Introduction to Ethics;* J. Trull (1997), *Walking in the Way: An Introduction to Christian Ethics.*

Ethnic Implications for Christian Education. Christian education has largely been developed in the West and exported to the two-thirds world through missionaries. Christian education was a key element in the Western mission endeavor and has been a very successful tool in converting non-believers. Particularly, two-thirds world women who had not been allowed to be educated welcomed a new opportunity to study in mission schools.

Education is a powerful tool in transmitting cultural values and heritage to succeeding generations. Western Christian education is not an exception. In fact, it serves as a powerful tool to enculturate non-Westerners. Niebuhr's models of Christ for culture, against culture, and above culture have rarely been sorted out in evaluating the impact of Christian education on non-Western groups.

While there is a universal message, the gospel also possesses particularity due to the cultural soil within which it is planted. But at the deeper level it has retained many of its cultural norms. In exploring ethnic implications of Christian education, it is important to ask some basic questions: What underlying theological paradigm does Christian education assume? What is the goal of Christian education? What outcomes does it seek? How does Christian education intersect with ethnicity? Christian education cannot be done in a culture-less vacuum. Christian education is not free from the influence of a particular perspective in its curriculum and delivery. It relies heavily on theology and culture. Thus, the person who delivers the educational content and the person to whom it is delivered are significant factors. The culture of the deliverer predetermines the content of the education and the learner's culture interprets the content of the education.

For example, a Korean who came from Korea to the United States in 1968 was newly married and was about to celebrate Thanksgiving Day in the American way for the first time. Close friends decided to get together at the home of the newlyweds and bought a big turkey. The newly wedded wife cut the turkey into Korean barbecued beef strips and baked them in the oven. The turkey strips came out of the oven as hard as cookies. It was an uneatable concoction—neither turkey nor barbecued beef. Eventually she learned how to cook turkey and to enjoy its taste.

Only when we understand the context of American culture can we know how to use the tools of the culture properly. Likewise Christian education cannot be done in a vacuum. Therefore, Christian education seeks how to integrate the gospel and culture, knowledge and deed.

For this reason, there has been a strong emphasis on practical theology in the West in the past two decades. This need for practical theology stems from the failure of dualism—the separation of idea from being. In the traditional Eastern mind the very essence of learning takes place when there is a fusion between the idea and being. Fung Yu-Lan states this as "sageliness within and kingliness without" (Yu-Lan, 1948, 8).

In the discipline of the sage the idea and deed are one. The Western quest for practical theology is a similar concept:

This-worldliness and other-worldliness stand in contrast to each other as do realism and idealism. The task of Chinese philosophy is to accomplish a synthesis out of these antitheses. That does not mean that they are to be abolished. They are still there, but they have been made into a synthetic whole. . . . According to Chinese philosophy, the man who accomplishes this synthesis, not only in theory but also in deed, is the sage. (Yu-Lan, 1948, 8)

Similarly, Western educator Parker Palmer merges theory and deed in education and inspires us in what theological education ought to be: "to teach is to create a space in which obedience to truth is practiced" (Palmer, 1993, xii). Palmer's emphasis on the fusion of mind and heart in education parallels the Chinese understanding of wholeness and health through the balance of *Yin* and *Yang*. The goal of theological education should be holistic spiritual formation which "seeks to be re-formed in our original, created image" (Palmer, 1993, 17).

Palmer brings soul back to education and moves us toward true theological education. Through an emphasis on transformational education, he brings mind and heart together in the educational process.

In summary, for an authentic Christian education to take place across all different ethnic groups, contextualization of the Christian message to each culture is crucial without diluting the essence of the gospel message, which also transcends cultural boundaries. This means we need educators with clear identity and integrity who are committed to process-orientation rather than outcome-orientation.

YOUNG LEE HERTIG

Bibliography. P. J. Palmer (1993), *To Know as We Are Known: Education as a Spiritual Journey;* F. Yu-Lan (1948), *A Short History of Chinese Philosophy: A Systematic Account of Chinese Thought from Its Origins to the Present Day.*

Ethnicity and Small Groups. Ethnicity can be defined as a group of people who share "common ancestry" and "memories of a shared historical past" (Schermerhorn, 1970, 53–67). Therefore, ethnicity has to be understood in historical context. However, preceding generations of immigrants often shatter the shared historicity because the offspring find themselves in historical limbo (Steinberg, 1981, 44–45). This creates a cultural tug-of-war between generations and among people of various ethnicities. Ultimately the cultural tug-of-war is a struggle for power to be.

Episcopal priest Eric Law (1993) builds upon Hofstede's concept of power distance to creatively equalize the role of power in multiethnic small groups. In a high power distance group the majority of people perceive that they have no power; in a low power distance group the majority of people believe they do have power. The higher the power distance of the ethnic group, the more the small group is needed to bridge the power distance. However, due to the consciousness of a hierarchy in the high power distance group, it takes a special method to create interaction in a multiethnic small group format.

Based on the theology of the cross and resurrection, Law developed the practice of "mutual invitation" for multicultural small group interaction. By using invitation, Law introduced an effective way of sharing power in a small group. The spokesperson shares first and then gives up his or her power by inviting another person to speak. The second person accepts the invitation or passes, and then invites another to speak. Thus power is accepted and then given out. The group thus experiences the sharing of power, the waiting, accepting, and giving out of power.

Law's method flows from the theology of the cross—the giving up of power in order to give out power. Talkative people who are not accustomed to waiting must accept the cross by giving up power. Less talkative people who are accustomed to waiting or staying silent are given power to speak, which flows from a theology of the resurrection. The invited person is always given the option to pass, if that person is formulating his or her thoughts.

Depending on what kind of power distance one's ethnicity practices, one has to either practice a theology of the cross or the resurrection. This mutual invitation is crucial in any small group interaction because there are always those who monopolize and those who are silent.

YOUNG LEE HERTIG

Bibliography. E. H. Law (1993), *The Wolf Shall Dwell with the Lamb: A Spirituality for Leadership in a Multicultural Community;* R. Schermerhorn (1970), *Comparative Ethnic Relations;* S. Steinberg (1981), *The Ethnic Myth: Race, Ethnicity, and Class in America.*

Ethnocentricity. Judging another's race, beliefs, or practices on the basis of one's own culture. Children grow up learning right and wrong ways of doing things in their own culture. These cultural practices are then used as standards by which to judge the beliefs and practices within one's culture and to measure outside cultures. Usually people judge another group favorably if they act similar to one's own culture and unfavorably if they do not. All human beings grow up naturally ethnocentric. Accepting different behaviors in another group or changing one's beliefs and practices is a difficult thing to do.

There are several examples of ethnocentric attitudes and behavior in Scripture. Jonah misinterpreted God's promise to bless Israel as an exclusive blessing for Israelites only. His ethnocentric beliefs led to an abhorrence of the Gentile Ninevites and a refusal to take the message of judgment and repentance to them for fear that God would bring them into the kingdom. Peter demonstrated ethnocentric behavior toward the Gentiles. The Holy Spirit gave Peter a remarkable admonition: "Do not call anything impure that God has made clean" (Acts 10:15), challenging Peter to leave his cultural superiority and take the gospel message to Cornelius and the Gentiles. Paul reminds us that ethnic and racial superiority has no place in the life of a Christian: in Christ, "There is neither Jew nor Greek, slave nor free, male nor female" (Gal. 3:28).

Van Rheenen (1994) suggests four areas Western people use to justify their ethnocentric feelings and behaviors. They use feelings of superiority in the areas of technology, education, culture, and theology to validate feelings of superiority. In each case the standard is derived from cultural values that might not be valid among other peoples.

Hiebert (1983) reminds us that it is wrong to make premature judgments of a people or group from an ethnocentristic mind-set. Evaluation of a culture is right, however, when done according to the Word of God. To make a proper evaluation, we must first recognize our own biases when we interpret Scripture and then genuinely study the behavior and values of other people. This he believes will result in more self-criticism and less ethnocentrism.

For the Christian educator ethnocentrism is an issue that must be addressed both personally and in the classroom. Personally, the educator needs to examine her or his own cultural attitudes through close personal contract with other cultural groups. The tension created in exposure to other groups enables one to see the strengths and weaknesses of a culture as well as one's own ethnocentric behavior. In the classroom, the Christian educator needs to value other cultural practices that are not sin, avoid stereotyping people, and not present one culture as the standard by which to judge others' behaviors or actions.

PHILIP BUSTRUM

Bibliography. P. G. Hiebert (1983), *Cultural Anthropology,* 2nd ed.; F. Van Rheenen (1994), *Missions: Biblical Foundations and Contemporary Strategies.*

See also ACCULTURATION; CULTURE; ENCULTURATION; ETHNIC IMPLICATIONS FOR CHRISTIAN EDUCATION

Ethnography. Methodology for research in social science for understanding the rich complexity of individuals, social groups, and whole cultures. It emphasizes looking at a particular social world from the perspective of insiders or members of that world. Its ultimate goal is to provide a comprehensive account or picture of the given social environment or phenomenon. Its primary methods include observation, interviews, and collecting documents, photographs, and videos. The scope of study varies from in-depth investigation into a single situation or case to many sites. It ranges in length from brief interviews to several years of observation. The design of ethnographic research is flexible and evolves as the research unfolds. The data generally take the form of field notes from observation or interviews. To collect these data the researcher enters into the world being studied in some role (usually unobstrusive) that is identifiable within the world's cultural framework. Data analysis is largely inductive and occurs concurrently with data collection. It involves looking for themes, patterns, anomalies, relating parts to the whole, and various forms of narrative analysis. Data analysis also often includes dialogue and feedback from key informants in the social world.

Christian education includes the practice of educational ministries of many kinds. Like other professional fields of practice (education, social work, health care) Christian education loosely rests on both theoretical and scientific foundations. Even though many practitioners may not understand or care about the philosophical or social scientific principles informing their practices, the quality of ministry and the vitality of the field depend on careful reflection on practice. As a field Christian education has not to date developed any significant social research base. Without such it remains captive to the exigencies of day-to-day ministry and to the shifting winds of cultural and social belief systems. Ethnography, part of the toolkit of social science, can provide significant insights for grounding Christian education more solidly in the lived realities of human persons and social groups and contexts.

Several purposes of ethnography in grounding Christian education can be delineated. First is the descriptive purpose of what actually goes on in Christian education programs. Accurate, complete descriptive accounts from participants in Christian education programs are needed. Both traditional and innovative programs need to be studied thoroughly in order to grasp the who, what, when, where, how, and why of educational ministries in churches, homes, colleges, camps, and so on. Second, ethnography can serve to foster theory building in Christian education. Grounding theories in real-world data can move Christian education beyond the realm of personal biases, traditionalism, and dogmatism. Third, ethnography can be used to evaluate the teaching and learning strategies in Christian education. Both summative and formative evaluations can be conducted in an ethnographic approach. To improve the effectiveness of any instructional method or curriculum, evaluative research is needed.

VERNON L. BLACKWOOD

Bibliography. R. Bogdan and S. K. Biklen (1982), *Qualitative Research for Education;* J. Goetz and M. LeCompte (1984), *Ethnography and Qualitative Design in Educational Research;* B. Webb-Mitchell, *Religious Education* 87, no. 2 (1992): 246–58.

Eucharist. *See* Communion.

Euthanasia. Term of Greek origin, literally meaning "good death," and referring to the act of inducing a gentle, painless death. The contemporary meaning of the word has reference to the deliberate termination of life in order to prevent unavoidable suffering. In 1937 the National Society for the Legalization of Euthanasia was founded in the United States, but it took nearly a generation before the subject claimed national attention. With the exception of the abortion question, no issue has sparked greater moral debate during the past two decades of the twentieth century. Even among its proponents there are two schools of thought. Advocates of *passive euthanasia* consider it ethical not to artificially prolong the life of a suffering person whose disease is inevitably fatal. Instead, comfort and relief are provided while the patient awaits death.

Aggressive life-support measures, such as the use of mechanical respirators with patients whose brain activity has ceased, are considered inhumane in the prolongation of life. A number of states have passed legislation granting patients the right to "death with dignity," by conferring the authority to withdraw life support upon a designated relative, friend, or legal advisor. In 1990 the United States Supreme Court declared that individuals who make their wishes known have a constitutional right to have life-sustaining treatment discontinued. Despite these recent legislative enactments, many physicians continue to struggle with the ethics involved in such decisions in light of their Hippocratic oath.

Much of the moral dilemma is the result of a clear definition of death. Whereas the cessation of breathing and heart activity was formerly considered the end of life, because these functions are able to be artificially maintained indefinitely, death is more widely accepted today as the lack of electrical activity in the brain. Supporters of *active euthanasia* urge taking proactive measures to terminate someone's life, and hence the colloquialisms "mercy killing" and "physician-assisted suicide." Although active euthanasia is considered a crime in the United States, Michigan pathologist Jack Kevorkian openly assisted in the suicides of dozens of purportedly terminally ill patients. In his 1991 book, *Prescription: Medicide—The Goodness of Planned Death,* Kevorkian spoke of the "stone-age ethics of space-age medicine," and of his personal crusade advocating physician-assisted suicide. By the end of 1997, he had defied numerous court directives and reportedly assisted in seventy-five deaths, but according to his attorney Geoffrey Fieger and assistant Janet Good (in whose death he also assisted), many other cases have been kept private. Although Kevorkian is the most visible of contemporary euthanasia activists, other less prominent voices with greater credibility are being raised in its support.

Foundations with links to health care enterprises currently fund programs with a distinct pro-euthanasia bias. Public opinion toward the issue has moved from strong opposition to a more neutral stance over the past quarter-century. In 1995 Australia's Northern Territory passed the "Rights of the Terminally Ill Act," which was heralded as the world's first law permitting euthanasia and suicide; but two years later the National Senate repealed it. A similar measure was passed in Oregon in 1994, but was challenged in court and never went into effect. Although euthanasia is widely practiced in the Netherlands, it remains technically illegal. Doubtless, the ethical debate surrounding euthanasia will continue well into the twenty-first century, as to whether "death with dignity" delivers what it promises.

DAVID GOUGH

Evangelicalism. The term *evangelicalism* virtually transliterates the Greek word *euangelion,* "gospel" or "good message." Though the history of *evangelicalism* as a distinct movement chronicles events within the present generation, its identifying traits, both doctrinal and experiential, extend much farther into the past. In fact, the earliest definers of its contemporary shape would see it merely as biblical Christianity thriving in contemporary cultures. Carl F. H. Henry (1979) identifies its positive tenets as "supplied by the apostolic preaching, at first in vocal and then in written form." Evangelicals should be defined in terms of their "devotion to the sure Word of the Bible" (361).

As a descriptive term, "evangelical" has been used since the Reformation of the sixteenth century to refer to doctrinal ideas distinguishing Reformation theology from Roman Catholic theology. Included were submission to Scripture as the final arbiter in all doctrinal formulation and theological dispute, the completeness of Christ's atoning work, justification by grace through faith founded on the imputation of Christ's righteousness by the forensic declaration of God, and the necessity of a sovereign, secret, regenerating work of the Holy Spirit to subdue and change the sinful propensities of the human heart. Eventually, Lutheran churches were called "evangelical" to distinguish them from Roman Catholic on the one hand and, on the other, from the "Reformed" wing of the Reformation. Reformed Christians, however, still used the term in its more specifically theological sense. The classis of Amsterdam, in about 1730, examined the preaching of Theodore Frelinghuysen because of complaints and found his sermons to be thoroughly "evangelical."

Since the 1940s, a generation of conservative Christians has consciously taken the moniker *evangelical* or *neo-evangelical*. Several formative silhouettes emerge as decisive in defining this movement. Among the first was the formation of the National Association of Evangelicals (NAE) in 1942. This organization served as an orthodox alternative for many to the liberal Federal Council of Churches (FCC) and the separatistic American Council of Christian Churches (ACCC). Many younger fundamentalists, disenchanted with endless schism and desiring a more pervasive and positive application of orthodox Christianity to the whole of society, began to seek ways of creative engagement with the culture as well as a rigorous and closely argued apologetic for orthodox Christianity. All of this was basic to an aggressive and far-reaching proclamation of the gospel. Harold John Ockenga (1905–85), the first president of the NEA, distinguished fundamentalism from evangelicalism by asserting, "The new evangelicalism embraced the full orthodoxy of fundamentalism, but manifests a social consciousness and responsibility which was strangely absent from fundamentalism." He argued that "orthodox Christians cannot abdicate their responsibility in the social scene " (Marty, 1977, 201, 202).

Among several highly qualified protagonists, Carl Ferdinand Howard Henry (b. 1913) emerged as a definitive thinker in the movement. His 1946 book *Remaking the Modern Mind* established a new tone for conservative interaction with intellectual thought and critique of the antisupernatural worldviews unchallenged by modernism. The tone was not strident and defamatory, but insistent upon a calm engagement with modern thought. Henry relied neither on caricature nor shallow presentation of an opponent's viewpoint but only honest, respectful analysis of contemporary philosophical and theological positions. This type of engagement did not signal a diminished commitment to orthodoxy or the clarity of one's affirmation of it. The purpose was to lay bare the emptiness of modernism and denude it of its pretensions to be the true heir of the Protestant spirit.

The new approach did not stop with scholarly engagement of secularism and liberalism, but was complemented by a rigorous self-critique of perceived fundamentalist failings. In 1947, in the book, *The Uneasy Conscience of Modern Fundamentalism*, Henry inserted a scalpel and "performed surgery" on fundamentalism. He knew that "revelational and non-revelational views" would always be in contrast and that redemptive aspects of Christianity should remain central to all evangelical concerns. Bible believers must not, however, sink into obscurantism or fail to challenge modern worldviews with the genius of the Hebrew-Christian outlook. Evangelicals need not embrace liberalism's defunct social gospel to cooperate in plans to improve society as long as warnings about the inadequacy and instability of such solutions are proclaimed clearly.

Academic, intellectual continuity for evangelicalism was to be provided by Fuller Theological Seminary, founded by Charles Fuller in 1947 in Pasadena, California. Ockenga served as its first president and Carl Henry was one of the first four faculty members. It was conceived to provide for the last half of the twentieth century the theological leadership provided by Princeton in the last half of the nineteenth century. Wheaton College (Illinois Institute, 1848; Wheaton College, 1860) emerged as the prototype evangelical college having among its graduates Harold Lindsell, Carl F. H. Henry, E. J. Carnell, Billy Graham, and Christian martyr Jim Elliott, a paradigmatic figure for unreserved abandon to missionary labor.

Evangelicalism implies a passionate and deeply biblical evangelism. According to Henry, evangelism as an activity and evangelicalism as a doctrinal system are inseparable. The New Testament envisioned no nonmissionary Christians and also knew of no nondoctrinal evangelism or acceptable evangelism consistent with defection from revealed truth. In God's providence this peculiarly defining moment for the evangelical movement came in the deeply private and personal struggles of Billy Graham. Billy Graham's Los Angeles crusade in 1949 was only the public evidence of the outcome of this struggle six weeks prior to the Crusade. Graham compared his narrowly preconceived views of God with the God of Scripture. His preaching lacked the authority that characterized preachers of other generations. His battle with the Bible led him to accept it as the Word of God "without reservations." Graham testified that he prayed that his preaching would bear the mark of biblical authority to convict him of sin and turn sinners to the Savior. Graham did not distinguish between the authority of God and the authority of the Bible; he was confident that God made His will known authoritatively in the Scriptures. The 1949 Los Angeles Crusade and the 1954 Greater London Crusade made Graham the most recognizable evangelical in the world. His influence triggered the 1956 beginning of *Christianity Today* and the 1966 Berlin World Congress on Evangelism.

Intellectual, social, and evangelistic voices needed the supplementary sustenance of a solid and insightful literary production. On October 15, 1956, volume 1, number 1, of *Christianity Today* came from the press. Its editor was Carl F. H. Henry and the executive editor L. Nelson

Bell, Billy Graham's father-in-law. Graham's article "Biblical Authority in Evangelism" was carried in that issue. G. C. Berkouwer, Addison Leitch, and Henry also had articles. In addition, Henry's editorial, "Why *Christianity Today*?" defined the magazine's purpose. He spoke clearly on the failure of liberalism to "meet the moral and spiritual needs of the people." He commended the work of Karl Barth in attacking liberalism and bringing in a "religious springtime after the long, cold, winter of Liberalism." He also made it clear, however, that if one cannot discern the difference between the views of the Bible represented by Barth's theology on the one hand and that of evangelical theology on the other, he "stands in need of theological lenses." Henry was clear that the evangelicalism espoused by *Christianity Today* would be confident in both the authority and clarity of Scripture. Too often had twentieth-century Christianity been disappointed by the reality that "A half-hearted confidence in the reliability and authority of Scripture faces the opportunities of evangelism with self-defeating uncertainties." The magazine would affirm the wrath of God, the propitiatory atonement, eternal punishment, a unity between what the Bible says in its words and propositions and what God says, "the great emphases of the historic creeds," the "reasonableness and effectiveness of the Christian evangel," and would impose a vision "of the sovereign God, of a sovereignty which is universal, unlimited and immutable." With Carl Henry as editor, *CT* became a voice of theological depth, integrity, and challenge. Large numbers of contemporary thinkers shared this vision.

Twenty years after the founding of *Christianity Today* saw 1976 dubbed "the year of the evangelical." Two presidential candidates, James Carter and Gerald Ford, identified themselves as evangelical Christians. This apparent success led to a massive surge in interpretations of the evangelical phenomenon and a corresponding confusion concerning its leading principles and historical sources. That same year saw Harold Lindsell's *Battle for the Bible* calling attention to, and warning against, divergence across the evangelical world over the nature of biblical inspiration and authority. Donald Dayton's *Discovering an Evangelical Heritage* (1976) sought to establish a historical perception of a more radical socially active foundation for evangelicalism. The original emphases on the inerrancy of Scripture, the historic creeds, and the material and formal principles of the Reformation have been challenged by advocates of a more subjective experiential model.

The first major evidence of fissure within the new evangelicalism came in December 1962, when Daniel Fuller's return from sabbatical to become dean of Fuller Seminary revealed a division in the faculty over inerrancy. Fuller pushed the school toward a limited inerrancy viewpoint. Bernard Ramm's general summary of evangelical principle in *The Evangelical Heritage* (1973) that any system that emphasizes subjective response over objective truth is a "fatal reconstruction of the Christian faith" (14) had been challenged. Ramm himself shifted notably in *After Fundamentalism* (1983) when he recommended Barth's theological methodology to evangelicals. In *Revisioning Evangelical Theology* (1993), Stanley Grenz argues that Henry's view of propositional revelation must be abandoned. Grenz favors a consensus-oriented methodology in *Theology for the Community of God* (1994). The historical and confessional basis is extended by Donald W. Dayton and Robert K. Johnston in *The Variety of American Evangelicalism (*1991). Dayton even called for a moratorium on the use of the word *evangelical* because of the great difficulty he had in locating a unitive principle for it. Clark Pinnock, an early champion of confessional evangelicalism, advocated wider latitude in the theological parameters of the movement. He pressed for acceptance of a theology of God whose nature would contradict both eternal wrath and knowledge of all future events. Theology should be governed by an anthropology centered on "significant freedom" for human beings. In light of all these falling boundaries, Millard Erickson published a discussion with the revealing title *The Evangelical Left* (1997). His last chapter poses the much-needed question as to how much movement may occur and one still be within the evangelical camp.

Several attempts at tightening definitions have been made. In 1977 the International Council on Biblical Inerrancy began a series of publications and conferences based on the commitment that the "defense and application of the doctrine of biblical inerrancy" is an "essential element of the authority of Scripture and a necessity for the health of the church." Conferences on biblical authority, hermeneutics, application, and doctrine produced monographs (e.g., *Scripture and Truth* [1983], *Hermeneutics, Authority, and Canon* [1986], *Applying the Scriptures* [1987], and *Evangelical Affirmations* [1990]) and succinct statements such as the "Chicago Statement on Biblical Inerrancy" (1978). Many groups to define theological expectations have used these statements.

At the same time, the evangelical tent continues to extend quite broadly. It is even a matter of dispute as to whether evangelicalism is a doctrine or a mood. Timothy Weber, who lists the four kinds of evangelicals as classical, pietist, fundamentalist, and progressive, reflects the theological vagrancy that has produced the lack of doctrinal consensus at the close of the twentieth century. He characterizes some as wanting "to force a kind of theological uniformity on evangelicalism" which Weber says never existed, while others "speak almost exclusively of an evangelical spirit, without specifying any theological boundaries." David Wells (*No Place For Truth or Whatever Happened to Evangelical Theology?* [1993]) gave documentation and considerable reflection to this disturbing trend. Wells questioned the evangelical resolve to recapture the centrality of confessional objective theology for the being and mission of the church.

The word *evangelical* has too long a pedigree to pass away from the theological world. In a movement purposefully transdenominational, intricate difficulties naturally attend attempts at drawing lasting definitions or even isolating dominant principles. If the movement, however, follows the general course of Christian history and maintains an identifiable presence in the Christian world, a clearly stated, coherently arranged, and confessionally important doctrinal silhouette will emerge. It will take an identifiable posture on the nature of biblical authority in religion, the existence and attributes of God, and the character of the redemptive message and experience.

TOM J. NETTLES

Bibliography. D. A. Carson and J. D. Woodbridge (1983), *Scripture and Truth; Christianity Today,* October 15, 1956, pp. 5, 6; D. Dayton (1976), *Discovering an Evangelical Heritage;* D. W. Dayton and R. K. Johnston (1991), *The Variety of American Evangelicalism;* C. F. H. Henry (1979), *The New International Dictionary of the Christian Church;* idem (1947), *The Uneasy Conscience of Modern Fundamentalism;* B. Ramm (1973), *The Evangelical Heritage;* D. Wells (1993), *No Place for Truth or Whatever Happened to Evangelical Theology?;* D. Wells and J. D. Woodbridge (1977), *The Evangelicals;* J. D. Woodbridge, M. A. Noll, and N. O. Hatch (1979), *The Gospel in America: Themes in the Story of America's Evangelicals.*

Evangelical Training Association (ETA). Nonprofit association, headquartered in Wheaton, Illinois, consisting of two hundred schools of higher education in three divisions: Graduate/Seminary, Undergraduate, and Adult Education. The mission of ETA is to provide programs and materials to churches and educational institutions which will help equip lay people for ministry and promote excellence in every aspect of Christian education. ETA has a broad interdenominational constituency, distributing its materials to churches in over ninety denominations.

ETA was founded in 1930 as the International Bible Institute Council of Christian Education (IBICCE) by five schools of higher education: Moody Bible Institute, Northwestern College, the Bible Institute of Los Angeles (now Biola University), Columbia Bible College, and Toronto Bible Institute (now Tyndale University).

The purpose of the organization was twofold. First, IBICCE sought to bring together schools of higher Christian education in an attempt to stan-dardize the curriculum used to train Bible teachers. Second, the founding schools desired to provide an alternative to evangelicals who were concerned about the predominance of liberal theology in the Religious Education Association (founded in 1903) and the International Council of Religious Education (founded in 1922). These two organizations produced Bible teacher training materials as well as outlines used by Sunday school curriculum publishers.

In 1931, the name was changed to Evangelical Teacher Training Association (ETTA), which reflected more accurately the purpose of the organization. Clarence H. Benson, professor of Christian Education at Moody Bible Institute in Chicago, Illinois, was the guiding force behind ETTA from 1930 until his death in 1954. One of Benson's strongest contributions was the writing of eight ETTA textbooks which sold a combined total of over 1 million copies.

ETTA quickly grew from a membership of 59 schools in 1935 to 164 schools in 1955. Its current membership is 200 schools. In 1988, the name was shortened to ETA by dropping the first "T"—"Teacher." This was done to emphasize a broadened commitment to provide programs and materials to a wider range of leaders in the local church in addition to Bible teachers.

ETA has developed a comprehensive adult education curriculum consisting of 19 core courses in four subject areas: Bible and theology, ministry skills, leadership skills, and outreach skills. Each course follows the CEU (Continuing Education Unit) pattern of 10 classroom hours per course. Since 1930, ETA has distributed over 3.5 million textbooks and its materials have been translated into over 25 languages. In addition, ETA has produced a number of audio and video training courses. ETA publishes a newsletter *Profile* (quarterly) and the *Journal of Adult Training* (twice a year).

Students in local churches and Bible institutes may earn ETA credit when the course is taught by an ETA-approved teacher, the course textbook is read, eight of ten classroom hours are attended, and a test or project is successfully completed. As students accumulate individual courses, they may apply course credits toward the earning of ETA certificates, which honor the student's educational achievement. ETA grants certificates on four levels, each of which requires the completion of four courses following a prescribed sequence.

A person becomes an ETA-approved teacher in one of two ways. First, ETA member schools award the ETA diploma to their graduates who complete a concentration in Christian education/church ministry courses. Diploma holders receive lifetime approval to teach courses for ETA credit. Over eighty thousand diplomas have been awarded since 1930. Second, individuals who are gifted, qualified to teach, and in agreement with the ETA doctrinal statement can be approved for a three-year period.

ETA has made at least four lasting contributions to evangelical Christian education. First, it provided a rallying point for schools of higher Christian education who are theologically conservative. Second, it provided a standardized training curriculum which helped raise the level of Bible teacher preparation at the institutional level. Third, it developed (and continues to do so) a comprehensive teacher/leadership training curriculum which is widely used in thousands of churches and Bible institutes. Fourth, it continues to provide opportunities for fellowship and cooperation across denominational, racial, and ethnic lines among a variety of evangelical churches and schools.

JONATHAN N. THIGPEN

Evangelism. Calling persons to repentance from sin and acceptance of the gospel. The gospel or the Good News is that God has sent his Son, Jesus Christ, to earth in order to redeem persons and bring them into a personal relationship with himself. In such biblical passages as John 3:16 God's love for all humanity is expressed, along with his desire that all persons will come to him through faith in the redemptive work of Jesus Christ on the cross and through the resurrection.

Evangelism is a work performed by the Holy Spirit through the testimony of Christian believers, who witness to a lost world about the Good News that God loves them. Evangelism takes place when a pastor reaches converts through evangelistic preaching in a local church or through the witness of a missionary to a national in the jungles of Southeast Asia. Evangelism may take place when one Christian believer shares personal faith with a business associate or with a neighbor.

Even though evangelism is ordinarily considered a New Testament concept, there are instances where it was apparent in the Old Testament as well. God's concern for all humanity was evident in his intention to bless other peoples through his people, Israel. Consider 1 Kings 8:41–45, Psalm 22:27–28, and Isaiah 2:2–4.

Evangelism was endemic to the Christian church from its inception. In the Great Commission (Matt. 28:18–20) Jesus prepared his disciples for an evangelistic thrust throughout the world by instructing them to be his witnesses. In the New Testament church evangelism first appears on the day of Pentecost (Acts 2). The apostle Peter proclaimed the story of God's dealing with the people of Israel and the coming of Christ as redeemer. The message ended with a call to repentance and faith in him. A multitude of persons responded to the message and followed Jesus.

From that point, the disciples continued to evangelize and the church continued to grow. Among the early converts were the Roman sol-dier, Cornelius, and his family. Peter led them to faith in Christ. These were Gentiles. It was evident that God's purpose included bringing people from all ethnic and racial groups to salvation through faith in Jesus. Scripture makes it clear that God is still concerned to bring all people to himself.

After chapter 12 of Acts, the evangelistic emphasis through the missionary journeys of Paul is described. He traveled throughout the Roman world, leading persons to faith in Christ. In each age since, missionaries have witnessed to peoples around the globe. They continue to retell the gospel of salvation in Jesus Christ. These ambassadors for Christ have not come exclusively from the ranks of professional evangelists. Rather, most are ordinary persons who experienced an intimate relationship with Christ. They share the message of salvation with persons who lack the inner joy and peace that Christ can provide. Through the centuries, personal evangelism has been the primary means for church growth.

Implicit within the gospel is the expectation of living a godly life. The early Christians were known as the people of the Way. The Christian life is a way of life, not simply a religion. The moral precepts need to be taught and followed in obedience to the precepts and commands of Jesus.

In the New Testament there are five words that describe the task of evangelism. Together these words assist in providing an appreciation for the breadth and scope of evangelism. The first of these is found in Matthew 4:23. Jesus went through Galilee "proclaiming the gospel of the kingdom." The Greek term for "proclaim" is *kerusso*. It carried the idea of one who was a herald of the good news.

Related to that term is the term *evangelist*. The Greek root for this term, *euangelion*, provides the basis for the English equivalent, *evangelism*. As it is employed in Acts 21:8, *euangelistes* also refers to the person who is the evangelist. This person brings good tidings or the message that salvation may be found through Jesus Christ.

The next term also identifies the persons who proclaim the gospel. The term is *martus*, and it means "witnesses." This term may be found in Acts 1:8. This passage recounts the words of Jesus prior to his ascension into heaven. He told the disciples that they would be his witnesses locally and to the ends of the earth.

Perhaps the essence of evangelism is captured best by Jesus in his use of two words in the Great Commission (Matt. 28:19–20). The first of these words, from verse 19, is disciple or *matheteuo*. It describes the one who becomes a follower of Christ. This word carries the idea of teaching and instruction. It connotes a disciple who is taught the precepts of Jesus. To become a Christian requires some knowledge of the teaching and precepts of Christ. It is clear from some of the early writings that the disciples in the early church carefully studied and learned his words.

This idea is further supported by the term *didasko*, which means "to teach," in verse 20. *Didasko* means imparting instruction to the follower and even goes so far as to suggest indoctrinating the disciple. Serious study of the words of Jesus and the material covered in the Bible needs to be high on the agenda of both newly evangelized and mature Christians. Evangelism without teaching leads to an emotional experience that lacks the depth needed to carry one through the vicissitudes of life.

The early church took the teaching seriously. The Didache, a very early manual for the church, suggests that there was a waiting period between the time of making a profession of faith and baptism. During this period the new convert was taught the content of Christian faith through catechism. The new believer was also guided to adopt a new and Christian lifestyle. This teaching period lasted for two to three years, culminating in baptism and church membership. With the nominal acceptance of Christianity, after A.D. 313, infant baptism and confirmation gradually brought an end to the catechumenate. Families assumed more responsibility in evangelizing and teaching their children.

If one examines the content of the evangelistic messages of Peter and Paul and others, they always point to Jesus. The Good News always focuses upon Jesus Christ, God's Son. He came to earth as God and through his birth, identified with humanity. He lived, taught, and ministered in his home country of Palestine. At the end of his ministry he went to the cross and died for the sins of the whole world. He arose the third day and is now seated at the right hand of God the Father Almighty. The Good News is that all who will trust in Jesus' sacrificial death and resurrection will find new life here and eternal life in the hereafter.

Evangelism may be done on a mass basis, as in the Billy Graham evangelistic crusades. Or evangelism may be done at the interpersonal relationship level, in which a believer shares the faith with someone who does not know Christ. Programs like Evangelism Explosion, the Navigators, and Campus Crusade for Christ provide instruction for Christians to develop their skills for personal evangelism. Most denominations also provide instruction for their members in ways to evangelize.

EDWARD A. BUCHANAN

Bibliography. M. Green (1970), *Evangelism in the Early Church;* P. Little (1988), *How to Give Away Your Faith.*

Evangelism, Child. Because the sin of Adam has been passed on to all of humankind (original sin), children are born separated from God and under his condemnation as sinners. Therefore, it is incumbent upon Christian parents and the church to evangelize children so that they might put their faith in Christ for salvation. How children are to be evangelized has been understood historically in a variety of ways.

Horace Bushnell (1861) argued that children of believers are to be raised in the faith, having never known a time when they were not believers. For Bushnell, evangelization was to be a natural process, taking place through the relationships between believing parents and their children. He believed that children who were raised in a Christian home should not have to go through a technical conversion experience, but should quietly come to faith through the nurturing efforts of their parents. Bushnell was reacting against the Revivalists, who believed that children could not be candidates for salvation until they reached the *age of accountability*, making them capable of understanding Christian faith. Their practice was to stress to children their need for a savior, but to withhold the possibility of salvation until the child was capable of a wholehearted commitment to the teachings of Christ.

Child evangelists base their efforts on an understanding of faith in Christ, which is primarily cognitive, presenting the Christian faith as a set of propositions to be accepted as true. Evangelization is a matter of inviting children to believe that Jesus died for their sins. Therefore, the task of evangelism is to present this content in ways that are understandable to children. Through symbols and stories, children of believers and unbelievers alike are presented with the same message. Unlike the Revivalists, these child evangelists believe that salvation comes through decision rather than through radical commitment to the teachings and authority of Christ.

Building upon the cognitive development theories of Jean Piaget, some believe that children cannot understand the content of the gospel, and therefore should not be taught religious truths. Ronald Goldman and John Peatling exemplify this position, arguing that theological constructs should not be taught until the child has reached *full cognitive maturity*, about the age of 12.

Two theological solutions to original sin are infant baptism and age of accountability. Both are designed to allow for infants who die prior to faith commitments to be able to enter heaven. Roman Catholics believe that infant baptism removes original sin and allows the child to return to a state of innocence. Lutherans believe that infant baptism is a means of grace, whereby God works faith into the heart of the child. Faith is understood as relational trust in God, similar to the trust children have in their mother. The Reformed position is that baptism is the sign of the covenant made between parents and God. Just as circumcision was a sign of commitment and consecration under the old covenant, so now baptism is of parallel significance under the new covenant, indicating commitment to raise the child to follow Jesus and trust in God to regenerate the child and bring him or her to faith.

Age of accountability is the second mode of making the child eligible for heaven. This doctrine asserts that until children reach an age of moral responsibility for their sins, God will not hold them accountable for their own sin, or the imputed sin of Adam. Therefore, children who die prior to the age of accountability go to heaven. Both infant baptism and age of accountability are theological responses to the problem of original sin.

A balanced perspective on the evangelization of children must be respectful both of biblical teaching on the nature of faith (having a content to be believed, requiring a heart response to God, and choosing to live in obedience to biblical teaching), and of the ability of children to believe the gospel. While making every effort to avoid trivializing the gospel message, the child evangelist must be able to explain the gospel in ways that are comprehensible to children, fulfilling our Lord's command to ". . . Let the children alone and do not hinder them from coming to me; for the kingdom of heaven belongs to such as these" (Matt. 19:14). Like all of humankind, children are in need of redemption, and the gospel is for them, too.

PERRY G. DOWNS

Bibliography. H. Bushnell (1861 reprint), *Christian Nurture;* P. G. Downs (1994), *Teaching for Spiritual Growth;* R. Goldman (1964), *Religious Thinking from Childhood to Adolescence;* J. Peatling (1981), *Religious Education in a Psychological Key;* G. T. Sparkman (1983), *The Salvation and Nurture of the Child of God.*

Evangelism, Youth. Evangelism means "bearing a message of good news." Practically, as Jesus himself demonstrated, it is an enterprise that encompasses everything from verbal proclamation of the Good News of Christ's coming to hanging out with a student on the basketball court, to sitting with some kids in a McDonald's, to harboring in your home a student whose body is reacting violently to too many bad decisions and too much alcohol. In short, as it was for the first Evangel, it is a ministry of making God's love "become flesh," giving a visible, understandable expression to the invisible God.

In the arena of youth ministry, evangelism is a process of bringing young people along on a journey from a point of nonawareness ("I don't see why people make such a big deal about God and religion"), to a point of awareness ("Okay, if God is your thing, that's cool; but I couldn't care less"), to a place of interest ("Are you saying that this God really loves me?"), to the milestone of acceptance ("I don't understand all of this stuff, but I understand enough to know that I need to receive Christ as my Savior"). It is a journey that

may take only weeks, or it may take months or years. As with Bunyan's *Pilgrim's Progress*, it is a journey fraught with pitfalls, snares, setbacks, temptations, and, by God's grace, occasional forward movement.

To fully appreciate this journey and invite students to make it is to understand some very basic truths about evangelism in the context of youth ministry. Few people make this journey alone. Too often, the church has approached the task of youth evangelism by using what one writer described as "the Little Bo Peep" approach: leave them alone and they'll come home wagging their tails behind them. Jesus' approach to lost sheep (Luke 15:4–7) was quite different. His model reminds us that Christian education is not a neat, clean, classroom enterprise. It is characterized less by chalk and a lectern, and more by dirty sandals and a shepherd's staff.

The universal characteristic of authentic, fruitful evangelism is that it is marked by relationships. Evangelism seldom happens at a distance. We cannot embrace those to whom we are not first willing to draw near. And any persuasive embrace always includes the personal touch (see John 1:14, literally "Jesus tabernacled or pitched his tent among them"). Even in those cases at a youth rally or a concert or a crusade where a student responds to an invitation from the front, it is almost always partially due to the influence of someone who has been traveling beside (see also 1 Thess. 2:8).

Proclaiming the gospel begins before we proclaim the gospel. Jesus called his followers to be fishers of men. It is obvious to even the novice fisherman that fish rarely lunge up out of the water and jump into a net sitting on the dock. Any youth ministry evangelism is going to have to set some hooks to bait youth with no spiritual background.

Some will argue that "the time is too short and the need is too urgent to waste time on youth ministry fun and games. . . . Our mandate in Scripture is not to make Christians; it is to make disciples." And it's true. The time is short and the need is urgent. But we cannot disciple believers until first they become believers. We cannot nurture the plant into fuller fruitfulness without first going through the painstaking work of preparing the soil, planting the seed, waiting out the seasons of gestation, and then nurturing the first appearance of young shoots.

Proclaiming the gospel must include a proclamation of the gospel. Evangelism is more than simply speaking the gospel, but it certainly is no less than speaking the gospel. Timing is critical, sensitivity is vital, credibility is essential, but there must be some point in the journey where we explain to our fellow travelers where it is we hope to be taking them. We need to explain to them the way of salvation so that they might choose to walk the road for themselves. Until we have made this proclamation, we have not fully proclaimed the gospel.

In some quarters there is such fear of turning off our youth that we never turn them on. No one is suggesting that we be rude or pushy. Explaining the gospel must be done in an attitude of humility and honesty, with an attitude that says, "My love for you is not dependent on your love for Jesus." But somewhere in the journey, we must explain the essential elements of the gospel, the bad news about sin and its consequent penalty of death, the Good News about the cross and how Jesus died to pay that penalty of death on behalf of all who will accept this free gift, and the best news that he arose again to raise us with him to a whole new life (Rom. 3:23–26).

Evangelism is not the end of the journey, it is the beginning of the rest of the journey. Just as a harvest cannot begin without the preparing of the soil, and the planting of the seed, likewise there can be no long-term fruit without growth, pruning, nurture, and developing roots. One of the common mistakes in youth evangelism is to treat it as an end in and of itself. It is not (cf. Col. 2:6–7). When we stress "come forward" more than we stress "press onward" we short-circuit the deeper work God desires in the life of a student and we turn what could have been a milestone into a tombstone.

DUFFY ROBBINS

Bibliography. R. Coleman (1972), *The Master Plan of Evangelism;* D. Fields (1998), *Purpose-Driven Youth Ministry;* D. Robbins (1991), *The Ministry of Nurture.*

Evil. *See* Sin.

Excellence. Surpassing or doing better than others. Excellence has two important connections with regard to Christian education.

First, it is the goal of all conscientious Christian educators that their students should excel in their Christian character. Teaching, leading, nurturing, discipling, and other tasks of Christian education are all directed toward the goal of Christ-like living.

Second, a conscientious Christian educator is one who seeks to excel in his or her Christian education ministry. It would not be a goal to excel so that one may boast of his or her excellence; rather to excel in one's ministry is a means of rendering effective service to the Lord. Scripture encourages Christians to do the things they do as unto the Lord so that he gets the glory. Scripture also indicates that God does take pleasure from the excellent service rendered by his servants (Luke 19:11–27).

KEN GARLAND

See also TOTAL QUALITY MANAGEMENT

Exceptional Persons. *Background.* An exceptional person is one whose special abilities or disabilities place him or her outside developmental norms. Physical impairment, a learning disability, or a mental handicap can cause an individual to be considered "exceptional." Those who are gifted in a particular area, such as creativity, can also be labeled "exceptional." Both heredity and environment play a role in the lives of all exceptional people. Some disabilities can be traced to genetic defects, while others are related to injury, disease, or environment. Similarly, giftedness depends on a combination of genetics, environment, and training. To what extent each factor influences development is still under debate.

Historically, disabled people were dependent on charity and often isolated from society. In some cultures, an impairment was a sure sign of divine disfavor. When a blind man was brought before Christ, the crowd asked whose sin had brought on his handicap (John 9:1–2). Mentally handicapped individuals have been considered untrainable, untreatable, and soulless. Impaired newborns were often left to die. Gifted children were often singled out for special training, as was the case with the prophet Daniel and his companions in the royal Babylonian court. During less enlightened times, intellect was considered exclusive to privilege, and only high-ranking children were offered educational opportunity. Today, efforts are being made to provide all exceptional people with opportunities to develop their potential and be mainstreamed into society. Medical advances, adaptive teaching methodology, public access laws, and growing public awareness make it possible for impaired people to make their contribution to the community. Disabilities that once meant lifelong institutionalization can now be treated in ways that allow individuals to live with a minimum of assistance. Special schools and programs for gifted children help identify and develop special abilities early in the lives of these exceptional people.

Gifts and Disabilities. The traditional measure of intellectual ability is the IQ (intelligence quotient) test. In recent decades, researchers have recognized the test's inability to accurately measure an individual's ability to adapt and thrive in her or his surroundings. Other types of tests for children involve standards for language acquisition, physical dexterity, and other age-level characteristics. Even though individuals progress at different rates, these age group norms make it possible for doctors and therapists to identify children who need early intervention and training.

Physical disabilities can be neurological, orthopedic, or related to other aspects of health, such as heart disease. Their impact can be mild or severely limiting. A category of disability that has only recently come under serious scrutiny is the area of learning impairments. Thanks to refined testing tools, symptoms once thought of as mental retardation have been recognized and successfully treated as a separate problem.

Implications for Education. Because care of at-risk newborns has dramatically improved many individuals reach adulthood with impairments that once would have been fatal in infancy. Because children are mainstreamed, many who would be home schooled or institutionalized are attending public school. Because laws encourage or guarantee wheelchair access, public transportation, and a welcome for canine helpers, many doors once literally closed to physically disabled people have been thrown open. While not legally subject to the same requirements for access, Christian educators must act under the moral obligation to open hearts and facilities to ministry to exceptional persons.

In rare cases, a class may be exclusively for learners with similar disabilities or gifts. Typically, a class will include only a few learners with special needs. Their gifts or disabilities may be obvious or hidden. In the case of hidden disabilities, the family of a learner may be reluctant to make them public for fear of rejection or simple denial that the disabilities exist. Open communication between parent and teacher is particularly important when a child's handicap can be overlooked or misunderstood. Blind individuals often find themselves shouted at by well-meaning people who assume all blind people must also be deaf. A neurological problem that causes a speech impediment can be mistaken for mental retardation instead of a simple problem in communication.

In general terms, good teaching methodology for the average learner is good methodology for the special learner. Multisensory activities make learning more effective for everyone, but are especially helpful for learners who have lost the use of one or more of the senses. A choice of activities will provide the gifted learner with stimulation and the challenged learner with the chance to choose an activity that will maximize his or her strengths. The traditional lesson format of listening, reading, and writing presents monumental stumbling blocks to a learner with problems processing written or aural input. Lessons that take into consideration the attention span of the learner's age level will deter misbehavior by minimizing boredom among typical learners and will greatly benefit the learner burdened with attention deficit disorder. ADD children and adults also benefit from subdued lighting, orderly surroundings, and a soft background of instrumental music.

Talented storytellers use voice inflection, gestures, visuals, and eye contact with their listeners. These techniques are doubly important if the listeners are hearing- or vision-impaired or are mentally retarded. Repetition is an aid to any learner, but crucial to one who must work harder than the rest to remember, understand, and apply a lesson. Memorization will be particularly difficult for those with certain learning problems. Teachers need to emphasize comprehension of Bible truth over exact recitation. Teachers of exceptional learners must recognize and capitalize on their strengths, and provide the degree of challenge that will result in success and improved self-confidence. Teachers of intellectually gifted learners, hyperactive learners, and ADD learners should be prepared with alternate and supplementary activities that are more than just busy work. Research materials, resource people, and other lesson-related projects can focus on learners' special interests and enrich the lesson for everybody.

The open space so important to active young learners and easy transition from small to large groups is also vital to the learner who must maneuver a wheelchair, oxygen tank, or canine helper. Desks, playground equipment, and ordinary school supplies such as crayons and pencils have been adapted for special needs and are available through institutional suppliers.

Firm, age-appropriate discipline is basic to any class, but especially in a class where learners need constant reminders and clarification of the rules. Correction must be educational rather than punitive. Teachers can minimize disruptive behavior by using learners' names often, limiting distracting elements, and providing a program with dependable structure.

Spiritual Considerations. Every exceptional person, whether gifted or challenged, has a spiritual nature. The intellectually gifted learner will be able to grasp abstract concepts earlier than the average learner of the same age group, but teachers must be wary not to equate intellectual capacity with spiritual maturity. Readiness for salvation will be most difficult to ascertain among those learners whose physical disabilities involve communication problems and among those whose mental limitations may lead a teacher to doubt their ability to comprehend the gospel message. Whatever their limitations or gifts, exceptional people need Christian education on a level commensurate with their ability to learn and respond.

ROBERT J. CHOUN

Bibliography. D. G. Benner, ed. (1999), *Baker Encyclopedia of Psychology*; R. J. Choun and M. S. Lawson (1993), *The Complete Handbook of Children's Ministry*; R. E. Clark, J. Brubaker, and R. B. Zuck (1975, 1986), *Childhood Education in the Church*; I. V. Cully and K. Brubaker Cully, eds. (1990), *Harper's Encyclopedia of Religious Education*; J. Kessler, R. Beens, and L. Neff, eds. (1986), *Parents and Children*; K. Klein (1982), *How to Do Bible Learning Activities*; R. P. Lightner (1977), *Heaven for Those Who Can't Believe*; C. S. Schuster, ed. (1985), *Jesus Loves Me, Too: The State of America's Children* (Yearbook, 1997); S. Sunderlin, ed. (1979), *The*

Most Enabling Environment; P. Warren and J. Capehart (1995), *You & Your A.D.D. Child.*

See also ATTENTION DEFICIT DISORDER (ADD); CHILD DEVELOPMENT

Executive Pastor. With the advent of large, multistaff churches in the 1980s came the need for a full-time pastoral staff member charged with coordinating the complex administrative needs of local congregations. Thus the position of "executive pastor" was created to coordinate all management concerns, including personnel, finances, and facilities. Rather than being the visionary leader, the executive pastor is most commonly a gifted administrator charged with implementing the vision offered by the senior pastor or church board.

The executive pastor serves a coordinating role between board and staff. The job description generally involves office administration, including overseeing the hiring of new personnel, supplying them with appropriate technology, and ensuring staff development. Policies and procedures are also a common part of the executive pastor's portfolio, as churches learn to cope with complex employment laws and building codes. Many churches use the executive pastor to facilitate ministry cooperation, establish and manage the budget, work closely with a lay board to ensure financial accountability, and create a master plan to chart future staff and facility needs. The role continues to evolve as churches begin focusing on previously neglected areas such as marketing and communications, and it is finding acceptance by smaller churches in need of a professional administrator on staff.

JERRY CHIP MACGREGOR

See also CLERGY; MINISTER; SENIOR PASTOR; SPAN OF CONTROL; TEAM; TEAM MINISTRY

Exegeting the Learner. Exegeting the learner correctly is almost on par with proper exegesis of Scripture. Teachers must read out of Scripture what the text says, not what teachers want it to say. Likewise teachers must read out of learners what learners need from teachers' lessons. Teachers need to read learners as carefully as they would read the text that they teach because they teach learners, not merely a biblical text apart from learners' life situations. Therefore careful exegesis of both text and learners is required of effective leaders and teachers.

Exegesis of learners covers five areas. First is *developmental exegesis* which determines the levels/stages of the development of learners. Six developmental areas are physical, cognitive, social, affective (emotional/psychological), moral, and spiritual/faith. Developmental stages will strongly

suggest appropriate texts to teach, approaches, strategies, methods, and materials depending on the levels/stages of development of learners. Developmental exegesis is undoubtedly the most important exegesis of learners. Ineffective learning will occur if this area is ignored or slighted. Children cannot be taught as little adults. Youth must not be taught as almost adults. Adults must not be treated as children. Each age group has definite developmental characteristics and therefore needs that come from being on certain developmental levels/stages. Developmental stages are described in various textbooks in child, adolescent, and adult development.

Values and beliefs exegesis seeks to discover espoused social, cultural, and moral values. What do learners say they value and believe? What are their cultural norms? It also asks the valuation and importance of these beliefs/values and norms. This area covers values and beliefs regarding life, morality, God, society, material possessions, value of earning money, family, vocation, importance of church, spiritual beliefs, attitudes toward worship, ministry, views of sex, drugs, alcohol, leadership, group identity, and many others both private and public, Christian and secular.

Practice/Action exegesis examines what learners actually do, not just what they espouse. The outcome is to determine the degree of congruence between espoused values/beliefs and actual life. Teachers must know if learners are actually living what they profess and to what degree learners are conformed to cultural values. Teachers cannot assume that just because learners can articulate Christian answers and Christian perspectives that they also live those in their daily lives. Knowing this helps teachers to focus learners' attention on bringing actions into agreement with scriptural values and beliefs.

Geographic/topographical exegesis determines where people actually live. Are they from rural or urban locations? Are they from the North, East, West, South? Do they live on the Great Plains or by one of the oceans, on a Great Lake or a small pond, along a mighty river or by a creek in Appalachia, in the Rocky Mountains or the coastal plains of the East, etc.? Their actual geography will help teachers understand how learners view life. People in various areas of the country have different values, perspectives, and practices.

Demographic exegesis looks at typical demographic data available in various governmental reports (national, state, county, city). Many of these data are also available by asking learners about themselves. Areas for examination are socioeconomic status, educational level, vocation, languages spoken/understood, contacts with other cultures, travels to other parts of the country and to other countries, marital status, number of children, divorced, remarried, widowed, own/rent house, relative ease of access to and use of various mass media (cable, TV, Internet, movies, magazines, newspaper, books), etc. There are predictable attitudes, values, beliefs, and practices that are associated with these various demographic characteristics that help teachers to construct their lessons so that they make sense to learners.

Awareness of these factors will help teachers know how to shape their lessons to fit the learners. The goal is to focus on the needs of the learners. Once valid exegesis of learners has been completed, teachers can turn to Scripture to determine what in the text connects with the learners. This avoids teaching what is incomprehensible or irrelevant to learners. It helps focus tightly on the needs of the learners and therefore provides teachers with helpful information to develop intended outcomes for their lessons. Without proper exegesis of the text, teachers are apt to misinterpret or make gross errors in the teaching of Scripture. Without proper exegesis of learners, teachers court teaching to unknown needs, something that is foreign to all of the New Testament documents that all show that the writers of Scripture had specific needs of the learners in mind as they wrote, under the Spirit's inspiration, to specific needs of the intended recipients. Teachers today need to do the same thing.

JOHN M. DETTONI

Bibliography. J. Fowler (1981), S*tages of Faith: The Psychology of Human Development and the Quest for Meaning;* K. Issler and R. Habermas (1994), *How We Learn: A Christian Teacher's Guide to Educational Psychology;* W. Yount (1996), *Created to Learn: A Christian Teacher's Introduction to Educational Psychology.*

Existentialism and Education.

Existentialism refers to a diverse philosophical family distinguished by the view that personal existence precedes essence. Educators, regardless of their philosophical orientations and religious convictions, can benefit from the contributions of existentialist thought.

Existentialist ideas have been ascribed to numerous persons from as far back as Descartes and Pascal to more recent thinkers, including Camus, Marcel, Merleau-Ponty, Husserl, Dostoevsky, Jaspers, Barth, Bultmann, Brunner, and Tillich. Among the most commonly mentioned existentialist philosophers are Kierkegaard, Nietzsche, Sartre, and Heidegger.

Kierkegaard theorized that reality proceeds from individual existence, in opposition to Hegel's concept that reality comes from ideas. This attack on idealism represented a challenge to the predominant views, conventions, and authorities of his day. In contrast with the teachings of many existentialists, Kierkegaard held to what he considered to be core Christian beliefs. But his innovative epistemology has given rise to mixed reactions among Christian thinkers. Many believe that Kierkegaard abandoned the essence of Christian teachings, while others place him "within the mainstream of the Christian tradition both in terms of the content of historic orthodoxy and in terms of the patristic and pietistic insistence that the truth is to be lived and not just believed" (Westphal, 1996, 1).

On the other hand Nietzsche, an atheist, openly declared that "God is dead." Rejecting the beliefs, values, and ethics of Christianity, "Nietzsche takes the will to power as the necessary and abiding source of all possible values" (Blackham, 1959, 33). He believed that authentic human existence is achieved by the "liberating, life-affirming strength of conviction, the acceptance of life's good and bad, and autonomy from religion" (Monaghan, 1997, 1). Nietzsche considered the values that individuals create for themselves to be the only adequate source of meaning and purpose in life.

For Sartre, also an atheist, there are no universals or a priori essences. In other words, our "human nature is basically undefined." Waking up one day to find out that we are here, we must begin the task of figuring out what we are and creating the meaning of our own lives (Peterson, 1986, 63).

Heidegger, who also denied the existence of a personal God, nonetheless addressed a number of transcendent concerns. He was critical of the trivial preoccupations of contemporary living and suggested instead that authentic existence can only be realized by coming to grips with our finitude and ultimate death. Furthermore Heidegger, in contrast with Nietzsche, considered the analytical and positivistic mind-set of modern science to be incompatible with the existential quest for authentic truth and meaning. Heidegger greatly influenced neoorthodoxy with his idea that truth is to be lived rather than known in an objective sense.

Even though existentialists make up an extremely diverse group, they share at least three basic perspectives that follow from the premise that existence precedes essence. First, reality is encountered subjectively in the person's life and experiences, rather than conceived of as something objective and universal. Each individual must formulate one's own truth, meaning, and values. Second, due to the existentialist denial that reality has universal rationality or order, comprehensive philosophical systems and worldviews are rejected along with claims to external sources of absolute truth, authority, moral values, and codes of conduct. Third, authentic human existence depends upon personal choice and action in the face of problems without easy and clear-cut solutions. A person's own truth, meaning, and values are to be applied boldly to life's situations. One cannot resolve the enduring problems of separation—of the mind and the body, of the citizen and the city, of the person and the world—by means of universal theories. Instead one must confront life's uncertainties and ambiguities, experience the anguish and despair, live with courage, conviction, and commitment, and thereby discover what it means to be human (Blackham, 1959, 150).

Surprisingly Christians share several similar themes with existentialists. For example, both groups take life experiences seriously, both are concerned with the crucial nature of the human situation, and both advocate personal involvement through choice and action. Admittedly, many are disquieted by the existentialist attack on the certainties of the faith. The skepticism of existentialism regarding spiritual realities is especially unsettling to believers who define their faith in terms of a personal relationship with God. Evangelicals in particular are offended by the challenge to the authority of Scripture. Notwithstanding these negative reactions, existentialist ideas can stimulate critical thought about numerous issues and result in significant insights regarding both educational theory and practice.

First, by questioning the universal applicability of traditional philosophies, existentialists can prompt Christian educators to consider the influences of a person's cultural heritage and contemporary environment on one's epistemological assumptions and worldview. For example, logical positivism has had an overwhelming influence on educational theory and practice in the West throughout the twentieth century. Society's faith in the scientific method continues to be seen in the natural, social, and behavioral sciences (Peterson, 1986, 65). In contrast, existentialists believe that a person comes to know truth primarily through faith and action, rather than as a predominantly cognitive activity. A critical examination of these distinctive ways of coming to know truth can enable educators to develop a Christian hermeneutic that is in greater harmony with biblical principles and more appropriate for the contemporary world.

Furthermore, the suggestion that traditional ways of thinking might not be universally applicable is a call to take into account the partiality and fallibility of human perspectives and understanding. The primary point here is not the validity of biblical truths per se, but rather the way they are perceived, interpreted, and represented to others. This reminder is also an invitation to Christian educators to practice greater humility and dependence on God, regarding both what and how one teaches.

Finally, existentialists and Christians alike endeavor to facilitate inward growth, reflection, self-knowledge, ethical development, decision making, and courageous action. Existentialists prefer teaching methods that begin and end with the learner's situation. Person-centered teaching approaches are also useful resources for Christian educators. Storytelling, role-playing, simulations, and discovery experiences are just a few educational strategies that can enable students to develop their imagination and awareness. But they must be balanced by other methods and subordinated to the broader educational objectives of the church and Holy Scripture.

NORMAN G. WILSON

Bibliography. H. J. Blackham (1959), *Six Existentialist Thinkers;* C. Guignon and D. Pereboom, eds. (1995), *Existentialism: Basic Writings;* G. Kneller (1958), *Existentialism and Education;* P. Monaghan, *The Chronicle of Higher Education* 43, no. 49 (1997); M. L. Peterson (1986), *Philosophy of Education: Issues and Options;* M. Westphal "Kierkegaard as Religious Thinker." *Theological Studies* (December 1996), 57(4). Available FTP: Hostname: umi.com

Experience and Theology. The relevance of religion in general, and Christianity in particular, to the meaning of life and the dynamic relationship between religious experience and dogmatic theology were the driving concerns of Friedrich Schleiermacher (1786–1834), a German Protestant theologian who is considered the father of modern theology and liberal Protestantism. His work has affected much of Christian theology since the nineteenth century since his central concerns permeate theological conversations well beyond liberalism. As with many theological constructs, the seeds of Schleiermacher's thought grew from the soil of his own experience. Born into the home of a Reformed minister, Schleiermacher was cradled in the pietistic movement and had a datable Christian conversion experience while attending a Moravian boarding school. His letters to his parents during this period mention his own sense of the inadequacies of faith, the Savior's gracious love, and his longing for deeper spiritual experiences of faith and piety. This Moravian community, which cultivated a distinctive religion of the heart, stamped an indelible, lifelong mark on the impressionable boy. Following graduation, Schleiermacher enrolled in a Moravian seminary to prepare for a life of ministry. While there, his intellectual questions led to a skepticism concerning the efficacy of salvation through Christ and his apparent abandonment of faith in God. He found that his teachers intentionally ignored the realties of the new intellectual life of Europe. Consequently, he broke from his family and his Moravian roots. In a letter to his father, he wrote, "I cannot believe that he who called himself the Son of Man was true, eternal God; I cannot believe that his death was a vicarious atonement" (Gerrish, 1984, 25).

Schleiermacher withdrew from seminary to study philosophy at the University of Halle, where he encountered the works of Kant and Plato. He immersed himself in his intellectual pursuits and a dispassionate course toward ordination. He graduated and accepted employment as a tutor and pastor. It was during his pursuit of the meaning of reality in the preparation for parish preaching and his encounter with the vital simplicity of faith evident in a Christian family for whom he tutored, that he began to reconstruct his understanding of Christian faith, and subsequently, his own personal experience of God. While he did not return to the simplicity of faith and morality of his Moravian tradition, he did regain the vitality of his awareness of need for God and the pietistic assurance of his salvation. On visiting the Brethren community, he expressed his gratitude for the strength of the religious experience of his youth which had seen him through the skepticism of his intellectual struggle. He declared, "I have become a Moravian again, only of a higher order" (Gerrish, 1984, 27). Following this renewal of faith, he served faithfully as teacher, preacher, and political activist until his death.

Schleiermacher's theological legacy is articulated in his two most widely read works, *On Religion: Speeches to Its Cultured Despisers* (1821) and *The Christian Faith* (1830). *Speeches* is addressed to the romanticists of Berlin's intellectual society who had rejected religion as being irrelevant to the emerging sophistication of the science and art of modernity. Schleiermacher suggested that what they had rejected was not vital faith, but static dogmatism. He argued that the nonrationalistic influence of religion lies at the foundation of all empirical life, that foundation being a self-conscious sense and taste for the infinite in science, art, and philosophy. He declared that life uninformed by personal religion and the religious community was artificially sterile and out of joint with creation and the Creator (Niebuhr, 1965, 19). Though not explicitly Christian in his arguments, Schleiermacher laid the groundwork in *Speeches* for his later developments in *The Christian Faith*, in which he systematically explored the experiential awareness of God through the present redemptive work of Christ. He understood this awareness (or intuition, to use his terms) to be that of self-conscious finitude in absolute dependence on the infinite God. In Christ and his demonstrated inner-awareness of God, Christians find both the way and means to overcome their own inadequate self-dependency and experience a vital union with God, just as Christ does.

Schleiermacher's primary legacy for Christian education is his concern for the integration of experience and theology. While one might cite several specific propositions of his experiential the-

ology, his most helpful contribution may be the process by which he approached the integrative task.

1. He took seriously the vitality of the nonrational, experiential character of theology. In the post-Enlightenment era with its disdain for traditional or imposed authority, Schleiermacher sought to reframe Christian theology in relevant terms. Central to his theology was the definition of religious experience as the feeling of absolute dependence on God and the sense of redemption through an existential relationship with God mediated by the living Christ and modeled by the church. He resisted every temptation to appeal to dogmatic theology which did not have direct bearing on human experience. Hence, his doctrine of creation takes precedence over the doctrine of the Trinity, a discussion he considered to be speculation divorced from piety. Further, the nature of redemption as the lived experience of the church was of greater importance than the paradoxical divine/human nature of Christ. For Schleiermacher, the search for theological truth was never a search for abstraction, but for the lived reality that shaped the daily expressions and thoughts of Christians. The final test of theology was its vitality within the Christian community. Theology that cannot be experienced is powerless, and experience that has no theological grounding is simply experience with no connection to ultimate reality.

2. Schleiermacher chose to engage rather than run from the cultural context of post-Enlightenment Europe. He took seriously the challenge of engaging the philosophical and scientific developments of his era. He adopted what he could, given his theological framework. Hence, he could not deny the empirical data of science and the ever developing understandings of human experience. Yet he challenged that which was inconsistent with his commitment to God's imminent presence in the world (e.g., the emerging individualism of existential philosophy and the reductionism of science to mere rationality). Schleiermacher sought to be intellectually responsible to the faith and to the cultural context. He pursued the integration of theological and scientific truth, yet retained the supremacy of theology whenever they were in conflict.

3. Schleiermacher understood that theology is communal and confessional, that is, it belonged in the daily experiences of the church. He taught that theology rose from and gave expression to the communal life of the worshiping community. The task of theology in all its forms (e.g., biblical, historical, philosophical) was to serve the practical needs of the Christian community for personal and corporate worship, morality, and service. The best theology is that which can be preached and taught at the most basic levels of understanding. The ideal parish leader is a pas-

tor who is resident theologian, making theological reality live in practical terms. Schleiermacher modeled this commitment as a parish preacher for most of his adult life.

While much of his work is to be commended, Schleiermacher is not without his critics. His focus on the existentially redemptive work of Christ discards much of classical Christology, which serves as a foundation for the efficacy of the atonement. Consequently, the importance of the death and resurrection of Jesus is reformulated in his theological system. Further, his existential soteriological focus based in the God-consciousness of every person eventuates in universalism. His biblical hermeneutic, which argued for reaching beyond the objectivity of the language of Scripture into the experience of the human author, often calls into question the objectivity of the biblical text. Further, the centrality of religious experience opens Schleiermacher to the criticism of subjectivism and the primacy of meaningfulness over objective truth. Many see his focus on human religious experience as eventuating in the anthropocentric theology of early-twentieth-century Protestant liberalism. It was against this anthropocentrism that neoorthodox theologians and Christian educators spoke so powerfully. Yet, even with these critiques, Schleiermacher cannot be dismissed summarily. While his specific theological propositions may leave much to be desired for the evangelical educator, his example of serious engagement in the dialogue of experience and theology does not.

Experience has always been central to the concerns of Christian education. Religious education as a modern discipline was born in the mid-nineteenth century as Horace Bushnell inquired concerning the conversion experience of children nurtured from infancy in the context of the Christian family. Christian education continued and expanded this inquiry to include the full range of human experience with God, self, others, and nature. Consequently, few arenas, including theology, are left untouched by this experiential perspective. Evangelical theology has long pressed for the experiential dimension of faith so that knowing God is more than cognitive assent to a theology formula. Faith is only complete in the direct experience of a vital personal relationship with God in Christ, by the Holy Spirit. Many religious educational theories promote the idea that direct religious experience and theologically grounded reflections on that experience enhance spiritual nurture. Most Christian denominations and publishers strive to develop educational curricula that are experientially relevant and press the integration of biblical truth and lived experience. The centrality of human experience to Christian education is undeniable.

Yet, as Schleiermacher discovered, personal religious experience alone cannot define the central focus of the Christian education. Experience must be in dialogue with the corporate experiences of the church and Christian theological foundations to avoid the fallacy of subjective relativism, interpreting meaning and ultimate truth through the narrow lens of one's own experience. Christian theology must serve as the foundation for the meaning of religious experience.

EDWIN ROBINSON

Bibliography. H. Bushnell (1984), *Christian Nurture;* C. W. Christian (1979), *Friedrich Schleiermacher;* B. A. Gerrish (1984), *A Prince of the Church: Schleiermacher and the Beginnings of Modern Theology;* R. C. Miller (1952), *The Clue to Christian Education;* R. R. Niebuhr (1964), *Schleiermacher on Christ and Religion: A New Introduction;* idem (1967), *Handbook of Christian Theologians;* M. Redeker (1973), *Schleiermacher: Life and Thought;* L. O. Richards (1975), *A Theology of Christian Education;* F. Schleiermacher (1958), *On Religion: Speeches to Its Cultured Despisers;* idem (1976), *The Christian Faith.*

Experiential Learning. Learning defined as "experiential" derives from the active participation of learners in events or activities which leads to the accumulation of knowledge or skill. Experiential learning is associated with the following key principles: (1) the environment consists of open space and people in groups, (2) the focus is helping learners to experience for themselves the meaning of content, (3) the goal is helping participants apply new principles to real-life situations, (4) the process emphasizes interaction, movement, awareness of one's own feelings, and developing a team spirit with other learners. At the heart of experiential learning lie the methodologies of games, simulations, and role-play.

Games are competitive encounters between groups of individuals (teams), such as a relay race or tug-of-war or building models of principles (Tinker Toys or Legos are building tools). Sometimes gaming involves a marketed product consisting of playing board, tokens, and money. Learning games have been developed for a wide variety of subject areas. One example is Adelle Carlson's *Harvest: A Fun Game About Retirement,* a card game structured around decisions persons must make in and before retirement.

Simulations are educational tools for helping people learn by experiencing common situations in different ways. By simulating situations, leaders help learners "play" with alternative decisions and see the consequences of their actions safely. The attempt is to help learners experience in a simulation what he or she will later experience in the real world. Some aspects of reality can be omitted while others are emphasized. For example, a man and a woman in a team play husband and wife in a situation concerning the household budget, while team members evaluate the interchange.

Role-playing is an unprepared, unrehearsed dramatization in which a learner assumes another's identity and makes decisions as that identity. Using the example above, the man would play the role of "wife" and the woman the role of "husband."

The antithesis of experiential learning is found in the traditional classroom: chairs in rows facing the blackboard, an expert teacher-teller, learner-listeners with notebooks and pens in hand, content structured and organized, methodology limited primarily to lecture, question-and-answer, and teacher-student interaction.

The History of Experiential Learning. Experiential learning grew out of principles of John Dewey's educational pragmatism and twentieth-century existentialism, reaching its peak during the 1970s' emphasis on humanistic education. John Dewey emphasized child-centered instruction and learning through activity. Dewey structured his methodology around projects which posed a problem to be solved.

While Dewey emphasized cognitive (thinking, problem-solving) involvement over affective (personal experiences), he focused educators' attention on student interests and abilities, participation, games and play, and self-expression (Smith, 1979, 186–89).

Existential philosophy holds that reality is unique to each individual, created out of each person's own choices. Reality is not an objective state of being, but a process of personal becoming. Existentialists believe the individual is a choosing agent, unable to avoid choosing his or her own way through life; a free agent, absolutely free to set the goals of his or her own life; and a responsible agent, personally accountable for his or her free choices. Existentialism was translated into educational thought by the humanistic philosophers Carl Rogers and Abraham Maslow. Rogers emphasized self-directed learning. Maslow emphasized self-direction and personal choice as key ingredients to the process (Reed and Bergemann, 1995, 233–34). One can readily see the framework these modern views of education provided for the experiential movement: student participation, activity learning, solving problems, building models, developing team spirit, student interests and abilities, and self-expression.

The Methodology of Experiential Learning. Direct, purposeful experiences involve the senses, minds, and bodies of learners. They include the freedom of creating an idea, designing a plan, pulling together the resources, and assuming the responsibility for putting all the parts of the project together. Intense involvement is a key ingredient to experiential learning: relational, face-to-face, back and forth shared experience. Leaders design environments for the creative use of open space and time in which objective content, personal activity, and group reflection cycle learners through the integration of personal views and new discoveries.

Drawbacks of Experiential Learning. Experiential learning requires more time than traditional approaches to teaching. Learners who prefer structure and order may find experiential learning confusing. Learning is difficult to evaluate as attitudes and behaviors change gradually over time. Large, open spaces for maximum freedom of movement are required. The "learning noise" of experiential learning can disturb other groups in the building. Competition between teams can become more important than understanding the subject clearly. This last drawback led to the demise of humanistic education in the late 1980s and early 1990s.

In summary, the "group encounter" phenomenon of open classrooms and individual choice of the 1970s has given way to the more structured approaches to teaching. The overemphasis on personal affect diminished the importance of content mastery, rendering learners more confident but less skilled. Still, the positive legacy of experiential learning lives on in contemporary practice: basing instruction on student needs and abilities, allowing students to make choices among assignments, cooperative learning, and self-reinforcement. One fundamental principle remains: it is students who must learn.

RICK YOUNT

Bibliography. D. G. Benson (1971), *The Fine Art of Creating Simulation Learning Games for Religious Education;* M. Gredler (1994), *Designing and Evaluating Games and Simulation: A Process Approach;* J. and L. Hendrix (1975), *Experiential Education;* A. Reed and V. Bergemann (1995), *In the Classroom: An Introduction to Education;* S. Smith (1979), *Ideas of the Great Educators;* K. Yardley-Matwiejczuk (1997), *Role Play: Theory and Practice;* Internet Sites: (Simulations and Games) http://picce.uno.edu/SS/TeachDevel/Teach Methods/SimulationGames.html; http://www.pastpers. co.uk/homepage.htm; http://www.learninglandscapes. com.

See also DEWEY, JOHN; HUMANISM, CLASSICAL; HUMANISM, CHRISTIAN; ROGERS, CARL

Experimentalism/Pragmatism/Progressive Education. Clarifications necessarily distinguish the subtle nuances of these terms: *pragmatism* is a particular branch of philosophy, a theoretical framework for viewing a given issue; *experimentalism* is a method of applying this philosophy; attempts to instill this philosophy and methodology into schooling is known as *progressive education.* Progressive education, simply put, is the designation of an educational movement that protested against formalism; arose in Europe and America during the last two decades of the nineteenth century; was associated with the philosophy of John Dewey; and emphasized commitment to the democratic idea, the importance of creative and purposeful activity and the real-life needs of students, and closer relations between school and community.

Pragmatism (sometimes called instrumentalism, experimentalism, or progressivism) is a uniquely American contribution to Western philosophy. Its introduction to American thought is often associated with mathematician Charles Sanders Peirce (1839–1914). He published an article in an 1879 *Popular Scientific Monthly* called "How to Make Our Ideas Clear." The gist of his notion is that the *meaning* of any idea or conception lies in the *consequences* that flow from it. The way to get a clear conception is by the difference that would be made if an idea is true or valid. In short, pragmatism is action-oriented and tests truth in terms of consequences.

Perhaps because he published little, Peirce is lesser known. More notable early proponents of pragmatism are William James (1842–1910) and John Dewey (1859–1952). Peirce was a Harvard University colleague of philosopher-psychologist James (perhaps best known for his *Varieties of Religious Experience*). Philosopher and educational theorist Dewey, Peirce's student at Johns Hopkins, has been called "one of the most influential American philosophers of the twentieth century."

The American progressive education movement, rooted in pragmatism, likely rose in popularity due to several concurrent events: (1) a national call for social reform (including curtailment of child labor practices); (2) demographic changes (most notably urbanization, industrialization, school population growth); (3) growing dissatisfaction with the schools' traditional curriculum; and (4) the writings of educational reformers, such as Francis W. Parker (1837–1902), whom John Dewey called "the father of progressive education" (Dejnozka, 1982).

Progressivism describes a movement that sought to extend the myth of the American dream to a nation of immigrants struggling with industrialization. Boys (1989) observes: "Its humanitarian impulse quickened by democratic ideals, progressivism charted a way of reconstructing American society through education" (46). Cremin (1961) summarizes its threefold motif as social reform, reform through education, and reform of education.

Childs (cited in MacDonald, 1972) characterizes progressive education as the work of educators "who have combined the psychological principles of child growth with the moral principles of democracy and have developed the conception that the supreme aim of education should be the nurture of an individual who can take responsibility for his [sic] own continued growth" (1).

In short, one may readily observe the pragmatist as primarily concerned with the process of knowledge, and the relationship of ideas to ac-

tion. Today, American educational philosophy is generally inclined toward pragmatism.

Perhaps the monumental contributions of James and Dewey to educational theory and practice will serve as a representative survey to the salient themes of pragmatism.

William James's views resounded with the practical bent of the American fiber. He spoke of truth as "what works"—a very individualistic perspective. He advocated the primacy of one's experiences as a determinate of reality. In concert with the democratic spirit, James asserted that values come from society.

Plainly, individualistic experience and flexible truth as a philosophy is a problematic topic for many. For example, time-honored tradition ceases to function as a reputable guide to truth. Confusion about educational aims and methods is inevitable. Experimentalism endeavors to adapt to the changing conditions of life. Truth is always in flux. A changing civilization produces the need for new, dynamic principles, or a reinterpretation of old principles. Experimentalism denies the existence of absolute truth, and in its place, substitutes relative truth or "progressive truth." Truth can only be accepted if it meets the test of experience; a supernatural base for truth is therefore untenable.

James's notions had substantial consequence on Dewey's call for radical reform in education. Repeatedly John Dewey attacked what he called "the spectator theory of knowledge" (which is typified by Plato's image of the prisoners in the cave, who passively observe the shadows without becoming aware they are not reality). Dewey (1916) wrote: "In schools, those under instruction are too customarily looked upon as acquiring knowledge as theoretical spectators, minds which appropriate knowledge by direct energy of intellect. The very word 'pupil' has almost come to mean one who is engaged not in having fruitful experiences but in absorbing knowledge directly" (164).

Dewey was critical of the traditional way of educating, since schools were isolated from the struggle for a better life and dominated by a medieval conception of learning. Instead, he argued, schools should be a genuine form of active community life, not a place set apart for the learning of lessons. Schools must be social in orientation so as to teach students the processes necessary for the workings of democracy. Dewey devoted himself to fashioning an alternative form of schooling, one in which passivity, mechanical massing of children, and uniformity of curriculum and method were replaced by activity, group participation, and adaptation to the needs of the student (Boys, 1989).

In his writings on education Dewey criticized the dualisms that underlay much of the previous conceptual work in the field. Indeed, his most notable books had as titles the dualisms Dewey was hoping to overthrow: *The Child and the Curriculum, The School and Society, Interest and Effort in Education,* and *Experience and Education.* In *Democracy and Education* (1916) he examined more than three dozen dualisms covering a vast range of topics—activity versus mind, authority versus freedom, body versus soul, capital versus labor, emotions versus intellect, individuality versus institutionalism, method versus subject matter, and so on. He contended these dualisms should be replaced by synthesis.

Several key components characterize pragmatism, described most accessibly for the lay reader in Dewey's less scholarly classic monograph *Experience and Education* (1938): growth, democracy, and activism. Growth is the universal criterion of education; democracy is the cultural condition of such growth; activism is the means for attaining this growth.

Growth. As humans encounter life, obstacles (or problems or challenges) arise. Growth occurs as people use their rational capacities to investigate solutions to problems. The chief means of working toward growth, promoted by Dewey, was the *scientific method* (or the *project method*). The five-step process used in Dewey's famed Laboratory School at the University of Chicago, was as follows: (1) encounter a problem, (2) diagnose the situation, (3) compile possible solutions, (4) hypothesize a reasonable solution, and (5) test the solution by taking action.

Dewey held certain key theses of growth. First, experience is an *interaction* between the individual and the environment. Second, experience generates *habits* that temper the character of subsequent experience; hence, experience is *continuous.* Third, not all habits are manifestations of growth, but a person may be said to be growing as she or he secures from experience *certain sorts of habits.* Fourth, these habits enable one to clarify and cope with the problems one's environment poses and which lead to additional habits for understanding and coping with new problems as they occur. Fifth, therefore, the mission of the school is to provide experiences that promote the growth of each student. Concretely and specifically, schools must have: (1) knowledge of the problems students have and are likely to have; (2) knowledge of habits useful in clarifying and coping with those problems; and (3) knowledge of the sorts of experiences that will bring about those habits.

Democracy. Dewey, although raised in a religious home, developed a naturalistic philosophy that regarded belief in the supernatural as a remnant of a more primitive outlook. Consequently, supernaturalism was incompatible with democracy, because it too often legitimized the authoritarian rule of an elite (Boys, 1989). True education, Dewey contended, is violated by religion. When one makes religion an absolute, people settle for security in fixed doctrines rather than risk discovery of truth by way of experimental methods.

Influenced by Thomas Jefferson, Dewey carried this hallmark of American nationalism—democracy—into the educational realm. He insisted the classroom be a microcosm of a democratic society. Teachers are not to be more highly regarded, but must participate on equal footing with students in the educational process. Knowledge is not unwelcomely imbued upon students; it is to be sought alongside the teacher-guide. Meaningful learning is not imposed from an outside source, but nurtured from within. Growth is cultivated in a democratic context. Boys (1989) concludes: "In the [pragmatists'] championing of immanence and denial of transcendence, they had replaced the cosmic source of human worth with the less forceful notion of the intrinsic worth of personhood in a democratic society" (69–70).

Activism. Activism is the essence of pragmatism—in contrast with learner passivity. Although experience and education are not equated (certainly there are bad experiences and miseducation), education rarely occurs without experience. Experience, Dewey writes, is both the means and goal of education. Experience is not undertaken on its own account or because it is merely developmental, but because it has a unique function to perform in inquiry.

Skeptics of Dewey dispute the role pragmatists assign traditional knowledge in educating people into a culture. Pragmatists respond that neither the emphasis on freedom nor the focus on creativity necessarily points to a disregard of tradition. The culture of the past indeed enters the curriculum, not as an end in itself, but because it is instrumental in the solution of some contemporary problem. It is out of these problems, furthermore, which the aims of instruction arise. Rivlin (1943) opines: "Education in general has no aims; pragmatically, only teachers, parents, and pupils have aims. Educational aims are instrumental to nothing outside of the educational process; in fact, education is subordinate to nothing except more education" (598).

Pragmatism has had a checkered history, and for a time it was blamed for producing serious defects in the American education system, defects that became matters of controversy when the former Soviet Union took the lead in the space-race with the launching of *Sputnik.*

Three major events served to strengthen and expand the progressive education movement: (1) the creation of the Progressive Education Association in 1919; (2) the Eight-Year Study, a research project sponsored by the Association that indicated successes of progressive-educated youth; and (3) the emergence of a "second-generation" of experimentalists, particularly William Heard Kilpatrick and Boyd H. Bode.

Ironically, in spite of his atheistic tendencies, Dewey had a role in the founding of the Religious Education Association in 1903. Although his participation was short-lived, his influence, chiefly through his writings, would have a profound effect not only on the REA but upon virtually all who sought to educate its members in religion.

Boys (1989) describes the quintessence of religious education from the first third of the twentieth century onward as the wedding of classic liberal theology and progressivist educational thought. "[L]iberal theology can be described most simply as a reconciliation of the scientific spirit of the late nineteenth and early twentieth centuries with traditional Christianity; it is a rethinking of Christianity in light of science . . . [L]iberalism counseled tolerance for divergent views and accepted the situation of religious pluralism" (45).

Though liberal religious educators did not reject the Scriptures or traditional forms of worship, neither played an important role. They disapproved of too much focus on the Bible, since they feared it would distract people from reality, and regarded true worship as seeing life objectively. Progressivist religious educators had little enthusiasm for theology; they were more preoccupied with education, including psychology and sociology. Again, Boys (1989) observes: "Conversion . . . was incompatible with these theorists' view of the divine-human relationship, since it rested on an authoritarian God and a passive creature. . . . [G]rowth replaced conversion as the key emphasis. . . . [W]ords such as sin and guilt nearly fell into disuse. . . . [C]onversion became a subject of empirical study" (57).

In the popular theological parlance of the era, liberal religious education exemplified Niebuhr's category of "Christ of culture," a cultural Christianity allied with self-reliant humanism. Education was tantamount to salvation.

More conservative Christian educators not only had serious theological grounds to critique the progressives but had suspicions about their entire educational stance as well. Their high view of God's revelatory Word suggested a view of *teaching as telling;* experiments and discovery seemed too random, too unpredictable, and baldly stated, too risky for wholesale acceptance.

Evangelicals wondered with Gangel and Benson (1983) if "it was legitimate to separate Dewey's [enticing] educational theory from his [naturalistic] philosophy?" As a philosophy, they concluded, pragmatism can never be acceptable to evangelical educators. Nevertheless implications for practice in Christian education are indisputable. "Pragmatism as a philosophy," Clark contends, "leads to a strengthening of secularism, a worship of science, a belief in the inherent goodness of persons, the rejection of absolutes and fixed truth, no genuine goals for education

outside of the individual and society" (Gangel and Benson, 1983, 303).

In sum, the legacy of pragmatism in Christian education is (1) an insistence upon the interrelatedness of doing and knowing engendered by a new enthusiasm for "learning by doing"; (2) an articulation of a child-centered curriculum which accordingly replaced creed-centered curricula; and (3) a progressivist emphasis on the whole child and on formation rather than conversion.

That contemporary evangelical Christian education has been deeply influenced by pragmatism in terms of both philosophy and program is unambiguous. Since the mid–1950s, however, new directions have appeared, particularly stimulated by neoorthodox theology. The church has been challenged to reaffirm a deeper biblical and theological grounding. The truth revealed in Jesus Christ is normative in relation to the "truth" that may be apprehended and tested pragmatically. The starting point for Christian education is not general experience, but the specific experience of the learner in relation to God's revelation in Christ. This is not to say pragmatism has been summarily repudiated but been guided toward a more biblical orientation.

MARK A. LAMPORT

Bibliography. M. C. Boys (1989), *Educating in Faith: Maps and Visions;* J. L. Childs (1931), *Education and the Philosophy of Experimentalism;* L. A. Cremin (1961), *The Transformation of the School: Progressivism in American Education, 1876–1957;* E. L. Dejnozka and D. E. Kapel, eds. (1982), *American Educators' Encyclopedia,* pp. 407, 416; J. Dewey (1916), *Democracy and Education;* idem (1938), *Experience and Education;* K. O. Gangel and W. S. Benson (1983), *Christian Education: Its History and Philosophy;* W. D. Halsey, ed. (1989), *Collier's Encyclopedia,* 8:576–78; T. Husen and T. N. Postlethwaite, eds. (1985), *The International Encyclopedia of Education,* 7:3859–77; W. James (1907), *Pragmatism;* G. R. Knight (1982), *Issues and Alternatives in Educational Philosophy;* J. B. MacDonald (1972), *A New Look at Progressive Education (1972 Yearbook);* H. N. Rivlin, ed. (1943), *Encyclopedia of Modern Education,* pp. 597–99, 612–14; J. E. Smith (1978), *Purpose and Thought: The Meaning of Pragmatism;* G. M. Wingo (1965), *The Philosophy of American Education;* J. P. Wynne (1963), *Theories of Education: An Introduction to the Foundations of Education;* A. Zilversmit (1993), *Changing Schools: Progressive Education Theory and Practice, 1930–1960.*

See also DEWEY, JOHN; JAMES, WILLIAM

Expiation. *See* Atonement.

Expository Teaching. Teaching, like preaching, has a structural variety that provides strengths for different purposes and occasions. The expository format centers its purpose, structure, illustrations, and application directly from one passage of Scripture. The exposition of a text provides scriptural principles to be learned, and is focused on learning Scripture itself. It exposes the truth within the context and culture of the text, occurring within the life-space of the biblical writer. Good exposition allows the student to place his or her own life in parallel to the biblical truth and ask significant questions like "What about me?" or "How should that experience change my own?"

The task of teaching is not just to observe the text of the Bible, but to know God and the relevance of truth through that text. Expository teaching looks beyond the person and skill of the teacher. It focuses on the structure of communication and the exposition of Scripture. The task of expository teaching is to portray the accuracy, clarity, and relevancy of a specific biblical text.

Accuracy. Meaning of specific words and word pictures: Since a word can have various meanings and may have changed from its original meaning, the good expositor must search for the biblical intention. This may involve studying the original language or searching several translations for the inference of definition. *Contextual accuracy:* The expositor must ask how each word fits into the phrase or paragraph, or how the phrase or idea fits into the topic or into the whole of revelation. *Cultural accuracy:* Just as words can change, the expectation and experience of cultures are different. What did these people know from daily experience about the word or analogy to understand the spiritual truth of this teaching? The question of accuracy is not concerned with what the reader thinks about its meaning, but rather with what the author intended for the reader to understand.

Clarity. The purpose of the text: There is a primary textual intention to every passage, even though there may be secondary applications. The stated purpose, grammatical structure, physical circumstances, or parallel accounts help clarify the writer's purpose. *The problem being addressed:* A teacher must often distinguish between the author's presented problem and the problem perceived by the listener. When Jesus addressed the possibility of freedom, his hearers responded, "We are Abraham's offspring, and we have never been enslaved to any one . . ." (John 8:33). *The major meaning:* The marvel of the Bible is that it tells a consistent story of God's character and his redemptive love for humankind. The exposition of meaning must harmonize with this consistency.

Relevancy. Expository teaching is not just relating the text with historical accuracy and clarity. Jesus and his apostles taught for revolutionary life-change in their day. Eternal truth must produce the same life-change in every era. *For decision making:* Learners must be confronted with the nugget of eternal truth in each lesson that will direct their daily walk. The expository teacher leaves the student with both the story of Scripture and the application it imposes on life today. *For life direction:* Not only does an expository study of Scripture give principles for making wise daily choices, but for setting goals and determining a path compatible with the general will of God. Expository teaching must present the relevancy for developing a pattern of life. Biblical truth makes a constant reference to Christ-likeness. Expository teaching must maintain a consistent reference to the values and lifestyle taught and modeled by Jesus, if it is to have true biblical relevancy.

If Jesus had come in our day to our culture, his illustrations would undoubtedly have dealt with cars and planes, TVs and computers, satellites and space, instead of sheep and goats, fishing and farming, or fig trees and vineyards. Yet the God he came to reveal is eternally the same, yesterday, today, and forever (Heb. 13:8). Expository teaching seeks to take timeless truth and translate it into the life stories of today. Transformation of sinful people into potential saints is to be the goal of all teachers of biblical truth.

An expository lesson must involve a paragraph or perhaps a whole chapter focused on a single theme or topic. A biblical writer is not forced to write a whole letter or book on a single topic, but expository teaching addresses at least one of those single topics as the major form and foundation of the lesson.

Expository teaching may also involve the sequence of expository lessons covering an entire book of the Bible. This method gives not only the advantage of exposing the major sections and themes of the book, but of the whole book itself. No student would expect to understand an author by reading only one page or one paragraph of his book. Therefore, it is desirable to include a balance of expository teaching in the learning experience of every student of the Word of God. Expository teaching has value for all things, holding promise for both the present life and the life to come.

GORDON R. CLYMER

Extended Family. Any blood or marriage relationship that goes beyond the nuclear family (defined as a wife, husband, and nonmarried children). The extended family includes relatives from previous generations such as grandparents, the nuclear family's generation such as aunts and uncles, and the most recent generations' additions such as the spouses of children and grandchildren. Depending on culture, race, and societal norms, extended families have varying degrees of influence on the nuclear family unit. Some cultures have highly integrated extended family units in which closeness is experienced in multidimensional planes, including emotional bonding, geographical proximity, and financial interdependence. Even within any given culture, each particular family unit defines its own level of involvement and expectation for the members of the group.

In a nontraditional definition of extended family, Christians also include the concept of the family of God in the paradigm. Extended family is part of the God-given structure to give support and health to each individual, moving beyond individualism to community. The extended family is part of that structure where humans develop most completely and wholistically. By including the members of the body of Christ (locally or universally) who encourage and support the carrying out of each person's unique story, the extended family has been given by God to serve our health and welfare.

JUDY TENELSHOF

Extremist. *See* Cult.

Extrinsic Motivation. There are two kinds of motivation, intrinsic and extrinsic. Extrinsic motivation comes from outside the person while intrinsic motivation comes from within.

A person's motivation in biblical terms refers to one's heart. That is why Paul writes, "The love of Christ controls us . . ." (2 Cor. 5:14). Other versions use "constrains," or "controls and urges us." In the case of extensive motivation the controlling force, the constraint, or the urging comes from outside the person and not from his or her "heart." In Christian education we refer to "team" effort and "playing along." Granted there must be a degree of internal motivation to participate in this but the major effort occurs from outside the person urging him or her toward a common task or goal. The bottom line may be "peer pressure."

The two primary ways external motivation is applied in Christian education is by (a) appreciation and (b) recognition or rewards. We have public installation services in which we consecrate ourselves and others to a particular task. This is an external way of telling those involved that we are all working toward the task or goal to be achieved. In essence we seek to elevate the ministry involved to the level of worship. We also have recognition times during which we publicly announce the achievements of those who have been successful. These external motivations are successful because human nature desires a degree of appreciation and recognition.

External motivation does not meet the basic needs of humankind such as physical or security needs (the lowest levels of Maslow's "hierarchy of needs"). They do help a person have a sense of belonging or a sense of self-esteem (internal, emotional needs).

In Christian education we need to be careful how we use external motivation. We acknowledge that love for God and humankind (Matt. 22:35–40) must be internally motivated and they cannot be legislated or mandated through any external motivation. Therefore we understand that external motivation is to lead toward glorifying God or it is unworthy of our efforts. We do not want to be like the "Gentiles" and use external motivation to "lord" it over those we are supposed to serve (Matt. 20:25).

ROY F. LYNN

Ff

Facility. Internal and external state of a church building. Churches have become more aware of the message communicated by their facilities. The philosophy and theology underlying the ministry of the congregation is conveyed by the building, as is seen in the difference between an Eastern Orthodox edifice and a local nondenominational community church. The church must establish its mandate and mission in order to best utilize its facilities and to be certain the facility portrays the intended message.

The ministry priorities of the church, when clearly understood by the membership, will alleviate problems related to the utilization of the facilities. Is the church accessible to the public, or does it appear to be a private club? The size and color of a room, comfort of the chairs, and lighting will all be elements that will enhance or hinder the teaching/learning experience.

How does the current facility adequately convey the theology of ministry and purpose of the church? How does the community see the building? Is the building being adequately utilized to the glory of God?

ELAINE BECKER

Bibliography. W. Graendorf, ed., *Introduction to Biblical Christian Education.*

See also ENVIRONMENT; RESOURCES

Faith. Reliability, trustworthiness, confidence (from Latin, "with faith") in or toward an object, exemplified in the common legal expression, "acting in good faith." Although "faith" receives bad press in popular parlance—akin to burying one's head in the sand like an ostrich and ignoring the obvious—the concept of faith is central for Christianity. "Without faith it is impossible to please [God]" (Heb. 11:6). In the New Testament, Christians are often called "believers" (Acts 10:45; 1 Thess. 1:7), and littleness of faith is Jesus' frequent criticism of the disciples (Matt. 8:26; 14:31; 16:8; 17:20). Scripture speaks of "the faith" (i.e., what is believed, 1 Tim. 4:6; Jude 3), initiatory saving "faith" (Acts 15:9; Eph. 2:8), as well as "faith" as a manner of Christian living (Rom. 1:17; 2 Cor. 5:7). This latter type of faith is primarily treated in the article.

Faith and Sight. A fundamental contrast posed by Scripture is between faith and sight: "We look not at the things which are seen, but at the things which are not seen; for the things which are seen are temporal, but the things which are not seen are eternal" (2 Cor. 4:18). Humans are part physical and part immaterial soul and spirit. And thus we live in two kinds of realms, a physical world of twenty-four-hour days, and an invisible, almost timeless world inhabited by angelic and demonic spirits and a supernatural divine Being. During our growing-up years, we learn to improve our eyesight so we can observe physical reality—noticing details, large and small. Similarly, believers growing in faith learn to "see" and tap into this spiritual reality that is just as real, except it is invisible. God's Word introduces the principles for successful living—principles not normally practiced by neighbors and fellow employees. But abundant living is accessible to those willing to keep trusting in God and to learn how to "walk by faith, not by sight" (2 Cor. 5:7). Christian faith is primarily a relational concept, involving a relationship with God and the implications that ensue. "Belief is commitment to God himself, and consequently to 'content'—to what God guarantees as his truth" (O'Brien, 1979, 1309).

Cognition and Affect in Faith. A traditional threefold analysis suggests that "Faith involves knowledge (*notitia*), persuasion (*assensus*), and commitment (*fiducia*). These three elements of faith are operative, not only when one first believes the gospel and trusts the Savior, but also in a growing faith throughout the Christian life" (Lewis and Demarest, 1987, 169). These elements may be illustrated by this mundane example: A general claim is made that chairs can safely hold the weight of people—knowledge of what is to be believed. Based on my critical observation at the library, I am persuaded and accept the claim as true, seeing the evidence of many people safely

283

seated in chairs—intellectual acceptance or assent of its truth. Then I act on this truth and sit in a chair, letting my full weight rest on the chair—personal commitment or trust in that truth.

Thus, faith involves both cognitive (knowledge and assent) and affective (trust) aspects—a matter of both the head and the heart. In the following discussion, these two main components are elaborated, describing faith's relationship to reason, to will, to affect, to action, and to Christian spirituality.

Faith and Reason. What are the basic tenets of the faith? Various syntheses of Christian doctrine have arisen in the form of creeds (from Latin, *credo*, "I believe") and confessions (e.g., Apostles' Creed [390], Westminster Confession [1646]). Near the beginning of this century, "The Fundamentals" (1910–15), a twelve-volume series, was published to define orthodox Christianity against liberal trends in the church—from which the term *fundamentalism* derived. Today, evangelical Christianity continues to affirm the following basic truths highlighted during the Reformation: unique authority of Scripture, salvation through faith alone, pursuit of holy and practical living, and evangelism to all nations.

How do reason and faith relate? To believe with certainty, is any evidence or validation needed? Or do we simply assent to and rely on the words of Scripture, regardless of our own questions or doubts? Packer (1984) suggests that "Beliefs, as such, are convictions held on grounds, not of self-evidence, but of testimony. Whether particular beliefs should be treated as known certainties or doubtful opinions will depend on the worth of the testimony on which they are based. The Bible views faith's convictions as certainties and equates them with knowledge . . . because they rest on the testimony of a God who 'cannot lie' (Titus 1:2) and is therefore utterly trustworthy."

It may be helpful to distinguish between the certainty of "the faith which was once for all delivered to the saints" (Jude 3 NASB) and our own human faith experience, of trusting more and more, and with greater certainty, in "the faith." It is here a paradox emerges: Some measure of certainty is needed to have faith, and yet faith also requires uncertainty—evidence may not be available and faith must move into realms even reason cannot go. And doubts can surface. Habermas (1990) identifies three kinds of doubts (factual, emotional, and volitional) and suggests ways for handling these.

Basinger (1997) offers a fourfold typology to explain the differing options for how necessary reason and rational evidence are to validate one's beliefs—particularly in relation to non-Christians. At one end of the continuum, reason is totally unnecessary ("hard fideism or anti-evidentialism," as represented by Barth, Kierkegaard)—faith alone, beliefs are immune from any critique by non-Christians. On the other end, reason is absolutely necessary ("hard rationalism or evidentialism")—beliefs must be capable of being conclusively proven to any rational person (e.g., Swinburne, Aquinas). The two middle-of-the-road positions take a softer view on these extremes. The main difference is that in "soft fideism or anti-evidentialism" (e.g., Plantinga), "reason can and must be used to defeat objections to religious belief; reason must at least show that one's beliefs are rationally possible" (Basinger, 1997, 71) and not internally inconsistent. Thus a defensive case is needed. For "soft evidentialists or rationalists" (e.g., Mitchell), some sort of positive argument must be offered, given the pluralism and diversity of worldviews in the marketplace.

Faith and Will. We cannot change our beliefs at will—we do not have direct control over our beliefs—we cannot believe in anything we want to. We acquire our beliefs passively over time, formed by the evidence we confront in life. "We believe our beliefs to be true because we know that we do not choose them, but we believe that they are forced upon us by evidence from the outside world" (Swinburne, 1986, 127). "Truly to believe in—as really to love—a person, or ideal or Faith is to be overtaken by it" (Astley, 1994, 211). Although beliefs cannot be changed directly at will (i.e., we lack "inner" freedom), we can indirectly influence our beliefs by freely placing ourselves in situations that permit attending to new or additional evidence (i.e., we have "outer" freedom) (Astley, 1994, 218).

Many of the beliefs that we arrive at are finally the results of our policy decisions. Although believing itself is not an act, our acts determine the sorts of beliefs we end up with. It is primarily because we judge that our beliefs are to some significant degree the indirect results of our actions that we speak of being responsible for them. . . . If we had chosen differently, if we had been better moral agents, paid attention to the evidence, and so forth, we would have different beliefs than in fact we do have (Pojman, 1974, 180).

Thus, not only are students responsible for giving themselves to acquiring new beliefs, but teachers also carry great responsibility since they decide which beliefs to expose their students to.

Faith and Affect. Faith also has an experiential side, an important component of faith often neglected in the discussion. Maybe the "objective" and cognitive aspect is easier to evaluate. Yet this subjective aspect of faith is essential for Christian living. These synonyms encompass this nonrational aspect: desires, convictions, readinesses, tendencies to act, given favorable opportunity. Like beliefs, we develop these passively, but can cultivate such affections over time, since we must learn to "hunger and thirst after righteousness" (Matt. 5:6). In response to the revivals of the Great Awakening, Jonathan Edwards identified standards to guide believers in discerning genuine religious affections. McDermott (1995) offers a contemporary version and presents twelve unreliable signs (e.g., frequent and passionate praise for God, time-consuming devotion to religious activities) and twelve reliable signs (e.g., seeing the beauty of holiness, humility). Unbelief is depicted in Scripture as a hardness of heart, stiff-necked, uncircumcised (Acts 7:51)—graphic images of pride and arrogance. Yet "God is opposed to the proud, but gives grace to the humble" (James 4:6 NASB). Cultivating a tenderness and humility before God implies a posture of trust in God that he loves us, cares for us, and will guide our paths.

Faith and Action. Genuine faith is a way of living and issues in noticeable actions and behavior, for "faith without works is dead" (James 2:26), as illustrated by the plagues in Egypt. For the seventh plague of hail, Moses warned them to save their livestock from the hail that would kill anything in the open field. "The one among the servants of Pharaoh who feared the word of the LORD made his servant and his livestock flee into the houses; but he who paid no regard to the word of the LORD left his servants and his livestock in the field" (Exod. 9:20–21 NASB). Some Egyptians evidenced faith in God's word.

Faith is known by its deeds. Later, Israel was given an opportunity to display its faith: "The LORD your God has led you in the wilderness these forty years, that He might humble you, testing you, to know what was in your heart, whether you would keep His commandments or not" (Deut. 8:2 NASB). When God tests our faith, the resulting actions display the convictions of our heart. After Abraham climbed the mountain and was about to sacrifice Isaac, God remarks, "Do not stretch out your hand against the lad, and do nothing to him; for now I know that you fear God, since you have not withheld your son, your only son, from Me" (Gen. 22:12 NASB). Through testing, God intends to purify our faith and nurture our growth in maturity (James 1:2–4; 1 Peter 4:12–19).

Faith and Christian Spirituality. Faith involves both thoughtful and experiential commitments. "To articulate the faith and to engage in the quest [to attain union with God] were twin aspects of a single enterprise. Only with the Enlightenment did it become at all commonly thinkable to reflect on God in a spirit of detachment, skepticism and even disbelief—and . . . in the context of a life in which prayer and worship played only a formal part or, eventually, no part at all. . . . Even committed Christian theologians, however, often came to share something of this separating off of Christian thought from the intensity of the quest for God" (Houlden, 1995, 512). Too often this important experiential side was devalued, even denounced, defaulting to a primarily cerebral faith as the norm. Yet throughout church history, periodic movements surfaced to reclaim a warm, heartfelt Christianity. During the 1700s and 1800s, pietism represented an attempt to emphasize practical, even mystical, Christian living, in lieu of a formal orthodoxy. In our own day, the term *Christian spirituality* carries the notion of wedding orthodox belief with a vibrant spiritual experience. Seeking God is a continuing quest of faith, both of mind and heart.

KLAUS ISSLER

Bibliography. J. Astley (1994), *The Philosophy of Christian Religious Education;* R. Basinger, *Christian Scholar's Review* 37, no. 1 (1997): 62–73; G. Habermas (1990), *Dealing with Doubts;* L. Houlden (1995), *Companion Encyclopedia of Theology;* K. Issler (forthcoming), *Seeking the God Who Hides: Welcoming God's Transforming Presence into Our Daily Lives;* C. Jones, G. Wainwright, and E. Yarnold, eds. (1986), *The Study of Spirituality;* G. R. Lewis and B. Demarest (1987), *Integrative Theology,* vol. 1; G. R. McDermott (1995), *Seeing God: Twelve Reliable Signs of True Spirituality;* T. C. O'Brien (1979), *Encyclopedic Dictionary of Religion,* vol. 2; J. I. Packer (1984), *Evangelical Dictionary of Theology,* pp. 399–402; L. Pojman (1974), *Religious Belief and the Will;* R. Swinburne (1986), *The Evolution of the Soul;* idem (1981), *Faith and Reason.*

Faith Community. *See* Fellowship.

Faith Development. Faith development theory contends that faith emerges through predictable stages that can be identified and defined. As with all developmental theories, the stages of faith are believed to be invariant (all people progress through identical stages) and sequential (all persons experience the stages in the same order). There is neither regression nor is it possible to skip stages in the developmental process.

The leading theorist in the area of faith development is James W. Fowler (1940-), who began his exploration into how human beings make meaning of life while at Harvard University. He continued his research at Candler School of Theology, Emory University, where he currently directs the Center for Research in Faith and Moral Development. A colleague of Lawrence Kohlberg, Fowler extended the cognitive-developmental research begun by Jean Piaget (1896–1980) and expanded by Lawrence Kohlberg (1927–87). While Piaget established the stages of cognitive development through which children progress in their epistemological frameworks, and Kohlberg focused on the development of stages of moral judgment, Fowler explored the possibility of stages of faith.

His seminal work is presented in *Stages of Faith* (1981) and has now been extended into five books. There are many who disagree with the theory at a fundamental level, arguing that faith is too mysterious a process to be reduced to developmental stages. However, others agree that, because there are clear developmental patterns in other aspects of the human personality (the physical, cognitive, affective, social, and moral), it is not unreasonable to believe that faith might also progress through predictable stages.

It must be clearly understood that Fowler understands faith to be a human phenomenon, not only a religious one. That is, he believes that all people have faith, whether they are religious or not. Faith, according to Fowler, is a means of making meaning of life; a hermeneutical framework through which persons interpret and understand life. According to Fowler, faith is a composing, a dynamic and holistic construction of relations that include self to others, self to world, and self to self, construed as all related to an ultimate environment (1991).

His definition of faith is clearly existential, tied to how a person composes meaning through the construction of relationships, and evolving in that it progresses through life. Hence, it fits clearly into a developmental framework. He focuses upon a triad of relationships—self to self, self to others, and self to world—all understood in relation to an ultimate environment. Self-to-self relationships focus on the development of the interiority of the person, moving from lack of self-awareness to an almost abnormal absorption with oneself and finally, to a decentralization of self. Relationship to others moves from complete dependency and identification with others to a more mature sense of being in relationship with and serving others. Self to world moves from the focused egocentrism of childhood to a much more wholistic view of the world and one's actual place in it. Relationship to ultimate environment (God and his kingdom) grows first from magical thinking about reality to very literal understandings of spiritual truth, and then to absorption with the values and concerns of the kingdom of God.

Fowler draws his theological grounding from Paul Tillich and H. Richard Niebuhr, and his philosophical grounding from Immanuel Kant's critical philosophy. As such, his orientation on several levels will put him at odds with evangelical theorists. With certain modifications, however, his theory can be helpful for understanding the complex phenomenon of faith. Moreover, his desire has been to identify the structures of faith that are compatible with all theological orientations and a variety of worldviews, both religious and nonreligious.

Fowler's theory is most clearly rooted in the works of Jean Piaget, Lawrence Kohlberg, and Erik Erikson. While Piaget and Kohlberg were clearly cognitive-developmentalists, Erikson was an epigenetic stage theorist, whose insights into psychosocial development yielded stages different in kind from the developmental stages of Piaget and Kohlberg. Erikson's stages offer perceptions into the development of the psychology of the person, but allow for lower stages to remain unresolved even as the person moves into higher stages of psychosocial development. The blending of the two kinds of stages adds both texture and, at times, a certain confusion to Fowler's work.

As with all developmental theorists, Fowler attempts to separate content (what a person believes) from structure (how a person holds his or her belief). Therefore, faith development theory is not concerned with the object of faith, but rather with the nature of the faith exercised by the individual. For Fowler's purposes, conversion is a change of faith content, moving from one set of beliefs to another. Conversion may enhance or inhibit faith development, depending on the nature of the content adopted. Moreover, when persons experience a conversional experience, they are likely to revisit the earlier stages in light of their new beliefs. The revisiting is not regression, but rather a reexamination of the issues of faith in reference to the new body of belief.

Fowler has suggested six stages through which human faith may progress. Because structural developmental stages are not controlled exclusively by chronological growth, not all people progress to the later stages. People may settle at a lower stage and remain there for the rest of their lives. Moreover, people will progress at different rates in relation to a variety of life experience issues. Therefore, the ages associated with the stages are only approximate.

Primal Faith (a prefaith stage), associated with infancy, forms the predisposition to trust, necessary for later faith development. Primal faith is formed through relationships with parents and others as a way of offsetting the anxiety that results from separations that normally occur during infant development. It is a prestage because it cannot be identified through the normal procedures for empirical research used for faith-development research. This prefaith stage is clearly influenced by the tension Erikson sees between the trust-mistrust at the forming of the human personality.

Intuitive/Projective Faith (stage one) is the highly imaginative stage when the young child is being strongly influenced by images, stories, and symbols, but is not yet disciplined by logical thinking. Perceptions and feelings are powerful teachers for those parts of life that are both protective and threatening. Images of faith are formed by the significant adults in the world of young children. Children raised in Christian homes may not yet be able to adequately articulate issues of faith, but they have learned certain realities about the world through the faith environment established by their parents.

Mythic/Literal Faith (stage two) appears in later childhood and beyond. Emerging cognitive abilities allow children to think logically and order their world according to categories of causality, space, and time. This stage is *mythic* in that it captures life's meanings in stories, but also *literal* in that it is generally limited to concrete thinking. Because of a lack of development of the interiority of the person, this stage is limited in its self-awareness and its capacity to understand the perspective of another person. God is understood in terms of moral reciprocity, keeping score of who must be forgiven and who must be held accountable. The lack of serious understanding of grace causes persons at this stage to either ignore or deny various segments of their life experience. At this stage the child is unable to see spiritual realities apart from literal constructs and is therefore limited in the way he or she can think about and respond to biblical truth. The possibility that "In my Father's house are many rooms" (John 14:2) is referring to spiritual reality rather than to a real mansion in the sky is not an option for stage two faith. An all-important task of mythic/literal faith is to sort out reality from make-believe. While mythic/literal faith is developmentally appropriate for children, its inherent limitations make it inappropriate for adults. However, Fowler suggests that it can be the modal faith stage of some religious groups.

Synthetic/Conventional Faith (stage three) will not appear before adolescence. Growing out of the strong relational orientations of adolescence, this stage is *synthetic* in that it synthesizes beliefs and values from the earlier stages into a coherent perspective. It is *conventional* in that it tends to adopt the belief systems and values of a larger community. An emerging sense of selfhood develops, with self-identity being constituted by roles and relationships within the larger community. Stage three people are highly committed to their group (i.e., their church) because the group becomes an idealized extended family. Because of extreme identity with the church, conflicts and controversy within the faith community tend to be highly threatening. The modal question of stage three is, "What do we believe?"

God is now perceived as an extension of interpersonal relationships, and is understood as a "best friend" whose primary role is to make life better for me and my community of faith. Absent is any real sense of paradox and mystery. Rather, life is defined according to one's own community, with God watching over and caring deeply for all within it.

A limitation of this stage is an overdependence on significant people within the community of faith, expressed in striving only to bring one's own beliefs into compliance with the beliefs of those in leadership. Any real sense of "third-person" perspective is lacking, and susceptibility to the "tyranny of the they" is highly probable.

Individuative/Reflective Faith (stage four) will not appear until young adulthood, if at all. It is marked by a double development of self and religious thinking. An experience of selfhood emerges which is in contrast to the community self of stage three. Self-authorization now creates the possibility for making decisions based solely on the self, apart from the expectations of the group. Third-person perspective makes it possible to see the self and the group from the perspective of the larger society as a whole. This stage is *individuative* in the sense that the person now individuates from the group with a much deeper sense of selfhood.

The stage is *reflective* in that the person can now reflect upon the religious convictions of the group, asking why the group believes as it does. It will demythologize religious rituals, asking for the meaning behind the rituals. The quest for deeper understanding and authenticity in faith may also cause a sense of loss or guilt as the comfort and safety of stage three is left behind. The modal question of stage four is "What do I believe?"

The primary limitation of stage four faith is its overreliance on its own perspective. There is a certain arrogance that allows the person to stand in judgment of a group and critique it. It can lead to such privatized faith that no external judgment is tolerated. However, stage four critiques can be most helpful for maintaining the integrity of a faith community, helping to avoid the danger of the nonreflective faith of stage three.

Conjunctive Faith (stage five) only appears in midlife or beyond. With conjunctive faith one becomes less sure of the judgments and assessments made in stage four and becomes much more open to insights and perspectives from others. Both divine immanence and transcendence are appreciated in new ways, and it becomes axiomatic that truth is multidimensional. Because it is now assumed that further understanding can be attained from others, significant encounters with other persons and groups are sought and valued, as a new quest for understanding is undertaken. The self-assurance of stage four is replaced with a deeper and more humble self-awareness accompanied by greater tolerance for outside perspectives from others. The modal question of stage five is "What can I learn from others?"

Universalizing Faith (stage six) is very rare, requiring a radical decentralizing of self and a radical new participation in the kingdom of God. Fowler contends that few people ever attain the fullness of stage six, where all that matters are issues of justice and love, with the self wholly identified with God and his kingdom. The modal question of stage six is "What is just and loving?"

Fowler attempts to separate the content of faith (*what one believes*) from the structure of faith (*how one experiences faith*). In attempting to describe his suggested faith stages, he tries to avoid theological concerns, focusing only on the human side of faith. It is impossible for theories of faith development to be completely scientific and value-free. The researcher cannot avoid bringing his or her own theological perspective into the analysis. However, faith development theory has done much to expand our understanding of why people believe differently at different stages of their development.

Christian educators are wise to consider the faith stages of the persons with whom they are working. Faith stage theory can provide some important clues as to why persons react the way they do or can help the educator anticipate potential opportunities for educational interventions in the lives of students.

Fritz Oser, a Swiss researcher, is expanding on faith development theory by exploring a stage theory of religious judgment, using analysis of religious dilemmas as a research tool. He analyzes responses to dilemmas according to three foci. (1) Does the subject perceive God as more transcendent or more immanent, seeking to understand how the person understands God's intervention in the world? (2) Does the subject perceive his or her relationship with God as more free or more dependent, seeking to understand how the person understands the balance between human freedom and human dependence? (3) Does the subject relate to God in a fearful or in a trustful way, especially in relation to the normal crises of life? Oser is seeking to understand the logic of religious development and has posited five stages through which religious judgment and understanding may emerge. At the time of this writing the stages have only broad descriptions and are still in the formative process. As with most developmental research, the problem of content and structure is quite complex, and Oser has been reluctant to claim universality for his theory until this difficult problem can be solved. He is fearful that theological content is being woven into the structural analysis of the stages of religious judgment he is attempting to define.

PERRY G. DOWNS

Bibliography. P. G. Downs (1994), *Teaching for Spiritual Growth;* J. W. Fowler (1981), *Stages of Faith;* idem (1987), *Faith Development and Pastoral Care;* J. W. Fowler, K. E. Nipkow, and F. Schweitzer, eds. (1991), *Stages of Faith and Religious Development: Implications for Church, Education, and Society;* S. Parks and C. Dykstra (1986), *Faith Development and Fowler.*

See also FOWLER, JAMES W., III; KOHLBERG, LAWRENCE; OSER, FRITZ K.

Family Camp/Retreat. Intergenerational event that offers the possibility of developing the family spiritually and relationally, housed in an outdoor setting. It combines the uniqueness of a camping experience with the dynamics of the most common unit of lifestyle relationships—the family constellation.

Although some camps offer opportunities for all family members to spend time simultaneously in activities with their peers, the true family camp incorporates experiencing, practicing, and sharing truth while relating with the family unit as a whole. It may also include some opportunity to do all of the above with peers, with other family units, and with other generations. Special emphasis may be given in peer units such as parenting issues for all adults or teen/family struggles targeted to that peer group. Interfamily insight, information, and support can be experienced by combining family units. Exposure to all generations offers varied perspectives and rich contributions.

Because of the combined assets of the camping lifestyle (slower pace, simplified living, natural surroundings) and the assets of family dynamics (real life, relationships already built, all members interacting with known issues) family camping permits the combining of strengths from both of these settings (camping and family) for learning. All family members are exposed to the same truth. Each has opportunity to apply that truth immediately in his or her relational environment. Such interaction offers the possibility of building relationships on a deeper level and practicing skills of living while in the process of learning. Not to be underestimated are the chance to have fun together as a family and the potential for follow-through in the home setting on truth learned in this togetherness experience.

There are essentially two basic philosophies of family camping in vogue with numerous varieties of combination, the centralized and decentralized concepts. The centralized plan brings family units together to enjoy large group activities planned by program directors. They eat together, play together in camp-organized activities, are taught by a speaker in a large group, and keep the same schedule. The decentralized model is more informal with units making their own choices of activities, teaching done through small group experiences with families designing their own schedules as meets their needs with only a few times (such as meals) scheduled in common.

While family camping offers many unique benefits, it also presents numerous challenges. One of the greatest is appealing to all generations at the same time, providing something special for each so a fulfilling time is had by all. Another factor is cost. Because the expense of paying for numerous family members is high, most churches build into their budgets a subsidy for campers for this type of camp. Younger children must be cared for if adults are to be free to gather with peers. Some churches meet this need by taking along "extended family" of singles, collegians, and grandparents who enjoy the connection with families afforded by this opportunity. Activities are conditioned by the participants' age-level limitations and by family values the camp seeks to endorse. This means competition within families is not fostered (avoiding everyone yelling at the 4-year-old who drops the ball), and activities must allow for all to participate and succeed.

For all its challenges, many have found family camping the most memorable and rewarding group learning experience they've had. It can strengthen family awareness and skills and offers opportunity for the church to model what it is calling parents to do in their homes.

JULIE GORMAN

Bibliography. C. M. Sell (1981), *Family Ministry.*

Family Life Education. Family life education consists of two related processes: teaching people the knowledge and skills necessary for successful family living and training parents to nurture their children's faith. Both are intricately tied together since parents' family living skills enable them to model Christian principles, necessary to their teaching them to their children.

In the twentieth century, Christian churches have been inconsistent in their emphasis on family life education. During the first few decades, churches ignored the family's role in Christian education and relied mostly on numerous church-related programs: vacation Bible school, camping, release time instruction, weekday clubs, and Sunday school. After the economic Depression of the late 1920s, churches turned to the family for the nurture of children because they could not afford Christian education directors to keep all their programs functioning and they were concerned about the decline in the quality of family life. In 1937 Regina Wieman warned: "The family is going through a long and perilous crisis. Nobody noticed just when it started; nobody can say just how long it will last; nobody knows what the outcome will be" (Wieman, 1937, 18).

In 1931 church leaders announced that the year 1934–35 would focus on the Christian home; then in 1937 three major books appeared, each calling for strong family life education programs (Carrier, 1937; Wieman, 1937; Sherrill, 1937).

The mainline church surge of interest in family life education reached a crescendo when the Faith and Life Curriculum of the United Presbyterian Church of the U.S.A. appeared in 1948. Hailed as the first serious attempt to implement the reserves of home and church through a common curriculum, other denominational publishers followed the same pattern. But, because most parents refused to cooperate, the strategy was

dropped. Since then, mainline churches have centered their faith nurture on children in the church.

In the late 1980s, a large-scale survey of the denominations of the National Association of Evangelicals revealed churches were doing little to aid families. It has been suggested that the large number of parachurch agencies attending to the family may be influencing the decision of many churches to provide the needed resources.

This "hands off" approach, however, seems to be changing. Published in 1989, a book by Charles Sell, *Family Ministry*, provided church leaders, seminary students, and others with a comprehensive view of how churches could enrich the life of families. Since then, a second edition has appeared along with several other volumes on the same subject. In a novel book, *Family-Based Youth Ministry*, Mark DeVries challenges youth leaders to modify their philosophy of youth ministry to include ministering to families. Numerous children and youth ministers are also being assigned the task of doing family ministry and, for the first time ever, in 1998 a professional organization of family pastors was formed.

The rise of these efforts appear to be prompted by the recognition of the plight of families. Social experts warn, "The nuclear family . . . needs massive help" (Yorborg, 1973, 204). Believing the institution of the family has been created by God, most church leaders are concerned about its continued existence and health.

Yet the summons to do family life education is not merely based on concern for the family. Advocates believe it is also for the sake of the church. Family ministry is church ministry because families do part of what the church is called to do.

Family life education is evangelism in that it trains parents to lead their own children to Christ. It is discipling because when parents are taught to develop their children's faith, they are doing the work of the church. In fact, children and youth leaders are beginning to claim that church-based Christian education efforts are failing because of the lack of Christian training in the home.

Another reason for family ministry is that it is crucial to the church's moral and spiritual ministry. Competency in the functioning of husbands and wives will inhibit divorce and adultery, major Christian concerns. Three of the ten commandments regulate family life. Some of today's major moral issues, such as child neglect and abuse, homosexual marriages, premarital and extramarital sex, and abortion are family matters. Besides these, a major argument is that church life and family life are systemically tied together. "As goes the family—so goes the church" (Rose, 1972, 188–89; Friedman, 1985, 36).

Several paradigms of family life education have emerged. Foremost among them is a program model. Events for family life education are planned by a family life task force, often under the direction of a staff member assigned the role of family minister. A second model is one where an age-group ministry extends its ministry to the church families. A third approach is one where a church organizes its whole life around family unit events and worship, including a great deal of intergenerational participation. Whatever the model, there are a number of strategies employed. Besides the mention of family-related subjects in sermons and Sunday school classes, churches conduct courses and seminars on marriage and family, including parent-child relations. In addition, there are attempts to bring generations together from time to time to improve the skills of family members and enhance the quality of their relationships. At times, the sessions may include just two generations, such as parents and teens; at other times, all generations participate.

The curricula for family life, ideally rooted in theology, deals with instrumental and expressive aspects of family. Instrumental includes those matters related to the somewhat external operation of a family: financial and time management, disciplining, teaching children, and leading family worship, as well as the carrying out of various duties and roles of family members. Expressive functions deal with so-called internal matters: sharing feelings, listening, affirming, being intimate, loving, and other competencies of interpersonal relating.

In training sessions, experiential strategies are often employed, such as testing to analyze strengths and weaknesses, role-playing, and participating in exercises that enable the practice of skills that are being taught.

Efforts to produce printed curricula integrating church and family nurturing have not been extensive. Apart from materials produced in the 1970s by innovator Larry Richards, publishers of Sunday school curricula have done little to move in this direction.

Guidelines for family life education include the following. It should be integrated into the life of the congregation. Not merely the adding of new programs, family issues must be dealt with in the church's existing agencies and ministries.

Further, family life education should involve people of all ages; children and youth need to be taught knowledge and skills related to family living. Also, people in so-called families in transition should not be left out: the separated, divorced, widowed, and their children need to be taught and supported.

When stressing family life education, churches should be careful not to neglect single adults. Efforts must be made to help them with their family issues (relation to parents and other relatives),

and strategies must be implemented to include them in the life of the church "family."

The congregation, seen as a "family," will be the most effective context for family life education. The church itself should operate on the basis of healthy interpersonal relationships, demonstrating to family members how to resolve conflict, to be intimate, to communicate, and to care for one another. In addition, the church should provide small group experiences where people, including single adults, can experience familylike intimacy and interaction. Many people in the church, having grown up in dysfunctional families, need, most of all, to be part of such a community. It is for this reason that the church is most suited to work for family wellness.

CHARLES M. SELL

Bibliography. B. Carrier (1937), *Church Education for Family Life;* M. DeVries (1994), *Family-Based Youth Ministry;* E. H. Friedman (1985), *Generation to Generation;* K. O. Gangel and J. C. Wilhoit, eds. (1996), *The Christian Educator's Handbook on Family Life Education;* D. W. Hebbard (1995), *The Complete Book of Family Ministry;* R. Rose (1972), *Christian Bible Teacher;* L. Sherrill (1937), *The Family and Church;* C. M. Sell (1995), *Family Ministry;* R. W. Wieman (1937), *The Modern Family and the Church;* B. Yorborg (1973), *Changing Families.*

Family Morality. C. S. Lewis defined morality in *Mere Christianity* (1952) as concerned with three things. First, with fairness and harmony between individuals. Second, with harmonizing the things inside each individual. And third, with what man was created for or the purpose of life as a whole. The first has to do with relationships between people, the second has to do with being aware and understanding oneself, and the third has to do with purpose in relationship to the Creator. How a person responds throughout life to these three components forms his or her character. These components cannot be separated. Each one affects the other. Being fair and honest in our relationships with others is embedded in the foundation of the self and relationship with God.

The field of "prosocial behavior," and in particular James R. Rest, suggests four human acquisitions that show morality formation as being deeply rooted in the human psyche. The first acquisition is empathy, which is acquired very early, if not genetically wired into human nature, and needs to be modeled and nurtured by parents or primary caretakers. Second is a primary human value, namely, a caring and mutually supportive relationship with another person, again needing to be established first with primary caretakers. Good relationships with other people are the most important outcome of a social system. Third, people basically want to think of themselves as being decent, fair, and moral as their self-concept within their personality system develops and that is at least part of their motivation to be moral. Children not only need a sense of belonging, which is developed in the first two acquisitions, but they also need a sense of value or worthiness. This will then lead to the fourth acquisition, developing an increasingly richer, more penetrating picture of the social world by reflecting upon their own social experience. Some even develop ideal visions of society based on their own more complicated inferences and encompassing plans.

These four acquisitions show that there are natural tendencies in individual human development in which moral development is rooted. These tendencies can support moral development or can be channeled by parents in other directions, become distorted, or be preempted by other tendencies. For example, Rest (1986) says, "Empathy can become prejudice, intimate relationships can become constrictive, the evolving self-concept system can organize itself around nonmoral values, and sophistication in social cognition can be used for exploitation as well as for moral purposes" (2–3). The family is key in the development of morality.

These four foundational acquisitions set the groundwork for the four psychological processes of Rest's model that occur in order for moral behavior to take place; namely, moral sensitivity, judgment, motivation, and implementation skills. Moral behaviors are not then the result of any single process but rather an interaction of the four components. Any one of the components may be demonstrated as a strength for a person, who may demonstrate a weakness in another component. Some people may be able to make sophisticated judgments but never take action. Or someone might take action, but his or her judgment may have been too simple. This is the reason it is so important for parents and the community in which children are raised to model moral behaviors.

Rest's four-component model is valuable for families to consider, particularly because of the integration of the cognitive, affective, and behavioral components. It moves families away from either a head or heart approach to parenting and helps them with their children to look at each decision to evaluate how the choice was made. This makes the model both practical and less controversial.

JUDY TENELSHOF

Bibliography. C. S. Lewis (1952), *Mere Christianity;* J. R. Rest (1986), *Moral Development.*

Fantasy. *See* Imagination.

Feedback. Final step in the communication transaction whereby the listener or message receiver responds to the speaker or the individual sending the message. Feedback in small group discussions and classrooms plays an important role in the communication process for at least three reasons. First, feedback is necessary in eliminating unintentional cues and ambiguous communication signals. For example, a group member who heard a speaker but is not sure how to interpret the statement might say something like, "Do you mean to say . . . ?" The more feedback that exists between a speaker and a listener, the more accurate the interpretation of the listener. Second, feedback encourages other members and sends the message to them that they and their thoughts are valued. Lack of feedback is demoralizing and discouraging; it disconfirms the speaker's significance to the group and lessens one's sense of self-worth. Finally, feedback helps complete the communication loop. A complete communication transaction occurs when a receiver verifies a sender's intent during interaction. When a receiver responds to an initial message and the sender in turn acknowledges that response, both parties can determine whether they have communicated as wished (Galanes and Brilhart, 1995, 46–48).

To be most effective, feedback should include several components. First, it should be clear and concise. Second, it should be open and honest, but tempered with sensitivity. Third, feedback must be constructive and meaningful to the sender. On occasions, feedback may be honest and open but have a negative effect on the speaker and lead to termination of the interaction (Wolvin and Coakley, 1992, 137–39).

HARLEY ATKINSON

Bibliography. G. Galanes and J. Brilhart (1995), *Effective Group Discussion;* A. Wolvin and C. G. Coakley (1992), *Listening.*

Fellowship. When this term is used to describe the church, it reflects what a church is, not what it does. Too often it appears in a description of the basic activities of a church with little regard for its use as a definition of a church.

Its meaning is best reflected in 1 John 1:3: "We proclaim to you what we have seen and heard, so that you also may have fellowship with us. And our fellowship is with the Father and with his Son, Jesus Christ." Therefore, the church is a fellowship of believers who are working together to make known to others the good news of Jesus.

The function of education is essential to the concept of fellowship. It is important for church members to understand the meaning of the word as a descriptive term for the church. In Bible study and discipleship activities the fellowship purpose must be identified and explained. Many churches are never as effective as they could be because members do not understand the true nature of fellowship.

The New Testament concept of fellowship provides a significant picture of caring and concern for other believers. Phrases from Scripture that illustrate this concept include, "They had all things in common," "Behold how they love one another," "Stir up one another to love and good works," "Be devoted to one another in brotherly love," "Live in harmony with one another," and "Serve one another in love."

It is no wonder that people who were described this way had such a profound influence on the people around them. The fellowship of which they were a part provided the stimulus for their efforts to evangelize others.

It is also evident that their practice of ministry to believers would have carried over into a concern for the welfare of those in their communities. It is easy to project a spirit of ministry to unbelievers when it has been practiced with believers.

Perhaps one of the most important concepts of fellowship relates to the relationship with God. One who trusts Christ as Savior enters into a fellowship relationship with God as well as other believers. The understanding of this relationship is heightened in community with fellow believers. Learning more about God encourages the spirit of fellowship and service with others. The opportunity to worship God with the fellowship enhances the experience.

The concept of fellowship undergirds all that a believer should know in becoming more like Christ. A major focus of any educational emphasis in a church should be to help believers understand the concept of fellowship in church life. It is only when this concept is understood that a church can do all that God intends for it to do.

WILLIAM G. CALDWELL

See also CHURCH; COMMUNITY, CHRISTIAN; KOINONIA; SUPPORT GROUP

Feminism. System of social, economic, and political thought that seeks justice in gender relationships. Feminists believe that women have been systematically devalued and disempowered, and they work to counteract this process. The influence of feminism has been felt in the economic sector (i.e., "equal pay for equal work"), political arena (i.e., female representation at all levels of government and legislation which is "woman-friendly"), and social relationships (i.e., equal access in education and egalitarian marriages).

David Diehl (1990) writes of five theological responses to feminism: strict hierarchicalism, moderate hierarchicalism, biblical feminism, mainstream feminism, and radical feminism (36–40).

Strict hierarchicalists believe the infallible Scripture teaches a hierarchicalist relationship between man as leader and woman as subordinate. They believe this to be a norm that transcends culture and time. Therefore, only men can serve as ministers and leaders in the church. Women are encouraged to participate in positions of service but cannot have authority over or teach men. Stephen Clark (*Man and Woman in Christ*), George Knight (*New Testament Teaching on the Role Relationships of Men and Women*), Susan Foh (*Women and the Word of God*), and C. C. Ryrie (*The Role of Women in the Church*) all represent a strict hierarchicalist position.

Moderate hierarchicalists echo the strict hierarchicalist's belief in the infallible Word of God's teaching regarding a hierarchy between men and women. They contrast their approach to hierarchy with the authoritarian patriarchy present in New Testament culture. Moderate hierarchicalists have been more recently self-named "complementarians," emphasizing the complementary roles of women and men. The leadership of the man is to include service to his wife, while the wife chooses willing and loving submission to her husband. Within the church, women are encouraged to be involved, but they are always to be under the headship of male elders or pastors. John Piper and Wayne Grudem espouse a complementarian viewpoint in *Recovering Biblical Manhood and Womanhood*. Donald Bloesch is an advocate of the moderate hierarchicalist position in *Is the Bible Sexist?* The Council on Biblical Manhood and Womanhood is an organization that supports this viewpoint.

Biblical feminism, sometimes called evangelical feminism, approaches the Bible as the infallible Word of God. However, their hermeneutic sees mutuality between the sexes as the God-ordained order of creation. Hierarchy is perceived to be a consequence of sin and can be overcome through the person and work of Jesus Christ. Egalitarianism in society, the church, and the home is advocated. Inclusive language is advocated in worship and educational materials. Bible translations which seek to reclaim the original intent by becoming more gender-inclusive are endorsed. Christians for Biblical Equality is an organization that supports this viewpoint. Gretchen Gaebelien Hull (*Equal to Serve*), Alvera and Berkeley Mickelson (*Women, Authority and the Bible*), Mary Stewart Van Leeuwen (*Gender and Grace* and *After Eden*), and Stanley Grenz and Denise Muir Kjesbo (*Women in the Church*) are representatives of the biblical feminist position.

Mainstream feminism believes the Bible contains the Word of God but is not itself the infallible Word of God. They believe that the Word is especially found in the person and work of Jesus Christ, the Redeemer of all oppression, including patriarchalism. Mainstream feminists advocate the use of inclusive language in Bible translation (even if it means rewriting the original to be more inclusive of women), worship resources, and educational materials. They embrace both masculine and feminine metaphors for God. Representatives of this view are Rosemary Radford Ruether (*Sexism and God Talk*), Phyllis Trible (*God and the Rhetoric of Sexuality*), and Sallie McFague (*Metaphorical Theology: Models of God in Religious Language*).

Radical feminism is expressed in two forms: Christian and post-Christian. The Christian expression believes patriarchalism and a male-centered bias have so pervaded the Bible that revelation cannot be centered in the Scriptures. Instead, revelation emerges from the experience of "woman-church," a community of women-affirming Christians who seek liberation from patriarchal oppression. Elizabeth Schussler Fiorenza (*In Memory of Her*) is an advocate of this position. Some of the mainstream feminists such as Rosemary Radford Ruether, have hinted at a more radical feminism in their later writings.

Post-Christian radical feminism believes that Christianity as a whole must be rejected in order for women to be liberated. Women must name their own religious experience, which is totally free of men. Lesbianism and witchcraft may be included in this "religious expression." Mary Daly (*Beyond God the Father: Toward a Philosophy of Women's Liberation*), Naomi Goldberg, and Starhawk are proponents of this viewpoint.

This overview of five theological responses to feminism demonstrates that feminism is a complex movement and cannot be dismissed or thoughtlessly categorized as anti-Christian. Feminism must be taken seriously by Christians and responded to with thought and critical reflection.

DENISE MUIR KJESBO

Bibliography. G. Bilezikian (1985), *Beyond Sex Roles*; D. Bloesch (1982), *Is The Bible Sexist?*; S. Clark (1980), *Man and Woman in Christ*; M. Daly (1973), *Beyond God the Father: Toward a Philosophy of Women's Liberation*; D. Diehl (1990), *Gender Matters: Women's Studies for the Christian Community*; E. S. Fiorenza (1983), *In Memory of Her*; S. Foh (1980), *Women and the Word of God*; S. Grenz and D. M. Kjesbo (1995), *Women in the Church*; G. G. Hull (1987), *Equal to Serve: Women and Men in the Church and Home*; G. Knight (1977), *New Testament Teaching on the Role Relationships of Men and Women*; S. McFague (1982), *Metaphorical Theology: Models of God in Religious Language*; A. Mickelson, ed. (1986), *Women, Authority and the Bible*; J. Piper and W. Grudem (1991), *Recovering Biblical Manhood and Womanhood: A Response to Evangelical Feminism*; R. R. Ruether (1983), *Sexism and God Talk: Toward a Feminist Theology*; C. C. Ryrie (1970), *The Role of Women in the Church*; Starhawk (1979), *The Spiral Dance: A Rebirth of the Ancient Religion of the Great Goddess*; P. Trible (1978), *God and the Rhetoric of Sexuality*; M. S. VanLeeuwen, ed. (1993), *After Eden: Facing the Challenge of Gender Reconciliation*; M. S. Van Leeuwen, (1990), *Gender and Grace: Love, Work and Parenting in a Changing World*.

See also DEACONESS; WOMEN IN MINISTRY; WOMEN, LEADERSHIP ROLE OF; WOMEN, ORDINATION OF

Fetal Alcohol Syndrome. Fetal alcohol syndrome (FAS) is a birth defect involving permanent brain damage caused by prenatal alcohol exposure. There are four diagnostic criteria for FAS: prenatal exposure to alcohol, prenatal and/or postnatal growth deficiencies, a certain pattern of facial features (although these features are frequently outgrown before or during adolescence), and central nervous system damage that is evidenced by behavior problems and may involve learning disabilities, mental retardation, and other mental deficits. FAS may also cause a myriad of physical defects. Fetal alcohol effects (FAE) is a term used to describe the same disability without the facial features or growth deficiencies. FAE is sometimes considered more devastating because these individuals are not physically recognized as being disabled and yet their behaviors can lead them into trouble in school, in society, and even with the law.

Many people think that all individuals with FAS/E are mentally retarded, but researchers now estimate that 75 percent of the individuals with FAS and 90 percent of those with FAE have normal IQs (Streissguth, 1997, 103). This was first thought to be an advantage, but it has become evident that a normal IQ hides the disability and helps those with FAS/E learn more and have more ideas without having the judgment and wisdom to use the information and ideas to make good choices. Their behavior is predictably unpredictable.

If undiagnosed, individuals with FAS or FAE (FAS/E) are misunderstood as rebellious, uncooperative, lazy, stupid, and selfish instead of being understood as disabled. Typical behaviors associated with FAS/E include not connecting cause and effect, having difficulty learning from experience, lacking remorse, and having a genuine innocence while repeatedly becoming involved in the same unacceptable or unlawful situations. These individuals can be extremely vulnerable to peer influence and are easily victimized. But they are also very manipulative and can be emotionally volatile. Although they are typically charming, they are very frustrating to live and work with. Several families report their children with FAS/E were kicked out of Sunday school or a church youth group. Families struggle to raise these children and don't know why their consistent love and discipline doesn't work. Many of these parents feel there is never enough time, love, and attention to fulfill their children's insatiable needs (Waller, 1998, 35–37).

Many doctors are reluctant to diagnose FAS/E for various reasons. A large number of children with FAS/E are underdiagnosed or misdiagnosed with attention deficit/hyperactivity disorder (ADHD or ADD). This can be a coexisting condition with FAS/E, but basic issues and deficits cannot be untangled until FAS/E is ruled out or confirmed. If the disability remains undiagnosed, these individuals have great difficulty getting the services they need to be safe and reach their potential.

There is a growing focus of attention on FAS/E in the United States and around the world. Hopefully a better way to diagnose FAS/E will be discovered and more effective means to serve these disabled individuals will be developed in the future.

GARY WALLER AND ANN WALLER

Bibliography. D. Davis (1994), *Reaching Out to Children with FAS;* A. Streissguth (1997), *Fetal Alcohol Syndrome;* A. Streissguth and J. Kanter, eds. (1997), *The Challenge of Fetal Alcohol Syndrome;* A. Waller (1998), *Preacher's Magazine* vol. 73, pp. 35–37; A. Waller and J. DeVries, eds. (1999), *The Best of FAS Times.*

See also ALCOHOLISM

Field Theory. Kurt Lewin's field theory attempts to explain personal motivation as behavior that is a function of an individual's life space, or psychological reality. Behavior is viewed as a function of the total personal and environmental perceptions by an individual. Lewin's theory stands in contrast to psychoanalytic thought in which behavior is a function of the history of the individual. In his thinking a person's past may influence only indirectly. Behavior is primarily a function of the current and immediate life space.

Life space refers to the totality of all psychological facts and social forces that influence an individual at a given time. It is usually divided into two parts: person and environment. Each part can be differentiated into boundaries. The personal region includes goals, needs, hopes, or aspirations. Profession, family, social taboos, and cultural expectations are some of the facets of the environment.

Lewin's theory differed from behaviorism in two key dimensions. First, it emphasized the subjectivity of the psychological field. To predict behavior one needs to describe the situation from the viewpoint of the individual whose behavior is under consideration, not from the viewpoint of the observer. Second, it highlighted that behavior must be understood as a function of the life space, or situation as a whole. In essence, behavior is motivated by a multitude of interdependent forces affecting an individual, as opposed to one or two salient rewards or reinforcers that may be present.

Field theory was born on the battlefields of World War I. Lewin's paper "The War Landscape" described the battlefield in terms of life space. The solder's needs determined how the landscape was perceived. When miles from the front it was peaceful on all sides for great distances. As the front approached, the landscape took on another perspective, becoming elements of battle (i.e., rocks and trees became places to hide).

After the war Lewin's appointment to the Psychological Institute of Berlin led to further development of field theory. Upon emigrating to the United States, he established the Center for Group Dynamics at MIT. Lewin's American research concentrated field theory applications upon the social problems of prejudice and internal group conflict.

The strengths of field theory include the structural concepts and insights it provides about the nature of conflict situations, the necessity of viewing the situation holistically from the participant's perspective, and the dynamic equilibrium between the person and the environment.

Field theory has had wide-ranging influence on group dynamics. Additional research by Lewin's colleagues and students has created a formidable array of concepts in the literature. Prominent are the areas of group cohesiveness, group communication, and influences from social pressures. Several dominant theories have emerged. Atkinson's achievement motivation, Heider's cognitive balance, and Festinger's dissonance theory are only a few. The famous T-group training (laboratory training in groups) spawned a movement of greater group sensitivities and understandings. It is estimated that over half of all social psychologists today can trace their intellectual roots to field theory.

JAMES A. DAVIES

Bibliography. A. Marrow (1969), *The Practical Theorist: The Life and Work of Kurt Lewin;* S. Patnoe (1988), *A Narrative History of Experiential Social Psychology: The Lewin Tradition;* B. Weiner (1972), *Theories of Motivation.*

See also GROUP DYNAMICS; PARENT EFFECTIVENESS TRAINING

Field Trip. Opportunity for students to learn aspects of the curriculum by going outside the classroom to see or experience something that could not be experienced within the confines of the classroom setting. Educational theorist/practitioner Johann Pestalozzi (1746–1827), an early advocate of the importance of field trips in education, believed curriculum should be organized around "sensate" activities—direct experiences that stimulate the senses. He maintained that these types of experiences have a tremendous effect on determining positive opinion, conduct, duties, and even virtue. Both secular and Christian education have been influenced by his ideas (Gangel and Benson, 1983). In Christian education, field trips are commonly used as an opportunity to enhance student learning about elements of worship, other religions, community concerns, matters of church history, or biblical materials through an activity outside the Sunday school classroom or church setting. These "hands-on" experiences allow class members to learn about Christianity in a more wholistic and three-dimensional manner. Visits to observe other ministry styles or to see other Sunday school teachers in action can be used as field trips to enhance the training leaders. Field trips may vary in time and distance traveled. They may be as short as a trip from one part of the church to another (such as an elementary Sunday school class visiting the sanctuary to learn about the symbols of worship) or as far and lengthy as a trip to another region (such as an adult Sunday school trip to Israel to learn about the geography of the Bible). To be most effective, a field trip should be carefully researched and planned, have distinct learning goals, be connected to the current curriculum, and allow for debriefing of the group experience and discussion of what has been learned.

JANA SUNDENE

Bibliography. K. Gangel and W. Benson (1983), *Christian Education: Its History and Philosophy.*

See also EXPERIENTIAL LEARNING; OBSERVATIONAL LEARNING; PESTALOZZI, JOHANN HEINRICH

Financial Plan. *See* Budget.

Finger Painting. Direct application of paints to paper, canvas, or another surface using the fingers or other parts of the hands or arms. It is considered a form of self-expression that is commonly used in education at the preschool and early elementary levels, but can be used at any level of Christian education.

Finger painting—or any drawings made by students—can reflect the individual's level or manner of understanding of a subject. Researchers such as Coles (1990) and Heller (1986) have assessed children's perspectives of God and religious faith through careful evaluation of what is drawn and how it is depicted. The direct involvement of the body in finger painting allows a relatively free and potentially cathartic expression of ideas and feelings that may not otherwise have an outlet. Thus finger painting is potentially useful for assessing understandings of, and feelings about, a wide variety of ideas and activities in Christian education. It is also an enjoyable experience.

DONALD E. RATCLIFF

Bibliography. R. Coles (1990), *The Spiritual Life of Children;* D. Heller (1986), *The Children's God.*

Fishbowl. Methodology utilized in group dynamics training experiences. A small, select group sits in a circle within a larger group and participates in a discussion while being observed by those who surround them. This allows for a "live demonstration" of group process, which can lead to a discussion about meanings of actions experienced in the inner circle as observed by onlookers and participants alike. The group leader

or any participant may call for a "freeze" in the action in order to inquire into the process as it is impacting the members involved. A fishbowl may be used as a stimulant by allowing outer observers to sporadically replace the members in the inner circle when they want to get into the conversation. Fishbowls also allow those with particular expertise in either subject or process to move the whole group to deeper levels of insight and skill development.

JULIE GORMAN

Flake's Formula. The phenomenal growth of the modern Sunday school movement has been attributed in part to what has become known as Flake's Formula. This organized approach to Sunday school growth was developed by Arthur Flake. Born in La Grange, Texas in 1862, Flake lived until 1952. Converted as an adult at the age of thirty-one, Flake soon became involved as a layperson in his local Baptist church at Winona, Mississippi. Flake was active in the Mississippi Baptist Young People's Union, where he served as president. He learned the basics of Sunday school by serving as superintendent in his local church. Using his business background in sales and administration, Flake developed a Sunday school which became a model for other churches in Mississippi.

The Sunday school success which Flake had as a layperson in Mississippi ultimately led to his being placed in charge of the Department of Sunday School Administration at the Baptist Sunday School Board in 1920. In this strategic position, Flake made several important contributions which include: development of the Standard of Excellence as a guide for Sunday schools, perfecting the Six-Point Record System, stressing the cause of weekly officers' and teachers' meetings, using the association to foster Bible study in the churches, and creating Sunday school enlargement campaigns (Taylor, 1994, 43).

Flake's greatest contribution to the kingdom of God may have come through the development of his five-step process referred to as Flake's Formula. The formula includes the following elements: know your possibilities, or sometimes stated as "discover the prospects," expand the organization, enlist and train the workers, provide the space, and go after the people.

Flake had a strong belief that a Sunday school should not be considered great unless it was attempting to reach a large majority of the people who should be attending the Bible study. The first step in reaching people would be to know your possibilities. The process could begin by making sure that the Sunday school roll had a number equal to the resident church membership. Flake stressed that every church member should be in Sunday school. This meant that a good place to find prospects would be to compare the Sunday school roll with the church membership roll. Individuals who are church members but not attending Sunday school are then placed on a list to become prospects for Sunday school (Flake, 1922, 20–21).

Another method utilized by Flake to discover prospects was to take a religious census. Flake stated that a religious census should occur at least annually in every community. He gave further instruction that in growing communities a census would be necessary at least twice a year and in rapidly changing neighborhoods a census may be needed every three months. The purpose of the religious census is to gain information in building the Sunday school and ultimately winning people for Christ (Flake, 1922, 21–22).

After a director had been selected to lead the census, Flake supported the following steps to help ensure a successful house-to-house survey. First, it is necessary to define the territory. If an exact territory is not determined, it would be difficult to evaluate the process. The next step in the process is to prepare the assignments. The preparation of the territory for assignment requires careful clerical attention. It may be necessary to divide the territory into districts which can be subdivided into blocks or sections that a worker could canvass in a two-hour time period. The number of the blocks will determine how many workers are needed for the survey. A capable person familiar with the territory should be selected to be in charge of each of the districts (Flake, 1922, 22–23).

Next, it will be necessary to enlist the workers for the canvass. Goals should be established in each age group which will give direction in helping to enlist the necessary number of people that are needed. The pastor and Sunday school superintendent may also encourage participation in the survey from their respective positions of authority. A public call for workers must be followed by personal enlistment. Once the workers are committed, it is important to provide them with sufficient materials to complete the canvass. This will include basic materials such as assignment envelopes, census cards, and pens. Flake suggested that the best time to complete the canvass would be on a Sunday afternoon since it is an easier time to get workers and the people contacted usually have a leisure attitude (Flake, 1922, 23–24).

After the census has been completed, it is necessary to put the information in a convenient, usable form. The prospects gained from the census should be age-graded so that future visitation assignments can be made by an age-appropriate Sunday school teacher or class. The census cards will become the foundation for a permanent prospect file. A list of the prospects should be given to the pastor, superintendent, department director, and teacher. In order that the Sunday school teacher is not overwhelmed by a large prospect list, it may be necessary to assign only a few prospects each week with the understanding that the prospects are to be visited by the class workers during that specific week. Accountability is established when the reported visits are turned in at the weekly officers' and teachers' meeting (Flake, 1922, 25–27).

The next step in Flake's Formula is to enlarge the organization. Flake believed that unless the Sunday school organization was expanded, all of the work done in taking the census would be useless. There would not be permanent growth in the Sunday school unless there was an organization strong enough to reach, teach, and hold the people. This type of organization requires a large committed group of workers. Flake stressed that there should be at least one worker for every ten people enrolled in Sunday school.

The only place to find new Sunday school teachers and workers is to look within the membership of the church. Both public and private prayers should be used to ask God to provide laborers for his harvest. While continual prayer is being given to the effort, a list of prospective workers and teachers can be made. Flake indicates that the pastor and Sunday school superintendent go over the church roll name by name to develop a list of prospective leaders. Many people are not involved in the work of Sunday school because they have never been asked. When enlisting workers, the Sunday school superintendent should show the prospective teacher a list of people who can be won to Christ and involved in Bible study. Persistence may be necessary as the prospective teacher is helped to see his or her obligation to serve Christ (Flake, 1922, 28–30).

The third step in Flake's Formula is to provide the space. Flake believed that it was impossible to build a large Sunday school from small, cramped facilities. A suitable place for Sunday school also must include proper equipment for each class. Flexibility is an important component in providing the space because adjustments may have to be made as a result of accessing the needs of the organization. For example, an adult class might be meeting in a large room when a smaller room would serve the same purpose. If the current church facility is still unable to handle the growth, another possibility would be to secure outside space such as a lodge or public school building. From the standpoint of efficiency and economy, it may be necessary for the church to engage in a building program and erect new buildings. According to Flake, a church must take care of its home base as a necessary part of fulfilling the Great Commission (Flake, 1922, 30–31).

The fourth step in Flake's Formula is to enlist and train the workers. Once the workers are enlisted as previously discussed, it is essential to furnish ongoing training. Flake stressed the necessity of providing a functioning weekly workers' and teachers' meeting. According to Flake, there are four well-defined purposes of the weekly officers' and teachers' meeting. The first is to promote study of the lesson for the following Sunday. When the lesson is discussed in the weekly workers' meeting, there is an incentive for teachers to prepare early, resulting in higher quality lesson preparation. Next, teachers should be instructed in how to best teach the lesson. A goal of the training will be for teachers to depart with practical ideas on how to teach the lesson. The third purpose is to consider briefly the problems and issues facing the Sunday school. Teachers should be given the opportunity to make announcements, ask questions, and make explanations when necessary. Last, the weekly officers' and teachers' meeting must involve prayer. There are some prospects for Sunday school who can be reached only through prayer (Flake, 1922, 109–11).

If the church decides to not have a weekly workers' and teachers' meeting, Flake suggests that a monthly workers' conference be provided. For churches which have weekly meetings, a monthly conference can be held in lieu of a specific weekly meeting. The monthly workers' conference is a place where officers and teachers can make and receive reports, determine policies, and assist in planning the work of the Sunday school. Flake stresses that a monthly workers' conference is a great Sunday school builder, but it should not be substituted for a weekly officers' and teachers' meeting (Flake, 1922, 108–20).

The final step in Flake's Formula is to go after the people. Flake believed the absence of a regular visitation program leads to discouragement and ultimately to a ineffective organization. A planned program of visitation should focus on both prospects and absentees. To have an effective ministry of outreach it is suggested that a regular weekly or monthly visitation day be reserved. A regular visitation day will help establish the foundation for a growing church. If people are left to visit on their own, the visitation will probably never take place. Flake indicates that a personal visit is the best approach to reach new pupils for the Sunday school and recover absentee members. Visitation also provides the opportunity to enlist youth as a part of a visitation team. To stress the importance of a regular program of visitation, the pastor should make frequent reference to it from the pulpit. When the pastor, Sunday school superintendent, and teachers all participate in visitation, it will be a success (Flake, 1922, 32–39).

J. GREGORY LAWSON

Bibliography. A. Flake (1922), *Building a Standard Sunday School;* B. Taylor (1994), *21 Truths, Traditions, and Trends.*

Flannelgraph. Means of bringing Bible characters and scenes to life by placing felt or felt-backed figures on a felt background. Some sets have as many as six hundred characters and objects. Illustrating a Bible story with these bright, finely detailed characters helps to hold the interest of children.

Flannelgraph is a teaching tool used primarily in a teacher-centered learning situation. It is greatly limited in its use with preschoolers, whose attention span precludes group learning for the longer periods of time necessary for a story to unfold through the use of flannelgraph. It allows for interactive learning of a limited nature when some of the children help place the figures on the background scene.

Although flannelgraph may appeal to the visual learner and reinforce teaching for the audio learner, it falls short of attending to the variety of learning styles and developmental stages that any group of children represents.

BARBARA WYMAN

Focus Group. Group in which members come together because of a particular issue, area of interest, need, or task. The focus is normally determined prior to the beginning of the group and will flow out of the group's clearly defined purpose. Because the group members have a good understanding of the nature of the group and what the group needs to achieve, it becomes much easier to evaluate whether the group is meeting its goals and objectives.

In the Christian education context, focus groups have been developed which emphasize such subjects or areas of interest as evangelism, discipleship, missions, Bible book studies, leadership training, and advocacy of contemporary social and religious issues. Since these groups revolve around a common theme or purpose, there is normally a high degree of participation and commitment to the group. Once the goals and objectives of the group have been met, the members feel free to either leave the group or redefine the purpose of the group.

J. GREGORY LAWSON

Focus on the Family. Focus on the Family, a nonprofit evangelical organization founded in 1977, is "dedicated to the preservation of the home." James Dobson, Ph.D. in child development and author of over 90 books, initiated his crusade for the family with a 25-minute weekly radio program broadcast over a dozen stations, and a single book on child discipline. Today Focus on the Family employs a variety of media formats to fulfill its mission through more than 70 different ministries.

Five guiding principles direct the ministries of Focus on the Family: knowing God begins through salvation in Christ; marriage between a man and a woman was ordained by God as a life-long relationship; children are a heritage from God; human life is of inestimatable worth; family, church, and government are basic institutions ordained by God, each with a specific purpose.

The "Focus on the Family" radio program continues as one of the most well-known of the organization's ministries. It is broadcast daily on over 4,000 facilities in more than 70 countries. Hosted by Dr. Dobson, these programs explore a significant number of family issues. Focus on the Family values also reach more than 2.5 million households through *Focus on the Family* magazine and a monthly newsletter, "Family News from Dr. James Dobson."

Other Focus on the Family ministries reach special interest groups through a variety of media forms. Some of these include: *Focus on the Family Clubhouse Jr.* magazine for children ages 4–8; *Focus on the Family Clubhouse* magazine for children ages 8–12; McGee and Me! and Adventures in Odyssey video series and radio broadcasts for children; *Breakaway* and *Brio* magazines for teens; Sex, Lies & . . . the Truth and Life on the Edge, video series for adolescents and young adults; *Boundless*, a webzine for college students; *Citizen* magazine and "Citizens Issues Alert" provide current information on social issues; *Single-Parent Family*; Armed Forces Radio and Television Services broadcasts; *Physician* magazine; "Pastor's Weekly Briefing" faxletter.

Education, a vital element of each ministry, is the primary focus of *Teachers in Focus* magazine, *Boundless* webzine, the Focus on the Family Institute, and the Counseling Enrichment program. Focus on the Family Institute offers a personalized undergraduate semester studies program, "committed to teaching and research programs which defend and support the family from a distinctively Christian base with modern cultural relevancy and practical application." The Counseling Enrichment seminar program supports Christian counselors in the integration of psychological and biblical concepts.

Focus on the Family offers professional counseling and referrals, responds to all inquiries for information and advice under Dr. Dobson's direction, and supports Crisis Pregnancy Centers.

KAY M. LLOVIO

Bibliography. *Boundless* webzine, *http://www.boundless.org*; J. Dobson (1992), *Dr. Dobson Answers Your Questions* vols. 1 and 2; idem (1977), *The New Dare to Discipline*; Focus on the Family website: *http://www.family.org.*; *Teachers in Focus* magazine and website: *http://www.family.org/forum/teachersmag*; R. Zettersten (1992), *Dr. Dobson: Turning Hearts toward Home*.

Follower. *See* Disciple.

Foresight. *See* Vision.

Formal Education. Approach to learning focused on acquiring skills, knowledge, attitudes, and values growing out of planned, intentional learning experiences. While more informal modes of education stress student interactions with experiences or environments, formal education is characterized by classroom sessions, learning agendas, teacher-directed methodologies, and required courses of study. There is a tendency toward a planned curriculum, leading to a completion of a block of study. It is often more linear than global in course and subject requirements.

Learning outcomes (sometimes known as goals, objectives, learning indicators, or aims) are important components of the curriculum plan in formal education. The teacher or learning leader sets out with some idea of what the student can be expected to learn in a certain block of time, whether in a lesson, a unit, a course, or the span of an academic degree. The topic, course, content, or contract, along with the student's needs and goals, govern the learning agenda.

The content of formal education is often comprised of required blocks, with some room for optional studies. While the student may bring to the learning environment life experiences or additional readings and research, the subject matter is generally teacher-directed rather than student-directed. The student's personal needs, priorities, life experiences, and goals enhance rather than dictate the daily directions of this approach to learning.

The majority of formal education is delivered in a classroom setting, in established blocks of time, via instructional media, books, video, lectures, speakers, and audiovisual methodologies. While the classroom provides the major environment of formal education, this does not rule out field trips, internships, laboratory work, and other practical, experiential forms of learning.

Formal education may be class- or group-oriented, or it could be individualized instruction. In church or congregational settings, formal education most likely is seen in the form of Sunday school and Bible study classes, structured groups with stated learning agendas, seminars, and one-to-one pairings in which there are intentional learning agendas.

Christian elementary and secondary schools, parochial schools, academies, Bible schools, Christian colleges and universities, and seminaries, among others, fall into the category of formal education, especially as it relates to Christian education. Some have attempted to delineate the distinctives between church-based religious instruction and school-based studies (for example, distinguishing between the term *religious education* and the term *Christian education*). In either case, however, the approach is generally more toward formal education in the school-based settings.

WESLEY BLACK

Formal Operational Thought. Children do not think like adults. As the young mature, their cognitive capacities go through a number of different phases. These stages involve both quantitative and qualitative changes. According to cognitive structural developmentalist Jean Piaget (1896–1980), the Formal Operational stage represents the last phase of thinking and begins appearing at approximately eleven years of age.

Formal operational thought opens new vistas to the participant. The beginnings of full adult reasoning powers become available. The young person begins to think *logically* by considering, connecting, and coordinating multiple perspectives of a variety of persons. In this stage mental actions are not limited to concrete experience but can be performed on *ideas and propositions*. Formal operators can reason logically about *abstract and hypothetical* processes or events that have no basis in reality. Many researchers suggest that the use of hypothetical-deductive reasoning is the surest way of determining whether a preadolescent has crossed over into the stage of formal operational thought.

Formal-operational thinking is succinctly described by three terms: rational, systematic, and abstract. The individual can now "think about thinking" and performs complex mental processes on ideas as well as tangible objects and events.

A distinction must be drawn between the capacity for formal operational thought and its performance. Although adolescents and adults have the potential to practice complex thinking levels, not all of them do. This inability may be due to variations in personal maturation, experience, or circumstantial demand. The difference between personal capacity and capacity to perform with *assistance* is called the ZPD ("zone of proximal development") by Vygotsky (1986). Tharp and Gallimore (1988) remind us that healthy teaching consists of assisting students' performance through the ZPD.

The Christian educator can find much value from the research on formal operational thought and its variants. It is a complex thinking task to help people grow into a scriptural worldview and divine viewpoint. Teachers can encourage such development via structured experiences and questioning strategies that provide for organizational clustering and retrieval of appropriate information.

JAMES A. DAVIES

Bibliography. K. Issler and R. Habermas (1994), *How We Learn;* D. R. Shaffer (1994), *Developmental Psychology;* C. Smokehouse (1998), *Joining Children on the Spiritual Journey.*

Foster Care. *See* Divorce, Children of.

Fowler, James W., III (1940–). Educator and minister. Fowler is recognized for his defining conceptualization of faith development. He conceives of faith generically as a universal, innate experience by which meaning is made and sustained. Thus, his concern is not with a specific religion but with the patterned process of growth that may take place in any religion. Faith development involves deep mental structures that underlie religious beliefs. Fowler views faith as relational, involving a triad of mutual, trusting relationships with others and with an ultimate center of power and value (God, in Christian faith). It is an integral process of centering that serves as foundational for beliefs, values, and meanings. Faith gives direction and coherence to life. Conceiving of faith as a verb, Fowler sees it as more than mere theoretical propositions. Rather, it involves active being and committing. Although Fowler's concern is with the human psychological side of faith, rather than the theological, his approach is informed theologically by Paul Tillich and by H. Richard Niebuhr's "transformational theology."

Psychologically, Fowler draws on the developmental theories of Piaget, Kohlberg, and Erikson and addresses the entire life span. Fowler conceptualizes epistemological concerns, identifying how faith comes to be known through a sequence of six developmental stages. Each stage represents a "structure" of faith, a way in which faith is thought of and a means by which faith meaning is made, a form of worldview. At each stage there is an integration of knowing and valuing. The stages are invariant in sequence, and each successive stage integrates previous stages while expanding one's faith capacities. Development is not automatic and may be arrested at any stage. For example, an individual may reach chronological adulthood while remaining in the faith stages of childhood or adolescence. Progression through the stages occurs as a result of complex interaction among biological growth, emotional development, cognitive development, psychosocial development, and the influences of religion and culture. In his most recent description, Fowler does not consider faith stages to be universal. That is, he does not view them as necessarily applicable to all cultural contexts.

Transitions between stages may be long and painful, although they do not necessarily involve change in content. Stage change is precipitated by disruptive experiences or by the realization that the present means of making meaning of life are inadequate.

For more than a decade, Fowler has worked to relate faith development theory to Christian faith. He acknowledges the limitations of his understanding of faith development in light of the reality of God's sovereignty in faith. Much of his attention is directed to church praxis, or practical theology, considering areas such as pastoral care, counseling, church education programs, family ministry, and so on. Specifically, Fowler sees compatibility with evangelical Christian faith in that characteristics of a given stage are thoroughly interwoven with particular content and consciousness of biblical faith. Salvation may occur at any stage. Each succeeding stage then deepens one's understanding of and commitment to faith in God and awareness of the needs of others. On the other hand, development for several stages may continue to be self-serving, with greater separation from God and an erroneous form of autonomy.

Development toward biblical wholeness depends on a dynamic combination of God's grace and human potential with openness to a deepening relationship with God. Movement through the stages involves a process by which believers become more and more subject to God's direction and in closer relationship with him. Sin results in arresting development as a result of self-centeredness. This may show itself as refusal to consider perspectives of others, as holding to a formula-based faith, or as following authoritarian leaders. At times, Fowler blends developmental theory with aspects of Christian faith in ways that fail to preserve core meanings of biblical/theological concepts. Significant distinctions sometimes fall away to accommodate assumptions of faith development theory, rather than allowing differences, for the present at least, to remain in dynamic, unresolved tension.

DENNIS DIRKS

Bibliography. J. W. Fowler, *Stages of Faith: The Psychology of Human Development and the Quest for Meaning;* idem, *Becoming Adult, Becoming Christian: Adult Development and Christian Faith;* idem, *Christian Perspectives on Faith Development: A Reader,* pp. 370–83; idem, *Christian Education Journal* 13:1 (1992): 13–23; idem, *Faithful Change: The Personal and Public Challenges of Postmodern Life;* J. W. Fowler, K. E. Nipkow and F. Schweitzer, eds., *Stages of Faith and Religious Development: Implications for Church, Education, and Society.*

See also BELIEF; COGNITIVE DEVELOPMENT; ERIKSON, ERIK HOMBURGER; FAITH; KOHLBERG, LAWRENCE; PIAGET, JEAN; STAGES OF LIFE/ADULTHOOD

Frames. The term *frame* has several meanings that can apply to Christian education. In behavioral psychology, a frame refers to a single step in the learning of a skill. At the conclusion of each frame of a behavioral program, immediate feedback is provided to each student. If students succeed in performing the task in the frame, they are rewarded and move to the next step. If students do not succeed, they are given correction and are provided either with the same frame a second time—in linear programs—or given an alternative form of the frame that was failed—in branching programs (Yount, 1996). Behavioral programs are believed to have a broad range of applicability in Christian education (Collins, 1969).

Sociologist Erving Goffman (1974) uses the term *frame* in a very different manner. Goffman, using a symbolic interactionist orientation, considers frames to be general understandings people have of a given situation. David Elkind (1994) believes frame analysis to be an important theoretical perspective in understanding the overall development of children. Difficulties in learning often occur when the teacher and student understand a given event from a different frame; there is "frame clash." This can be the result of differing cultural backgrounds, or simply alternative perspectives of the situation—such as the contrast between the rules of teachers and the "peer culture" that encourages the breaking of rules. These are alternative frames—perspectives and sets of actions—that also exist in Christian education contexts (Ratcliff, 1998). Frames of this sort can be "spoiled" or left incompleted. They can also be acquired, and people also learn to "switch" rapidly from one frame to another in an educational setting (Elkind, 1994), as when adults move from lecture to small group discussion in a Bible study.

Yet another use of the word *frame* is the "play frame" of preschoolers. Youngsters are able to mentally transform a given environment into two areas: that of play, and that of nonplay. The play frame includes the assumption of pretense, the use of toys, and the ascription of roles by those who are playing together. The real-world environment of the child is considered to be outside the play frame. As children grow older, they become able to "decontextualize" the play frame; they can describe it in detail and are able to change the frame at will.

The play frame is important not only in the flexibility with which youngsters can see themselves in that frame, but also because the play frame is the basis for acquiring aspects of the "story frame"; the distinction between events in a story and the actual environment of the child (Ratcliff, 1988). Examples of the story frame include the telling of a story about self in the third person, and the stereotypical beginnings and endings of stories (i.e. "once upon a time" and "lived happily ever after") that constitute the frame or boundary between story and the real world. These implicit structures in stories—the story frame—are important aspects of Christian education, particularly since these structures can vary across cultures, subcultures, and even between individuals. The Bible uses stories to communicate essential aspects of faith, and thus story frames appropriate to learners can enhance reception of story content.

Donald E. Ratcliff

Bibliography. G. Collins (1969), *Search for Reality: Psychology and the Christian;* D. Elkind (1994), *A Sympathetic Understanding of the Child;* E. Goffman (1974, 1986), *Frame Analysis;* D. Ratcliff (1988), *Handbook of Preschool Religious Education;* idem (1998), "Peer Culture and School Culture Theory: Implications for Educational Ministry with Children," presented at the annual conference of the North American Professors of Christian Education; W. R. Yount (1996), *Created to Learn.*

Franke, August Hermann (1663–1727). German Pietist and educational reformer. Born into a prosperous, pious family, he was first educated through private instruction before going on to the gymnasium at Gotba. At fourteen he enrolled at the University of Erfurt, studied at Keil, and earned a degree from Leipzig. In 1689 he became a committed Pietist and returned to Leipzig to teach. Forced to leave there, Franke served as a pastor in Erfurt for a year until his Pietist learnings again caused his departure.

In 1691, Spener was instrumental in getting him a nonpaying teaching position at the University of Halle as professor of Oriental language. Seven years later he became the chair of the Department of Theology. Along with these positions he served as a pastor at Glaucha. He continued to teach at Halle until his death. Franke's aim in education was to honor God. This was to be accomplished by the transformed life rather than by dogma. The transformed life was characterized by active love, the realization of the kingdom of God as present, the terrible depth of sin, and the richness of God's grace. Franke insisted on theology being channeled into practical forms. Holy Scriptures provided the core of the curriculum at every level of educational endeavor. In seminary, he emphasized the study of biblical languages with the direct application of that study to preaching and pastoral care.

Franke's emphasis in theological education shifted from doctrine to right action, from theological speculation to devotional earnestness, from the intellectual to the experiential, from systematic theology to biblical exposition, from what God did in history to what God wants humans to do today, from passive reliance on God's initiative to human responsibility. Franke believed that education should be home-centered. The teacher was a replacement for the parent. Therefore, the example of the teacher was primary. Classes were to be small, and the relationship between teacher and student was to be characterized by love. Discipline was stringent, but physical punishment was rare.

The accomplishments of Franke are considerable. In 1692, he established a school for the children of poverty, believing that all should have the opportunity for education. In 1695, he founded an orphan school. In 1697, he opened a Latin school for college preparation. In 1705, he began a boarding school for the wealthy and nobility. He was involved in training teachers. He recruited as many as 250 of his college students to teach in the above school in exchange for their board. He began a publishing institute for biblical literature, provided an infirmary, and sent preachers and missionaries to America and Asia. In contrast to Luther, he didn't expect the state to support these educational ventures. They were provided for by faith offerings at the university and the church and from other donors.

At his death 2,200 children were being taught at his institutes, 134 orphans were in his schools, and 167 teachers were employed for this task in addition to 250 college students.

Richard E. Allison

See also Family Life Education; Modeling

Frankena, William Klaus (1908–94). American philosopher. He was acknowledged by many as a "philosopher's philosopher" (Goodpaster, 1976, vii). After he earned degrees from Calvin College, the University of Michigan, Harvard, and Cambridge, his career spanned twenty-four years of teaching as well as the chairmanship of the Department of Philosophy at Michigan.

Frankena was primarily recognized as a moral philosopher and secondarily as a philosopher of education. His early writings (1939–50) demonstrated respect for philosophers with varied ethical viewpoints. Later works provided his conclusions concerning the basis and character of what is right in human conduct. In a 1969 article, "Ought and Is Once More," he stated, in characteristic fashion, that major moral philosophies are various combinations of four statements: (1) judgments of obligation and value (Oughts) are rationally justifiable, objectively valid, and so on; (2) judgments of obligation and value cannot be logically inferred from factual ones (Ises); (3) judgments of obligation and value cannot be rationally justified, objectively valid, and so on, unless they can be logically inferred from factual ones (Ises); and (4) judgments of obligation and value are intuitive, self-evident, and self-justifying.

Frankena's moral philosophy was a combination of statements #1 and #2, distancing him from conservative Christian viewpoints, which combine #1 and #3 with reference to created laws of logic and propositional revelation of truth in Scripture. Frankena's "ground" of oughtness was a moral point of view that "lies in a (shared) de-

301

partment of our conative makeup as humans" (Goodpaster, 1976, ix).

Educators have found Frankena's conceptual analysis process useful in relating theory and practice for education in general and Christian education in particular. Frankena proposed that an adequate philosophy of education has at least three branches: a descriptive branch concerned with facts, a normative branch concerned with values, and an analytic branch concerned with analysis.

Frankena's *analytic* model is a web of five boxes. The left side of the model (Boxes A, C, and E) is a *normative* sequence, concluding with a set of practical precepts about educational practice (E). The right side of the model (Boxes B and D) is *descriptive*, containing beliefs to which an educator appeals to justify a normative educational process.

Box C represents excellences (abilities, traits, etc.) that are the outcomes of an educational endeavor. Box A represents the ethical and social ends that require the cultivation of these excellences. Box E is the conclusion of the analytic model. It represents practical precepts about what should be done—how the excellences should be produced. These ethical ends, educational excellences, and instructional methods are normative. They are what an educator believes an educational process *ought* to be.

Box B represents empirical and other beliefs and knowledge showing what excellences in C are necessary for carrying out the ethical ends in A. Similarly, Box D represents facts of psychology, sociology, and the science of education that show what means should be used to produce the excellences in C.

Frankena further concludes that a normative philosophy of education has two parts: "(1) a comparatively philosophical and theoretical line of reasoning, involving A, B, and C, to show what excellences are to be cultivated by education, and (2) a comparatively empirical or scientific and practical line of reasoning, involving C again and D and E, to show how and when they are to be cultivated. The conclusions of the first part become premises of the second part" (Frankena, 1965, 8–9).

Frankena's model is appropriate for analyzing the educational thought of others and for developing a personal philosophy of education. It leads an educator to be logical, consistent, and thorough as reasons for both effective methods and appropriate objectives are established in a well-ordered educational progression with superior ethical consequences.

DANIEL C. STEVENS

Bibliography. W. K. Frankena (1965), *Philosophy of Education;* K. E. Goodpaster, ed. (1976), *Perspectives on Morality: Essays by William K. Frankena;* R. Habermas and K. Issler (1992), *Teaching for Reconciliation: Foundations and Practice of Christian Educational Ministry.*

Freire, Paulo (1921–97). Brazilian educator. As a young boy, he learned to read and write informally from his parents. Throughout his childhood he was fascinated with the meaning of words and language and the reality of the world they represented. When he was age eight his comfortable, middle-class world was forever shattered by the worldwide economic convulsions of the Great Depression. The experience of poverty changed his life forever. He dedicated himself to overcoming poverty and oppression at the age of eleven. He came to believe that literacy was the primary means of empowering poor people to free themselves from the bonds of the culture of oppression and to participate in their own liberation within a truly democratic political process. From 1947 to 1964 (when he was imprisoned and later exiled as a threat to the state) Freire engaged in literacy education for justice in northeast Brazil. In exile he worked for UNESCO in Chile doing literacy work. After a interim year teaching at Harvard, Freire went to work for the World Council of Churches, helping churches around the globe pursue a vision of prophetic justice through education. From 1980 until his death Freire worked in his native Brazil, establishing and coordinating a variety of educational projects for all ages.

Freire's starting point for education is the concrete historical situation. Small groups of people meet together in culture circles to reflect and act together on the social reality in which they are immersed. Everyone is an active participant in reading and naming the world in which they live through democratic dialogue. Key words and issues, called generative themes, emerge from this critical dialogue. Critical reflection and action (or praxis) on the social reality fosters deep transformation of the participant, known as conscientization. In this process the mind-set or consciousness of the dominant, oppressive class in society is replaced by one's own critical consciousness or perspective on the world with an awareness of the contradictions and injustices in it. This internal transformation is also referred to as humanization, in which people become alive or fully human as they are freed from bondage to the dominant culture and worldview. The essence of education for Freire is the overcoming of the banking model of education, which seeks to deposit the knowledge of the dominant culture into the pupil who is unchanged, by means of dialogue and critical praxis. The role of the teacher is transformed into a questioner, problem poser, and fellow agent in praxis. Education by its very nature as critical praxis engages the elements of social injustice present in the world and thus works for social transformation for both the oppressed and the oppressor.

Freire's educational experience and model are informed throughout by his Christian faith.

Freire's parents instilled in him a deep Roman Catholic faith. Freire recognizes that much of the church is traditional and conservative regarding the status quo. Other churches are modernizing and reformist in nature. But only the prophetic church seeks true liberation through critical analysis of social structures that oppress and dehumanize. The prophetic Christian educator par excellence is Jesus Christ, who enfleshed the Truth by denouncing inhumanity and announcing the transforming Word of God for all people, especially social outcasts. Freire believes that the church is one the few institutions in society that can practice popular, holistic, liberatory education with integrity. Out of this framework the work of base ecclesial communities and liberation theology in Latin America is best understood. These grassroots groups of Christians are in essence culture circles of radical Christians who are called by God to transform the church and the world in the name of Jesus.

VERNON L. BLACKWOOD

Bibliography. P. Freire (1973), *Education for Critical Consciousness;* idem (1994), *Pedagogy of Hope;* idem (1970), *Pedagogy of the Oppressed;* idem (1985), *The Politics of Education;* M. Gadotti (1994), *Reading Paulo Freire: His Life and Work;* D. Schipani, (1984) *Conscientization and Creativity: Paulo Freire and Christian Education.*

See also ENCULTURATION; ETHNIC IMPLICATIONS FOR CHRISTIAN EDUCATION; MORAL DEVELOPMENT; ROMAN CATHOLIC EDUCATION

Freud, Sigmund (1856–1939). Originator and pioneer of psychoanalysis. Freud was born to Jewish parents in Frieberg, Moravia (now Pribor, Czech Republic), spent most of his life in Vienna, and died in London, England. He studied medicine at the University of Vienna, graduating in 1881, at which time he entered private practice as a clinical neurologist. In the early 1900s Freud became keenly interested in psychoanalytic theory and practice and along with Alfred Adler, Otto Rank, and Carl Jung, formed a weekly discussion group that became known as the Vienna Psychological Society. In 1910 he broadened his efforts to promote psychoanalysis and formed the Vienna Psychoanalytic Association. Freud has had a significant influence on psychology and education, and has also indirectly impacted Christian education. The primary contribution of Freudian psychology is the attempt to understand the internal forces that shape the activity and personality of an individual (Downs, 1994, 71).

While Freud was a physician by profession, his specialization was what would today be called psychiatry. His scientific interests led him into the clinical theory of psychoanalysis, an approach to therapeutic treatment of psychological problems which places major emphasis on unconscious feelings and thoughts. The interpretation of dreams and understanding dream symbolism were critical keys to exploring his patients' unconscious thoughts and neurotic symptoms.

While Freud was an avowed atheist, he demonstrated an intense interest in religion and has had an indirect influence on Christian education, although his impact on pastoral care has been far more conspicuous. One marked area of influence occurs in the sphere of personality development. Freud's impact emerges primarily through the writings of Jung, whose personality schema is, in turn, employed by Christian writers to better understand spiritual formation.

A second indirect influence of Freud on Christian education takes its course in the discipline of human development. James Loder (1981), for example, has reinterpreted certain key elements of Freudian theory in terms of stage structure and transformational occurrences. Freud also profoundly influenced Erik Erikson (1982), whose theory of psychosocial development in turn serves as a helpful basis for faith development (Fowler, 1981).

While Freud was a pioneer in understanding human nature and a significant contributor to the field of psychology, his theory of psychoanalysis has not been totally absorbed into mainstream psychological thought. Furthermore, his works have generally not been well accepted by conservative Christians.

In addition to his medical and psychiatric work, Freud was an extremely productive author. In sixty-three years of writing, he published over six hundred papers and books. His most important works include *The Interpretation of Dreams* (1900), *Group Psychology and the Analysis of the Ego* (1921), *The Ego and the Id* (1923), and *On Creativity and the Unconscious* (1925).

HARLEY ATKINSON

Bibliography. P. G. Downs (1994), *Teaching for Spiritual Growth;* E. H. Erikson (1980), *Identity and the Life Cycle;* J. W. Fowler (1981), *Stages of Faith;* E. J. Jones (1964), *The Life and Works of Sigmund Freud;* J. E. Loder (1981), *The Transforming Moment;* P. Vitz (1988), *Sigmund Freud's Christian Unconscious.*

Friendship Evangelism. "If there is one God, Creator, Redeemer, Judge, as the early Church passionately asserted, then those who have been brought back from their rebellion against him into fellowship with him cannot but pass on the knowledge of that rescue to others; the new life cries out to be shared" (Green, 1970, 78).

Friendship evangelism does what Michael Green has suggested. It is evangelism that is committed to passing on the knowledge of rescue. It is evangelism by way of lifestyle rather than confrontation. Out of a life of gratitude to God an individual shares her or his story of redemption. It is based on loving rather than converting a person to a particular point of view or lifestyle. This does not mean that conversion is not important, but rather the method that is used is the method of love. The example of Christ is important to remember. His ministry was one of establishing relationships of love, care, and concern. As we read the stories surrounding his life, we come away with a sense of his compassion for everyone.

This method of evangelism is based on the idea that people are drawn to Jesus by what they observe in the lives of others. Jerry Cook says of this, "We are to not simply to 'be a Christian' but we are to 'be Christian'" (Cook, 1984). People are more likely to be converted to Christianity by a relationship than through a confrontational approach. They are often watching with hopeful eyes for something that is true and genuine and real. As they watch the Christian being Christian, hope can be restored and lives changed."

Friendship evangelism is a very attractive model of outreach. One reason is that it is much easier to train the congregation to the principles of friendship evangelism than to make personal evangelists out of them. Another is that, assimilation and follow-up are very natural because they are done with people with whom a relationship already exists.

The major drawback of friendship evangelism is that it takes time to build bridges of friendship, to establish trust, and to "salt" the relationship enough for the individual to become thirsty for the "living water" of Christ. It takes a lot more energy and time than short-term commitments do. It takes time to get acquainted and really know people. It takes time to build trust. This time is not just a surface "howdy" but means doing things together. This use of time must be viewed positively with the idea that one is investing his or her life in the life of another, and that is never a waste.

Friendship evangelism has the benefit of a sense of family. When people commit to Jesus Christ as Savior, they become part of his family, and it is a family in which they are not total strangers. They know people. They have friends in the church. They are not alone; they have someone with whom to walk this new life journey. Friendship evangelism has a high retention rate because it is based on and nutured in relationship.

GARY WALLER

Bibliography. J. C. Aldrich (1981), *Life-Style Evangelism*; R. Becton (1997), *Everyday Evangelism: Making a Difference for Christ Where You Live*; J. Cook, (1984), *Leadership*; G. Crossley (1994), *Everyday Evangelism*; M. Green (1970), *Evangelism in the Early Church*; L. Pointer and J. Dorsey (1998), *Evangelism in Everyday Life: Sharing and Shaping Your Faith*; T. Rainer (1996), *Effective Evangelistic Churches*; D. Salter (1997), *American Evangelism: Its Theology and Practice*; J. M. Terry (1994), *Evangelism, A Concise History*; T. Wardle (1990), *One to One: A Practical Guide to Friendship Evangelism*.

Fundamentalism. As a movement, fundamentalism began within early-twentieth-century Protestantism as a defense of historic orthodox Christianity. Historians find it helpful to center understanding of the peculiar dynamics of this phenomenon mainly on the organized resistance to the encroachment of modernist thought. Its leaders contended that the Bible, Christian doctrine, and Christian experience did not need to be redefined in light of the scientific, philosophical, and literary assumptions of modern culture, but rather reaffirmed as the only legitimate challenge to its arrogance. Fundamentalism continued throughout the twentieth century as a major player in American Christianity, continually developing a religious, social, moral, and political agenda from its understanding of a core of doctrinal beliefs central to orthodox Protestant Christian witness. Fundamentalism, broadly conceived, has experienced a number of changes in its interaction with society and in its internal relations.

As a concept, fundamentalism emerged in the publication of twelve small volumes entitled *The Fundamentals* from 1910 to 1915, and later published in a small, four-volume edition by the Bible Institute of Los Angeles in 1917 (later named Biola University). R. A. Torrey (1856–1928), former pastor of Chicago Avenue (Moody Memorial) Church and then dean of the Bible Institute of Los Angeles, and A. C. Dixon (1854–1925), successor to Torrey at Chicago Avenue and then pastor at Spurgeon's Tabernacle in London, edited the volumes.

As a self-conscious movement focused on a reduced number of clearly identified issues, the terms *fundamentalism* and *fundamentalist* appeared in the *Watchman-Examiner* on July 1, 1920, announcing the intention "to do battle royal for the fundamentals."

Periodization of fundamentalist development takes various forms, but the differences between interpreters are minor. In the last half of the nineteenth century, prior to any attempts at formal organization, orthodox Christians observed with caution, or alarm, emergent worldview challenges. Prominent in this incipient stage was the conflict between R. L. Dabney and James Woodrow over the relation between science, specifically geology and evolution, and Scripture. Charles Hodge (d. 1878) and George F. Wright (d. 1921) took different approaches, but both challenged the philosophical naturalism implicit in evolutionary theory. The Toy controversy (1879) at The Southern Baptist Theological Seminary and the Briggs controversy (1881–93) within Presbyterianism highlighted the issue of how biblical criticism and evolutionary philosophy altered historically orthodox ideas of biblical authority and inerrancy.

Next, in the first two decades of the twentieth century, conservative Protestants began to identify specific issues around which they would be willing to form a united front. As evidenced in *The Fundamentals,* contributors to the early movement came from a great diversity of denominational backgrounds including leaders in major denominations and Christian organizations in America, England, and Canada. The subject matter for discussion was broad. The relation of higher criticism to biblical inerrancy, specific theological issues (theology, Christology, hamartiology, and soteriology), preaching, evangelism, missions, the threat of Romanism, "Modern Thought," the cults, and a variety of articles largely concerned with Christian experience constitute the volumes. The articles indicated serious work and even some diversity of approach on the part of the contributors. Concerns were focused but not narrow; the purpose was apologetic and dogmatic, but the engagement was informed and genuine.

The World's Christian Fundamentals Association, an organization that encouraged programmatic cleansing of denominations, colleges, and theological seminaries, developed from a 1919 meeting in Philadelphia. Prominent in it were William Bell Riley, John Roach Straton, I. M. Haldeman, J. Frank Norris, and others.

From the mid-1920s to the mid-1930s several confrontations over evolution and increasing liberalism in denominations failed to root out the growing prominence of those who followed modernist thinking. Paradigmatic to the flow of controversy was Harry Emerson Fosdick's (1878–1969) sermon preached May 21, 1922, at First Presbyterian Church of New York City entitled "Shall the Fundamentalists Win?" Using Gamaliel's advice to the Jews in Acts 5, he admonished fundamentalists to tolerate liberals. While characterizing the "fundamentalist programme" as "one of the worst exhibitions of bitter intolerance that the churches of this country have ever seen," he proceeded to tell his congregations why belief in inerrancy, the virgin birth, substitutionary atonement, and a literal return of Christ were static, uneducated, irrational, and crude. Clarence Macartney (1879–1957) answered with a sermon eventually published as "Shall Unbelief Win?" He affirmed that toleration of liberalism would eventuate in a new kind of Christianity. The most thorough protagonist for orthodoxy among the Presbyterians was J. Gresham Machen (1888–1937), a professor at Princeton Theological Seminary. His critique of liberalism in *Christianity and Liberalism* (1923) sought to demonstrate that orthodoxy and liberalism were two different religions.

The climax of the growing conflict over evolution came in the Scopes trial in Dayton, Tennessee in 1925. William Jennings Bryan, a prominent Presbyterian layman and political defendant of the common man, fell victim to a reservoir of elitist journalistic antagonism to conservative Christianity. The downward spiral of the fundamentalist image subsequent to the Scopes trial and the attending characterization of William Jennings Bryan as an obscurantist fool is typical of the public treatment of fundamentalism. Bryan's objections to evolution involved social, ethical, and civic concerns as well as scientific and theological ones. He perceived men like Clarence Darrow and H. L. Mencken as elitist naturalistic determinists. They were held back from social application of the principle of the *survival of the fittest* only by the residual elements of a Christian worldview. Bryan believed that evolutionary thought would destroy the Christian underpinnings of society and with it the compassion necessary for maintaining democratic ideals. The belittling of Bryan carried with it an attempt to marginalize Christian thought to the level of a barely tolerated private superstition.

Whether or not fundamentalists themselves believed the propaganda that they were defeated and could be considered irrelevant may be debated. They responded, however, with the formation of denominations and organizations composed only of those untainted with modernist thought. The documents do not prove that this represented a retreat as some historians have indicated, but rather a preparation for engagement with culture in a way acutely relevant to their worldview. In 1932 the General Association of Regular Baptists seceded from the Northern Baptist Convention by way of the Bible Baptist Union. The Presbyterian Church of America, eventually the Orthodox Presbyterian Church, was formed in 1936 under the impetus of J. Gresham Machen's leadership when Machen's credentials were suspended by the General Assembly of the PCUSA. Disagreement over premillenialism led to a division within that group and the formation of the Bible Presbyterian Church in 1937 under the leadership of J. Oliver Buswell and Carl McIntire. Northern Baptists saw a second exodus in 1947, when participants in the Fundamentalist Fellowship formed the Conservative Baptist Association. Disagreement over foreign mission support figured largely in the OPC and the CBA divisions. In addition to the formation of new denominations, thousands of independent churches and scores of missionary societies arose from the energies of the controversy.

Separation forced increased aggressiveness and a reinterpretation of role. Stronger emphasis on evangelism, missions, and controlled education led to steady growth of the fundamentalist groups. The Bible college and Bible institute movements, already clearly established by Moody Bible Institute and Nyack College, grew rapidly. These schools provided not only a formidable mission force and large numbers of trained Christian workers, but an active and effective shaping of educational options in America. In addition, 1926 marked the beginning of the most rapid growth in church adherence and attendance since the Revolutionary War. The increase was due entirely to those groups aligned with fundamentalist doctrinal and ethical perceptions. The modernist-tolerant mainline churches underwent consistent decline.

By the mid-1940s, a number of influential thinkers emerged within fundamentalist ranks that sought a corrective to what they perceived as an increasing social and intellectual narrowness in the movement. Out of this uneasiness emerged the neo-evangelical movement under the initial leadership of E. J. Carnell, Harold Ockenga, and Carl F. H. Henry. Other fundamentalists, such as Methodist evangelist and educator Bob Jones Sr. (1883–1968), continued to define themselves with strong convictions of separation, sometimes with increasing strictness, from moral degradation in society and liberalism in churches.

Throughout the history of fundamentalism, several factors facilitated the cartoon genre of its public image. Its submission to the authority of Scripture in opposition to the antiauthoritarianism of the naturalistic scholarship of the post-Darwinian era has made it appear hopelessly out of touch with reality. Its relentless evangelism has brought in masses of people who gladly support strong personalities who appear to have deeply felt, biblically founded convictions. Personal idiosyncrasies, internal feuds, an increasingly narrow moralistic focus, and appeal to the masses have provided a large arena for caricature by the critics of fundamentalism. People like J. Frank Norris, Billy Sunday, and John R. Rice provided energetic leadership and appealed to a large segment of conservative Christians, but also presented an acute profile easily highlighted in comic-strip colors.

Many interpretations have minimized if not ignored the religious element in fundamentalist development. Stewart G. Cole (1931) saw the conflict as a city mouse/country mouse dynamic, while Norman Furniss (1954) saw fundamentalism as an anti-intellectual reaction. Richard Hofstadter continued the anti-intellectual theme and depicted fundamentalists as anxious, if not paranoid, over a loss of status in society. Ernest Sandeen (1970) rightly embraced a theological interpretation of the phenomenon but may be challenged on his presentation of both the character and history of the theological issues involved. George M. Marsden (1980) greatly expanded the interpretive scope and gave a highly inflected narration of the theological and intellectual pedigree of fundamentalism. In the end, however, he reduces "fundamentalism" to a generic form manifest in America in a certain

subset of Protestantism not unlike the isolationist and reactionary mind-set contributing to Islamic fundamentalism.

Fundamentalist style so easily dismissed by opponents should not obscure the fact that theological substance has remained relatively constant and, in the fundamentalist self-consciousness, preeminent. From Machen to Rice to Jerry Falwell, the line of fundamentalist thought has adhered amazingly well to the original agenda. The observable intervention of God into this world in the miraculous and revelatory, the inerrancy of Scripture, the tri-unity of God, the deity of Christ, the virgin birth of Christ and his true humanity, his perfect obedience and substitutionary atonement, the necessity of the personal work of the Spirit, the fall of Adam and the resultant sinfulness of humanity, the necessity of the new birth, justification by faith, the surety of Christ's return, and the reality of heaven and hell have enjoyed constant adherence and proclamation.

While these controversies resulted in the eventual separation of conservatives from the main denominational body among Presbyterians and Baptists in the North, theological changes occurred more slowly in the South. By 1969 graduated theological shifts with the PCUS, the former Southern Presbyterian Church, and proposed alliances with the National and World Council of Churches, the UPCUSA, and COCU led a group within the church to separate. In 1973 in Augusta, Georgia, they formed a new body that in 1974 at the second general assembly took the name Presbyterian Church in America. While these churches more readily identify themselves with neo-evangelicalism than with fundamentalism, ecclesiological and theological dynamics and a Machenesque commitment to Scripture and Confession were reminiscent of those forty years earlier.

Although Southern Baptist J. Frank Norris initiated controversy within their ranks and influenced a number of ministers and churches to follow his lead, the massive majority of Southern Baptists shared all the doctrinal concerns of the early fundamentalist movement. Absence of doctrinal aberration in the early days of the conflict and heightened denominational concentration kept them out of the mainstream of the movement. The entire controversy, however, repristinized in Southern Baptist churches and institutions beginning with the Elliott controversy (1959–63). Major confrontations beginning in 1979 led to leadership shifts in all the Convention-wide agencies and institutions. Instead of the separation of the orthodox, however, the movement toward separate organizations had to be done by those more accepting of the modernist agenda.

Other denominations, such as Wesleyan/holiness groups and several immigrant denominations, share fundamentalist convictions and concerns, but absence of the modernist challenge within their ranks kept them away from the peculiar dynamics of the controversy.

Tom J. Nettles

Bibliography. V. L. Brereton (1990), *Training God's Army: The American Bible School, 1880–1940;* S. G. Cole (1931), *The History of Fundamentalism;* R. Finke and R. Starke (1992), *The Churching of America 1776–1990;* N. Furniss (1954), *The Fundamentalist Controversy, 1918–1931;* J. B. Longfield (1991), *The Presbyterian Controversy;* J. G. Machen (1923), *Christianity and Liberalism;* G. Marsden (1980), *Fundamentalism and American Culture;* E. R. Sandeen (1970), *The Roots of Fundamentalism: British and American Millenarianism 1800–1930.*

See also BIBLE COLLEGE MOVEMENT; EVANGELICALISM; HIGHER EDUCATION, CHRISTIAN; NATIONAL ASSOCIATION OF EVANGELICALS

Gg

Gaebelein, Frank Ely (1899–1983). Education and biblical scholar. Gaebelein was a graduate of New York (1920) and Harvard (1921) Universities. Ordained as a minister of the Reformed Episcopal Church and recipient of honorary doctorates from Wheaton and Houghton colleges, his rich heritage in Christian education began as the founding headmaster of the Stony Brook School (1922–63). It was at Stony Brook that Gaebelein developed a highly respected model for Christian secondary education and became active in both the Council for Religion in Independent Schools and the Headmasters Association.

A prolific writer, Gaebelein became coeditor of *Christianity Today* magazine in 1963 and served in that capacity until 1966. A passion for integrating Christian commitment with every facet of life fueled his diverse literary work of sixteen books, numerous magazine and journal articles, and a lifetime of preaching and speaking engagements at colleges, universities, and seminaries worldwide. He also served as general editor of *The Expositor's Bible Commentary*. While Gaebelein's writings included several books of theology and biblical commentary, he is best known among Christian educators for two books, *Christian Education in a Democracy* (1951) and *The Pattern of God's Truth* (1954). In these two books, he establishes the importance of Christian teaching in a pluralistic society and his concern with integrating Christian faith and academic excellence, respectively.

The integration of faith and learning drove both Gaebelein's desire for educational excellence and his insistence upon an education consistent with Christian faith. As he said, "At the heart of all thinking about education, whether Christian or secular, lies the problem of integration. Education is a living thing; no less than the individual it must have a philosophy. . . . To declare allegiance to an educational point of view is one thing; to integrate a school or college in all its parts—curriculum, student activities, administration, and everything else—with that point of view is another thing" (Gaebelein, 1954, v). Although Gaebelein was committed to high doctrine and a view of the world based upon biblical truth, he was convinced that much of Christian education falls short of living up to this expectation. Much of his ministry career and life echoed a call to every facet of Christian education to both uphold and practice the lofty principles of theological and biblical orthodoxy.

A breadth of education, personal interests, and creative skills gave way to varied expressions of his profound personal faith. As a skilled communicator, he became a distinguished lecturer on Christian campuses throughout North America and earned a reputation as an elder statesman and twentieth-century leader in American evangelicalism.

WILLIAM F. FALKNER

Bibliography. F. E. Gaebelein (1946), *The Christian Use of the Bible;* idem (1954), *The Pattern of God's Truth.*

Gangs. Term used to refer to a group (usually adolescent or young adult) who meet regularly, have a common name, and share common rules, signs, colors, and/or symbols. Individually and collectively, most or all of the members participate in illegal activities. A known propensity for illegal activities sets gangs apart from groups of adolescents or young adults who join together simply to find a sense of identity or belonging. Gangs are considered the fastest growing small groups in America.

Gangs have existed for hundreds of years. Most modern-day gangs however, had their beginnings in either Los Angeles or New York during the 1920s. These early gangs were seen largely as a bunch of kids with chains, zip-guns, or baseball bats fighting other gangs over turf areas. However, the introduction of crack cocaine into American society in the early 1980s drastically changed the nature and activities of gangs. Gangs discovered this drug to be a source of escape for their members and also a relatively simple means of bringing a vast quantity of money into their gang family. It has been estimated that the annual profit made from cocaine in the United States alone runs as high as $150 billion, much of which is a direct result of gang involvement.

Until recently most gangs began in lower socioeconomic communities and consisted primarily of ethnic minorities. Today, however, gangs cross all ethnic, financial, and social barriers. Traditional black and Hispanic gangs now openly accept white members. Nor are gangs restricted to inner-city areas. More and more gangs are now being found in the suburbs, smaller communities, and rural areas. A United States Department of Justice study reports that 38.7 percent of small cities indicate the presence of gangs. Fifty percent of mid-sized cities and nearly 84 percent of large cities also report the presence of youth gangs.

Gangs within the United States are identified under eight major groupings.

Crips	Bloods
Folks	People
Hispanic	Asian
Southeast Asian	Mexican

Additionally, there exists a general classification for miscellaneous gangs such as white supremacist and neo-Nazi groups. While there are no exact figures for the number of young people who have joined gangs, it is known that in Los Angeles County alone there are now over 650 sets of gangs with an estimated membership totaling between 70,000 and 100,000 youth. These sets are smaller clusters of male and/or female youth associated primarily with the Crips and the Bloods, the two largest gang groupings.

The presence of gangs in American society presents a vexing problem for law enforcement, which now maintains special divisions charged with the responsibility of curtailing gang activity. They also present a major challenge for Christianity, whose "charter" encompasses most of the concerns that prompt gangs (identity, community, belonging, sense of significance and value, purpose or cause, etc.), and whose lifestyle struggles to live out the realities of these issues.

RICK GRAY

Bibliography. B. Larson and W. Amstutz (1995), *Youth Violence and Gangs.*

Gender Differences. *See* Communication, Styles of.

Gender Identity. *See* Gender Roles.

Gender Roles. Identification of specific traits and qualities as masculine or feminine. Since the Industrial Revolution in the United States, gender roles have been tied to a fixed division of labor. Men worked outside the home and provided for the family's economic needs, while women worked inside the home, providing home management and child care. To be masculine meant exhibiting qualities of leadership, strength, and stoicism. Femininity was characterized by nurturance, tenderness, and support.

The clearly defined gender roles of the past meant specific expectations. Everyone knew what a man was to supposed to be and do and what a woman was to be and do. However, there was a downside to fixed gender roles. The role expectations for men to provide for their families and to be in control at all times put pressure on men to prove their worth, and may have led to feelings of inadequacy or fear of failure. Traditionally men were to hide their feelings, which resulted in their being emotionally distant from their wives and children in the home and in relationships outside the home. Women were dependent on the men in their lives for economic support and social status. This began with their fathers, continued with their dependence on their husbands, and sometimes carried into a dependence upon their sons. Women were to give their lives in support of others with little thought to personal development and achievement.

Gender Role Socialization. Winston Johnson in *Gender Matters* (228–29) describes four basic theories of gender role socialization:

1. *Identification theory*—This theory was developed by Freud and stated that children identify with the same-sex parent, thereby learning their gender roles. It describes the difficulty that young boys have since typically both boys and girls begin life more closely identified with their mothers. The task for the young boy is to differentiate himself from his mother and identify with his father.
2. *Social learning theory*—This theory states that behaviors which are rewarded and reinforced tend to be repeated and those behaviors that are ignored or punished tend to be extinguished. Boys and girls are rewarded and punished differently for the same behaviors. Children sense what is wanted and try to provide it because if they act in unacceptable ways they may be ignored, discouraged, or even punished.
3. *Modeling theory*—This theory states that children imitate adults they admire, especially same-sex parents and friends. As children imitate same-sex role models they construct an appropriate gender role.
4. *Cognitive development theory*—This theory states that individuals strive to live a life of

consistency between what they believe, what they value, and how they act. Little boys try to learn the "right" way to behave as a boy, and little girls learn the "right" way to behave as a girl.

Critics of sex role theory identify six areas for discussion (Van Leeuwen, 1993, 227–33):

1. An unchanging "essence" of masculinity and femininity cannot explain deviations within individuals and variations from person to person.
2. The assumption that masculine and feminine traits are valued equally is unfounded. Society places greater economic and cultural value on characteristics and activities deemed masculine than on those ascribed to females.
3. Sex-role theory does not explain why and how certain characteristics became dichotomized as masculine and feminine in the first place. Gender roles are viewed differently by those in different cultures and generations.
4. The assumption that gender forms the core of one's identity is simplistic. It downplays the part that race, ethnicity, class, and religion play in shaping an individual's identity.
5. Sex-role theory endorses a passive mode of learning, assuming that we unreflectively imitate others and accept what we are told.
6. The assumption that masculine and feminine sex roles are equally constricting has been criticized. Sex-role theory fails to take into account the structural imbalance of power and unequal access to resources that exist between the sexes.

Contemporary Approaches to Gender Roles. There is a steady movement toward valuing the same qualities in both men and women (i.e., strength coupled with nurturance). This has led some to state that there has been a blurring of gender roles, which has led to confusion between the sexes and in society at large. Others believe the new approach to gender roles with fluid boundaries allows for greater valuing of people independent of their gender and fuller self-expression for all people. The challenge for the future will be to balance past experience and contemporary realities in the field of gender roles.

DENISE MUIR KJESBO

Bibliography. J. S. Hagen (1990), *Gender Matters: Women's Studies for the Christian Community*; G. G. Hull (1987), *Equal to Serve: Women and Men in the Church and Home*; M. S. Van Leeuwen (1993), *After Eden: Facing the Challenge of Gender*.

General Education. *See* Liberal Arts.

Generalization. In behavioral psychology, *classical conditioning* refers to the association of a stimulus and response. In the classic experiment by Ivan Pavlov, a dog learned to salivate in response to the ringing of a bell because of the association of the bell and food. Pavlov discovered that ringing a smaller or larger bell than the originally conditioned bell would also produce the conditioned response of salivation, a phenomenon termed *generalization*. The generalized response could be encouraged by the ringing of the second bell with food, or conversely generalization could be decreased by ringing the bell without food. This decrease of generalization is termed *stimulus discrimination*.

Psychologists often consider fears and phobias to be the result of similar conditioning. For example, children may come to fear the dark because they associate darkness with frightening stories told by an older sibling. Fear from the stories is conditioned with the darkness of the room. This might then generalize to a fear of dark closets, dimly lit automobiles, and other dark places.

Another branch of behavioral psychology, *operant conditioning*, emphasizes the consequences of behavior. A specific action learned in one context may occur in other situations because it has been generalized. This can be encouraged by supplying a reinforcer, a reward such as praise or candy. Generalization explains the actions of people in unfamiliar situations; the tendency is to act the same as in previous, similar contexts.

Christian educators often emphasize the importance of generalizing actions learned at church to everyday life. Applying the Bible to issues at home and work is as important as using the Bible to answer teachers' questions. Skills such as the use of a concordance can be taught in a Bible study methods class at church, then generalized to personal Bible study.

Children sometimes associate church with fear or boredom when they are given an inappropriate curriculum or overly restrictive rules. This can generalize to all church activities, and—as adults—they may avoid churches altogether because of the associated negative emotions (Ratcliff, 1986).

The principle of generalization can be applied for effective disciplinary procedures in Christian education contexts (Ratcliff, 1982), understanding prejudices in cross-cultural ministry (Ratcliff, 1997), and as an important aspect of educational ministry in general (Yount, 1996).

The term *generalization* can also refer to creating statements of intention derived from more specific goals and objectives, an important aspect of theological education (Ford, 1991).

DONALD E. RATCLIFF

Bibliography. H. Atkinson, *Christian Education Journal* 14 (1993): 58–72; R. K. Bufford (1981), *The Human*

Reflex: Behavioral Psychology in Biblical Perspective;
L. Ford (1991), *A Curriculum Design Manual for Theological Education;* K. Issler and R. Habermas (1994), *How We Learn: A Teacher's Guide to Educational Psychology;* P. Meier et al. (1991), *Introduction to Psychology and Counseling;* D. Ratcliff, *Journal of Psychology and Christianity* 1 (1982): 26–29; idem (1997), *Multicultural Religious Education;* R. Yount (1996), *Created to Learn.*

Generational Impact. A *generation*, as the term is commonly used today, refers to individuals of somewhat similar age, often grouped in spans of about twenty years. Four commonly described generations include the builders (born 1930–45), baby boomers (born 1946–64), busters (born 1965–81), and the millennial generation (born 1982–2000). Generation specialists Strauss and Howe believe these generations represent four parts of a cycle that recurs throughout history, particularly American history.

One can take the characteristics of any generation and identify specific Christian education strategies that best fit those characteristics. Leith Anderson (1990) states that members of different generations have difficulty understanding the perspectives of other generations, and thus they will be attracted to different kinds of churches. Builders, for example, are likely to visit a church on Sunday morning and be attracted to churches of under three hundred members, while boomers are attracted to services other than Sunday morning and prefer churches of one thousand or more. Builders are more faithful to a specific church and denomination, while boomers are more likely to attend churches that meet specific felt needs—such as ministries for their children or youth—regardless of denomination and without long-term loyalty. Anderson fears that many churches and religious organizations that thrived with builder assumptions, such as the value of hierarchy in church leadership, may meet disaster when that constituency dies off because they refused to reorganize according to the assumptions of later generations, such as the egalitarian team leadership.

What specific generational distinctives need to be addressed? Hundreds of ideas have been suggested that can only be sampled here. Anderson (1990), for example, recommends that baby boomers can be reached by high quality programs, dropping denominational links in church names, having high expectations regarding the spiritual disciplines and volunteer service, anonymity of visits, inclusion of a variety of music styles, and emotionally stirring, participatory worship. In contrast, Mahedy and Bernardi (1994) propose that busters be viewed as traumatized victims of boomer selfishness and irresponsibility, sometimes requiring therapy but more often just needing friendship and faith. Feelings of abandonment in busters should be met with active participation in a radically committed lifestyle centered on community life and led by people who desire intensive relationships with one another. Ford (1995) points out that the rationalistic approach to evangelism that appeals to many boomers often fails to reach busters, and similarly Celek and Zander (1996) emphasize that boomers often want church to be a gourmet meal while busters may prefer a potluck. Millennials, in Zoba's (1997) opinion, are most likely to be reached through peer ministry that occurs in unusual places or unconventional times, establishing new rites of passage similar to the Jewish bar mitzvah, and mentoring by older adults.

While many experts recommend changes in the church to accommodate the demands and needs of different generations, some recommendations are similar regardless of the generation described. For example, Anderson (1990), Barna (1994), and Zoba (1997) each emphasize the importance of relationships in effective generational ministry, with small group activities as imperatives for boomers, busters, and millennials. Similarly, all three writers describe a common distrust of institutions, including church and denominational organizations. Perhaps, as some have suggested, this is because all three generations—and perhaps builders as well—have come to a point where they are dissatisfied with who they are as generations and can only find their fulfillment in God and one another.

Rather than overemphasizing generational distinctives, perhaps the church needs to consider the potential for intergenerational ministry, an option encouraged even by some generational specialists in Christian education such as Leith Anderson. He also advocates "generational balance" in church activities. The assumption is that the strengths of one generation can be used to help meet the needs and compensate for the weaknesses of other generations. It is also important to note that the needs and characteristics of any generation tend to change with time; a generation in its teen years will not remain exactly the same through middle age. There are also important individual differences between members of the same generation. Targeting ministry to the supposed characteristics of a given generation may, in fact, result in ministry that overlooks geographic, ethnic, and gender distinctives; or it may be irrelevant to the majority who already attend a given church for some other reason. Generational trends may provide direction in some situations, yet the specific characteristics of those to be reached must be of prime concern.

DONALD E. RATCLIFF

Bibliography. L. Anderson (1990), *Dying for Change;* G. Barna (1994), *Baby Busters;* T. Celek and D. Zander (1996), *Inside the Soul of a New Generation;* K. Ford (1995), *Jesus for a New Generation;* W. Mahedy and J. Bernardi (1994), *A Generation Alone;* W. Strauss and N. Howe (1997), *The Fourth Turning: An American*

Prophecy; idem (1991), *Generations;* W. M. Zoba (1997), *Christianity Today,* February 3, 1997.

See also BABY BOOM GENERATION; BUILDER GENERATION; BUSTER GENERATION.

Genetic Engineering. *See* Bioethics.

Gerontology. *See* Aging, Ageism.

Gestalt Psychology. The word *gestalt* comes from the German word meaning "form" or "configuration." Gestalt theory adds a distinctive contribution to the study of how people learn and organize perceptions and it creates openness to new insights. Thus, Gestalt is a theory based on organizing different perceptions or parts into a unity greater than the individual parts. In this way Gestalt theory can potentially open humans to new insights and paradigms.

Gestaltists developed five major laws that govern perception. The law of Pragnanz is the most basic law. This primary law identifies the human tendency for organizing perceptions using regularity, simplicity, and stability into a good gestalt. Other specific laws that explain how people typically reach a gestalt include the following: (a) law of similarity—an organization of perceptions into similar categories; (b) law of proximity—the association of perception according to the sameness of parts which can be facilitated by such things as arrangement, place, or time period; (c) law of closure—a motivation to discover closure with incomplete figures, ideas, or series as a way to achieve satisfaction; and (d) law of good continuation—organization by learners that stresses continuation in the same mode until the introduction of new information creates a new perspective (Koffka, 1935).

In Gestalt psychology learning also employs problem-solving methods expressed through a goal of transposition. The practice of learning in Gestalt has the goal of involving the whole person—the cognitive, affective, and physical. In a Gestalt approach to learning there are no logical, vertical organization schemes producing one conclusion; to the contrary, one discovers a process that stimulates participants to draw their own conclusions.

A brief history documenting the emergence of Gestalt psychology is informative. In 1890, Christian von Ehrenfels, a nineteenth-century Austrian philosopher, introduced the word *gestalt* into the English language. Ehrenfels's research differed vastly from then-prevailing conventional "atomistic" studies that failed to recognize that the whole is much more than the sum of the parts. His conclusions were novel enough to establish a precedent for a Gestalt theory.

In the first quarter of the twentieth century, Gestalt psychology challenged the American associational psychologies of structuralism, functionalism, and behaviorism. At this time, there was a rejection of adding to or reconstructing older theories and an insistence, especially in the Gestaltist movement, on "demolishing the old systems, and building anew from the foundation up" (Helson, 1917, 345).

Subsequently, during the 1920s and 1930s Gestalt theory, considered a psychology of protest, was in its heyday. Although perceived as a system of confused and cloudy ideas, Gestalt psychology sought to clarify knowledge about human perception. Besides Karl Duncker and a few others, this theory did struggle to attract a substantial second-generation following. Since the 1950s forms of Gestalt psychotherapies pioneered by Friedrich S. (Fritz) Perls (who sought to mesh mind and body as a way to deal with the whole human organism as a holistic concept) found many expressions.

Gestalt psychology, as introduced into America by Max Wertheimer, Kurt Koffka, and Wolfgang Kohler, authenticated many formerly neglected aspects of visual perception (Perls, Hefferline, and Goodman, 1951). The original work of this scientific trio inscribed a mark upon psychological history.

Max Wertheimer, a meticulous genius, is chiefly acknowledged as the founder of Gestalt psychology (Koffka, 1935). Although he never wrote a systematic treatise, Wertheimer, the oldest, was the "originator and leader, and the other two [Kohler and Koffka] promoted his preeminence" (Boring, 1950, 594).

The youngest and perhaps best known member of the original trio, Wolfgang Kohler, can easily be considered the evangelist of Gestalt psychology. Kohler's famous work, *The Mentality of Apes,* "brought the notion of insightful learning into the foreground, as an alternative to trial and error" (Hilgard and Bower, 1966, 229), demonstrating novel problem solving independent of prior experience. His model remains considerably influential to this day.

Koffka's work establishes that he was the systematizer for the entire Gestalt movement. His work *Principles of Gestalt Psychology* (1935), the only systematic collection of Gestalt psychology, discusses issues of learning and memory that are central to Gestalt theory. The world owes a debt of gratitude to these three thinkers who originated and inspired Gestalt psychology.

JERRY BOWLING

Bibliography. E. G. Boring (1950), *A History of Experimental Psychology;* H. Helson, *The American Journal of Psychology* 28 (1917): 538–66; E. R. Hilgard and G. H. Bower (1966), *Theories of Learning;* K. Koffka (1935), *Principles of Gestalt Psychology;* Fredrick S. Perls, R. F. Hefferline, and P. Goodman (1951),

Gestalt Therapy: Excitement and Growth in the Human Personality.

See also FIELD THEORY; LEWIN, KURT

Gifted. *See* Exceptional Persons.

Gifted Children. Interest in the study of gifted individuals is generally considered to have begun with the work of Lewis Terman at Stanford University. Terman published the first widely used intelligence test for children, the Stanford–Binet Intelligence Scale, in 1916. Since the early years of defining giftedness as a measure of intelligence (IQ), the term has been expanded to include areas outside the more traditional intellectual and academic abilities.

Researchers have developed a variety of descriptive traits. Preschool children considered to be gifted may exhibit early and advanced development in such areas as language acquisition, fine and gross motor skills, reading, memory, self-confidence, creativity, and music ability. A typical list of gifted abilities which a schoolage child might exhibit includes such characteristics as the following:

A gifted individual—
1. is curious;
2. is persistent in pursuit of interests and questions;
3. is perceptive of the environment;
4. is critical of self and others;
5. has a highly developed sense of humor;
6. is a leader in various areas;
7. understands general principles easily;
8. often responds to the environment through media and means other than print and writing;
9. sees relationships among seemingly diverse ideas. (Tuttle and Becker, 1983, 13)

In general, for children of any age, giftedness is usually considered to be present when there is evidence of some trait or ability which stands out as being particularly remarkable, or different in kind or intensity, as compared to the average developmental characteristics for that age group.

As with all developmental characteristics, several cautions should be considered when consulting lists of traits. First, lists do not always indicate specific situations or different types of giftedness. Second, even if children are gifted, they may not always display evidence of their giftedness. The home, play, or learning environment, including the individuals found in those environments, must provide a safe and inviting atmosphere for the gifted child to express his or her giftedness. Finally, most lists do not make provision for cultural differences.

Sometimes, the expression of giftedness may be perceived as deviant and a challenge to authority. For teachers working with potentially gifted children in their ministries, discernment must be exercised in separating misbehavior from indications of giftedness. In discussing Bible topics, a gifted child may provide what appears to be a wrong answer, but has actually approached the subject from a different direction. Gifted children can become bored and may need to be challenged to go deeper. They are often highly critical of themselves and of others and place high expectations on their work product. In learning situations, gifted individuals need the freedom to express themselves through a variety of modes. They are persistent, and may sometimes be viewed as obnoxious and rude in their pursuit of a goal.

Gifted children are sometimes rejected by peers and teachers. The gifted do not need special attention, just understanding and acceptance. They need to be challenged to offer their gifts to the Lord as instruments for his service to be used however he chooses and with his blessing.

SHELLY CUNNINGHAM

Bibliography. F. B. Tuttle and L. A. Becker (1983), *Characteristics and Identification of Gifted and Talented Students.*

Gilligan, Carol (1936–). Professor at Harvard School of Education. She is an educator noted for her groundbreaking work in women's development. Her book *In a Different Voice: Psychological Theory and Women's Development*, published in 1982, is a major contribution to moral development theory and to understanding women's ways of thinking. This book presents a sharp challenge to prevalent moral theories based on abstract principles and universal gender-blind understandings of human development. Gilligan's feminist approach suggested the existence of many moral voices, created by gender as well as race, culture, and class. She defined moral "voice" as the product of relationships with others, and proposed a female "ethic of caring." This radical vision of morality has prompted extensive debate.

Gilligan began work in moral reasoning as a research assistant to Lawrence Kohlberg in the 1970s. She began to question his methods and conclusions, and went on to conduct her own research to focus on women's development. Kohlberg had developed a rule-governed model of moral development in six stages, based on a study composed entirely of male participants. Kohlberg's model is still widely used today.

Gilligan charged that these stages were based on justice-centered thinking, and were derived from research which neglected to consider context. For example, Kohlberg presented people with a "simple" moral dilemma to resolve, then created his model from the various responses people gave him. Here is one of the dilemmas: A man's wife is dying of a rare medical condition. The drug she needs is available at the local pharmacy, but the man can't afford the drug. Should he steal the drug to save his wife?

Gilligan found that women scored lower than men on Kohlberg's moral reasoning test because they were concerned more with maintaining the relationships involved in the dilemma than arriving at a judgment of right and wrong from a detached perspective. Women ask questions about the context: What is most important to each of the people in the situation? Who else may be affected by the situation? What cultural and religious values are at stake? What is the circumstance of the pharmacist, and the relationship of pharmacist to the couple? What consequences to the many relationships would ensue from different actions? Gilligan goes on to ask "what if" questions, which challenge the possibility of determining one universal judgment for this dilemma: What if the husband and wife roles were reversed? What if the pharmacist were poorer than the couple? What if the person dying were only distantly known to the person who might obtain the drug?

Gilligan found a distinct difference between the way women and men framed and resolved moral dilemmas. Women spoke of caring, connection, and peace. Men spoke of justice, equality, reciprocity, and rights. These two different voices, claims Gilligan, represent two very different worldviews, neither being superior, but both requiring effort to hear and understand the other. Feminine ways of thinking about moral decisions tend to eschew universal abstract principles in favor of sensitivity and responsiveness to the particularities of the situation; opportunities to express care and concern for others; and no right or wrong answers, only solutions that need to be worked out in ways that maintain stable interpersonal relationships

Gilligan concluded that women's orientation to moral decision making is more focused on care than justice, with ideals of attention and response to need. Gilligan went on to show how girls develop a morality of care through their continued identification with and attachment to their mothers. Because boys must individuate from their mothers, this early separation heightens their awareness of the power differentials between themselves and adults. This contributes to males' more principle-based thinking and preoccupation with fairness issues.

Gilligan's critics have argued that the ethic of care is not adequate for a moral theory. Care is a multilayered, complex experience, and Gilligan's work overlooks its dialectical nature. Some write that justice and care are not sharply different, but are complementary dimensions of morality. Other theorists have suggested that justice and care are not necessarily gender-based, as Gilligan claims. Subsequent studies have suggested that both males and females reason based on both justice and care. Some have argued that the "care" perspective is more descriptive of moral thinking among certain cultures or people located in a particular historical time than among women treated as a universal group. Still other critics maintain that Gilligan's work masks the diversity of women's experiences and moral voices.

Gilligan's recent work explores adolescent girls' development of self. Using "voice-centered" (listening to) research, she concludes that girls experience a developmental crisis and lose a sense of self. Her latest book *Between Voice and Silence: Women and Girls, Race and Relationships* (published in 1997 with J. M. Taylor and A. M. Sullivan) examines the self-silencing that occurs among grade 8–9 girls who are at risk of dropping out of school or entering abusive relationships and early motherhood.

Lively debate created by Gilligan's critics continues. Meanwhile, educators make extensive use of her emphasis on listening to "different voices." Her feminine model of care inspires many efforts to foster greater empathy and care responses among students. Gilligan's research continues to contribute to understanding of care as an integral aspect of moral reasoning.

TARA J. FENWICK

See also GENDER ROLES; KOHLBERG, LAWRENCE; MORAL DILEMMA; MORAL EDUCATION; MORAL REASONING, THEORY OF

Goal. A statement of intent. Goals can be established for student behaviors or teacher activities, or as statements of desired outcomes in an organization or program. Goals involve measurable behavior, progress, or learning in cognitive, affective, psychomotor, or response domains. Goals are general statements with varying levels of specificity. Sometimes the term is used synonomously with other descriptors, such as purpose, objective, aim, or outcome.

Goals can also be evaluated in terms of specificity. Purposes tend to answer "why?" Goals tend to answer "what?" Objectives tend to answer "how, when, and where?" To be sure, these are arbitrary divisions, and historical analysis provides evidence that educators will not agree on the use of these three terms. Understanding of a hierarchy within the goal structure assists in pinpointing the needed discussion in this area. Clarification of whether the goal is on an organizational, program, or instructional level will help avoid confusion. Also, goals can be too broad (e.g., "Students should learn about salvation") or too narrow (e.g., "Each student will compare Calvinistic and Arminian concepts of salvation to determine their own personal confidence of their salvation experience"). However, a balance of intent and process is most desirable in writing goals (e.g., "Students will compare their belief regarding salvation as explained in class and analyze their acceptance of it").

Purposes seem to refer to overarching principles of program or instruction; the direction or aim, something that one wants to achieve (e.g., "Students will grow closer to the Lord through having a quiet time"). These kind of goals indicate an intended direction or path. When measuring something that has already happened, a goal is more akin to an end, an outcome, or an objective (e.g., "Each student should organize a regular personal time of Bible reading and prayer").

Sources for goals will vary according to the educational philosophy of the writer. Group consensus, preparing students for life situations (scientific method), and outlining goals according to Christian ideals and biblical imperatives (philosophical) are three methods for determining goals. When writing good or effective goals, Edge's (1956) guidelines prove helpful. Goals or aims should be (1) brief enough to be remembered, (2) clear enough to be written down, and (3) specific enough to be attainable.

Goals provide many benefits. For example, they demonstrate present and future awareness; enthusiasm; the basis for evaluation; forced planning; an emphasis on productivity; and a reduction in conflict. Some of the best aspects of goal setting are that goals provide an opportunity to celebrate past accomplishments. Goals provide clarity of activity in the present. Goals afford cause for cooperation in the future. Establishing goals is worth the investment of time and energy.

GREGORY C. CARLSON

Bibliography. F. B. Edge (1956), *Teaching for Results;* K. O. Gangel (1997), *Team Leadership in Christian Ministry;* J. F. Sellars, *Christian Education Journal* 14, no. 1 (1993): 92–93.

See also LESSON PLAN; STRATEGIC PLANNING; VISION

Godless. *See* Atheism.

Good Boy/Nice Girl. *Good boy/nice girl* refers to the Conventional stage of moral development in which individuals conform to the standards of their family or group in order to be approved and accepted. Pleasing and helping others has become important. The factor of good intentions comes under consideration

This term describes a stage of moral development as described by psychologist Lawrence Kohlberg. In his work, Kohlberg divides the process of moral development into three sequential stages. In the Preconventional stage, an individual will define right and wrong according to the reward or punishment that follows the behavior. At this stage, authority figures are assumed to be

right and must be obeyed. At the second, Conventional stage, the individual has learned to value the standards of his or her family or group and is willing to act for the welfare of the group. Most individuals at this level are already adolescents. At the third, Postconventional stage, values are recognized as universal principles, independent of authority. Basically, these three stages describe a journey from the belief that "might makes right" to "right is above might." Obedience to avoid punishment becomes obedience to an ethic regardless of personal loss or gain.

One of Kohlberg's tests to assess his subjects' level of moral development was a story of a man who steals an unfairly high-priced drug to save the life of his dying wife. Preconventional perspectives focused on the amount of damage done to the pharmacy during the robbery. Conventional thinkers at the good boy/nice girl stage considered the noble motives of the thief and worried about the opinions of his family and neighbors.

Although Christian educators can profit from an awareness and understanding of Kohlberg's work, they should keep in mind that Kohlberg saw no connection between religion and moral development. Viewing these stages from a Christian perspective that acknowledges the role of God's Holy Spirit, educators can see that Kohlberg's work simply observes what is God's own design for moral growth. Studied with discernment, Kohlberg's stages offer helpful teaching guidelines:

1. At the good boy/nice girl level, children will benefit from role plays that put them in other people's shoes. Teachers should ask subjective questions about the moral dilemmas faced by Bible characters, and help learners identify motives behind deeds.

2. Discipline must be fair and consistent, and learners should be able to understand how rules benefit their entire group. When administering correction, teachers should pay attention to the intentions behind the actions. To reinforce good behavior, teachers should be specific with praise and encouragement. God's laws must be presented as absolutes, not options.

3. Adults must strive to be models of Christlike behavior, because children and adolescents at this level are ready to differentiate between authority and right.

Kohlberg's description of the process of moral development can be a helpful resource to Christian educators when examined and applied according to a biblical perspective.

ROBERT J. CHOUN

Bibliography. B. Clouse (1993), *Teaching for Moral Growth;* L. Kohlberg (1998), *Essays on Moral Development:* vol. 1, *The Philosophy of Moral Development;* B. Munsey (1980), *Moral Development, Moral Education.*

See also FAITH DEVELOPMENT; KOHLBERG, LAW-RENCE; MORAL DEVELOPMENT

Gospel. The word *gospel* comes from the Greek word *euangelion*, which refers to glad tidings, or good news. In the Old Testament references to the gospel were associated with sharing the glad tidings of God's intervention with his people (1 Sam. 31:9; 2 Sam. 1:20; 2 Kings 7:9; Ps. 96:2–3, 11–12; Isa. 40:9; 52:7; Nah. 1:13, 14). In the context of the New Testament, gospel has two uses: the sharing of the good news about Jesus Christ's arrival and message, and, the record of the life of the incarnate Christ.

The Gospel Message. The message of hope and redemption is indeed good news when one considers the fate of nonregenerate people. The good news of salvation in Christ is available for everyone who believes (Rom. 1:16). What is needed is a response to the invitation, for one must appropriate the gift for it to be meaningful. Once we accept this invitation we become the recipients of peace, hope, and God's love. This provides courage to endure hardships amid the many misunderstandings encountered in life. But beyond this life there is the hope and security of knowing that our future is secure in Christ. We have heaven to look forward to as believers.

The coming of Jesus Christ was cause for rejoicing, for it represented the culmination of hundreds of prophetic teachings. Jesus arrived on the scene as the ultimate messenger from God to proclaim the "glad tidings" to the meek, freedom for the captive, and release to those in bondage (Isa. 61:1).

The Gospel Record. During the second century the term *gospel* also came to refer to the recorded life of Christ. We have four recorded Gospels (records) of Christ's life. The Gospels of Matthew, Mark, Luke, John describe eyewitness accounts of the life of Christ (e.g., "The beginning of the gospel of Jesus Christ, the Son of God." Mark 1:1 NASB). The term was also used in the second century to refer to some apocryphal records written by various church leaders.

MICHAEL J. ANTHONY

Bibliography. J. K. Champlin (1996), *The Evangelical Dictionary of Biblical Theology;* E. A. Livingstone (1997), *The Dictionary of the Christian Church;* W. E. Vine (1966), *An Expository Dictionary of New Testament Words;* M. G. Watkins and L. I. Watkins (1992), *The Complete Christian Dictionary for Home and School.*

Govern. *See* Control; Management.

Great Awakenings. The First Great Awakening in America occurred in the first part of the eighteenth century, primarily between 1720 and 1750. While names like Jonathan Edwards, George Whitefield, and William Tennant were promi-nent, the Awakening was much more than the activity of a few public leaders. The Awakening could be termed "Great" because it was general and wide-reaching. People from a broad spectrum of American life were impacted by the movement. There is no doubt that the Awakening played a large role in developing a national consciousness among the different colonies, binding people together in a common belief that God had a special destiny for America.

The Great Awakening added new churches across all denominations. This growth of churches resulted in a movement to provide educational opportunities for the growing number of ministerial recruits. The forerunners of many present-day eastern universities were born during this period of time, with William Tennant's "Log College" representative of the educational initiative begun in this period. Basic schools also emerged for Indians, Negroes, and the children of indentured servants.

Until the Great Awakening, American religious life reflected the assumptions of Geneva and Calvinism. What emerged in the Great Awakening was not so much a substitute theological system, but a new mood. If anything, it was a revolt that replaced a view of Christian life focused on an outward observable formulation of religious life with a deference toward personal religious experience. This shift of priority in American religious life came with accompanying controversy. The Great Awakening was not only a renewal movement that called for conversion, but a renewal movement that challenged the standing religious assumptions about the very nature of Christian life itself.

The growth of American churches and the political independence reflective of the American Revolution significantly impacted American Protestants. As 1800 approached, churches became aware that the peace after the Revolution had caused a general dereliction of national and personal spiritual disciplines. The perceived need for religious renewal now had the historical precedent of revivalist preaching and religious experience from which to draw. The Second Great Awakening, which stretched through the first half of the nineteenth century, featured the assumption that religious leaders could create a revival by utilizing means that were focused on influencing hearers to make a decision for Christ. Revivals ensued under leaders like Timothy Dwight (Jonathan Edwards's grandson), president of Yale College. The frontier version of this kind of revivalist initiative is exemplified in the camp meetings led by ministers like James McGready. Charles Finney personifies this revivalist tradition born out of the First Great Awakening of the previous century. He no longer viewed revival as an end in itself, but as a part of a renewal of vital religious life in perpetuity.

A person whose life exemplifies the Second Great Awakening's impact on Christian education is Horace Bushnell. Bushnell is known as the father of the religious education movement. As a pastor in Connecticut, Bushnell used revivalist tactics to impact his community, with diminishing returns. After several years he confessed that the most disheartening expectation of the Christian minister was the thought that vibrant Christianity depended primarily on revivals. Bushnell's subsequent response to the revivalist mode of the era is his idea of Christian nurture. He focused his attention on the home as the primary place of nurture based on the thesis that children should grow up as Christians and never know themselves as being otherwise. Bushnell was far ahead of his time in advocating a religious experience that was psychologically positive for the child. Bushnell saw proper education and responsible Christian families as the greatest opportunity for perpetuating Christian life.

The Second Great Awakening's proactive entrepreneurial character exemplified American Christianity throughout the nineteenth century. Whether liberal or conservative, new structures and programs grew quickly. The Sunday school movement became an aggressive evangelistic tool on the American frontier and a stabilizing force in the American church throughout the century. The Chautauqua movement emerged as a training program for lay teachers of the Bible, using extension education principles popularized in England. The Chautauqua movement is the forerunner of a variety of adult education initiatives that take learning to the grassroots of America.

The Young Men's Christian Association (YMCA), with its aggressive evangelism and solid Bible study approach, was the training grounds for Christian leaders like D. L. Moody. Moody, in turn, championed the Bible school movement, which made basic theological training accessible to the laity, empowering thousands to serve God faithfully.

The aggressiveness of Christianity born out of the Second Great Awakening yielded incipient women's movements as women found ways to participate in ministries and Christian training outside the home. Female seminaries emerged, offering women entrance into formal education. Women became involved extensively in the great century of missionary effort.

The contiguous Great Awakenings of the eighteenth and nineteenth centuries clearly reflected the political order of America and the ecclesiastical priorities of Protestants. The religious paradigm shift that occured, for better or worse, during this period has had ongoing and significant impact on American church life and the character of educational endeavors (secular and Christian) that have subsequently emerged.

BYRON D. KLAUS

Bibliography. E. Cairns (1986), *An Endless Line of Splendor;* K. Gangel and W. Benson, eds. (1983), *Christian Education: Its History and Philosophy;* W. Hudson, *Religion in America* (1965); M. Noll (1992), *A History of Christianity in the United States and Canada;* J. Reed and R. Provost, eds. (1993), *A History of Christian Education.*

See also BUSHNELL, HORACE; COLONIAL EDUCATION; EDWARDS, JONATHAN; SUNDAY SCHOOL; SUNDAY SCHOOL MOVEMENT

Great Commission. In each of the Gospels and in Acts we find a version of the Great Commission (Matt. 28:19–20; Mark 16:15; Luke 24:25–27; John 20:21–23; Acts 1:7–8). Some scholars believe that each of these commissioning speeches is spoken at a different time and with a different emphasis during the forty days between Jesus' resurrection and ascension. The Great Commission is in reality a "Great Summation." Matthew's version of the Great Commission has its roots in Isaiah 49:6, where God's people are called to be a light to the nations, that is, all people outside the household of Israel. The heart of this Commission is its stated goal to make "disciples of all nations." The purpose of making disciples is to build an ever-increasing community of people who understand that their eternal destiny lies in representing the claims and cause of a redemptive God. Such evangelization assumes not only initial conversion, but also intentional long-term incorporation into a maturing process. The strategic object of this stated goal is "all nations."

Luke's record of the Great Commission in Luke 24:45–47 makes quite clear that Jesus is succinctly stating that the message of repentance and forgiveness to all nations "is written" in the Old Testament Scriptures. The "all nations" (*panta ta ethne*) usage that Jesus surely would be alluding to in the Lukan version of the Commission, would include referencing such passages as Genesis 18:18; 22:18; 26:4; Isaiah 2:2; 25:7; 52:10; 56:7. Thus Jesus' command carries with it the undergirding of the Old Testament and is not some new directive, but a command that restates for emphasis the mission of a redemptive God that's been enfleshed by Jesus Christ and is for all peoples/nations (*panta ta ethne*).

"Making disciples of all nations" necessitates teaching that goes beyond the mere transmission of information. Christ's command was specifically to teach people to obey everything that he had commanded. The Greek verb used is *matheteusate*. The term focuses on the concept of repentance, radical conversion, and submission to the lordship of Jesus Christ. A disciple was not merely a learner who examined random bits of information hoping one day for it to be useful. The verb *to disciple*, in the context of this Great Commission, clearly meant to acknowledge the lordship of Jesus Christ in repentance and faith and to submit oneself to a continuing process of learning which had as its focus the radical altering of lives. The process that the disciples were instructed to participate in clearly intended for the disciples to instruct converts in the same way that Christ had instructed the disciples during his earthly ministry. The idea that one could lead a person to call Jesus "Lord" without knowing and doing the things he taught would have been an unthinkable distortion. Jesus made quite plain that a faith commitment would be one of the unalterable conditions of discipleship because he called people to radical allegiance and constant obedience. He didn't ask for a generalized emotional response or a reckless pledge of loyalty. Jesus the Teacher demanded nothing less than knowledge of and obedience to his teaching.

Jesus' training of the twelve disciples really was a crucial dimension of preparing his small band to be able to carry out the mandate given to them after his ascension. They were really the only link between the historical Jesus and successive generations of disciples, and therefore the structure and the content of the discipleship process between Jesus and his disciples was absolutely critical. The task of these disciples was not to teach on their own or make their own disciples of the nations. The disciples, and subsequently all generations of the church, entered into this mandated effort realizing that the empowerment to go into all the world was through the Holy Spirit. In addition, they were not to teach their own agenda, but faithfully replicate what they had been taught in word and deed by the Teacher himself.

BYRON D. KLAUS

Bibliography. L. Coleman (1989), *Why the Church Must Teach;* F. Dubose (1983), *The God Who Sends;* D. Filbeck (1994), *Yes, God of the Gentiles, Too;* R. Hedlund (1991), *The Mission of the Church in the World;* J. Piper (1993), *Let the Nations Be Glad.*

See also DISCIPLE; DISCIPLING; EARLY CHURCH EDUCATION; EDUCATION IN THE EPISTLES; EDUCATION IN THE GOSPELS AND ACTS; GOSPEL; MISSION; MISSIONS EDUCATION

Greek Education. The Greek educational system rose to prominence in the fifth and fourth centuries B.C. but its roots go back several centuries earlier. As such it was the second time in history that a civilization developed a thorough system of literacy for the young (free males primarily). The Hebrew educational system, where literacy was almost universal (at least for males), had been instituted by about 1000 B.C. if not earlier. One of the critical factors in the rise of the Greek educational system was the writing of Homer's two classic works, *The Odyssey* and *The Iliad* (approximately 850 B.C.). "As Plato said, Homer was in full sense of the word educator of Greece" (Marrow, 1956, 9). These two literary works established the concept in the Greek mind of the ideal citizen. Whether the ideal citizen was a soldier or an artist depended on the individual city state, but *paideia* became the Greek educational concept for learning about culture and citizenry. Greek education had one purpose: to produce the ideal citizen, and this was considered primarily the state's responsibility.

By the fifth century B.C. there emerged in Athens an educational system intended for all free males which was by necessity of a collective character, and this led to the creation and development of the school (Marrow, 1956, 39). Until the age of 7 boys were tutored at home by a pedagogue who was usually a slave. Then at the age of 7 the boy was escorted to the public schools. There he continued to study the three classical areas of art, letters, and physical education until the age of 15 or 18 (depending on the situation). Education was not considered a practical preparation for life. At the age of 18 government or military service was often required.

Beginning in the fifth century B.C. traveling tutors known as sophists tutored young adult men in rhetoric and other skills. These sophists were universally received with great enthusiasm by the young men (Walden, 1909, 15). However, it was in opposition to these that Socrates (469–399 B.C.) raised the accusation that the educational ideal (*paideia*) was being lost for the sake of mere pragmatism. Socrates became an innovator in educational methodology that included dialogical learning called the Socratic method. His pupil Plato (427–347 B.C.) founded a school of higher learning in Athens and became the father of philosophical idealism. At the same time frame as Plato, Isocrates founded another school of higher learning in Athens which had more of a practical bent since Isocrates was an educator and not a philosopher. Plato's student, Aristotle (384–322 B.C.), continued higher education in Athens and became the father of philosophical realism. Greek higher education utilized formal instruction but also considered that tutoring by a qualified mentor was a critical component in the full-orbed education of the student. During the golden era, lasting at most two hundred years, many modern educational subjects were established such as geometry, history, and physical education. This period of Greek history was one of the greatest periods of human culture in all of history.

Concurrent with this educational system in Athens a very different state-sponsored system developed in the rival city-state of Sparta. Sparta's renowned educational system known as the *agoge* (meaning "rearing") lay at the heart of the Spartan ideal (McKennell, 1995). Boys at age 7 were sent to live in a harsh military training environment until the age of 18, whereupon they entered military service. The training was intended to produce soldiers. Girls also had some training with the goal of producing wives and then mothers for future procreation and rearing of Spartan warriors. At age 30 a Spartan man could then marry and produce more boys who would themselves be sent off at age 7 to years of harsh physical and military training. These Spartan boys became models of courage, virtue, and obedience (McKennell, 1995).

Aristotle's pupil Alexander founded an empire. At this time two philosophies called Epicureanism and Stoicism became the predominant worldviews in Greece. Rome conquered Greece in the second century B.C. and imported many Greek slaves to Rome where they became tutors, thereby deeply impacting Roman education. During the next few centuries Christianity began and spread. Eventually there were clashes between the education of Rome which was now highly influenced by Hellenism, and Christian education concepts, which were much more like Jewish education. In the third and fourth centuries A.D. very few Christians were educated in Roman or Greek schools. Augustine, Origen, and Clement were a few of the notable exceptions. However, after Constantine Christianized the Roman Empire, Greek educational ideals eventually went into eclipse. Books were burned and even the famous university at Athens was closed in the sixth century. Greek education lay largely dormant in the West until the twelfth century.

During the twelfth century a movement called scholasticism began to recover Greek educational ideals primarily by rediscovering Greek literature which had been preserved in large Muslim libraries such as the one at Cordoba, Spain. With the emergence in Europe of the dual movements of Renaissance and Reformation, both Greek and Hebrew learning styles were reinstituted with vigor. Modern Western education is largely a curious mix of these Greek and Hebrew learning systems. The Greek model began to dominate more in the West during the second half of the twentieth century as Protestantism and biblical education have diminished somewhat in influence.

DAVID J. SEIVER

Bibliography. F. A. Beck (1964), *Greek Education 450–350 BC;* K. J. Freeman (1922), *Schools of Hellas: An Essay of the Practice and Theory of Ancient Greek Education;* W. Jaeger (1943), *Paideia: The Ideals of Greek Culture;* H. I. Marrow (1956), *A History of Education in Antiquity;* N. McKennell (1995), *The Gymnasium of Virtue: Education and Culture in Ancient Sparta;* J. W. H. Walden (1909), *The Universities of Ancient Greece.*

See also ACADEMY; ARISTOTLE; PLATO; SCHOLASTICISM

Grief. Psalm 23, a poignant portrait of the caring shepherd, has brought comfort to millions of Christians as they grieve. Christians and non-Christians grieve in similar ways, especially when one understands grief as a normal, appropriate human response to significant loss. This loss may be of a person, a physical or mental capacity, a relationship, or a material possession to which the person has formed a major attachment. The intensity of one's grief is normally in direct proportion to the degree of attachment to the person or object of the loss. Ability to manage grief varies according to one's personality, circumstances, the nature of the loss, and the person's prior experiences with loss.

Grief is most often associated with the death of a loved one. Patterns of grieving have changed sharply in North America over the past century. Whereas a century ago one would wear black and withdraw from normal societal functions for at least a year, in contemporary society very little opportunity is given to the bereaved to withdraw. The general expectation is to "get back to normal" as quickly as possible. Christian pastors and friends occasionally add to this myth by downplaying the reality of grief. Using various passages of Scripture, pastors and friends often confuse the comfort of knowing that the deceased may be in heaven with the need to provide support and help for the bereaved who remains behind.

It is imperative that the bereaved intentionally face the loss and accomplish a number of tasks associated with grieving. While a certain passage of time is necessary to grieve properly, time alone does not heal. The survivor needs to accept the reality and permanence of the loss. The bereaved must experience all of the feelings and emotions associated with the loss. One must find a way to summarize the memories of the survivor's relationship with the deceased so that those memories can be treasured without holding the bereaved back from moving on in life. The survivor must also discover afresh who he or she is as an individual, what God has in mind for them, and how they can reaffirm their own individual identity. At that point the survivor needs to be able to reinvest in life and feel complete again.

C. S. Lewis (1961) says in *A Grief Observed* that "grief is like a long valley, a winding valley where any bend may reveal a totally new landscape" (47). There is no quick answer to grief, nor do Christians have some special power to avoid it. The power available to Christians is to endure grief with a sense of hope that others may not have. But grief is still grief. It is normal and healthy. Even Christ himself grieved at the death of Lazarus (John 11:35), and he grieved his own pain and impending death in the Garden of Gethsemane (Matt. 26:36–46). Christians must always remember that God doesn't want people to die. He created them to live. Death is an intrusion, a result of the brokenness of sin in this world. So death rarely comes when we want it to. Those who are bereaved must remember that death is not God's fault. On the contrary, death cannot thwart God's plans (Rom. 8:38–39). God understands the agony of death; Christ endured death on the cross (Phil. 2:8). But God can rebuild the survivor's life. God opens new doors, presents new opportunities, and gives new challenges if the survivor has the courage to face grief and work through that grief to a full resolution.

The term *grief work* was first used by Freud to denote the intentionality that someone must use to cope with this emotional period in one's life. Grief can be divided into three categories: anticipatory, acute, or complicated (delayed) grief. Kübler-Ross (1970) popularized anticipatory grief in her work with terminally ill patients, identifying the five stages of accepting one's death as denial/isolation, anger, bargaining, depression, and acceptance. Anticipatory grief does not mean that when the loss occurs the grieving process has been completed or even made easier. Anticipatory grief flows into acute grief which is brought on by the loss itself. During this period of bereavement the survivor should be encouraged to work through the various tasks of grieving identified earlier in this article. If grief is avoided, denied, or the person is distracted from the process, the grief becomes delayed, or complicated, often resulting in more enduring negative consequences. Some factors that serve to complicate grief are an ambivalent relationship with the deceased, a prior mental illness, the absence of a support network, or a sudden, untimely death with inconclusive information concerning the nature of the death.

Under normal circumstances, however, a person can move through to a full resolution of grief. By full resolution, we mean the absence of the emotional pain that intrudes into one's life or holds one back from moving forward fully in one's life. Instead of deciding merely to make the best of a bad situation, the bereaved should be encouraged to recognize that even in the face of death God is giving the person an opportunity for a new beginning. When handled in a healthy manner, a person can discover through his pain and trauma a new sense of self, a new sense of purpose, a deeper relationship with God, and a new vision for one's life and ministry.

ROBERT C. DEVRIES
AND SUSAN J. ZONNEBELT-SMEENGE

Bibliography. J. Bowlby (1980), *Attachment and Loss: Loss, Sadness, and Depression;* S. Freud (1917), *Mourning and Melancholia;* E. Kübler-Ross, (1970), *On Death and Dying;* C. S. Lewis (1961), *A Grief Observed;* S. Zonnebelt-Smeenge and R. DeVries (1998), *Getting to the Other Side of Grief: Overcoming the Loss of a Spouse.*

Groome, Thomas H. (1945–). Irish-American Catholic educator. Born in Dublin, Ireland, in 1968 he left Ireland and came to the United States. His formal education includes St. Patrick's College (M.Div., 1968); Fordham University (M.A., 1973); Teachers' College, Columbia University, and Union Theological Seminary (D.R.Ed., 1976). During the 1975–76 academic year he taught theology and religious education at Catholic University of America in Washington, D.C. The following year he accepted a position in the Department of Theology at Boston College, where he served as professor of theology and religious education.

Groome's story as an educator began in the fall of 1966, when, as a third-year seminary student, he was assigned to teach a religion course to a group of junior boys at a Catholic high school. After a disastrous attempt to instruct his class through prepared lectures, Groome discovered that the students, given a chance to ask questions, were interested in their faith. This caused him to examine how he was attempting to accomplish the work of Christian religious education.

The result of his continued reflection and practice formed the basis for his book *Christian Religious Education: Sharing Our Story and Vision* (1980). Groome presents in it an approach to Christian education in which the educational process becomes more humanizing and liberating for all of the participants. He refers to this approach as a shared Christian praxis. By using this term, Groome identifies an underlying assumption. He defines praxis as "reflective action, that is, a practice that is informed by theoretical reflection, or conversely, a theoretical reflection that is informed by practice" (xvii). His choice also reveals the influence of Paulo Freire, about whom Groome observes, "Freire is the most significant exponent of a praxis approach to education today" (175).

The elements of Groome's approach (he purposely avoids calling it a theory) are outlined in chapters nine and ten of his book. He suggests that shared praxis involves six components (present action, critical reflection, dialogue, the "story," the "vision," and present dialectical hermeneutics) and five movements. However, he would reject any attempt to systematize his work. His components provide a guide and a process for engaging participants in the story and vision of the faith community. Groome has won praise for his comprehension, his insight, and his reminder that Christian education should focus on the participants while remaining true to the content of the message.

DOUGLAS BARCALOW

Bibliography. T. H. Groome (1980), *Christian Religious Education: Sharing Our Story and Vision;* idem (1991), *Sharing Faith: A Comprehensive Approach to Religious Education and Pastoral Ministry—the Way of Shared Praxis.*

See also CHRISTIAN EDUCATION; FREIRE, PAULO; MODELING

Group Dynamics. The study of the nature of groups, the laws of their development, their internal and external communication patterns, and their interrelations with individuals, other groups, and larger authorities. It is a wide-ranging field of study concerned with both the process and product of groups. As a branch of the social sciences the field has focused on the techniques for social change, on the procedures for observing and recording group interaction, and on improved understandings of the forces that influence group success or failure.

Foundational work in the field began at the turn of the twentieth century with Charles H. Cooley. An increasing number of empirical studies on group dynamics was undertaken at the University of Iowa, the University of Michigan, and M.I.T. during the second quarter of the century. Grant monies for this research were funded by multiple interest groups and reflected the climate of the times—business wanted to employ scientific management more efficiently, the military desired to train people more quickly, and educators aspired to improve social behavior of the citizenry.

The field studies of Kurt Lewin (at the University of Iowa and later at M.I.T.) led him to establish the National Training Laboratory for Group Development at Bethel, Maine, in the late 1940s. Here leaders practiced techniques arising from the research in order to use the insights later at their businesses or schools. A number of denominations imitated these training labs. The goal was to assist clergy in becoming more sensitive to the positive and negative forces involved in church group life. The National Council of the Churches of Christ held the first interdenominational group development laboratory in 1956.

During the 1960s and 1970s much of the energy of group dynamics carried into the encounter group movement. At the same time, educational structures were dissolving in many mainline churches, whose attention turned to the needs of the inner city and to the poor.

One of the first contemporary researchers to investigate a group's interaction was Bales (1950). He identified two primary foci with which a group must deal. First, a group must give attention to the kinds of interpersonal relationships it develops and uses. These *socioemotional concerns* exhibit a powerful influence on members as they provide stability and harmony, and allow the group to function smoothly. Expressing care and concern for each other, welcoming new members, and surmounting tension with humor are elements often found in this rubric. The concepts of pastoral care and Chris-

tian community form solid theological bedrock for such a relational emphasis. It should receive high priority in any type of church organization.

Second, *task concerns* involve attention to the group's designated goal or purpose. Achievement of goals, clarification of each member's individual aims and common stake in the group, and the establishment of priorities are cited under this heading. In bipolar fashion a group will oscillate between maintenance and task functions. Wise leadership attends both to the fulfillment of the group's primary task and to the nurturance of its membership.

Later researchers discovered a third function addressed by successful groups. Boundary functions are concerned with developing and sustaining group and members' relationships with relevant individuals and systems outside the group. These include activities related to the members' behavior, developing supportive relationships, and changing social conditions. A critical principle of group practice is its ability to carry out the functions of maintenance, task, and boundary spanning.

One of the most researched technical aspects of group dynamics is the analysis of human spatial behavior (*proxemics*). Territories can be classified as primary (exclusive, long-term, such as a home), secondary (social or work areas used on an intermittent basis), or public (areas open to anyone on a short-term basis). Conflicts are more likely to arise in secondary areas, such as a church classroom or social hall. Personal space is culturally oriented. In the United States interpersonal distance can be intimate (0–1.5 feet), personal (1.5–4 feet), social (4–12 feet), or public (over 12 feet). Group participants should practice the appropriate level of intimacy for the type of interaction.

Seating arrangements vary with the type of task and the degree of closeness desired. For casual conversation, seating at right angles or face to face is preferred. For cooperation, the seating format should be side by side. A competitive environment is fostered when seating face to face or directly across from another. For boards and committees central seats are close to and in full view of others. Eye contact is most easily maintained. Persons who take more prominent positions are perceived as leaders.

Religious educators can rely heavily on the knowledge gained from group dynamics. Groups that become positive, cohesive units can exert a strong influence on members, facilitating achievement of goals and promoting mutually satisfying relationships. Conversely, ignoring group forces may cause negative effects such as premature personal disclosure or the suppression of opinions. Understanding group maintenance (nurture), task and boundary functions is another critical principle. The group climate, its structure, and the processes that develop have a significant impact on the achievements of the group. These principles may be applied to board or committee work, or when working with family systems. Awareness of group dynamics helps members become more sensitive to one another and to ways in which group processing can be facilitated.

JAMES A. DAVIES

Bibliography. H. J. Bertcher (1994), *Group Participation;* D. Cartwright and A. Zander, eds. (1968), *Group Dynamics: Research and Theory;* E. Griffin (1982), *Getting Together;* A. P. Hare, H. H. Blumberg, M. F. Davies, and M. V. Kent (1995), *Small Group Research: A Handbook.*

See also LEWIN, KURT; SMALL GROUP

Grouping and Grading. Issues related to grouping and grading play a significant role in the philosophy of a Christian education program. While *grouping* relates to how the various age groups are divided and organized, *grading* relates to the design of the curriculum across the various groups. Decisions relating to the various options of organization and curriculum are based on issues of grouping and grading.

Traditional Sunday schools are often divided into divisions, departments, and classes. Divisions are broad categories usually including early childhood (birth–5), children (grades 1–6), youth (grades 7–12), and adults. The way children and youth divisions are designed may vary depending on whether or not the local public school system has a middle school. When there is a middle school, the children's division typically includes grades 1–5 and the youth division grades 6–12.

Divisions are divided into departments as the Sunday school grows. Departments are usually made up of two or more classes. The recommended teacher/student ratio in each class is limited to 5 in early childhood, 6–8 with children, 8–10 with youth, and 25–40 with adults. As attendance increases, new classes and departments are formed. Early childhood departments ideally have no more than 15 children. As the number of young children increases, there are separate departments for babies, toddlers, 2s, 3s, 4s, and 5s. In the children's division, classes are normally divided into primary (grades 1 & 2), middler (grades 3 & 4), and junior (grades 5 & 6) departments. In the youth division it is advisable to separate junior and senior high as soon as attendance grows to five or six regular attenders in each group. Departments do not usually exceed 30–40 students.

In addition to this traditional approach to grouping, some churches have had a great deal of success with a "rally" format for both children and youth. This format usually involves large groups of between 50 and 300 persons meeting together in a large group, then separating for more intimate reflection in small groups with trained leaders.

Adults may choose to organize themselves into traditional age groupings, or into elective classes for those desiring variety. Some of the more creative approaches to adult groupings include developmentally based groups with classes offered for believers at various stages of spiritual growth and commitment.

Closely related to grouping is grading. Grading refers to the way the curriculum is correlated throughout the Christian education program. With *uniform grading* the same Bible text is studied in all classes throughout the Sunday school. *Unified grading* focuses on the same theme throughout the various classes. Sunday schools with 150–400 students often use *departmental grading* which allows each department to have a different theme or topic suited to their particular age group. Larger programs often use a *closely graded* curriculum in which each grade in the Sunday school focuses on a different theme and text.

With the rapid changes occurring within church programs we can expect to see even more creative options for grouping and grading in the future.

GARY C. NEWTON

Group Stages. A number of researchers have found that groups develop and change over time in relatively predictable phases (Farrell, Heinemann, and Schmitt, 1986; Davies and Kuypers, 1985; Hare and Naveh, 1984). These patterns of behavior often happen gradually, without distinct separation and clear lines of demarcation. Depending on the group and the types of people involved, different kinds of interactions and behaviors can be used to identify the phases.

Current research suggests that a typical pattern of development for many groups includes five phases: first, the purpose of the group is defined and the commitment of the members is secured; second, necessary resources or skills must be acquired or provided; third, appropriate roles are developed or learned and a satisfactory level of morale is achieved; fourth, the group works at carrying out the task with the coordination of leadership; fifth, the terminal phase, during which the group redefines the relationships between members as it disbands (Berman-Rossi, 1992; Brower, 1989; Galinsky and Scholper, 1989). These five phases have been popularized by Tuckman and Jensen (1977) as forming, storming, norming, performing, and adjourning. In essence, groups move from a building stage in which they begin to bond as a group to a period of possible conflict about purposes, activities, and relationships. They then move to a more mature phase of self-directed action-toward-goals. Evaluation of the group's work and members' joint experience provides the foundation for ending.

Some sages eliminate the last phase, preferring a four-phase approach. They reason that some people may drop out of a group at the end of the first phase if they are not committed to the idea of the group, or at the end of the second phase if they judge that resources are inadequate. Evidence suggests that it is equally likely that dropout will occur near the end of the third phase if members are dissatisfied with the leadership or role distribution.

While group stages are presented as an orderly and sequential process, it must be noted that the process is often cyclical, with groups returning to earlier stages along the way or skipping certain stages. A number of studies do not report well-defined phases in group development. They have found continued growth related to some type of interpersonal behavior as the group becomes more cohesive and better able to handle the task (Davies and Hazewinkel, 1986; Doreian, 1986; Boyd, 1984).

Other researchers suggest that there may be no phases in group development that apply equally to all types of groups. They maintain that it is more essential to focus on the significant differences between various types of groups and relate these to primary group results (Cissna, 1984; Hirokawa, 1983).

The implication of these findings for Christian educators is that groups need different things at different times. Good leaders will make sure that groups get what they need when they need it through awareness, cooperation, and accommodation.

JAMES A. DAVIES

Bibliography. A. P. Hare, H. H. Blumberg, M. F. Davies, and M. V. Kent (1995), *Small Group Research: A Handbook;* P. B. Paulus (1989), *Psychology of Group Influence.*

Guidance. *See* Counseling.

Guide. *See* Direct.

Hawthorne Effect. An observed change in the behavior of subjects in a research investigation based upon their awareness of participating in an experiment, their knowledge of the researcher's hypothesis, or their response to receiving special attention. This phenomenon was discovered in 1927 when worker productivity was studied under the monotonous working conditions of factory personnel at the Western Electric Company's Hawthorne plant in Cicero, Illinois. Elton Mayo and his investigative team were surprised to learn that productivity increased not only with improved working conditions (such as an increase in the number of breaks and better lighting conditions), but also when such conditions were made worse (reduction in the number of breaks and dimmed lighting). The researchers concluded that the fact of being studied, rather than the experimental factors being manipulated, had caused the workers to react as they had.

In any experiment, improved performance that can be attributed to the increased attention and recognition which subjects receive has subsequently come to be known as the *Hawthorne effect*. Whenever this occurs, the external validity of the experiment is jeopardized, because the behavior of the subjects is affected not by the treatment *per se*, but by their knowledge of being participants in a research study.

DAVID GOUGH

Bibliography. F. S. Roethlisberger and W. J. Dickson (1939), *Management and the Worker.*

Healing Ministry. *See* Recovery Ministry.

Hebrew Education through Feasts and Festivals. Feasts and festivals were regular assemblies of Israel at scheduled periods in the year for joyous feasting and thanksgiving to commemorate both civil and religious events. Israel's three major annual feasts, also known as the three pilgrim festivals (Exod. 23:14–19; 2 Chron. 8:12–13), include the Passover/Feast of Unleavened Bread (Exod. 12:1; 13:16; 34:18–20, 25; Lev. 23:4–8; Num. 28:16–25; Deut. 16:1–8), the Feast of Weeks/Harvest (Exod. 23:16; Lev. 23:15–21; Num. 28:26–31; Deut. 16:9–12), and the Feast of

Tabernacles/Ingathering (Exod. 23:16; Lev. 23:33–41; Num. 29:12–38). The other festivals were the New Moon festivals (Exod. 40:2, 17; Num. 10:10; 28:1–10; 1 Sam. 20:18; 1 Chron. 23:31) and Sabbaths (Exod. 16:22–30; 20:8–11; 23:12; 31:12–17; 34:21; 35:2–3; Lev. 23:3; 26:2; Num. 28:9–10; Deut. 5:12–15).

In Judaism, as in Christianity, renewal is often accomplished through rediscovery. In celebrating the various feasts and festivals, Israel returns to neglected roots and rediscovers a fresh understanding of God's power, purposes, and presence as creator and sustainer of the nation. Thus, Hebrew festive celebrations were purposeful educational events for the whole community.

Feasts and Festivals as Educational Events. The Passover feast had specific educational goals. The rich imagery of the celebrations evoked the curiosity of inquisitive children to ask questions about the historical event (Exod. 12:26–27; 13:8, 14–16). Blood-sprinkled doorposts recalled the original signal to the angel of death to "pass over" their homes. Israel's firstborn males must thus be consecrated and redeemed, for God spared them from death that fateful night when all Egypt's firstborn were slain (Exod. 13:11–16). Fully dressed to go, the whole family ate the meal in haste. They even baked bread without yeast, illustrating the urgency of that moment. Bitter herbs reminded them of their harsh and brutal sufferings in Egypt. Through this yearly festival, the nation thus returns to its roots, and commemorates the exodus from Egypt as an act of God's mighty deliverance (Josh. 5:10; 2 Kings 23:21–23; 2 Chron. 30:1–5, 13–20; Exod. 6:19–21).

The Feast of Unleavened Bread was celebrated concurrently with the Passover. All yeast was removed from the home during this period and violators were excommunicated (Exod. 12:1–20; Lev. 23:4–8; Num. 28:16–25; Deut. 16:1–8). The seven day celebration was marked by holy convocations and no work was allowed. During this period, the whole community ate bread without yeast, reminding them of their affliction in Egypt. Unleavened bread is the bread of affliction, eaten in haste on that night of departure (Deut. 16:3).

The Feast of Weeks took place on the 50th day after the offering of the barley sheaf at the Feast of Unleavened Bread. It began with a sacred assembly and no work was to be done. The nation offered the first fruits of the wheat harvest to God as freewill offerings and in proportion to the harvest (Num. 28:26; Deut. 16:10). Burnt offerings and sin offerings were also made (Lev. 23:18–20; Num. 28:27–30). The nation was to rejoice in God's presence for the land God had given, and to share this joy not only with their children, menservants, and maidservants, but also with the aliens, fatherless, and widows in their midst (Deut. 16:11–12). This feast was also known as the Feast of Harvest or Pentecost. It was at this feast that God poured out his Holy Spirit upon the New Testament church in a miraculous way (Acts 2:1–4).

On the fifteenth day of the seventh month, the nation celebrated the Feast of Tabernacles or Ingathering where crops were gathered from the field (Lev. 23:33–36; Exod. 23:16; Deut. 16:14). This seven day festival was marked by holy convocations where no work was allowed. Animal sacrifices and grain and drink offerings were offered (Lev. 23:33–36; Num. 29:13–38). The people were to celebrate with joy and to include the menservants, maidservants, aliens, fatherless, and widows (Deut. 16:14). During this period, all native born Israelites were to live in booths to remember their days of sojourn in booths when God led them out of Egypt (Lev. 23:40, 42–43). This feast was celebrated throughout Israel's history (2 Chron. 8:12–13; Ezra 3:4; Neh. 8:13–18; John 7:2–3, 37–38).

As required under Mosaic law, Israel consecrated itself to God each new month during the New Moon festivals (Num. 28:11). Normal work ceased and the celebrations were marked by blowing of the trumpets (Num. 10:10) and offerings and sacrifices (Num. 28:11–15; 1 Chron. 23:30–31; 2 Chron. 2:4; 8:12–13; 31:3). Wrong attitudes during New Moon festivals incurred God's wrath (Isa. 1:13–14; Hos. 2:11; 5:7). Observation of the Sabbath was a distinctive of the people of God. Every seventh day was to be a holy day of rest to remember God's work in creation (Exod. 20:8–11; Lev. 23:3; Gen. 2:2–3). Servants, aliens within the community, and even animals were to cease from labor, and violation was punishable by death (Exod. 31:14; 35:2; Num. 15:32–36).

The most holy day of Israel's year was the Day of Atonement (Exod. 30:10; Lev. 16; 23:26–32; 25:9; Num. 29:7–11). On the tenth day of the seventh month, Israel sought forgiveness for her sins through complex sacrificial rites. After the high priest sanctified himself through ceremonial washings and the sacrifice of a bullock, he would sacrifice a goat for the sins of the nation. Finally, a scapegoat bearing the sins of the people was sent into the wilderness, symbolizing God's pardon for the sin of the nation (Lev. 16:20–22; Gal. 3:12; 2 Cor. 5:21). This was a day of public fasting preceded by special Sabbaths.

Pedagogical Insights. Hebrew celebrations of feasts and festivals provide some interesting pedagogical insights. First, learning was fully experiential. Burnt offerings, animal sacrifices, harvest offerings, and lavish feasts evoked the full senses of sight, sound, touch, taste, and smell. The festivals often required cessation from normal life and labor and sometimes called for a radical change of lifestyle (Feast of Tabernacles). Second, learning occurred within communities. The Passover was celebrated within families who encouraged free participation of children. Other feasts frequently involved the nation as a whole. Third, learning focused on God as the source and sustainer of the nation. The great feasts were often occasions of covenant renewal, calling the nation back to its roots and beginnings in God. Not surprisingly, reading and teaching of the Law accompanied the other festivities (Deut. 31:9–13; Neh. 8). Last, but not least, learning encompassed the whole of life with its varied needs. Through a system of elaborate celebrations, the people remembered their humble beginnings (Passover/Feast of Unleavened Bread), celebrated God's sustaining grace (Feast of Weeks, Feast of Ingathering), received cleansing (Day of Atonement), and regularly consecrated themselves to holy service (Sabbath, New Moon).

YAU-MAN SIEW

Bibliography. J. C. Rylaarsdam (1962), *The Interpreter's Dictionary of the Bible;* C. M. Williamson and R. J. Allen (1991), *The Teaching Minister;* D. Ng and V. Thomas (1981), *Children in the Worshiping Community.*

Hendricks, Howard (1924–). Chairman of the Center for Christian Leadership at Dallas Seminary. Born into a broken home with parents already separated, Hendricks recalls that the only time he ever saw them together was 18 years later when he was called to testify in a divorce court. These early struggles afford one of the motivations for his commitment to strengthening the family through his public ministry. He earned the A.B. and D.D. degrees from Wheaton College and a Th.M. degree from Dallas Theological Seminary. In addition to pastoring Calvary Presbyterian Church in Fort Worth from 1950 to 1952, Hendricks also taught at Southern Bible Training School in Dallas and the Fort Worth Bible Institute before becoming a teaching fellow in practical theology at Dallas Seminary in 1951. In 1958, he became the founding chairman of the Department of Christian Education at Dallas Seminary and currently holds the rank of Distinguished Professor of Christian Education.

His board memberships include Multnomah School of the Bible, Search Ministries, the Navigators, Walk Thru the Bible, and Promise Keepers. He has also authored numerous books including *Say It with Love, Heaven Help the Home,* and *Teaching to Change Lives.* In 1995, he coauthored *As Irons Sharpens Iron* with his son William. In 1997 Hendricks coauthored *Values and Virtues,* a collection of more than 2000 quotes on a wide variety of subjects such as adversity, family, honesty, leadership, and perseverance. He serves as general editor of *A Life of Integrity,* a collection of essays from respected Christian leaders.

Probably best known for his plenary session addresses at conventions and conferences around the world, he has been listed in *Who's Who in American Education* and has been widely published in periodicals such as *Decision, Moody,* and *Christianity Today.* He can be heard on the *Art of Family Living* radio program. He and his wife, Jeanne, live in Dallas and are the parents of four children and the grandparents of six granddaughters.

Hendricks has been a frequent speaker at conferences on Christian education, as well as at teacher and parent training classes, and he continues to be in wide demand for pulpit supply and Bible teaching ministries. He has ministered in over seventy countries and served as the chaplain of the Dallas Cowboys from 1976 to 1984.

Hendricks is considered by virtually all who know him to be one of the most articulate spokesmen for biblical Christianity, and especially for Christian education, during the twentieth century. He has mentored dozens of contemporary Christian leaders, among them Charles Swindoll, the current president of Dallas Theological Seminary. About his former mentor Swindoll says, "For more than thirty-five years I have known, loved, and admired Howie Hendricks. I am not alone. He has left his mark on thousands of lives. In a real sense, only he knows the mentoring secrets that have marked men for a lifetime."

KENNETH O. GANGEL

Herbart, Johann Friedrich (1776–1841). German philosopher of education. In 1802 he received his doctorate at Göttingen, where he subsequently taught for seven years. He later held Immanuel Kant's chair of philosophy at Königsberg for twenty-four years. There, Herbart established a teacher training program and demonstration school that became a pattern for schools of education in Europe and in the United States. He then returned to Göttingen, where he actively taught until his death. Early in his career, while tutoring in Switzerland, Herbart visited Johann Pestalozzi's school at Burgdorf. He was affected by the educational reformer's zeal, and his approach to schooling manifests awareness of Pestalozzi's work. Some have declared that Herbart became the philosopher of education that Pestalozzi was not. Herbart's pedagogy was exquisite, while Pestalozzi's was, at many points, peculiar.

Herbart was intent on attaining educational objectives and committed to goals that accommodate individual differences and academic potential. This personal concern was in accord with Herbart's belief (diverging from Kant and Johann Gottlieb Fichte) that the *sole* aim of education is the development of moral character. His pedagogical motto was "How can a person be educated morally?" Adopting a modified form of mental realism led Herbart to attribute as much significance to relational training of feeling and doing as to deliberate transmission of knowledge.

In Herbart, there is a strong educational connection between knowledge of that which is good and the will to do it. However, he rejected pendulum swings toward either mere instruction (indirect influence of morality by developing the mind) or elaborate education (direct influence of morality by training the will). Herbart's writings display a well-developed experiential and psychological conceptualization of cognitive, affective, and psychomotor domains of education that parallel personality components of intellect, emotion, and will. Herbart characterized this as unified and moral educational instruction.

Herbart resisted traditional education in which a teacher determines the action of the student. Rejecting idealism, he embraced associationism, which later characterized the philosophy of John Stuart Mill. Herbart developed a philosophical approach to education that conceived of the mind (knowledge and understanding) as a constantly changing product of interaction between and assimilation of "presentations" (conceptual events related to concrete experience). In his view, the cognitive impact of new presentations is affected, but not determined, by a student's current set of accumulated concepts. New ideas emerge from material previously mastered.

This dynamic developmental construct was formalized in an educational model that emphasized sequential stages of moral development. Herbart proposed a four-step approach to teaching composed of clearness, association, system, and method. The Herbartian pedagogical movement that arose in the late nineteenth century preferred various forms of a five-step approach composed of preparation, presentation, association, generalization, and application. Later, these approaches to the inculcation of virtue and character eroded into popular curriculum outlines often adopted by inadequately trained teachers.

At the turn of the twentieth century, German educational theory and Herbartian methodology influenced educational trends in the United States. As early as 1895, American educators established a National Herbart Society for the Scientific Study of Education. Soon, however, this organization evolved into the National Society for the Scientific Study of Education, indicating fascination with non-Herbartian systems of education. Influence of Herbart (certainly through John Stuart Mill, but radically simplified) can be detected in the student-centered progressivism of John Dewey (a National Society board member). However, Dewey attacked aspects of Herbart's educational theory related to the nature of child development.

Herbart taught in the context of institutionalized German Christianity, and recognized a place for religious influence in childhood education. He encouraged religious educators to avoid formal theological instruction apart from relational guidance in the home and church. Humanistic and naturalistic perspectives were prevalent in Herbart's philosophy and methodology. However, absence of antireligious jargon paved the way for moderate impact on European and American Christian education. As early as 1860, normal school (later, teachers' college) students affected by the methods and theories of Pestalozzi, Friedrich Froebel, and Herbart carried psychological methods into the Sunday school movement. Religious educators were attracted to Herbart's emphasis on moral development and training in virtue—even though his own concept of virtue was personal moral freedom rather than Christ-likeness.

Herbartian concepts in accord with contemporary Christian education and religious instruction are multiple:

- The aim of education is character development rather than mere transmission of content.
- Virtuous content is a critical component of relational education.
- Personal judgment is a crucial factor in the capacity of a student to develop as a noble person.
- Quality education is best conducted in natural circumstances rather than in classroom settings.
- Systematic instruction is compatible with life-related character formation.

Herbart insisted that an adequate educational theory must include a comprehensive analysis of the aims, intended outcomes, and means of education. This is a balance that contemporary Christian educators have discovered and appre-

ciated in the analytic educational philosophy of William Frankena.

DANIEL C. STEVENS

Bibliography. H. B. Dunkel (1969), *Herbart and Education;* idem (1970), *Herbart and Herbartianism: An Educational Ghost Story.*

See also COGNITIVE DEVELOPMENT; FRANKENA, WILLIAM KLAUS; MORAL EDUCATION; PESTALOZZI, JOHANN HEINRICH; SUNDAY SCHOOL MOVEMENT

Hermeneutics and Exegesis in Teaching. Hermeneutics is the science and art of interpretation. The word comes from the Greek noun *hermeneutikos,* meaning "of or for interpreting." The verb form, *hermeneuo,* means "to explain, interpret, or translate." Interpretation is essential to understanding the will of God. From its traditional meaning as a set of rules governing exegesis of Scripture, interpretation has been widened to include communicative, epistemological, and ontological dimensions, all essential to the teaching task of the church.

From earliest times, the preaching and teaching tasks of the Christian church focused on the essential gospel as well as on the whole counsel of God as revealed in Scripture. Precisely because the Scriptures came to people within different locales and distinct cultures at particular times in history, principles of interpretation have been employed in the discovery of the meaning of the text. That is to say that in attempting to understand the original intent of a particular author, the student of Scripture needs to employ methods that account for the entire historical, critical, and cultural milieu that surrounded the Word in its original formulation as well as in its communication and reception.

Before the nineteenth century the term *hermeneutics* was used almost exclusively to mean a science of interpreting the Jewish and Christian Scriptures. Since that time it has been used more broadly to explain the principles used in the interpretation of any text or situation.

Possession of the Bible does not in itself assure knowledge of the Bible. On this premise the Bible student, preacher, or teacher approaches the task of interpretation with whatever textual, historical, grammatical, and critical methods are available to seek understanding. For believers, faith always seeks understanding.

One of the important biblical texts where the word *hermeneutics* is used is Luke 24:27. On the Emmaus road, Jesus reportedly "explained" the Scriptures to the disciples. The incident of Philip and the Ethiopian eunuch (Acts 8:26–40) illustrates the necessity of interpretation in learning. Upon finding the Ethiopian reading Isaiah the prophet, Philip asked: "Do you understand what you are reading?" The reply was an invitation to bring meaning and application to the text: "How can I unless someone explains it to me?"

Strategic use of sound hermeneutical principles helps bridge the linguistic and cultural gaps between the ancient and modern worlds so that the learner may be able to understand the Scriptures. The New Testament can be understood as an interpretation of the Old Testament.

The same hermeneutical principles apply whether one preaches or teaches the Word of God. It is important to grasp the essential meaning of any given text before applying the text to the present situation.

It is the particular task of pedagogy to allow both instructor and learner to interact with the biblical text. The dialogical nature of effective teaching differs from the more declarative means of communicating biblical understanding through preaching, yet the same hermeneutic applies to the study of the text. Such a dialogical motif, accompanied by the declarative approach, assures that audiences and learners grasp what the authors of the divine text intended for their readers or hearers.

Historically, the church has relied upon two chief functions or means of communicating the Word of Truth—preaching and teaching. Neglect of either is unfaithfulness to God. In recent years the position of C. H. Dodd (*Apostolic Preaching and Its Development*, 1936) has dominated Protestant understanding of the essential message of the faith, but it has also tended to separate the two functions of preaching and teaching. Dodd viewed apostolic preaching as including an ordered corpus of Christological truth (*kerygma*) while teaching was essentially moral instruction (*didache*). James Smart (1954), Robert Worley (1958), Robert Mounce (1960), and others have viewed the two functions as more similar than dissimilar. A unified view is based upon such texts as Acts 5:42 where the words *teach* and *preach* refer to the same christological content of the Christian message. The objectivity of the biblical message, whether heard from preacher or teacher, is essential. If faith comes by hearing and hearing by the Word (Rom. 10:17), then it follows that the communicator of the Word proceed with both caution and boldness. Caution is needed to guard against undue subjectivism and conjecture as to the meaning of the text. Boldness is a natural outcome when a sound hermeneutic is accompanied by reliance upon the Spirit of God who alone illumines the Word and enlightens the minds of both teacher and learner.

A Spirit-enlightened Word in no way negates scholarship. History has revealed that where rigorous attention has been given to the text in the discovery of its meaning, the church is renewed. Evangelicals have been known as "people of the book." This rich tradition mandates a thoughtful

hermeneutical approach to the study of the text of Scripture.

Hermeneutics in History. While modern hermeneutical theory and practice date to the late nineteenth century, work with the text of Scripture is as old as the text itself. In Talmudic tradition many modes of interpretation, perhaps as many as thirty-two, were distinguished, but even the early rabbis taught that nothing can override the plain meaning of the text. Origen (185–254), in the early Christian era, identified three senses of the Bible to which humans correspond: the fleshly, the psychic, and the spiritual. His hermeneutic relied upon the allegorical meaning of the text. Early church fathers used typology and related techniques of numerology along with the dominant allegorical method. More clearly, since the rise of the catechetical schools at Alexandria and Antioch in the postapostolic period, the tension between the allegorical and historical approaches became dominant. In both cases appeals were made to the text of Scripture. Unable to resolve these tensions and polarities, the councils of the church moved away from the dependence upon the biblical text for clues of a hermeneutic toward traditional teachings of the church as normative and authoritative.

When the Latin Vulgate was produced by Jerome in the fourth century, the church tended to depend upon that translation as arbiter in all doctrinal matters. Augustine (354–430), whose insight and scholarship fundamentally affected the direction of the church, offered three criteria for determining meaning: (1) the rule of faith taught in the clearer passages of Scripture, (2) the authority of the church, and (3) the context of the passage. In time, tradition took precedence over reasoned study of the Scriptures.

The medieval period solidified tradition, introduced the textual gloss (marginal readings treated as valid Scripture), elevated allegory as the primary approach, and, to a lesser degree, kept alive the literal-historical method. Scholasticism freed the church from reliance upon allegory but elevated reason and philosophy.

The Reformation, with its renewed sense of the importance of direct study of the Bible, Bible translation, and the recovery of the central role of preaching the Word, rejected the allegorical method of interpretation. Reformers opted for the plain, simple, and literal sense of the text, emphasizing the right of private judgment but avoiding idiosyncratic interpretation. Commentaries produced by Luther and Calvin are still prized as models of exposition based upon a grammatical, literal, and historic approach to the text with reliance upon the Spirit uniting believers in affirming the great doctrines of the faith.

Post-Reformation Christians fractured over subjectivism and rationalism. Pietists and others relied more on experiential understandings than on the clear meaning of the text. The introduction of higher criticism of the text with later adaptations of reductionism left a trail of destruction in the churches. With historicity questioned and a mythological overlay of the text, the direct study of the Bible was weakened. Despite this, a renewed interest in the study of hermeneutics was spawned by efforts to demythologize the text, basing interpretation on a mix of rationalism and existentialism. Proponents of this approach place emphasis upon contemporization of the text over the grammatico-historical approach used by evangelicals.

The twentieth century saw the rise of numerous translations of the Bible and evangelical advances in Bible interpretation, as well as expansion in transcultural missions. The latter efforts are forcing a new look at culturalisms and contextualisms (i.e., liberation theology, black and feminist hermeneutics, ethnicity, and efforts to recover gender-neutral understandings of the Scriptures).

For evangelicals who hold to a divinely inspired and authoritative text, the subject of hermeneutics becomes vitally important. Efforts to understand the historical, linguistic, and cultural nature not only of propositional truth, but also of the very words of Scripture, calls for a sound hermeneutic.

Postmodernism continues the tradition begun by Bultmann, Pannenberg, and others to remove everything that speaks rationally of God and his activity in our world in order to make the Bible understandable to modern society. Modern critics increasingly deny the possibility of discovering the original or intended meaning of a text. Such a relativistic approach is considered invalid by evangelicals. While admitting to a genre-driven interpretation, they deny making the Bible a text of individual or personalistic meanings.

The genre, or type of literature, provides helpful clues in textual understanding (e.g.: prophetic, poetic, gospel narrative). It has been generally accepted that there are multiple genres or types of literary material in the Bible, perhaps as many as eight: (1) law, (2) historic narrative, (3) gospel narrative, (4) parables, (5) prophetic/apocalyptic, (6) wisdom, (7) poetic, and (8) epistolary. The serious teacher or student will seek to understand these and other literary formulations in any search for meaning.

Deconstruction and postmodern theories pose a challenge to the autonomy of the text. Modern communications theory with its basic model of sender, message, and receiver interfaces with hermeneutics and the related methods of exegesis. In practice, however, the biblical text mediates between the events of understanding, one produced by the text itself and the others from interaction with it. Since the texts are historical, literary in composition, cultural in their context

as well as divinely inspired, every method may be used to understand the Word of God so long as it is consistent with a sound biblical hermeneutic.

Recent evangelical authors have developed useful guides to interpretation. Osborne (1991) identifies ten stages of interpretation that move from induction to deduction. Klein, Blomberg, and Hubbard (1993) place major emphasis upon various rules governing the genre or type of literature. Regardless of type, if any interpretation is to be true, it must be consistent with (1) the obvious sense in the literary context, (2) the facts of the historical-cultural background, (3) the normal meaning of the words in the context, and (4) the proper grammatical relationship between words.

Exegesis. Exegesis is the process of drawing out of a text its intended meaning. From the Greek word *exegeomai*, the word is used to describe the disclosure or description of a document, statement, or incident. Where found in the New Testament, it appears to be a term interchangeable with hermeneutics. In the Johannine text of John 1:18 the word explains how God made himself known to human beings by exegesis or "declaration" of the Son of God. In Luke 24:35 the two disciples "exegeted" or told what had happened to them on the Emmaus road.

The relationship of exegesis to hermeneutics is one of kind and degree. Hermeneutics may best be viewed as the umbrella under which exegesis fits. Hermeneutics deals with broad principles or rules of interpretation governing biblical exegesis. The Word of God, properly understood in various cultural settings, prompts both teacher and learner to search for proper meanings employing historical, critical, linguistic, and cultural understandings. Both in hermeneutics and exegesis, evangelicals have relied upon what is now known as the literal-grammatical-historical method. Exegesis is the more exact science to unlock these meanings.

Exegesis, as contrasted to *eisegesis* ("to read into"), forms the heart of hermeneutical theory. Exegesis employs three approaches to the text: (1) understanding the grammar of a text, (2) understanding the meaning of individual words in a sentence, and (3) understanding the message as a whole in the context of a paragraph, chapter, individual Bible book, and the entire text of Scripture. These are interdependent upon one another.

Exegesis may involve a Scripture translation, paraphrase, or commentary, its overall rules being governed by hermeneutics and a biblical theology. In other words a text cannot stand alone in meaning but fits within the entire structure of revealed truth.

Exegesis involves a process: (1) examining the text itself, its origin and wording, (2) scrutiny of translation, (3) discovery of historical context—authorship, setting, and dating, (4) analysis of literary context, (5) determining the genre or literary type, (6) outlining and diagramming structure, (7) classification of grammar and syntax, (8) systematically studying a given truth in the setting of all revealed truth, and (9) applying the text.

In short, three basic questions may be asked of any text: What does it say? What does it mean? How does it impact me? Care must be given, however, not to shortchange all the steps of exegesis lest a learner rush to a personal application that is totally unwarranted from the biblical data.

There are two misapplications of the text to avoid: moralizing the Word and personalizing the Word. Christian education has been guilty of both and is often viewed as inferior compared with other methods of transmitting and appropriating truth. Moralizing the Word involves applying a particular moral framework to a truth viewed from a particular vantage point in time. Personalizing a text is similar in that an individualistic world and life view dictates meaning and application. Both moralizing and personalizing a text may be avoided by applying sound hermeneutics and exegesis theory.

First, it must be understood that the reading of any biblical text assumes that the present reader is not the original reader. Effort should be made to determine how the text may best have been understood by the original reader. Second, the interpretive community of believers (the *ekklesia*) constitutes the context of the reading. Third, since the original authors and hearers are no longer participants in the process, the interpretive interaction takes place between text and learner. Since the text is historical in its composition and presentation, every method must be used to understand its meaning in that light before a rush to application.

Finally, the witness of the Holy Spirit figures prominently in an evangelical understanding of biblical exegesis. Calvin and other Reformers rejected external authority as the basis for understanding truth and substituted the witness of the Spirit (i.e., John 14:26; 16:13–15). The Christian is not unaided in teaching the Word of God. Ultimately it is the Holy Spirit that sheds light upon divine truth. While unbelievers may gain understanding of a text, apart from the work of the Holy Spirit who enlightens the mind they may never come to truth that is "spiritually appraised" or examined (v. 14). The text of 1 Corinthians 2:6–16 is important in that essential wisdom comes from God.

EDWARD L. HAYES

Bibliography. D. A. Carson (1992), *Exegetical Fallacies;* F. L. Cross (1997), *The Oxford Dictionary of the Christian Faith;* G. D. Fee (1983), *New Testament Exegesis;* D. N. Friedman (1992), *The Anchor Bible Dictionary;* W. Kaiser and M. Silva (1994), *An Introduction to Bible Hermeneutics: The Search for Meaning;* W. Klein, C. Blomberg, and R. L. Hubbard (1993), *Introduction to Biblical Interpretation;* A. B. Mickelson (1963), *Interpreting the Bible;* C. F. D. Moule (1982), *Essays in New Testament Introduction;* G. R. Osborne (1991), *The Hermeneutical Spiral;* M. Silva (1987), *Has the Church Misread the Bible?;* B. Ramm (1970), *Protestant Biblical Interpretation;* R. C. Worley (1958), *Preaching and Teaching in the Earliest Church.*

Heterogeneity. A diversity of social, ethnic, intellectual, and economic backgrounds among members of a population group. Congregational theorists use the term to describe the potential diversity of congregations, or of groups within a particular congregation, which share similar theological convictions and administrative oversight (Nelson, 1988). Educational leaders use the term in addressing an educational setting that contains a diverse array of cultural backgrounds and expectations (Breckenridge and Breckenridge, 1995), as well as various learning styles (Gardner, 1983; LeFever, 1995).

Christian educators believe that the educational environment is richer when there is a large diversity of cultural backgrounds and learning styles present within a group. The assumption is that this diversity will provide a new perspective for each learner. Christian educators should recognize and address the level of heterogeneity within any teaching situation, in the potential social and ethnic diversity represented in the group and in the various learning styles present.

DEAN BLEVINS

Bibliography. J. Breckenridge and L. Breckenridge (1995), *What Color Is Your God?: Multicultural Education in the Church;* H. Gardner (1983), *Frames of Mind: The Theory of Multiple Intelligences;* M. LeFever (1995), *Learning Styles;* C. E. Nelson, ed. (1988), *Congregations: Their Power to Form and Transform.*

See also ETHNIC IMPLICATIONS OF CHRISTIAN EDUCATION; MULTICULTUALISM

Heterogeneous Quality. *See* Heterogeneity.

Heteronomous Morality. Heteronomous morality has both a broad and narrow definition. In the broad sense, heteronomous morality is the acceptable ethical behavior of a diverse group in society; this is sometimes referred to as social morality. Social morality addresses the contemporary social issues of a society, identifying moral and immoral behavior. At the end of the twentieth century in North America, these issues included abortion, war and the ethical protest of war, euthanasia, penal reform, welfare programs, prayer in school, genetic cloning, homosexual marriage, and surrogate parenting, to name a few. John R. Stott (1975) describes this level of moral discussion as "macro-ethics."

Closely associated with this broad definition is *personal morality*, which identifies and categorizes moral and immoral behavior for an individual; this may be described as "micro-ethics." Personal morality addresses the acceptable ethical behavior of an individual on such issues as lying, stealing, cheating, defaming, and murdering. Within the moral development literature, beginning with Jean Piaget (1932), research suggests that personal moral reasoning includes two vitally important developmental processes: heteronomy (externally imposed morality) and autonomy (internally reasoned morality). Thus, a narrow definition holds that heteronomous morality and heteronomy are synonyomus terms. In this definition, heteronomous morality involves those external moral structures necessary for a child to understand legal systems. By age 8, according to Piaget, the transition to autonomy begins. Autonomous morality focuses on equity, responsibility, group consensus, mutual respect, and individual motives determining morality rather than on simply objective adherence to established rules.

When using the term in its narrow sense, autonomous morality virtually eliminates the broader perspective of moral standards for society. Piaget's emphasis on development toward autonomy minimizes the value of externally imposed moral standards beyond childhood; this seems counter to Scripture's presentation of moral standards for adults who seek to obey God. While Kohlberg's moral development theory suggests stage development in moral reasoning in individuals, Kohlberg recognizes that moral developmental takes place in the context of social relationships.

A variety of sources may be used to establish heteronomous morality in the broad sense. A religious belief system is the most common source for heteronomous morality. Around the world, a variety of religious systems influence societal morality in various cultures: Islam, Hinduism, Confucianism, and animism are examples. Other sources contributing to moral structure in a heteronomous world include (1) decision making by the people in a democracy, or by elected representatives of the people, as in a republic, (2) political power centered in an individual or belief system and enforced by force (i.e., Marxism), (3) cultural traditions, or (4) challenges to moral reasoning including cognitive disequilibrium.

A Christian worldview suggests that (1) God established the standards for acceptable ethical behavior and revealed it to men and women through the Holy Scriptures, and (2) the Scriptures serve as an objective standard by which an individual or any Judeo-Christian society acknowledges such a divine ethical standard for behavior. A snapshot of Jesus' values for society are found in his Sermon on the Mount (Matt. 5:1–7:29).

When a society recognizes divine principles for morality such as a Judeo-Christian moral structure, or when a heteronomous group seeks to establish its own principles for moral governance, issues regarding authority and credibility of the moral source must be established as well as issues related to the authority and role of institutions to enforce the moral code. Within societies, these institutions are (1) the family unit, (2) the church or religious groups, (3) all levels of government, and (4) educational systems whereby moral values are taught.

Any study of social morality and ethics should include a detailed study of personal morality as well as the extensive research literature associated with stage development theory of moral reasoning (e.g., Jean Piaget) including moral development theory (e.g., Lawrence Kohlberg) and faith development theory (e.g., James Fowler).

PATRICK A. BLEWETT

Bibliography. B. Clouse (1993), *Teaching for Moral Growth;* J. W. Fowler (1981), *Stages of Faith;* K. O. Gangel and J. C. Wilhoit (1994), *The Christian Educator's Handbook on Spiritual Formation;* L. Kohlberg (1963), *Child Psychology: 62nd Yearbook of the National Society for the Study of Education;* J. Piaget (1932), *The Moral Judgment of a Child;* J. R. Stott (1975), *Balanced Christianity.*

Hidden Peoples. Groups of people who have little or no knowledge of, or access to, the gospel. According to Winter (1984), the term was first used by Robert Coleman to refer to unevangelized people who are overlooked by the church. Generally, it centers around people from the three major non-Christian religions—Islam, Hinduism, and Buddhism.

The roots of the hidden peoples movement are based in the work of Cameron Townsend, founder of Wycliffe Bible Translators, and Donald McGavran, church growth specialist from the Fuller School of World Mission. From his experience in South America, Townsend set out to translate the Scriptures into the language of the unreached tribal groups of the world, identifying five hundred, then one thousand, and finally over five thousand such groups. About the same time, McGavran, from his work in India, identified homogeneous units of people as the means of planting churches and spreading the gospel. Ralph Winter of the U.S. Center for World Mission is credited with taking these concepts and applying them to missions. He envisioned focusing on unreached or hidden people groups who were similar in culture or social status as a means of fulfilling the Great Commission. The hidden peoples movement shifted the emphasis of missions from the traditional geographical or national fulfillment of the Great Commission to an emphasis on taking the gospel to tribes or people groups. This happens as churches are planted in each unreached people group.

As the movement began to gather momentum in the 1970s, it struggled to find an acceptable definition for hidden peoples or unreached people groups. The Lausanne Committee for World Evangelization and the 1980 Edinburgh Conference wrestled with the problem and suggested similar definitions. The Edinburgh Conference defined hidden peoples as "those cultural and linguistic sub-groups, urban or rural, for whom there is as yet no indigenous community of believing Christians able to evangelize their own people" (Starling, 1981). Missiologists also have struggled with criteria for an unreached people group. The minimum percentage of Christians within an unreached group has ranged from 0 percent to 20 percent. Definition and criteria problems have resulted in a wide variance in the reported numbers of unreached people groups.

Luis Bush, at the 1989 Lausanne II Congress in Manila, was the first to label the 10–40 Window, the geographical area stretching from 10 to 40 degrees north of the equator from the western edge of North Africa and Spain across the Middle East and southern Asia to Japan, as the place where most of the world's unreached people live. He identified them as the Muslim, Hindu, and Buddhist blocs. This has been a valuable point of reference in the hidden or unreached peoples movement.

One of the main benefits of the unreached peoples movement has been to give Christians an awareness of the number of people who do not have a gospel witness within their social/cultural group. Proponents of this movement have noted that 90 percent of the world's missionaries and mission resources are used to take the gospel to the 10 percent of the world's population which is most evangelized. Further, only seven out of every hundred missionaries work in the most unreached areas.

Three projects within the unreached peoples movement have served to educate the church in missions. AD 2000 and Beyond has encouraged the church to see the urgency of the missionary task, the Adopt-A-People Campaign has served to increase prayer and identification with unreached groups, and the Joshua Project 2000 has centered on providing the church with much needed data on people groups around the world.

Efta (1994) called attention to three weaknesses of the hidden peoples movement. First, the Bible divides the world into the saved and unsaved, not reached and unreached. Second, there is the danger of making the unreached people the only priority instead of seeking the leading of the Spirit. Third, there is the danger of calling some groups Christian who do not subscribe to salvation by faith in Christ alone.

A hallmark of the unreached peoples movement is the sense of urgency to complete the task of world evangelism by taking the gospel to every unevangelized people group. This is a model for Christian educators to emulate.

PHILIP BUSTRUM

Bibliography. D. Efta, *Evangelical Missions Quarterly* 30 (1984): 28–32; R. Winter (1984), *Reaching the Unreached: The Old-New Challenge.*

See also CULTURE; ENCULTURATION; HOMOGENEITY; MISSION; MISSIONS EDUCATION

Hierarchy of Needs. Abraham H. Maslow was born in a suburb of Brooklyn, the son of a Jewish businessman. As a youth he had an inward focus and expressed himself through his studies and by working in the family business. He studied behaviorism and experimental psychology at the University of Wisconsin. In 1934 he received his doctorate in primate sexuality and dominance under the direction of Harry Harlow. His early publications were on animal studies. As he read more in psychoanalysis and Gestalt psychology his viewpoint began to change. The psychological subject matter and method he saw as being of most importance was beginning to consider the complexities and uniqueness of the human experience.

Maslow's early career was spent at Brooklyn College, New York. He continued his intellectual growth by contacts with leading psychologists and social scientists of the time. At that point he began to put together his theory of human motivation. His focus on positive elements of human psychology furthered his goal of understanding human potential and its motivation.

These early efforts were communicated in his book, *Motivation and Personality* (1954). This was a rather far-reaching analysis of human motivation in terms of a hierarchy of inherent needs (Arkes and Garske, 1982). He extended these motivation concepts and their implications for well-being and human functioning through his publications over the next decade and a half. He moved to Brandeis University and founded, in 1962, the Association of Humanistic Psychology. This is sometimes identified as the formal beginning of the "third force" in psychology. Maslow was elected president of the American Psychological Association in 1967. He died in 1970.

Maslow's theory is based on a series of multiple motives which are arranged in a hierarchy. All but the top motive in the hierarchy, self-actualization, that is, striving for psychological growth and fulfillment, are organismic needs. This striving is only one of the human needs identified by Maslow. He is clear that the other needs must be attained before behaviors motivated by self-actualization will occur. He gives self-actualization the status of a determinant of behavior. It causes a specific domain of behavior to occur when operative (Årkes and Garske, 1982).

Beginning at the bottom of the hierarchy, the needs are more physiologically innate and stronger. As the hierarchy proceeds upward they become more psychologically learned and weaker. Biological needs such as eating, drinking, and breathing are identified by Maslow as *instinctoid;* they are universal and given and their effects on behavior can be modified. They do not drive behaviors, but persons select from several behaviors that are need-satisfying.

Basic needs share several characteristics: (1) failure to gratify results directly in dysfunction, (2) restoration remedies the dysfunction, (3) continued presence of gratification prevents dysfunction and brings on health, (4) when choice is operative, gratification of one basic need will be preferred over another, and (5) prolonged gratification will reduce demand.

The hierarchy of needs is divided into five classes as follows: physiological needs, safety needs, belongingness and love needs, esteem needs, and self-actualization need. Maslow discusses cognitive needs and aesthetic needs, but he did not include them in his hierarchy (Maslow, 1968). Rather he calls them preconditions of motivation or adjustive tools. He does see aesthetic needs in *some* people (1970). As a lower need is gratified the next up the hierarchy becomes the most dominant source of motivation. This continues up to self-actualization. This sequence is typical but not unchangeable. Two kinds of behavior may be unmotivated. Some needs may become functionally autonomous. An example is eating for reasons other than to satiate hunger, such as social pleasure. Also some behavior is, according to Maslow, expressive. It is merely a reflection of the person.

The strong physiological needs are relatively independent of one another and of other motivations and have some specific physical base. Safety needs, security, stability, dependency, protection, structure, and order, are often manifested in ideologies that make one feel safe. These are pronounced in children. Needs for belongingness and love produce striving for affectionate relationships, both giving and receiving. Esteem needs have two subsets; self-esteem and esteem of others. The first set includes strength, achievement, competence, and so on. The second set includes status, prestige, recognition, attention, and appreciation. Deception would not satisfy these needs. Satisfaction of all these needs leads to the top of the hierarchy, the self-actualization need, to become everything that one is capable of becoming.

The mechanisms of motivation in the Maslow theory are two: One is deficiency motivation (*D-motivation*) which is operative when there is a deficiency in satisfaction, an unfulfilled need. It suggests a need for equilibrium or tension reduction. It is operative for the four lower basic needs. Growth or being motivation (*B-motivation*) operates only at the self-actualization level. Here there is no lack of satisfaction or urgency, but a steady progress toward potential. This might be viewed as metamotivation, beyond the need gratification. One is in a state of being, rather than a state of deprivation. The D-motivated and the B-motivated needs divide the hierarchy into two distinct parts.

Maslow's theory of the hierarchy of needs as the basis of human motivation is complex. It tends to be communicated by others in simplified ways. This is probably necessary. As a result the content of the theory is broken out into a hierarchy that varies in levels. Sometimes it is articulated in the original five, but often in seven with "To Know and Understand" as level five and "Aesthetic Appreciation" as level six. William R. Yount (1996) provides an excellent brief but thorough description of all needs. He also adds "transcendence" as an eighth level.

Transcendence is important in Maslow's scheme of needs. Some interpret it to be an aspect of self-actualization. Maslow also refers to transcendence as being, perfection, or ends of psychology: it conveys the ability to transcend time and space, self, others, and it includes the spiritual, broadly defined. "Transcendence refers to the very highest and most inclusive or holistic levels of human consciousness, behaving and relating, as ends rather than a means, to oneself, to significant others, to human beings in general, to other species, to nature, and to the cosmos" (Maslow, 1971, 279).

There are nontranscending and transcending self-actualizers. The nontranscenders share all the characteristics of self-actualizing, but have less peak experiences and fewer B-cognitions. They are also less spiritual and holistic.

The need-hierarchy theory is a comprehensive, humanistic, developmental theory of motivation. It has implications for counseling and education, but has found much application in the field of organization and management. Its limitations seem to be in the lack of clarity about how the basic needs were selected and ranked and why others were not included. Also, the body of clinical or experimental data supporting it is sparse.

EUGENE S. GIBBS

Bibliography. H. R. Arkes and J. P. Garske (1982), *Psychological Theories of Motivation;* A. H. Maslow (1954), *Motivation and Personality;* idem (1968), *Toward a Psychology of Being;* idem (1970), *Motivation and Personality;* idem (1971), *The Farther Reaches of Human Nature;* R. C. Sprinthall, A. Norman, and S. N. Oja (1998), *Educational Psychology: A Developmental Approach;* W. R. Yount (1996), *Created to Learn.*

See also FIELD THEORY; GESTALT PSYCHOLOGY; HUMANISM, CLASSICAL; MOTIVATION, THEORIES OF

Higher Education, Christian. Colleges and universities in America are unique among the systems of higher education found throughout the world. While maintaining many of the characteristics of their English and German antecedents that contributed so much to their origins, America's colleges and universities nonetheless evolved as unique institutions. From the smallest sectarian college to the largest, most complex public university, the landscape of American higher education is replete with institutions of virtually every size, type, and philosophical orientation imaginable.

Practically every college founded in America from the colonial period to the Civil War was organized, supported, and controlled by religious interests. Since the mid-nineteenth century, many more institutions have been founded by a diverse assortment of churches and religious denominations. Although some relationships between sponsoring religious bodies and their colleges have been minimized or even severed over the years, there are currently more than seven hundred religiously affiliated colleges and universities in the United States.

Religiously affiliated colleges and universities can be found in every sector of American higher education. While virtually all church-related colleges and universities began as liberal arts colleges, more than 60 percent could be legitimately classified as comprehensive institutions today. Liberal arts colleges and comprehensive institutions can be differentiated by the percentage of their graduates receiving undergraduate degrees in the traditional disciplines known as the arts and sciences. In comprehensive institutions, many graduates obtain degrees in professional areas such as business or engineering, and graduate programs are prevalent.

The largest percentage of church-related institutions are Roman Catholic (33 percent), Methodist (16 percent), Baptist (11 percent), and Presbyterian (10 percent). Collectively, these institutions enroll approximately 1.4 million undergraduates, about 10 percent of the total undergraduate enrollment in the United States (Sandin, 1991).

A taxonomy of denominational higher education is instructive in understanding the religious nature of church-related institutions. Sandin's (1990) model identifies four categories of religiously affiliated institutions: pervasively religious, religiously supportive, nominally church-related, and independent with historical religious ties.

In applying this taxonomy to the 720 church-related institutions in the United States, Sandin (1990) found that about 16 percent (117) of the institutions could be considered pervasively religious, 38 percent (273) religiously supportive, 41 percent (293) nominally church-related, and 5 percent (37) historically religious. Denominational groupings with a majority of their institu-

tions in the pervasively religious or religiously supportive categories are Independent (100 percent), Wesleyan/Holiness (100 percent), Lutheran (80 percent), Baptist (76 percent), Pietist (67 percent), and Catholic (54 percent). Denominational groups with a majority of their institutions in the nominally church-related or historically religious categories include Congregational (73 percent), Methodist (72 percent), Presbyterian (71 percent), and Disciples of Christ (61 percent).

DENNIS A. SHERIDAN

Bibliography. R. T. Sandin (1990), *HEPS Profiles of Independent Higher Education,* vol. 1, no. 1; idem (1991), *Autonomy and Faith: Religious Preference in Employment Decisions in Religiously Affiliated Higher Education.*

High/Low Context Groups. *High-context* and *low-context* are terms used to describe differences found in individuals and cultures relative to the degree of sensitivity to their immediate context.

Educators accept the fact that individuals have different ways in which they perceive, learn about their world, and demonstrate what they have learned. Further, it is generally accepted that these differences have been influenced by early socialization experiences. Research has shown a relationship between culture and cognitive styles in that socialization practices of a particular culture have a definite role in determining learning behavior preferences.

Historically, the identification of high/low context groups is often traced back to studies by Witkin and his associates during the 1950s when cognitive style was researched in terms of the field-dependent and field-independent dimension. Field-dependent learners were viewed as high-context (also called *global* learners) and field-independent learners were considered low-context (*analytic* learners). High-context individuals were especially sensitive to the immediate concrete context, whereas low-context individuals were especially interested in issues that are broader and more abstract than the immediate context.

General characteristics have been associated with the two designated types of learners. Low-context learners tend to be more skilled at abstract analytical thought but are considered less sensitive to the feelings of others and are thought to have less developed social skills. They often are more intrinsically motivated and less influenced by social reinforcement. Conversely, high-context learners are very much in tune with their social environment and have highly developed social skills. Accordingly, they are more extrinsically motivated and influenced by their social environment.

Low-context learners find nonsense memorization of little value but will value opportunities for critical thinking. They enjoy working independently and prefer academic courses to the more practical subjects. Frustrations include generalities, hearing opinions expressed as fact, not understanding the purpose of what they are doing, and being asked to move to another task before the present task is completed. They find it hard to work with interruptions, and feel more efficient when tasks or assignments can be categorized or when some sort of system is available. Their strengths are the ability to attend to details, to remember specifics, to show consistency, objectivity, and a sense of justice (Tobias, 1994).

High-context learners value cooperative learning. They enjoy testing what is learned in the real-life setting. Relationships are more important than the task. They often think about many things at one time, find it somewhat difficult to be disciplined to an organizational system, and feel frustrated if they are forced to show the steps used to get an answer. Their strengths are in seeing the big picture, their sense of fairness, their ability to do several things at once, and their high value for relationships (Tobias, 1994).

The learning situation is strengthened by both low-context teachers and learners and high-context teachers and learners. In reality, both contexts bring strengths and challenges to the learning situation. The most effective teaching-learning setting is one in which low-context teachers and learners also strive to balance their preferred style with high-context characteristics. The same is true for high-context teachers and learners as they strive for a balance between their preferred style and low-context characteristics.

LILLIAN J. BRECKENRIDGE

Bibliography. T. Armstrong (1987), *In Their Own Way;* C. Fuller (1994), *Unlocking Your Child's Learning Potential;* H. Gardner (1983), *Frames of Mind: The Theory of Multiple Intelligences;* J. E. Plueddemann (1991), *Christian Education;* C. U. Tobias (1994), *The Way They Learn;* L. V. Williams (1983), *Teaching for the Two-Sided Mind: A Guide to Right Brain/Left Brain Education.*

Hints. *See* Cues.

History of the Christian Education Profession. Christian education has roots that extend to the time of Jesus; but as a distinct profession, it is a twentieth-century development.

Events during the first quarter of the twentieth century were the formative influences for the profession. Faced with moral and ethical problems in society, pressures from World War I, and growing social needs, the nation sought quick answers to bring about an ideal democracy. The means for achieving this national destiny were sought through modern approaches to education. The perception was that education would answer all of society's problems.

In the religious sector, there were new approaches to Bible study, grading plans for organizing the Sunday school, and fresh curriculum materials. There were additional needs related to age groups, and churches had to renovate or construct facilities to accommodate the new programs. Churches, along with society, were quite optimistic about solving problems through the new educational methods and social approaches to ministry. It was out of this milieu that vocational positions developed that evolved into directors and ministers of education.

Early leaders came primarily from the clergy and served as associate ministers responsible for various functions not cared for by the senior pastor. Increasingly, due to the influence of the Sunday school movement, leaders came from a lay orientation with a background in secular education, and served churches as paid Sunday school superintendents or educational workers.

By the mid–1920s, it was clear that the new field was here to stay, but what was not clear was the role that the new workers would fill. Following the early blooming of the profession, work in most churches declined from the depression through World War II. Many churches had to combine positions or release staff persons they could not pay. This resulted in numerous combination positions involving anything from secretarial work to janitorial duties. Indeed, the title *educational secretary* became common, and anyone filling an educational position was expected to do office work and provide other support services such as maintaining bulletin boards and keeping supply closets organized.

There were other forces that contributed to the decline and redirection of the profession. The most important was that church and denominational leaders began to realize that educational workers were not a cure-all for problems in the church and in society. Expectations had been too high and persons filling the positions were inadequately prepared.

Training Opportunities. The earliest professional training for religious educators began in 1903 with the organization of the Hartford (Connecticut) School of Religious Pedagogy, later changed to Hartford School of Religious Education. Although not specifically for ministers, many major universities had begun programs in religious education by 1915, notably Columbia University (New York), University of Chicago, Yale, and Boston College.

The key development for evangelicals was the establishment of a religious education department at Southwestern Baptist Theological Seminary (Ft. Worth, Texas) in 1915, which became the School of Religious Education in 1921. Under the leadership of J. M. Price, this school became the largest producer of religious educators. The school's founding purpose was to supply the increasing demands for church educational directors, elementary educational directors, social and young people's directors, field workers for Sunday school and youth work, teachers of religious education, student secretaries (campus ministers), and kindergarten workers.

The Profession Takes Hold. By 1930, the profession had substantial support in seminaries, educational and publishing agencies of major denominations, and churches. The primary reason for this support was an increasing clarity in the role and function of the educational worker as an organizer and program leader.

Although evangelicals were increasingly supportive, the historical distinctions between clergy and lay continued to plague the profession. The focus at some schools was on laity ministers who would serve primarily in the tradition of the Sunday school movement, as either paid or volunteer workers. The emphasis at others, while not opposed to the lay leader tradition, focused more on clergy who, in the tradition of the pastor-teacher, would teach and equip laypersons who would then provide specific leadership for church programs.

Decline and Recovery. Between 1930 and 1945, the profession declined and there was much soul-searching regarding the proper role of staff ministers. For example, in a history commissioned by the Christian Educators Fellowship (Furnish, 1976), there were about 800 educational ministers in all of the major denominations at the beginning of this period and only about 1,000 educational ministers fifteen years later. By the mid 1960s, however, there were around 11,000, illustrating the tremendous recovery that the churches and the profession experienced following World War II.

By the mid-1960s, vocational preparation had developed significantly with degree programs at the master's level on many campuses. In recognition of the need for a strong theological orientation among educators, schools gradually developed a three-year theology degree with an educational ministry specialty to supplement the older master of religious education degree.

The current trend is to provide competency-based education based on job expectations, and to focus on the distinctly Christian dimension of religious education as reflected in additional areas of study related to faith development and in changes in degree nomenclature from religious education to Christian education.

Evolution of Job Duties. In the lay ministry tradition, job duties have expanded beyond Sunday school and related activities to coordination of all church programs involving reaching, teaching, and developing persons as Christians. In the clergy tradition, duties have expanded beyond general pastoral leadership to include specific functions such as administration of educational programs, ministry to a particular age group, or church administration.

Job duties are clearly delineated in the lay ministry tradition between pastoral duties and staff duties. Educational workers have always been expected to provide direct leadership by promoting, evangelizing, enlisting, organizing, staffing, and training for Sunday school and related programs.

Duties are more functional in the clergy tradition, with pastoral and staff ministers focusing on areas of individual specialization. Ministers of education usually are responsible for a portion of pastoral duties, plus specific responsibility for general administration of educational programs. Ministers of education in this tradition are expected to be the equippers and enablers of lay persons who, in turn, provide direct leadership throughout the church.

These two traditions have blurred as positions in churches have tended to focus on similar Bible study, Christian development, and age group programs, and as seminaries have developed standardized curriculum offerings based on job functions. The profession today includes persons vocationally involved in many facets of Christian teaching and nurture, recognizing that Christian educators serve in all types of church and denominational staff positions, teaching and administrative positions, missions, and related nonprofit Christian institutions.

BRUCE P. POWERS

Bibliography. D. J. Fournish (1976), *DRE/DCE—the History of a Profession;* B. W. Kathan, *Religious Education* vol. 73, no. 5-S (1978); C. M. Maguire (1960), *J. M. Price: The Portrait of a Pioneer;* H. C. Munro (1930), *The Director of Religious Education;* K. R. Stoltz (1931), *Studies in Religious Education.*

History of the Sunday School. Perhaps no other nonprofit institution has had so great an impact on the North American scene as the Sunday school. Impacting the lives of generations, it was the basis of educating the masses in the early colonial period of American life. Today, it continues to have an influence in the lives of millions of church attenders each week.

Old Testament Roots. The Sunday school, as we have come to know it today, traces its roots directly to the late eighteenth century. Certainly there were prototypical programs that we could consider forerunners of the Sunday school movement. When Israel was entering the Promised Land, God reiterated the mandate that parents were responsible for teaching their children God's laws (Deut. 6:1–9). Unfortunately, those parents often abdicated their responsibility, and so the nation of Israel apostatized (Judg. 2:10–11).

Synagogue Schools. Following Israel's return from captivity, the nation's spiritual leaders recognized that families were not teaching their children effectively. And so they established synagogue schools to supplement temple worship.

Five hundred years before the time of Christ, a school system was established to teach children systematically beginning at age five. When a Jewish community numbered ten or more families, a volunteer teacher was assigned to teach a class of up to twenty-five pupils. When the number exceeded twenty-five, an assistant was provided. Obviously, these were not Sunday schools, but they offered instruction similar to what would develop centuries later.

Early Christian Roots. Following the ascension of Christ, New Testament church leaders were concerned about instructing new converts in Christianity. The early church established schools that were amazingly similar to Sunday schools today. They taught biblical truth as well as the application of these principles to life.

In the fourth century, following his conversion to Christianity, Gregory the Illuminator established schools in Armenia to teach new converts. The sixth Council of Constantinople (c. 680) decreed that schools should be established to teach Christianity in small towns, just as they had been in large cities.

Following the bleak educational vista of the Middle Ages, Martin Luther recognized the importance of religious education. Philip Melanchthon, the theologian Reformer who worked closely with Luther, suggested that one day a week be set aside for religious instruction, establishing schools similar to Sunday schools. "After one recitation, the master should explain in a simple and correct manner the Lord's Prayer, the creed, and at another time the Ten Commandments. And he should impress upon the children the essentials, such as fear of God, faith, and good works" (Clyde Manschreck, *Melanchthon: The Quiet Reformer*, 1958, 141).

The concept of schools for religious instruction spread. Recognizing the effectiveness of the Reformers, the Jesuits established schools to provide religious instruction to children. Count Nikolaus von Zinzendorf, leader of the Moravians, in the mid-1700s grouped converts into small bands or societies for the purpose of biblical instruction. Teaching children was a strong emphasis in the groups.

Robert Raikes and the Sunday School of Today. The Sunday school movement, as we know it, began in 1780. There is little question that Robert Raikes of Gloucester, England, is the father of the Sunday school. Sunday school did not grow out of a revival, although it coincided with one. Raikes was not a religious leader, and he did not recruit teachers with formal theological training. In fact, part of the genius of the Sunday school movement is that it was a lay movement, organized and staffed by lay people. And it has impacted lay people more than any other lay movement in history.

Robert Raikes, a newspaper man, was deeply concerned about the working and living conditions of the lower classes, and for twenty-five years he struggled unsuccessfully to address his concerns. He had assumed that vice, crime, immorality, and poverty in the ghettos of Gloucester resulted from ignorance. He therefore established a program to work with prisoners after their release, attempting to educate them out of their poverty and crime. But he finally concluded, after twenty-five frustrating years, that this program had accomplished virtually nothing.

It finally dawned on Raikes that he was waiting too long to address the problem. He decided that children were the logical starting point, and so he established the first Sunday schools for them. His initial attempts had a somewhat different focus from schools that evolved over the next few years. Raikes was concerned about the children of Gloucester who worked six days a week in the mills and factories of the city. Children as young as 8 were forced to work in the pin factories. (Factory owners reasoned that children's tiny fingers could pick up pins more easily than adults' could.)

But Sunday was something else. The "day of rest" was the only day that the children were free. And with parents relaxing or sleeping off a drunken stupor from Saturday night revelry, the children ran wild. "Sunday being a day of rest and the mills and factories closed, the children ran the streets and spent the day in immorality and vice. In the agricultural districts of England, farmers were forced to take special precautions on Sunday to protect their places and crops from the depredation of juvenile offenders" (*The History of Education*, 1948, 617).

These unruly children were prime candidates for "Sunday schools." Raikes's program, which he described as "botanizing in human nature," was not intended as a tool of the local church. Rather he was concerned about rescuing the dregs of society, having concluded that ignorance was their greatest liability. So Raikes envisioned a program that would teach children to read and write, and which also included instruction in morals and manners. While he may not have realized it at the time, the emphasis on morals and manners, relying upon the Bible as his textbook, probably was the secret to his success.

Raikes was able to convince a Mrs. Meredith, who lived on Sooty Alley, to teach the children of chimney sweeps. According to some reports, the children were so obstreperous that they had to be marched to Sunday school with logs tied to their legs to keep them from running off. Although Mrs. Meredith gave up in despair, another woman, a Mrs. King, agreed to allow a school to be taught in her kitchen by May Critchley. This school fared somewhat better and lasted for almost two years.

In his first few schools Raikes hired four women at a weekly wage of one shilling each (about 25 cents) to teach 90 children on Sundays from 10:00 A.M. to noon, and from 1:00 to 5:00 P.M. In order to attend, the children needed only to have clean hands and faces, and their hair combed (probably the only time all week that this occurred). The curriculum for these children, whom Raikes described as "miserable little wretches," consisted of reading and writing, good morals, and religion. There is little question that the four ladies earned their weekly shillings.

After his initial success, Raikes organized one Sunday school after another. Of course not everyone encouraged Raikes in his project. Even friends mocked him, calling him "Bobby Wild Goose and His Ragged Regiment." Raikes actually waited to publicize his endeavors until he was fairly sure of the outcomes. And when he did announce his project, it was a simple paragraph in the November 3, 1783 *Gloucester Journal* (his own newspaper):

> Farmers and other inhabitants of the town and villages complained that they received more injury to their property on the Sabbath than all the week besides. This in a great measure, proceeds from the lawless state of the younger class, who are allowed to run wild on that day, free from every restraint. To remedy this evil, persons duly qualified are employed to instruct those that cannot read, and those who may have learned to read are taught the Catechism and conducted to church. In those parishes where this plan has been adopted, we are assured that the behavior of the children is greatly civilised.

In the first decade of Sunday school many changes occurred. Once Queen Charlotte became a supporter of Sunday school, it became much more fashionable, and the upper class began getting involved. Persons such as John Newton (slave trader-turned-preacher), William Cowper (poet and hymn writer), and theologian Thomas Scott supported Raikes's program. Soon curriculum materials were published and distributed by the Society for the Support and Encouragement of Sunday Schools in the Different Counties of England. This was followed by the London Sunday School Union, which printed guidebooks for teachers and a curriculum for instruction. John Wesley also played a key role in promoting Sunday schools as an integral part of his revival movement, and subsequently as a key element in the growth of Methodism.

Within four years of the 1783 announcement, Raikes claimed an enrollment of 250,000 students. By 1835 (after just 50 years) it was reported that more than 1,500,000 students were attending Sunday schools in England. For many of these, Sunday school was their only educational experience. More than 160,000 lay teachers instructed these children.

The first American Sunday school organization was the First Day or Sabbath School Society, founded in Philadelphia in 1790. The American Sunday School Union played a vital role in expanding the Sunday school to America, even as it was exported to countless nations around the world.

Historians have identified at least five major contributions that the Sunday school movement made to England.

- It triggered revival and supported the revivals of Wesley and Whitefield. One historian has insisted that the Sunday school movement is what spared England the horrors of revolution that France experienced.
- It stimulated persons to recognize the need for free public education for all classes of society.
- It awakened the middle and the upper classes to their responsibility to make meaningful contributions to society, triggering dramatic social reform.
- It stimulated the production and distribution of quality religious literature designed to be understood and used by lay persons.
- It stimulated a desire for adult education. Although children were the original focus, adults soon came to recognize that they too needed schooling.

Unquestionably, Raikes was God's man for his time. When he died in 1811, more than 400,000 were attending his Sunday schools. He was mourned throughout the land as few kings have been mourned. And as Raikes—a man who loved and invested his latter years in children—instructed prior to his death, each child attending his funeral received one shilling and a plum cake.

WESLEY R. WILLIS

Bibliography. A. M. Boylan (1988), *Sunday School: The Formation of an American Institution, 1790;* C. B. Eavey (1964), *History of Christian Education;* K. O. Gangel and W. S. Benson (1983), *Christian Education: Its History and Philosophy;* G. E. Knopf (1979), *The World Sunday School Movement;* B. D. Lockerbie (1994), *A Passion for Learning: The History of Christian Thought on Education;* J. E. Reed and R. Prevost (1993), *A History of Christian Education;* W. R. Willis (1979), *Two Hundred Years and Still Counting.*

See also RAIKES, ROBERT; SUNDAY SCHOOL

HIV. *See* Acquired Immunodeficiency Syndrome.

Holistic Education. Holism is a concept which sees people as whole beings, consisting of integrated, coordinated parts, and recognizes that this whole is greater than the sum of its parts. Humans are composed of six separate parts that form this integrated whole: physical, cognitive, social, affective, moral, and spiritual. Although these are identifiable as separate entities, none can exist apart from the others. How one develops in one area will directly and indirectly affect all of the other five. We do not live a two-storied life: the spiritual which is the higher and most important followed by all the other less important areas. Each area informs, impacts, and helps to determine development in all other domains. Paul observes this in 1 Corinthians 12:12: "The body is a unit, though it is made up of many parts; and though all its parts are many, they form one body." Each part or domain of human development needs to be integrated into a spiritual whole. We can see scripturally how these parts relate in Luke 2:52: "And Jesus grew in wisdom and stature, and in favor with God and men." The boy Jesus developed in all the areas of humanness, just like any other human. These areas were integrated into the whole person that became the mature person, Jesus.

Often Christians think of the spiritual as a totally separate entity, unrelated to the other domains of life. This leads to a bifurcated existence and often opens the door to sin because the spiritual has not been integrated into the whole person. The spiritual becomes so separate from normal life that people actually live a type of schizophrenic life, that is, two separate lives. What they do in their spiritual life is disconnected from their everyday life—office, school, recreation, home. Eating, drinking, reading, watching television and videos, caring for their bodies, feeling emotions, making moral decisions, and taking moral actions are unrelated to their spiritual life. They live disjointed, segregated, noncongruent, and separated lives which are not whole lives. Often churches encourage this perspective by teaching to the mind in hope of achieving a change of beliefs, attitudes, and behaviors. Unfortunately, this approach is nonholistic. It relegates changes of the majority of what it is to be human to only one approach, the cognitive or mental.

When we speak of holistic education, we focus on teaching that helps to integrate all of life into a whole. Scripture speaks definitively and positively about wholeness in learning and teaching. Jesus told us, "Love the Lord your God with all your heart and with all your soul and with all your mind and with all your strength'" (Mark 12:30). The implication is that we are more than spiritual beings. As humans we are physical (strength), cognitive (thinking), feeling (affect), spiritual beings, as well as moral and social beings. One's love for God cannot be contained in just one domain. It permeates all that a person is. The psalmist exclaims that his whole being, not just his heart or soul, will exclaim "Who is like you, O LORD?" (Ps. 35:10) Heart, mind, soul, spirit, and a physical voice proclaim praise to God. Proverbs states that the word of wisdom is

to reside in one's heart; this wisdom is life and health to a person's whole body (Prov. 4:20–23). Thus the Word of God is not merely for one's spirit but for one's whole being. Romans 12:1 states that we are to give our whole bodies to God as living sacrifices. Paul is not talking about just our physical bodies but our whole selves: the physical to be sure, and all the other domains that constitute our being. All of these are to be given to God and to be transformed by God's Spirit. Paul summarizes this teaching in 1 Thessalonians 5:23 by praying that God will sanctify Christians completely, "through and through." He adds, "May your whole spirit, soul and body be kept blameless at the coming of our Lord Jesus Christ." Again, Paul's emphasis is on the totality of the person, even naming "spirit, soul, and body".

Paul states a similar idea in Romans 12:1–2 by exhorting Christians ". . . to be transformed . . . by the renewing of . . ." their minds in order to approve God's perfect will for their lives. Transformation is the living out of God's will for the Christian in every aspect of life. The purpose of teaching is transformation of the person, not merely to inform the mind. Christian teachers are sadly mistaken when they teach only for information and not transformation, too. Scripture was not given merely to inform us about God. Rather, Scripture is that two-edged sword, "sharper than the sharpest knife" (Heb. 4:12 NLT) that insightfully distinguishes between and perceptively analyzes our very innermost thoughts and desires. The reason for this action by the Word of God is ". . . to teach us what is true and to make us realize what is wrong in our lives. It straightens us out and teaches us to do what is right" (2 Tim. 3:16 NLT). In other words, Scripture and the human teacher who is directed by the Holy Spirit do not merely inform us about God; Scripture also stimulates us to be different people in the areas of life, love, faith, and purity (1 Tim. 4:12–13).

In order for this transformation to occur, teachers must aim at delivering more than just biblical information and truth in the hope that these will somehow catch the attention of learners. Teachers must purposefully structure their lessons to involve the learners interactively, involving them cognitively, affectively, and behaviorally so that they will be different people (existentially). Teachers use these four areas—cognitive, affective, behavioral, and existential—as the means for structuring their lessons so that the whole person is transformed and not merely informed.

The way to reach the whole person is to engage the whole person. This engagement occurs when teachers teach to the whole person in the teaching-learning process. Teaching to the whole person so that the whole person is transformed means that teachers do not deliver information alone. Nor do they merely tell. Nor do they merely reinforce memorization of Scripture, as wonderful as Scripture is. Stories, memorized Scripture, and information are insufficient to provide for transformation. By merely teaching to the cognitive, the remainder of the person is ignored.

Transformation occurs in the whole person, not merely in the mind or feelings. Teaching that does not result in the reformation of the whole person is truncated teaching, faring no better than traditional education that requires memorization of data to pass teachers' tests in order to get promoted.

Teaching holistically means that Christian educators work with the Holy Spirit to reach the whole person. Teachers must focus their lesson preparation on teaching not only to the cognitive domain but also to the other five domains of humanness. This is done by asking for affective responses, discussing how a particular biblical truth could and/or should affect one's life, asking for a commitment to make behavioral changes in one's life based on the knowledge received from the biblical instruction, and encouraging each other in making the changes. Holistic education begins with information but ends only when the whole person has been transformed in areas that are germane to each learner.

If we do not teach holistically, people will become well educated, biblically literate, but immature Christians who cannot conduct their daily lives in an integrated, holistic manner. They instead live like two different people, seldom allowing the gospel to permeate their everyday life. By teaching holistically a teacher teaches the whole person—body, mind, soul, and spirit—in the physical, cognitive, social, affective, moral, as well as spiritual domains.

JOHN M. DETTONI

Holy Spirit. Jesus introduces us to the Holy Spirit as teacher in John 14:26—"But the Counselor, the Holy Spirit, whom the Father will send in my name, will teach you all things and will remind you of everything I have said to you." After Pentecost, when the Holy Spirit was historically given to the church, his role became central in teaching the disciples and reminding them of all the things that Jesus taught them while he was on earth. His ministry actually expanded the ministry of Jesus by making Jesus' Spirit accessible to any of his disciples willing to be filled with his presence and power. This is at least in part what Jesus meant when he said that it was to the disciples' advantage that he go to be with his Father (John 16:17). Jesus goes on in this same passage to say that when "the Spirit of truth comes, he will guide you into all truth. He will not speak on his own; he will speak only what he hears, and

he will tell you what is to come. He will bring glory to me by taking from what is mine and making it known to you" (John 16:13–14).

The Holy Spirit is the catalyst in the teaching-learning process in Christian education. His work and ministry provide the spiritual distinctive that separates Christian education from education in general. The Holy Spirit as teacher is not limited by time or space. His role as teacher permeates every aspect of the teaching-learning process. He is the agent who guides the teacher and learner into all truth. The Holy Spirit is ultimately responsible for all learning, leading people to know and apply truth. He ministers primarily through five elements of the teaching-learning process—the teacher, the learner, the curriculum, the participants, and the environment—to enable persons to mature in Christ.

The first avenue through which the Holy Spirit works is the teacher. The spiritual gift of teaching is included in each of the lists of spiritual gifts in the New Testament (Rom. 12:3–8; 1 Cor. 12:27–31; Eph. 4:7–13; 1 Peter 4:10–11). In Ephesians 4:11, the gift of teaching is closely related to the gift of pastoring. The Holy Spirit uses gifted teachers/pastors to prepare, equip, and train believers to serve one another within the body of Christ. Spiritually gifted teachers seem to have a holistic ministry in Scripture, teaching God's Word in a way that changes both lives and communities. "The spiritually gifted teacher helps the Spirit-directed learner to understand and apply the Word of God in the context of the community of other spiritually gifted Christians" (Plueddemann, 1989, 308). Such a teacher must possess not only a thorough knowledge of God's Word but also an ability to communicate it to people in such a way as to equip them to apply the Word within their lives and their relationships. The Holy Spirit uses the spiritually sensitive teacher to orchestrate every aspect of the learning experience toward the Spirit's goals. As Plueddemann states, the gift of teaching is the "art of compelling interaction" between the various elements within the teaching-learning environment (308).

The second area of the Holy Spirit's ministry related to the teaching-learning process is that of the learner. No matter how gifted a teacher may be, learning and growth toward Christ-likeness will not take place unless the Holy Spirit is free to work within the heart of the learner. According to Roy Zuck in his classic study on the work of the Holy Spirit in teaching, the Spirit of God is actively involved in the learner's heart in three ways: conviction, indwelling, and illumination (Zuck, 1972, 45–52). When a learner's heart is open to God, the Holy Spirit instigates the conviction of sin (John 16:8). Through the indwelling of the Holy Spirit a believer may learn the things of God, even without a teacher present, as needs arise (1 John 2:27). Although this text may be misinterpreted to insinuate that believers have no need for human teachers because of the Holy Spirit's direct teaching ministry, this is not the intent of the text. This text merely affirms the fact that even believers who are walking in the Spirit have to be careful not to be seduced into following false teachers who violate the Word of God. Since the purpose of the Holy Spirit is to glorify Jesus Christ, and Jesus Christ is the incarnate Word, the Spirit's voice cannot contradict the Word of God (John 1:1; 16:14–15).

Indwelt by the Holy Spirit, believers are taught through the illumination of the Holy Spirit. In Ephesians 1:18, Paul prays concerning the believers "that the eyes of [their] heart may be enlightened" so that they may know on an experiential level the blessings of Christ. This illumination or enlightenment is "the supernatural work of the spirit whereby he enables man to apprehend the already revealed truth of God" (Zuck, 1972, 52).

This revealed truth of God (Scripture) is the third element in the teaching-learning process. In a broader sense, the curriculum is the larger rubric for which Scriptures play the most critical role. Because of its objective nature, Scripture provides the foundation for the work of the Holy Spirit. Second Timothy 3:16–17 states that "All Scripture is God-breathed and is useful for teaching, rebuking, correcting and training in righteousness, so that the man of God may be thoroughly equipped for every good work." Inspiration relates to this initial act of God's sharing his truth in the original writings of Scripture. This objective revelation of God "never had its origin in the will of man, but men spoke from God as they were carried along by the Holy Spirit" (2 Peter 1:21). Because Scripture is directly inspired by God, it must be used as the final test of truth, by which believers distinguish truth from error. In using the term "sword of the Spirit" to refer to God's Word (Eph. 6:17), Paul emphasizes the Holy Spirit's aggressive use of the Word in accomplishing God's purposes. Growth takes place as both teacher and learner interact with and obey the Word of God. Scripture serves as the foundation for all curriculum issues.

The fourth element of the teaching-learning process that the Holy Spirit works through is the interaction between the participants in the learning situation. The nature of the church as the "body of Christ" suggests that it grows through its ability to learn and work together (Eph. 4:11–16). A major part of the Holy Spirit's teaching ministry relates to the interpersonal relationships within the church and other learning environments. An interesting phrase, "with all the saints," found in verse 18 of Paul's prayer in Ephesians 3 makes this point very clear. This phrase is crucial to understanding Paul's prayer, that the believers may be able to comprehend "with all the saints . . . how wide and long and high and deep is the love of Christ, and to know this love that surpasses knowledge" (Eph. 3:18–19). Interaction among all the saints is critical to the Ephesians' comprehension of both the power of the Holy Spirit and the love of Christ.

The fifth dimension of the Holy Spirit's work in the teaching-learning process is the environment. Environmental or contextual factors in Christian education may include such things as seating arrangement, lighting, temperature, visuals, room location or size, colors, distractions, or smells. While some of these elements may seem too "common" to relate to the supernatural work of the Holy Spirit, we must remember that God has used such physical elements to set the environment for spiritual learning throughout history. Learning experiences such as Moses by the burning bush, Jews in the tabernacle or the temple, Jesus and his disciples at the Sea of Galilee, the early disciples in the upper room, Paul and Silas in the jail at Philippi, or Paul and the philosophers in the midst of the Areopagus illustrate the importance of the environment related to the learning of truth. Both the teacher and the learner cooperate with the Holy Spirit by strategically designing the physical and aesthetic aspects of a learning environment to allow the Holy Spirit freedom to accomplish his purposes.

Thus the Holy Spirit works through each of these five elements of the teaching-learning process. He is the catalyst for learning truth, no matter where it is found. Although we may never totally understand the complexity of his role in the teaching-learning process, we must continue to depend on his wisdom and power to teach and learn God's truth.

GARY C. NEWTON

Bibliography. C. F. Dickeson (1991), *Christian Education; Foundations for the Future*, pp. 121–35; R. Habermas and K. Issler (1992), *Teaching for Reconciliation;* R. Pazmiño (1988), *Foundational Issues in Christian Education: An Introduction in Evangelical Perspective;* J. E. Pleuddemann, *Education That Is Christian*, pp. 105–10; J. Wilhoit (1986), *Christian Education and the Search for Meaning;* W. Yount (1996), *Created to Learn: A Christian Teacher's Introduction to Educational Psychology;* R. B. Zuck (1972), *Spiritual Power in Your Teaching.*

See also LESSON PLAN; INSTRUCTIONAL THEORY; CONTEXT IN TEACHING CHRISTIAN EDUCATION; CURRICULUM

Home Bible Studies/Groups. *See* Adult Christian Education.

Home Church. *See* House Church.

Home Education. *See* Discipline; Family Life Education.

Home Fellowships. *See* Cell Church; House Church.

Home School Movement. The education of children conducted primarily in the home by one or both parents has increased over the past decades. This alternative to parochial, private, and public schooling provides an important parental option, as do charter schools, school-choice programs, and vouchers. Home schooling is primarily practiced with younger children. As students become older, they sometimes transfer to formal schools as the academic demands move beyond the resources and abilities present in the home. Estimates place 1.5 million students involved in home schooling at the end of the 1990s in the United States.

Reasons for Home Schooling. People choose to home school for a variety of reasons. These include: (1) maintaining family closeness and allowing for additional bonding and nurturing time; (2) offering individualized learning and addressing the special needs of gifted, disabled, or emotionally challenged children; (3) providing a safe haven from the alcohol, drugs, negative peer pressure, sex, and violence associated with public schools; and (4) addressing content from particular pedagogical, philosophical, political, or religious perspectives. Home schooling is sometimes selected over other alternatives due to financial reasons or geographical considerations.

Parental views on public school alternatives involve concerns about low academic standards and poor teaching. Others see government schools as having a restrictive environment with a politically repressive agenda. A major consideration for Christian parents has been the way religious issues are addressed in a school's curriculum. They feel that certain important values foundational to learning and life are missing. Some Christian beliefs are openly ridiculed in the classroom and hostile assumptions are substituted. Schooling at home provides parents opportunities to instill the unique perspectives of the Christian worldview throughout a child's learning program. Some who oppose home schooling charge parents with being reactionary, separatist, or racist.

Biblical Basis for Home Schooling. The parental responsibility to educate children can be traced back to Old Testament times (see Deut. 6:7). The Book of Proverbs includes examples of a father's teachings to a son (1:8–9). Many in the Christian community choose to practice home schooling as a means of fulfilling their parental task of faithfully raising their children (see Eph. 6:4). Parents who choose this educational option require a special motivation, endurance, and ability. For many it is an economic hardship since it usually requires one parent to remain at home.

Historical Development of Home Schooling. In the United States, home schooling has its roots in the colonial period. Colonists primarily educated their children at home and through community apprenticeships. In Massachusetts during the 1640s, authorities set guidelines for parents to follow in teaching their children. As a result, some communities organized town schools to assist in meeting these requirements. The colony later mandated that schools be established in every community, but attendance remained voluntary. Later, during the 1800s, the idea of a common school for all American citizens was developed and attendance became compulsory. Those who oppose these required government schools on various grounds have sometimes opted for home education.

Many famous Americans have been schooled at home, including George Washington, Abraham Lincoln, Booker T. Washington, Thomas Edison, and Florence Nightingale.

Since 1993, all 50 states allow for home schooling and most have home school coordinators. Some states set standards for home schooling and require annual testing; others only specify material to be covered in a given period. Most states do not specify any teaching qualifications for parents.

Critique of Home Schooling. Critics of home schooling argue that students who are not in a traditional school setting will not adequately develop socially. They believe that the limited involvement home schoolers have with other children will negatively affect their ability to interact successfully with others in the future.

Supporters of home schooling point out that healthy socialization can be achieved in other ways. Students interact with other home schoolers involved in home school cooperatives. They play with other children in assorted dance, music, and sports activities. A variety of groups such as scouts, 4-H, YMCA, and camps provide numerous relational opportunities. Community-based service learning projects get students involved with people of various ages. Older students employed outside the home become familiar with the social demands of a work setting. Many home schoolers are actively involved in the life of a local church. Current research indicates that most home schoolers are comparable socially to conventionally schooled students.

Those opposed to home schooling also claim that it is academically inferior and assert that untrained parents are unable to instruct as well as professional teachers. Defenders of home schooling emphasize the value of personalized instruction and point to studies which indicate that home schoolers are equally or better prepared academically than their public school counterparts regardless of a parent's educational background or certification. Many home school graduates are accepted to college and attend distinguished universities.

Resources Available for Home Schooling. A wide variety of educational curricula and resource materials has been produced specifically for the home school market. Area educational fairs targeting this group feature training seminars and related material sales. Parents sometimes band together in home school cooperatives to share resources and teaching responsibilities. In some communities, public schools actually provide home schoolers with access to certain facilities and materials. Further support and related information is available through state home school organizations and a growing number of websites. Two national organizations providing important support include the Home School Legal Defense Association and the National Home Education Research Institute. A search of the Internet will also reveal countless resources for the home school parent.

ROGER WHITE

Bibliography. S. Card and M. Card (1997), *The Homeschool Journey;* L. Dobson, ed. (1998), *The Homeschooling Book of Answers: The 88 Most Important Questions Answered by Homeschooling's Most Respected Voices;* M. P. Farris (1997), *The Future of Home Schooling: A New Direction for Christian Home Education;* C. J. Klicka and C. Klicka (1994), *The Right Choice: The Incredible Failure of Public Education and the Rising Hope of Home Schooling;* B. D. Ray (1997), *Strengths of Their Own—Home Schoolers across America: Academic Achievement, Family Characteristics, and Longitudinal Traits;* J. W. Whitehead and A. I. Crow (1994), *Home Education: Rights and Reasons.*

Homogeneity. Similarity of social, ethnic, or economic background in a population group. Church growth experts have used this concept as a descriptive statement that people are best evangelized into churches with similar social and cultural backgrounds (Hunter, 1990). Within education the term describes an implicit teacher expectation that all student learning will naturally match the dominant academic culture, which actually may contain biases in learning style, ethnic interpretation, and social influence (Bowers and Flinders, 1990).

Christian educators use the term to describe characteristics of a given congregation while also acknowledging the potential diversity of learning styles and values that may still be located within the group. The level of homogeneity within a population may lend to the stability of the group. Accurately assessing homogeneity will also assist the teacher in assessing student culture, readiness for learning, and the formative socialization power of the group.

DEAN BLEVINS

Bibliography. C. A. Bowers and D. J. Flinders (1990), *Responsive Teaching: An Ecological Approach to Classroom Patterns of Language, Culture and Thought;* K. R. Hunter, *Global Church Growth* (January–March 1990).

See also CHURCH GROWTH; ETHNIC IMPLICATIONS OF CHRISTIAN EDUCATION; ETHNOCENTRICITY; HETEROGENEITY; LAW OF READINESS

Homosexuality. Sesame Street's Bert and Ernie hold a same sex-wedding. During a demonstration a man raises a placard reading "My boyfriend and I have traditional values." To respond well in such situations, churches must understand that the landscape surrounding homosexuality is shifting. Due to the spread of AIDS and the gay agenda, people have increased awareness of same-sex preference. An acceptance of homosexuality as an alternative lifestyle is becoming more common among youth. Many adolescents know at least one friend who is openly gay. Legal battles are intensifying. Challenges across the country are occurring over same-sex marriage, spousal benefits (insurance, visitation rights), custody, and adoption. Increased vocalization is creating more polarization. Conservative Christians who espouse a traditional view, as opposed to those who maintain that same-sex preference is God-given, are becoming more confrontive, aggressive, and political in pushing their agenda. The latter group is doing a particularly good job of convincing people in the neutral middle ground that homosexuality is of God. In response to these movements an increasing number of churches are now "mainstreaming"—helping homosexuals who are seeking change.

Homosexuality is not widespread. A figure often quoted since the methodologically flawed Kinsey Report is that 10 percent of the population is homosexual. But the landmark study by researchers at the University of Chicago, *Sex in America: A Definitive Study* (1994), found that only 1.4 percent of women and 2.8 percent of men identified themselves in this way. While a larger percentage reported having had homosexual experiences in their lifetime, only this minute percentage described themselves as gay.

Several principles are important when ministering to those with a same-sex preference. (1) Stress biblical authority. Teach the biblical worldview on sexuality in general, and based on that, the Bible's stance on homosexuality. Emphasize reading of the text—not reading between the lines (Lev. 20:13; Rom. 1:22–27; 1 Cor. 7:2–7). (2) Wrap the message in a blanket of love, acceptance, and encouragment. Homosexuality is one sin among many. In *Counseling and Homosexuality* (1988), Wilson reminds us that the capacity for same-sex love is essentially the love-need of the child for the parent. Often there is great agony and hurt. Both the homosexual and his or her family members need caregiving and pastoral concern. Providing nonsexual friendships with persons of the same sex is highly important. (3) Church education must be two-pronged. First, internal social stigmas must be accurately addressed. These include prejudice, shock, and homophobia. They serve as a militant force against positive ministry with homosexuals. Second, Christians need to be educated about the pain that exists in the homosexual lifestyle: haunting loneliness, anguish, jealousy, anger, and hatred are often aggravated by a childhood conversion and an innate awareness that their actions conflict with God's will. (4) Give realistic hope. Homosexuals are often without hope. Through open discussion about their struggles, genuine love, support, and prayer, change can occur. Some church ministries are seeing 40 percent of those seeking change move into full heterosexuality, with another 40 percent achieving consistent celibacy.

Current resources for churches serving the homosexual community are Bergner's *Setting Love in Order,* Schmidt's *Straight and Narrow?,* and Riley and Sargent's *Unwanted Harvest.* Redemptive and recovery programs include One by One and Transforming Congregations, both from the Presbyterian Church (USA). Exodus International is a fine organization providing information on ex-gay ministries worldwide.

The true orientation of Christians is not what we are by constitution, but what we are by choice and God's power. The church that takes its mission seriously will seek out those persons who may be the most needy and will encourage them in the things of God.

JAMES A. DAVIES

Bibliography. M. Bergner (1995), *Setting Love in Order;* B. Sargent and M. Riley (1995), *Unwanted Harvest;* T. E. Schmidt (1995), *Straight and Narrow; One by One,* Presbyterian Church (USA); *Transforming Congregations,* Presbyterian Church (USA); *Exodus International.*

Horne, Herman Harrell (1874–1946). Horne was born in 1874 in Clayton, North Carolina. His early education included the local public school and Davis Military Academy in Winston-Salem. He graduated from the University of North Carolina with A.B. and A.M. degrees in 1895. Continuing his graduate work at Harvard, he graduated with an S.M. degree in 1897 and a Ph.D. degree in 1899. He also studied at the University of Berlin.

His first teaching assignment came as an instructor in French at the University of North Carolina. His next appointment came at Dartmouth College, where he taught philosophy and achieved the rank of professor. In 1909 he became professor of philosophy at the school of pedagogy at New York University. In 1922 the school of pedagogy was renamed the school of education. Horne served there as professor and chairman of the Departments of Educational Philosophy and the History of Education. He also helped to establish the Department of Religious Education. He died in 1946.

Horne was an idealist educational philosopher. He was a prolific writer in the fields of educational philosophy, psychology, pedagogy, and religious education. His philosophy stemmed from a firm belief in the immortality of the soul and the ideal of Jesus as the incarnation of a model toward which each person should strive.

He authored twenty-six books and numerous articles. He was the first professor in the United States to deliver a classroom lecture on the radio in 1923. During his productive career, Horne received four honorary degrees. He was a fellow of the American Association for the Advancement of Science and the Society for the Advancement of Education.

While John Dewey was expounding his pragmatic philosophy of education at Columbia University on Morningside Heights, Horne was teaching in the same city at Washington Square. Horne was providing a significant idealist alternative to Dewey. Though never caustic in his opposition to Dewey, Horne responded in the framework of one who was dedicated to Christ. Horne believed that the purpose of education would lead a person toward virtue as one created in the image of God. This is in stark contrast to Dewey's idea of education as "the reconstruction of experience." Dewey focused upon the scientific method; Horne believed that content, particularly moral and Christian content, needed to be transmitted to the student. While Dewey denied God, Horne believed that God was the primary educator.

Horne's primary method of teaching was Socratic. He believed that the teacher must know well both the subject and the student. The teacher must awaken in the student the desire to learn and must be a true friend to the student.

EDWARD A. BUCHANAN

Bibliography. H. H. Horne (1910), *Idealism in Education.*

See also DEWEY, JOHN; IDEALISM; INTERACTIVE LEARNING; SOCRATIC METHOD

House Church. Over the past thirty years, house churches have emerged as a vital form of small group life both within and alongside congregations. House churches have some similarities with small groups that meet for prayer, study, and fellowship. They also have some similarities with cell groups in newer style congregations who sometimes celebrate the Lord's Supper together and are strongly oriented to people outside the group, though mostly only with a view to evangelism. But they tend to differ from such groups in several basic respects:

- They regard themselves not just as part of the church but as church—as "little churches within the larger church" if they exist within a congregation, or as a small church that meets as a larger group with other small churches if they are part of an independent cluster of house churches.

- They include children and teenagers as well as adults, and seek to include them as much as possible in what they do. House churches usually meet each week for several hours, and include weekly singing, praying, learning, having a meal, sharing, playing, and planning.
- They view their common meal as the Lord's Supper. In this they not only remember Christ's death and resurrection but anticipate God's coming kingdom and, during the meal, conscious of the Spirit's presence, talk about and enter into each other's lives and activities.
- Leadership is vested in the whole group, so that all basic decisions are made by consensus, and whoever is contributing helpfully at the time is regarded as leading the meeting. Yet within the group, several people will always emerge who have more maturity and experience, as well as a capacity to build and maintain community.
- There is a strong concern to integrate what happens in the house church with people's responsibilities outside the group in their families, workplaces, neighborhoods, cities, and wider world. The group assists each of its members to discern their calling and ministry, and then supports them, prays for and with them, and holds them accountable to it.
- The group encourages all its members to develop a way of life, both communally and individually, that reflects the values of the kingdom. Among other things, this affects issues of time, money, mobility, parenting, and lifestyle.

House churches provide a context in which nonformal, holistic Christian education takes place. For example, children learn how to relate to other children through play and common activities, as well as with adults, sometimes in a mentoring relationship. Teenagers are given a range of Christian role models to choose from and have the opportunity to hear adults discussing their doubts and certainties, hopes and disappointments, and how faith relates to their everyday lives. Married couples observe the ways other married couples communicate, discipline their children, engage in spiritual disciplines, and undertake ministry. Younger Christians see and experience at close range how leadership is exercised and nurtured, and are given the opportunity to take on increasing responsibility in the group as they grow older.

Since, as mentioned, everyone helps to make major decisions that affect the life of the group, all learn what is involved in discerning God's will and taking responsibility. Everyone also contributes to the learning that goes on in the group—informally through what they model or say in conversation; through facilitating a Bible study, coordinating discussion of a book, or interpreting Scripture; through leading a guided meditation, giving testimony, articulating their experience, or sharing a parable—and in this way develops the gifts given them by the Spirit. As, from time to time, each member assists others in practical ways to deal with difficult personal issues or external situations, all develop skills in learning the art of love as well as in counseling and pastoring others.

Given all these advantages, it is not surprising that house churches are growing throughout the world. This is also partly because they are not so much a new strategy for deepening or extending the church as they are a rediscovery of an old practice that goes back to New Testament times. Meeting together in this way was at the center of early church life, and tends to resurface whenever there is a genuine desire for renewal in the church or for a profound impact on the world around it.

ROBERT BANKS

Bibliography. R. Banks (1994), *Paul's Idea of Community;* R. and J. Banks (1997), *The Church Comes Home: Bringing Community and Mission through Home Churches;* L. Barrett (1986), *Building the House Church;* M. A. Cowan and B. J. Lee (1997), *Conversation, Risk and Conversion: The Inner & Public Life of Small Christian Communities;* C. Smith (1992), *Going to the Root: Nine Strategies for Church Renewal.*

Human Development. *See* Adult Life Cycle.

Humanism, Christian. The influx of humanistic methodology into the American educational system has given rise to considerable tension within the Christian community in recent years. Schools serve the people of this country by educating its students in the basic disciplines of math, science, literature, and the arts. However, schools play a much larger part than the mere transmission of cognitive information. In a very real sense they are also involved, whether by design or not, in the teaching of values, morals, ethics, and social standards of our society. As Blake (1986) writes, "In the most fundamental sense, schools exist to transmit the values of society. To do this teachers must cultivate certain attitudes and values . . . Therefore, to be effective, the teacher must make a moral commitment that goes beyond the simple formulation of a professional ethic" (100).

The question, however, is who determines such values and attitudes and on what basis will such ideas be formulated? For the past four decades there has been a heavy emphasis upon humanistic models of education in our public classrooms. This educational trend has influenced many of our church schools as well, thus causing a significant debate regarding its inherent good or evil. An intelligent response requires a close look into the definition, historical development, and current practices of humanistic educational methods employed in America today.

As defined by Corliss Lamont (1980), one of America's leading humanists, "Humanism is a philosophy, the guiding principle of which is concentration on the welfare, progress, and happiness of all humanity in this one and only life" (vii). Taken by definition alone, the uninformed could quickly reach the conclusion that such a philosophy is inconsistent with Biblical teaching. This is not the definition espoused by the individual who created humanism but rather a definition given by one who has advocated, in this author's opinion, the misuse of such an educational philosophy.

Origins of Humanistic Thought. The historical development of contemporary humanism can be traced back to Democritus and Aristotle of ancient Greece (Lamont, 1982, xl). "Its tie to Greek culture resulted in pagan features such as the glorification of humankind" (Dodgen, 1986, 195). "The Greek set about humanizing everything. He humanized God. He humanized nature. He humanized his daily life. So great-minded men measured all things and gave a firm and noble body of standards to the human life which came after them" (King, 1931, 20).

In 146 B.C. the Romans conquered Greece, and the Greek teachers and the entire educational system were quickly absorbed into the Roman Empire. In fact, it is generally concluded that many of the educational and philosophical advances that were made at that time in the Roman Empire were actually made by enslaved Greeks (Johnson, et al. 1969, 204). One such Roman educator was Lucretius, who continued Aristotle's humanistic philosophies (Lamont, 1982, xl). In its heyday humanism drew heavily upon the Stoicism of Cicero and the sophist approach of Quintilian. These two ancient Roman humanists did much to solidify and build upon early Greek humanistic thought (Gueber, 1961, 69–70).

Rome was destroyed by Alaric in A.D. 410 and with its destruction came the end of Greek and Roman influence for many hundreds of years. It was not until the fall of Constantinople in 1453 that Greece returned to Western Europe as a significant factor in educational thought. At that time that there was a resurgence in Greek teachers, manuscripts, and spirit. Students returned to the classics—especially those produced in fifth and fourth century B.C. Athens—to find a spirit and a code of understanding. These individuals were known as humanists (King, 1931, 22–23).

A change took place when Western civilization came out of the Middle Ages. In 1459 the popular writer Battista Guarino summarized his treatise on this new form of educational curriculum by stating, "Learning and training in Virtue are peculiar to man: therefore our forefathers called them Humanitas, the pursuits, the activities, proper to mankind. And no branch of knowledge embraces so wide a range of subjects as that learning which I have now attempted to describe" (Monroe, 1905, 370).

During the period of the Renaissance, several scholars were significant in their quest for humanistic models of education. One such leading educator was Desiderius Erasmus (1466–1536). Erasmus believed that man was the center of the universe. He had a notable faith in God and a disdain for human forms of government since he believed them to be hypocritical in nature. Thus, the aim of education for Erasmus was that the student learn to develop independent judgment (Mayer, 1966, 183).

Erasmus is referred to as the "prince of humanists." The Greek New Testament was to him a thing to be conjured. Erasmus was a unique individual because of his ability to integrate humanistic philosophy with the Christian faith. However, this integration did not have a lasting influence on humanism (King, 1931, 23). He was acclaimed as a scholar for his emphasis upon subjects such as rhetoric, poetry, moral philosophy and history, and the study of Greek and Roman classics. This group of disciplines were termed the *humanities* and those who espoused their virtues were called humanists (Pratte, 1971, 40).

Humanistic educational theory at this period of time was based upon a foundational study in Greek and Latin literature aimed at producing "the Renaissance man." This person was a cultivated gentleman, a *homo universalis*. Thus humanistic education denoted a specific preference for classical values, and challenged the student to rediscover himself as a distinctly free being (Pratte, 1971, 41).

It is difficult to distinguish between the Renaissance and the Reformation movements in terms of years and geographical setting. In the same way it is difficult to draw a distinction between religious educators and humanistic educators during this period of educational history. "In fact, it was a consequence of the character of the later Renaissance movement that all the religious leaders seized upon education as the chief instrument for bringing about the reforms which they desired. On the Protestant side, the great leaders are naturally Luther and Melanchthon" (Monroe, 1905, 409).

Martin Luther (1483–1546) is known as the father of the Reformation because of his stand on individualized faith, vernacular education of the masses, and his opposition to the hypocritical church system then in force. He urged the study of the ancient languages in order to achieve a sincere piety that would lead to the establishment of a Christian community (Gruber, 1961, 77–78). Although not an educator *per se*, he heavily influenced the educational system of his day. Because most education at that time was controlled by the Catholic church, Luther's condemnation of the church brought about a virtual closing of many great schools. Although it would be inaccurate to label Luther as a Reformation humanist, as some so espouse, no one can deny the significant role he played in the development of humanism by preparing the way for Philip Melanchthon (1479–1560) as the "Preceptor of Germany," for he was to Germany in educational reform what Luther was in religious reform.

Melanchthon was a scholar by anyone's definition. At the age of sixteen he wrote the Greek grammar which became the universal text for the German schools. His Latin grammar, written a few years later, likewise achieved a similar reputation. His textbooks on dialectic theology, rhetoric, ethics, physics, and history were seen as the foundational books of study for any learned man. "Through his influence the university was soon remodeled along humanistic and Protestant lines" (King, 1905, 419).

By the close of the sixteenth century, western Europe had been irrevocably changed. The past two hundred years had been monumental in its religious, cultural, social, and educational reforms. Religion and education had become inseparably bound as the ideals of one depended on the methods of the other. "The Protestant Reformation was in large measure dedicated to showing the greatest concern for restoring Christianity to its original and unsullied state. In effect, this type of humanism sent men in search of original Greek and Hebrew forms of the Scripture to determine which church teachings truly had been given to man through revelation and which had been admitted in error" (Pratte, 1971, 43).

Thus, in education, Protestantism demonstrated humanist influences by creating an atmosphere that was conducive to academic adventure, challenge, and scholarship. Its emphasis upon Greek and Hebrew, together with the Latin of its day, played a large part in opening up the works of Plato, Aristotle, and Cicero to eager minds. To this degree, the Reformation played a key role as a transition from the stagnated Middle Ages to the Modern period.

During the period of the Enlightenment, there were a number of significant humanist educators. Among such notables were Sir Francis Bacon (1561–1626), Thomas Hobbes (1588–1679), René Descartes (1596–1650), Baruch Spinoza (1632–1677), François Voltaire (1694–1778), David Hume (1711–1776), and Jean-Jacques Rousseau (1712–1778). Each played a role in furthering humanistic principles of education. Perhaps one of the most significant was the Swiss-French moral philosopher Jean-Jacques Rousseau. Pestalozzi, Froebel, and Dewey were to a large degree products of his thinking. It is not an exaggeration to say that our contemporary educational system is to a large degree indebted to this man.

John Dewey (1859–1952) is seen as the Father of Progressive Education. He was an astute man with a highly trained mind. He served for ten years as the chairman of the Department of Philosophy, Psychology, and Pedagogy at the University of Chicago (Barlow, 1985, 326). However, most of his career as a philosopher was spent at Columbia University.

At the heart of Dewey's belief system was the notion that humans are free agents in a world still in the making. They must, therefore, be free to make decisions, and their wants and desires must count ultimately in determining the nature of the universe (Gruber, 1961, 197). Dewey advocated an educational system that posited a child-centered curriculum (Gangel, 1983, 301). School was seen as a miniature society in which democracy must prevail. This allows for freedom on the part of the learner, but not uncontrolled freedom. Dewey advocated that the student play an active part in his or her own learning process. Dewey comments on the importance of this point when he states, "Freedom and restriction, the negative side, is to be prized only as a means to a freedom which is power: power to frame purposes, to judge wisely, to evaluate desires by the consequences which will result from acting upon them; power to select and order means to carry those ends into operation" (Dewey, 1938, 74).

Carl Rogers has also become a notable contemporary humanist. He asserted that teaching is a vastly overrated function, because the emphasis should rather be on the process of learning. His contribution to educational humanism can best be summarized as follows: (1) teachers must enter the teaching-learning relationship without fear, front, or facade. They must be real persons by being their real selves; (2) learning is facilitated when the pupil is prized, valued, and respected by the teacher who can care without being possessive; (3) empathic understanding, an awareness of how the pupil is feeling about the situation, facilitates learning; (4) trust facilitates learning processes because it permits the three foregoing characteristics to emerge. It consists of believing that the learner need not be crammed with information that is of the teacher's choosing but that the pupil has capacities for developing his own potential (Bernard, 1974, 17).

Numerous are the background influences that have affected the development of humanism over the years. Numerous too, is the spectrum of those who have made these influences. It should be clear, therefore, as we endeavor to examine the background influences of humanism and their foundational philosophies, that humanism is not a creed or a dogma. Although it is true that the majority of humanists share the same view of man in relation to his universe; are critical of supernaturalistic attempts to deemphasize man's meaning for today; and have similar moral commitments to free thought, to the fulfillment of human potentialities and to the democratic manner of organizational and governmental structures as a whole, they nevertheless represent a wide range of opinion (Kurtz, 1973, 7).

Principles of Educational Humanism. When discussing humanistic education it is important to remember that it is not the product of any one person or school. It did not receive its birth from a conference, educational reform, or a legislative act. It has, however, been influenced by people from a variety of fields. This section will present the views and assumptions of a variety of authors, educators, and psychologists.

As applied to education, humanism encompasses a variety of assumptions about the teacher, learner, curriculum, and context of learning. Each principle will be highlighted to aid the reader in gaining an understanding of the principles of educational humanism.

1. Central to the humanistic movement in education is a desire to create a learning environment which is free from fear, punishment, harsh discipline, and manipulative instructional methods. This is done in order to move away from the adversarial role of teachers in the traditional approach. The humanist's desire is to create an atmosphere that facilitates a free flow of discussion. This would in turn create educational relationships permeated with trust and a sense of security (Knight, 1980, 99).

2. Teachers should be trusting, sincere, and empathetic with their students. They should prize their students and hold them in high regard (Biehler, 1980, 399). Rogers (1967) concluded that such an attitude on the part of the learning leader would set the stage for successful experiences and that students would become more self-accepting and aware of themselves (43–54).

3. Affective factors should be explored as much as the cognitive dimension of classroom instruction (Biehler, 1986, 399). Research by Bayer (1986) indicates that children who are taught in an atmosphere which is conducive to affective learning will also have a more positive self-concept (130–131). Weinstein and Fantini (1970) make an impassioned plea for educators to include the affective domain in the writing of educational curriculum and instructional objectives when they write, "The pervasive emphasis on cognition and its separation from affect poses a threat to our society in that our educational institutions may produce cold, detached individuals uncommitted to humanitarian goals. . . .

Knowledge can generate feelings, but it is feelings that generate action. . . . Unless knowledge is related to an affective state in the learner, the likelihood that it will influence behavior is limited" (27–28).

4. The relationship between the teacher and the pupil has an important impact on the learning process. Thomas Gordon (1974), a popular humanist educator, describes a healthy teacher-student relationship as follows: The relationship between a teacher and a student is good when it has (1) openness or transparency, so each is able to risk directness and honesty with the other; (2) caring, when each knows that he or she is valued by the other; (3) interdependence of one on the other; (4) separateness, to allow each to grow and to develop uniqueness and individuality; (5) mutual needs meeting, so that neither's needs are met at the expense of the other's needs (24).

5. How students feel about themselves will greatly influence the manner in which they learn. This principle is closely related to the third principle as it acknowledges the relationship between self-concept and learning.

William Purkey (1978) calls attention to the relationship between a student's self-concept and scholastic achievement and recommends that instructors develop and use skills of "invitational learning." Such skills as learning students' names, having one-on-one contact with them outside of class, praising and affirming them, demonstrating personal and classroom discipline, and being transparent with personal feelings will help the child recognize his value and capabilities.

6. Teachers should use techniques to encourage pupils to explore their feelings and emotions. This can be done through the use of sensitivity training and encounter groups. There is a degree of concern in the literature about this particular principle because of the need for trained counseling techniques with such an approach. The danger is far too great that a teacher with insufficient training may do more harm than good through inexpert and ill-advised attempts to implement growth group methodologies in the classroom.

7. Teachers should use techniques for encouraging students to identify with others, empathize with them, and relate their feelings to the feelings of others (Beihler, 1986, 400). Such suggested techniques include the use of role play, psychodrama, sociodrama, and simulation games.

8. Teachers should use techniques that would help students become more aware of their own attitudes and values. Values clarification was a popular concept in the late 1960s and early 1970s. Done in moderation, this technique can help students apply biblical content using higher levels of learning such as analysis, synthesis, and evaluation.

Humanistic Techniques in Christian Education. As one reads through this list of humanistic principles it becomes clear that many of these are based upon sound principles of learning. Indeed it would not be difficult to cite biblical references to demonstrate examples from Scripture where many of the principles can be seen. That is not to say that educational humanism has its roots in Scripture. Such a statement would be based upon faulty methods of hermeneutics. However, many churches would do well to incorporate these principles into their learning environment. The following suggestions should help the Sunday school teacher use the benefits of educational humanism while refraining from any detrimental elements.

1. Try to remain aware of the extent to which you direct learning in the classroom. Whenever possible, allow students to share in the choices about their instructional activities.

2. Establish a warm, positive, accepting atmosphere.

3. Where it is appropriate, function as a facilitator, encourager, helper, or friend. Before functioning in this capacity, however, be sure and consider any possible complications. Young children, for example, may not be able to handle such a role on the part of their teacher.

4. If you feel comfortable doing it, occasionally open up and share your own personal feelings about what you are teaching.

5. Do your best to help your students develop positive feelings about themselves and their individual stage of development.

6. If appropriate, ask students to participate in role playing or simulation games. Such games challenge students to think beyond the limits of the Bible lesson to practical application for today.

7. Do your best to provide learning experiences that will lead to development of the habits and attitudes you want to foster.

8. Make use of object lessons. When illustrative incidents occur (teachable moments), take advantage of them.

9. Set a good example yourself.

10. Don't be afraid to teach absolutes and demonstrate the importance of moral standards. Remember, teaching virtue was one of the first reasons for the creation of humanism in Greek education.

It is imperative to bear in mind that humanism is not a specific educational technique. In essence, "Humanism is an educational philosophy characterized by admirable attitudes toward students and toward educational goals that should be characteristic of *all* teachers" (LeFrancois, 1988, 136). It has as its presuppositional base such philosophies as naturalism, progressivism, and existentialism and has been heavily influenced by the disciplines of psychology, sociology, and religion. Some of these disciplines and influences have had a positive effect on its development and some of them have been negative. Each has played a role in shaping a particular emphasis. For this reason there is a great deal of confusion regarding its definition and contribution within society as a whole. Nowhere is this felt more than in our churches and Christian educational institutions. Both liberal and highly conservative educators have debated the merits of such an educational philosophy. The result has been that educational humanism has been viewed with suspicion by those Christian educators who have not bothered to determine its value for themselves. Relying rather on the judgements of others many have failed to critique its presuppositions for themselves. What is needed is an attitude of tolerance and an open mind toward demonstrating the higher levels of learning such as evaluation and synthesis. Without such abilities many Christian extremists are guilty of ignorance and academic bigotry.

MICHAEL J. ANTHONY

Bibliography. D. L. Barlow (1985), *Educational Psychology: The Teaching-Learning Process;* D. L. Bayer, *The School Counselor* (1986): 123–34; H. W. Bernard and W. C. Huchins (1974), *Humanism In the Classroom: An Eclectic Approach to Teaching and Learning;* R. F. Biehler and J. Snowman (1986), *Psychology Applied to Teaching;* J. J. Blake, *Sociology of Education* 59 (1986): 100–113; W. H. Burns and C. J. Brauner (1962), *Philosophy of Education: Essays and Commentaries;* R. J. Calsyn, C. Pennell, and M. Harter, *Elementary School Guidance and Counseling* (1984): 132–39; D. H. Clark, L. Asya, and A. L. Kadet (1971), *Humanistic Teaching;* G. H. Clark (1960), *Dewey;* J. Dewey (1963), *Experience and Education;* D. J. Dodgen and M. R. McMinn, *Journal of Psychology and Theology* 14, no. 3 (1986): 194–202; R. P. Fairfield (1971), *Humanistic Frontiers in American Education;* R. Farmer, *Education* 105, no. 2 (1986): 162–71; K. Gangel and W. Benson (1983), *Christian Education Its History and Philosophy;* T. Gordon (1974), *T. E. T.: Teacher Effectiveness Training;* P. Gay (1969), *The Enlightenment: An Interpretation;* F. C. Gruber (1961), *Foundations for Philosophy of Education;* J. A. Johnson, H. W. Collins, V. L. Dupuis, and J. H. Johansen (1969), *Introductions to the Foundations of American Education;* W. P. King (1931), *Humanism: Another Battle Line;* G. R. Knight (1980), *Philosophy and Education;* P. Kurtz (1973), *The Humanistic Alternative;* C. Lamont (1982), *The Philosophy of Humanism;* D. K. Lapsley and S. M. Quintana, *Elementary School Guidance and Counseling* (1958): 246–57; G. R. LeFrancois (1985), *Psychology for Teaching;* J. Locke and P. Gay (1964), *John Locke on Education;* F. Mayer (1966), *A History of Educational Thought;* R. K. Mills, *Education* 105, no. 4 (1986): 408–10; P. Monroe (1905), *History of Education;* V. C. Morris (1969), *Modern Movements in Educational Philosophy;* R. Osborn (1970), *Humanism and Moral Theory;* R. Pratte (1971), *Contemporary Theories of Education;* C. Rogers (1967), *The Problem of Being Human;* C. Weinberg (1965), *Humanistic Foundations of Education;* G. Weinstein and M. D. Fantini

(1970), *Toward Humanistic Education;* R. Weller (1977), *Humanistic Education: Visions and Realities.*

Humanism, Classical. Emerging during the latter half of the fourteenth century in Italy, classical humanism offered the invigorating combination of three noble goals: a revived study of the Greco-Roman civilization; a renewed interest in and hope for humanity; and a revitalized approach to a value-based education.

First, the rebirth of classicism concentrated on the ancient treasures, derived from the original meaning of humanism, as found in the phrase *studia humanitatis,* or human studies, a concept primarily fashioned by Cicero. As they recaptured the essence of a liberal arts curriculum, specific interest in these two early civilizations focused on subjects like grammar, rhetoric, history, poetry, and moral philosophy.

Second, a new and heightened interest in people arose as Protagoras's slogan "Man is the measure of all things" was resurrected. Contrary to many conservative critiques, historically such a motto did not necessitate the abandonment of faith, though it did set the stage for multiple forms of rebellion against traditional religious positions. For instance, under the ever-broadening umbrella of classical humanism, on the one hand, there existed the powerful influences of both Desiderius Erasmus (1466–1536), who sought reform from within the Catholic Church; and Thomas More (1478–1535) who, in his *Utopia,* called for a society based on natural reason—believed to be shared by all human beings—without the need for supernatural revelation. But, on the other hand, one could also locate the more conventional Christian views of the English humanist John Colet (1467–1519) who, in his lectures on Romans, reaffirmed the paired doctrines of personal sin and divine forgiveness. Indeed, classical humanism spanned such a wide range of ideologies and religious beliefs that it capably provided a haven for an unusual mixture of groups, including portions of the Roman Catholic Church (represented by the ideas of Erasmus and More), divisions of Protestantism (adherents to the ideas promoted by Luther and Melanchthon), independent philosophers (represented by particular works by Spinoza and Kant), specific features of German pietism, the moderates of the Church of Scotland, and the "Broad Church" school of Anglicanism. Furthermore, this sweeping movement incorporated a growing number of people who totally rejected Augustinianism (on the issue of human will) along with anything that even sounded religious.

Third, a variety of worthwhile educational outcomes served as a significant consequence of classical humanism, a variety that consisted of elevating teaching to a divine vocation; exchanging the elitist position of schooling for compulsory education for all boys and girls; establishing numerous secondary schools and universities; returning to the knowledge of the biblical languages and focusing on the Bible's original source material; increasing the use of the printing press; and advancing the vision for academic freedom. In fact, based upon the secondary understanding of the Latin word *humanitas* ("the human race")—which identifies moral human behavior—humanism, for all intents and purposes, was equated with the Greek concept *paideia,* yielding the meaning of "polite (or humane) education."

But by the mid-nineteenth century, nothing was left of humanism's religious foundation. Though it began with such a noble purpose, it soon fell victim to the influences of an increasingly secular society. As confidence in humanity and human potential surged ahead, so did skepticism of all theist-based systems. The term *humanism,* for the most part, was now employed to denote self-sufficiency apart from God. Creation was consciously pitted against Creator. Most, if not all, who label themselves humanists today are atheist, or at least agnostic. Thus, the term *secular humanism* was coined.

The landmark document that sprang from this pattern of secularization was the *Humanist Manifesto I,* composed in 1933. Among the notables who signed this document was John Dewey. Among the outstanding features within the document was the renewed claim of humans to be self-sustaining, evolutionary beings. Doctrines of creation, supernaturalism—even deism—were disposed of. Complete realization of the human potential was humanity's ultimate goal according to this treatise.

The year 1973 brought an update to this cause, suitably called *Humanist Manifesto II.* While reaffirming the original commitment of forty years earlier, this latest document raised the corporate level of consciousness by emphasizing the need for personal responsibility toward all humankind. A prominent figure within this contemporary movement is Paul Kurtz, who has participated in numerous ventures for humanitarian causes, such as providing leadership as editor of *The Humanist* and as founder of Prometheus Books. A quarter century ago, Kurtz also helped create the Committee for the Scientific Investigation of the Paranormal, which fostered the *Skeptical Inquirer,* a resource which discredits information circulated by psychic and paranormal advocates. Less than a decade later, Kurtz also assisted in the formation of two groups: the Academy for Humanism, an organization that dispenses humanist views and agendas, and the Religion and Biblical Criticism Research Project, which publicizes pertinent discoveries in religion, particularly those relating to beliefs which humanists dismiss (e.g., supernatural phenomena and the historicity of Jesus).

Much like its predecessor, classical humanism, present-day humanism reveals a broad spectrum of support from a diverse scope of disciplines. For instance, a handful of contemporary ideologies which sense some degree of welcome from this accommodating movement include Dewey's pragmatism, Jacques Maritain's personalism, Jean-Paul Sartre's atheistic existentialism, and Karl Marx's communism.

In sum, humanism is steeped in godlessness. *Homo sapiens*-centeredness thinly veils its self-worship. Yet the humanist movement does provide the church with some rich resources, not the least of which embrace valuing the individual, prizing human abilities and potentials, tolerating a breadth of viewpoints, expressing dignity toward people, supporting human rights, and emphasizing personal responsibility.

RONALD T. HABERMAS

Bibliography. M. J. Anthony, *Christian Education Journal* 12, no. 1 (1991): 79–88; A. Flew (1983), *The Westminster Dictionary of Christian Spirituality;* G. M. Marsden (1990), *Dictionary of Christianity in America;* L. W. Spitz (1987), *The Encyclopedia of Religion.*

See also CHRISTIAN HUMANISM

Hume, David (1711–76). David Hume was a noted British empiricist of the eighteenth century often regarded as one of the finest philosophical minds of his era and a key figure in the Enlightenment. His influence is still seen in modern empiricism, pragmatism, and philosophical skepticism. Some opposed to theistic belief find support in the arguments of Hume, particularly regarding the implausibility of miracles or other occurrences contrary to a naturalistic understanding of the universe.

Born in Edinburgh, Scotland, he attended the university there and later served professionally in such positions as a librarian, military aide, and diplomat. While still in his teens he began intense thinking and writing concerning what was to become a complete philosophical system published in 1739 as his first work, *A Treatise of Human Nature.* When this first work went largely ignored, he wrote *An Inquiry Concerning Human Understanding* (1748) as one attempt to make portions of his initial work more understandable. Some of his arguments against traditional theism are contained in *Dialogues Concerning Natural Religion*

(1779), published posthumously. The importance of his philosophical thought was noted only after his death; he was known by his contemporaries more for historical writings.

Hume attempted to apply Newtonian methods to a scientific study of human nature. Following British empiricists Locke and Berkeley, he opposed the deductive reasoning of the rationalists and instead emphasized the role of experience in acquiring knowledge. The empiricists maintained that the mind could know nothing of the outside world except what is conveyed to it through sensory experience. Yet Hume's epistemology also consciously incorporated skepticism to show the limits of all reasoning and knowledge. Skepticism, Hume maintained, was the only alternative if the empirical method was pushed to its ultimate conclusions. One could not prove that anything outside the self existed, and he even questioned the existence of the continuing self. Surprisingly, he argued skeptically against the traditional view of causation, a vital foundation of all scientific study.

Hume viewed theistic faith as a product of superstition. Morality for him was essentially naturalistic, with no absolutes. He contended against miracles, not so much on the basis that they could not have happened, but that their occurrence is scientifically improbable. His use of scientific law to deny the miraculous is only one example of inconsistencies in his thought, since he had elsewhere argued against the basis for such natural laws.

Hume's arguments, taken to their logical conclusions, sometimes defy logic and appear self-defeating. For example, philosophical skepticism, taken to the extreme he proposed, undermines the possibility of all rational thought, including his own. Probably the most powerful effect Hume has had on modern thinking results from his contention that one can say nothing meaningful about things beyond the sensory world. As such he has had widespread influence on modern agnostic and materialistic systems of belief which question the supernatural and spiritual realities.

RICHARD LEYDA

Bibliography. C. Brown (1968), *Philosophy and the Christian Faith;* D. Hume (1888), *A Treatise of Human Nature;* idem (1748), *An Inquiry Concerning Human Understanding;* idem (1779), *Dialogues Concerning Natural Religion.*

Hypnotic Regression. *See* Regression.

Ii

Idealism. Oldest Western philosophy, first finding full expression in Socrates and his pupil Plato. As a philosophy, idealism emphasizes the world of the mind. Reality is regarded as being both conceptual and ideal. For this reason, ultimate reality is expressed in spiritual or intellectual nomenclatures.

Idealism stands opposite of realism, with its attention given to the physical world as a source of truth and knowledge, which idealism regards as an obstacle to pure reason and contemplation. Idealism's epistemology emphasizes the existence of truth that is universal, internally consistent, and absolute. This truth originates in the Supreme Being, who possesses the ultimate mind, which we are to imitate or reflect.

Idealism's axiology stems from its perception of reality and truth. Ethical and aesthetic values are to imitate and reflect the ideal. The theme of character and cultural development is expressed on both an individual and social level in idealism's axiological convictions.

Educational Implications of Idealism. As an educational philosophy, idealism focuses on the student's development of character, particularly in the cognitive domain, so as to make a positive contribution toward the advancement of culture and society. The educational goals of idealism are simple: (1) preservation of culture, (2) promotion of the contemplative life, and (3) development of the ideal individual for the ideal society.

The person of the teacher is central, both personally and intellectually, in idealism. The teacher is paradigmatic of ideal truth, ethics, and cultural excellence.

The curriculum of idealism is cognitive in focus, emphasizing the development of the intellect and character. Common instructional methods consistent with idealism are lectures, reports, contemplative questions, and dialogue. Curricular content is typically comprised of wisdom literature, cultural heritage, classical literature, and symbolic or idealistic literature. Students are viewed as minds in microcosm, waiting to be developed by the teacher.

Adherents to idealism as an educational philosophy include Socrates, Plato, St. Augustine, Berkeley, Kant, Hegel, Froebel, Royce, Hocking, Whitehead, J. D. Butler, Antz, and Castell. Early in the twentieth century idealism gave rise to a new philosophy of education, essentialism, which stood opposed to Dewey's progressive-pragmatic philosophy of education.

Critique of Idealism. Evangelicals will find some affirmations in common with idealism, such as the existence of God and the nature of truth as being absolute and "revealed" by God and "knowable" to humanity. During the history of the early church, Platonic idealism influenced such educators as Clement of Alexandria and Origen in the third century A.D., as well as St. Augustine (fourth to fifth century), who based his ontological argument for the existence of God on Platonic thought.

However, while these general affirmations are valuable, several aspects of idealism as a philosophy of education are untenable to evangelicals:

(1) The metaphysic of idealism denies the general revelation of nature. The Scriptures affirm the revelatory worth of the physical creation (Ps. 19:1–4; Rom. 1:16–20). As previously noted, while realism places value on the study of nature as a means of discovering truth, idealism rejects this notion and hence devalues God's general revelation.

(2) Idealism is concerned with preservation of the status quo. While for some this would be an acceptable stance for Christian education, any stance that *only* preserves the church's culture rather than *professing* the faith *to* the culture in which the church exists is not only inadequate, but compromises the mission and educational emphasis of the church.

(3) While idealism does affirm the existence of a Supreme Being/Mind, it "is an intellectualized one which excludes concepts of grace and redeeming love" (Peterson, 1986, 30). Hence, while the existence of "god" is acknowledged, the god of idealism is not equivalent in attributes to the God of Scripture.

(4) Idealism advocates the detachment of faith and reason. While evangelicals acknowledge the difference between faith and reason, they likewise maintain a symbiotic connection between the two. Yet, this connection is denied by many adherents to idealism, e.g. Blanchard and Kant.

Finally, (5) idealism posits "the dichotomy of the spiritual and the material" (Knight, 1989, 64), forming a quasi-gnostic perspective on spirituality. Such a dichotomy can only lead to the loss of Christian spirituality as being a holistic life-view. Hence, while idealism does provide some beneficial perspectives, it is inadequate as a sole basis for education that is Christian.

JAMES RILEY ESTEP

Bibliography. J. Donald Butler (1951), *Four Philosophies and Their Practice in Education and Religion;* G. L. Gutek (1988), *Philosophical and Ideological Perspectives on Education;* G. R. Knight (1989), *Philosophy and Education;* M. L. Peterson (1986), *Philosophy of Education.*

Identity Achievement. The identity achievement individual is one who has experienced an exploration (crisis) period and is committed to self-chosen ideological and occupational goals. This individual has seriously considered various occupational alternatives and has made his own decision, even though it may be influenced by parents. He or she has evaluated past beliefs and resolved issues so as to act responsibly and would be capable of handling unexpected responsibilities or a sudden change in environment (Marcia, 1966, 551–52). This is the desired status of the four degrees of identity formation.

JAY SEDWICK

Bibliography. S. L. Archer, *Journal of Adolescence* (1989): 345–59; E. Erikson (1963), *Childhood and Society;* idem (1968), *Identity: Youth and Crisis;* idem (1968), *International Encyclopedia of the Social Sciences;* pp. 61–65; J. E. Marcia, *Journal of Personality and Social Psychology* 3, no. 5 (1966): 551–58; idem (1980), *Handbook of Adolescent Psychology;* pp. 159–87; R. E. Muuss (1996), *Theories of Adolescence;* J. W. Santrock (1996), *Adolecence.*

See also IDENTITY DIFFUSION; IDENTITY FORECLOSURE; IDENTITY MORATORIUM; IDENTITY STATUS

Identity Diffusion. The identity diffusion individual has no set occupational or ideological direction, even though he may have explored alternatives extensively. The individual lacks commitment in both areas and is not very concerned about it. He or she may indicate an occupational leaning, but would easily switch to something else more appealing if there were an opportunity. He or she is either uninterested in ideological issues or takes a "smorgasbord" approach where every position and cause is of equal value (Marcia, 1966, 552).

JAY SEDWICK

Bibliography. S. L. Archer, *Journal of Adolescence* (1989): 345–59; E. Erikson (1963), *Childhood and Society;* idem (1968), *Identity: Youth and Crisis;* idem (1968), *International Encyclopedia of Social Sciences,* pp. 61–65; J. E. Marcia, *Journal of Personality and Social Psychology* 3, no. 5 (1966): 551–58; idem (1980), *Handbook of Adolescent Psychology,* pp. 159–87; R. E. Muuss (1996), *Theories of Adolescence;* J. W. Santrock (1996), *Adolecence.*

See also IDENTITY ACHIEVEMENT; IDENTITY FORECLOSURE; IDENTITY MORATORIUM; IDENTITY STATUS

Identity Foreclosure. The identity foreclosure individual is committed to occupational and ideological positions, but has not experienced any crisis or exploration of alternatives. This person's choices have been made by parents or other influential persons. He or she is becoming what others have intended for him or her to be. The individual's personality is characterized by rigidity. If a situation is encountered where parental values are challenged or are not adequate, the individual feels severely threatened (Marcia, 1966, 552). Identity formation should move from moratorium to achievement as youth mature through late adolescence (18–21 years).

JAY SEDWICK

Bibliography. S. L. Archer, *Journal of Adolescence* (1989): 345–59; E. Erikson (1963), *Childhood and Society;* idem (1968), *Identity: Youth and Crisis;* idem (1968), *International Encyclopedia of Social Sciences,* pp. 61–65; J. E. Marcia, *Journal of Personality and Social Psychology* 3, no. 5 (1966): 551–58; idem (1980), *Handbook of Adolescent Psychology,* pp. 159–87; R. E. Muuss (1996), *Theories of Adolescence;* J. W. Santrock (1996), *Adolecence.*

See also IDENTITY ACHIEVEMENT; IDENTITY DIFFUSION; IDENTITY MORATORIUM; IDENTITY STATUS

Identity Moratorium. The identity moratorium individual is currently struggling with occupational and ideological issues. He is in an "identity crisis." He is actively involved in the struggle to make commitments in both areas. Adolescent issues preoccupy him as he attempts to compromise between his parents' wishes, his own capabilities, and society's expectations. He is vitally concerned and often consumed with what seem to him to be unresolvable questions (Marcia, 1966, 552). This is the most common status of adolescents.

JAY SEDWICK

Bibliography. S. L. Archer, *Journal of Adolescence* (1989): 345–59; E. Erikson (1963), *Childhood and Society;* idem (1968), *Identity: Youth and Crisis;* idem (1968), *International Encyclopedia of Social Sciences,* pp. 61–65; J. E. Marcia, *Journal of Personality and Social Psychology* 3, no. 5 (1966): 551–58; idem (1980), *Handbook of Adolescent Psychology,* pp. 159–87; R. E. Muuss (1996), *Theories of Adolescence;* J. W. Santrock (1996), *Adolecence.*

See also IDENTITY ACHIEVEMENT; IDENTITY DIFFU-SION; IDENTITY STATUS

Identity Status. The fifth stage of Erik Erikson's (1963) eight stages of human development is the tension between identity versus identity confusion commonly encountered during adolescence. *Identity* is "an internal, self-constructed, dynamic organization of drives, abilities, beliefs, and individual history" (Marcia, 1980, 159). The major task for adolescents according to Erikson's research is to form a coherent, integrated, and workable identity that will guide them into young adult life, adult responsibility, and successful task completion in later stages. To be sure, the question of identity is much more involved than "Who am I?"

Identity does not originate in adolescence. From birth onward the child learns what is important and valued in his culture as he and the community respond to one another's behavior. "Identity formation employs a process of simultaneous reflection and observation, a process taking place on all levels of mental functioning, by which the individual judges himself in the light of what he perceives to be the way in which others judge him in comparison to themselves and to a typology significant to them; while he judges their way of judging him in the light of how he perceives himself in comparison to them and to types that have become relevant to him" (Erikson, 1968a, 22). Identity formation builds to an "identity crisis" during adolescence which is dealt with in various ways, depending upon societal influences (Erikson, 1968b, 62). By crisis is meant "a necessary turning point, a crucial moment, when development must move one way or another" rather than an impending catastrophe (Erikson, 1968a, 16). Identity formation continues throughout later adult life as individuals continue to adjust the way they relate in a changing world (Marcia, 1980, 160).

Identity formation involves an exploration of and a commitment to an ideological position and an occupational direction (Marcia, 1980, 160). Exploration (crisis) refers to the assessment of alternatives by engaging in activities which provide the knowledge to make an informed decision. It is either absent, present, or ongoing. Commitment refers to an investment in the decision with consideration as to how the choice will be integrated with other goals (Archer, 1989, 346).

James E. Marcia (1966) built upon Erikson's theories and research by formulating four distinct identity statuses for the purpose of studying the degree of identity formation. The four statuses are identity achievement, identity diffusion, identity moratorium, and identity foreclosure.

One caveat to Erikson's and Marcia's early research—it was primarily completed with male subjects and male identity issues. Some researchers have questioned the validity of the statuses for adolescent girls and their particular identity formation. However, the statuses have proven useful, in spite of the differences in content areas for girls. The descriptive information for each status would be different for girls because they sometimes struggle with different issues. The primary concern which needs to be resolved for adolescent girls is the establishment and maintenance of interpersonal relationships (Marcia, 1980, 179).

JAY SEDWICK

Bibliography. S. L. Archer, *Journal of Adolescence* (1989): 345–59; E. Erikson (1963), *Childhood and Society;* idem (1968a), *Identity: Youth and Crisis;* idem (1968b), *International Encyclopedia of Social Sciences,* pp. 61–65; J. E. Marcia, *Journal of Personality and Social Psychology* 3, no. 5 (1966): 551–58; idem (1980), *Handbook of Adolescent Psychology,* pp. 159–87; R. E. Muuss (1996), *Theories of Adolescence;* J. W. Santrock (1996), *Adolescence.*

See also IDENTITY ACHIEVEMENT; IDENTITY DIFFUSION; IDENTITY FORECLOSURE; IDENTITY MORATORIUM

Ignatius of Loyola (1491–1556). The youngest of thirteen children, Iñigo de Oñaz y Loyola was born in the family castle of Loyola in the Pyrenees. Soon into his childhood years Iñigo latinized his first name to Ignatius. Beginning his career of public service, Loyola served as a page for Queen Isabella. It was here that he learned to read and write. He soon entered the Spanish military and served under the command of the duke of Najera. During the siege of Pamplona (1521) his legs were injured by a French cannonball. During the long period of recuperation Ignatius sought release from tedious hours of boredom by reading numerous books. Two of these volumes were *The Life of Christ* and *The Lives of the Saints.* Touched by the sacrificial manner in which the characters of these books lived their lives, Ignatius's heart was stirred. Shortly thereafter he left his military career to become a soldier in Christ's army.

During this period of time, Pope Paul III had mounted a response to the significant losses which the Roman Catholic Church had suffered during the initial years of the Reformation movement. The pope's strategy was fourfold: stronger preaching in the local congregations, reinforced mandatory use of the confessional, missionary expansion, and educational reform. It was this latter facet which received Ignatius' attention. Since much of the cause of the demise of the Catholic Church at this time could be attributed to the lack of training in the preparation of the clergy, Ignatius sought to bring about educational reform in the church.

Together with a group of six colleagues, he founded a new Catholic order in Italy known as the Society of Jesus (later known simply as Jesuits) in 1540. These religious leaders set out to expand the church through the means of religious schools. They sought to educate youth in Catholic doctrine by establishing schools where they could receive religious and secular instruction. His approach was highly successful and the heritage of Catholic education traces itself back to the foresight of this religious leader.

One of his central themes in religious instruction was a lifestyle of integrity. He taught his students how to live by offering his own life as an example. He sought to have his students imitate his values, worldview, and spiritual disciplines. He pioneered Catholic religious instruction outside of Italy by starting schools across Europe. He died in 1556 and was canonized in 1622. More than four hundred years after his death, the impact of his life on Catholic religious instruction continues to this day in many parts of the world.

MICHAEL J. ANTHONY

Bibliography. F. L. Cross and E. A. Livingstone (1997), *The Oxford Dictionary of the Christian Church;* C. B. Eavy (1964), *History of Christian Education;* K. O. Gangel and W. S. Benson (1983), *Christian Education: Its History and Philosophy;* J. E. Reed and R. Prevost (1993), *A History of Christian Education.*

Illustration. *See* Demonstration.

Imagination. Imagination sparks such wild ideas. Green eggs and ham! Cats in hats! Wardrobes that lead into Narnia! Attached to mystery, to newness, to creativity, it is a posture of openness to wonder—to vision—to intuition. Imagination finds its creative juices in the unheard of, the unseen, the previously unconnected. Urban T. Holmes (1981) writes, "The very nature of the imagination requires that no preconditions be set on what is possible within our experience" (88). He goes on to identify imagination cultivation as a primary agenda for ministry today in order to recover the meaning of what it means to "be-in-the-world-as-one-who-images," as one who breaks out of the perfunctory "linear logic of causality" and moves into intuitive thinking (90).

Imagination must be distinguished from fantasy. The latter escapes from the sphere of reality and facts while the former utilizes facts, discovering new meaning and perspective in them through treating them as symbols that give to the intuitive more than meets the eye. The Scriptures are filled with symbols meant to convey more than simply facts. The tabernacle was rich in imagery; events such as the exodus imaged far more than an exit; the faithful are purveyors of the "aroma of Christ" (2 Cor. 2:15), a fragrance that conjures up life at its best and death at its worst.

While children, with their openness to believe and to see beyond the veil of the opaque, seem to thrive naturally in the realm of imagination, the ability to see images as representing more than surface realities typically becomes veiled with years. We call the world of imagination by an interesting referent, "the world of make believe." Tom Beaudoin (1998), in his provocative tracing of Generation X's irreverent quest for spirituality, proclaims the imperative of reclaiming imagination within religion for connecting with Xers. Writing as an Xer himself, he states, "Our popular culture is heavily image oriented and iconographic. From music video to cyberspace to fashion, image is our story as much as text was the story for past generations. The icon is the common currency of our popular culture" (156). The symbolic speaks to his generation—whether on screen, in vogue as "style," or appearing within a religious context. As such these symbols purvey an overabundance of meaning that stimulates imagination and meaning in the receiver. "Imagination allows us to make and receive infinite interpretations of how symbols represent God's presence in the world" (156). This concept helps to explain this generation's responsiveness to *story*, a means of conveying vast meaning through narrative symbols and characters.

A sense of wonder, of living intuitively in openness to newness of the Spirit is an essential ingredient in Christian education—at home in creativity and faith. It is constructed on facts but is reflective of an infinitely creative God who excites our being with such words as "no eye has seen, no ear has heard, no mind has conceived what God has prepared for those who love him" (1 Cor. 2:9). The ministry of Christian education is empowered with imagination.

JULIE GORMAN

Bibliography. T. Beaudoin (1998), *Virtual Faith: The Irreverent Spiritual Quest of Generation X;* J. W. Berryman (1991), *Godly Play;* U. T. Holmes (1981), *Ministry and Imagination.*

See also BUSTER GENERATION; CREATIVITY, BIBLICAL FOUNDATIONS OF

Imbalance. *See* Disequilibrium.

Immersion. *See* Baptism.

Immigrant Family. If it takes a village to raise a child, then migration puts the family in a cultural and social vacuum. The interrelationship between the host society and immigrant family is key to the degree of the immigrants' assimilation into mainstream culture.

There are several variables which are crucial in dealing with immigrant family ministry issues. They include structural, situational, and psychological variables (Hurh and Kwang, 1984, 207). Structurally, socioeconomic and cultural differences between the host society and immigrants affect immigrants' adaptation to the host society. If the host society has a culturally open but socioeconomically closed structure, immigrants experience segregation despite their desire to assimilate. On the other hand, immigrants may have high socioeconomic backgrounds but limited cultural adaptive capacity due to a language barrier, thus hindering adaptation.

Situational variables include the host society's demographic, socioeconomic, and ecological conditions. In the case of a large influx of immigrants, ethnic confinement in social relations and in the labor market determine the degree of the immigrants' adaptation. Psychological variables which determine the degree of social distance include both the dominant group's and the immigrants' perception of the situation.

Due to both external and internal variables, the immigrant family undergoes disruptive changes. Often the offspring of immigrants become enculturated through mainstream education while immigrant parents feel the need to cling to the old values in the midst of sudden changes all around them. In addition to the generation gap which the mainstream family experiences, the immigrant family faces intense worldview conflict both in family and community life, and this affects the host society's communication with them (Hertig, 1991, 244).

In the United States, the marital relationship may change drastically due to a two income structure. The gender gap between the husband and the wife widens when the wife begins working. No matter how much the husband holds onto patriarchal values, day-to-day life experience does not convey his traditional values. The wife, meanwhile, likely encounters sexual prejudice from her culture and racial prejudice from the host culture. Among siblings, assimilation patterns vary depending on their own internal and external interactions with the dominant culture. Christian education must therefore be aware that family life may be quite chaotic.

The immigrant family finds its own substitute community in a country where not many extended families and social connections are established. The ethnic enclave is an example of how immigrants form social networks by offering helping hands financially and emotionally.

YOUNG LEE HERTIG

Bibliography. Y. L. Hertig (1991), "The Role of Power In the Korean Immigrant Family and Church"; W. M. Hurh and C. K. Kwang, *International Migration Review* 18, no. 2 (1984).

Imprinting. In the study of mammals, this refers to the instinctive learning response of young animals as they attach themselves to the first object with which they have contact. Attention is focused on this object, which then becomes the pattern for their behavior. Studies of birds indicate that though this connection would normally occur with the mother, it could also be with a human being or an object such as a clock.

Used in psychological theory, the term refers to modeling, or observational learning. In this way values are taught by people (parents, teachers, clergy, public leaders), as well as by movies, television, and books. One of the leading proponents of imprinting is Albert Bandura, whose observation of the ways children mimic aggressive behavior in adults has sparked debate about the influence of violence observed in movies and television, or reading or hearing about violent acts. Another suggested area in which this type of learning occurs significantly is that of sexual conduct.

Imprinting has the benefit of allowing a person to learn without ever performing the behavior or experiencing the consequences of the action. For example, a child may avoid hot stoves if he or she has observed another child burn his or her hand on one. Seeing other children rewarded for good behavior in church or getting good grades for studying may be enough to motivate similar behavior.

The biblical pattern is that the life of the teacher is in some way replicated in students. Thus Jesus admonishes, "A pupil is not above his teacher; but everyone, after he has been fully trained, will be like his teacher" (Luke 6:40). Paul challenges and commends Christians for imitation of godly characteristics of fellow believers (1 Cor. 4:16; 11:1; Phil. 3:17; 1 Thess. 1:6; 2:14; Heb. 6:12). Modeling in the context of close relationships remains one of the most significant tools of the teacher.

THOMAS HUTCHISON

Bibliography. A. Bandura (1973), *Aggression: A Social Learning Analysis;* idem (1985), *The Social Foundations of Thought & Action: A Social Cognitive Theory.*

See also BANDURA, ALBERT; OBSERVATIONAL LEARNING; SOCIAL COGNITIVE THEORY

Independence. *See* Autonomy.

Individual Differences. The concept implies that no two individuals are alike. Each person is unique with regard to motivation, knowledge, aptitude, interest, ability, and many other variables. Educational psychologists analyze ways people differ on characteristics that can be measured in tests of factors such as intelligence, personality, attainment, and attitude.

It should be noted that this is a shift in focus from the earliest forms of psychological testing.

The primary goal of the early nineteenth century experimental psychologists was to develop generalized descriptions of human behavior. Their concern was not measuring individual differences, but rather identifying the uniformities. The differences between responses were either ignored or considered an unfortunate form of error that limited applicability of the generalizations. A dissertation on individual differences in 1888 by American psychologist James McKeen Cattell signaled a change in direction. From this beginning, testing procedures were standardized, and the areas of assessment expanded to include a wide range of variables, such as memory, imagination, attention, comprehension, or suggestibility.

Currently there is widespread recognition and extensive research devoted to identifying and understanding the differences between individuals. Pedagogically, in contrast to entire school features like whole classroom instruction, annual promotions, age-related grade placement, and common assignments, the uniqueness of each student is the basis for alternative strategies like individualized instruction, child-centered progress, and elective courses.

Developmental psychologists have suggested that growth is sequenced, with each person developing in a prescribed manner physically, cognitively, emotionally, affectively, morally, and even spiritually. While there are general patterns to the growth of people in these areas, it must be noted that wide variability is found among individuals at each level. Therefore, it is important to consider the uniqueness of each individual when assessing and determining learning strategies.

Differences in the area of intelligence are formed by a combination of hereditary and environmental factors. Recognized as a very complex variable, intelligence is generally described as the capacity to do things such as learn from experience, adapt to new situations, understand abstract concepts, or apply knowledge. Scales such as the Stanford-Binet Intelligence Scale and the Wechsler scales are examples of tests used to quantify intellectual ability based on the statistical distribution of scores. Gardner (1993) has proposed a theory of multiple intelligences, suggesting that differences are due to expression rather than possession of intellectual capacity.

Personality describes the unique behavior of a person in interaction with the environment and other people, including moods, attitudes, and opinions. Tests have been devised for the classification of certain personality traits, such as introversion or extroversion, or task or relationship focus. These assessments address a wide range of factors which include motivation, response to stress, and most comfortable pattern of behavior in work or social contexts.

Learning styles reflect the thesis that individuals vary in how they learn. Through a combination of hereditary and environmental influences a person develops "modality strengths" or preferences for learning. Those who learn best by seeing words or pictures are called visual learners. Those learning best by hearing are referred to as auditory learners. Tactile/kinesthetic learners learn best when they are able to touch manipulatives, or are active (dancing, etc.). Brain and learning styles research suggests that students are thought to be primarily one of these three types, or a mixed modality.

The New Testament expands on the contemporary educational discussion in reference to spiritual gifts. These are the enablement of the Holy Spirit for every believer to minister within the body of Christ for the spiritual benefit of others. Paul's illustration of the functioning human body demonstrates that each person is uniquely gifted by God, depending on others for the joint exercise of these gifts to produce individual and corporate spiritual maturity (1 Cor. 12; Eph. 4:1–16).

THOMAS HUTCHISON

Bibliography. A. Anastasi (1988), *Psychological Testing;* A. K. Ellis and J. T. Fouts (1996), *Handbook of Educational Terms and Applications;* H. Gardner (1993), *Frames of Mind: The Theory of Multiple Intelligences;* H. Gardner, M. L. Kornabery, and W. K. Wake (1995), *Intelligence: Multiple Perspectives;* K. Issler and R. Habermas (1994), *How We Learn: A Christian Teacher's Guide to Educational Psychology;* G. A. Kimble (1998), *Human Learning and Cognition: Theories of Learning: Major Themes and Issues: Contemporary Trends in Learning Theory;* M. D. LeFever (1996), *Learning Styles: Reaching Everyone God Gave You to Teach.*

Individualism and Groups. Individualism is the self-centered pursuit of personal rights and autonomy that supersedes concern for the well-being of others or for the good of the larger community. Robert Bellah and his associates describe it as "a belief that the individual has a primary reality whereas society is a second-order, derived or artificial construct" (1985, 334). Simply put, individuals and their self interests have priority over others and relationships are formed to maximize self interest (Gorman, 1993, 61). From a biblical perspective, individualism stands in sharp contrast to the interdependence illustrated by the divine persons of the Trinity (John 5:19; 8:28; 14:24; 16:7, 13) and the numerous "one another" passages found in the epistles (e.g., Gal. 5:13; 1 Thess. 5:11; Eph. 5:21) that encourage the edification of others.

Social scientists argue that the interdependence and other-centeredness of the Bible is lost to contemporary society. Bellah and his colleagues suggest that individualism lies at the very core of American culture which has pursued individual rights and autonomy to ever new realms (1985, 142–43). Christopher Lasch describes "the culture of competitive individualism, which in its decadence has carried the logic of individualism to the extreme of a war of all against all, the pursuit of happiness to the dead end of a narcissistic preoccupation with the self" (1979, 21). Allan Bloom, in a sweeping analysis of American students, describes them as being preoccupied primarily with themselves (1987, 83).

Observers of the small-group movement are concerned that radical individualism is certain to pervade small groups (Gorman, 1993, 60; Wuthnow, 1994, 27). William Dyrness states, "In general, Americans do not join groups for what they can contribute, but for what they can get out of them" (1989, 98–99). Individualism has a number of detrimental effects on small groups and on small-group interaction. Individualism impacts a group negatively when each individual remains more committed to his or her personal needs and interests than to the life of the group (Gorman, 1993, 76). This leads to relationships that tend to be superficial, temporary, and unsatisfying.

How can a small group resolve the tension between allowing members to focus on personal growth while at the same time meeting the needs of others? One helpful way by which group participation contributes to personal growth is by giving individuals feedback about who they are. Such other-centered interaction provides individuals "with a mirror in which to reflect upon their lives and reaffirm their self-definition" and the opportunity "to grow because of the interaction and support found in small groups" (Wuthnow, 1994, 210).

HARLEY ATKINSON

Bibliography. R. M. Bellah, W. M. Sullivan, A. Swindler, and S. M. Tipton (1985), *Habits of the Heart;* A. Bloom (1987), *Closing of the American Mind;* W. Dyrness (1989), *How Does America Hear the Gospel?;* J. Gorman (1993), *Community That Is Christian;* C. Lasch (1979), *The Culture of Narcissism;* R. Wuthnow (1994), *Sharing the Journey.*

See also GROUP DYNAMICS; GROUP STAGES; SMALL GROUP

Inductive Bible Study. A methodological approach to the study of Scripture. After previewing the whole passage, the student observes with careful focus the exact words and phrases of a biblical text and proceeds to logical, generalized conclusions based on examination of those observed particulars. This procedure is opposite of the deductive method, which begins with a generalization and marshals validity for that generalized statement by looking for particulars that support it.

In the early 1900s Wilbert W. White, founder of Biblical Seminary in New York (now New York Theological Seminary), developed this method to help students study the Bible for themselves. This basic three step process has become a popular study methodology for enabling persons to understand Scriptural truth (without needing to know the original languages) and to recognize its relevance for application to their lives.

The inductive process consists of three major steps: observation, interpretation, and application. In observation, priority is given to accurate firsthand examination of what is actually said by carefully focusing on the words of the text. This includes noting which words are used (who? what? when? where?), tenses of verbs, relationships between terms (contrasts, comparisons, repetitions), and phrases indicating cause and effect, means to an end, and timing. The first phrase in Mark 1:14 ("After John was put in prison," followed by "Jesus went into Galilee, proclaiming the good news of God. 'The time has come,' he said. 'The kingdom of God is near. Repent and believe the good news!'") gives an interesting perspective on timing. If the phrase had been cause and effect ("Because of John's imprisonment"), the meaning of the text would be different. Jesus specific declaration of "the time has come," includes John's being placed in prison. Likewise the contrast of John's being incarcerated in a prison followed by Jesus moving in and proclaiming good news helps to frame the information in counterpoint.

Interpretation searches for meaning in and from the text. The first responsibility in interpretation is to seek to understand what the text would have meant to the hearers in the context in which it was written. This is accomplished by defining words used, asking the question "why?" and thinking through special implications connected to the speaker or listeners in the original setting. For example, in Mark 4:38 when Jesus was sleeping through the severe storm while in a boat with the disciples, they awoke him with the words, "Teacher, don't you care if we drown?" The meaning of those words is heightened by connections and questions. Those who suggest drowning included seasoned fishermen who knew this lake. The phrase "don't you care" comes from those who had experienced the extreme caring of his nature. What were they asking? Does sleep mean not caring? What did they want Jesus to do? What expectations did they have of him? Would Jesus drown, too? Such questions probe the meaning behind the text.

The learner, in doing interpretation, must always search the text for information that affects interpretation. Often another phrase of the passage will shed further light on how a particular phrase is to be interpreted or will give parameters to which the explanation must be confined. Where no definitive information is directly given, the student then moves into suggesting a logical meaning. It is important in projecting these hypothesized interpretations to emphasize the tentative nature of these answers by using the phrase "It may be . . ." or "This could mean . . . ." It is also wise to give more than one of these "possible" interpretations to avoid skewed application.

The other half of the interpretative process is to interpret truth personally in life. After first seeking to understand as accurately as possible the meaning this text would have to the hearers, inductive methodology moves learners to interpret meaning for their lives in this present century. Again, this "personalizing" of truth is often brought about through questions. "In what way am I experiencing what the character or writer is describing?" "What situation do I face where this truth could make a difference?" "How can I respond in a manner that obeys this text today?" Personalizing involves seeing several possible significances for my life today that carry the truth of the interpreted text into relevant situations in life. Careful interpretation of the text is prerequisite to accurate response. These potential responses are all cognitive "could," "should," and "can" kinds of responses. For transformation to take place the will must be involved.

Therefore, the final step of the process is actual commitment to a specific chosen response in regard to the discovered truth. Inductive study becomes formational when learners are called to respond with, "I will . . . as a result of what I now know." Good inductive Bible study always leads to life change between the learner and God. As persons interact with the Word of God, the Spirit speaks to them of specific issues affected. The formational leader nurtures that process and watches God at work in a transformational encounter between life, truth in God's Word, and God's power.

JULIE GORMAN

Bibliography. G. D. Fee and D. Stuart (1982), *How to Read the Bible for All It's Worth;* R. A. Traina (1980), *Methodical Bible Study;* O. Wald (1975), *The Joy of Discovery in Bible Study;* J. Wilhoit and L. Ryken (1988), *Effective Bible Teaching.*

See also BIBLE STUDY METHODS; HERMENEUTICS AND EXEGESIS IN TEACHING

Inductive Learning. Process of induction that involves reasoning which progresses from the particular to the general. Inductive learning is closely associated with the scientific method of drawing conclusions from data which have been gathered and analyzed.

In educational terms, inductive learning is largely experiential and empirical. The gathering and analysis of data are used to develop theories; learners are encouraged to infer conclusions from the facts. Discovery learning and positivism are popular educational theories which are closely associated with inductive learning. Teachers who use the inductive process believe that learning is cumulative; they believe that it is important to begin with what students know and

understand and then to move to more complex levels of knowledge and understanding.

The use of inductive learning in Christian education can be found in the study of the Bible utilizing inductive methodology. In this approach to Bible study the learner begins by examining a passage of scripture with an effort to discover what the author intended to say to the first readers. This exegetical work requires an examination of the historical context, the literary context, and a careful, methodical study of the content. The basic structural relationships of the text are explored and the design of the text is identified. From there the learner seeks to develop an understanding of the potential relevance of the text for contemporary life. This process of interpretation is often referred to as hermeneutics. The learner who follows this process gathers a specific set of facts (data gathering), analyzes those facts in light of the original intent (analysis), and seeks to develop or identify applications or truths which are relevant for contemporary life (conclusions). These are the basic elements of inductive learning.

Critics of inductive learning point out the benefits of logical (deductive) inference, which has been used so successfully in many disciplines. They argue that insight or understanding is the product of deductive (not inductive) processes and that the inductive process typically utilizes prior knowledge (inference) in the pursuit of data. Inductive learning is also criticized for the pursuit of knowledge without the benefit of a meaningful context

Supporters of inductive learning insist that, if left alone, facts and information can speak for themselves and that preconceived ideas of truth (typically used in the deductive process) may be biased and untrustworthy. Learners should be allowed to make inferences from the facts and then to test those inferences in new situations. They further argue that the inductive process is really the only manner in which new knowledge can be discovered.

Inductive learning is frequently contrasted with deductive learning, the process of moving from general truth to specific facts. Most Christian educators would agree that induction and deduction can be complementary and that learning is a complex phenomenon that may be understood as utilizing both inductive and deductive processes.

DENNIS A. SHERIDAN

See also DEDUCTIVE LEARNING

Inerrancy of Scripture. For nearly a quarter of a century, the issue of inerrancy has represented a major intramural problem among evangelicals. Battered and challenged in speeches and books, the argument may lead some Christians in the twenty-first century to conclude that the doctrine of inerrancy is some recent invention concocted by fundamentalists to thwart the dilution of inspiration. So before we go any further in this brief review, we do well to note again the words of Princeton's distinguished B. B. Warfield:

> The Church, then, has held from the beginning that the Bible is the Word of God in such a sense that its words, though written by men and bearing indelibly impressed upon them the marks of their human origin, were written, nevertheless, under such an influence of the Holy Ghost as to be also the words of God, the adequate expression of His mind and will. It has always recognized that this conception of co-authorship implies that the Spirit's superintendence extends to the choice of the words by the human authors (verbal inspiration), and preserves its product from everything inconsistent with a divine authorship—thus securing, among other things, that entire truthfulness which is everywhere presupposed in and asserted for Scripture by the Biblical writers (inerrancy). (Warfield, 1948, 173)

Over two decades ago, Harold Lindsell authored *The Battle for the Bible* in which he referred to inerrancy as both "an evangelical problem" and "a doctrine of Scripture." He emphasized with Warfield the absolute centrality of Scripture as the basis for Christian faith and knowledge. Indeed, in the field of education one's position on the Bible becomes the dividing line between an evangelical view of truth and anything less. The doctrine of Scripture is the veritable foundation upon which Christian educational philosophy unfolds. Lindsell affirms Warfield's view that inerrancy has been the singular view of orthodox Christians from the days of Jesus himself: "From the historical perspective it can be said that for 2000 years the Christian church has agreed that the Bible is completely trustworthy; it is infallible or inerrant" (Lindsell, 1976, 19).

Readers should understand that this article deals with inerrancy alone; it does not treat revelation, inspiration, authority, canonicity, illumination, or hermeneutics. Even with that narrowing, we can scarcely grasp the strategic important of this concept in a few short paragraphs.

What is inerrancy? Some would insist upon a difference between the terms *inerrancy* and *infallibility*. In point of fact however, they are identical. The only possible distinction Bible scholars have made is the application of infallibility to the scriptural message about a salvific relation to God, and the use of inerrancy to focus on the words of the text. That seems confusing however, and the writings of both Warfield and Lindsell seem to use the terms synonymously.

One could even conclude that attempts to find different meanings in these two crucial words stem from the desires of some theologians to re-

tain the term *infallibility* while rejecting *inerrancy*. But neither the testimony of the Scriptures themselves nor of orthodox theologians of the past will allow that kind of distinction. In the words of Saucy, "*Inerrancy* means, simply, that the Bible is without error; it does not contain mistakes. All its statements accord with the truth"(Saucy, 1978, 78).

Pinnock warns that "the result of denying inerrancy, as skeptics well know, is the loss of a trustworthy Bible. Limited inerrancy is a slope, not a platform. Although we are repeatedly assured that minor errors in unimportant matters would not greatly affect the substance of the Christian faith nor the authority of Scripture, this admission has the effect of leaving us with a Bible which is a compound of truth and error, with no one to tell us which is which. What is lost when errors are admitted is divine *truthfulness*. Evangelicals confess inerrancy because it is biblical to do so" (Pinnock, 1971, 80).

We should ask what the Bible affirms about its own inerrancy. Though the word itself does not appear, the concept comes to us from passages such as Matthew 5:17–18; John 10:33–36; 1 Timothy 5:18; 2 Timothy 3:16–17; 2 Peter 1:19, 21; 2 Peter 3:16. What follows is a sampling of modern evangelical theologians on the Bible's testimony to itself:

> Clark Pinnock: It is an incontrovertible historical fact that Paul held to the plenary inspiration of Holy Scripture. His was the doctrine of God speaking in *all* the sacred writings. (Pinnock, 1971, 56)

> B. B. Warfield: Inspiration is, therefore, usually defined as a supernatural influence exerted on the sacred writers by the Spirit of God, by virtue of which their writings are given divine trustworthiness. (Warfield, 1948, 131)

> Charles C. Ryrie: The only way the Scripture can lose its authority is if it contains errors, but Christ taught that the Scripture cannot be broken. Thus He must have believed it did not contain errors. (Ryrie, 1986, 94)

> Philip E. Hughes: Throughout the New Testament, indeed, the whole of Christ's life, death, and resurrection is seen in the light of the fulfillment of Holy Scripture, and therefore as a vindication of the Bible as the inspired Word of God. (Henry, 1962, 16)

Can one be Christian, even evangelical, and deny the doctrine of inerrancy? Certainly, though the former represents a considerably wider playing field than the latter. Christians are defined by their relationship to Jesus Christ and acceptance of his death on the cross in their behalf. *Evangelical* is the contemporary adjective we use to specify historic orthodox theology. Yet there are modern evangelicals that do deny inerrancy so one must agree with the possibility. Nevertheless, doctrine is important and the denial of biblical truths such as the virgin birth represents an aberration in orthodox Christology. Certainly we can also affirm an orthodox doctrine of Scripture which takes its stand on an error-free Bible, affirming not only inspiration, but also inerrancy (infallibility).

KENNETH O. GANGEL

Bibliography. C. F. H. Henry (1962), *Basic Christian Doctrines;* H. Lindsell (1976), *The Battle for the Bible;* C. H. Pinnock (1971), *Biblical Revelation—The Foundation of Christian Theology;* C. C. Ryrie (1986), *Basic Theology;* R. L. Saucy (1978), *Is the Bible Reliable?;* N. B. Stonehouse and P. Woolley, eds. (1946), *Infallible Word;* B. B. Warfield (1948), *The Inspiration and Authority of the Bible.*

Infancy. The term *infant* is generally used to describe a child between birth and about eighteen months of age, although historically it has also been used to describe children up to about five years of age. The end of infancy is somewhat vague, as it can be marked by speaking in sentences, being potty trained, or walking. Sometimes infants are differentiated from toddlers, the latter denoting children who walk freely without assistance.

Too often infants are relegated to the periphery of Christian education; some believe that churches *teach* children but only *baby-sit* infants. While babies may not be able to comprehend theology, important precursors to child and adult faith can be encouraged.

Trust and Faith. Well-known developmentalist Erik Erikson (1963) emphasized the importance of infant trust as the root of faith, even religious faith. This trust comes as a result of living in a trustworthy environment, where the needs of the child are quickly and consistently met by loving adults, whether they be parents or parent-substitutes.

The church can help meet the needs of children, and thus help build strong foundations for faith, by encouraging parents to give infants adequate time and attention and by providing parent-like care of children in the church nursery. The church can provide day care for children in single parent families and others who cannot give full-time care for their children. Christians can also provide assistance to parents who choose full-time care through Bible study programs with child care and the like.

Several specific guidelines for encouraging trust in children are recommended by Caldwell (1989). Church programs for babies must be led by people who are trustworthy, in an environment that is interesting yet predictable. Having the same caregivers is the ideal, yet often difficult to achieve in churches. Those who care for infants need to have training in basic health con-

cerns such as disinfecting play spaces and using care in diaper changing. Continuity between church and home can be encouraged by exchanging notes with parents and keeping careful records. Older babies and toddlers may cry when separated from parents during church activities. A possible solution is to institute a policy that if children do not stop crying within a few minutes of the parents leaving, the parents will be summoned. What is most important is that discomfort not be associated with the church, as repeated feelings of anger, boredom, or fear in the church setting may unconsciously influence childhood and adulthood perceptions of that context.

Honig (1989) encourages adults to "read" an infant's nonverbal communications as the youngster signals interest or disinterest in activities. It is important for nursery workers to follow those signals and provide changes in activity when boredom is indicated. She believes that altruism may be encouraged by prohibiting aggression and minimizing the potential for conflict by "baby-proofing" the church nursery.

The Beginning of a Concept of God. Stern (1985) speaks of the infant internalizing repeated interactions with others so that these general patterns of activity will be recalled in the form of an "evoked companion." Thus the child may sense a person being present and playing with the baby merely upon sight of an object associated with such play. The evoked companion precedes the "numinous," the sense of the presence and relatedness with God (Fowler, 1989) which is powerfully influenced by the baby's images of parents. Rizzuto (1979) believes the infant's rudimentary idea of God functions as a transitional object between children and parents, much as blankets and teddy bears can function as parent-substitutes and thus encourage individuation and separation.

Infants are thought to perceive parents as having divine attributes, and only later being able to separate parents from God (Goldman, 1965). This underscores the importance of parental interactions in the development of an accurate concept of God. Anxiety and feelings of abandonment in relation to parents may negatively influence the understanding of God, at least at an affective level of experiencing. Church leaders thus need to encourage supportive and positive parental interactions with babies through classes for prospective and current parents of infants, thus encouraging a positive affective foundation for the child's view of God.

Baby Games and Interactions. Beginning just days after birth, babies participate in repetitive actions, termed by Piaget (1963) *circular reactions.* Activities such as banging toys and moving arms back and forth produce learning and understanding. Later in infancy these become more social and interactive in games such as "peekaboo" and nursery rhymes with associated activities. It may be that these encourage object permanence, the realization that something continues to exist even when not immediately observed, which can be compared with the biblical definition of faith (Heb. 11:1). These can be foundational for later ritualistic and interactive activities within the faith community (Fowlkes, 1989; Fowler, 1989).

Churches should encourage parents to have these playful interactions with their children, as well as teach nursery workers the importance of such activities. Simple and brief activity-based stories and music are also important, particularly with older infants. These also help form positive associations with the church environment, which—at an affective level—may last a lifetime.

Babies' Ministry to Adults. Infants can teach adults by example, as when Jesus used an infant as an object lesson (Luke 18:16–17). Christians are to realize their own helplessness and become as infants in their dependence upon God for nourishment and removal of waste (sin). Infants can teach adults a deeper understanding of the new birth symbolism, such as prebirth development, the importance of delivery—conversion—as decisive change, the immaturity of the newborn, and growth as a natural process given adequate sustenance. The birth of a baby produces joy in most parents, just as God and the angels rejoice over a new convert (Luke 15:7).

DONALD E. RATCLIFF

Bibliography. B. Caldwell (1989), *Faith Development in Early Childhood;* E. Erikson (1963), *Childhood and Society;* J. Fowler (1989), *Faith Development in Early Childhood;* M. Fowlkes, *Religious Education* 84 (1989): 338–48; R. Goldman (1965), *Readiness for Religion;* A. Honig (1989), *Faith Development in Early Childhood;* J. Piaget (1963), *The Origins of Intelligence in Children;* M. Rizzuto (1979), *The Birth of the Living God;* D. Stern (1985), *The Interpersonal World of the Infant.*

Infancy/Toddler. *See* Early Childhood.

Informal Education. An approach to learning focused on acquiring skills, knowledge, attitudes, and values growing out of student interactions with experiences or environments. While more formalized education incorporates classroom sessions, learning agendas, teacher-directed methodologies, and required courses of study, informal education offers an alternative approach. Informal education tends to be less structured, with less emphasis on required courses leading to the completion of a plan of study. It is generally more global and less linear in learning approaches.

Informal education is also more experiential than intentional in regards to learning outcomes. Learning grows out of student experiences or student interactions within an environment, either intentional or spontaneous. The field or environment drives the learning rather than the classroom.

The content of informal education is often derived from experiences or casual readings done by the student. This normally leads to a student-directed rather than a teacher-directed form of learning. The student's personal needs, priorities, life experiences, and goals dictate the daily directions of this approach to learning.

It would be a mistake to assume that all informal education is nonstructured (inductive) and without some aspects of deductive approaches. A skillful mentor, for example, might plan a series of experiences or assignments in which an apprentice will gain certain types of knowledge or skills. While the outcomes may not be clearly predictable, the student is likely to gain valuable insights into approaches that will be required in the future.

Informal education may be class or group oriented, or it could be in a one-on-one format, the most popular form of apprenticeship. In a class or group setting, students are in a cohort that works through a set of assignments or experiences leading to a variety of learning outcomes. The emphasis is heavily weighted toward application and personal learnings rather than toward assimilation of a body of content.

In church or congregational settings, informal education most likely is seen in the form of mission or ministry projects. These activities may have stated purposes and prescribed goals, but a parallel track of learning, with less predictable outcomes, often takes place. People learn valuable lessons about Christian service and ministry, gain appreciation for those they have ministered to, and develop more thoughtful lifestyles following mission or ministry projects.

Church leaders often use one-to-one pairings—a leader with a less mature Christian—to guide students in matters of spiritual growth. This approach, with less structured goals, informal meeting times, and casual meeting places, opens a rich reservoir of learning possibilities. The student learns more than the content of a lesson. The student has the opportunity to observe the teacher react and interact, gain from chance encounters, inject personal experiences into the discussion, and personalize the content in a way often missing in more formal approaches.

In a similar way, home Bible studies are popular forms of informal education. A group can interact with the biblical content and gain insights from personal experiences shared by group members. The outcomes of such a group may be different for each member of the group.

Home Bible study or discipling approaches often fall into the informal education camp. Parents' discipling of their children follows the model of Deuteronomy 6:6–7 in which parents are admonished to diligently teach their children the things of God. Further, Ephesians 6:4 directs parents to bring their children up in the training and instruction of the Lord. This is accomplished most often through modeling, casual learnings, and informal education in the everyday routines of parents and children. Children observe their parents attending church services, praying before meals, ministering to friends and neighbors, reading the Bible, and living out their Christian faith. Parents are informally teaching their children, whether they plan to do so or not.

WESLEY BLACK

See also MENTORING; NONFORMAL EDUCATION; OBSERVATIONAL LEARNING; TEACHABLE MOMENTS

Information Processing. How do people learn? Why do people forget what they learn? How do people store and retrieve the information, concepts, and associations that they accumulate as they develop from infants into adulthood? What kinds of cognitive teaching strategies can be employed to enhance the learning process? These are the types of questions which researchers in the area of information processing theory attempt to answer.

The information processing model of cognitive psychology is the dominant model among learning theories. According to this theory, information is "processed," or organized, analyzed, and synthesized, in steps or stages.

Information processing theory identifies learning as an interaction between environmental stimuli and the learner. The information to be learned is the stimulus and the learner is the processor or transformer of information. To assist in describing this exchange, information processing uses the computer as a metaphor. Like computers, people take in or input information, the information is manipulated and coded, and people output information.

In this computer metaphor of information processing, there are three types of information storage: sensory memory or sensory register, short-term memory or working memory, and long-term memory. The sensory register stores information received from the senses (sight, sound, taste, touch, smell). Also called echoic or iconic memory, the data retrieved at this stage is brief and almost unconscious. It is a momentary impression or sensation lasting from a fraction of a second to no more than three or four seconds. Sensory information is highly limited and almost all of it is permanently lost unless the data is recognized and attended to and transferred to short-term memory.

Short-term or working memory consists of information a person is currently conscious about. It lasts approximately twenty seconds and can hold about seven unrelated items of information at any given point in time. In order for items to be maintained in working memory, they must be rehearsed or repeated.

Finally, long-term memory is the permanent and relatively stable record of everything a person has learned. The storage capacity for this stage appears to be unlimited. Long-term memory is passive and unconscious and not easily disrupted. Although information stored in long-term memory may be considered permanent, not all stored knowledge is easily retrieved. Stored material is organized according to relationships, and recall involves searching for connections or associations.

In our teaching of the Bible, the goal is to move information that can lead to transformed lives from the sensory register stage of memory into long-term storage. Learning is easier and remembered longer when the material is rehearsed, well organized, related to old information, and perceived as meaningful and significant by the learner.

SHELLY CUNNINGHAM

Bibliography. K. Issler and R. Habermas (1994), *How We Learn: A Christian Teacher's Guide to Educational Psychology;* W. R. Yount (1996), *Created to Learn.*

Inner City. *See* Urban Christian Education.

Inner-City Family. *See* Urban Family.

Inner-City Youth Ministry. Ministry efforts directed at youth who reside within the core or central areas of our nation's cities. *Inner-city* youth ministry acknowledges that the context within which youth ministry occurs is an important consideration.

The inner city can be defined as that part of the city which by virtue of age and neglect has undergone physical deterioration and may be occupied primarily by persons in the lower economic strata of society. Today, youth make up the greatest percentage of almost every inner-city community due to the large number of single-parent homes and the large size of many of those families.

Youth who grow up in poverty in inner-city areas tend to share common attitudes and behaviors. These include a limited amount of time spent in the home; a lack of appreciation for time-oriented routines; involvement in antisocial activities such as gangs, drugs, and illicit sex; and fatalistic expectations. Outsiders are often surprised to discover young people and even little children playing out on the street well after dark. They observe youth living out their lives in the streets and substituting unwritten street codes for the rules and values usually taught within the home. Much of this behavior can be attributed to a lack of adequate playthings, overcrowded apartments, and inadequate adult role models.

Left unchecked, these factors produce the feeling that life beyond the streets offers little hope. This hopelessness has helped to make the inner city fertile ground for the message of a gospel of hope and love.

A popular axiom holds that ministry directed at youth is impossible apart from relationship. Nowhere is this more true and important than among inner-city youth. Experienced youth workers have determined that one of the most effective means for building relationships is through a process called person-centered ministry. Person-centered ministry requires that three key considerations be understood before attempting to build meaningful relationships with youth.

Consideration One: Minister in their world, not yours. By learning the culture, customs, norms, and habits of young people who live in inner-city communities, the youth worker will be more effective at bridging cultural and generational gaps.

Consideration Two: Minister to their needs, not yours. For all young people adolescence is a time of confusion, separation, and independence. In the turmoil of moving from adolescence to adulthood, youth have to wrestle with physical changes occurring in their bodies, pressure from society to begin to make a meaningful contribution as an individual, and peers who push for conformity to their norms. At this time in their lives, inner-city youth welcome positive Christian role models who communicate to them that they will help them to successfully navigate this period.

Consideration Three: Begin at their starting point, not yours. Life in the inner city tends to cause youth to grow up quickly—but not all young people respond to the demands of the inner city in the same way. The effective youth worker must be sensitive to meet the youth at his or her own individual level of maturity.

Person-centered ministry enables the youth worker to invest himself or herself in the life of the young person on a one-on-one basis. The accomplishment of this type of personal relationship demonstrates youth ministry at its very best.

RICK GRAY

Bibliography. W. S. Benson and M. H. Senter (1987), *The Complete Book of Youth Ministry;* D. Claerbaut (1983), *Urban Ministry;* J. M. Dettoni (1993), *Introduction to Youth Ministry.*

Input. Material that is presented to the learner during each unit or "frame" of instruction. Also called *stimulus* from its original use in operant and differential psychology, input is the first of three steps in a cycle of instruction. The cycle begins with the presentation or input of information to the learner. This may occur in many forms, including: speech, print, audio or video tape, still or moving film, computer graphics and sound, etc. The content of input is usually a single, clearly defined proposition or concept. It may also be an expansion of a concept that has been previously presented. Input usually builds sequentially upon itself, frame by frame, exposing the learner to more and more complex concepts as the instructional program unfolds.

The second step of the cycle involves an activity designed to help the learner interact with the input. An activity may be answering a question, filling in a blank, manipulating an object, or any other action that enables the learner to respond to the material in some way.

The final step gives feedback about the learner's activity response. This step determines how the learner responded, and provides the learner with reinforcement, remedial help, additional input, or another activity depending upon the results.

In computer terms, input refers to the information given to a computer system by a user through any kind of input device. Common input devices include keyboard, light-pen, touch screen, mouse, joystick, microphone, touch pad, and pedals. The computer uses this kind of input in its calculations, data manipulation, and logical functions.

ROBERT DeVARGAS

See also BRANCHING PROGRAMMING; COMPUTER-ASSISTED INSTRUCTION; COMPUTER-ENHANCED LEARNING

Insight. The idea of attaining a particular knowledge state or moving from confusion to comprehension remains central to the meaning of insight (Dominowski and Dallob, 1995). Advancements in understanding the scientific concept of insight began with the pioneering and visual perception research developed by the Gestaltists back in the 1920s and 1930s. Gestalt psychologists provided at least a half-dozen classical views of insight based on problem solving. Today, cognitive psychologists conclude that although the Gestaltist contributions posed numerous questions that remain unanswered, a fair assessment of this early work classifies it as anecdotal rather than experimental and not specific enough to permit direct experimentation (Perkins, 1981).

Insight, as with a lightning stroke, is a complex and not a singular concept. In a general overview from the recent literature, researchers do establish some consensus when identifying components of the insight process. First, there is a preparation period when the problem is identified or arrival at an impasse (failure to reach a solution) occurs. Next comes an incubation period consisting of time away from the problem serving as a transition to a solution. Third, the hallmark activity is the suddenness or the "Aha!" experience with an accompanying affective dimension that can be either a positive emotion such as joy or a negative groan of "Why didn't I see this before?" Finally comes the insight experience or illumination. The process should encourage subsequent elaboration and evaluation where one completes the hard work necessary to bring the insight to a productive end state. The insight process assumes that each moment of insight has its own internal structure—its affective and cognitive microgenesis.

Where does insight come from? In the literature there are two or three agreed-upon conventional approaches for explaining insight as well as a host of recent developments. The former view mentioned is the *special-process view,* or Wizard Merlin perspective, that includes bursts of inspiration and sudden restructuring. A contrasting approach is the *"nothing special" view,* or business as usual view, which endorses insight as a normal mental process in human learning and perceiving (Perkins, 1981). A third conventional perspective for insight is called the *prepared mind perspective*, ascribing insight to a researchable information processing procedure.

Present cognitive investigation into the nature of insight continues to progress toward consensus building, and agreement about several components such as suddenness, incubation, and spontaneity find solidarity in the reviews. Current research presents challenging ideas, controversy, and heated debate about the concept of insight. Acknowledging the social context, exploring a systems view, and reconstructing Don Campbell's evolutionary paradigm are a few of the other research possibilities under development. Insight is a common mode of learning for adults and differs radically from rote learning.

JERRY BOWLING

Bibliography. R. L. Dominowski and P. Dallob (1995), *The Nature of Insight;* D. Perkins (1981), *The Mind's Best Work.*

Instinct. *See* Insight.

Instrumental/Relativist. The terms *instrumental* and *relativist* are associated with an ancient dilemma, namely, the nature of truth and reality. Plato, in opposition to the Sophists, asserted an absolute reality—one that existed independent of humankind's construction of reality. Christians who accept Scripture as God's revelation also accept the objective or absolute nature of truth. Reality is a consequence of God's creative and redeeming activity. Reality exists independently of one's perception of that reality.

The issue of relativism is not, however, a simple one. Certain distinctions must be maintained between the nature (essence) of reality/truth and how one perceives and responds to that truth. Even within Scripture, Paul acknowledges a certain form of "relativity" (not "relativism") in how one honors God. In Romans 14:5–8 Paul allows

for a variety of approaches in honoring God, as long as each one is "fully convinced in his own mind." Christians experience a certain form of freedom (relativity) but only within the context of an absolute truth (reality). Just as a fish has the freedom to swim wherever it will within the medium of water, so the Christian is free to live individually and uniquely within the medium of being "in Christ."

The issue of relativism and instrumentality, therefore, is an issue of philosophy, morality, and faith commitment which has implications for the educational ministry of the church. A pure relativist would nurture students to create truth for themselves. A Christian educator who is committed to God's Word as truth would, on the other hand, help a student name the reality (absolute) of the Word and discern how that Word might come to expression within an individual's life (relativity).

A similar discussion could focus on the word *instrumental.* Milton Rokeach (1968) popularized the term in distinguishing between "terminal" and "instrumental" values. Astley (1994) defines an instrumental value as "the value something has as a means to something intrinsically good." Most people may know this issue as the "means vs. ends" debate. For the Christian, the "ends" are established. Phrases like "seek first his kingdom" (Matt. 6:33) and "fix our eyes on Jesus" (Heb. 12:2) define the end or goal of the Christian life. In so far as one maintains that focus, one may select any number of "means" (or instrumentalities) to achieve that end, taking into account a number of variables including culture, environment, and personality. In lesson planning, the teacher must be clear about the truth which is to be conveyed in that lesson (absolute) but is free to select a number of methods in pursuit of that goal.

ROBERT C. DE VRIES

Bibliography. J. Astley (1994), *The Philosophy of Christian Religious Education,* pp. 257–89; M. Rokeach (1968), *Beliefs, Attitudes, and Values.*

Integration of Faith and Science. Integration is the process of bringing together the knowledge discovered through the search for truth (science) with the special revelation of truth through God's communication with humans (faith). The inclusion of this article in this dictionary implies that science (particularly the social sciences) is useful to and compatible with our goals in Christian education. However, Christians throughout history have struggled with just how to integrate faith and science and occasionally have questioned the theological validity of such integration (Niebuhr, 1951).

Only after we have sufficient knowledge of science in its varied forms can we consider how or if we should attempt to integrate this knowledge into our faith. Further, only those who are committed to Christian maturity will reflect upon the degree to which their faith is influenced by the assumptions implicit within scientific inquiry.

We acquire knowledge as frequently and unconsciously as we breathe. The drive to understand ourselves and the world is God-given (Gen. 1:28) yet the pursuit of such knowledge apart from God's guidelines brings sin and death (Gen. 3). Whether we are referring to Freud's defense mechanisms or Jung's concept of the introvert, Skinner's laws of learning or Piaget's cognitive development theory, we sample freely from the social sciences, yet few would uncritically accept all that the social sciences present as fact or theory. Our assumption is that we can discern the useful from that which is incompatible with our faith, yet exactly how we accomplish this and what principles guide us is sometimes unclear.

Niebuhr presents three basic models of integration (Niebuhr, 1951). "Christ against culture" is a view held by those who are generally suspicious of humans' efforts to help themselves and who affirm special revelation (Scripture) as sufficient for any knowledge we need to live a healthy and productive life (2 Tim. 3:16–17). Proponents are normally most critical of the social sciences, which are often seen as promoting philosophy rather than faith (Rom. 1:21). Those who hold a "Christ of culture" perspective are focused on a transformation of culture more characteristic of liberal Christianity. Science and its methods are generally embraced to the degree that they don't conflict with the basic goals of Christianity. The "Christ above culture" model and its three variations account for the majority of Niebuhr's work as he summarizes Christian thinkers who attempt to maintain a primary loyalty to Christ (Isa. 55:8–9; Matt. 6:24) but recognize the theological necessity to utilize man's knowledge in this pursuit (John 17:15).

Jones's paradigm is somewhat different as he suggests three specific ways in which science and faith may be integrated (Jones and Butman, 1991). "Ethical integration" is an attempt to evaluate science by religious moral principles, while "perspectival integration" would suggest that faith and science are independent disciplines most appropriately utilized when we address an issue from different perspectives. The "Christianizer of science integration" reviews science in light of scriptural absolutes and principles with a strong commitment to Scripture as inerrant while seeing scientific vocabulary and methods as useful in God's kingdom (1 Cor. 9:22).

DAN E. CLEMENT

Bibliography. S. L. Jones and R. E. Butman (1991), *Modern Psychotherapies: A Comprehensive Christian Appraisal;* H. R. Niebuhr (1951), *Christ and Culture.*

Integration of Theology and Educational Philosophy. Not to be confused with ethnic or gender integration, this term used in the context of educational philosophy refers to the teaching of all subjects as part of the total truth of God, thereby enabling students to see the unity of natural and special revelation. Christian teachers are committed to the authority of the Bible, the teaching role of the Holy Spirit, the centrality of Scripture at the heart of curriculum, and the development of the Christian world-and-life view on the part of both faculty and students.

It stands to reason that faculty must have a highly developed biblical and theological awareness to be able to integrate scriptural truth in whatever disciplines they serve. In much the same way the Great Books became the organizing principle of curriculum at the University of Chicago several decades ago, the Bible stands at the center of curriculum for any evangelical institution wishing to pursue integration. God's revelation—personal, written, natural—stands as the foundation for a Christian philosophy of life and education. Effective Christian teachers at any level of evangelical education must carry a two-edged sword. With one sharp edge they slice through specialized disciplines, and with the other they grasp and apply biblical answers to academic and cultural questions.

Integration in educational philosophy begins with the authority of Scripture. It moves quickly to a recognition of the contemporaneity of the Bible and the Holy Spirit. Evangelical educators recognize the role of the Holy Spirit in interpreting and applying Scripture.

> But when he, the Spirit of truth, comes, he will guide you into all truth. He will not speak on his own; he will speak only what he hears, and he will tell you what is yet to come. He will bring glory to me by taking from what is mine and making it known to you. All that belongs to the Father is mine. That is why I said the Spirit will take from what is mine and make it known to you. (John 16:13–15)

The integrative process provides a clear understanding of the nature, source, discovery, and dissemination of truth. Evangelical educators affirm that *all truth is God's truth.* But what does that mean? Simply that wherever truth is found, if it is genuine truth, one can ultimately trace it back to the God of the Bible. And since the God of the Bible is also the God of creation, the true relationship between natural and special revelation begins to emerge at the junction of epistemology.

Integrative process in educational philosophy assumes the designing of a curriculum overtly constructed upon the centrality of special revelation. In the integration of faith and learning, each subject relates to Scripture and no area remains untouched. In a very real sense, integration takes place like the two cells of a battery—negative and positive. Christian educators integrate faith and learning by recognizing basic ways in which the subject fits into or is congruent with God's revelation, and by noting and demonstrating how the facts, theories, and implications of any given subject have been negatively affected by sin and, therefore, distorted.

Integration of truth and Christian education also demand the development of the Christian world-and-life view. No dichotomy exists between the sacred and secular for the thinking Christian. The teacher who genuinely understands Christian education will work courageously at developing an internalization of God's truth, not just acquiring cognitive knowledge.

We must also affirm that bibliocentric education extends to all areas of student life. Christian faith relates to every activity on the distinctively Christian campus, or for the Christian on a secular campus. Christian education which speaks openly of its integration of faith and learning assumes the accompanying responsibility to demonstrate how that philosophical posture is implemented in the lives of students at all times and in all places. In the words of John Westerhoff,

> Education involves critical reflection on every aspect of our life of faith in the sight of the Gospel. It is a reforming process that assumes and necessitates growth and change. Education, in his sense, needs to be a natural part of our personal and communal lives. Without faithful education or critical reflection as believers in Jesus Christ and members of his church, we would be unable to engage in the faithful formation of Christ-like persons and communities. (Lockerbie, 1994, 404)

The central issues of philosophy (metaphysics, epistemology, anthropology, axiology) are also the central issues of theology. Gaebelein argues that learning unrelated to life is no better than faith without works, and that though natural truth may be of a different order than revealed truth, it is nonetheless God's truth. Christian teachers do not make up truth; it always surrounds us. We experience it formally or informally and then, based on our understanding of special revelation, we ascertain through the Holy Spirit's assistance how precisely truth fits into life.

In a Christian philosophy of education, the prepared mind of the Christian student becomes fertile ground for experiencing truth both formally and informally. Consider Gaebelein's words:

> On the one hand, God's truth is external to Christian education in that it is not dependent upon what education is or does. On the other hand, there is, as integration proceeds, a merging of the internal into the external, thus the internal, though always subordinate to the external, joins in living union with the external, which remains transcendently beyond it. This is the heart of integration and the crux of the matter. (Gaebelein, 1954, 8–9)

Evangelical educational philosophy emphasizes process in integration. We do well to remember Lois LeBar's distinction between philosophy and process: "We evangelicals concur wholeheartedly on the *place* of the Bible in teaching, but we have given little thought to the *use* of the Bible" (LeBar, 1995, 122). Holistic Christian thinking does not just happen; effective Christian teachers deliberately design it. An evangelical philosophy calls Christian educators to bring culture and Christ into close union without fearing that culture will destroy truth. But such practice can only happen if teachers approach the procedure with a careful balance between open-mindedness and unchallenged doctrine. An unwarranted dogmatism which offers regimented indoctrination as a religious sop to a student who really comes for rational inquiry and learning finds no serious place in a distinctly Christian classroom.

Christian teachers and students who wish to develop their minds in an evangelical world-and-life view by thinking Christianly about the surrounding culture, discover that at least three steps seem essential: knowing the Scripture intimately; studying the culture diligently; and analyzing events and issues theologically. About every issue we face in life (as well as in the classroom) we ask several crucial questions:

1. Does the Bible speak to this issue?
2. Are there general Christian principles which apply?
3. Have Christian scholars, past or present, dealt with this issue?
4. Does this position or theory defy absolute standards of morality or value?
5. Is the Holy Spirit leading me to a definitive viewpoint on this matter?

Christian integration rests on spiritual-mindedness. It reveres not dogmatism but tolerance; not shouting but reason. And perhaps teachers should never view it as an accomplished ideal. At best we can point to some position along the journey and trust by God's grace that it will be more advanced than positions at previous points of evaluation. Integrating faith and learning falls within the boundaries of that magical word *liturgy*—it is both worship and service (Gangel and Hendricks, 1988, 85).

KENNETH O. GANGEL

Bibliography. F. E. Gaebelein (1954), *The Pattern of God's Truth: Problems of Integration and Christian Education*; K. O. Gangel and W. S. Benson (1983), *Christian Education: Its History and Philosophy*; K. O. Gangel and H. G. Hendricks (1988), *The Christian Educator's Hand-*

book of Teaching; P. A. Kienel, O. E. Gibbs, and S. R. Berry, eds. (1995), *Philosophy of Christian Education;* L. E. LeBar (1995), *Education That Is Christian;* B. D. Lockerbie (1994), *A Passion for Learning.*

Intellectualism. The term *intellectualism* is used in at least two senses. First, it is used in a positive sense to refer to the vital role of the intellect and reason in the life of faith. Second, it is used in a disparaging sense to refer to the attitude which exaggerates the role of the intellect over against the role of the will and emotions.

Intellectualism in the positive sense refers to the significant place Christian faith gives to the exercise of human intellect and scholarly endeavor. In this constructive role, the human intellect or reason reflects on the nature and meaning of God's revelation in history. It supports or confirms faith, for example, by demonstrating the manner in which Christian faith offers a compelling vision of reality. It orders and arranges various truths of revelation into logically coherent systems or doctrines. It further clarifies the implications of revelation for life and relates the truths of revelation to other areas of human knowledge.

The work of Christian scholars, as E. Harris Harbison (1956) observed in his classic work, is "to purify the religious tradition itself, to relate it to the surrounding culture, and to take account of scientific discovery." He added, however, that scholars "are never the motive power of Christianity; they are rather the governor on the driving shaft" (2–3).

A proper Christian intellectualism recognizes both the high role of human intellect and reason and its limits. From a biblical perspective, two observations regarding the human intellect are important. First, the intellect is subject to and limited by the conditions of human finitude. Some things are simply beyond comprehension by the human mind. Consequently, it should not be surprising that the Bible states that God's ways are inscrutable (Rom. 11:33) and that the world does not know God through human wisdom (1 Cor. 1:21). Second, the intellect is also subject to the distorting pressures of human sin. Reason can become a tool of the prideful self, succumbing to the sin of pride.

These limitations of human intellect do not at all commit Christians to abandoning belief in objective reality or giving up the quest for truth. Nor does it commit the Christian to irrationalism or subjectivism. The issue is not *whether* one uses reason but the *proper* use of reason.

Intellectualism in the negative sense arises out of the prideful, improper use of reason. Søren Kierkegaard (1960), one of the keenest observers and sharpest critics of such intellectualism, called it the "theoretical attitude," a kind of disengagement from God that turns God and Chris-tian faith primarily into an object of critical investigation and debate and that hangs back from intimate relationship with him.

Helmut Thielicke pointed out in his classic booklet, *A Little Exercise for Young Theologians* (1962), that the early warning signs of this form of intellectualism appear in one's language. One begins to shift from the first person to the third person. One talks less about "the will of God for my life" and more about "the implications of the biblical message," less about "Christ in my life" and more about Christology. Personal address *to* God gives way to technical discussion *about* God. This way of speaking and thinking easily becomes a way of life.

The Scriptures do not separate doctrine from spiritual life. As Jaroslav Pelikan put it, "When the Old Testament speaks about 'instruction' or the New Testament about 'doctrine,' this includes both confession and conduct, both theology and ethics." He adds that a "separation between them is fatal" (1971, 169). But fairly early in Christian history they began to be wedged apart.

Theologians began to distinguish "the precision of dogmas" from "the ethical part." Though both were viewed as important, doctrinal precision took its place well above ethics as a measure of orthodoxy; the correct profession of truth superseded the practice of truth. Throughout the succeeding centuries Christians have tended to separate belief and practice, doctrine and life.

The secularization of the academy since the Enlightenment, with its sharp division between "sacred" and "secular" learning, has raised this separation to a new and more pervasive level in the modern period. The modern academy has tended to train its members to back off from things in order to view them coolly, to distance themselves from passionate commitments for fear of losing their objectivity. For Christians immersed in this environment, the fear of being unscholarly easily looms larger than the fear of being unholy; passion for God gets replaced by descriptions of passion.

Both forms of intellectualism abound. Some Christians use their intellect in order to fathom God's depths and find clues to the biblical mysteries. Others substitute intellectualism itself, their study about God, for life in God. The difference is, as in most things Christian, a matter of the heart.

HOLLY ALLEN

Bibliography. E. H. Harbison (1956), *The Christian Scholar in the Age of the Reformation;* A. Holmes (1977), *All Truth Is God's Truth;* S. Kierkegaard (1960), *The Diary of Søren Kierkegaard;* M. Noll (1993), *The Scandal of the Evangelical Mind;* J. Pelikan (1971), *The Christian Tradition: A History of the Development of Doctrine,* vol. 1; H. Thielicke (1962), *A Little Exercise for Young Theologians.*

Intentional Processes. One use of the term *intentional processes* is found in the writings of M. M. Bakhtin (1981). In this regard Bakhtin's work is often related to that of L. S. Vygotsky. Bakhtin focused his linguistic analysis on "utterance" and the principles that organize utterances within their contexts. The way people make utterance has an intention associated with it. Therefore, it is not random. Nor is utterance mere selection. The intention is the speaker's making a word or other part of language (utterance) her or his own from the language heard from someone else. When the word is appropriated it is adapted to the speaker's own semantic and expressive intention.

Another use of the term is in the information processing theory of learning where it is sometimes called *attentional processes* (Sprinthall, Sprinthall, and Oja, 1994, 304). When a person experiences environmental input through the senses, it is sent into a sensory register in the brain. This lasts for one-half to four seconds. If the individual is paying attention to the input it is encoded and moved into storage. If the input information is not attended to immediately, it will probably be lost. If attended to, it will move into short-term memory, sometimes called "working" or "active" memory. Short-term memory can hold about seven separate items and for only a few seconds to around a minute. Sometimes the items in short-term memory may be linked or "chunked" to expand capacity. Next the memory item can be passed into long-term memory. This may take a second or up to twenty minutes. Long-term memory has the potential of holding the item for a lifetime. The key to moving items from short- to long-term memory lies in being motivated to engage in rehearsal from one to the other.

The two types of rehearsal are "maintenance" and "elaborative." Maintenance is rote repetition in short-term memory, such as repeating a telephone number. Elaborative rehearsal is based on expanding, embellishing, and relating other items or concepts already in long-term memory to the new item. Taking notes and immediately using the items are rehearsal strategies. The term *permastore* is being used to describe these strongly durable items stored in long-term memory that can be recalled with facility over long time periods. Whether one remembers things very well or not well at all is greatly dependent upon appropriate attention to the intentional processes.

EUGENE S. GIBBS

Bibliography. M. M. Bahktin (1981), *The Dialogic Imagination;* N. A. Sprinthall, R. C. Sprinthall, and S. N. Oja (1994), *Educational Psychology: A Developmental Approach.*

See also CHUNKING; INFORMATION PROCESSING; MEMORY

Interactive Learning. Methods that engage the learners with the teacher, with one another, and with the instructional content. They emphasize the relational, cooperative, dialogical aspects of teaching. Interactive methods stand in contrast to transmissive methods, which emphasize the flow of information from a knowledgeable teacher to the empty vessel: the student. The difference is between *learning by impression* (lecture, object lessons, viewing videos) in which the student's role is to sit quietly, observe, listen, and learn, and *learning by expression* (role playing, group discussion, and individual and group projects) in which the student is actively involved through speaking, writing, or physical movement (Mustazza, 56).

The rationale for interactive learning methods includes increased retention, involvement of various learning styles, enhanced student-teacher relationships, and enriched classroom experiences.

DENISE MUIR KJESBO

Bibliography. M. LeFever (1996), *Creative Teaching Methods;* C. Meyers and T. B. Jones (1993), *Promoting Active Learning;* T. Schulz and J. Schulz (1993), *Why Nobody Learns Much of Anything in Church and How to Fix It.*

Interdependence in Small Groups. The principle of *interdependence* states that individual members of a small group or community do not operate in isolation but continuously affect each other, as well as the group as a whole. Interdependence in small groups is contrasted to the negative factors of individualism, which puts self at the center of an individual's world and exalts personal rights and self-gratification over the well-being of others.

Interdependence was the practice and apostolic expectation of the small house groups of the early church. From the initial beginnings of the church, Christians "had everything in common" (Acts 2:44 NIV) and there was an assumption by the apostles that believers would minister to one another as they grew in their knowledge of Jesus Christ (Rom. 12:5; 10:24; James 5:16; 1 Peter 1:22; 4:9). The type of interdependent life together that the early church practiced was proclaimed by Jesus Christ (John 13:34–35) and modeled by him in the context of his small group, the Twelve. Many, if not all, of the profound lessons the disciples learned from Christ unfolded out of their intimate relationships with one another (see John 13:14) (Gorman, 1993, 49–50).

How can interdependence be nurtured in small groups? First, for true interdependence to exist and flourish there must be a putting aside of individualism that focuses on self and the advancement of personal interests. Second, man-made barriers of nationality, race, class, education, and gender must be overcome. One mark of a small group moving toward Spirit-empowered interdependence is the way members of different backgrounds experience a sense of belonging and freedom to relate to each other. Third, interdependence can be nurtured by practicing corporate experiences. For example, the new believers in Jerusalem continually devoted themselves "to fellowship, to the breaking of bread and to prayer" (Acts 2:42 NASB). As small group members participate with one another in disciplines such as prayer for one another, singing, sharing burdens, and even eating together, a sense of unity and oneness will be generated.

HARLEY ATKINSON

Bibliography. J. Gorman (1993), *Community That Is Christian;* G. Icenogle (1994), *Biblical Foundations for Small Group Ministry.*

See also INDIVIDUALISM AND GROUPS.

Interference in Learning. This is also known as *inhibition theory.* Within the study of transfer of learning, interference or inhibition theory emphasizes that forgetting occurs because of interfering effects of new learning and prior learning. Learning new material that is similar to previously learned material may result in forgetting some of the previously learned material (called *retroactive* interference or inhibition). Likewise, the remembrance of the previously learned material may make learning the new, similar material more difficult (called *proactive* interference or inhibition). Retroactive and proactive interference apply only when the two sets of information or tasks have interference potential, that is, when they are similar enough to cause the inhibition. Interference or inhibition is most frequently observed in situations in which students are required to memorize lists or specific facts.

For example, having memorized a list of things that occur at the point of salvation (justification, regeneration, adoption, sanctification, etc.) a student may later find it difficult to memorize a list of the Holy Spirit's ministry (convicting, regenerating, indwelling, baptizing, sealing, filling, etc.) because the two seem similar. This would be an example of proactive interference. On the other hand, after having memorized the list of the Holy Spirit's ministry, the student finds it difficult to recall accurately the previously learned list of things that occur at the point of salvation because he or she is confusing the two lists. This would be an example of retroactive interference.

There are several practical suggestions for students seeking to minimize transfer of learning interference. The first step would be to recognize and acknowledge that the phenomenon may become a problem in a specific learning situation and take specific steps to minimize the interference. One specific step would be to highlight the differences between the two sets of similar tasks. By concentrating on what the differences are, it will be easier to see the similarities in perspective to the whole. A second suggestion is to initially overlearn the material. The greater the degree of original learning, the greater the retention of the originally learned task. Third, if two tasks that are known to produce interference are learned in different environments, such as different rooms, then less interference is produced by environmental or contextual cues. An additional suggestion to avoid retroactive inhibition would be to study right before bedtime. Sleeping immediately after learning prohibits the opportunity for any additional stimulus from interfering with the retention of the material.

Teachers can assist learners in minimizing proactive inhibition by making them aware of what to expect. If students are told that learning a second task will be hindered by some specific previously learned material, they can take the positive steps mentioned above to minimize retroactive inhibition.

DALE L. MORT

Bibliography. H. C. Ellis (1972), *Fundamentals of Human Learning and Cognition.*

Interference Theory. In our teaching of the Bible, the goal is to move information that can lead to transformed lives from the barely conscious, sensory register stage of memory into long-term storage. Unlike the sensory or short-term memory stages of information processing, long-term memory appears to be almost limitless in the amount of information which can be stored and the length of time it can be stored. However, difficulties in learning and retaining new information and retrieving old information are often experienced. One of the most common proposed theories for this difficulty is interference.

According to interference theory, information may be forgotten when learning one thing interferes with, detracts from, confuses, or replaces the learning or remembering of something else. There are two types of interference: *proactive inhibition* and *retroactive inhibition.* In proactive inhibition, what was learned earlier interferes with recalling new material. For example, in a Bible survey course, after mastering the first several books, learning about subsequent books may become more difficult. In contrast, retroactive inhibition happens when new material interferes with recalling or remembering what was learned earlier. Using the same example mentioned previously, while learning about a new book of the Bible in this week's survey course, it becomes difficult to remember the details learned about earlier books.

Interference as a cause of forgetting in the learning process can be lessened by working to organize the material in such a way that related ideas are connected or taught close together and comparisons and contrasts are noted. During the Bible survey course, teach the four books which make up the Gospels together so that similarities and contrasts may be identified. Stress the distinctions and work hard to encourage overlearning of new concepts which may interfere with the old. Regular and active review will also help to prevent the "forgetting" of either old or newly learned information.

SHELLY CUNNINGHAM

Bibliography. K. Issler and R. Habermas (1994), *How We Learn: A Christian Teacher's Guide to Educational Psychology;* W. R. Yount (1996), *Created to Learn.*

Intergenerational Approach to Learning.

Traditionally, churches have provided all sorts of events and activities that bring the generations together: eating meals, service projects, parent-child banquets, and the like. Today, there are promising new approaches for keeping family units together and mixing people of various ages in multigenerational learning activities.

An intergenerational learning event is one that includes two or more generations interacting together for the purposes of nurture, discovery, or training (Koehler, 1977, 4). The benefits are many. These include receiving affirmation from others, helping people understand each other, providing for modeling to take place, obtaining points of view different from one's own, and fostering communication and relationships among family members and others.

Educational objectives for intergenerational learning are similar to those of other learning contexts: content objectives such as learning biblical concepts about death; affective objectives including shaping values and attitudes toward death; or skill-building objectives such as developing listening skills.

There are any number of church settings for these events. Basic settings incorporate ongoing church services or activities, such as a Sunday school class, midweek meeting, Sunday evening service, or a "fifth Sunday" morning or evening session. Short-term settings include occasional basic church settings such as holding a multigenerational Sunday school for one month in place of regular Sunday school; adult small groups focusing on two or four intergenerational sessions a year, or once a month in place of a regular meeting; Wednesday evening intergenerational events replacing midweek meetings during the summer months, with one quarter's Sunday school classes for fourth to sixth graders and parents; or structuring a one-day, three- to four-hour celebration with meals, replacing all Sunday morning activities.

Elective, short-term settings offer another option: a six-week elective intergenerational Sunday morning class; a teen and parent course on teen-parent relationships; an intergenerational vacation Bible school; an eight-week family cluster dealing with family life skills; or a Lenten home Bible study for all ages.

Elective, ongoing settings suggest further opportunities. Examples include a Sunday school class for elementary school children and their parents, elective classes for teens and adults or for all age groups, or a home group that is intergenerational (meeting perhaps once a month or weekly).

When an intergenerational event includes all generations—children, youth, and adults—educators propose following a number of principles. (1) Design activities for all to participate in. (2) Devise methods geared to children of about 8 years old, with provision for those unable to read. Use action learning such as drawing, drama, role play, and so on, rather than a heavy emphasis on verbal presentations. (3) Explain clearly the aim of each activity. (4) Use visual aids as much as possible. (5) Plan to change activities about every ten minutes. (6) If the group is large, break it down into small groups. (7) Conduct discussions to cause learners to think about what they have experienced. (8) Plan activities that build relationships. (9) If you use games, try to make them purposeful and related to the main theme. (10) Determine to keep the adults from dominating the discussions.

Multigenerational learning sometimes meets with resistance. Adults may not value creative learning activities, nor do they at times feel challenged. Besides these obstacles, people must overcome the threat of discussing issues with people of other age levels. Integenerational learning is unique and novel. Participants don't know what to expect or how to act in such situations, and leaders often are not sure how to conduct them.

The availability of appropriate literature is changing that. Both White's *Intergenerational Religious Education* and Miles's *Families Growing Together* are complete and practical guides for this type of ministry. The book *Families Growing Together* has an up-to-date listing of the resources available for launching and sustaining exciting and meaningful intergenerational events.

CHARLES M. SELL

Bibliography. G. E. Koehler (1977), *Learning Together: A Guide for Intergenerational Education in the Church School;* M. S. Miles (1990), *Families Growing Together: Church Programs for Family Learning;* J. W. White (1988), *Intergenerational Religious Education.*

Intergenerational Learning.

A learning experience in which two or more generations participate at the same time. However, defining a generation is hard to do. One method of identifying a generation uses the groups of younger children, older children, youth, young adults, middle adults, and older adults (Kohler, 1976). In their significant book about the cycle of generations throughout America's history, Strauss and Howe (1991) define a generation as "a special cohort-group whose length approximately matches that of a basic phase of life, or about every twenty-two years over the last three centuries" (34). With this definition in mind, intergenerational learning is not a learning experience shared by children, youth, and adults. It is an experience shared by children, parents, and grandparents.

James White, author of *Intergenerational Religious Education* (1988), observes that "however one chooses to define generation, the point is that there are important differences in people brought about by the years lived and social/cultural/historical events in those years" (21). Intergenerational learning helps generations of people involved learn about each other and from each other.

White also observes that intergenerational learning takes place when the following factors are present: common experiences, parallel learning, contributive occasions, and interactive sharing. In order to learn from others, everyone involved must be present at the same time. Because people learn differently at different ages, the same material must be presented in several age-appropriate ways for parallel learning to take place. After parallel learning takes place, everyone must contribute something to the whole experience. Finally, interactive sharing is necessary to learn from one another and gain everyone's perspective.

Goals of Intergenerational Learning. The main goal of intergenerational learning is interaction among the generations. There are other basic objectives that are similar to those of other learning experiences involving new ways of thinking, feeling, or doing. Sell (1995) noted that "the value of intergenerational education is located in the process itself, which becomes both the means of learning and the occasion of gaining certain learning by-products" (187).

Grouping Generations. White (1988) lists five options for grouping intergenerational learning: family cluster groups/extended spiritual families; one-day workshops; special events; workshop service and related activities; and annual family camps. These groups are easily organized using familiar paradigms such as family group, weekly class, workshop, worship service, or camp.

There are many themes appropriate for intergenerational learning. Work projects, family issues/problems, Bible study, celebrations, and missions studies are appropriate points of common focus. The actual content and curriculum does vary widely among denominations and congregations.

A wide variety of methods is useful in intergenerational learning situations. Sell (1995) provides nine useful principles in selecting methods. Sell states that "methods should (1) provide for intergenerational interaction, (2) allow nonreaders to participate, (3) challenge adult thinking, (4) provide for physical movement between approximately ten-minute segments, (5) offer variety, (6) creatively involve the various senses, (7) make the experience enjoyable, (8) stimulate in-depth relationships, and (9) provoke interaction with God and His truth" (194). A variety of methods should be used at any intergenerational learning event. Therefore, useful methods include, but are not limited to, drawing, simulation games, small group discussion, camping, role play, film, video, puppets, storytelling, illustrated lecture, pantomime, posters, singing, and cooking.

One specialized approach to intergenerational learning is the "family cluster" approach. Grouping, goals, and methods all focus on the concerns of family life. In this approach, a number of complete family units regularly meet together for an extended period of time. The overall goals of the family cluster approach are for participants to support one another and learn how to deal with family problems. Among the unique methods involved in family clusters is the use of a contract. Each family signs a contract committing each member to active participation in the learning experience (Miles, 1990).

RONNIE J. JOHNSON

Bibliography. G. E. Koehler (1976), *Learning Together: A Guide for Intergenerational Education in the Church School;* M. S. Miles (1990), *Families Growing Together: Church Programs for Family Learning;* C. M. Sell (1995), *Family Ministry;* W. Strauss and N. Howe (1991), *Generations: The History of America's Future, 1584–2069;* J. W. White (1988), *Intergenerational Religious Education.*

See also CONTEXT IN TEACHING AND MINISTRY; CONTRACT LEARNING; FAMILY LIFE EDUCATION

Internal Rewards. *See* Intrinsic Rewards.

International Council on Religious Education. The International Council on Religious Education (ICRE) was organized in 1922 and functioned as an independent body until 1950, when it became part of the Commission on General Education of the National Council of Churches. The purpose of the organization was to foster American religious education, which was accomplished through a number of vehicles, including publishing uniform and graded curricula, offering a leadership training program, publishing a journal, hosting religious education conferences, and encouraging religious education during and after school.

The roots of the Council emanate from the American Sunday school movement and the American Sunday School Union. In America, Christian education was initially housed in public schools and in postsecondary institutions. The Bible was a primary focus of the curriculum and a primer for learning reading and values. When the Bible lost its place in public education, the Sunday school movement filled the educational void.

Taking its cue from Robert Raikes in England, Sunday school was a laity-led movement. With the founding of the American Sunday School Union in 1824 the movement became organized. The Union wrote and distributed curriculum, aggressively founded Sunday schools, evangelized thousands of students, and, despite a lack of formal clergy or denominational support, became the central agency in the progress of Sunday school for more than forty years.

However, the Union and church leadership recognized that the movement was not addressing four educational needs: an effective curriculum; properly trained teachers; an educational philosophy and teaching methods that were effective and appropriate; and a general professional oversight that could evaluate and renew the church's educational program. In 1832, the Union recommended and facilitated a national convention, which eventually became international conventions and at the 1922 convention in Kansas City the ICRE was formed. By then the international conventions were in the hands of those to the left of evangelicals theologically.

The conventions were attended by well-known church leaders within and outside main denominations. Initially, actions taken by the convention were brought to the convention floor for approval of the delegates. Gradually, the conventions lost legal control to an organizational committee and its director. Along with this development, denominations formed their own Sunday School Council, causing a schism in the church's educational progress. At the 1922 convention all factions, denominations, independents, a few evangelicals, and liberals agreed to a merged organization.

The process of the merger raised a debate over whether the Council should be called "religious" or "Christian." Some conservatives felt that the term *religious* would diminish the amount of Bible in the curriculum and allow it to include secular literature, psychology, and other general education subjects. In reality, there were a number of conflicts between the conservatives and liberals over questions relating to the infallibility of the Bible (authoritative or a guide?), the degree of Bible content within a curriculum (primary or secondary?), the natural state of man (sinful or good?), and the outreach emphasis of Sunday school (evangelistic or the general development of religious character?).

Eventually, the conservatives broke from ICRE, forming their own organizations including the Evangelical Teacher Training Association (today, Evangelical Training Association) in 1930, and

the National Sunday School Association in 1946. These were begun by those affiliated with the eventual formation of the National Association of Evangelicals.

MICHAEL J. KANE

Bibliography. C. B. Eavey (1964), *History of Christian Education.*

InterVarsity Christian Fellowship. InterVarsity emerged out of the student university movements in Britain and particularly from a group of committed students at Cambridge University in England. Student-initiated Christian societies were known in Britain as early as the 1600s (Johnson, 1979, 26). With the expansion of universities in the late 1800s, a student movement committed to the Bible, evangelism, and mission grew, with significant impact locally and globally. Christian unions were pioneered by students on university and college campuses throughout Britain.

By the early 1900s, however, many of the student groups under the umbrella of what became known as the Student Christian Movement (SCM) had become so theologically inclusive that evangelical students began to withdraw from SCM because of doctrinal issues and their concern for biblical truth and a clear witness to the student world. With a concern to bring together evangelical students from various campuses, the first InterVarsity Conference for university students was held in December 1919. This became an annual event, and by 1925 a doctrinal basis for the conference was articulated in order to clarify what was essential to Christianity (Hill, 10).

In April 1928 evangelical student groups were formally formed into the InterVarsity Fellowship of Evangelical Unions (which was known as IVF). From the beginning IVF was influenced by the Keswick movement, with its emphasis on the lordship of Christ, personal holiness, the work of the Holy Spirit, and the importance of outreach to people around the world. In 1933 further developments occurred with the establishment of the Theological Students' Fellowship to assist students to stand firm in their faith in the university environment. Concurrently, a Missionary Fellowship presenting the missionary challenge to the students and a Prayer Fellowship to encourage former members who were now in ministry developed.

At the same conference as IVF's formal founding, international expansion was promoted when Norman Grubb, a missionary leader and a British university graduate, returned from Canada in time for the annual IVF conference in 1928 requesting that a representative from the British InterVarsity pioneer the work in Canada because the state of Christian unions on campuses in Canada and the United States was so weak. Rowland Bingham, a Canadian leader who was the founder and director of the Sudan Interior Mission (SIM), was in attendance at the same conference. He also encouraged IVF to consider Canada. Howard Guinness was chosen to go to Canada and left in November 1928. He traveled throughout the country for over a year with a clear vision to establish an evangelical witness on university campuses. He also initiated a Pioneer Camp for senior high school boys during this time before leaving for Australia at the end of 1929 to further the IVF ministry. In 1930 Noel Palmer resigned his pastorate so that he and his wife, Josie, could become the Canadian team leaders of InterVarsity (Donald, 1991, 121).

Upon Guinness's return from Australia and New Zealand in 1930, he and Palmer agreed to immediately launch the Inter School Christian Fellowship (ISCF) in Canadian high schools. Later the first Pioneer Girls Camp was held in the summer of 1933. To this day the two fundamental strategies for InterVarsity Christian Fellowship (IVCF) of Canada continue to be student groups on campuses and Pioneer Camps, though the ministry has been expanded to include various vocational fellowships as well.

In 1934 Stacey Woods, originally from Australia, came to head the Canadian IVF, and in 1936 he invited Charles Troutman Jr., an American, to join the Canadian staff. In 1938 the InterVarsity Fellowship of Canada board approved work in the United States, appointing the first three workers in 1939. Although there had been Christian students meeting on various U.S. campuses, Woods and Troutman gave focus to these fragmented groups by linking them to a mushrooming international movement. Finally, in 1941 the first official meeting of the U.S. board was convened with its own constitution.

In the same year (1941) the United States InterVarsity started *HIS* magazine in order to assist students in becoming what God wanted them to be (Hunt and Hunt, 1991, 94). *HIS* Magazine continued until it was renamed *U* magazine in 1987, but this ministry ended for IVCF in 1988.

With the rapid growth of the movement, training became an important component. Key national leadership development camps were developed to train students in off campus training centers. The first student training camp opened in 1945 for Canadian and United States IVCF staff north of Toronto and was known as Campus-in-the-Woods. These training camps expanded to various strategic areas in the United States as IVCF grew.

Motivating students to world missions was a vital part of InterVarsity's heartbeat, and in 1945 another student movement, Student Foreign Missions Fellowship (SFMF), merged with IVCF. The first Urbana missions conference attracted 576 students and took place at the University of Toronto in Ontario, Canada, December 27, 1946–January 2, 1947. Key speakers at that conference included Bakht Singh of India, Rev. L. E. Maxwell, president of Prairie Bible Institute, Rev. Robert McQuilkin, president of Columbia Bible College, Dr. Harold Ockenga, pastor of Park Street Church in Boston, and Dr. Samuel Zwemer, a missionary pioneer to the Muslims.

With rapid growth in the U.S. movement, the second student missionary conference was held at the University of Illinois, Urbana, December 27, 1947–January 1, 1948, with the theme "From Every Campus to Every Country" (Hunt and Hunt, 1991, 129). Now this missions-focused conference is held on a three-year cycle at Urbana, with over 19,000 in attendance in 1996.

Right from the beginning, with InterVarsity's focus on witnessing, inductive Bible study, and global missions, literature that was appropriate to the student world became an obvious need. Bible study aids, books relating to apologetics and theology, as well as evangelistic materials became strategic. As a result, the InterVarsity Press was born in England. At first the North American InterVarsities used many of the materials from IVP in Britain. In 1947–48, however, InterVarsity Press in the United States became the official publishing arm of the IVF in that country (Hunt and Hunt, 1991, 115). The publishing arms in both countries still share titles at times, and numerous titles have been translated into a multitude of other languages. In 1963 the British InterVarsity Press even assisted in establishing the Africa Christian Press with a focus on encouraging African literature rather than merely translating Western materials.

As InterVarsity expanded in Canada and the United States, the Nurses Christian Fellowship became part of IVCF. Special programs for professional groups, such as the Teachers Christian Fellowship, as well as educational opportunities for leadership and cross-cultural ministries were developed.

Early in its existence, the British IVF (in 1974 the name was changed to the Universities and College Christian Fellowship for Evangelical Unions, UCCF, and included the United Kingdom and Ireland) and later the Canadian IVCF had a concern to reach out to students in other countries. This became the foundation of a global fellowship formalized in 1947 as the International Fellowship of Evangelical Students (IFES) with Stacey Woods as its first leader. Today the IFES represents more than 130 countries with indigenous student groups as members.

InterVarsity continues to provide Christian witness and discipleship to the world's universities and their students. Encouraging student initiative and student leadership with the constant changeover of students entering and graduating is an ongoing challenge. Establishing witnessing communities of students and faculty on high school, college, and university campuses throughout the world with a clearer partnership with the local church remains the passion of InterVarsity as each country seeks to fulfill its mandate of evangelism, discipleship, caring support, truth, and mission with students and alumni.

CHARLOTTE K. BATES

Bibliography. M. V. Donald (1991), *A Spreading Tree: A History of Inter-Varsity Christian Fellowship of Canada, 1928–1989, Sixty Years;* R. Hill, *For the Faith of the Gospel, 1928–78: The IVF/UCCF Story; Honouring God's Faithfulness in the Student World;* K. Hunt and G. Hunt (1991), *For Christ and the University: The Story of InterVarsity Christian Fellowship of the U.S.A./1940–1990;* D. Johnson (1979), *Contending for the Faith: A History of the Evangelical Movement in the Universities and Colleges.*

Intimacy. Although the word *intimacy* is used extensively in counseling circles, it is rarely found in most psychological dictionaries. In Webster's thesaurus, the word is synonymous with *acquaintance.* Other related words are *familiarity* and *inwardness*.

The word *intimate* comes from the Latin word, *intimus,* which means "innermost." Intimacy suggests a very strong personal relationship, a special closeness that suggests a mutual understanding of one another. Ferguson (1994) sees it as a wordless gnawing of the soul for emotional and spiritual connectedness with our Creator and also with other human beings.

Chafetz (1989) describes intimacy as relatively open communication on a broad range of topics salient to the lives of each spouse, including substantial empathy for one another's joys, concerns, and problems. He views it as being based upon deep communication and established relationships. He recognizes that intimacy is a development in the relationship governed by the couple's ability to communicate with and express empathy for one another.

Lamanna and Riedmann (1994) define intimacy (as related to love) as the capacity to share one's inner self with someone else and to commit oneself to that person despite some personal sacrifices. They recognize the necessity for communication and self-disclosure, but they introduce the idea of commitment that leads to trust and selflessness as important elements in the development of intimacy. Their definition also suggests that intimacy is directly related to a person's capacity/ability to share his or her innermost being with another person.

It is suggested that there are two levels of intimacy: sexual intimacy and psychic intimacy. Sexual intimacy references two people who share their bodies sexually, while psychic intimacy implies two people sharing their minds and feelings. Sexual intimacy is experienced as two individuals give themselves to one another as an act of communicating affection and caring through intimate physical contact.

While the sexual and psychic are both referred to as intimacy, they can exist simultaneously and still maintain their individual identity. Others have suggested that these concepts are actually two separate components of intimacy.

Some of the defining features of intimacy might include openness, honesty, mutual self-disclosure, caring, warmth, protecting, helping, being devoted to each other, mutually attentive, mutually committed, surrendering control, dropping defenses, becoming emotionally attached, and feeling distressed when separation occurs.

JAMES A. HEADRICK

Bibliography. J. Chafetz (1989), *Marital Intimacy and Conflict: The Irony of Spousal Equality in Women: A Feminist Perspective;* D. and T. Ferguson and C. and H. Thurman (1994), *Intimate Encounter;* idem (1994), *The Pursuit of Intimacy;* M. A. Lamanna and A. Riedman (1994), *Marriages and Families: Making Choices and Facing Change;* J. Trent (1996), *Love for All Seasons: Eight Ways to Nurture Intimacy;* H. N. Wright (1992), *Holding on to Romance: Keeping Your Marriage Alive and Passionate After the Honeymoon Years are Over.*

Intrinsic Rewards. In contrast to an extrinsic reward where a student receives something external, such as a good grade, a star, or verbal praise, an intrinsic reward refers to an internal satisfaction on the part of the student. The thrill that accompanies the discovery of something new, or the excitement of finally understanding a concept, or even the achievement of a personal goal are all examples of intrinsic rewards. Because extrinsic rewards may not always be present in every learning situation, intrinsic rewards provide a more effective and longer lasting motivation to learn.

Intrinsic rewards are usually associated with the cognitive learning theories and Jerome Bruner's Discovery Learning, or the humanistic philosophies of Abraham Maslow and Carl Rogers. According to Bruner, all students have an innate will to learn that stems from their own curiosity, their drive to achieve, and their desire to work cooperatively with others (Yount, 1996). The fulfillment of these desires is rewarding in itself. In Maslow's hierarchy of needs, the achievement of intrinsic rewards motivates the individual toward self-actualization. It is the feeling of accomplishment and the sense of well-being that causes individuals to strive to become the best they can be as persons and to take the fullest advantage of their potential as human beings.

The Scriptures are filled with examples of how the Word of God should be an intrinsic reward in and of itself. Psalm 119 speaks often of how God's Word is a delight to those who read and study it (vv. 16, 35, 47, 70, 77, 92, 143, and 174). In the New Testament, Paul also refers to the joy that the law of God brings to the inner person (Rom. 7:22). Many times God links present intrinsic rewards with future extrinsic rewards. In Colossians 3:22–25, Paul promises servants that if they serve their masters for the intrinsic reward of pleasing God and not for the extrinsic reward of pleasing men, they will eventually receive the extrinsic reward of a future inheritance.

DALE L. MORT

Bibliography. W. R. Yount (1996), *Created to Learn.*

See also HUMANISM, CLASSICAL; MASLOW, ABRAHAM

Intuitive Conceptualizing. The way in which children from approximately 4 to 7 years of age form concepts. Children this age begin to see relationships and to use numbers. However, these capacities are said to be intuitive because the children usually cannot explain the concept. They have an intuitive grasp of an idea, but not the mental capacity to explain it logically.

Even if children do not fully understand a concept so they can explain it, the concept may be functional. The concept guides actions and choices. For example, children will not be able to explain the theological concept of the omnipresence of God. However, if the concept is explained and experienced in units understandable to them, children are intuitively aware of God's presence everywhere; they function as if they could explain the concept.

The idea of intuitive conceptualizing has immense importance for Christian educators of children. Christian educators should plan and teach with the following principles in mind: (1) Much of children's faith response is intuitive. Children do not usually master biblical concepts and their application on the formal level. Understanding this prevents educators from expecting children who respond appropriately in one situation to respond the same way in another situation. (2) Translate faith concepts into children's experiences to communicate effectively. (3) Communication of biblical concepts requires situation-specific instruction. (4) Children are constructivist learners. They think about those things with which they have had experience. (5) Much of what children understand about faith they learn by imitating significant persons in their lives. Teachers who model appropriate responses are as important as the words they speak and the experiences they plan.

If these principles are observed, children who conceptualize intuitively can and do learn biblical concepts and faith responses.

ELEANOR A. DANIEL

Bibliography. L. O. Richards (1983), *Children's Ministry;* J. Westerhoff (1976), *Will Our Children Have Faith?*

James, William (1842–1910). American psychologist and one of the founders and proponents of pragmatism. He was educated by tutors and at private schools in the United States and Europe. In 1869, after having twice interrupted his studies at Harvard to do research in Brazil and to study physiological psychology in Germany, he received his medical degree. Possessing a deep interest in the relationship between the mind and the body, he began teaching psychology at Harvard in 1876 and philosophy three years later. James remained at Harvard until his retirement in 1907.

Among his most noteworthy students were G. Stanley Hall, the first individual to earn a Ph.D. in psychology at Harvard, and Gertrude Stein, who credited his mentoring influence in her first book, *Three Lives.*

James's writing career began with book reviews in popular magazines and philosophical journals. He gained some notoriety abroad for a series of philosophical essays he composed for a French publication. Although he wrote at length on the subject, James never developed his own systematic philosophy. To him asking the right questions was of greater value than arriving at answers. Furthermore, he purposely shunned dogmatism, preferring to write for popular rather than professional audiences. At times unsettled in his approach to the study of psychology, he taught it as a natural science, and concluded a twelve-year writing project by publishing his two-volume *Principles of Psychology* (1890).

James taught that consciousness functions in an active, purposeful manner to relate and organize thoughts, thus giving them a "streamlike continuity." This theory further stated that the validity of an idea is supported by its utilitarian character (it has come to be known as functionalism). *Principles,* which was subsequently abridged into one volume, was acclaimed as both an academic and stylistic success and became the leading psychology text in both Europe and the United States. Combined with his *Talks with Teachers* (1899), which was a volume of earlier lectures he had given on the subject, it influenced the introduction of scientific and experimental psychology into the theory and practice of education.

Thinking, according to James, is always personal and subjective, occurring as a reflexive action and not as some mechanical and determined process. He referred to the "fringe of consciousness" out of which the will makes selections by preferring one stimulus over another. Such is the manner, as James saw it, in which organisms adapt themselves for survival. This formed the basis of James's psychological theory, as well as of his pragmatic philosophy. After he had established an international reputation in psychology, he focused his later works on philosophy. It is not surprising, therefore, that many of his philosophical views find their roots in his psychological studies.

James elaborated his theory of pragmatism in works such as *Pragmatism: A New Name for Some Old Ways of Thinking* (1907) and *The Meaning of Truth: A Sequel to Pragmatism* (1909). He considered pragmatism to be both a method for analyzing philosophical questions as well as a theory of truth. He further saw it as an extension of empiricist thinking in that it departed from abstract theory with absolute principles to concrete theory with relative principles. "Truth happens to an idea," he declared. "It becomes true, is made true by events." If a notion of truth is useful, it is pragmatic; it is true because it works, not the other way around. Theories, James would contend, were useful only so far as their utilitarian value was determined. But, he would add, as human experience changes, truth may also change.

Although he belonged to no church or organized religious group, James regarded a religious faith as beneficial. In *The Varieties of Religious*

Experience (1902), he examined the issue of belief in cases in which no immediate evidence exists on which to base one's belief. As a strong advocate of free will, he concluded that in the area of religious commitment, belief can create its own truth through the effects created in the experience of the believer by his or her "willing nature." He did not define "religion" as such, but rather the "life of religion," which "consists of the belief that there is an unseen order, and that our supreme good lies in harmoniously adjusting ourselves thereto." Doubt and uncertainty produce neuroses, and faith is able to provide a curative effect. Belief in God, then, is pragmatically justified if it makes a positive difference in the experience of the believer. Consequently, James extended this principle by giving similar credence to individuals who participated in clairvoyance, mental healing, and other practices that defied scientific explanation, thereby making enemies in both the medical-scientific and orthodox religious communities.

Although such tolerance damaged his professional reputation, James established himself as a pioneer in the field of psychic research and bolstered the discussion of psychic phenomena in legitimate circles. In the field of education, his influence on twentieth-century pragmatic theorists, most notably John Dewey, continues to the present. During his latter years he came to be accepted as the foremost American philosopher of his time.

DAVID GOUGH

Bibliography. G. W. Allen (1967), *William James;* H. M. Feinstein (1984), *Becoming William James;* W. James (1907), *Pragmatism: A New Name for Some Old Ways of Thinking;* idem (1902), *The Varieties of Religious Experience.*

See also DEWEY, JOHN; PSYCHOLOGY OF RELIGION

Jesuits and the Counter Reformation. The Society of Jesus (*Societas Jesu*), whose members are called Jesuits, is the largest Roman Catholic male religious order in the world. It was founded in Paris on August 15, 1534, by a Basque nobleman named Ignatius Loyola (c. 1491–1556) and six of his companions, all of whom took vows of poverty and chastity in the hope of serving the Catholic Church as missionaries to the Muslims of Palestine. In 1537 these men traveled to Venice in order to secure safe passage to the Holy Land. While there, they attracted three additional followers but, because the republic of Venice was then at war with sultan Soleiman II, they were unable to set sail. Consequently, they journeyed to Rome in order to present themselves to the pope, offering to serve as itinerant ministers wherever he would direct them, and always for the greater glory of God (hence the Jesuit motto, *ad majorem Dei gloriam*). Pope Paul III welcomed

them warmly, giving them each local assignments, and approved them formally as a Catholic order in September 1540.

As the Jesuit order grew, so did the influence of Ignatius's now-classic work, the *Spiritual Exercises*. Begun in the early 1520s and revised throughout his lifetime, the *Spiritual Exercises* offered a four-week course of study and contemplation in Christian perfection. Encouraging readers to mortify the things of the flesh and give themselves over entirely to the service of God, the *Spiritual Exercises* served as the founding document of Jesuit life and mission. Each new recruit was required to undertake this four-week course upon entering the order and, by 1570, most Jesuits performed the exercises on an annual basis as well, contemplating their sin (week one), the kingdom of Christ (week two), and Jesus' passion and resurrection (weeks three and four). Before long, the Jesuits used this book in their missions among the people, holding retreats and encouraging devotions that continue to this day.

After taking their first steps along Ignatius's road to Christian perfection, Jesuit missionaries were eager to fulfill their vow to serve wherever the pope would direct (a vow unique to the Jesuit order). Many early Jesuits, most notably Ignatius's closest colleague, Francis Xavier (1506–52), served as itinerant evangelists in far-off places like India and Japan. As time went on, however, most of the Jesuits' missionary labors were spent on the founding of schools and the task of promoting Christian education. Ignatius insisted that even his greatest missionaries and theologians spend time catechizing the young and working to educate the poor. And by the time of Ignatius's death (1556), nearly three-fourths of his order was involved in some way in Christian education (roughly the same percentage of Jesuits has been involved in education ever since).

While the Jesuits were not the first monks to distinguish themselves as teachers, they were the first for whom pedagogy was a stated part of their monastic mission. By the time of Ignatius's death, there were already 46 Jesuit colleges. By 1579, there were 144. And in 1599 the Jesuits codified their pedagogy in the well-known *Ratio Studiorum*, which not only established curricular aims, but set forth teaching methods and standards of scholarly life for their schools as well. In fact, the Jesuits played such a major role in early modern education that, before the Enlightenment, they were often referred to as the "schoolmasters of Europe." All the Jesuit schools were open to people of every class and their instruction was always offered tuition-free. The most famous of these schools was founded in 1551 and was known in its early years as the Roman College. Since the time of Pope Gregory XIII (1572–85) it has been called the Gregorian University and is known as the school that produced the first modern seminary. To this day, education is so important within the Jesuit order itself that its novitiates must undergo several years of study before ordination. Working first in the liberal arts, and then philosophy and theology, they often take up several more years of study in pursuit of advanced degrees.

Such a heavy emphasis on education both within and outside the order has led quite naturally to a high level of theological sophistication. And, while anti-Protestant dogmatic efforts had only an incidental place on the original Jesuit agenda, they proved a major part of the sixteenth-century work of these papal servants. Indeed, it was often the Jesuits who took the lead in shoring up the Catholic Church by revivifying and codifying its theology. Both at the Council of Trent (1546–63) and in subsequent Catholic debates on the doctrines of grace (particularly the *de auxiliis* controversy of the late sixteenth and early seventeenth centuries), Jesuits made major contributions to the Counter-Reformation. In response to Protestant claims that Scripture alone (*sola Scriptura*) was normative for Christian doctrine, the Jesuits argued that Catholic tradition was a necessary guide for interpreting Scripture. And in the face of Protestant claims that justification comes only through faith (*sola fide*), the Jesuits claimed that saving faith must always be shaped by meritorious acts of love. Such prominent Jesuit theologians as Peter Canisius, Robert Bellarmine, and Francisco Suarez led the way in this Catholic countermovement and established a long tradition of first-rate Jesuit theological reflection.

The area in which the Jesuits have left their greatest mark in the history of scholarship is in a field of study they helped to create, moral theology. Having taken a special interest in the Catholic sacrament of penance early on, the Jesuits soon became famous for their lectures on "cases of conscience." Tackling very specific and thus quite difficult moral issues with great precision (some would say too great) and logical consistency, they pioneered in the field of moral casuistry. And as moral theology became a separate field of study in the sixteenth century, the Jesuits often led the way in its development. They became famous (and often notorious) for their advocacy of "probabilistic" moral reasoning, which allowed for moral liberty in the most difficult cases of conscience. And while ridiculed by Blaise Pascal and others for their excessive (and thus legalistic) ethical precisionism, their painstaking work in this field of study has raised the scholarly standard throughout the discipline.

As well-known experts in cases of conscience, the Jesuits were often sought after to serve as confessors to kings and noblemen. Indeed, throughout middle Europe during the early modern period, it was the Jesuits who most frequently filled such roles. Not surprisingly, they aroused much jealousy by assuming these positions of privilege, particularly among those Catholics (such as the Jansenists and the Gallican nationalists of France) who already resented their theological stance. By the first half of the eighteenth century, Enlightenment philosophies, as well, attacked the Jesuits on secular grounds, ridiculing their ethical and theological precisionism. By the late 1750s, the Jesuits had become so unpopular that various European rulers began to expel them from their territories.

By the year 1773, opposition to the Jesuits had become so strong that Pope Clement XIV, under pressure from the French courts, officially suppressed the Society of Jesus by papal edict. While a complete eradication of the order never actually took place (mainly because the Russian empress Catherine II refused to enforce the edict, allowing the Jesuits to carry on their work throughout her territories), this papal suppression decimated the Jesuits and their ministry. Pope Pius VII did restore the order on August 7, 1814, after Napolean fell and the pope himself was released from captivity in France. But it would take another century before the Jesuits had regained the numerical strength and the influence that they had lost in the difficult years of the mid-eighteenth century.

Today the Society of Jesus is as strong as it ever was and it continues to further its mission of Christian education. There are now Jesuits hard at work in most countries throughout the world. And there are roughly one million students enrolled in literally thousands of Jesuit schools. Having become especially strong in the United States, the Jesuits' best-known universities now include Fordham, Georgetown, Loyola, and Marquette. And while in 1749 (the last year prior to their suppression for which there are extant records) the Jesuits numbered 22,589, in 1990 they numbered approximately 24,500. It is the Society of Jesus that now runs the Vatican Radio Station. The Jesuits now edit several leading religious journals including *Gregorianum*, *Biblica*, *Etudes*, *Civilita Cattolica*, *The Heythrop Journal*, and *Theological Studies*. And the Jesuits have made a greater contribution to theological scholarship in the twentieth century than probably any other single religious order or denomination (their leading theologians in this century have included such luminaries as Karl Rahner, Jean Danielou, Henri de Lubac, Bernard Lonergan, and Teilhard de Chardin). Clearly, then, the Society of Jesus has borne more fruit in the field of Christian education than its founding fathers ever imagined. Despite their controversial reputation in many non-Jesuit Christian circles, they have often succeeded in setting the pace of Christian learning.

DOUGLAS A. SWEENEY

Bibliography. A. M. de Aldama (1990), *The Formula of the Institute: Notes for a Commentary;* D. Alden (1996), *The Making of an Enterprise: The Society of Jesus in Portugal, Its Empire, and Beyond, 1540–1750;* W. V. Bangert (1986), *A History of the Society of Jesus;* J. Brodrick (1940), *The Origin of the Jesuits;* J. de Guibert (1964), *The Jesuits: Their Spiritual Doctrine and Practice: A Historical Study;* K. Hengst (1981), *Jesuiten an Universitaten und Jesuitenuniversitaten: Zur Geschichte der Universitaten in der Oberdeutschen und Rheinischen Provinz der Gesellschaft Jesu im Zeitalter der konfessionellen Auseinandersetzung;* Gabriel C. Mir (1968), *Aux sources de la pedagogie des jesuites: Le "Modus parisiensis";* J. W. O'Malley (1993), *The First Jesuits;* L. Polgar, ed. (1981–90), *Bibliographie sur l'histoire de la Compagnie de Jesus, 1901–1980,* 3 vols.; A. Scaglione (1986), *The Liberal Arts and the Jesuit College System;* C. Sommervogel et al., eds. (1890–1960), *Bibliotheque de la Compagnie de Jesus,* 12 vols.

See also IGNATIUS OF LOYOLA; REFORMATION, THE; ROMAN CATHOLIC EDUCATION

Jesus Christ. The Lord Jesus Christ was the greatest teacher who ever lived. A large portion of the Gospels is taken up with the teaching methods and materials of Jesus. What the Lord taught and how he taught it are vital to Christian educators, for they reveal a pattern to follow in helping learners move toward maturity in the faith.

The Teaching Matter of Jesus. It is extremely difficult to summarize what Jesus taught, but there are at least five themes the Bible clearly reveals the Lord repeating in his teaching.

First, Jesus spent considerable time teaching about *the Father.* Christ made sure his listeners saw God as a personal Father (John 14:23–24), a holy King (Matt. 6:33), and a mighty Creator (Mark 13:19). The Lord wanted his followers to understand that God loves humankind (John 3:16), cares for each individual (Matt. 10:31), and watches over all the earth (Matt. 6:25–26). Christ's teaching on the Father was quite unique, since up until that time the Jews did not conceive of a personal relationship with God, but a national relationship. Christ's closeness to the Father, and his use of familiar terms, reshaped the traditional view of God. Those accustomed to approaching an almighty God in fear were amazed that a teacher could talk gently and lovingly about a God who cares for them. Throughout his ministry, from the Father's blessing at his baptism to the day he ascended to the Father's right hand, Jesus helped people think about the Father in a new way.

Second, Jesus had much to teach about *the Son.* It is interesting that Christ gave himself a number of names, including the "Good Shepherd" and the "I Am," but the title he used most often was "Son of Man," which reflects both his humanity and his representation of all human beings through judgment. Jesus regarded his mission in life to be a sacrifice for the sins of all humankind, and much of his teaching directly reflects that (see Mark 9:12; Luke 24:25–27; Matt. 26:24). Jesus explicitly taught the disciples that his death was a sacrificial offering instituting a New Covenant with God (Matt. 26:26–28), and that it was substitutionary in that he died on our behalf (Mark 10:45). He also taught that through his death God triumphed over evil (John 12:31), and everyone must repent and believe if they are to receive the benefit of his substitutionary death (John 5:24). Through his teachings on the Son, Christ's followers found out about their own sinfulness, the coming kingdom, and the rest that awaits those who know the Lord.

Third, Jesus was the first teacher to teach clearly about *the Holy Spirit.* Christ described the person and work of the Spirit to his followers, and explained that he had the power of the Holy Spirit at work within himself. Jesus taught that the Spirit guides Christians (Matt. 10:19–20), regenerates believers (John 3:5), and helps us to worship God (John 4:24). His greatest teaching on the Spirit occurs in the Upper Room discourse, in which Jesus describes the Holy Spirit as the Counselor (John 16:7) and explains how the Spirit helps Christians learn and grow (John 16:13–15).

Fourth, Jesus spent a great deal of time teaching his followers about *the kingdom.* Some scholars think this was Christ's most important theme, for in it Jesus explains that God is not only king over the present world, but will also be sovereign over a coming kingdom of righteousness. The Lord made clear that the kingdom of God had come to earth—a new concept to his listeners. They were encouraged to become members of God's kingdom by receiving the free gift of salvation, and exhorted that to take part in the kingdom would result in living a new life. The lives of his hearers were changed forever when Jesus taught that humility, love, and godly character would mark those who live for the kingdom, rather than obedience to a set of religious rules. Then, using both parables and prophetic language, Jesus taught of the future kingdom, in which those who believe will reign with him.

Fifth, the Lord spent much time teaching about *the new life.* His listeners were largely Jewish, raised to think and act in a particular pattern, but Christ's coming heralded an entirely new way of life. He was the initiator of the New Covenant; the old way of living had passed away. When Jesus spoke of using a "new wineskin" (Matt. 9:17), he was trying to get people to see that following him would mean leaving the old ways and developing an entirely new pattern for living that included a personal relation with God. Without the theme of a new life, Christ's teaching would have been merely a study in theology. As it is, his teaching was the impetus for changing the lives of men and women the world over.

The Teaching Methods of Jesus. A close examination of the Gospels reveals a myriad of methods that Christ used in teaching people. Each method had the same goal—to move people toward spiritual maturity. Those who were far away needed to be introduced to the truth, and those who were near were encouraged to grow deeper in their faith. His methods included the following:

1. *Stories and Drama.* The first thing that leaps out at the reader of Christ's words is the natural drama he practiced. Stories were the Lord's most common method for helping people understand his message. In his stories we find drama, conflict, and insight. Stories are effective because they help us to see ourselves objectively through the eyes of another, taking bits of a complex world and making them easy to understand. Children come to understand the larger world through stories, and Jesus helped his hearers comprehend the great truths of eternity by regularly telling stories that illustrated his points.

2. *Parables and Vivid Language.* It is impossible to look at the teaching of Jesus and not be impressed with the colorful characters and images he used. His characters were clearly drawn (the good Samaritan, the prodigal son), and he frequently used striking metaphors to illustrate his point (the Vine, the Shepherd, the Door). Christ's vivid language is evident throughout the Gospels, whether he is telling the disciples they will be "fishers of men," or calling the Pharisees a "brood of vipers." The Lord also used paradoxical language ("Those who would become great among you must become slaves"), humor ("How can you worry about the speck in your neighbor's eye when you have a beam in your own eye?"), and contradiction ("I came not to bring peace but a sword") to keep his students' attention and get them to think. The Teacher never allowed himself to be dull, but made his words interesting.

3. *Reason.* Jesus used logic to cause those around him to reflect on his teaching. For example, in the Sermon on the Mount, he detailed God's care for the birds, then asked, "Are you not more valuable than birds?" He also forced his hearers to think through the logic of their reasoning. When charged with casting out demons by satanic power, the Lord got his audience to think about the impossibility of the devil warring with himself. It was Christ's ability to get Nicodemus to reason through the new birth that moved him toward salvation. Even as a boy, Jesus' ability to reason from the Scriptures amazed those around him. By forcing people to reflect on truth and reason it out, he helped people mature in their understanding of God.

4. *Emotional Appeal.* Many of the stories and principles Christ used were meant to move people emotionally as well as logically. Most of his hearers could relate to the humility of the repentant tax collector in Luke 18, and understood the joy of finding the lost coin in Luke 15. But the emotion Christ stirred up was not always sympathetic. He deliberately upset the chief priests and Pharisees with his story of the tenants (Matt. 21), and his direct rebuke to the people of Nazareth (Luke 4) created a firestorm. The Lord understood that people do not simply respond to cold logic, for the Creator designed them with emotions in order that we can respond personally and emotionally to him. Christ's emotional appeals, along with his personal relationship, drew people toward himself.

5. *Rhetoric and Argumentation.* Rather than simply standing and lecturing, Jesus found ways to naturally teach those around him. He regularly dialogued with others, sometimes posing questions and sometimes responding to the questions of others. He often relied on the Old Testament, citing references and relating them to his present situation. The Sermon on the Mount is a classic case of an orator using a variety of rhetorical methods to relate truth, mixing principles with illustrations, all surrounding one theme, and moving the entire speech toward a conclusion. In some cases Jesus changed from the gentle persuader to a fiery preacher, such as in his eschatological sermon of Matthew 23–25. Using emotional illustrations, quotations, and repetition, he argued fiercely for each of his listeners to make an immediate decision to follow God.

6. *Repetition.* Christ understood the importance of repeating key themes so that his points would stick in the minds of his listeners. For example, at the beginning of the Sermon on the Mount, Jesus phrased the Beatitudes in a repetitive way, making it easy to follow and easy to understand. Similarly, in the prophetic message of Matthew 23, Christ used seven "woes" to create an outline for his followers. Repetition helps the listener follow along and acts as a memory aid. Profound truth is often not comprehended with one hearing, so the Lord repeated his principles over and over, which may be one reason why there is variation in some of the Synoptic Gospel quotations.

7. *Authority.* Scripture records that many people regarded Jesus as a rabbi, and he accepted that term for himself. But both his methods and his materials were considerably different from that of the typical first-century Jewish teacher. For one thing, he didn't simply appeal to other teachers for confirmation, but claimed to have a message directly from God. When he cited the Old Testament Law, he claimed the authority to go beyond its direct message. The people certainly were able to discern something unique about the teaching ministry of Jesus, for Scripture regularly reminds us that the people of his day recognized that Christ was one who taught with authority, unlike the other teachers of the day.

8. *Variety.* Jesus adapted his teaching to his audience. When speaking to a group of common la-

borers, He used parables to which they could easily relate. When debating the temple scholars, He used solid biblical examples and logical arguments. When teaching the twelve disciples, Jesus became personally involved with each man, answering their questions and preparing them for leadership in his new church. And when talking with one man, the Lord set aside speeches in order to deal with the unique needs of the person facing him. Christ seized teachable moments, using every opportunity to illustrate truth, be it a question from a rich young ruler, an angry mob with an adulteress, or a storm at sea. His adaptability and variety of teaching methods set a standard for all teachers.

9. *Skill Development.* Christ had a plan for his disciples. Rather than assuming they would all learn, he taught them principles, then sent them out to minister. In Luke 9 we are told that Jesus sent out the Twelve, then gathered them back together in order to discuss their adventures. He explained his parables to them in private, so that they could see the truth of his words, and he helped shape the character of each man through his example of love and service. Christ's demonstration of humility in washing the feet of each disciple reveals a wise teacher who understood what his students needed to see in order to grow. By the time of his resurrection, the disciples were prepared to lead the New Testament church. Jesus understood that a teacher is a disciple-maker, moving students not just toward more knowledge, but toward a deeper walk with God.

10. *Faith Building.* The miracles of Jesus were done to minister to people and to reveal himself as the Messiah, but also to build the faith of the believers. Sometimes a teacher needs to help nurture the faith of students by encouraging them to trust God. Christ routinely used faith-building exercises to help his followers grow spiritually, for he knew that God would be faithful. Teachers must be willing to help students learn how to step out in faith.

The Teaching Ministry of Jesus. No study of Christ's teaching would be complete without an evaluation of its effectiveness. All one must do to see the results of Christ's ministry is to look at the lives of the disciples. Before spending time with Christ, these fishermen, tax collectors, and political extremists were selfish, brash, and proud. After spending time with him, they were selfless, courageous, and humble. Men who had little schooling and no social position suddenly had wisdom, power, and strong faith in God. After having spent three years with the Lord Jesus, men who had done nothing more significant than catch fish were able to preach to kings, persuade the masses, and turn the world upside down. Jesus' teaching helped shape the disciples into world-changers whose influence extends to our own day. Christ molded the character of the

disciples, and in doing so he set his plan in motion to establish his church and take the good news into all the world. No teacher can hope to do more. The Lord left a model of materials and methods for all Christian educators to follow.

JERRY CHIP MACGREGOR

Bibliography. W. Barclay (1978), *Jesus as They Saw Him;* A. Edersheim (1990), *The Life and Times of Jesus the Messiah;* C. Evans (1993), *Jesus;* D. Guthrie (1982), *Jesus the Messiah;* B. Hull (1990), *Jesus Christ Disciple-maker;* D. Prime (1993), *Jesus: His Life and Ministry;* P. Smith (1994), *Jesus: Meet Him Again for the First Time;* G. Stowell (1982), *Jesus Teaches.*

See also EDUCATION IN THE GOSPELS AND ACTS; EDUCATION OF THE TWELVE; TEACHABLE MOMENTS; TEACHINGS OF JESUS CHRIST

Jewish Education. Jewish education has influenced Western thought from its infancy. In ancient times, Jewish parents taught children in their homes. Wholeness of heart was cultivated and passed on from parents to children as the sacred trust of a people in covenant relationship with God. For thousands of years, this trust was accepted without question. In the past two centuries, however, beginning with the post-Enlightenment generations, radical change has fragmented the Jewish consensus concerning the role of education. Today, Jewish education addresses a multitude of interests, not only spiritual and religious in nature, but also cultural, social, political, national, and even academic.

Ancient Times. In ancient times, the Torah was considered sacred, the very word God spoke and Moses preserved. God had kept his four hundred year promise to the patriarch Abraham by freeing his descendants from slavery to forge a nation in covenant with himself. God then ordained the passing on of these words as an oral history and lasting heritage, commanding, "You shall teach them diligently to your sons and shall talk of them when you sit in your house and when you walk by the way and when you lie down and when you rise up" (Deut. 6:7 NASB). Parents took this command to heart, and thus began child-centered education in the home.

Parents watched with loving eyes as their children developed. No fewer than eight Hebrew names describe childhood development, from *newborn* to *suckling* to *weaned one* to *clinger,* and on to later stages of *the one who shakes off* and *the ripened one.* Education preceded formal instruction. For example, upon each doorpost hung a mezuzah, a shiny metal case with the above-quoted words of Deuteronomy written on parchment and inserted within. As the *suckling* was carried from room to room, the parent would extend a finger to kiss the mezuzah attached to the door post between the rooms. Soon the child would be reaching for the mezuzah too. Next, the parent would add a benediction from the Psalms, "The LORD shall preserve your going out and your coming in" (Ps. 121:8 NKJV). Not long after, the child could be heard uttering the benediction too. Praxis (learning by doing) led to internalizing *mitzvoh* (good deeds, as commanded by God). Thus, values were caught long before being taught in formal instruction.

At Passover, all leaven was purged from the home and an unblemished firstborn lamb was sacrificed. Just before the family ate the lamb, the father would tell the youngest child the Passover story, starting with the tears of slavery, then the plagues including the slaying of the firstborns, and concluding with the great exodus to freedom: "With a powerful hand the LORD brought *us* out of Egypt" (Exod. 13:14 NASB). Year after year, the story was retold, passed on from father to son as an everlasting heritage.

Eventually, parent-based education slackened, and a national crisis resulted. Uneducated youth were unqualified and uninterested in the academies of higher learning. Simeon the high priest addressed the problem by legislating universal elementary education. Schools were to be funded by the local communities, with no more than twenty-five children per schoolmaster. The mandate, in A.D. 64, became the first instance of compulsory public schooling in history. For precocious children, the Sayings of the Fathers summarized the traditional curriculum as follows: Torah at age 5, Mishnah (Oral Law) at 10, the mitzvoh (bar mitzvah) at 13, and Talmud at 15.

Jewish Education in the United States.
The earliest Jewish settlers immigrated to New Amsterdam in 1654 from Brazil. In all, twenty-three Sephardic Jews settled, pooling funds to purchase a burial ground. The settlers viewed education as a parental responsibility. As in the ancient days, congregational involvement became necessary only when parents failed to meet their obligations. It was not until 1760, in New York, that a Sephardic congregation, Shearith Israel, hired the first schoolmaster to teach Hebrew and English to its children.

Ashkenazi Jews changed the colonial pattern. They built well-organized, communally supervised and financed educational facilities for both rich and poor, including the heder (private elementary school), the Talmud Torah (community supported elementary school), and the yeshiva (higher education). Day schools reaffirmed the role of education in training and mentoring. The Orthodox Torah Umesorah schools trained children to pray, wear *tefillin* (phylacteries with parchments inserted), practice kosher eating habits, keep the Sabbath and festivals as holy days, and shun intermarriage. Learning was considered the highest form of worship, and the Bible remained the centerpiece of education until the nineteenth century.

In contrast, Reform Jews desired Americanization. In 1850, Elizabeth Gratz built Philadelphia's first Sunday school. Then, early in the twentieth century, led by Samson Benderly and his followers, the Reform adopted five assumptions that differed from those of traditional Jewish education. These included a bicultural model for Jewish communal life, a belief in the unique quality of Jewish experience in America, a conviction that acculturation could be accomplished without assimilation, a belief that an Americanized form of cultural Zionism should form the basis of communal and educational life, and the use of education to ensure socialization in a democratic society.

From 1880 to 1920, the Jewish population of the United States quadrupled, buoyed and overwhelmed by mass immigration from Russia and Eastern Europe. The Reform practices sought to educate Jewish children to be good citizens, motivated by a sense of civic duty and responsibility. The rise of centralized agencies, the Jewish Federations, resulted from Benderly's efforts to acculturate Jewish immigrants. The Federations actively promoted the training and licensing of teachers, the development of methodology, and the standardization of curriculum. In a parallel development starting in 1922, Mordechai Kaplan, leader of the Reconstructionists, integrated the assumptions of modern naturalism into the practice of Judaism. Though small in numbers, Reconstructionists have introduced normative ideas such as the synagogue center, the havurot (warm fellowship groups for study or social activity), and the bat mitzvah. As with the Reform, the religious and spiritual precepts of traditional Jewish education are replaced by cultural and national practices designed to socialize Jews and foster democracy in American society.

Jewish Education Today.
According to Reisman (1979), only 46 percent of American Jews have membership in a Jewish denomination, and 55 percent did not attend services except on holy days. A Hebrew University study (1997) reported that 45 percent of Jewish children participated in Jewish education programs in the United States, contrasting sharply with enrollments of 65 percent to 85 percent in day schools in Canada, Mexico, and Australia.

The data show a steep drop-off for American enrollment occurring after bar/bat mitzvah. The National Jewish Population Survey of 1990 reported that only 15 percent of the day school students continue on to grades 9–12. The great majority of the 115,000 students who attended day schools received a traditional education at Orthodox Hebrew day schools (55 percent), Traditionalist yeshivahs (20 percent), or Hasidic day schools (13 percent). Most recently, in 1997 the enrollments of children in nontraditionalist day schools are booming, with the overall student population growing by an additional 70,000 students.

Data on the day schools are not easily obtained. In 1996, Drachler attempted an extensive survey of day schools and located information in 37 doctoral dissertations, 10 master's degrees, 50 periodicals in English, Hebrew, Yiddish, and Latino. In all, Drachler found a total of 700 items, 400 of which were in periodicals, and the rest being scattered in books, proceedings, reports, and pamphlets.

New sources of Jewish education are growing on the Internet. Trends are explosive, with the sheer volume of information growing at exponential rates. Levin (1996) has called the Jewish network on the Internet "the greatest compilation of Jewish law, fact, history, opinion, news, tradition, belief, and culture since the Talmud." The Jewish International Association Against Assimilation is the Jewish network's watchdog, with stated goals to strengthen ties to Israel, offer a Jewish information service within the Jewish world, and assist individuals in using the web.

As of 1997, several thousand locations exist on the World Wide Web. Information can be obtained by gopher menus, Internet Relay Chat rooms (IRC), mailing lists (e-mail clubs with themes and topics), and newsgroups (listed by file name and message). Web sites proliferate for Jewish Studies programs, public and private agencies, corporations, publishers, and not-for-profit institutions. A sampling of education-related listings on the web gives information on almost anything imaginable, including Hebrew software, Hebrew fonts, Israel, games, bar/bat mitzvah lessons, Torah and grammar discussions, magazines, children's books, conferences, ethics, fellowships, festivals, graduate programs, home schooling, high schools, Judaism, law, liturgy, online classes, orthodoxy, and even Israeli television.

Conclusions. Jewish education has evolved from ancient times. Traditional methods continue, with parents mentoring children to walk wholeheartedly in covenant relationship with God. New complexities have entered the environment, however, through the Enlightenment, the mass immigrations of the nineteenth century, the rise of the state of Israel, and the Internet. Nevertheless, Jewish education still retains its place not only for articulating Jewish identity, but also as a means for individuals and, perhaps, nations to seek the face of the Almighty.

JEFFREY E. FEINBERG

Bibliography. W. Barclay (1959), *Educational Ideals in the Ancient World;* H. H. Donin (1977), *To Raise a Jewish Child;* N. Drachler, ed. (1996), *A Bibliography of Jewish Education in the United States;* A. Edersheim (1982), *Sketches of Jewish Social Life in the Days of Christ;* I. Goldman (1975), *Life-long Learning among Jews: Adult Education in Judaism from Biblical Times to the Twentieth Century;* L. P. Gartner, ed. (1969), *Jewish Education in the United States: A Documentary History;* W. B. Helmreich (1982), *The World of the Yeshiva: An Intimate Portrait of Orthodox Jewry;* J. Kaminetsky, ed., *Hebrew Say School Education: An Overview;* S. L. Kelman, ed. (1992), *What We Know about Jewish Education: A Handbook of Today's Research for Tomorrow's Jewish Education;* M. Levin (1996), *The Guide to the Jewish Internet;* J. Pilch, ed. (1969), *A History of Jewish Education in America;* D. Romm (1996), *The Jewish Guide to the Internet;* A. I. Schiff (1988), *Contemporary Jewish Education: Issachar American Style;* B. L. Sherwin (1987), *Contexts and Content: Higher Jewish Education in the United States;* N. N. Winter (1966), *Jewish Education in a Pluralist Society: Samson Benderly and Jewish Education in the United States.*

See also HEBREW EDUCATION THROUGH FEASTS AND FESTIVALS; JUDAISM

Job Description. Written document summarizing the duties and responsibilities required of a specific position within an organization. The job described may be a volunteer or paid position. The job description does not outline what the worker actually does, but what the organization expects the worker to do. It is the job description that sets the standard for the performance of the worker/volunteer, not the other way around. Job descriptions outline the work to be done, but not how it is to be accomplished.

Well-written and well-used job descriptions greatly enhance the functioning of any organization. Job descriptions help distinguish one job from another and clarify duties so that conflict arising from assumptions or misinformation can be minimized. They aid in recruitment, training, and personnel evaluation. Since ambiguous duties adversely affect worker performance, job descriptions play a crucial role in the motivation of workers, whether paid or volunteer.

There is a distinction between a job specification and a job description. A job description details the work to be done, while a job specification lists the skills, abilities, and knowledge required by the person(s) performing the job. In practice, job specifications are often included in job description documents.

Although the format, terminology, and components of job descriptions widely vary, the following sections typically need to be considered: title, purpose, duties and responsibilities, contexts, accountabilities, and training provided. The dates the description was written and all subsequent revision dates should also be recorded. Each job within an organization needs to be given a unique title, which is specified in the job description. The purpose stated in the job description explains the rationale for the position.

The major component of a job description is the listing of duties and responsibilities. In the literature, as well as in practice, the terms *duties, tasks*, and *responsibilities* are often used interchangeably, as is the case in this article. One way they are sometimes distinguished is to define tasks as the smallest unit, duties as multiple tasks, and responsibilities as work that may be delegated to others but for which the worker is ultimately responsible. The duties and responsibilities section of a job description covers all dimensions of the job. Depending on the complexity of the job being described, the tasks are sometimes categorized. Some organizations find it beneficial to prioritize the list of duties, with the most important tasks listed first. While job descriptions are intended to be comprehensive, every job involves unplanned activities and every organization experiences change that influences the work required. Thus many job descriptions include an "other" category to allow for unforeseen responsibilities.

Sometimes to further clarify the distinction between jobs within an organization, it is helpful for the job description to include a section detailing some duties that are *not* included in the job being described.

Some job descriptions incorporate details about the social and physical environments in which the work is to be performed. Time requirements or descriptions of the workload may also be included. Job descriptions for volunteer positions or temporary jobs need to include the duration of the assignment.

To remain effective, job descriptions need to be reviewed and revised on a regular basis. Preparing to write a job description requires collecting data from a variety of sources. Data collection methods can include questionnaires, open-ended interviews, group interviews, direct observation, work logs, expert panels, and a review of the literature.

While many churches and religious organizations make widespread use, though in varying degrees, of job descriptions for employees, the value of job descriptions for volunteers in the church is less commonly understood. Well-written and frequently revised job descriptions for church volunteers help prevent leader burnout because volunteers know exactly what is expected of them and the duration of their term of service.

NANCY L. DEMOTT

Bibliography. J. Ghorpade (1988), *Job Analysis: A Handbook for the Human Resource Director;* P. C. Grant (1989), *Multiple Use Job Descriptions: A Guide to Analysis, Preparation, and Applications for Human Resources Managers;* M. Wilson (1983), *How to Mobilize Church Volunteers.*

Job Interview. See Job Description.

Johari Window. Model designed to illustrate awareness in interpersonal relationships. It is named after its creators Joseph Luft and Har-

rington Ingham (a combination of first names Joe and Harry—Johari). The model consists of four quadrants of awareness: *open, blind, hidden,* and *unknown.*

The *open* area represents behavior, motivation, and feelings that are known to both self and others. The *blind* quadrant includes feelings, behaviors, and motivations that are known to others but of which the self is unaware.

The *hidden* quadrant includes areas of life known to ourselves but not revealed to others. It represents feelings about ourselves that we know but find difficult to reveal to others. It might include fears, past experiences we would prefer to forget, and our fantasies.

The area of the *unknown* contains the behaviors, feelings, and motives of which neither the individual or others are aware. Yet we can assume they exist because eventually some of these behaviors, feelings, and motives become known, and we then realize they were significantly influencing relationships all along. This quadrant represents areas of potential growth or self-actualization.

The Johari Window is most helpful in illustrating and promoting self-disclosure in small groups. The size of each quadrant increases or decreases according to changes in relationships. For example, as disclosure takes place in a hidden area, the open area increases while the hidden quadrant decreases. Luft (1984) advocates changing the shape of the models so that the open quadrant increases while the other areas become smaller. The larger the first or open quadrant, the better the communication will be. When the open area is small, however, there may be a high threat level, and communication is usually poor. As trust is developed among group members, awareness of hidden, open, and blind facets of relationships increase. Along with this awareness is a desire to move items from the hidden and blind quadrants into the open quadrant.

HARLEY ATKINSON

Bibliography. J. Gorman (1993), *Community That is Christian;* J. Luft (1984), *Group Processes: An Introduction to Group Dynamics.*

Journal Writing. Activity of recording one's thoughts, feelings, ideas, and events on paper. This written record may be complex—even in outline form—or quite simplistic without any specific organization. In 1966 Ira Progoff, a professor and psychologist at Drew University, developed the Intensive Journal which has five major divisions with sixteen subdivisions. At the other end of the spectrum is a journal with no visible organization but merely a straightforward flowing of thoughts.

Examples of journal writing exist throughout history. The Psalms give evidence of their writers' feelings and thoughts, angers and confusions, praises and thanksgivings. The gospel writers provide journals of Jesus' life and actions. St. Augustine's *Confessions* and John Wesley's *Journal* reflect personal thoughts of the authors. Dag Hammarskjold's *Markings* is an intimate account of his dialogues and questionings in relationship to a being other than himself. Henri J. M Nouwen's *The Genesee Diary: Reports from a Trappist Monastery,* Etty Hillesum's *An Interrupted Life,* and *The Journals of Jim Elliot* are contemporary examples of written recordings of the lives of these diverse people.

A journal used for spiritual formation and growth is an active tool encompassing every dimension of one's life, a spiritual discipline offering a way to interact with Jesus. Journaling is a living process, "one important place where I can gather all of me together to bring my total being before God" (Kelsey, 1980, 72). One does not grow in one area of life without affecting, either positively or negatively, each other area. Keeping a journal puts one in a position to record both outer events and inner thoughts and reactions. This process of recording one's life is intimately related to God's love for each person, to the responsibility to love God, oneself, and one another as God loves us. "God loves you and his relationship with you cannot exist apart from you revealing yourself in his presence" (Kelsey, 1980, 71). In addition, the journal offers a means of recording God's action in one's life as a person records responses to God's activity and to God's Word. "It is by means of journal reflection that we get in touch with our past, recognize what is happening to us in the present, and develop a sense of where our future lies. . . . It focuses mind and heart on the issues of growth with the aim of discerning what God is doing in one's life" (Peace, 1995, 9).

Elizabeth O'Connor suggests three tools for growth when involved with journal writing: reflection, self-observation, and self-questioning. A fourth tool, important for spiritual growth and direction, is action-application. In Christian journaling "every inward work requires an outward expression" (O'Connor, 1980, 41). "Whenever one's record of the inner life takes the place of human relationships, one is in danger. . . . Our journaling should make us more outgoing, loving, and relatable. . . . A journal is no substitute for living" (Kelsey, 1980, 97). By taking time to reflect and question, to wrestle and struggle, to be joyful and thankful, to praise and worship, a person becomes clearer in direction and action. One does not write to focus on oneself. The focus is on God within and one must follow this introspection with an outward expression of God's will as it is understood.

A journal's inner journey of exploration is not for every person. It requires a conscious, unswerving commitment to honesty with oneself, putting down one's thoughts and feelings without judgment, trusting God for revelation on the journey. Journaling is one tool for growth in relationship to God and in relationship to other people as one is involved in ministry.

DIANNE WHITING

Bibliography. M. Kelsey (1980), *Adventure Inward: Christian Growth through Personal Journal Writing;* E. O'Connor (1980), *Letters to Scattered Pilgrims;* R. Peace (1995), *Spiritual Journaling: Recording Your Journey Toward God.*

Judaism. Commonly known as the religion of the Jews, Judaism draws its teachings from the Old Testament, especially from Exodus 20 through the end of the Pentateuch. However, it also leans heavily on the traditions of the elders (Mark 7:3–13), which may or may not reflect Old Testament support. According to Graybill, "The principal elements of Judaism include circumcision, a strict monotheism, an abhorrence of idolatry, and Sabbath-keeping" (Tenney, 1963, 455). From Abraham to Jesus, the people of God were known as Israelites who spent fifty years in captivity in Babylon and were conquered by one nation after another, from Assyria to Rome.

Hebrews (Jews) were primarily a nomadic people who immigrated from Mesopotamia. After Moses, they were led by judges until the appointment of Saul as the first king. Under Solomon (ca. 970–930 B.C.) Judaism reached its zenith of wealth and power but the golden era ended with Solomon's death. The northern kingdom of Israel was captured by the Assyrians in 722 B.C. and the Babylonians took Jerusalem in 587 B.C. As the Books of Ezra and Nehemiah describe it, Israel returned to Palestine in approximately 536 B.C.

Many scholars believe that the Old Testament represents the most significant collection of writings produced by the ancient world. Certainly the people of Judaism dominated the culture of their immediate surroundings, constantly fighting off alien cultures to protect their exclusive monotheism. No other ancient nation displayed such a commitment to ethical and moral behavior along with a judicial system based on justice and mercy. Ellison argues that the term *Judaism* stands in contrast with the religion of the Old Testament, from which it was derived.

> During the intertestamental period, in which Judaism was developing, various directions became obvious—e.g., Pharisees, Sadducees, Essenes, Zealots, Hellenists—but the situation created by the destruction of the Jewish state in A.D. 70 and confirmed by the crushing of the Bar-Kochba revolt in A.D. 135 left a pharisaic interpretation of Judaism without rivals. It reached its full development by A.D. 500, its authoritative documents being the Talmud, composed of the Mishnah and Gemara, and the Midrashim (official interpretations of the OT books). (Douglas, 1978, 552)

The New Testament bears many marks of the Hellenistic culture of the Roman world, but it is unmistakably linked to the Old. Just over fifty years before Jesus' birth, Israel was still under control of the Maccabees, but in 63 B.C. Pompeii claimed Jerusalem for Rome. With respect to worship, ancient priestly pomp had been replaced by readings and prayers in the synagogues and the respective right-wing and left-wing theology of the Pharisees and Sadducees.

Serious Christians have always understood the absolute link between the Old and New Testaments as well as the dependence of Christian theism upon the rigid monotheism of Judaism. The great Yahweh of the Old Testament is addressed as *Father* by Jesus. As Marty (1962) puts it, "The high theology of St. Paul's letter to the Colossians sees in Christ the dwelling of the fullness of the godhead bodily, and the Fourth Gospel speaks of Jesus as the eternal word of God made flesh. But neither these writings nor the sayings of Jesus are intended to contradict the monotheistic pattern. 'He who believes in me, believes not in me but in him who sent me' (John 12:44)" (19).

KENNETH O. GANGEL

Bibliography. J. D. Douglas, ed. (1978), *The New International Dictionary of the Christian Church;* A. Edersheim (1954), *The Bible History of the Old Testament;* B. Lockerbie (1994), *A Passion for Learning;* M. E. Marty (1962), *A Short History of Christianity;* E. J. Young (1958), *An Introduction to the Old Testament.*

See also EDUCATION IN THE MONARCHIES AND PROPHETS; EDUCATION IN THE PENTATEUCH; EDUCATION IN THE PSALMS AND PROVERBS; JEWISH EDUCATION

Jung, Carl Gustav (1875–1961). Founder of analytical psychology. Born in Kesswil, Switzerland, to a clergyman of the Swiss Reformed Church, he studied at the University of Basel (1895–1900), majoring in medicine and specializing in psychiatry. Upon obtaining his medical degree he worked at the psychiatric clinic of the University of Zurich, where he also served as an assistant professor in psychiatry. In 1906 Jung began a collaboration with Sigmund Freud that ended in 1913 due to disagreements over psychoanalytic theory. Jung was the founder and first president (1911–14) of the International Psychoanalytical Association. In 1913 he resigned his lectureship at Zurich in order to concentrate on clinical practice, and to explore and research various dimensions of psychology, personality, and religion. For much of his life Jung demonstrated a strong interest in the occult, mysticism, and mythology.

Jung's work intersects Christian education and spiritual formation with his widely accepted classification of personality types. According to this typology human personality moves in one of two directions, either extroverted or introverted. The extroverted personality tends to move toward people and action, while the introverted personality moves in the opposite direction, to a quiet, introspective world, free from people. In addition to extroversion and introversion, Jung identified three sets of polaric functions or ways people relate to the world: intuiting and sensing; feeling and thinking; judging and perceiving. Out of the two major attitudes and contrasting functions, Jung fashioned a classification of personality types. According to the theory individuals tend to prefer certain modes of behavior over others, according to their personality types.

Extensive research and testing has led to the development of the Myers-Briggs Type Inventory, which is used to construct profiles of sixteen personality types. One of the interest areas impacted by these personality types is religious education, especially in the realm of spiritual formation. For example, Mulholland (1993) uses Jung's expanded model of human personality to explore holistic spirituality and examine the insights analytical psychology can bring to one's spiritual pilgrimage.

In addition to his psychiatric work, teaching, and research, Jung was a prolific author. His numerous writings include *The Theory of Psychoanalysis* (1915), *Psychology of the Unconscious* (1925), *Modern Man in Search of a Soul* (1933), *Psychological Types* (1933), *Psychology and Religion* (1938), and *The Integration of Personality* (1939).

HARLEY ATKINSON

Bibliography. L. T. Bischof (1964), *Interpreting Personality Theories;* M. R. Mulholland (1993), *Invitation to a Journey;* R. M. Ryckman (1989), *Theories of Personality.*

See also FREUD, SIGMUND; JAMES, WILLIAM; PSYCHOLOGY OF RELIGION

Justice. *See* Law and Order.

Juvenile Delinquency. Legal term first used in 1816 when Illinois passed a law defining juvenile delinquency. Since then, every state has passed juvenile delinquency laws. However, states differ in their criteria for delinquency. The legal definitions have evolved over time as well. For example, *juvenile offender* or *youthful offender* are viewed as more "politically correct" and acceptable terms today.

Due to the scope of the problem and the differences between children and adults, there is a separate justice system for juveniles. Separate courts were created to remove children from the criminal courts. Usually, the age limit for designation as a juvenile is between ages sixteen and eighteen. During 1994, there were over 1.5 million delinquency cases in courts with juvenile jurisdiction. Of these, almost 855,000 were formally processed in the juvenile justice system (Scalia, 1997). Delinquent behavior is either violation of the law by juveniles, or status offenses. Status offenses apply to juveniles only and include behavior such as truancy, gang activity, and antisocial acts. In some cases involving a violent crime, juveniles may be transferred to adult status; however, this happens in relatively few cases (Scalia, 1997).

Causes of Delinquent Behavior. Theories explaining delinquent behavior usually fall into one of three general categories: physiological, psychological, or sociological. Physiological theories explain delinquency as the result of inherited genetic traits. Psychological theories focus on individual development and disjunction. Sociological theories, involving the effects of society on the individual, have become increasingly preferred in explaining delinquency. Sociological theorists have established bases for explaining and predicting delinquent behavior. Sociological theories view the nature of the home environment, the quality of the neighborhood, behavior in school, and labeling as contributing to delinquent behavior. However, it has never been conclusively proven that delinquency can be predicted or prevented. Unfortunately, delinquency is looked upon as an integral part of society (Cavan and Ferdinand, 1981). Significant social factors involving delinquency include gender differences and social class. More boys than girls exhibit delinquent behavior, although the number of girls has risen dramatically since the 1980s. Most delinquents, especially in the United States, come from the middle and lower classes. Low self-esteem, unchallenging schools, and rebellion against authority have been suggested as reasons juveniles from these classes become involved in delinquent behavior. Violence in movies, television, music, and even comic books are often cited as a factor in causing delinquent behavior.

Treatment and Prevention. The major emphasis of the juvenile justice system is not punishment but rather treatment, supervision, and rehabilitation of juvenile offenders. Disposition of a case is usually made in one of the following ways: dismissal of the case, referral to an adult court for trial, placement on probation supervision, placement in foster care, or commitment to a residential facility. One of the newest options is the so-called boot camps, where juveniles are submitted to a military model of discipline and work (Siegel and Senna, 1997).

Prevention of delinquent behavior is obviously preferable to rehabilitation. Curfew laws, gun laws, and drug and alcohol laws are legal means that have been tried to curb delinquent behavior. Community programs involving mentoring at-risk juveniles, strengthening families, and providing recreational activities for juveniles have been tried with varying degrees of success. Nevertheless, juvenile delinquency remains a significant problem (Siegel and Senna, 1997).

Juvenile Delinquency and Christian Education. Churches are in a position to play a significant role in the prevention of juvenile delinquency. Many of the programs designed to prevent delinquent behavior can be provided by churches (Watkins, 1994). Churches already provide recreational and social opportunities for adolescents in addition to regular educational activities. Mentoring programs are similar to some discipleship programs. Strengthening families is one of the most significant services a church can provide to prevent delinquent behavior. Parents play a fundamental role in the lives of their children. This applies to every family regardless of its social station in the community, income, or educational background. Because parents command the greatest influence in a young person's life, churches need to provide support and/or consider organized parenting classes.

RONNIE J. JOHNSON

Bibliography. R. S. Cavan and T. N. Ferdinand (1981), *Juvenile Delinquency;* L. J. Siegel and J. J. Senna (1997), *Juvenile Delinquency: Theory, Practice and Law;* J. Scalia (1997), *Juvenile Delinquents in the Federal Criminal Justice System;* D. R. Watkins (1994), *Christian Social Ministry: An Introduction.*

See also ADOLESCENT DEVELOPMENT; DYSFUNCTIONAL; EARLY ADOLESCENCE

Kk

Kant, Immanuel (1724–1804). German philosopher. Born the son of a poor saddlemaker, he knew poverty personally and intimately. Deeply attached to his mother, who was given to strong religious convictions, Kant was reared by a strict Lutheran creed in puritanical form. A rigidly structured personal life resulted in daily routines of rising, tea drinking, writing, lecturing, eating, and walking, each with its own fixed time. His inner life stands in stark contrast, as he is known for world-altering thoughts.

Highly influenced by Rousseau's *Emile*, Kant significantly impacted both ethics and epistemology. His *Critique of Pure Reason* (1781) effectually dethroned reason and ushered in the Enlightenment. Kant understood the mind as an essential tool but also emphasized its limitations. He espoused man's emergence from immaturity to think for himself without relying on the authority of the church, the Bible, or the state to tell him what to do. His epistemology combined rationalism and empiricism.

Living as he did in the time of the French and American Revolutions, Kant acknowledged the problems of government, power, and law. Key themes in his writings are the means by which to preserve peace and freedom. He supported the democratic movement and as an adult had no interest in church services, detesting the rigorous regulation and mechanization of religion. He was deeply in favor of religion based on doing good for its own sake rather than a contrived system of extrinsic rewards.

Having experienced severe discipline in his eight years at Gymnasium Fridericianum, he spoke out on the evils of such discipline in school. He advocated school systems based on moral law and the dignity of the individual, coupled with work and discipline as a means of reaching the highest goal. Further, autonomy was the process of gradually freeing a student's will from external control to the subjection of internal control. The best morality, said Kant, was principled and made on the basis of universal ethical principles or guides. Men were to act not as they want but as they ought.

A voluminous writer, he is best known for his trilogy of critiques of human knowledge (*Pure Reason*, 1781), ethics (*Practical Reason*, 1788), and aesthetics (*Judgement*, 1790). Beginning at age sixteen and continuing for a lifetime, Kant was insatiably interested in the scientific realm and in its epistemology. His defense of a priori concepts were applied to the disciplines of math, physics, morality, and everyday experiences. Time, space, number, and cause and effect were among his a priori givens.

CHERYL L. FAWCETT

Bibliography. P. G. Downs (1994), *Teaching for Spiritual Growth;* C. J. Friedrich, ed. (1949), *The Philosophy of Kant: Immanuel Kant's Moral and Political Writings;* K. Gangel and W. Benson (1983), *Christian Education: Its History and Philosophy;* I. Kant, *Education;* P. Wolff, ed. (1970), *The Essential Kant.*

See also COLONIAL EDUCATION; EPISTEMOLOGY; ETHICS; ROUSSEAU, JEAN-JACQUES

Kerygmatic Theology. *Kerygma* is a Greek word meaning "proclamation" or "preaching." The usage of the term within the New Testament makes no distinction between the act of proclamation and the content of that proclamation. Current scholarship employs the term to describe the content of the early Christian message. The theological debate around the term *kerygma* has focused on the relationship of the early church's proclaimed message to the historical Jesus.

The "historical Jesus" is the person who lived in the realm of time and space, including everything he actually said and did. The "kerygmatic Christ" is the person proclaimed by the apostles and worshiped by the early church. The "kerygma" consists of the church's testimony concerning Jesus Christ, such as the sermons in the Book of Acts, and the theological interpretations in Paul's letters. Kerygmatic theologians assert that the basis of Christian faith and commitment is the early church's witness concerning Christ, not the historical record of Jesus' words, deeds, and experiences found in the Gospels. They conclude that the historical record concerning Jesus is too scant and fallible to legitimize faith in him.

The issue hinges on these questions: Does faith in Christ need reliable historical data as its basis? Or, regardless of the Gospels' authenticity, is faith legitimized only by the witness of his first followers, on whom he exerted a powerful influence? To what extent does the early church's testimony about Christ depend on actual occurrences for its validity? Which is the more satisfactory basis for Christology: the Bible's historical record of his life and work, or the early church's interpretation and proclamation? Are the words and facts in the New Testament God's revelation, or merely a human witness to God's revelation in Jesus Christ?

Historical Development. During the first half of the twentieth century, Karl Barth, Rudolf Bultmann, and Emil Brunner were among the scholars who constructed a Christology on the kerygma, or the church's proclamation about Jesus. Whether the Gospels' information about Christ was accurate was inconsequential. They concluded that the early church's report of Jesus' impact cannot, with certainty, be connected to the earthly life of Jesus of Nazareth. In contrast to liberal scholars, these kerygmatic theologians presupposed Jesus' divinity, accepting it by faith, because that was the early church's interpretation of Jesus' life and work. Instead of grounding faith in the rational probability of historical evidence, they based it on the apostles' conclusions about Christ.

The most prolific example of a theologian who disagreed was Wolfhart Pannenberg. He believed that historical inquiry behind the kerygma of the New Testament is both possible and necessary. Persons who rest their faith upon the kerygma alone, and not upon the historical facts of Jesus' life as well, cannot escape the suspicion and fear that their faith is misplaced. When one researches the New Testament with the same historical method employed in the investigation of other past events and personalities, what the early church believed about Jesus appears reasonable. Theological conclusions not rooted in rational proof, or confirmed by historical research, are hollow and excessively subjective. Without an empirical reference, the kerygmatic Christ is somewhat vague and unreal. Pannenberg contended that faith in Christ is still a gift of the Holy Spirit, not merely a product of reason. Yet he stated that knowledge of the historical revelation is a logical precursor to faith.

An Evangelical Synthesis. Millard Erickson (1985) agrees with Pannenberg's concern over the substantiality of belief. Yet he is not in complete agreement with Pannenberg. Erickson concludes that Pannenberg's Christology hinges on establishing its historical contentions with objective certainty, which is difficult to achieve. If the facts of Christology yield objective history that is read-

ily verified by historical inquiry, then Jesus' divinity ought to be apparent to any honest investigator. Yet some who have examined the historical evidence remain unconvinced. Erickson also questions Pannenberg's distinction between the role of God's Spirit, and reason, in producing faith. If the Spirit must employ historical evidence to create faith, is the source of that faith truly vertical (God), or is it one's own subjective response to the evidence?

Erickson posits an alternative Christology rooted in an evangelical understanding of biblical revelation. Rather than base commitment to Christ *either* on the church's witness (faith), *or* on historical confirmation (reason), he retains both approaches. Revelation is *both* the historical events *and* their interpretation by the early church. These are two harmonious and complementary means by which God discloses himself.

Erickson's starting point for faith is the kerygma. The church's proclamation about Jesus offers a hypothesis and provides a framework for examining and integrating the historical data. More than any other hypothesis about Jesus, the apostles' interpretation makes sense of the historical phenomena. The "kerygmatic Christ" and the "historical Jesus" are together in a mutually dependent fashion. Increased familiarity with the church's witness enhances understanding of the historical information about Christ. Discovering facts about Him can more fully persuade inquirers that the apostles' interpretation is true.

Implications for Christian Education. Debate on the legitimate basis for Christology raises an issue that is integral to Christian education: biblical revelation. Is the New Testament merely an apostolic witness to divine revelation in the person of Christ? Or does divine revelation include the actual words and historical information in the New Testament record?

How educators answer those questions determines how they approach the teaching of Scripture. The ultimate goal of Bible study is to experience the person of Jesus as did his first followers. Yet that is more likely to occur when teachers dignify the Bible's information about him. If students' views of Christ are not rooted in observation of and confidence in biblical data, their "Christ" is one of personal invention instead of divine revelation. Why engage in inductive Bible study if the record of Jesus' words and deeds is unreliable? Educators must assign meaning to the passages that speak of Christ *before* they can conceive of him or derive meaning concerning him (Richards, 1970). Unless the locus of authority is God's Word, no one can discover truth.

TERRY POWELL

Bibliography. M. Erickson (1985), *Christian Theology;* L. Richards and G. Bredfeldt (1998), *Creative Bible Teaching.*

Kierkegaard, Søren (1813–55). Kierkegaard was born in Copenhagen, Denmark, the last of four sons. He had three sisters. He lived under the shadow of his father, Michael Pedersen Kierkegaard. As a young man Michael cursed God for his life of poverty and hard work. He was convinced that he had committed the unpardonable sin. To him, the retribution for his sin seemed to come true when Søren's mother and five of his siblings died by the time he was 22.

Though Kierkegaard suffered from melancholy and was not strong physically, he entered the University of Copenhagen to study theology in 1830. Kierkegaard's call was to help people become Christians. He believed that Christ alone should be the example for life. He did not want to be seen as the focal point of instruction, so to guard against this he used indirect communication. This involved the use of stories and fictional, but realistic, characters. His main theme was that Christianity was not a doctrine to be learned but a life to be lived.

One of Kierkegaard's personal heroes was the Old Testament patriarch Abraham. Abraham was willing to sacrifice his only son Isaac to God. This demonstrated an irrational "leap of faith." Not marrying his fiancée may have been Kierkegaard's sacrificial leap of faith.

Kierkegaard attacked the Danish state church for gaining much from the culture but losing the true Christianity of the Bible. He said Denmark was not a Christian nation. He criticized Danes who falsely thought being Christian meant being nice persons and conforming to the social norms. Being a true Christian meant standing before God and striving to follow Christ.

Besides attacking the institutional church, Kierkegaard also attacked Hegelian idealism. This was a leading rationalism. Kierkegaard's message was that human experience and rationalism were not to be taken as ultimate authorities in spiritual matters. For it was a pagan perspective that viewed humanity as basically good and capable of knowing God on its own. This is counter to the Christian perspective, which sees humans as sinners, lacking truth and the capacity to know God apart from revelation. This revelation reached its high point when God came to humanity in the person of Jesus Christ.

Kierkegaard is sometimes referred to as the father of existentialism. If so, it is only indirectly. He very much rejected the idea that the gospel needed rational proofs. They seemed to him to give the impression that faith in Christ was a doctrine or a system of thinking. This led people away from simple faith in Christ. To keep himself from being taken as an exemplar of Christianity, he led the public life of a man about town.

A contribution to the contemporary evangelical scene is Kierkegaard's recognition that Christianity and contemporary culture can become confused. Today commitment to Americanism is often seen as commitment to Christianity. Kierkegaard was against the culture influencing Christianity. He believed that Christianity should influence the culture.

Eugene S. Gibbs

Bibliography. S. Kierkegaard (1957), *Attack upon Christendom;* idem (1946), *Works of Love.*

Kinesthetic Learners. Kinesthetic learners have a preference for taking in information and remember best by becoming physically involved and interacting with what is being learned. These learners are extremely energetic, take frequent breaks, keep on the move, and shift positions often. The kinesthetic learner is well coordinated and often enjoys participating in sports or outdoor activities. Hand gestures or other forms of body language are frequently used when conversing. Their best ideas often come when engaging in a walk or other kind of physical activity. They need methods that allow them to engage learning by touching, feeling, and manipulating things.

The effective Christian educator shows sensitivity to communicate the truth of the Gospel to others in a language that is relevant and "connects" the truth in powerful and personal ways. The awareness of the preferred style of learning of a particular student is a vital element in reaching those within our realm of influence. Diversity is a distinct characteristic of all that God has created. That diversity is no more apparent than in God's highest act of creation. Research clearly indicates that people have a variety of ways in which they learn and process information.

Howard Gardner, a Harvard professor and eminent researcher, released compelling evidence that each human being possesses more than one type of intelligence. He describes at least seven different intelligences: linguistic, logical-mathematical, spatial, musical, bodily-kinesthetic, interpersonal, and intrapersonal. Gardner believes that all seven of the intelligences are equal in impact although the first two have traditionally been valued more in our society. Gardner asserts that the other five intelligences are consciously discriminated against by traditional schooling. His research supports the contention that each individual has a different profile of strengths and talents among these domains. Teachers who recognize these unique qualities provide learning experiences that allow students to access their special strengths in learning. When students are taught with methods that use their preferred strength, they learn more and enjoy learning more.

Many traditional approaches to Christian education lack balance in providing more active learning experiences for kinesthetic learners.

These individuals need to engage information with their bodies by modeling, acting out, or pantomiming the material they are learning. An increased awareness and use of kinesthetic methods in the church and home could encourage these learners to feel more valued by God, their families, and the church. The Christian educational process would become more engaging and relevant to those who may need it most.

How can you help kinesthetic learners blossom in the home, at school, or at church? Evaluate the methods used in learning activities and plan for a balance of auditory, visual, and kinesthetic modalities in your lesson plan. Do you intentionally plan for ways to channel the energy of a kinesthetic learner with active, hands-on activity? Participating in a drama, project, painting, or sculpting clay to illustrate the lesson would be engaging to all learners, especially the kinesthetic. Use the energy of a kinesthetic learner to run errands and keep on the move. Help to find as many ways as possible to keep moving in any given situation without causing disruption or misbehaving. Allow as much variety as possible. Many kinesthetic children find it difficult to do the same thing longer than ten minutes. Design homework and study time to be as flexible and as movable as possible. Do not expect your kinesthetic child to look at you when talking. Allow the student to pace, wander, and recite. Praise your kinesthetic learner for his or her strengths. Reading and researching more about the kinesthetic learner will increase your awareness and appreciation for this special person that God has "fearfully and wonderfully made" (Ps. 139:14).

DAVID WINE

Bibliography. T. Armstrong (1993), *7 Kinds of Smart;* D. Kolb (1984), *Experiential Learning: Experience as the Source of Learning and Development;* H. Gardner (1993), *Frames of Mind: The Theory of Multiple Intelligences;* M. D. LeFever (1995), *Learning Styles: Reaching Everyone God Gave You to Teach;* C. U. Tobias (1995), *The Way We Learn: How to Discover and Teach to Your Child's Strengths;* idem (1996), *Every Child Can Succeed.*

See also KOLB, DAVID; LEARNING STYLES

Knowles, Malcolm S. (1914–). American adult educator. Born in Florida, he completed a B.A. at Harvard and obtained an M.A. and a Ph.D. from the University of Chicago. In 1940 he became the director of adult education for the Boston YMCA, and formulated much of his theory of informal education and self-directed adult learning during his years of practice there. In 1951 he became the founding executive director of the national Adult Education Association, and in 1960 he was asked to establish a new graduate program in the field of adult education at Boston University. The program prospered and student numbers proliferated, but conflict about his ideas of adult learning with the senior administration led to Knowles's movement to North Carolina State University at Raleigh in 1974, where he continued to teach, write, and deliver presentations about andragogy around the world until his mandatory retirement in 1979.

Knowles was introduced to the term *andragogy,* a concept current in Europe in the late 1960s, by a visiting Yugoslav adult educator, Dusan Savicevic. Andragogy was defined by Dr. Knowles to mean "the art and science of helping adults learn," and it swiftly became an enormously popular theory among adult educators and trainers throughout North America. Knowles's theories of self-directed learning and andragogy have influenced research and practice in adult education since the first publication in 1970 of his landmark book *The Modern Practice of Adult Education: Andragogy vs. Pedagogy.*

Knowles outlined five key characteristics defining adult learners: (1) As a person matures, his or her self-concept moves from that of a dependent personality toward one of a self-directing human being. (2) An adult accumulates a growing reservoir of experience and needs an opportunity to use experience in learning activities. (3) An adult's readiness to learn is closely related to the developmental tasks of his or her social role. Adults need to see the relevance between instructional content and the issues in their everyday lives. (4) There is a change in time perspective as people mature—from future application of knowledge to immediate application. Thus an adult is more problem-centered than subject-centered in learning. 5) Adults are motivated to learn by internal factors, such as increased self-esteem, rather than by external ones, such as an instructor's praise, grades, or punishment. (This fifth principle was added in Knowles's later revision of andragogy.)

Knowles went on to elaborate an entire system of techniques for instructing adults based on his five principles of andragogy. In *Andragogy in Action: Applying Modern Principles of Adult Learning* (1984), he suggested that adult educators should follow these six suggestions for improving their practice: (1) Set a warm, welcoming, pleasurable classroom "climate," both physical and psychological. (2) Involve learners in the mutual planning of objectives and activities for the instruction. (3) Involve learners in diagnosing their own learning needs. (4) Involve adults in designing their learning plans, ideally through individualized "learning contracts," where learners identify resources and benchmarks to assist their learning process. (5) Help learners carry out their learning plans by being a "facilitator" or guide, rather than a "teacher." (6) Involve learners in evaluating their own learning progress, as well as the effectiveness of the learning process, materials, activities, and the adult educator.

Knowles's theory of andragogy, with its prescription for a participative, learner-centered, self-directive instructional approach, has raised much controversy since 1970. Some critics are concerned that it is unclear whether andragogy is a theory of learning or teaching. Others have charged that Knowles has not made an adequate case, either through argument or empirical research, for the validity of his principles of andragogy. Some critics take exception to Knowles's description of the adult as problem-centered and interested primarily in learning with immediate relevancy and application to his or her life: this presents a narrow and reductionist view, say critics. Others challenge Knowles's continuing emphasis on self-direction as a key characteristic of the adult learner. Self-direction, maintain some adult educators, is more a desired outcome for adults than a given condition of how adults operate. Some theorists challenge the accuracy of the assumption that all or even most adults are self-directed in their learning. Finally, many writers have taken exception to Knowles's "one size fits all" approach to describing adult learners, maintaining that adults are highly unique and diverse. Adult learners cannot be described separately from their individual contexts, because no person learns the same way in different settings, different types of content, or at different ages and stages of their adulthood. Furthermore, claim many critics, Knowles's theory is rather Western in its cultural bias, stressing individualism and self-esteem.

Knowles modified his theories over the years in response to these criticisms. In his 1980 revision of *The Modern Practice of Adult Education*, he retracted his earlier claim that andragogy was diametrically "opposed to" pedagogy (the art and science of helping children learn), and instead theorized that pedagogy and andragogy were on a continuum. Later, Knowles admitted that four of the five principles were applicable in many cases to children as learners. Still later, Knowles described andragogy as a "model of assumptions" of adult learning rather than a "theory," and qualified it further as a "situational" model that was subject to contextual differences among learners. Most recently, Knowles began extending his notion of self-directed learning to create a conception of community learning centers as new kinds of educational facilities where lifelong learning can take place. What Knowles continues to emphasize, however, is the importance of life experience as a key source of learning for adults. He also stresses, as he has since 1970, the need for an andragogical approach in certain situations with adults. In this respect, he has helped move adult education methods away from a methodology-centered instructional design approach, to more human, more holistic, and more sensitive approaches. Most adult educators, even Knowles's

critics, credit him for calling attention to the needs and interests of the learner and thus fundamentally changing the field of adult education.

Knowles was an inductee of the inaugural Human Resource Development Hall of Fame, and is still active consulting and writing in the field of adult education. Other books he has written include *Self-Directed Learning* (1975) and *The Adult Learner: A Neglected Species* (1984).

TARA J. FENWICK

See also ADULT DEVELOPMENT; ADULT CHRISTIAN EDUCATION; ADULT LIFE CYLE; ANDRAGOGY; CONTRACT; CONTRACT LEARNING; LIFELONG LEARNING; PEDAGOGY

Kohlberg, Lawrence (1927–87). Psychologist and educator. Kohlberg is known for his cognitive theory of moral development, which drew on philosophical reflection and empirical psychological research. Countering prevailing psychoanalytic and behavioral thought, which held that morality is absorbed from and reinforced by aspects of one's surroundings, Kohlberg rejected socialization and other influences as being inadequate for moral development as he defined it. Instead, he believed that individuals develop internal moral structures (ways of thinking) to make meaning of life and its moral concerns. Nearly thirty years of longitudinal and other empirical studies and interaction with researchers validated and refined his understanding of the development of moral reasoning.

Influenced by Kant, Baldwin, Piaget, and Dewey, Kohlberg was concerned with questions such as "What is virtue?" and "What is justice?" His theory of moral development was shaped around the universal moral principle of justice, which he defined as recognition of an individual's rights as well as the individual's acknowledgment of the rights of others. In later years, Kohlberg indicated that justice includes concerns for empathy and caring as well. Moral development in its basic pattern proceeds from heteronomous moral judgment (which depends on parents, teachers, and other authorities) to autonomous judgment in which responsibility for moral decisions based on justice rests within the person. Kohlberg's concept is interactional in that mere biological maturation does not account for development. Rather, development occurs as the result of interaction between a person's cognitive moral capacities and the influences of significant persons, ideas, and contexts.

Expanding on Piaget's two-stage model of moral judgment development, Kohlberg identified six stages of development, each of which represents qualitatively distinct moral reasoning. The stages are invariant in sequence and no stages may be skipped. While the pace of development varies by individual, development may cease at any stage. There is greater congruence between moral conviction and moral behavior at higher stages of moral reasoning. That is, persons in the upper stages are more likely to practice moral behavior than persons at lower stages. Higher stages are more effective because they offer capacities for resolving moral issues and come closer to the justice ideal. While growth in stages is essential for moral action, cognitive moral growth does not explain moral behavior. Rather, affective processes such as will or ego strength are also necessary.

Kohlberg focused on practices of moral education that encourage development. He used a modified form of Socratic questions and answers dealing with hypothetical moral dilemmas and actual classroom situations. These dialogues are intended to create dissatisfaction in the minds of students with their current levels of understanding, and expose them to thinking one stage higher than their own. Kohlberg's educational approach, growing out of conviction that development of internal thought patterns is essential, was a reaction against relativistic values clarification and indoctrination of specific moral virtues. However, he believed it necessary to begin by communicating certain virtues to provide a basis for moral reasoning. Kohlberg emphasized the importance of providing opportunities in the classroom for role-taking or seeing things through the eyes of others. He likewise accentuated the significance of the moral environment, or aspects such as group or institutional norms and structures, which serve as a bridge between moral judgment and action. In fact, such "hidden curriculum" itself represents a stage of moral development that tends to prompt moral judgment and action in participants accordingly.

Kohlberg believed that there are relationships between moral stages and religious thinking in that religious thinking depends on moral structures. Hence, development of moral reasoning is necessary for development of religious thought, but is not sufficient since religious thinking involves other dynamics.

He likewise believed that religious thinking supports moral development by providing reasons for being moral. Indeed, Kohlberg understood religious beliefs to provide *content* for moral decision making. He proposed a sequence of stages of religious thought that parallel stages of moral reasoning. Development of religious thinking is a rational process, although love is seen as an essential component. At various points in the refinement of his theory, Kohlberg postulated a seventh "faith" stage, the highest stage of religious judgment dealing with cosmic or infinite issues.

Potential conflict between evangelical Christian theological convictions and Kohlberg's theory exists in one crucial area. Kohlberg rejected what he described as "divine command" bases for moral development. By this, he implied Christian claims concerning the authority of scriptural teachings in the life and moral decisions of believers. His concern, though not focused on truth claims of Scripture, was that biblical commands represent absolutes that are not universal and that tend to inhibit growth in moral reasoning. However, it appears legitimate to suggest that Kohlberg's concern was more with how Scripture is at times taught. When teaching involves reasons for biblical instructions and consideration of moral dilemmas in which they are to be applied, it is reasonable to conclude that moral development theory may be applied to the experience of believers.

DENNIS DIRKS

Bibliography. L. Kohlberg (1969), *Handbook of Socialization Theory and Research;* idem (1981), *Essays on Moral Development,* vol. 1; *The Philosophy of Moral Development: Moral Stages and the Idea of Justice;* idem (1984), *Essays on Moral Development,* vol. 2, *The Psychology of Moral Development: The Nature and Validity of Moral Stages;* L. Kohlberg and D. Candeeidem (1976), *Moral Development and Behavior: Theory, Research, and Social Issues;* L. Kohlberg et al. (1987), *Child Psychology and Childhood Education: A Cognitive-Developmental View.*

See also CHRISTIAN EDUCATION; DEWEY, JOHN; FAITH, FAITH DEVELOPMENT; FOWLER, JAMES W., III; GILLIGAN, CAROL; MORAL DEVELOPMENT; MORAL DILEMMA; MORAL EDUCATION; PIAGET, JEAN; ROLE PLAY; SOCRATIC METHOD

Koinonia. The term *koinonia* has two prominent meanings: (1) participation in the act of establishing relationship or covenant; and (2) gathering together as a community for mutual fellowship and maturation.

Background. The concept of gathering together, or *koinonia,* grew out of ancient meal customs, which placed a high value on the symbolism of fellowship as denoted by the gathering around a table, an understanding lost to much of the Western world. In ancient civilizations, sharing a meal with someone was an honor and an act of veneration. Such occasions were conducted in a variety of social and religious associations. These activities, therefore, contributed to the development of early Christian communal meals (Freedman, 1992).

Old and New Testament Uses. The Hebrew mind recognized fellowship as something that transpires between individuals. The Greek mind primarily thought of *koinonia* as a personal relationship to deity. This personal relationship was a foreign concept to Old Testament Israel because of the distance that the individual Jew felt separated him or her from God. The righteous individual of the Old Testament regarded herself or himself as in a relationship of dependence upon God and belonging to Him, as opposed to a relational fellowship. Smith (1965) confirms the notion that *koinonia* was never expressed in the Old Testament in the same way as in the New Testament, even in the Septuagint, which was influenced by Greek thinking. The most similar situation in the Old Testament were the meals shared by those entering a covenant (Gen. 26:26–31), as a consummation ceremony of the newly established relationship. They did, however, exhibit an interpersonal relationship within the confines of the faith community for each other and common meals were often the result of this expression.

The New Testament expression of possessing a commonality of nature within the faith community lies fundamentally in our personal relationship with Jesus Christ. The basis of this relationship is delineated from the standpoint of our salvific interaction with Christ himself (1 John 1:5–10). As Christians, our nature becomes the same as that of Jesus, and as long as we remain in fellowship with him, in his nature, we "walk in the light, as he is in the light" (v. 7). When our nature is such that we love what is not within his nature, we "walk in the darkness" (v. 6). The idea of *koinonia* within the early church is grounded in the premise that the nature of Jesus Christ himself is the fiber that binds individuals together, even to the point of having all things in common.

This concept, then, of "having in common" is possible within the fellowship of an exclusive community of believers centering around Jesus, since this is the only place, or common arena, in which we are gathered. It does not specifically relate as only a relationship of one believer to another, but also that this interpersonal relationship is entered into through the person of Jesus, thus inspiring a reciprocal relationship. This type of relationship, bound by the Spirit, is the essence of the Acts 4:32–37 account, in which personal possessions were sold and then brought to the apostles for distribution within the faith community. One understanding we do receive from the Acts account is insight into the manner in which this unique community expressed their love for one another. On one hand, it was a continuation of the love that was modeled to them by Christ himself (Luke 8:1–3; John 12:4–8; 13:29), while on the other hand it was a fulfillment of what was prophetically declared as a sign of the end times (Deut. 15:4) (Kittel, 1965).

Usage in Christian Education Today. The concept of *koinonia*, or "experiencing genuine fellowship through the common bond of Christ," is duty-bound to "knit believers together in love, stressing social/moral maturity in the church" (Habermas and Issler, 1992). Habermas and Issler continue by listing some of the practical instructional activities that promote community within the life of the church: sharing with prayer partners; bearing one another's burdens; helping others develop their gifts; eating together; going on a church retreat; interceding for others; rejoicing with others; participation in meaningful leisure activities; developing accountability partners; studying a controversial issue with those who hold alternative views; learning to disagree; counseling others; and providing services to the needy.

RONALD W. FREEMAN

Bibliography. D. N. Freedman (1992), *The Anchor Bible Dictionary;* R. Habermas and K. Issler (1992), *Teaching for Reconciliation: Foundations and Practice of Christian Education Ministry;* G. Kittel (1965), *Theological Dictionary of the New Testament;* W. R. Smith (1965), *Theological Dictionary of the New Testament.*

Kolb, David (1939–). American educator and social psychologist best known for his theory of experiential learning and the Learning-Style Inventory (LSI). Prior to receiving his Ph.D. (1967) in social psychology from Harvard University, Kolb earned an M.A. from Harvard and an A.B. from Knox College. From 1965 to 1975, he taught organizational psychology and management at the Massachusetts Institute of Technology. Since 1976 Kolb has taught in the Department of Organizational Behavior at the Weatherhead School of Management, Case Western Reserve University.

Kolb's primary contribution to Christian education lies in the domain of learning process. Drawing heavily from the works of John Dewey (philosophy), Kurt Lewin (social psychology), and Jean Piaget (developmental psychology), he describes his own theory of experiential learning and proposes a model of the structural foundations of the learning process.

For Kolb, the process of experiential learning can be described as a four-stage cycle involving four learning modes: concrete experience, reflective observation, abstract conceptualization, and active experimentation. The model is further constructed of two distinct, intersecting axes. One is a preference for grasping through either concrete experience or abstract conceptualization; the other is a preference for transforming knowledge either through active experimentation or reflective observation.

The central notion of Kolb's model is that learning requires both a pool of experience and some transformation of that experience into knowledge. The simple perception of experience alone is not sufficient for learning; similarly, transformation by itself does not represent learning, for there must be something to be transformed.

Kolb elaborates his structure of the learning process into a dual-axis model of learning styles. Four basic styles of learning emerge: accommodation, divergence, convergence, and assimilation. *Accommodators* are oriented toward concrete experience and transform knowledge through active participation. *Divergers* are also oriented toward concrete experience, but transform knowledge through reflective observation. *Convergers* rely primarily on abstract conceptualization and active experimentation. Finally, *assimilators* are oriented toward abstract conceptualization and reflective observation.

To measure an individual's learning style and personal strengths and weaknesses as a learner, Kolb designed the Learning-Style Inventory (LSI). With the use of a questionnaire and diagram in which the four learning styles are visualized, the LSI measures an individual's major emphasis in the four learning styles. The purpose of the LSI is to better understand the different ways people learn and do problem solving, so as to help them be aware of the consequences of their own learning style and to design learning experiences that take these learning style differences into account.

Kolb is the author of numerous journal articles, chapters in books, technical reports, and test materials. In addition to writing *Experiential Learning,* he has coauthored *Innovations in Professional Education: Steps in a Journey from Teaching to Learning* (1995), *Organizational Behavior: An Experiential Approach to Human Behavior in Organizations* (1995), and *The Organizational Behavior Reader* (1995). Kolb has been a significant member of numerous major research projects in areas such as management, career development, learning process, experiential learning, and motivation. Finally, he has served as a consultant to a number of major business corporations and government organizations on issues such as career development, problem management, management training, achievement motivation, and staff training.

HARLEY ATKINSON

Bibliography. D. Kolb (1984), *Experiential Learning: Experience as the Source of Learning and Development;* idem (1999), *The Learning Style Inventory.*

See also ABSTRACT THINKING; ACCOMMODATION; ASSIMILATION; CONVERGENT/DIVERGENT THINKING; JOHN DEWEY; INDIVIDUAL DIFFERENCES; LEARNING STYLES; KURT LEWIN; PIAGET, JEAN; TACTILE LEARNERS; VISUAL LEARNERS

Korean Christian Education. It was 1884 when Protestant missionaries first entered Korea, even though Roman Catholic missions had begun in that nation a hundred years before. Protestants were not allowed to proselytize per se, but they could establish Western education and medical services. This could be considered as preevangelism. Dr. H. W. Allen, a medical missionary, built the first Christian hospital, *Kwang-Haewon,* the predecessor of Yunsei Medical School. Rev. H. G. Appenzeller founded Bae-Jae Mission School in

1885; Mrs. W. B. Scranton founded the first girls' mission school, *Ewha,* in 1886; and Rev. H. G. Underwood founded Yunhee Mission School in 1887. Approximately 39 mission schools were founded between 1885 and 1909 (Son in-Soo, 1987), the year before the Japanese annexation ushered in the persecution age of Korean Christianity. Significantly, the history of Korean Christianity began with Christian education. From 1887, when the first five Sunday schools had begun in Pyongyang (Clark, 1973), until 1990s, Korean church schools could be divided into four periods: beginnings of the Sunday school (1887–1922); growth of the Sunday school (1922–45); recovery of church education (1945–60s); and professionalization of church education (1960s–90s) (Kim Hee-Ja, 1989).

The Beginnings of the Sunday School (1887–1922). After the first five Sunday schools were begun in 1887 at Pyongyang, many Sunday schools were planted in Seoul and other cities. Korean mission churches focused on adult education, and the education of children emerged along with adult Bible classes. Even before the first missionaries entered and worked in Korea, the Bible had been translated into Korean by Rev. Ross and Mrs. Mackintyre with the help of the first Korean baptized in Manchuria. In 1882 the Gospel of Luke was translated, and the whole New Testament was translated in 1887. The Korean Bible was the major curriculum for church education for both adults and children. The zeal for learning the Bible spread widely in the Korean church. Wherever churches were planted, Bible classes were opened for new Christians.

In 1905, the Federal Council of Mission or The General Council of Protestant Evangelical Missions was organized for the fellowship of missionaries and the publication of Sunday school curriculum. They translated the American version of the Unified Sunday School Lessons into Korean. In 1911, five Korean Christian educators joined the Council. In 1913, Mr. H. J. Heinz, the general secretary of World Sunday School Association, visited the Korean Sunday School Convention, where 14,700 members gathered (Kim Yang-Sun, 1971). By 1915 there were many "Sunday School Extensions" into the rural areas. In 1919, the March First Movement encouraged millions of Koreans to take to the streets in nonviolent demonstrations for independence, but the movement was quickly suppressed. In the following years Japan tightened its control in Korea, suppressing other nationalist movements. As a result, people increasingly came to church hoping that through education they might gain independence from Japanese rule. Therefore, the Sunday school played an important role in the country. In time, there were over 10,000 Sunday schools. By 1922, the Chosun Sunday School had been organized by Korean church educators as the umbrella organization for the Korean Sunday school.

The Growth of the Sunday School (1922–45).
In 1922, the first vacation Bible school (VBS) was held during summer vacation. Mrs. Moffet organized the vacation Bible school, which grew rapidly. In 1930, there were 36,239 children in VBS and this increased to 128,926 by 1934. In 1925, there were 5,601 Sunday schools and 107,350 children attending. Around 20 percent of them came from non-Christian families and about 10 percent of those were converted and grew to be adult Christians. Sunday school had proven to be a strong vehicle for evangelism in Korean churches.

In 1930, Francis Kinsler founded the Children's Bible Club as a charity school for poor children. He taught three hours a day, five days a week, with curricula in the Korean language, mathematics, geography, natural science, and the Christian life. Many children who attended made professions of faith. In fact, over 60 percent of the students became Christians. In 1937, the Chosun Sunday School Association was liquidated by the Japanese. They forced the Korean people to worship their Japanese god, *Shinto*. Koreans were forced to change their names into Japanese, and they were not allowed to use the Korean language at school or in the church. Many mission schools were closed.

American-made Sunday school curricula were found to be insufficient due to ethnic, cultural, political, and ideological identification issues. However, they did meet Korean needs and concerns of the day. Koreans were angry about the inhuman physical, mental, and spiritual torture by the Japanese. Out of this frustration and emotional, physical, and spiritual exhaustion, Koreans had desperately turned to the Christian faith for strength, for answers to painful questions in life, and for a hope of independence from Japan. The great needs of the day contributed to the rapid growth of Sunday schools and churches.

The Recovery of Church Education (1945–60).
On August 15, 1945, Korea regained its sovereignty from Japan. In 1948, the previously abolished Chosun Sunday School Association was re-organized with a new name, the Korean Council of Christian Education, which encouraged the development of church education beyond Sunday school boundaries. There were great efforts to improve and increase church education by thoughtful church and denominational leaders. In 1950, however, the Korean War broke out and many church buildings were completely destroyed. There were 1,312,836 Korean military casualties, including 415,004 dead; the estimated communist casualties were 2 million (*Encarta*, 1997, 98). Hardly any community escaped at least one serious casualty from the horrors of the armistice. After the Korean War, people worked hard to rebuild their lives and churches. Major denominations undertook great efforts to remove all scars from the war. They worked hard to evangelize people through Christian education. Emphasis was put on the development of Christian education directors in the churches. From the control of laity in the church schools, the profession was born out of the desperate need for church education. The first Korean scholars who went abroad to America to do Christian education studies returned with masters or doctoral degrees, ready to train disciples in their churches.

The Profession of Church Education (1960s–90s). Around 1960, the title of "educational evangelist" was used by those who were in fact Christian education specialists. Some of them came from Korean seminaries. Their churches often provided scholarships. Some were part-time workers while in seminary. It is true that this unique position contributed to the development of church education, but it is also true that problems of inconsistency in church education arose due to the short and temporary nature of these jobs. Some did their Christian education work on a part-time basis before they took a pastorate. Enormous numbers of people came to church to find meaning in life after all the hardships through which Koreans had suffered and from the political turmoil of those days.

From the 1980s, Korean economic prosperity abounded. Many church leaders became serious about the need for educational ministry to bring revival in the Korean church. Much money was invested in educational facilities, new curriculum development, and electronic media, which made an impact on classroom teaching and worship in the church sanctuaries.

For the profession of church education, the first Christian education department was established at Soong-Sil University, followed by most theological seminaries and Christian colleges, which initiated Christian education majors at the undergraduate and graduate levels. In 1961, the Church Education Conference was begun. Presently it has developed into an association with a hundred Christian education scholars as members. Hundreds of books have been published by Korean scholars. Books were translated and introduced to the laity and Christian education students as well. Many journals—*Friends of the Teacher, Christian Education, New Family, Educational Church, Christianity and Education*—have been published monthly and subscribed to by many church school teachers, students, and ministers. Thoughtful church and denominational leaders have developed many teacher training and teacher education programs. Major denominational and nondenominational published curricula have been revised through complete reorganization to communicate the relevance of the Christian faith to the contemporary needs and concerns of the people.

It has been over 114 years since the first Protestant missionaries came to Korea and established Christian education. In the twenty-first century, Korean Christian education should seriously consider the integration of professionalism and spirituality. Church education has been taken care of by the laity and by part-time educational evangelists as a means for the revival of the church. Yet church education has not been considered seriously by senior ministers. The church has been separated into pastoral ministry and teaching ministry for more than a century. The future of the Korean church should be changed into the new paradigm of the teaching church rather than just the preaching church.

HEEJA KIM

Bibliography. A. D. Clark (1973), *The History of the Church in Korea;* W. S. Jung (1991), *The Task and Methods of Modern Christian Education;* H. J. Kim, *Presbyterian Theological Quarterly* 56, no. 2 (1989); Y. S. Kim (1971), *Research on History of Korean Christianity: Microsoft Encarta 98 Encyclopedia* (1997); S. H. Moffett (1962), *The Christians in Korea;* In-Tak Oh, ed. (1994), *The History of Church Education;* I. S. Son (1987), *The History of Korean Education II.*

Laissez-Faire Approach. The term *laissez faire* is French for "let do" or "let people do as they please." Leaders who exercise a laissez-faire approach are characterized by being passive but giving assistance or ideas if requested by others. This approach to group organization and leadership occurs when the group's leader does not exert much influence on the group and makes little effort to lead (Engel and Snellgrove, 1989).

In a well-known study, Kurt Lewin et al. (1958) studied the impact of different kinds of leadership on group behavior. Lewin asked 11-year-old boys to participate in some after-school clubs. The adult using the laissez-faire approach allowed the group complete freedom in decision making in regard to activities and group procedure. The leader gave neither positive nor negative evaluation though he was friendly to the participants. As a result, the boys were relatively unproductive when the adult was present and spent most of the time asking questions. The researchers found that the boys were most active when the adult was absent.

For an example of this approach to parenting and its destructive results, examine Eli and his sons in 1 Samuel 2.

KENNETH S. COLEY

Bibliography. T. L. Engel and L. Snellgrove (1989), *Psychology: Its Principles and Applications;* R. Lippitt and R. K. White (1958), *Reading in Social Psychology,* pp. 446–511.

Laissez-Faire Leadership. Originally an economic philosophy, this term now also represents a particular attitude or style of leadership and classroom management. Laissez faire or *laissez nous faire* (French for "leave us alone") represents a popular intellectual eighteenth-century philosophy that government should remove all regulatory control of trade and prices. This economic policy was conceived in the then highly restrictive business environment of England and Europe and was an influential policy in the early United States before giving way to regulatory control at the beginning of the twentieth century. Within education, laissez faire may be used to characterize certain administrative policies, such as school-based management, which are designed to return school policy decisions to the local school level (Odden and Wholstetter, 1995).

Laissez-faire leadership assumes that specific direction should not be given to program goals or methods. In Christian education such an approach is often confused with collegial or team-centered leadership, styles that do require some sense of shared purpose or agreed-on goals. Age-level leaders and teachers operating under laissez-faire leadership often become isolated in their own area of educational ministry. Educational philosophy and teaching methods usually vary from classroom to classroom. Some classes may actually use approaches that are antithetical to each other. Students moving from one area of age-level ministry to another may experience "gaps" in their education regarding the Bible and the Christian faith while addressing certain themes in a repetitive but inconsistent manner.

Within the classroom, laissez-faire teachers rarely provide direction concerning curriculum design or actual student interaction with the material. Children's teachers that seek to simulate an "open classroom" setting might not provide direction in either the selection of topics or the degree of interaction between the student and the material. A youth ministry preoccupied with topical studies or adult classes that focus only on specific issues or student-felt needs may also betray a laissez-faire approach by the teacher. Students within such classes often do not receive an education that addresses the full scope of biblical teaching or an education of sufficient depth to ensure proper understanding of these teachings.

Laissez faire then is often descriptive of an organization (congregation, age level ministry, or Sunday school) that does not seek to provide a comprehensive approach to educational ministry. While such an approach might be embraced for a short time (primarily in reaction to oppressive leadership or a previous rigid curriculum), the lack of specific direction may ultimately lead to a disinterested student population with a truncated view of the Christian faith.

DEAN BLEVINS

Bibliography. J. Dettoni (1993), *Introduction to Youth Ministry;* P. Hersey and K. H. Blanchard (1964), *Management of Organizational Behavior: Utilizing Human Resources,* 7th ed.; J. M. Burns (1978), *Leadership;* E. Odden and P. Wohlstetter, *Educational Leadership* 52 (1995): 32–36; W. A. Sabin and N. Warren (1965), *The McGraw-Hill Dictionary of Modern Economics,* pp. 199–200; R. C. Whorley (1976), *A Gathering of Strangers: Understanding the Life of Your Church.*

See also AUTHORITARIAN APPROACH; CLASSROOM SETTING; DEMOCRATIC APPROACH TO GROUPS; LEADERSHIP; LEADERSHIP DEVELOPMENT; SERVANT LEADER

Laity. Nonordained members of a church. Ministry is usually the context for the term, and it is normally used in contrast to the clergy, or ordained members of the body of the church. Common usage refers to a specific set of people of a religious faith as distinguished from its clergy. Laity also could refer to a group of people in contrast to those of a particular profession or those with specialized training. Thus, we sometimes use the term *lay pastor* when referring to a person who has not received specific pastoral or theological training. This contrast between an untrained, nonprofessional volunteer in the church and its paid staff often fails to provide an accurate picture and is therefore unfortunate. It needlessly differentiates between members of Christ's body.

Considerable controversy arises when the distinction between clergy and "laity" is stressed. In fact, Hendrik Kraemer, in his definitive book *A Theology of the Laity* (1958), describes a "clericalized lay people." His argues that to create such a gulf between clergy and laity is to do damage to the church. "The laity, its place, its responsibility, its ministry is as essential an aspect of the Church as that of the clergy. The laity should therefore . . . be appealed to . . . simply on the basis of what they are by the nature and calling of Christ's Church as the 'people of God,' sent into the world for witness and service" (Kraemer, 1958, 167).

The laity might best be understood as those members of the body of Christ who are not ordained, yet may actively be called the people of God (*laos theou*). George Laird Hunt summarizes the biblical concept: "God's people are his by his choice and call and that he chose a people for mission, to make his name and his Word known. The term was applied to Israel and then to the inclusive church. The phrase carries none of the distinction between clergy and laity known today" (Culley, 1967, 377).

The exact term *laity* does not occur in the Bible. However, the word *laos* in the New Testament (occurring 140 times in the New Testament, eight of these in the plural) builds on the Old Testament idea of God's people being separate from the peoples of the world who do not know God. The missionary nature of making God known to the world is inherent in being God's people. This important understanding then shapes our present practice in regard to the difference between clergy and lay people in ministry functions. The practice of keeping nonordained lay people away from God-ordained ministry needs to be examined.

One may justify a separation from the Old Testament distinction between the priesthood and the people. And the New Testament makes a division between leader and follower, with higher standards applied to leadership (see 1 Tim. 5:17–20; Titus 1:5–9). Acts 5:12–13 does seem to indicate a respect for the apostles, but as a rule the early church did not seem to practice such distinctions. *The people of God* (1 Peter 2:9, 10) is a phrase used to include all those who follow Christ. But the term does not seem to refer to the difference between priesthood (clergy) and laity, but rather between those who are of God's family and unbelievers. Therefore, biblical usage would indicate a close understanding of the Protestant concept of the priesthood of the believer.

Historical Perspective. There does not seem to be undue separation between clergy and laity in the New Testament. All believers are members of one body (Rom. 12:4, 5) and are gifted for ministry (1 Cor. 12, 14). While Christ did give gifted people to the saints to equip them, the emphasis seems to be on that "which every joint supplies" (Eph. 4:11–16 NASB).

By the time of the Middle Ages, a sharp division between the general congregation and the priesthood arose. The special functions of the clergy took precedence over the degraded ministry of the common people. During the Reformation, the concepts of the New Testament were revitalized, to a degree. The priesthood of the believer was a fruitful call to broad involvement from God's people. Simply stated, the priesthood of the believer means that "each person is capable of relating to God directly" (Erickson, 1983, 1085–86). The evangelical movements of the eighteenth and nineteenth centuries continued to stress lay involvement based upon their theology. The Laymen's Missionary Movement of the late 1800s is a particular example. In contrast, segments of the church, notably the Roman Catholic, Anglican, and other mainline denominations, have struggled with the place of lay people in ministry.

Contemporary Perspective. Several questions remain regarding the Christian educator's understanding of the lay movement. Volunteerism is enjoying a resurgence, and a number of evangelical writers address concerns in this area. As mentioned above, the emphasis on lay people in missionary involvement has revitalized this church endeavor. Lay counseling is a powerful phenomenon, but structures for this infant field have not been established and tested to an adequate degree. Worship and liturgy have enjoyed only small movements to becoming more congregationally led, as most corporate services are still planned and controlled solely by the clergy. Witness and outreach have become more broadly based as Lay Witness Weekends and Evangelism Explosion as well as other methods have made significant impact on the work of the church. The church's role of instruction still lies in the hands of millions of faithful lay people who teach weekly.

The ordination of clergy, and their training to be equippers for ministry instead of doers only, are challenges for the future evangelical church. Gender and race inclusion are still, unfortunately, issues which have either not been examined by many churches, or have even been opposed. In a society that is increasingly secularized, the church will see more of its work outside its walls. Thus the mobilization of the laity is essential. The typical skepticism toward authority and the busyness of the normal lay member will continue to frustrate Christian educators who seek to enlist and encourage the laity of their church. Simple, meaningful structures that promote unity will need to be designed and implemented. Releasing lay people to ministry still needs creative endeavor if the church is to be what the New Testament intends it to be. Christian educators do well to address the ministry of the laity.

GREGORY C. CARLSON

Bibliography. K. B. Culley (1967), *The Westminster Dictionary of Christian Education;* M. J. Erickson (1983), *Christian Theology;* H. Kraemer (1958), *A Theology of the Laity;* G. Kittel, ed. (1967), *Theological Dictionary of the New Testament;* D. Williams and K. O. Gangel (1983), *Volunteers for Today's Church.*

Language, Inclusive. An approach to writing and speaking that attempts to use the English language in a way that is inclusive of all people. It is typically associated with issues of sexism, but can be broadened to include ageism, racism, nationalism, and classicism. Other terms that can be equated with inclusive language are nonsexist language, nondiscriminatory language, or nongendered language.

Advocacy of inclusive language has been common in stylistic writing manuals since the 1970s. Examples of changes are:

man, mankind	becomes	human, humanity, humankind
chairman	becomes	chair, chairperson, moderator
salesman	becomes	salesperson, sales representative
stewardess	becomes	flight attendant
fireman	becomes	firefighter

The English language has only gendered third-person pronouns, "he" and "she." Attempts to use inclusive language with these pronouns include use of "he or she," alternating female and male pronouns within the writing, rewriting in the plural, writing in a passive voice, or completely rewriting and eliminating the pronoun.

Discussion of inclusive language within the Christian community has been a subject of great debate in recent years. Several denominations have convened task forces and issued statements regarding the use of inclusive language (for example, the Presbyterian Church in the USA, the United Methodist Church, and the Episcopal Church).

Controversy has swirled around the publication of the Inclusive Language Lectionary (National Council of Churches, 1983), the rewriting of hymnbooks and liturgies, and inclusive Bible translations. Several Bible translations have chosen to use inclusive language in an attempt to be true to the meaning in the original text (the New Revised Standard Version, the New Living Translation, the Contemporary English Version, the New Century Version, and the New International Version Inclusive—available only in England).

At the root of the discussion regarding Bible translation is the question of whether

formal equivalence or functional equivalence, as Bible translation theories, produces the best translation for our day. Formal equivalence (sometimes called "literal translation") believes that the original wording, grammar, and syntax should be retained so long as the resulting translation is understandable (KJV, NASB, and RSV are examples). Functional equivalence (also called "dynamic translation") believes that the text should have the same impact on the modern reader that the original had on the ancient reader. According to this approach, it is not the *original terms* but the *meaning of the whole* that is important . . . (the Good News Bible, and the NLT are examples; NIV and NRSV are sometimes literal, sometimes dynamic). The first is a "word-for-word" translation and the second is a "thought-for-thought" translation. (Grant Osborne, *Christianity Today,* October 27, 1997, 33)

The use of inclusive language has the potential for empowering evangelism to a world whose use of language has changed. Nancy Hardesty (1987) states:

Thus, using inclusive language is not merely a matter of taste or literary sophistication but a matter of faithfulness to God and to our moral responsibility for our neighbors. As the report on "Language About God" to the former Presbyterian Church in the United States says, "Language about God commonly used only a decade ago has now become for many an impediment to communication, community, and to faith itself" (p. 7). To speak accurately about God and lovingly to our neighbor requires the use of inclusive language. (15)

One area of controversy which is emotionally *and* theologically laden concerns the language we use for God. Typically the language used for God includes primarily masculine metaphors (Father, Son of God). There are both masculine and feminine images of God in Scripture and God is obviously neither male nor female.

God, by any orthodox definition, transcends human masculinity and femininity. Therefore, even core terms like "Father" cannot reduce God to our concepts of manhood. If there is a problem with such terminology, it does not lie in the nature of God nor in the words of Scripture, but in any meaning we ascribe to them that goes beyond the biblical intention and restricts God to human categories. Correspondingly, metaphors that ascribe feminine characteristics to God should be recognized as descriptive instruments to help us understand the depths of God's character and care for us. Pagan deities were either masculine or feminine. God is infinitely greater than such categories. (Tucker and Liefeld, 1987, 450)

DENISE MUIR KJESBO

Bibliography. J. S. Hagen, ed. (1990), *Gender Matters;* N. Hardesty (1987), *Inclusive Language in the Church;* R. Tucker and W. Liefeld (1987), *Daughters of the Church;* M. S. Van Leeuwen, ed. (1993), *After Eden: Facing the Challenge of Gender Reconciliation.*

Latchkey Children. Children who have a key to their home when they leave for school in the morning because they are in a self-care arrangement before and/or after school while their parents are at work.

An estimated two million school-age children in the United States take care of themselves after school. The average time alone is less than two hours per day, although some are without supervision for the entire day during summer months (Cole and Rodman, 1987).

In studies comparing latchkey kids with children who have a parent available when they get home from school, results were similar on measurements of self-esteem, locus of control, and teachers' ratings of social adjustment (Cole and Rodman, 1987). Negative aspects were that some unsupervised children were frightened or used television viewing for companionship. One study identified a majority of the juvenile delinquents in detention as latchkey kids (Long, 1983). Positive characteristics for latchkey kids were greater independence, self-reliance, and more resourcefulness. Latchkey kids were also found to hold fewer gender-role stereotypes (Robinson, 1986).

Authorities recommend that children under 8 years of age should not be left home alone. Even then, not all 8-year-olds are capable of adequate self-care. Parents should assess their children relative to readiness for self-care responsibilities.

An assessment plan to determine readiness for self-care should include physical, emotional, cognitive, and social aspects. Physical concerns would include the child's ability to avoid personal injury when moving around the house, the ability to lock and unlock doors, and the ability to safely operate specified household equipment. Emotional concerns include the child's ability to handle unexpected stressful situations, the ability to follow rules, and the degree to which the child is comfortable being alone without feeling lonely or fearful. Cognitive abilities include problem-solving skills, the ability to take telephone messages, and adequate understanding of oral and written instructions. Socially, the child should be able to relate to other children and adults and be able to summon help from neighbors and community resources should it become necessary.

LILLIAN J. BRECKENRIDGE

Bibliography. C. Cole and H. Rodman (1987), *When School-age Children Care for Themselves: Issues for Family Life Educators and Parents;* T. Long and L. Long (1983), *Latchkey Children;* B. E. Robinson, B. H. Rowland, and M. Coleman, *Family Relations* 35 (1986): 473–78.

Late Adolescence. The life passage immediately preceding young adulthood; typically defined as ages 18–21 in North American culture, descriptions of late adolescence may include a range of ages from 17 to 24.

Developmentally, the late adolescent passage provides opportunity for youth to put into place the final pieces of the mosaic of their personal identity as they prepare to assume the responsibilities of adulthood. Arthur Chickering's (1978) *Education and Identity* identifies seven vectors of growth that occur during this transitional phase: *achieving competence, managing emotions, becoming autonomous, establishing identity, freeing interpersonal relationships, clarifying purposes,* and *developing integrity.* This growth results in late adolescent interest in issues such as identity, sexuality, family, dating and marriage, ethics, vocation, mission, stewardship, and life planning.

The late adolescent transition is also a particularly pivotal stage in spiritual formation. James Fowler (1981) describes the shift as being from a *Synthetic-Conventional* adolescent stage of faith to an *Individuative-Reflective* adult stage. Transition from a faith that conforms to its peer context to a faith able to stand on its own is not fully accomplished within this short period of life. The transformation does, however, find its genesis during late adolescence.

Descriptively, therefore, the latter stage of adolescence is characterized by entertaining new ideas, examining previously held beliefs, exploring new questions about one's self, experimenting with new roles, relationships, and opportunities, and establishing a baseline of values for living as an individual in the adult world. Consequently, the late adolescent is not typically inclined to conform to traditional institutional and relational norms.

Given these characteristics of late adolescents, it is not surprising that this age group is one of the most challenging for the Christian educator. The late adolescent is engaged in a quest for spiritual understanding, experiences, and applications that will survive the tests of his emerging adult world. Furthermore, the late adolescent seeks learning experiences that transcend conventional educational methodologies. Perhaps the greatest challenge in Christian education during this crucial age, however, is the realization that within each of these learners is a wealth of potential ready to be mined through effective Christian nurture.

Educating late adolescents for spiritual growth is best facilitated in a relational context where learners encounter meaningful fellowship, ownership, and discipleship. Meaningful fellowship is critical because the late adolescent seeks intimate relationships that go beyond the casual and often fickle relationships of earlier adolescent stages. This age group wants to develop trust through mutual self-disclosure and shared experiences. Meaningful ownership of the ministry is important to late adolescents because they desire to find places to contribute, to see their gifts and talents expressed in ways that make a significant impact. Finally, meaningful discipleship implies that there is a purposeful, intentional investment in their spiritual lives. The late adolescent is impatient with religious routine, and is also discontent when the content of the teaching fails to be relevant to the significant life questions which are emerging in their world.

One of the focal points for such an educational ministry among late adolescents must be recognition of their expanding worlds. Many are leaving parents and homes for the first time. They are discovering the broader realities of their world through educational and vocational experiences. Late adolescents are also forming relationships that require greater levels of personal identity, security, and sharing. They are exploring a world of options for where they will live, what they will do, and how they will relate. Acknowledging and responding to these broadening horizons requires educators who are flexible, able to explore issues from multiple perspectives, patient with the investigative and experimental processes of discovering one's place in the world, and capable of providing both challenge and support for the journey into young adulthood.

Historically, local churches have struggled in their attempts to program educational ministries for late adolescents. In addition to the inherent challenges of their developmental stage, there are many practical difficulties in building effective ministries among this group. First, many of them leave their home communities to go to college. Because of distance and their disinterest in traditions and institutions, late adolescents may find themselves feeling detached from their home churches and unmotivated to get involved in a new church near their school. The hectic, less structured, and more stressful schedule of college life contributes to the difficulty. Meanwhile, the home church may find itself with a large population of late adolescents for a few weeks during school breaks and with almost none during the rest of the year. Second, because of the need for less traditional, more intentional learning environments and experiences, finding leadership for late adolescent educational ministries can be perplexing. Not as compliant and easily satisfied as older adults, not as simplistic and readily accepting as younger teenagers, the group's needs may appear intimidating. Third, churches tend to be geared toward children, youth, and adults with families. Many late adolescents simply feel that once they have graduated from the high school youth program there is no place for them in the church until they are married and have children of their own. Though this is unintentional, it is nevertheless a commonly shared perception among late adolescents and young adults.

For the above reasons, parachurch organizations have proven more effective at reaching and nurturing late adolescents than churches have. Campus organizations and community ministries have often proven more attractive to this age group. The flexibility, lack of traditional trappings, the capacity for creating unique late adolescent experiences, the competencies of staff leadership, and the presence of ministry within their immediate relational contexts are just some of the reasons why the parachurch has been so successful.

Late adolescents are the fast-approaching crest of each generation's next wave of leadership in the church and the community. Their spiritual maturation during this transitional period of life is crucial both for their individual lives and for the ministry of the gospel in each successive generation. For these reasons, it behooves local congregations and communities of believers to examine ways to bridge the educational ministry gap between youth ministry and adult ministry.

RICHARD R. DUNN

Bibliography. W. Crain (1992), *Theories of Development: Concepts and Applications;* E. Erikson (1968), *Identity, Youth and Crisis;* J. Fowler (1981), *Stages of Faith;* S. Garber (1996), *The Fabric of Faithfulness;*

J. Loevinger (1976), *Ego Development;* S. Patty (1997), *Reaching a Generation for Christ*, pp. 45–86.

Late Adulthood Ministry. Chronological age is one way of defining the older, or senior adult. Some writers and organizations choose the half-century age as a starting point. Others choose 60 or the more commonly accepted 65-year retirement mark as the defining age. Actually, the entry point is probably 50 to 70 years, with the time a person enters retirement as a more useful benchmark. After all, old age is really a matter of perspective. A 20-year-old is an old person in the eyes of a 5-year-old!

One thing that is demonstrable is that with the advances in medicine and nutrition, people are living longer and more productively. The over 65 population in the United States has increased to the point where, as we pass the year 2000, almost 1 in every 5 Americans is 65 years or older. At the same time the over 75 group is approaching 7 percent of the population. With the increase in life expectancy, senior adults are more active, more independent, and are working longer to offset the greater costs connected with longevity. Retirement homes and villages, now big business, are more security and life-care oriented, providing many of the services that the family and church once provided.

Older adults are valuable people in the sight of God. In an age that celebrates youth, it is important for the church to have a balanced view of ministry that includes all ages. The Bible underscores the value of senior adults. "A gray head is a crown of glory; it is found in the way of righteousness" (Prov. 16:31 NASB). "You shall rise up before the grayheaded, and honor the aged, and you shall revere your God; I am the LORD" (Lev. 19:32 NASB). "Honor your father and your mother, as the LORD your God has commanded you, that your days may be prolonged, and that it may go well with you on the land which the Lord your God gives you" (Deut. 5:16 NASB). The righteous man will "still yield fruit in old age; they shall be full of sap and very green" (Ps. 92:14 NASB). Finally, "You younger men, likewise, be subject to your elders; and all of you, clothe yourselves with humility toward one another, for God is opposed to the proud, but gives grace to the humble" (1 Peter 5:5 NASB).

The first educational experience recorded in Scripture was an adult experience; God was the teacher and Adam and Eve were his students. The perfect Teacher, with his innocent creations, formed the foundation for all knowledge that was to come through the ensuing ages. It was a unique beginning based on a personal relationship, a process guided by God, wide-ranging in content.

In the New Testament picture of Christian education, similar elements are in place with a perfect Teacher, the Holy Spirit (John 16:13), guiding a human teacher and redeemed people into all truth. The essential focus of the educational ministry of the church is to present mature, Christ-like believers to God (Eph. 4:11–16). Since maturation is a lifelong process, and since people come to Christ at different ages and mature at varying rates, it is important for the church to have a well-designed and functioning educational program that embraces all ages that are part of the local fellowship.

The church or Christian organization concerned about older adults sets a high standard for ministry. To love, respect, and honor older adults is a commitment and enduring value of the Christian faith. Scripture is the guiding authority. Beginning in Jerusalem (Acts 1:1–7) and over the centuries, the church has been a leader in caring ministries that provide food, clothing, medical, and spiritual assistance where needed. It is important that church and parachurch ministries continue to meet the practical needs of senior adults. This includes physical facilities that will not endanger or discourage older adults from full participation in the life and ministry of the church. Things like difficult stairways, dimly lit halls, slippery floors, inaccessible restroom facilities, or acoustical problems need to be addressed to make the ministry setting both safe and comfortable. Scheduling is also of concern as many older adults have increased difficulty with night travel due to declining eyesight.

The content of church ministry, from the pulpit to the classroom, must be reviewed. With important emphasis on family ministry, the older adult, who may be alone due to the death of a spouse, can feel excluded unless careful plans include them. The needs and focus of senior adults do not always coincide with the needs of younger and middle-aged adults. Social and political concerns often take a backseat to personal significance and survival concerns such as loss of leadership roles, increased available time, health or money matters, and anticipating the reality of death. Inspiration and assurance of purpose and worth are of greater importance to older adults than many other matters.

A significant change occurred in adult ministry (especially church ministry) in the last half of the twentieth century. The paradigm or grid of values and rules through which life is interpreted and understood is now remarkably different. The old paradigm portrayed retirement as play time; volunteering as sacrifice of self; worship as intellectual and spectator-oriented; facilities as a simple auditorium and classroom structure; and teachers as dispensers of propositional knowledge. The present paradigm projects retirement as a time of learning, serving, working, and playing; volunteering as maximizing abilities; worship as participative and experiential; facilities as multipurpose; and teachers as facilitators. In the midst of this change the viewpoints of middle and older adults may differ greatly in scope and style. It is important that the church or adult ministry organization recognize the differences and seek to bridge the gaps with love and sensitivity.

In ministering to and teaching older persons the following should be considered:

1. Establish ministry to older adults as a core value for your church or organization. Agree with God that senior saints are a great reward and resource and make it a part of your mission/vision/values statement.
2. Pray for the older adults in your ministry. They are often viewed as prayer warriors but they also need prayer support. Enlist them and engage them in a ministry of prayer.
3. Identify the existing needs and available resources for older adults in your area and ministry. Establish some study groups to research the matter. Conduct a survey of facilities and programs and devise a plan for matching resources to needs.
4. Review your organization's paradigm for older adult ministry by creating a focus group to study the results and make recommendations for improvement. Investigate the methods and materials used in evangelism, instruction, worship, fellowship, and service programs.
5. Provide high-level and direct leadership help for older adult ministry. Encourage seniors to use retirement time more effectively, share their life lessons more broadly, and use their God-given resources more productively.

GILBERT A. PETERSON

Bibliography. W. and C. Arn (1993), *Catch the Age Wave;* B. E. Brown, *Christian Education Journal* 4, no. 1 (1983): 18–25; W. M. Clements (1989), *Ministry with the Aging;* W. C. Graendorf, *Christian Education Journal* 4, no. 1 (1983): 38–43; R. M. Gray and D. O. Moberg (1977), *The Church and the Older Person;* M. D. Hiett and E. Whitworth, *Christian Education Journal* 4, no. 2 (1983): 13–23; R. J. Johnson, *Christian Education Journal* 4, no. 16 (1983): 37–45; J. W. McCant, *Christian Education Journal* 4, no. 1 (1983): 26–37; D. O. Moberg, *Journal of Christian Education* 3, no. 1 (1982): 51–64; T. B. Robb (1991), *Growing Up: Pastoral Nurture for the Later Years;* J. J. Seeber (1990), *Spiritual Maturity in the Later Years.*

Late Childhood. The grade school years preceding early adolescence, generally ages 6 to 12. Some authorities narrow the focus to ages 9 to 12. The developmental tasks of late childhood include making friends, team play, learning skills, self-efficacy, and self-evaluation.

Friends provide peer relationships that enable problem solving and challenge children to new levels of accomplishment through friendly rivalry. By playing and interacting with peers whose perceptions differ from theirs, children learn to see the world from other points of view. They learn the importance of compromise, and they will often change or modify rules in order to maintain friendships. Peer approval is a strong factor in late childhood, and many children are willing to engage in antisocial behaviors such as cheating, stealing, and trespassing in order to maintain friendships. Children who are unsuccessful in establishing relationships may experience feelings of rejection and loneliness. They may act out by being disruptive, withdrawn, or aggressive with their peers. Christian education can minimize negative experiences by developing ministries that encourage the formation of healthy friendships in a safe environment.

In addition to personal success, children enjoy team success through play such as sports. With team membership, there is the possibility of winning or losing, and children learn that their actions contribute to either the success or failure of the entire group or team. These concepts are inherent in ministry, and Christian athletic groups are excellent teaching vehicles that can nurture cooperation and teamwork. With division of labor, children learn that each position on a team is important even though it has a specific function that may differ from a fellow team member's position. Cooperation through sharing of resources and assisting other members, along with competition to attain better positions within the team, are learned through team play. The subordination of personal goals to group goals, the principle of division of labor, the value of competition, and even learning how to lose are significant lessons relevant to this developmental stage.

Skill development is vital during late childhood. Learning a skill such as reading, for example, enables children to access new information, use language differently, and develop new forms of thinking. Reading, probably the most important skill learned during late childhood development, may be encouraged through church tutoring programs. Involved parents are vital for assisting in the development of reading skills because they encourage good study habits and proper classroom behavior. Incorporating parent participation in Christian education can be accomplished by asking parents to bring their students' report cards home for display and by providing incentives for those parents who annually visit their child's school. Teacher expectation also influences student performance. Churches can assist teachers by establishing small groups such as a "Teachers Nurturing Teachers" ministry, designed to challenge and inspire teachers.

In addition to skill building, children focus on self-evaluation. They receive messages from parents, teachers, and peers that shape how they view themselves. Children who are told that they are cooperative, intelligent, and creative often include these descriptions in their self-evaluation. From this evaluation comes confidence or self-efficacy, which is the assurance that tasks can be performed well. According to Albert Bandura (1982), there are four sources of information that contribute to self-efficacy. If tasks have been completed successfully in the past, these *enactive attainments* are a source of self-efficacy. Failing early in the process of learning a task, such as learning how to play tennis, for example, can discourage children from proceeding with that task. *Vicarious experiences* are also a vehicle of self-efficacy. If children see others succeed or fail in performing a task, their own perception about success or failure at that task is shaped. Through *verbal persuasion*, children can be encouraged to believe in themselves, which can help them experiment with new tasks. This is dependent, however, on *physiological* judgments, which are based on the level of anxiety or anticipation over succeeding at that new task. Overly tense children may not perceive themselves as successful. Excitement and interest provide a better balance for positive self-efficacy.

Metacognition is Piaget's concept of how children come to know and learn. The ability to learn new techniques, recall information, organize, and engage in training are cognitive tasks. Effective strategies that nurture and stimulate children so that doubt is minimized and feelings of knowing are fostered increase self-efficacy. During late childhood, children are involved in concrete operations. Conservation, classification, and combinatorial skills help children develop logic and order their physical world. Through problem solving, generalizations of principles are made and applied to peer relationships, skill attainment, team play, and self-evaluation.

Erickson defines the psychosocial crisis as "industry versus inferiority" during the late childhood years. Children evaluate their success in acquiring skills and performing meaningful work and relate it to their ability to contribute to the social community at large. External rewards such as grades, praise, and privileges increase self-confidence, foster independence, and promote skill development. Feelings of inferiority or worthlessness come from the self as well as from the social environment. Parents and teachers who compare children to one another, or who criticize their motivation or ability, contribute to a sense of failure and to the shaping of a pessimistic view. For most children success or failure in the school environment determines whether the psychosocial crisis of industry versus inferiority will be successfully resolved.

Additional factors that contribute to a positive identity include developing a healthy relationship with God, unconditional love from parents, feeling good about one's ethnic identity, and preliminary college plans or career goals. Since the best contributor to self-esteem is a healthy relationship with God, church-based Christian education

programs must minister to children in ways consistent with their developmental needs. Having fun, taking field trips, engaging in games and sports, and addressing the musical interests of children in late childhood are vital. Activities should involve students' free time—after school and weekends—but this demands committed workers who are also good role models.

LaVerne A. Tolbert

Bibliography. J. Dobson (1978, 1989), *Preparing for Adolescence;* B. M. Newman and P. R. Newman (1991), *Development Through Life: A Psychosocial Approach;* L. Tolbert (1999), *Teaching for Heaven's Sake.*

See also Early Adolescence; Erickson, Erik Homburger; Metacognition; Piaget, Jean

Lateral Thinking. A thinking process closely related to insight (restructuring) and creativity (provoking new patterns) developed principally by Edward deBono. A central idea with lateral thinking is being flexible and overcoming old ways of thinking. Lateral thinking also embraces the idea of challenging assumptions, not for creating chaos or doubt, but for upgrading outdated information, concepts, or problems. In this approach to thinking there are conscious attempts to move away from rigid patterns leading in definite directions toward reforming the patterns (thinking outside the box). In this way it is similar to brainstorming or to J. P. Gilford's concept of divergent thinking.

Two aspects of lateral thinking characterize its usefulness: a provocative use of information, and challenging accepted assumptions (deBono, 1973). Essentially, the most basic principle of lateral thinking is that any particular way of looking at things, problems, or situations is only one from among many other possible ways. Thus, "lateral thinking is also concerned with the breaking out of the concept prisons of old ideas" (deBono, 1973, 11). What occurs in lateral thinking is achieving insight by creating new patterns out of available material.

Fundamental differences exist between lateral and conventional vertical thinking. Edward deBono (1973) identifies several distinctives: (a) lateral thinking is generative searching for repatterning, embracing richness, and even delaying judgment, while vertical thinking seeks the best approach while being right at each step when looking for a solution; (b) lateral thinking makes jumps (a→e→d→c→b→a), welcoming unlikely provocative intrusions, while vertical thinking follows a sequential path (a→b→c→d→e), looking for the most predictable pathway by chiefly searching for what is a correct current pattern. At the same time, lateral thinking should not threaten the validity of vertical cognition. On the contrary, "the two processes are complementary not antagonistic" (50).

Essentially, lateral thinking is more concerned with change than with proof, which often invites volatility in matters of Christian dialogue. When Christian education is soundly based upon the need to be right all the time one risks sacrificing the development of new ideas. Arrogance, fear of making mistakes, premature discarding of ideas, and blocking a potential better pattern or effective communication possibility are all dangers encountered in nonlateral thinking (deBono, 1973). Lateral thinking resembles the functional image of the visionary, while vertical thought more accurately characterizes the managerial role.

A primary application for lateral thinking includes problem solving from various perspectives that break paradigms and empower people. Since its inception lateral thinking has gained a worldwide acceptance with specific lateral thinking techniques such as CoRT and the six thinking hats.

JERRY BOWLING

Bibliography. E. deBono (1973), *Lateral Thinking: Creativity Step by Step;* idem (1992), *Serious Creativity: Using the Power of Lateral Thinking to Create New Ideas.*

Law. *See* Constitution, Church.

Law and Order. Rule systems designed to benefit society and regulate the behavior of its citizens. Law and order was given by God to Moses in the commandments and interpreted by prophets and priests. The law of the Lord is "perfect" (Ps. 19:9) and finds its ultimate fulfillment in the person of Jesus Christ (Matt. 5:17). We are also told in 1 Corinthians 14:33 that God is not the author of confusion but of order and peace.

Most laws are of human construction, and attitudes toward them are less exalted than attitudes toward the law of God should be. Perspectives vary depending on the situation a person is in at the time and the understanding of the person as to how the law affects self and others.

Lawrence Kohlberg (1927–87), director of the Center for Moral Education at Harvard University, observed a developmental hierarchy of ways that people view law and order. At the lowest stage (stage 1) the person believes it is all right to disobey the law as long as you are not caught. It is only wrong if punishment follows the act. At the next stage a person will follow a rule in order to reciprocate for past or present favors, for example, "I'll do what you tell me because you're nice to me." At stage 3, the person believes law and order should be maintained because it makes for good relationships with significant other people such as family and friends.

Stage 4 is usually dubbed the "law and order" stage because the person who reasons at this stage says that the law should be obeyed for its own sake. All of us are protected by the law and

obligated to the law. Those who have progressed to Kohlberg's stage 5 believe that when laws conflict, some will take precedence over others and sometimes laws should be changed for the benefit of people who are not presently receiving fair treatment. At the sixth and final stage, the concern is for laws that will bring justice to every person. A person operating in stage 6 believes that everyone is to be treated equally without regard to nationality, ethnicity, gender, ability, age, or economic status.

BONNIDELL CLOUSE

Law of Effect. Thorndike's recognition that the consequences to a response will either strengthen or weaken the connection between the stimulus and the response. It is also known as the "pleasure-pain principle." Thus if a response is followed by a satisfying consequence the connection will be strengthened; however, if it is followed by an annoying consequence the connection will be weakened. Thorndike states "[a] connection being made between an S and an R and being accompanied with or followed by a satisfying state of affairs man responds, other things being equal, by an increase in the strength of that connection. To a connection similar save that an annoying state of affairs goes with or follows it man responds, other things being equal, by a decrease in the strength of the connection." The law of effect broke with the theory of frequency of occupancy as the determiner of the strength of association. In later years Thorndike added the idea of "spread of effect" to this law. Reinforcement not only increases the probability of a reinforced response but also increases the probability of neighboring responses. The law stresses that rewards strengthen learning behaviors and was the forerunner of Skinner's reinforcement theory.

CHARLES H. NICHOLS

Bibliography. E. Thorndike (1911), *Animal Intelligence.*

Law of Exercise. Thorndike's recognition of the repetitive nature of learning. He states, "Other things being equal, exercise strengthens the bond between situation and response" (Thorndike, 1912, 95). Thus, connections between a stimulus and response are strengthened as they are repeated, and conversely, connections between a stimulus and response are weakened by discontinuance or if a neural bond is not used. These two concepts are also called the *law of use* and the *law of disuse.* Strengthening to Thorndike meant an increase in the probability that a response will be made when a similar stimulus occurs. By weakening he meant a decrease in the probability that the next time the stimulus occurs the response will occur. The law of exercise is most effective when the practice leads to the maintenance of a pleasurable state and when the elements of the practice go together logically (sense of belongingness). This law does not teach that practice makes perfect; it stresses that practice makes permanent. After the 1930s Thorndike did abandon this law. However, he still maintained that practice leads to minor improvements and the lack of practice leads to slight forgetting.

CHARLES H. NICHOLS

Bibliography. E. Thorndike (1912), *Education;* idem (1932), *The Fundamentals of Learning;* idem (1940), *Human Nature and the Social Order.*

Law of Good Continuation. This law reflects a progress of perceptual organization on the cognitive plane, which allows the whole to emerge. Since we tend to see things as ending up consistent with the way they started, we perceive more quickly patterns that are smooth and continuous rather than discontinuous. Koffka states, "A straight line is a more stable structure than a broken one, and that therefore organization will, *ceteris paribus*, occur in such a way that a straight line will continue as a straight line" (Koffka, 1935, 153). Good continuation means that when connected points or lines result in straight or gently curving lines, they are seen as belonging together and as following the smoothest path. Where continuation is present learning proceeds more easily. In education this law stresses that better reception and retention will occur when the curriculum or learning situation proceeds in an orderly, consistent manner. This law also suggests that there is a tendency to organize our perceptions about people in the same way. What is noted about a student at the start of the process might be carried through to its logical conclusion. If a student starts poorly, it is surmised he will end poorly.

CHARLES H. NICHOLS

Bibliography. K. Koffka (1935), *Principles of Gestalt Psychology.*

Law of Membership Character. This law acknowledges that a single part of a whole does not have fixed characteristics; it gets its characteristics from the context in which it appears. Since parts get their significance from the whole, individual concepts are only truly understood in the light of the gestalt or total field. The total field does not get its significance from the parts, as emphasized by structuralism. Thus experiences cannot be broken down into elementary parts in order to understand them, because the whole is not just the sum of its parts; it is more—it is itself. "Sets of stimuli produce effects not derivable from the effects of the single stimuli. These effects, observable only in extended wholes, are depend upon strictly objective conditions namely, specific geometric relations between stimuli"

(Asch, 1968, 160). A trunk, a head, a body, and a tail have no connection unless one understands an elephant. In the same way students must see how various courses or lessons relate to other courses or lessons. This law also related to teachers and the class. The total class persona is more than the individuals that make it, so a teacher needs to understand the class atmosphere before looking at individual students.

CHARLES H. NICHOLS

Bibliography. S. E. Asch (1968), *International Encyclopedia of the Social Sciences.*

Law of Pragnanz. This law is the core of Gestalt psychology, which emphasizes the perception of pattern between an individual and the environment. The law can be formulated like this: "Psychological organization will always be as good as the prevailing conditions allow" (Koffka, 1935, 110). The term *good* is not specifically defined but it does not refer to moral goodness. It seems to allude to such qualities as simple, concise, symmetrical, or harmonious. An organism, since it desires this pragnanz, will use regularity, consistency, and uniformity as means of making the psychological organization "good." Thus when a person first experiences a perceptual field it is disorganized, but it is pregnant with ideas on which the person will impose an order in a predictable way. That predictable way includes five other laws: similarity, closure, good continuance, proximity, and membership character, and is unique to each individual. Every individual desires stability or equilibrium, and when faced with a situation that offers disequilibrium will endeavor to impose their order on that situation. The circumstances (environment) in which the individual must function will determine what is psychologically good at any particular moment. Thus the "good" response is produced and therefore allows the conceptualization of gestalt, a pattern or wholeness.

CHARLES H. NICHOLS

Bibliography. K. Koffka (1935), *Principles of Gestalt Psychology.*

Law of Proximity. This law acknowledges the special relationships of perceptual groups. The closer the distance between fields of observation the more stable the "whole" will become, because things that are near to each other appear to be grouped together. Koffka (1935) acknowledged that the law of proximity is not easy to define, but that "we have demonstrated that when the field contains a number of equal parts, those among them which are in greater proximity will be organized into a higher unit" (164–65). Thus elements which are proximate to one another tend to go together in a pattern to achieve a configurational whole. The mind sets boundaries that it perceives belong together and interprets data in accordance with those boundaries. There are limits to this law. When the special distances become too great, unification will probably not occur. Thus the shorter the intramembral distance the more stable the relationship becomes. Secondly, it seems that individuals see special distances differently. What seems a whole to one may not appear so to another. This law also acknowledges the timing of events. The more recent events will be retained easier than those which occurred long ago. Thus an educator must be concerned with timing and distance when helping students receive and retain information.

CHARLES H. NICHOLS

Bibliography. K. Koffka (1935), *Principles of Gestalt Psychology.*

Law of Readiness. Thorndike's recognition that an individual will learn more quickly if the individual is ready to learn. His early idea of this law contained three parts that he laid out in *The Original Nature of Man.* Basically the parts state: when a conduction unit is ready to conduct, conduction by it is satisfying; when a conduction unit is ready to conduct, not conducting is annoying; and when a conduction unit is not ready for conduction and is forced to conduct, conduction by it is annoying. A conduction unit is the establishment of a specific bond or connection between a neuron (neurons) and a synapse (synapses). Thus, as in the structure of the nervous system, in a given situation certain conduction units are more predisposed to operate than others. The phrase "when a conduction unit is ready to conduct" refers to readiness for action, while "satisfying" and "annoying" refer to actions of nonavoidance and avoidance. If a class is conducted in such a manner as to have the students anticipating the situation, they are more apt to learn. However, if the student's anticipations are not realized or they are not ready for the learning situation, there is frustration and anger.

CHARLES H. NICHOLS

Bibliography. E. Thorndike (1913), *Educational Psychology:* vol. 2, *The Original Nature of Man.*

Law of Set or Attitude. Thorndike's recognition of the individual learning differences that each learner brings to the learning situation. He stated the law this way:

It is a general law of behavior that the response to any external situation is dependant upon the condition of the man, as well as upon the nature of the situation; and that, if certain conditions in the man are rated part of the situation, the response to it depends upon the remaining conditions in the man. Consequently, it is a general

law of learning that change made in a man by acting on any agent depends upon the condition of the man when the agent is acting. The condition of the man may be considered under the two heads of the more permanent or fixed and the more temporary or shifting, attitudes, or sets. (Thorndike, vol. 1 [1913], 24)

Permanent sets include culture, hereditary traits, and physical limitations. Temporary sets include fatigue, emotional status, deprivation, and gratification. Thus the set or attitude (also called disposition or preadjustment), which depends on the organism's background and its current physical condition at the time of the learning situation, will determine whether a learning situation is satisfying or annoying, successful or frustrating.

CHARLES H. NICHOLS

Bibliography. E. Thorndike (1913), *Educational Psychology:* vol. 1, *The Psychology of Learning.*

Leadership. "In our search to understand the intricacies of leadership," write Clark and Clark (1994), "reading popular books and articles about leadership provides little help and can be confusing. We are left with many questions" (17). These authors go on to define leadership as "an activity or set of activities, observable to others, that occurs in a group, organization, or institution involving a leader and followers who willingly subscribe to common purposes and work together to achieve them" (19). Though this definition seems too narrow, it does emphasize the relationship between leaders and followers and the central issue of leadership: organizational purpose.

Barna (1997) prefers a definition that includes five key attributes. A leader is one who mobilizes; whose focus is influencing people; who is goal-driven; who has an orientation in common with those who rely upon her or him for leadership; and who has people willing to follow (23). Most experts in the field make a significant distinction between leadership and management, the former emphasizing people skills and the latter organizational skills.

One prominent author in the field of leadership emphasizes leadership as a fourfold balancing act.

First, you must be able to relate skillfully to the managers and workers inside your organization who look to you for guidance, encouragement, and motivation. Second, you must be able to take full advantage of the external environment and relate skillfully to people outside your organization who are in a position to influence its success. Third, you must be able to shape and influence all aspects of the present operations of your organization including the development of products and services, production processes, quality control systems, organizational structures, and information systems. Finally, you must be highly skilled in anticipating the future—that is, in assessing and preparing for developments . . . that are likely to have critical implications for your organization in the coming decade. (Nanus, 1992, 11–12)

Scripture tells us that Christian leadership must be different from leadership in the world (Luke 24:22). Leaders do many important things, but the character of the Christian leader is always more important than any activity. Leadership can be viewed as the exercise of one's spiritual gifts under the call of God to serve a certain group of people in achieving the goals God has given them toward the end of glorifying Christ.

Much has been written about leadership style with words like *transactional, servant,* and *visionary* commonly appearing as descriptive adjectives. Though Christian leadership is grounded in spiritual gifts and the call of God, one cannot deny an axiom obvious in Scripture and almost all recent secular research on this topic· leadership is learned behavior.

Today we see a newly emerging language of leadership and organizational behavior. Blind obedience is out; involvement is in. Titles such as manager and supervisor are being replaced by team leader, project coordinator, and facilitator. The latter terms imply a more shared approach to governance. Handy books about the attributes necessary for leadership list a belief in oneself, a passion for the job, a love of people, and a capacity for aloneness. In pondering where these qualities may be found, Hesselbein (1996) comes up with a fascinating conclusion: "Unless and until business creates a cause bigger and more embracing than enrichment of the shareholders, it will have few great leaders. We are more likely to find them in the non-profit arena. If that is so, then that sector may yet become the training ground for business and perhaps even politics" (9).

Christians who read the current literature find it interesting that the best elements of research regarding leadership style, which evolves from multimillion-dollar inquiry on the part of industrial science, concludes what is already common knowledge among those who have explored what Scripture teaches on the subject. The New Testament recognizes the inherent value of the individual and the worth of human relations not only as a means to an end, but as an end in itself and the Christian community. In a very real sense, the church should be the most person-centered organization in the world. Indeed, a congregation that has its vertical relationships in order (theocentricity) will generally follow with proper horizontal relationships (anthrocentricity).

In some Christian organizations today, a one-person ministry looks much like the worldly leadership condemned by our Lord in Luke 22. If we serve our own generation with power and effectiveness, we must stop pretending that Christian leadership resembles the kings of the Gentiles.

> Biblical team leadership takes place when divinely appointed men and women accept responsibility for obedience to God's call. They recognize the importance of preparation time, allowing God's Holy Spirit to develop tenderness of heart and skill of hand. They carry out their leadership roles with deep conviction of God's will, clear contemporary issues which they and their followers face. Above all, they exercise leadership as servants and stewards, sharing authority with their followers and affirming that leadership is primarily ministry to others, modeling for others and mutual membership with others in Christ's body." (Gangel, 1997, 64)

KENNETH O. GANGEL

Bibliography. G. Barna (1997), *Leaders on Leadership;* K. E. Clark (1994), *Choosing to Lead;* L. Ford (1991), *Transforming Leadership;* K. O. Gangel (1997), *Team Leadership in Christian Ministry;* F. Hesselbein, M. Goldsmith, and R. Beckhard (1996), *The Leader of the Future;* B. Nanus (1992), *Visionary Leadership.*

See also LEADERSHIP DEVELOPMENT; LEADERSHIP NETWORK; LEADERSHIP PRINCIPLES; MANAGEMENT

Leadership Development. Leaders influence other people toward a shared vision. The call and development of other leaders is intimately connected to the sovereignty of God, discipleship, and spiritual giftedness. Discipleship is how one lives out his or her call to be a Christ-follower. The process of making a disciple is seen as a leader's influence over those in his or her sphere of influence. The disciple maker seeks to move them toward a close biblical and personal commitment to Jesus Christ. This lifestyle is marked by obedience to the Word of God and the demonstration of a distinctively Christian lifestyle (Gangel, 1985). Being a person clearly marked by the character of Christ constitutes the first step in leadership development, since no one can teach another to be or do what he or she has not first done.

Leadership development is further connected to spiritual gifting. After exhorting believers "in view of God's mercy, to offer your bodies as living sacrifices, holy and pleasing to God" (discipleship), the apostle Paul then declares, "We have different gifts, according to the grace given us . . . let him use it [his gift] in proportion to his faith" (Rom. 12:1, 6). A spiritual gift is to be cultivated and invested in kingdom activity, whether teaching, helping, or governing.

Leadership development requires defining where a person is, identifying where to take him or her, and providing the opportunities and resources for growth needed to reach the desired end point. Hersey and Blanchard (1982) identify three key elements in leadership behavior: relationship behavior, task behavior, and maturity of followers. The developmental cycle is a growth cycle which moves an individual or group beyond the level previously reached. The first phase of the cycle, High Task-Low Relationship ("Telling"), involves providing specific instructions and closely supervising the performance of an individual. At the second phase, High Task-High Relationship ("Selling"), the leader explains his or her decisions and provides opportunity for clarification. In the third phase of the cycle, High Relationship-High Task ("Participating"), a leader shares ideas and facilitates in making decisions. Finally, in the fourth phase, Low Relationship-Low Task ("Delegating"), a leader turns over responsibility for decisions and implementation. Maturity among followers involves both ability (possession of the necessary knowledge and skill) and willingness (the necessary confidence and commitment) to do a job.

John Maxwell suggests beginning with an inventory of Five A's: *assessment* of needs (What is needed?); *assets* on hand (Who are the people already in the organization who are available?); *ability* of candidates (Who is willing?); and *accomplishments* of candidates (Who gets things done?). Maxwell then relies upon BEST, an acronym to remind him of a strategy to follow: **B**elieve in them, **E**ncourage them, **S**hare with them, and **T**rust them.

Leslie A. Andrews

Bibliography. K. O. Gangel (1985), *Church Education Handbook;* P. Hersey and K. Blanchard (1982), *Management of Organizational Behavior: Utilizing Human Resources;* B. P. Powers (1981), *Christian Education Handbook: Resources for Church Leaders.*

Leadership Network. An organization founded in 1984 by two entrepreneurs, Bob Buford and Fred Smith Jr., as an effort to link the leaders of large churches (1,000+) throughout the United States. Today the network includes mainline, evangelical, and independent churches characterized by their innovation, desire to be on the cutting edge of ministry, and entrepreneurial leadership.

Leadership Network focuses on the practice and application of life-changing biblical faith at the local church level. It targets leaders who are lifelong learners and are in a position to influence the greatest amount of change.

> The mission of Leadership Network is to accelerate the emergence of the 21st century church. We believe the emerging paradigm of the 21st century church calls for the development of new tools and resources as well as the equipping of a new type of 21st century church leader, both clergy and laity. This new paradigm is not centered in theology but rather it is focused on structure, organization, and the transition from an institutionally based church to a mission driven church.

> We value innovation that leads to results and working with Kingdom perspective church leaders. We value seeing the fruit on other people's trees. And finally, we value getting it "right" for those we serve as well as for our team. (www.lead net.org)

Leadership Network has developed four services to accomplish their mission:

1. Learning events consisting primarily of forums for invited leaders of large churches. Occasional special conferences, summits, and forums center on twenty-first-century church issues.

2. Information services. The gathering, analysis, and distribution of relevant information is a major initiative of the Leadership Network. They accomplish this task through their quarterly publication *NEXT,* their biweekly NetFax, their *Intro Action* newsletter, and a copublished book series with Jossey-Bass Publishers.

3. Incubation Center for New Initiatives. Leadership Network has helped to initiate other organizations that serve the local church—for example, Leadership Training Network (LTN), which provides training and products for local churches. The Church Champions Network connects leaders serving the needs of local rather than institutional churches. The Teaching Church Network provides local churches with learning and mentoring opportunities. And the Social Entrepreneurs Network links business, community, and church leaders seeking to make a difference within their communities and churches by addressing social issues.

4. Innovation and Research involves pilot projects undertaken by Leadership Network alone or in partnership with other organizations.

Leadership Network, believing that networking is the defining organizational form of the twenty-first century, is structured as a "network of networks" composed of three core groups. The Church Leader Network consists of "innovative and early adopter" local church leaders who seek to identify "best practice churches" to determine the principles behind their success. They then seek to translate these principles into processes that can be adopted by other churches. The Interventionist Network seeks to educate and equip those who help local churches. The Information Network explores futuristic trends, concerns, and ideas occurring within innovative churches. This material is synthesized and broadcast through their information services.

Contact information: Leadership Network, 2501 Cedar Springs LB–5, Suite 200, Dallas, TX 75201. Via the Internet: www.leadnet.org.

Bruce R. McCracken

Leadership Principles. Leadership within educational ministries relates to a person's ability to provide vision and direction. While some aspects of leadership relate to management, the two are distinct. Leadership establishes the purpose of a ministry, while management enables the ministry to accomplish the purpose. As Warren Bennis (1989) explains, "Leaders are people who do the right thing but managers are those who do things right" (18).

In order for Christian leaders to do the right things, they must base their leadership strategies on a solid biblical and theological foundation. Although successful leaders in Scripture displayed different styles of leadership, they possessed a similar attitude of servanthood to both God and the people they serve. Jesus explains this distinctive of leaders in Matthew 20:25–28 (NASB):

> You know that the rulers of the Gentiles lord it over them, and their great men exercise authority over them. It is not so among you, but whoever wishes to become great among you shall be your servant, and whoever wishes to be first among you shall be your slave; just as the Son of Man did not come to be served, but to serve, and to give His life a ransom for many.

While some authors (Youssef, 1986) refer to *servant leadership* as a leadership style, it is more accurately considered as an *attitude* of leadership. Christian leaders should display this servant attitude regardless of their particular style of leadership. The most foundational principle of Christian leadership is that in all situations leaders must display a servant attitude. Such an attitude is rooted in a person's character or heart. People must have a single-minded heart to serve God and others before they can effectively lead others in ministry.

A second biblical principle of leadership relates to the functional role of the leader as an equipper of believers for ministry (Eph. 4:11–12). In such a role the Christian leader serves as a catalyst to encourage people within a church or ministry to develop and use their gifts and abilities to serve others. Stevens and Collins (1993) suggest that church leaders need to create an environment conducive to the mobilization of laypersons. When a church or organization is a healthy system, its members grow and reach out to one another (xv). Thus a major role of the leader relates to orchestrating a healthy climate in a church or organization.

Both secular and Christian authors uphold the principle that effective leadership is built upon a disciplined inner life and solid character. The first three habits of Covey's *Seven Habits of Highly Effective People* (1990) deal with the inner life of a person. The first habit relates to a leader's ability to be proactive in taking the re-

sponsibility within one's circle of influence. The second habit relates to a leader's ability to articulate and follow a principle-based personal mission statement. The third habit relates to a leader's ability to practice self-management. Maxwell (1993) explains that integrity is the most important component of leadership (38). This principle is also reinforced by Paul in his description of the qualifications for church leaders. The majority of the qualifications he mentions relate to character rather than skills (1 Tim. 3:1–10; Titus 1:7–9).

Based upon a solid foundation of integrity of character, several skills are necessary for the leader in Christian ministry. The literature identifies at least seven categories of skills for the effective leader: (1) vision/mission building, (2) empathetic listening, (3) empowering/delegating, (4) team building, (5) problem solving/conflict resolution, (6) systems monitoring, (7) flexibility in style.

Barna (1992) defines vision as "a reflection of what God wants to accomplish through you to build His kingdom" (29). He makes a distinction between vision and mission. Vision relates to the unique, strategic distinctive of the ministry. It is articulated in a clear, catchy statement that is able to provide a focus for all persons related to the ministry. The mission statement, on the other hand, is more of a general, philosophical statement about what the ministry is about and how it will accomplish its purpose (38). In order to encourage ownership, a leader needs to involve as many persons as possible in developing a statement of vision and purpose. People tend to take more responsibility in following a vision they help to create.

The second skill of a leader relates to empathetic listening. Since leaders, by nature, tend to be directive and goal-oriented, one of the most important skills they must learn is what Covey (1990) defines as the ability to "seek first to understand, then to be understood" (237). If leadership flows out of a person's character, then people will tend to follow leaders who demonstrate their character through genuine interpersonal empathy. Such empathy involves looking at issues and concerns from other persons' perspectives. Paul challenges believers to practice this skill in Philippians 2:3–4 (NASB): "Do nothing from selfishness or empty conceit, but with humility of mind let each of you regard one another as more important than himself; do not merely look out for your own personal interests, but also for the interests of others." Although it takes time for leaders to genuinely get to know their fellow workers, the investment of time will reap rich dividends of loyalty and commitment. People follow those who care for them.

The third skill necessary for effective leadership is the ability to empower others and to delegate. Maxwell (1995) defines this skill as the ability to instill in others the desire and ability to minister, and then to "lead, teach, and assess the progress of the person being equipped" (84). This skill is directly related to one of the major roles of a church leader mentioned in Ephesians 4:12: to equip people in the church to minister to others. While a leader may be tempted to use delegation as a tool to dump undesired tasks on others, this is not the purpose of delegation from a biblical perspective. Delegation is based on the biblical premise that every believer is a minister, gifted in some unique way to serve within the body of Christ. Thus, delegation is empowering others to use their God-given abilities and talents. By giving away both the responsibility and the rewards of ministry, leaders allow their people to enjoy the satisfaction of serving God and others.

The fourth skill of effective leadership is team building. This skill relates to a person's ability to inspire others to work together in ministry as a cohesive team. DePree (1989) states that "the most effective contemporary management process is participatory management" (24). Since the church, by nature, is an interconnected body, one of the most important skills of its leadership is the ability to encourage the body to function as a unified team. As Stevens and Collins (1993) explain, "One of the greatest challenges of equipping the saints is to help the church discover itself as the church by cultivating interdependence—together with diversity" (38).

The fifth skill of effective leadership relates to problem solving and conflict resolution. One of the major reasons people leave ministry is because of their inability to deal redemptively with interpersonal conflict and disagreement. Covey (1990) identifies three habits of highly effective people relating to this skill of conflict resolution: Habit four—"Think Win-Win"—deals with a leader's ability to see problems from others' perspectives, to identify the major issues related to the problem, to determine what an acceptable solution would look like, and to identify all the possible options for arriving at an acceptable solution (233). Habit five—"Seek First to Understand, Then to Be Understood"—deals with a leader's ability to empathize with other persons' perspectives. Habit six—"Synergize"—deals with a leader's ability to orchestrate a process of conflict resolution that values both the individual and dynamic interaction between individuals to produce a mutually enriching solution.

The sixth skill relates to a leader's ability to monitor the various systems making up the church or Christian organization and to coordinate their interactions to fulfill the overall vision and mission. Stevens and Collins (1993) explain that the pastoral leader's "most productive direction will be to work with the culture and the systemic organization of the church rather than to

deal exclusively with individuals" (xviii). This skill relates directly to Covey's sixth habit of synergy based on the principle that the whole is more than the sum of its parts. Success often depends on a leader's ability to see beyond the provincialism of particular problems, issues, and agendas, to visualize the larger, more comprehensive picture. The leader needs to be able to get various people together to strategize how the various subgroups within a church or organization can fit together to accomplish their vision.

The seventh and last leadership skill relates to a leader's ability to be adaptable and flexible in utilizing various styles of leadership. Blanchard, Zigarmi, and Zigarmi (1985) term this skill *situational leadership*. In order to master this skill, leaders must practice three competencies: (1) flexibility—the ability to utilize various leadership styles depending on the demands of a situation; (2) diagnosis—the ability to assess the level of competency and commitment of various persons; and (3) contracting—the ability of leaders to establish specific goals with people and then match their style of leadership to people's level of competence and commitment. This adaptable leadership approach seems consistent with the leadership strategies of leaders from the Bible. Jesus continually adapted his style to meet the needs of various persons in a variety of situations (Matt. 23:14–36; John 13:1–20; 21:15–22). Paul also adapted his style of leadership depending on the situation he was in and the developmental level of those he was working with (2 Cor. 2:5–11; 1 Thess. 1:7, 11). A real test of leadership seems to be related to a person's ability to maintain a consistent, servant's heart no matter what leadership style is demanded by the situation.

GARY C. NEWTON

Bibliography. G. Barna (1992), *The Power of Vision;* W. Bennis (1989), *Why Leaders Can't Lead;* K. Blanchard, P. Zigarmi, and D. Zigarmi (1985), *Leadership and the One Minute Manager;* R. C. Covey (1990), *The 7 Habits of Highly Effective People;* M. DePree (1989), *Leadership Is an Art;* J. C. Maxwell (1993), *Developing the Leader Within You;* idem (1995), *Developing the Leaders Around You;* R. P. Stevens and P. Collins (1993), *The Equipping Pastor;* M. Youssef (1986), *The Leadership Style of Jesus.*

Learning Atmosphere. *See* Learning Climate.

Learning Centers. A method of organizing a classroom in which the teacher arranges materials, content, and experiences in such a way that learners pursue a learning task individually or in small groups. These are sometimes described as learning activities. Although learning centers can be used with any age group, educators usually consider them most appropriate for preschool and elementary school learners.

The use of learning centers as a teaching method is based upon two primary assumptions: (1) each learner is unique and has a preferred learning style; and (2) learning is active. Learning centers are not new in the sense that historically, teachers in multiple-grade classrooms have often organized children into small groups to pursue their own learning while the teacher works with another age group on a different learning task. It is relatively new in that teachers have come to understand that, even in a single-grade classroom, learners are diverse and need opportunities to pursue learning tasks the ways they learn best.

Learning centers can be used to teach a variety of outcomes. Their use is limited only by the teacher's outcome priority, by the creativity of the instructor, and, to some extent, by the classroom.

Learning centers permit flexibility in the classroom. Not all children must do the same thing at the same time. Not all children learn at the same speed. Learning centers allow children to spend at least a portion of a class session learning in the ways they learn best. The use of learning centers also permits learners to make choices, a factor that usually increases motivation for learning. Learning centers provide a greater variety of activities available to learners, and they make learning enjoyable. They also provide a structure for the development of relationships.

The use of learning centers requires that adequate time be available in the session to provide a balance of small group and large group experiences. Learning centers may require more leadership in the classroom, especially when they are for preschoolers or young elementary learners.

Good use of learning centers depends upon careful planning. Teachers will find the following factors helpful as they choose learning centers for a teaching session:

1. Available leadership and the skills required of those guiding a center.
2. Teaching objectives. The center should be designed to guide learners to achieve specific objectives.
3. Learners' preferences for types of activities.
4. Available materials and equipment.
5. The space in which the class meets. Some centers require special arrangement of facilities.
6. Available equipment.
7. Place in the teaching session to use the centers. Some learning activities can be used only when prior knowledge has been achieved. Some are best designed to introduce concepts and content.

Most current curriculum materials suggest possible learning centers to develop the lesson. Even then, the teacher must take into account the seven factors stated above in order to make the best choice of centers for specific learners and sessions.

Teachers who choose to use learning centers should have good observational skills. They must watch what students are doing and listen to what they are saying if they are to derive maximum learning from the center. They need to maintain a good balance between the use of learning centers and large group experiences. They need also to ask good questions to encourage learners to think and to gain maximum insight and benefit from a learning center.

ELEANOR A. DANIEL

Bibliography. R. G. Lee (1982), *Learning Centers for Better Christian Education;* R. Isbell (1995), *The Complete Learning Center Book.*

Learning Climate. Spatial, material, and psychosocial context of the educational experience. The combination of these various conditions either enhances or distracts from the educational experience. Teachers and learners both contribute to learning climate. The challenge for the teacher is to design the learning climate to be optimally effective in gaining specific learning objectives. The learning climate may take shape in a traditional classroom setting, a nontraditional educational context, or in a simulation that provides gamelike experiences to direct the educational experience.

Spatial planning incorporates the control and arrangement of furniture, and the use of architecture. Tables, chairs, and desks can be arranged to support or discourage teaching exercises and strategies. For example, an auditorium with stationary seating does not readily permit small discussion groups. Furniture arrangement also contributes to traffic patterns in the classroom and influences social interaction. Desks in rows prohibit free movement among learners, while groupings of desks in tables of four facilitate small group interaction. Seating arrangement density also influences a sense of privacy and large group cohesiveness.

Other physical contributors to the learning climate include lighting, both natural and artificial. Acoustics affect whether learners can readily hear the teacher and other learners, and control the influence of distracting noise. Heat and cold contribute to attentiveness.

Contemporary architects are aware of spatial needs in the educational environment and design educational facilities with these requirements in mind. A first major departure from the traditional classroom setting was the open space school concept of the early 1970s. These design plans varied widely but most were characterized by the absence of full walls between rooms and a large common area where learners could interact.

Learning climate is influenced by material availability and placement. Learner behavior can be positively affected when educational materials are within eyesight, reachable by the learner, neatly arranged, and in working condition. Learner curiosity is engaged when information is readily available and access to it does not distract from learning objectives. For example, if an assignment requires access to a computer, but none is available, or if the teacher controls its use by lock and key, the learners may become distracted as they await access. Learning centers providing alternatives and ready access to a variety of educational experiences are now used in many church and public classrooms.

The psychosocial context of the learning climate includes both teacher and learner. Attitudes and expectations that contribute to the learning climate are influenced by culture, social dynamics, familial situations, psychological adjustment, health, speech, physical characteristics, and many other items. Teachers must be aware of both their own contribution to the psychosocial context and that of each learner. The words spoken in the learning environment greatly influence learning. Praise and criticism for educational tasks shape the self-concept of the learner and the general climate of learning.

Tension is often present in the contributions of social science and theology to the development of learning climate. Social science can help provide valuable facts to develop the learning climate. Theology also contributes to learning climate by assisting in the setting of an atmosphere where the Spirit can operate as Teacher.

Christian educators must realize that creating a learning climate will happen whether by intent or default. Competence in setting, identifying, and adapting varied learning climates is the mark of a good educator. The ability to change and work in a variety of learning climates, depending on the learning objectives and methods employed, permits a well-rounded educational plan that can meet the educational needs of diverse learners.

JAMES R. MOORE

Bibliography. C. E. Loughlin and J. H. Suina (1982), *The Learning Environment: An Instructional Strategy;* G. F. McVey (1985), *The International Encyclopedia of Education: Research and Studies,* 5:2953–61; H. C. Waxman, *Journal of Classroom Interaction* 26, no. 2 (1991): 1–4; C. S. Weinstein, *Review of Educational Research* 49, no. 4 (1997): 577–610; C. S. Weinstein and T. G. David (1987), *Spaces for Children: The Built Environment and Child Development.*

See also CLASSROOM SETTING; CLIMATE, CLASSROOM; CLIMATE, SMALL GROUPS

Learning Cycle. *See* Kolb, David.

Learning Disabilities. *See* Learning Disorders.

Learning Disorders. The term *learning disorders* or *learning disabilities* is used when there is a dysfunction in one or more of the basic psychological processes involved in understanding or in using the spoken or written language. The disorder may manifest itself in imperfect ability to listen, think, speak, read, write, spell, or calculate mathematics. Children with learning disabilities may have average or above average intelligence as measured by IQ scores. Although physically healthy, and possessing good overall learning potential, these children may fail in the educational arena because of a problem that interferes with their normal learning process. Because learning disorders are difficult to define, they are usually identified by what they are not. A child who is disadvantaged environmentally, culturally, or economically, for example, is not automatically classified as having a learning disability; neither is a child with visual, hearing, or motor disabilities, mental retardation, or emotional problems.

The most common forms of learning disabilities are reading disabilities. Children with the reading disorder called *dyslexia* have a language disorder and therefore have a specific reading problem. Dyslexia may be categorized into three subgroups: *dyseidetic, dysphonetic,* and *mixed.* Children who are dyseidetic read very slowly because they must sound out each word; they cannot rely upon a repertoire of visually recognized words. Children who are dysphonetic are unable to relate symbols to sounds and make bizarre spelling errors. Although these children may read at their grade level, they remain very poor spellers. Children with a mixture of several kinds of dyslexia have the most severe reading/spelling problems.

Children who have difficulty expressing their thoughts in writing have the learning disability called *dysgraphia.* Unreadable penmanship and difficulty grasping a pencil or writing on the lines may accompany dysgraphia. *Dyscalculia* is the inability to comprehend simple mathematical functions. These children can't perceive differences in shapes and tend to confuse mathematical symbols. Difficulty in several areas such as reading, handwriting, and arithmetic is categorized as a global learning disability.

To help these children succeed in school, early diagnosis is important, but labeling children too early may be counterproductive. Problems with visual-perceptual skills such as drawing circles at age 3, for example, and difficulty with perceptual-motor tasks like tying shoes at age 6, may indicate developmental delay rather than a learning disability. Hyperactivity, impulsivity, and clumsiness may indicate a learning disorder. Federal regulations require that school districts assess every child who may be identified as possibly requiring special education services. Although IQ testing may be perceived as a culturally biased assessment for poor and minority students, it is usually the measuring rod for learning disabilities. When there are discrepancies between IQ scores and academic achievement, a learning disorder may be indicated.

Children ages 3 to 21 who, through a series of formal testing and academic assessment have been diagnosed as having learning disorders, are protected under the 1975 Education for All Handicapped Children Act, renamed the Individuals with Disabilities Education Act (IDEA) in 1991. IDEA protects the educational rights of children with disabilities by promoting their education in the classroom alongside their nondisabled peers. In addition, schools must provide special services such as transportation, mental health services, and physical therapy. Special education programs which use promising educational practices, materials, and technology are also mandated by law. Once a child is assessed and identified as learning disabled, the program is to be tailored to the child's individual needs and should include vocational training as well as career counseling.

School districts accomplish the above through the following procedure. Within thirty days after the assessment, an educational program meeting, which is called an Individual Education Program (IEP) meeting, is held. IDEA provides children, parents, and caretakers with a system that safeguards their right to select the special educational service, which the public school must provide, by requiring that a parent or caretaker participate in the IEP meeting. In addition to the parent or surrogate parent, the team consists of the child's teacher, the school psychologist or therapist, a district representative qualified in special education, and the child when appropriate. This team devises the child's educational program which is to be updated annually with a reassessment of the child every three years. Parents have the right to appeal if they disagree with the results of the IEP assessment.

Depending upon the severity of the disability, a small percentage of children with learning disorders may retain the disability into their adult years. Many, however, are able to complete college and enjoy successful careers.

LaVerne A. Tolbert

Bibliography. Alliance for Children's Rights, *Special Education Handbook*; M. L. Batshaw and Y. M. Perret (1992), *Children with Disabilities*.

Learning Maturation. *See* Learning Readiness.

Learning Pattern. *See* Learning Styles.

Learning Readiness. Given that the Christian teacher's main concern is for the learner, and thus for having each lesson planned and taught to meet spiritual needs, readiness is of utmost consideration. Effective teaching and learning will be geared to the readiness level of the child, youth, and adult. To the church in Corinth, the apostle Paul wrote, "I gave you milk to drink, not solid food; for you were not yet able *to receive* it. Indeed, even now you are not yet able" (1 Cor. 3:2 NASB). Along with teacher readiness factors such as competence, enthusiasm, teacher-student relationship, and expectation of students, discerning the learner's readiness is a fundamental principle of education.

Philosophical and Theological. A clearly understood Christian view of human nature, ontological and behavioral, is basic. Behaviorally, "all have sinned and fall short of the glory of God" (Rom. 3:23 NASB). Ontologically, all are in the "image of God," which includes not only our spiritual and eternal nature but also our volitional freedom of choice of behavior including willingness or unwillingness to learn.

Educational Psychology. Learning Theories. Linked with a conception of human nature, the theorist asks whether humans are innately good, evil, or neutral; and, in relation to their environment, are they active, passive, interactive, or reactive? For the Christian teacher, the question is, Will the learner choose to be any one of these as well as eventually mature his or her ability to introspect (with himself or herself in light of God's will) and then decide to act positively with respect to the learning environment?

Learning Levels. Educators regularly recognize three learning domains: cognitive, affective, and psychomotor, or more simply, head-thinking (acquaintance and understanding), heart-feeling (insight and decision), and, hand-acting—or, should it be feet-walking?—(living and empowered). When reviewing the six learning levels within these three domains, note how they sequentially as well as interactively (learning is too dynamic to think any one of these levels is going on without the others) build upon each other. Level six, empowered, is God's doing as is stated in Colossians 1:11. (Each of these levels is given or implied in vv. 9–11.)

Developmental Psychology. Several stages of child development have been proposed by Piaget: sensorimotor thought (0–2 yrs.) as inborn reflex schemas; preoperational thought (2–7 yrs.) with preconceptual followed by intuitive thought (2–4 and 4–7 yrs.); operational stage (7–16 yrs.) with substages concrete operations (7–10 yrs.), and formal operational thought (11–16 yrs.). The latter ages can deal with reflective thinking, theorizing, and hypothesis structuring. The upstart of understanding Piaget's stages is the importance of the teacher's realizing that no two learners are alike.

Developmental Physiology. The brain scanning technique has led psycholinguists to determine early stages of infant recognition of spoken communication. Developmental disabilities such as attention, memory, and motor deficits are also identified with deficiency of brain development. Neuropsychiatrists, with the help of biochemistry and imaging devices, attempt to analyze spiritual activity and to detect a distinction between mind and soul—a humanistic approach.

GEORGE W. PATTERSON

Bibliography. R. L. Hotz (1998), *Of Neurons and Spirituality;* J. Piaget (1952), *The Origins of Intelligence in Children;* B. Patterson (1980), *The Growing Christian Teacher.*

See also ADOLESCENT DEVELOPMENT; ADULT DEVELOPMENT; HUMANISM, CLASSICAL; LEARNING THEORIES

Learning Styles. People process information in amazingly diverse ways. Not surprisingly, as brain research expands so does our understanding of what intelligence really is and the limitations of using a single measurement to identify who is smart and who is not. When brain and learning research work together, the resulting theories are often called learning styles.

A person's learning style includes how the student perceives things best and then processes or uses what has been seen. Each person's individual learning style is as unique as a signature. When a person has something difficult to learn, that student learns faster and enjoys learning more if his or her learning style is honored in the classroom.

When Christian educators teach to students' learning styles, they make it possible for all students to get more excited about learning, explore and better understand the facts, enjoy grappling with the implications, and most importantly in the Christian context, be more willing to put what they have learned into practice.

Successful teachers no longer believe that what is good for one student is good for all. A knowledge of learning styles helps teachers value student differences rather than seek conformity. Using multiple methods for instruction is one important way students' diverse styles are honored. Learning style research helps teachers reach every student God gave them to teach, not just the ones who learn in traditional ways.

Three secular educators have added significantly to what we know about the learning process. Rita Dunn (1992, 1993) has been a pioneer in isolating elements of learning and testing their classroom implications. Howard Gardner (1993) in his theory of multiple intelligences enlarges what we view as intelligence. His research, dealing with "intelligence" rather than learning styles, demands that teachers rethink classroom processes that facilitate learning, especially among those students who learn in wildly different ways. Bernice McCarthy (1987, 1996) has researched a learning cycle that allows students who think in very different ways to be successful within the same class hour.

Each researcher adds to the body of learning styles knowledge. Marlene LeFever (1995) has combined the work of Dunn and McCarthy and applied their work for use by Christian education volunteers, teachers, and pastors.

21 Elements of Learning. Rita Dunn's research is centered around 21 elements of learning. Not every student is affected by each of the 21, however most are affected by between 8 and 12. When the elements that are important to a student are present in the learning situation, the student will succeed. When too many are missing, the student may fail.

The 21 elements are:

Environmental Stimuli
- Sound
- Light
- Temperature
- Learning Space Design

Emotional Stimuli
- Motivation
- Persistence
- Responsibility
- Structure

Sociological Stimuli
Groupings in which students do their best work include
- Self
- Pair
- Peers
- Team
- Teacher
- Varied

Physiological Stimuli
- Perceptual (senses or modalities through which students take in information, usually the auditory, visual, and tactile/kinesthetic senses)
- Intake
- Time
- Mobility

Psychological Stimuli
- Global/Analytic
- Hemispheric
- Impulsive/Reflective

Each of these 21 elements is a study of its own. For illustrative purposes, we'll consider just one: learning space design. Some students work best at desks or tables, but a surprising number learn best when they are allowed to spread out on rugs or couches. (The need for informal design increases with adolescence.) Educators need to look at classroom design in terms of what needs to be accomplished by the people in that setting, rather than in terms of how learning spaces have traditionally looked.

One teacher discovered that when students who needed informal design had their needs met, they tested 20 percent higher than when they were in a formal setting (Shea, 1983). Students who respond to a more formal desk-and-chair setting are able to adapt to informal situations much more easily than those who need an informal setting are able to adapt to the formal. A boy who does his best work at a desk can just put his back up to the wall and make a desk from his lap. A girl who learns best when her body is stretched out and relaxed has much more difficulty making a beanbag chair out of her traditional desk.

Multiple Intelligences Theory. Howard Gardner's theory of multiple intelligences (MI Theory) suggests there are at least seven intelligences. Each of these intelligences refers to a student's ability to solve problems or do something that is valued in his or her culture. Students will have varying abilities in each of the seven, perhaps actually being brilliant in one or two. If the one or two are used and affirmed in the classroom, wonderful. If they are not, the child may be labeled a poor student or even mentally disabled.

The Seven Intelligences. *Linguistic Intelligence:* The capacity to speak or write effectively; the intelligence of words. *Logical Mathematical Intelligence:* The capacity to use numbers and reason well; the intelligence of pictures and images. *Spatial Intelligence:* The ability to perceive and act upon the visualspatial world accurately; the intelligence of pictures and images used in both the arts and sciences (IQ tests rate students on these first two intelligences, and occasionally on the third, spatial intelligence. But consider what they don't rate and the number of students who are educationally undervalued because of teachers' limited view of intelligence). *Bodily Kinesthetic Intelligence:* Expertise in using the whole body to express ideas and feelings; the intelligence of the whole body and the hands that students can use to solve problems, perform or make something. *Musical Intelligence:* The capacity to understand and use musical forms; the intelligence of tone, rhythm, and timbre, allowing students to hear patterns, remember them, and often manipulate them. *Interpersonal Intelligence:* The ability to understand moods and motivations of other people; the intelligence of social understanding. *Intrapersonal Intelligence:* The intelligence of self knowledge; knowing who you are and what you want to do.

When teachers accept the idea of multiple intelligences, the way they teach will change. No longer is there one right way to teach, but rather many ways to teach any concept or skill.

According to Gardner's research, all students should demonstrate at least some dimension of all seven intelligences. Some, of course, will have developed more highly than others. For example, a child with a highly developed spatial intelligence may show a preference for learning about new things through pictures, art, photography, three-dimensional building, etc. (Armstrong, 1994). This same child may have difficulty socially because he or she can't read social cues communicated through gestures and facial expressions. Classroom methods and materials will help this student excel in areas of strength and improve in those areas where intelligence is not as high.

Methods need to be selected to engage a variety of intelligences. Educators have long recognized someone who can solve logical problems as being smart, but what about the person who is sensitive to color, line, shape, and form?

Gardner's work, like the work of many researchers who are exploring how the brain functions, is enlarging the definition of the intelligent person. When more students see themselves as competent or even gifted, they will be willing to attempt greater things for the Lord. Their internal "brain police" will no longer tell them, "You're not smart enough. You're not really gifted. You have limited abilities with which to serve Jesus."

Success in any learning style requires a new look at methods: mime, music, painting, role play, simulation, mapping, sculpting, drama, discussions, moviemaking, pictorial writing, and the list goes on and on. Classroom methods are limited only by the teacher's imagination. Gardner's work puts flesh on Plato's admonition: Do not then train youths to learn by force and harshness, but direct them to it by what amuses their minds so that you may be better able to discover with accuracy the peculiar bent of the genius of each.

Cycle of Learning. What is lacking in the two patterns already discussed is a way for professional and volunteer Christian education teachers to implement learning style concepts in a consistent, ongoing way. Research educator Bernice McCarthy provides that pattern. She suggests that there are four basic learning style patterns, and while no student learns exclusively in one pattern, he or she usually identifies most strongly with one or perhaps two. When the student's strongest, easiest way of learning is included in the lesson plan, the student feels intelligent and affirmed. During that section of the lesson, he or she is often freed to take a class leadership role. The teacher's responsibility is to structure class so that every student has a chance to shine every time the class meets. A basic four-step pattern can help the teacher accomplish this goal.

This four-step pattern becomes a cycle of learning that can be followed over and over again. Starting with step 1 and progressing to step 4, all students participate in all four steps. Different students will be smartest during different parts of the lesson because each step spotlights students with different learning styles.

Step 1: Students who take the leadership here are excellent with broad overviews of content, and often inadequate with details. They can help the whole class focus on the importance of what will be studied. They answer the questions: "Why should we study this? Why is this important?" These students bring their prior knowledge into the classroom and use it as the basis for new learning.

Step 2: Students preferring this step are excellent analytic, sequential learners. They are the students who have traditionally taken home the most A's on their report cards. They answer the content question, "What do we need to know? What does the Bible say?" Students who enjoy Step 2 learning are often seen as smartest because school values and tests for the answers to "What?" questions, and underrewards those who excel in answering the other steps' questions.

Step 3: These students are excellent at testing the lesson's content. Often they are good with their hands and appear smarter when they can move as part of the learning process. They answer the question, "How does this work?" They are disinterested in any learning that doesn't have practical implications.

Step 4. These students are creative in the traditional sense. They are able to see future implications of what they have learned. They answer the questions: "What can this become? How can we add something unique of our own to what we've learned and practiced?"

Different methods can be used in all four steps. A teacher might refer to Gardner's Seven Intelligences and try to incorporate methods that encourage musical abilities or interpersonal skills. Dunn's research on classroom design will help the teacher create a setting where the environment facilitates rather than interferes with learning. Elements such as room setup, lighting, and time of day from the Dunn research add additional areas of consideration.

When implemented learning styles research will not make the teachers' job easier—just much more effective. It's a growing body of research that God has given to this generation. The challenge to Christian teachers is to find better ways to use it because they touch the future: they teach!

MARLENE LEFEVER

Bibliography. T. Armstrong (1994), *Multiple Intelligences in the Classroom;* R. Clark, L. Johnson, and A. Sloat, eds. (1991), *Christian Education: Foundations for the Future;* R. Dunn and K. Dunn (1992), *Teaching Elementary Students through Their Individual Learning Styles;* idem (1993), *Teaching Secondary Students through Their Individual Learning Styles;* H. Gardner (1993), *Multiple Intelligences: Theory and Practice;* M. LeFever (1996), *Creative Teaching Methods: Be an Effective Christian Teacher;* idem (1995), *Learning Styles: Reaching Everyone God Gave You to Teach;* B. Mc-Carthy (1996), *About Learning;* idem (1987), *The 4 MAT System Teaching: Learning Styles with Right/Left Mode Techniques;* M. Scherer, ed. (1997), *Educational Leadership: Teaching for Multiple Intelligences;* Tom Shea (1983), "An Investigation of the Relationship among Preferences for the Learning Style Element of Design, Selected Instruction Environments, and Readers' Achievement with Ninth Grade Students to Improve Administrative Determination Concerning Effective Educational Facilities" (Ph.D. Dissertation, St. John's University).

Learning Theories. Various theories concerning the way people appropriate, comprehend, and retain new information. While deeply indebted to contemporary psychology, theories addressing how people learn best are as old as Christian education. Augustine, in his sermon "The Teacher" (A.D. 389), emphasized the nature of the learner. J. A. Comenius (17th cent.), through his writings and his textbook *Orbis Pictus,* as well as J. Pestalozzi (18th cent.), emphasized forms of teaching that took seriously the learner's need to connect knowledge with personal sense experience. Historically, philosophers such as Locke and Kant (18th cent.) have struggled over how much of our knowledge is determined by purely external empirical data or how much our learning is influenced by our own internal presuppositions. The birth of learning theory as a psychological discipline occurred in the late nineteenth and early twentieth centuries with the work of pioneers like H. Ebbinghaus and E. Thorndike, and with the development of the Stanford-Binet test of IQ (intelligence quotient) in individuals. Other theorists, such as B. F. Skinner, J. Piaget, J. Bruner, A. Bandura, E. Erikson, M. Belensky, and L. Vygotsky demonstrate how the complexity of learning has since been seriously explored.

Learning theories attempt to address a number of key questions concerning how we receive and retain personal and objective knowledge. The central issues often include the following questions: How are we able to receive and discriminate between different types of information (data) as we receive it through our senses? What conditions (internal and external) enhance our ability and desire to learn? How are we able to process new information along with previous information and incorporate it into our lives? How are we able to retrieve and utilize information when it is needed?

Each question reveals several major issues that learning theories attempt to address through studies of sensory perception, association, information processing, memory, and motivation.

Large Traditional Families. Specific learning theories tend to fall into broad categories or "families" that share similar assumptions about the nature of people and the importance of the surrounding environment. The largest families lie along a continuum between extremes that stresses either the impact of the environment in shaping how we act (behavioral learning) or our individual personal ability to filter and organize information that we receive (primarily cognitive learning). Many theories combine these two emphases, acknowledging the influence of society (either certain communities or particular people) in dialogue with the individual's personal abilities. These theories are often grouped into social or relational learning theory.

Behavioral Learning. Behavioral learning theories emphasize how external stimuli (S) can cause a reflexive response (R) within a living organism. Living organisms, including humans, can then be conditioned to associate certain stimuli with a pattern of similar responses (S-R). S-R conditioning may be described in a number of forms, including classical conditioning, operant conditioning, and reinforcement theory. The primary assumption of these theories is that ultimately external forces can be manipulated to the point that the person "learns" by association to respond/behave in a predictable manner. Psychologists such as I. Pavlov, B. F. Skinner, and J. Watson have championed this approach. Skinner advocated an approach called operant learning—learning determined progressively through scheduled exercises that reinforced certain responses by the learner. Motivation was determined either by creatively rewarding the learner (positive reinforcement) or by intentionally eliminating any obstructions to learning (negative reinforcement). Personal punishment as a form of reinforcement was discouraged.

Behavioral theories tend to have a rather passive or antagonistic view of persons, which is often contradictory to Christian anthropology. Extreme behaviorism contradicts a Christian's assigning value to the worth of individuals based on God's continuing love for people. Beyond this limitation there are certain important aspects to consider for Christian education. Behavioral models take seriously the power of actions, such as worship or patterned prayer, to shape our understanding and practice of the Christian life. Recognizing that teachers need to remove environmental barriers to learning (negative reinforcement) and that teachers need to praise students (positive reinforcement) are sensible insights from behavioral learning. Behavior modification, far from manipulation, may help persons leave older, destructive behaviors by helping them to "act" into new ways of behaving that are much more healthy.

Cognitive Learning. Cognitive learning theories tend to emphasize the individual's capacity to selectively accept and organize information in the mind. Cognitive theories vary according to the theorist's conception of how the information is processed and stored. Motivation for learning is determined less by external factors and more through personal curiosity and the pleasure (or frustration) that occurs in understanding new information. Emotion, or affect, is assumed as a personal trait that may either encourage or prohibit the learning process.

The most prominent cognitive theory, information processing, treats the mind like a computer or huge filing system. Sensory information is sorted, processed, stored, and retrieved along lines of cognitive association with other similar bits of stored data. Learning occurs best when new information is well organized so that it "connects" (or is cognitively associated) with previous data that the learner already knows, through an appropriate mental structure. Theorists like R. M. Gagne emphasize advanced organizers such as a comprehensive introductory outline, fill-in-the-blank guides, or simple alliteration to assist guided learning.

Another learning theory, Gestalt (German for "form" or "shape"), assumes that different lines of association may emerge as the learner creates a new, larger pattern based upon seemingly disparate units of thought. Theorists advise persons to seek information inductively, bringing smaller ideas together to determine the larger concepts. Learners may also use inquiry or problem solving as a strategy to allow different ideas to emerge around a central issue. Discovery learning, another strategy, is similar to problem solving and assumes that new knowledge can be discovered or even created through exploration and analysis.

One prominent theorist, Jean Piaget, links cognitive learning to personality development. Piaget notes that new information may be stored in older, familiar patterns of thinking (*assimilation*) or require new structures of thought to adapt to the new data (*accommodation*). Learners' ability to assimilate or accommodate new information is often connected to their age and level of maturity (Gallagher and Reid, 1981). Theorists like Piaget and R. Keagan see people's ability to think and to learn as a basic form of human development. The learner's ability to accept data and create new mental structures becomes an indicator of maturity.

Christian educators, when dealing with cognitive learning, must first balance their understanding of human limitations (due to sin and human finiteness) with their understanding of human capabilities (based upon their creation in the image of God and their current lives under God's grace and influence). Cognitive theorists assist in Christian belief and discernment. Data, whether from the Bible or from other sources of Christian thought and practice, can be analyzed, organized, stored, and used to inform and enrich Christian discipleship. Information processing provides a way to develop structures of thought known as convictions, beliefs, or doctrines. These doctrines can represent God's expansive and complex revelation in concise forms, so that people can have a better and more coherent understanding of God. One caution is that these formulations cannot fully replace God's revelation since they are created by human effort and are thus limited. Analytical skills, however, are helpful in analyzing and comparing current beliefs and formative practices with the Bible, Christian history, and contemporary experience to make sure that those doctrines and practices are consistent with the purposes of the gospel.

Social Learning. The third large learning theory family is social or relational learning. The primary assumption of this approach is that people learn in community as they observe, copy, and replicate other persons' explicit behaviors as expressions of thought and emotion. This theory, advocated by A. Bandura, is often conceived as a mediation between behavioral and cognitive learning, respecting both external influences (particularly people as role models) and internal thinking processes. Persons may perceive and choose to imitate behaviors based on personal preference, but their imitations are reinforced in personal interactions with the role model or in public interactions within the community. Teaching is emphasized as a form of modeling, where the whole person or the collective action within a community is seen as a source of learning.

A broad understanding of this approach acknowledges the relationship between the learner and broader social structures. E. Erikson emphasized that affective learning occurs in relationship to the broader culture. Our ability to emotionally learn from and cope with internal stresses ("crises") is often mediated through social institutions (parents, school, church, work, marriage, etc.). L. Vygotsky and P. Freire have also noted that cognitive and behavioral processes, including language acquisition, cannot be separated from social relationships and cultural influences.

Christian formation, as a broad category of discipleship, recognizes that many behaviors may be taught or modified through personal or group relationships. Formation, although combined with theories of behavioral and cognitive learning outlined above, acknowledges that people are shaped or patterned into a large part of what they assume is Christian behavior. Responses to religious experience as well as personal assumptions about spirituality and worship are often deeply influenced by significant role models and larger communities. Christian educators must take seriously and utilize every activity within a church for the sake of discipleship. Christian educators must also be aware of the dangers of any formation that is inconsistent or even contradictory to the gospel. The shaping process of authentic formation can help learners to tacitly respond to new situations in ways that are consistent with the Christian message.

Alternative Approaches. Beyond the larger learning families there are also other special considerations prompted by learning theory. Learning theories inspire a large body of literature on individual learning preferences or styles. These learning styles may be based upon our preferences in how we receive data, either through different senses (visual, aural, kinesthetic, or even intuitive) or through how much data we prefer to receive, either in large blocks or in smaller units. Other learning styles tend to focus on our preferences in processing the data, whether imaginatively considering many options at once, or analyzing particular data, or seeking immediate application (Kolb, 1984). In each of these preferences or styles of learning, theorists acknowledge the variety of differences in how people learn best.

Learning theorists also explore how certain approaches to learning may be emphasized by certain cultures. These cultures influence what people value as authentic knowledge (the sociology of knowledge) and value as appropriate "ways of knowing" or learning. Women's psychology, through theorists such as M. Belenky et al. (1986), note that often women value learning that is based on relationship and that helps to "connect" people with the subject they are studying, whereas other learning theories have favored a more detached, scientific stance. Theorists have noted that some cultures see knowledge as a gradual yet steady accumulation of data while others value learning via conflict (Pazmiño, 1997, 192–94) or through sudden leaps of insight and imagination (Loder, 1989). H. Gardner (1983) posits that persons may have more than one type of intelligence based upon how they employ linguistic, musical, spatial, analytical, body-kinesthetic, or interpersonal capabilities. J. Bruner and others (Eisner, 1985) have noted that the way persons understand data and organize it (whether in static, discrete propositions or in fluid, contextual narratives) also influences learning. Each of these alternative approaches illustrates the complexity behind current learning theory.

Theological Considerations. Christian educators can appreciate the variety of learning theories but, as noted, each theory family brings certain limitations so educators must be cautious in their evaluation and use. Certain assumptions behind each theory, when not subjected to Christian discernment, may actually prove detrimental to the gospel. Maintaining a balanced view of the learner and a complex understanding of God's revelation is important. Often the role of the Holy Spirit is least understood in the process of learning. Problems arise when the Holy Spirit is seen completely independent of the learning process, so that attention to different learning styles or fostering a positive learning environment is seen as irrelevant. At the other end of the spectrum the Holy Spirit might be considered only after all other learning strategies are employed (much like a relief pitcher at the end of a baseball game) so that the Spirit's role is not taken seriously in the entire learning process. A better way of understanding the Holy Spirit is to see the Spirit participating and working through the various approaches to learning. Learning then becomes a means of grace, a way by which the Holy Spirit may truly communicate grace through existing human structures and practices. Ultimately, the diversity of learning theories reveals the complexity of God's creation (including human beings) and the variety of ways to approach God's truth. Careful attention to these theories will help Christian educators broaden their teaching methods to reach more people for the kingdom of God and deepen the faith of existing believers.

DEAN BLEVINS

Bibliography. M. F. Belenky, B. M. Clinchy, N. R. Goldberger, and J. M. Tarule (1986), *Women's Way of Knowing: The Development of Self, Voice and Mind;* E. Eisner, ed. (1985), *Learning and Teaching the Ways of Knowing;* J. M. Gallagher and D. K. Reid (1981), *The Learning Theory of Piaget and Inhelder;* H. Gardner (1983), *Frames of Mind: The Theory of Multiple Intelligences;* D. Kolb (1984), *Experiential Learning: Experience as the Source of Learning and Development;* J. E. Loder (1989), *The Transforming Moment,* 2nd ed.; R. W. Pazmiño (1997), *Foundational Issues in Christian Education,* 2nd ed.

LeBar, Lois E. (1907–) Professor of Christian education and chairperson of the Christian Education Department at Wheaton College from 1945 to 1975. Her vision for a Word-centered, learner-focused, Spirit-filled Christian educational ministry was far ahead of her time and is still deeply relevant today.

LeBar received her teaching certificate from Geneseo Normal and Training School (now SUNY Geneseo) in New York State and earned her B.A. from Roosevelt University, her master of Christian education degree from Wheaton College, and a Ph.D. in religious education from New York University.

In addition to inspiring generations of students at Wheaton, her lasting contribution to Christian education was the publication in 1958 of her magnum opus, *Education That Is Christian.* This book was republished in 1989 with an introduction and notes by James E. Plueddemann, a former student of LeBar who succeeded her as chair of the Christian Education Department at Wheaton.

LeBar laid out a comprehensive philosophy of Christian education. She called for a Christian education practice and program that found a balance between educational ministry related to "outer factors" such as knowledge of the facts of the Bible and "inner factors" such as the felt needs of the learner. She called for a balance between a "back to basics" approach of facts learning and a creative, student-centered approach.

LeBar focused on Jesus as a teacher. She emphasized the fact that Jesus' main mode of teaching was not lecture but a person-centered, needs-meeting, interactive style. Her discussion of Jesus' use of parables as a call to dialogue, to faith, and to discovery initiated by the learner is richly insightful. She found examples of this learner-centered discovery style of teaching in the rest of Scripture also.

The learner was also in focus. LeBar found in the Scriptures a developmental picture of the learner who must internalize, act on, and participate in the learning if there is to be a lasting effect. The teacher's primary role is to be a facilitator and guide. Learning is active and arises from the needs of the learner.

LeBar viewed curriculum not as a body of content but as "those activities that . . . bring pupils one step closer to maturity in Christ." The Bible needs to be the content of the curriculum, but the Bible as the living Word of God, not as a dead letter to be memorized and its facts repeated by rote. The Bible must be taught, learned, and discovered as the Word of God written in light of the Word of God incarnate to enable it to light a fire in the learner's heart. LeBar strongly emphasized the work of the Holy Spirit in this process.

As biographer Plueddemann concludes, "Long before James Fowler studied faith development, LeBar discussed stages of faith in Jesus' healing of the blind man. Before Thomas Groome popularized the concept of 'shared praxis' in education, LeBar pleaded that the educator move from life to truth. . . . Before the research of Piaget became popular in Christian education, LeBar was pointing out the radical implication of inner, active, and continuous learning. . . . She anticipated much of the problem-posing methodology of Paulo Friere. LeBar practiced what she preached, and the past thirty-five years have shown her method to have significant merit" (LeBar and Plueddemann, 1989, 12–13).

PERRY G. DOWNS

Lectionary Curriculum. A set of biblical lessons that are systematically appointed to each day of the year. From ancient times, particular lessons were appointed for Jewish festivals. The early Christian church adopted this practice. In the ninth century, these were standardized by the Roman Church. The lectionary has historically been used by the Lutheran, Roman Catholic, and Anglican churches. More recently, interest has grown among other Protestant churches, culminating in a "common" lectionary now used widely throughout the world. This lectionary follows a three-year cycle, each year emphasizing a different synoptic gospel, with the Gospel of John interspersed throughout all three years. The term *curriculum* refers to the teaching plans, materials, and lessons used to achieve educational goals and objectives. Several publishing houses have developed curricula that follow the common lectionary.

A lectionary is holistic in its approach, covering God's activity in the Old Testament through the life of Jesus. The lectionary curriculum, then, provides opportunity to examine the entire story of God's love and action in the world. When the educational emphasis within a congregation follows the same pattern, congregational members gain a more thorough understanding of the passage. Worship becomes more meaningful when education and worship are intertwined. Families, in particular, often benefit from this structure. Spiritual conversations become more common at home when all members of a family experience the same lessons through both education and worship opportunities.

SUSAN L. HOUGLUM

Lecture. From the Latin word *legere* (to read), an oral presentation of facts or concepts. Lecturing enables an instructor to convey a significant amount of information within a prescribed or limited period of time.

When to Employ a Lecture. This teacher-centered method is most effective when learners need background information that is not readily available to them; when class members encounter a "problem text" that requires extrabiblical insights or interpretive framework; or when there is a high degree of motivation for the speaker. Lecture facilitates learning when combined with discussion methodologies.

Components of a Lecture. The three elements of a lecture are *content, form,* and *delivery.* Content consists of what the lecturer says, suggesting that expertise in one's field and mastery of one's message are integral to effectiveness. The *form* of a lecture refers to how the speaker organizes or structures the presentation. Does the talk begin with a compelling anecdote or thought-provoking quotation? Are the speaker's main points clearly discernible? Do the main points reveal uniformity? Other characteristics include points in a logical sequence; simplified vocabulary; illustrat-

ing truths conveyed; and organizing material around a single theme.

Delivery refers to the vocal and nonverbal characteristics exhibited by lecturers: varying tone and volume, changing the rate of speaking, and body language (facial expressions and gestures) to reinforce and give significance. The primary factor separating highly evaluated college teachers from low-rated instructors is enthusiasm, or expressiveness, during lectures (Weimer, 1993).

Increasing Attention During Lectures. Students' attention increases when lecturers appeal to two or more senses, as when key concepts are visualized. Their perception of the content's relevance to their lives is also a crucial motivational variable. Studies suggest that students' attention increases from the beginning to ten minutes into the lecture, and decreases after that point. When tested after a lecture, students recalled 70 percent of material covered in the first ten minutes, but only 20 percent of material covered in the last ten minutes (Hartley and Davies, 1978).

TERRY POWELL

Bibliography. P. E. Abrami, L. Leventhal, and R. P. Perry (1982), *Review of Educational Research* 52:446–64; J. Hartley and L. K. Davies (1978), *Programmed Learning and Educational Technology,* 15:207–24; M. Weimer (1993), *Improving Your Classroom Teaching.*

Lee, James Michael (1931–). American theorist of religious education. Born in New York City, he attended Catholic schools and received degrees from Saint John's University (A.B.) and Columbia University (A.M.; Ed.D.). For a short period of time he taught in New York City high schools, followed by teaching positions at Seton Hall, Hunter College, Saint Joseph College, and the University of Notre Dame.

Following the liquidation of the religious education program at Notre Dame, Lee joined the education faculty at the University of Alabama in Birmingham. In Birmingham, he founded and remains president and general editor of Religious Education Press, a nonprofit organization committed to publishing scholarly academic books related to the discipline of religious education.

While Lee has edited or authored a number of scholarly books and numerous articles, he is best known for the trilogy of books that set forth his social science model of religious instruction: *The Shape of Religious Education* (1971), *The Flow of Religious Education* (1973), and *The Content of Religious Education* (1985).

Lee's social science model is based on the assumption that religious learning is no different from any other type of learning. Religious instruction employs the same theories, concepts, laws, and procedures that apply to general instruction. It is through the social sciences that religious instruction is best understood and instructional strategies are developed.

Concerning the purpose of religious instruction, Lee proposes what he calls the integralist position. This stance regards the primary purpose of religious education "as the fusion in one's personal experience of Christianly understanding, action, and love coequally" (Lee, 1973, 11). He further believes that the integralist position will enable the learner to effectively actualize a five-dimension pattern of Christian living: religious belief, religious practice, religious feeling, religious knowledge, and religious effects.

Lee takes special care in distinguishing between religious content and theological content. Theology, he argues, is the speculative science that investigates the work and nature of God. Religion, by contrast, comprises a lifestyle, a lived experience. Theology is abstract; religion is concrete. Consequently, theological instruction is concerned with enabling the learner to theologize, while religious education facilitates religious behavior in the life of the learner.

As a publisher, educator, author, and the father of the social science approach to theorizing about religious instruction, Lee has had a profound impact on religious education. His treatment of religious education is ecumenical in nature and he endeavors to appeal to Roman Catholics, mainline Protestants, and evangelicals.

HARLEY ATKINSON

Bibliography. H. W. Burgess, *Models of Religious Education;* J. M. Lee (1971), *The Shape of Religious Education;* idem (1973), *The Flow of Religious Education;* idem (1985), *The Content of Religious Education.*

See also CHRISTIAN EDUCATION; ECUMENICAL EDUCATION

Legal Dissolution. *See* Divorce.

Lesson Plan. A teacher's guide to development of a class session. It serves as a road map for the session. As teachers develop lesson plans, they take into account the needs of those in their class, the appropriate teaching and application of the Scripture passage, and the resources available to them in presenting the lesson. Good lesson planning begins with prayer, and moves to study of the Scripture passage and selection of the central truth, which provides the focus for the lesson. The central truth is a statement of the key idea that the teacher will emphasize during the lesson.

The teacher then selects the specific learning objectives for the session. Outcomes are stated in terms of content to be learned, attitudes to be formed, or actions to be taken as a result of the lesson. The teacher then selects the teaching methods by which the content will be communicated and the objectives achieved. Methods for a session are chosen on the basis of the interests and abilities of learners, intended teaching outcomes, time and resources available, and feasibility in the classroom in which the group meets. This plan is then written and taken to class as a guide for developing the session.

The written lesson plan for teaching a Bible session contains the following elements: (1) the title of the lesson, (2) Scriptural basis, (3) the central idea of the lesson, (4) learning objectives, (5) needed materials, (6) a plan for gaining the attention of the class, (7) an outline of the Bible content and how it will be presented, (8) suggested application(s) of the lesson material and means of presentation, and (9) a way to draw the lesson to a close and draw out the response of the learners.

Teachers may or may not use printed curriculum materials to develop a lesson plan. However, even if they are using an established curriculum, they follow the same procedure. They consider and sometimes choose from suggestions made in the teachers' guide. At other times, they design activities of their own.

Following the session, teachers evaluate the effectiveness of the lesson plan, noting what went well and what can be improved. This allows for better lesson planning for the future, especially in classes for children and youth when the same lesson may be used again later with a different group.

ELEANOR A. DANIEL

Bibliography. L. O. Richards (1970), *Creative Bible Teaching;* R. E. Rusbuldt (1997), *Basic Teaching Skills.*

Levinson, Daniel Jacob (1920–94). Social psychologist. Born in New York City, he is best known for his work espousing the existence of adult developmental stages in men. He received a B.A. from the University of California–Los Angeles in 1940 and an M.A. and Ph.D. from the University of California–Berkeley in 1942 and 1947. He began his teaching career at Western Reserve University in Cleveland, Ohio, as an assistant professor of psychology in 1947. In 1950, he moved to Harvard to work as assistant professor of social relations, and became a research associate in social science and psychiatry five years later. In 1960 he became an assistant professor of psychology and psychiatry. In 1966 he went to Yale, where he taught as professor of psychology and conducted research until his retirement in 1990. He continued his research and finished a draft of his last book only weeks before he died in New Haven, Connecticut.

The author of numerous books and articles in the fields of psychology and social science, Levinson became widely known with his groundbreaking book *Seasons of a Man's Life* (1978). Based on a new method of research he called *intensive biographical interviewing,* Levinson and his team interviewed forty men ages 35–45, looking at their life structures from three perspectives: sociocultural world (i.e., social class, religion, family, occupation), aspects of a man's self (i.e., talents, moral values, character traits, wishes), and his participation in the world. The research indicated that men go through definable stages in their life structure, just like children develop in stages.

These periods are: early adult transition (ages 17–22), terminating adolescence and making preliminary choices for an adult life; entering the adult world (ages 22–28), becoming independent and creating a stable life structure; age 30 transition (ages 28–33), refining that life structure; settling down (ages 33–40), establishing a niche in society and working at obtaining goals in areas of importance to him; midlife transition (ages 40–45), evaluating life in relation to his goals and deciding what he really wants for himself and others; entering middle adulthood (ages 45–50), creating a new life structure and making choices based on what emerges from the previous stage; age 50 transition (ages 45–50), similar to the age 30 transition; culmination of middle adulthood (ages 55–60), similar to the settling down stage; late adulthood transition (ages 60–65), preparing for the final stage; and late adulthood (ages 65 and older).

Immediately after the publication of *Seasons of a Man's Life*, Levinson began a similar study of women. His research showed that women go through the same age-related stages although they operate differently in each one due to gender differences.

LIN JOHNSON

Bibliography. D. Levinson with C. Darrow, et al. (1978), *The Seasons of a Man's Life;* D. Levinson with J. Levinson (1996), *The Seasons of a Woman's Life.*

See also CAROL GILLIGAN

Lewin, Kurt (1890–1947). American social psychologist. Born in Mogilno, Prussia, he received his Ph.D. in 1914 from the University of Berlin, where he later taught psychology and philosophy. In 1932, he sojourned to the United States and served briefly as visiting professor at Stanford University. A year later he emigrated to the U.S. and was professor of child psychology at Cornell University (1933–35) before becoming professor of child psychology at the University of Iowa. In 1945, he moved to the Massachusetts Institute of Technology, where he founded the Research Center for Group Dynamics. He served as director of the center for two years. In 1947, Lewin helped establish the National Training Laboratory, to help teach methods of group dynamics to members of the academic and business worlds. Among his early associates were Max Wertheimer, the father of Gestalt psychology, and Wolfgang Kohler, another Gestaltist.

Over three decades of research, Lewin's theoretical interests shifted numerous times, but he is noted primarily for his extensive study in human motivation and group dynamics. Lewin derived his theory of motivation from principles initially expressed in Gestalt psychology. Central to this theory, known as "life space" or "field theory," is the notion that there is a psychological field or space in which a person moves. This *life space* or *force field* is constituted of the person (including goals, aspirations, values, attitudes, and ideas), as well as the psychological environment (people, events, ideas, and so forth) that influence or determine that individual's behavior at any given time. Lewin believed that the greater knowledge or understanding an individual had of one's life space and the interaction between self and the psychological environment, the more effective that person would be in predicting or explaining his or her own behavior.

In the mid–1930s Lewin expanded his theory to include the behavior of groups and is considered the founder of modern group dynamics. Just as the individual operates in a personal life space, so the group exists in a *social field* or space. The group is characterized by a dynamic interdependence of group members and an intersection of individual life spaces. As a result of his research studies, Lewin found that certain types of discussion and group decision techniques were superior to lecturing in transforming ideas and changing social conduct patterns.

Lewin was an inspiring teacher and considered by many of his peers to be one of the most brilliant figures in contemporary psychology. His influence in a variety of social psychological realms, such as sensitivity training, group processes, learning theory, personality theory, and management theory, lives long after his death. His numerous writings include *A Dynamic Theory of Personality* (1935) and *Principles of Topological Psychology* (1936).

HARLEY ATKINSON

Bibliography. C. Hall and G. Lindzey (1957), *Theories of Personality;* K. Lewin (1935), *A Dynamic Theory of Personality;* idem (1936), *Principles of Topological Psychology;* A. Marrow (1969), *The Practical Theorist: The Life and Work of Kurt Lewin.*

See also FIELD THEORY; LIFE MAP

Lewis, Clive Staples (1898–1963). C. S. Lewis was born in Belfast, Northern Ireland. He suffered many disappointments during his early years: his mother died when he was 9 years old; his father was aloof and distant; he was tyrannized by his experience in the English public schools. Comfort came to him through a lifelong close relationship with his brother Warnie, a few intimate friends, and a love of literature. He spent a couple of idyllic years under the private instruction of W. T. Kirkpatrick as he prepared for entrance exams to Oxford University. He went up to Oxford during World War I, joined the Officers Training Corps, and reached the trenches of France on his nineteenth birthday. He was wounded in battle by an English round that fell short of its mark and killed some of his friends.

When he returned to Oxford after the war, Lewis accomplished the remarkable feat of winning three Firsts in classics, English literature, and philosophy. He taught philosophy at the university for one year before settling into a fellowship in English language and literature at Magdalen College, Oxford, in 1925. His academic reputation was established by the publication of *The Allegory of Love* in 1936. Lewis was a popular lecturer and respected scholar. He was elected a fellow of the British Academy in 1955. He never held a professorship at Oxford but was elected to the chair of medieval and Renaissance literature at Cambridge in 1954, a position that the university created for him. Throughout his years at Oxford and Cambridge Lewis remained at the center of an informal literary society called the Inklings. The group included J. R. R. Tolkien, Charles Williams, Neville Coghill, Lord David Cecil, and other friends of Lewis.

Lewis was an adult convert to Christianity. He spent many years as an atheist, later an agnostic, materialist, Hegelian idealist, then a theist, and finally, on September 28, 1931, he became a Christian. His conversion to Christianity was influenced by several things. First, he was profoundly aware of a deep sense of longing within him. The object of this desire eluded him and drove him through a long pilgrimage he would later describe as "the Dialectic of Desire." Lewis would tether his desire to something he believed was its object. His expectations would be raised and then disappointed. He would untether himself from the thing he thought would fulfill him and the search would begin again. Second, though he was skeptical of Christianity, he found himself attracted to Christian authors. He was imaginatively captured by the writings of George MacDonald and impressed by the reasonableness of G. K. Chesterton, and he discovered himself wondering if the Christians were, in fact, all wrong. A late night conversation with Hugo Dyson and J. R. R. Tolkien was the concluding factor sealing his conversion.

While Lewis regularly published scholarly works throughout his academic career, he also wrote popular books of Christian apologetics. His well-reasoned arguments in *The Problem of Pain* resulted in an invitation to deliver a series of broadcast talks over BBC Radio during World War II. These talks were later published as *Mere Christianity*. He began preaching to RAF airmen during the war and speaking with greater frequency at churches and university chapels. He also helped start the Oxford Socratic Club, which opened up dialogue between Christians and skeptics. Here too Lewis's evangelistic concern was evident. His popularity as an author grew significantly after the publication of *The Screwtape Letters*. He was even featured on the cover of *Time* Magazine, September 8, 1947. He wrote science fiction, children's stories, and novels, all charged with spiritual significance. His fiction was not preachy, but Lewis was convinced that "any amount of theology can now be smuggled into people's minds without their knowing it" (*Letters of C. S. Lewis*, July 9, 1939). Since his death five volumes of his letters have been published which reveal an almost pastoral concern for people.

Lewis's entire professional life was invested in education. Though he wrote articles concerning teaching English language and literature in the University, he only wrote one book on education, *The Abolition of Man or Reflections on Education with Special Reference to the Teaching of English in the Upper Forms of Schools*. The book grew out of Lewis's Riddell Memorial Lectures delivered at the University of Durham in 1943. Lewis sets forth a defense for belief in objective value (what he calls the "Tao"). Consequently, ideas and sentiments can be considered true or just when they are congruous with the Tao. The justice of an idea is manifest in rendering to the thing itself, its due. Rejection of the "Doctrine of Objective Value" leads to an arbitrary innovation of value, which may result in the destruction of a society settled on subjectivism, and risks the "abolition of man."

Lewis was a bachelor most of his life. He married Helen Joy Davidman in 1956. Joy was dying of cancer at the time of their wedding. She recovered briefly and their three and a half years together ended with Joy's death, June 13, 1960. Lewis chronicled his grief in *A Grief Observed*. The last book that he prepared for publication was *Letters to Malcolm: Chiefly on Prayer*. It is a book of rich personal devotion and worship.

JERRY ROOT

Bibliography. R. L. Green and W. Hooper (1974), *C. S. Lewis: A Biography*; C. S. Lewis (1947), *The Abolition of Man*; idem (1936), *The Allegory of Love*; idem (1964), *A Grief Observed*; idem (1964), *Letters to Malcolm*; idem (1966), *Letters of C. S. Lewis*; idem (1952), *Mere Christianity*; idem (1943), *The Pilgrim's Regress*; idem (1943), *The Problem of Pain*; idem (1942), *The Screwtape Letters*; idem (1955), *Surprised by Joy*.

Liberal Arts. Central to a traditional liberal arts education is the cultivation of both character and mind. Its aim is to help persons become more fully human. Although rooted in ancient Greek philosophy, the liberal arts approach to education has deeply influenced Christian education today. Christian liberal arts colleges have become some of the most successful institutions of learning within the Christian community.

The earliest roots of liberal arts education are found in the writings of Plato and Aristotle that deal with the questions of virtue, ethics, and truth. Grammar, logic, and rhetoric were established by these early Greek philosophers as the basic subjects for the truly educated person. Even the power and force of the Roman Empire was unable to squelch the superior Greek educational ideals. By the early Middle Ages the classical liberal arts curriculum was established, made up of the trivium (grammar, logic, rhetoric) and the quadrivium (arithmetic, geometry, astronomy, music).

Augustine (354–430), bishop of Hippo in North Africa, had a profound impact in channeling Plato's philosophical and educational ideas into the Middle Ages. In the classic *On Christian Teaching*, Augustine introduces the concept "all truth is God's truth," a theme that has been repeated countless times in present-day Christian liberal arts colleges. Another interesting contributor to liberal arts was early-fifth-century African pagan educator Martianus Capella. In his treatise *The Marriage of Philology and Mercury*, he introduced the seven liberal arts as nuptial presents from Mercury to his bride. This treatise on the liberal arts was one of the most widely used textbooks on learning during the Middle Ages. Building on the educational ideas of Augustine, Boethius (ca. 480–524) kept the classical studies of the liberal arts in focus during the early Middle Ages.

As the Roman Empire began to decline in the fourth and fifth centuries, so did public education. Monasticism became the primary means of education as the church increased its domination of the culture. In its attempt to separate itself from the world and secular society, the church made religion the major focus of education in the monastery. Although initially established to train boys for the ministry, monasteries eventually accepted boys for general learning by the ninth century. Between the sixth and eleventh centuries, monasteries perpetuated the classical educational tradition with its focus on Latin and the seven liberal arts.

With the growth of the church as an institution in the fourth and fifth centuries also came the establishment of cathedral schools led by the bishops. These bishops eventually hired teachers, many of whom were recruited from public education. Along with subjects like Scripture and theology, students also learned the classical liberal arts. Eventually, toward the end of the first millennium, the cathedral schools became more prominent than the monasteries as centers of learning.

The cathedral school evolved into the university as cathedral schools such as those at Paris and Bologna hired chancellors to supervise the teaching faculty. These schools eventually formed guilds or *universitas* of faculty and students. Based on the classical liberal arts subjects, these institutions gained greater freedom to specialize. While most universities focused on the "queen" of all the disciplines, theology, other schools specialized in law or medicine. During the Renaissance and the Enlightenment the focus at the university moved from theology to humanism to science. While the liberal arts disciplines remained central to university education during these centuries, there was a distinctive movement away from theology toward natural science.

The establishment of Harvard College (1636) in Boston was an attempt by the Puritans to reestablish a Christian liberal arts institution to train ministers and Christian teachers. Returning to the classical liberal arts distinctive of the Middle Ages, Harvard attempted to gain ground lost to the secularization of society over the previous five hundred years. Its curriculum included all the liberal arts subjects (except music), along with Latin, Greek, Hebrew, and theology. Soon other religiously oriented liberal arts colleges were established in America, including William and Mary and Yale. Although they began with clear Christian distinctives, it did not take long for each of them to accommodate to culture and lose their commitments to biblical orthodoxy. Most if not all of the liberal arts schools that began in America in the seventeenth and eighteenth centuries slowly lost their evangelical distinctive. Enlightenment philosophies of rationalism, deism, naturalism, empiricism, and humanism began to infiltrate the universities and undercut the biblical foundation of truth. Classical liberal arts disciplines were soon displaced by practical disciplines focused more on preparing students for jobs than on shaping the mind and character.

Allan Bloom (1987), in reflecting on the state of the university today in America, states: "The university now offers no distinctive visage to the young person. . . . The student gets no intimation that great mysteries might be revealed to him, that new and higher motives of action might be discovered within him, that a different and more human way of life can be harmoniously constructed by what he is going to learn" (337).

While not necessarily articulating a "Christian" perspective on liberal arts education, Bloom, in *The Closing of the American Mind*, traces America's movement away from its liberal arts heritage toward relativism and pragmatism.

From a distinctively Christian perspective, Arthur Holmes (1987), in *The Idea of a Christian College*, challenges the university to return to the classical distinctive of a liberal arts education "to form the mind, to stretch the understanding, to sharpen one's intellectual powers, to enlarge the vision, to cultivate the imagination, and impact a sense of the whole" (30). Rather than indoctrinate, the task of a Christian liberal arts education is to "fan the spark and to ignite our native inquisitiveness" (30). Instead of merely reflecting the trends and ideas of our culture, a true liberal arts education should challenge students to critically examine themselves and their culture against the standard of biblical truth.

There seems to be some indication that this approach to education is being resurrected. Within the past 150 years there has been a growing number of distinctively evangelical Christian liberal arts schools established across North America. The continuing challenge will be for such institutions to maintain both their distinctive "Christian worldview" and "liberal arts" philosophy.

GARY C. NEWTON

Bibliography. W. Benson and K. Gangel (1983), *Christian Education: Its History and Philosophy;* A. Bloom (1987), *The Closing of the American Mind;* A. Holmes (1987), *The Idea of a Christian College;* P. Johnson (1995), *Reason in the Balance;* R. Orrill (1995), *The Condition of American Liberal Education;* J. Reed and R. Prevost (1993), *A History of Christian Education;* E. Trueblood (1959), *The Idea of a College.*

See also HUMANISM, CHRISTIAN; HUMANISM, CLASSICAL; MEDIEVAL EDUCATION; REFORMATION, THE; RENAISSANCE EDUCATION

Liberalism. In general terms, to be liberal is to favor progressive change and individual freedom. Liberalism in political thought, for example, gave momentum to the American and French Revolutions. Liberalism in Christianity has been characterized by a willingness to compromise traditional doctrine in order to bring the faith into line with contemporary science and philosophy.

Christian liberalism had its beginnings in the new learning of the Enlightenment. Influenced by German philosopher Immanuel Kant, theologians changed their focus from God to man. Biblical critics denied the doctrines of revelation and inspiration. Science overruled Scripture. Emphasis on God's benevolence began to cloud the necessity to fear his wrath. The model of Christ's life took on greater importance than his death and resurrection. Sin was reinterpreted as mere ignorance. Darwinism cast doubts on the biblical account of creation. In liberal thought, Christianity had to be reevaluated in the light of each new advance in science and philosophy. The Christian faith was reduced to being only one among a selection of religions. Christ was considered not as God incarnate, but as a man who had fully realized his inner potential.

Albert Ritschl, a nineteenth-century German theologian, rejected everything supernatural about Christianity and proposed that the Christian faith be based solely on its historic foundations. Traditional creeds were distrusted. Instead of Christianity shaping culture, culture was to reshape Christianity.

Critics of Ritschl maintained that the liberal emphasis on culture and human potential made the concept too dependent on cultural norms. They proclaimed the whole idea overly optimistic in its view of humanity and labeled it "cultural Protestantism." Swiss theologian Karl Barth sought to counter liberal thought by reaffirming Christianity. He began a comparatively conservative movement that became known as neoorthodoxy.

Liberal theology began to exert its influence in America in the post–Civil War years. Americans began to demand social relevance from religion. Churches became heavily involved in humanitarian efforts to improve social conditions. Their motivation was noble—the gospel was intended to be applied to life—but there was an underlying problem. While the "social gospel" created activism, the theology behind it unfortunately tended to downplay the basic sinfulness of humanity. It was believed that trust in the "brotherhood of man under the Fatherhood of God" would bring about social justice for all. A benign but unbiblical view of humanity insinuated that humankind was evolving into a more moral being. Wait long enough, the liberals predicted, and society would be perfect.

Liberalism faltered in the wake of two world wars and the Depression. People found it hard to believe that humankind was basically benevolent. A new movement called neoliberalism grew in status under the banner of Harry Fosdick of New York City's influential Riverside Church and Henry Van Dusen of Union Theological Seminary. Neoliberalism, like its predecessor, stressed ethics over doctrine. In the 1950s and 1960s, neoliberalism was championed by theologian Paul Tillich. In the 1960s and 1970s, it found expression in the "God is Dead" theology and several other splinter groups.

Although membership in liberal churches has declined, liberal thought is still around, especially in academic circles. Today's postliberals teach that Christian revelation is not unique, that the New Testament must be demythologized, and that the Bible is basically flawed. The postliberalist aim is to re-create Christianity as a middle ground between traditional Christianity and total abandonment of the faith.

The liberalist movement that had begun with a generation of misguided conservatives was passed on to a generation with no orthodox foundation to curb its enthusiasm for modern thought. David Smith (1992), in his *Handbook of Contemporary Theology* (85), compares neoliberals with the foolish man who "built a house on the ground without a foundation" (Luke 6:49). Smith predicts that the next generation of liberalists will have become so secular that they will make no claim to Christianity at all.

Liberalism may have influenced religious educators to some extent by encouraging the design of curriculum that aims at the application of Scripture to daily life. Aside from the compromising of basic doctrine, perhaps the most detrimental aspect of liberal thought with regard to education has been the removal of moral absolutes. Within more liberal churches and many public education institutions, children are being taught that situational ethics are easier to apply than divine mandates.

ROBERT J. CHOUN

Bibliography. I. Cully and K. B. Cully, eds. (1990), *Harper's Encyclopedia of Religious Education;* K. B. Cully, ed. (1953), *The Westminster Dictionary of Christian Education;* D. F. Ford, ed. (1997), *The Modern Theologians;* E. F. Harrison, ed. (1972), *Baker's Dictionary of Theology;* A. E. McGrath (1997), *An Introduction to Christianity;* A. Richardson, ed. (1969), *A Dictionary of Christian Theology;* D. L. Smith (1992), *A Handbook of Contemporary Theology.*

See also CULTURE; ENCULTURATION; NEO-ORTHODOXY

Liberal Theology. "Iconoclastic reorientation" from the "historical perspective to the scientific" in Christian theology (Burgess, 1996, 77). In this instance, *liberal* is not used as an adjective; rather, it denotes a theological movement within Christianity that peaked in the first quarter of the twentieth century.

Tenets of Theological Liberalism. The advent of liberalism in America followed the basic pattern of its European predecessor. American liberalism was heavily influenced by Schleiermacher's existentialism and the German theologians (e.g., Ritschl and Harnack), who rooted Christianity in pragmatic and radical higher critical studies. European liberalism first entered the American scene through divinity schools, seminaries, and graduate schools.

Burgess (1996, 76) summarizes the tenets of liberalism into four points: (1) Theological constructs are open to continual change, hence doctrine is not composed of unalterable expressions of truth, but simply contemporary articulations and applications. (2) Religious education is essentially concerned with social and cultural reconstruction, not with individual salvation. (3) Liberal theology seeks to create social consciousness via intentional social interaction, replacing evangelical commitment to holiness and righteousness with a social agenda and cause. Finally, (4) Christian personality and lifestyle arises from the development of latent personal and religious capacities. An additional observation is added by Boys (1989), who notes liberal theology's advocacy of "religious pluralism" (45). This advocacy becomes evident in their education agenda, as Pearson (1958), commenting on Athearn's definition of religious education, notes,

"This definition is broad enough to include Jewish, Mohammedan, Hindu, and all other non-Christian religions, as well as the Christian" (16).

While liberalism maintains the same categories as classical theology, the contents of these categories are significantly different. The extreme immanence of God is affirmed by liberalism, minimizing his transcendence and sovereignty. God is seen as working through the natural realm in its processes, not via miracle, which would constitute an affirmation of transcendence. The universal "Fatherhood of God" is foundational in liberal theology, but this is not a scriptural affirmation, since the Bible speaks of God as the Creator of all, but the relation of "Father" is reserved only for those within the community of faith.

Within liberalism, human nature is determined primarily by the findings of the social sciences, especially anthropology. Humanity is regarded as being essentially good; hence human sinfulness is denied. The "brotherhood of man" is affirmed, though such a concept is unscriptural, since brotherhood (and sisterhood) are reserved for the community of faith, not humanity in its sinful state.

Jesus and Christ are regarded as two separate issues in liberal theology. Jesus was the historical Palestinian Jew upon which the title and place of Messiah or Christ was given posthumously by the early Christian community. Hence, liberal theology does not reconcile the historical Jesus with the Christ of faith.

Salvation is seen as gradual personal and social transformation and evolution, not a radical or sudden conviction or conversion. Salvation is not regarded as the restoration of a relationship with God, but as following the social ethics of Jesus. Hence, education is essential to the process of salvation as a means of personal and social transformation.

Scripture is regarded as being primarily a human production, as *one* religious text among other sacred bodies of literature. Similarly, revelation is seen as progressive, the development of human reflection on the divine, devoid of objective content and information as maintained by the evangelical community. The Old Testament is regarded as representing the cultic religion of a primitive Palestinian culture, and the New Testament as the "religion of Jesus." Hence, Burgess (1996) comments regarding the liberal theological approach to education, "The Bible . . . becomes, *at best* a resource," being considered inadequate to aid the task of liberal religious education (95, emphasis added).

Liberal Religious Education in the Twentieth Century. "Religious education is a classic expression that weds classic liberal theology and progressivist educational thought" (Boys 1989, 39). The proponents of liberal religious education were numerous during the first half of the twentieth century, but they are now all but extinct from the evangelical educational landscape.

Horace Bushnell's (1802–76) *Christian Nurture*, with its emphasis on gradual transformation over sudden conversion and redefining of human nature, served as the prototype of American religious education (Burgess 1996, 78–79; Boys 1989, 40–44). The rise of Darwinism in the mid-nineteenth century likewise significantly contributed to the advent of liberal religious education in twentieth-century America.

George Albert Coe (1862–1951), founder of the Religious Education Association, is paradigmatic of the liberal model of religious education. He asserted the concerns of social reconstruction over the individual, and the necessity of reframing Christianity in a modern, liberal expression (e.g., he used the phrase "democracy of God" rather than the scriptural "Kingdom of God" to describe the church).

Other contributors to liberal religious education include Sophia Lyon Fahs (1876–1978, Unitarian), William Clayton Bower (1878–1954, Disciples of Christ), Adelaide Teague Case (1887–1948, Episcopalian), Walter Scott Athearn (1874–1934, Methodist), and Ernest John Chave (1886–1961, Baptist). Perhaps the last significant work of liberal education was written by a student of Coe's, Harrison S. Elliot, entitled *Can Religious Education be Christian?* (1940). It was this text that signaled the eventual collapse of the theological liberal model of education.

The demise of liberal theology occurred in the 1940s with the rise of neoorthodoxy and process theology, both of which challenged the legitimacy and value of classical liberalism. Neoorthodoxy found expression in Barth and Bultmann, but it was H. Sheldon Smith's *Faith and Nurture* (1941), written in direct response to Elliot's work, that raised the educational challenge to the established liberal approach. Similarly, process theology was introduced by Whitehead and N. S. Ferré, but reached its full educational expression within the mainline churches in Randolph Crump Miller's *The Clue to Christian Education* (1950) and *The Theory of Christian Education Practice* (1980).

JAMES RILEY ESTEP

Bibliography. M. C. Boys (1989), *Educating in Faith;* H. W. Burgess (1996), *Models of Religious Education;* G. A. Coe (1923), *A Social Theory of Religious Education;* idem (1929) *What Is Christian Education?;* D. E. Miller (1981), *The Case for Liberal Christianity.*

Liberation Theology. An overarching term for a group of theologies, based on socialistic assumptions, that concern themselves primarily with economic injustice and social oppression. Generally linked to Roman Catholicism in Latin America, liberation theology emphasizes the deliverance of people from economic, political, and social bondage of an institutionalized nature in place of the primary emphasis on personal redemption from sin that is central to evangelicalism. In terms of salvation, liberation theology tends to highlight liberty not by placing one's faith in Christ but by working for the reconstruction of persons and societies according to the liberationist version of a politicized kingdom of God. Much has been made of liberation theologians' Marxist thought and the option of a "systematic recourse to violence."

Brief investigation of three major proponents will add clarity to this theological movement.

Gustavo Gutierrez (1928–). Gutierrez is the preeminent Latin American liberation theologian and his book, *A Theology of Liberation: Perspectives,* is frequently considered the basic text to understanding the liberationist perspective. In the 1960s, perceiving that his theology—formed significantly at the University of Lyons in France—was inadequate to deal with downtrodden parishioners in Lima, Peru, Gutierrez began forming a new system of thought. Believing that capitalism brought progress and riches for the few and poverty for the many, Gutierrez moved from a biblical theology to a "critical reflection on liberating praxis" which he said eventuated in liberation from private poverty, that is, socialism. Gutierrez, although a parish priest, celebrated author, professor, and visiting lecturer, lives in a slum area of Lima where his quarters are simple. His concern for the impoverished is apparently genuine as he, in his words, lives, writes, and teaches "from the underside of history."

Gutierrez attempts to mix Marxism with Christianity and even seems to suggest that the entire world will experience eschatological salvation as Marxists work for political and temporal liberation. How this all results from a biblical hermeneutic too often seems inconsequential to Gutierrez; indeed, he has reached his conclusions by reacting to conditions as they exist in Latin America and equating the mission of the church with necessary political revolution. The Catholic priest has, in essence, reduced the gospel to serve myopic and partisan ends, that is, the interpretation of the Word of God is subjugated to a commitment to Marxist revolution.

Necessary correctives to Gutierrez's thought include a hermeneutic that must allow Scripture to have the last and defining word; emphasis that heaven cannot be made here on earth no matter which paradigm—Marxist or capitalist—prevails; recognition that sin, evil, and salvation belong primarily to people, not to systems and institutions; that orthopraxis (right action) must not be exalted at the expense of orthodoxy (right belief which, of course, informs right action); and that "universalism" is an erroneous element in a biblically responsible theological construct.

Leonardo Boff (1938–). Once a member of the Franciscan order in Brazil, Boff resigned from the priesthood in favor of standing as a layman. He sees the theology of liberation arising out of a biblical perspective of justice and an ethical indignation at the poverty and marginalization of the great masses of people. He is the most prolific of the liberationists, having penned many well-known works, and is editor of *Revista Eclesiastica Brasiliera,* an important Brazilian theological periodical. He is said to be the most prominent and talented theologian in the Portuguese-speaking world but has also been twice "silenced" by the Vatican for challenging the authority of the Roman Catholic Church.

Boff is among some of those in liberationism who have been critical of Marxism, seeing major problems in the dogma that Christianity must correct. Even so, a basic acceptance of foundational Marxist tenets gives his theology an undeniable Marxist flavor.

He is perhaps best known as one of the leading theologians dealing with Christology in liberationism (cf. *Jesus Christ Liberator,* 1972). In Boff's understanding, Jesus came to earth to usher in the kingdom of God, which has both future and present implications. When Christ announces the kingdom, it is a call against principalities that oppress the disenfranchised.

Boff is also known for his development of the exodus of Israel from bondage as a paradigm for liberation theology. He believes that the same God who took sides with the oppressed against the pharaohs of this world is still available to come to the aid of the oppressed today.

Boff also writes enthusiastically about "base communities"—small groups of Christians (consisting of fifteen to thirty people), who meet once a week or so to discuss local problems and possible solutions to various predicaments. Scripture study, song, and intercession for one another are typical components of such meetings, and the Eucharist is served if a priest is present. These communities are not meant to rival the church but to serve as a more intimate and active way of being the church. Estimates are that some eighty thousand base communities have existed in Brazil and one hundred thousand across Latin America. Women tend to be the instigators and perpetuators of these groups, asserting themselves in this setting where the church has frequently subjugated them elsewhere.

The "base" of these communities derives its name from the members of the units; they are made up almost entirely of the "base" (or poor) of their locales. Boff sees a vital "ecclesiogenesis" in worldwide progress as today's church is born out of the faith of the poor. Base communities excite Boff because of his critical view of hierarchical authoritarianism and clericalism, which he thinks should be less important as "new min-istries and a new style of religious life incarnated in the life of the people" arises.

Boff's use of Scripture differs from that of evangelicalism, as from Gutierrez. The task of the Christian faith is not so much found in an interpretation of the Scriptures, but rather in the interpretation of life itself. The Bible is thus full of myths (which Boff accepts as the best way to relate religious precepts) and is a result of speculation and theologizing of religious men. The Christian faith, therefore, does not prescribe concrete applications but a general mode of attitude.

Boff's interest in his later years has centered on the use of social trinitarianism as a model for liberationist thought and speculation that Mary was the hypostatic incarnation of the Holy Spirit.

Juan Luis Segundo (1925–). Segundo is a Jesuit from Uruguay notable for attempting to cover the expansive range of Christian doctrine, much of this before recent articulations of liberation theologies. Segundo has thus made his mark across a theological landscape that has no systematic theology to represent its views.

Segundo's provocative writing style unites religion and life, the transcendent and the natural, the church and the secular into a cohesive whole. When talking of the many forms of liberation theology in Latin America, Segundo views men and women who construct the kingdom of God within a contemporary framework on a political as well as an individual basis.

Segundo may be best known for his "hermeneutical cycle," which contrasts substantially with the traditional approach. Traditionally, an approach to truth and praxis begins biblically and theologically, proceeds to interpretation and construction of a worldview, and then continues to application. Segundo proposes that the starting place is reality itself, or the way things are. Move from this to critical reflection, that is, what is to be done, a process that utilizes the tools of sociology and economics. The third step wrestles with the Word of God before moving to a commitment to action, or truth applied.

The reason that liberation theology is difficult to define with precision is testimony to Segundo's hermeneutic. Liberationists seem to suggest that if one's theology is not achieving the objective, then that theology must change. Hence, liberation theology is a constantly changing dynamic.

Third World or Latin American liberation theology has given rise to many other forms in the First World. Black African liberation theology can be found in South Africa, black liberation theology has been trumpeted by James Cone in the United States, feminist liberation theology applied similar theological precepts to perceived oppression of women, homosexual groups have attempted to glean from similar perspectives, and others have tried to "domesticate" Latin American liberationism for their own version of the victimized poor.

Liberation theology appeals to those who feel victimized and seek a worldview that meets their need for relief; desire a more integrated faith that speaks to the vital issues of contemporary society and the responsibility of a compassionate faith; see "liberation" as a central conceptual framework for organizing Scripture; desire an effective marriage of evangelistic and social action concerns; and recognize the need for a critical analysis of capitalism as a system of social and economic organization.

MATT FRIEDEMAN

Bibliography. L. Boff (1981/1985), *Church, Charism and Power: Liberation Theology and the Institutional Church;* G. Gutierrez (1971/1988), *A Theology of Liberation;* J. L. Segundo (1968/1972), *A Theology for Artisans of a New Humanity;* R. C. Hundley (1987), *Radical Liberation Theology: An Evangelical Response.*

Library/Resource Center. A collection of print and media materials that supplement and complement the Christian education program of the church. The library/resource center becomes a teaching center in its own right by providing books, videos, computer programs, and other resources that may be checked out and used at home for those involved in individual learning projects. It complements the Christian education program by providing commentaries, teaching resources, and other materials useful to teachers as they prepare and teach their Bible classes and study groups. Some libraries also contain curriculum materials and visual aids useful to teachers and youth coaches.

If it is to be a viable ministry, the library/resource center must have a director or a team of leaders responsible for its operation. The first task of the library/resource center leadership team is to develop a statement of mission. The mission statement should include a general statement regarding whom the library is to serve, the kinds of materials to be included, and the purposes to be achieved by its existence. This mission statement will enable the leadership team to develop a collection policy, set guidelines for how and what materials may be donated to the center, plan for space and equipment, determine what services to provide, promote the use of the center, and set hours of operation.

No longer should a library be limited to print materials, but should instead include a variety of media—video, computer, visual, tape, and CD, as well as books.

Although the library is a valuable resource for adult education and for assisting teachers in their ministry, the leadership team should consider the value of extending the collection of materials and services to include children. If library services are planned for children, computer games, children's

books and videos, and children's Bible study resources will be added.

One of the most important decisions the leadership team must make is how to develop the collection. The library should be a budget item for the Christian education budget. But not many churches have unlimited funds to buy everything that is needed.

Additional ways of acquiring materials need to be identified. Some Christian bookstores have a program to provide a percentage of purchases to be credited toward the development of library resources for the buyer's church. If so, the library leadership team must communicate this to church members, informing them what stores provide this service and how to take advantage of it. Many churches also promote the idea of memorial gifts to the church library. Some individuals will also be willing to pass along their used books to the library. Be sure, however, to have a set of guidelines to clearly communicate what kinds of materials are added to the library and to indicate that the leadership team reserves the right to dispose of materials not accepted for the library. These materials can often be sold at used bookstores, leaving some cash to be used for more appropriate materials.

ELEANOR A. DANIEL

Lifelong Learning. Person's continual attempts at processing information, while developing purposefully and systematically throughout all of life.

Formal discussion of the concept began in the 1930s. Because of a growing understanding of human development and cultural change, educational theorists began to understand that the acceleration of cultural change required educational methodologies that did more than transmit static information. What was needed was a strategy that equipped learners throughout the life cycle to think and function in the dynamic climate of social and cultural change.

Lifelong learning is integrally related to life experience. As an active participant in learning, the learner becomes increasingly self-directed as he or she engages in the dynamic process of growth.

Dave (1973) outlined a number of characteristics of lifelong education that help clarify various dimensions of the use of the term *lifelong learning.* Lifelong learning is characterized by variety, flexibility, diverseness, adaptation, innovation, and continual change. This distinctly personal process has as its goal the maintenance and improvement of the quality of life. It includes the realms of formal, informal, and nonformal education, going beyond intentional education to include spontaneous learning such as that which occurs in the family and the community.

Considering the sustainable habits of learning required to meet the challenges of a changing culture, Knowles (1972) identified a number of crucial learning competencies. They include the development of curiosity in learning; the ability to formulate questions answerable through inquiry; to identify and locate relevant and reliable sources of information; to analyze, organize, and evaluate data; and to generalize, apply, and communicate answers to the questions raised.

Though the concept is very broad, one is attracted to the wholeness that encompasses the totality of the learning process and sees it as what Dave (1973) identified as "an organizing principle" for all of education.

MARI GONLAG

Bibliography. R. H. Dave (1973), *Lifelong Education and School Curriculum;* M. S. Knowles (1978), *The Adult Learner: A Neglected Species.*

Life Map. A counseling and personal enrichment tool. A life map is a way of visually exploring one's life journey, anticipating better self-understanding. Mapping is used as a technical term in the counseling field (Minuchin, 1974).

Life-mapping includes reflection on one's past, identification of key events, persons, and feelings, then evaluation of one's present situation to face the challenges of the future. Though the Bible includes no visuals, the apostle Paul furnishes a life critique in Philippians 3:4–14, reviewing his family background and religious experience, then comparing them to his present understanding of God's mercy and grace.

The use of graphic expression helps a person draw on insights from the brain's right hemisphere, often leading to deeper personal insights than simply using words and concepts.

Life-maps are best utilized within Christian education among adults who have lived long enough to identify trends, turning points, and so on, in their lives. Teenagers might also find life maps valuable in assessing their childhood experiences.

DANIEL C. JESSEN

Bibliography. S. Minuchin (1974), *Families and Family Therapy.*

See also COGNITIVE FIELD THEORY; LEWIN, KURT

Lifestyle. Lifestyle is often defined by externals: clothing, housing, possessions, use of time and money, selection of friends, and so on. Lifestyle is grounded, however, in a person's core values, a result of decision-making capacities God has given to humankind. The Bible teaches divinely ordained values, thereby bringing a Christian's lifestyle under God's scrutiny. The Christian educator, being concerned about the integration of biblical values with daily life, must therefore study both the Bible and the lifestyle of the learners to be effective. In fact, when a Christian educator seeks to link the lives of learners with the eternal truths of the Bible, the educator/teacher's lifestyle awareness becomes a major factor in the success of the teaching-learning process.

Lifestyle influences the teaching-learning process as follows:

Needs Assessment. A study of the lifestyles of the learners often enables the teacher to assess the spiritual condition of their hearts and lives, to discover to what extent there is a commitment to biblical values. Additionally, this exploration of the learners' lifestyles enables a teacher to start with their felt needs in the approach to the teaching topic (LeBar, 1989, 191), thereby increasing learner motivation.

Goal-setting. Because Jesus Christ desires to be Lord of all of life, the Bible should be taught in such a way that it leads to changed lives (LeBar, 1989). Goals for Christian education are therefore often most effectively stated in terms of anticipated impact on the learners' lifestyle.

Application. An understanding of the learner's lifestyle is essential for suggesting possible application of biblical truth to daily life. Larry Richards's four-step teaching design (Richards, 1970, 110) culminates in the "look/took" steps, wherein teacher and students speculate on potential ways the biblical text applies to their lives (look), which is followed, hopefully, by implementation in lifestyle (took).

In terms of age-level differences, the lifestyle of children is usually dictated by authority figures. Even so, children may exert pressure on parents to purchase certain clothing, toys, fast foods, and the like. Thus, children do govern their own lifestyle to some extent, so they should be helped to examine lifestyle issues from a biblical perspective. Youth and adults have considerable personal freedom, which allows them to choose a lifestyle of their own making. A key part of Christian education is, therefore, helping youth and adults clarify and measure their values and lifestyles against biblical standards.

DANIEL C. JESSEN

Bibliography. L. E. LeBar (1989), *Education That Is Christian;* L. O. Richards (1970), *Creative Bible Teaching.*

Lindeman, Eduard C. (1885–1953). American philosopher of adult education. Born in St. Clair, Michigan, his Danish immigrant parents died while he was still a child. He did not receive any systematic education as he drifted among a variety of jobs in agriculture, shipbuilding, and construction. In spite of his illiteracy, Lindeman was accepted at the Michigan Agricultural College, which later became Michigan State University. Receiving help, he was an able learner and soon was writing essays, poetry, and editorials for the newspaper. He graduated in 1911 and married the daughter of the chairman of the horticultural department in 1912.

Lindeman was a significant leader in the philosophy of adult education. He wrote about social and democratic directions that adult education should take. Maintaining that adult education does not have the same purpose nor can it use the same methodology as pedagogy, he developed the concept of andragogy. He stressed the use of small groups and informal educational approaches.

After graduation, Lindeman served in various roles. One of his jobs involved editing *The Gleaner*, an agricultural newspaper. Concurrently, he served as an assistant minister of the Plymouth Congregational Church in East Lansing, extension director for the 4-H Club, and an instructor for the YMCA. In 1920, he landed his first teaching position at the North Carolina College for Women. By 1924, he was teaching at the New York School of Social Work, which was later called Columbia University School of Social Work, from which he retired in 1950.

His primary ideas for adult education were stated in his 1926 book, *The Meaning of Adult Education*. In this work he clarified his goals for adult education. He enunciated the idea of andragogy as the best approach to adult learning. Andragogy views learning from an adult position of personal discovery across the life span, rather than simply the transmission of factual content. Almost half a century later, the concept was further developed by Malcolm Knowles.

Lindeman was interested in the curriculum of adult education and insisted that there was a close relationship between the discussion of issues in small groups and an effective democratic society. He insisted that adults be confronted with real-life issues, reflect on those issues and beliefs, and as a result, take social action. His ideas have permeated such groups as the Study Circles Resource Center and the National Issues Forum.

The imprint of Lindeman's ideas on methods may be clearly seen in adult-oriented college programs across this country. Learner-centered lessons for adults that draw on their life experiences and receive attention through group discussion are prevalent. Instructors are facilitators of groups, rather than the transmitters of information.

EDWARD A. BUCHANAN

Bibliography. E. C. Lindeman (1926), *The Meaning of Adult Education.*

See also ADULT CHRISTIAN EDUCATION; ADULT DEVELOPMENT; ANDRAGOGY; LIFELONG LEARNING; KNOWLES, MALCOLM S.; PEDAGOGY; TEACHABLE MOMENTS

Line and Staff Chart. *See* Organizational Chart.

Linear Programming. Early form of programmed instruction that gradually emerged from the work of B. F. Skinner. In 1943, Skinner successfully trained a pigeon to roll a ball around its cage by using operant conditioning. He gave reinforcements to the animal when it demonstrated very small actions that were similar to the desired behavior. Within a short period of time these small steps, which Skinner called successive approximations, conditioned the pigeon to perform its new task flawlessly.

Linear programming is similar in structure to Skinner's work with the pigeon. Once an educator identifies a desired learning outcome, he or she divides the instructional material into very small units or "frames" which are presented one at a time to the learner. Each frame is then followed by either: (1) a more difficult frame; (2) an informational or reinforcement frame; or (3) a review or test frame. During the presentation of these frames the learner is encouraged to respond to each unit through some action such as answering a simple question or rephrasing given information. If his or her response is incorrect, then the same unit of information is presented once again to the learner. He or she will then have another opportunity to respond to the material. This loop of successive approximations continues until the learner responds correctly. Once the learner has responded successfully to a particular unit, the program leads the learner to interact with new or expanded frames of information. This process continues step by step, frame by frame, until the learner has successfully demonstrated the desired learning outcome.

The term *linear* refers to the direct, lockstep method by which each learner advances toward the desired learning outcome. Although the speed at which different learners arrive at the learning outcome may vary, this extrinsic programmed approach requires that all students move through each and every frame in a specific and predetermined sequence.

ROBERT DEVARGAS

See also BRANCHING PROGRAMMING; COMPUTER-ASSISTED INSTRUCTION; COMPUTER-ENHANCED LEARNING

Line-Staff Relationships. As organizations grow and develop, they discover that at a certain point they need to define the working relationships that exist among individual members. One popular way to do so is to draw a diagram that shows the relationships.

This diagram usually consists of the titles, or positions, of the organization's members (sometimes the names of the persons who hold each position are added, usually in a smaller font). Generally the title is in a box, and each box is connected to one or more other boxes by lines to indicate the kinds of relationships that exist among the various positions.

Most line-staff relationship diagrams indicate authority, responsibility, and lines of reporting. For example, the president of the organization might be at the top of the chart, indicating that ultimate authority resides in that office. There might be one or more vice presidents, each one under the president and connected to the president with vertical lines. This indicates that the vice presidents derive their authority from the president, are responsible to the president, and report to the president. Under each vice president might be several committee chairs. The lines connecting the vice president to the chairs indicate the same things about authority, responsibility, and reporting. In addition to vertical lines, most line-staff diagrams include a number of horizontal lines. Horizontal lines show the relationships that exist among the various officers and program units of the organization. For example, there might be horizontal lines connecting all of the vice presidents to each other, indicating that they meet together, work together, and share information in support of each other.

Many organizations have moved away from the traditional vertical (hierarchical) line-staff relationship in favor of a more collegial paradigm in which authority and responsibility rests in a group. Such a diagram is more circular in appearance, with curved lines. The authority might be in a small group in the center of the diagram. Other members of the organization are connected directly to those in the center, and to each other, indicating mutuality and collegiality. This type of diagram looks more like a web than the traditional diagram.

JOHN H. AUKERMAN

See also ADMINISTRATION; LEADERSHIP; MANAGEMENT; SPAN OF CONTROL

Little, Sara Pamela (1919–). American professor of Christian education. Born in Charlotte, North Carolina, she received an A.B. degree from Queens College (1939) in Charlotte, an M.R.E. degree (1944) from the Presbyterian School of Christian Education in Richmond, Virginia, and a Ph.D. (1958) from Yale Divinity School. In addition, she did postgraduate work at Harvard (1965).

Little was professor of Christian education at Presbyterian School of Christian Education from 1944 to 1950. At the same time she served as the assistant to the regional director of Christian education for the Synod of North Carolina. From there she taught at Union Theological Seminary in Richmond, Virginia, from 1951 to 1976. In addition, she taught occasionally at Union Theological Seminary in New York and at Princeton Theological Seminary. A highly respected educator, she lectured and led seminars worldwide. Since 1973 she has been an elder in Grace Cov-

enant Presbyterian Church of Richmond. She has been active in the Religious Education Association, serving on the editorial board of *Religious Education*.

Her early writings include *Learning Together in Christian Fellowship* (1956) and *The Role of the Bible in Contemporary Christian Education* (1961). Little's concern early on was the relationship between theology and education. She believes that Christian education should not function apart from theology. God's revelation as found in the Bible is to be the "determinative principle" for the character of the curriculum of Christian education. While many fields of knowledge contribute to understanding, Little is committed to a dialogical approach with a confessional flavor that respects the individual and her or his freedom. The purpose of this process is to enable the learner to become a participant in the faith community. Anything that assists in the development of the community enhances the learning experience.

Her other writings include *The Language of Christian Community* (1965), *Youth, World and Church* (1968), and *To Set One's Heart: Belief and Teaching* (1986). In addition, she has written chapters in many publications such as Marvin Taylor's *Foundation for Christian Education* and Jack Seymour's *Contemporary Approaches to Christian Education* as well as articles for the journal *Religious Education*.

RICHARD E. ALLISON

Liturgy. A term used to denote a particular manner of relating to God. Although it has undergone major shifts in modern expression, the essential elements have remained the same.

Background. In Old Testament usage, liturgy (*latreuein*) related to the religious conduct of worship by the people to a particular deity or god figure, especially in the area of cultic sacrifice. The same meaning is evident in sacrificial worship to Molech (Lev. 18:21), any of the Baals (Judg. 2:11), or any of the Astoreths (Judg. 2:13). It can also include the worship of human images such as Nebuchadnezzar's gold image (Dan. 3:1–18).

The requirement placed upon Israel was to worship Yahweh alone, and thereby recognize his position as Lord. This defines the people's primary responsibility, which is to worship, although the meaning goes deeper when referring to Yahweh worship. A primary component in the relationship of the Hebrews to Yahweh is contained in their attitude, in addition to service. Included in this is the disposition of the heart along with the demand for right demonstration of this attitude in the whole of religious and moral conduct, which defines the true uniqueness of the religion of Israel (Kittel, 1965).

Early Christianity. Early Christianity brought about a significant change in liturgy as it moved away from the more ritualistic service of the priests accompanied by the specific actions of the people, especially concerning the times of prayer and sacrifice, to a more flexible manner of worship. As Christianity separated itself from Judaism, the individual gained an increasingly important role. With this, the primary focus on prescribed liturgical action gave way to a redefined personal relationship with God through the person of Jesus and by the Holy Spirit. Christians did have religious gatherings where various types of rituals were practiced. They gathered to eat together, to celebrate the Lord's Supper, to baptize new members, to read Scripture, to listen to God speak to them through other believers, to experience healing, to pray and sing hymns of praise and thanksgiving to God. These activities were not tied to particular places or times but could be practiced virtually anywhere since the unifying feature was temporal rather than spatial (Freedman, 1992).

Within the first two hundred years of Christianity, the groundwork was being laid for a new concept of liturgy. Liturgy became more narrowly defined. It was used as a method of structuring worship, since the action of worship was becoming increasingly expressive of either a personal, individual, or group relationship to God. J. E. White goes one step further in defining the relationship between liturgy and worship by stating, "Liturgy is a work performed by the people for the benefit of others . . . the essential outward form through which a community of faith expresses its public worship" (1980, 23–24).

RONALD W. FREEMAN

Bibliography. D. N. Freedman (1992), *The Anchor Bible Dictionary;* G. Kittel (1965), *Theological Dictionary of the New Testament;* J. E. White (1980), *Introduction to Christian Worship.*

See also ORTHODOX CHRISTIAN EDUCATION

Locke, John (1632–1704). English philosopher. Born in Wrengton, Somerset, England, he learned temperance and simplicity from his Puritan family. At Westminster, Locke studied the classics, Hebrew, and Arabic. He later criticized the school for its narrow emphasis and harsh discipline. At twenty, Locke entered Oxford. He stayed on after earning a bachelor's degree to complete a master's and join the faculty. Locke lectured on Latin and Greek and was later appointed censor of moral philosophy.

When his father's death left him an inheritance, Locke had the freedom to expand both his education and his circle of friends. He studied medicine but did not actively practice or teach for years. In 1665 Locke's interest in politics led him to join a diplomatic mission to Germany. On his return to the university, Locke began to study philosophy. His study of Descartes led him to question the Scholastic views that he had been taught. Philosophy mixed with politics when Lord Ashley, earl of Shaftesbury, invited Locke to London to be his personal physician.

The earl managed affairs for the colony of Carolina, and Locke became his advisor in the framing of the colony's constitution. While Locke was on a trip to France to rebuild his failing health, England suffered political turmoil. Locke returned to find his friend on trial for treason because of his opposition to the Crown. Linked to the earl, Locke himself was kept under close watch. Tried but found innocent, the earl grasped the opportunity to sail to Holland. Locke soon followed. James II of England tried to have Locke extradited, but Locke managed to stay in Holland and pursue his writing. Once again Locke's interests turned to politics and he became involved in the plan to place William of Orange on the English throne. When William became king, it was John Locke who escorted William's Queen Mary to England.

Living with friends in England, Locke continued to write and served the government as a commissioner. During these productive years Locke published his *Essay Concerning Human Understanding* and *Two Treatises of Government.* These were followed by *Some Thoughts Concerning Education* and the *Reasonableness of Christianity.* Locke died in 1704 while at work on commentaries on the Pauline Epistles.

Locke's main contribution to education were the views expressed in *Some Thoughts Concerning Education,* in which he shows a sympathetic understanding of children. Remembering how he hated the rote learning of his own education, Locke proposed a curriculum tailored to the needs and aptitudes of the individual child. His medical background and perhaps his own poor health led Locke to recommend lots of fresh air, exercise, and a healthy diet for children. Good health and good character, Locke maintained, were to be valued over intellectual learning.

As incentives to learning, good examples and life-applications were promoted over numerous rules and severe punishment. Parents were urged to maintain their authority, but not with harsh discipline. More would be gained through praise. Remembering the relationship he had with his own father, which started out cold and warmed with the years, Locke advised parents to develop a warm, affectionate relationship with their children. Parents should spend time with their children, getting to know them and teaching them by example. Encourage curiosity. Teach through play. Make learning fun. The primary aim of early education, according to Locke, was simply the development of virtue.

Locke recommended a varied curriculum that would include history, law, ethics, music, the sciences, and a manual trade. He believed in the educational benefits of travel and the importance of learning a second language in childhood. Opposed to the emphasis on classical languages and grammar that dominated his studies at Westminster, Locke promoted training in a modern language with an emphasis on conversation. Although common practice today, Locke's ideas were in direct opposition to the educational methods of his own time.

In his religious writings, Locke said that belief was the private business of the individual and God. In an era of intense religious persecution, Locke preached tolerance. A forced belief could only result in hypocrisy. The state, Locke insisted, had no right and no power to compel belief. If the strongest power can impose its own religion on the weak, can that make those beliefs true? Locke argued that shifts in political power prove that truth cannot be equated with a position of strength. As a Christian, Locke believed in the divine inspiration of Scripture. He longed for a return to the simplicity of the New Testament church. He declared that the claims of Christianity were consistent with reason and that revelation can be trusted in areas where reason is insufficient.

ROBERT J. CHOUN

Bibliography. R. I. Aaron (1971), *John Locke,* 3rd ed.; J. F. Bennett (1971), *Locke, Berkeley, Hume: Central Themes;* M. W. Cranston (1957), *John Locke, a Biography;* C. B. Eavey (1964), *History of Christian Education;* P. Edwards, ed. (1967), *The Encyclopedia of Philosophy,* vol. 4; K. O. Gangel and W. S. Benson (1983), *Christian Education: Its History and Philosophy;* J. W. Gough (1961), *John Locke's Political Philosophy, Eight Studies;* J. Locke (ed. J. W. Yolton) (1961), *An Essay Concerning Human Understanding;* idem (ed. J. W. Gough) (1946), *The Second Treatise of Civil Government and a Letter Concerning Toleration;* idem (trans. P. Abrams) (1967), *Two Tracts on Government;* J. W. Yolton (1956), *John Locke and the Way of Ideas.*

See also COLONIAL EDUCATION; PURITAN EDUCATION

Loder, James Edwin (1931–). American professor of philosophy of Christian education. A Presbyterian minister with Ph.D. from Harvard University, he took clinical training at Massachusetts Mental Health Clinic in Boston, researching the relationship of theology and psychiatric theory at Menninger Foundation. He has conducted postdoctoral work at Piaget's Institut des Sciences de l'Education in Geneva.

Loder's writing intertwines his interests in theology, philosophy, and psychology. Noting the tendency of theology and psychology to move in separate orbits, his passion is for the formal integration of the two disciplines.

Loder authored several books and book chapters, including *Religion and the Public Schools* (1965); *Religious Pathology and the Christian Faith* (1966); "Fashioning of Power: A Christian Perspective on the Life-style Phenomenon" in *Context of Contemporary Theology* (1974); "Creativity in and beyond Human Development" in *Aesthetic Dimensions of Religious Education* (1979); "Incisions from a Two-edged Sword: The Incarnation and the Soul/Spirit Relationship" in *The Treasure of Earthen Vessels* (1994). Loder's best known and widely reviewed works are *The Transforming Moment: [Understanding Convictional Experiences]* (1981) [omitted in the second edition] and *Knight's Move: The Relational Logic of the Spirit in Theology and Science* (1992) coauthored with physics professor Jim Neidhardt.

The Transforming Moment opens with a personal incident from 1970, in which Loder, while attempting to assist a stranded motorist, nearly lost his own life. Another vehicle collided with and pinned him under the stranded car. The event proved to be transformational in his life. He describes the relationship of human spirit and Holy Spirit by weaving human sciences and theology. Loder observes five steps in the transformational event: (1) personal conflict, (2) internal scanning for integrative solutions, (3) imaginative joining of two or more incompatible frames of reference, (4) personal release and openness, and (5) integration of experience, which forges past and future into a new meaningful whole. Loder's focus is on the epistemology of conviction, and he highlights the process of changing stages familiar to developmental stage theories. Four dimensional contexts of world, self, void, and the Holy provide the setting in which convictional events occur. *Void* is, for Loder, that reality which takes meaning out of self and the world and manifests itself in absence, loss, shame, guilt, hatred, loneliness, and the demonic. Critics maintain that Loder's approach is "too individualistic and unappreciative of the nurturing powers of traditional communities" (Dykstra 1982).

The basis of epistemology employed in *Knight's Move* is drawn from a geometric referent (the Möbius band) and is presented through a Kierkegaardian perspective. The authors illuminate the relational nature of all reality—physical and spiritual—including the role of the knower. This relational epistemology is offered as an alternative to the postmodern rejection of objectivism and relativism.

CHERYL L. FAWCETT

Bibliography. G. J. Dorrien, *Sojourners* 12 (1983): 36–38; C. Dykstra, *Princeton Seminary Bulletin* 3, no. 3 (1982): 339–41; J. W. Fowler, *Religious Education* 77, no. 2 (1982): 133–48; R. A. Hunt, *Pastoral Psychology* 30 (1982): 194–96; M. Palmer, *Paraclete* 28 (1994): 30–32.

See also CRITICAL REFLECTION; INTEGRATION OF THEOLOGY AND EDUCATIONAL PHILOSOPHY; TEACHABLE MOMENTS

Loneliness. "A state of feeling that one does not belong or is not accepted. It could imply intense emotional pain, an empty feeling, a yearning to be with someone, or a restlessness" (Carter, 1982, 89).

Loneliness is a common experience to millions who live in the United States. It is often characterized by the feeling that no one cares. Lonely persons may think that their world would somehow be all right—if only someone cared! Those who experience the most intense feelings of loneliness are often people who are guilty of relationship sabotage. They are afraid of intimacy and so they sabotage relationships in order to minimize risk. The cost is a high level of loneliness and a reinforcement of the idea that nobody cares (Carter, 1982, 65).

Human relationships are a safeguard given by God to eliminate the potential for loneliness. Early in creation God determined that "it is not good that man should be alone" (Gen. 2:18 NKJV). Therefore, God created Eve for Adam. The need for relationships has not diminished since that time but is part of the very fabric of that which makes us human. If a person were stranded alone on a deserted island one could legitimately ask whether that person, without other human contact, could indeed be fully human. To be human is to be in community, in relationship. It might be argued that loneliness could also be defined as an experience of isolation resulting from an individual's separation from God, separation from others, and displeasure with self. It is accompanied by a lack of inner peace and contentment (Carter, 1982, 65).

Anda LaRoux states that there is a link between the strength of an individual's faith and the depth and frequency of feelings of loneliness. This may imply that the lonelier the student is, the weaker his/her faith is in Jesus as the Redeemer, and vice versa. These findings support the views held by many who maintain that the deepest cause of loneliness may be sought in religious uprooting and severance of an individual's vertical relationship with God (LaRoux, 1998, 174–80).

There are two needs that seem to be part of the human experience. One is the need to feel loved and valued, and the other is a need for social belonging. If either of these needs is not met there is a great possibility that the result will be a deep sense of loneliness. Lonely people seem to have a common foe, the feeling of separation. They feel they are different; one of a kind. This brings a sense of displeasure with self and intensifies the isolation that they feel causing a tragic downward spiral. They desire relationships, and yet they may either destroy them or remain aloof from forming such relationships, deepening the feelings of loneliness. In an attempt to counter their loneliness many have turned to singles bars, encounter groups, drugs, free sex, Eastern religions, and the cults. Others have withdrawn into depression, anger, self-hatred, overeating, and isolation.

What is the suggested solution? "Any accepting the truth that a measure of loneliness, or separateness, is natural for all people, it is possible to take some important steps toward developing a realistic philosophy of living." Carter, Meier, and Minirth assert "that loneliness is a problem that can be overcome" (1982, 123).

Therefore we need to learn to assess our present situation, determine if we are sabotaging our relationships, learn to be in control of our own negative emotions, and try to see our problems for what they really are—simply problems. Sometimes the only way out of loneliness is to get up and make friends. At other times it is simply telling ourselves that it is okay to be alone.

Rokach and Brock (1998) conclude, "Loneliness, despite its pervasiveness, can be successfully addressed and its pain reduced. If one subscribes to the belief that loneliness is as natural and integral a part of being human as are joy, hunger, and sorrow, it stands to reason that the aim is control rather than prevention of loneliness" (107).

GARY WALLER

Bibliography. L. Carter, P. Meier, and F. B. Minirth (1982), *Why Be Lonely? A Guide to Meaningful Relationships;* A. LaRoux, *South African Journal of Psychology* 28, no. 3 (1998): 174–80; A. Rokach, *Journal of Social and Clinical Psychology* 17, no. 1 (1998): 75–88; A. Rokach and H. Brock, *Journal of Psychology* 132, no. 1 (1998): 107.

Love. In the Bible, love is expressed primarily as an action through a variety of terms. In the Old Testament the root *ahb* denotes love for people, for God, for things and actions, as well as God's love for humanity. In the Septuagint and the New Testament, the concept of love is expressed primarily by two terms—*phileo* and *agapao.* Classical Greek had other expressions for love, such as *stergo,* meaning love between parents and children or love between rulers and people, and *erao* and *eros,* denoting desire, longing, and sexual love, though the terms also had a mystical understanding. These terms, however, do not find expression in biblical usage. In the biblical context, *phileo* and the cognate noun *philia* convey fondness, friendship, brotherly love, or affection for others. The most distinct Christian usage is that of *agapao* and *agape;* however, *agapao* denotes sacrificial and deliberate action on behalf of another, particularly in reference to God's love toward humanity. The foundation for love (*ahb, agape*) is the character of God.

Old Testament Usage. God's love is demonstrated through his redeeming activity in salvation history through his electing of Israel (Exod. 15:13) and establishing a covenant with them (1 Kings 8:23). God's love is described as an everlasting love (Jer. 31:3), as the basis for God's actions toward humanity (Deut. 7:7–8), as gracious and kind (Pss. 103:11; 117:2), as steadfast and unfailing (Ps. 32:10; Isa. 54:10), and as faithful (Pss. 88:11; 89:33). The message of the prophets declares that, even in the midst of judgment, God's elective love bestows grace, mercy, and forgiveness on his people, with whom he is in covenant relationship.

New Testament Usage. The essence of God's character is expressed in the declaration "God is love" (1 John 4:8, 16). This declaration does not deny God's attributes of holiness and righteousness, but, rather, adds to the understanding of God's being. God's love is to be understood in the context of righteousness and justice. God's love does not overlook the sinfulness of humanity; rather, God's love is the motivation behind the salvific activity in Christ on behalf of humanity (John 3:16; Rom. 5:8; Eph. 2:4–7; 1 John 4:10) with God's love being extended to all humanity (1 Tim. 2:4). Further, God's present relationship with redeemed humanity through Christ is characterized by love (Rom. 8:38–39; 2 Cor. 5:14).

God's loving is the basis for human loving. Humanity, in responding to God's love, is to love as God loved (1 John 4:11) and as Christ loved (John 13:34). Jesus stated that love summed up all the commandments (Matt. 22:40) and that there are no greater commandments than the ones that call persons to love (Mark 12:31). The greatest commandment is "Love the Lord your God with all your heart and with all your soul and with all your mind and with all your strength" and the second is "Love your neighbor as yourself" (Mark 12:30–31). Such a human love is enabled by God's love because God first demonstrated his love to humanity (1 John 4:19). The person changed by God's love in Christ is to display a "habitual attitude of love" (Morris, 1981, 229).

Human *agape* love is to display the characteristics of compassion, kindness, bearing with one another, forgiving one another—summed up in the charge to "put on love" (Col. 3:14). Further, Paul, in 1 Corinthians 13, expresses the nature of this love by describing how love is to act. Such love is to be patient, kind, forgiving, protective, trusting, hopeful, enduring. It is not to be envious, boastful, proud, rude, self-seeking, not easily angered, not delighting in evil; rather, it is to rejoice in the truth. Christian love is not primarily a feeling or an emotion; rather it is an intentional involvement in the lives of others. Christian love is to be directed to God (2 Thess. 3:5), to one's neighbor (Gal. 5:14), to other believers (Gal. 6:10), to one's spouse and family (Eph. 5:26), and to one's enemies (Matt. 5:43–48). *Agape* love has implications for Christian education. Scripture points out that love is to be normative of the Christian way of life (1 Cor. 16:14; Eph. 5:2; Col.

3:14; 2 Pet. 1:7). Love, therefore, ought to be integral to the content, process, and purpose of Christian education. First, love is to be taught; it is the content of Christian education. Christ commanded his disciples to "obey everything I have commanded you" (Matt. 28:20). In heeding this command, followers of Christ are to obey the command to love as he loved (John 13:34). Paul also indicates that "the goal of this command is love" (1 Tim. 1:5). Learning to love encompasses love of self, family, neighbor, other Christians, strangers, and those who are enemies. The teaching of love is a mandate for Christian education. Second, love is to describe the process of Christian education. The practice of Christian education must be carried out in love with respect to the learner. As Christ modeled love in relation to those he taught by having compassion and concern for their welfare, so ought Christian educators to model the same love in relation to those whose learning they are facilitating. Love is to be the way of life for the Christian educator and therefore is to guide the educational process (Eph. 5:2). Third, love is to guide the purpose of Christian education. Paul's attitude in presenting everyone complete in Christ (Col. 1:28–29) depicts a self-giving, sacrificial love on behalf of believers in order to accomplish his purpose. Educators are to disciple believers and to educate Christianly because God commands the love of one another, and the building up of one another in love (Eph. 4:16). Love in the educational process is no mere abstract concept; rather, it provides a foundation upon which effective Christian education is accomplished.

ROLAND G. KUHL

Bibliography. W. Günther, and H.-G. Link (1975), *The New International Dictionary of New Testament Theology*, 3:538–51; G. Johnston (1962), *The Interpreter's Dictionary of the Bible*, 3:168–78; L. Morris (1981), *Testaments of Love*; A. Nygren (1932–39), *Agape and Eros*; L. Smedes (1978), *Love within Limits*.

Love and Belonging. One of the stages of Abraham Maslow's hierarchy of needs, *love and belonging* speaks to man's need to feel loved by others and to belong to a group. Maslow (1970) has postulated that after an individual has basic physical needs met and has a sense of safety and security, the need to be loved and to belong becomes a primary goal in life.

The need to feel loved and to have a sense of belonging to a group of some sort is definitely God-given. In Genesis 2:18, God saw that it was not good that Adam was alone, so he created Eve. Throughout all of the Old Testament we see the importance of the family and the source of love and belonging to be found there. In the New Testament, we can see how the local church becomes a place for Christians to find true Christian love and the support that comes from belonging to a group with shared values and interests.

Before students can reach their full learning potential, they must first have basic needs met. A vital part of the learning process then is to instill in students a sense that they are accepted and loved for who they are in Christ, and then to create an atmosphere of oneness within the group so that each individual student feels that he or she belongs.

DALE L. MORT

Bibliography. A. H. Maslow (1970), *Motivation and Personality*.

See also MASLOW, ABRAHAM HAROLD

Luther, Martin (1483–1546). German Protestant Reformer. Born in the small mining town of Eisleben, Thuringia, Germany, the very next day he was baptized in the Church of St. Peter and Paul and given the name Martin, in honor of the saint on whose day he was baptized. His parents moved to nearby Mansfeld when he was about six months old, and it was in this setting that he spent his childhood. His early years in the Mansfeld school grounded him in the central truths of the Christian religion, gave him a solid foundation in his native language, and provided fundamental training in music. At age fourteen he was sent to Magdeburg for a year of schooling, followed by enrollment in the School of St. George at Eisenach, where he remained until he completed the course of study preparing him for entry into the university.

Educational Influences. In 1501, at the age of eighteen, Luther enrolled as "Martinus Ludher ex Mansfeld" at the renowned University of Erfurt. He did not go by the name of Luther as we know it today until as late as 1519. Various forms of his surname can be found in his earliest correspondence and other signed documents (Bruce, 1928). Medieval university structure in Luther's time did not require students to complete a set amount of course credits, but to pass certain oral examinations. In September 1502, less than two years after enrolling at Erfurt, Luther received his bachelor's degree. He then devoted the next few years to earning his master's degree, receiving it in the minimum time required in January 1505 (Kolb, 1991). His next pursuit, following his father's wishes, was the study of law. This course of direction however, would be drastically altered, as would the direction of the church and of Western culture in general.

On one July day in 1505, Luther was caught in a violent thunderstorm. Fearing possible death, he sought the assistance of one of the most popular saints of the day, and cried out, "Help me, Saint Anne! I will become a monk" (Kolb, 1991). Although the thunderstorm soon passed, the spiritual storm within Luther continued for years. He kept his promise by leaving the study of law and entering the Augustinian monastery of Erfurt. This brought great disappointment to his father, who had supplied him with books and even had gone so far as to arrange a marriage for him.

Priest and Professor. As an Augustinian monk, Luther lived a life of piety, seeking to find the assurance of his salvation through works and personal sacrifice. He persisted in his craft of menial labor by even going house to house begging for the benefit of his cloister. Upon entry to the monastery, Luther was given for the first time his own copy of the Bible. On May 2, 1507, Luther was consecrated a priest and celebrated his first Mass. As a priest, he did not remain a recluse in the monastery. His earlier training in philosophy enabled him to receive an appointment as an instructor in philosophy at the recently established University of Wittenberg in 1508. Two years later, he was assigned to make a journey to Rome representing the reorganization plan of the Augustinian Order. He returned from Rome around February 1512, and was made sub-prior of the Augustinian monastery at Wittenberg. He devoted himself to the study of theology, and in October 1512, was awarded the degree Doctor of the Bible. In 1515, he became the district vicar of his order and had general supervision of the all monasteries within his region.

The publishing of the Ninety-Five Theses on the subject of indulgences on October 31, 1517, propelled Luther to the center stage of European Christendom and provoked discussion that initiated massive religious and societal change, which later became known as the Reformation. It was through debate and continued study that Luther's theological understandings finally came together. He came to believe that Christians are not saved through their own good works, but by God's grace. The grace of God is not earned, but received in faith.

Influences on Education. Perhaps the most influential work of Luther in terms of education is his translation of the Bible into the German language. This gave common persons direct access to God's Word and allowed them to read for themselves about the abundant love and mercy of God. The text of the Bible in German, and the recent invention of the printing press, helped pave the way for an educational reformation in Germany. Luther authored such works as *To the Councilmen of All Cities of Germany That They Should Establish and Maintain Christian Schools* (1524) and *On Keeping Children in School* (1530) to encourage the state to develop schools for all children. He suggested a curriculum that included Latin, Greek, music, history, mathematics, physical training, and instruction in the practical responsibilities of living.

Luther also modeled another form of education—home schooling. Luther's domestic life helped remove the requirement of clerical celibacy and paved the way for Protestant clergymen to take on the responsibilities and duties of marriage and family. This most practical protest against the doctrine of celibacy, taking Catharina von Bora for his wife, allowed Luther to experience the family as one of the foundational opportunities for teaching the Christian faith. His *Small Catechism*, written in 1529, was designed to be used by the head of the household, to teach his family the chief parts of Christian doctrine.

STEVEN CHRISTOPHER

Bibliography. R. H. Bainton (1950), *Here I Stand: A Life of Martin Luther;* G. M. Bruce (1928), *Luther as an Educator;* F. Eby (1931), *Early Protestant Educators;* R. A. Kolb (1991), *Luther: Pastor of God's People.*

See also BIBLE TRANSLATIONS; CHRISTIAN HUMANISM; CLERGY AS EDUCATORS; MEDIEVAL EDUCATION; PHILIP MELANCHTON; REFORMATION, THE

Lyceum. The Lyceum generally has two references: first, it was the gymnasium on the east side of Athens where Aristotle held his classes; second, this term is also used synonymously for his school of thought. Later it came to represent a form of adult education in the United States originating during the colonial period (Good, 1973).

By 600 B.C. Athens had a population of well over 200,000 people (65,000 slaves, 45,000 foreigners, and 100,000 citizens). Athens was ruled by the aristocracy until after the Peloponnesian War, at which time a trend developed toward a more democratic form of political order. Aristotle (384–322 B.C.) was convinced that the middle class should have some control of their destiny and supported these social changes. Aristotle was convinced that man's greatest service was to his country. As such, a sound education was needed in order to guarantee the future stability and success of Athenian society.

Between the ages of 8 and 13 most boys attended a public school for learning elementary subjects such as reading, writing, and counting. The secondary level of education was available for boys between the ages of 14 and 18. Here they learned history, drama, poetry, grammar, science, and public speech, and had a rigorous physical education requirement in the gymnasium. Further studies were available for military training at the university level. Higher education was limited due to the high cost and lack of teachers.

Since Aristotle believed that the quality of society depended on the quality of education available to its citizenry he developed the Lyceum school for this purpose. His curriculum included a heavy dose of science and philosophy for all of his students (Johnson et al., 1970).

In the tradition of Aristotle's Lyceum school, there came a movement in early colonial America known as the Lyceum Movement. A lyceum was an institution through which lectures, dramatic performances, and debates were presented. There are records dating back to 1786 that refer to the use of lyceums in the education of the public (Bode 1956). Skilled experts traveled from institution to institution providing lectures. These schools were important to the early adult education movement in America at that time.

MICHAEL J. ANTHONY

Bibliography. C. Bode (1956), *The American Lyceum;* C. B. Eavy (1964), *History of Christian Education;* E. F. Frost (1966), *Historical and Philosophical Foundations of Western Education;* K. O. Gangel and W. S. Benson (1983), *Christian Education: Its History and Philosophy;* C. V. Good (1973), *Dictionary of Education;* J. A. Johnson, H. W. Collins, V. L. Dupuis, and J. H. Johansen (1970), *Introduction to the Foundations of American Education;* M. Mayer (1966), *A History of Educational Thought;* J. E. Reed and R. Prevost (1993), *A History of Christian Education;* A. E. Sanner and A. F. Harper (1978), *Exploring Christian Education.*

Mm

Mainline Denominations. According to Richard Hutcheson Jr. (1981), this phrase has only come into widespread usage recently. It implies that denominations so designated are somehow more central, or are to be identified with the historical mainstream of American Protestantism. However, as the phrase is being used today, it carries many other connotations, from theological posture to attitude toward culture to commitment to missions and evangelism. Hutcheson offers the following as a definition of mainline denominations, which will serve as an outline for this article: "The large historical denominations having memberships reflecting great diversity, but leadership and official positions putting them generally in the liberal, ecumenically inclined and socially concerned wing of Christianity" (39).

Mainline denominations are usually seen as large or major denominations. Examples would include the American Baptist Convention, the Church of Christ (Disciples of Christ), the Episcopal Church (USA), the Evangelical Lutheran Church of America, the United Presbyterian Church, U.S.A., the Reformed Church of America, the United Church of Christ, and the United Methodist Church. It should be noted, however, that there are some large denominations that do not fit all of the traditional characteristics of mainline denominations. The Southern Baptist Convention, for instance, is the largest Protestant denomination in the United States. However, it would not be called mainline by most observers, nor by most Southern Baptists, because they do not fit other connotations associated with the term. The same could be said for the Lutheran Church, Missouri Synod.

While the mainline denominations are large in the sense of being well-established, most have been and continue to experience numerical decline. Naturally, this has caused a great concern to mainline denominational leaders. According to a 1997 article in *Christianity Today*, in the years 1965–94 the combined memberships of the mainline denominations decreased by about 20 percent, while many evangelical and charismatic/Pentecostal denominations experienced significant growth.

The use of the term *mainline* would seem to identify these denominations with the historical mainstream of American Protestantism, and this would have been true of the mainline denominations fifty or perhaps even thirty years ago. With the explosion of the fundamentalist-modernist controversy of the 1920s, many of those regarded as extremists or fundamentalists withdrew from the major denominations, leaving the control of the denominations to those regarded as liberals. The majority of the rank-and-file members of those denominations, however, were conservative in their beliefs. The development of neoorthodoxy enabled the mainline denominations to retain many of those conservative members, and to claim to be the mainstream of American Protestant Christianity, well into the 1950s or 1960s. But as these denominations have continued to drift to the left, their claim to be centrist or in the historical mainstream has been increasingly difficult to maintain.

Today, the mainline denominations, at least in terms of their leadership, are associated with the left wing of American Protestantism, while many of their members individually identify with the evangelical or more conservative wing. This diversity in membership, while allowing the denominations to be inclusive, has been the source of great stress as well. For example, many denominations have struggled to come to a position on homosexuality that meets the satisfaction of all their members. The more conservative members have at times been distressed by the official position of their denomination, and have in some cases formed smaller advocacy groups within the denomination to argue for more conservative positions on social issues (e.g., Good News Methodists, United Church People for Biblical Witness, Presbyterians United for Biblical Concerns).

"Ecumenically inclined" is an apt phrase for contemporary mainline denominations. Another way to identify them has been to refer to those aligned with the National Council of Churches (NCC) or the World Council of Churches (WCC). The fact that many of the mainline denominations have the word "United" as part of their names shows that their present form is the result of uniting elements that had been separate in the past but have now been brought together.

While "socially concerned" would once have characterized mainline denominations more than evangelical ones, that distinction no longer holds true. Rather, they differ in what they are concerned about. The eruption of the culture wars reflects the differing visions of what American society should be. In fact, James Davison Hunter (1991) has argued that the major division in American society today is no longer between the various Protestant denominations or even among Protestants, Catholics, and Jews, but between those he calls "the orthodox" (evangelicals and traditional Catholics and Jews) and "the progressives" (many, but far from all, in the mainline churches, along with moderate to liberal Catholics and Jews, and most secularists).

Mainline denominations face a number of pressing problems in the years ahead. Yet many individual congregations retain spiritual vitality; there are people being reached and ministry going on, and there are resources within their individual denominational traditions capable of renewing and sustaining them. According to a recent forum of evangelicals who remain significantly involved in and committed to these mainline denominations, "The Spirit hasn't left the mainline" (Campolo, Frey, Hestenes, and Willimon 1997).

JOHN S. HAMMETT

Bibliography. T. Campolo, W. C. Frey, R. Hestenes, and W. H. Willimon, *Christianity Today* 41 (August 11, 1997): 14–20. J. D. Hunter (1991), *Culture Wars: The Struggle to Define America;* R. G. Hutcheson Jr. (1981), *Mainline Churches and the Evangelicals: A Challenging Crisis?;* M. Marty (1981), *The Public Church: Mainline-Evangelical-Catholic;* J. Mulder and L. Weeks (1996), *Vital Signs: The Promise of Mainstream Protestantism;* R. Wuthnow (1988), *The Restructuring of American Religion.*

Maintenance Rehearsal.

Maintenance Rehearsal. An operation within information processing theory (IPT). IPT's theoretical framework is based on a computer model of information processing. As such, it has three stages: sensory register, short-term memory (STM), and long-term memory (LTM). The operation labeled *maintenance rehearsal* is a function of short-term memory. Information is gathered from environmental stimuli through the sensory register. If data is given attention by the STM, the mind can choose to ignore and reject it or intentionally process it toward LTM. If information is determined to be meaningful, through active repetition and rehearsal it can be encoded and sent to LTM.

Maintenance rehearsal involves recognition, association, and repetition of information with intention to remember. Encoding by rehearsal or repetition involves four basic approaches: activity, organization, elaboration, and mnemonics. *Activity:* learners are actively involved in the encoding. It may be as simple as singing the alphabet song, or as complex as associating similarities of a new alphabet to one already learned. *Organization:* information is grouped into categories or patterns, or arranged in some logical form to aid encoding. Organization is enhanced using charts, tables, or time and procedural sequences. *Elaboration:* new information is encoded by linking it to information already in LTM. Interconnection with meaningful information gives older students an advantage simply because of the volume of information already learned. *Mnemonics:* this artificial way of organizing and attaching meaning to new information provides structure for rehearsal. Mnemonic devices, such as associations with observable objects, acrostics, acronyms, or key words and phrases are popular artificial associations.

The purpose of maintenance rehearsal is to give attention to new information, to give it structure and meaning long enough to encode and associate it with information already stored, and to send it to LTM. It is also used to reinforce information retrieved from LTM to refresh and expand it with new associations.

GORDON R. CLYMER

Bibliography. W. Yount (1996), *Created to Learn: A Christian Teacher's Introduction to Educational Psychology.*

Maladaptation. Any organism must adapt to the reality of its environment and circumstances if it is to continue to exist. For people, adaptation occurs at a biological level and also at social and emotional levels. Maladaptation occurs when this adaptive process goes awry, i.e., results in what are considered negative patterns of either beliefs or overt behavior. Particular concern is appropriate for children with such maladaptive behaviors as substance abuse, sexual promiscuity and teen pregnancy, suicide, academic underachievement, dropping out of school, and criminal behavior. Some question exists as to whether such behaviors are disruptive or disturbed.

Maltreatment is often cited as a precursor to maladaptation, and multiple victimization places children at greater risk of maladaptation. Children who have fetal alcohol syndrome, who are victims of abuse, and who experience chronic exposure to stressful situations. They are also more prone to maladaptation than those who do not experience chronic exposure to stressful situations, are more prone to maladaptation than those who do not experience such trauma, violence, and stress.

Regardless of the cause of maladaptation, people who exhibit such patterns present problems for religious educators in terms of learner readiness and classroom management. Development of adequate coping skills is often pursued in attempts to solve the problem of maladaptation whether the focus is on prevention or treatment. Other prevention efforts include such widely diverse strategies as prenatal care and cognitive problem-solving.

CLAIR ALLEN BUDD

Bibliography. G. W. Albee and T. P. Gullotta, eds. (1997), *Primary Prevention Works;* R. D. Ketterlinus and M. E. Lamb, eds. (1994), *Adolescent Problem Behaviors: Issues and Research;* A. K. Yancey (1992), *Identity Formation and Social Maladaptation in Foster Adolescents.*

Malign. *See* Abuse.

Maltreatment. *See* Abuse.

Management. "Process of evaluating, planning, organizing, staffing, leading, and directing the efforts of colleagues, and of employing all other resources in achieving stated goals" (Benson, 1990, 392). Management bridges policy and practice. From a biblical perspective, based on Jesus' teaching on servant leadership in Matthew 20:20–28, it is also "meeting the needs of people as they work at accomplishing their jobs" (Rush, 1983, 13). Olan Hendrix defines management as "the stewardship of the talents of the persons entrusted to our care" (Hendrix, 1987, 3).

Although the word *management* is often used interchangeably with *leadership,* it is a broader term of which leadership is a part, as seen in Benson's definition. Management or administration focuses more on the task while leadership concentrates more on the person.

Biblical Examples. Among the many models of management in Scripture are God, Joseph, Moses, and Jesus. God delegated authority to humans to rule the earth after he had created it (Gen. 1:28; Ps. 8:3–8). After Joseph was put in jail because he refused to sleep with Potiphar's wife, he managed the prisoners for the jailer (Gen. 39). Later, when he became Pharaoh's right-hand man, he managed the resources of Egypt in order to provide food for the people when famine struck (Gen. 41). Acting on the advice of his father-in-law, Moses delegated a portion of his responsibilities for managing the Israelites to capable men (Exod. 18:13–26). Jesus managed twelve disciples, training them to take responsibility for evangelizing and discipling people after he left the earth.

The Five Functions of Management. Taking a system approach to understanding the functions of management will help the learner gain a more comprehensive assessment of the details associated with the management process. A manager is involved in many tasks. The five major ones are outlined below along with principles for handling conflict, which may arise during any or all of them. The job is a blending of these, however, not an orderly progression through them.

Planning. Planning is the process of implementing goals by evaluating the past and present and formulating steps to achieve those goals. Premising data reflect what has been done in the past which may impact future planning. Based upon an understanding of the past, and equipped with the mission of the organization, plans are developed which help the organization attain its mission.

Organizing. Organizing is grouping people and tasks to accomplish specific goals. For example, a church's educational ministries may be organized by appointing directors for each ministry (e.g. children's ministry, youth ministry, adult ministry, etc.). A reporting structure is developed and instituted to keep these areas coordinated. Managers must write well-developed job descriptions for each position.

Staffing. In this function, the manager seeks to recruit the right person for the job. Assisted by a detailed job description, the manager advertises the opening, screens the initial applicants, interviews prospective candidates, hires the best person for the job, and then begins the long-term process of orientation and training.

Directing. Directing is the work of inspiring and motivating people to act. The best leadership is done by example rather than dictatorship. It involves identifying problems and then solving them, making decisions, and communicating clearly with people as well as working with the Holy Spirit to stimulate people to act, selecting the right people for various tasks, and equipping them to do the work. Additional tasks within this function include delegating assignments and distributing appropriate authority to accomplish these assignments.

Controlling. Holding people accountable for their work is a critical element of effective ministry. After delegating, the manager oversees those under him or her to monitor the accomplishment of goals and objectives. Evaluation is always based upon known standards of measurement (i.e., plans and objectives). A manager works with employees to define the goal and then uses that goal as a basis of measuring performance. Where there are deviations from the prescribed plan, corrective action or termination is required.

A note regarding conflict management: no manager can avoid conflict, but when it arises, there are some scriptural steps to take to deal with it.

1. Pray for wisdom and guidance in the situation and that the people involved will want to work with you to resolve the conflict.
2. Get the facts straight; don't act on opinions or gossip (Deut. 19:15).
3. Deal with the matter as soon as possible (Eph. 4:26–27). Waiting only intensifies the conflict instead of resolving it.
4. Don't wait for the other person to come to you; take the initiative to try to solve it (Matt. 18:15).
5. Go to the person or persons who are involved in private (Matt. 18:15; Prov. 25:9–10).
6. Focus on the issue, not the person. State the conflict without making accusations.
7. Be willing to forgive—more than once if necessary (Luke 17:3).
8. If step 5 doesn't resolve the situation, go to the person again, taking someone else with you (Matt. 18:16).
9. If necessary, dissolve the relationship (Matt. 18:17).

LIN JOHNSON

Bibliography. W. Benson (1990), *Harper's Encyclopedia of Religious Education;* R. Bower (1964), *Administering Christian Education;* K. Gangel (1989), *Feeding and Leading;* C. George and R. Logan (1987), *Leading and Managing Your Church;* O. Hendrix (1987), *Management for the Christian Leader;* B. Powers, ed. (1997), *Church Administration Handbook;* M. Rush (1983), *Management: A Biblical Approach.*

See also ADMINISTRATION; JOB DESCRIPTION; PLAN, PLANNING; PREMISING DATA

Management, Biblical Basis of. The study of management, though relatively new to the industrialized world, has been around since the dawn of humankind. It is unfortunate that management is viewed by so many people in the church as secular, humanistic, and nonbiblical. Scripture is full of examples to help us comprehend the nature of management. What is usually lacking is an understanding of what Scripture has to say about the topic. As Rush (1983) states so well, "People involved in leading and managing God's work need to develop a biblical philosophy of management. There is an increasing awareness among Christian leaders that God's people need to become more effective in managing His work" (17). Perhaps a better term for describing management is stewardship. In essence, a manager is a steward of resources that belong to another individual or group.

Scripture states that "[God] is not a God of confusion and disorder but of peace and order" (1 Cor. 14:33 Amplified). It should come as no surprise, then, to realize that God desires us to be well managed as well—in our personal lives as well as in the manner in which we oversee the affairs of his church. Management in this article refers to the process and activities of planning, organizing, staffing, leading, and evaluating. These have been referred to collectively as the management process. Although espoused by many secular authors (Koontz and O'Donnell, 1974) these elements can be clearly seen throughout the pages of Scripture.

Planning. The activities associated with planning include setting objectives and goals, developing strategic plans, analyzing premising data, and making decisions. All of these elements are seen throughout both Testaments. Examples of planning in the Old Testament include Noah's preparation of the ark, the collection of food by the Hebrews in the wilderness, the manner in which King David set aside supplies for the building of the temple, Nehemiah's plans for the building of the Jerusalem walls, God sending Jesus at a time which was foreordained before the foundations of the world were laid, and also Paul's church planting activities. Each example helps us understand that planning is biblical and an important dimension in the management of God's resources.

Organizing. The activities associated with organizing include the development of job descriptions, developing a structure by which people relate to one another, and determining how many people one manager can effectively supervise. Examples of these activities are seen in the way God directs his prophets to select and anoint the kings of Israel, and the way Paul dictated job qualifications and responsibilities for leaders of the church (pastors, elders, deacons, etc.—in 1 Tim. 3:1–13; Titus 1:6–11). The process of organization ensures the proper stewardship of God's ministry resources.

Staffing. This element of management requires the proper screening, recruitment, and training of leaders. It is clear throughout the Old Testament that only those selected by God were allowed to be his representatives. Regarding the tabernacle and temple worship, only those from the lineage of Aaron and tribe of Levi were allowed into the priesthood. Jesus was selective in his choice of the twelve apostles. These fortunate few would be the recipients of three and a half years of close training by the Master Teacher. Likewise, Paul was careful in choosing his traveling companions and those to whom he delegated leadership responsibilities.

Directing. This dimension of management speaks of the interpersonal skills that are necessary for effective management. The ability to recognize and resolve conflict is at the heart of this managerial function. The Old Testament is full of examples of broken family and social relationships. Supervision of workers as seen in the training of the twelve disciples by Jesus is a critical component of providing direction. Paul and Peter were often called upon to settle disputes in the early churches. The study of leadership styles is critical to the managerial activity of direction and this is addressed numerous times in both Old Testament and New Testament teachings. God desires for those who provide direction to do so with a servant's heart, not lording over the flock. A servant leader is the supreme example of effective direction.

Controlling. Another way to describe control is *evaluation*. This is the ability to determine whether you are conducting yourself within the parameters of God's will. It is the ability to measure progress and take appropriate means to stay on track or return to the original plan. Activities are controlled by controlling people and careful attention must be given to the attitude in which people are controlled.

Using just the Book of Proverbs an individual interested in the biblical basis of management could develop a fairly comprehensive list of biblical citations regarding issues relayed to management. Such a list is provided below to help illustrate just how much content there is in the Scriptures relevant to the study of management:

Walking with Integrity: 2:7; 6:16–19; 10:9; 11:1, 3, 20; 14:2, 16; 15:22; 16:6, 12; 19:1,23; 20:6–7; 22:1; 28:6

Guidance and the Value of Counselors: 2:1; 10:17; 11:14; 12:15; 13:10, 18, 20; 15:22; 19:20; 20:18; 24:5, 6; 27:17

Wisdom and Diligence: 2:15, 12; 8:12–16; 10:45; 12:14, 23, 24; 14:23; 15:1; 16:10, 12, 21; 17:2; 19:11; 21:5, 22; 28:20

Planning, Goal Setting, Vision, Prioritizing: 1:17; 11:14; 16:14; 21:5, 30; 4:25–27; 12:5; 19:21; 24:7

Interpersonal Relationships/Conflict Management: 10:5; 15:22; 20:5, 18; 29:18; 10:11–13; 12:20; 15:1, 18, 21; 16:7, 21, 28; 17:9, 14; 18:1; 20:3, 22; 27:17–18

Self-Control in Leadership Character: 5:23; 10:19; 11:13, 17, 24–26; 12:12, 16; 13:3; 15:18, 23, 28; 16:32; 17:27; 18:7, 13, 21; 20:1; 25:8, 11, 15, 20, 28

Investing Wisely in Others: 9:7–9; 27:17; 11:25; 26:10

Being Humble: 3:7; 8:13; 11:2; 12:9; 15:25, 33; 16:5, 18; 18:12; 25:6, 7, 27; 27:2, 21; 29:23

Affirmation of Others: 3:27; 12:25

Justice and Mercy, Partiality: 3:3; 11:17; 14:21; 20:28; 21:3; 24:23–25; 28:21; 29:14

Mentoring/Being Mentored: 1:28; 2:1; 3:1, 11; 4:1; 9:9; 13:1; 31:28

Skill in Knowledge/Administration: 1:7; 10:14, 21; 19:2; 27:23 ; 28:2

Friendships: 17:9, 17; 18:24; 27:6, 9, 10, 17

Watching Your Speech: 2:11, 12; 10:14, 19; 11:32; 12:18, 27–28; 13:3; 14:5; 15:1, 23, 28;

16:13, 21; 17:9, 27–28; 18:4, 7, 13, 21; 19:1; 25:8, 11, 15

Following God to Receive Favor: 3:14; 4:14

Obeying God's Word Results in Peace: 3:21–24; 6:20–23; 7:13; 8:32–36

Accountability to God: 5:21

Principles of Finance: 6:15; 10:2; 11:4, 15, 25; 13:11, 22; 15:27; 17:8, 18; 21:6; 23:4

Not Being Lazy: 6:10–11; 13:4, 18; 24:30–34

Being Self-Motivated: 6:6–8

Ill-Gotten Gain: 10:2, 4, 26; 14:23; 15:27; 16:8; 28:16

Speaking the Truth: 11:13; 12:24, 27; 14:25; 15:4; 16:24; 19:9, 22; 20:19, 28

Being Honest: 16:11

Gathering the Facts First: 13:10

Not Seeking Material Rewards: 15:27; 18:13, 17; 21:17; 23:45

MICHAEL J. ANTHONY

Bibliography. M. Bechtle (1992), *Foundations of Ministry: An Introduction to Christian Education for a New Generation;* P. Hersey and K. Blanchard (1977), *Management of Organizational Behavior;* H. Koontz and C. O'Donnell (1974), *Essentials of Management;* M. Rush (1983), *Management: A Biblical Approach;* idem (1989), *Managing to Be the Best;* J. O. Sanders (1980), *Spiritual Leadership.*

See also ACCOUNTABILITY; LAISSEZ-FAIRE LEADERSHIP; LEADERSHIP; LEADERSHIP NETWORK; LEADERSHIP PRINCIPLES; MANAGEMENT

Management by Objectives. An administrative philosophy originated by George Odiorne but associated with Peter Drucker, initiated in the 1950s and popularized in the 1960s. Migliore and Gunn (1995) define management by objectives (MBO) as a comprehensive approach for identifying or developing an organization's purpose, objectives, strategy, desired results, and forms of evaluation. MBO involves a nine-step process: (1) defining the organization's purpose and reason for being; (2) monitoring the organization's environment; (3) realistically assessing its strengths and weaknesses; (4) making assumptions about unpredictable future events; (5) prescribing written, specific, and measurable objectives in the major areas of the organization; (6) developing strategies for using available resources; (7) making long- and short-range plans to meet objectives; (8) appraising the organization to determine whether it is meeting the desired pace and consistency with the objectives; and (9) reevaluating purpose, environment, strengths, weaknesses, and assumptions before setting objectives for the next performance year (27).

MBO theory is a mechanistic philosophy that assumes a routine, efficient, reliable, and predictable organization (Morgan, 1997, 13). As applied to Christian education, MBO strengths are its ability to define, evaluate, and reach specific ministry goals. Similar approaches have developed in church management (known as *ministry by objectives*—MBO), school administration (known as *education by objectives*—EBO), and curriculum design (*Tyler method*).

MBO leadership does risk becoming a rigid, autocratic bureaucracy if initial communication and feedback are poorly implemented. Individuals may often be seen as interchangeable "parts" within the machine and the hidden curriculum often includes a socialization toward conformity for the sake of the goal. MBO leadership may also overlook the more organic and unpredictable nature of many congregations. It has also been seen as quite time-consuming.

MBO, however, does provide a strategy for implementing structure and focus in ministry leadership. Contrasted to other nondirective management approaches, such as laissez-faire leadership, MBO provides distinct advantages for administering Christian education. MBO is a particularly successful strategy in areas where administration has been haphazard in an otherwise stable organization. MBO, done well, ensures that all levels of ministry have input and ownership of the common ministry goals, providing a sustained administrative approach in stable congregations.

DEAN BLEVINS

Bibliography. P. Mali (1986), *MBO Updated: A Handbook on Practices and Techniques by Objectives;* R. Migliore and B. Gunn, *Hospital Topics* 73, no. 3 (1995): 72–79; G. Morgan (1986), *Images of Organization;* J. R. Turner (1993), *The Handbook of Project-Based Management: Improving Processes for Achieving Strategic Objectives.*

See also ACCOUNTABILITY; ADMINISTRATION; EVALUATION; LAISSEZ-FAIRE LEADERSHIP; LEADERSHIP; MANAGEMENT

Mann, Horace (1796–1859). American educator. Born in Franklin, Massachusetts, he was an early advocate of public education. He believed that education should be free, universal, nonsectarian, centered on motivating the learner rather than on rote memory, and reliant on well-trained teachers.

Growing up in a poor and harsh environment, Mann split with his strict Calvinist upbringing around age 12 and moved toward the Unitarianism popular at the time. He had little formal schooling as a boy and managed to educate himself by reading as many of the 116 volumes in the Franklin public library as he could. Through his own studies and the help of a few tutors, including a local pastor, he was able to gain admission at the age of 20 to Brown University in Providence, Rhode Island, where he distinguished himself. He gave the valedictory address, which was filled with nineteenth-century optimism concerning the way education could advance the human race with dignity and happiness.

He chose law as a career, studied at Litchfield (Conn.) Law School, and settled in Dedham, Massachusetts, where his legal acumen and popularity won him a seat in the state House of Representatives. There he led the movement that established the first state hospital for the mentally ill in the United States. From 1835 to 1837 he served in the Massachusetts Senate, becoming its president.

In 1837, after much soul-searching, he switched careers and moved into the world of public education when he became the first secretary of the newly formed Massachusetts board of education. Massachusetts boasted a public school system going back to 1647, but by the 1830s the quality of education had deteriorated noticeably and all control had slipped into the hands of economy-minded local school districts. The state board of education was established to collect and publish school information. It had no authority except its moral suasion.

For eleven years Mann used the position as his personal pulpit to give moral leadership, persuade, and educate the public as to the vital importance of a strong, nonsectarian public school system. His annual reports to the board on the state of education are masterpieces of educational philosophy and vision in which he identified and discussed foundational problems in education that are still relevant today.

His message centered on six fundamental propositions: (1) a republic cannot remain ignorant and free, hence the need for universal "common" education—not meaning the education of commoners as opposed to the rich, but a quality education common to all; (2) the public should pay for, sustain, and oversee such education—the public needs to be intimately involved in education as a trust for future generations and for the future of the country; (3) education is best provided not in private schools, which serve only one segment of children, but public schools embracing children of all religious, social, and ethnic backgrounds; (4) education must be profoundly moral but not sectarian, not favoring one denomination's or religion's expression (he took much criticism for this from clergy, each wanting the schools to teach the doctrines of his own denomination); (5) education must reflect a free society even in its pedagogy, which should be free from harshness and should infuse the learner with a desire to learn; (6) education should be provided by well-trained, professional teachers.

Mann resigned in 1848 to take the seat of former President John Quincy Adams in the U.S. Congress, where he promoted the abolitionist cause with the same fervor as his predecessor. In 1853 he became president of Antioch College in

Yellow Springs, Ohio, a new college committed to coeducation, nonsectarianism, and equal opportunity for African Americans. He died two months after a famous speech to graduating students in which he said, "Be ashamed to die until you have won some victory for humanity."

PERRY G. DOWNS

Maritain, Jacques (1882–1973). Catholic philosopher. He attempted to interpret the philosophy of Thomas Aquinas in twentieth-century terms at a time when Thomistic influence within the Roman Catholic Church was being challenged. It was his desire to readdress Thomism in terms of the practical and intellectual dilemmas facing the modern world.

Born into a French Protestant family, he embraced scientific materialism as a student at the Sorbonne. There he met his wife Raissa, a Russian-born Jew. In exchanging marital vows, the couple also made a pact to commit suicide if within a year they had not discovered the meaning of human existence. Shortly thereafter, however, their fatalistic plans were abandoned largely due to hearing lectures on metaphysics by the popular Henri Bergson. Maritain was intrigued by Bergson's emphasis on the value of intuition in scientific thinking and his contention that reality is beyond rational understanding. Thus ended Maritain's short-lived affinity with science.

He was led to convert to Catholicism in 1906 by the mystic poet Leon Bloy. With Raissa at his side as both companion and sometime co-spokesperson, Maritain devoted his entire life to lecturing and writing more than fifty philosophical books and countless articles expounding the role of human intuition as the path to spiritual discovery and greater knowledge. Despite being unconventional and at times admittedly nonprofessorial, he served on university faculties in both France (Institut Catholique in Paris, 1913–40) and Canada (Institute of Medieval Studies in Toronto, 1940–60) and lectured extensively in the United States.

According to Maritain, philosophy begins with what he called the "intuition of being." But intuition, he held, must be linked with other forms of knowledge. In his most influential work, *The Degrees of Knowledge*, he contended that humanity's knowledge of the universe falls under three categories: nature ("mobile being"), mathematics ("quantity"), and metaphysics ("being as being"). In this magnum opus attempt at synthesizing science, philosophy, and theology, Maritain reasoned that within nature were many phenomena that went beyond experimentation and mathematical analysis. He meticulously restated Aquinas's relationship between divine revelation and human reason in modern terms, incorporating what came to be seen as fresh knowledge into

traditional philosophic reasoning. The influence of Maritain's thought reached nearly every area of human life, as evidenced in his voluminous works: history (*On the Philosophy of History*, 1957), science (*Science and Wisdom*, 1940), education (*The Education of Man*, 1962), politics (*True Humanism*, 1936), aesthetics (*Creative Intuition in Art and Poetry*, 1953), and morality (*Moral Philosophy*, 1960). Like Thomas, his was a belief system in which the spiritual and the intellectual were interwoven, impacting the cultural and political issues of the present.

DAVID GOUGH

Bibliography. J. M. Dunaway (1978), *Jacques Maritain;* J. Maritain (1937), *Degrees of Knowledge;* idem (1962), *The Education of Man;* idem (1964), *Moral Philosophy.*

See also AQUINAS, THOMAS; INTEGRATION OF THEOLOGY AND EDUCATIONAL PHILOSOPHY; METAPHYSICS; NEO-THOMISM

Marker Events in Adult Development. Periods of change, growth, and disequilibrium that bridge two distinct periods in personal development. A great deal has been written about these transitions. Some of the more notable authors on this subject are Daniel Levinson (*Seasons of a Man's Life*, 1978), Erik Erikson (*Childhood and Society*, 1993), Roger Gould (*Transformations*, 1975), and Gail Sheehy (*New Passages*, 1995).

In its most simplistic form, most adult transitions may be placed in one of two categories: *common* or *uncommon* marker events. The common marker events are those transitions that almost everyone experiences in North America. Due to societal norms and expectations, persons will experience these marker events at a particular time in their adult life. The uncommon marker events, in contrast, are not directed by societal norms or expectations. They are distinctly individual, unpredictable, and not universal.

To illustrate, common marker events include the following: becoming independent from parents, marriage, choosing a career, the birth of a child, becoming an empty-nester, grandparenthood, and retirement.

Uncommon marker events would include separation, divorce, adopting a child, discovering one has cancer or another debilitating disease, "coming out" as a gay man or lesbian, death of a child, winning the lottery, saving someone's life, developing a mental/emotional disorder, experiencing war, rape, molestation, menopause, midlife reassessment, experiencing and coping with death.

In most textbooks, religious marker events are not included. Yet religious markers can be some of the more pivotal transitions in adulthood. Religious marker events (most of which are "uncommon") include embracing a faith of your own, adult baptism, discovering your life's calling, discovering (and first utilizing) your spiritual gifts, fasting, personal revival/renewal, and meaning-making during tragedy.

All of these marker events (individually and collectively) mold us into the persons we are becoming in Christ.

MARK BUSHOR

Marketplace Ministry. The words *marketplace ministry* generally conjure up one of the following images: a Christian employee counseling a fellow employee or sharing the gospel informally with him or her; a lay business association that encourages believers to invite nonbelieving colleagues to a meal where someone will give a testimony; a group of Christian professionals meeting regularly for fellowship and nurture; a city church that provides midweek opportunities for Bible study and prayer for its members; a training program to disciple marketplace believers and challenge them to consider undertaking missions as tentmakers.

All of these—counseling and evangelism, study and prayer, testimony and fellowship, discipleship and mission—are valid dimensions of marketplace ministry. But there is more to it than these. Indeed, these miss out on what is at the core of such a ministry. Work should provide more than a context for these forms of ministry. It can be a ministry in its own right. When this is the case, these other forms of ministry that take place around one's work possess more credibility and influence. So the first responsibility of believers in the marketplace is to discern in what ways and by what means their work is itself a divine ministry.

Good examples of this understanding of marketplace ministry include the efforts by businesspeople such as Max De Pree, former CEO of Herman Miller Furniture, or Bill Pollard, present CEO of ServiceMaster, to pattern the goals, values, structures, operations, and ethos of their companies according to a Christian view of people, community, empowerment, and service; and the activities of such professional associations as the Christian Legal Society or the Nurse's Christian Fellowship, who reflect on their workplace responsibilities from a biblical perspective and by this means seek to integrate their work into their faith.

A proper understanding of marketplace ministry begins with a sense of calling. Business consultant and lay author William Diehl (1987) discovered that Christians who have a sense of calling to the marketplace were more spiritually committed, ethically responsible, financially generous, and active in the church than their believing colleagues. But this sense of calling rarely came via a dramatic encounter with God. Mostly it emerged as they followed through on their basic responsibilities, were responsive to circumstances, discerned their gifts and others' needs, and had a growing inner conviction that they were where God wanted them to be.

In tandem with this sense of call comes deepening insight into the way their work forms part of God's ongoing activity and purposes. They may see connections between their work and some of the theological categories used to describe God's work in the world—in creating, providing, revealing, teaching, caring, bringing justice, and transforming (Banks, 1993). They may see reflections in their work of some of the biblical images drawn from the world of human work that are used to portray God at work—as builder, potter, refiner, farmer, winegrower, garment-maker, musician (Banks, 1993).

Often these people receive further light on the divine character of their work by reflecting on stories about marketplace believers—from Joseph to Esther to Aquila and Priscilla—in the biblical writings. Also they may consciously view their work as a service to Christ (Eph. 5:7–9), as linked with the gifts of the Spirit (Exod. 31:1–2), as enabling them to support others (Acts 20:34), and as qualifying them for responsibility in the church (1 Tim. 4:7).

To say that work can and should be a ministry does not mean that all work is equally meaningful, fulfilling, significant, or beneficial. Nor does it mean that it is only our work in the marketplace and church that can be a calling. We also have our family, neighborhood, and civic responsibilities to consider. Our calling and ministry can even include our leisure activities. The particular vocational mix for each person differs, and differs even for the same person at different stages in life; but broadening the way marketplace ministry is understood would make a real contribution to individuals' estimate of what they do and to their impact upon the world around them. Christian education can play a seminal role in instructing and equipping God's people for their various ministries of daily life outside the church, including the marketplace.

ROBERT BANKS

Bibliography. R. Banks, ed. (1993), *Faith Goes to Work: Reflections from the Marketplace;* W. Diehl (1987), *In Search of Faithfulness: Lessons from the Christian Community;* idem (1991), *The Monday Connection: A Spirituality of Competence, Affirmation, and Support in the Workplace;* D. F. Crabtree (1989), *The Empowering Church: How One Congregation Supports Lay People's Ministries in the World;* J. Haughey (1989), *Converting 9 to 5: A Spirituality of Daily Work;* D. Sherman and W. Hendricks (1990), *Your Work Matters to God.*

Maslow, Abraham Harold (1908–70). Humanistic psychologist and founder of the Association for Humanistic Psychology. Born in Brooklyn,

New York, he became a leading theorist and advocate of the human potential movement, the so-called third force that provided an alternative to the dominant psychological theories of behaviorism and psychoanalysis.

He was educated at the City College of New York, Cornell University, and the University of Wisconsin, from where he received his Ph.D. When Brandeis University was established in 1948, he was named the founding chair of that institution's psychology department, a position he held for more than two decades. He also served as president of the American Psychological Association.

Maslow attained notoriety in his seminal work, *Motivation and Personality* (1954). Therein he explored "the hierarchy of potency" in human motivations, observing that "man is a wanting animal"; no sooner is one desire satisfied than another takes its place. But Maslow also noted sense and order in the succession of motives. According to his theory of self-actualization (a term actually coined by Carl Jung), there is a hierarchy of basic instinctual needs common to the human condition. As lower needs are met, the individual proceeds up the ladder to higher needs. At the bottom of the hierarchy are basic physiological needs, followed by the needs for safety and security, love and affection, achievement and self-esteem, and self-actualization. Finally, at the top of the ladder are aesthetic needs, the craving to experience beauty.

Interest in higher levels of motivation led Maslow to the study of self-actualized individuals, who differ from most people in possessing an unusually high degree of psychological health, having marked ability to free themselves from stereotypes, and being able to perceive everyday life realistically and accept it without defensiveness. Such individuals are characterized by an efficient perception of reality, acceptance of self and others, sensing a purpose or mission in life, independent thinking, an empathetic understanding of others, moral and ethical convictions, and creativity. It is such people, Maslow wrote in his *Toward a Psychology of Being* (1962), who appear to have "peak experiences" of joy, insight, or intense awareness.

Having identified the potentiality of humankind, he expounded a school of psychological thought that emphasized values such as trust, openness, risk taking, acceptance of self and others, capacity for joy, and empathy. An understanding of the fully actualized person, therefore, would provide direction for those who were less so. Man is basically good, according to Maslow, and needs only to reach the limits of his potential without appeal to outside sources. In his final work, *The Farther Reaches of Human Nature* (1971), published shortly after his death, he delineated between two types of self-actualizers. Transcendent actualizers tend to be more mystical and contemplative in their insights, whereas nontranscendent actualizers are more pragmatically oriented.

Although much of Maslow's work has been molded into varieties of educational theory, it is not without criticism. His belief in man's intrinsic goodness offers what many consider an inadequate answer to the evil that is prevalent in society. To Maslow, evil is the result of the frustration of man's basic nature by a corrupt society. In denying man's depravity, he saw no conflict between reason and instinct, stating the maxim, "Be healthy, and then you may trust your impulses." By rejecting divine revelation and any notion of dependence on a divine being, Maslow's theories have more forcefully illustrated the distinctions that exist between natural humanism and classical Christian humanism.

DAVID GOUGH

Bibliography. F. G. Goble (1970), *The Third Force: The Psychology of Abraham Maslow;* A. H. Maslow (1970), *Motivation and Personality,* 2nd ed.; idem (1982), *Toward a Psychology of Being,* 2nd ed.; idem (1971), *The Farther Reaches of Human Nature.*

See also HIERARCHY OF NEEDS; HUMANISM, CLASSICAL; JUNG, CARL GUSTAV; LOVE AND BELONGING; SELF-ACTUALIZATION

Mastery Learning. A process of learning that allows students with different histories, abilities, and motivation sufficient time to master a given curriculum (Bloom, 1976). During the middle 1960s Bloom suggested that, while students learn at different rates, all can learn and master the material if given ample time and the right learning conditions (Guskey, 1995). Therefore, learning is not bound by time constraints nor a teaching methodology. What is needed is a strategy that clearly states the intended objectives and allows for each student to spend the needed time to master the material.

If a student is having difficulty learning the curriculum the teacher should allow more time for mastering subject material, or reduce the amount of material to be learned. Bloom claimed that 95 percent of the students could achieve the essential learning objectives as opposed to 20 percent of the students involved in a traditional norm-referenced classroom (Livingston, 1996).

Affect and motivation interact with student learning preferences. When students are provided instructional support sufficient to master the objectives, they (1) feel better about school, self, teacher, and curriculum, (2) learn to persevere on task completion, and (3) are better prepared for subsequent learning tasks (Livingston, 1996).

Another term for mastery learning is *learning for mastery* (LFM). Normally, (1) specific objectives would be selected and clearly communicated to the student, (2) a standard would be established for measuring the mastery of material, and (3) feedback would be given along with individualized instruction prescriptions for achieving the objectives.

A teacher would divide the curriculum into small units. After instruction, the unit would conclude with a form of testing to measure whether the unit objectives have been mastered. If mastery has occurred the same process will be followed for the next unit. Nonmastery of the objectives would result in the teacher evaluating the students' weaknesses that need to be strengthened to allow for mastery of the unit.

Curricular options would be prescribed based on individual student needs. Prescriptions could include, but not be limited to additional lectures, small-group instruction, different reading assignments, multimedia, study guides, and computer-assisted instruction (Fagan, 1996).

Formative evaluation should not be part of the grading process but provide information to the student and teacher about the material that was learned well and what was not. Corrective learning activities are made specific to each item or part of the test so each student works only on skills or concepts that were not mastered. Activities are designed to present the material differently to enrich the mastery experience (Guskey, 1995).

Bloom's position was that mastery was more than learning the basics; it involved enrichment exercises to go beyond to application and higher order thinking regarding the mastery objectives (Livingston, 1996). A teacher should design the learning experience to go beyond the knowledge level. Mastery will occur when the student is able to surpass mere reciting of facts.

There is some doubt as to whether mastery learning is equally appropriate for high-ability and low-ability students. At issue is placing students of different levels in the same class. If the objectives must be mastered for the unit before the class moves to the next unit, what are high-ability students doing while low-ability students are working toward mastery? The teacher is faced with two options: (1) allow high-ability students to move to the next unit (more work for the teacher), or (2) assign enrichment activities that allow the student to achieve higher levels of learning (will students stay motivated?).

Research has generally concluded that mastery learning is effective with both fast and slow learners. Educators involved with mastery learning commonly believe that there is a greater benefit for slow learners. Since the goal is mastery, time to mastery becomes less a factor. The student continues with the unit until the objectives have been achieved.

When mastery learning is done correctly, students should be normally distributed with pretest scores. By the end of the program the distribution should be negatively skewed. Since all have mastered the curriculum most should perform at a high level, resulting in little variation in test scores. The implication is that correlation between initial aptitude and final score should be near zero. Research has revealed that students tend to approach this kind of profile on locally prepared as opposed to standardized tests (Fagan, 1996).

Research conducted by Livingston, involving graduate students, studied whether under favorable conditions of mastery learning, differences in faster and slower learners would decrease over successive units. Results of the study revealed there was no change over time. The differences remained the same at the start of each unit. Although the findings did not support smaller variances, the study did reveal that mastery learning is an effective approach to teaching to achieve a course's objectives. Mastery learning can produce a positive attitude toward the course, subject matter, and teacher. Students rated the course and instructional procedures as one of the top courses in their studies (Livingston, 1996). Additional research has revealed similar findings for grade school students.

Teachers desiring to assist all their students to be successful in learning can find that mastery learning offers a means by which this goal can be accomplished. Mastery learning can generally be implemented with only minor changes to teachers' methods. This approach does not make teaching easier but it does allow for more students being helped in the learning process.

GARY WALLER

Bibliography. B. S. Bloom (1976), *Human Characteristics and School Learning;* K. S. Bull (1996), *Historical Encyclopedia of School Psychology* pp. 201–2; T. R. Guskey, P. Passaro, and W. Wheeler (1995), *Teaching Exceptional Children;* J. A. Livingston and J. R. Gentile, *The Journal of Educational Research* 90, no. 2 (1996): 67–74.

Maturation. *See* Aging, Ageism.

McGuffey Readers. To many, William Holmes McGuffey (1800–1873) is the most important person in the history of American public school education—yes, "THE schoolmaster of the nation."

At his death, the National Education Association passed this resolution:

In the death of William H. McGuffey, late Professor of Moral Philosophy in the University of Virginia, this association feels that they have lost one of the great lights of the profession whose life was a lesson full of instruction; an example and model to American teachers.

His labors in the cause of education, extending over a period of half a century, in several offices as teacher of common schools, college professor and college president, and as author of textbooks; his almost unparalleled industry; his power in the lecture room; his influence upon his pupils and community; his care for the public interests of education; his lofty devotion to duty; his conscientious Christian character—all these have made him one of the noblest ornaments of our profession in this age, and entitle him to the grateful remembrance of this Association and of the teachers of America. (Elmira, New York, August 7, 1873).

The New England Primer of the eighteenth century and the *McGuffey Readers* of the nineteenth century were the most widely read and best known in the history of American education. Henry Steele Commager said of the Readers: "They played an important part in American education, and helped to shape that elusive thing we call the American character" (Commager, 1962).

Robert Wood Lynn (1973), an important historian of religious education, contended that they were "more than a textbook; they were a portable school for the new priests of the republic." They "embodied a vision of piety, justice and the commonwealth, a form of *patriotic piety* which still appeals to some folk living amidst our current *crisis of loyalty*" (10, 23).

Of the six editions of *McGuffey's Reader*, William Holmes McGuffey compiled and edited the first four. He was not responsible for any edition beyond that of 1857. "By 1879, the theistic, Calvinistic worldview so dominant in the first editions had disappeared, and the prominent values of salvation, righteousness, and piety were entirely missing. All that remained were lessons affirming the morality and life-styles of the emerging middle and those cultural beliefs, attitudes, and values that undergird American civil religion" (Westerhoff, 1978, 19).

WARREN S. BENSON

Bibliography. H. S. Commager (1962), *The Commonwealth of Learning*; R. W. Lynn (1973), *Religious Education*; J. H. Westerhoff III (1978), *McGuffey and His Readers: Piety, Morality and Education in Nineteenth-Century America*.

Meaningfulness. The level of significance that persons may assign to things such as Bible study. The level of meaningfulness of any specific passage of Scripture will depend on various factors, such as Bible study skills, previous life experiences, the views of significant others, and the perceived relevance of the passage to current issues in life. Growing people to maturity in Christ requires that instruction must make the Christian faith meaningful to students' lives.

Meaning is usually the domain of semantics. Meaning can be derived from the basic elements of a word or from the best examples of a concept. Communication between two people begins with a shared language. Language is based on an arbitrary but common understanding of symbols and their referents. Different meanings can occur due to varying word orders and the context in which the language is used.

Meaning is also determined by one's view of interpretation. God chose to communicate using human language in order to relay meaning. Scriptural truth is not dependent upon human interpretation of it, but the purpose of Scripture is to communicate meaning relevant to the experience of human beings. Three different but interactive components of meaning are envisioned when Scripture speaks of meaningful faith.

The cognitive aspect (*notitia*) reminds instructors that there is an element of knowledge to meaningful faith. There is specific biblical content to be understood and believed (1 Thess. 4:14).

Meaningful faith also demands an active emotional embrace (*assensus*). This relational aspect involves capturing the believer's heart passion. One assents to the truthfulness of the object of faith and to having one's heart controlled by him. Consequential faith believes in (*pisteuo eis*) Jesus. This linguistic construction is unique to the New Testament. Downs (1994) suggests that this implies a different kind of belief from the Hellenistic notion that separated belief from commitment.

The crowning element of making Christianity meaningful translates into lifestyle. True faith causes people to volitionally act (*fiducia*) on that which they know and to which they have committed. Conscience, purpose, and determination are involved. The litmus test for the significance of one's faith is its being expressed by good works and obedience (Eph. 2:8–10). Faith that justifies must have some aspect of this desire for obedience resident within it (James 2:26).

Orthodox teachers can glean and apply the best technical insights about teaching and age appropriateness and still miss the mark. To enhance meaningful Christianity, personal contact and relationship are ultimately more powerful than good organization and formal techniques. The discipline of prayer and the power of the Holy Spirit must be invoked or it is likely that little of permanent, meaningful value will be accomplished.

The work of Eric Klinger (1978) shows the importance of meaningfulness for people's lives. People will be motivated to pursue things that are emotionally important to them. Such incentives include personal compassion for others, commitment to a purpose greater than self, and serving others. These inducements are best found only in the Christian faith.

The prayer for illumination is asking the Holy Spirit to open our eyes to the meaning of the Bible passage we are studying. It is God's book and he provides the "eyes" to see and "ears" to hear what God knows will be meaningful to us.

JAMES A. DAVIES AND ROBERT J. RADCLIFFE

Bibliography. R. Beechick (1982), *A Biblical Psychology of Learning;* R. W. Pazmiño (1997), *Foundational Issues in Christian Education;* J. Wilhoit (1991), *Christian Education and the Search for Meaning.*

Mears, Henrietta Cornelia (1890–1963). Henrietta Mears has been acclaimed by many as one of the most influential Christian female leaders and educators of the twentieth century. As a pioneer of the contemporary evangelical movement, her example of personal evangelism and vision for global mission and leadership inspired many who were to follow. The modern Sunday school and its curriculum have been revolutionized by her biblically and educationally sound approach and methods.

Born in Fargo, North Dakota, she was tutored in the Christian faith by her mother, from whom she learned a disciplined devotional life and an effective presentation of the gospel. Trained as a teacher, she received her bachelor's degree from the University of Minnesota in 1913. From this time until 1928 she taught and administrated in Minnesota public high schools, while also volunteering leadership among Baptist Sunday schools. The First Presbyterian Church of Hollywood, California, then persuaded her to become director of Christian education, a role in which she was to serve for the next thirty-five years. Under her direction, the Sunday school grew from 450 to over 4,000 in only two and one-half years and eventually trained tens of thousands of young people in the Scriptures. Dissatisfied with the materials being used, she wrote closely graded lessons for all levels which were sought by churches nationwide. To meet this demand, she founded Gospel Light Publications along with Cyrus Nelson in 1933. Her materials evidenced strong continuity between lessons and a biblical focus, and emphasized the student's personal commitment and life application. These productions maintained a high quality, were attractive, and included pictures.

"Teacher," as her students called her, was noted for her Sunday school teacher training program and development of leadership from the College Department. Her avowed purpose was to train Christian world leaders for the next generation. She personally led thousands of young people to faith in Christ and sent over four hundred into vocational ministries around the world. Convinced of the spiritual and educational power of the Christian camp, she founded Forest Home Christian Conference Center in southern California in 1938. Spiritual revivals occurred there as a result of the College Briefing Conferences of 1947 and 1949. These events had a major impact on a number of parachurch and missions organizations which were then in their formative stages. Evangelist Billy Graham; Jim Rayburn, founder of *Young Life;* and Bill Bright, founder of *Campus Crusade for Christ;* among others, attest to her critical impact on their lives and ministries. A co-founder of the National Sunday School Association, she lectured widely on behalf of the Sunday school movement as one who raised that institution to a new level. In recognition of her leadership in Christian education, she was awarded an honorary Doctor of Humanities degree by Bob Jones University in 1949. She founded GLINT (Gospel Literature International) in 1961 to translate Gospel Light literature, being convinced of the urgency of international missions and world evangelization. She continued in vital ministry until her death.

The core values of her philosophy of education were to honor Christ and to remain faithful to the Scriptures. While her central purpose never changed, she believed methods should change to meet contemporary needs. Her teaching and curriculum writing combined sound educational and human development theory with biblically derived principles for conducting Christian education and training. Her disciplined life, hard work, vision, enthusiastic attitude, and love for students made her a compelling model and mentor. She had a unique ability both to see leadership potential and to challenge students to develop it. Her most enduring writing is *What the Bible is All About (1966),* a survey of the whole of Scripture taken from one year of her high school lessons. Among her greatest contributions to the field were the enduring impact she had on the lives of others, the ongoing ministries she helped to found, and her innovative approach to Sunday school curriculum.

RICHARD LEYDA

Bibliography. E. O. Roe, ed. (1990), *Dream Big: The Henrietta Mears Story.*

Measurement and Christian Education. Measurement refers to differentiating people, constructs, or objects using labels, ratings, or numbers. Measurement often involves testing, surveys, systematic observation, or interviews. Measurement can be used in Christian education to assess people prior to teaching to determine individual needs and desires, readiness for instruction, and prior levels of understanding or skills in a given area (Tamminen and Ratcliff, 1992). The results of Christian education activities may also be measured, and sometimes results are compared with entry-level measurements to determine if learning has occurred. Measurement is also an important component of research design in Christian education. Measurement may be used in the assessment of individual learners, a group, a program, a church, or even an entire denomination.

Measurement is integrally related to objectives and application of learning theory. Before assessment of a program can begin, for example, goals and purposes must be determined since these reveal what is to be measured. In research, implicit or explicit theories about a phenomenon influence the design of measurement instruments. Theories and objectives specify what is important for a given context or purpose and thus what is to be measured.

Two important concepts in measurement are reliability and validity (Starks and Ratcliff, 1988). The first of these involves the consistency with which an instrument measures something. For example, if a measure of spiritual maturity was given to an individual on three successive days, producing very different results on each occasion, the instrument would not be considered trustworthy because it was not consistent. Yet even if a test produces consistent results, and is thus reliable, that does not assure that it is measuring what it was intended; it is not necessarily valid. A test that measures attitudes about music may produce consistent results, and therefore be reliable, yet if the goal of that measurement is to determine how much a person has learned in a lesson on Amos, the test would not be valid for assessing that goal.

As noted earlier, Christian educators can use measurement to determine if their students have learned what was intended, whether results are determined formally with a paper-and-pencil test, or informally through verbal discussion or questions and answers (Ferro, 1995). When the desired outcomes do not occur, this suggests that either students did not possess prerequisite abilities prior to instruction, instruction was not sufficient or appropriate, or there were problems with the measuring instrument, such as inappropriate phrasing of questions (Stych, 1994b).

Measurement is also important in determining preexisting characteristics of groups that may influence what should occur in churches and other Christian education contexts. Inventories of spiritual gifts, for example, may indicate the roles and offices individuals can best fulfill in a Christian organization. Scales of spiritual development might reveal areas of weakness that need more attention in Christian education programs, and inform theories of spiritual growth. Surveys of church attenders may reveal preferences and needs that are inadequately being met (Engel, 1991). It is important that instruments are developed and validated in a manner that ensures trustworthiness (for example, see Benson and Clark, 1982).

DONALD E. RATCLIFF

Bibliography. H. E. Barnett, *Christian Education Journal* 4 (1983): 63–75; J. Benson and F. Clark, *The American Journal of Occupational Therapy* 36 (1982): 789–800; J. F. Engel (1991), *Handbook of Youth Ministry;* T. Ferro (1995), *Handbook of Family Religious Education;* D. Sappington and F. Wilson, *Christian Education Journal* 12 (1992): 46–68; D. Starks and D. Ratcliff, (1988), *Handbook of Preschool Religious Education;* B. E. Stych, *Christian Education Journal* 14 (1994a): 9–18; B. E. Stych, *Christian Education Journal* 14 (1994b): 36–45; K. Tamminen and D. Ratcliff (1992), *Handbook of Children's Religious Education.*

Media. Tools of communication that, when used educationally, can enhance the achievement of instructional objectives. In recent years primary classroom media have included printed materials, video and audio recordings, computers, overhead projectors, films, and filmstrips.

The original word in the Latin, from which the English is derived, means "middle." Forms of media constitute the link between the sender and the receiver of a message. As technology expands in future years the church, like society at large, may be tempted to overemphasize the link or the middle ground of communication at the expense of the message itself. But it is the message of Scripture—literally, the gospel or "good news"—that is central to Christianity, not the choice of media itself. As exciting as technological advances are and will be, they are to be subordinated by Christian educators to the message of Jesus Christ and Christian orthodoxy. Media must be held firmly in place as a means to an intimate relationship with the loving and holy God, the unqualified end.

Brisk advances in coming years between the television and computer and the increase of sophisticated and advanced audio-visual resources will likely constitute the coming waves of technological advance in educational media. But other forms of relatively unsophisticated media presentation will continue to be utilized effectively—homemade visuals and audiovisuals, story books, overhead projectors, puppets, music, symbols, and so on. Sophisticated and unsophisticated means of communication will always work concomitantly to play an important role in Christian education.

The challenge ahead for the religious educator will be to adapt the older methods for constant and ongoing use in the church and stay apprised of the new trends in order to effectively appeal to a culture that is experiencing rapid technological advance.

MATT FRIEDEMAN

Medieval Education. Medieval education began with the decline of the early church catechumenate at the end of the fourth century and ended with the birth of the Reformation in the sixteenth century.

Baptism, Confession, and Worship Rituals. The ancient catechumenate practices faded as the emergence of infant baptism became common, due in part to the legalization of Christianity. The rise of infant baptism along with the decline of the catechumenate brought about the need for godparents who, along with parents, were responsible for teaching the faith.

Because parents, godparents, and clergy were usually poorly educated, formal teaching centered on the Apostles' Creed, the Lord's Prayer, and the Ten Commandments, along with some moral instruction. Since bishops were responsible for Christian indoctrination, the priests instructed the people from the pulpit and admonished parents to instruct children in the home. Catechetical manuals, written during the medieval period, assisted clergy with religious instruction. The *Elucidarium*, an anonymous eleventh-century work, provided a simplified and systematic explanation of church doctrine. The *ABC des simples gens*, a fourteenth-century work of Jean de Gerson, outlined church teachings and practices in the vernacular for "simple folk."

The church practice of confession served as another avenue of Christian indoctrination. Since it was determined that only priests could absolve sin, the Fourth Lateran Council required annual confession for church members. Along with preaching, priests were appointed to hear confessions, prescribe penances, and instruct individuals on their Christian responsibilities.

As Christianity spread, popular practices of piety such as holy days, processions, wayside shrines, pilgrimages, and adoration of saints became pervasive formative forces of religious culture. Processions and passion plays, along with other forms of religious drama, were significant means of religious education. In northern Europe, stained glass windows in churches displayed biblical scenes, and carved illustrations from the Old Testament and the life of Christ could be found in Romanesque churches and Gothic cathedrals. Medieval visual art communicated the Christian faith through images and was often referred to as the "Bible of the poor."

Monasticism. The monasteries, schools of asceticism and Christian life which emerged during the Middle Ages, served to preserve and develop catechesis. Along with monks and clerics, monasteries instructed children of nobility and of the poor. Monastic instruction, guided by moral and religious purposes, included reading, writing, arithmetic, singing, and the elements of Christian doctrine.

Monasticism originated in the East and implanted itself in the West during the fourth century. Monastic training in the East was ascetic and moral while the focus was spiritual rather than intellectual. Monasteries in the West emphasized the written word and, due to the threat of barbarism, insisted that every monk and nun be able to read and be devoted to Scripture. The monastic schools had two departments, one for interns, those intending to be monks, and another for externs, those intending to return to secular life upon completion of their education.

St. Benedict founded the famous monastery of Monte Cassino in A.D. 529, known for adapting monasticism to the Western mentality. The Rule of St. Benedict, which emphasized poverty, chastity, and obedience, also included guidelines for reading and for educating children. The Benedictine monastery stressed the value of labor, which allowed the Benedictines to become teachers of crafts and agriculture as well as spiritual guides. St. Benedict emphasized Christian practice more than theory and literature. Cassiodorus, in the sixth century, provided the first Benedictine scholarly contribution in his *Institutions*, which included the study of Christian theology, history, and liberal arts.

Religious orders were common and influential during the Middle Ages. "Canons Regular," communities of clerics leading a common life, existed throughout Europe and engaged in the education of secular students as well as clergy. Although neither the thirteenth-century Franciscans nor the Dominicans were established for educational purposes, both advanced the cause of learning through their support and use of schools.

Cathedral Schools and Religious Movements. Cathedral schools, located in each cathedral seat and in smaller communities as well, trained priests but were intended to provide education for all people in the community. Along with teaching the facts of the Christian religion, instruction included grammar, rhetoric, dialectic, music, arithmetic, geometry, and astronomy. Cathedral schools were both places of worship and social gathering places for young people. Other church schools included song schools, parish schools, and chantry schools.

Toward the end of the eighth century, Charlemagne, also known as Charles the Great, influenced the improvement of education in Western Europe by establishing schools in every monastery or bishopric, and by decreeing the use of the vernacular by priests, making prayer and Scripture accessible to common people. Alcuin of York was chosen by Charlemagne to lead his palace school. Alcuin employed new teaching methods which included positive motivation, simplification of complex concepts, valuing individual gifts, and conversation. Alcuin promoted educational reform through his students such as Charlemagne and Rabanus Maurus (776–856).

Religious movements such as the Friends of God and the Brethren of the Common Life promoted a pious religion of the heart and made religious instruction a high priority. These groups sought to educate school boys of common people and contributed to the gradual transition from medieval ecclesiasticism to scholasticism. Martin Luther was a student of the Brethren of the Common Life.

Scholasticism. The scholastic movement emerged via church leaders who attempted to synthesize Christian theology and secular philosophy by combining Aristotle's deductive dialectic with the authoritarian theology of the Catholic Church. The scholastic movement withstood opposition because it appealed to the intellectual interests of the time. Although scholastic philosophers displayed little concern for the education of common people, scholasticism influenced the development of medieval universities.

Johannes Scotus Erigena (815–877) is considered the "first scholastic." Peter Abelard (1079–1142) wrote *Sic et non*, which included questions regarding beliefs and dogmas of the church. Abelard accepted only matters of faith that were confirmed by reason, and encouraged his students to think for themselves through a process of questioning and doubt. Thomas Aquinas (1225–74), the leading scholastic thinker, developed the basic doctrinal framework of the Catholic Church through his work *Summa Theologica*, a masterpiece in the art of dialectics. The epistemology of Aquinas embraced both faith and reason while Aquinas held that faith is always superior.

Medieval Universities. Cathedral schools and scholasticism were contributing factors to the development of the medieval universities that emerged during the twelfth century. The popular teaching of scholastic scholar Peter Abelard at the cathedral school of Notre Dame facilitated the establishment of the University of Paris. During the twelfth century, the term *university* signified a school-related corporation which included a society of students and masters. Universities were organized according to a guild system in which the corporations were formed by groups of craftsmen, monks, or cathedral chapters. Medieval universities were influential centers of culture and education, giving shape to the modern university system.

BEVERLY JOHNSON-MILLER

Bibliography. P. J. Marique (1924), *History of Christian Education;* H. L. Marrou (1956), *A History of Education in Antiquity;* J. E. Reed and R. Prevost, (1993), *A History of Christian Education.*

See also AQUINAS, THOMAS; MONASTICISM; SCHOLASTICISM

Meditation. Reflection upon, pondering, thinking about. In meditation one meets with God and learns what God wants of his people.

Though meditation is commonly associated with Eastern religions, it is a Christian practice advocated in Scripture. Foster (1978) notes that in Eastern forms of meditation the emphasis is on detachment from the world, from oneself, and from God; however, Christian meditation involves attachment, in which there is "detachment from the confusion around us in order to have a richer attachment to God and other human be-

ings" (15). Though Christian meditation has come to involve many practices, such as clearing and centering of one's mind and developing concentration through focusing on some aspect of creation, the practice of meditation in a biblical context, primarily in the psalms, centers on God (Ps. 63:6), the law of the Lord (Pss. 1:2; 119:148), and the works of God (Ps. 77:12). Though there is no mention of the term in the New Testament, the spiritual practice of meditation is implied, as in Paul's admonition in Philippians 4:8 to "think about" excellent and praiseworthy things and in Jesus' command in Matthew 28:20 to teach new disciples "to obey everything I have commanded you" because the practice of obedience necessitates the discipline of meditation.

In the Psalms meditation is primarily concerned with the intentional, directed engagement of the Word of God as the means for coming into God's presence. The psalmist declared one blessed whose "delight is in the law of the LORD" and who meditates on it day and night" (Ps. 1:2). The purpose of meditation on God's Word is described in Joshua 1:8 as an intentional focusing on the will of God in order to do it. Meditation is not passive, but it requires one to be actively engaged in listening to God, opening oneself to the will of God as revealed in Scripture, reflecting on it, permitting it to become the basis for judging one's own character and actions and to lead to decisions regarding living out the Christian life. Meditation is a focusing on Scripture for internalizing and personalizing the will of God in one's own life, for one's own discipleship and spiritual growth, rather than a preparation for preaching or teaching. Such a focus often necessitates dwelling on Scripture with one's whole being—not merely on the meaning of the text, but on its mood, in order to make it present to oneself. This requires reading Scripture slowly, with intentionality and deliberateness, so that when a passage makes an impression the reader is prepared to stop in order to reflect on and ponder it. So vital is such meditation that Bonhoeffer remarked that "every day in which I do not penetrate more deeply into the knowledge of God's Word in Holy Scripture is a lost day for me" (1986, 30). Therefore, meditation takes seriously the role of Scripture as being "useful for teaching, rebuking, for correcting and training in righteousness" (2 Tim. 3:16). Often the discipline of prayer accompanies effective meditation. Willard (1988) notes that "our prayer as we study meditatively is always that God would meet with us and speak specifically to us, for ultimately the Word of God is God speaking" (177).

The spiritual discipline of meditation also has implications for Christian formation and educational practice. Fundamental to Christian growth is knowing Scripture, yet, as Downs (1994) notes, "there is an increasing deemphasis on Bible teaching in the educational programs of our churches, with growing emphasis on meeting felt needs" (135). Christian education in holding Scripture as foundational for Christian development must foster the practice of meditating on Scripture in order for persons to know, understand, and obey Scripture so that their living is in accordance with God's will. Scripture must not merely be transmitted as content to be learned, but it needs to be recognized as living and dynamic (Heb. 4:12), as something on which Christian growth is dependent. Therefore, the practice of meditation is essential in educating persons for discipleship so that the Word of God may be integral to spiritual growth. Persons are only able to grow spiritually as they know and live the Word of God.

ROLAND G. KUHL

Bibliography. D. Bonhoeffer (1986), *Meditating on the Word;* P. G. Downs (1994), *Teaching for Spiritual Growth;* A. Brooke, *Learning and Teaching Christian Meditation;* R. J. Foster (1978), *Celebration of Discipline;* M. T. Kelsey, *The Other Side of Silence: A Guide to Christian Meditation;* D. Willard (1988), *The Spirit of the Disciplines.*

See also CRITICAL REFLECTION; SOLITUDE

Meeting. *See* Conference.

Melancholy. *See* Depression.

Melanchthon, Philip (1497–1560). Lutheran Reformer and theologian. Born in Bretten, Baden, he altered his family name, Schwarzerd (meaning "black earth"), to its Greek form, Melanchthon. He is best remembered as the successor to Martin Luther and the systematizer of Lutheran theology during the Reformation. Small of stature and unimposing in speech, by external appearances Melanchthon was the antithesis of Luther.

Educated at Heidelberg and Tübingen, where he was trained in the classical languages and Hebrew, he was named the professor of Greek at Wittenberg at the age of twenty-one. Less than a year later, Luther nailed the Ninety-Five Theses to the church door. Greatly influenced by Erasmus, Melanchthon found humanism and Luther's thought compatible and was soon won over to the evangelical cause.

In 1521, under Luther's influence, he composed a short but important work in Latin on the theology of the Wittenberg reformers entitled *Loci Communes Rerum Theologicarum* ("Common theology"), the first theological treatise of the Reformation. Here Melanchthon addressed "the most common topics of theological science" in an effort to "incite people to the Scriptures."

Melanchthon is credited with establishing the German school and university system, and has been called *Praeceptor Germaniae* ("Germany's Principle Teacher"). When Charles V, the emperor of the Holy Roman Empire, convened the Diet of Augsburg in 1530 in an attempt to unite his people and defend his territory from the impending danger of Turkish invasion, he charged the Lutheran nobility to explain their religious convictions. Melanchthon was called on to draft a common confession of Lutheran doctrine. The resulting document, the Augsburg Confession, was presented to Charles V on June 25, 1530, and became the official creed of the Lutheran Church.

In 1537 Melanchthon wrote *Treatise on the Power of the Papacy,* which became a part of Luther's Schmalkaldic Articles. Following the death of Luther in 1546, he translated, and somewhat modified, the Augsburg Confession into Greek and presented it to the patriarch of Constantinople. Interpreted by some Lutherans as a corrupt perversion of the original Confession, it resulted in division rather than the unity Melanchthon had hoped to create. His desire for peace within Christendom resulted in charges of compromise and landed him in dogmatic controversies with his former allies. His humanist training never left him, and even in his later years he sought to repair the breech between Roman Catholicism and Protestantism. Less dogmatic and assertive than Luther, he died amidst charges of compromising Lutheran doctrine.

DAVID GOUGH

Bibliography. C. L. Manschreck (1958), *Melanchthon: The Quiet Reformer.*

See also ERASMUS, DESIDERIUS; HUMANISM, CHRISTIAN; LUTHER, MARTIN; REFORMATION, THE

Memorization. In Deuteronomy, God directs the Hebrews to keep his commands upon their hearts (Deut. 6:6). Although memory is generally thought of as an intellectual function, research bears out the Bible's assertion that meaningful memories have an emotional connection. We will remember a fact or concept if it is indeed "upon our hearts." A lesson with personal relevance will be retained long after algebraic formulas and the capitals of foreign nations have been forgotten. Retention also escalates when more than one physical sense is actively involved.

Factors like repetition, multisensory input, and personal relevance affect the depth at which a memory will ultimately be stored. The initial storage level is the sensory stage. The brain sifts and evaluates input and selects certain memories for storage. Useful input goes into short-term memory storage, where it can be kept handy for current purposes. If a short-term memory receives enough reinforcement, it may be passed along to long-term memory storage. Long-term material usually has personal relevance. Long-term memories can seemingly be "forgotten" but can be retrieved by the trigger of circumstances similar to those surrounding the making of the memory. The smell of cookies baking can revive the memory of a long-forgotten Christmas and bring it into sharp focus.

What we have learned about memory has implications for education. One of the goals of Christian education is that learners know and apply the Word of God. By relating lessons to everyday experience, teachers can push Scripture memorization and comprehension from the limits of short-term storage into the long-term level. To facilitate Scripture memorization and understanding, verses for memorization should be correlated to lessons. Verses should be age-appropriate in content, length, and vocabulary. Because the ability to memorize is sharpest in childhood, these years are a critical time to learn Scripture. Educators must be careful that the urgency to memorize verses is not served at the expense of comprehension. Understanding can easily be checked by asking a learner to rephrase a verse using her or his own vocabulary. Some educators employ mnemonic devices such as symbolic images, music, or games.

The value of Bible memorization is indisputable. What must be reconsidered in the light of research and Scripture itself is the method by which it can best be taught. To teach Bible truth in real-life application encourages greater retention than rote memorization of verses unrelated to further study.

Any form of active learning increases the ability to remember. An effective method for Scripture memorization is drama. By relating Scripture to simulated everyday experience, teachers increase the likelihood that similar real-life occurrences will trigger memories of the Scripture lesson. Another powerful aid to memorization is storytelling, which places a piece of information into a sequence of facts or events from which it can be easily retrieved.

By monitoring brain activity during sleep, researchers have discovered that the brain uses rest periods to edit and sort memories. Teachers can respond to this finding by preparing lesson schedules with varied activities that provide brain "rest stops."

ROBERT J. CHOUN

Bibliography. D. G. Benner, ed. (1985), *Baker Encyclopedia of Psychology;* R. J. Choun and M. S. Lawson (1993), *The Complete Handbook of Children's Ministry;* R. E. Clark, J. Brubaker, and R. B. Zuck (1975, 1986), *Childhood Education in the Church;* I. Cully and K. B. Cully, eds. (1990), *Harper's Encyclopedia of Religious Education;* R. Slywester (1995), *A Celebration of Neurons: An Educator's Guide to the Human Brain;* E. Towns (1993), *Town's Sunday School Encyclopedia.*

Memory. Memory is fundamental to all of life. The encoding, storage, and retrieval of skills, behaviors, and pieces of information are marvelous attributes of our brain. Compared to computers, any human brain is able to exceed them in speed and number of activities. Human memory is durable, but elusive. Memory is affected by mood (one aspect of emotion), the context or environment in which the memory was formed, and the environment in which the attempt to recall is made. Loss of memory is called amnesia.

Memory may be grouped into three broad categories: active, short-term, and long-term. Active memory provides recall for day-to-day activities. Short-term memory provides recall of recent events. Being able to remember a Bible verse until class is over, and forgetting it thereafter, demonstrates how short-term memory needs to become long-term memory. Bible verses that are memorized may not become a part of long-term memory. It is not a foregone conclusion.

Some of the things that help to place something in long-term memory are individual desire, a person's age, and the frequency of rehearsal. Memory cues are most effective when the individual creates them and when encoding is specific. As events become older, and rehearsal of them declines, our memory of them decays. Some persons who have some type of change in their mental processes often find long-term memories reappearing after years of absence. Short-term memory may not be very active at all with these types of people.

There should be a distinction between recall and recognition, with the latter being easier. There is a discrimination between explicit (conscious) and implicit (unconscious) memory as well as procedural and declarative knowledge.

The role of memory in Christian education has often been limited to certain things, such as Scripture verses, the order of Bible books, names of people, and events of Scripture. The term *rote* has often been used with the term *memory* to indicate a wooden or slavish adherence to text without understanding. Memorization does not have to be without understanding, but if it is, memory alone is a poor method of teaching.

Various ways of memorizing have been invented to help people remember important things. Teachers have employed such devices to help their students remember facts that are important. The use of drills and other repetitive teaching activities should be matched with activities that help students understand the information being memorized.

ROBERT J. RADCLIFFE

Bibliography. D. A. Norman, ed. (1970), *Models of Human Memory.*

See also MNEMONIC DEVICES

Memory Cues. *See* Chunking.

Men's Ministry. Men deserve leadership that will call out their spiritual gifts to minister in the world as well as within church activities. Scripture provides support for men's ministry: "Iron sharpens iron, so one man sharpens another" (Prov. 27:17 NASB). "Husbands, love your wives, and do not be embittered against them" (Col. 3:19 NASB).

Lay ministry, including the men's movement, has an impressive heritage. As early as 1226, Francis of Assisi organized the Franciscans, originally an order of the laity. In the fourteenth century the Lollards arose in England, insisting that laypersons have the right to preach and teach, and stressing the priesthood of the believer. This trend has strong roots in the Reformation as well. Perhaps the strongest movements of the sixteenth century were the Anabaptists or Mennonites. Because of their strong convictions about the laity, they rejected an official clergy. For two centuries they did not have an institution for training preachers. Much of the impetus for lay ministry in the twentieth century grew out of the leadership of John Mott, who popularized the watchword "the evangelization of the world in our generation." Marshall Hudson began the Baraca Sunday school movement, comprised initially of men, in Syracuse, New York, in 1890. More recently, Elton Trueblood focused on lay ministry, especially in his book *Your Other Vocation* (1952).

Most historians of the movement point toward the Layman's Missionary Movement as the precursor of men's ministry in the twentieth century. Begun in 1906 on the one hundredth anniversary of the famous Williams College "Haystack Prayer Meeting," it combined a new interest in men's self-consciousness about religion with a zeal for foreign missions.

Unmistakably, the men's movement of the 1990s has been fueled by the remarkable rise of Promise Keepers. Promise Keepers describes itself as a "Christ-centered ministry dedicated to uniting men through vital relationships to become godly influences in their world." Men pledge to follow seven promises connected to their relationship to Jesus Christ, other men, their wives and children, and persons of other races and denominations. Several hundred thousand men gathered on the Washington mall on October 4, 1997, to hear challenging messages and engage in protracted prayers of repentance. This movement has spawned both denominational and parachurch imitations. Several women's groups have begun that support their "promise keeper husbands." A number of denominations have renewed their attention toward men's ministries.

Men's ministry has followed a version of men's service clubs with a meal and speaker on a week-

night. A growing number of churches have established units for disaster relief, church building, and special support groups in the church and community. Some men have dedicated themselves to working with boys and have participated in lay-led revivals. The lay renewal movement that began in the 1970s was spearheaded by Christian men. Some churches have experimented with small group Bible studies, prayer groups, men's retreats, and monthly or weekly luncheons primarily for men. Many men participate in men's prayer breakfasts and church sports teams. Another popular strategy is accountability groups that help men keep their spiritual edge.

Several parachurch organizations have historically focused on men, such as the Gideons, a worldwide Bible distribution organization, and the Navigators, which began as a ministry to servicemen on ships in the Western Pacific during World War II.

As men's ministry moves into the twenty-first century, several relevant questions deserve attention: First, what model should Christian men emulate—warrior, paternal caretaker, servant-leader, pastor's helper, or lay Christian in the world? Second, how can Christian men find meaningful ministry in the church? Third, what is the role of so-called amateur Christians in today's church, which is increasingly dominated by clergy? Fourth, can men find meaningful Christian service in teaching small children in the Sunday school, as well as in men-only activities? Fifth, does a church men's ministry depend on faith stirred in a stadium event to maintain its momentum? Sixth, is men's ministry a discipleship approach, a missionary support and educational emphasis, an activist group, or a parachurch organization? Finally, can men's ministry establish links with other historical men's/lay movements?

JIM WALTER

Bibliography. J. Carter (1996), *Living Faith;* H. Kraemer (1958), *A Theology of the Laity;* S. C. Neill and H. R. Weber, eds. (1963), *The Layman in Christian History;* E. Trueblood (1952), *Your Other Vocation.*

Mentoring. The term is first seen in ancient classical Greek literature in Homer's epic, the *Odyssey.* In this story, Ulysses asks a wise man by the name of Mentor to oversee the administration of his household, especially his son Telemachus, while he is away fighting in the Trojan War. The relationship between Mentor and Telemachus becomes a lasting bond. It is interesting to note that at times the goddess Athena inhabits Mentor in order to provide Telemachus with wise counsel and advice. In this capacity then, the concept of a mentor-protégé relationship is gender-inclusive. Mentor guides Telemachus in his journey to be reunited with his father. He helps him find a ship, accompanies him on the first leg of his journey, and then departs until the end of the story, when he returns to help Telemachus, his father, and his grandfather connect in family heritage and return home together.

It would seem from this story that mentoring has something to do with the maturation process, helping a young man or woman through the perilous journey toward adulthood. A mentor is one who helps shape the character and identity of the child and protects her or him during the journey. Indeed, the Latin term for protégé literally means "to protect." The mentor serves to guide, nurture, protect, and facilitate the learning of one under her or his tutelage.

To many, mentoring is closely aligned with discipleship. Although similar in many ways, there are some important differences between the two. Discipleship is concerned with the quality of relationship which exists between the new believer and the Lord. It is focused on character development, since out of one's character behavior emanates. It is, in essence, a spiritual dimension of development. Mentoring, on the other hand, is more global in nature. It deals with training in character but also concerns itself with issues related to vocational preparation (i.e., apprenticeship), developing healthy interpersonal relationships, fostering life skills, systematic academic training, and values formation. Mentoring is preparing someone for life in its multifaceted dimensions.

The Bible speaks of mentoring relations in both the Old and New Testaments. Howard and William Hendricks (1995), in their book *As Iron Sharpens Iron*, provide an excellent overview of these relationships (180–81).

In the Old Testament. Jethro and Moses (Exod. 18): Jethro taught his son-in-law the invaluable lesson of delegation. Moses and Joshua (Deut. 31:18–29): Moses prepared Joshua to lead Israel into Canaan. Moses and Caleb (Num. 13; 14:6–9; 34:16–19; Josh. 14:6–15): It appears that Moses groomed Caleb for leadership, and inspired in him an unswerving faith in the Lord's promises. Samuel and Saul (1 Sam. 9–15): Samuel tried to shape Saul's character as king. Even when Saul rebelled against the Lord, Samuel kept challenging him to repent and return to God. Samuel and David (1 Sam. 16; 19:18–24): Samuel anointed David as king and gave him refuge from Saul's murderous plots. Jonathan and David (1 Sam. 18:11–4): An outstanding example of peer mentoring, Jonathan and David remained loyal to each other during the troubled days of Saul's declining reign. Elijah and Elisha (1 Kings 19:16–21; 2 Kings 2:1–16): The prophet Elijah recruited his successor Elisha and apparently tutored him in the ways of the Lord while Elisha ministered to Elijah's needs. Jehoiada and Joash (2 Chron. 24:1–25): The priest Jehoiada helped Joash, who

came to the throne of Judah when he was only seven years old, learn to rule according to godly principles. Unfortunately, Joash turned away from the Lord after his mentor died.

In the New Testament. Barnabas and Paul (Acts 4:36–37; 9:26–30; 11:22–30): Barnabas opened the way for Paul to associate with the church after his dramatic Damascus road conversion. Barnabas and John Mark (Acts 15:36–39; 2 Tim. 4:11): Barnabas was willing to part company with Paul in order to work with John Mark. Later, Paul came around to Barnabas's point of view, describing John Mark as "useful to me for ministry." John Mark is believed to have been the primary author of the Gospel of Mark. Priscilla and Aquila and Apollos (Acts 18:13, 24–28): Tentmakers Priscilla and Aquilla served as spiritual tutors to Apollos at Ephesus. As a result, Apollos became one of the early church's most powerful spokesmen for the gospel. Paul and Timothy (Acts 16:13; Phil. 2:19–23; 1 and 2 Tim.): Paul invited Timothy to join him during one of Paul's missionary journeys. Timothy eventually became pastor of the dynamic church at Ephesus. Paul and Titus (2 Cor. 7:6, 13–15; 8:17; Titus): Paul, along with Barnabas, apparently won this Greek-speaking Gentile to the faith and recruited him as a traveling companion and coworker. Titus became a pastor and, according to tradition, the first bishop of the island of Crete.

Mentoring is a concept and process that every responsible Christian who is serious about passing on the faith should be involved in at some point. It is a critical component of parenting as a parent guides, nurtures, and prepares a child for life. As believers, we should be committed to the process of mentoring another in order to ensure the ongoing success of the church.

Michael J. Anthony

Bibliography. L. A. Daloz (1987), *Effective Teaching and Mentoring;* T. W. Engstrom (1989), *The Fine Art of Mentoring;* H. Hendricks and W. Hendricks (1995), *As Iron Sharpens Iron.*

Mentoring in the Family. There is a decline in the strength of the American home today. The future effectiveness of the church depends on how well we raise a family, and on how well our children are mentored in this generation. The good influence of mentoring is assumed; everyone is aware that mentoring takes place, but too little attention is given to the high value—the necessity even—of mentoring and to the difference between mentoring and parenting. There should be frequent real-time instruction in Christian education departments in reference to the possible spheres of influence the mentor may have and in how one's special skills can be shared with a young adult through establishing relationships. We might cite Barnabas and Paul in Acts, then the Pauline letters, as exemplary of a mentoring relationship we call discipleship. Doesn't the one doing the discipling help to clarify issues and model the right attitudes and behavior with admonitions to follow Christ in the one doing the discipling? Doesn't the discipling model provide features of a relationship we sometimes call mentoring? Christian education must include greater emphasis on mentoring as a calling and as a means to strengthening this generation of youth to the degree that they will in turn become good leaders and parents of the next generation.

While the church and other well-intentioned character training organizations willingly seek to serve the present generation of preadolescents and adolescents, they will do well to set their sights on the next generation, too. This can be done by giving prominence to training in Christian parenting and to instruction in mentoring as a necessary adjunct to parenting's influence on spiritual growth. Christian education should be ready—and this need not be on a big scale, rather on a one-to-one or small-group basis—to include more frequent, ongoing training in how to mentor for spiritual growth. A given congregation could choose to mentor one or two young people as prototypes of what can happen through mentoring. Others in the congregation would then see that mentoring is an art and a skill that all are capable of using, both with their own children once they reach adulthood and with other young people who are not part of the immediate family.

While the mentor may be in relationship with the protégé as a parent, by way of instructing, training, teaching healthy boundaries, and providing a loving environment based on scriptural principles, nonetheless the mentor's role is most likely to be a more generalized one of helping to clarify and evaluate issues, of affirming and supporting the protégé's good choices and values, of talking less and listening more, of relating to the young person as another adult who can be sincerely impacted and impressed by the protégé's original ideas and discoveries. The mentor has a role to play that differs somewhat from the parent's day-to-day role. If there is genuine relationship, then the influence will follow in a natural sort of way, not as a kind of teaching. For Howard and William Hendricks (1995, 231), mentoring is not a program but a relationship.

Another difference between parent and mentor is that the protégé voluntarily selects the mentor as one out of many possible models to relate to and to emulate. Similarly, when adult children seek advice from their parents after having made the separation from home, we see again that it is by selective choice that they seek mentoring from parents whom they now appreciate as having spiritual values similar to the ones they have adopted as their own, from parents who now seem to be full of useful know-how and practical experience, from parents who now can, in their different role as mentors, give more acceptance and validation than criticism. Much like athletic coaches, the mentors cheer their protégés onward in their own particular journey.

Parents can first set up potential mentors with easy access to their children, even before they reach adolescence, so that the mentors will already be in place when the parents' authority ceases to be the only authority. Figures such as church leaders, sports coaches, extracurricular directors, specially regarded teachers, and the like, serve as bridges to the outside world (Durfield, 1995) and as a secondary safety net that earlier was provided almost exclusively by the family. Guidance is given and Christian values and spiritual principles are imparted, visions of possibilities are suggested, encouragement to develop a healthy identity that is wholly his or hers alone, creativity and individualism is fostered—all to the end that a healthy separation from parents may take place.

In addition to the so-called outside mentors, there can also be another fruitful source of mentoring: the parents themselves. In the process of letting go of the young adult, the parent is no longer the one who grants permission; rather he or she begins to entrust the adolescent child with more and more responsibility for the outcome of his or her choices. Now there is enthusiastic "coaching" and encouragement as the young adults begin to find the way they want to live, how they will treat others, how they will choose a spouse and create their own family, how they will discover a useful profession.

How difficult it is at times to let go of the control and let mistakes occur, when all that the parent sees ahead is the proverbial "empty nest" and feels a sense of sadness about losing the children to their independence. Often parents are accused of interfering with the lives of their adult children, perhaps out of fear of being permanently deleted from the children's lives. How much easier to let go if there is the anticipation of still enjoying a continuing presence in the adult child's life in the role of a mentor who functions now in a less intense way and with greater objectivity—provided of course there has truly been a letting go and a taking care of any unfinished business in the way of broken relationships or long-standing hurts or misunderstanding. Parents are clearly still the parents, yet are now more mentors whom the adult children may seek out voluntarily, perhaps for advice, perhaps just to be with people whom they know understand them, perhaps simply for their good company. The parent-as-mentor will now strengthen the family ties in a perhaps unexpected way that will bring joy to all. It's not a matter of losing a child, it's gaining an adult.

Robert Clinton (1988) describes the mentor as a developer of leadership qualities; he or she is an

461

encouraging and serving person who promotes the realization of potential for leadership in the still-to-be-developed person (217). Durfield (1995) observes that the mentor does not substitute for the parent, implying that mentoring is concerned with a different role—although in the absence of a parent in the home, a mentor may at times step in to serve as a surrogate parent (23).

Perry Downs (1994) points out that besides theology, a productive educational ministry will also include an understanding of how people learn and what motivates human behavior. The process of educating for spiritual growth cannot be a mere pouring of scriptural information into empty vessels. There must also be a respect for human growth and development (69). Valuable depictions of the different stages of human growth, with the attitudes and activities that most characterize each of these stages, are found in Erikson's (1982) widely accepted analysis of the human development life cycle (32–33). Further sources for how people learn and develop are works by Piaget, Kohlberg, and Fowler.

Relevant scriptural passages are the Book of Deuteronomy and the Wisdom literature of the Old Testament as a sources of life principles and mentoring advice. The Gospel of John provides a model of a loving father and by analogy could also give some clues as to the tone and attitude of an effective mentor. The Matthew version of the Beatitudes models Christian character. The Scriptures describing discipleship, especially in Acts and in the Pauline letters, give models of Christian mentoring and modeling. An excellent parable that shows parenting and mentoring is the story of the prodigal son in Luke 15:11–32. In this passage we see how the father moved from parent to mentor in letting go and allowing for the son's voluntary selection of the father's values.

If each church trained parents to parent, parents to mentor, and other men and women to mentor, that would be of great importance to the advancement of the Kingdom. Someone has said that the Christian church is only one generation away from extinction. It may be that society itself, as we know it today, is also one generation away from extinction. What will make the difference? I believe it will be the church renewing its call to mentoring children and youth and helping them to grow into being the leaders and models of right in their homes, churches, and communities.

GORDON L. COULTER

Bibliography. R. J. Clinton (1990), *The Making of a Leader;* P. G. Downs (1994), *Teaching for Spiritual Growth;* idem (1995), *The Power of Fowler;* R. C. Durfield, *A Model for Mentoring and Surrogate Fathering for African American Males;* T. W. Engstrom (1982), *The Fine Art of Mentoring;* E. H. Erikson (1982), *The Life Cycle Completed;* H. Hendricks (1995), *As Iron Sharpens Iron.*

Mercy Killing. *See* Euthanasia.

Metacognition. The process of thinking about the thought process. One way used to categorize thinking considers various patterns or styles a person prefers when learning something new. Bernice McCarthy's 4MAT system is such a pattern. Howard Gardner from Harvard presents another cognitive pattern. Gardner postulates seven ways of thinking and learning that he calls Multiple Intelligences. Another way to think of thinking is its source of motivation, from others or self. Self-directed learning is usually associated with adults and other-directed thinking is often associated with children. Another way to think of thinking is developmentally, or in terms of various ages exhibiting different stages of thinking.

One of the first and most famous metacognition theories from a developmental point of view is the theoretical taxonomy presented by Jean Piaget (1896–1980). He described the qualitative differences as two main processes that develop between children and youth. First, he claimed there is a tendency to organize mental processes into coherent systems. Organizational systems develop as a person ages. His second principle of cognitive functioning is adaptation. Adaptation takes place through two complementary processes: assimilation and accommodation. Assimilation involves the person's dealing with the environment in terms of mental structures, while accommodation involves the transformation of mental structures in response to the environment. Piaget's description included infants through adults, although the last stage optimally begins at older childhood.

The type of cognitive development Piaget describes begins with Sensorimotor and proceeds to Preoperational, Concrete Operational, and finally, Formal Operational stages. In brief, Sensorimotor employs imagination and fantasy. Preoperational thinking is associated with the distinction between categories of information such as conservation and seriation. The third stage, Concrete Operational, refers to thinking that has tangible or sensible referents. The last stage Piaget calls Formal Operational; it is associated with thinkers who can hypothesize about issues and think abstractly.

One of the advantages of focusing on the process of thinking for the Christian educator is increased creativity. Following Piaget's theory, it is possible for Formal Operational thinkers to consider "what if" scenarios. Most Bible teaching uses a form of application that requires transfer of a principle into a totally different setting. Any kind of thinking below formal operations would have more difficulty making that transfer. This is only one reason why metacognition is an important area of study for Christian educators and the teaching of the Bible.

ROBERT J. RADCLIFFE

Bibliography. H. Gardner (1983), *Frames of Mind;* H. Ginzberg and S. Opper (1979), *S. Piaget's Theory of Intellectual Development.*

See also PIAGET, JEAN; COGNITIVE DEVELOPMENT

Metamessage. A change-altering component that impacts understanding of the content that has been shared. Communication involves sending messages at two levels: the informational level and the metamessage level. Metamessages "frame" information to help the communicants know how to interpret what is being said. Responses usually issue from these interpretations more than from the data alone. Subtle, underlying material that accompanies mere words becomes important when seeking to understand a person. Nonverbal communication plays a large part in metamessages. Vocal pitch, volume, rate of speech, body language, and facial clues reveal moods, attitudes, and feelings that impact interpretation. Factors that influence communication include distance between communicators, immediacy, touching, environment in which information is shared, credibility of speaker, previous relational history, and gender (women generally appear to be more attuned to reading metamessages). The metamessage lends understanding (or misunderstanding) to mere words. Checking in with the communicator to clarify or "reframing" (asking, "Is there any other way this statement could be interpreted?") helps keep open channels of understanding. Because conversation maintains relationship as well as gives information, a person wanting to be understood or to understand must cultivate awareness of underlying clues that compose the metamessage.

JULIE GORMAN

Bibliography. J. Gorman (1993), *Community That Is Christian;* D. Tannen (1986), *That's Not What I Meant;* idem (1990), *You Just Don't Understand.*

Metaphor. *See* Parable.

Metaphysics. One of three broad subdivisions of philosophy. The other divisions are epistemology, which investigates the nature and validity of knowledge, and axiology, which answers the question, "What is of value?" The goal of metaphysics is to identify the nature and structure of all that is. As traditionally defined, metaphysics probes the nature of reality to say how things are. Unlike science, which investigates natural phenomena, metaphysics asks questions about the ultimate reality behind the natural world. It is concerned with the nature of reality of the nonphysical world. Metaphysics claims to: (1) tell us what really exists or what the real nature of things is; (2) be fundamental and comprehensive in a way no individual discipline is; and (3) reach conclusions that are intellectually impregnable and thus possess a unique kind of certainty.

The questions probed by metaphysics are arranged into four subsets. First are cosmological questions that address the theories of the origin, nature, and development of the universe as well as its purposefulness. This would include such questions as "How did the universe originate and develop?" and "Is there a purpose toward which the universe is moving?" Also included here are questions regarding the nature of space and time. The second subset of questions are theological questions regarding the nature and being of God. These questions would include "Is God one or more than one being?", "What is the nature of God's attributes?", and "Are there other heavenly beings and if so, what is the nature of them?"

A third subset of metaphysical questions is anthropological. These are questions regarding the nature of human beings. Such questions would include "What is the nature of free will?", "To what extent are human beings truly free?", "What is the relationship between the mind and body?", "Is the mind more fundamental than the body?", and "Are human beings born good, evil, or morally neutral?" Finally, metaphysics includes ontological questions. These are questions related to the nature of existence or what it means to be. Such questions would include "Is reality only of the natural realm?", "Is it composed of both the natural and the supernatural?", and "Is reality orderly and fixed, or is change a central feature?"

Metaphysical questions have direct relevance to the educational practices of Christian educators. Within the mind-set of each Christian educator are metaphysical beliefs that are implicitly expressed in one's educational practices. In addition, educational practices themselves reflect particular answers to many of these questions. A critical challenge for the Christian educator is to (1) carefully examine one's own metaphysical beliefs in order to determine where there may be distortions of the biblical truth regarding these questions, and (2) thoughtfully choose educational practices that are consistent with a biblical response to these metaphysical questions. For example, Christian educators believe in a reality that is both natural and supernatural. Yet historically, Christian educational practices have tended to give greater emphasis to the intellectual process of learning Bible knowledge than to experiencing the supernatural Holy Spirit.

MERILYN J. MACLEOD

Bibliography. W. Hasker (1983), *Metaphysics: Constructing a World View;* G. R. Knight (1989), *Philosophy and Education: An Introduction in Christian Perspective;* T. V. Morris (1991), *Our Idea of God: An Introduction to Philosophical Theology.*

Methodology (Teaching and Research). Norman and Richard Sprinthall (1990) give three broad models of teaching methodology. Other authors (Joyce and Weil, 1996; Wittrock, 1986) suggest families of teaching methods.

Teaching Methodology. A model is a cluster of strategies that are consistent with certain assumptions about learning. The first is "transmitter of knowledge." This view assumes that out of a body of knowledge teachers can select facts and concepts for students. The teacher digests these and makes them understandable to the students. Emphasis is on facts and information, which must be mastered before students can think for themselves. They need to know what is already known before creating new ideas.

New knowledge is set out in a linear, step-by-step sequence. The teacher sometimes uses a generalization of the lesson's main points, or concepts, given at the outset of teaching. This helps create expectations for the students and allows them to focus on what is most important. Next come concrete examples of the generalized concept. These are connected to the concept for the students. This is followed by a restatement of the concept. Expression of the concept and delivery of the fact-laden examples aim to reduce ambiguity and lead all students to the same point of understanding.

The lecture format is the strongest method for this model. Its advantages are that much can be communicated and a whole class is kept together. Its disadvantages are that students may think all learning calls for passivity. The teacher must keep students involved in the lecture to prevent this. Visuals and rhetorical questions help. It also assumes that one approach to learning fits everyone.

Model two is "inductive inquiry." Teachers try to reveal the fundamental structure of a discipline. They work with concepts or the process of inquiry. Once students understand these structures, they can be given tasks using them. The method leads to discovery of new insights. This can result in intellectual excitement that motivates students. The teacher analyzes content and asks questions, rather than simply giving answers.

There are several forms of inductive inquiry. In each, the teacher arranges content in an open-ended fashion to stimulate students to ask questions and explore. This method can be difficult for young children, although it has been shown that elementary students can benefit from it. Teachers must be very clever to mix communication of facts to the inexperienced student while allowing for discovery. An important component of the inductive method is developing the student's potential to reason independently. Cueing in questioning, use of structure or close organization, and advance organizers may be necessary when students lack experience.

The third model is "interpersonal learning." This approach looks at creating an environment of learning based on a warm relationship between teacher and student stemming from genuine affection, empathy, sincerity, and honesty. These positive conditions result in the possibility of experiential learning. Carl Rogers has been the leading proponent of this method (1969). The conditions make students free to learn. Emphasis is on human interaction, not facts or concepts. Where stress levels are high learning declines. Teacher warmth can create a learning-positive climate. However, a warm climate may not be enough to promote learning.

While most teachers probably have limited teaching styles, some synthesis of methods needs to be the goal. Differing skills and experiences of teachers and students, differing demands by varying academic disciplines, and differing available resources help to drive such syntheses.

Research Methodology. Research in education and Christian education has been influenced by social science research methods. These can be divided into three categories: quantitative, qualitative, and historical. Philosophical argumentation and biblical/theological inquiry are also important. However, the influence of the social sciences has increased in the past several decades. Social science research may be longitudinal, spread over time; or cross-sectional, one or few measures at a particular point in time.

Quantitative, sometimes called *positivist,* research assumes that the environment, both physical and social, has an independent and relatively constant reality. These researchers collect numerical data on observable behaviors of large samples of people and conduct mathematical analyses with the numbers. They usually begin with a theoretical position and test hypotheses based on the theory.

One approach to quantitative research is experimental design. This requires the use of random subject selection and comparison with a control group. Quasi-experimental designs lack one or both of these. Descriptive design simply seeks to find out what is. Correlation design wants to know how two variables are related. Causal-comparative design tries to discover possible causes and effects of behavior patterns or personal characteristics by comparing individuals in whom a phenomenon is present with those in whom it is not. The only way to find cause and effect is through the use of rigorous experimental studies.

Qualitative (postpositivist or interpretive) research assumes that environments are transitory and situational. How life is viewed is based on personal interpretations. These researchers primarily collect verbal data through intense case studies and then subject them to analytic induction. The cases usually involve one person or a small group. Based on the analyses, theoretical positions may be developed.

Qualitative traditions include ethnography, which studies characteristic features and patterns of a culture, and phenomenology, which is interested in reality as it appears to individuals. Emancipatory action research is where practitioners' self-reflective efforts to improve the rationality and justice of their work is the focus. Symbolic interactionism considers the influence of social interactions on structures and self-identity. Narrative analysis studies organized representations. Semiotics looks at signs and their meanings (Gall, Borg, and Gall, 1996, 593). Some authorities think that qualitative research is best used to discover themes and relationships, while quantitative research best plays a confirmatory role (Biddle and Anderson, 1986).

Historical research consists of "systematically searching for data to answer questions about past phenomenon for the purpose of gaining a better understanding of present . . . issues" (Gall, Borg, and Gall, 1996, 644). Historical researchers acknowledge human bias and fallibility of sources, but believe it is possible to discover what "really" happened at a given time when appropriate methods and analyses are used. Interpretation is important as is finding reliable sources.

EUGENE S. GIBBS

Bibliography. B. J. Biddle and D. S. Anderson (1986), *Handbook of Research on Teaching* pp. 320–52; M. D. Gall, W. R. Borg, and J. P. Gall (1996), *Educational Research: An Introduction;* B. Joyce and M. Weil (1996), *Models of Teaching;* C. Rogers (1969), *Freedom to Learn;* N. A. and R. C. Sprinthall (1990), *Educational Psychology: A Developmental Approach;* M. C. Wittrock, ed. (1986), *Handbook of Research on Teaching.*

Middle Adolescent Youth, Ministry to. Ever since psychologist Gordon Hall introduced the term *adolescence* in the 1920s to try to define and describe a developmental stage of life somewhere between childhood and adulthood, scholars have debated the ages of beginning and ending of adolescence. Additionally, further studies have identified significant developmental differences within the stage of adolescence, leading some to make even more narrow definitions and descriptions.

It is common today to see adolescence in three distinct stages. Early adolescence is most often seen as the years between ages 11 and 13. Middle adolescence is defined as the years between 14 and 16, and later adolescence includes students between ages 17 and adulthood.

Middle adolescence is often a difficult time in a student's life. Some of life's greatest developmental physical and social changes are taking place during these years. For most, the physical body is undergoing a rapid growth spurt, which may continue even into young adulthood. For others, growth has already been under way for as long as two years and they are beginning to realize that the bodies they now have represent what they will look like throughout adulthood.

Second, the transition from middle school to high school takes place for most of these students sometime during middle adolescence and that transition is viewed by many with a great deal of apprehension and sometimes fear. They tend to view high school as the last phase of youth before the pressures of entering college or the workforce beyond.

A traditional approach to youth ministry may cause church youth leaders to ignore or be unaware of the differences in development among the phases of adolescence. Grouping students in the traditional junior high and high school format may make it impractical to be able to deal with needs unique to the middle adolescent students.

Several years ago, very large churches attempted to deal with this issue and others by having a separate department for ninth-graders often referred to as "The Niners." While that enabled leaders in those ministries to deal with significant issues facing the ninth grade students, it often left them feeling shut off from the rest of the youth group.

Designing a ministry for middle adolescent students involves consideration of the following developmental characteristics.

1. Middle adolescents have begun to develop a deeper understanding of gender and sex issues than they had as young adolescents, but have not yet matured to the point where they begin to be concerned with the underlying personal and moral issues involved.
2. They desire more freedom from their parents than previously desired, but that desire is also frightening to them.
3. They struggle at times with intense feelings of loneliness, confusion, and low self-esteem, which were not problems for most of them during early adolescence.
4. They are not yet preoccupied with questions of life choices such as marriage, career, and college studies as they will be in later adolescence.
5. Not only are they not prepared to enter the world of adulthood, they have no desire to enter that world.

Some questions to guide the design of ministry to middle adolescents are:

1. What needs do these middle adolescent students have that are unique to their age group and how can those needs best be addressed with the resources available in a church for youth ministry?
2. What approaches for building relationships with middle adolescent students will be most effective?

3. What are the best ways to introduce middle adolescent students to a relationship with Jesus Christ?

Recently, successful youth programs in some larger churches are attempting to deal with the need for a developmental approach to ministry to youth without disrupting the traditional groupings of junior high and high school. These program distinctives will only work in a larger church, however.

In the approach used by these churches, there is a traditional junior high group made up of students in the seventh to eighth grades and a traditional high school group made up of students in grades 9 to 12. However, in both programs there is an associate youth director for students in each grade. This associate person is recruited for seventh-graders or ninth-graders and stays with his or her students until they graduate from the junior high or high school program. This associate leader is responsible to get to know the students in his or her charge and to lead a team of volunteer small group leaders in ministering to the needs of the students in their grade for two full years (junior high) or four full years (high school).

In at least one of these churches, small group leaders (called core leaders) are encouraged to stay with students through the transition from eighth to ninth grade (junior high to high school) so that the fears and apprehensions the students have about that transition can be dealt with by a core leader whom they all know and with whom they have an ongoing relationship. The feeling is that having a relationship with a leader already established during this transition year, greatly reduces the stress and anxiety experienced by the students as they move into high school.

There are those in youth ministry who believe that dividing young people into three categories by age unnecessarily complicates the ways in which ministry is delivered to students. In response, the following information might be helpful.

Students in the adolescent stage of life are putting significant effort into identity formation. Much, if not most, of what they say and do and how they respond to adults, peers, and others relates to their attempts to answer the question, "Who am I?" Middle adolescents have almost completed the process of discovering identities; and later adolescents are busy experimenting with the several identity ideas they have discovered. During middle adolescence, workers have opportunities to help them sort through the discovered identity ideas and distinguish between healthy and unhealthy models.

Because adolescence is a stage of formation where so much change is taking place at such a rapid pace, more narrowly defined age distinctions can help youth workers focus on very specific developmental issues with smaller groups of students.

Because middle adolescence is a time of great personal uncertainty, it is also a time when high levels of cognitive dissonance (disequilibrium) are in place and disequilibrated students are primed for learning. There are many exciting teachable moments with middle adolescents that weren't present a year earlier and will be gone, sometimes forever, a year later.

KEN GARLAND

Bibliography. R. R. Dunn and M. H. Senter (1997), *Reaching a Generation for Christ;* L. Parrott (1993), *Helping the Struggling Adolescent;* W. Rice (1990), *Junior High Ministry;* D. R. Veerman (1990), *Reaching Kids before High School.*

Middle Adulthood. Ministering to and with middle adults is a relational enterprise for mature Christians who serve as knowledgeable resources and experienced examples. Exceptions abound in the actual practice of Christian education, but middle adult learning focuses upon advanced biblical understanding, rich spiritual discernment, and the development of servant leaders.

Much of what is written concerning middle adult ministry reflects conclusions of scholarly research and change theory related to family relationships, career development, community participation, and church involvement. In a now classic article, Chickering and Havighurst reviewed many of these broad-based, sometimes longitudinal, and frequently anecdotal studies concerning adult life experience. They identified typical developmental tasks that appear in successive age categories.

Life stage analysis deals with patterns—characteristics not present in every individual or church population. These patterns are starting points for understanding key concerns, obstacles, and opportunities that must be accommodated in middle adult Christian education.

Midlife Transition: Ages 35–45. Following turbulent early adult years, there is a widely recognized intermediate period that is comparable to a great canyon filled with obstacles. Midlife transition is an arduous climb up multiple impediments toward higher ground—a plateau for some and a summit for others. This is an achievement-intensive era of changed time perspectives, revised career plans, and redefined family relationships.

Midlife transition learners possess wide-ranging knowledge and competence. Educational practices that tap prior learning become important. Instructional materials that clarify values and lifestyle preferences are central. Significant exchanges with fellow students and instructors are desired, and educational opportunities that correspond with individual needs are appreciated.

Middle Adulthood: Ages 45–57. After negotiating midlife transition, many adults enjoy a satisfying and creative life. They are sure of themselves, and know what they want and what they can and cannot do. After multiple changes over fifty years, they possess a full repertoire of coping strategies. They know what will and will not work in most situations. However, this "wisdom" is only as genuine as its value base.

Concerns of middle adulthood include sustaining careers, restabilizing family relationships, making meaningful contributions to a community, and adjusting to biological changes.

Middle adult learners value education, but demand a larger measure of self-determination. Recognition of prior learning and integration of new knowledge with current experience is vital. Educators must incorporate shared insight. A collegial relationship between instructors and learners is crucial.

Levels of Middle Adult Ministry. Because middle adults are found at various stages of spiritual development, Christian educators must establish appropriate educational objectives.

Individuals in the secular *community* must be introduced to Christians or to biblical truths that God uses to produce serious seekers of faith. This is remedial ministry for middle adults who have avoided the church.

Many of these individuals become *curious.* Here, they join middle adults who have experienced sterile religion or have been sidetracked by sectarian or divisive issues. These nonbelievers need to hear the simple gospel message and have specific questions answered as the Spirit of God draws them toward genuine belief.

Foundational Christian education to and with middle adults involves strengthening those who are *convinced* of the truth of the gospel, but struggle with the lordship of Jesus Christ. This learning stage, characterized by basic teaching, in-depth discussion, and initial ministry participation, is normally experienced in early adulthood.

The primary focus of ministry to and with middle adults is continuing education for the *committed,* whose minds, hearts, and lives are being transformed by the revealed truth and behavioral directives of the Bible. God expects all believers to attain this level of Christian maturity. These strong Christians are examples for both younger and older, but less mature, believers in everything they say and do (speech, conduct) in their relationships with God (faith) and his people (love) as well as in their personal moral purity (1 Tim. 4:12).

The most advanced form of middle adult ministry (reflecting the developmental strategy in Eph. 4:11–12) encompasses training for men and women who aspire to ministry leadership in accord with the gifts of the Holy Spirit (1 Tim. 3:1). In terms of spiritual maturity, they are committed believers. However, these *commissioned* individuals are servant leaders who promote unity and stability in the body of Christ.

Centrality of Instruction. High-level knowledge and reasoning based upon the truth of God's Word is a primary objective of Christian education ministry to committed and commissioned believers. Middle adult Christians ought to be teachers who have mastered elementary principles (Heb. 5:12) and have progressed to full mental maturity. Christian educators must teach middle adults to know truth and to practice the behavioral implications of God's Word. Christian education for convinced and committed Christians must be solid food that trains the senses to discern good and evil (v. 14).

Necessity of Transformation. In order to provide the breadth of ministry required to support the full range of middle adult spiritual needs, multiple levels of educational outcomes related to knowledge and perspective as well as behavior are required. Only educational programs that include all three elements can sufficiently nurture the depth of Christian maturity that must be attained. Middle adulthood is the stage during which the thinking, reasoning, and speaking patterns of childhood must be fully done away with (1 Cor. 13:11).

Comprehensive personality change is in view here—global change involving intellect, emotion, and will. Consequently, a unified array of cognitive, affective, and conative (behavioral) objectives must be employed in order to support transformation toward Christlikeness (v. 12).

The result of complete ministry is conscious assent to scriptural truth concerning God and his will. This *faith* manifests itself in a biblical perspective of *hope* as well as ethical behavior toward all God's children in the form of *love* (v. 13).

Believers of all ages must navigate the Christian life in a culture characterized by agnosticism, despair, and postmodern abandonment of a ground of morality. Faith, hope, and love abide as solid indictors of effective teaching and strong Christian education ministry to and with middle adults.

DANIEL C. STEVENS

Bibliography. L. Aden, D. G. Benner, and J. H. Ellens, eds. (1992), *Christian Perspectives on Human Development;* A. W. Chickering and R. J. Havighurst (1981), *The American College;* K. O. Gangel and J. C. Wilhoit, eds. (1993), *The Christian Educator's Handbook on Adult Education;* R. E. Y. Wickett (1991), *Models of Adult Religious Education.*

Middle Childhood. The developmental period between early childhood and the beginning of adolescence. Though the boundaries are fluid, the span usually includes ages 6 to 11, generally from first through fifth grade. It is sometimes referred to as the elementary school years. (Some authors limit middle childhood to age ten and add an in-between period before adolescence called late childhood or preadolescence.)

Physical and Cognitive Change. Physical growth during this period is usually stable and consistent, sometimes described as a latent period before the rapid physical changes of early adolescence. Children grow an average of 2 to 3 inches a year. Their legs become longer and their trunks slimmer. They gain 5 to 7 pounds per year, mainly because of increased size of muscles and the skeletal system. They double their strength capacity during these years. Toward the end of this period, immense physical changes occur, especially in girls, as children move from childhood to preadolescence and on to adolescence.

Motor skills become more coordinated than they were in early childhood. If children have no physical disabilities and, at the same time have opportunity to practice, they master most skills such as climbing, skipping rope, swimming, bicycle riding, and skating.

Children this age need to be active. Sitting for long periods of time produces more fatigue than rigorous large muscle activity.

Middle childhood is a time when most children master fundamental skills necessary for academic achievement. Though children can achieve a sense of their competency in other ways, academic skills, or lack of them, profoundly affect their sense of self-esteem. Piaget describes this as the Concrete Operational period—mental actions now allow them to do mentally what was done physically in early childhood. With this increased mental capacity, memory becomes keen.

Children vary in the ways they acquire and process information. Howard Gardner (1983), a Harvard psychologist, asserts that as many as seven different kinds of intelligence can be identified: (1) linguistic, the use of words; (2) musical, the use of rhythm and tones; (3) logical-mathematical, the use of symbols; (4) spatial, which is the ability to deal with shapes, colors, and other artistic concerns; (5) bodily-kinesthetic, small and large muscle use; (6) personal self-knowledge and insight; and (7) social, the ability to interact effectively. Gardner believes that every child possesses at least one of these intelligences; many children possess more than one. Teachers would do well to recognize that different children prefer different approaches to learning, based on the kind of intelligence(s) they possess.

Social and Emotional Climate. Middle childhood is a time when children's social horizons widen beyond the family. The family remains the primary social focus for children. But teachers and peers become quite important in their social system and contribute to their self-understanding and self-esteem. Those children who are not popular with their peers often become disruptive and aggressive, leaving them vulnerable to delinquent behavior.

Children's friendships are important. They provide companionship, stimulation, physical support, ego support, social comparison, and intimacy/affection. Friendships are more momentary in nature up to age 7. But these relationships become lasting during the latter part of this period.

Erikson described the psychological task of middle children as industry versus inferiority—children weigh their academic success and social capability to assess their personal competency. They are also interested in how things work. Encouraged to explore, they learn how to solve problems and discover how the world works. This, too, contributes to their sense of competency. Those who assess these factors positively attain what is commonly called good self-esteem; those who are unable to make a positive judgment regard themselves as inferior.

Moral and Spiritual Change. Morally, children at this age are in the stage defined as conventional by Kohlberg. They abide by certain internal standards, but they are the standards of others, such as parents or teachers. They often adopt their parents' moral standards.

In terms of faith, children are usually at what Fowler calls the mythic-literal stage. This means that they work hard at sorting out the real from the make-believe. They can create a narrative of their own life meaning. They are interested in stories of individuals and communities. Their concept of God moves from a purely anthropomorphic understanding to a rudimentary understanding of his qualities. God is still communicated to them through their social systems such as family and church. They come to understand that sin separates them from pleasing God. But they often have difficulty understanding grace, mainly because they are bound by the law of reciprocity and the idea of immanent justice—and they see God in the same way. Children begin to take on for themselves the stories, beliefs, and observances that symbolize belonging to their faith community.

Christian Education in Middle Childhood. Those who organize Christian education experiences for children this age must remember the wide range of abilities that are represented in any one- or two-year age span. Closely grouped classes for each year of school is an ideal. However, the size of some churches mandates class groups that include multiple grades. In those cases, the church should plan for groups as closely homogeneous as possible. Class groups are most productive when the teacher/pupil ratio is one teacher for each six to eight children.

Teachers of children in the middle childhood range need to recognize the variety of learning styles represented in their class and provide a variety of activities to appeal to and provide for successful learning ventures for all who are in the class. They must also recognize the importance of their own relationship to the children as a way of teaching faith. Children learn many of the lessons of faith from intergenerational relationships. They imitate the faith and actions of those older than themselves. Administrators of Christian education programs need to plan a combination of graded and intergenerational experiences for children to learn faith best.

ELEANOR A. DANIEL

Bibliography. J. Fowler (1981), *Stages of Faith;* H. Gardner (1983), *Frames of Mind;* L. O. Richards (1983), *Children's Ministry;* J. Santrock (1995), *Life-Span Development.*

Middle School. The level of schooling that targets youth in early adolescence. Although different grade level combinations exist, generally middle schools educate students between the ages of 10 and 15. The concept of the middle school, which was first introduced in the 1960s, was an attempt to be developmentally responsive to students facing the challenges of early adolescence and to create a better transition from elementary school to high school. This is accomplished by moving away from the traditional junior high structure (similar to high school with a different teacher for each subject) to a structure that combines the nurturing elements of the elementary school with the easing of controls common in the high school environment. Characteristics of intellectual, physical, moral, emotional/psychological, and social development are identified that are unique to this stage of young adolescence. Strategies such as creating smaller learning environments, providing adult advocates for students, and partnering with families and the community are engaged in order to foster a positive school climate.

JANA SUNDENE

Bibliography. National Middle School Association (1995), *This We Believe: Developmentally Responsive Middle Schools.*

Midlife Crisis. A life transition that carries with it several familiar characteristics. The terminology as well as the concept is new, brought about, in part, by increasing longevity whether one can detect a crisis or not. Sell talks about the kinds of changes crisis can bring: "Extroverts want to be more introverted, turning to reading, gardening, or painting. Introverts may want to pop out of their shell more, sharing feelings and thoughts more openly. A man or woman may be compelled to jog or join a health club, as if suddenly discovering he or she has a body" (Sell, 1991, 123). He also argues that a midlife crisis, genuinely so understood, must be marked by two criteria: the first is trauma and the second the concern for possible outcomes. Regarding his own research, Levinson (1978) writes,

For the great majority of men—about 80% of our subjects—this period evokes tumultuous struggles within the self and the external world. Their mid-life transition is a time of moderate or severe crisis. Every aspect of their lives comes into question, and they are horrified by much that is revealed. They are full of recriminations against themselves and others. They cannot go on as before; they need time to choose a new path or to modify an old one. (42)

Response to the midlife crisis calls Christians to focus on God's Word and relationship with other believers. Sell (1991) suggests themes for several doctrinal studies such as "Theological Themes for Midlifers: Theology of Suffering, Doctrine of Maturity, Doctrine of Grace, Theology of the Church, Theology of Society, and Theology of Hope." He concludes his brief study with the words, "If the mid-lifer finds himself in the woods, God's Word will be the light that will show him the path through it" (156).

KENNETH O. GANGEL

Bibliography. J. Eisenson (1991), *Growing Up While Growing Older;* D. J. Levinson (1978), *Seasons of a Man's Life;* K. O. Gangel and J. C. Wilhoit, (1993), *The Christian Educator's Handbook on Adult Education;* C. Sell (1991), *Transitions Through Adult Life;* R. E. Y. Wickett (1991), *Models of Adult Religious Education Practice.*

Millennial Generation. The Millennial Generation, or "Generation Y," refers to the final generation born in the second millennium. The most commonly cited birth years are 1982 to 2000, thus denoting everyone 18 and younger at the turn of the millennium. The Millennial Generation includes the "Baby Boomlet" of children born between 1989 and 1993, years when the number of children born equaled the peak years of the Baby Boom.

Generational historians Strauss and Howe describe Millennials as most likely becoming a "Civic Generation," a consistent recurring generational pattern within history. This generation grows up in homes where they are increasingly protected and treasured. The adults around them tend to define social issues in terms of how they will affect their children. Strong principles and rationality are increasingly emphasized in the training of Millennials, as well as the virtues of cooperation, equality, and community, powerfully influencing who Millennials will become. Strauss and Howe claim that Civics, in each cycle of history, become adults who are concerned about others and the world in general as they work in teams to overcome major crises in society. They mature to become dominant, heroic achievers who build social institutions during their middle-age years and remain busy in old age.

Wendy Zoba (1997), summarizing survey results, describes Millennials quite differently. Millennials see themselves as inattentive, feeble, and ignorant because everything has been handed to them, letting change occur without becoming involved, being easily swayed by others' opinions, lacking honor, feeling that nothing is secure, not believing in anything or anyone, and just "coasting." Summarizing the thinking of numerous experts on the subject, she typifies Millennials as being fast-paced with a fragmented focus, living for the present, jaded so that nothing surprises them, constantly searching for indications of insincerity in others, and not trusting adults. Yet Millennials are also interested in religion and can be influenced positively by peer pressure. As with the Buster Generation, Millennials desire strong relationships, but unlike Busters they are not as materialistic and are not rebellious. Zoba has hopes, as Strauss and Howe predict, that previous generations will encourage civic resolve and team-centered purpose in the Millennials, producing a strong sense of community and Millennials who become the heroes they wanted but did not find in childhood.

There is considerable diversity within the Millennial Generation; like all generations, individuals may or may not approximate the trends that have been documented because of personal choices and unique circumstances. Even the expected trends may be mistaken; Strauss and Howe note the unlikely possibility that Millennials might develop characteristics of an "Adaptive Generation," as did the Builder Generation of the 1930s and early 1940s, instead of fitting the Civic Generation pattern. Ultimately, people—even generations of people—make choices that produce unexpected changes.

DONALD E. RATCLIFF

Bibliography. W. Strauss and N. Howe (1997), *The Fourth Turning: An American Prophecy;* W. Strauss and N. Howe (1991), *Generations;* W. M. Zoba (1997), *Christianity Today,* February 3, 1997.

Miller, Randolph Crump (1910–). American education theorist. Born in Fresno, California, into the family of an Episcopal priest, a calling he would one day himself accept, he began his education at Pomona College, where he received his bachelor's degree in 1931, and completed his education at Yale Divinity School, where he was awarded a Ph.D. in 1936. The next year, 1937, Miller was ordained as an Episcopal priest.

Miller's professional involvement in the field of Christian education spans three generations. He started his teaching career at Church Divinity School of the Pacific (Berkeley, Calif.) in 1937 and taught there for fifteen years (1937–52). From 1952 to 1982 Miller held the Horace Bushnell Chair of Christian Nurture at Yale Divinity

School. He also regularly taught a class at Harvard on Christian nurture. His popularity as a writer and lecturer in the field of Christian education has been accented by his service with the Religious Education Association. He served as coeditor of *Religious Education,* REA's main journal, from 1956 to 1957, and later as editor from 1958 to 1978. After his retirement from Yale in 1982, Miller assumed the role of executive secretary of REA, holding that position through 1985. Even while in retirement he continues to contribute to the field of education, his most recent editorial work being *Theologies of Religious Education* (1995).

During the first half of the twentieth century, Christian educators debated the role of theology (particularly the role of the Bible) in education. Miller's academic predecessors (George A. Coe, Harrison S. Elliot, Shelton Smith) questioned whether theology should ever influence Christian education, but Miller argued that the place of theology in Christian education was indispensable. For Miller, education was primarily a theological discipline. Perhaps his most recognizable statement in this regard is "theology in the background, grace and faith in the foreground" (Miller, 1982).

While he gained a reputation for being one of the foremost Christian education theorists in the twentieth century, Miller is also recognized as an eminent theologian and sought to establish a satisfactory link between content and method. In his most fundamental contribution to the field of Christian education, Miller argues that the "clue to Christian education" is a rediscovery of a relevant theology that bridges the gap between content and method. Consequently the task of Christian education is to make theology relevant, realizing that the goal of Christian education is Christian truth.

It was Miller's combination of Deweyan progressive education with an existential process theology, rather than classical liberalism or neo-orthodoxy, that drew attention to his approach to Christian education. Miller's self-imposed challenge was "Someone has to make a Christian out of John Dewey." Miller hypothesized that Dewey's process education could be effectively merged with a Christian process theology, coalescing into a process oriented theory of Christian education. It is Miller's reliance on process theology that poses the most significant challenge for evangelical educators to utilize his educational theory.

While teaching he began his writing career, and he is noted for four main works. *The Clue to Christian Education* (1950) was the first full expression of Miller's conviction concerning the role of the Bible in the process of "doing theology." He argued that the missing component of mainline Protestant religious education in the twentieth century was, quite simply and profoundly, the

Bible. *Biblical Theology and Christian Education* (1956), which presents the "biblical drama" systematically, relates each major episode to learners of various ages. *Christian Nurture and the Church* (1961) details how the church is the permanent institution and context for Christian nurture and central to the process, with attention given to other institutions that have profound influence on Christian formation (the family, school, and community). *The Theory of Christian Education Practice* (1980) deals with the practical implications of his three former works.

Miller is a self-avowed empiricist and liberal, and has profoundly influenced mainline Protestants. He aligns himself closely with process theology and seeks to apply process thinking to religious education. He is influenced primarily by the theology of H. Richard Niebuhr and the philosophical thought of Alfred North Whitehead.

The published works of Randolph Crump Miller are numerous. He has written over 150 magazine and journal articles, edited or written approximately twenty books, and contributed more than fifteen articles to edited works.

JAMES RILEY ESTEP AND HARLEY ATKINSON

Bibliography. I. V. Cully and K. B. Cully, eds. (1978), *Process and Relationship;* K. O. Gangel and W. S. Benson (1983), *Christian Education: Its History and Philosophy;* S. Little, *Religious Education* (special issue, 1961); S. Little (1961), *The Role of the Bible in Contemporary Christian Education;* R. C. Miller (1950), *The Clue to Christian Education;* idem (1974), *American Spirit in Theology;* idem (1980), *The Theory of Christian Education Practice;* idem (1983), *Modern Masters of Religious Education;* idem (1982), *Religious Education and Theology.*

See also DEWEY, JOHN

Minister. The common theme surrounding the term *minister* is service. It has been used in the public arena to identify those who hold certain public offices that are intended to serve the people. It should be noted that pagan religions such as Baal worship also had ministers (1 Kings 10:19–23). In the Old Testament, which clearly differentiates between professional and general religious service, *minister* referred primarily to the religious responsibilities of the Levites and priests (Exod. 28:42–43; Num. 3:5–10; Deut. 10:8).

However, this situation changed dramatically in the New Testament. The term *minister* grew primarily out of the word *diakonos,* which Vine (1981) notes is translated most often as servant, attendant, minister, or deacon. While in the Old Testament only certain people were ordained or set apart for priestly work, in the New Testament all members of the body of Christ were considered part of the holy priesthood (1 Pet. 2:5, 9–10) and ministers before God and his church. However, a select or specified priesthood was maintained for many years through the Catholic Church, which allowed only certain individuals to provide the religious services. The Reformation attempted to refocus attention on the priesthood of all believers, but as Ogden (1990) states, it never fully delivered what it promised.

It appears that one contributing factor to this has been the professionalization of ministry. With the proliferation of specialized fields of study that grew out of modernism came an increase in schools to prepare people to fulfill these occupational positions. Examples include senior minister, youth minister, minister of Christian education, children's minister, singles minister, and so on. Although the local church did not outwardly espouse a different class of believers, Ogden and others believe this has occurred nonetheless.

There appears to be a renewed effort among Christians to once again espouse and act upon the concepts of the priesthood of believers and every member ministry. Evidence of this includes a new emphasis on volunteer mobilization and training, identification and utilization of spiritual gifts, and entrusting more significant responsibilities to nonvocational ministers. Many churches are also focusing on helping all believers realize that, as members of God's priesthood, they are "created in Christ Jesus for good works, which God prepared beforehand, that we should walk in them" (Eph. 2:10 NASB).

JAY DESKO

Bibliography. G. Ogden (1990), *The New Reformation;* W. E. Vine (1981), *An Expository Dictionary of New Testament Words.*

Minister of Christian Education. A professional church leader hired by a local church to oversee the congregation's educational ministry. As a profession, the minister of Christian education position in Protestant churches originated in the early twentieth century with the formation of the Religious Education Association in 1903, and grew with the trend to pay the Sunday school superintendent, whose title was changed to director of religious education. The profession was born out of a desire to bring more focused attention and increased quality to the educational efforts of local churches. Initially, the term *religious education* was used as a way of distinguishing education that had a religious purpose from general education, and was inclusive of persons from all faiths. However, the modifier *religious* became associated with liberalism and was replaced in most Protestant churches with *Christian education.*

Evangelical Christian educators left the Religious Education Association (REA) because they felt the REA was too heavily influenced by progressive education and liberalism. A professional organization for Evangelical Christian educators, the National Association of Directors of Christian

Education (NADCE), grew out of the National Sunday School Association to promote the growth of evangelical Christian education (Koyzis, 1995).

Traditionally, the roles of the minister of Christian education have frequently included, but are not limited to, administrator, teacher, recruiter and trainer of volunteers, program planner and promoter, evaluator, faith interpreter, education consultant, and learning specialist.

Since the advent of the Christian education professional, there has been discussion of the appropriate training required to adequately prepare persons to direct the church's educational ministry. As early as 1915, a study by the Religious Education Association concluded that the proper academic preparation for directors of religious education should include a graduate degree in religious education. In practice, Christian education has been a profession of widely differing professional standards and educational requirements. While many Christian educators have master's degrees, these degrees include master's in Christian education, master's in secular education, master's of divinity with no specialization in Christian education, a master's of divinity with a concentration in Christian education, and a master's of theology with a concentration in Christian education.

Lack of specific educational requirements is not the only factor contributing to the rocky development of the profession. Other factors include the status of the profession, and gender issues. Studies repeatedly reveal that ministers of Christian education do not feel that their profession receives the status it deserves.

Gender-related imbalances appear to affect the Christian education profession in many Protestant denominations. Particularly in evangelical denominations, the majority of full-time positions are held by men, while women occupy the majority of part-time Christian education jobs. Women in evangelical churches are also more likely to be given the title of director of Christian education, while men are titled ministers of Christian education.

Minister or director of Christian education is one of several titles used to designate the Christian education professional in the local church. Recent studies have revealed an increasing number of titles, including associate pastor, children's minister, program director, minister of family life, and director of discipleship. Over thirty titles have been documented.

Increasingly, full-time professional Christian educators in the local church are required to take on roles beyond the traditional Christian educator roles. These expanded roles can include preaching, visitation, counseling, and worship leadership, among others. In 1989, the name of NADCE was changed to PACE (Professional Association of Christian Educators) to reflect the increasing diversity of roles and job titles used in educational ministry.

The crucial role of education in the growth and mission of the church mandates that the profession continue. The future of the profession would be greatly strengthened by renewed cooperation among practitioners, theorists, denominational leaders, and theological institutions working to enhance the status of the profession, standardize educational requirements, and erase gender discrimination.

NANCY L. DEMOTT

Bibliography. D. G. Emler (1989), *Revisioning the DRE;* A. A. Koyzis, *Christian Education Journal* 15, no. 2 (1995): 69–87; K. E. Larson, *Christian Education Journal* 16, no. 1 (1995): 9–27; K. E. Larson, *Christian Education Journal* 16, no. 2 (1995): 46–64; K. E. Larson, *Christian Education Journal* 16, no. 3 (1996): 95–109; J. M. Stubblefield, (1993), *The Effective Minister of Education: A Comprehensive Handbook.*

Ministry. Few terms resonate with as many connotations as ministry. The word is integral to seminary course titles ("Strategy for Youth Ministry"); to book jackets (*The Complete Handbook of Children's Ministry*); and to interaction among church leaders ("Tell me about your ministry"). Some Christians associate the word with their volunteer efforts. For others, ministry connotes the roles of vocational Christian workers.

To grasp the significance of the term requires an exploration of its New Testament usage; discussion of who is responsible for ministry; and the concept's practical implications for laypersons as well as for vocational leaders.

The Greek word for minister is *diakonos.* This noun is translated "servant," "attendant," or "deacon." The verb form means "to wait upon" or "to serve." A glance at selected verses reveals the broad spectrum of activities covered by the word, and the variety of people who were involved in its implementation.

New Testament Usage. (Italics indicates a form of the word.) After Jesus healed Simon's mother-in-law, "she began *to wait on* them" (Mark 1:31). During a public discourse, Jesus said, "If anyone *serves* Me, the Father will honor him" (John 12:26 NASB). Jesus "did not come *to be served,* but *to serve*" (Mark 10:45 NASB). Jesus equated taking care of the poor, the sick, and prisoners with ministry rendered unto him (Matt. 25:42–45). Phoebe was a "*servant* of the church" at Cenchrea (Rom. 16:1 NASB). Paul lumped Corinthian believers with his own team of workers when he wrote, "God [has] reconciled us to Himself through Christ, and gave us the *ministry* of reconciliation" (2 Cor. 5:19 NASB). In the same letter, Paul labeled the church's planned financial gift to Jerusalem a "*ministry* to the saints" (2 Cor. 9:1 NASB). God gave the church pastor-teachers "for the equipping of the saints for the work of *service*" (Eph. 4:12 NASB). Paul disclosed the qualifications for the office of *deacon* (1 Tim. 3:8–13). During Paul's second Roman imprisonment, he complimented Onesiphorus for refreshing him, telling Timothy "you know very well what *services* he rendered at Ephesus" (2 Tim. 1:18 NASB). Jewish Christians were told that God would remember "the love which you have shown toward His name, in *having ministered* and in *still ministering* to the saints" (Heb. 6:10 NASB). In reference to God's enablement of church members, Peter wrote, "as each one has received a special gift, employ it in *serving* one another" (1 Peter 4:10 NASB).

From those representative verses one can gain a basic assumption of Christian education: *ministry is the privilege and responsibility of every Christian, not merely the domain of professionals.*

Conclusion of Contemporary Authors. Contemporary churchmen steeped in ecclesiology echo this conclusion. Ray Stedman (1972), in a treatise on Ephesians 4, declared that the ultimate work of the church is to be implemented by the saints—plain, ordinary Christians—and not by a professional clergy or a few select laypeople. He asserted that the four offices of apostle, prophet, evangelist, and pastor-teacher exist for one basic function: equipping common Christians to do the tasks assigned to them. John MacArthur Jr. (1982) echoed Stedman's conviction. He lamented that for many Christians church is a place to go to watch professionals perform and to pay the professionals to carry out the church program. MacArthur called this scheme a violation of God's plan, a hindrance to the growth of God's people, and an obstacle to the evangelistic outreach of the church into the community.

According to Norman Harper (1981), every Christian has a ministry for which he or she is accountable to God. When the layperson is confronted with the opportunity to serve in the church, the question is not whether he or she has a ministry, but whether that particular form of ministry is the one to which God is calling him or her. Harper rejects the notion of "voluntarism" in regard to ministry, since it promotes the notion that ministry is optional. Elton Trueblood (1983) did not call church members "laypersons." A layperson in regard to law has not passed the bar exam and is not qualified to practice. In contrast, Trueblood insisted that there is no place in the church of Jesus Christ for those who cannot practice. Instead of "laypersons," he called church members "ministers of common life" (24).

The Priesthood of All Believers. A biblical concept that reinforces every Christian's identity as "minister" is the priesthood of all believers. This doctrine announces every believer's direct access to God, without the necessity of a human priestly mediator (Heb. 4:14–16; 10:18–22). Yet the priesthood of all believers also suggests a priestly function for God's people.

Peter reminded church members of the ministerial mandate stemming from their noble identity: "You are a chosen race, a royal priesthood . . . a people for God's own possession, that you may proclaim the excellencies of Him who has called you out of darkness into His marvelous light" (1 Pet. 2:9 NASB). When he called the church a "holy priesthood," Peter urged readers to "offer up spiritual sacrifices acceptable to God" (1 Pet. 2:5 NASB). Similarly, Paul told Roman Christians to "present your bodies a living and holy sacrifice, acceptable to God, which is your spiritual service of worship" (Rom. 12:1 NASB). As the "great high priest" (Heb. 4:14), Jesus gave his own life as the ultimate sacrifice for sin. Findley Edge (1971) insisted that Jesus' example of *the priest as the sacrifice* clarifies the implication for his followers. What is the "sacrifice" that the Christian, as a priest, is to offer God on behalf of a sinful world? According to Edge, he is to offer himself, his life in ministry.

Role of Vocational Leaders. The identity of church members as ministers elevates, rather than diminishes, the role of vocational Christian leaders. God gives them a distinct call and commensurate authority "for the equipping of the saints" (Eph. 4:12 NASB). The Greek term translated "equipping" is *katartismon*, from which the English word *artisan* is derived. It was used in the apostle Paul's day of a fisherman *mending* a net and of a physician *resetting* a broken bone. The idea couched in the word is that of "preparing for usefulness." The varied activities of vocational workers should have an enabling outcome, motivating and training church members to fulfill their distinctive ministries within the church program and within their spheres of influence in the community. Though God calls every Christian into some form of ministry, he does not call everyone to leadership. The New Testament clearly differentiates between saints (church members) in general, and leaders in particular (Acts 15:22; 1 Thess. 5:12–13; 1 Tim. 3:1–13; Heb. 13:7, 17; 1 Pet. 5:1–5).

Resources for Ministry. Along with his mandate for ministry, God provides resources that facilitate success. To each believer he gives at least one *spiritual gift*, or capacity for service (1 Cor. 12:7). The Holy Spirit helps teachers, as well as their students, to understand Scripture (1 Cor. 2:10–14). It is the Holy Spirit who opens the hearts of persons responsive to the gospel (John 16:8; Acts 16:14). Since positive ministry outcomes depend on divine as well as human endeavor, persons involved may tap into God's power through prayer (Eph. 6:19; 2 Thess. 3:1). God's written Word also has innate power to change people's lives (2 Tim. 3:15–17; Heb. 4:12).

Practical Implications. From the fertile soil of the Bible's teaching on ministry sprout practical implications for laypersons, church staff, and professors who train future vocational leaders.

God's call for all believers to be involved in ministry should infuse church members with a sense of meaning and purpose in life. Knowing they are "ambassadors for Christ" (2 Cor. 5:20) who represent him in every sphere of activity gives significance to what they may otherwise perceive as routine or mundane. They should view ministry opportunities as privileges with eternal significance, rather than as burdensome religious obligations.

Church leaders should plan their schedules, the church's calendar of activities, and its budget in light of God's equipping mandate. To what extent do their relational contacts result in members' expanded ministry? Do church organizational structures encourage rather than stifle lay involvement in God's work? Does the church budget allocate funds for the training and ministry mobilization of church members? Bruce Wilkinson (1983) employed a sports analogy in advocating a training mentality among professional clergy. He said it would be ridiculous if football coaches yanked their starting lineup off the field and inserted themselves into the game to run the plays. Yet he believes that is what many church leaders do. Wilkinson likens staff members to star players who pass, block, and kick—while spectators watch and clap. He urges leaders to fulfill the role of coaches who help church members get into the game and succeed. According to Wilkinson, church leaders succeed when they prepare others to do the job.

Bible colleges and seminaries should prepare vocational leaders who are conversant with ecclesiology and familiar with concrete strategies for lay participation in ministry. Students' future implementation of a biblical philosophy of ministry depends on how they are taught to think about the church. Bill Hull (1993) expressed concern about the weakness of evangelical schools in providing students a scripturally based philosophy of the church. He questioned whether the typical graduate walks into his first pastorate with a philosophical framework by which to understand his work and God's objectives for the people seated before him in the pew. Hull said that a typical graduate knows little about vision, or about training others in ministry skills (30).

In the Bible, God provides a cogent articulation of "ministry." He reveals who is expected to minister, how he empowers for ministry, and whom he has called to prepare his people for ministry.

TERRY POWELL

Bibliography. F. Edge (1971), *The Greening of the Church;* N. Harper (1981), *Making Disciples: The Challenge of Christian Education at the End of the 20th Century;* B. Hull (1993), *Can We Save the Evangelical Church?;* J. MacArthur Jr. (1982), *Body Dynamics;* T. Powell (1987), *Welcome to Your Ministry;* R. Stedman (1972), *Body Life;* E. Trueblood (1983), *A Time for Holy Dissatisfaction;* B. Wilkinson (1983), *Talk thru Bible Personalities.*

Ministry-Based Evangelism. The God-directed attempt by Christians to truly care for those in need, realizing that as we care for others we care for Jesus (Matt. 25:31–46). Rather than forcing a choice between meeting people's spiritual needs or physical and emotional needs, ministry-based evangelism imitates Jesus by ministering to the whole person (Matt. 15:32).

Whatever temporal, physical, or emotional needs people have, the ultimate goal of ministry-based evangelism is to fulfill their eternal need for a relationship with Jesus Christ (Rom. 6:23). Ministry-based evangelism is done because God cares about people in need and because He desires for people to come to salvation (Rom. 10:1), not just because of cutbacks in government welfare. Ministry-based evangelism provides opportunities to teach people God's ways as they move from dependency on public assistance to dependency on God.

Jesus taught that the greatest and foremost commandment is "to love the Lord your God with all your heart, soul, and mind" (Matt. 22:37–38 TLB). Obeying this commandment is the key to all ministry.

Those who practice ministry-based evangelism strive to develop a relationship with those to whom they minister that mirrors God's relationship with His people. When Christians sin there are consequences, but they are still God's children. God convicts and teaches so that His people may learn and come back to Him in repentance.

Those practicing ministry-based evangelism find that those they help also fail. In ministry-based evangelism, consequences are not eliminated or relationships ended, but attempts are made to teach and confront people with Scripture so that God may bring growth out of failure.

Jesus saw the multitudes and was moved with compassion to help them (Matt. 9:36; 14:14; 15:32; Mark 6:34; 8:2). More than that, in the midst of the multitudes He also saw and had compassion for individuals (Matt. 20:34; Mark 1:41; Luke 7:13). It was compassion and action that set the Samaritan apart from the priest and Levite on the road to Jericho (Luke 10:33).

Jesus said that the second greatest commandment is to love one's neighbor (Matt. 22:39), and that Christians will be known as His disciples if they love one another (John 13:34–35). This is not the feeling-oriented love so prevalent in society today, but an active love that calls Christians to do good even to their enemies (Luke 6:27, 35).

Prayer is a vital component of ministry-based evangelism. Those practicing ministry-based evangelism pray for salvation of souls (Rom.

10:1), as well as for the direction and wisdom of the Holy Spirit. Prayers are also made for the resources needed to meet the needs encountered, with a dependence on God's provision rather than humankind's or government's. Psalm 50:10 reminds God's people that the Father owns the cattle on a thousand hills. He can certainly provide for the "least of these" (Matt. 25:40).

Historically, Christians ministering to those in need have most frequently focused on meeting physical needs. Clothing closets and food pantries are examples of this focus. These approaches fall under the heading of emergency assistance. While the gospel may be presented, the long term effectiveness of emergency assistance is minimal. Ministry-based evangelism goes beyond emergency assistance to minister to the whole person.

Recently, ministry-based evangelism has begun to emerge as a formal discipline within the field of Christian education. Ministry-based evangelism and ministry-based discipleship are the two avenues of ministry that originate from the field of biblical social work. Biblical social work is biblical, relational, and holistic.

Biblical social work is founded on the belief that Scripture is sufficient to solve people's problems in daily life. Passages that teach sufficiency of Scripture include: Isaiah 55:11; 2 Timothy 3:16–17; Hebrews 4:12; and 2 Peter 1:3. Based on this perspective of the sufficiency of Scripture, biblical social workers rely on God's Word for all aspects of their ministry. Formal educational opportunities and research are becoming available for Christians to develop skills in biblical social work. Biblical social workers must be in a dynamic, growing relationship with Christ. Based on this strong relationship with Christ, they are enabled to help others within the context of a loving relationship. Biblical social work is also holistic, and based upon the realization that we must minister to the whole person. When people are in need and/or crisis it is crucial for the biblical social worker to understand that they are effected physically, spiritually, and emotionally. Biblical social work attempts to bring the healing of Christ to all areas of their lives.

A study of the Gospels reveals that Jesus, the Word of God, was concerned about the whole person and developed strong relationships with those around Him. As Christians reflect on the question "What would Jesus do?", Scripture reveals ministry-based evangelism as an effective means of carrying out the Great Commission and reaching the world for Christ.

JOHN E. BABLER

Bibliography. D. A. Atkinson and C. L. Roesel (1995), *Meeting Needs, Sharing Christ: Ministry-Evangelism in Today's New Testament Church*; C. G. Ward (1996), *The Billy Graham Christian Worker's Handbook*; D. R. Watkins (1994), *Christian Social Ministry*.

Miracles. *See* Signs and Wonders.

Misconception. *See* Distortion.

Misrepresentation. *See* Distortion.

Mission. The mission of a church must be clearly defined and members of the body must be led to understand and accept the mission. There needs to be a basic understanding of the essential character of a church before its mission can be described. Biblical phrases help in developing this understanding. The church is described as "the people of God," "a new creation," "the bride of Christ," "the body of Christ," "a branch of the vine," "a fellowship." All of these terms are useful in shaping an understanding of mission.

Individuals are called to discipleship when they accept Christ as Savior. They become a part of the church to develop as disciples and to help the body to accomplish what it needs to be doing. It is essential that all members of the body understand their responsibility to grow as individual believers and also to accept their part in growing the church.

The word *mission* implies that there is something to be done, a work to be accomplished. In the church, it is understood that this is to be accomplished by the members of the body. The body is to carry out the commission of Christ. This is rooted in what the church is, its nature.

In Ephesians 3:9–10 Paul describes the "manifold wisdom of God." As an individual comes to know the "mystery," a response of faith can be made and the person becomes a child of God. Those who have received Christ can then be used by God to make known the wisdom of God to others. Christ charged his followers to let the gospel be spread. This is a significant privilege that has been given to believers, but it carries with it a significant responsibility as well. It is to this privilege and responsibility that all believers are called in accomplishing the mission of the church. The proclamation of the gospel is shared by all believers as they act on this assignment.

There is a sense in which the mission of the church is fairly simple: share the gospel and make disciples. The difficult part comes when the church begins to determine its strategy for accomplishing this mission. It is in this setting that individuals begin to think about what *they* want to do instead of what *Christ* wants done. Perhaps the greatest test of fellowship in a church comes when its members are faced with trying to describe and then carry out the mission of the church. Education plays a vital part in helping believers understand and determine that they will seek the mind of Christ and not pursue their own agendas in accomplishing the mission of the church.

WILLIAM G. CALDWELL

See also CHURCH; FELLOWSHIP; KOINONIA; MISSIONS EDUCATION

Missions, Methods of. The history of effective Protestant missions traces its roots to the sixteenth century. With great anticipation and dedication, mission groups exploded their way first across Europe and later through the United States, Africa, India, and South America. With one goal in mind, these early missionaries went out to reach unreached people groups (Kane, 1982, 76). Some of these early mission groups included the Danish-Halle mission, the Moravian missions, and the Netherlands Missionary Society (Kane, 1982, 80).

As with any human endeavor, there are always some approaches that succeed and some that miss the mark. Unfortunately, some even cause damage to their mission enterprise. What follows are effective and ineffective techniques that have been used for evangelism over the past few centuries.

Effective Missionary Methods. The most prominent method that has proven to be highly successful is the translation of Scripture into the common language of indigenous people groups. Historically, missionaries worked with little or no modern resources, painstakingly translating each word and syntax into previously known written languages. After this daunting challenge, they subsequently taught the inhabitants to read this newly written text. Some of these translators were members of the British Bible Society, the Foreign Bible Society, and Wycliffe Bible Translators. Nothing could be more effective than having God's active and living Word available in one's mother tongue.

Also noteworthy are the efforts of radio evangelism. Using this evangelistic method, missionaries are able to go inside walls they could not otherwise penetrate. The radio ministries of the FEBC (Far East Broadcasting Company) and HCJB (based in Quito, Equador) are fine examples of what radio ministries are doing today to access people behind closed geopolitical borders. This is especially important in communist countries and in Muslim countries where the freedom to study God's Word is far too risky. The use of Bible correspondence courses and distance learning instructional methods are also effective tools for the same reasons aforementioned.

During the early decades of the twentieth century Christian mission schools began to make their contribution to mission expansion. Especially in rural, poor, and illiterate societies, there is no better venue to influence a community for Christ than through education. Mission agencies had as their goal not only the teaching of reading and writing, but also influencing young minds of the next generation with biblical truths. It is noted that "with so many people being exposed to Christianity over such a long period of time

during the most formative years of their lives it is no wonder that so many of them embraced the Christian faith in one form or another" (Kane, 1982, 142).

Ineffective Missionary Methods. In contrast to the victories of effective Christian evangelism through Bible translations and radio broadcasts are the problems with other missionary approaches.

Unfortunately, many of the first missionaries were either unaware of or condescending in their attitude toward the cultural distinctives found on the foreign field. Often communicated, sometimes without intent, was an attitude of superiority regarding the ways of Western civilization. This "superiority complex" resulted in a barrier between the missionary of Western origin and the host national. Because these missionaries were not successful in separating Christianity from its setting in Western culture this attitude produced a truncated paradigm of Christian beliefs. Thus, Western-looking buildings, services, and dress were instituted while drums, dancing, and indigenous styles were seen as taboo. "In so doing, they placed on the necks of their converts a yoke that was more than they could bear. Christianity as it was developed in the Third World ended up with a 'Made in the USA' stamp on it" (Kane, 1982, 162). The missionaries were shortsighted in not creating an indigenous church in a non-Western form.

At the point where many missionaries were able to enter into otherwise closed regions or states came the emergence of colonization as well. Because of the missionaries' timing, they were seen as part of the same entity. Therefore, where the colonial system was productive and positive (e.g., Black Africa), the efforts of the missionaries were also. However, where the colonization was abusive or repressive (e.g., India), then the missionaries unfortunately were included in the natives' distrust toward the foreigners (Kane, 1982, 129). The drive for colonizing foreign soil and for propagating the gospel were seen as one and the same by many foreign nationals.

One other failed methodology stems from the inability of the Roman Catholic Church and the Protestant churches to systematically work together in regions where one was present before or more strongly represented than another. Although these two churches share notable differences, these certainly pale in comparison to the actual threats to Christianity posed by Hinduism and Islam.

Although Protestant missions originated in the 1600s, there remain timeless principles that we as Christians in the twenty-first century, can apply in our evangelicalistic approaches today—for example, the correlation between one's own spiritual maturity with his or her burden for reaching the lost. Any significant missionary movement was first launched following a revival or awakening. It is imperative for the church to maintain personal spiritual vitality and to be dedicated to prayer for the ongoing revival of the universal church if the fields are to be harvested any further.

The church must continue to embrace the breadth of God's plan and his ability to use peoples, practices, and denominations that are foreign to her. It will be of great importance in the decades ahead, where little or nothing is considered absolute, to find areas of agreement and commonality (e.g., with our Catholic brothers and sisters) rather than areas of dispute. Similarly, the church must recognize how Satan can prevent us from accomplishing the Great Commission through denominational distractions over petty issues of little eternal consequence. Ultimately, we must remain focused on the serious task of evangelizing the largest population in history with the message of Christ.

Finally, a mission work is most effective when it meets the needs of the whole person, encompassing spiritual, emotional, physical, medical, and educational areas. Mission efforts which have maintained this have evidenced a higher degree of significant indigenous growth and longevity. Effective stewardship requires careful attention to the use of methods which have proven beneficial in the past while still seeking to remain on the cutting edge by exploring new methods for reaching the lost.

MICHELLE D. ANTHONY

Bibliography. J. H. Kane (1982), *A Concise History of the Christian World Mission;* idem (1971), *A Global View of Christian Missions: From Pentecost to the Present;* K. S. Latourette (1937–94), *A History of the Expansion of Christianity;* R. Winter (1970), *The Twenty-Five Unbelievable Years 1945–1969.*

Missions and Children. Children are encouraged to move beyond self-centeredness to a focus on others when they are introduced to missions. Missions as an outward ministry of evangelism and service beyond the local church body is of primary importance. At the same time, the attitudes of altruism and globalization deserve consideration as well. Altruism is an attitude demonstrating unselfish interest in helping someone else. The goal of globalization is to develop an awareness and appreciation of global interconnectedness and interdependence as it relates to the mission of the church.

The missions experience is nurtured through the community of the church. A Christian education program is foundational in developing a child's interest in missions. The primary goal for such a program is to teach mission attitudes and concepts. Although traditional programs may focus on overseas missionaries and projects, there is a movement toward a more inclusive concept of missions in which one's own culture and society is included within the missions perspective.

Missions programs seem to be fairly uniform in that they include the following in various degrees of emphasis in their statement of missions education for children: (1) an awareness that God loves children and adults everywhere; (2) an awareness of the responsibility of the church in the worldwide outreach ministry; (3) personal involvement in communicating the gospel everywhere; and (4) mission involvement in one's own setting or in the world beyond this immediate setting (ACMC, 1988).

Missions awareness begins at home within the family unit. Conversation around the table or as a planned part of family devotions stimulates children's interest in both home and international mission efforts. This openness to missions is further encouraged through the children's ministry in the local church.

Missions becomes an integral part of church life as it is integrated into the total educational program. Childhood years are especially important, as foundational values and life perspectives are developed. During this time, both home and church influence later decisions for missions involvement. In a survey of missionaries, 16 percent made their commitment to become a full-time career missionary before the age of 13, 43 percent had parents who were career missionaries or who invited missionaries into their homes, 42 percent were affected by missions conferences, and 58 percent cited direct contact with missionaries and the mission field and reading missions books as influencing them (Campbell, 1991).

A comprehensive missions program will include missions information, motivation for missions, and opportunities for direct involvement. Activities include visits by missionaries, service opportunities, studies of mission countries, and special projects that allow the child to be directly involved in giving and praying for others. The curriculum for weekly programs often includes mission stories, games, crafts, prayer, and music. Methodology and aids that are especially conducive for teaching missions include visuals, videos, audiotapes, global awareness center, letter writing, drama, exhibits, and field trips.

Intentional activities to promote prosocial behaviors such as helping, sharing, comforting, cooperating, and showing empathy provide a foundation for a "mission spirit." Parents and teachers can foster such behaviors by demonstrating them within their own lives. Missions education is most effective when integrated into the immediate context rather than existing peripheral to the child's everyday experiences.

LILLIAN J. BRECKENRIDGE

Bibliography. B. Campbell (1991), *I Don't Want to Wait until I'm Grown Up;* G. Dueck (1990), *Kids for the World: A Guidebook for Children's Mission Resources;*

J. L. Gibson (1975), *Childhood Education in the Church;* *Missions Education Handbook* (1988).

Missions Education. The foundation of missions education was established by the apostle Paul. Jesus gave his disciples and the early church the task of world evangelism and discipleship in the Great Commission. It was not, however, until the era of the apostle Paul that the church began to take the gospel to other places and peoples. Paul not only did missions, but also took it upon himself to educate the church about missions. He did this in several ways. First, he shared his missionary vision with the members of the Antioch church. Under the direction of the Holy Spirit, the Antioch church then sent Paul and Barnabas to minister (Acts 13:1–3). Second, Paul reported personally to the church about his mission endeavors when he returned from his mission work. He took this opportunity to educate the church in the task and opportunity of mission evangelism (Acts 14:28–29). Third, Paul wrote letters to churches while doing mission work. While the primary purpose of these "prayer letters" or epistles was doctrinal, they also served to acquaint people with his missionary work. Finally, Paul invited the church to participate financially in his missionary endeavors through their support of needy people (1 Cor. 16:3) and on at least two occasions received personal financial support from the church at Philippi (Phil. 4:14). These seeds of missions education planted by Paul came to life during the modern missionary movement.

Between the time of Paul and the modern missionary movement of the eighteenth century, missions work moved in a slow and halting fashion. There were exceptions along the way such as the movement involving Patrick of Ireland. In the 400s he established monasteries as a base of missionary education and outreach. These monasteries developed into training institutions in evangelism from which missionaries were sent out and where they returned for rest and renewal. However, missions education did not gain a foothold until the advent of the modern missionary movement in the eighteenth century. The foundation for the modern missionary movement was laid in the Reformation and in the spiritual revivals of the eighteenth century. The Reformation grounded the church in the Word of God and spiritual revivals fostered a desire in people to take the gospel to other peoples and lands.

William Carey (1761–1834), known as the father of modern missions, was a leader in missions education. In 1792 he wrote his influential book *An Enquiry Into the Obligation of Christians to Use Means for the Conversion of the Heathens.* His book changed the thinking of people toward missions and stirred many to commit themselves to the task of the Great Commission. Later in 1792 Carey, along with other Baptist ministers, started the Baptist Missionary Society. Almost immediately, Carey applied to the society for missionary service in India. He resigned his pastorate and after months of deputation sailed for India with his wife and family in 1793. Although he never returned home, his letters from India over thirty-nine years were a tremendous influence in educating and motivating many to missions service. As a result of his influence, mission societies such as the London Missionary Society (1795), Church Missionary Society (1799), Baptist and Foreign Bible Society (1804), and the American Baptist Missionary Union (1814) came into being.

In the early days of the modern missionary movement, it was mission societies that led the way in educating Christians about missions. At first, these missionary societies only worked to obtain support for missionaries on foreign fields. Gradually, however, they recognized the direct relationship between education and serving, and incorporated missionary education programs into their structure. The London Mission Society, for example, realizing the need to educate people about missions began sending teams of representatives to churches to inform the members about the work of their missionaries in foreign lands. Soon, prospective and veteran missionaries were speaking in churches to inform people about the biblical reasons for missions work, acquaint them with the needs of the foreign field, and request their financial aid. These speaking engagements served to educate people about missions and raised money for support. About this time, mission agencies began using the printed page to educate their constituency about missions. The *Mission Register,* started in 1813, was a monthly journal sent to interested people and churches reporting on the activities of missionaries. This was a forerunner of many other mission journals (Dunstan, 1963).

As the mission societies grew, denominations, beginning with Wesley and the Methodist movement in the early nineteenth century, formed their own mission organizations. Denominations played an important role in mission education and soon created their own mission boards and eventually their own missions departments to educate their constituency about missions.

Mission societies eventually gave way to faith missions like the China Inland Mission, founded in 1865 by Hudson Taylor. Other nondenominational mission groups like the Sudan Interior Mission (1893) and the Africa Inland Mission (1895) followed in quick succession. Each of these groups promoted missions education in churches as they recruited volunteers and raised money. At the same time Bible institutes began to emphasize foreign missionary service and developed curriculum to prepare students for missionary service. Schools such as Columbia Bible College, Nyack College, Multnomah School of the Bible, Prairie Bible Institute, Briercrest Bible Institute, and Lancaster Bible College played a large role in missions education.

In England and the United States during the latter half of the nineteenth century, large missionary conferences were held to educate people about missions. Missions-sponsored conferences were held in Liverpool, England (1860), London (1880), and New York (1900). They attracted a wide audience of pastors, missionaries, and missions personnel. Pastors were thought to be the key to missions education within the church. The main focus of the conferences was to discuss means of educating people about missions. As a result of these conferences, organizations for missions education were formed within the churches. Women's missionary groups as well as children's missionary organizations were formed. It was during this time that many churches developed missions courses for their members. Literature also played an increasingly major role in missions education. Mission societies published regular news sheets, reports, and magazines to inform people about missions and to encourage support and giving. The London conference listed over one hundred missions publications for Europe and America.

At this time, student mission organizations were also being formed. The Student Volunteer Movement for Foreign Missions held quadrennial missions conventions beginning in 1891 in Cleveland, Ohio, to educate students about missions. Their motto was "The evangelism of the world in this generation." An educational department of the movement printed textbooks on missions topics. In their fifty-year history, the Student Volunteer Movement saw 20,500 students sent to the foreign fields.

As the church entered the twentieth century, missions education was undertaken in local churches by specific groups such as women's missionary circles, Sunday school lessons produced by denominational and independent presses, and missionary deputation. Independent mission groups have used the media to educate their constituency about missions.

On a global scale, two international evangelism conferences helped to educate people about the goals, purposes, and plans of world missions. The first conference, the Lausanne Conference held in Switzerland in 1974, was attended by 2,500 participants from over 150 nations. Sponsored by the Billy Graham Evangelistic Association, the conference served to motivate and educate attendees concerning world evangelism. The second conference, called Lausanne II, was held in Manila, Philippines in 1989, bringing together 4,000 participants from 170 countries. This conference focused on the task of evangelism and reaching the unreached peoples of the world by the year 2000.

On a national level in the U.S., Urbana has fostered missions education among university students. Following the pattern of the Student Volunteer Movement, the Urbana missions conference began in 1946 at the University of Toronto. Over its years of existence it has served to educate and motivate many to missions. Sponsored by InterVarsity Christian Fellowship, these triennial events attract nearly 16,000 university students. Over the years, nearly 200,000 students have attended. Urbana, which is held at the University of Illinois in Urbana, features dynamic speakers and opportunities for students to consider the challenge of a Christian lifestyle, praying for missions, and committing to mission endeavors. The purpose of the five-day conference, held between Christmas and New Year's, is to educate university students about God's heart for the world and their role in the great commission. Over 250 different mission agencies are represented at the conferences. In recent years over 20 percent of the attendees have committed themselves to short or long term mission service, and over half committed to support mission endeavors as part of their Christian lifestyle.

On a local level, missions education has been furthered through the Perspectives on World Christian Movement course, an intense missions education course developed by Ralph Winter of the U.S. Center for World Mission. Influenced by the Urbana conference of 1973, Winter developed a course in 1974 to help students make effective choices in missions. Winter was concerned that the gospel be taken to all the nations, particularly unreached people who have no viable church. The course covered the biblical, historical, cultural, and strategic aspects of the missions movement. The forty-five-hour course has been taken by over thirty thousand people and has been extremely effective in changing lives and motivating churches to become involved in the Great Commission.

PHILIP BUSTRUM

Bibliography. R. A. Tucker (1983), *From Jerusalem to Irian Jaya: A Biographical History of Christian Missions;* R. D. Winter and S. C. Hawthorne, eds. (1992), *Perspectives on the World Christian Movement: A Reader;* W. N. Wysham (1963), *The Westminster Dictionary of Christian Education.*

Misuse. *See* Abuse.

Mnemonic Devices. Techniques used to increase memory skills. There are various types of mnemonic devices, some of which employ words, pictures, or any of the other senses to help people recall information. Some mnemonic devices depend on organization of information into meaningful pieces.

The first category of mnemonic devices is *clustering*. This means grouping the items to be remembered into more meaningful classifications. Another type is *interactive images*. The item to be remembered with this device is associated with a picture created to recall the words originally linked with it. A similar device is a *pegword system*, where a new word is associated with a word on a previously memorized list. The method of *loci* uses visualization of an area with landmarks (such as a house) to link with items to be remembered.

Another example of a mnemonic device is an *acronym*. Here a word or expression is formed whose letters stand for a certain other word or concept. Similar to an acronym is an *acrostic*, but here a sentence is formed rather than a single word to help remember the new words. For example, to help remember the names of the lines in the treble clef, music students memorize the acrostic phrase "Every good boy does fine." Another type of mnemonic device is the *keyword system*, an interactive image that links the sound and meaning of a foreign word with the sound and meaning of a familiar word.

There are many examples of how mnemonic devices can be used in Christian education. For instance the books of the Bible have often been set to music. In this type of memory cue, the tune provides the mnemonic device for the names of the Bible books.

The interactive image has been used to help people memorize Scripture verses. The idea in this type of mnemonic device is that a contrived picture will bring to mind the aspects of the Bible verse it was designed to recall. Since texts of Bible verses are usually more than one word and sometimes more than one concept, the pictures can become very detailed and, in some cases, bizarre. If people create their own pictures for the Bible verses they intend to memorize, the verse or content to be memorized would most likely be more memorable.

The potential application of these mnemonic devices to Christian education is great. In fact, even the few examples given here can be applied to the great wealth of Bible facts that would be beneficial to have in memory for recall and use.

ROBERT J. RADCLIFFE

See also INFORMATION PROCESSING; MEMORY

Modality. A main avenue of sensation. Learning modalities are the various sensory channels through which learning occurs, such as sight, sound, and touch/motion.

The premise behind modalities is that individuals vary in how they learn. Through a combination of hereditary and environmental influences a person develops "modality strengths" or preferences for learning. Thus, people are generally classified as visual, auditory, or tactile/kinesthetic learners.

Modality teaching, or modality-based instruction, involves the practice of using a variety of strategies, activities, and means of explanation for the same content. This approach contends that individuals have a preferred style of learning, and the most effective teaching approach matches the modality of presentation with the preferred style of the learner.

This perspective is debated, as some argue that different modalities are most effective for particular content. Others suggest that involving multiple modalities in each lesson is most effective for all learners.

THOMAS HUTCHISON

Bibliography. R. and K. Dunn (1992), *Teaching Elementary Students Through Their Individual Learning Styles;* M. D. LeFever (1995), *Learning Styles: Reaching Everyone God Gave You to Teach;* B. McCarthy (1987), *The 4MAT System: Teaching to Learning Styles with Right/Left Mode Techniques.*

Modeling. Structured and unstructured efforts of an observed model to elicit new and desired patterns of behavior in the observer. Modeling should be a planned element of education to enable intentional behavioral outcomes. The informal aspect of modeling also plays a vital role in the learning process, as the desired objectives demonstrated spontaneously in life context by those involved in the instructional process provide a formidable educational tool.

Although modeling was a typical rabbinic pattern in contemporary Palestine, Jesus excelled in its effective application with his disciples. As noted by Lawrence Richards: a student should have continuous, long-term contact with the model in a wide array of life situations; the model should be consistent over a long period of time; the model should engage the student in both planned and spontaneous demonstrations of preferred outcomes; the model should assure that his or her verbal lessons are congruent with the modeled behavior; and a caring relationship with the student should encompass the educational environment (Richards, 1975, 84–85).

In Jesus' challenge to "follow me," all of Richards's emphases seem to be present. An example of this dynamic is the disciples' desire to learn more about prayer. "Lord, teach us to pray!" they beg one day after observing Jesus in prayer. Modeled behavior elicits a desire for learning and results in a teachable moment.

The apostle Paul uses explicit modeling language when he exhorts recipients of his epistles to "Be imitators of me, just as I also am of Christ"

(1 Cor. 11:1 NASB) and "For you yourselves know how you ought to follow our example" (2 Thess. 3:7 NASB).

Researchers Bryan and Walbek conducted a study that illustrates the power of modeling. Each child who participated in the study played a game with an adult model. The point of the game was to win money. As part of the experiment, a box requesting donations for the poor was placed in the room where the game was played. Each adult model made mention of the box; some spoke in favor of donating and the value of giving, while others maintained that their winnings should be their own and nobody should ask them to give the money to someone else. Regardless of their stated position, each group of adults only gave from their winnings half of the time. The results of the experiment demonstrated quite dramatically that the children's benevolent behavior was affected much more by what the adults did than by what they said. If, for instance, an adult spoke against donating but gave anyway, the children were more likely to give. If the adult spoke in favor of giving but didn't contribute, the children were more likely to imitate the adult's actions than her or his advice.

In recent years, Stanford educational scientist Albert Bandura has noted specific differences between modeling (acquisition of new responses), the inhibitory-disinhibitory effect (respectively, ceasing or starting some deviant behavior as a result of seeing a model punished or rewarded for similar behavior), and the eliciting effect (engaging in behavior related to that of a model).

MATT FRIEDEMAN

Bibliography. A. Bandura (1969), *Principles of Behavior Modification;* idem (1977), *Social Learning Theory;* L. Richards (1975), *A Theology of Christian Education.*

Monasticism. Soon after the early church grew in influence, it began to experience social, economic, and political persecution. In addition, society was becoming more pagan and multicultural, accepting a broader range of religious practice. Fearing persecution and wanting to remain unstained from the world (James 1:27), believers sought to escape the secularization associated with life in society. Coupled with a desire to return to the simplistic lifestyle modeled by Jesus and his apostles, Christians left the security of city life and took up residence in mountains, in huts along the banks of rivers and lakes, and in caves in the wilderness. Having stripped themselves of any vestige of human comfort, these hermits, or monks as they later came to be called, were free to meditate and commune with God without the distractions and constraints of city life.

One such individual who lived an ascetic life was an Egyptian Christian by the name of Anthony (251–356). When he was five his parents died, which resulted in his receiving a sizable inheritance. Fifteen years later he gave his fortune away and departed for a solitary life in the Egyptian desert. While living in a hut on the banks of the Nile River, Anthony is said to have fought numerous spiritual battles with the devil. Following the example of Christ, Anthony wrestled with the powers of darkness as he sought to live a pure life. He is reported to have castrated himself in an effort to fulfill the literal instructions of Matthew 18:9.

Anthony's wisdom spread throughout the region and in time he gathered around himself a group of individuals who were attracted to his teaching. This gathering became known as the first monastery. The communal living arrangement did not have much structure and those who associated with him were free to work, worship, or study as they wished. Most preferred to live solitary lives but would come together occasionally to worship. Anthony left this communal living for a more solitary experience on a mountain near the Red Sea. There he remained until shortly before his death at the age of 105 (Frost, 1966).

The monastic movement was started out of a growing desire to retreat from the evil effects of society under the premise that only when one was far removed from the damaging effects of pagan society could one be free to draw close to God. These groups often formed small communities around the leadership of a wise teacher. Prominent monastic leaders of this era include Pachomius, Basil, Benedict, and Augustine of Hippo.

In order to be a knowledgeable disciple, a monk was required to learn to read, copy the Scriptures, memorize large portions of it, sing, meditate, and pray. A monk took three vows, also known as rules of conduct—vows of chastity, poverty, and obedience. Each was critical to the success of the disciplined monastic lifestyle. Life was simple in the monastery. "The monastery despised the broadening of culture. Monks aspired to be saints, not scholars; they valued prayers more than poems. Many monks tried to forget what they had learned about poetry, philosophy, and other secular knowledge. Early followers were generally suspicious of the world's knowledge. Memorizing scripture and the ascetic alphabet produced spiritual knowledge" (Reed and Prevost, 1993, 115).

At first the monastery allowed for two types of students: those who wanted to become monks (*interni*), and those who simply wanted to receive an education yet remain in their chosen vocational field (*externi*). At first their curriculum was similar except for that which was needed for those choosing to become monks (Frost, 1966). Eventually, however, the curricular needs of each were so distinct that monasteries specialized in only one of these forms of education. These schools were the primary means by which a young man could receive an education between the sixth and eleventh centuries. The only other schools which were operational during the Middle Ages were the cathedral schools or Episcopal schools (Eavey, 1964).

The monastic educational system was harsh and highly disciplined. The primary focus was on religious instruction, and the content of the curriculum was controlled by the pope. Fasting and prayer were required of all students and classes were taught in Latin. The students progressed through the seven liberal arts: grammar, rhetoric, dialectic, arithmetic, geometry, music, and astronomy (Gangel and Benson, 1983).

Many of the monasteries had large libraries. This was due in part to the careful dictation and copying of books. One monk would recite a book while several others would carefully write down what was heard. Another group of monks would check what was written to ensure accuracy. Once they finished, the monks traded manuscripts with other monasteries, thereby increasing their library holdings. It was this academic resource which produced so many outstanding thinkers and scholars during the Middle Ages. Leading thinkers from across Western Europe received their education in monasteries (Reed and Prevost, 1993).

MICHAEL J. ANTHONY

Bibliography. C. B. Eavy (1964), *History of Christian Education;* E. F. Frost (1966), *Historical and Philosophical Foundations of Western Education;* K. O. Gangel and W. S. Benson (1983), *Christian Education: Its History and Philosophy;* F. Mayer (1966), *A History of Educational Thought;* J. E. Reed and R. Prevost (1993), *A History of Christian Education;* A. E. Sanner and A. F. Harper (1978), *Exploring Christian Education.*

See also MEDIEVAL EDUCATION; SCHOLASTICISM

Monogamy. Marriage relationship with one mate. *Monogamy* is rooted in two Greek words combined to mean "one woman" and refers to the nature of a marriage relationship. The antithesis of monogamy is polygamy, which is rooted in the concept of many or multiple wives; thus, it is defined as a marriage relationship with multiple partners.

Biblically, the concept of marriage is first mentioned in Genesis 2:22–25. Inferred from the Genesis passage is the concept of monogamy in the language of one man—one woman—one flesh. This is God's ideal. Yet, polygamy appears to be a common practice in the ancient Middle East. Often, multiple marriages were politically expedient for the king (2 Sam. 5:13), and some viewed the taking of foreign wives as part of the spoils of war to be acceptable under the Law (Deut. 21:10–14). Examples of Old Testament polygamous marriages include those of Jacob, David, and Solomon even though Moses warned that

taking many wives was a dangerous thing (Deut. 17:17). Monogamy seems to have become the ethical standard for Israel after the exile, forcing Malachi to address divorce issues.

The desired duration of a monogamous relationship throughout Scripture is life. When a life partner dies, the marriage vow is terminated allowing the surviving spouse to marry another person (1 Tim. 5:14). The concept of a second, subsequent marriage is called *serial monogamy.*

The New Testament references monogamy as the normal practice among believers. Scripture is filled with references prohibiting adulterous or extramarital relationships. Among the Jewish people of Jesus' day, divorce was commonplace, providing a mind-set for serial monogamy. Paul addresses monogamy by listing it as a positive character trait essential for leadership in the church (1 Tim. 3:2, 12; Titus 1:6). There is considerable debate over whether Paul's instruction to Timothy and Titus was intended to eliminate serial monogamy among church leaders or whether his purpose was to eliminate polygamy. Both sides of the debate agree that being "a one-woman man" is the heart of this essential character trait for church leaders.

In any biblical discussion of biblical monogamy, research must include the concept of divorce and remarriage. In other words, does Scripture allow for serial monogamy when divorce is the cause? In the Old Testament, consideration must be given to Moses' granting a certificate of divorce in Deuteronomy 24:1, and to God's hatred of divorce in Malachi 2:16. In the New Testament, emphasis is placed on Jesus' teaching in Matthew 5:31–32; 19:9; and Luke 16:18; and Paul's instructions in 1 Corinthians 7:1–15.

Finally, in examining biblical monogamy, Scripture provides no evidence to support any definition of marriage that would join individuals of the same gender together in marriage. In fact, Scripture suggests that any form of sexual relationship outside of heterosexual union within species is an abomination and sin—not a marriage relationship (Lev. 18:22–23; Rom. 1:26–27). Thus, monogamy is a moot point outside heterosexual marriage.

PATRICK A. BLEWETT

Montessori, Maria (1870–1952). Pioneer in modern education and originator of the progressive educational method that bears her name, the "Montessori Method." Maria Montessori was born in the Italian village of Chiaravalle in the province of Ancona. As an adolescent in Rome she demonstrated a great aptitude in mathematics and considered a career in engineering, but later turned her interests toward biology and medicine. She gained entrance to the University of Rome and in 1896 distinguished herself as the first woman to graduate with a degree in medicine, doing so by obtaining a double degree as Doctor of Medicine and Doctor of Surgery.

Upon graduation, Montessori worked in the psychiatric clinic at the University of Rome. Her clinical experience with retarded children led her to a study of the educational problems of the mentally handicapped and subsequently she founded a school for them. In 1907 she extended her methods to normal children by opening her first *Casa dei Bambini* (Children's House) in a Rome slum for some sixty children, ages 3 to 6. Later that year she opened a second Children's House in the same district, and in the following year another was opened in Milan. In 1909 she published her monumental *The Montessori Method* (translated into English in 1912) and her educational approach began to attract worldwide attention. Many Montessori schools were established in a number of countries between 1910 and 1920.

In addition to her work with children, Montessori held the Professorial Chair of Hygiene at Magistero Femminile in Rome, served as professor of anthropology at the University of Rome, and for a time was government inspector of schools in Italy. Wars and civil unrest forced her to move from country to country. Her efforts in Italy were halted when the fascist government shut down her schools. She moved to Barcelona, Spain, and worked there until the Spanish Civil War forced her to move to the Netherlands. She was uprooted again with the onset of World War II and spent time in India and Ceylon. After the war, she returned to the Netherlands where she taught and lived until her death.

The Montessori method of education is best understood in light of a triangle of critical components: the child, the environment, and adults. The method is based on the child's growing awareness of the world as perceived through the senses, as well as on natural development. Teachers are encouraged to observe the natural and spontaneous behaviors of children and then arrange learning experiences that arouse the interest and nurture development in them. Montessori education emphasizes learning in the formative years of birth to age 6; children schooled by the method often read and write before age 5.

The Montessori educational environment is a wall-to-wall totality in which every object, every piece of furniture, even the decor itself, is the product of careful preparation and thought-out design. Furthermore, the environment provides an open atmosphere of freedom tempered with structure and order. For example, children are free to move about the classroom from one set of specially designed materials to another but knowing that their boundaries of work space will be respected by others. Children also have freedom in selecting and using materials, but there is a sense of order and structure in how the materials are arranged.

The teacher or "directress" of a Montessori classroom serves as an observer, facilitator, preparer of the environment, and introducer of new material. Since self-motivated and individualized learning is at the heart of the method, the teacher guides and facilitates as the learner explores and discovers information in the prepared environment. Parents play an active role in the school by communicating with the teachers, visiting the classroom, reinforcing the philosophy in the home, and taking part in school activities.

The Montessori method of education has been used in thousands of schools around the world, although it has gained only limited acceptance in the United States. The first American public Montessori school was opened in 1975, and the number of public schools offering Montessori programs in this country now number about one hundred. The method has been embraced in the United States by private institutions and home school teachers as well. The influence of Montessori in Christian education is found in Sonja Stewart and Jerome Berryman's *Young Children and Worship*.

Montessori toiled in the fields of psychiatry, hygiene, and anthropology in addition to being a crusader for the emancipation of women. But first and foremost she was an innovative and revolutionary educator. Her own genius spawned an international educational movement which in turn inspired gifts and abilities inherent in countless children. Montessori also involved herself in the writing of books and papers. In addition to her initial and best-known work, *The Montessori Method*, she authored *Pedagogical Anthropology* (1913), *The Child in the Church* (1929), *The Secret of Childhood* (1939), and *The Absorbent Mind* (1949).

HARLEY ATKINSON

Bibliography. M. H. Loeffler (1992), *Montessori in Contemporary American Culture*; M. J. Montessori (1976), *Education for Human Development*; S. M. Stewart and J. W. Berryman (1989), *Young Children and Worship*.

Moody, Dwight L. (1837–99). One of the greatest Christian leaders of the nineteenth century. Dwight Lyman Moody is synonymous with evangelism, church growth, the revival movement, and Christian education. Born in Northfield, Massachusetts, Moody lived a life of meager existence. Growing up in a relatively poor farming area, Moody did not receive much formal education. His stature as a dynamic Christian leader is testimony to how God can change the world through an individual dedicated to serving God's purposes.

His father was an alcoholic and died when Moody was just 4 years old. Moody's disdain for life on the farm led him to join his uncle as a shoe salesman in Boston at the age of 17. He came to faith in Christ on April 21, 1855, while attending Sunday school. Shortly after his conversion, he moved to Chicago and continued his career as a shoes salesclerk. His enthusiastic personality brought him success as a salesclerk and he prospered at a young age. However, his heart's desire was to see young people give their lives to Christ and experience the life-saving grace of God. He was so committed to ministry that he soon left the security of his job and became the director of the local YMCA while receiving no financial remuneration. Though not well educated, he was a gifted orator and his ability to take the Word of God and apply it to the needs of common people were uncanny. His popularity as a preacher soon grew and his Sunday morning service began to attract a great deal of attention.

Moody soon found himself preaching evangelistic crusades to audiences in England, Ireland, Scotland, Canada, and across the United States. He was concerned for the spiritual growth of his converts and wanted to ensure their ongoing spiritual formation. As a result, in 1886 Moody cast his vision for the establishment of the Chicago Evangelization Society. Growing out of this organizational structure would come the Moody Bible Institute and Moody Press.

Most of the seminaries of his day were preparing men for the senior pastorate. Few were concerned about helping the average layperson grow in personal faith. Since he had experienced a fruitful ministry as a simple salesclerk, he understood the need for other laypeople to receive quality Bible instruction. Moody began a school in 1889 to assist in the training of the laity. His primary concern was that the students be equipped to do evangelism, but soon the curriculum expanded to include additional studies. The Moody Bible Institute was committed to preparing what Moody referred to as "gap men" (Bailey, 1959).

Moody's emphasis on lay training and his subsequent Moody Bible Institute began a trend in Christian education that spread all across North America. The Bible Institute Movement was born and soon it would shake the very foundation of all church life in America. Moody died after a series of heart ailments. Not letting his health troubles impede his work for God, Moody was committed to showing the world what God could do through the life of one man who was wholly committed to him.

MICHAEL J. ANTHONY

Bibliography. F. C. Bailey (1959), *D. L. Moody: The Greatest Evangelist of the Nineteenth Century;* K. O. Gangel and W. S. Benson (1983), *Christian Education: Its History and Philosophy;* J. D. Woodbridge, ed. (1988), *Great Leaders of the Christian Church.*

Moral Development. Morality is a central value in the Judeo-Christian faith. Concern for moral instruction and moral development has taken persons down different paths of exploration and action. Some invested their energy in teaching moral content—what is right and what is wrong. Others, such as Jean Piaget and Lawrence Kohlberg, have tried to understand the processes of moral reasoning, while still others, including Sigmund and Anna Freud and Eric Erikson, examined the moral affects—emotions and values—motivating moral behavior. Are the varied perspectives simply conflicting viewpoints, or are they parts of a whole that need integration? If they are parts of the whole, what role does each element play in moral development? The remainder of this article will explore moral reasoning, moral affect, and moral behavior.

Moral Reasoning. Building on the work of Piaget, in 1955 Kohlberg began to study the moral reasoning of ninety-eight American boys ages 10 to 16. For thirty years he followed those subjects, interviewing them every three years. Out of that longitudinal study he formulated and refined his theory of cognitive moral development. Cross-cultural studies and research conducted by colleagues also fed into the critique and refining of the theory (1991, 15).

Basic Assumptions. It is important to examine cognitive developmental theory against the backdrop of some basic assumptions.

1. Various aspects of human development are interrelated. Physiological development is the basic prerequisite for cognitive development, and moral reasoning uses cognitive skills already developed. Piaget and Kohlberg believed that the brain must reach a particular level of development before it can process certain kinds of thinking. However, other factors must also be at work for cognitive and moral development to occur.

2. Cognitive developmentalists distinguish between the content and the structure of thinking. The content of moral reasoning is *what* one believes to be right or wrong. The structure of moral reasoning is seen in *why* one judges something right or wrong. It is development in the structure of moral reasoning that Kohlberg described.

3. Each stage of moral development is normal for a particular period of life and therefore worthy of celebrating. The reasoning of each stage provides crucial building blocks in the moral foundation and therefore cannot be skipped.

The Pattern. From his research Kohlberg identified three levels of moral reasoning:

Level I—Preconventional
Level II—Conventional
Level III—Postconventional

The labels given to the levels indicate how persons using each form of moral reasoning relate to the moral conventions or standards of their society. Persons using preconventional moral reasoning are not aware of the society's standards and therefore do not consider them in judging right and wrong. Conventional moral reasoning highly values the standards of the society, or a subculture to which the person belongs, and looks to those standards for moral guidance. Postconventional moral reasoning allows one to go beyond conventions, not to abandon them for a new personalized moral code, but to use moral principles to evaluate the culture's laws and their application. Jesus criticized the Pharisees for being so locked into their moral conventions that they had lost sight of the heart of God's law. "[You] hypocrites!" Jesus charged. "You tithe mint and dill and cummin, and have neglected the weightier provisions of the law: justice and mercy and faithfulness" (Matt. 23:23 NASB).

Within each of the three levels Kohlberg identified two stages of moral reasoning. For the purpose of this brief article, however, Table 1 summarizes the characteristics of each level of moral reasoning, noting progression within a level without differentiating among the stages.

It is important to note that Kohlberg believed most children reason at Level I; older children and adolescents begin to move into Level II, and many adults continue to use Level II moral reasoning. Moral development is a lifelong concern, not just something important for children and youth.

Piaget found that the path of moral development begins in egocentrism and leads toward perspectivism—the ability to see things from another person's point of view. The ongoing challenge of moral development is to be able to put ourselves in the shoes of an ever widening variety of persons. Kohlberg's model reflects this idea. Level II moral reasoning calls for understanding the perspectives, first of friends and family and later, of our society. Level III requires that we see things from the perspective of those who are different from us and become the voice that speaks for minorities and the powerless who cannot be heard speaking for themselves. The possibility for development never ends. There are always others with whom we can gain greater empathy as we get to know their joys, sorrows, and challenges.

Table 1
Kohlberg's Levels of Moral Reasoning

	Egocentric Level I	Level II	Perspectivistic Level III
Source of Authority	Self-interest	External standards—models and rules	Internal principles
Definitions	Right is what adults command or what brings reward.	Right is what good people do or what the law says one should do.	Right is living out moral principles and being just.
	Wrong is what I am punished for—what brings pain.	Wrong is what good people do not do or what the law says one should not do.	Wrong is violating a moral principle and being unjust.
Intentions	Oblivious to intentions.	Makes allowances for intentions. Lenience tempered by sense of duty.	Considers intentions but also concerned about justice.
Justice	What adults command. Later, equal treatment.	Defined by society.	Equal consideration for all.
Value of Persons	Valued in material terms. "Persons are valuable for what they do for *me*."	Valued because of relationships of affection and for their contribution to society.	Valued because they are persons. Human life is sacred.
Stimulus to Right Actions	Fear of punishment and desire for reward.	Desire to please important persons and perform one's duty to society.	To be true to oneself one must act upon the moral principles to which one is committed.
Ability to Take Another's Perspective	Understands the perspective of persons in situations which he or she has experienced.	Understands the perspective of friends, family, and eventually society.	Understands the perspective of a wide range of persons, including minority groups.

Kohlberg saw justice as the central concept influencing the structure of moral reasoning. Children first believe justice is whatever adults command, and then, in the process of development, come to understand it as absolute equal treatment. In Level II people accept society's definition of justice and value laws designed to administer justice. But in Level III persons move on to believe that justice is equity, equal consideration for all, even minorities. The principle of justice, as equal consideration for all, becomes the moral judge of personal and public decisions and actions.

Carol Gilligan, a colleague of Kohlberg, began noticing a difference between the responses given by men and women in research interviews. This led her to study the moral development of women (1982). Gilligan found that women as well as men move through preconventional, conventional, and postconventional phases in moral reasoning. The central developing concept in the moral reasoning of many women, however, is care and responsibility rather than justice. They base moral decisions on their understanding of their responsibility to care for others in a given situation. Rather than objectively trying to apply principles of fairness and equity, women want to find a solution that causes the least hurt and offers as much care as possible. Women may delay making a decision as they seek for a more "care-filled" plan of action.

When asked, "Which is the great commandment?" Jesus responded, "'You shall love the Lord your God with all your heart, and with all your soul, and with all your mind.' This is the great and foremost commandment. The second is like it: 'You shall love your neighbor as yourself'" (Matt. 22:36–39 NASB). Jesus spoke to the moral perspective of both women and men. He gave us principles, not a specific priority rule, but the principles are the principles of love for God, self, and others, principles that incorporate both care and justice.

Factors Influencing Development. Piaget identified four necessary but insufficient causes of development: heredity and maturation, direct experience, social interaction, and the process of equilibration. No single factor is sufficient to cause development; all four must be at work. These factors, I believe, point to what parents, teachers, and friends can do to enhance the moral development of one another.

Heredity and maturation are inner factors beyond our control, but it is important that we accept, celebrate, and patiently work with what heredity and a person's rate of maturation make possible at any given time. Parents and teachers can provide an environment rich in opportunities for direct experience and social interaction. New experiences and interacting with people whose life situations and viewpoints differ from ours raise questions about the adequacy of our understandings and approaches to life. These questions cause an inner uneasiness or disequilibration that must be resolved. Our inner questions cause us to look at our perspectives, discover their limitations, and make necessary changes, while keeping the understandings we discover were correct. This process is what Piaget calls *equilibration,* "the motor of development." Parents and teachers can support others as they struggle to resolve their inner conflict and gain new ground in their moral development. If we welcome questions and treat them with respect, our children and friends will know they can bring their most troubling perplexities to us, not for pat answers, but for support and direction in the process of finding new, more adequate understandings.

Moral Affect. Mentored by Anna Freud and Eric Erikson, and having worked with children over several decades, Robert Coles is well equipped to articulate a psychoanalytic perspective on moral values and affects and how they influence moral development. In his book, *The Moral Intelligence of Children,* Coles addresses the concern of raising good children. Good children take goodness seriously and desire to live the Golden Rule: they respect and are committed to others. They know that being good is a struggle and that one must wrestle with complex moral tensions (1997, 17–20). Coles notes two characteristics of the "not so good" child: a stony heart and self-absorption. Building on Erikson's understanding of psychosocial development and his own extensive conversations with children, Coles points to the experiences that influence the moral formation or development of children and adolescents. Different experiences are crucial for children during various periods of development. Also, Coles makes clear that adults who take seriously their role as moral instructors and are open to learn and be challenged by children will continue to grow in their moral integrity.

Early Childhood. Moral formation begins very early, even before birth. The way in which parents prepare for the arrival of their baby surrounds the child with values. As prospective parents make their first lifestyle adjustments, they are preparing for their role as moral educators.

According to Erikson, the first crisis of life is one of trust versus mistrust. Learning that it is safe to trust is foundational to healthy development. Well-meaning parents who gratify their baby's every desire instantly, without consideration for their own needs, fail to teach the child another crucial lesson. Children must learn to manage a legitimate amount of frustration for the sake of being considerate of others. They need to accept the fact that they are not the center of the universe around which everyone else must move. Babies begin to learn this lesson when parents respond to them, not always instantly, but soon enough; when they are allowed to cry a bit before going to sleep or to entertain themselves for a while.

When 2-year-olds begin asserting their autonomy by declaring, "No," they are ready to begin work on another important moral lesson, the meaning of both "yes" and "no." If parents always give in to the child's pressure, "no" is meaningless, but "no" must be balanced by "yes." While children are learning what they may not do, parents can help them discover all the wonderful things they *may* do—to experience the fun of "yes." Coles says that not to say "no" in the first months of life is to teach children lessons in indifference and inattention, and to set the stage for moral confusion. To avoid moral confusion, children need parents who have values and ideals and who practice those values in the presence of their child (1997, 84, 93).

Babies and toddlers learn to love in the process of being loved. They learn what pleases their parents and enjoy pleasing them. As parents establish boundaries based on the values of the family and the abilities of the child, and as children respond by living for the most part within those boundaries, they experience mutual respect. Such children have abandoned a great deal of self-absorption before starting kindergarten and demonstrate noteworthy goodness (1997, 94–96).

Elementary School Age. The elementary school years are a time of curiosity when children try to figure things out and make sense of their world. Their curious minds take on issues of right and wrong, trying to decide how they should behave and why. Anna Freud believed that these are the years when the "child's conscience is built—or it isn't" (Coles 1997, 98). Conscience is the inner voice that, having heard what others say, now declares what should or should not be done and guides in making moral choices.

Children between the ages of 7 and 10 begin raising moral and ethical questions, giving the adults close to them opportunities to engage them in moral discussions. We can tell stories that clarify a moral issue, share our own experiences of moral struggle and decision, offer suggestions, and above all, give them an example of moral behavior to observe. Through such means, whether planned or unplanned, we can help children develop morally.

There is a danger, Coles notes, in parents becoming too zealous in their moral instruction. Children may become uptight, judgmental, and self-righteous when overtaught. Healthy moral instruction comes in the flow of life through parents and teachers who know and live their values; from adults who regularly reflect on whether or not they truly live those values in everyday, sometimes complex, situations and who are open to receive moral insights from their children.

Coles discovered that a group of children in a classroom discussion could come up with deep moral insight when given time to reflect, listen to one another, and follow the ideas that came to mind. Such discussions, however, are most likely to grow out of reflections on a story, an event from history, or the children's lives, without a lot of effort on the teacher's part to formally direct their thinking. Children are best served by letting them enter the story with their imagination, live the event, and then begin to talk about it (1997, 121).

Adolescence. As adolescents try to break away from their parents and establish their identity, some reject the moral values of the family. But in this time of pushing away, young people also need something to hang onto. Although teenagers may seem to want no rules or restrictions, many have a strong conscience that creates inner anxiety and loneliness when they fail to control their urges and actions. All persons, including adolescents, need standards and values to give them structure and strength. Coles believes that parents, teachers, and other adults can assist young people in developing their moral values even when they do not seem to want adult advice. He identifies several means by which adults contribute to the moral development of adolescents.

Adults who care about young people will listen to their perspectives, objections, and defenses, but in the discussions the adults will also clearly articulate their values. Teens need to know what we believe is right and wrong and why we expect certain behaviors from them. When adolescents begin choosing wrong, they need persons in authority not to turn a blind eye, but to care enough to confront them with the destructive nature of their actions.

As adults working with teens, we need to reflect on our experiences as adolescents and be willing to share some of our struggles. Such sharing may create an important connection with young persons as we empathize with their struggles and they realize we have been there too. Many adolescents long for a moral companion, an older person who connects with them and with whom they can honestly discuss moral questions and issues relating to the meaning of life. The adults whom teenagers accept as moral guides are those whose words and lives are consistent. Sometimes a parent can be his or her child's moral companion, but not in all cases. Families are blessed to be part of a faith community where their children can find wise, caring companions to support them in their moral development.

Our most powerful moral teaching tool comes through the lives our children see us live. Before Moses instructed the Israelites to teach God's commands to their children, he first instructed them to love the Lord their God with their whole being and have God's commands upon their hearts (Deut. 6:5–6). When love for God permeates our being and God's laws are not external rules to be obeyed through great effort, but are written on our hearts, our children see a winsome value system.

Moral Behavior. From his research on moral action, Kohlberg found that two factors working together tended to predict whether children would act morally. Those factors were moral reasoning and ego strength (1972, 459, 476). The intellectual ability to assess a situation and predict the likely consequences of an action, the tendency to choose long-term greater good over immediate gratification, and the ability to attend or focus on a task contributed to what Kohlberg called ego strength, or what might be identified as a strong will. Ego strength gives the power to do what one believes is right.

Moral reasoning influences how we interpret a situation. Whose perspective we can or do take colors our perception of the dynamics at work and our decision regarding what is the right thing to do. Our level of moral reasoning also influences our assessment of whether it is our responsibility to act. People can, however, decide what is the morally right thing to do and that they ought to take that right action, but then not act. They may choose not to pay the price of being moral.

Kohlberg acknowledged that his theory of cognitive moral development did not answer the question, "Why be moral?" and that religion or faith gives one a reason to be moral (1981, 321–22, 336). Coles was amazed by the moral strength of some children with whom he worked. As he listened to them he came to believe that their religious faith contributed greatly to that strength. Moral development and spiritual development are not the same, but they are intertwined.

CATHERINE STONEHOUSE

Bibliography. M. Belenky, B. Clinchy, N. Goldberger, and J. Tarule, eds. (1986), *Women's Ways of Knowing: The Development of Self, Voice, and Mind;* R. Coles (1997), *The Moral Intelligence of Children;* idem (1986), *The Moral Life of Children;* C. Gilligan (1982), *In a Different Voice: Psychological Theory and Women's Development;* L. Kohlberg (1972), *Curriculum and the Cultural Revolution;* idem (1981), *The Philosophy of Moral Development: Essays on Moral Development;* idem (1991), *The Kohlberg Legacy for the Helping Professions;* L. Kuhmerker with U. Gielen and R. Hayes, eds. (1991), *The Kohlberg Legacy for the Helping Professions;* J. Piaget (1965), *The Moral Judgment of the Child;* C. K. Sigelman and D. R. Shaffer (1995), *Life-span Human Development;* C. Stonehouse (1998), *With Children on the Spiritual Journey;* J. Wilhoit and J. Dettoni, eds. (1995), *Nurture That Is Christian: Developmental Perspectives on Christian Education.*

See also GILLIGAN, CAROL; KOHLBERG, LAWRENCE; MATURATION; PIAGET, JEAN

Moral Dilemma. In common language, moral dilemma can refer to almost any kind of moral problem. In the more specified domain of philosophy, it is when unresolvable conflicts between moral obligations or requirements occur. Thus, when two situations exist in which the agent morally ought to adopt each of two alternatives separately but cannot adopt both of them together, that individual is in a moral dilemma. If one of the conflicting moral requirements is overridden by another, a moral dilemma does not exist.

Most moral theorists agree that no such situations exist. Immanuel Kant is numbered among this group. Utilitarians try to avoid all moral dilemmas by claiming that when alternatives tie, neither maximizes utility, so there is no moral obligation to adopt either alternative separately. Others try to avoid moral dilemmas by constructing moral principles that never conflict or by giving ranking such that one conflicting moral requirement always overrides the other.

In 1950 Lawrence Kohlberg employed moral dilemma as a method of determining the level of moral reasoning in his longitudinal research regarding moral development. Based on the concept that moral reasoning unfolds as one develops mentally, Kohlberg posed to children of varying ages a situation in which they had to make a choice between two conflicting moral values. The reasoning behind the choice expressed by the respondent revealed the level of moral reasoning. Such dilemmas involved analysis, interpretation, selection of relevant data, evaluation, and choice.

There are many moral dilemmas that take exception to Kohlberg's theory, and research claims that such levels of moral reasoning are universal, arguing that they are more reflective of late-twentieth-century Western social development and masculine ways of thinking. "All major theistic religions, however, would require much greater consideration of the place of divinely-revealed ethics and morality derived from theological reflection" (Bridger, 1995, 608).

CHERYL L. FAWCETT

Bibliography. D. Atkinson, D. F. Field, A. Holmes, and O. O'Donovan, eds. (1995), *New Dictionary of Christian Ethics and Pastoral Theology,* pp. 122–27; F. W. Bridger (1995), *New Dictionary of Christian Ethics and Pastoral Theology,* p. 607; B. Clouse (1991), *New Twentieth-Century Encyclopedia of Religious Knowledge;* W. Sinnot-Armstrong (1992), *Encyclopedia of Ethics.*

Moral Dilemmas, Use in Ministry. Many teachers choose to use a moral dilemma when they want to test the degree to which previously learned materials can be applied in real-life settings. It is also a popular method used by instructors to determine a student's motivation, values, and basis of moral reasoning. They can be brought into the classroom in the form of a thought-provoking question, case study, or experiential learning activity. Because they require careful thought to develop, many teachers do not use them. In addition, if used inappropriately, they can threaten a student's thought process and social standing, and create a significant degree of personal disequilibrium.

Moral dilemmas were used extensively by Lawrence Kolberg as a means of assessing one's moral character and judgment. Moral dilemmas deal with not only the "What would you do in the following scenario?" but also allowed the researcher to examine the "Why would you do it?" This method allowed Kolberg the opportunity to look inside the reasoning ability of his subjects.

As one examines the manner in which Jesus trained his disciples it must be concluded that he also used this method of instruction. It was not enough for Jesus to know that his disciples had a head knowledge of a particular theological truth. Indeed, the Pharisees and religious leaders of his day had plenty of that. What he wanted to know was the why of his disciples' actions. A classic example of this approach to his training can be found in Matthew 12:10–14.

MICHAEL J. ANTHONY

Moral Education. Process of helping individuals attain a level of reasoning and behavior that is based upon mutually agreed-upon standards of conduct that contribute to the greater good of humankind and society. *The American Heritage Dictionary* (1992) defines that which is moral as something that is "concerned with the judgment of the goodness or badness of human action and character." It includes the conscious sense of what is right or wrong and what conforms to the standards of just behavior. As such, morality—behavior that reflects the Ultimate Good (God)—is most clearly revealed in the context of social relationships. Wolterstorff (1980) acknowledged this context in recognizing moral responsibilities as "our responsibilities for how we treat human beings" (33).

Biblical Perspectives. A biblical and theological approach to moral education must begin with the goodness of God. Actions that are good and moral are those that are "godly," reflecting the very nature of the One who is himself the source of all goodness (Gen. 1; Ps. 100:5; Mark 10:18; John 10:11). Because God is the Ultimate Good, all that is good finds its source in him. According to Psalm 119, God has made his ways known to us through his laws (i.e. commands, statutes, precepts, etc.). These laws, then, become the source and content of moral education, what Wolterstorff (1980) identified as moral law.

Jesus decreed that the greatest commandment (i.e., moral law) called humanity into a right relationship with God: "Love the Lord your God with all your heart and with all your soul and with all your mind and with all your strength" (Mark 12:30). The second great commandment (Mark 12:31) describes the outworking of the first within the social context: "Love your neighbor as yourself."

C. S. Lewis (1952) noted the limitations of a definition of morality that grew solely out of the realm of social interaction. Since we are created in God's image to serve God's purposes, Lewis proposed, moral behavior is not limited to interactions with others but also includes the integration of the human personality and relationship with God, who gives purpose and meaning to life.

Yet despite morality's broader definition, it is external behavior that testifies to morality most clearly. Thus, it is that behavior which has traditionally been the focus of both secular and Christian educational efforts. While the content of moral education begins with God's law, the process is influenced significantly by our understanding of human development. Clouse (1993) provides valuable insight for the theory of moral education by identifying four divergent psychological approaches to human personality.

Overview of Moral Development Theory. The psychoanalytic approach, rooted in Freudian psychology, sees moral growth as the outcome of a child's early interaction with the expectations and demands of society, primarily mediated through parents. Since humanity is by nature depraved, moral growth is the result of the struggle to conform to society's expectations by conquering natural, self-centered desires. According to this approach, moral education would focus on self-discipline (Clouse, 1993).

The learning approach, rooted in behaviorism, views moral growth as the result of the imitation of examples and rigorous training in good behavior through the use of rewards and punishments. According to this approach, moral behavior is the result of environmental conditioning. A person is morally good if he or she behaves in ways that benefit society. The focus here is almost exclusively on behavior—also referred to as character education (Clouse, 1993).

The humanistic approach understands moral growth as a process that springs from within the individual and moves toward realization of the full potential of human nature. Since human personality cannot be compartmentalized, moral development is part of the holistic development of the individual and leads toward a mature personality which is "generous, altruistic, and cooperative" (Clouse, 1993, 316). Morality finds its truest expression in relationships, so educational strategies such as values clarification, transactional analysis, and other relationship-intense techniques help people develop their full moral capabilities.

Perhaps the most prominent approach today is that of the cognitive theorists, especially Jean

Piaget and Lawrence Kohlberg. This approach to moral development views moral growth as a process of moving through progressively more complex stages of moral reasoning. In this process, the individual moves from being totally egocentric to being increasingly responsive and responsible to society (Clouse, 1993). The challenge of moral education is to provoke learners to achieve more and more sophisticated moral reasoning in order to solve moral dilemmas.

Fundamental to the topic of moral education is the clarification of the goals that such education pursues. Various approaches mark the attempt to clarify goals. One approach identifies key moral values that provide the content for moral education. In the 1980s, the American Institute for Character Education (Goble and Brooks, 1983) developed a list of values supposedly shared by all cultures. These values included such characteristics as courage, personal conviction, generosity, kindness, helpfulness, honesty, honor, justice, tolerance of those who are different, the stewardship of time and talents, freedom of choice, freedom of speech, good citizenship, the right to be an individual, and the right of equal opportunity.

Two major movements have characterized the traditional approach to moral education. The character education movement is built upon the concept of teaching children moral values through the monitoring of behavior, including rewards for appropriate moral behavior and punishment for inappropriate behavior. Typical throughout much of recent educational history, character education is demonstrated in such concrete ways as the teaching of good behavior on the school playground, right conduct regarding truthfulness in the classroom, proper respect for teachers, and other virtues of life especially cultivated in the socialization process of childhood. Underlying the character education movement is the concept that adults know the standards of proper behavior and can teach them to children. The obvious shortcoming of this approach is that knowing the right or moral behavior often fails to generate moral actions. In answer to this problem, the social adjustment approach developed (Clouse, 1993).

The ability to get along well with family, peers, authority figures, and others depends upon a person's healthy and well-developed self-image. Thus moral education seeks first to help persons love and respect themselves. Social adjustment (i.e., the ability to operate morally in a social context) will be the natural result of the normal moral growth of emotionally healthy people. Here moral education attempts to develop self-esteem rather than to dictate moral behavior.

Believing that the task of teaching morality begins at home, Ward (1989) suggested a number of tasks that encourage moral development in children. These tasks include stimulating inquiry into moral issues, encouraging verbalization concerning moral conflicts, asking "why?" questions, sharing and discussing experiences where moral concerns are at stake, listening responsively in honest dialogue about moral issues, exploring understanding in situations that upset moral belief structures, and standing beside—in the ministry of presence—those persons experiencing moral conflict (117–18).

MARI GONLAG

Bibliography. The American Heritage Dictionary of the English Language (1992); ASCD Panel on Moral Education, *Educational Leadership* 45, no. 8 (1988): 4–8; B. Clouse (1993), *Teaching for Moral Growth: A Guide for the Christian Community—Teachers, Parents, and Pastors;* F. G. Goble and B. D. Brooks (1983), *The Case for Character Education;* C. S. Lewis (1952), *Mere Christianity;* T. W. Ward (1989), *Values Begin at Home;* N. P. Wolterstorff (1980), *Educating for Responsible Action.*

Morality. *See* Virtue.

Moral Reasoning, Theory of. Thinking and judgmental processes that occur when a person is faced with a moral problem. Moral reasoning is one of three major areas in the study of morality, the other two being moral behavior and moral emotions. Moral reasoning is based on what a person thinks or says is right or wrong. This is in contrast to the behavioral dimension, which observes what a person does, and to the affective dimension, which seeks to determine how a person feels. Studies show that these three areas are interrelated. To act without thinking and to feel without being aware of the consequences of emotions is to act irresponsibly and to experience sentiment without the benefit of informed judgment.

Moral reasoning develops as the child matures in cognitive understanding. Swiss philosopher Jean Piaget in *The Moral Judgment of the Child* (1932) compared younger and older children in their responses to stories involving a moral dilemma. Younger children judge an act according to the objective consequences of the act, with no regard to whether the culprit intended to cause harm. They also see an act as good or bad in terms of whether it violates a rule and not in terms of how relationships between people are affected. They will advocate severe forms of punishment for even minor infractions, and they immediately link misfortunes with personal inadequacies rather than with natural events. But as children mature in understanding they realize that accidents should not be dealt with in the same way as deliberate acts even though the same amount of damage may occur. They begin to see that the same deed may help one person and harm another. Punishment should fit the crime, and if punishment leads to reform of the culprit or restitution for the victim, this is better than punishment just for the sake of hurting the offender. Furthermore, misfortune may come upon good people as well as on wrongdoers. Adversity is not always an act of God on those who have displeased him.

American psychologist Lawrence Kohlberg (1984), building on the work of Piaget, is considered by many to be the foremost authority on the development of moral reasoning. Like Piaget, Kohlberg maintained that a person passes through earlier or lower stages of development before going on to later or higher stages, but his research focused on the adolescent and young adult in contrast to Piaget's studies of children between the ages of 4 and 12. By observing young people at a higher level of cognition, Kohlberg was able to expand Piaget's original two level system to a six-stage sequence that extends from early childhood through adulthood. Each stage occurs in an invariant sequence, is qualitatively different from the one preceding it, and represents a more comprehensive system of intellectual thought.

A key term used by Kohlberg is *conventional,* which means that right and wrong are determined on the basis of convention or what society expects of its members. The conventional level is at the midpoint of moral reasoning and includes the two middle stages (stages 3 and 4) in the hierarchy of moral thought.

Stage 3 thinking equates good behavior with whatever pleases or helps others. Attitudes of significant other people such as family, friends, and neighbors determine what is right. Stage 4 reasoning says that obeying the law, doing one's duty, and maintaining the given social order is what one must do to be a good person. Most adult Americans make statements at stages 3 and 4 although the same person will often make statements at different stages depending on the situation.

At the earlier *preconventional* level (stages 1 and 2) right and wrong are judged not in terms of what society says is right or wrong but in terms of consequences to the self. A person reasoning at stage 1 will follow a rule in order to avoid punishment, such as a child obeying the parent or an adult driving the speed limit to avoid being arrested. At stage 2 a person is still concerned with personal needs but views human relations in terms of the market place, as in "I'll scratch your back if you'll scratch my back."

Those who progress to the *postconventional* level (stages 5 and 6) expand their ideas of right and wrong to include not only a desire to enhance self (preconventional) and to conform to social expectations (conventional) but to a concern for the rights and humanity of every person. Stage 5 thinkers will seek to change a rule or law that violates the well-being of a group of people, and those who have reached stage 6 say that

morality is grounded in abstract principles of justice and respect for every individual.

The application of moral reasoning theory to Christian education may be found in a number of sources including the use of Piagetian techniques at different age levels (Foster and Moran, 1985), the employment of Kohlberg's paradigm to explain church conflict as a function of church members reasoning at different stages (Clouse, 1986), an application of Kohlberg to the Christian liberal arts college (McNeel, 1991), and a demonstration of how Bible stories can be used in Sunday school to move children to higher levels of spiritual and moral understanding (Clouse, 1993).

BONNIDELL CLOUSE

Bibliography. B. Clouse, *Journal of Psychology and Christianity* 5, no. 3 (1986): 14–19; idem (1993), *Teaching for Moral Growth: A Guide for the Christian Community—Teachers, Parents, and Pastors;* J. D. Foster and G. T. Moran, *Journal of Psychology and Theology* 13 (1985): 97–103; L. Kohlberg (1984), *Essays on Moral Development: The Psychology of Moral Development;* S. P. McNeel, *Journal of Psychology and Christianity* 10 (1991): 311–22; J. Piaget (1932), *The Moral Judgment of the Child.*

See also KOHLBERG, LAWRENCE; MORAL DEVELOPMENT; PIAGET, JEAN

Moravian Education. The Moravians are spiritual descendants of the Hussites, who were followers of the Bohemian Protestant martyr John Hus (1371–1415). Hus taught that the Bible should be available in the vernacular and that both the Bread and the Cup should be served to congregants. As the Hussites before them, the Moravians stressed the primacy of the Bible in matters of faith and conduct, a holy lifestyle, and a commitment to practicing neighborly love. The Moravians were also influenced by the pietist movement, characterized by Philip Jacob Spener (1635–1705) and August Hermann Francke (1663–1727). Spener started a home Bible study movement known as *collegia pietatis.* Francke had organized an elementary school for children, a secondary school, and an orphanage.

The Moravians were formally organized in 1457 as the *Unitas Fratrum,* the "Unity of Brethren." Under the leadership of Gregory the Patriarch, the *Unitas Fratrum* emphasized the threefold concept of faith, fellowship, and freedom. They stressed practical Christian living over doctrine or church tradition. The Moravians were also deeply concerned about the education of children. One of their bishops, John Amos Comenius (1592–1670), was perhaps the most important educator of his day and has been called "the father of modern education." The teaching of Comenius motivated the Moravians to establish schools as well as churches.

After a time of extreme persecution, the Moravians were given refuge on the estate of Count Nikolaus Ludwig von Zinzendorf (1700–1760) in Saxony. The movement was on the verge of extinction but under Zinzendorf's leadership the Moravians were revived. Zinzendorf has been called "the greatest evangelical since Luther and probably the most ecumenical thinker of his day" (Gangel and Benson, 1983, 181). At an early age, Zinzendorf chose as his life-motto, "I have one passion; it is He, He only."

Zinzendorf had studied under Francke, a family friend and Zinzendorf's godfather, for six years in Halle. There is no doubt Zinzendorf's passion for childhood education was fueled by his time with Francke.

Zinzendorf's estate was running out of room to accommodate the rapid growth, so a town, Herrnhut ("the Lord watches over"), was built nearby. The community practiced spiritual disciplines such as extended times of prayer and fasting. In addition, Zinzendorf emphasized evangelism, encouragement, and accountability.

The education of the children of Herrnhut was a priority to Zinzendorf. Following the pattern he learned from Francke, children were brought up and educated apart from their parents. The community even sought to control the selection of marriage partners.

There were three main components to the Moravian education system under Zinzendorf—the Bible, the catechism, and the hymnal. The Bible was held to be the only rule of faith, doctrine, and practice. The Moravians believed the Bible should be translated into the tongue of the people and read on a daily basis. They tended to shun detailed doctrinal statements but did acknowledge professions of faith such as "Jesus Christ is Lord!" and the early creeds of the church.

Moravian worship was liturgical. Moravian liturgies contained prescribed hymns and readings for the leader and congregation. Christmas and Easter were the most important times of Moravian worship. One of Zinzendorf's customs was to give his congregation at Herrnhut a "watchword" for the next day. This "watchword" consisted of one or more Bible verses, one or more hymn stanzas, and a brief prayer. This practice continues to the present in the annual publication of the *Moravian Daily Text*. Zinzendorf was a prolific hymn writer, and hymn singing, both public and private, was an integral part of Moravian worship.

The Moravians also had a vision to reach the world with the gospel. In 1732 the first Moravian missionaries, John Dober and David Nitschman, sold themselves as slaves to travel to the West Indies. In 1735, August Spangenberg was sent to America, where he founded churches in Georgia, North Carolina, and Pennsylvania. By 1738, communities had been established in five European countries. The missionary fervor of the Moravians continues to the present with an estimated ration of missionaries to congregants of 1:60 compared with 1:5000 for Protestantism at large. Zinzendorf himself visited the colonies of America in 1741 in a failed attempt to achieve union of the churches there. John Wesley traced his conversion to observing the composed spirits of a group of Moravians during a stormy transatlantic passage. A few days later Wesley's heart was "strangely warmed" after hearing a Moravian read the preface to Luther's commentary on the Book of Romans. Current membership in the Moravian Church is over 700,000 worldwide.

JONATHAN N. THIGPEN

Bibliography. K. O. Gangel and W. S. Benson (1983), *Christian Education: Its History and Philosophy;* T. F. Kinloch (1975), *A History of Religious Education;* J. E. Reed and R. Prevost (1993), *A History of Christian Education;* W. Walker (1959), *A History of the Christian Church.*

Mormon Education and the Family.

The origin of The Church of Jesus Christ of Latter-day Saints lies in the teachings of Joseph Smith, who claimed to discover *The Book of Mormon: Another Testament of Jesus Christ* in 1823 with the aid of the angel Moroni in upstate New York. Smith proclaimed himself a prophet of God and sought to restore the true church of Jesus Christ, which he claimed had been lost with the death of the apostles. Subsequent supposed revelations to Smith revealed that "the glory of God is intelligence" and the quest for learning became essential to spiritual progress for both this life and the life to come. The Latter-day Saints' educational philosophy is rooted in their desire for eternal spiritual progress.

The family provides the context for educational praxis. One of the Articles of Faith of the church states: "We believe in being honest, true, chaste, benevolent, virtuous, and in doing good to all men. . . . If there is anything virtuous, lovely, or of good report or praiseworthy, we seek after these things." Educational progress is seen as enabling the perfectibility of individuals to ever-higher moral, spiritual, and intellectual levels. Education results in righteous living and growth of knowledge of both religious and secular subjects.

High moral standards accompany Latter-day Saints and include temperance in all things. This is evidenced by total abstention from alcohol, tobacco, coffee, and tea, and opposition to pornography, gambling, and other social ills. The church is outspoken on moral issues and expects parents to live and teach moral values to their children. The Sabbath is kept as a day of worship to concentrate on Christ-centered interests. Morality, church support and participation, civic service, and strong family ties are apparent in active Latter-day Saints families.

The family, including husband and wife, children, and parents—present, past, and future—may be "sealed for time and eternity" in temple ordinances where "families can be together forever." The eternal temple sealing may be received in this life or, if one has not had opportunity, by proxy after death. The church teaches that those who lived before the time of Christ, or between the death of the apostles and the restoration of the church through Joseph Smith, have died without opportunity of salvation. Temple sealing is followed by faithful obedience to the commandments. The family unit provides education, familial and social support, historical awareness, and genealogical information necessary to complete temple ordinances for dead family members.

Formal education generally takes place in the family home, in the local congregation, and in higher education. The family early begins to emphasize education and children begin a period of preparation and practice where they learn to distinguish good and evil until they reach an age of accountability (about 8 years) when they are baptized into the church. Subsequent to baptism they are expected to adhere to the teachings of the church to obtain salvation.

Children take active part in the religious life of the family through family prayers, daily reading of Scripture, the taking of sacraments, bearing testimony to the congregation, and receiving priestly blessings. One distinctive of the family is weekly "family home evenings," a night free from church meetings and set aside for in-home family instruction on living gospel principles, and the duties of children to parents, the home, church, society, and the nation. Family home evenings were instituted in 1965 and manuals, resource materials, and videos are produced to assist parents in this responsibility.

Family education is also strengthened through the home teaching program where home teachers go in pairs to each Latter-day Saint's home at least once per month. The home teachers represent the bishop or leader of the local congregation and bring messages of inspiration, guidance, and goodwill for the family.

In the context of the local congregation, the Sunday School Union provides education classes on Sundays for all ages. The Primary Association provides religious instruction together with games and art activities for children ages 8 through 12 years. Its purpose is to teach children the tenets of their faith and to help children learn to live while preparing for church baptism. Children over 12 years participate in the education programs of the Mutual Improvement Association. The Boy Scouts of America, while not specifically a part of the Church, enrolls a larger percentage of Latter-day Saints boys than any

other religious group in their civic-minded education program. The church also provides a varied educational program for 17- to 24-year-olds.

The lack of public education facilities in Utah in the late 1800s, together with the large influx of new settlers, caused the church to initiate educational academies for instruction in elementary subjects. After the turn of the century secondary courses were added culminating in a standard four year high school curriculum after 1910. When public schools increased and economic hard times hit, education was turned over to the state. Three of these academies survive today in different forms—Brigham Young University, Ricks College, and Juarez Academy in Mexico.

Today Brigham Young University, with its main campus in Provo, Utah, and a campus in Laie, Hawaii, is the largest private university in the United States with over 27,000 students. The church also operates the Jerusalem Center for Near Eastern Studies in Israel, Ricks College in Rexburg, Idaho, and the Latter-day Saints Business College in Salt Lake City, Utah.

While public education is encouraged, the church sponsors elementary or secondary schools in less developed countries including Mexico, Kiribati, New Zealand, Tonga, Western Samoa, and Fiji. The efforts of these schools are largely limited to work toward literacy and basic education so that the Mormon teachings might be understood.

Accompanying public education, the Church Educational System operates throughout the United States and in over 100 other countries and territories. While public and private schools provide secular education, the CES emphasizes religious instruction alongside the secular experience. Its purpose is to assist students in understanding what Mormons call the restored gospel of Jesus Christ. Such high school students are enrolled in seminary classes, and young adults and college age students in institutes of religion. These weekly classes are often held in the local Church meeting house or in buildings owned and operated by the Church near school campuses. Currently, institutes of religion serve students in 1,230 U.S. and Canadian colleges and universities. The curriculum focuses on reading and study of the Church's scriptures—*The Holy Bible* (King James Version), *The Book of Mormon, The Doctrine and Covenants, The Pearl of Great Price*—and on church history.

JAMES R. MOORE

Bibliography. D. Bitton (1994), *Historical Dictionary of Mormonism;* The Church of Jesus Christ of Latter-day Saints official Internet site. *http://www.lds.org.* The Church of Jesus Christ of Latter-day Saints (1986), *Gospel Principles;* E. Decker and D. Hunt (1984), *The God Makers: A Shocking Exposé of What the Mormon Church Really Believes;* D. H. Ludlow, ed. (1992), *Encyclopedia of Mormonism.*

Multiculturalism. Multiculturalism is not an end in itself, but a means to more effectively contribute to the kingdom of God in a multicultural world. We live in a society shared by many cultures. Leaders in Christian education face the task of developing multicultural sensitivity in order to more effectively relate to all persons. In addition, church leaders share the responsibility of Christians in general to effectively communicate the gospel message to all cultures. Finally, the Christian response to multiculturalism calls us to an affirmation of the personal worth of each person in our society.

Multicultural education within the public sphere has not shown a consensus relative to either definition or goals, even though it emerged as a developing field of study in the 1950s. Goals have included a number of approaches such as an understanding of and sensitivity to other cultures, the development of a society that more equally shares power, or a radical critique of Western culture (Bullard, 1992). In more general terms, the major goal of multiculturalism might be stated as changing the total educational environment to promote a respect for diversity. Although such a statement would certainly apply to Christian education, a more specialized Christian perspective might be stated as *the personal application of Christian life and thought to all social groups that seek their spiritual identity in the church.*

In its broadest sense, multiculturalism in the church should be viewed as a process that affects the structural organization of the church, pastoral/instructional strategies, and personal values of members. As church leaders strive to become informed regarding the cultural diversity of our society, they should also identify areas in which Christian traditions have been affected by culture. Organizational approaches and personal attitudes that are ethnocentric in nature should be discouraged.

Christian educational specialists will encourage the development of positive interethnic relationships as they demonstrate the same within the church community. Cross-cultural skills in teaching are needed so that provision is made for various learning styles. When the identity of the church is socially inclusive, all members will be able to integrate their ethnic/social culture with that of the church culture. All within the constituency should be encouraged to appreciate their own ethnicity as a part of identity formation.

Relationships that represent cooperation, openness, interest in others, and inclusiveness should be fostered in the church. Parents, as primary models of these characteristics, may need the assistance of church programs in their task of rearing children to appreciate diversity. People of all ethnic backgrounds, living and working together, provide a message to be "caught" as parents and teachers are observed in their everyday relationships. Goals for spiritual development and Christian service can be realized in efforts to empower members of minority groups and in the commitment to correct injustices.

Church educational programs can enable members to see themselves as part of a larger society and to be able to identify, empathize, and relate with members of diverse groups from this larger society. Negative attitudes about ethnic groups often accompany a lack of knowledge of or contact with specific ethnic groups. Members should be encouraged to appreciate and celebrate diversity within the local church. Attention should be given to the harm caused by stereotyping, prejudice, and discrimination.

A number of guidelines should be kept in mind when planning a multicultural curriculum. Group interaction and reflection should be included so that experiences and biases can be considered in an open atmosphere. Curriculum materials utilized should truly reflect the diversity of America. Physical aspects of rooms and teaching aids should represent various cultures in books, interest centers, and wall hangings. Lessons and small group sharing can focus on similarities as much as differences between groups.

When a church is designing a Christian education program specifically for an ethnic group, the needs and concerns of the group represent the beginning step. As a minority group, there may be specific needs in the areas of education, housing, or employment. In addition to this, many will have painful experiences as a result of unfair judicial practices and racism. Education as a living experience should be the focus. The principles of Christ relate to both joyful and painful aspects of our lives in ways that are different across cultures and, at the same time, are similar. Mentoring should be encouraged. Although primarily applied to children and youth, the concept is of importance to all ages.

As a social institution, the church functions as either an open or closed system. As a closed entity, new ideas and different people are not readily accepted. Outside influences do not easily permeate the boundaries of the social group. On the other hand, the church as an open system embraces diversity in individuals and views. New ideas and different ways of functioning are not perceived as threatening but as enriching to the total community. When openness characterizes the church and its educational ministry, people from all cultures are welcomed.

LILLIAN J. BRECKENRIDGE

Bibliography. D. Augsburger (1986), *Pastoral Counseling across Cultures;* J. Breckenridge (1995), *What Color Is Your God? Multicultural Education in the Church;* S. Bullard, *Educational Leadership* 49 (1991–92): 3, 5; J. L. Gonzalez (1992), *Out of Every Tribe and Nation: Christian Theology at the Ethnic Round-*

table; S. G. Lingenfelter and M. K. Mayers (1986), *Ministering Cross-Culturally;* M. Ortiz (1996), *One New People: Models for Developing a Multiethnic Church.*

See also CULTURE; ENCULTURATION

Multiple Intelligences. Traditional views of intelligence ask "How smart is that person?" and attempt to answer by the assessing of a single ability. Proponents of the concept of multiple intelligences ask "How many ways is that person smart?" in acknowledgment of the complex nature of intelligence.

British psychologist and statistician Sir Francis Galton (1883) and American psychologist James McKeen Cattell (1890) created the first mental tests based on a concept of intelligence which was revealed by simple tests of sensory acuity and speed of reaction. By the early 1900s, the French psychologist Alfred Binet and his colleague Theodore Simon discovered the first effective way to measure intelligence. Believing that intelligence involved sophisticated mental powers of reasoning, good judgment, memory, and abstraction, Binet devised a test of "general mental ability" that included a diverse array of complex verbal and nonverbal reasoning tasks.

Binet's test was adapted in 1916 by Lewis Terman of Stanford University and the American version known as the Stanford-Binet Intelligence Scale. The current Stanford-Binet deals with four content areas: verbal reasoning, quantitative reasoning, abstract/visual reasoning, and short-term memory (Santrock, 1992).

To resolve the dilemma of whether intelligence really was an all-inclusive entity that could be represented by a single score, or whether it was a collection of many different abilities, the statistical technique of factor analysis was used to understand the correlation of various identifiable abilities. Charles Spearman (1927) used factor analysis and found that all of the test items correlated to a greater or lesser extent to one another. He proposed that they had in common an underlying general factor or what he called "g." Since the test items were not perfectly correlated, he suggested that each also measured a specific factor called "s" which was unique to the task. His development of a two-factor theory of intelligence was called into question by his own research, which indicated that some subsets of test items correlated more highly with one another than they did with other items. This finding led him to add to his theory a set of group factors that were of moderate degrees of generality. He identified four such group factors: verbal, visual, and numerical abilities, and another factor that was social in nature.

An American contemporary of Spearman, Lewis Thurstone, did not originally view intelligence as unitary. He concluded that intelligence was composed of seven primary mental abilities: verbal meaning, perceptual speed, reasoning, number, rote memory, word fluency, and a spatial or visualization factor. He later found that his primary mental abilities correlated moderately with one another and acknowledged the existence of "g" as well as second-order group factors fewer in number than the seven primary factors. Thurstone's research underlined the notion that intelligence tests were mixtures of very diverse mental tasks, and a single, composite score could conceal important information about a person's pattern of abilities.

The use of factor analysis resulted in J. P. Guilford's (1967, 1985) "structure-of-intellect" model, which generates a total of 150 possible separate ability factors. His model includes a "behavioral" content category that is responsive to the possibility of "social intelligence" and he added tests of creative thinking. From that concept emerged his description of divergent and convergent thinking. *Divergent production* involves fluency in thinking of a wide number of alternatives to meet a particular need, in contrast to *convergent production* which involves arrival at a single best answer.

In 1963, R. B. Cattell described fluid intelligence (primary biological and/or neurological functioning) and crystallized intelligence (life experience and education). Horn (1980) argued that crystallized intelligence (based on cumulative learning experiences) increases throughout the lifespan while fluid intelligence (the ability to perceive and manipulate information) steadily declines from middle adulthood.

An elaborate model was introduced by Howard Gardner (1983, 1993) which involves seven types of intelligence: language, logic and mathematics, spatial, music, movement, self-understanding, understanding of others. Gardner's approach has impacted assessment and teaching (Lazear, 1991, 1994; Armstrong, 1994) and frequently represents what many refer to as *multiple intelligences.*

The psychometric approach to defining mental abilities may have limited value if it is not combined with an understanding of the dynamics of mental processes. An information processing approach sees performance on mental tests as related to a number of basic, underlying information processing components: sensory apprehension, attention, memory strategies, symbolic comparison and transformation, metacognitive processes, and others. Investigators believe that individual differences in such processing components lie at the heart of varying performances on intelligence test items.

The influence of the information processing approach is seen in the triarchic theory of Robert Sternberg (1990, 1997), who described intelligence as having three factors. He describes analytical thinking and abstract reasoning as *componential intelligence* which is closest to what is commonly measured by intelligence tests. Insightful and creative thinking is labelled *experiential intelligence*, "street smarts," and practical know-how is called *contextual intelligence*. Successful intelligent people know how to capitalize on their strengths and compensate for weaknesses. They achieve a balance among the "triarchy" of abilities. A fundamental idea underlying this view is that conventional notions of intelligence and tests of intelligence miss important kinds of intellectual talent and overweigh what are sometimes less important kinds of intellectual talent.

Continued research and interest in other areas such as emotional intelligence (Goleman, 1995) and moral intelligence (Coles, 1997) are evidence that the understanding of multiple intelligences may still be incomplete.

BARBARA WYMAN

Bibliography. T. Armstrong (1994), *Multiple Intelligences in the Classroom;* A. Binet and T. Simon (1916), *The Development of Intelligence in Children;* J. M. Cattell, *Mind* 15 (1890): 373–81; R. B. Cattell, *Journal of Educational Psychology* 54 (1963): 1–22; R. Coles (1997), *The Moral Intelligence of Children;* F. Galton (1882), *Inquiries into Human Faculty and Its Development;* H. Gardner (1983), *Frames of Mind: The Theory of Multiple Intelligences;* idem (1993), *Multiple Intelligences: The Theory in Practice;* D. Goleman (1995), *Emotional Intelligence: Why It Can Matter More Than IQ;* J. P. Guiliford (1967), *The Structure of Intellect;* idem (1985), *Handbook of Intelligence,* pp. 225–66; J. L. Horn and G. Donaldson (1980), *Constancy and Change in Human Development;* D. Lazear (1994), *Multiple Intelligence Approaches to Assessment: Solving the Assessment Conundrum;* idem (1991), *Seven Ways of Teaching: The Artistry of Teaching with Multiple Intelligences;* J. W. Santrock (1992), *Life Span Development;* C. Spearman (1927), *The Abilities of Man: Their Nature and Measurement;* R. J. Sternberg (1985), *Beyond IQ: A Triarchic Theory of Human Intelligence;* idem (1997), *Successful Intelligence;* L. L. Thurstone (1938), *Primary Mental Abilities.*

Music. Organized sound or a combination of rhythm, beat, and message is the universal language of the soul and a response of believers to their Creator. Music is a powerful communicator, taking participants through a wide range of emotions and creating a variety of moods.

Music in the Bible. With about five hundred references to music in the Bible, it is evident that music was an important part of the total lives of believers. Especially in the Old Testament, it was predominantly used in worship services to express devotion and praise to God. Corporate and public worship included both vocal (solos, groups, choirs) and instrumental music. (See, for example, Hebrews 2:12 and Psalm 150.) In fact, the Book of Psalms is the Jewish hymnbook.

The key passages for a biblical basis for music are Ephesians 5:18–19 (NASB), "Be filled with the Spirit, speaking to one another in psalms and hymns and spiritual songs, singing and making melody with your heart to the Lord," and Colossians 3:16 (NASB), "Let the word of Christ richly dwell within you, with all wisdom teaching and admonishing one another with psalms and hymns and spiritual songs, singing with thankfulness in your hearts to God." Paul taught that singing is an evidence of being filled with the Holy Spirit and that we are to teach and encourage one another through singing. Such use of music results from knowing and meditating on God's Word. Early believers sometimes communicated biblical truth by setting it to music since they did not have the written New Testament. Also indicated in these two passages is the fact that there is variety in music and that music is to be directed to one another as well as to the Lord, both done with a right heart attitude.

In 1 Corinthians 14:15, Paul says to sing with the Spirit and understanding, thus underscoring the right heart attitude. Songs are meant to be sung with the mind, implying that the words are clear and meaningful. But they also express our emotions. Furthermore, singing is used to build up believers: "What is the outcome then, brethren? When you assemble, each one has a psalm, has a teaching, has a revelation, has a tongue, has an interpretation. Let all things be done for edification" (1 Corinthians 14:26 NASB). Plus music expresses joy: "Is anyone cheerful? Let him sing praises" (James 5:13 NASB).

Music in Education. As an instructional method, music is a powerful way to teach students and help them remember biblical truth and testify about God. Songs can tell a Bible story, explain doctrine, teach Scripture verses, suggest ways to live biblical truth, challenge listeners and singers to act on what they know, relate testimonies, and be prayers. Music also promotes spiritual growth through praising God in worship and ministering to others while developing musical talents. However, singing should not be used merely as a time filler or for entertainment. When choosing music for educational purposes, there are a number of criteria to keep in mind:

1. Will the song help accomplish the aim of the lesson or the purpose for using music?
2. Are the words scripturally accurate and theologically correct? Unfortunately, a number of songs and hymns used in churches teach unbiblical information that has to be corrected later.
3. Are the words and the length of the song appropriate for the age group? Too often, teachers select songs with symbolism or abstract concepts that children are not capable of understanding, or the words are too childish for older children and teens. And the younger the age group, the shorter the attention span is.

4. Are the words easy to understand, or do teachers have the time to explain them so students are singing with understanding?
5. Is the melody appropriate for the age group? The younger the child, the simpler the melody needs to be, the more important repetition is, and the more limited the vocal range is.
6. Do the words follow the guidelines of Philippians 4:8 (NASB): "Finally, brethren, whatever is true, whatever is honorable, whatever is right, whatever is pure, whatever is lovely, whatever is of good repute, if there is any excellence and if anything worthy of praise, let your mind dwell on these things"?
7. Is the song easy to sing, or will students stumble over notes and words, thus taking their attention off the message of the song?
8. Is the score appropriate for the mood or emotion you want to emphasize? A boisterous melody, for example, will not create a quiet mood.
9. Does the song represent quality? Does it have depth of meaning and artistic quality?
10. Is there variety in the styles of music chosen? Because personal tastes vary from hymns to contemporary Christian music, from choruses to worship songs, it is important to vary the selections. Teachers and leaders may need to help groups learn to appreciate music they normally do not listen to.

LIN JOHNSON

Bibliography. C. Johansson (1984), *Music and Ministry: A Biblical Counterpoint;* K. Osbeck (1975), *The Ministry of Music;* E. Routley (1978), *Church Music and the Christian Faith;* D. Thiessen (1994), *Psalms, Hymns and Spiritual Songs;* V. Whaley (1995), *Understanding Music and Worship in the Local Church.*

Nn

Narrative Theology. *See* Storytelling.

National Association of Evangelicals (NAE). "The NAE is a voluntary fellowship of evangelical denominations, churches, organizations, institutions, and individuals, demonstrating unity in the body of Christ by standing for biblical truth, speaking with a representative voice, and serving the evangelical community through united action, cooperative ministry, and strategic planning" (Melvin, 1997, www.nae.net). Currently claiming 43,000 congregations, 49 member denominations, and an impact on 27 million constituents, the NAE is one of 117 national fellowships that belong to World Evangelical Fellowship.

Its history dates back to the early twentieth century. Having lost prominent positions of influence and leadership among many mainline denominations, conservatives in the 1920s and 1930s established their own schools, mission societies, radio ministries, camps, denominations, and church associations. While effective on a local basis, these independent groups lacked sufficient clout in influencing appropriate state and national government agencies and media groups. The need for a unified voice for conservatives became clear when the Federal Council of Churches (FCC) mounted an attempt to convince ABC and NBC radio networks not to sell air time to conservative religious radio ministries. This and similar threats set the stage for a new partnership.

Under the leadership of J. Elwin Wright of the New England Fellowship, and Will Houghton, then president of Moody Bible Institute, a group of conservative leaders gathered in Chicago in 1941. There they formed the Temporary Committee for United Action Among Evangelicals and planned another meeting for April 1942 in St. Louis. Delegates at this meeting made history by forming the National Association of Evangelicals for United Action—later shortened to NAE. Harold J. Ockenga was appointed as their first president and J. Elwin Wright as promotional director. During the discussions held at St. Louis, the NAE defined itself separately from the FCC and, much to the dismay of the impassioned Carl McIntire, separately from McIntire's conservative group, the American Council of Christian Churches (ACCC). In response to McIntire's style and mood, the newly founded NAE wanted to positively position itself within the religious community and to focus on spreading the gospel and less on the sometimes negative spirit of the ACCC and its stated main goal of opposing the FCC.

Throughout its fifty-five-year history, the NAE has served as a forum, voice, and resource for the evangelical church. Building cooperation between denominations and groups that represent the diversity and independent spirit of American evangelicalism is a major accomplishment. NAE's numerous subsidiaries, commissions, and affiliates have organized evangelical leaders throughout America to make a major impact on humanitarian aid, families and children, Christian education in the church and Christian schools, and various evangelistic efforts like the Evangelical Fellowship of Mission Agencies (the world's largest).

Some critics question the future impact of NAE, citing the apparent absence of young leaders within its ranks, the perceived lack of participation from the so-called megachurches of America, and the decline in many member denominations. While a strategy for soliciting the involvement of today's younger leaders may help, NAE's future may lie in continued efforts to build coalitions among diverse evangelicals and in rallying them in their shared desire to fulfill the Great Commission.

G. CRAIG WILLIFORD

Bibliography. *An Evangelical Manifesto: A Strategic Plan for the Dawn of the 21st Century* (1996); A. H. Matthews (1992), *Standing Up, Standing Together: The Emergence of the National Association of Evangelicals;* D. Melvin (1997), *About the National Association of Evangelicals.*

National Catholic Educational Association. Founded in 1904, the National Catholic Educational Association represents approximately two hundred thousand Roman Catholic educators who serve students in Catholic elementary and secondary schools, in religious education programs, in colleges and universities, and in seminaries. Their mission is to advance the educational mission of the church and to provide leadership and service to its members. Because almost 50 percent of Catholic schools are located in urban, inner-city, and rural areas serving children from low-income families, the NCEA has a special concern for these children.

The NCEA provides many special services that are outlined below:

Annual Convention and Exposition. This is the key service provided by NCEA, in which members receive spiritual and professional guidance. Typically it is attended by 14,000 to 20,000 delegates who can select from hundreds of workshops conducted by the various departments of the association.

Summer programs. Summer programs are held in addition to the annual meeting to allow members to keep up their skills and technological knowledge. One example is a four-day intensive program to foster leadership and promote involvement in local and national educational issues.

Publications. The association conducts extensive research and publishes a variety of reports and handbooks related to each membership category. They also publish *Momentum,* a professional journal.

Special Events. The NCEA designs the National Marketing Campaign for Catholic Schools as well as Catholic Schools Week and National Appreciation Day for Catholic Schools.

Departments. The association is divided into seven departments, each with an executive director and other professional staff.

Elementary Schools. NCEA provides services for students and school administrators, teachers, early childhood educators, development directors, parents, and pastors. They also provide grants to teachers for innovative practices in values and global education.

Secondary Schools. NCEA conducts research and serves administrators, teachers, and staff for Catholic secondary school students. The "Shepherding the Shepherds" program fosters spiritual development of the leaders through a two-day retreat that encourages prayerful reflection, journal writing, and sharing with peers.

Religious Education. NCEA publishes research and offers two national assessment tools. Assessment of Catholic Religious Education (ACRE) measures the religious knowledge, beliefs, attitudes, and practices of students in elementary and secondary schools and parish programs. Information for Growth (IFG) is an adult self-assessment instrument that assesses the adult participant's images of God, religious beliefs, attitudes, and spirituality. They also conduct the annual National Association for Parish Coordinators and Directors of Religious Education (NPCD) convocation, which runs concurrently with the national convention.

Chief Administrators of Catholic Education (CACE). CACE comprises three divisions: Division of Total Catholic Education, Catholic Schools, and Religious Education and a separate section of Supervision, Personnel, and Curriculum (SPQ). They, too, offer an annual meeting and leadership institute.

National Association of Boards of Catholic Education (NABCE). NABCE offers training and guidance to board, commission, and council members. Through sponsoring and conducting research on what makes boards more effective and successful, they then provide publications and workshops for members for in-service planning, building consensus, and making decisions.

Association of Catholic Colleges and Universities (ACCU). ACCU serves Catholic colleges and universities through publications and an annual winter meeting.

Seminary. NCEA aims to increase the effectiveness of seminaries through networking, publications, and a convocation.

Their address is: National Catholic Educational Association. 1077 30th Street NW, Suite 100, Washington, DC 20007–3852. Home page: http://www.ncea.org.

SARA ANNE ROBERTSON

See also ROMAN CATHOLIC EDUCATION

National Council of Churches (NCC). The NCC was founded in 1950 with an impetus from twenty-nine denominations and twelve existing ecumenical agencies, each with differing foci and some whose roots go back to the nineteenth century. These organizations joined together to communicate ideas, work together on programs and projects, express a common unity and mission, and accomplish those things which could better be done united than separate.

The NCC is comprised of a great variety of Protestant denominations, Orthodox, and Anglicans, but has few evangelical denominations and no Roman Catholic members in contrast to the World Council of Churches.

Rewritten in 1981, the preamble to the constitution of the NCC seeks to reflect a community of Christian communions rather than a council. It reads, "The National Council of the Churches of Christ in the U.S.A. is a community of Christian communions which in response to the gospel as revealed in Scriptures, confess Jesus Christ, the incarnate Word of God, as Savior and Lord. The communions covenant with one another to manifest ever more fully the unity of the Church. Relying upon the Holy Spirit, the Council brings these communions into common mission, serving in all creation to the glory of God."

In 1997, with a staff of 317 and a budget of $61,000,000, the NCC was comprised of thirty-three communions representing a membership of fifty-one million. The organization of the Council has recently been simplified to include the General Secretariat, Church World Services and Witness, and National Ministries. Church World Services and Witness and National Ministries are composed of representatives from member communions and include such activities as providing worldwide aid to the needy, such as disaster relief, refugee assistance, technical assistance, and reconstruction; promoting global education, monitoring human rights and international economic and political issues; promoting the use of the New Revised Standard Version of the Bible and the Revised Standard Version; strengthening and enriching family life; promoting peace and justice, interfaith activities, and theological discourse; and providing resources in areas such as education for missions, literacy, and higher education. Other activities include advocating racial, economic, and environmental justice; stewardship; religious liberty of women and children; relating the Christian gospel to community media; interpreting the work of the NCC through various forms of media and providing information in technology and statistics; training leaders in writing, publishing, and distributing reading, literacy, and religious education materials; producing Christian broadcasting programs and literature.

Funding for the NCC is varied and complex, but the chief sources of finances are public appeals and the contributions of church and member agencies. The cost of materials produced by the Council is usually covered by their sale, but the sale of the NRSV and the Uniform Lesson Series of Bible studies are substantial and help support related programs. Church World Services and Witness obtains funding from individuals and churches, government payments for certain programs involving refugee resettlement, and other sources which amount to approximately 70 percent of the total NCC budget. NCC itself is the preeminent expression of the movement toward ecumenical Christian unity in the United States.

DORIS BORCHERT

National Sunday School Association. Organized in 1945, the National Sunday School Association (NSSA) was an interdenominational, Protestant evangelical organization committed to the revitalization of Sunday school.

From the early 1900s the Sunday School Movement in the United States was in sharp decline. One reason for the decline was the theologically liberal influence on the curriculum materials provided in the uniform series produced by the International Council of Religious Education. A liberal theology and the social gospel, with little if any reference to the Bible, were unacceptable to conservative Christians. Also, after the turn of the century, the leadership of the Sunday School Movement was taken out of the hands of the key lay leaders and given to more liberal "professional" educators. Finally the national Sunday school conventions and rallies were no longer providing leadership and enthusiasm as they had in the past.

The National Association of Evangelicals (NAE) recognized the importance of a strong educational component to undergird the evangelism efforts of the churches. They also recognized the seriousness of the decline and the need to produce theologically acceptable resources. In 1944 the president of the National Association of Evangelicals called a meeting of representative publishers, editors, and Christian education leaders in Columbus, Ohio, to consider what might be done about the situation. From this meeting two committees were appointed; one to proceed in the development of a new Uniform Bible Lesson Outline Series, and another to organize an evangelical National Sunday School Association.

The following year, on May 1, 1945, a group of conservative leaders met in Chicago. They were called together by the commissions appointed in Columbus, and they organized an association to produce new uniform Sunday school lessons and to spearhead Sunday school revival through Sunday school conventions.

Their first Sunday school convention was held in Moody Church, Chicago, October 2–6, 1946. A board of directors was elected and an executive secretary was secured. From the beginning the purpose of the organization was to bring about a revitalization of the Sunday school with emphasis on biblical teaching and evangelism. They adopted the National Association of Evangelicals' statement of faith and became affiliated with that organization in 1946.

Charged with the strategic challenge to revitalize the nation's dying Sunday schools, this organization significantly contributed to Sunday school growth. The period from 1945 to 1960, as reported in the *Yearbook of American Churches*, indicated that Sunday school enrollment practically doubled to over 41 million students in fifteen years.

A national Sunday school convention was held each year from 1946 to 1954. Then, from 1955 to 1968, twin conventions were held in the East and the West. Regional and local associations were organized and some sponsored conventions as large as the national meetings.

The National Sunday School Association organized commissions and groups on youth, denominational Sunday school secretaries, research, camping, publishers, and the National

Association of Directors of Christian Education. These groups met prior to the national Sunday school conventions and provided resource people for platform speakers and the many workshops held at the convention. The groups developed their own identity as well and made significant contributions to the field of Christian education and to the Sunday School Movement.

By 1969 NSSA began to promote national leadership seminars rather than major conventions. Leadership in the organization was not as strong as it had been under the capable leadership of executive secretary Dr. Clate Risley and some of these seminars were poorly organized and suffered from low attendance. Financing for NSSA came primarily from the income of the national conventions and with these no longer held, economics also contributed to its demise.

The National Association of Evangelicals tried to keep the organization going, but it eventually died. NAE organized the National Christian Education Association in 1976 and this organization tried to carry on the work of revitalizing the Sunday school through special seminars. It did not receive the enthusiastic support of the churches or of the leadership in the field that NSSA received when it began. It ceased to exist in 1996.

In addition to the significant increase in Sunday school attendance during the early years of NSSA, the organization's contributions to Christian education continue to this present day. Over two hundred Sunday school conventions are held all over the United States each year. Some of the NSSA commissions are now full-fledged organizations such as the North American Professors of Christian Education, The Association of Christian Schools International, Christian Camping International, and the Professional Association of Christian Educators.

DENNIS E. WILLIAMS

Bibliography. E. A. Sanner and A. F. Harper, eds. (1978), *Exploring Christian Education;* B. L Shelley (1967), *Evangelicalism in America.*

See also NATIONAL ASSOCIATION OF EVANGELICALS; RAIKES, ROBERT; SUNDAY SCHOOL; SUNDAY SCHOOL, HISTORY OF

Navigators. International nondenominational Christian organization with the expressed purpose of "To know Christ and to make Him known."

Dawson Trotman, founder of the Navigators, began teaching a sailor by the name of Les Spencer principles of Christian living. One of Spencer's shipmates asked him about his changed life. Spencer brought his friend to Trotman and said, "Teach him what you taught me!" Trotman's response—"You teach him!"—was the beginning of the Navigators.

Spencer began to teach his friend what Trotman had taught him. Soon, 125 sailors on the USS *West Virginia* were growing in Christ. By the end of World War II, men on a thousand ships and military bases had become Christians and were discipling others. In 1948, China became the destination of the first overseas Navigator missionary. Presently, more than two thousand Navigator missionaries minister in over eighty countries. Thousands have been trained to develop intimacy with Christ and help others do the same.

Navigator staff are specialists in one-to-one and small group interactions. Individualized training produces a certain type of Christian—a laborer who has learned to evangelize the lost, establish young believers in their faith, and equip them to promote the kingdom of God regardless of their vocation, location, and circumstance of life.

Common characteristics of Christians trained by the Navigators include proficiency in Bible study, a strong devotional life, Scripture memory, ability to share the gospel, and serving in a local church while having a vision to disciple others.

The following is a brief overview of the different types of ministry entities the Navigators engage in worldwide:

African-American. Ministry occurs through rehabilitating old homes and playing sports with gang members to achieve relevant contact with individuals.

Business and Professional. B&P staff influence the global market by training professionals to lead others to Christ in their own spheres of influence.

Church Discipleship. This service assists local churches through various means such as "The 2:7 Series." This practical discipleship program enables churches to disciple and mobilize the laity.

Collegiate. These staff are raising up laborers who will impact the world for Christ. Ministers in this field of service focus on college students, faculty, and staff.

Community. This versatile entity reaches out to a broad spectrum of people by ministering within focus groups entitled Friendship, Marketplace, MetroNet, Rural and Small Town, Three "E" (evangelism, establishing, and equipping), and YouthNet.

Hispanic. Ministry occurs among Spanish-speaking, bilingual, and bicultural individuals, emphasizing multiplication among Hispanic laborers throughout the United States.

International Ministries Group. This service ministers to international students and scholars, expatriates, and nonresidential missionaries traveling from the United States to other countries.

Military. Ministry occurs among United States military both at home and abroad. The intent is to train individuals to walk with Christ and serve him throughout all of life.

Navigator Women's Ministries. This international ministry exists to equip and edify women regardless of their age and context of life. This service is fostered by encouraging women to utilize their gifts for the promotion of God's kingdom. A quarterly newsletter and mentoring relationships are important elements of this personalized ministry.

Research and Innovation. This ministry's primary functions include stimulating innovation, initiating, and fostering new Navigator ministries, and arousing further research and development.

NavPress. NavPress publishes books, videos, tapes, and Bible studies that foster intimacy with Christ, and culturally relevant materials to minister to others.

Glen Eyrie. Glen Eyrie is The Navigators' Conference Center, which offers conferences regarding practical issues of life. The facility provides an environment for nurturing depth with Christ and others.

Leadership Development Institute. Located at Glen Eyrie, the LDI is designed to train individuals to be lifelong laborers by equipping them in the direction of their God-given design and fields of influence.

Eagle Lake Camp. Eagle Lake is a 700-acre wooded adventure land located north of Glen Eyrie. This ministry offers youth and adults experiences such as fishing, canoeing, mountain biking, horseback riding, and wilderness backpacking, all designed around biblical teaching.

National Services Center. The NSC is located in Colorado Springs, Colorado, and provides accounting, administration, communications, development, and leadership for Navigator staff.

MICHAEL F. SABO

Bibliography. R. D. Foster (1983), *The Navigators;* B. L. Skinner (1974), *Daws.*

Needs, Maslow's Theory of. Abraham Maslow is considered to be the father of humanistic psychology, which centers on human beings and their values, capacities, and worth. His 1954 book *Motivation and Personality* joined Carl Rogers's *Counseling and Psychotherapy* (1942) in introducing many of the basic tenets of humanistic psychology. Humanism reflects Jean-Jacques Rousseau's romantic view of human nature as intrinsically good, but corrupted by society. It developed in reaction to Freud's view of human nature as problematic and tinged with intrinsic evil and to the behaviorists' view of human behavior as determined solely by environmental influences.

Maslow believed that all human beings have an innate drive for self-realization, self-fulfillment, or self-actualization. Self-actualization is the unfolding and fulfillment of one's personal potential. People move toward that fulfillment through the meeting of seven levels of basic needs. This hierarchical model is expressed as a pyramid, with basic needs on the bottom and self-actual-

ization as the culminating point of the pyramid. Each level of the pyramid is dependent on the previous level.

The first four levels deal with deficiency or basic needs. These include *survival* (needs for shelter, warmth, food, water, and sleep); *safety* (concern for tomorrow's needs, security and freedom from threat in an orderly, predictable environment); *belonging and love* (receiving love and acceptance from family and peers, establishing relationships); and *self-esteem* (recognition and approval, self-respect, competence and mastery). Of these basic needs the physiological needs are the strongest because if deprived of these, the person would die.

Beyond these basic needs exist growth needs. *Intellectual achievement* (the need to know and understand) and *aesthetic appreciation* (experiencing and understanding beauty, order, truth, justice, and goodness) exist and may lead to *self-actualization* (development of one's talents, capacities and potential). It is, according to Maslow, "the desire to become everything that one is capable of becoming." Characteristics of the self-actualized person include such things as acceptance of self and others, spontaneity, openness, democratic relations with others, creativity, positive humor, and independence. Clouse (1993) includes these characteristics as well: self-actualized persons are realistic, resist conformity, have a high sense of ethics, and center on work rather than on themselves. Maslow embraced the concept of self-actualization both as an empirical principle and as an ethical ideal.

Yount (1996) refers to Maslow's later work (1968) and defines an eighth level called *transcendence.* This is defined as the spiritual need for broader cosmic identification. Yount indicates that this level is included in only one text, indicating that it seldom receives attention.

Educators make application of Maslow's theories by realizing that if basic needs are not being met, students will have difficulty focusing on growth needs, including the need to know and understand. Maslow believed that children make wise choices when given the opportunity. When children are in attractive learning situations, they will choose from the offerings they find personally valuable. The learning experience becomes its own reward.

The humanistic educator sees the child as a whole person, a totality composed of many interrelated parts. Basic skills of learning are important, but must not exclude human relations. Moral learning is a part of understanding what makes other people unhappy and of learning to act in socially acceptable ways. Morality is internal, rather than imposed by external forces. Humanistic themes such as accepting self and others, understanding one's own feelings and the feelings of others, achieving mastery and competence, setting purposeful goals, and dealing with choice and the consequences of choice, are a part of the educational process.

The influence of humanism is somewhat moderated today by a society disillusioned by the hope of creating a better world through a humanistic educational program. The emphasis on personal self-fullfillment seen in Maslow's model may have led to too much emphasis on the individual and too little emphasis on the good of the society. Clouse (1993), in a balanced examination of humanism, also indicates that the rise of cognitive psychology has overshadowed the humanist approach.

Some religious organizations have been critical of the tenets of secular humanism—the self-sufficiency of man, the rejection of religion as little more than superstition, acceptance of the scientific method, and placing primacy on values of academic freedom and civil liberties. Their criticism has been broad-based and condemnatory of all forms of humanism.

Yet humanism as a concept continues to influence educators, both secular and religious, who view pleasant methods, trained teachers and attractive classrooms, and a focus on the learner as essential to the learning experience. Maslow's emphasis on human potential continues to define many aspects of the postmodern society, emphasizing attention to the inner self, awareness of cultural limitations, pleasure in beauty and nature, and wise decision-making.

BARBARA WYMAN

Bibliography. B. Clouse (1993), *Teaching for Moral Growth;* A. H. Maslow (1954), *Motivation and Personality;* idem (1968), *Toward a Psychology of Being;* C. Rogers (1942), *Counseling and Psychotherapy;* W. R. Yount (1996), *Created to Learn.*

See also HIERARCHY OF NEEDS; HUMANISM, CHRISTIAN; HUMANISM, CLASSICAL; JUNG, CARL; MASLOW, ABRAHAM HAROLD; ROGERS, CARL

Neonates. *See* Infancy.

Neoorthodoxy. Twentieth-century theological movement based in Europe and North America which rejected classical liberalism and attempted to reaffirm the *orthodox* teaching of the Christian community (such as those articulated by Paul, Augustine, Luther, and Calvin), but in a *new* or modern voice. As such, neoorthodoxy drew critics as well as converts from the theological left and right, and signaled a fundamental shift from the human-centered theology of classical liberalism to a God-centered theological position. However, neoorthodoxy as a movement lacked long-term viability. Sara Little (1995) describes neoorthodoxy as a "momentary manifestation" (14) of the Reformed tradition, since its measurable effect diminished in the early 1970s.

Origin and Development of Neoorthodoxy. Existentialism is the philosophical basis for neoorthodoxy. Søren Kierkegaard (1713–55), the father of existentialism, postulated a "leap of faith," wherein the basis or object of faith is not necessarily intellectually or rationally discernible; hence separating faith and reason. This separation becomes the fundamental assumption in neoorthodox theology. Existentialism was advocated in the twentieth century by such philosophers as Martin Heidegger, Karl Jaspers, and Jean-Paul Sartre.

The father of neoorthodoxy was Karl Barth (Swiss Protestant, 1886–1968), who influenced a generation of theologians (e.g., Paul Tillich, Reinhold Niebuhr, H. Richard Niebuhr, Emil Brunner), New Testament scholars (e.g., Rudolph Bultmann, Friedrich Gogarten), and scholar-pastor Dietrich Bonhoeffer. Barth's theology was a fusion of the Reformers' theology and Kierkegaard, adapted to the cultural setting of the early twentieth century. Hence, the historical circumstances of Barth's life gave rise to neoorthodoxy as much as did his acquaintance with existentialism and his rejection of classical liberalism.

Neoorthodoxy is also known by three other titles: (1) Initially, it was known as *Theology of Crisis,* since the "Fatherhood of God and Brotherhood of Man" attested to by classical liberals no longer seemed viable in light of the atrocities of World War I and social chaos of the Depression. Barth's *Romans* (1919) is perhaps the earliest and fullest expression of crisis theology, which led to its rapid acceptance among European theologians. (2) *Dialectical Theology,* reflecting the idea of the diverse nature of truth in existentialism and classical liberalism, which must be determined through dialogue. (3) More recently, it has made its advent into Roman Catholicism in the form of *Kerygmatic Theology.*

Theological Tenets of Neoorthodoxy. Neoorthodoxy's theological position is decisively to the right of the classical liberalism to which it responded. (1) *God* is viewed as being transcendent from his creation and humanity, and consequently possesses the quality of Otherness. Only God can transverse this transcendence, and this necessitates revelation, intervention in history, and grace. God is viewed in a quasi-traditional Trinitarian fashion, and is regarded as Creator, Revealer, and Redeemer; but stress is on the christological element. (2) The *Scriptures* are regarded as God's Word (incarnated in Christ, attested to by Scripture, and proclaimed by the church) and are authoritative. However, the Bible is not the *content* of God's revelation, but is regarded as a witness to divine revelation. For example, the Bible records the interventions of God in human history, but it is not an intervention itself. Hence, it is not the revelation itself, but one step removed from the revelatory event. (3) The

Christ of faith is the basis and object of faith, as opposed to the historical Jesus of classical liberalism's quest. The miracles surrounding his life are reinterpreted for modern significance (demythologized), but not affirmed as actual historical events. Hence, Christology is stressed in neoorthodox theology. (4) *Salvation* is viewed as both personal redemption and historical, through redemptive history and eschatology. The atonement is viewed as broadly, almost to the point of universalism. (5) *Humanity* is affirmed as being the *imago dei*. Sin is regarded as rebellion against God due to human freedom. This sinfulness is manifested in self-centeredness and alienation from others, and hence is psychologically and sociologically understandable.

Assessment of Neoorthodoxy. (1) Neoorthodoxy did acknowledge and indict classical liberalism as being inadequate and fatally flawed, as would evangelicals. (2) Despite its rejection of classical liberalism, neoorthodoxy did accept its radical modern critical methods of biblical criticism. Hence, underlying its "orthodox" theological appearance, its basis was the higher criticism of classical liberalism. (3) Neoorthodoxy was indeed a theological step toward the right, but did not step far enough to the right to be considered traditionally evangelical. As Gangel and Benson (1983) surmise, "Barth was couching the ideas of critical scholars in the terminology of fundamentalists to arrive at a compromise which was certainly to the right of the old liberalism, but did not return the church to biblical Christianity" (316). Hence, it did not deliver that which it promised. (4) Finally, neoorthodoxy is theologically "gray," neither conservative nor liberal, but both and neither simultaneously. While this may sound contradictory, it reflects the internal contradictions within neoorthodoxy which ultimately led to its demise.

Neoorthodoxy and Education. The theological departure from classical liberalism to neoorthodoxy produced reappraisals within the church's education community. H. Shelton Smith's *Faith and Nurture* (1941) was the first to advocate neoorthodox theology's educational potential and implications. He directly challenged classical liberalism's educational approaches as articulated by its champion George Albert Coe, and more specifically Harrison Elliot's *Can Religious Education be Christian?* (1940).

According to Sara Little (1995), theology is both source and norm in neoorthodox education. These roles are reflected in the educational endeavors of mainline Protestant denominations of the mid-twentieth century. For example, James Smart's *Teaching Ministry of the Church* (1948) advocated the Bible serving as both content and "watchtower" of Christian education. Lewis Sherrill, who was heavily influenced by Tillich, developed the "Covenant Life Curriculum" for the Presbyterian Church U.S.A. throughout the 1950s. Similarly, Paul H. Vieth's *The Church and Christian Education* (1947), which summarized the "Study of Christian Education" sponsored by the National Council of Churches, reflects a neoorthodox stance in both theology and education. Neoorthodoxy in both Christian theology and education is regarded as a past movement which has since ceased.

JAMES RILEY ESTEP

Bibliography. K. O. Gangel and W. S. Benson (1983), *Christian Education: Its History and Philosophy;* S. Little, *Theology of Religious Education* (1995): 11–34; D. C. Wyckoff, *Christian Education Journal* 15, no. 3 (1995): 12–26.

Neo-Thomism. Modern revival of medieval scholastic theology and philosophy, of which Thomas Aquinas (1225–74) was the primary thinker and spokesman. Also called neo-scholasticism, the contemporary movement traces its beginnings back to an 1879 encyclical of Pope Leo XIII which praised Aquinas as the foremost of all the Doctors of the Church and commanded that his teachings be propagated to the fullest extent. Further encyclicals in the last century have attempted to reestablish the authority of Thomism in Roman Catholicism as *the* philosophy underlying all areas of knowledge and all educational pursuits.

Jacques Maritain was perhaps the most well-known Neo-Thomist educational theorist of recent times. His book, *Education at the Crossroads* (1943), is the classic statement in English of this movement. At the same time there has developed a secular type of Neo-Thomism, represented by the thinking of such individuals as Mortimer Adler (*The Paideia Proposal*, 1982) and Robert Maynard Hutchins.

As the term suggests, Neo-Thomism has resurrected the Aristotelian rationalism of Aquinas with its unified worldview based on the metaphysics of realism. For Thomism, reality is a knowable totality, a combination of the natural, knowable by reason, and the supernatural, knowable by faith. According to Aquinas, faith and reason are both given by God and need never conflict. Thus, philosophy and theology, while distinct, form an inseparable whole.

Both branches of Neo-Thomism, the religious and the secular, emphasize reason, logic, and first principles. For education, this has certain consequences. The teacher is responsible for the content of learning, and the mind and will of the student are the primary foci of the teaching process. Student desires are important but secondary. The mental capacities of the learners must be disciplined to analyze and understand the unalterable truth of reality.

This approach places subjects that deal with the exercise of reason on the basis of first principles at the center of the ideal curriculum: mathematics, languages, and, for the religious Neo-Thomist, the revealed truth of doctrine. From these durable truths, the student then attempts to understand the lesser-known aspects of reality. In this quest, it is important that the student become skilled at reading, writing, and speaking. Practical skills are also to be included, but are seen as secondary to the most important aims of education, namely, the cultivation of rationality and spirituality.

All Christians can appreciate much of the philosophical underpinnings of Neo-Thomism, with its emphasis on the existence and knowability of truth, the existence of God, the validity and importance of reason, and the like. On the other hand, this movement has been criticized by some Christians for its fixation on the works of Thomas Aquinas, its tendency to minimize human depravity, and its tendency to intellectualize faith. Beyond this, educators of many different persuasions see at least some Neo-Thomist educators as overemphasizing the cultivation of the intellect in the educational process, while at the same time neglecting the importance of such things as the affective realm of life, learning by doing, and the practical application of truth to contemporary problems.

MARK H. HEINEMANN

See also ADLER, MORTIMER; AQUINAS, THOMAS

Neugarten, Bernice L. (1916–). American gerontologist. Born as the daughter of a Jewish Lithuanian immigrant father, she grew up in Norfolk, Virginia, where she excelled as a student. Skipping several grades brought her to the attention of the superintendent of schools, who encouraged her to study at the University of Chicago. She was only seventeen when she arrived at the university. She completed her B.A. degree at twenty and finished her master's at 21. While studying at the university, she met a businessman, Fritz Neugarten. They were married in 1940 and he supported her academic career.

Neugarten has contributed to the field of life-span education and aging. She was one of the first to study the second half of life for adults. She integrated insights from several disciplines, including economics, psychology, sociology, anthropology, and education. She has been influential in developing public policy for older persons.

Through the Committee on Child Development she was offered assistance to study for her Ph.D. While participating in a research project in the community study of Morris, Illinois, she completed her doctoral research on friendship patterns and social class. Meanwhile, her committee was expanded to human development

and, at age twenty-seven, she received the first Ph.D. in human development awarded in the United States.

She taught at the University of Chicago until 1980, when she retired. She was invited to start a doctoral program in Human Development and Social Policy at Northwestern. After eight years she returned to Chicago as Rothschild Distinguished Scholar at the Center on Aging, Health, and Society.

She has written or edited eight books and 150 articles and monographs, and delivered numerous lectures. She guided 150 doctoral students in the field and served as a chair on the White House Conference on Aging. She has challenged many of the prevailing notions about aging, such as the trauma of menopause and the universality of the midlife crisis. She maintains that need, not chronological age, is the issue that should be addressed in public policy. She has also insisted that "development" may be a misnomer in adult aging, since people grow old in many different ways.

EDWARD A. BUCHANAN

Bibliography. B. L. Neugarten, ed. (1968), *Middle Age and Aging.*

See also ADULT DEVELOPMENT; ANDRAGOGY

Nomothetic Dimension. Term used in administrative (or leadership) philosophy. It is a combination of the Greek words *nomos* (law, rule) and *thetos* (that which is set up, put in place, or adopted). *Nomothetic* then, in an organizational sense, refers to the rules and values set up by an organizational system for its maintenance and growth. Administrative philosophy brings to light the tension between the organizational system and the needs, desires, and values of the individual. This tension is a major dilemma for many involved with organizational leadership. The needs of the individual are referred to by the term *idiographic* (Greek *idios* = individual). Thus, administrative philosophy assists leaders in properly reconciling the interactions between the nomothetic and idiographic dimensions of organizational life.

KENNETH HAMMONDS

Bibliography. C. Hodgkinson (1978), *Toward a Philosophy of Administration;* idem (1983), *The Philosophy of Leadership.*

Nonformal Education. Term first coined in 1970 to describe an educational approach used since the beginning of history. Research by Philip Coombs in the late 1960s found that this form of education was related to the growth of developing societies. Ted Ward, through his research and teaching at Michigan State University, is one of the most prominent evangelical educators to popularize the term.

Nonformal education can be understood best as we compare and contrast it to both "formal" and "informal" education. While formal education typically relates to structured educational experiences like school, informal education relates to the learning that happens naturally during the normal routines of living. Formal education is highly structured, built on a traditional social structure, and intentional in its goals. Informal education is similar to formal education in that it is built on a traditional social structure. It is different in that its goals are not intentional but based on the informal social relationships within a culture. Informal education happens naturally without deliberate planning. The distinctive of nonformal education is that it is both intentional and need-based, thus salvaging the benefits from the other forms of education without being limited by their traditional ties to culture. This unique feature of nonformal education allows it to be a change agent within a given culture. While formal education focuses on the traditional schooling approach to education and informal education focuses on the process of socialization in learning, nonformal education relates to deliberate educational strategies based on meeting people's needs outside of the formal schooling model. Since it tends to be highly functional, change-oriented, and learner-driven, nonformal education is a versatile educational approach.

Nonformal education is especially suited to the mission of Christian educators, whose task it is to equip persons to use their gifts and talents to minister to other people. While some aspects of this task can be accomplished within educational institutions, there is a growing consensus within both the school and church that such training needs to be more "field-based." More and more pastoral, ministry, and missionary training programs are being developed around the world that would fit the category of nonformal education. Such programs are designed with intentional goals to meet specific needs within a given culture. Although a variety of teaching methods may be used, the structure is flexible enough to continually adapt to the changing needs within the culture. Nonformal education is thought by many Christian educators to provide a most effective means by which the church can develop strategies to train disciples of Jesus Christ in a constantly changing world.

GARY C. NEWTON

Nonprofit Organizations. A government designation for a group of people who come together around a mutual interest in order to perform some sort of service outside the realm of business. NPOs differ from for-profit businesses by ensuring that no moneys earned go toward the enrichment of any individual. An NPO generally develops from a mission that draws like-minded people toward the cause and leads to the development of an organization with a unique name, identity, purpose, and staff or membership. They may work with children, the elderly, the mentally and physically handicapped, or the underprivileged. Some promote the arts, others promote special interests, and still others work to protect consumers, taxpayers, and the environment. There are more than 6 million NPOs in the United States, working with hospitals, colleges, museums, symphonies, chambers of commerce, and a myriad of causes. Some of the largest NPOs include the Girl Scouts, the American Medical Association, and various religious denominations.

The Church as NPO. Nearly every church in the United States is a nonprofit organization, with a board, bylaws, and a budget. Its nonprofit status makes the church exempt from corporate or property taxes, with the understanding that the organization is not in business to turn a profit, must submit an annual financial report, and does not exist solely to benefit a few individuals. NPOs get their funding through private donations, and gifts given to them may be written off one's taxes, so a church member's tithe is tax-deductible as a charitable donation.

Though most churches don't realize it, the U.S. government is actually a partner with every NPO. The government subsidizes their mail by offering NPOs lower postage rates; foregoes collecting corporate, utility, and sales taxes from them; and promotes giving by individuals, thereby lowering the overall taxable income of millions of people. In turn, the government keeps some control over NPOs, granting or taking away nonprofit status and requiring that certain criteria be met annually. Currently the criteria include an organizational name, a board of directors, bylaws by which the NPO functions, an annual budget, and articles of incorporation that must include a statement of purpose, a membership list, and some sort of program plan.

JERRY CHIP MACGREGOR

Bibliography. T. Connors (1988), *The Nonprofit Handbook;* Corin et al. (1995), *The Nonprofit Board: Strategies for Organizational Success;* D. Gies et al. (1990), *Nonprofit Organizations: Essential Readings.*

Nonverbal Communication. Only 10 percent of what a listener understands from a speaker comes through the verbal portion of communication. Research studies over several decades approximate this ratio, but attribute the remaining 90 percent to various forms of nonverbal communication. The most frequently listed media are the body (including legs and hands), the face (including mouth and eyes), audible vocalizations (including sounds and inflections), and external entities (including space, time, and physical objects).

In a sense, verbal communication is *what* we say. Nonverbal communication is *how* we say it. These combine within information contexts to produce most of the meaning that is transferred through informal conversation and prepared speech.

Educators must learn to control nonverbal communication in order to reduce gestures and movements that interfere with intended meaning. They must practice nonverbal cues that contribute to understanding. Educators must also become sensitive to nonverbal behaviors transmitted by others. Using all five senses, skilled instructors monitor audience pleasure and pain, interest and boredom, readiness and lack of preparation.

Technically, nonverbal communication includes everything that informs apart from encoded language (words). In practice, forms of nonverbal communication are windows to the hearts of both speakers and listeners. The best control of nonverbal communication is sincerity.

DANIEL C. STEVENS

Nonverbal Language. *See* Body Language.

Norming. Norms are informal ground rules that provide guidelines concerning appropriate and inappropriate behavior in a group. These implicitly understood substrata form the "character" of a group. Rarely do norms specify absolutes. Rather, they indicate ranges of acceptable and unacceptable boundaries of behavior.

Norms are not, as a general rule, determined by an authority outside the group but are imposed by members on each other. These behaviors frequently mirror general cultural beliefs. Studies suggest norms can be clustered into two different categories: conformity by *commission* (emitting behavior) and conformity by *omission* (omitting behavior) (Kumar and Sharma, 1981; Bradley, 1978; Otani and Dixon, 1976).

During the developmental stage of a new group, norms are developed quite rapidly, often without members realizing what is occurring. Unless challenged, practiced behaviors become norms. A group is often not consciously aware of a norm until someone questions, violates, or challenges it.

When there is conflict between how an individual wishes to act and how the norms prescribe that he or she "should" behave, peer pressure is invariably placed on the individual to change and adapt to the group.

This can range from slight frowns to ostracism. Conversely, positive reinforcement can be given when members act in accordance with expectations. While important to all group members, newcomers must work extra hard at being aware of implicit norms because to violate them may

mean punishment, loss of influence, and perhaps exclusion from the group.

Direct frontal assault on a group norm is rarely successful. The person desiring the change is often viewed as deviant. Still, established group norms can be successfully changed. The following guidelines are suggested. First, the member must be viewed as loyal and committed to the group's well-being. Second, careful observation of the offending behavior should be documented, including its effects. Third, constructive clarification should address the concern, at an appropriate time. Fourth, use an inclusive question as a precursor to discussion: "Does anyone else share my concern?" (Brilhart and Galanes, 1992).

Norms have a tremendous impact on the processes and the outcomes of a group. They can be used both positively and negatively throughout the course of a group.

JAMES A. DAVIES

Bibliography. J. Brilhart and G. Galanes (1992), *Effective Group Discussion;* J. Davis (1969), *Group Performance;* R. Guzzo and E. Salas (1995), *Team Effectiveness and Decision Making in Organizations.*

Nouthetic Counseling. Counseling based on the Greek word *noutheteo,* which is translated "admonish" in English New Testaments. This English word is inadequate to completely describe the Greek term. *Noutheteo* includes the sense of confronting with the truth of Scripture. A. T. Robertson paraphrases it as "putting sense into" someone. Nouthetic counseling presupposes an obstacle to be overcome and a need for change in the person being counseled.

Nouthetic counselors believe that Scripture is not only inerrant, but that it is also sufficient to deal with the problems of everyday living. Passages that support this position include Psalm 19:7–9 and Psalm 119. The position is specifically addressed in key passages such as Hebrews 4:12, 2 Timothy 3:16–17, and 2 Peter 1:3.

Love and concern that others grow and ultimately glorify God are primary motivators in nouthetic counseling. Nouthetic counselors believe that it is vital to confront sin with the truth of Scripture. This directive approach takes seriously the biblical mandate to speak the truth in love.

A biblical example that illustrates this balance is found in Acts 20. As Paul was returning to Jerusalem, he sent for the elders of the church at Ephesus. The description of their emotional meeting includes Paul's statement that "for a period of three years I did not cease to admonish [*noutheteo*] you night and day with tears" (20:31). Earlier in the encounter Paul stated, "I have not shunned to declare to you the whole counsel of God" (v. 27). While Paul declared God's truth unashamedly, he did it with love and concern.

This biblical example shows the strong love that marks nouthetic confrontation in verses 37 and 38: "They all wept freely and fell on Paul's neck and kissed him, sorrowing most of all for the words which he spoke, that they would see his face no more." While on earth, Jesus did not hesitate to confront sin. He also taught that the most important commandments are to love God and love neighbor (Matt. 22:37–40). Following Jesus' example is the task of nouthetic counseling.

JOHN E. BABLER

Bibliography. J. E. Adams (1972), *Competent to Counsel;* H. R. Brandt and K. Skinner (1995), *The Word for the Wise: Making Scripture the Heart of Your Counseling Ministry;* J. R. MacArthur Jr. and W. A. Mack (1994), *Introduction to Biblical Counseling: A Basic Guide to the Principles and Practice of Counseling.*

Nursery. Nurseries are often paradoxical places where the workers are given the least amount of respect and the most responsibility. It is also a place where children often cry at the start of the first visit and then cry when they have to go home after their experience is over.

Nursery is a cooperative venture between the Christian educator and the parents, focusing on the growth and development of the most impressionable of all church attenders. Caring for physical needs is the chief task of the infant nursery. The nursery should be a safe, caring place to sleep, crawl, drink a bottle, have clean diapers, and experience loving interaction with men and women who love God.

Adequate staffing is necessary. The more permanent the staff, the more effective the learning environment is for the child. One adult for every three children under age one and one adult for every four to five toddlers is desirable. Ample floor space is critical to the young child's need to explore and move around. A five by seven foot area is needed for each child equaling about 25 to 35 square feet per child. Proper equipment includes a changing table, rocking chair for adults and children, sink, cribs for sleeping infants, and cabinets mounted to the walls for storage of personal belongings. An ample supply of age-appropriate toys, books, and cassette tapes is also necessary. If space is available, an area for nursing mothers with newborns is helpful. Cleanliness is vital, and so toys should be washable. Bed sheets should be washed after each use, as should smocks used to protect workers' clothing.

Safety issues in nursery have become increasingly important. Dutch doors for bathrooms, background checks on potential workers, wearing of plastic gloves to do diaper changing, and check-in and check-out systems so that children are not released to the wrong adult are all becoming standard procedure. Some churches have developed extensive child safety policies including procedures for what to do in case of a charge of child abuse against a nursery worker.

Because the child's first and most lasting impressions of God are formed in the nursery experience, the staff and the activities of the nursery should be positive, loving, and nurturing.

Large blocks of unstructured time are preferable for free play by children, in tandem with guided conversation. Singing, storytelling, reading, eating snacks, and other educational efforts must be informal and one-on-one due to the social development of the children. When all such activities are focused around a theme or emphasis, the child will go home with concrete learning having taken place.

Parents are ultimately responsible for the spiritual rearing of their offspring but the church is an incredibly important partner in the process by both caring for the needs of children and providing spiritual educational assistance for parents in the process of accomplishing their goals. The nursery is also used as an outreach opportunity as contact is made with couples of newly arrived children in the community, offering assistance both physically and spiritually.

CHERYL L. FAWCETT

Bibliography. R. Choun and M. Lawson (1993), *The Complete Handbook for Children's Ministry: How to Reach the Next Generation;* W. Haystead (1989), *Everything You Want to Know About Teaching Young Children: Birth to Six Years;* V. A. Wilson (1986), *Childhood Education in the Church,* pp. 83–97.

See also DAY CARE CENTERS

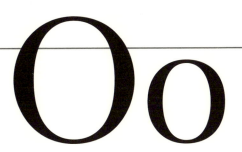

Objective. A clear, concise, specific statement used in a planning process to describe intended outcomes. It is a written statement that briefly details the direction a group, organization, or learner is going and how they will know when they have arrived. Objectives precede and guide program development. Although objectives state the desired outcome, they do not indicate how the outcome will be achieved.

In the literature and in practice the terms *objective* and *goal* are often used interchangeably. Both provide focus and direction for planning actions. More precisely, a goal is a broad, general statement of the desired outcome. Therefore, its achievement is difficult to measure. An objective, on the other hand, is more specific and measurable. Objectives are defined operationally, not in abstract terms. Thus *goal* and *objective* can be distinguished by the degree of specificity, with an objective being the more specific of the two. In some of the literature this distinction is made with the terms *general objective* and *specific objective*.

Mager (1984) delineated several characteristics of effective objectives that have been widely used and subsequently translated by various authors into the "ABCD" formula for evaluating the usefulness of objectives: **A**udience—who is going to exhibit the performance; **B**ehavior—the stated performance; **C**onditions under which the performance will be observed; and **D**egree—the standard against which the performance will be judged. In practice, not all four of the above components must be used when writing program or educational objectives. By definition, however, an objective requires that an outcome be stated.

Educational objectives have been categorized into several domains. The cognitive domain deals with the knowledge, information, and thinking outcomes of education. The affective domain encompasses attitudinal, emotional, value-laden, or feeling outcomes. And the psychomotor domain is performance that requires physical activity.

Learning theory influences the way objectives are written for instruction. Behavioral learning theory, with its emphasis on learner response to specific environmental stimuli, dictates prespecified performance objectives that are stated in terms of what the learner will be able to do when the teaching session is completed. On the other hand, constructivism is a learning theory which emphasizes the role of the learner in constructing meaning from his or her experience. In this case performance objectives are not prespecified by the curriculum or the teacher. Instead, process objectives may be stated. A process objective states the experience or process the learner will engage in, but not what he or she will be able to do at the conclusion of that process.

NANCY L. DeMOTT

Bibliography. R. F. Mager (1984), *Preparing Instructional Objectives.*

See also LESSON PLAN

Object Lesson. A teaching methodology that utilizes some tangible object to reveal insight and understanding of a concept that is intangible. Usually a quality of the item selected portrays a similarity to the truth the teacher wishes to explain or communicate. Because object lessons are most frequently used with children, care must be taken to help them see clearly the "likeness" in the symbolic object. Including many different avenues (pictures, questions, stories) leading to grasping meaning of the same truth help the child understand the desired significance. Object lessons often miss the mark because they neglect the careful construction of these bridges to a child's understanding. Children find it easier to connect concrete objects with concrete understanding (e.g., a box can become an imaginary car) than connecting concrete objects (symbols) with conceptual ideas (e.g., money representing security). Words with double meanings and plays on words which sound like each other only confuse the child's limited thinking (e.g., using the "sun" to represent Jesus the Son or confusing "holey" and holy). Careful questioning and varied reinforcement of the same truth is necessary to assure mental grasp. In object lessons that demonstrate magic or surprise, the child's focus is often on "how did you do that" rather than internalization of the truth being taught. Because of their ability to conceptualize, adults are often better suited to learn from this method than are children. Jesus' use of objects (lilies of the field, lambs, seeds) were always directed to adults.

JULIE GORMAN

Observational Learning. Learning, according to Albert Bandura (Eggen and Kauchak, 1994), is more strongly affected by watching and thinking about the behavior of others than by focusing on consequences. Whereas traditional behavioral learning theories concentrate primarily on consequences, Bandura believed that they were incomplete. In his social cognitive theory the focus is on both the internal and external forces affecting learning. Environmental events, personal factors, and behavior all influence and are influenced by each other. Bandura calls this *reciprocal determinism*.

Observational learning occurs in two forms: modeling and vicarious conditioning. In the former, the learner imitates the behavior of the model even though the model receives no reinforcement or punishment while the observer is watching. A child will learn appropriate behavior in church by observing the modeling of persons the child considers as role models. Types of modeling include direct modeling (imitating a parent's behavior); symbolic modeling (imitating behavior of characters in the Bible, books, television, movies); synthesized modeling (classroom behavior based on observations of teacher, older students); and abstract modeling (inferring a system of rules for playground behavior by observing others in the playground).

Vicarious conditioning occurs when one observes the behavior of others and adjusts one's own behavior accordingly. When Jennifer hears the teacher praise Marie's good behavior, Jennifer's good behavior is vicariously reinforced.

The elements in observational learning include paying attention, retaining information or impressions, producing behaviors, and being motivated to repeat the behaviors. The learner will pay attention to the person who embodies what is considered popular, attractive, admired, and competent, whether in church, sports, interpersonal relationships, or in popular culture. Retention occurs when that behavior is rehearsed mentally or by actual practice. Once the behavior has been rehearsed and practiced it may be performed smoothly with feedback and coaching. However, the behavior may not be practiced until there is some motivation or incentive to do so.

ELEANOR M. LOEWEN

Bibliography. P. Eggen and D. Kauchak (1994), *Educational Psychology: Classroom Connections;* A. E. Woolfolk (1998), *Educational Psychology.*

Open Classroom. A concept that became popular in the early 1970s, when educators began capitalizing on the fact that children learn best by doing. Instead of working in structured environments, children were given the freedom to make choices concerning what they would study, work on, and learn during the school day. Classrooms were divided into small units using bookshelves. Bean bag chairs and pillows provided comfortable areas for reading and studying. Educators assumed that the children would be motivated to learn at their own pace, stay on track, and accomplish even more than if they were placed in "traditional" classrooms, sitting at desks listening to teachers lecture.

Ideally, the open classroom concept placed more emphasis on the learner and his or her needs rather than on the subject matter to be learned. Emphasis was to be placed on successes of the student rather than failures and on making the learning environment a happy and satisfying experience for both the teacher and the pupil. Teachers provided students with individual help as it was needed. Students worked on projects and individual workbooks based on their own specific learning goals.

Unfortunately, as educators came to the realization that not all students can learn in an unstructured environment and that they do not possess unlimited quantities of self-motivation, the open classroom concept began to wane in popularity. Bookshelves were replaced by walls, and teachers began to take charge of learning goals for specific content areas. Very few open classrooms exist in our schools today.

MARCIA MACQUITTY

Operant Conditioning. B. F. Skinner developed into a precise science the experimental analysis of behavior known as operant or Skinnerian conditioning. Skinner observed that real-life behavior consists largely of an operant emitting behavior (response) subsequently reinforced by the environment (reinforcing stimulus) which increases the probability that the emitted behavior will be repeated. Whereas in respondent/classical conditioning a reinforcing stimulus elicits a response, in operant conditioning the operant first emits a response.

Because the operant emits a response upon the environment rather than the environment eliciting a response, the recurrence of an undesirable response can be decreased by withholding a reinforcing stimulus (extinction), removing a reinforcing stimulus (punishment Type II), or presenting an aversive stimulus (punishment Type I).

Behavior is shaped by identifying an initial response already emitted by the operant that is as topographically similar to the desired terminal response as possible, conditioning the initial response to regularity, and switching reinforcement to a new response one step closer to an approximation of the terminal behavior and repeating the process until the terminal behavior is conditioned to regularity.

Although much of Skinner's research into operant conditioning involved the study of animal response to reinforcement, he labored to apply his findings to the field of education. By arranging contingencies of reinforcement in the classroom, Skinner asserted that the technology of behaviorism would radically improve the effectiveness of teaching-learning situations. Educational practices such as performance objectives in instructional planning, computer-assisted instruction (teaching machines), programmed instruction, and competency-based teacher education are applications of behavioral technology.

Critics of operant conditioning argue that manipulating the behavior of others destroys human freedom and dignity, degenerates motivation of behavior to mere reward-punishment contingencies, and dismisses the role of values. Christian educators also question Skinner's view of the nature of man and the role of the environment in determining behavior.

MARK E. SIMPSON

Bibliography. M. J. Boivin, *Journal of the American Scientific Affiliation* 37, no. 2 (1985): 79–85; B. F. Skinner (1938), *The Behavior of Organisms: An Experimental Analysis;* idem (1968), *The Technology of Teaching;* idem (1972), *Beyond Freedom and Dignity;* D. L. Whaley and R. W. Malott (1971), *Elementary Principles of Behavior.*

See also OPERANT LEARNING; SKINNER, BURRHUS FREDERIC; SR BONDS

Operational Thinking. Within Jean Piaget's theory of cognitive development, a rather remarkable shift occurs about the time a child moves into elementary school. Piaget describes the thinking of young children as "pre-operational" while older children possess the capability of performing "concrete operations." As persons move into adolescence they typically develop the capacity for "formal operations." Operations are "actions of a certain kind, interiorized actions coordinated in well-defined structures . . ." (Piaget, 1973, 65).

Two characteristics separate operational thinking from what precedes it. First, the child becomes capable of a certain logic, such as class inclusion (mothers + fathers = parents), indicated by reversibility (parents – fathers = mothers). Second, the child approaches problem-solving in a systematic way, rather than by trial-and-error. In addition, "decentering" (centering is the tendency of the child to focus on only one property of an object at a time) is considered necessary for the formation of operations (Piaget and Inhelder, 1969).

In concrete operations, the child is able to perform these mental activities but is dependent on concrete objects. This logic is one of "classifications, relations, and numbers" (Piaget, 1973, 21). Operations here are coordinated within a comprehensive system of internalized mental structures. Operations in the period of formal operations are qualitatively different—the older child or adolescent begins to be able to manipulate propositions rather than only objects, and to work with multiple variables at the same time.

Frequently in Christian education, teaching of young children employs abstract concepts and generalizations, and uses verbal propositions. However, understanding that operational thinking doesn't begin until about age seven should encourage preschool teachers to teach more through concrete activity and experience than through only abstract symbols (words). Children in elementary school are capable of learning definitions of theological terms and statements of belief. The more sophisticated operations of adolescents and adults enable them to compare belief systems and struggle with the question of why one belief is more consistent with Scripture than another.

CLAIR ALLEN BUDD

Bibliography. R. W. Bybee (1982), *Piaget for Educators;* B. Inhelder and J. Piaget (1958), *The Growth of Logical Thinking;* idem (1973), *The Child and Reality;* J. Piaget and B. Inhelder (1969), *The Psychology of the Child.*

Ordination. Recognition by the church that a person has been called into and is qualified for full-time professional ministry for Christ. Should a director of Christian education or a youth director be ordained? This issue is relatively simple to decide. Are those persons committed to minister as good shepherds of the flocks given to them? Are they truly shepherds in heart and action (see 1 Peter 5), or do they merely operate a program? If the former, then they are pastors and should be ordained. If they are merely program operators, then ordination is not necessary.

Denominations and local churches vary in their requirements for ordination. Often youth workers and directors of Christian education have been systematically excluded from ordination by many denominations or local churches because they have not had sufficient "training," meaning that they have not graduated from a theological seminary with an M.Div. degree. Often these people are looked down on by those with the requisite degrees as being somewhat inferior.

The issue should not be academic degrees or ecclesiastical requirements, but personal and spiritual competencies along with the Lord's call to minister. Receiving an M.Div. degree and passing an ordination exam do not guarantee competency. The need is for a series of truly qualifying requirements that are meaningfully related to full-time ministry. These requirements would include academic competencies and the validity of the call to minister. They should affirm the suitability and ability to be a pastor for the church. The questions should be: Does the person truly attest to a divine call to ministry? Does he or she evidence both the gifts and calling to minister? Is this an unchallengeable and irrefutable call that the ordaining body can also affirm? The church does not rubber stamp an individualistic call. Rather, it determines whether or not the person is truly qualified and called.

Competencies are critically important in any professional area that deals firsthand with people's lives. These competencies should include being able to understand proper Old Testament and New Testament biblical exegesis, basic biblical, historic, and systematic theology, counseling, nurturing-servant-leadership development, and effective teaching and preaching. An equally important competency is the ability to exegete people: to understand their developmental needs, their sociology, culture, values, socioeconomic status, and so on. Pastors need a solid grounding in understanding both theological/biblical and people issues and in knowing how to be nurturing-servant leaders (see 1 Thess. 2:3–13).

The call to ordained ministry should not be considered a call to a special age group or demographic entity. It is the recognition by the church that a person has been ordained already by God to ministry for the Lord in a professional capacity for which she or he is to receive remuneration.

Ordination should not be limited to those who preach on Sunday mornings, baptize, officiate at the Lord's Supper, and conduct weddings and funerals. To be ordained is to be commissioned for the full-time ministry of the Word and the sacraments/ordinances to the people of God and to the world that God so loved. Ordination should not be to a special demographic group or churchly function. Each ordained person and each local church or denomination should determine where one's combination of gifts, talents, abilities, and proclivities are best used in the light of the local congregation's situation.

God calls people into a professional capacity of ministry. This position is first a call from God and then recognized by the church. Without both, one should question the validity of any purported call to professional ministry. Christian educators, youth pastors and youth directors, and other assistant/associate pastors are equally called to full-time ministry and should be given the recognition by the church that they are indeed pastors, worthy of ordination, of being set apart for professional ministry. Calling, giftedness, and recognition of both by the church are the issues for ordination (Acts 13:2–4).

JOHN M. DETTONI

See also ASSOCIATE PASTOR; CLERGY; LEADERSHIP; MINISTER; WOMEN, ORDINATION OF

Organism. A living element mutually dependent on other living elements for meeting certain needs and contributing to its survival. Organisms are part of an open system and are therefore in a continual exchange with other systems and subsystems. Organisms have the ability to adapt to certain changes and have needs that when met result in survival and growth (negative entropy). On the other hand, when organisms' needs are not met, deterioration and death result (entropy).

In Christian culture, the term *organism* has been used as a way of describing the nature of the universal church and local church. This description grows out of the New Testament, where the church is referred to as a "body." The most thorough example is found in 1 Corinthians 12, where Paul uses the metaphor of a physical body having many parts to help the Corinthian believers understand the nature of the local church. Each part is important to the overall function of the whole body and if one part of the body suffers, the whole body suffers as a result. Additional teaching on this topic is found in Romans 12:4–5 and Ephesians 4:15–16.

JAY DESKO

Bibliography. G. Inrig (1975), *Life in His Body;* G. Morgan (1986), *Images of Organization.*

See also CHURCH

Organization. One of the five major functions of administration (the others are planning, staffing, directing, and evaluating). Throughout Scripture it is clear that God is interested in organization in all of these respects. From the creation of the universe he set in motion a plan by which his creation would have fellowship with him. He set administrators over particular tasks and has coordinated the management of the body of Christ.

The second half of the twentieth century has seen an increased dependence on large business organizations for the production of needed goods and services to replace smaller family businesses. The church has moved toward megachurches rather than smaller denominational congregations. Sociologists endeavor to understand the workings and dynamics of organizations, including their culture, climate, and the maturing process by which the health and age of any given organization can be determined. Church organizational growth and development can be examined in a similar fashion.

Traditionally, organizations have been understood in terms of the division of work, delegation of authority, chain of command, and span of control. Concern has also been given to human relations, showing interest in the attitudes of personnel as well as in their productivity.

The church maintains a unique balance between being organization and organism, for while the church is the body of Christ, a living organism, it requires some form of organization, ranging from intricate hierarchical structures to a minimum of formal structure. Church organization must be examined with this twofold nature in mind in order to be effective. The Great Commission of Matthew 28:19–20 is pertinent, as is the injunction of Ephesians 4:11–16. Not only is the church to evangelize the world; it is also to nurture its own members until the entire body is presented mature before Christ.

Many congregations are benefited by setting out clearly the organizational structure of the leadership and decision making process, diagrammed through a simple organizational chart. The lines of communication and the areas of responsibility of the various committees and leaders are set forth. Time spent in planning and management will in the end add to the unity experienced in the local congregation and will enhance the achievement of goals and objectives.

ELAINE BECKER

Bibliography. E. H. Schein (1985), *Organizational Culture and Leadership.*

See also ADMINISTRATION; GREAT COMMISSION; LEADERSHIP; MANAGEMENT; ORGANISM; ORGANIZATIONAL CHART; SPAN OF CONTROL

Organizational Chart. The authority and relationships within most organizations are shown in an organizational chart. In order to know what and where things are being done, organizations require a blueprint showing the division of work, chain of command, and departmentalization of various activities. It may also be likened to an X-ray showing the organization's skeleton, an outline of the planned, formal connections among various units. This blueprint provides all employees or members with a visual statement of these relationships, enabling them to see how their work relates to the overall operation of the organization and to whom they report.

Because the organizational chart specifies each area of responsibility and authority, it can also help managers coordinate activities. However, since the chart reflects the organization during only one period of time, it is recommended that it be updated periodically to reflect changes.

Organizations can be classified into at least four main types according to the nature of their internal authority relationships: line, line-and-staff, matrix, and network or virtual organizations. These categories are not mutually exclusive. In fact, most of today's organizations, whether they be business, educational, or ministry, combine elements of one or more types of organizational structure.

The line organization, the oldest and simplest form of organizational structure, is based on a direct flow of authority from the chief executive to subordinates. The line organization is simple. The chain of command—the set of relationships that indicates who gives direction to whom and who reports to whom—is clear, so "buck-passing" is extremely difficult. Decisions can be made quickly because the manager can act without consulting anyone other than an immediate supervisor. However, an obvious defect exists within line organizations: each manager has complete responsibility for a number of activities and cannot possibly be an expert in all of them. This defect is very apparent in medium- and large-sized organizations, where the pure line form fails to allocate specialized skills so vital to modern organizational success. There is a tendency for those in upper management positions in line organizations to become overburdened with administrative details and paperwork, and to have little time for planning.

The line-and-staff organization combines the direct flow of authority present in the line organization with staff departments that serve, advise, and support the line departments. Line departments are involved directly in decisions affecting the operation of the organization. Staff departments tend to lend more specialized technical support.

The major difference between a line manager and a staff manager is in authority relationships. A line manager forms a part of the main line of authority that flows throughout the organization. Often, line managers are involved directly with the critical functions of the organization. A person in a staff management position would provide information, advice, or technical assistance to aid line managers. Staff managers do not normally possess the authority to give orders or to compel line managers to take action, although they do have the necessary line authority to supervise their own departments.

A growing number of organizations are using the matrix or project management organization—a structure in which specialists from different parts of the organization are brought together to work on specific projects. The matrix organization is used typically as a subform within the line-and-staff structure.

The matrix organization is built around specific projects or problems. Employees with different areas of expertise gather to focus on these specific problems or unique issues. An identifying feature of such organizations is that some members of the organization report to two supervisors instead of one. Project members receive instructions from the project manager (horizontal authority), but maintain membership in their permanent functional departments (vertical authority). The term *matrix* comes from the cross-referencing of the horizontal authority-responsibility flow over the vertical flows of the traditional line-and-staff organization.

The primary benefit of the matrix structure lies in its flexibility and in the potential it offers to focus resources on major problems or projects. However, the project manager must be able to mold individuals from diverse parts of the organization into an integrated team, and team members must be comfortable working for more than one boss.

The project-team approach offers built-in flexibility for adapting to the changing needs in the environment that the organization is seeking to service. It also provides an outlet for employees' creativity and initiative by gathering handpicked groups of employees—and at times outside consultants—who possess the right skills for a particular project. When the problem is solved or the project ends, the group dissolves and the employees return to their regular jobs. In the future, as the need arises, they may become part of a different group assembled to solve a different problem. The trend here is a move toward what is referred to as *boundarylessness*. Boundarylessness is the ability to work up and down the hierarchy of the organization, across functions and geographies of the organization, with all levels of those stakeholders affected by the organization.

A network or virtual organization is one in which the major functions are broken up into strategic business units or organizations that are brokered by a small headquarters or core organization. The virtual organization is built around information networks, flexible workforces, outsourcing, and various webs of strategic partnerships. Kiechel (1993) predicts that the virtual organization will become the predominant organizational structure of the next millennium, since network or virtual organizations: (a) promote greater flexibility—the vertical division of labor will be replaced by a horizontal division; (b) reduce bureaucratic inefficiencies because staff overhead and administrative costs are much lower relative to a traditional organizational structure; (c) improve an organization's competitiveness; (d) promote efficiencies through outsourcing; (e) shift the emphasis from making or producing a product to providing a service; and (f) redefine work itself, emphasizing constant learning and high-order thinking and deemphasizing set work hours (39).

In summary, the line organization is a form that has typically been used by smaller organizations. Line-and-staff and the newer matrix structures are the main forms of organizational structures for medium and large-sized organizations. In theory, they combine the line organization's rapid decision-making capability and effective, direct communication with the staff specialists' expert knowledge needed to direct diverse and widespread activities. The matrix or project management organization has distinct advantages when used in combination with committed teams. The network or virtual organization is the newest form of organizational structure, used especially by many high-growth organizations. This virtual concept lends itself to reduced labor and administrative costs in addition to increased flexibility.

ELLERY G. PULLMAN

Bibliography. W. Kiechel, *Fortune* 5, no. 27 (1993): 39.

See also JOB DESCRIPTION; PLAN, PLANNING; SPACE OF CONTROL

Organize. To function with effectiveness and efficiency in accordance with one's reason for being. Thus, for a church, denomination, or parachurch organization to be organized is an act of stewardship in the effective and efficient deployment of people, time, finances, and other resources in order to bring glory to God and to fulfill its raison d'être.

Scripture is filled with examples showing that God is concerned with organization. He is not a God of chaos, confusion, disorder, or disharmony. He does not create and sustain creation in vain (Isa. 45:18–19). From Creation on, Scripture shows that he is the God of organization, unity, purpose, direction, and harmony. Paul's instruction to the Corinthians (1 Cor. 14:40) is classical: "but all things should be done decently and in order" (NRSV). Orderly fashion requires organization.

Both God and his earthly leaders plan in order to carry out his mission. Scripture is filled with demonstrations of this fact. God is characterized in Scripture as one who plans (e.g., Ps. 33:11; Jer. 29:11; Eph. 1:11). God expects his followers to use their God-given wisdom to plan and organize in order to carry out his purposes (e.g., Prov. 2:6; 16:3; 20:18). Scripture also provides examples of planning and organizing in order to achieve what God wants accomplished (e.g., 2 Cor. 1:15–17).

Organization is to serve the organism, the church, not vice versa. Too often organizational structures dictate the functioning of that organism. Organizing should occur with several principles in mind. It should follow the nature, function, and purpose of the church. It should be flexible. It should provide for the development of leaders. It should be reviewed periodically in order to make changes according to the changing needs of the organism. It should be efficient and effective.

Church history is replete with many different forms of organizations for both local churches and denominations. There is no one biblical organizational structure. Battles have been fought over what leaders thought was the biblical organizational structure. Most leaders today see various possibilities in Scripture, depending on the needs of the church within a given culture and society. It is crucial that the church be organized, keep itself renewed in its structures, and go about doing the tasks assigned to it by the Lord of the church.

The leaders of God's people, pastors and churchly officers, function as administrators, not bosses of the organization. They provide the impetus so that the people within the organism function "decently and in order," avoiding chaos, disorder, and confusion, and functioning in a harmonious unity. Church leaders are responsible to help keep the organization flexible, focused on the mission of the church.

JOHN M. DETTONI

See also ADMINISTRATION; EVALUATION; LEADERSHIP; MANAGEMENT; ORGANIZATIONAL CHART; PLAN, PLANNING; SPAN OF CONTROL; STAFF, STAFFING

Organizing Principle. The rationale curriculum designers use to ensure that the elements of curriculum design are properly related to each other (Colson and Rigdon, 1981, 50). The organizing principle attempts to answer the question, "How can the elements of curriculum design be brought together in proper synthesis?" There are five elements of curriculum design. They are: objectives, scope, methodology, learners, and context. The element called *objectives* attempts to answer the question of "Why?" The element *Scope* seeks to answer the question "What shall we study?" *Methodology* answers the question "How shall we study?" The element called *Learners* answers the question "Who will learn?" *Context* seeks to answer the question: "Where will learning take place?"

The organizing principle is like a recipe. A recipe ensures that all of the ingredients are brought together in proper relationship to each other. The organizing principle states that an effective curriculum involves somebody (the learner), in learning something (the scope), in some way (methodology), somewhere (the context), for some purpose (objectives) (Ford, 1991, 50).

An example of an organizing principle for a church's curriculum is, "The involvement of learners in a meaningful exploration of the realities of the Christian faith and life in such a way that they move toward attending the educational objective. This is done in the context of the church's life and work" (Colson and Rigdon, 1981, 50–51).

DARYL ELDRIDGE

Bibliography. H. P. Colson and R. M. Rigdon (1981), *Understanding Your Church's Curriculum;* L. Ford (1991), *A Curriculum Design Manual for Theological Education;* R. Tyler (1949), *Basic Principles of Curriculum and Instruction.*

See also CONTEXT IN TEACHING AND MINISTRY; CURRICULUM; METHODOLOGY (TEACHING AND RESEARCH); OBJECTIVE; SCOPE; SEQUENCE

Originality. *See* Creativity, Biblical Foundations of.

Orthodox Christian Education. Education in the Orthodox tradition attempts to integrate the areas of worship, school, and community. Characteristic of Orthodox theology itself, educators in this tradition tend to emphasize a holistic, almost cosmic, approach to the Christian faith. Teaching and learning occur within the community of believers, which views education "as a lifelong process, everyone as student and teacher, and every place as school" (Boojamra, 1989, 13).

The Orthodox faith traces its history directly to Christ and his apostles. During the early centuries of the church, a division grew between the Western (largely Roman) church and the Eastern (largely Greek) church. The rift culminated in a split between Rome and Constantinople traditionally dated at A.D. 1054 when Pope Leo IX excommunicated Michael Cerularius and his followers for having closed the Latin-speaking churches in Constantinople. The Greek church from that point on developed independently from the Latin (Roman Catholic) Church, placing more emphasis on cosmology and Christ's incarnation than did their Western counterpart.

Stepping into a typical Orthodox church often feels like entering God's grand world, standing beneath a domed, vaulted ceiling representing the cosmos of God's creation. All that God created is holy. Christ's work, symbolized by his incarnation, is to redeem this world to its rightful place in the cosmos.

Education in the Orthodox tradition, therefore, places heavy emphasis on community, on an awareness of the world in which we live, and on an awareness that everything in this cosmos is of God. For example, a person in the Roman tradition might consider certain water "holy" because it was consecrated and set aside by the priest. This "holy water" differs from all the rest because it has taken on peculiar characteristics. In the Eastern tradition, any water that might be designated as "holy" is done so to remind the believer that all water is holy.

Education, therefore, is not so much talk about God or the things of God as it is the experience of God as the Holy Redeemer. Developing a theory revolving around the three aspects of worship, teaching, and praxis, Constance Tarasar (1995) described how the primary method of religious education is that of socialization. Worship is an essential component for socializing children into the faith. Appreciative of John Westerhoff III's emphasis on enculturation, the Eastern tradition not only uses a plethora of icons, symbols, and images in worship, but tends to emphasize the mystical, intuitive, and affective as well. Picture, music, ritual, and art play an important part in the educational process.

Teaching, or more formal instruction, may involve an emphasis on concept development, analysis of texts, and the development of theology. But the heart of this activity is, according to Tarasar (1995), to reflect together on life as a community. "Here we can discuss the relationship between words and actions, examine alternatives for our behavior, and set goals based upon our knowledge and experience. Formal teaching is a necessary part of our church life; but it can neither be replaced by, nor should it be allowed to become a substitute for, the other dimensions of worship and praxis" (112). Teaching, therefore, tends to engage persons in critical reflection on experience rather than on some form of indoctrination or rote memorization of creeds or doctrines.

The area of praxis refers to the learning that occurs as people live their faith together in daily activities. Tarasar (1995) suggests that "if worship is the 'What' and the teaching the 'Why' of our life as Christians, the dimension of Christian praxis is the *'How'*—the realization, assimilation, and application of the faith and belief of the community as lived-out daily through the practice of Christian ethics" (112). The goal is *theosis*, a process of deification, of moving progressively toward eternal salvation. Theologically, the doctrine of conversion tends to be minimized while the doctrine of sanctification, or the movement toward holiness, is more prominent.

The Eastern tradition is dominant in a number of geographic areas, not the least of which are the Middle East, Greece, Eastern Europe, and the former Soviet Union. In recent years, a number of revivals or renewals have led many of these churches toward an approach that involves the total church. A number of youth movements in Western Europe and the Middle East have also influenced the Orthodox churches.

Since the demise of the Soviet Union and the apparent lessening of restrictions on the expression of religious freedom in these countries, the Orthodox churches in these areas have faced a tremendous crisis. Church attendance has become popular, but educational resources are extremely scarce. This factor not only challenges them to develop their own materials, but also makes them susceptible to the influence of Western Protestants. The World Council of Churches, concerned with this phenomenon, has attempted to support the Russian Orthodox Church by holding various consultations to assist them in developing their own indigenous material. Like other churches in the Orthodox tradition, the Russian Orthodox Church seeks to develop material that will integrate worship, teaching, and practice for persons of all ages.

ROBERT C. DE VRIES

Bibliography. J. Boojamra (1989), *Foundations for Orthodox Christian Education;* C. J. Tarasar (1995), *Theologies of Religious Education;* M. Van Elderen, *One World* 195 (1994): 12–15.

Oser, Fritz K. (1937–). Dr. Oser served for many years in a variety of administrative positions at the University of Fribourg, Switzerland (1978–89). In addition, in 1982 he was a convenor/organizer at the International Symposium on Moral Education held at the University of Fribourg. Later in his career he was a Fellow at the Center for Advanced Studies in Berlin, Germany (1994–95).

Oser identified five stages of religious judgment or reasoning that form a pattern of cognition, language, feeling, and action in dealing with life experiences in relation to God. Although religious judgment involves reasoning, its concern is with the whole personality. Oser categorized these stages within the general field of structural developmental theories but found that religious structures, or ways of making religious decisions, are distinct from cognitive or moral structures. Oser was influenced by the developmental understandings of Piaget, Kohlberg, Fowler, and Goldman. His approach to religion is generic and not associated with a specific religious tradition. Religion, to Oser, is a means of making meaning of life in light of the reality of God. He assumes that religious reasoning follows similar patterns in all religious traditions or denominations, although each religion deals with different content.

Oser found the stages of religious reasoning to be sequential and, until age 66 years, irreversible. Development tends to parallel chronology until age 25; stage 1 is most prominent at ages 8–9 years, stage 2 at 11–12 years, and stage 3 at 20–25 years. Thereafter, age is less a factor in stage development. Each stage is qualitatively different from other stages, increasingly complex, and involves greater integration of a person's religious perspective with all of life. Progress through the stages involves increasing maturity in religious judgment. Oser reasons that significant religious life issues are viewed differently at each stage, much like the apostle Paul described the thinking process of the adult differing from that of children (1 Cor. 13:11). The higher stages involve greater flexibility, or an ability to apply religious reasoning to a wide variety of concerns. Growth to the higher stages comes only after significant reflection regarding the issues of one's faith and life. Oser believes the stages to be universal; that is, they apply to all persons in all cultures, although specifics of making religious decisions differ in various cultures and religious traditions.

Development in religious judgment, according to Oser, involves a deepening relationship with God. It is a process of repeated times of feeling distant from God followed by new understandings and a deepened relationship with him. It begins with a sense of inadequacy in making meaning of life events. There is a growing dissatisfaction with one's current understandings of God and a need for more comprehensive understandings. This leads to a rejection of the current structure of religious reasoning and the creation of a new structure that explains life more adequately. Development of the next stage involves losses such as prior bases for security, images of God derived from one's parents, and so on. But there are also gains such as greater depth of knowledge and wisdom, sense of direction for life, and increased thought concerning life and its meaning.

Religious instruction can be made more effective as teachers connect new information with students' existing structure (stage) of religious judgment. Failure to do so risks rupturing the learning process. Development requires that all religious knowledge be reprocessed at each stage, necessitating that content be presented to students in ways that address the perspective of each stage. This can be done through use of role plays and discussions of religious dilemmas that expose students to religious reasoning one stage higher than their own. Instruction cannot be simply dispensing information. Students must be led to develop their own understanding of the meaning of faith teachings, a process that inevitably will lead to some misinterpretation. However, Oser views this as inevitable since doctrines are framed at the highest stages of religious judgment. Furthermore, development through the stages will tend to correct minor misunderstandings at lower levels.

DENNIS DIRKS

Bibliography. F. K. Oser (1980), *Toward Moral and Religious Maturity: The First International Conference on Moral and Religious Development*, pp. 277–315; idem (1991), *Religious Development in Childhood and Adolescence*, pp. 5–25; idem (1991), *Stages of Faith and Religious Development: Implications for Education and Society*, pp. 37–64; F. K. Oser and A. Schlaffi (1985), *Moral Education: Theory and Application;* F. K. Oser and P. Gmtinder (1991), *Religious Judgment: A Developmental Perspective.*

Outdoor Activities. *See* Camping Facilities.

Outdoor Ministries. The out-of-doors setting has a long history as a venue for educational activity. It should come as no surprise to learn that outdoor ministries have a varied and valuable role for those who seek to bring about Christian maturity in the life of believers.

Many Christians, when asked about significant events in their spiritual journey, will recall a time at a retreat, a decision made around a campfire, or a speaker at a youth camp. People have formed friendships while struggling with a tent in a storm or exploring a trail into a quiet woods. Experiences such as discovering a new wonder of God's creation or meeting a physical challenge have proven to be timeless opportunities for instruction and faith-building. As a result, the Christian community has learned to utilize outdoor ministries as a means of enhancing the educational efforts of the church.

From very modest beginnings almost two centuries ago, to the most advanced year-round Christian camps and conference centers of today, outdoor ministries have played a significant role in the life of the church.

Historical Development. Anyone who examines the history of Christian education in the United States will eventually recognize the manner in which outdoor ministries have influenced, either directly or indirectly, the spiritual formation of young people and adults.

In addressing the development and history of youth camps, one author acknowledges organized youth camps as being uniquely American in their origin, having "no precedent in other countries for this program for youth" (Eells, 1986, v). Youth, however, were not the only ones being served by outdoor ministries.

Adults have been a part of the outdoor ministries movement from the very beginning. Most histories of American revivals will include reference to the "camp meetings" of the late eighteenth and early nineteenth centuries. Such meetings were for the purpose of evangelism to be sure, but they also provided adults with the opportunity to gather for social and educational purposes. The most famous camp meeting was held in Cane Ridge, Kentucky, in 1801, and crowds were estimated to be as large as 25,000.

Another distinctly adult-oriented movement was established in 1884 by John H. Vincent and William Rainey Harper at Lake Chautauqua in New York. Concerned for the improvement of the Sunday school, Vincent began offering training for teachers. The Chautauqua Movement provided adults with the opportunity to get away from home and attend training sessions in a relaxed, outdoor setting.

Having noted the early opportunities for adults, it should be acknowledged that it was the effort to involve children and youth that helped develop outdoor ministries. By the middle of the nineteenth century, various individuals were active in taking youth out of the formal classroom and leading them in organized expeditions to the outdoors. The earliest organized camping program to be held on a regular basis dates to 1861 and is credited to Frederick William Gunn, a headmaster in Connecticut who saw the camping experience as an opportunity to develop both physical skills and Christian character in the boys of his school.

By the 1870s outdoor ministries were being offered through several organizations which, in the spirit of the era, viewed the Christian mandate in such a way that the betterment of society was a natural outgrowth of Christian education. The YWCA began a camping program for young girls in Philadelphia in 1874. One year later the "Country Week" was initiated in Philadelphia, followed by the "Fresh Air" movement in New York in 1877. These organizations sought to take youth out of their urban environments and, through a week in the country, introduce them to the benefits and wonders of God's creation.

It was the twentieth century before churches began to see the benefits of having their own camping facilities to offer programs specifically designed for outdoor ministries. In 1923 the Salvation Army opened the Star Lake Music Camp in Bloomingdale, New Jersey. Other organizations followed, including the Christian Service Brigade (1937) and Pioneer Girls (1939, now Pioneer Clubs).

In the 1940s there was sufficient interest in camping and other forms of outdoor ministries that directors of campgrounds in regions around the United States and Canada began informal associations to explore ways of cooperating. The first regional organization was the Western Conference and Camp Association, formally established in 1951 at Hume Lake Christian Camps, Hume Lake, California, under the leadership of Walter Warkentien.

By 1963 several of the regional associations had joined together to form the Christian Camp and Conference Association International, and in 1968 the name was shortened to Christian Camping International (CCI). Currently CCI serves over nine hundred member camps and conference centers in the United States and has member organizations on six continents.

Purpose of Outdoor Ministries. From the very beginning, there have been commonly recognized purposes which have added to the growth of these programs. While outdoor ministries take many forms and offer a variety of experiences, four common elements provide the initiative behind them.

The most obvious component of outdoor ministries is the physical dimension. Participants are not only moved out of the church/classroom and into creation, they are also given opportunity to engage in physical activities that do not lend themselves to a formal setting. Thus, team sports, waterfront activities, hiking, camping out, gathering wood, and even just walking from one's cabin to the dining hall provide many opportunities for youth (and adults) to become involved in physical activities.

Along with the physical activity, there is the intentional effort to get participants to step out of their daily environment and become conscious of the world around them. This provides opportunity for reflection on God as Creator, the world as he created it, and one's own role within it. Common activities such as stargazing on a clear summer night, the care and feeding of animals at a nature center, and discovering the many wonders within a pine forest can often be used to evoke praise and wonder from small children and adults.

Closely related to the previous purposes is the time element. Participants are engaged in physical activities within a different environment—as well as involved in the learning experience—twenty-four hours a day. For many, involvement in outdoor ministries is viewed as a break from their normal calendar of events. In one sense, they are allowed to leave the place of stress, schedules, and tension, and retreat away from all of that. It is while they are away that outdoor ministries can provide opportunity to reflect upon life and those things which are important.

The fourth purpose of outdoor ministries is to provide opportunity for learning to live within a community. This is the social aspect of the program, and it is what pulls the previous purposes into a program of Christian education. All of the previous purposes can be accomplished by an individual going out alone. The communal living aspect of outdoor ministries provides the means by which participants can learn to live interdependently.

Forms of Outdoor Ministries. The most obvious form for outdoor ministries today is the residential youth camp. This is the setting where parents send their children to a camp, entrusting them into the care of the camp staff. However, this is only one of many forms. Just as the field of Christian education has become more specialized, so have the options in outdoor ministries.

In addition to the residential summer youth camps, there are year-round camps that offer specialty camps for youth. Sports camps, academic camps, horsemanship camps, and winter camps can all be part of a camping program.

Besides the residential format, programs are available in a wide range of trip camping. Examples of trip camping would include canoeing, biking, rafting, backpacking, sailing, and bus trip camping. Stress camping or survival camping is another means of engaging participants in the outdoors while pushing them to their limits.

For adults, outdoor ministries can range from family camping to Caribbean cruises. Many churches have learned the value of retreats for their adults. Retreats can provide opportunities to grow spiritually, enrich marriages, or increase skills.

Another growing area for adults is a work camp. In this setting participants, often owners of recreational vehicles, travel to a work site and join together in building, remodeling, or cleaning a home or project.

With the growth of the recreational industry and America's fascination with new forms, the opportunities to develop new programs of outdoor ministries is limited only by one's imagination.

Issues and Concerns. The potential for outdoor ministries is great. A rich history, combined with creative programming, provides many options. However, anyone becoming involved in outdoor ministries must also give consideration to issues that must be faced.

The financial cost of doing outdoor ministries must be considered. As participants grow to expect greater specialization, more comfortable environments, and trained leadership, the planners of outdoor ministries will have to find ways to keep their programs affordable. A hidden cost is the requirement for insurance, particularly as programs involve greater risks for participants, and planners have to protect against litigation.

Related to financial concerns is the growing demand for quality facilities. Planners of adult programs must consider their audiences. Items such as handicap accessibility, private baths, and menu options are concerns for those who are trying to involve adults today.

Other areas of concern include government regulations, finding quality staff, changing constituencies, and concern for the environment. In spite of these, outdoor ministries continue to grow and involve the participants in God's creation. As long as the heavens continue to declare the glory of God (Ps. 19:1), we can be confident there will be outdoor ministries.

DOUGLAS BARCALOW

Bibliography. American Camping Association, 5000 State Rd. 67 North, Martinsville, IN 46151. Phone: 317/342–8456; fax: 317/342–2065. Christian Camping International, PO Box 62189, Colorado Springs, CO 80962. Phone: 719/260–9400; fax: 719/260–6398; E. Eells, (1986), *History of Organized Camping: The First 100 Years.*

See also CAMPING FACILITIES; CHRISTIAN CAMPING INTERNATIONAL

Outreach Group. A group of Christians who join together to bring the gospel to non-Christians. The New Testament frequently records individuals working corporately in evangelistic and other ministries, for instance, the missionary team of Paul, Barnabas, and other associates.

Outreach groups are organized under the auspices of a local congregation or a parachurch organization to follow up with church visitors, to reach special interest groups (such as Young Life Club, M.O.P.S. for mothers of preschoolers), or to conduct preevangelism projects (such as Prison Fellowship's Angel Tree).

At its heart, an outreach group is composed of growing Christians who are not only burdened to reach out to unsaved persons, but are also Holy Spirit empowered and gifted. Its purpose is to show and tell the love of God to those outside the Christian community through mercy ministries, educational efforts, or direct personal evangelism.

DANIEL C. JESSEN

Overgeneralization. Overgeneralizations occur when we "generalize beyond the facts" (Barzun and Graff, 1970, 139–41). "Bad generalizations are often the result of careless language . . . [the interpreter] says 'all' or 'every' or 'never' when the evidence goes but a little way toward such a universal proposition" (139–41). The old anecdote about the English traveler illustrates this. He saw three red-headed girls in the inn where he stopped and wrote in his diary: "All the women in this country have red hair."

It is all too common to hear the word *sabbath* used in reference to the Lord's Day, Sunday, when sabbath literally means "rest," and that was in regard to Israel's memorial of being delivered out of Egypt (Deut. 5:15). The Christian's rest is yet to come (Heb. 4). Overgeneralization is also sometimes the result of poor translation (Good, 1946). James 3:1 is frequently mistranslated, "Let not many of you become teachers, . . ." when it should be, "Let not many of you continue to be teachers . . ." (Dana and Mantey, 1948, 301). This overgeneralization contradicts the universal that, "by this time you ought to be teachers" (Heb. 5:12) as well as the expectation that all Christians are to grow. (vv. 12–14; 2 Pet. 3:18).

GEORGE W. PATTERSON

Bibliography. J. Barzun and H. F. Graff (1970), *The Modern Researcher;* H. E. Dana and J. R. Mantey (1948), *A Manual Grammar of the Greek New Testament;* C. V. Good (1966), *Essentials of Educational Research.*

Overseas Theological Education. Formal and nonformal theological education outside North America. Theological education is the intentional and supervised equipping of the church's leadership. As such, theological education is and always has been an essential task of the church. From the apostolic band of the New Testament age and the catechetical schools of the postapostolic period to the cathedral schools of the late medieval period and the Bible schools scattered throughout the contemporary world, theological education is central to the life of the Church in every culture.

In Europe, cathedral schools of the eleventh and twelfth centuries were established as centers for training priests for parishes under the care of a local bishop. As the curricula of cathedral school expanded and faculties grew, the first modern universities were born. The University of Bologna, dating from the late eleventh century, and the University of Paris, founded about 1150, are generally considered the earliest. Despite the breadth of their curricula, however, the study of theology and clergy training long retained a position of prominence.

Today, European state churches continue to require university theological degrees for ordained ministry, but the theology faculties of European state universities are overwhelmingly liberal in their approach to the Bible and life. Parallel to the university system, evangelical Christians have founded Bible schools to prepare graduates for nonordained ministries in parish education and missions. Many of these Bible schools combine excellent training in the Scriptures with immersion in the formational life of a ministering community. Although generally unrecognized by educational authorities, some Bible colleges in England have attained government recognition through the former Council for National Academic Awards and, more recently, through affiliation with regional universities. The effectiveness of European Bible schools and colleges is evidenced in the spiritual life of the churches in which graduates serve, and in the significant contribution these churches continue to make to the task of world evangelism.

Theological education also has been a principal concern throughout the expansion of the church in the non-Western world. As Roman Catholic missionaries of the sixteenth century followed the Conquistadors to the New World and beyond, they established universities for training native priests, on the model of those in Europe. Early Protestant missionaries took apprentices whom they trained as "evangelists." During the nineteenth and twentieth centuries other missionaries founded hundreds of Bible schools in the non-Western world, beginning with Carey's College of Serampore. Lacking the skills needed to design culturally appropriate educational programs, Protestant missionaries, like Catholics of an earlier era, replicated (with minimal adjustments) the European and North American schools in which they trained.

Efforts toward "renewal of theological education" have most often been focused on and fostered in overseas contexts. Perhaps the best known and most far-reaching renewal movement in overseas theological education is theological education by extension (TEE). TEE typically employs self-study material and peer tutoring to take theological education to church leaders in their ministry contexts. Born of frustration with the ineffectiveness of Western theological education in Guatemala in the early 1960s, TEE programs have multiplied throughout Latin America, Africa, Asia, and the former Soviet Union. Only in North America, Western Europe, and Northeast Asia (i.e., Korea, Japan, and Taiwan),

where formal education traditions are strong, has TEE been largely ignored.

The growing missionary vision of overseas churches throughout the 1990s gave rise to widespread recognition of a need for missionary training. Unlike the North American church, where missionary training has been seconded to Bible schools and seminaries, mission agencies and churches in Africa, Asia, and Latin America typically have established missionary training centers parallel to national Bible schools. Although primary emphasis is placed on forming the life of the missionary, on a theology of mission, and on principles of cross-cultural life and ministry, many missionary training centers also provide instruction in the Bible and doctrine. The Missions Commission of the World Evangelical Fellowship (WEF) has provided networking and training services for this expanding movement.

Theological education institutions overseas, like those in North America, seek recognition and affirmation through accrediting structures. Where excluded from government recognition, theological educators have established agencies for peer accreditation. During the early 1970s, the Theological Education Fund (TEF) stimulated overseas theological schools affiliated with the World Council of Churches to organize regional associations to regulate academic standards.

Within the evangelical church overseas, national and regional theological education associations were also formed and assumed accrediting functions. One of the earliest was the Philippine Association of Bible and Theological Schools, founded in 1968. Asia Theological Association (ATA) and the Accrediting Council for Theological Education in Africa (ACTEA), founded in 1977, were the first regional associations of evangelical overseas schools.

In 1980, evangelical educators founded the International Council of Accrediting Agencies for Evangelical Theological Education (ICCA) as a project of the Theological Commission of the World Evangelical Fellowship. Renamed the International Council for Evangelical Theological Education (ICETE) in 1996, the agency exists to network, coordinate, and serve evangelical theological educators and their schools through regional accrediting agencies. In addition to ATA and ACTEA, current membership in ICETE includes the Caribbean Evangelical Theological Association (CETA), the European Evangelical Accrediting Association (EEAA), the South Pacific Association of Bible Colleges (SPABC), and Asociación Evangélica de Educación Teológica en América Latina (AETAL). The Accrediting Association of Bible Colleges (AABC) is the only North American accrediting agency with membership in ICETE. The World Conference of Associations of Theological Institutions (WOCATI), founded in

1996, pursues similar objectives among schools affiliated with the World Council of Churches.

ROBERT W. FERRIS

Bibliography. *Evangelical Review of Theology* 19, no. 3 (1995); R. W. Ferris, ed. (1995), *Establishing Ministry Training: A Manual for Programme Developers;* D. G. Hart and R. A. Mohler Jr., eds. (1996), *Theological Education in the Evangelical Tradition;* C. Lienemann-Perrin (1981), *Training for a Relevant Ministry: A Study of the Contribution of the Theological Education Fund;* R. V. J. Windsor (1995), *World Directory of Mission Training Programs.*

See also BIBLE COLLEGE MOVEMENT; BIBLE EDUCATION BY EXTENSION; THEOLOGICAL EDUCATION BY EXTENSION

P p

Paideia and First-Century Education. *Paideia* is a Greek term literally meaning "the art of child rearing and education." Eby and Arrowood (1940) describe it as one of two terms the Greeks used to express their idea of education, the other being *agoge*. *Paideia* can be generally defined as the sum of all physical and intellectual achievement to which humanity may aspire. *Paideia* represents the ideal perfections of mind and body. It comes from the word *pais*, meaning child, which was connected with the word *paidia* meaning a child's sport or play. According to Eby and Arrowood (1940) *paideia* was a process of guiding the child's "spontaneous activity into artistic and graceful forms." Greek educators saw it as a harmonious synthesis of the child's physical and intellectual powers. The expected result was the perfection of character. Character was formed and perfected through strict guidance of the child's activity and through keeping a tight rein on the child's emotions. In Greek thought this character formation was necessary for the child's eventual participation as an upstanding citizen. It was necessary to serve the state first and the individual subjugated his needs to the state.

Later, Athenian teachers approached education and *paideia* in a more systematized fashion. Bowen (1972) finds that these early educators developed a system that would train young men to learn the arts of effective citizenship. The philosopher Plato layered the meaning of *paideia* and made it an intellectually respectable term. He used it to describe the process of intellectual achievement and the pursuit of truth. Plato believed that character and intellect could be formed through proper education.

An essay called "The Education of Children" written by an unknown author in the first-century Christian era clearly outlines this form of Greek education. The essay defines the goal of education as moral excellence. All instruction was to be directed to that end. The environment of the child must be of excellent moral quality. The father must be an example of a person with high character and the mother must be of good birth. This gave the child a better chance through heredity of achieving moral excellence.

The child's training began at birth. It was essential that the child was breastfed and entrusted to the care of good slaves (*paidagogai*). All the child's activities were directed toward the development of a life of moderation and of aesthetic discipline. Because wisdom and character, in this traditional Greek view, were thought to come from training and instruction, great care was taken in the selection of the teacher. He had to be of good moral character, skilled, and good with children. The content of the instruction followed the pattern of general Greek education (*enkylios padeia*). The use of this concept in the essay indicates the universal acceptance of *paideia* by the first century A.D.

In the Athenian system the child's education was not directed to a particular role as citizen, as with the Greeks, but to a more personal cultivation of the moral life through right thought and action.

The Greek *paideia* is similar to Cicero's *humanitas*, which he used to describe the end product of an orator's education: ethical character. The Roman orator and educator Quintillian used these principles to usher in the golden age of Roman education in the first century A.D. His philosophy of education is outlined in his discussion of the education of an orator, *De Institutio Oratoria*. His ideas on education influenced educational theory from the fifteenth through the eighteenth centuries. The dominant school of the renaissance was the Latin grammar school.

Quintillian divided oratorical education into three stages: early education, grammatical education, and rhetorical education. Children should be taught to read at an early age, learning Greek first and then Latin. Education was to be interesting, allowing the child to feel encouraged and capable. The main course of study was literature accompanied by music, astronomy, and philosophy. He advocated the use of memorization because an orator needed to know many facts. But above all, the orator was to be a good man. For these Greek and Roman educators character was, indeed, the measure of a man.

IVY BECKWITH

Bibliography. J. Bowen (1972), *A History of Western Education,* vol. 1; J. Cogan, A. Ellis, and K. Howy (1981), *Introduction to the Foundations of Education;* F. Eby and F. Arrowood (1940), *History and Philosophy of Education: Ancient and Medieval.*

Panel Discussion. Large group teaching method that provides a healthy balance of orderly conversation and audience interest. The setting for a panel includes a central or raised area in which a group of four to eight individuals explore an announced issue through discussion. The audience faces the panel, but may surround it as a horseshoe or circle. For audiences of fifty or more, raised platforms and microphones are helpful.

Unlike a symposium, in which expert participants deliver prepared speeches for the entire session, a panel discussion follows a speech, media presentation, or demonstration. Members should be knowledgeable outsiders, but not necessarily experts. If audience participation is desired, a panel may be followed by a forum, which calls for comments and questions from the floor. A colloquy is a modified version of panel in which half of the members are experts and half represent the audience.

Introduction of panel members by a moderator is normally the first step. Opening statements, if allowed, should be limited to two or three minutes. An orderly exchange of viewpoints should characterize a panel discussion. In Christian education, panels are particularly useful for controversial and divisive issues. They are excellent means for exploring sensitive issues by including panel members who have experienced the topic at hand.

The purpose of a panel discussion is to inform an audience of various aspects of a problem or issue. Because participants often disagree, advantages and disadvantages of alternative actions are revealed. Since panel members are not skilled speakers or subject authorities, a panel is not a preferred method for thoroughly covering topics.

Participants may attempt to monopolize the discussion or introduce unrelated issues. A skilled moderator will maintain dialogue and nudge discussion back on track. It is the "back and forth" character of panel discussion that maintains audience interest and stimulates individual thought.

DANIEL C. STEVENS

Parable. The meaning of the word *parable* is somewhat elusive. However, most biblical scholars agree that a parable is a story that has only one point, a particular religious or ethical purpose, is always thought-provoking or challenging to action, and is a distinct literary form.

While parables appear in both the Old and New Testaments, the predominant scriptural user of parables to teach was Jesus. Some estimate that fully one-third of all the utterances of Jesus in the Gospels are parabolic. In the Gospels there is the similitude, which is a brief narrative of a typical or recurrent event from real life (the lost sheep, the lost coin); the parable, which is a somewhat longer story of fictitious or true-to-life events (the sower, the talents, the prodigal son); and the exemplary story, which is an example illustrating a general principle (the good Samaritan, the rich fool).

Parables are not allegorical; that is to say, not every name, place, or feature of the story is symbolic and demands an interpretation. However, parables do embody metaphors and similes while never removing themselves from reality or conveying fictitious or untrue ideas.

Parables typically have three components. There is a *setting,* usually a fictitious or true-to-life event with a time and place. Then there is a *central character or group of characters.* Finally, there is *a dilemma to be faced,* a decision to be made, or a problem to be solved in which the listener or reader is encouraged to make application of the story in his or her own life.

With regard to Christian education, it has long been something of an informal maxim that telling a compelling story is always a good way to teach. Several modern-day Christian educators have chosen parable as a teaching technique (see *I Love to Tell the Story* and *How Silently, How Silently and Other Stories* by Joseph Bayly as examples). Storytelling as a form of communication is taught in some college Christian or religious education curricula.

Parables take on different shades of complexity depending on the age group targeted as the audience. With children, parables are often used to make a complex idea easier to understand. With youth and adults, the same purpose can be accomplished; however, parables can also be used effectively with those age groups to encourage higher levels of critical thinking about one's Christian life and relationship with the Lord. When used by a skilled storyteller, parables can enrich one's teaching ministry, encourage higher levels of student involvement in teaching, and enable students to learn and retain a higher portion of that which they learn.

KEN GARLAND

Bibliography. D. Bayly (1978), *I Love to Tell the Story;* idem (1973), *How Silently, How Silently and*

Other Stories; W. Harrington (1987), *The New Dictionary of Theology,* pp. 739–42; S. J. Kistemaker (1984), *Evangelical Dictionary of Theology.*

See also EDUCATION IN THE GOSPELS AND ACTS; EDUCATION OF THE TWELVE; JESUS CHRIST; METHODOLOGY; STORYTELLING; TEACHINGS OF JESUS CHRIST

Paradigm. Set of rules that (1) establish or define boundaries; and (2) tell one how to behave inside the boundaries so as to be successful.

Thomas Kuhn (1962) coined the term *paradigm.* He outlined the concept in terms of the scientific process. Kuhn felt that "one sense of paradigm is global, embracing all the shared commitments of a scientific group; the other isolates a particularly important sort of commitment and is thus a subset of the first" (Hloyningen-Huene, 1993, 134). Using this observation, a global paradigm consists of theories, laws, rules, models, concepts, and definitions that go into a generally accepted fundamental theory of science and a local paradigm is more specialized and focused in nature.

Education as a concept is global in nature. It focuses on acts of teaching (objectives, method, and evaluation) as well as learning. It is from this global paradigm that a more local paradigm emerges. For example, when one speaks about educating people a global paradigm is imagined. Yet when that same individual begins to describe the learner, a more local paradigm such as the major historical philosophical paradigms of idealism, realism, scholasticism, behaviorism, humanism, and cognitivism come into focus.

An even more specialized paradigm comes into focus in describing the practice of Christian education. Below is a chart that compares the two most frequently used paradigms in contemporary Christian education.

Behavioral	Cognitive
Learning is passive.	Learning is active.
Students must learn the correct response.	Students explore various possible response patterns and choose between them.
Learning requires external reward.	Learning can be intrinsically rewarding.
Knowledge is matter of remembering information.	Knowledge is a matter of acquiring information.
Understanding is a matter of seeing existing patterns.	Understanding is a matter of creating new patterns.
Teachers must direct the learning process.	Students direct their own learning. Applications require the learner to see relationships among the problems.

Once a problem can no longer be solved within the existing paradigms, new laws and theories emerge to form a new paradigm which, if accepted, overthrows the old. To abandon one paradigm for another is to alter the entire intellectual basis of a community whether it be scientific, political, or otherwise.

RONALD W. FREEMAN

Bibliography. J. A. Barker (1992), *Future Edge: Discovering the New Paradigms of Success;* F. Capra (1982), *The Turning Point: Science, Society and the Rising Culture;* P. Hloyningen-Huene (1993), *Reconstructing Scientific Revolutions;* T. Kuhn (1962), *The Structure of Scientific Revolutions.*

Parent Education. *See* Parent Effectiveness Training.

Parent Effectiveness Training. Parenting skills enhancement program popularized by Thomas Gordon in the early 1970s through his book entitled *Parent Effectiveness Training.* Gordon's premise is that parents need assistance to be most effective in raising their children. Beginning in his own community of Pasadena, California, in 1962, he designed a course and invited a few parents who were having problems with their children. Approximately eight years later, two hundred communities within eighteen states were using Parent Effectiveness Training (PET). The program of training expanded in its appeal to parents in general, not just those with troubled children. Couples also participated prior to having their children.

Parent Effectiveness Training assumes that "parents and their children can develop a warm, intimate relationship based on mutual love and respect" (Gordon, 1970, 2). PET focuses upon such things as skills for effective communication and conflict resolution, while assisting parents to encourage their children in accepting responsibility for solutions to their own problems.

According to Gordon, parents fall into one of three groups: (1) "winners"—those who are authoritative over their children; (2) "losers"—those who give their children considerable freedom; and (3) "oscillators"—those who vacillate back and forth between the above—the category in which, Gordon states, the majority of parents fall. Parent Effectiveness Training, however, presents an alternative. The "heart and soul" of PET is found in the "no-lose" method of conflict resolution where both parent and child win because solutions are mutually agreeable.

Many churches today also provide parent training programs to enhance parental effectiveness. Some churches are more deliberate and organized in their efforts than are others. Efforts may range from the provision of periodic literature helps—those which raise parents' awareness levels regarding their children's developmental characteristics—to more advanced, ongoing programs and seminars/workshops utilizing the expertise of qualified professionals—dealing with a teenager's drug problem. Churches which employ training for parents or are planning for such should take into consideration and provide for all family types—single-parent families, blended families—and dysfunctional family situations where appropriate, as some situations will require referral. Even young, newly married couples should be considered for training, since many of these will in all likelihood become parents.

The psalmist realized that parenthood is one of the greatest privileges God grants humanity and declared, "Behold, children are a gift of the LORD; the fruit of the womb is a reward" (Ps. 127:3 NASB). Christians recognize that while parenthood is no easy task, it is one of life's most rewarding and significant opportunities. For these reasons, a church's Christian education program necessitates some degree of parental training.

MARTHA S. BERGEN

Bibliography. K. O. Gangel and J. C. Wilhoit, eds. (1996), *The Christian Educator's Handbook on Family Life Education: A Complete Resource on Family Life Education in the Local Church;* T. Gordon (1970), *Parent Effectiveness Training.*

Parenting Models. Approaches caregivers use in raising children. Particular patterns of relating develop into styles of parenting. Parenting models become the philosophy and method parents use to nurture the human spirit within their children to live according to biblical standards. The importance of having a biblical model of parenting is underscored by the fact that the family is the child's primary and most influential experience of God's nature. The way a parent deals with a child will shape the future of that child's perception of any relational patterns with God. The approach a parent takes in raising a child greatly impacts the child's view of God, self, and others. The first definition of parenting models deals with support and control variables, while the second part analyzes parenting through a content and action grid. Both angles are helpful in defining different parenting models and can be integrated with a biblical perspective.

Parental interaction with a child has varying levels of support and control. Support is defined as making the child feel loved. This goes beyond mere words, involving the creation of a relationship that communicates value and acceptance which is understood from the child's own perspective and experience. Control is defined as facilitating, through obedience, desired behavior in the child. This control comes about through many techniques, ranging from coercion to logical reasoning. The healthiest forms of control

are found in the establishment of firm boundaries, appropriate consequences, and empowering choices for the child to take responsibility for her or his own behavior. Four types of parenting models have been identified using the support and control variables: authoritarian, permissive, neglectful, and authoritative.

Authoritarian parents are high in control but low in support. This type of family has a definite hierarchy of control and runs the household with rigid rules and regulations. The enforcement of rules is swiftly carried out by adults who are feared by the children. Children learn that love is highly conditional and based on performance and conformity to set standards. Authoritarian parents use an aggressive style of interaction with children to control their behavior. Osborne (1989) describes this as using personal attacks and threats to punish and intimidate children into compliance. Phrases like "Don't ask questions, just do it!" and "Because I said so" are often used to give parents a sense of control. The basis of this model is the parent's need to "win" or break the spirit of the child.

The second model, a permissive parenting style, offers a high degree of support but is low in control. This model has no recognizable structure in place to establish or enforce rules or guidelines. Punishment and rewards are arbitrary and inconsistent, leaving a child unsure of the consequences of any given behavior. Emotions rule the behavior of parents, thus creating a sense that love is highly conditional. Permissive parents have an unassertive style of interaction using indirect or emotional pleas to manage a child's behavior. This can often come in the form of a rhetorical question such as: "Why don't you come in early tonight?" These parents express what they want in a subtle way that makes them feel kinder but leaves a child feeling indirectly obligated (Osborne 1989).

The third style of parenting is neglectful. This model offers low support and low control. Of all the models, this is the one that devastates the spirit of a child most. The lack of nurture and guidelines devalues the child so she or he turns to outside forces to find security and significance in life. The need to feel loved and have a sense of belonging is a driving urge that will force a child into compliance to any authority, whether good or bad.

The fourth model is an authoritative parenting style, which combines a high level of control with a high level of support. This style has the greatest possibility of producing healthy, well-adjusted adults who have the ability to be responsible for their own actions. This model develops a network of supportive interaction, thus creating an atmosphere that is flexible and conducive to creative, constructive, and responsible activity (Coloroso, 1990). Rules are explicitly and clearly stated. Consequences are logical, realistic, and palatable. Discipline is carried out with loving authority for the purpose of future maturity in the child. Children feel accepted and loved unconditionally because they have inherent dignity and worth. This encourages competency and cooperativeness, which empowers a child to think for himself as he grows into adulthood.

Authoritative parents use an assertive style of interaction to manage a child's behavior. They directly state what they want, taking ownership for their preferences and wishes (Osborne 1989). They use phrases such as "I like it when . . . ," "I need . . . ," and "I will not . . ." Authoritative parents expect a change of behavior by stating their demands clearly and in a way that does not force victory or defeat for either parent or child. This empowers children to make their own choices and to reap the benefits or consequences of their behavior.

Guernsey suggests effects of these parenting styles as evaluated in four relevant categories: self-worth, conformity to authority, religiosity, and identification with a counterculture. With a Christian worldview in mind, biblical parenting should seek to develop the whole child. Attempting to meet the spiritual, social, psychological, physical, and moral needs, a parent models the nature of God to a child.

Authoritative parents raise children with the highest sense of self-respect and security. Permissive parents rate second, while authoritarian parenting styles produce the third highest level of self-worth in children. Neglectful parenting styles are the most harmful to children's sense of self-worth and security.

In regard to conformity to authority, authoritative parents generally develop children who are able to follow the norms of society and be responsible adults. Permissive parents are second, neglectful parents third, and authoritarian parents rate last in the ability to facilitate a child's obedience to appropriate forms of authority.

Parents who successfully pass on their religious beliefs to their children tend to have an authoritative parenting style. Permissive parents have the second greatest influence, while neglectful and authoritarian parents are third and fourth, respectively.

The last category, identification with the counterculture, is an undesirable trait where authoritarian and neglectful parenting styles scored the highest, with permissive parents third. Authoritative parents showed the highest success at keeping their children from joining a subversive counterculture.

This research, along with an understanding of the effects of different parenting models, helps establish the concept that growth and health are connected to high levels of support and control. Children need to be taught that rules are established for their own good because they are dearly

loved. Consequences and rewards of choices have an empowering effect on children because they experience the impact their decisions and behaviors make on the well-being of themselves and others.

This second part of the definition of parenting models incorporates concepts introduced by Balswick and Balswick (1989). Their study revolves around the variables of action and content. Parents who are high in action live out the behaviors and values they want to see in their children. Parents who are high in content verbalize and teach these behaviors and values. The four styles of parenting that arise through the interaction of action and content are described as neglecting, teaching, modeling, and discipling.

Neglectful parents are low in action and content, giving no direction or demonstration of desired values or behaviors. This style of parenting gives children no example to follow and no truth to guide them as they grow into adulthood.

A teaching parental model is also low in action, but high in content. The phrase "Do as I say, not as I do" would symbolize the messages the child receives from parents. Children often feel "preached at," which may cause them to lose respect for their parents when they see the discrepancies and inconsistencies. The neglecting and teaching models of parenting generally have ill effects on children and misrepresent the relating pattern that God has with his children.

Modeling parents are high in action, demonstrating the expected behavior, but are low in content. For these parents, the verbalization of values is not as important as modeling because they believe that a lifestyle is caught, not taught. The only drawback to this model is that the child is given no guiding principles by which to make his or her own decisions when faced with new experiences.

Discipling takes this same high level of action but combines it with a high level of content, giving a child the model and the direction necessary for desirable behavioral patterns in life. This is the most desirable parenting model because it not only articulates the values and beliefs desired by the parents, but integrates those into a consistent story for the child to experience. Therefore, before children understand the "why" behind an action, they will experience the "how," and will have the background to make positive choices based on past experience. As a child grows, parents explain the reasoning behind particular lifestyle choices so that a coherent philosophy of life is established.

This discipling concept is important considering the impact parents have on the child's experiential knowledge of God. More than intellectual content, a child needs to experience the relational aspect of deep and secure connection with God who models to his children the very standards he asks of them. As children experience that type of high support, control, action, and content from their parents, they can transfer the love and trust they have experienced to their Heavenly Father.

JUDY TENELSHOF

Bibliography. J. O. and J. K. Balswick (1989), *The Family: A Christian Perspective on the Contemporary Home*; B. Coloroso (1990), *Kids Are Worth It!*; P. Osborne (1989), *Parenting for the 90s.*

See also DISCIPLINE; MODELING

Parent Involvement Program. Organized effort to involve parents in their children's education. Several private denominational schools, as well as various public schools, currently employ some type of parent involvement program (PIP). Such schools recognize the positive connection between parental involvement and a child's success in the educational process. Through PIP the base of support is broadened beyond school personnel to include parents as partners in a child's education. As such, parents take an active role investing resources of time and talents, as well as money, toward the attainment of a quality education for their children. Moreover, a sense of bonding develops as students, school personnel, and parents work together to achieve educational goals.

Parents are assumed in the Scriptures to be the primary educators of their children. The biblical model attests to the duty and blessing that belong to parents for teaching and modeling a lifestyle which honors God. The Old Testament writer expressed this when he penned God's instruction, "And you shall teach them [*God's laws*] diligently to your . . . [*children*] and shall talk of them when you sit in your house and when you walk by the way and when you lie down and when you rise up. . . . And you shall do what is right and good in the sight of the LORD, that it may be well with you . . ." (Deut. 6:7, 18 NASB).

Some churches have incorporated parental involvement as part of their Christian education curriculum, for example, with activities for parents and children to accomplish together. Thus, churches encourage and assist parents in their God-given role as the primary religious educators of their children. Christian parenthood should help bring children into a mature relationship with God and others. Without parental involvement, success is less likely to occur in any realm of a child's life.

MARTHA S. BERGEN

Bibliography. W. Mitchell and M. A. Mitchell (1997), *Building Strong Families: How Your Family Can Withstand the Challenges of Today's Culture*; Tampa Catholic High School (1998), *Parent Involvement Program*, <http://www. tampacatholic.com/parent.htm>.

Participation. *See* Active Learning.

Pastor. *See* Clergy as Educators; Minister.

Pastoral Counseling. *See* Biblically Based Counseling.

Patriarchal. *See* Authoritative Approach.

Patriarchal Family. Family structure of Israel's founding fathers, Abraham, Isaac, Jacob, and Jacob's twelve sons. The word *patriarchal* combines the Latin word *pater*, "father," with the Greek verb *archo*, "to rule." The patriarch is thus a ruling ancestor who may have been the founding father of a family, a clan, or a nation. It is used less frequently in a wider reference to David (Acts 7:8, 9).

The patriarchs lived seminomadic lives in the land of the Fertile Crescent, from Ur in Mesopotamia to Egypt. These biblical families journeyed with their flocks and herds, never owning property except for a burial field purchased by Abraham. The narratives of the patriarchs are recorded in Genesis 12–50. Their society was both village and pastoral, tribally organized into interrelated extended families.

The Israelite society was highly patriarchal and so even though the major content of the narrative revolves around the sons, it is properly the story of the patriarch because he is still alive and functioning as the head of the family. It is thus the father's story because it is the father's family.

The patriarchal period centers on the covenant with God and relates to the promise of the blessing, the promise of prosperity, and the promise of a land. While promised many descendants, at the time the promise was given Abraham had not even one. While promised a land, he continued to wander like a resident alien.

The Genesis narrative focuses on the theological purpose of man responding to the divine call and promises and their subsequent fulfillment and nonfulfillment. The patriarchal God was the clan's patron deity. Each patriarch referred to its deity by a special name indicating the close personal tie between the two. Patriarchs worshiped God as "El," which is a generic name for "god" in all Semitic languages. El was the preeminent god, or head of the pantheon in the Canaanite literature who reigned over the divine assembly in the farthest north. None of the mythical aspects or other characteristics of the Semitic reference was adopted by Israel.

God associated himself with persons, not with places as in Canaanite religious conceptions. Thus, He was the God of Abraham, the God of Isaac, and the God of Jacob. Patriarchal narratives are a family's history and are ultimately tied to the redeemer Jesus Christ, the son of God, who would provide the blessing for all the families on earth.

CHERYL L. FAWCETT

Bibliography. F. W. Bush (1986), *The International Standard Bible Encyclopedia*, vol. 3; R. K. Harrison (1991), *Holman Bible Dictionary;* C. F. Pfeiffer (1975), *The Zondervan Pictorial Encyclopedia of the Bible*, vol. 4.

Pauline Theology. *See* Education in the Epistles.

Pedagogy. Art, science, practice, or profession of teaching, especially systemized learning or instruction in principles and methods of teaching.

When Paul referred to the Law as "our schoolmaster" (Gal. 3:23 KJV) he was eliciting an image common to the Greek world of the *paidagogos*, the slave-tutor who supervised an upper-class boy's activities and was responsible for his moral and intellectual training. The term "pedagogue" came to be applied to teachers generally, and "pedagogy" to systems of instruction.

Adult educators draw distinctions between pedagogy (teaching the immature) and andragogy (teaching adults). Recognizing the dependency status of the child in relation to the teacher, and the contrasting egalitarian relationships required in adult education, andragogy stresses self-directed and participative methodologies. However, these methodologies can also be used with children. The term *pedagogy* continues to refer generally to the science and function of teaching.

The church fathers from Augustine to Luther used largely transmissive, "theory-to-practice" pedagogies, which stressed verbal knowledge of doctrine, exemplified in the memorization of catechisms and Scripture. In the seventeenth century an inductive pedagogy of experiential knowledge for learning Christian faith was developed by the Moravian educator John Amos Comenius. However, in much of church education, both Protestant and Catholic, the traditional pedagogical approach has prevailed, based on the assumption that cognitive "knowing" leads to behavior.

Ideally, a pedagogy emerges from educational philosophy, guiding professional preparation and practice. In the late twentieth century many educational philosophies espoused an *experiential* or *democratic* pedagogy that develops content in collaboration with the needs and activities of learners. *Culturally relevant* pedagogies aim to empower students by using cultural referents to engender knowledge, skills, and attitudes. *Critical or radical* pedagogies arising from neo-Marxist theorists question the traditional school culture as one that confirms the status and privileges of dominant classes at the expense of subordinate groups.

Christian educators have often borrowed from general education in an effort to train volunteer teachers in pedagogy. In the heyday of the Sunday school at the turn of the nineteenth century, John Vincent and other religious educators founded the Chautauqua adult education movement for that purpose. In 1950 Clarence Benson assured Christian teachers that they could have a successful teaching experience if they were willing to give careful attention to the recognized principles of pedagogy. Many Christian educators might disagree about the specifics of those principles, but they continue the effort to construct a systematized pedagogy in response to the call of discipleship and current theories of teaching and learning.

BARBARA WILKERSON

Bibliography. C. H. Benson (1950), *The Christian Teacher;* T. H. Groome (1991), *Sharing Faith.*

Peer Ministry. Peer ministry is built on the assumption that Christian adults, youth, and children at similar phases of their lives can minister effectively to one another as colleagues.

Peer ministry has its roots in the New Testament doctrine of the priesthood of all believers, so emphatically emphasized by the Protestant Reformers. In the last third of the twentieth century, the priesthood doctrine was energized by a movement in the ecclesiastical world toward a renewed ministry of the laity. Clergy were encouraged to undergo a massive paradigm shift, specifically, to focus more on equipping believers for ministry than doing it themselves. Within this church renewal movement, attention was focused on the "one another" passages of the New Testament, as the basis for mutual building up of believers within the body of Christ, resulting in the spread of the gospel to those outside Christ. The charismatic movement added strength to the concept of peer ministry through its emphasis on the gifts of the Holy Spirit, divinely distributed among believers in the body of Christ. Moreover, some Christian leaders such as Larry Crabb have questioned the evangelical church's heavy reliance on mental health professionals, to the diminution of the role of "ordinary Christians." They are espousing peer ministry, specifically, that the hurting members of the local congregation be cared for through the networking of supportive peers and elders, "where trusting strugglers lock arms with others as together they journey on" (Crabb, 1997, xvii).

A variety of visible expressions of adult Christians ministering to one another have grown out of these theological roots. Organizations such as Stephen Ministries proposed the idea that "ordinary church members" become "lay pastors," that is, take over pastoral tasks that had traditionally been reserved for the clergy, such as visitation of the sick. The training of women and men to become "lay counselors" is another expression of peer ministry.

Within youth ministry, the concept of peer ministry is well over a hundred years old, originating in the pioneering work of Christian Endeavor. Youthful members of Christian Endeavor are designated to serve as music, devotional, and prayer leaders for their meetings. Around 1960 a "planning group" model was proposed for weekly youth fellowship meetings, incorporating the youth in both planning and conducting the program. About a decade later, Larry Richards (1972) advocated a shift away from having youth undertake program responsibilities. Rather, he suggested that youth should undertake active person-to-person ministries with their peers.

Today an increasing emphasis is being made in youth ministry on the development of mature teenagers who are able to minister to other adolescents. In some cases this focuses on peer evangelism, seeking to empower teenagers to witness to their friends at school. In other cases, youth are being trained to come alongside their friends as listeners and encouragers in the role of peer helpers.

At the children's level, some churches, particularly those charismatic in nature, are seeking to enable children to find and exercise their spiritual gifting among other children. Thus, peer ministry is often expressed in prayer, healing, and evangelistic efforts.

DANIEL C. JESSEN

Bibliography. L. Crabb (1997), *Connecting;* D. Detwiler-Zapp and W. C. Dixon (1982), *Lay Caregiving;* L. O. Richards (1972), *Youth Ministry;* M. J. Steinbron (1987), *Can the Pastor Do It Alone?;* B. Varenhorst and L. Sparks (1988), *Training Teenagers for Peer Ministry.*

Peer Pressure. Influence that age-mates exercise on one another in the formation of perceptions, attitudes, and behaviors. While this social psychological phenomenon is applicable for all ages, it is particularly acute during adolescence and young adulthood.

Adolescent concerns for social acceptance and identity formation make peer pressure a significant factor in the developmental process. The increasing awareness of the adolescent's social context and others' perceptions of the self that accompany the social cognition of formal operational thought heighten the adolescent's desire to "fit in" to a preferred peer group. In the transition between childhood and adulthood, adolescents often turn to their peers to define the socially acceptable norms.

On a more practical level, teenagers spend more time with their peers than do younger children. The early adolescent begins withdrawing from adults and spending increasing amounts of time with selected peers. Middle adolescents spend about twice as much time with peers as they do with parents or other adults. Adolescent peer groups receive increasingly less adult supervision and control. They often seek out locations in public and at home where adults will not watch them closely. This natural separation process

from parents and adult figures increases both the likelihood and intensity of peer pressure.

Some sociologists argue that peer pressure replaces familial influences as the primary reference group for youth attitudes, values, and behaviors. More recent studies have indicated a more moderate understanding in which adolescents function with significant connection to both parents and peers, rather than making definitive choices between the two. Others suggest that parents retain primary influence for significant spiritual values, moral commitments, and career plans while peers influence perceptions regarding interpersonal relationships outside the family and adolescent cultural trends.

Many adolescents choose speech patterns, hair and clothing styles, music preferences, and friendships based on peer pressure or group conformity. This conformity is often perceived as negative and harmful. Teenagers may be influenced to participate in antisocial or delinquent behaviors like substance abuse, premature sexual activity, reduced academic effort, and rebellion against authority. This negative impact may be the result of the personal insecurities, inadequate communication skills, poor parental relationships, lack of assertiveness, and immature perspectives of reality.

An increasing number of researchers have found that poor relationships with parents are directly related to negative peer relationships. Poor communication between parents and youth, permissive home environments or extreme authoritarian control, and estrangement from parents and siblings encourage the likelihood of antisocial or deviant peer influence. Conversely, parents who encourage appropriate communication skills, teach self- and other-awareness, model appropriate social relationships, and effectively resolve conflict are more likely to have adolescents who are able to keep peer influences in proper perspective.

The desire to conform to group standards can be positive. Many teenagers have been influenced by their friends to engage in positive behaviors, such as joining a school club, attending church, studying the Bible, or engaging in compassionate service activities. This proactive approach enables churches, schools, and youth organizations to have significant impact on adolescents through group activities and positive friendships. When an adolescent who has been negatively influenced by peers becomes involved in a community or Christian group, the sense of acceptance, security, and recognition provide an opportunity for the development of a healthy self-concept and appropriate social status. In recent years, mass movements encouraging prayer, sexual purity, and reflective Christian decision-making (WWJD?) have relied heavily on positive potential of peer pressure.

There is little doubt that peer pressure is a major theme for adolescents. The results of peer pressure can be seen in the choice of friends, fashions, speech, recreation, and values. Parents, teachers, youth workers, and significant adults can assist teenagers in dealing with peer pressure by modeling self-control, providing opportunities for open communication about the positive and negative realities of social influences, and encouraging the teenagers' personal control over their actions and positive influence of others.

EDWIN ROBINSON

Bibliography. J. S. Coleman (1961), *The Adolescent Society;* G. K. Olson (1984), *Counseling Teenagers;* L. Parrott (1993), *Helping the Struggling Adolescent;* J. Santrock (1998), *Adolescence: An Introduction.*

Penance. *See* Confession.

Pentecost. The word *Pentecost* derives from the Greek *pentekostos*—"fiftieth." In the second or third century B.C., the Greek-speaking Jews used the term to refer to an annual Old Testament religious festival, Feast of Weeks. This feast (also known as Firstfruits or Feast of Harvest) was a one-day feast that took place the fiftieth day after the wheat harvest. It was a time for offering the firstfruits (first portion) of the harvested grain to the Lord (Exod. 34:22; 23:16; Lev. 23:15–22).

When the Jewish temple was destroyed by the Romans in A.D. 70, temple worship and sacrifices ceased. The Jews then aligned the Feast of Weeks (Pentecost) with the giving of the Law to Moses on Mount Sinai. The rabbis then taught the view that the Law was given fifty days after the exodus. The Old Testament doesn't confirm this view.

This simple ancient Hebrew Feast of Harvest was transformed by the supernatural events of Acts 2 into the birth of a new international move of God—the formation of a new community. The 120 Jewish disciples who received the promised Spirit (Luke 3:16; 24:49; Acts 1:4–8) were empowered to pray, proclaim, and praise the resurrected Savior in a new way.

This fiftieth day after Easter (Day of Pentecost) marks what many call the "birthday of the church." This new "church" became the firstfruits of a new people who would later expand into an international and multiethnic universal church with millions of believers in Christ (Gal. 3:26–28; Col. 3:10–11).

The early church fathers of the second to fifth centuries like Athanasius, Tertullian, and Augustine observed the Christian Pentecost as a celebration of Christ's resurrection—firstfruits of the Christian's resurrection. They worshiped with Scripture readings; praise songs; standing prayer—no kneeling (thus standing in anticipating of the general resurrection); no fasting (thus recognizing the heavenly banquet with Christ); and water baptism for the newly instructed converts.

Today, the modern church is yet empowered by the early Pentecostal power. It too is challenged to pray, proclaim, and praise Jesus Christ in a new way. Not as a homogenous racial or ethnic group, but as a new "called out" body and community—a body that includes all varieties of humankind. The modern church's spiritual power and witness; fervent worship and praise; and its empowerment with spiritual gifts, all result from the supernatural birth beginning with Pentecost, A.D. 33.

KENNETH HAMMONDS

Perception. Cognitive picture stored in the brain. Perceptions develop as a result of a complex combination of elements, including concrete experiences, cultural beliefs, and social influences. Over a period of time perceptions develop into mental maps that help people make sense of their experiences and their world, ultimately resulting in behavior that is compatible with their perceptions. In addition, because the brain does not tolerate discontinuity, people will often unconsciously force their experiences into categories that already match their deeply held models. People often, but not always, see only what their mental models allow. Such perceptions and their related mental models are often treated as "the only truth" from the person who holds them, even if the perception is inaccurate. As a result, diverse opinions and, at times, significant conflict, can result. Since people often associate with those who hold to similar models, it is very difficult to change the perception of another without a safe environment for exposure to differing perceptions and disconfirming data.

JAY DESKO

Bibliography. E. DeBono (1990), *I Am Right You Are Wrong;* V. Satir and G. Bateson (1975), *The Structure of Magic.*

See also INSIGHT; JOHARI'S WINDOW; LIFE MAP; SELF-CONCEPT

Perceptive. *See* Insight.

Perry, William G., Jr. (1913–). Developmental psychologist. Perry is known for identifying patterns of thought and moral development in college students, ages seventeen to twenty-two, thus challenging contemporaneous wisdom that cognitive development reached its peak prior to the college years. Changing forms of thought are mental "structures" by which students make meaning of knowledge, values, and responsibilities. The pattern of development follows a logical sequence that allows for a greater degree of complexity.

Development involves a sequence of nine positions (stages), or three general categories. First, *dualism* (dualistic thinking) characterizes the beginning college student. Life is understood in absolute terms of right or wrong, good or bad, we versus they. Problems have correct answers and authorities know the right answers. Students are to engage in the hard work of memorizing correct answers, choices, commitments, and so on that authorities should provide. Second, thought becomes characterized by *multiplicity*. In areas of knowledge where right answers are not yet known, the student believes diverse opinions and values are appropriate. Third, thought forms develop to *commitment*, a rather complex thought process in which the student chooses to affirm certain knowledge and values while fully recognizing that other choices exist. Commitments are made based on reflection, unlike earlier stages in which careful consideration is absent. Without clear understanding of the diversity of perspectives, true commitment cannot be reached. Responsibility for maintaining affirmations is within the individual, rather than resting on others.

Development is prompted by exposure to a wide variety of perspectives in peers, faculty, and content of study. However, development involves significant investment of energy in response to internal urges toward growth, which is perceived as normal and natural. At the same time, there is an opposing drive to conserve past development without risk. Still, the strongest urge in most students is toward growth.

Most students develop to the commitment level, though some choose from three alternatives to growth. First, temporizing is a pause in growth of a year or more. This alternative may involve consolidation of previous growth or may simply reflect hesitation to develop further. Whether growth is again assumed, or escape (see #2 below) is chosen instead, depends on attitude. If personal responsibility is acknowledged, resumption of development is likely. If, on the other hand, the student waits for someone/something outside of self to prompt growth, further development is unlikely, and alienation and the irresponsibility of escape occurs. A second alternative to growth, retreat, involves regression, which may occur anywhere along the developmental path. Some abandonment of responsibility occurs as the student moves backward to a previous position. If the retreat is to dualism, the student's dichotomous perspective tends to seek "enemies" representing opposing viewpoints. Allegiance may be given to an authority or absolutes that reject other perspectives, or the student may adopt an opposition to authorities. Third, a student may escape, a growth alternative that takes one of two forms: (1) disassociation, or passive drifting, in which life is given over to "fate"; or (2) encapsulation, in which escape is sought from demands of dealing with diverse viewpoints.

According to Perry, development in religious faith from simple beliefs to mature, committed faith requires a period of doubt. Perry emphasizes the necessity of doubt, not in the sense of denial, but sincere questioning to establish faith's validity and reasonableness.

Educationally, Perry was concerned that his descriptive scheme not be treated as prescriptive to force development. Instead, he emphasized the need to view it as a means of improving teachers' ability to communicate with students by corresponding with students' ways of making meaning. Rather than devising strategies to cause growth, teachers encourage development when they expose students to diverse thinking.

DENNIS DIRKS

Bibliography. W. G. Perry (1970), *Forms of Intellectual and Ethical Development in the College Years;* idem, *The Counseling Psychologist* 6, no. 4 (1977): 51–52; idem (1978), *Encouraging Development in College Students;* idem (1981), *The Modern American College: Responding to the New Realities of Diverse Students and a Changing Society.*

See also CRITICAL THINKING; EARLY ADULTHOOD; MORAL DEVELOPMENT; MORAL DILEMMA

Perversion. *See* Distortion.

Pestalozzi, Johann Heinrich (1746–1827). Swiss educator. The early death of his father left Pestalozzi and two siblings to be raised by their mother. The family's poor economic situation created a lonely childhood, a condition to which he remained sensitive and which helped shape his later educational posture. Greatly influenced by Rousseau's *Emile,* Pestalozzi was a naturalist who believed that individuals learn primarily through sensory perceptions. He saw human beings as naturally good but spoiled by a corrupt society. His ideas and practices led to the reform of traditional schooling, which had been characterized by dull memorization and deadening recitation. Greatly concerned with the plight of the poor, he established a school for disadvantaged children in Neuhof, Switzerland, in 1773. Although financial problems forced its closure within five years, the experience was crucial in the formulation of Pestalozzi's educational posture.

In 1780 he wrote *The Evening Hour of a Hermit,* a book of aphorisms that clearly revealed the influence of Rousseau and expressed the heart of his educational philosophy. The following year he began work on what would become his most widely read book, *Leonard and Gertrude,* an *Emile*-like novel that attempted to demonstrate how changes in the pedagogical pattern could lead to social, moral, and political reform. It laid the basis for Pestalozzi's emphasis on a secure, loving, and homelike learning environment. Teachers, he proposed, should not only be concerned with academic instruction, but should encourage the development of the whole child. Despite fighting intense feelings of guilt for neglecting his duties to his own family in order to pursue his educational experiments, Pestalozzi argued that children needed to be raised in a stable family and community in order to develop their personalities and values to the fullest.

He founded an institute in Burgdorf to educate children and prepare teachers and a boarding school in Yverdon. There he worked to develop a method of group instruction that used natural objects to foster the learning process in gradual and cumulative steps. The school's atmosphere was generally permissive, and included physical exercises, play activities, and nature walks. Its success attracted students and visitors from across Europe. Among those influenced by what they observed were Friedrich Froebel (the founder of the kindergarten) and Johann Friedrich Herbart (who formalized the theory of apperception), both of whom drew heavily on Pestalozzian concepts.

Pestalozzi's principles of instruction can be divided into two categories, the "general" and the "special." The general method involved teachers' providing an emotionally warm and secure climate in which the student could feel safe. Once this predisposition was established, the special method was employed. This involved sensory learning through the use of natural objects in what Pestalozzi called the "object lesson." Like Rousseau, he urged that lessons be based on the sensory experiences with which the child was familiar. As students progressed in their learning, Pestalozzi further employed a set of learning strategies that summed up his approach. Instruction, he urged, should (1) begin with the concrete before introducing abstract concepts; (2) begin with the learner's immediate environment before dealing with what is distant and remote; (3) begin with easy exercises before introducing complex ones; and (4) always proceed gradually, cumulatively, and slowly. Pestalozzi believed strongly that all children had an equal right to education and possessed the inherent capacity to profit from it.

In attacking conventional educational forms as excessively verbal and lifeless, he held that the innate faculties of a child were best developed in accordance with natural principles. Such an educational pattern would be successful only to the extent that teachers were adequately prepared to carry it out. Thus, to Pestalozzi, training teachers in naturalistic principles was of primary importance. The schoolmaster, he argued, should be one of the most important persons in the community. He was to be a person of strong emotional and ethical character and capable of loving children from every strata of society.

Frequently criticized and considered revolutionary in his day, the educational concepts of Pestalozzi subsequently exerted great influence on the development of progressive pedagogy in Europe and the United States in the twentieth century. His emphasis on learning by natural principles and human emotions paralleled the earlier thought of Rousseau. But whereas Rousseau proposed abandoning the school concept, Pestalozzi sought to reform it. Ever the champion of the underprivileged, when he died his grave was marked only by a rough stone and a single rose bush. On the one hundredth anniversary of his birth a monument was erected at his burial site, which read in part, "All for others, nothing for himself."

DAVID GOUGH

Bibliography. R. B. Downs (1975), *Heinrich Pestalozzi: Father of Modern Pedagogy;* G. L. Gutek (1968), *Pestalozzi and Education;* K. Silber (1960), *Pestalozzi: The Man and His Work.*

See also HERBART, JOHANN FRIEDRICH; LEARNING THEORIES; OBJECT LESSON; ROUSSEAU, JEAN-JACQUES

Peter Principle. Description of how people are gradually promoted until they reach a level of incompetence. Although there is little scientific research to document this phenomenon, many people in human resource management of organizations refer to it and its ultimate outcomes.

A brief, hypothetical example of the Peter principle would be as follows. A new attender at church volunteers to assist in the children's Sunday school program. The Sunday school director notes how well he or she works with children. As a result, he is asked to teach a class. During this time the volunteer leads six children to a personal relationship with Jesus, resulting in another success, and then as a result, receives praise from parents, children, and other volunteer staff. Because of this continuation of success, the volunteer is asked to help train other Sunday school teachers. Up to this point, he or she has been perceived as a "success" in helping children, teaching the Bible, training others, carrying out personal evangelism, and encouraging others. When the Sunday school director retires, who better to ask to take his or her place than this "successful" individual? However, there is not always a correlation between what skills contributed to the success of the individual at other levels of involvement and what it will take to be successful at the next level of service. In this case, the volunteer had not demonstrated skill or passion for organization and administration, volunteer recruitment, or strategy and policy development. At times, the very skills or competencies that are necessary to do a good job in one task or area may be the very behaviors that lead to incompetence in another task or area.

JAY DESKO

See also ADMINISTRATION; EVALUATION; LEADERSHIP; MANAGEMENT

Phenomenology. Although the term dates back to 1765, as a philosophical movement phenomenology finds its roots in Edmund Husserl (1859–1938), the most prominent of a group of philosophers who described themselves as phenomenologists. Husserl's first major philosophical work, the *Logical Investigations* (1900/1901), perhaps best illustrates the phenomenological method in practice, while later texts such as *The Idea of Phenomenology* (1907) and *Philosophy as Rigorous Science* (1910) attempt to articulate his phenomenological philosophy. Frustrated with what he saw as philosophical speculation, Husserl called for a return to the things themselves, a new beginning in which philosophers first focus on the relevant phenomena and only then construct theories.

So radical is this beginning that, in contrast to the natural sciences, which operate from the standpoint of what Husserl calls the natural attitude (in which metaphysical commitments are assumed without examination), Husserl insists that philosophy must become a truly rigorous science by abandoning all presuppositions and returning to the basic data of consciousness. To reach this level of original intuition (where phenomena are directly available to consciousness), Husserl suggests both the phenomenological reduction in which we bracket all metaphysical assumptions about reality and the eidetic reduction in which we reduce all particulars to the essential features. In effect, Husserl takes the modern ideal of detached scientific objectivity to its ultimate extreme. Although Husserl's early thought makes no clear commitment to either realism or idealism, by *Ideas I* (1913) he had clearly moved to idealism and remained an idealist throughout his lifetime. A significant development in his later thought, evidenced in such texts as *The Crisis of European Sciences* (1934), is an increasing shift of interest. From the concern for epistemic justification to what he terms the *Lebenswelt*, the cultural and historical life-world of everyday human existence. Of all Husserlian notions, that of the life-world has had the greatest impact on phenomenology of education.

Despite the fact that Husserl had hoped for his assistant Martin Heidegger (1889–1976) to continue his work, Heidegger's much greater focus on the historicity and contextuality of human existence proved a major source of disagreement. Given his goal of scientific objectivity, Husserl's phenomenological method attempts to reduce all particularity in favor of the essential and universal. However, since Heidegger argues that human knowledge is thoroughly historical, cultural, and tied to particular linguistic expression, the goal of objectivity ends up being neither possible nor even desirable. Heidegger replaces Husserl's phenomenological method with hermeneutic phenomenology, which affirms the phenomenological project of returning to the phenomena but likewise recognizes that our apprehension of the phenomena is always historically and culturally conditioned. Moreover, while phenomenology for Husserl was designed to bracket metaphysical questions about what things are, all of Heidegger's philosophy is ultimately concerned with the question of being. In *Being and Time* (1927), Heidegger attempts to explicate the meaning of being by concentrating on human being, what he terms *Dasein*. In later texts, Heidegger increasingly moves from scientific analysis to thinking about being poetically. Although Heidegger explicitly repudiated the label of existentialist, the existential aspects of his thought have had a great impact on a wide variety of disciplines.

Avowed existentialists Jean-Paul Sartre (1905–80) and Maurice Merleau-Ponty (1908–61), both heavily influenced by Husserl and Heidegger, were widely read in the 1950s and 1960s, yet they have since been eclipsed by two contemporary phenomenologists, Hans-Georg Gadamer (b. 1900) and Jacques Derrida (b. 1930). Having studied with Husserl and Heidegger, Gadamer was particularly influenced by Heidegger's hermeneutical turn. Thus, Gadamer's *Truth and Method* (1960), the most significant text of this century on hermeneutics, is a phenomenology of understanding. By way of the metaphor of the fusion of horizons, Gadamer argues that genuine understanding can still take place despite historical and cultural distance. Less sanguine than Gadamer, Derrida tends to focus on the limits of language and concepts. In *Speech and Phenomena* (1967), Derrida argues against the Husserlian assumption that language can—at least in principle—adequately communicate thought. Derrida is best known for deconstruction (a term which he borrows from Husserl), a method of analyzing philosophical and literary texts which seeks to expose unstated metaphysical commitments.

BRUCE E. BENSON

Bibliography. C. Macann (1993), *Four Phenomenological Philosophers;* J. Weinsheimer (1985), *Gadamer's Hermeneutics;* J. Caputo, ed. (1997), *Deconstruction in a Nutshell.*

Philosophy of Christian Education. The philosophy of Christian education wrestles with questions related to designing a cohesive educational strategy based on distinctive Christian presuppositions that effectively help people within a given cultural context become more like Jesus Christ. While the tendency in Christian education seems to be either to do it the way it has always been done, or to do it any way that works, these two options may not always be wise. The discipline of philosophy can add wisdom to the practice of Christian education. The word "philosophy" means the "love of wisdom." Paul, in summarizing his purpose in life, affirms his commitment to educate with wisdom in the following passage: "We proclaim him, admonishing and teaching everyone with all wisdom, so that we may present everyone perfect in Christ" (Col. 1:28). In order to teach with wisdom, Christian educators must base their methods on well-thought-out philosophical presuppositions.

While secular philosophers today have all but abandoned the idea of absolute philosophical presuppositions, they are the foundation of the Christian educator's philosophy of education. Absolutes relating to metaphysics, epistemology, and axiology are at the core of the Christian educator's belief.

Metaphysics relates to the issue of "what is real and the nature of reality." This branch of philosophy deals with speculative questions relating to four areas: cosmology—the nature of the universe; theology—the nature of God; anthropology—the nature of human beings; and ontology—the nature of being. Each of these areas relates directly to one's philosophy of Christian education.

Significant cosmological issues for the Christian educator include how the universe began, whether there is a design to the universe, and what its destiny is. The clear declaration in Scripture of the purposefulness of the universe has direct implications on how Christian educators should plan their ministries and teaching experiences.

A significantly important aspect of metaphysics for the Christian educator is theology. Theology deals with issues relating to the nature of God. Since Christianity revolves around God, his Son, Jesus Christ, and the supernatural work of the Holy Spirit, this area of study is of crucial importance for the Christian educator. This focus is seen clearly in Colossians 2:2, 3, where Paul expressed that his purpose in ministry is to help others to know Christ. An intimate, personal knowledge of Jesus Christ is the only way to know God and all the riches of the knowledge of him and his creation.

The third aspect of metaphysics is anthropology, which focuses on the study of human beings. Issues related to anthropology for the Christian educator include how we view the various aspects of the person. For example: How should we divide up the various aspects of the person? Are there three or four aspects of the person? Is the person primarily controlled by the mind or the will? How do the various aspects of the person interact with one another? A major distinctive of a Christian understanding of the person relates to the nature of the person regarding good and evil. While the various denominations focus on different emphases, the Christian educator cannot ignore the two fundamental doctrines found throughout Scripture. While humankind was created perfect in the image of God, man and woman sinned and distorted that image, resulting in radical consequences. How the Christian educator defines this key issue will determine how the educator views the student and how much freedom the teacher gives the student within a learning context.

The fourth aspect of metaphysics is ontology. Ontology relates to the nature of "being" itself. Ontological issues for the Christian educator include questions such as: Are there higher forms of spiritual service within the church? Is a member of the clergy more spiritual than a common lay person? Is the spiritual world completely separate from the physical world? Are physical needs and desires real? Tackling these issues is becoming even more important for Christian educators in the light of influx of Eastern religious ideologies into Western culture.

Epistemology is another branch of philosophy that has direct implications for the field of education. Epistemology deals with the major questions of "the nature of truth" and "how we know." Other issues related to this branch of philosophy include questions such as: Is truth relative or absolute? Is knowledge objective or is it somewhat subjective, based upon the perspectives of the teacher or learner? Is knowledge true by definition or only after it is experienced by a subject? The answers to these and other epistemological questions drive both our content and our methodology as Christian educators. Arthur Holmes (1977) challenges Christian educators to articulate a view of truth that "combines universal truth (metaphysical objectivity) with free personal commitment (epistemological subjectivity)" (7). We see this balance between objective knowledge of God and the personal experience of the knowledge clearly throughout Scripture. Paul speaks of both the objective and subjective understanding of God's love in Ephesians 3:17, 18.

The third branch of philosophy, axiology, answers the question "What is of value?" in education. Issues of both ethics, what is right, and aesthetics, what is beautiful, are dealt with within this category. Axiology provides many of the Christian educator's goals within a philosophy of education.

William Frankena (1965, 4–10) gives us one of the most helpful models for integrating our philosophical beliefs into a coherent philosophy of Christian education. His model is made up of five boxes, each representing an aspect of one's philosophy of education. Each of the boxes relates systematically to another box, thus ensuring a certain cohesiveness to the overall philosophy. This helps to prevent the Christian educator from uncritically borrowing presuppositions or methods from non-Christian worldviews.

Box A in Frankena's model contains a statement about the ultimate purpose of humankind. Choices for this box usually include humankind's responsibility to glorify, serve, love, honor, obey, or worship God. The statement in box A provides thematic unity to the other four boxes.

Box B includes both philosophical and empirical premises about human nature, life, and the world. Included in this box are the foundational beliefs that undergird one's philosophy of education. Often included in this box are the educator's beliefs concerning the Bible, the Godhead, the church, the family, principles of human development, the role of the Holy Spirit, and other important theological and empirical foundational beliefs.

There is a direct connection between "Box A—Ultimate Purpose" and "Box B—Premises," and the next category, "Box C—Excellencies." *Excellencies* refer to the characteristics one's educational philosophy is designed to produce, based upon the foundational ideas mentioned in the *Ultimate Purpose* and the *Premises*. The excellencies, collectively, paint a picture of the ideal person. Christian educators often draw on Jesus' teachings from his "Sermon on the Mount" or Paul's teaching on "the fruit of the spirit" to describe their excellencies.

Box D contains explanations based on empirical and scientific theory about how to produce the stated excellencies. The learning theories explained in this box are derived primarily from social science research. Care must be taken to critically evaluate the presuppositions of the theories used before applying them within a Christian context.

Box E contains the specific educational strategy with goals and objectives related to every aspect of the educational practice. The details described in this section, related to curriculum, methods, and organizational structure, are based on the data from the first four boxes, thus ensuring a cohesive educational philosophy.

The "Frankena Model" helps the Christian educator to integrate theory and practice in articulating a statement of philosophy of Christian education. This guards against one of the greatest dangers in educational ministry, that of utilizing methods that are not well thought out philosophically, theologically, and educationally.

GARY C. NEWTON

Bibliography. W. Frankena (1965), *The Philosophy of Education;* T. H. Groome (1980), *Christian Religious Education;* A. F. Holmes (1977), *All Truth Is God's Truth;* G. Knight (1998), *Philosophy and Education;* R. Pazmiño (1997), *Foundational Issues in Christian Education: An Introduction in Evangelical Perspective;* M. L. Peterson (1986), *Philosophy of Education: Issues and Options;* J. Wilhoit (1986), *Christian Education and the Search for Meaning.*

See also EPISTEMOLOGY; EXISTENTIALISM AND EDUCATION; FRANKENA, WILLIAM KLAUS; PRAGMATISM

Philosophy of Education. Everybody involved in education has some understanding of what education should be and how it should work. Expectations people hold about the purpose, goals, and methods of education vary a great deal. These beliefs about the nature of education exist at different levels of a person's awareness and regardless of whether the ideas have been consciously considered, everyone operates from some basic set of assumptions about the subject. These beliefs and how they are lived out make up one's personal philosophy of education.

Looking across the wide range of personal philosophies of education one can identify some common concerns and themes. Philosophers of education formally study these same issues and suggest preferred approaches for looking at education. This academic field is called philosophy of education. A traditional task of professional educational philosophers has been to analyze and then organize the major understandings about education into broad groupings. These categories or major schools of thought are also known as philosophies of education. Examples include idealism, realism, pragmatism, reconstructionism, behaviorism, and existentialism.

Regardless of whether one is referring to the formal academic study, a personal outlook, or a specific school of thought, all philosophy of education arises from a general philosophy of life. What one believes about life informs how one understands education. Questions about one's identity, the problems of living, and remedies for the human condition are at the base of everyone's view of life. How one addresses concerns about reality, the world, humanity, death, knowledge, ethics, and history defines a person's foundational perspective or worldview. From this frame of reference people formulate and practice a philosophy of education.

The major branches of formal philosophical study consider the nature of the world (metaphysics), knowledge (epistemology), value (axiology), and beauty (aesthetics). Understandings in these areas provide the groundwork upon which specialized philosophies are built. A general philosophy about the world and life yields a specific philosophy of education. That in turn directs the development of educational policy and informs education practice.

The broad scope of education practice overlaps concepts like learning, schooling, training, and indoctrination. Philosophies of education in turn address issues related to the purpose of education, the nature of the learner, the subject matter, the learning process, and the teacher. Most educational concerns can be traced to these critical themes.

Concerning the purpose of education, questions are asked about the aims, goals, and objectives of the educational endeavor. Toward what end do we educate? What do we hope to accomplish? What kind of product are we trying to create? How does education relate to society and what part do schools play? Philosophies look to different sources for authoritative answers to these questions, and the answers tend to revolve around the roles assigned to the family, community, church, government, and school. Decisions about the purpose of education have a major influence on the design, development, and direction of educational practice.

Related to this first theme are considerations about the nature of the learner. What does it mean to be human and how are students to be perceived? Some view the student as a higher form of animal to be trained, while some see the child as a product of the state to be controlled. Others see the pupil as a machine to be programmed, a plant to be tended, or an empty vessel to be filled. Understandings on the nature of the learner are crucial because they indicate how the student will be treated in the learning environment.

In the area of subject matter, concerns turn to the content of the curriculum. What should be taught to students? Who makes the decision, and how is it determined? In light of all the knowledge that exists, what is most worth knowing? Some conclude that a specific collection of information needs to be passed down from generation to generation. Other philosophies advocate that students should determine their own subject matter. Still others emphasize the process of learning rather than any specific content. Studies in this area define the relevancy of specific curricular topics.

Regarding the learning process, attention centers on educational psychology and how people learn. Attempts are made to define intelligence, the stages of human development, and which educational activities yield particular outcomes. Focus is placed on the importance of reason and behavior as well as the emotional and social dynamics of learning. Some believe that learning is primarily cognitive and that a rational approach is to be preferred. Others choose to emphasize behavioral conditioning with a system of rewards and punishments. Still others point to the importance of nurturing the emotional world of the child and the cooperative aspects of learning in community. Since people have different learning styles, many teaching methods arise from understandings in this area.

Looking at the teacher, philosophies consider the role of the instructor. Who should assume or be given this responsibility? Should this person be viewed primarily as a transmitter of knowledge, a socializing agent, an exploratory guide, or a behavioral engineer? Within the Christian tradition, educational philosophers draw from biblical themes related to the creation of the world, the sin of humanity, and the process of redemption. The Bible is viewed as a revelation through which one may see God's character and come to realize his ultimate intent for humanity and the world. The purpose of education is to help fulfill God's revealed plan for creation and thereby please him. Humans are uniquely created for relationship with God and to be responsible stewards of the world. Since learners suffer from the consequences of living in a fallen and damaged world, education is to align itself with the restoring work of the Holy Spirit. Those redeemed by Christ need equipping to faithfully fulfill their responsibilities, while those apart from Christ are to be served in love with the hope that they too might come to know him and live God-honoring lives.

Regardless of the philosophy of education one embraces, practice does not always reflect theory. Neither educators nor educational institutions are always consistent with stated beliefs, and ongoing consideration of the themes of education is needed. While schools may have an official philosophy represented in their mission statement and related documents, schools are also made up of individual educators who hold a variety of personal views related to their work. Over the past several decades American public schools have generally reflected philosophical beliefs associated with pragmatism and postmodernism.

ROGER WHITE

Bibliography. L. Berkhof and C. Van Til (1990), *Foundations of Christian Education: Addresses to Christian Teachers;* G. H. Clark (1946, 1988), *A Christian Philosophy of Education;* N. DeJong (1969), *Education in the Truth;* K. O. Gangel and W. S. Benson (1983), *Christian Education: Its History and Philosophy;* G. R. Knight (1998), *Philosophy and Education: An Introduction in Christian Perspective;* C. S. Lewis (1947), *The Abolition of Man: How Education Develops Man's Sense of Morality;* H. A. Ozmon and S. M. Craver (1998), *Philosophical Foundations of Education;* R. W. Pazmiño (1997), *Foundational Issues in Christian Education: An Introduction in Evangelical Perspective;* M. L. Peterson (1986), *Philosophy of Education: Issues and Options;* N. P. Wolterstorff (1980), *Educating for Responsible Social Action.*

See also EXISTENTIALISM; IDEALISM; PRAGMATISM; REALISM; RECONSTRUCTIONISM

Philosophy of Ministry. The "why"and "how" of ministry. The "why" is concerned with the biblical, theological, historical, and social science bases of ministry. The "how" is concerned with the praxis of ministry. Consistency between one's understanding and doing of ministry is essential. Working with a broad definition of ministry, an examination is in order of the descriptor "philosophy of ministry" in light of its attributes, characteristics, and relevance for Christian education.

Ministry is caring for others in the name of Christ. Within the church it includes the strengthening and equipping people for service as part of the body of Christ (Eph. 4:7–16; Rom. 12:3–8; 1 Cor. 12:12–31). Ministry is always purposeful. Philosophy, the love of wisdom, is a critical approach to life that seeks to make sense of life and order the world in which we live.

The descriptor "philosophy of ministry" indicates that one has deliberately sought to understand coherently both the nature and practice of ministry. Developing a philosophy of ministry is a critical undertaking pursued in an attempt to remain faithful to Scripture and relevant to the cultural setting in which one ministers.

A philosophy of ministry possesses five attributes. (1) It must be biblically consistent. It should seek to say no more than Scripture or no less then Scripture. (2) It should be theologically consistent. Identification and acknowledgment of the unique contributions of one's particular theological tradition to a "philosophy of ministry" is essential. (3) It should engage and mine the depths of other disciplines. If all truth is God's truth then truth, which is always consistent with God's character and Scripture, must be recognized and inform both the understanding and practice of ministry. To neglect the findings of other disciplines when consistent with Scripture is a denial of common grace and undermines one's ability to faithfully fulfill the creation mandate. (4) A philosophy of ministry must be relevant. It must address the target setting as it is, not as it is perceived to exist. It should enable one to engage others and live transformationally within a culture rather than rescuing people and escaping from that culture. (5) A philosophy of ministry should be proactive rather than reactive. It should promote constructive engagement, an offensive position, rather than a defensive posture. It should be aware of the challenges a ministry will face and provide a guide for facing them.

A philosophy of ministry can be broad or narrow. It is written to guide a church or parachurch's ministry or a target ministry. The philosophical nature of this inquiry means that a philosophy of ministry will have three distinct characteristics.

A philosophy of ministry seeks to *describe* what one believes about ministry and explains the rationale for one's approach. This descriptive characteristic is concerned with the assumptions, facts, and theories that inform one's understanding of ministry.

A philosophy of ministry is also a *normative* statement about the "why" and "how" of ministry. In other words, it consists of enduring propositions about the values a ministry should incul-

cate and its ends. A normative statement seeks to state which elements of a philosophy ministry transcend culture, and are true and applicable regardless of the setting or context.

A philosophy of ministry should also be *analytical*. It should seek to ensure that the assumptions, concepts, statements, methods, and theories employed are coherent and consistent with each other. This also includes ensuring that one's ministry practice is consistent with one's rationale, and that one's rationale informs the practice of ministry.

Developing, revising, and maintaining a philosophy of ministry is not an esoteric exercise. It is pursued either implicitly or explicitly. By making it explicit, one becomes aware of the assumptions, beliefs, and experiences that shape understanding and practice of ministry.

Varieties of models for developing and organizing a philosophy of ministry are available. The philosopher William Frankena developed one of the best. It is a comprehensive model that encourages the "why" and "how"—the theory and practice of ministry—to constructively dialogue with each other. The "why" part of the model is composed of three related components or boxes.

The first box, Box A, is concerned with the ultimate ends of ministry. It contains a description of how the world *ought* to be. For example, in light of Genesis 1–3 Box A may include statements such as, "The human person will be in a right relationship to God, self, others, and the created order."

The second box, Box B, is comprised of the beliefs that inform one's understanding and interpretation of life. These beliefs are rooted in Scripture and informed by one's theological tradition. For example, the belief that human beings are totally depraved would be located here. Drawing on the vision in Box A and the understanding of the world, including the human person in Box B, one then seeks to articulate the excellences to be formed. Excellences are those attributes, traits, and beliefs one desires to inculcate in the learner (Box C). One should seek to form in the learner a set of beliefs that enable him or her to understand and interpret life, and make decisions in a biblically consistent fashion.

The "how" part of the model is also composed of three boxes, although, it shares Box C in common with the "why" part. The purpose of this part is to describe the actual practice of ministry in a manner consistent with one's theoretical rationale. The fourth box, Box D, contains a description of the methods one will employed. The methods, which should be consistent with Box B, are drawn from Scripture and complemented by truths discerned from other disciplines. For example, does one assume that people naturally desire to know God's Word? No, because of our sinful nature it is necessary to motivate people to study the Bible. One's understanding of the nature, role, and place of motivation fits here. Box E, the fifth one, contains statements about how one will actually minister to facilitate the excellences listed in Box C. Or how does one minister? Will the Bible study be didactic or discussion-oriented and why? Will Sunday school be organized by age groups or intergenerational in character? Box E is concrete in character.

A philosophy of ministry is essential to pursuing one's vision, planning, and evaluating the effectiveness of a church or parachurch's program. It is always present and thus when acknowledged, developed, and revised it serves as an instrument for discerning the priorities and character of a ministry in a clear and consistent manner.

DARWIN K. GLASSFORD

Bibliography. J. I. Packer (1993), *Hot Tub Religion;* W. K. Frankena (1965), *Philosophy of Education.*

See also FRANKENA, WILLIAM KLAUS; PHILOSOPHY OF CHRISTIAN EDUCATION; PHILOSOPHY OF EDUCATION

Philosophy of Religion. Branch of philosophy that focuses in a general way on philosophical questions that can be raised concerning religious belief and practice. Philosophy of religion is closely related to the more narrowly focused discipline of philosophical theology, which characteristically explores in philosophical fashion the logical, metaphysical, and epistemological relations that hold among the various elements of a particular religious perspective, such as Christianity or Islam. In the Western part of the world, philosophy of religion has traditionally been confined to exploring the philosophical dimensions of theistic perspectives, since these (and especially Christianity) are most prominent in the West. More recently, however, due largely to the greater contact that exists between people of differing faiths, the philosophy of religion as conducted in the West has devoted more attention to issues of religious pluralism and interreligious dialogue.

The philosophy of religion, though specialized, overlaps in significant ways many other branches of philosophy. For example, many of the most fundamental questions in the philosophy of religion are epistemological: Is belief in God justified? What is the special character of religious belief? What are the sources of religious knowledge? How is faith related to the exercise of reason? The question, "What sort of being is God and what properties must God have in order to be God?" is a question in the philosophy of religion that overlaps with issues in metaphysics or general ontology. The question, "What is a miracle?" is also ontological or metaphysical, but it relates as well to the philosophy of science. The concept of a miracle must be understood in relation to the concept of a law of nature, which falls within the purview of philosophy of science.

The question, "Does an identifiable miracle count as evidence for certain religious propositions?" is epistemological. But what about the question, "Have miracles happened?" It might be thought that this is a question for historians rather than philosophers. But here we meet with concerns about whether the methods of the historian are suitable for determining whether miracles have happened. And these concerns belong to the philosophy of history.

Consider the question, "What is the relationship between the existence and will of God and the normative force of moral principles?" Here is a question both for the philosopher of religion and for the moral philosopher or ethicist. Some questions in political philosophy, especially questions about the relation between church and state, are of interest to philosophers of religion. For example, is there a religious justification for civil disobedience, and does this sort of justification differ in salient ways from other sorts of justification for the same type of behavior? There is even overlap between philosophy of religion and aesthetics. For example, the philosopher may wish to know whether religious icons are more than mere works of art, or whether they are members of a special class of works of art that differ from all other works of art in important ways.

Clearly, the philosopher of religion must be knowledgeable about many different specialized areas of philosophy. And though the philosophy of religion is interesting in its own right, it is also valuable for its fruitfulness for exploring many other fields of knowledge.

During the past three decades, the philosophy of religion has been restored to a place of genuine respect, as evidenced by marked increase in activity on the part of sophisticated philosophers. In the United States alone there are three significant professional societies that specialize in the philosophy of religion (each with its own professional journal, as identified in parentheses): the Society of Christian Philosophers (*Faith and Philosophy*), the Evangelical Philosophical Society (*Philosophia Christi*), and the Society for Philosophy of Religion (*International Journal for Philosophy of Religion*). Most other professional journals in philosophy regularly feature essays in philosophy of religion, and lectures in philosophy of religion are routinely scheduled during the large annual meetings of the American Philosophical Association. This development has drawn philosophers and their methodologies into dialogue with theologians and fostered engagement with the efforts of organized religion.

Naturally, Christian philosophers of religion have been especially interested in exploring Christian belief and practice. Much energy has been concentrated on developing a satisfactory account of justified belief in the Christian theistic scheme and on assessing the case against Christian theistic belief. Many Christian philosophers today are sympathetic with the enterprise of natural theology, the development of extrabiblical evidence in support of belief in God. There are influential contemporary versions of cosmological and design arguments for the existence of God. One especially favored version of cosmological argument, called the *"kalam* cosmological argument,"* reasons that the universe must have had a beginning and that it must therefore have been caused by a personal being of great power and intelligence that has always existed. The most influential versions of design argument emphasize the delicate balance of numerous cosmic constants that make life in our universe possible. Contemporary Christian philosophers have also developed sophisticated arguments based on moral experience, the nature of human minds, the existence of evil, and other phenomena.

Other Christian philosophers have laid greater stress on the value of religious experience in providing grounds for Christian belief. Some of these philosophers, especially those who have come to be called "Reformed epistemologists," have sought to integrate this emphasis with the doctrine of the testimony of the Holy Spirit.

The case against Christian theism has also been multifaceted. Some "atheologians" have reasoned (1) that in the debate about God's existence, there is an initial presumption of atheism that can only be overcome with evidence sufficient to justify belief in God, and (2) that there is not sufficient evidence to justify belief in God. A related strategy holds that if God existed, then the evidence for God's existence would be greater than it is, for God would desire that humans believe in him and God would satisfy this desire by providing greater evidence of his existence. The problem raised here has been called the problem of "divine hiddenness." It is inspired by the judgment that there are many intelligent people of good will who do not believe in God. (Of course, it may seem equally surprising to nonbelievers that there should be so many intelligent, well-informed, and morally admirable believers in God.)

The most direct argument for the nonexistence of God, or for the irrationality of belief in God, is the argument from evil. According to this argument, the existence or amount or kinds of evil in the world make it unreasonable to believe in God. In response, Christian philosophers have countered with evidence for the existence of God, explained the role of human freedom in causing much of the evil in the world, developed various accounts of morally sufficient reasons that God may have for permitting the evils there are, and argued that it is not reasonable to suppose that

humans would know or understand all of the reasons which justify God's permission of evil.

The philosophy of religion is an engaging area of study that deserves a greater place in the educational program of the church, at every level. Not only does it promise to enrich the lives and faith of believers, but it also provides a means of meaningful engagement with nonbelievers in the contest of ideas, which is part of the mission of the church.

R. Douglas Geivett

Bibliography. K. J. Clark, ed. (1993), *Philosophers Who Believe;* N. Geisler and W. Corduan (1988), *Philosophy of Religion;* R. D. Geivett (1993), *Evil and the Evidence for God;* R. D. Geivett and G. R. Habermas, eds. (1997), *In Defense of Miracles;* R. D. Geivett and B. Sweetman, eds. (1992), *Contemporary Perspectives on Religious Epistemology;* D. Howard-Snyder, ed. (1996), *The Evidential Argument from Evil;* T. V. Morris, ed. (1994), *God and the Philosophers;* A. Plantinga and N. Wolterstorff, eds. (1983), *Faith and Rationality;* L. P. Pojman, ed. (1994), *Philosophy of Religion: An Anthology;* P. L. Quinn and C. Taliaferro (1997), *A Companion to Philosophy of Religion;* W. L. Rowe (1993), *Philosophy of Religion;* J. F. Sennett, ed. (1998), *The Analytic Theist: An Alvin Plantinga Reader;* R. Swinburne (1977), *The Coherence of Theism;* idem (1979), *The Existence of God;* idem (1981), *Faith and Reason;* idem (1996), *Is There a God?;* C. Taliaferro (1998), *Contemporary Philosophy of Religion;* W. J. Wainwright (1999), *Philosophy of Religion;* K. E. Yandell (1999), *Philosophy of Religion: A Contemporary Introduction.*

Piaget, Jean (1896–1980). Noted Swiss experimenter and theorist in the fields of developmental psychology and human intelligence. He is best known for his theory of intellectual development and studies of how children learn. His scholarly contributions to academia were enormous and his theoretical offerings were remarkably insightful.

In his childhood years Piaget showed an intense interest in science and nature, and at age 10 he published his first paper, a description of an albino sparrow he discovered in a park near his home. During his adolescence, however, Piaget was introduced to his godfather, Swiss scholar Samuel Cornut, who acquainted him with the issues of philosophy, particularly epistemology. Piaget maintained an interest in both epistemology and biology but determined that in and of themselves, the disciplines of science and philosophy were too narrow and what was needed was a synthesis between the two. Initially, however, he focused his attention on biology, completing his undergraduate studies in natural sciences at the University of Neuchatel. He received his Ph.D. in 1918 at the same university, writing his dissertation on mollusks.

In 1920, Piaget accepted a position at the Binet Laboratory in Paris, where he was given the task of developing a standardized instrument for measuring intelligence. In the course of his work, Piaget became intrigued with the discovery that children of the same age often gave the same incorrect answers and that there were similar wrong answers given at different ages. This marked the genesis of his lifelong efforts to identify the changes in the manner in which children think and perceive their world. By now Piaget had discovered the key to bridging the chasm between biology and philosophy—psychology. Through the integration of the three disciplines he became a pioneer in the field of study he termed *genetic epistemology*.

In 1921 Piaget was invited to become the director of research at the Jean-Jacques Rousseau Institute in Geneva. His studies there led him to write a number of research articles and the first of numerous of books on children, *The Language and Thought of the Child* (1926). In 1929 he began teaching at the University of Geneva, and in the decades following he taught a wide variety of subjects at universities in Geneva, Lausanne, Paris, and Neuchatel. Other positions he held before his death in 1980 included director of the Rousseau Institute, director of the International Center for Epistemology, and chair of the International Bureau of Education (later affiliated with UNESCO).

Germane to Piaget's theoretical framework is the assumption that there are two basic functions which affect intelligence: organization and adaptation. *Organization* is the tendency to systematize and combine processes into coherent systems. *Adaptation* is the tendency to adjust to the environment and is to be considered in terms of two simultaneous operations: accommodation and assimilation. *Accommodation* occurs when individuals modify their conceptions and alter their responses to the environment, while *assimilation* takes place when perceptions of sense data are changed to fit the mental conceptualization.

Equilibration is the natural tendency to balance assimilation and accommodation or to maintain harmony between what one already knows and what one experiences. When this balance is disturbed or when one experiences something that does not fit what he or she knows, *disequilibration* (anxiety, discomfort, or confusion) exists.

Piaget's theory of cognitive development divides intellectual growth into four sequential stages: Sensorimotor (birth to 2 years); Preoperational (2 to 7 years); Concrete Operational (7 to 11 years); and Formal Operational (11 years and older). (These ages are only rough estimates and vary from culture to culture and individual to individual). Piaget hypothesized that human thinking progresses from the innate reflexes of infants to the abstract logical reasoning of adolescents and adults. Each stage of development represents thinking skills that are qualitatively distinct from other stages.

In the *Sensorimotor* period the child proceeds from instinctive reflexive actions at birth to the ability to separate self from the environment. Cognitive ability is limited, by and large, to immediate experiences encountered through the senses.

Preoperational thinking is characterized by what Piaget calls the *semiotic function*, the ability to use mental symbols. In other words, the child can utilize a mental picture of a "car" or "house" to represent the real object which is not in immediate view. This ability frees the child somewhat from the here and now, although reasoning skills are still limited. Preoperational thinking is intuitive and highly imaginative; the significant growth of language skills is pertinent to this phase.

During the period of *Concrete Operations*, the child develops the ability to perform more complex thinking skills, including *reversibility* (the ability to reverse the mental process), *conservation* (the ability to see that while the appearance of an object changes the other essential characteristics remain the same), and *classification* (the capability to order by number, size, or other common characteristics). The capacity to relate to time and space also increases during this time.

While children in the first three stages are bound cognitively to the physical realities of the here and now, *Formal Operations* affords the individual the capability of more flexible thought. The adolescent can now create hypothetical situations, imagine possibilities, engage in abstract thought, and test ideas. Reasoning skills come to maturity.

To psychologists, developmental theorists, educators, and those in related disciplines, Piaget is often considered the foremost contributor to the domain of cognitive development. Religious educators have also endeavored to apply his theory of development to religious education. Ronald Goldman (1968), for example, applied Piaget's stages to religious thinking and raised questions concerning children's ability to comprehend religious ideas. James Fowler (1981) has incorporated Piaget's epistemological focus into his structure of faith development.

Christian educators can benefit from an understanding of cognitive development in at least three ways. First, awareness of different characteristics of thought processes at each stage of development provides teachers with insights for creating age-appropriate learning experiences and choosing suitable teaching techniques. Second, Christian educators are reminded that religious teaching must take into account the intellectual abilities of learners at various stages of growth. The teacher must neither overestimate nor underestimate the cognitive ability of the student. Third, effective teachers actively engage students (especially children) in the teaching/learning process.

Although Piaget has had a prodigious impact on educational practice and Christian education, his ideas have come under criticism. Some of the most common charges against him are that he underestimates the abilities of young children, his lower stages are described in negative terms, he overestimates the formal thinking skills of adolescents, and the stages are not as distinct as he proposes. Nonetheless, in spite of the criticism, Piaget's theory of cognitive development is held in high regard as an explanation of the development of mental capacities and functions (Yount, 1996, 92–93).

In addition to being the foremost contributor to the field of cognitive development, Piaget is second only to Sigmund Freud in sheer volume of written contributions to the broad field of psychology. His publications include over forty books and more than a hundred articles on child development. His major books include *The Child's Conception of the World* (1929), *The Moral Judgment of the Child* (1932), *The Psychology of Intelligence* (1950), *Play, Dreams and Imitation in Childhood* (1951), *The Child's Conception of Number* (1952), and *The Origins of Intelligence in Children* (1952).

HARLEY ATKINSON

Bibliography. J. W. Fowler (1981), *Stages of Faith;* H. Ginsburg and S. Opper (1979), *Piaget's Theory of Intellectual Development;* R. Goldman (1968), *Religious Thinking from Childhood to Adolescence.* J. Piaget (1926), *The Language and Thought of the Child;* W. R. Yount (1996), *Created to Learn.*

See also COGNITIVE LEARNING, THEORIES OF; FOWLER, JAMES W., III

Pioneer Ministries. Pioneer Clubs is a church-sponsored weekly club program for boys and girls, age 2 through grade 12. The organization began in 1939 as a Wheaton College Christian Service assignment. Betty Whitaker Bouslough and several other students developed a girls club which they called Girls Guild. They wanted to involve club members in activities that would give them godly role models, help them see their God-given talents, and help them learn to live for Christ in every activity of every day. They coined the phrase "Christ in every phase of life," which is still Pioneer Clubs' focus today.

In 1941 the name changed to Pioneer Girls, with a theme of pioneering and adventure. The camping phase of the ministry, known as Camp Cherith, began with a three-day camp in Volo, Illinois. Today there are twenty camps in the Association of Camp Cherith Camps in the United States and six in Canada.

As students graduated from college, they took the concept of the club with them. With the help of many volunteers, Pioneer Girls spread throughout the United States and into Canada. Churches in over sixty denominations appreciated the goal of ministering to every part of children's lives. Pioneer Girls complemented their Sunday schools, giving children opportunities to apply truths learned on Sunday to everyday situations.

In 1981, in response to requests from many churches and denominations, boys' clubs began, and the organization became Pioneer Clubs. It is designed in seven age groups to (1) integrate spiritual and personal development, (2) emphasize evangelism and discipleship, and (3) give children opportunities to learn new skills, make friends, have fun, and develop Christian values.

Pioneer Clubs' Goals. (1) To enable children to enter into a personal relationship with Christ and to know his Word; (2) To enable children to form healthy relationships; (3) To enable children to grow as whole persons; (4) To enable adults to understand children and help them develop.

Pioneer Clubs' Distinctives. Christ in Every Phase of Life. The Pioneer Clubs program is Christ-centered and Bible-based. Through club activities, members have opportunities to learn principles of Christian living, practice these principles in everyday situations, and see adults model Christlike behavior.

Meaningful Bible Memory and Bible Study. Understanding and application are essential to making Scripture memory a time to know God and his Word. Rather than merely a rote exercise, memory verses come directly from the weekly Bible study. Applications grow out of this inductive Bible study, where club members search Scripture themselves rather than just listening to a story or devotional. The Bible study time is called Bible Exploration to convey the excitement of discovering how God's Word applies to their individual lives. Thus there are options given for application, and members choose for themselves how they will carry out what they're learning to do.

Participative Learning. Since learners retain more when they are involved, the Bible studies and activity times encourage active participation.

Emphasis on Cooperation. Club members earn awards together as the requirements are built into meeting plans. Thus they all gain skills with an emphasis on self-improvement rather than on trying to outdo others. Similarly, when playing games, the goal is to create a fun experience and build unity. Leaders are encouraged to use cooperative games where the emphasis is on teamwork rather than winning.

Relationship Orientation. Teaching that God created us to be interdependent helps children see the need for relationships. Curriculum materials deal with family, peers, and other adults.

Spiral Curriculum. Pioneer Clubs' curriculum has been designed by curriculum specialists. The same concepts are dealt with at each age level, but in ways that fit children's increasing physical, intellectual, emotional, and spiritual capabilities.

Variety. Variety is expressed, not only in the activities, but also in the teaching techniques employed. This adapts to children's different learning styles.

Service to the Local Church. Pioneer Clubs believes the church is God's main means for evangelizing and nurturing, so they encourage any church which wishes to utilize the program to do so flexibly and within their own format which fits their own situation best. Pioneer Clubs provides program and training materials to equip the church to carry out its mandate of bringing its people to maturity in Christ. Pioneer Ministries, P.O. Box 788, Wheaton, IL 60189–0788. (630) 668–9674. Pioneer Clubs Canada, Box 5447 Burlington, ON L7R 4L2.

SARA ANNE ROBERTSON

Plan, Planning. Planning is the process of implementing future goals by evaluating the past and present and formulating steps to achieve those goals. It is a means to an end, not an end in itself. A plan helps a group or congregation move from the way things are to the way they ought to be in order to accomplish their mission.

Biblical Basis for Planning. The Bible has much to say about planning. For instance, Nehemiah planned to rebuild the wall of Jerusalem; the Book of Nehemiah is a record of how he carried out that plan in spite of opposition. Dozens of proverbs deal with the topic of plans and the planning process. An example would be Proverbs 15:22 (NASB): "Without consultation, plans are frustrated, But with many counselors they succeed." God himself had a plan to save people from their sins and carried it out in specific way and at a specific time: "But when the fulness of the time came, God sent forth His Son, born of a woman, born under the Law, in order that He might redeem those who were under the Law, that we might receive the adoption as sons" (Gal. 4:4–5 NASB).

Importance of Planning. It is unfortunate that so many ministry leaders view planning as a secular process which should be avoided while doing God's work. They mistakenly believe that planning takes away from the freedom of the Holy Spirit to provide input. However, such a philosophy shows a blatant disregard for the numerous commands and examples given to us in the Scriptures. The Holy Spirit can also guide during the planning process. Planning provides direction and purpose, is a means to establish goals and steps to achieve them, helps us to be good stewards of the resources (people, money, and things) God has given us, and helps us avoid crisis management.

Basic Steps in Planning. Bower outlines a general pattern for planning (1964, 61–65). The stages are: (1) Define the problem. (2) Suggest possible solutions. (3) Gather relevant data about the past and present (i.e., survey the group involved, interview people, study records) to confirm or reject solutions. (4) Forecast the future. What will the situation be fifteen years from now? Where do you want to be or what do you want to accomplish? (5) Make the decision based on the results of the previous steps. (6) Prepare your plans by stating objectives that are specific and measurable and determining when to evaluate progress along the way. (7) Accept the plans. The board, committee, group, or congregation should vote or agree on the plans so they have ownership of them. (8) Secure necessary funds and personnel to carry out the plans.

LIN JOHNSON

Bibliography. R. K. Bower (1964), *Administering Christian Education;* K. Gangel (1989), *Feeding and Leading.*

Plato (427?–346 B.C.). Greek philosopher. Born in Athens to aristocratic parents, from 407 to 399 he was a student of Socrates. His early writings, *Dialogues,* are a dramatic presentation consisting of an informal conversation involving several people. Early on, Socrates is the principal character who shows how inadequate the views that are proposed are.

At the death of Socrates, Plato became disillusioned with politics and spent the next few years traveling, as tradition has it, in Egypt, Cyrene, Sicily, and parts of Italy. He returned to Athens in 387 and founded the Academy in the garden of a gymnasium. Plato spent the rest of his life teaching at the Academy except for two trips to Syracuse. This was upon invitation with the intent of creating the philosopher-king. He believed that all kings should be philosophers.

The *Dialogues* culminate in the *Republic.* For Plato, the ideal state parallels the tripartite arrangement of the soul. First, there are the workers who provide economic necessities. Next are the guardians who defend the state. Third, those with elite knowledge are the rulers. The cooperation of the parts leads to justice. Government and medicine are for experts. A few persons through education will be elevated so as to understand the "good" and this will give them the duty if not the will to rule.

For Plato, forms are distinct from things. Objects of sense perception are not real. It is the objects of thought, the forms, that are completely true. Apprehension of forms is knowledge. Knowledge comes from recollection rather than teaching. The things we see remind us of the forms. Very little worth is attributed to sense in the creation of knowledge. Thus there is a dualism in which the person is composed of soul and body. The soul is the form and the body is corporeal. The soul consists of appetites, spirit, and reason. Reason is the "god within man," and thus the person is able to contemplate the forms. Concerning the world, Plato describes in *Timaeus* how the Maker of the World created the world having both body and soul. Thus rationality is inherent in the world, which has always existed and always will. Since the Maker is good, the world also participates in the good.

Plato's Academy lasted over five hundred years and his philosophy endures to the present day. Many, such as Philo, Clement of Alexandria, Origen, Gregory of Nyssa, and Augustine, were helped in their understanding of theology by Plato. Plato went on to dominate Christian philosophy in the early Middle Ages until Aristotelian thought supplanted Platonism in the thirteenth century. The Renaissance brought a revival of Platonism. To this day, the teachings of Plato are utilized to harmonize reason and religion.

RICHARD E. ALLISON

See also ACADEMY; ARISTOTLE; AUGUSTINE; LIBERAL ARTS; MEDIEVAL EDUCATION; RENAISSANCE EDUCATION

Play, Role in Childhood Education. Play is an activity that proves productive for children. The past twenty years have been consumed in unabated scientific research on the subject in an attempt to understand the dynamics of development at work in children at play. The resulting literature base is voluminous, complicated, and at times conflicting in its reported findings.

While the processes of children's play are still being scrutinized, the results are solidly established. What is known is that play assists the development of prosocial attitudes, and can be instrumental in the formation of moral character.

Play for most children is the opposite of work. Thus play is characterized by being active, pleasurable, voluntarily chosen, episodic, meaningful, and at times, for older children, symbolic (in the sense of "this stick represents a horse").

Play is the chief way infants and young children learn. According to Piaget, children pass through predictable and increasingly complex patterns of play. Beginning with the sensorimotor stage, the infant learns through *senses* of smell, taste, touch, sound, and sight. They move through *practice play* (ages 2–7), to *symbolic play*, finally to *games with rules* (ages 7–11).

The central role of play in the educational process was established as early as Froebel (1887). Time and further research have only intensified that conclusion. Children learn not only cognitively from play but also experience significant growth socially as they learn to play with and not just alongside others. James Johnson (1990) describes play as not only contributing to the consolidation of recent learning for children but also as providing opportunity for new masteries and the acquisition of novel insights. Problem-solving skills can be developed through play.

Piaget described children's play as being predominately assimilation. On occasion when existing structures prove inadequate, the child is forced to accommodation, a process whereby reality is accounted for and structures are changed.

Skills learned in play provide a foundation for all future learning (Swedlow, 1986). Children learn to classify objects, make shapes, solve problems, develop eye-hand coordination, develop and refine gross and fine motor skills, and refine social and communication skills. Most important, they see themselves as learning

Play also serves as a window to a child's development. An observant adult can learn much about the life and issues of a child by examining choices, activities, and conversational patterns while children are engaged in free play. Emotional and mentally healthy children, even during a crisis, will play spontaneously and freely, expressing anger, sadness, and aggression toward inanimate objects like trucks (McFadden, 1986, 76). The abused or victimized child will hide to play, more often conceal anger until he or she erupts violently, appear untrusting of adults, and will display aggression and violence toward toys that represent people or loved objects (McFadden, 1986, 76).

The wise Christian educator will tap into this rich learning resource of play and design learning environments that are full of materials and experiences that are familiar to children's home and preschool life.

Christian education preschool classrooms will include blocks for building, books for exploring, puzzles, a learning center with objects from God's creation, along with a home living center and art activities. The home living center should include appliances found in homes, dolls and doll beds, dress-up clothes, and small child-size tables and chairs (Choun and Lawson, 1993).

The way children play develops according to social developmental stages. Children first play *solitary* (age 2), next *parallel* (age 3) alongside but not with others, then *associatively* (ages 3–4) exchanging ideas but still doing their own thing, and finally *cooperatively* (age 4–5) (McCandless, 1990).

The Christian teacher's role in using play is a purposeful one. Designing an activity based on an aim or outcome, the teacher actively participates in the play process. Guided conversations, initiated by the teacher, lead the student to discover and respond to truth. Linking words with actions maximizes learning and applying of biblical truth to practical real-life situations.

CHERYL L. FAWCETT

Bibliography. R. Choun and M. Lawson (1993), *The Complete Handbook for Children's Ministry;* J. Johnson (1990), *Children's Play and Learning,* pp. 213–34; J. B. McCandless (1990), *Harper's Encyclopedia of Religious Education,* p. 489; E. J. McFadden (1986), *Play: Working Partner of Growth;* R. Swedlow (1986), *Play: Working Partner of Growth,* pp. 29–34.

Policy. Statement of procedures or rules that guide decision making. Formulated by leaders, it is a general guide which is not designed to cover all the specific details of a situation. Broad in its application, it provides principles of operation. For example, the education committee may write a policy statement for teachers of children and teens, outlining several ways to deal with students who need to be disciplined during class sessions.

The purposes of policies in education include guidance for making decisions; answers to general questions that may arise; stability within a ministry; consistency and fairness so decisions are not impulsive or arbitrary; prevention of problems; and prevention of favoritism and capriciousness.

LIN JOHNSON

Postmodernism. While the label *postmodern* is often applied to anything which overturns traditional standards and is thus perceived to promote relativism (moral or otherwise), postmodern thought is much too varied and amorphous to count as a well-defined ism. The standard history of the term dates back to the 1950s, when literature and architecture that broke modern conventions began to be called postmodern. By the 1980s, the term was being applied to such contemporary continental European philosophers as Jacques Derrida, Michel Foucault, Hans-Georg Gadamer, Martin Heidegger, Emmanuel Levinas, and Jean-François Lyotard, as well as the American philosopher Richard Rorty. Curiously overlooked is the fact that the use of the term in theology dates back at least as far as the 1928 book by the Methodist bishop Bernard Iddings Bell entitled *Postmodernism.* Arguing that modern (or "liberal") theology was at that point already dead, he spells out his version of what comes after theological modernism in a way which remarkably prefigures current attempts at postmodern (or postliberal) theology.

What unites postmodern thinkers, however loosely, is their reaction to modern (which is to say Enlightenment) thought, a reaction which often takes the form of a simultaneous continuation of the modern project and the calling of that project into question. Thus it is difficult to draw a clear line between postmodern and modern philosophy, for modern thinkers often have postmodern aspects to their thought and postmodern thinkers often sound remarkably modern.

Modernity. Modern thought can be characterized by three closely connected elements. First, modern thinkers place a great emphasis on the *autonomy of the individual,* assuming that human beings both are and ought to be free to define themselves. The result is that modern thought significantly degrades tradition and authority. Second, modern thought tends to have *strong confidence in the powers of reason* in general and the rationality of the specific individual. Third, *reason is usually taken to be pure and objective.* One might not always reason in an objective way, but objective reason is an achievable goal.

All of these aspects are strikingly evident in the thought of Immanuel Kant. In what might be termed the "modernistic manifesto," the essay *What Is Enlightenment?* Kant tells us that the motto of the Enlightenment is *sapere aude,* loosely translated as "have the audacity to think for yourself." In place of the authority of tradition, one should set up one's own rationality as the authority. Even though Kant speaks of the limits of reason (and even of limiting reason to make room for faith), he still makes reason the supreme test. Thus, in *Religion Within the Bounds of Reason Alone,* Kant reconfigures Christian belief in a rationalistic way which reduces Christianity to little more than its moral claims. Since he conceives reason to be objective, Kant assumes that one is able to make rational decisions concerning philosophical and religious belief in an objective and detached manner.

Kant describes his basic philosophical reorientation as a Copernican Revolution but it really has exactly the opposite effect, for Kant puts human rationality, and thus the human subject, at the center of the universe. Instead of seeing the mind as a sponge that soaks up data, Kant depicts the human mind in the *Critique of Pure Reason* as organizing (and thus interpreting) our experience by way of basic ideas and concepts. In calling his philosophy transcendental, Kant implies two things: (1) that the organization by way of thought is necessary for there to be any experience at all (thus making human interpretation central to knowledge); and (2) that this structure of knowing is universal for people in all times and places. Of course, if we always interpret the world in a particular way, then we never know it as it really it is. Hence Kant makes his famous distinction between the phenomenal world (the world as it appears to us) and the noumenal world (the world as it is in itself apart from human interpretation). In effect, the emphasis in Kant is moved from truth in itself to truth as we know it.

Although Kant maintained that the mind's structure is universal and unchanging, during Kant's lifetime Johann Fichte argued that there can be many different ways of viewing the world and no one way can be declared correct. Thus our interpretation of the world is crucial to making the world what it is and the subject becomes absolutely central. The claim that there are different and changing ways of viewing the world is further radicalized by G. W. F. Hegel, who argues in the *Phenomenology of Spirit* that history can be viewed as a progression of various worldviews, none of which are absolutely true or false even though each reveals a certain degree of truth (some being more true than others). Truth is thus the sum total of perspectives.

Postmodernity. It is not without precedent, then, that Friedrich Nietzsche, who is arguably the first postmodern, puts the very notion of truth as universal and immutable into question at the beginning of *Beyond Good and Evil* when he writes, "Supposing truth to be a woman, what?" While Nietzsche can rightly be accused of being sexist, the implications of this statement are profound not only for our ability to know truth but also for the very definition or essence of truth. Nietzsche thinks that the claims of philosophy to give us truth have been pretentious and unfounded. At best, says Nietzsche, human knowledge of truth can be no more than simply a "perspective," not "the Truth." Yet, if there is only a multiplicity of perspectives or interpretations, does not Nietzsche effectively jettison the notion of truth and end up being incoherent, claiming something like the truth is that there is no truth? While Nietzsche makes extreme claims in his early philosophy, in his later works (e.g., *Twilight of the Idols*) it seems that his attack is directed more specifically toward truth in a Platonic sense, truth as defined in terms of simple essences removed from history and life. The result is that truth becomes contextual, historical, and empirical.

However postmodern Nietzsche is in regard to questioning the truth and rationality, he is perhaps the apotheosis of the modern view of the self. Nietzsche's exultation of the self can be seen as partly in reaction to the decline of Christianity. On the one hand, by pronouncing the death of God in *The Gay Science* he sees himself as simply stating the fact that Christianity is no longer a vital cultural force. While Nietzsche vehemently criticizes Christianity (particularly in *Antichrist*), it is not always easy to tell how much those criticisms are directed against Christianity itself or a weak version of Christianity (influenced by Kant) which held to its forms without holding to its substance (for a critique of theological liberalism, see Nietzsche's essay on David Strauss in *Untimely Meditations*). On the other hand, Nietzsche sees this decline as the opportunity to replace Christianity with something which affirms life by promoting the will to power (an idea introduced in *Thus Spoke Zarathustra* and developed in *The Will to Power*). Christianity squelches our innate desire to have power over everything around us,

but proper human flourishing for Nietzsche results when we unleash this will. The masters or overmen are precisely those who choose their own values and appropriate whatever they desire, while slaves are those who adopt such values as sympathy and humility. Nietzsche's view of the overman is essentially the romantic conception of the artistic genius, the lone creator who flaunts all societal conventions and answers to no one.

Although Martin Heidegger intended in *Being and Time* to concentrate on the question of the meaning of being, his unusual portrayal of the human person has actually had more influence. Heidegger emphasizes the historical and cultural aspects which permeate understanding and knowledge, as well as seriously undermines such basic philosophical dualisms as subject/object and realism/idealism. Since human beings for Heidegger are always connected to the world around them so that each helps define the other, neither realism nor idealism adequately describes their relationship. In his later texts, such as *The Onto-theo-logical Constitution of Metaphysics*, Heidegger makes the distinctly postmodern move of questioning the very project of metaphysics (theorizing concerning being), arguing that it has been characterized by what he terms ontotheology.

Although Heidegger's own religious beliefs were not exactly clear, his comments on ontotheologizing are instructive. Virtually all Western metaphysicians have placed God at the end of the chain of being, says Heidegger, taking God to be the greatest being upon which the entire foundation rests. While this move might seem admirable, the problem for Heidegger is that it ends up being a way to control God by making him into an explanation to fit the philosopher's purposes and thus ends up being the ultimate expression of the will to power. In the *Letter on Humanism*, Heidegger expands his critique of metaphysics to reason in general, claiming that what philosophers have termed reason turns out to be a way of controlling the world and elevating human beings. In place of this setting up of the self as autonomous and almighty, Heidegger suggests a heteronomous or de-centered self. In place of philosophizing (the claim to give us the world as it really is), Heidegger suggests a kind of poetry which thinks about being and truth but neither attempts to control them nor makes pretentious claims to know them.

Although Heidegger was concerned with language, in Hans-Georg Gadamer and Jacques Derrida this emphasis becomes central. Whereas Derrida focuses more on the problems of language, Gadamer is optimistic about the prospects of understanding and truth. Explicitly reacting to the modern move which makes the individual into the sole authority, in *Truth and Method* Gadamer suggests the need for a rehabilitation of the concepts of tradition, authority, and prejudice. Kant's ideal of thinking for oneself, says Gadamer, is both impossible and undesirable, for we are highly dependent upon the judgments and ideas passed on to us by tradition. Thus the self never stands alone. Further, there may well be authority (such as the Bible) that can and should be recognized as legitimate, rather than being simply rejected in order to set oneself up as the authority. Although we must always be willing to examine the assumptions and prejudices of our culture, Gadamer recognizes that our thinking is always closely connected to our own historical and cultural horizon, meaning that reason and understanding are never pure. The fact that understanding is always contextual means that we will never be able to understand ancient texts or the thought of other cultures in precisely the same way as the author and original audience understood them (since our context is not the same), but we can understand in a way which is similar enough (through what Gadamer terms a fusion of horizons) to permit genuine understanding. Gadamer does not think that reason's dependence upon culture and tradition is necessarily to be lamented; it is simply the way the human mind works.

Derrida's early texts such as *Speech and Phenomena* and *Of Grammatology* focus on the ideality of linguistic meaning and the relation of language to things. By way of his extremely careful method of reading known as deconstruction, which is designed to illuminate the assumptions and values implied by a text, Derrida questions the ideal of knowing things just as they are and shows that the mediation of knowledge by language makes this ideal impossible. Thus language presents us not with the thing in its fullness (either as phenomena or noumena) but with only a "trace" of it. Derrida's deconstruction of binary oppositions (e.g., subject/object, male/female) and his assertion that language refers to nothing outside itself has caused some to conclude that his theory of language results in utter equivocation. While this charge may well be laid against some of his followers (who have often used deconstruction as a tool against all absolutes), Derrida himself seems to hold that meaning is constituted both by the thing (through the trace) and by the context of signifiers, resulting in meaning which, though never purely univocal (since it partially relies on the play of signifiers), is still stable enough to make communication possible. Given this conception of meaning, any knowledge of truth for Derrida must inevitably be contextual and historical (and the implication would seem to be that the idea of truth itself as ideal and immutable could no longer be held).

In a surprising move for both his followers and critics, Derrida's later philosophy turns to questions of morality and faith (though he claims that the early work makes way for these later reflections). In *Force of Law: The Mystical Foundation of Authority*, Derrida claims not only that justice is beyond deconstruction but that deconstruction is justice, since deconstruction illuminates the aporia (or ultimate undecidability) of all decisions. Every instance of justice, says Derrida, both instantiates and does injustice to the ideal of justice, since all human attempts at justice fail when held up to the ideal of justice. Derrida turns to negative theology and the aporia of God-talk in *How to Avoid Speaking: Denials* by considering the ability of human speech to capture God. Using the notion of the trace (which makes something partially but never fully present), Derrida argues that there is a strange logic at work in talk about God. While we want to affirm certain things about God, there is a danger of taking those affirmations too seriously, for all human statements made about God fail to describe him adequately. Derrida continues these themes in *The Gift of Death*, where he argues that true morality (which he takes to be exemplified by Christianity) demands a sacrifice of oneself for the other (thus the idea of dying for the other). Using the account of Abraham and Isaac as a basis, Derrida reconfigures moral responsibility in terms of responsibility to persons rather than rules, arguing that truly moral action can give no ultimate justification of itself and so ends up being a gift to the other.

As a devout Jew, Emmanuel Levinas counters the centrality of the self in modern thought by claiming that morality requires decentering the self and placing the other first. A truly ethical relation to the other is noneconomic or nonreciprocal in that one expects nothing in return. In *Totality and Infinity* (and in *Ethics and Infinity*, a book of interviews with Levinas), he depicts not only modern thought but the entire Western philosophical project as exemplifying the desire to control or totalize everything (whether truth, other people, or the ultimate Other, God) by making them mere components of one's own conceptual system. Yet Levinas argues that the other always ultimately escapes our grasp and that our attempts to master the other result in injustice. Whereas philosophy has traditionally seen either metaphysics or epistemology as foundational, Leinvas thinks that ethics is truly first philosophy. Thus reason for Levinas is not something possible on our own but arises only in the context of community with the other. In response to the assumed objectivity of reason by modernism, the thought of Michel Foucault focuses on the cultural, temporal, and institutional particularities of rationality. Arguing that concepts and ways of thinking are intimately connected to our interests and purposes (a thesis reminiscent of Fichte), Foucault is particularly concerned with how knowledge relates to power (e.g., in *Power/*

Knowledge). The problem, for Foucault, is that knowledge is a dangerous tool (as Foucault puts it, "everything is dangerous") which can be used for both good and bad purposes."

For instance, societies establish power by dividing practices such as the separation of the normal from the abnormal and thus are able to promote a particular vision of society. Foucault argues that even what we consider to be objective criteria develop over time as the result of chance and particular interests. Thus Foucault's method of philosophizing (described and illustrated in *The Order of Things* and *The Archaeology of Knowledge*) is to provide a history of thought and practices. The question which disturbs Foucault is not that of whether human knowledge can be said to have progressed in any significant sense, but what the effect of that quest for knowledge has been. Although Foucault is (rightly) criticized for assuming that a power play lies behind everything, his philosophy is an important reminder that the quest for knowledge has not always been inspired by pure motives. Whether Foucault was a moral and epistemological relativist (however aberrant his personal life) is open to debate, though his way of philosophizing need not necessarily lead to that result.

In the American context, many of the preceding themes can be found in the thought of Richard Rorty. In *Philosophy and the Mirror of Nature* he attacks the idea that human knowledge can mirror nature and dismisses foundationalism (the ideal of providing a foundation for human knowledge) as a vain hope. Often quoted as defining truth as "what our peers will let us get away with saying," Rorty speaks of himself as an ironist, someone who holds to certain beliefs all the while knowing that they are not true in any sense other than the pragmatic sense of "useful for the moment." Whereas in his early philosophy Rorty still held to the idea of philosophical argumentation, in his later philosophy (e.g., *Contingency, Irony, and Solidarity*) he claims that there can be no real arguments but simply "redescriptions" of things, poetic metaphors that make positions seem appealing. Although Rorty is usually (and rightly) labeled a relativist, he thinks any such terms as true rationality or relativism ultimately make no sense in a context where there is no God and nothing is sacrosanct because there is no meaningful alternative (which the term *relative* requires). Rorty's postmodern view of the self takes over the Nietzschean idea of poetization of the self but without the romantic overtones. The self can never be completely oneself, for the self is but a tissue of contingencies which are highly dependent upon the influences of one historical and cultural context. Yet Rorty thinks that the result of this recognition of contingency is the need of a solidarity which promotes community.

Probably the most prominent Christian postmodern philosopher is Jean-Luc Marion, who provides a fine example of how postmodern insights can be applied to Christian thought. In *God without Being*, he considers what kind of talk about God is appropriate. Given that God can never be fully present to consciousness, Marion argues that our claims to knowledge of God always run the risk of placing a conceptual schema on God which creates him in our own image. Arguing that God is above even being (so that God is not defined as the greatest possible being), Marion affirms not the God of the philosophers but the God of faith. While idols are our pictures or concepts of God which reflect us rather than God, icons point us beyond ourselves to God. For Marion, any concept of God which claims to present us with God in his fullness is idolatrous, for God always escapes our grasp. In contrast to idols, icons give us a trace of God, who is the ultimate saturated phenomenon in the sense that there is so much there that no concepts could capture him. God exists, says Marion, but not as we exist: his being is love and he is beyond the realm of being (*ousia*) and predication. In effect, Marion attempts to steer a middle course between bad silence (when all talk about God is silenced) and unguarded chatter. A wise silence recognizes the limitations of one speech and attempts to say only what one can legitimately say, the question being not so much what one says of God but how. Writing from a Catholic sacramental perspective, Marion makes the Eucharist central: we meet Christ in the breaking of the bread, where Christ is present to us as a gift of which we are not the authors and which we do not possess.

Conclusion. One must beware of any simple acceptance or rejection of either modern or postmodern thinking. On the one hand, the legacy of modern thought has probably been more negative than positive for Christian belief. While the Enlightenment emphasis on critical inspection of one's beliefs is admirable in a sense, the goal of thinking for oneself has often been linked to an agenda. As Gadamer bluntly points out, Enlightenment critique is primarily directed against the religious tradition of Christianity, the Bible. Further, not only does the modern conception of the self as autonomous seem incorrect descriptively, it also is incompatible with a Christian view of the person in which individuals find their identity as members of a community. Finally, although Scripture clearly affirms the value of human rationality as part of what it means to be made in God's image, the modern confidence in human reason is deeply at odds with the biblical emphasis on the limits of human ability.

On the other hand, the postmodern reaction is sometimes equally as questionable and incompatible with Christianity. We have seen that some postmodern thinkers, such as Nietzsche, take the modern conception of the self to its absolute extreme. Moreover, the rejection of the modern pretentions of human reason is sometimes so severe as to eliminate the possibility of knowing truth at all. Yet, while postmodern thought has elements which are not supportive of Christian belief, there are others which are of significant value for Christians. In particular, Marion, Gadamer, Levinas, and Derrida (at least in his later thought) have much to offer. Their emphasis on a decentered self is a helpful corrective to the presumptuous claims of modernity and resonates with Christian teachings concerning the danger of pride. Even a thinker like Nietzsche, however antagonistic he may be toward Christianity, can be instructive, for his penetrating critique of the failings of Christians is sometimes all too true. Further, the postmodern denial of the pure objectivity of reason is not so far away from the Christian idea that knowing the truth is closely linked to being a virtuous person, since sin can easily cloud our minds. While the questioning of the power and purity of reason by postmodern thinkers is appropriate, one need not go to the extreme of concluding that there is only contingency. There is a great difference between the idea that all human reason is permeated by contingency (or historicality) and the idea that human reason is merely contingent and in no sense universally valid. Christians can heartily endorse the postmodern recognition of the limits of rationality (and the humility of spirit that recognition should entail) without concluding that there either is no truth or that we are incapable of knowing truth.

BRUCE E. BENSON

Bibliography. D. A. Carson (1996), *The Gagging of God;* D. Lyon, *Postmodernism;* J-F. Lyotard (1984), *The Postmodern Condition;* idem (1993), *The Postmodern Explained;* C. Norris (1990), *What's Wrong with Postmodernism?;* R. C. Solomon (1988), *Continental Philosophy Since 1750.*

Practicum. Complement to theoretical instruction that seeks to test classroom ideas and insights in vocational or subject-related life situations. The practicum is frequently deemed a necessary component for a balanced educational approach and as a general concept seems congruent with the ancient Semitic understanding of learning. In ancient Hebrew, the connotation of *yada* (know) was "to experience, to encounter." Indeed, the concept embraced the whole understanding of personhood, intimating the intellect, emotions, and psychomotor facets.

Recognizing the limitations of mere classroom-related content, many contemporary educators in church and formal classroom settings have attempted to develop instruction that intersects with application. A class with a biblical compassion component, for instance, might reinforce its curriculum by taking students to the inner city to build affordable housing for the poor. Christian education degree programs frequently seek to offer students opportunities for educational service in local churches. A class with a social action emphasis might encourage the student to become politically active in a nearby locale.

In some educational programs theoretical and practical aspects of the curriculum are almost wholly segregated. Many of the courses deal with theoretical or theological aspects of reality, while a few will actually engage the majority of student time in a field of practical application, using concepts discovered in the classroom in settings of performance. In recent years there has been much criticism of the isolation of practical application of theory from theory itself. The integration of thinking and doing is considered critical in some burgeoning paradigms of education and is viewed by a growing number of educators as a frontier for improvement in Christian education at all age levels.

In practicum situations, the mentor or field supervisor is critical to the process of learning and in the best situations observes, critiques, encourages, and instructs to help the student improve performance skills. Furthermore, another key component of such praxis is the opportunity to reflect on the practicum at various intervals in order to consider revisions of opinion and update perceptions. Group discussions and conversations with the mentor or teacher frequently provide such reflection, and today many Christian education programs have implemented the repetition of classroom-practice-reflection in an effort to effectively equip students for service in the local church.

MATT FRIEDEMAN

Bibliography. W. L. Bateman (1990), *Open to Question: The Art of Teaching and Learning by Inquiry.*

Praxis. Way of knowing; an epistemology that links both theory and practice, and requires critical reflection upon the past, present, and future. Understanding praxis is made more difficult when some use the English word *practice* as its translation.

Primarily, praxis is an adult education approach because it requires critical thinking and problem posing on the part of the student. In adult education circles there is continuing debate over what the role of adult education should be: a largely cognitive process, or a means for social and societal change? In the latter, praxis is a critical examination of a historical struggle for freedom. This involves unmasking assumptions and analyzing power relationships. In the past, adult education has been a force for social equity. That debate has not generally entered discussions of evangelical Christian education, where Christian applications are largely confined to the individual or to one's own family.

In the twentieth century Paulo Freire, a Brazilian educator, renewed interest in praxis as an educational approach. He criticized what he called the "banking" concept of education, in which the teacher as well as the student thought of education as imparting knowledge from a superior to an inferior. Two other terms associated with Freire were *conscientization*, a process of examining closely sociocultural reality, and *praxis*, a term meaning the polarity between theory and practice. Accordingly, education must include both *praxis* and *conscientization* to change consciousness. Why this emphasis on the educational context? It is illusionary that women and men can be transformed through educational processes while oppressive social structures remain intact.

Clearly Freire emphasizes the practice of freedom and emancipation in education activity. The intention is no less than the transformation of society as well as individuals.

The Roman Catholic religious educator Thomas Groome is the foremost proponent of praxis as a religious education process. He calls his five-movement process *shared praxis*. Accordingly, religious education is a life pilgrimage in which we assume responsibility for appropriating our past and purposefully set out to create our future as we struggle and live together in the present.

According to Groome, religious education follows five movements: naming present action, sharing the participants' stories and visions, comparing the Christian community's story and vision, and a dialectical hermeneutic between the community and individual's story and vision. In this process Christians dynamically engage in their own and the church's past, present, and future.

Accordingly, the values of praxis support a biblical form of "knowing," form a bridge between the past and future, and address both the individual and society, making a strong ethical statement through educational processes.

How is this different from what we have been doing all along? First, ask probing, insightful questions. Second, ask questions that lead class members to search within their minds and experiences. Third, include in the process both thoughts and feelings.

JIM WALTER

Bibliography. P. Freire (1972), *Pedagogy of the Oppressed;* T. H. Groome (1980), *Christian Religious Education: Sharing Our Story and Vision.*

Prayer. Prayer is a universal practice of all religions. Christian prayer, however, is distinctive since it is prayer in Christ that rises out of an understanding of the Triune God. It is profoundly theological, requiring growing knowledge of God, and practical, affecting the way a person lives. Prayer requires both thinking about the nature of prayer, and engaging in the practice of prayer.

Understanding the Nature of Prayer. From a general perspective, prayer can be described as the human response, made in various ways, to God's Word and has both a broad and narrow meaning.

In its broad sense "prayer refers to the Christian's fundamental attitude toward and relationship with God" (Chan, 1998, 127). The essence of prayer is the person's relationship with God, self, and others, rather than with asking or pleading with God to give and to act. Prayer, as Clement of Alexandria maintained, "is keeping company with God" (Houston, 1996, 9). Its purpose is to know God in a growing relationship of loving obedience. Therefore, prayer is sharing in the divine nature, and being transformed into the image of Christ. Prayer is a way of life lived in intimate relationship with God, resulting in transformation. In this sense, the person can "pray without ceasing" (1 Thess. 5:17 NRSV), since prayer is far more than taking time out of each day to converse to God. As such, it is an ongoing relationship with God, requiring a growing knowledge of God. Prayer, therefore, is intensely theological and personal.

In the narrow sense, "prayer refers to specific acts of the soul in communion with God" (Chan, 1998, 128). It is what the Christian says and does when she or he prays. Acts of prayer have been classified as adoration, including praise, confession, thanksgiving, and supplication or petition. However, these acts are always a response to first hearing God speak or seeing him act. This is clearly the nature of prayer in the *Psalter*, and thus Peterson (1989) perceptively entitled his book on Psalms, *Answering God.* The Psalmists first perceived God speaking and acting in the daily experiences of life and answered in honest and humble speech. Understanding prayer in both this broad and narrow sense has obvious implications for the practice of prayer.

Engaging in the Practice of Prayer. Because prayer is both relationship with God and specific acts, its practice involves both thinking and doing. Teresa of Àvila insisted that "If it is prayer at all, it must be accompanied by thought" (1988, 6). Paul made the same point when he claimed, "I will pray with the spirit, but I will pray with the mind also" (1 Cor. 14:15 NRSV).

Thinking about prayer begins not with thoughts about prayer itself, but with thoughts about the character of God, about the person of the prayer, and about the content of the prayer. True Christian prayer begins with theology, what the person thinks and believes about God. Devotion to God, an essential requirement for the life of prayer, will only grow out of our theological understanding of God. This means that prayer is related to God's revealed Word and should, therefore, arise out of that Word as the prayer prayerfully reflects and wonders, "Who are you, God?" True Christian prayer begins with the desire to know God and humbly submit to him.

Thinking about prayer, however, is no substitute for practicing prayer. Experienced prayers have consistently maintained that a person learns to pray by praying. For this reason it is helpful for people to make use of written prayers, both in Scripture and in the Christian tradition. The Book of Psalms is recognized as the prayer book of the people of God. Peterson (1989) describes the Psalter as "God's gift to train us in prayer that is comprehensive and honest" (3). Praying systematically and regularly through the Psalter teaches God's people how to pray, and also about God. For centuries, Christians have prayed Scripture, turning what they learned into a matter of prayer and meditation before God. Numerous Christian traditions have recorded prayers published in various forms that continue to teach people to pray. Praying written prayers, either from Scripture or the Christian tradition will enhance extemporaneous praying and will guard prayers from trivializing speech to God, helping them to heed the warning of Ecclesiastes to "let your words be few" when entering God's presence (5:1–2 NRSV).

While prayer is a universal human activity and can arise spontaneously, it still needs to be taught. The disciples recognized this and thus requested "Lord, teach us to pray." It is the task of the Christian educator to take up the challenge and teach others to pray.

JACKIE L. SMALLBONES

Bibliography. S. Chan (1998), *Spiritual Theology;* J. Houston (1996), *The Transforming Power of Prayer;* K. Leech (1980), *True Prayer;* E. H. Peterson (1989), *Answering God;* St. Teresa of Àvila, edited by H. Backhouse (1988), *Interior Castle.*

Prayer, Teaching of. Prayer is an essential part of the Christian life that is best taught by modeling and learned by practice (Luke 11:1). The numerous references in the Bible to prayer (mentioned in sixty-two of its sixty-six books) attest to its importance for the believer (Constable, 1995, 5). However, in spite of its importance and wide usage, there is no single passage of Scripture that specifically defines prayer. Nevertheless, from the many different references to prayer, two distinct but related understandings surface.

The first and most common understanding is that prayer is an activity in which the believer communicates with God (Matt. 6:6–13). This communication is to be two-way, involving both speaking and listening. These two qualities are essential for the development of a healthy relationship between the believer and God. When prayer is reduced to one-way communication, the growth of the relationship is stunted. Furthermore, the Bible teaches that this two-way communication is to be characterized by the believer's willingness to approach God in an attitude of humility and dependence. Such an attitude is best accomplished when the believer remembers that the very desire to pray is but a response to God first initiating the relationship (1 John 4:10). A correct concept of God also enhances this attitude of dependence and humility. Jesus taught his disciples to imagine God in a very intimate and personal manner, as "Abba" or in contemporary English, as "Daddy," when they prayed (Luke 11:2). For first-century Jewish believers, imagining God in such a personal and intimate manner was not only new, but necessary for the growth of their relationship with God.

Another characteristic of this two-way communication with God is the believer's uncensored honesty in expressing needs, feelings, and desires while at the same time recognizing with thankfulness God's grace, mercy, and majesty. David exemplified this characteristic when he expressed his feelings of love, anger, thankfulness, loneliness, fear, and repentance (Pss. 62:1–2; 74:1). Dishonesty in communication with God is the opposite of this characteristic and is a hindrance to building a healthy relationship with him (Matt. 6:7–8).

The second understanding of prayer that surfaces in the Bible is that it is an attitude or way of life oriented toward God (1 Thess. 5:17; Col. 4:2). This kind of prayer entails learning how to live with an awareness of God's constant presence. This second understanding of prayer is related to the first in the sense that prayer as a way of life is dependent upon two-way communication. The primary characteristic of this second understanding of prayer is the replacement of monologue with dialogue in the mind of the believer. The believer learns how to constantly converse with God in her or his mind throughout the activities of the day rather than live in monologue with self (Nouwen and Foster, 1997, 118).

The above understandings of prayer remind the believer that it is not an end in itself. Prayer serves as a vehicle to cultivate and enhance the believer's relationship with God. It allows the believer to grow in companionship with God. In prayer, God transforms the believer to think his thoughts and to desire what he desires (Foster, 1978, 33). As this kind of growth occurs, the believer can make requests fully knowing that she or he is asking according to God's will (Matt. 7:7).

A final important teaching about prayer covers those things that hinder prayer. Dishonesty on the part of the believer has already been mentioned. Another hindrance to prayer is wrong motive (James 4:3). Wrong motives indicate that the believer is seeking to bring God into line with her or him will rather than letting God bring her into line with his. Closely related to wrong motive is unbelief (James 1:6; Mark 5:25–34). Unbelief is self-defeating because it indicates that either the believer is not seeking God's will or else lacks confidence that God is able to answer the prayer. A final barrier to prayer is a lack of compassion (1 Cor. 13:1). The failure to empathize with those for whom the requests are made is not the kind of supplication that grows out of a believer's intimate relationship with her heavenly Father (Foster, 1978, 35).

DAVID BRISBEN

Bibliography. H. T. Blackaby and C. V. King (1994), *Experiencing God;* D. A. Carson (1984), *Teach Us to Pray: Prayer in the Bible and the World;* T. L. Constable (1995), *Talking to God: What the Bible Teaches about Prayer;* R. Foster (1978), *Celebration of Discipline;* R. Foster and H. Nouwen (1997), *Leadership* 18, no. 1 (1997): 112–18.

Preaching. Proclaiming the Word of God in order to inspire belief. The Old Testament records that the law was read to the people of Israel during the Feast of Tabernacles every seventh year (Deut. 31:9–13). The purpose of this proclamation of God's Word was so that the people of Israel, as well as Gentiles living among them, would "listen and learn to fear the Lord your God and follow carefully all the words of this law" (Deut. 31:12). God-fearing kings of Israel commanded public reading of the law. Jehosophat sent officials and Levites to teach "throughout Judah, taking with them the Book of the Law of the Lord; they went around to all the towns of Judah and taught the people" (2 Chron. 17:9). The Old Testament also records that once the people of Israel were settled into the rebuilt Jerusalem, Ezra gathered them to hear a reading of God's law. "They read from the Book of the Law of God, making it clear and giving the meaning so that the people could understand what was being read" (Neh. 8:8).

The New Testament uses various terms to describe preaching, including "to herald," "to proclaim," and "to teach." Paul affirmed the importance of preaching the Word in his letters to the churches in Colossae and Thessalonica, in which he urged that his messages be read to the believers (1 Thess. 5:27; Col. 4:16). In his letter to Timothy, Paul urged him to entrust what he had heard from Paul "to reliable men who will also be qualified to teach others" (2 Tim. 2:2).

In A.D. 150, Justin Martyr recorded that preaching based on Scripture was a regular feature of Sunday worship. Preaching fell in and out of fashion through the centuries. Notable preachers included such men as Origen, Augustine, and Thomas Aquinas. Reformers, including Luther, Calvin, and Zwingli, required that public worship services include preaching.

Today, a sermon is featured in most Sunday worship services. The typical sermon explores a biblical passage and applies it to the lives of the listeners. Church growth expert Elmer Towns (1995) describes preaching as either positive or negative motivation. A prophecy-oriented preacher will tend to lead a church according to the law that says "that which gets inspected gets done." The preacher who emphasis is exhortation will motivate because "that which gets rewarded gets done." Both preaching orientations are needed, says Towns, if the local church is to grow (317).

Along with the adult-level sermon, some churches choose to feature a "children's sermon." Usually based on a story or object lesson, the children's sermon is designed to instruct on their own level children who attend adult worship services. At its best, the children's sermon reaches not only the youngsters but also the adults. At worst, the children's sermon becomes merely entertainment.

ROBERT J. CHOUN

Bibliography. T. Cully and K. B. Cully, eds. (1990), *Harper's Encyclopedia of Religious Education;* E. F. Harrison, ed. (1960), *Baker's Dictionary of Theology;* E. Towns, ed. (1995), *Evangelism and Church Growth.*

Prejudice. Judgment based on a limited number of observations, generalized to all members of a group, resulting in consistent behavior toward the group. It is based on unsupported judgment and usually carries an emotionally negative connotation. Allport says prejudice occurs when one meets the conditions of overcategorization and irreversible misconceptions. Overcategorization is attributing to all members of a group the characteristics of a few. Irreversible misconceptions occur when a person persists in those beliefs after receiving evidence to the contrary. In other words, prejudgment has turned to prejudice. Types of prejudice include ethnic, racial, religious, social class, and gender.

Scripture gives several examples of prejudice. Jesus told the story of the priest and Levite who passed by a wounded man in the story of the good Samaritan (Luke 10:29–37) to illustrate ethnic or social class prejudice. The Holy Spirit rebuked Peter in Acts 10 for his racial and ethnic prejudices against the Gentiles. Jesus countered the gender prejudices of his day when he defended a woman caught in adultery (John 8:3–11). The apostle Paul summarized the position of the church and the task of Christian education when he said, "You are all one in Christ Jesus" (Gal. 3:28). Oneness in Christ rules out prejudice in the life and teaching of the Christian educator.

PHILIP BUSTRUM

Bibliography. G. Allport, *The Nature of Prejudice.*

Premarital Sex. *See* Abstinence.

Premising Data. Term used in the field of planning management to describe key elements of an organization's internal and external environment for the purpose of making well-informed assumptions or forecasts about future planning.

Both internal and external environmental factors include prevailing policies and existing plans that control the basic nature of the organization. For example, Christian education program planning is, among other things, affected internally by a group's doctrinal distinctives and polity and externally by the legal mandates of its community.

Koontz and Weihrich (1993) write, "A distinction should be drawn between forecasts that are planning premises and forecasts that are translated into future expectancies, usually in financial terms, from actual plans developed" (185). For example, demographics and growth projections of one's external community provide premises upon which future plans can be developed in Christian education programming. An internal decision to expand Christian education facilities, budget, or staffing translates planning into expectations. In the first case, the forecast is a prerequisite of planning; in the second case, the forecast is a result of planning.

RONALD W. FREEMAN

Bibliography. H. Koontz and H. Weihrich (1993), *Management: A Global Perspective.*

Presbyter. *See* Elder.

Preschool Education. *Biblical and Historical Background.* In one of his letters to Timothy, the apostle Paul urges the young man to continue in what he has learned, saying that "from infancy" Timothy had known the Holy Scriptures (2 Tim. 3:15). Like many children of his time, Timothy received home schooling in religious matters beginning at an early age. Parents are commanded in Scripture to take charge of the religious education of their sons and daughters. In Deuteronomy 6:6–7, Moses' instructions are for parents to talk about God in connection with everyday experiences from morning until night. In the centuries that followed, religious instruction in early childhood was to become a controversial subject.

With the opening of the New World, European educational traditions came to America. The education of children, except for privileged families, was an informal arrangement. Middle-class families had to join forces to employ teachers. A one-room schoolhouse could include 3-year-olds along with 18-year-olds. For many, education was strictly vocational. Children of poverty, including preschoolers, were pressed into the labor force. In nineteenth-century America, a child of 5 or 6 might be expected to work a sixteen-hour day in a factory.

Because so many children were working six days a week, special schools were opened on Sundays for instruction in religion and basic literacy. The concept of this Sunday school began in England and quickly spread to America, where it could focus on the Bible. By the turn of the century, the United States had a system of public education, but it did not officially include preschoolers.

The early church, whose views on the sanctity of life helped curb widespread infanticide, was responsible for the founding of many Christian schools. In colonial America, the labor force was supplemented by young orphans sent from England against their will. The Puritan understanding of the young child was that he or she was inherently sinful and incapable of conversion until the age of accountability. Until that point, the extent of the child's religious instruction was to be focused on the miserable state of his or her hopeless condition. With the rise of romanticism, the pendulum of thought on the subject swung to the opposite extreme. Children, as part of nature, must be inherently good. This benevolent view brought childhood education into the spotlight. Philosophers and educators studied not only the content of learning, but also the process. The special needs of children and the importance of play in education came into focus.

The first kindergartens began in Germany in 1837. The concept spread to the United States, where private organizations sponsored kindergartens to teach the children of German immigrants. Waves of immigration at the turn of the century brought families whose young children had to work or remain at home unsupervised while parents worked. Charitable organizations opened kindergartens to provide these children with literacy and care. In 1873, the kindergartens were made part of the public school system. In the early 1900s laws limiting child labor and requiring school attendance boosted school enrollment.

Early childhood education achieved new status. Researchers and educators made improvements in curriculum that tailored content and methods to the special needs of young children. Day nurseries and nursery schools opened in the 1930s to provide care and instruction for children too young for kindergarten. Today many churches, even those who do not sponsor elementary schools, provide nursery school and kindergarten.

Understanding the Preschooler. Far from being a miniature adult, the preschooler is an individual with special needs and tremendous potential. Structured programs for early childhood education usually begin at age 3, but research shows that age-appropriate instruction is crucial right from infancy. Lifelong attitudes toward God and his church are formed during the early childhood years.

Intellectually, the child is a literal thinker. Because abstract terms can easily be misunderstood, teachers must avoid symbolism and link abstract concepts to real-life experiences. Lessons with layers of meanings, such as parables, will prove difficult for young children who can consider only one concept at a time. Programs that are scheduled back-to-back, such as Sunday school followed by children's church, should focus on the same theme. Because many preschoolers will be able to repeat a concept or word without grasping its meaning, teachers must ask questions that check understanding. Repetition of verses, songs, and stories that grow tedious for adults are helpful to preschoolers with short memories. Like learners of any age, preschoolers learn best by doing. They must actively participate in the learning process. Models of behavior are especially important at this age. Teachers can even model correct speech patterns. Because they have little understanding of history or geography, lessons that require any grasp of biblical chronology will prove too difficult for preschoolers.

Emotionally, preschoolers are egocentric. Things are important only if they relate directly to the children and their needs. One of the challenges facing preschool teachers is the socialization of the child. Preschoolers find it difficult to consider the viewpoint or welfare of others. Sharing is a major issue. Another challenge of early childhood is the delay of self-gratification. New feelings of independence clash with adult-imposed restrictions that require self-control. Teachers must set firm but reasonable limits on behavior and try to affirm and encourage good behavior through specific praise. Even the concept of guilt is difficult for a child of this age group. To a preschooler, guilt is not associated with bad intentions, but only with getting caught in the act and punished. By relating morality to age-appropriate situations, teachers can guide children beyond this stage to the level where right and wrong are recognized as moral absolutes. The level beyond that applies those absolutes to behavior, a stage few adults reach.

The rapid physical growth of infancy and the toddler years slows down during the preschool years. The brain and the connections between its cells continue to develop as the brain becomes more specialized. Large muscles come under control, even though fine motor skills are not yet developed. Preschoolers have improved eyesight and eye-hand coordination.

Play, although it appears purely physical, serves many developmental needs. As preschoolers move from solitary play to cooperative play, they develop communication and socialization skills. They practice problem solving, exercise creativity, and play adult roles. Through dramatic play, they may be able to see a situation from another's viewpoint. Play is basically the business of childhood.

The Scriptures tell us that each of us must become as a child to enter the kingdom of heaven. This is obviously not a reference to physical stature, mental development, or sociability, but to a trusting nature and humble state. Although young children will have an incomplete knowledge of doctrine, they are in a unique position to experience complete reliance on someone other than themselves. The child's view of God will be drawn from human models. God's spiritual nature, a tough concept even for an adult, is incomprehensible. God's omnipresence is another challenge for the child who must reconcile God being in heaven with God being everywhere. Preschoolers can have difficulty distinguishing miracles from magic. When children of this age pray, they encounter another problem. Because they pray for their wants, it can be disturbing to them when God furnishes their needs instead. Seemingly unanswered prayer can be a stumbling block.

The Learning Environment. Preschoolers need stimulating environments if they are to learn at their full potential. Child-scale furnishings, interesting activity centers, physical comfort, and room to move around are all important. Curriculum must be designed specifically for these unique age-group characteristics. All the games, activities, songs, and stories presented in a given session should focus on a single theme. Any element of a teaching session that does not point learners toward the learning aim distracts them from it. Activities should take full advantage of the young learner's tendency to use every sense to learn. Teachers should be warm and accepting, because much of the young child's attitude toward the church will be a reflection of this attitude toward the teacher. Because so much depends on the student/teacher relationship, the class must be limited in size. In a 5-year-old group, approximately six children to one teacher is ideal. Additional teachers are necessary for even younger learners.

Lessons must be simple and emphasize real-life application. Concepts are to be taught in a reasonable sequence so that later lessons build on a solid foundation. Methods must be appropriate to the abilities, interests, and attention span of the preschooler. Storytelling, drama, art, blocks, books, puzzles, and music can all be directed at the lesson aim and serve a span of learning styles. Dress-up dramatic play, especially in the setting of a home-living activity center, lends itself to many lesson aims for the preschool age group.

Conclusion. Often the most neglected age group when it comes down to funding and facilities, the preschool department of a church's educational ministry is, along with the nursery, its most important area. It is during these formative years that an individual develops the attitudes toward God and his church that will last a lifetime. Visiting young families judge a church on the basis of its ministry to young children. Without a quality program they will not return.

ROBERT J. CHOUN

Bibliography. R. Beechick (1980), *Teaching Kindergartners;* idem (1979), *Teaching Preschoolers;* L. Brown (1986), *Sunday School Standards;* R. J. Choun and M. S. Lawson (1998), *The Christian Educator's Handbook on Children's Ministry;* W. Haystead (1995), *The Twenty-First Century Sunday School;* K. Klein (1982), *How to Do Bible Learning Activities: Ages 2–5;* K. D. Osborn (1980), *Early Childhood Education in Historical Perspective;* D. Ratcliff, ed. (1988), *Handbook of Preschool Religious Education;* J. C. Wilhoit and J. M. Dettoni, eds. (1995), *Nurture That Is Christian;* S. C. Wortham (1992), *Childhood 1892–1992.*

Preservation. *See* Conservation.

Price, John Milburn (1884–1975). Price was born near Fair Dealing, Kentucky. He was converted in a revival meeting on Friday, August 11, 1899. Price earned his bachelor of science degree from Western State Kentucky, the bachelor of arts degree from Baylor University (Texas), the master of arts degree from Brown University, and the master of theology, doctor of theology, and doctor of philosophy degrees from Southern Baptist Theological Seminary. "Until he entered Brown University in 1911, he was preparing to enter the pastoral ministry, but it was in this environment of liberal thinking that God directed Price's talents to the educational field. Price recalls that he "studied Hebrew under a Reformed Jewish Rabbi, who preached on Browning the night I went to hear him at his synagogue, Greek under a liberal Episcopalian, and sociology under a materialistic evolutionist." These experiences caused him to realize the deadness of liberal thinking and religion. Price's reconsidering of his calling resulted in his turning to religious education" (Briggs 1964).

Price was a true pioneer in the field of religious education among Southern Baptists. There are a number of "firsts" associated with his career. Among these include the first department among Baptists to offer vocational training in religious education in 1915 at Southwestern Baptist Theological Seminary in Fort Worth, Texas. Under his leadership, his school was also the first in America to offer a religious education diploma (1917); first in America to offer a doctor's degree with a major in religious education (1919); first in requiring supervised field work as a requirement for a degree (1920); first to initiate a Baptist Sunday School Superintendents' Conference (1920); first to coordinate a vocational conference in religious education (1921); first to offer a demonstration kindergarten in a Baptist seminary (1921); first to require academic prerequisites for degrees from Baptist seminaries (1922); first and oldest to teach vacation Bible school among Baptists (1922); first to offer special seminary courses for noncollege graduates (1923); first building in America designed exclusively for teaching religious education (1950); first School of Religious Education among Southern Baptists to be accredited (1951); first school among Southern Baptists offering credit courses in age group work (1919), recreational leadership (1921), vacation and weekday schools (1921), secretarial training (1922), religious publicity (1922), craft work (1923), church finances (1923), Baptist Student Union work (1923), religious drama (1924), visual aids (1926), religious counseling (1933), and church library work (1948).

Price pastored in Kentucky and Rhode Island, and was the first salaried association worker in the South, serving the Blood River Association (Kentucky). He taught school and served as a principal in Indian Territory. In 1915 he accepted the director of religious education position at Southwestern Baptist Theological Seminary. While directing the school and teaching classes, Price pastored Webb Baptist Church for twenty-one years.

His books include *Christianity and Social Problems* (1928), *Vital Problems in Christian Living* (1942), *Jesus the Teacher* (1946), *Mastering Life's Problems* (1958), *Formative Factors in Christian Character* (1959), and *The Unfolding Life* (1963). Price retired in 1956 after forty-one years as dean of the school.

RICK YOUNT

Bibliography. P. Briggs (1964), *A Historical Review of Dr. J. M. Price.*

Priest. *See* Clergy.

Priesthood of Believers. The Bible is the essential foundation for all the issues pertaining to the church of Jesus Christ. The Bible is the Word of God, providentially inspired, and is provided for humankind as a source book regarding the Christian faith and theology. Therefore, it is absolutely necessary to explore the teaching of the Bible regarding the concept of the priesthood of all believers and its application to Christian education, specifically, lay leadership within the church.

The Old Testament Roots of the Priesthood of All Believers. In approaching the biblical-theological materials concerning the priesthood of all believers, it is appropriate to survey the Old Testament. By investigating relevant passages, we can provide conclusive evidence that the people of God were called to the priesthood of all believers.

Lea (1988) states, "There is evidence in the Old Testament that God called the people of Israel to a special ministry of blessing other nations for his glory" (16). This special and unique role of Israel as the people of God was based upon God's establishment of a covenant with Abram to the world through Abram's seed (Gen. 12). Being the people of God included their responsibility toward the other nations, not only the privilege that they possessed. This responsibility does not merely require the formal duty of sacrifice, rather it demands other types of sacrifice which included, primarily, obedience and humility (Ps. 51:17).

Lea (1988) claims that this status of being the people of God was intended to be applied to the nation collectively. Exodus 19:5–6 (NASB) reads, "Now then, if you will indeed obey My voice and keep My covenant, then you shall be My own possession among all the peoples, for all the earth is Mine; and you shall be to Me a kingdom of priests and a holy nation. These are the words that you shall speak to the sons of Israel." God promised the people of Israel that national obedience would lead them to be "a kingdom of priests and a holy nation." Eastwood (1963) describes "a kingdom of priests" as "a kingdom, because God had chosen them as the instrument of His purpose; priests, because they were to become servants of His will by revealing His purpose to the world" (3). He also adds that every member of the kingdom of priests was privileged to draw near to God in dedication, worship, and service, so that they might learn how their mission to the world was to be fulfilled.

A second Old Testament passage, which emphasizes the priestly function of Israel, is Isaiah 61:1–6. Crane (1994) states that "one of the most important composite promises for restoration heralds a jubilee celebration of the Lord's favor when the anointed one of the Lord will preach good news to the poor, bind up the broken-hearted, proclaim freedom to the prisoners, comfort the mourning, and restore ancient ruins" (25). And the recipients of this proclamation will be "called the priests of the Lord; you will be spoken of as ministers of our God. You will eat the wealth of nations, and in their riches you will boast" (Isa. 61:6 NASB). Lea (1988) and Ryrie (1974) both state that the context of this passage is eschatological. There is no doubt that the priesthood of all believers anticipated in the Old Testament is designed by God to reach its fullness with the coming of the Messiah. God's goal for the people of Israel was to make them into a nation that declared his will to the world.

While God desired that all his people be priests in the world, significant focus was placed upon a special Levitical priesthood within Israel. Within this priesthood there was a clearly defined, three-tiered hierarchy. The Levites, representing the firstborns of the Israelites, were set apart for sanctuary service and preparation. The sons of Aaron were personally responsible for the sacrificial offerings. The high priest was given special prominence above all others (Crane, 1994).

However, other priests and priestly activities involving sacrifice, mediation, and instruction are found in the biblical narrative. For example, Cain and Abel offered a sacrifice (Gen. 4:2–6). Noah built an altar and offered a burnt sacrifice described as pleasing to the Lord (Gen. 8:20). On numerous occasions, Abraham built an altar. After Abraham rescued Lot from the four kings, Abraham was blessed by Melchizedek, king of Salem, and responded by giving Melchizedek a tenth of all that he had (Gen. 14:20). Micah, an Ephraimite, consecrated one of his sons to serve as a priest (Judg. 17:5). David's sons served as priests (2 Sam. 8:18). Gideon offered a sacrifice (Judg. 6:26). These examples show that priestly activities were still carried out by ordinary people up until the time of the judges. While priestly activities were carried out within the other tribes of Israel, Levites were consecrated to serve in that capacity by the end of the period of the judges. Micah obtained the services of a Levite who had previously served in the tribe of Judah, which may hint at a traveling Levitical priesthood (Judg. 17:12). By this time in the Old Testament, the priests were a special group set aside by God to be his means of mediation with others.

Lay Leadership in the Old Testament: The Eldership. In the ancient Near East, including the nation of Israel, the concept of society being ruled by a body of elders was widespread. In Hebrew, the word for elder (*zaqen*) is the same word used to describe old or older men. Throughout the Old Testament, the term *elder* bears the twofold meaning of an age designation and a title of office. The majority of Old Testament occurrences of *zaqen* refers to a collective body of leading men with official, recognized status to act for the people, not just to all the society's old men (Strauch, 1986).

From the time they were slaves in Egypt, Israel was governed by a council of elders. God acknowledged the elders' place of leadership by sending Moses to them first to announce the people's deliverance (Exod. 3:16). The elders appeared as the people's chief representative leaders (Exod. 4:29–31) and as Moses' chief assistants—standing by his side when he confronted Pharaoh (Exod. 3:18) and assisting him as he prepared the people for the first Passover (Exod. 12:21).

According to Strauch (1986) the eldership was Israel's oldest and one of its most fundamental institutions. Throughout Israel's history, the elders appeared to exercise an important and pervasive influence over daily community life. The term *elder* is used predominantly in the Old Testament as a designation for an official community leader like a judge, officer, prince, or priest. Elders clearly represent a distinct governing body of men with certain political and religious functions (Strauch, 1986). The elders were men of counsel and wisdom. Many illustrations in the Old Testament reveal the elders' counseling role in the local community and entire nation. According to Ezekiel, visions belong to the prophet, law to the priest, and counsel to the elders (Ezek. 7:26). Jeremiah referred to the elders as the sages who give counsel (Jer. 18:18).

The New Testament Emphasis on the Priesthood of All Believers. The priesthood that was anticipated and promised in the Old Testament was fulfilled once and for all in the great High Priest, our Lord Jesus Christ. Those who believe in him join in his ministry. The priesthood and ministry of all believers is rooted and grounded in this continued ministry of Jesus through his people. The church exists as the continued incarnation of Jesus whose presence is truly with his people through the power of the Holy Spirit (Crane, 1994). Without Christ there is no church. Without Christ there is no identity as God's people.

In Paul's letter to the church in Colossae, a New Testament reference to priesthood is found which is closely linked to the issue of identity. Paul emphasizes the person of Christ and what he has done as being absolutely essential for understanding the identity of those who follow him. Although the letter does not specifically mention the priesthood, it does give a clear declaration of Christ's fulfillment of Old Testament types and the fact that the identity of the believer is tied to his identity. He emphasizes with clarity and power this new identity of Christ because, now, the believer's identity is completely based upon Christ. In Christ, believers come to their fullness; therefore there is no lack or inadequacy in what he has done or in who they have become through him. Colossians 1:17–18 exalts Christ by claiming "He is before all things, and in Him all things hold together. He is also head of the body, the church; and He is the beginning, the firstborn from the dead; so that He Himself might come to have first place in everything (NASB)."

Lea (1988) claims that the most important New Testament passages concerning the priesthood of all believers appear in 1 Peter 2:9–10; Revelation 1:5–6; and Revelation 5:9–10. It is quite clear in these passages, and furthermore it is vitally important for believers to realize that collectively all Christians have a marvelous privilege and standing before God. Regarding this passage, Leonard (1988) claims that "these words provide a foundation for that powerful concept of the priesthood of all believers. By God's calling and choice, all that belongs to Christ belongs to the priesthood."

There does not seem to be any difference between the reference to priests in Revelation 1:6 and Revelation 5:10. Both verses picture the ministry of the believer-priest as a service for God (Lea, 1988). Believers are a kingdom in both an eschatological and a present sense. Eschatologically, believers will fulfill a kingly function in reigning with Christ in his messianic kingdom. The passage underscores the privilege of believers in that they share the opportunity of reigning with Christ in his final reign. It also underscores the responsibility of believers in that they are to serve as priests (Peck and Hoffman, 1984). The New Testament priesthood of all believers is also reflected in the ministry activity of believers in the New Testament period, particularly in the Book of Acts and the Epistles of Paul and Peter.

At the birth of the early Christian church, Peter recalled Joel's words concerning the ideal ministry, calling, and mission, which characterized that new entity:

> "And it shall be in the last days," God says,
> "That I will pour forth of My Spirit upon all mankind;
> And your sons and your daughters shall prophesy,
> And your young men shall see visions,
> And your old men shall dream dreams;
> Even upon My bondslaves, both men and women,
> I will in those days pour forth of My Spirit
> And they shall prophesy." (Acts 2:17–18 NASB)

Almost immediately, however, disputes arose over the fair distribution of food to the widows. Wisely, the Twelve realized the urgent need for organizational change to relieve them from some of the heavy tasks. As a solution, they called the congregation together and explained the problem (Acts 6:1). Next, they proposed that the congregation select seven qualified men who were known to be full of the Holy Spirit and wisdom, whom the apostles would place in charge of handling funds and caring for the material needs of the poor. The apostles would then be free to devote themselves wholly to the Word and prayer (Acts 6:4). This process initiated the differentiation of functions of ministries by the people of God.

The letters of Paul and his associates also bear witness to the contributions made to the early church by various people who were not included in the official leadership of the church. In Romans 16, Paul mentions Phoebe, a businesswoman in Rome, and many others, including Andronicus and Junia, Paul's companions in prison in Rome. Others are mentioned in the other Epistles; for example, Zenas, a lawyer in Titus 3:13; and Onesimus, the runaway slave, and his owner, Philemon.

Lay Leadership in the New Testament: The Eldership. New Testament writings say that elders were present in the first Jerusalem church.

Having elders in the church followed a Hebrew tradition. Elders are first mentioned in relation to the collection at Antioch, which Paul and Barnabas brought to the elders at Jerusalem (Acts 11:30). The elders are then referred to in the account of the apostolic ground and the formulation of the apostolic decree (Acts 15:2, 4, 22f.; 16:4). Paul and Barnabas, in their missionary ventures, established many new churches. When they left those congregations they selected elders and commended them to the Lord with prayer and fasting (Acts 14:23). Paul, in his great address to the Ephesian elders (Acts 20:18–35), shows what significance he attached to them.

In the early church, Paul ordained elders to encourage the growth of the churches (Acts 14:23; 20:17; 1 Tim. 5:17; Titus 1:5; James 5:14; 1 Peter 5:1–5). Pastors were sometimes seen as both preachers and ruling elders (Eph. 4:11; 1 Cor. 12:28). The governing elders of the assembly or church were simply called elders (Acts 20:28; 1 Tim. 3:1). In James's letter he specifically exhorts the sick to "call for the elders" of the church. James' primary instruction to the elders is to pray, and this call was directed to the official body of elders, not just an individual elder. Indeed, James portrays an official church prayer gathering at the sick person's bedside (Strauch, 1986). In the New Testament, the types of ministry elders could engage were numerous. This diversity portrays the beautiful church of Christ, with every member engaging in different ministries, but built up by the edification of the church (Eph. 4:11–16).

Lay Leadership in the New Testament: The Deaconship. Biblical scholars disagree as to when and how the office of deacon was established and/or formed (Kung, 1967). Many church historians and biblical scholars trace the office of deacon back to the story found in the sixth chapter of Acts. However, many modern scholars do not refer to Acts 6:1–4 as the "election of deacons," but instead as the "selection of the seven." Some modern scholars list a couple reasons for the distinction. First, the name "deacon" is not given to these seven men who were chosen in Acts. This passage does say that they were charged "to deacon" (Acts 6:2) and to be involved in "deaconing" (Acts 6:4). Hans Kung (1967) is convinced that Luke purposely avoided the use of the title in reference to "the seven," a title which he must have known. Kung thinks that this is true not only in Acts 6:1–6, but also even more strikingly, in reference to Philip in Acts 21:8. It would have been just as easy for Luke to refer to Philip as "the deacon" as it was to call him one of "the seven," which he does. Kung thinks this distinction must have been a conscious choice made by Luke. Second, the duties of Stephen, Philip, and the other "seven" seemed to go beyond those which Paul describes for deacons in his writing.

"The seven" in Acts, in addition to caring for the poor, preached, baptized, evangelized, and performed miracles. The expansion of duties has caused some modern scholars to think of "the seven," mentioned in the Book of Acts, as the forerunners of later "presbyters," rather than as "deacons." (Kung, 1967). In either case Acts 1:1–6 provides a clear biblical basis for the servant ministry of the laity.

The priesthood of believers is an essential doctrinal teaching of the church. It was never the expectation of God that a select group of individuals would administrate and govern all of the affairs of the church. The passages related to the spiritual gifts confirm God's intention to have all men and women involved in ministry. As recipients of God's grace, we have been given a positional standing which allows us to represent both ourselves and our fellow man before God's throne. In this capacity as priests, we serve God as his representatives to a lost and needy world.

ESTHER YOU

Bibliography. G. J. Brooke, *The Modern Churchman* 32, no. 3 (1990): 32–40; J. J. Crane (1994), *The Ministry of All Believers;* C. Eastwood (1960), *The Priesthood of All Believers;* idem (1963), *The Royal Priesthood of All Believers;* J. L. Garett Jr., *Southwestern Journal of Theology* 30, no. 2 (1988): 22–33; H. H. Hobbs (1990), *You Are Chosen;* H. Kung (1967), *The Church;* T. D. Lea, *Southwestern Journal of Theology* 30, no. 2 (1988): 15–21; B. J. Leonard, *Review and Expositor* 85, no. 4 (1988): 625–34; S. J. Mikolaski, *Southwestern Journal of Theology* 30, no. 2 (1988): 6–14; P. N. Page (1993), *All God's People Are Ministers;* R. P. Stevens, *Crux* 31, no. 2 (1995): 5–14; A. Strauch (1986), *Biblical Eldership;* D. L. Young, *Southwestern Journal of Theology* 30, no. 2 (1988): 46–54.

See also DEACON; DEACONESS; ELDER; MINISTER; PASTOR

Prison Ministry. Each year over 1.5 million adults are incarcerated, with over 5 million either on probation, in jail, or on parole. While 97 percent will return to society, 78 to 93 percent will be back in prison within six months. The direct cost to society per inmate ranges from $20,000 to $60,000 annually. However, with inmates having approximately 1 million children under the age of 18, the indirect costs are much higher.

Prison ministry is not new, but today it has matured into a comprehensive ministry. Besides the traditional focus on inmates themselves, there are strategic ministries to ex-prisoners, spouses, children, victims, prison employees, the church at large, and public policymakers. Volunteers are involved in direct evangelistic and discipleship ministry in the system and as they reenter society. Others work with families, meeting practical and spiritual needs, such as providing Christmas gifts for prisoners' children, letter writing, and transportation for family visitation. Professional counselors are often utilized. There are opportunities for pastors to work with chaplains and to begin in-prison churches. Individuals are involved in lobbying to reform the justice system based on biblical teaching.

While anecdotal evidence has always indicated a successful role for religion with prisoner reform, today there is documented evidence. Studies with faith-based programs have demonstrated a reduction in prisoner offenses while incarcerated. One study found that prisoners attending as few as ten Bible studies per year had return rates of only 14 percent compared to 41 percent for those not attending. Programs using targeted core values can make a difference.

MICHAEL J. KANE

Bibliography. B. R. Johnson, D. B. Larson, and T. C. Pitts, *Justice Quarterly* 14 (1997); *Sourcebook of Criminal Justice Statistics 1995.*

See also ADULT CHRISTIAN EDUCATION; ADULT, MODELS OF CHRISTIAN EDUCATION; JUVENILE DELINQUENCY

Private Christian Schools. The popular perception of "private" schools is that they are not supported financially by public money. This is not precisely the case. Many states provide financial support to non-state schools for transportation of pupils, textbooks, speech and hearing diagnostic services, health services, guidance services, remedial teaching, standardized testing, services with handicapped and gifted children, "nonideological" equipment (computers, science, math, etc.), and administrative and clerical expenses of maintaining state-mandated files. This varies greatly by state and individual schools may volunteer not to receive such funds (Office of Policy Research and Analysis, 1997). The primary difference between private and public is control and purpose.

Some private Christian schools have had their enrollment ups-and-downs over the past thirty years. Currently all private schools in the United States enroll about 11.1 percent (5,033,908) of all students, grades K through 12. Public school enrollment stands at 45,162,026 (*U.S. Education Market Data Retrieval,* 1997). Home schooling accounted for approximately 854,111 in 1994 (*The U.S. Education Market at a Glance,* 1996). These figures include nonreligious and non-Christian private schools.

The largest number of students in private, religious schools are in Catholic schools (over 60 percent). Bishop John Carroll instructed Catholic parents about the importance of Catholic schools in 1792. By 1840 the differences between Catholic leaders and the growing public school movement over such issues as textbooks, funding, and Bible-readings reached the point that Bishop John Hughes in New York began the creation of an entire Catholic school system. He and others had rightly perceived that the public schools were essentially Protestant in character. The faculties of Catholic schools, until very recently, were almost always priests and members of Catholic religious orders, often from abroad. In 1964 Catholic schools had an enrollment of 5,574,354. This declined by 1989 to 2,551,119 but rebounded to 2,618,567 in 1993 (Cooper and Gargan, 1996). These changes seem to reflect broader changes in the Catholic Church over these years.

The next largest enrollments are seen in evangelical/fundamentalist schools. This group of schools has experienced phenomenal growth in the past thirty years. In 1964, with less than 7,000 schools, enrollment was 113,410. By 1989 this had grown to more than 8,000 schools with 944,975 students. In 1993 the number of schools had been reduced to 7,551 but enrollment had grown to 1,027,461 (National Center for Statistics, 1994).

These schools are quite varied. Most are single, independent schools. There are a few systems with several schools at various levels under the same administration. Most, however, are relatively small, with typical enrollments being between 100 and 200 students. About 70 percent of these schools have arisen through and continue to be sponsored by local congregations. Very often evangelical/fundamentalists parents and their churches are motivated to start a school or to send their children to Christian schools due to their objections to public school policy or environment. This might have been expected when a more pluralistic national population spelled the demise of the powerful Protestant influence in earlier public schools. Also, from about the 1960s on, there seems to have been a loss of consensus concerning American institutions, including the nature and function of schools. Many Christians choose religious, private schools because they support a worldview consistent with that of the parents. While some of the schools founded since the 1960s, especially in the South, could be characterized as "segregation academies," this is no longer the case (Nordin and Turner, 1980). Evangelical/fundamentalist schools reject formal state regulation and emphasize the centrality of Jesus Christ and the Bible. Most seem to provide a shared sense of mission and common values which appear to be characteristic of effective schools. Prominent amounts of Americanism and capitalism are to be found in the curricula of many of these schools. The two largest associations for these schools are the Association of Christian Schools International (2,000) and the more separatist American Association of Christian Schools (1,100 schools).

The rise of secularism, scientism, permissivism, perceived attempts at social engineering, textbook controversies, dissolution of cultural standards, the increase in drug and alcohol abuse, and uncertainty about sources of authority seem sure to promote the continued growth of evangelical/fundamentalist schools. Realizing that all education is value laden and that Christian nurture is a full-time endeavor, church members have increasingly supported schools which embody the biblical beliefs and values of the home and church.

The third largest Christian schools group is that with Lutheran identification. In the late 1700s Henry Melchior Muhlenberg organized schools, mainly among German immigrants in Pennsylvania, Maryland, and Virginia. By 1820 there were 342 Lutheran schools in America. With the decline in use of the German language these schools declined, but rebounded in the twentieth century. In 1964 there were 1,750 schools of the American Lutheran, Missouri Synod Lutheran, and Wisconsin Evangelical Lutheran denominations. They enrolled 208,209 students. They peaked in 1989 following the merger that formed the Evangelical Lutheran denomination with 299,592 students. In 1994 they had 206,728 in 1,523 schools (Cooper and Gargan, 1996). Lutheran schools tend to be very closely related to the church and very professional in faculty and administration.

The fourth largest private, religious schools in America are Jewish schools. They have grown from 72,912 students in 1963 to 171,324 students in 647 schools in 1994. Over 87 percent of these are Orthodox Jewish schools (Cooper and Gargan, 1996).

Schools related to the Episcopal Church form the fifth largest group. In 1994 some 349 schools enrolled 88,079 students (Cooper and Gargan, 1996). This is a near one-third increase in the past thirty years.

Number six in size are the Reformed/Calvinist schools. They enrolled 77,778 students in 270 schools in 1994. This is down from a high of 87,215 students in 1989 (Cooper and Gargan, 1996). These schools tend to be very well developed with denominational curricular work and teacher growth workshops. The Reformed (affiliated with the Reformed Church of America or the Christian Reformed Church of America) schools in this country and in Europe take philosophy of education very seriously. Their philosophical work is largely based on the Calvinist doctrine of the sovereignty of God in the totality of life. Reformed schools have a strong heritage of education from elementary to university levels going back to Holland in the 1500s. Many of these were open to the poor as well as to the rich. A sect of the Dutch Calvinist church, called "Seceders," were influenced by religious revival and pietism, and very interested in Christian education, left the Dutch state church and led emigra-tion to America. A revival in the Reformed church under Abraham Kuyper in the 1870s reemphasized the sovereignty of God and again boosted church interest in schools. Many Reformed schools are part of an association known as Christian Schools International, which is based in Grand Rapids, Michigan.

Seventh-day Adventists have, as of 1994, 67,034 students in 1,072 schools (Cooper and Gargan, 1996). This denomination has over 4,000 schools worldwide, including universities and a medical school. The first Seventh-day Adventist elementary school in America was founded in Buck's Bridge, New York, in 1853. At the secondary and college levels, school-operated industries help to support students. Seventh-day Adventist schools are usually very careful to represent such church values as noncompetitiveness, racial integration, and Bible-based curriculum.

The rest of private education in the United States is made up of Mennonite and Amish schools, Islamic, independent nonreligious, special education, alternative, and military schools, and Montessori schools. These schools enroll over half a million students (*The U.S. Education Market at a Glance*, 1996).

Private schooling in America, as we now know it, has tended historically to be associated with immigrant populations. These groups typically settled along the East and West coasts and the cities of the Great Lakes. However, currently they are well distributed across the country. As of 1994 the South led the nation in such schools with 28.7 percent of enrollment. The Midwest was next with 27.1 percent, followed by the Northeast with 26.3 percent and the West with 17.9 percent. This represents movement in growth away from the Northeast and Great Lakes and into the South and greater Midwest (Cooper and Gargan, 1996).

The information given here about private Christian schools only hints at the great resilience and dedication shown by these institutions, their teachers and administrators, and their constituencies. While parents send their children to Christian schools for many reasons, commitment to religious beliefs and values fuel the passion that sustain these schools.

EUGENE S. GIBBS

Bibliography. B. S. Cooper and A. Gargan, *Journal of Research on Christian Education* 5, no. 2 (1996); V. D. Nordin and W. L. Turner, *Phi Delta Kappan* 61, no. 6 (1980); National Center for Statistics (1994), *Private School Universe Survey, 1993–1994;* Office of Policy Research and Analysis (1997), *The Private School Landscape; The U.S. Education Market at a Glance* (1996), available Internet: www.schooldata.com; *U.S. Education Market Data Retrieval* (1997).

See also ASSOCIATION OF CHRISTIAN SCHOOLS INTERNATIONAL; HOME SCHOOL MOVEMENT

Private Religious Schools. Schools that are sponsored and funded by local congregations or independent boards for the purpose of providing general schooling in a religious setting. Sometimes called parochial schools, parish schools, day schools, Christian schools, or independent schools, they offer classes in such basic studies as mathematics, English, history, science, and religion.

Virtually every denominational group has conducted Christian schools, although the patterns of operation and purposes differ somewhat from group to group. Catholics have long operated private schools, commonly called parochial schools. These were begun to teach Catholic dogma to the millions of Catholic European immigrants to the United States in the nineteenth century. Catholic schools remain strong even to this day, though enrollment has decreased in recent years. Lutherans have also operated parochial schools, generally for the same reasons as the Catholics. Dutch Reformed and Seventh-Day Adventist schools were begun for similar reasons. Jewish day schools are rarely operated by only one congregation, but rather by independent groups.

Evangelical Protestants, who often confined their early schools to kindergartens or preschools, have actively formed many Christian schools in the past twenty-five years. A variety of factors have motivated the establishment of these schools: dissatisfaction with public schools, government standards for education, and a general concern about a materialistic and non-Christian culture. Individual congregations established many of these schools. Increasingly, however, independent schools, not associated with any one congregation and governed by a board representing Christians from many quarters of society, have emerged.

Religious schools are governed in a variety of ways. Catholic elementary schools are usually closely associated with a parish while secondary schools are either diocesan or private, the latter operated by a religious order. Lutheran schools are largely elementary and are supervised and financed by a single congregation. Many evangelical schools follow the same pattern as Lutheran schools, although private schools are increasingly popular.

Curriculum in Catholic schools includes preparation in the sacraments and systematic study of church history, Bible, and theology. Protestant groups differ somewhat in how religion is taught. Many of the conservative Christian schools utilize curriculum in all fields of study which has been integrated with clear biblical teachings and mainline doctrine. Many schools also include Bible classes in their curriculum. Less conservative schools offer foundational curriculum similar to or identical with that of the public school, supplemented with theological materials. A variety of Christian publishers provide curriculum materials for Christian schools.

Some congregations consider their Christian school a mission arm of the church. Many engage in evangelization, though this kind of religious assimilation is not the goal for all schools.

Christian schools, especially those established in the past twenty-five years, have been criticized because of selective admissions policies that, some say, promote an elitism and often racial exclusion. Some schools have had acrimonious relationships with state educational officials, though that seems to be less prevalent now than it was in earlier years.

Several agencies exist to provide support for evangelical Christian schools. The largest is the Association for Christian Schools International (ACSI), which provides alternative credentialing for teachers, accreditation for schools, curriculum materials, and significant support services for schools, most notably through several annual conventions at strategic locations throughout the United States and the world.

The advent of home schooling is perhaps the most recent development in alternative school patterns. Although the home school movement is by no means confined to the Christian community, many Christians have opted to home school their children for all or much of their educational experience. Home schooling associations and several publishers provide support for parents who choose this mode of education.

ELEANOR A. DANIEL

Bibliography. J. C. Carper and T. C. Hunt, eds. (1993), *Religious Schools in America;* A. Peshkin (1986), *God's Choice.*

See also ASSOCIATION OF CHRISTIAN SCHOOLS INTERNATIONAL (ACSI); HIGHER EDUCATION, CHRISTIAN; HOME SCHOOL MOVEMENT; PRIVATE CHRISTIAN SCHOOLS; ROMAN CATHOLIC EDUCATION

Proactive Inhibition. This is also known as proactive interference. Proactive inhibition refers to the difficulty students have distinguishing details of a new set of information due to any similarities among the new material and previously learned material. Proactive inhibition is most frequently found when memorizing lists of items. The degree of similarity between the items will determine the degree of difficulty in distinguishing between the two sets. The more similar the sets of information, the more the previous material will inhibit or interfere with the learning of the new material.

An example of proactive inhibition would be when an individual has memorized a verse from the King James Version but then tries to memorize that same verse in the New American Standard Version. Proactive interference will make it difficult for the individual to keep some of the

King James wording from creeping into the New American Standard rendering. Another example would be recounting the two miraculous feedings of the multitudes. Because the stories are so similar, a student would probably have trouble remembering the specifics of the Feeding of the 4,000 in Matthew 15 (4,000 men, seven loaves, a few fishes, seven baskets of leftovers) if he or she has previously memorized the details of the Feeding of the 5,000 in Matthew 14 (5,000 men, five loaves, two fishes, twelve baskets of leftovers).

DALE L. MORT

Problem Solving. One of the most important tasks of any leader is problem solving or decision making. In fact, problem solving and decision making are closely related conceptual skills. Problems call for decisions, just as opportunities do. Both processes call for the use of a general decision-making process and the application of information-gathering, analytical and creative thinking, and planning skills. Many organizations today that are being driven by the Total Quality Management movement are in fact training their employees in the essential skills of problem solving.

A very simple process is as follows.

Step 1. *Identify the problem.* The individual or group considers various ways of looking at the problem and chooses the one that is most helpful in solving it. This requires opening your mind to a myriad of new ideas, and then focusing in on the one best way to define the problem.

Step 2. *Analyze the problem.* Look for causes, issues, and questions that arise. Research and gather the information that is needed to understand the problem. Once again, start by being open to new potential causes of the problem that is being dealt with. Then close in on one or more key causes for action.

Step 3. *List possible solutions.* Be creative. Think of as many solutions as possible that might solve the problem. Then think about each option to make it as clear and as understandable as possible.

Step 4. *Select and plan one solution.* Which is the best way? Compare the options in as many ways as possible. Then focus on how to implement the one chosen.

Step 5. *Implement the solution.* Follow through on the plan to solve the problem or make the change.

Step 6. *Check the solution.* How well does it work? Identify any continuing problems and start the process again.

How many times does one stop to analyze a problem and redefine it? The problem-solving process allows anyone to stop and think before beginning a new project or to evaluate the progress of a venture already in process. This can save a lot of wasted effort later.

ELLERY G. PULLMAN

See also DECISION MAKING; TOTAL DUALITY MANAGEMENT

Process Observer. Designated person who fulfills a role in group dynamics by focusing on the interrelationship components in a group. Unless highly skilled, the observer usually sits apart from the group so as to be able to stay focused without becoming involved in the group activity. The agenda includes notation of who talks to whom, what kind of interaction takes place, roles embraced by group members, leadership actions, how decisions are made, awareness of climate, attempts at cohesion, body language, and feelings displayed. Process observers may call for a "freeze" in the group's action to inquire into deeper meanings inherent in participants' responses or to call attention to items to which members appear oblivious. Process observation is always framed in a "wondering," tentative questioning to prompt participants' increasing insight into significances in the process. The observer, if successful, becomes an enabler who helps the group clarify and improve their awareness of the way individuals and collective units function in that particular group.

JULIE GORMAN

See also GROUP DYNAMICS; SMALL GROUPS

Process Theology. The relationship of God to the created order (the cosmos) has always been a difficult topic, and one prone to error. Classical orthodoxy holds the doctrines of *divine immanence* and *divine transcendence* in tension, insisting that God is both immediately involved with creation and present (immanent), and yet he is simultaneously apart from and separate from creation (transcendent). An overemphasis on transcendence creates a God who is uninvolved, distant, and untouched by events in the created order. His love, if it exists, is a static, uninvolved sort of love. An overemphasis on immanence creates a God who is in everything, and may even be confused with creation itself, as in pantheism. An overemphasis on transcendence removes the possibility of supernatural intervention in the created order (miracles), and an overemphasis on immanence removes the possibility of natural order with everything that happens being understood as supernatural in origin. A balanced perspective recognizes both natural order and the possibility of miracles.

About 1600 a view called Socinianism (named for its founder Socinius) offered the idea that God does not determine our decisions outside of ourselves, and that "by making free decisions we give divine knowledge new content and thus change God" (Eliade, 1987, 168). This view made God contingent upon the decisions and events in human history, arguing that because God does not know everything that humans will do, nor does he control all that humans do, God is, in a certain sense, dependent upon human activity, and as the world changes, God changes with it. Hence, just as creation is in process, so God also is in process. Socinianism was deemed heretical by orthodox theologians and did not gain much interest or much of a following until much later when changes in philosophy made this view much more interesting.

Scripture affirms that God is constant and unchanging. "I the LORD do not change" records Malachi 3:6 (NRSV), and James writes that with God "there is no variation or shadow due to change" (James 1:17 NRSV). However, some interpretations of this doctrine have created a God who is static, immobile, and sterile, which is a misunderstanding of the doctrine of immutability. Such understandings are rooted more in the Greek notions of immobility and sterility than in the biblical images of God. But Scripture is making reference to God's character, his nature, and his dependability, not his actions, when it affirms that he does not change. The Bible teaches that God is trustworthy and actively involved in created order at the same time that he is unchanging and stable.

The "fundamental thesis of Process Theology is that reality is processive" (Erickson, 1986, 279). The philosopher Alfred North Whitehead opened the door to this view of reality when his organic philosophy argued that reality is *becoming* rather than *being*, dynamic rather than static. Newtonian physics saw reality as *substance* while Whitehead saw it as *event*. He believed that reality was in constant process, on both the micro-level, as in protons, neutrons, and even the quarks of quantum physics, and on the macro-level as in human beings, institutions, societies, and nations. Because things were constantly changing, and changing with great rapidity, Whitehead believed that the nature of reality had the character of fluidity rather than substance (Griffin, 1989, 7–8). Whitehead's philosophy was one of the foundations for what has become known as *postmodernism* and especially for its applications to theological understanding.

Whitehead saw reality as organic and therefore as interrelated. Rather than seeing and thinking about real events and concrete entities as separate and discrete, he believed that all of reality must be understood in terms of relationships to all that precedes and all that follows. Interdependence is given priority over independence as the ideal, and this understanding is raised to the level of ontology, as a fundamental characteristic of reality. It is regarded as an inescapable fact relative to the nature of things (Cobb and Griffin, 1976, 14).

God is not understood as immune to the law of interdependence; he, too, is understood to be interdependent with his creation. While his primary attribute is love, process theologians insist that his love is not impassive, as they understand orthodox theologies to present it. Rather, they insist, God's love is passionate, genuinely sympathetic, and responsive to those he loves. Because those he loves are in process, God must of necessity also be in process, changing as the new needs and interests of those he loves change. Just as we are emerging and constantly changing, so God too is emerging and changing.

Process theology understands God to be *in* everything he has created. It is not pantheism (God *is* everything), but rather is panentheism, God is in everything. Because of the view of reality as in process, it necessarily follows that God too is in process.

Process theology rejects notions of God as sovereign, omnipotent, and omniscient as inadequate for the modern world. If God is all powerful and all good, why then does he fail to intervene at times of terrible evil such as the Holocaust or in natural disasters? Rather, God is presented as "the poet of the world, with tender patience leading it by his vision of truth, beauty, and goodness" (Sherburne, 1981, 183).

Process theologians understand God as *dipolar*, having two poles or opposites both resident in his being simultaneously. The one pole is the mental or *primordial* aspect which is his abstract essence that is not influenced by anything else and which therefore makes him the ground of all reality. In this aspect of his essence, he is understood as the one Actual Entity who cannot be influenced by any other entity. The second aspect of God is his physical or *consequent* pole which is internally affected by all that happens in the world. God feels with us, he laughs, cries, rejoices, and grieves with us, and is even hurt when we are hurt or when we hurt others. Process theology sometimes even refers to the world as God's body, and God as the soul of the world, so interconnected are God and the cosmos (McFague, 1987, 69).

God's consequent nature makes him not only responsive and receptive to the processes of the world, it also renders him limited to these processes. His omniscience means that he can know at any given moment everything that can be known, but nothing more, because he does not know what will happen next. God is in constant reaction to the processes of the world. Things are constantly happening, and have always been happening, in the life of God, that are completely unforeseen, and only become knowable to God as they happen. Therefore theologies of omniscience, which affirm that God knows everything that will happen before it happens, and theologies of sovereignty, which affirm that everything that comes to pass does so at the will of God, must be abandoned for a view of God that sees him so intimately related to his creation that he is progressing with it. Humankind is now to be understood as participating with God in determining the future. God contains within himself all of the possibilities of the choices and patterns creation can take, but it is humankind which actually determines which choices will be made and what will actually come to pass. God knows all of the past intimately and exactly, but he does not yet know the future because the future cannot be known until it is actually taking place. God is understood as a tender companion, not as a "coercive power" controlling all that happens.

Process theology rejects images of God as king, judge, or military ruler, even though each of these are found in Scripture. Rather, it insists, God must be presented as a nurturer, counselor, participant, and friend. Some fear that the power images of God are the cause for oppressive and destructive behaviors of people, especially of men, because exercising power is understood as somehow a "godly" way of acting. The more gentle and participatory images of God presented by process theology allow humans to think in more interrelated ways regarding our contacts with others. Just as God relates to the world as the "loving persuasion of a tender companion" (Miller, 1982, 35), so we too must relate in these ways to others.

Process theology does not struggle with the problem of evil as does orthodox theology. Process theology sees evil as the natural outcome of humankind choosing not to actualize God's love and redemptive activity in our interactions with others. Because God is not understood as being in control of history, he cannot be held accountable for the many atrocities in human history. Process theologians believe that humankind is responsible for the events of history, not God; but God has always been present, urging us to better choices and more appropriate ways of dealing with one another. God grieves because of the choices we have made, but never withdraws his redemptive love from us.

Because God and his relationship to the world are redefined, it follows that the definition of evil and of redemption must also change. Process theology understands evil as a matter of broken relationships, not specific acts in violation of a moral code. Evil is determined to be evil only as it is seen in relation to other events; there cannot be a static moral code of right and wrong because situations, events, and relationships are always changing.

Whitehead said, "Religion is what we do with our solitariness" (Whitehead, 1926, 16). In process theology redemption is the activity of people to reestablish relationships, to come back to loving relationships. God desires that no one be lost, and offers his tender care to this end.

There are a growing number of writers who are building their approaches to religious education on the foundation of process theology. Randolph Crump Miller was the first to offer a carefully articulated approach to Christian education from the perspective of process theology (Miller, 1980). For Miller, and other Christian educators who accept process theology, all education is religious in that its goal is the communication of values that lead to redemptive purposes in the world. Teaching people to love, be kind, respect others, respect the environment, and do their best is what God's activity in the world is about. Whatever is happening in society that is positive and good is the work of God and is in fact, revelatory, because through these events God is speaking his will to the human family. Therefore the task of Christian education becomes helping people to hear the voice of God in all that is happening in the world, and to see all of life as engagement with God's creative, loving, and redemptive activity in the world. But the task is also leading people to function as cocreators with God and as coredeemers, helping to build the world into a new reality of love.

PERRY G. DOWNS

Bibliography. W. A. Beardslee and J. Holland (1989), *Varieties of Postmodern Theology;* J. B. Cobb Jr. and D. R. Griffin (1976), *Process Theology: An Introductory Exposition;* M. Eliade, ed. (1987), *The Encyclopedia of Religion;* M. Erickson (1986), *Christian Theology;* S. McFague (1987), *Models of God;* R. C. Miller (1982), *Religious Education and Theology;* idem (1980), *The Theory of Christian Education Practice;* D. W. Sherburne (1981), *A Key to Whitehead's Process and Reality;* A. N. Whitehead (1960), *Religion in the Making.*

Prochoice. *See* Abortion.

Professional Association of Christian Educators (PACE). PACE was formerly known as the National Association of Directors of Christian Education (NADCE). In 1961 Dr. Gordon G. Talbot, a director of Christian Education in a Baptist church in Des Moines, Iowa, asked Dr. Clate Risley, executive director of the National Sunday School Association, if an affiliate of NSSA could be formed for professionals in Christian education in local churches. NSSA was the Christian education arm of the National Association of Evangelicals based in Wheaton, Illinois.

Gordon Talbot, a dynamic and capable leader, provided great impetus to the launching of this organization. He was, in effect, its founder and first president. Well organized and assertive as a leader, he was the right person to provide initial leadership.

A coterie of gifted men and women were ready for such an organization and it grew with surprising swiftness and strength. The late Ray Syrstad was a pivotal figure in its early development. Other primary individuals were Rodney Toews, Richard Bunger, Julie Gorman, Sherwood

Strodel, Lewis Lawton, Winona Walworth, James Forstrom, Allyn Sloat, Lloyd Miller, Arnold Berntsen, Ronald Widman, Charlotte Ransom, Dale Gates, Elmer Taylor, Forrest Williams, Benjamin McGrew, and Warren Benson.

Professors such as Drs. Charles Schauffele of Gordon-Conwell Theological Seminary, Bill Bynam of Talbot School of Theology, and Howard Hendricks of Dallas Theological Seminary gave of their time and support to this fledgling enterprise. Dr. Roy Zuck of Scripture Press Foundation was a factor as well.

The very lengthy presidency of William Carson was initially effective for the National Association of Directors of Christian Education. The presidency of Dr. Michael Lawson, Professor of Christian Education at Dallas Seminary, brought new zest and strength to the organization. He and his cabinet changed the name to the Professional Association of Christian Educators (PACE), seeking a broader constituency. The field of Christian education in the churches was changing radically and the role of the director of Christian education was succumbing to the contemporary specializations arising in the churches.

PACE has been given vital leadership under Dr. Lawson. He has been supported by Robert Herrington, Karen Van Galder, Danny Mize, Roy Reiswig, Buck Oliphant, Miles "Skip" Lewis, Stanley Olson, Lynn Gannett, Bob Schroeder, Lin McLaughlin, and Jim Baird.

Currently, PACE is focusing its communication efforts on the Internet, establishing chat rooms, databases, and hot links to important educational sites (www.paceinc.org). PACE also promotes regional meetings targeting specialized topics.

WARREN S. BENSON

Program. Programs are the "what" and "how" of church operations. Prior to program planning there must be a theological and philosophical understanding as to why there should be any program. From these basic premises, a model of ministry should be developed that designates the major components of a program. Upon these two major analytic and systematic planning processes, the program is developed.

The program is the detailed, planned activities that are derived from the theology and philosophy and the model of a church's reason for being. Programs should not be developed until at least generally accepted principles have been discussed and agreed upon, and until some basic model of how the church will function has been worked out. Then the particulars of what to do and how to do it can be designed and developed.

Program particulars give in detail the answers to the following general issues: for whom the program is intended, what the intended outcomes are, when it will be held, how often it will operate, who is responsible to do what and by when to make sure the program details will be fulfilled, how much will it cost, what personnel are needed to operate the program, what leadership development needs to occur to ensure that leaders will function effectively, what nonhuman resources (including buildings, materials, equipment, etc.) will be needed, who will obtain these, how finances will be raised, what promotion will be necessary, and how to know if the program has met its intended outcomes.

Programs reflect the theological and philosophical perspectives of the sponsoring organization. To plan a program without doing the proper thinking and praying beforehand is to court disaster.

JOHN M. DETTONI

See also FACILITIES; RESOURCES

Project. Teaching method that involves students in a variety of learning experiences in a defined time period. A project enables students to learn information, to discover the personal meaning of that data, and to express information, meaning, and application.

The student is actually involved in the project—searching for information, constructing a model, researching Bible facts, or processing ways to utilize data in a practical manner.

Learning projects engage children, youth, and adults in activities that appeal to differing learning styles, call students to a high level of involvement, and allow for interaction among students. Examples include creating a music video, producing a newscast that reports a biblical event, writing missionaries on e-mail, or participating in a field trip in which students learn through firsthand experience and observation. One teacher took her class to a synagogue to learn how Jewish people worship, while another took his coed class on a tour of the local jail to survey ministry possibilities.

With children, projects often take several weeks to complete. The first week serves to introduce the project where children make plans and receive assignments. The following weeks are spent in active research, construction, and working together as a team. The last session may involve a report or presentation to the larger group. Projects require consistent attendance.

Jesus used the project method when he sent the twelve on the Galilean tour. (1) He aroused their sense of need through praying for workers as he commanded (Matt. 9:37–38). (2) The group followed a plan of action. (3) After the action was carried out, reports were made (Luke 9:10; Mark 6:30). (4) These reports revealed the need for further learning.

Whether building a model of the tabernacle, tracing and comparing genealogies, or developing a map of Paul's travels, learning projects can add zest and interest in Bible study. There are risks, however in conducting projects. Students may remember more about the process—how to construct the tabernacle—than they will about the Bible passages themselves. Effective use of the project requires careful planning and thorough preparation.

JIM WALTER

Bibliography. F. B. Edge (1959), *Helping the Teacher;* E. Rives (1969), *Guiding Children.*

Projection. Term used to describe the attribution of one's own thoughts and feelings to someone else. Although employed to some degree by all individuals, projection is the primary defense mechanism of paranoid personalities. Such attribution is unconsciously employed in order to protect the ego from acknowledging that undesirable characteristics actually exist within oneself. For example, individuals who have difficulty getting along with others often "project" the source of the problem onto others when the fault is actually their own. Jesus Christ presented a classic description of projection in Matthew 7:1–5. Frederick Perls's Gestalt therapy is largely based on the principle of projection, whereby clients are encouraged to engage their social environment by projecting their needs, fears, or desires onto what is "out there."

DAVID GOUGH

Promise Keepers. Christian outreach to men. Largely through stadium rallies, but also through conferences and resources, it encourages men to live godly lives and to keep seven basic promises of commitment to God, their wives and families, and their fellow men. It has sought to unite men of all races, denominations, and cultures, believing that accountable relationships among men are important in helping Christian men to follow the seven promises.

Bill McCartney, former head football coach at the University of Colorado, founded Promise Keepers in 1990. Known primarily for their stadium rallies, over 2 million men have participated in these events. Its headquarters is in Denver, Colorado. A singular feature of the events has been its interracial membership. Over 25 percent of its staff are of ethnic backgrounds, and stadium events also feature a variety of ethnic speakers and musicians, as well as participants.

On Saturday, October 4, 1997, Promise Keepers convened in Washington, D.C., in one of the largest gatherings ever held there. Several hundred thousand men participated in Stand in the Gap: A Sacred Assembly of Men, a day of personal repentance and prayer for the nation, and their families. The movement has spawned a plethora of men's ministry conferences, speakers, videos, and books about men's Christian living.

Promise Keepers has not been without its detractors, though. Some critics have linked the organization with the Christian Coalition and other far-right religious and political movements. They avow no such connection. At one time the organization marketed the book *The Masculine Journey* by Robert Hicks (1993). However, when it caused controversy, it was withdrawn. Women's groups have accused Promise Keepers of subjecting women under men. However, leadership of the organization have steadfastly denied that accusation. Others have been disturbed by the decidedly ecumenical and Pentecostal nature of the rallies.

From the beginning, Promise Keepers has focused on involving pastors and developing men's ministry in the church. They have provided leadership training conferences, books, and other products for that purpose. One of their promises is that "a Promise Keeper is committed to pursue vital relationships with a few other men, understanding that he needs brothers to help him keep his promises." They believe that the small group provides men with the opportunity to bear one another's burdens in a supportive, encouraging, accountable setting. A "key man" coordinates the work of the men's groups and serves as a link between Promise Keepers and the church. An "ambassador" is a volunteer representative of Promise Keepers who communicates the mission and heart of Promise Keepers to his community's churches.

JIM WALTER

Bibliography. E. Wagner, *Focusing Your Men's Ministry.*

See also MEN'S MINISTRY

Prophetic Teachings. *See* Education in the Monarchies and Prophets.

Protest. *See* Demonstration.

Protestant Reformation. *See* Calvin, John.

Prototype. *See* Paradigm.

Proximity. *See* Contiguity.

Psychoanalyst. *See* Freud, Sigmund.

Psychology. *See* Regression.

Psychology of Religion. Field of study that uses scientific research methodologies and psychological categories of thought to study human religious experiences, behavior, and beliefs. This study includes the relationship of individual religion to other aspects of one's psychosocial makeup. It may also include study that falls under the heading of "social psychology of religion," which focuses on shared beliefs and behaviors of religious groups. Of particular interest to researchers are such concepts as conversion, religious experience, religious attitudes, religion and psychopathology, and religion and well-being. Religious development across the life span is also a significant area of concern.

Psychology of religion as a field of special study appeared in the late 1800s. Prior to this time, one of the first pioneers was Jonathan Edwards, who spent most of his life as a minister of the Congregational Church of America. He witnessed several revivals of religion and systematically observed and analyzed the facts of religious experience. His book, *A Treatise Concerning Religious Affections* (1746), was the first important work on experiential religion ever published in America.

One hundred years later, G. Stanley Hall studied adolescent religious experiences using questionnaire techniques, and Edwin Starbuck wrote the first full-length book on the study of psychology of religion (*The Psychology of Religion* [1899]). But the classic early work responsible for elevating the study of psychology of religion to its prominence was William James's *Varieties of Religious Experience*, published in 1902. James drew heavily on Starbuck's research and added recorded cases, many of which were of extreme religious belief and behavior. He distinguished between institutional religion (a religious group or organization) and personal religion (the individual mystical experience). James was most interested in understanding personal religious experience.

Within psychological circles, Sigmund Freud and Carl Jung contributed to the exploration of religious beliefs and their effects on psychological health. Freud suggested that religious beliefs and behaviors develop in relationship to parental perceptions and are then projected onto a person's view of God. His work provided insight into the pathogenic religion that inhibits psychological growth and health for so many people. Jung, on the other hand, included religion in his psychology in a positive light, emphasizing that spiritual growth leads to a basic sense of identity and meaning.

Stimulated by the work of Freud and Jung, George Albert Coe, a leading religious educator, spent a lifetime studying the psychology of religion and produced books based on his study (*The Psychology of Religion* [1916]; *The Motives of Men* [1928]). He did more to consider the relation between the psychology of religion and religious education than any other researcher. Around this same time period, a few seminary departments of religious education began to include courses with a psychological orientation. A new field for research was introduced by Anton T. Boisen in *The Exploration of the Inner World* (1936). Boisen held that some forms of religious experience were related to mental illness, and presented many cases of both to demonstrate his hypothesis.

In the late 1940s and early 1950s, a renewed interest in psychology and its applicability to religious education and counseling became evident. Eric Fromm combined a psychoanalytic approach with a cultural orientation that he then applied to religion and ethics (*Psychoanalysis and Religion*, 1950). Gordon Allport's *The Individual and His Religion* (1950) explored the use of psychology in understanding individual religion. His religious orientation scales measured two approaches to religion: "mature" religion, described as dynamic, open-minded, and able to deal with inconsistencies, and "immature" religion, defined as self-serving and representative of the negative stereotypes people have about religion. His idea of religious orientation has remained a focal point in the psychology of religion, despite criticism of its use.

Other works on the psychology of religion are by Walter Houston Clark (1958), Paul E. Johnson (1959), and Orlo Strunk Jr. (1959). A new outgrowth of psychology of religion research has been "pastoral psychology," which studies the ways in which psychological principles can be applied to pastoral and church practices.

The plethora of research, theoretical papers, and books related to psychology of religion reveal an increasing interest in psychology of religion. Numerous symposia and conventions provide opportunities for researchers from both fields to exchange ideas and discuss the integration of psychology and theology. The rise of the field of pastoral counseling and an increased emphasis on the field of psychology in religious colleges and theological seminaries show increased interest, as well. A number of journals, such as *Journal for the Scientific Study of Religion, International Journal for the Psychology of Religion, Journal of Psychology and Theology,* and *The Journal of the Psychology of Religion*, publish psychology of religion research and many psychology of religion textbooks are readily available. In addition, Internet sites provide up-to-date research in this field as well as ongoing dialogue with researchers.

The past decade has introduced new theories, including attachment theory, role theory, developmental issues, and coping theory. Researchers in psychology of religion state that research and inquiry from both a psychological perspective and a religious perspective are needed in order to bring forth a more comprehensive understanding of the integration of psychology and religion.

NORMA S. HEDIN

Bibliography. A. R. Fuller, *Psychology and Religion: Eight Points of View;* H. N. Malony, *Psychology of Reli-*

gion; W. Oates, *The Psychology of Religion;* R. F. Paloutzian, *Invitation to the Psychology of Religion;* B. Spilka and D. N. McIntosh, eds., *The Psychology of Religion: Theoretical Approaches;* D. M. Wulff, *Psychology of Religion: Classic and Contemporary Views.*

See also ADLER, MORTIMER J.; EDWARDS, JONATHAN; FREUD, SIGMUND; JAMES, WILLIAM; JUNG, CARL GUSTAV

Psychomotor Domain. As you read this article you are functioning in the psychomotor domain. Holding a book, turning a page, or placing a book back on the shelf results from the collaboration of cognitive (thinking) and psychomotor processes. In the simplest terms, the psychomotor domain is the process wherein a sensory signal is sent to the brain and the brain sends a command signal to the muscles of the body that results in movement or reaction. These movements vary in complexity. Movements occurring in a specific order can be identified as a motor skill that denotes "an action or a task that has a goal and that requires voluntary body and/or limb movement to achieve the goal" (Magill, 1993, 7).

Movement is a fundamental part of life and educational practice. In the educational context, one tends to think of encouraging movement that is voluntary and purposeful. The relationship of physical activity to thinking, feeling, behavior, motivation, and the full range of experiences in the learning process led researchers and educators to seek a means of classifying psychomotor behaviors. Benjamin Bloom's *Taxonomy of Educational Objectives* is perhaps the best known attempt to classify learning objectives in the cognitive, affective, and psychomotor domains. This approach was perceived to be useful for educators in that a classification system could provide a framework for curricula, tests, and educational research. Bloom's work focused on the cognitive domain and at his encouragement, numerous other researchers and educators have expanded this taxonomy or classification to consider the affective and psychomotor domains as well.

Utilizing the taxonomy as a model, Anita Harrow (1972) identified six categories of psychomotor development: (1) reflex movements which are actions elicited without conscious volition in response to some stimuli, (2) basic-fundamental movements which are inherent movement patterns formed from a combining of reflex movements, (3) perceptual abilities which is the interpretation of stimuli from various modalities providing data for the learner to make adjustments to his environment, (4) physical abilities which are functional characteristics of organic vigor which are essential to the development of highly skilled movement, (5) skilled movements which demonstrate a degree of efficiency when performing complex movement tasks which are based upon inherent movement patterns, and (6) nondiscursive communication through bodily movements ranging from facial expressions through sophisticated choreographies (Harrow, 1972, 104–6).

The purpose of this taxonomy was to classify observable behaviors from simple to complex as a means of assisting curriculum developers in structuring education goals relevant to the needs of children. The psychomotor domain is primary in the development of speech, reading readiness, handwriting, keyboard skills, athleticism, and performance areas in science, art, and music. While much of educational endeavor has centered on thinking processes, motor skills are part of the total development of the person in the educational process.

Classifying motor skills on the basis of precision of movement is identified and distinguished as *gross* and *fine motor skills.* Gross motor skills are walking, running, jumping, and so on. Gross motor skills stress coordination and smooth movement without significant precision. Fine motor skills require precision and control of the small muscles of the body and require more cognitive development than gross motor skills. Writing, drawing, and sewing are examples of these more precise skills. Christian educators are faced with the challenge of ensuring that activities and movement are appropriate to the psychomotor skill level of their students. The physical growth and development of children in their progression through gross and fine motor skill competency varies significantly from individual to individual. Careful observation of students will assist teachers in selecting appropriate tests and challenges that allow for a range of psychomotor skill. A general understanding of motor skill development in relationship to age and/or ability is invaluable to the Christian educator.

Several basic concepts, principles, and assumptions concerning the psychomotor domain are helpful for those who teach. Skills are classified along a continuum moving from simple to complex. The simpler the skill, the less the strategizing required to accomplish the task. Simpler skills are more reflexive in nature and require less cognitive development than complex skills. For those who teach children, the difficulty of the skill on the continuum is a major determinant as to the amount of training required to accomplish it. A taxonomy of psychomotor skills can be useful as a framework for evaluating an individual's progress in the development of a skill. The acquisition of skills and knowledge, information processing, and motivation are important aspects of most psychomotor learning. While some teachers may assume that most of their efforts should be addressed to the cognitive realm, a wise teacher will realize that a well-rounded and fully functioning person needs development in all domains.

The relationship of the psychomotor domain to the learner and the learning environment is an important consideration for the Christian educator. Concerning the learner, important aspects of understanding motor skills include perception, controlling movement, attention, memory, and individual differences. Visual skills play an important role in many motor skills and vision is basic to the discussion of the psychomotor domain. When all sensory systems are available to us, we tend to trust vision the most. Perhaps this perception bias provides insight as to the power of visual cues in the learning environment. Magill (1993) suggests that vision is involved in the control of coordinated, voluntary movement "by searching the environment for information to provide advance information to enable a person to anticipate the action required in a situation." Structuring the learning environment to provide adequate visual information such as proper lighting, adequate space for movement, appropriate size and color visual materials, and colors and textures which are appealing should enhance learning by facilitating the psychomotor domain.

Two other forms of perception are important to the psychomotor domain. Auditory perception involves abilities concerned with hearing and differentiating pitch and intensity in sounds, locating and tracking sounds, and recognizing and reproducing past auditory experiences (Harrow, 1972, 183). Kinesthetic perception is the feel that goes along with any movement task or the learner's interpretation of the stimulus received through the organs in muscle (Harrow, 1972, 179). Visual, auditory, and kinesthetic perceptions are all essential forms of stimuli in psychomotor development and thus must be considered as integrated and in relationship when discussing the psychomotor domain.

The identification of "psychomotor" as a distinct domain in a classification is effective for research and study of the components of movement theory and the procedures relating to learning movement skills. In the classroom, the teacher can utilize such isolated information to assist in the development of learning and behavioral objectives and to structure the best environment to meet student needs. In the final analysis, all domains, principles, and theories inform an integrated approach that seeks to capture the best of educational practice.

PHILIP D. MCLEOD

Bibliography. R. Beechick (1982), *A Biblical Psychology of Learning;* B. S. Bloom, *Taxonomy of Educational Objectives Handbook I: Cognitive Domain;* A. J. Harrow (1972), *A Taxonomy of the Psychomotor Domain;* R. A. Magill (1993), *Motor Learning Concepts and Applications;* A. J. Romiszowski (1981), *Designing Instructional Systems.*

See also COGNITIVE THEORY; KINESTHETIC LEARNERS; LEARNING TAXONOMIES

Public Education. *See* Mann, Horace.

Punishment and Obedience. Punishment takes many forms and is often administered to encourage obedience. If a person knows that punishment will follow noncompliance he or she will be more apt to obey a rule or mandate. In both the Old Testament (Deut. 11:26–28) and the New (2 Thess. 1:8) punishment is the consequence of disobedience to God.

There are both external and internal forms of punishment. Behavioristic psychologists categorize external forms as either Type I or Type II, a Type I being the application of an aversive stimulus such as a spanking, scolding, or other threat to one's well-being and a Type II involving the removal of something desirable or rewarding such as a toy from a child, driving privileges from a teenager, or employment from an adult. Schools and homes are progressively using more Type II and less Type I punishment as studies show that Type II is just as effective and produces fewer undesirable side effects than Type I.

Internal forms of punishment are delineated in the psychoanalytic concept of the superego and the biblical teaching of the conscience. The feeling of guilt that follows wrongdoing comes from within the person and is accompanied by confession and a desire to change. The internal is preferable to the external as the conscience remains within the person making for stable and trustworthy behavior in contrast to the opportunistic and unpredictable actions that often accompany the anticipation of external consequences.

The same is true when it comes to obedience. An obedience to God that stems from the heart (Rom. 6:17) and is a witness to others (Rom. 16:19) takes precedence over an obedience based on fear. Love is from within, a desire to respond, inspired by gratitude to God and a sense of relationship to him. It is loving obedience and obedient love.

BONNIDELL CLOUSE

Pupil. *See* Disciple.

Puritan Education. The Puritans of New England understood education to be primarily a concern of the home and the church. They recognized, however, that such education was not always adequate and intimate ties between church and state quickly led to state involvement in education. Several attempts to establish public education were made in New England during the early seventeenth century, particularly in the Massachusetts Bay Colony. By the early 1640s, however, it had become apparent that these attempts were largely unsuccessful.

In May 1642 the General Court enacted the "Massachusetts Bay School Law," one of the earliest colonial laws concerning education. The law declared childhood education to be a parental duty. Parents who failed to provide adequate teaching in law, religion, reading, and vocational skills were to be fined. Local representatives were appointed to visit homes and did indeed fine many parents. Frequently, this resulted in private tutoring or apprenticeship positions. The vagaries of the law and difficulties in its enforcement made it insufficient as a means of providing uniform education. More than anything else this law proved to both local communities and colony leadership that adequate childhood education could not be provided in most homes. In spite of this realization, interest in forming public schools appears to have declined somewhat during the early 1640s. The General Court believed it necessary to make further legal provision for education.

On November 11, 1647, a new law was enacted, often termed the Old Deluder Satan Act, which was pivotal in the establishment of public education in the colonies. This new law was based on the belief that a chief goal of "that old deluder, Satan," was "to keep men from the knowledge of the Scriptures." Therefore, the law concluded, every township consisting of at least fifty households was required to appoint and support one teacher for the children of the town. Any town consisting of at least one hundred households was required to set up a grammar school capable of preparing children for university education. Each township was to raise the finances for these schools in any way they saw fit, provided that parents were not "oppressed by paying much more than they can have them taught for in other towns." Towns were to pay a fine for each year they failed to comply with this new law.

Within ten years of its enactment, all eight of the hundred-family towns in Massachusetts had established grammar schools and one-third of the smaller towns had provided their own schooling. Unfortunately, after that decade, compliance in new townships diminished rapidly. The real impact of the law must be viewed from a broader perspective. Public schools sprang up across New England as other colonies followed the example of Massachusetts Bay. By the 1650s schooling as an institution had become firmly established in America (Cremin, 1970). These schools were public in the sense that they were maintained by and under the authority of the township. Any parents were permitted to send their children. They were not, however, free, and with few exceptions, parents who were unable to pay tuition were forced to send their children elsewhere.

Steven White

Bibliography. L. A. Cremin (1970), *American Education: The Colonial Experience, 1607–1783*.

See also Colonial Education

Qq

Quaker Education. George Fox, founder of the Quaker denomination, advised in 1668 the setting up in England of a school for young boys and another for girls. These schools were to have two aims: (1) to instruct and train practically and vocationally so students might live in the world; and (2) to prepare students for their future state in life according to the religious faith of the Friends (as Quakers were also to be called). Brinton (1940) wrote, "The Quaker school prepared, not for the great secular society all around it with its many conflicting, changing standards or lack of standards, but for a special kind of life which was to some degree embodied in a special community—The Society of Friends. This way of life was the goal of Quaker Education" (22). From these early foundations Friends schools grew in level of education (elementary to college) and in number in England, the United States, and around the world.

As the Quakers became established in America so did their formal education. This growth may be divided into three stages, of which some form remains today. In the seventeenth and eighteenth centuries there developed elementary schools which provided many communities the basics of both education and the Friends' way of life. The elementary schools declined in number due to the rise of public education. Next grew the academy, coeducational boarding schools which retained the elementary school while teaching at a high school level of education. Most of these also closed when public education took their place. In the latter half of the nineteenth century came colleges, mainly begun in colonial days for the education of clergy. These were boarding schools that maintained a strongly religious education. Some of these early colleges have grown into respected academic institutions today, such as George Fox University, Whittier College, John Hopkins University, Cornell, and Brown.

Some of the Friends contributions to Christian education include providing a foundation for elementary schools in the United States, education for slaves after the Civil War, laying the foundations of education for Indians in America, and great promotion of the Sunday school movement both in England and the United States.

KEITH R. KING

Bibliography. H. H. Brinton (1940), *Quaker Education: In Theory and Practice.*

Quest for the Historical Jesus. From a Christian point of view the idea of a "quest" for Jesus is puzzling. Since its earliest existence the church has confessed Jesus Christ as the Son of God who came to earth seeking to save the lost. He is not lost; we are. There is no need for people to embark on a "quest" to find him, since he has already come and has made himself fully known.

But "the quest of the historical Jesus"—the phrase comes from the English translation of a book by Albert Schweitzer about nineteenth century study of the life of Jesus—is very much a part of the rhetoric of contemporary biblical scholarship. Likewise, Jesus himself, and theories about him as established by the "quest," continue to exert influence in both popular culture and academic disciplines across educational curricula. Scrutiny of the "quest" is therefore germane to Christian education.

Definition. The "quest of the historical Jesus" refers most directly to the attempts of scholars who reject creedal Christianity's ability to give a "historical" account of Jesus' life rather than a "theological" or "dogmatic" explanation along lines amenable to historic Christian confession. In other words, the quest has typically been dominated by a studied skepticism regarding the virgin-born, miracle-working, crucified-risen-ascended Jesus Christ presented in the New Testament. Instead, modern "critical" thinking in various forms demands a reconstruction of Jesus' life that will free him from the doctrines of the Bible and the church through the centuries. The "historical Jesus" in this understanding is not Jesus as the New Testament sources say he lived and taught in the first century. "Historical" rather signals allegiance to a naturalist worldview and therefore an *a priori* rejection of Jesus' divinity, bodily resurrection, and other aspects of his person or work that this worldview finds repugnant. Since the biblical sources present Jesus as the Messiah, the Christ of Old Testament promise who will appear as Lord and judge when he comes again, a "quest" is necessary to recover the real history of a figure who, from a naturalist point of view, could never have existed as New Testament documents present him.

Another less technical and corrosive definition of the quest is possible. Scholars throughout church history, especially in recent centuries, have been interested in the historical circumstances in which the life of Jesus took place. In this sense the "historical" Jesus is simply Jesus Christ as he lived, died, rose, and ascended in the days of Caesar Augustus and Pontius Pilate. The "quest" for this figure is nothing more than the perennial attempt of careful students of the New Testament in its first-century setting to reconstruct the ministry and meaning of Jesus in a way that will do the most possible justice to the extant historical evidence as it sheds light on the canonical Gospel narratives. These narratives are taken as God-given and as historically reliable, an inference for which Scripture's self-testimony, church teaching, and historical research furnish ample grounds. Since new knowledge of the first century is continually emerging, and since unfolding decades require continual rethinking of past understanding, there is need for an ongoing "quest" for a grasp of Jesus that will incorporate the full range of documentary evidence about the times and surroundings in which his life took place.

History. Historians of the quest now speak of it in three phases, though this partitioning is an oversimplification. The first quest was chronicled in 1906 by Albert Schweitzer, who surveyed a vast literary production spanning well over a century, from Reimarus (1694–1768) to Wrede (1859–1906). It should be noted that Reimarus did not actually originate the quest but made use of ideas already current in English Deism. This earliest phase of the quest was dominated by Enlightenment antisupernaturalism and responses to it, whether pro or con. D. F. Strauss in his 1835 *Life of Jesus,* for example, argued that the New Testament accounts were so overembellished that any methods, including rationalist ones, were doomed to fail in arriving at a reliable historical account of Jesus' life. His pessimistic conclusions met with spirited rebuttals by other scholars who were not convinced that New Testament claims are as unreliable as Strauss alleged. Most of the key figures of the first quest were German and therefore reflected the philosophical and theological movements peculiar to that country (but see, e.g., from France E.

Renan's 1863 *Life of Jesus,* which presented a nondivine, "simple peasant" portrait of Jesus).

Foremost among these movements was theological liberalism. A complex and varied religious posture, it involved at least two key convictions: religious teaching must conform to modern culture and modes of thought; religious authority takes second place to secular human reason and experience. Many corollaries spin off from these convictions, but in general it may be said that they demand the restatement of most traditional Christian teachings. Since Jesus is a factor in almost all such teachings, the nineteenth-century quest frequently involved the discovery of a Jesus with notable dissimilarity from the Jesus of classic Christian creeds. Even Schweitzer (1911), whose Jesus was a noble but tragic figure and not the Lamb that was slain for the sins of the world, pronounced the first quest a failure: "There is nothing more negative than the result of the critical study of the Life of Jesus" (396). Widely divergent results, due in part to liberalism's refusal to acknowledge Jesus' apocalyptic worldview and assumptions as undeniably part of his teachings and legacy, discredited the century-long first quest.

The years of the first quest saw notable contributions from scholars supportive of the historic Christian faith, not just from its detractors. Positive assessments of the biblical Jesus traditions were penned by Neander (1837) and Edersheim (1883), both converts from Judaism, along with numerous others. Capable, even sophisticated articulations of nuanced approaches to modern recovery of the meaning of the ancient Jesus traditions were put forward in the work of scholars like Martin Kähler (1835–1912) and Adolf Schlatter (1852–1938). The impression that the quest was the exclusive province of scholars who disparaged acknowledging Jesus as the Christ is mistaken.

In Schweitzer's wake came the Great War and the reconfiguring of theological scholarship. Until the mid-twentieth century the quest as such lay in relative dormancy. Leading New Testament scholar Rudolf Bultmann attributed most of the New Testament's Jesus material to early church creativity, not historical occurrence. Like D. F. Strauss in the previous century, he was highly pessimistic about what can be known about Jesus historically; like others in the liberal Lutheran tradition, he saw historical facts as playing no role in faith anyway (a position grounded more in Neo-Kantian philosophy than in Luther's teaching). But a "new" or second quest sprang to life among Bultmann's students beginning in 1953. Rebelling against their mentor at this point, they insisted that there is a definable tie between the Jesus of history and the exalted Lord of New Testament proclamation. Unfortunately, their work was consumed with esoteric methodological and hermeneutical positioning and failed to move far from beneath Bultmann's imposing shadow. The second quest was passing quietly from the scene within a decade of its onset. Perhaps its most notable production was G. Bornkamm's *Jesus of Nazareth* (1960).

In retrospect scholars look back to about 1980 as marking the rise of a third quest. It still dominates Jesus studies today and is characterized by bewildering diversity in approach and findings. For some (e.g., E. P. Sanders, J. H. Charlesworth, G. Vermes) the third quest involves the desire to do full justice to Jesus' Jewishness, often at the expense of central portions of Gospel testimony. For others (e.g., G. Theissen, R. A. Horsley) it means the attempt to view Jesus as a sociopolitical activist. Others (e.g., B. H. Mack, F. G. Downing) read the evidence as pointing to a Jesus who adopted a non-Jewish, Cynic philosopher modus operandi. Others (e.g., E. Schüssler Fiorenza) advocate the view that Jesus ought to be viewed most of all as a personification of divine wisdom (*sophia*), perhaps even in feminist style seeking to debunk patriarchal structures of his day. Some third questers (e.g., J. P. Meier) have amassed reconstructions of Jesus of imposing erudition. In Meier's case a Jesus of relatively traditional proportions has emerged (see also Bockmühl, 1994). A notable feature of the third quest is a solid core of scholarship arguing for a continuity between Jesus and the Gospel portraits of him (see Brown, 1997, 820, who mentions B. Witherington, M. deJonge, J. D. G. Dunn, P. Stuhlmacher, and N. T. Wright).

A small group within the third quest has sought and attracted popular media attention: the Jesus Seminar. Scholars associated with the group have made sensationalist claims based on dubious methods, typically issuing controversial press releases near the time of major Christian holy days like Easter. Their work is marked by an outmoded antisupernaturalism, excessive skepticism, and a decided animus toward historic Christian faith (see, e.g., the polemics in R. Funk, 1996). It is their belief that Christianity and traditional Christian believers are the source of much that is evil in the world and little that is good. Scholars associated with the Jesus Seminar over the years since its founding in 1985 include Funk, J. D. Crossan, and M. J. Borg. Although Jesus Seminar members portray those who disagree with their work as ignorant and dangerous fundamentalists, it is mainline scholarship that has most trenchantly denounced its claims and tactics (see, e.g., Brown, 1997; L. T. Johnson, 1995).

Findings. What have the various quests, viewed as a whole, achieved? Any response to this question must be an interim report, since the quest in its latest version shows no sign of having reached a final destination. But five results may be suggested. First, the quest has shown that scholars too often find no more in their subject matter than what their prior convictions allow. This does not mean that a measure of objectivity is impossible, but it does imply that highly skilled academicians may be woefully mistaken in their pronouncements about Jesus. In an age when everyone from preachers to presidents to physicists finds occasion to make pronouncements involving Jesus, this insight is salutary.

Second, the quest confirms that a knowledge of ancient history is necessary for adequate understanding of Jesus, whoever he was. Grasp of first-century language, culture, literature, politics, religion, and more furnishes a nexus apart from which interpretation of Jesus is bound to be skewed. At a time when theological educators are lowering standards of ancient language requirements and knowledge of first-century lore, and when modern learning theories or even sheer intuition seem to be replacing solid command of the Bible's content, it may be asked whether either the church or scholarship can afford these moves. Lessons learned from the quest suggest otherwise.

A third reminder of the quest is that Jesus is an appropriate and even necessary object of academic study. Banned from mention in many North American public schools, he is nevertheless recognized as a key figure in world history by upper-level academicians. Despite the arbitrariness and wild divergence of their theories about him over the past two centuries, their research and debate rightly place Jesus and traditions associated with him at the highest level of international intellectual attention and discussion. Fourth, the quest is a vivid reminder that not all claims made about Jesus are true, since so many of them have been in such utter conflict. Both the (often secularized) media and popular Christian piety would do well to develop more critical and informed mechanisms for assessing such claims than they currently appear to possess.

Fifth, the quest documents that believers in Jesus as Savior and Lord are not necessarily deluded fanatics or regressive anti-intellectuals. True, much evil has been said and done in the name of Jesus. Abuses by and in the church have often given a certain legitimacy to iconoclastic reconstructions of Jesus in the history of the quest. But it is just as true that anti-Christian intellectuals have enlisted Jesus to support their own agendas. Behind the horrors of twentieth-century Marxism was Karl Marx's New Testament professor Bruno Bauer (1809–82), a first-quester who argued that Jesus did not exist. Such "scholarship" is compromised by hidden presuppositions just as surely as the unreflected beliefs of conservative "Christian" bigots.

The fact is that questing scholars of excellent personal and academic reputation have concluded that the "historical" Jesus is precisely that Jesus whom the New Testament presents and whom

Christians have confessed over the centuries. Despite sensationalist claims to the contrary (e.g., by the Jesus Seminar), therefore, it continues to be the better part of intellectual honesty to bow before Jesus Christ as Lord rather than to dismiss his worshipers as unenlightened, ill-informed, and recalcitrant in the face of the latest "scientific" findings. Educational theories and practice that choose to proceed from a careful but trusting sifting of New Testament testimony about Jesus need fear no censure from the sometimes pessimistic and radical pronouncements generated by the current quest.

ROBERT W. YARBROUGH

Bibliography. P. Barnett (1997), *Jesus and the Logic of History;* M. Bockmuhl (1994), *This Jesus: Martyr, Lord, Messiah;* R. Brown (1997), *An Introduction to the New Testament,* pp. 817–30; C. A. Evans (1996), *Life of Jesus Research: An Annotated Bibliography;* R. Funk (1996), *Honest to Jesus;* L. T. Johnson (1995), *The Real Jesus;* J. P. Meier (1991–), *A Marginal Jew,* 3 vols.; A. Schweitzer (1948), *The Quest of the Historical Jesus;* R. B. Strimple (1995), *The Modern Search for the Real Jesus;* M. J. Wilkins and J. P. Moreland, eds. (1995), *Jesus under Fire: Modern Scholarship Reinvents the Historical Jesus;* B. Witherington III (1995), *The Jesus Quest: The Third Search for the Jew of Nazareth;* N. T. Wright, *Anchor Bible Dictionary,* 3:796–802.

Questions. Basic educational method and are essential for effective instruction.

Questions are used in the classroom to:

- Acquire information about the students. These questions must be used with sensitivity so that students do not feel they are being interrogated. Good teachers use questions for this purpose in order to build relationships and to plan for effective instruction.
- Evaluate, prior to instruction, what the learners already know. Questions used in this way may be presented orally or in writing. The intention is to use the answers to plan instruction.
- Evaluate, after instruction, to determine how much learners have learned. Questions are used in this way to ascertain what factual information, as well as higher cognitive levels have been learned.
- Stimulate discussion.
- Aid discipline. Teachers often direct questions to students who are not listening as a way to get attention and encourage listening.
- Involve students in their own learning.

Not every purpose is applicable to every age group. But good questions are used for one or more of these purposes with learners of all ages.

Three basic kinds of questions may be used for the purposes described. Each kind of question is used to accomplish specific purposes. All are essential to develop effective Bible discussions.

Information questions are simple factual questions prefaced with words such as who, where, when, and what. These questions query for specific information. The answer is in the Scripture text or has been covered in previous instruction. In Bible discussion, these questions are usually used first. Because the answers are in the text and the questions can be linked to the text, learners gain confidence in their responses.

Comprehension questions probe understanding and meaning. They are often prefaced with words such as why and how. Like information questions, they are linked to the Scripture text or previous instruction, but they ask the learner to move beyond simple recall to think of relationships, meanings, and interpretations. Questions of this kind are often used as follow-up to factual questions in developing a Bible discussion. After the facts have been ascertained, comprehension questions help learners probe meaning and make appropriate interpretations.

Application questions look beyond factual recall and comprehension to use of the information. These questions are linked to the text, but also to the life of the learners. They bridge the gap between text and life. Application questions may be general or specific. General application questions ask how people anywhere can apply the teaching of the text. Specific application questions ask the learner to make personal decisions and responses to the Scripture.

Guidelines for developing and using good questions:

- Plan and write questions before presenting the lesson. Information questions seem relatively easy to frame, but comprehension and application questions require thought to develop effectively. Good informational questions require thought so that the most important information is sought and so they are asked in the most appropriate order.
- Call on students in random order to answer questions. It is easy for the teacher to call on the student who always has the right answer or the one always eager to participate. But good questioning techniques will bring peripheral students into active participation in the class.
- When directing a question to a specific person, preface the question with the person's name.
- Do not use questions to embarrass or ridicule a student. Even when questions are used to call a student back to attention, the purpose should never be to degrade a student before the class.

- Accept any part of an answer to a question that is correct. Sometimes the answer is only partially correct. If so, take what is correct and move ahead in the instruction.
- Affirm students when they answer questions, even when they answer incorrectly. That can be done by providing verbal or nonverbal feedback to the learner.

ELEANOR A. DANIEL

Bibliography. R. Habermas and K. Issler (1992), *Teaching for Reconciliation;* R. W. Pazmiño (1998), *Basics of Teaching for Christians.*

See also SOCRATIC METHOD

Quiet Time. The Christian life is best understood as a personal relationship involving the sovereign, triune God and his people. One of the components of this living relationship is what is often referred to as the quiet time. Other terms for this vital component of the Christian life include personal devotions, private prayers, daily devotions, and solitude.

The quiet time is best understood as a time set aside for honest, open conversation alone with God. The use of Scripture reading, meditation, and prayer are all aspects of this intimate time of conversation between the believer and God. Another important aspect of the quite time is silence (Ps. 46:10). Silence allows the believer to learn how to listen to and hear God's voice as he or she meditates on God's Word (Foster, 1978, 86).

The quiet time as a component of the Christian life has marked the lives of believers throughout church history. Their testimony over the centuries has been that the quiet time serves as a means for believers to become more sensitive to God's constant presence and work in their lives and in the world, to evaluate their own lifestyles, and to listen to and apply God's Word.

However, even more important testimony as to the necessity and vitality of this discipline for the Christian life is that of Jesus Christ. Jesus, after whom the believer is to model his or her life, continually spent time alone with God. He withdrew from others to be alone with God in times of sorrow (Matt. 14:13), before making critical decisions (Luke 22:42), in times of intense ministry (Luke 6:12), and as a daily practice (Mark 14:23). Jesus Christ, who lived in perfect communication with God, required the silence and solitude of the quiet time in order to both talk to and listen to God. His example is to be followed (1 Cor. 11:1).

A danger about this vital component of the Christian life is that believers become legalistic about its form and practice. The Bible does not prescribe a form for quiet times. This absence does not, however, mean that believers can not learn from the accumulated wisdom of Christians over the past centuries. Some of the basic elements passed down over the centuries that

have helped to make the quiet time more fruitful include the following steps. First, the believer should begin this activity by centering his or her thoughts on God. Quoting a favorite verse, psalm, or hymn is often helpful for this first step. Second, time should be spent meditating on a text of Scripture. Quality, not quantity, is important at this stage. Often, it is as the believer meditates on God's Word that God speaks to a specific concern. Finally, time should be spent in communication and conversation with God. This time of conversation should be characterized by unguarded honesty in expressing feelings, concerns, sins, and desires, as well as humility in recognizing God's greatness and grace.

DAVID BRISBEN

Bibliography. R. Foster (1978), *Celebration of Discipline;* G. T. Smith (1994), *Essential Spirituality: Renewing Your Christian Faith Through Classic Spiritual Disciplines.*

Quintilian (c. 35–c. 99). Spanish rhetorician. Born in Calagurris, Spain, after elementary education, his study of rhetoric commenced in Rome. He was educated by the famed rhetorician and advocate of the court, Domitius Afer, and the renowned grammarian, Remmius Palaemon. While in Rome he also listened to Seneca, who at the time was at the peak of his power and influence. After the death of Domitius, Quintilian returned to Spain.

At a time when few teachers excelled, Quintilian was one of the world's great teachers and writers. His *Institutes of Oratory* set forth the educational ideal of ancient Rome, to develop the good orator. Quintilian stressed that moral virtue should accompany rhetorical excellence.

In 68 Emperor Galba brought Quintilian back to Rome. His successor Vespasian appointed Quintilian as a professor of Greek and Roman rhetoric. He continued to hold this position under Titus and Domitian. Along with the gifts from his wealthy and aristocratic students, Quintilian became wealthy and famous. One of his students was Pliny the Younger.

In middle age he married a young woman and they had two sons. Quintilian suffered a great loss when she and the sons each died prematurely. Somewhere around 90 he retired. Quintilian was appointed to tutor the grandnephews of Emperor Domitian. Their father, Flavius Clemens, helped Quintilian receive the privileges of a consul. He died toward the end of the first century.

Quintilian's goal for education was to assist students to develop the best oratorical skills and to complement those skills with good character. In the *Institutes* he describes the effectiveness of Cicero while using Seneca as an example of consummate oratorical skill, but one lacking in moral character. Book XII describes in detail the quality of moral integrity that should characterize students at all levels of Roman education. He stressed the importance of knowing and using the individual differences among students. He opposed corporal discipline and urged consideration of the pupil and rewards to encourage motivation.

EDWARD A. BUCHANAN

Bibliography. H. E. Butler, *The Institutio Oratoria of Quintilian,* 4 vols.

See also INDIVIDUAL DIFFERENCES; ROMAN CATHOLIC EDUCATION

Rr

Rabbi as Educator. Rabbi, literally translated "my great one," was a title bestowed on a teacher who possessed great knowledge and wisdom of *Torah* as a way of life. The term *Torah*, derived from a Hebrew root meaning "to shoot" or "aim," referred to the five books of Moses as God's aim or instruction for life with his nation. Only later, after the academies under Roman occupation in Palestine began ordaining rabbis to make decisions as legal experts, was Torah translated more generally as "law." In this context, the rabbis became purveyors of God's instruction, but also of the nation's laws and traditions as well.

According to Torah, study was encumbent upon all male Jews, and it was the parents' responsibility to pass the heritage to their children: "You shall teach them diligently to your sons," wrote Moses from the mouth of God (Deut. 6:7 NASB). A more literal understanding of the Hebrew states, "You shall prick into their hearts" the instruction of God. Thus, more than words or ideas, teaching connotes the internalization of God's Word. Every child is to experience being at Mount Sinai, personally receiving the words of the covenant from the mouth of God himself. Obedience to the covenant meant more than law in a society. It was a marriage between God and his people.

Ancient Times: 800 B.C.–A.D. 20. Initially, parents took their responsibilities seriously. Literacy was widespread during the period of the judges (Judg. 8:14). Households received additional help from the Levites, the priestly tribe (2 Chron. 7:7), up to the end of the first temple period. After the seventy-year exile to Babylon, Ezra renewed the obligation to transmit the Torah by calling for regular public readings of the Torah. A Talmudic reference indicates that the public readings were set for Mondays, Thursdays, and Saturday afternoons (Bav. Kamma 82a). The tradition became well established before the end of the Second Temple period (A.D. 70).

The term *rabbi* first appeared in Palestine under Roman occupation, and it was bestowed upon sages whom the people wished to honor for their knowledge of the Torah. As cultural literacy waned, the rabbis found it difficult to educate those who came to mentor and study with them.

Finally, in the first century B.C., Simeon ben Shetach, president of the Sanhedrin (the Jewish Supreme judiciary body), ruled that community education be universal and compulsory for all boys, regardless of social or economic status. This formal ruling shifted the task of transmitting Torah from the parents to community schools and academies, supervised by the rabbis.

The Rabbinic Period: A.D. 20–A.D. 1040. Shortly before the destruction of the second temple, Joshua ben Gamala ruled that all provinces and cities appoint teachers to instruct children starting at the age of 6 or 7 (Bav. Batra 21a). The Talmud tells stories of the rabbis' dedication to educating young children. Said Rabbi Chiyya, "I go up to the village, where there are no teachers, and I teach each of five children a different one of the five chumashim [Torah], and I teach each of the six other children a different one of the six orders of the Mishnah by heart. Then I tell them, 'During the time that I return to my place and come here again, teach Scripture to one another and teach Mishnah to one another.' In this way, I make sure that the Torah is never forgotten from the Jewish people" (Bav. Metz. 85b).

Compiled in A.D. 200, the Oral Law took the place of the destroyed temple. During this period, the Oral Law (Mishnah) was compiled, edited, and written down by Judah haNasi (Judah the Leader). For his work, the Talmud specially refers to Judah haNasi not by name but by the title Rabbenu haKadosh, "our most holy great one/teacher." The analysis of the Torah and the Oral Law became the passion of the rabbis. The Tannaim ("tellers") expanded on the Torah and Mishnah (A.D. 10 to A.D. 200), the Amoraim ("sayers") discoursed (A.D. 200 to A.D. 500), the Yeshiva heads (Geonim or "greats") wrote papers or "responsa" to the communities scattered throughout the world (A.D. 500 to A.D. 700), and the Savoraim ("reasoners") finished redacting all the material into the Talmud (A.D. 700 to A.D. 770).

The great academies of Babylon ruled Judaism and passed on the teachings of Talmud for several more centuries until the death of Hai Gaon, the last of the Geonim, in 1038.

Scholars and the Modern Period: A.D. 1040–Present. The Talmud had become a two-and-a half-million word curriculum of study and discussion, developed over eight centuries by the scholars of the entire nation. This scholarly feat was the fruit of the now defunct academies of Palestine and Babylon. The task of transmitting the Torah, along with Mishnah and Talmud, fell to the scholars. Rashi (Rabbi Shlomo ben Isaac, 1040–1105) founded a Talmud academy in Troyes, France. His concise, rational elucidation of the literal meaning of Torah became the standard for exegetical scholarship. His commentary on the Babylonian Talmud opened the convoluted arguments of the Talmud to the laity. Then came Rambam (Rabbi Moses Maimonides, 1135–1204) to systematize the Talmud as a logical code of fourteen divisions. Joseph Caro (1488–1575) closed the process of systematizing Talmud as a legal framework with his seminal work, the *Shulkhan Aruch* (1570). Thus, the rabbis evolved into scholarly legal experts, who ruled the community by knowledge of the Talmud.

Today, rabbis are still responsible for bar mitzvah (the task of passing the heritage of the Torah to the next generation). Now there is also bat mitzvah (training the girls in Bible study). Duties in the modern age have also expanded to include representing the Jewish community to the modern society. Rabbis require a broad knowledge of homiletics, history, Bible, theology, philosophy, ethics, liturgy, Hebrew literature, and knowledge of the general secular culture. Rabbis still educate, but they must adapt their methods and materials to a fast changing world.

JEFFREY E. FEINBERG

Bibliography. G. Bader (1988), *The Encyclopedia of Talmudic Sages*; A. Cohen (1975), *Everyman's Talmud*; R. H. Goldwurm, ed. (1991), *Art Scroll Series: The Schottenstein Edition*; B. Herring, ed. (1991), *The Rabbinate as Calling and Vocation: Models of Rabbinic Leadership*; G. Wigoder, ed. (1991), *Dictionary of Jewish Biography*.

See also BAR/BAT MITZVAH; HEBREW EDUCATION THROUGH FEASTS AND FESTIVALS; JEWISH EDUCATION

Racism. When speaking of persons, a *race* can be defined as a variety of humankind that is distinguishable by certain physical attributes, such as color of skin and eyes, stature, bodily proportions, and the like. The term is closely related to *ethnicity*, a word that is also used to categorize people into groups, as distinguished by customs, language, characteristics, and group history. Racism involves discriminating among or against persons based on the belief that one race is superior to another or that members of the various races must avoid certain forms of interrelationship with each other. Understood thus, racism can be numbered with other sins of injustice, such as sexism, xenophobia, and other forms of prejudice.

Racism can take various forms, can be overt or subtle, and can be practiced knowingly or unknowingly. On a personal level, it may mean that one thinks or acts in a certain way toward another simply because of that person's race. Perhaps a church member chooses to avoid sitting in a certain pew because of the skin color of one already seated there. There is also the phenomenon of what may be called "institutional racism." A local church may proclaim that their doors are open to all people, regardless of race or color. But, in subtle or not-so-subtle ways, the church may communicate to newcomers that genuine acceptance into the fellowship and real opportunity for service and leadership are dependent upon their willingness to lay aside key aspects of their own culture and behave as though they were members of the majority group.

Extreme cases of racism have marked human history, including, in the past century, Hitler's efforts to exterminate Jews (this is not to say that Jews are rightly to be regarded as a race, but only that they are often treated as such) and other groups of people. Even today, we witness horrific scenes of genocide from one corner of the world or another. Tragically, the church has not been immune from committing such sins. Indeed, the sin of racism seems often to be one of the last that believers confront with seriousness and resolve. Our Christian history is filled with stories of various expressions of racism. Blatant examples include centuries of anti-Semantic rhetoric and behavior from Gentile Christian leaders and, in recent American history, White Christians justifying the enslavement of Blacks by abusing or ignoring the testimony of Scripture.

In seeking to combat racism, some attempt to assume a position of neutrality, claiming that "we are color blind." Though often well intended, this posture is generally neither helpful nor biblically faithful. In the first place, it is probably impossible that we could *not* notice the color and culture of others. But, more important, to do so would be an insult to the Creator who, in sovereign wisdom, has created persons with diversity. As this is very evidently the design of our Maker, our most prudent choice will be to speak to understand and appreciate the diversity of persons, not to deny it. Furthermore, the "color blind" approach often bespeaks an unwillingness to deal with the facts of previous years of prejudice, injustice, and oppression.

The church should be concerned to faithfully teach the biblical stories of creation and redemption as they relate to anthropology. It is a fundamental truth that all persons are created in the image and likeness of God. It is equally fundamental that by the death of Christ the walls of sinful division between persons, erected by national and ethnic prejudice and pride, have been shattered. In Christ there is no East or West, no Gentile or Jew. This is not to say that such distinctions no longer exist in human reality, but that in Christ the ground has been completely leveled. Every oppressive system of prejudice that people have established is disarmed and condemned. The church must be committed to living out this new "in Christ" ethic, and not be conformed to the sinful patterns of this world. When we see fellow believers failing in this regard, we must be bold to rebuke them and call them to repentance, as Paul challenged Peter in Galatians 2:11–21.

Churches must also obey their own teaching in these areas, submitting themselves to examination in the light of God's Word. Is hospitality genuinely extended to all persons, regardless of race and ethnicity, or are people truly welcomed only if they are ready to leave their culture at the front door of the church? Are opportunities for leadership and service truly opened to all, or only to some?

In choosing curriculum materials for teaching in the church, Christian educators should look out for evidence of stereotyping of persons of a certain group, whether the stereotypes seem positive or negative. Rather, materials should seek to fairly and accurately represent all persons. Do our curriculum materials express an appreciation of the diversity God has created in people, or do they largely ignore this diversity?

Another positive step forward in the battle against the sin of racism is providing opportunities for members to hear from, and build relationships with, persons from a variety of racial and ethnic backgrounds. Lack of exposure often leads to ignorance and misunderstanding that may contribute to racist and prejudicial attitudes.

GARY A. PARRETT

Bibliography. A. Hacker (1992), *Two Nations*; D. L. Okholm, ed. (1997), *The Gospel in Black and White*; B. Wilkerson, ed. (1997), *Multicultural Religious Education*.

See also CULTURE; ENCULTURATION; MULTICULTURALISM

Raikes, Robert (1736–1811). Founder of the Sunday school. Born in Gloucester, England, the eldest son of a newspaper publisher, he received little formal education. When his father died, he inherited ownership of the *Gloucester Journal* at age twenty-five. Immediately he expressed concern for the children of poverty who worked twelve hours a day, six days a week in the mills, mines, and sweatshops. Discovering that the lack

of parental and societal control led to unruly behavior and landed many of them in the local prison, Raikes believed that vice could be better prevented than cured. He proposed an experimental idea to Rev. Thomas Stock, the vicar and headmaster of the local Cathedral school, of establishing a form of training for these children of the street. Raikes agreed to finance the project out of his own pocket.

In July 1780, the first school met on Sundays, the only day the children were not working, in the home of a Mrs. Meredith on Sooty Alley. Soon over one hundred boys between the ages of six and fourteen began attending. The only requirement for entry was a clean face and combed hair, but discipline was strictly enforced. Initially the Bible served as the only text, until four textbooks written by Raikes became a part of the curriculum. Lessons were taught in the mornings and early afternoons, after which the children were taken to church for instruction in the catechism. Within three years, eight such schools were opened in Gloucester. Decreasing crime among juveniles correlated with the establishment of the schools. Local factory owners, who employed many of the young men, marveled at the transformed character of those who were attending.

On November 3, 1783, Raikes published an account of the school's success in his newspaper, giving national exposure to the movement. Five years later, John Wesley endorsed the Sunday school, calling it "one of the noblest specimens of charity which have been set on foot in England." By 1830, a half century after their founding, it was estimated that 1.25 million British children were being reached through the Sunday school. Raikes died in 1811, insisting that all glory be given to God ("Providence was pleased to make me the instrument . . . unto Thy name be the glory") for the work he had accomplished.

DAVID GOUGH

Bibliography. A. Gregory, *Robert Raikes: A History of the Origin of Sunday Schools*.

See also COLONIAL EDUCATION; SUNDAY SCHOOL; SUNDAY SCHOOL, HISTORY OF; SUNDAY SCHOOL MOVEMENT

Rationalization. Attempt to justify a wrong behavior or attitude by substituting a safe but untrue explanation for it instead of giving the real reason. It is a psychological term describing one type of defense mechanism. Rationalization helps people cope with embarrassing or difficult situations, avoid looking like failures, or make themselves look better. For example, Dave calls his superintendent an hour before Sunday school starts to tell him he can't teach his class because he doesn't feel good. In reality, he went to bed very late and got up feeling groggy. Signs of rationalization include finding excuses or reasons for actions or attitudes other than the real ones, anxiety or anger when someone challenges those reasons, an inability to recognize inconsistencies in reasoning, and quite often deluding oneself into believing the cover-up story.

LIN JOHNSON

Realism. Word used philosophically, psychologically, and theologically. In the field of philosophy, the word reaches back all the way to Plato and Aristotle. In the debate involving the philosophies of idealism, realism, and nominalism, the issue centered on the essence of reality. Plato was known as the "idealist," positing that all individual objects were expressions of a reality, or "form," which gave meaning and essence to those objects. Aristotle, the "realist," on the other hand, suggested that one could know nothing except that which first came through the senses. For Aristotle reality consisted of the objects themselves. Universals were not "reality" itself, only an extension of the true reality residing in the objects.

This basic debate came to its fullest expression in persons such as Thomas Aquinas and his primary opponent, William of Ockham, the "nominalist," during the Middle Ages. Aquinas was known for his attempt to blend the Christian faith with the philosophy of Aristotle, representing a school of thought known as scholasticism. William of Ockham, on the other hand, developed an epistemology (philosophy of knowledge) which laid the foundation for the Renaissance. It allowed for a definition of reality that resided in individual objects or experiences. In an overly simplified form, this philosophy planted the seeds for subjective philosophies in which the individual person can determine what is, or is not, real.

The issue, however complex it may be, is of importance to Christian educators, particularly when one asks the question about the source of knowledge and truth. Theologically, one deals with the issue of realism in addressing the source of truth. In a postmodern era, many have the attitude that truth, or reality, consists in nothing more than a consensus of individual perceptions of truth. Each person is allowed to determine for himself or herself what is true. Society defines truth simply by listening to the consensus of thought on any issue. Claims to have truth or knowledge grounded in something outside personal perception is held suspect. Two excellent critiques of this modern philosophy are Bellah's *Habits of the Heart* and Carter's *The Culture of Disbelief*.

The term *realism* is often used in the field of psychology, usually in contrast to idealism and pessimism. The term is used interchangeably with *realistic*. The realist is said to see things that way they really are, whereas the other options exaggerate either the positive or the negative aspects of that reality. On the other hand, one subcategory of realism might be that often known as the scientific method. This approach to science, popular in the mid–1900s, asserted that one could have an objective perception of reality. A scientist was to be thoroughly objective in assessing the data discovered in the laboratory. Most scientists have come to accept the fact, however, that persons perceive all reality through certain worldviews or paradigms. Truth is not a matter of merely assessing facts, but learning to understand and interpret those facts in relationship to one another.

Religious educators in the evangelical tradition are likely to find themselves most comfortable in the realistic camp, at least in so far as they assert that reality (or truth) is objectively established and is not dependent for its truthfulness on our perception of it. God, in his very nature and in his revelation, provides the truth. Yet this truth has not come to us as pure, unbiased scientific data. The truth comes to us in the form of his Son—the Word become flesh. In encountering him we encounter the truth—the reality that governs all of creation.

ROBERT C. DE VRIES

Bibliography. R. N. Bellah (1985), *Habits of the Heart;* S. Carter (1993), *The Culture of Disbelief;* T. Kuhn (1962), *The Structure of Scientific Revolutions.*

See also EPISTEMOLOGY; IDEALISM; PHILOSOPHY OF CHRISTIAN EDUCATION; PHILOSOPHY OF EDUCATION; PHILOSOPHY OF RELIGION

Reasoning. *See* Enlightenment.

Rebellion. *See* Cults and Youth.

Recollection. *See* Memorization.

Reconstituted Family. Brought about by the high divorce and remarriage rate in the United States, the reconstituted family is becoming more and more common. The term is often used synonymously with blended, step-, remarried, binuclear, or new extended family. It seems most descriptive of family units formed of persons previously part of a family unit other than their biological family or family of origin. Most often this would include children of either the wife, husband, or both.

The range of reconstituted family types is large and may be complicated: divorced man-single woman; widowed man-divorced woman; divorced man-divorced woman, etc. All of this, plus the plight that brought the family into existence (divorce, death, and so on), add to the strain upon the family's members to make the usual adjustments all people must make when living together.

Families in American culture are expected to perform certain functions. These are reproducing, rearing children, providing economically for its members, and meeting the basic necessities of life for its members. These vary by ethnicity, social class, religion, philosophy, and geography, but must be met to the satisfaction of the law and community mores (Barker, 1992). The reconstituted family, unlike the nuclear family, has subsystems that must be dealt with in order to clarify relationships. These are the former spouse subsystem; the remarried couple subsystem, the parent/child subsystem; the sibling subsystems: step- and half-siblings; and the mother/stepmother-father/stepfather subsystems (Ahrons and Rodgers, 1987). All of these contribute to the stress and strain, the conflict, hostility, anger, and hurt that are common to all families.

EUGENE S. GIBBS

Bibliography. C. Ahrons and R. Rodgers (1987), *Divorced Families: A Multidisciplinary View;* P. Barker (1992), *Basic Family Therapy.*

See also BLENDED FAMILIES

Reconstructionism. Cultural or social reconstructionism claims to be the successor of progressivism and John Dewey's experimentialism. It unambiguously states that the chief purpose of education is to "reconstruct" society in order to deal with the cultural crises. Therefore, the school must reinterpret the basic values of our civilization in view of what we have learned from scientific information now available.

In the 1920s John Dewey wrote *Reconstruction In Philosophy,* suggesting a name for this movement. In the 1930s, a school of thinking arose, some of whose adherents were called Frontier Thinkers. They wanted to create a cooperative society that was loyal to the new social order and that would more equitably distribute the wealth to be shared. George S. Counts in his *Dare the School Build a New Social Order?* (1932) challenged the American school system. He attracted a number of progressive educators who desired to join this educational ideology that attempted to analyze society and establish a plan for social reform. They saw that public education was a strategy for ridding the society of ills and injustices and reconstructing it for a better day that they could affect for good.

In 1950 Theodore Brameld wrote *Patterns of Education* and in 1956 his *Toward a Reconstructed Philosophy of Education* produced a telling effect that would be this school of thought's strongest effort. Reconstructionists believed that educators, teachers, students, and school should:

- identify major social problems by critically examining the present condition of society;
- analyze social problems, issues, and controversies with the aim of resolving them in ways that enhance human growth and development;
- be committed to bringing about constructive social change and reform;
- cultivate a planning attitude among students that will be carried into adult citizenship activities; and
- join in promoting programs of social, educational, political, and economic reform. (Gutek, 1983, 65)

It was education that they saw had the potential of bringing in a new social order. As the depression hit in the bleak 1930s it was a difficult time to launch such a program but it was a period of great need in every area of life. The essentialists viewed the school as an instrument through which the excellent aspects of the culture could be preserved. In the 1960s and 1970s, "the currents of social discontent were directed with force against American public schools, their administrators, and their teachers. This discontent was not directed solely toward the educational system but was part of a larger dissatisfaction with the quality of American life. In particular, the perplexing problems of poverty, cultural deprivation, and racial discrimination which Counts talked about [sixty] years ago are still unresolved" (Gutek, 1974, 166).

"The social sciences of anthropology, economics, sociology, political science, and psychology form a helpful curricular foundation which reconstructionists utilize to identify major problem areas of controversy, conflict, and inconsistency." The ideal world society of reconstructionism would be "under the control of the great majority of the people who are rightly the sovereign determiners of their own destiny" (Knight, 1998, 122).

WARREN S. BENSON

Bibliography. G. R. Knight (1998), *Philosophy and Education: An Introduction in Christian Perspective;* G. L. Gluk (1983), *Education and Schooling in America;* G. L. Gutek (1974), *Philosophical Alternatives in Education.*

Recovery. Regaining of something which is lost, due to sickness, addiction, misfortune, or theft. In educational terms, it most closely aligns with synonyms like restoration, correction, reconciliation, and adjustment. It infers the return to a normal condition, as in, "I recovered from my cold" (a return to health.) Or it may refer to a recovery from an addiction, such as "I am a recovering alcoholic."

Questions as to the adequacy and completeness of a recovery are almost always associated with the successful disciplining of a believer. Is the person "over" whatever abnormal condition he or she was in—sin, mental illness, maladjustment, neurosis, or physical limitation or illness? These questions need biblical guidance.

Biblical Concepts. "Brethren, even if anyone is caught in any trespass, you who are spiritual, *restore* such a one in a spirit of gentleness" (Gal. 6:1 NASB). Restoration is a biblical concept which refers to the putting back into joint, mending, preparing, or equipping of the person for life with God. "Restoration is something that each of us can identify with. When we are ill, we yearn to be restored to health—when depressed, restored to joy. But only the coming of again of Jesus will restore all things and establish the harmony that God intended for his creation" (Richards, 1985, 527). When Paul encouraged the Corinthians to restore the erring member, he says in 2 Corinthians 2:6–8, "What the majority of you agreed to as punishment is punishment enough. Now is the time to forgive this man and help him back on his feet. If all you do is pour on the guilt, you could very well drown him in it. My counsel now is to pour on the love" (Peterson, 1995, 374).

Reconciliation can also be allied with the idea of recovery. In the Scriptures, one can be reconciled to God (2 Cor. 5:18, 20; Rom. 5:10), and also to others (Matt. 5:10). "Reconciliation involves both a resolving of differences and a restoring of harmony. Fundamentally, the term means to 'reestablish friendship'" (Habermas and Issler, 1992, 35).

Psychological Use. In counseling, the idea of recovery is masked in the expectation that a person will get better or return to a normal condition. As therapists, counselors describe the "recovery ratio": "The ratio of the number of patients discharged during the year, or another period, to the total number of patients" (Goldenson, 1984, 625). When counselors discuss the recovery of function they are stating that there is a "return to normal levels of performance" (Harre and Lamb, 1983, 521). Educators seem to mix their ideas between a biblical concept and a psychological one.

GREGORY C. CARLSON

Bibliography. R. M. Goldenson, ed. (1984), *Longman Dictionary of Psychology and Psychiatry;* R. Harre and R. Lamb, eds. (1983), *The Encyclopedic Dictionary of Psychology;* R. Habermas and K. Issler (1992), *Teaching for Reconciliation;* E. H. Peterson (1995), *The Message;* L. O. Richards (1985), *Expository Dictionary of Bible Words.*

Recovery Ministry. Movement within the Christian community that purposes to help people make positive, life-changing steps toward emotional, relational, and spiritual health. The movement seeks to integrate the latest psychological techniques into a uniquely Christian approach to help people deal with interpersonal and relational issues that not only have negative psychological repercussions, but hinder their relationship with God as well.

Recovery ministry marks a return to the type of holistic discipleship and pastoral care that was practiced by the Church prior to the twentieth century. The twentieth century, unlike previous periods of church history, witnessed a split between the arena of emotional health and spirituality in the Christian community. This split is often traced back to Sigmund Freud, the father of modern psychology. Freud was perceived as being antagonistic toward organized religion, including Christianity. He defined religion as a neurotic attempt to remain a dependent child with God as the parent. This understanding gave birth to a widening gap between the field of modern psychology and so-called religious issues (Propst, 1987, 21).

Recovery ministry, as a movement, is characterized by numerous programs that utilize different psychological techniques to help people proceed through life in a healthy way. An example of one of the psychological techniques employed by recovery ministry is the popular utilization of cognitive-behavioral therapy. This basic tenet of this psychological technique is that what people consciously and subconsciously think, believe, and tell themselves strongly influences their personal behavior and their feelings about life. Christian counselors, pastors, and lay leaders seek to help people control their thoughts, behaviors, and emotions through the use of rational strategies. This approach works best for specific and clearly defined problems such as phobias, anxiety, and mild depressions caused by negative thoughts (Vitz, 1992, 102).

Another popular example of recovery ministry is the utilization of group therapy. The Christianization of the twelve-step process that in the past has been associated with Alcoholics Anonymous often serves as a model for these groups. This approach has been employed by the Christian community to help people break behavioral patterns not only of substance abuse, but of other addictive behaviors such as eating disorders, sexual addictions, and abusive relationships. The basic tenet of these groups is that addiction is a disease that has its origin in early childhood experiences. A second dimension is that the participant takes a moral inventory of self along with a cognitive commitment to change. Finally, the person is supported in this commitment by other members in the group (Morgan, 1993, 14).

A final important example of recovery ministry is that which deals with dysfunctional family systems. Family systems theory claims that negative behavioral and relationship patterns are passed from one generation to the next. Recovery ministry seeks to help families break these negative patterns and replace them with biblical models of family relationships (Carder, 1991, 18).

Recovery ministry for the Christian community is quite arguably beneficial; however, caution is also in order. One caution is to recognize that the practice of constantly examining and talking about one's past can generate new problems and forms of psychopathology. A second caution is that encouraging people to constantly see themselves as victims of their past can result in deep resentment and hatred toward the perpetrator as well as give rise to self-pity, or in some cases, a strong sense of moral superiority (Vitz, 1992, 108). Scripture offers a corrective approach by encouraging people to not only recognize that they have been sinned against, but also to recognize that they themselves are sinners who sin against themselves, against others, and against God. This biblical corrective allows people in recovery ministry not only to acknowledge their past hurts, but also to take responsibility for present and future changes.

DAVID BRISBEN

Bibliography. D. Carder, E. Henslin, J. Townsend, H. Cloud, and A. Brawand (1991), *Secrets of Your Family Tree: Healing for Adult Children of Dysfunctional Families;* D. Morgan (1993), *Life in Process: Moving Beyond the Things That Hinder, Moving toward the Things That Help;* R. L. Propst (1987), *Psychotherapy in a Religious Framework: Spirituality in the Emotional Healing Process;* P. C. Vitz (1992), *No God but God: Breaking with the Idols of Our Age.*

Recreational. *See* Camping Facilities.

Recreation in Christian Education. Recreation is what one elects to do in his or her discretionary time. Appropriate recreation refreshes the human body, spirit, and mind. Inherent in the concept is the use of one's time once work and life responsibilities are completed. Involvement in recreation is by definition voluntary and pleasurable.

Establishing the creation pattern, God worked for six days and declared the seventh a day of rest. As his creatures, we are to do our work in six days and on the seventh take time for rest, restoration, reflection, and worship of our Creator.

Involvement in recreation is customarily associated with children and youth, but in the modern era it has become more evident that recreation is incumbent on every one of God's creatures. Each life stage presents its own tasks and challenges and, correspondingly, its own rewards.

Recreation yields rewards including fellowship opportunities, release of tensions and stress from work, the improvement of skills, opportunity for creative outlet, physical activity, and exercise, among others. While Scripture does not demand recreational activity, several biblical principles lend support to such endeavors. Human development when it is complete will include the physical, spiritual, social, and mental aspects, according to Luke 2:52. The apostle Paul makes a wide variety of references to athletic motifs, including boxing, running, and competing in the Olympic games of his day. In Paul's letter to Timothy, he mentions the benefit from physical activity and exercise (1 Tim. 4:8) but keeps it in perspective with spiritual pursuits. Jesus modeled the balance of work and rest with his disciples (Mark 6:31) as they took time away from ministry to be refreshed.

Every culture has engaged in recreational activity. When the balance between work and recreation was not properly maintained, the society suffered accordingly (Ryken, 1995). The waning years of the twentieth century have produced increases in discretionary time, affluence, and population growth, as well as new openness of recreational outlets for women—all of which tend toward increased activity.

Boston philanthropist Joseph Lee inaugurated the modern era of playgrounds in the United States. In the late 1880s, he financed playgrounds for underprivileged neighborhood children in his town. He found that children had to be taught how to play together without fighting and breaking the equipment. His playgrounds included gardens, concerts, ponds for wading and skating, coasting hills, storytelling, and more. From the mid–1940s until the 1970s, relative prosperity and optimism reigned and suburban recreational parks flourished. A major focus of the "war on poverty" provided recreational opportunities for economically deprived individuals. The 1960s and 1970s ushered in increasing outlets for minorities, women, elderly, and those with disabilities. The recession of the 1970s ushered in more austere government and cutbacks for recreational spending. By the 1980s, adults were working more and finding less time for leisure (Kraus, 1997).

Variety marks quality recreation. Pursuits include indoor and outdoor, active and quiet, outlets for creativity, and more structured activities. The number of individuals involved also includes variety, for maximum enjoyment. Some recreation is best enjoyed alone, some in small groups of three to six, some in medium groups of seven to twenty, some in large groups over twenty and less than one hundred. Mass group activity describes those with over one hundred participants.

Recreational activities include art, crafts, drama, music, individual, dual, and team sports, outdoor living skills, nature activities, board and table games, celebrations, festivals, guessing games, hobbies, parties, picnics, mixer games, and ice breakers, among the myriad of possibilities (Farrell and Lundagren, 1978, 142–206).

Recreation in and of itself does not lead to spiritual growth and development, but when properly planned, supervised, and administered, spiritual outcomes are possible. Decisions regarding choice of activity for the Christian are bounded by the injunction of 1 Corinthians 10:31 to do all to the glory of God.

CHERYL L. FAWCETT

Bibliography. G. D. Butler (1965), *Pioneers in Public Recreation;* P. Farrell and H. M. Lundagren (1978), *The Process of Recreation Programming: Theory and Practice;* R. G. Kraus (1997), *Recreation and Leisure in Modern Society;* R. E. Troup and J. O. Brubaker (1986), *Childhood Education in the Church,* pp. 307–30; L. Ryken (1995), *Redeeming the Time.*

Recruitment. Biblically, entrusting the gospel "to faithful men who will be able to teach others also" (2 Tim. 2:2 NKJV). Effective recruitment requires an ongoing plan to identify, secure, and support qualified people to serve in the church's teaching ministry. Most Christian educators call it their greatest challenge. Approached negatively, the task may feel like begging and burdening volunteers. Approached positively, the task calls out the gifts of people to extend Christian faith into the next generation.

Ongoing Plan. Recruiting requires an ongoing plan. Recruiting which begins when a ministry opening occurs begins too late. Part of recruiting involves creating a positive environment toward teaching and overcoming resistance to teaching. We create a positive environment for teaching when we raise the visibility and value of teachers and teaching within the faith community. No formula exists for accomplishing this goal; leaders must regularly ask, "What are we doing to raise the importance of teaching in our midst?" Teacher consecrations, sermons on teaching, service recognition, open houses, and publicity forms with classroom highlights are possible ways to raise the esteem granted teachers. A second part of the ongoing plan is to provide a positive, satisfying experience for those currently involved in the teaching ministry. Volunteer teachers today often feel isolated and underappreciated. An ongoing plan for expressing gratitude and assisting teachers meet the demands of their work helps them feel supported and connected.

Educators must also examine resistance to teaching and find ways to overcome the barriers. The pattern of involvement must roughly fit the pattern of people's lives. Consistent attendance at a home church seems less valued in today's mobile society. We may lament this change and wish for greater commitment, but we also need to have systems in place (e.g. team teaching and a good substitute network) that accommodate contemporary life patterns.

Identifying. Finding prospective teachers must be a shared responsibility. If a soccer team needs a goalie, the team has a problem, not the coach alone. Members of the current "team" can provide names of prospective teachers and, if prepared, invite prospects to volunteer. Most agree that an invitation to teach should include, at a minimum,

a position description, the time commitment required, and expectations for the position.

Securing. While recruiting involves creating a positive environment toward teaching, it also involves bringing people to a decision point: saying yes or no to an opportunity to serve. The person and the ministry are best served when the decision point is marked by the following: (1) the person is responding to a sense of God's call; (2) adequate time is allowed for considering the decision; and (3) the process is wrapped in prayer.

Supporting. Supporting volunteer teachers takes us full circle in the recruiting process. First, teachers feel supported when supervisors provide guidance, assistance, training, and encouragement. Teaching/learning settings tend to isolate teachers and may result in teachers feeling that "no one knows what I'm doing." Guidance from a supervisor through feedback and counsel tells teachers that their work matters to someone. Second, teachers also feel supported when they receive assistance carrying out their work. A current substitute list, a well-stocked supply room, easily accessible audiovisual equipment, and funding for special activities tell teachers help is available. Third, teachers feel supported when they are trained with the skills necessary for effective teaching. Fourth, teachers feel supported when they are encouraged. Thank-you notes, words of appreciation, awards, or a small gift or memento are ways of encouraging teachers to persevere.

Qualified People. Theological, educational, and legal reasons justify churches and Christian organizations being more intentional about what constitutes qualified volunteers. Qualifications serve a screening function and make recruiting more than issuing a public request for volunteers. For children's safety and the church's protection, some states mandate volunteers be screened for any prior criminal records. A church may require membership as a condition of volunteering. Active recruiting that results in particular people who are deemed qualified being asked specifically to serve offers the best path for churches to follow in securing apt teachers (2 Tim. 2:24).

ROBERT DROVDAHL

Bibliography. M. Senter (1983), *The Art of Recruiting Volunteers;* D. Williams and K. Gangel (1993), *Volunteers for Today's Church;* F. R. Wilson (1990), *Christian Education Journal* 11 (1990): 51–68.

Redistribution. *See* Decentration.

Reflection. Methodology that fosters personal formation. It is valuable in personal study as well as classroom experiences. Reflection encourages deep thinking about the meaning of a truth or passage of Scripture and is extremely useful in enabling connection between truth and life both through implication and application. This method can help a learner get in touch with feelings, previous experiences, and significances of integration. This process consciously brings together outer truth and inner reality.

Key factors inherent in effective use of this methodology are time, concentration, and freedom to process truth without the constant pressure to produce. Meditation is a cognate skill to reflection. Both of these are difficult for those who live a fast-paced life. Our culture also tends to value production over process. But wise use of this methodology can foster self-teaching and inner-activated learners who are not content to simply collect informative data, but who also work at the interface of such truth with personal meaning making and response.

Reflection is enhanced by journaling, meditation, and the use of questions. Mulholland suggests the following questions in response to the Scriptures to prompt a response in the deeper levels of being. "How do I feel about what is being said? How do I react? How do I respond down deep within? Why do I feel that way? Why am I responding in this manner? What is going on down inside me?" (1985, 24). Reflecting is a way of coming to know oneself, which is a major component in internalizing new truth.

Howard Gardner in *Frames of Mind* (1983) describes the person for whom reflection is natural. He calls this kind of intelligence intrapersonal. For those whose strengths lie in other intelligences or whose culture does not value this contemplative way as much as outer activity, this mode of learning will require practice and patience. Since God designed us for both inner wholeness and outer expression in activity, cultivating a balance in learning methodologies will facilitate formational learning. Focusing on this inner learning can help to break through outer habitual motions and initiate long-term transformation of the learner.

Not only is reflection foreign to U.S. culture and experience, it also places more responsibility on the learner for the learning and this may be resisted as too personal, too difficult to face, or too much work. Some trends in spirituality find even young children learn to value this opportunity to get in touch with who they are and to make meaning of life. Reflective feeling is a valuable ingredient in worship but reflection in general must be used with great awareness of cognitive limitations found in young learners.

Suggestions for use of reflection in teaching are: (1) Use pictures (words or graphics) and symbols to stimulate thinking. (2) Use a variety of questions that help the learner connect. (3) Give an example of the reflection process. (4) Play music that enhances thinking about the concept or text. (5) Suggest various ways the re-flection or response to it can be shared—journaling, drawing pictures, prayer and worship, verbalizing. Reflection as a teaching method should be in the repertoire of every teacher who wants to cultivate transformation through learning.

ROBERT J. RADCLIFFE AND JULIE GORMAN

Bibliography. H. Gardner (1983), *Frames of Mind: The Theory of Multiple Intelligences;* K. Leetch (1989), *Spirituality and Pastoral Care;* M. R. Mulholland Jr. (1985), *Shaped by the Word.*

Reformation, The. Events in the fifteenth through the seventeenth centuries aimed at reforming the Roman Catholic Church. Often it is called the Protestant Reformation because of the name given to the action of the German princes who formally protested to the Second Diet of Speyer (1529) its decision to uphold the edict of the Diet of Worms against the Reformation.

The religious reformation was preceded by a Renaissance of learning which began in Italy in the early part of the fourteenth century and which revived the study of Latin classics. The movement spread northward into France, Germany, and Holland, where the study of Hebrew and Greek was added. In the universities this brought more attention to the early church fathers and led to a fresh study of the Old and New Testaments.

Forerunners of the Reformation. John Wycliffe (1330–84) of Oxford bitterly attacked the pope, and all of the Church's leaders. He planned a translation of the Bible and an order of Poor Preachers who would take it to the people. The Lollards who propagated his views on personal faith, divine election, and the Bible did not win over the governing classes in strength, and so could not achieve the reformation unaided, but by popularizing Wycliffe's ideas, they prepared minds in Germany, Scotland, and Bohemia for later reformers.

John Huss (1372–1415), rector of the University of Prague, printed Scripture in the vernacular, emphasized practical Christianity, and made the university a stronghold of Wycliffe's doctrines.

Brethren of the Common Life, begun by Geert de Groote (1340–84), founded schools in the Netherlands which emphasized living a life of devotion based on teachings of the Bible. Among those they educated was Erasmus of Rotterdam, who edited the Greek text of the New Testament and published reliable texts of the Fathers. Erasmus's ideas about religious instruction were elaborated later by Comenius (1592–1670).

Girolamo Savanarola (1452–98) of Florence attacked sin in both the church and the world. Martin Luther called him the *proto martyr* of the Reformation.

Factors Leading to the Reformation. Papal power increased after the Council of Constance

(1414–18) ended the Great Schism, unifying the papacy once again. The influence of the Renaissance caused the papacy to become increasingly erudite and to desire to add to the cultural splendor of Rome. Failing to understand the office as a spiritual responsibility, the papacy became just one more worldly Italian court where everything could be bought. Money controlled the agenda. Dissatisfaction with simony, the sale of relics, and the wealth of the monasteries became widespread.

Other changes in the fourteenth and fifteenth centuries prepared the way for the Reformation in the sixteenth. Mysticism emphasized direct personal communion with God. The Black Death which killed a quarter of Europe's population opened the way for younger scholars with newer ideas. Humanism focused on earthly life in the present and urged humans to gain a balanced classical education to better understand their lives. The discovery of the magnetic needle and other navigational tools made possible extensive voyages of discovery which broadened the world of the Europeans. New scientific discoveries challenged the notion that the earth was the center of the universe. The invention of the printing press with movable type by Johann Gutenberg (c. 1400–1468) made knowledge more readily available. The invention of gunpowder and the development of commerce challenged knighthood and the power of feudal lords. The rising spirit of nationalism meant that national rulers began to see Rome as a symbol of foreign tyranny. Princes, free cities, and minor nobility in Germany were ready to support Luther when he took his stand against the church at Rome. Help from these political leaders made the success of the Reformation possible.

The Reformers. Martin Luther (1483–1546), professor of biblical literature in the small, new University of Wittenberg in Saxony, had struggled with anxiety over his own salvation, had been distressed by the corruption of Rome when on an official visit, and had come to the conclusion that the essence of salvation is justification by God through faith alone and without works. He had decided that the church and its priesthood had no role to play in mediating salvation. When he learned that Johann Tetzel was selling indulgences as a part of a scheme to raise money for the renovation of St. Peter's in Rome, he protested, and in 1517 posted on the Wittenberg church door a list of 95 theses dealing with the indulgences in preparation for a debate. From this modest beginning the controversy spread. Driven to open revolt when Rome failed to respond, Luther ultimately advocated, among other things, a national church and the right of priests to marry. Pope Leo X excommunicated him. In 1521 Emperor Charles V summoned Luther before the Diet of the German princes at Worms. He refused to recant and was condemned as a heretic, but the elector of Saxony kept him in hiding.

Luther's doctrines spread, and in 1530 he and his follower Phillip Melanchthon (1497–1560) presented a classic outline of Reformation faith to the Diet of Augsburg. Soon after, the rulers assumed the regulation of the churches within their territories and the Reformed faith became legal over half of Germany. The monarchs of Denmark and Sweden also declared their countries' churches to be reformed.

Huldrych Zwingli (1484–1531) led the reform in Zurich, Switzerland. Primarily a pastor and political leader, he used sermons, disputations (67 Artikel), tracts, and other writings to further his cause. In 1529 he got the Catholic faith prohibited in the canton of Zurich and formed the Christian Civic Alliance with Basel and Bern. The five Catholic forest cantons formed their own Union and Zwingli was killed in 1531 in the Second War of Kappel when he accompanied his forces into battle.

John Calvin (1509–64) was the youngest of the three great Reformers and lived to consolidate and unify their great themes. Moving from France to Geneva in 1536, the year the city declared for the reformed doctrines, Calvin established the first training school for ministers of the reformed church. The Geneva Academy trained those who came from many European countries.

The Reformation in England came for political rather than theological reasons. The Statute of Six Articles in 1539 clearly shows that Henry VIII did not mean to break with traditional Catholicism, but he overthrew papal supremacy in England and dissolved the monasteries. He had little sympathy for the continental Reformation, but endorsed an English translation of the Bible which was to be placed into every church for everyone to read. Calvinism came in as a radical movement within the national church, but after the Puritan Revolution (1640–60), the national church was restored.

Luther, Zwingli, and Calvin have been called magisterial Reformers because they worked through the system of government available to them and set up state churches in the Catholic pattern with which they were familiar. Knowing the people's love for tradition and habit, they wanted to retain everything which they did not think stood in the way of the gospel. Other believers, however, thought that the church of their day was apostate and beyond rescue. They wanted to restore original and primitive New Testament Christianity in which adults professed their faith and were baptized as a sign of that decision. Some of this diverse group also advocated pacifism and communal living. Called "deserting disciples" by the magisterial Reformers, they were cruelly persecuted by both Catholics and Protestants for a hundred years.

Educational Aspects of the Reformation.
Most of the leaders of the Reformation were either university teachers or were exceptionally well-educated pastors. The initial approach of the magisterial Reformers was typical of medieval scholasticism—publishing theses, debating them, and following up with published documents. The printing press made these publications impossible to stop. Pamphlets with pungent cartoons and simple language made the debate accessible to the masses. The Reformers also translated Scripture and wrote commentaries.

The Reformation doctrines of justification by grace through faith, the priesthood of all believers, and the authority of the Scriptures demanded universal education. If each individual is responsible to God, he or she must understand that responsibility in terms of the Word. This was a problem because only the well educated could read the Bible.

The extension of education at the elementary level was a major contribution of the Reformation. As a result, the vernacular language took on new importance, and a new pedagogy developed which realized the importance not only of books, but of learning a practical trade. This new idea in education was supported by the Protestant emphasis that God called everyone to his service, not just the clergy.

Luther emphasized the home, but did not believe that the teaching of the parents was sufficient to provide all the education necessary for the children. In his "Letter to the Mayors and Aldermen of All the Cities of Germany on Behalf of Christian Schools" written in Wittenberg in 1524, he urged schools to provide a well-rounded education including Latin, Greek, and Hebrew so students could properly understand the Bible for the sake of Christianity and the Scriptures. He also argued that the schools were needed because society, for the maintenance of civil order and good households, needed accomplished and well-trained men and women. The schools were to be financed by citizens' councils. Open to both boys and girls, the schools were also to be enjoyable.

Luther's coworker, Phillip Melanchton, concentrated almost entirely on education, creating a new educational system and setting up a secondary school system. At his schools at Eisleben he instituted a program of studies in which students moved from simpler to more complex subjects. He made the University of Wittenberg where he taught one of the centers of theological studies in Reformation Germany.

Each Reformer differentiated his doctrinal positions from those of the Catholics and from other Reformers by means of catechisms. Luther's *Small Catechism* (1529) was circulated more than any other book except the Bible. Luther also wished to warm the hearts of his followers and used a revised liturgy and hymns for this purpose. He also made the sermon central in worship, using it to teach the grace of God, to urge repentance and faith, and to shape the community by giving guidance for daily life.

Calvin was in favor of universal education with the cost borne largely by the community. His followers in the Netherlands in the Synod of The Hague in 1586 provided for setting up schools in the cities, and the Synod of Dort in 1618 decreed that free public schools should be set up in all villages. Influenced by Calvin, John Amos Comenius (1592–1670), a bishop among the Moravian Brethren, contributed to the extension of education at the elementary level by counseling leaders in several nations. His *Great Didactic* published in 1657 formed the basis of modern education.

Calvin himself concentrated on higher education in his academy. Strong Calvinist universities were established in Leiden (1575), Amsterdam (1632), and Utrecht (1636) in the Netherlands and the University of Edinburgh (1582) in Scotland. The Puritan, or English Calvinist, movement founded Emmanuel College at the University of Cambridge in 1584.

Because of their severe persecution and their doctrine of separation of church and state, the Radical Reformers at first made little lasting impact on the educational establishment of Europe. Their work was local. Anabaptist schools for children living in a Hutterite community in Moravia were described by a visitor in 1578 who noted that children of Radical Reformers received most of their education at home and at worship.

ROBERT L. LAMB

Bibliography. C. V. Anderson (1981), *Introduction to Biblical Christian Education*, pp. 36–52; F. L. Cross and E. A. Livingstone, eds. (1981), *A Faithful Church;* E. Daniel, J. W. Wade, and C. Gresham (1987), *Introduction to Christian Education;* F. Eby (1915), *Christianity and Education;* K. O. Gangel and W. S. Benson (1983), *Christian Education: Its History and Philosophy;* H. J. Hillerbrand (1964), *The Reformation, A Narrative History Related by Contemporary Observers and Participants;* K. S. Latourette (1953), *A History of Christianity;* J. E. Reed and R. Prevost (1993), *A History of Christian Education;* R. Ulich, ed. (1954), *Three Thousand Years of Educational Wisdom, Selections from Great Documents;* J. H. Westerhoff III and O. C. Edwards, eds. (1981), *A Faithful Church.*

See also BRETHREN OF THE COMMON LIFE; CALVIN, JOHN; MEDIEVAL EDUCATION; HUMANISM, CHRISTIAN; LUTHER, MARTIN; MELANCHTHON, PHILIP; ROMAN CATHOLIC EDUCATION; ZWINGLI, ULRICH

Regression. Term used in Freudian psychotherapy, closely related to the concept of fixation, which describes an individual's defense mechanism of reverting to behavior that characterized a previous stage of life in order to achieve sources of gratification or security experienced during that earlier period. In psychotherapy, regression is viewed as a means of coping with anxiety, conflict, fear, or frustration. Children may regress (e.g., sucking their thumbs, using baby talk) when a new baby is born into the family, attempting to regain attention and a sense of security. Regression can also occur in adults and may be brought on by severe mental disturbances. The concept of regression is also used in some stage theories of human development (e.g., Perry's [1970] theory of intellectual and ethical development; Erikson's [1982] theory of psychosocial development) to refer to an individual's reverting to thought processes and behaviors that characterized a previous stage or level of development.

KEVIN E. LAWSON

Bibliography. E. H. Erikson (1982), *The Life Cycle Completed;* W. G. Perry (1970), *Forms of Intellectual and Ethical Development.*

See also SIGMUND FREUD; WILLIAM G. PERRY JR.; PSYCHOLOGY OF RELIGION

Reinforcement Scheduling. Learning is "an enduring change in observable behavior that occurs as a result of experience" (Eggen and Kauchak, 1994, 255). One way learning takes place is through "operant conditioning" (changes that result from behavioral consequences). The work of B. F. Skinner is generally associated with operant conditioning. Skinner postulated that behavior is sandwiched between two sets of environmental influences: those that precede the influence (antecedent), and those that follow the influence (consequences).

In operant conditioning the individual has control over personal behavior. Consequences of actions influence subsequent behaviors. Change in behavior is indicated when the person repeats the action that led to the consequence. The reinforcement of the behavior is the key to changed behavior. Two types of reinforcers are positive reinforcement and punishment. Positive reinforcement is always associated with increases in behavior, and its effectiveness is demonstrated. Punishment involves decreasing or suppressing behavior. Consequences following an action may serve as reinforcement for one individual, or punishment for another.

The effectiveness of reinforcement on behavior will depend on the schedule of reinforcement. How frequently are reinforcers given? How much time elapses between opportunities for reinforcement? What is the predictability of reinforcement?

Teachers may control consequences of behavior by controlling the antecedents of behavior through cueing and prompting (Woolfolk, 1998). Cueing "sets up" the desired behavior and precedes the prompt. A cue would reinforce students' accomplishment in remembering. A prompt may be needed when learning a new behavior. The prompt should fade as soon as possible so that the students do not become dependent on the prompt. An example of cues and prompts is guidelines students use when working on group projects. When they no longer need the prompts, the teacher can assume they have learned proper responses for working in groups.

Reinforcement Schedules. Reinforcement schedules can be *continuous* (each desired behavior is reinforced) and *intermittent* (desired responses are reinforced intermittently).

1. Continuous Reinforcement. When approaching a new task it may be necessary to provide continuous reinforcement until the students are able to complete the task without reminders. For example, a teacher may need to repeat the guidelines for classroom conduct on a daily basis at the beginning of the school year through praise each time the guidelines are followed. This becomes inefficient over time. The goal should be to expand the reinforcement intervals to the point that the teacher only occasionally has to refer to the guidelines.

Continuous reinforcement encourages rapid learning of a response; however, the response may disappear rapidly when the reinforcement disappears. Rewards for desired behavior would fall into this category (e.g., stickers for perfect attendance). Once stickers are no longer provided, the student may not be as conscientious about attendance.

2. Intermittent Reinforcement. Two basic types of intermittent reinforcement schedules are interval schedules (based on the amount of time between reinforcers) and ratio schedules (based on the number of responses students give between reinforcers).

(a) Interval schedules can be fixed or variable. An example of a fixed interval would be a weekly quiz. Variable intervals would be unannounced quizzes. The fixed interval ensures an increase in the response rate when the time for the reinforcement approaches, however, it drops rapidly after the reinforcement. What is learned for a Friday quiz may not be remembered the following week. If a quiz is given at variable intervals students will demonstrate greater persistence in behaviors associated with the reinforcer (quiz). Behaviors learned through variable intervals are highly resistant to extinction of the behaviors.

(b) Ratio schedules can also be described as fixed or variable. A fixed-ratio reinforcer is given after a fixed number of behaviors. Students' performance will depend on the length of the pause related to the size of the ratio. There is little persistence in the behavior and a rapid drop in the response rate when the expected number of responses are given and no reinforcer appears. For example, when a teacher tells a student, "When you have completed the ten questions, you may go to the activity corner," the student expects the reward. Not receiving the reinforcer (reward) may discourage the student from completing designated tasks in the future.

Variable-ratio reinforcement tends to produce a steady rate of positive responses because of the unpredictability of the reinforcement. Response stays high and only drops off gradually when reinforcement stops. If students want to achieve high marks on quizzes they will maintain a regular study schedule because they do not know when there will be a quiz.

Types of Reinforcers. There are two types of reinforcers: *primary* and *secondary*.

1. Primary. Primary reinforcers satisfy inborn biological needs, such as food, warmth, sleep, or sex. Primary reinforcers are natural, unconditioned, or unlearned. They are automatic responses to basic life needs. Students will complete tasks much more rapidly if they get enough sleep. School breakfasts function as another example of primary reinforcers. Primary reinforcers can be effective when teaching a new behavior since they have a rapid effect on the rate or quality of a behavior.

2. Secondary. Secondary reinforcers (unconditioned) are those reinforcers that are initially meaningless, but acquire importance by being associated with primary reinforcers or already established primary reinforcers. Praise, grades, or completing a project acquire reinforcing value through learning.

Winzer (1995) describes three types of secondary reinforcers: *token reinforcers* (exchanging five tokens for free time); *activity reinforcers* (students work hard in order to have extra computer time); and *social reinforcers* (positive verbal and nonverbal messages when students do well).

One common reinforcer is the "Premack Principle." Activities which occur at a high frequency (more preferred) can be used to reinforce the completion of lower frequency (less preferred) activities. An illustration of the Premack Principle would be, "Finish your writing project and then you can go to the art center."

An important skill for a professor to master is the effective thinning, or reducing, of reinforcements. The desired behavior of chapel attendance is that students will see the value of chapels and will not need reinforcers.

Generally, in order to maintain the desired behavior, reinforcement should shift from continuous to a rich intermittent schedule in which reinforcement is given relatively frequently, and then continue on to thin, or reduce, the amount of reinforcement given. There is no specific formula that can guide the thinning process. Students' behavior is the only true measure of the reinforcer's effectiveness, so it is critical that the student behavior be carefully monitored.

Another way of using reinforcers in the reinforcement schedule is by "shaping" the student's behavior. Using writing skills as an example, one would begin with students' current level of writing proficiency as a starting point, move to a series of steps shaping the skills toward college level expectations, and, when those skills are achieved, provide reinforcement feedback indicating that the skills are well established.

Effects of Reinforcement Schedules. Understanding how schedules of reinforcement impact behavior can help teachers make more informed decisions as they work with students. Since reinforcement is dependent upon the behavior produced, both variable- and fixed-ratio schedules produce faster, longer lasting response rates than do interval schedules. Thus, if a college's goal is to have all students participate in chapel services, then variable schedules would be implemented.

Potency of a reinforcer will depend on the learner's situation. High grades, used as reinforcers for students, may lose their effectiveness when all students get high grades in a course. Even the source of reinforcers influence the potency of a reinforcer. A respected professor's praise and compliments may be more potent than those of one who is less respected.

The ultimate goal is for students to develop their own, inner behavior that motivates them toward appropriate social, academic, and behavioral performance.

ELEANOR M. LOEWEN

Bibliography. P. Eggen and D. Kauchak (1994), *Educational Psychology: Classroom Connections;* M. Winzer (1995), *Educational Psychology in the Canadian Classroom;* A. E. Woolfolk (1998), *Educational Psychology.*

See also EXTRINSIC MOTIVATION; INTRINSIC REWARDS; MOTIVATION

Relational Evangelism. *See* Friendship Evangelism.

Relativism, Religion, and Christian Education. Relativism is a philosophic position which denies that there is any absolute reference point or that there is any possibility of knowing anything as it is. Relativism affirms that one's knowledge and value judgments, that is, what one perceives as true or false, right or wrong, good or bad, are subject to one's perception and situation. Because perceptions and situations differ from place to place, time to time, person to person, and culture to culture, relativism concludes that no universal judgments can be made. While relativism may be related to pluralism, it should not be confused with it. Pluralism is a social reality and a political position, acknowledging differences, particularly racial, cultural, and religious differences, and affirming the right of most differences to exist.

A relativistic viewpoint (sometimes identified with skepticism) has a long history in philosophy. However, it had been a minor voice until the modern era when David Hume (1711–76) developed the notion that the only way we can know is through perceptions based on sensory input. Later, Immanuel Kant (1724–1804) attempted to protect science from relativism by postulating that the human mind had innate categories for sense perception, but he denied that ability to know anything nonmaterial, including God. It should be noted that Albert Einstein's (1870–1955) theory of relativity in physics has increased the popular sense that "all is relative," but in fact his theory includes the constant of the speed of light.

The relativist viewpoint now permeates secular societies. In a 1994 U.S. survey, George Barna found 72 percent of the respondents agreed with the statement, "There is no such thing as absolute truth; two people could define truth in totally conflicting ways, but both could be correct." (Barna, 1994, 155–56). Allan Bloom observed that "There is one thing a professor can be absolutely certain of: almost every student entering the university believes, or says he [or she] believes, that truth is relative" (1987, 25). However, many people have little awareness of the groundings, inner contradiction, implications, or consequences of relativism and they often apply it selectively.

Relativism is worked out in many areas of thought. Metaphysical relativism denies any objective absolute, including the eternal God portrayed in the Bible. Epistemological relativism, starting with finite, conditioned, and individual humans, denies the ability to know absolute truth.

Cultural relativism goes beyond the obvious recognition that cultures differ in many ways from one another. Cultural relativism holds that cultures are constructed by people according to their own values and needs and are not to be evaluated by the norms of any other culture of (nonexistent) absolute. If a group believes certain behavior to be right, then the act is right for them and there can be no justification for morally judging it. Cultural relativists cannot condemn slavery previously practiced in the Southern states, child and adult sacrifices of ancient religions, the genocide of the Nazis, or the recent apartheid of South Africa.

Ethical or moral relativism is related to cultural relativism. The idea of absolute criteria for values is rejected; universally binding categorical imperatives (such as the Ten Commandments) are denied. Values are only relative to the person or situation (situational ethics) or culture in which a person functions. Some implications of this position include the impossibility of judging any culturally accepted practice as immoral, the illusion of the idea of moral progress, the arbitration of

morals by public opinion, and the importance of defining the boundaries of the culture.

Religious relativism is another variation of cultural relativism. Kant argued that the transcendent dimension in religion is unverifiable and that at best it is allowable as an individual and private experience. Since there is no external or ultimate reference point by which religions may be judged or compared, people are left to choose a religion if they wish based on what seems best for them.

Apologists for the Christian faith have correctly identified relativism as one of the major mindsets which must be addressed in order for modern and postmodern persons to be able to adopt the Christian faith and life. Christians realize that human knowledge is limited by our finiteness in terms of the faculties we have to receive information, our ability to process that information, the accessibility of the object of our knowledge, and our location, space and time. We acknowledge the "relative relativeness" of many things, and accept that "we know only in part" (1 Cor. 13:9), but insist that we may know, as Francis Schaeffer (1972) said, "true truth" (18). We believe that at the heart of reality is the infinite, eternal, personal God who formed the universe, communicated moral laws to humankind, acts redemptively in history, and will be the arbiter of all creation.

Christian education must address not only the logic of relativism but also take into account its mood. Many people are attracted to relativism because it leads to tolerance of differing views. Relativistic thought also considers it inappropriate to make universal claims such as "Jesus is the way to God" or to try to persuade people to change their minds. Christian educators must show respect for all people, allowing them to state their views and listening empathetically to them, while lovingly challenging them with the message of the Bible. We can and must stress relevance and personal meaning without succumbing to the impoverishment of relativism.

PAUL BRAMER

Bibliography. G. Barna (1994), *Virtual America;* A. Bloom (1987), *The Closing of the American Mind;* F. Schaeffer (1972), *He Is There and He Is Not Silent.*

See also HUME, DAVID; KANT, IMMANUEL; PHILOSOPHY OF RELIGION; POSTMODERNISM

Religious Education Association (REA). The Religious Education Association was founded in Chicago in 1903. It was in its origin dominated by liberal Protestant academics disillusioned with the staid biblicism of the American Sunday school movement.

The founding convention of the REA was hosted by Wm. Rainey Harper, president of the University of Chicago. Early members of the association included many university presidents as well as major nationally known academics: G. Stanley Hall, Andrew Draper, Nicholas Butler, J. B. Angell, John Dewey, and a host of others. Evangelicals, Catholics, Jews, or conservative Protestants were not in evidence. What drew all these illustrious leaders of American higher education to Chicago was the liberal progressive vision of Harper.

Harper was a Baptist Scripture scholar, a linguist, and a dynamic administrator. He was the essence of a progressive educator, believing that education properly designed would save society and give meaning to the entire social enterprise. He saw the university as the "messiah" of society. The way to that salvation was by the scientific study of the Bible. Harper's REA was to be the institution which embodied this vision, a social vision of cultural redemption. Biblical values would lead to social growth and morality.

Harper died in 1906. His mantle of leadership was passed on to George Albert Coe. Coe, like Harper, believed in a social salvation. He coined the phrase "The Democracy of God" as a metaphoric vision of what religious education could do for the culture. Coe's leadership dominated the association for the next two decades. His *Social Theory of Religious Education* (1917) became the dominant liberal view on the proper role of religious education. Here was no understanding of personal salvation, no serious view of historical Christology, no understanding of the severity of human evil and sin, and no allowance for a theology of dialectical realism. There was no God of justice and mercy, rather a God of lived experience, incarnate in human experience, unrelated to historical Christian understandings, but open to those who were socially moral and loving.

The "Democracy of God" was such a vision of human redemption. Doctrinal issues, conservative views of Scripture, or the meaning of salvation were rejected. Catholics were unwelcome because of their "doctrinal" basis, few Evangelicals were welcome, hardly any Lutherans, and only token Jews. The REA held a worldly vision of human change, a progressive view of the meaning of education, as that action that transforms human persons into loving, kind, and intelligent persons.

The Religious Education Association grew and flourished until the late 1930s. Its growth parallels that of the progressive school movement. Major universities such as University of Chicago, Northwestern, Yale and Columbia/Union Seminary trained large numbers of religious educators during the early decades of the century. Hundreds of socially minded religious educators were formed in the vision of those early progressives. Here was a vision of public pedagogy designed to build a *paideia* of Christian virtues.

The decades after World War I and after the Depression were difficult for the association. Social liberalism waned, both as a serious intellectual value as well as a practical solution to the real needs of a people disillusioned by war and economic disaster. Gradually neoorthodoxy gained prominence in major Protestant seminaries. Social Gospel modernism was no longer respected or taken seriously. Voices from within the religious education movement were the most effective critics of the association. H. Shelton Smith, a religious education colleague at Union Seminary, New York, wrote his telling *Faith and Nurture* in 1941. It was a frontal attack on progressive liberal religious education, "divine immanence, growth, goodness of man, and the non- historical Jesus" were all components of theological romanticism. Smith called for a renewal of biblical faith, a strong Christology and a clear neoorthodox understanding of sin and grace. Liberals were in retreat, the REA declined in influence, and numbers of members dropped.

Herman Wornom was elected General Secretary in June 1952. He took leadership of a weakened association, battered and wounded, dispirited and disillusioned. His work over the next twenty years transformed the REA. Wornom solicited Evangelicals, invited Roman Catholics, and welcomed Jews. He revived the strong interest in research and social science insights related to teaching and learning. He traveled extensively and reestablished the pattern of national conventions after a twenty year period of absence. He was reasonable and balanced, a centrist who had a vision of ecumenical perspective and was open to voices once not permitted in the association. The REA grew under his guidance and was taken seriously by religious educators across the country.

Since Wornom's retirement in 1970 the REA has struggled to maintain a public viable presence. Individual judicatories now host national religious education conventions. Ecumenism is no longer a dominant theme in American church life. And clear national leadership has not emerged within the REA.

When the Association of Professors and Researchers in Religious Education (APRRE) formed in 1970 the REA experienced a serious blow to its intellectual leadership. Now the majority of the professors and teachers in Religious Education in most denominations have joined APRRE. It has become the major professional organization for most of the academic leadership in religious education throughout the United States. It is designed to meet the academic professional needs of seminary and university teachers in religious education. The intellectual energy and center of the field of religious education has shifted from the REA to the APRRE.

The present circumstance of the REA is delicate indeed. Regular national conferences are no longer widely attended. The Religious Education journal continues as the last important remnant of leadership of the REA. Yet the dominant shape of its content is largely academic, written for university and seminary usage, not parish religious educators. The future of the REA is in serious question. It may like other agencies of progressive education have had its day. Its legacy is secure, its contributions significant, but its usefulness no longer significant, it will die, or more likely be formed in a new fashion suited for this time and these challenges.

STEPHEN A. SCHMIDT

Bibliography. S. Schmidt (1983), *A History of the Religious Education Association;* J. P. Wind (1987), *The Bible and the University.*

Religious Publishing Companies. Religious publishing companies exist to provide publications for churches, particularly curriculum materials and other resources helpful in carrying out the teaching, worship, and leadership ministries of the church.

The church has always needed and produced books, even when books were difficult to reproduce. Many were beautifully illustrated. Most were copied and produced in monasteries. The invention of the printing press in the fifteenth century made possible a wider distribution of books. The Bible was the first book printed by Gutenberg, the inventor of movable type in the West. As the Bible was translated into the vernacular, it was printed and more readily distributed to the masses. Hymnals and other worship helps were commonly produced in early days.

Religious book publishers today produce a wide range of materials. Some companies are narrow in focus, publishing only a few kinds of curriculum and related resources. Others produce primarily religious books and Bibles. Still others publish a wide variety of materials, ranging from books to curriculum. Certain publishers produce scholarly works.

Curriculum publishers vary from denominational publishing concerns, such as LifeWay of the Southern Baptist Convention or Christian Board of Publication for the Disciples of Christ, to large, independent publishers such as Standard Publishing Company (Cincinnati), Gospel Light (Ventura, Calif.), Group Publishers (Colorado Springs), and David C. Cook (Colorado Springs). Some publish curriculum for Sunday school, children's church, small group Bible studies, Christian schools, vacation Bible school, and youth groups. Others focus on materials for only one or two programs and sometimes for a limited age range.

Religious book publishers produce a wide range of Christian reading materials for children, youth, and adults. The best-seller is still the Bible. Some companies focus primarily on publication of study helps, such as study Bibles, atlases, and commentaries. Others produce a variety of self-help and inspirational materials for children, youth, and adults. Some publishers, such as Religious Education Press (Birmingham, Ala.), produce books or materials for academic fields. Some publishers attempt to serve a large, diverse Christian market, producing curriculum and related resources, Bible study helps, and books on spirituality, biography, ministry, and other topics. Others focus primarily on a denominational market.

A rapidly growing segment of the Christian publishing effort is children's books. These are often Bible storybooks, but also include books teaching Christian concepts. A second rapidly developing segment of the market is Christian fiction for all ages.

Religious publishers have in recent years expanded their efforts to include nonprint media such as videotapes, CDs, tapes, and computer software. Some of these materials, such as videotapes, CDs, and audiotapes, are widely distributed while computer materials are less available. However, these nonprint media appear to have the greatest potential for expanding the market of religious publishers.

The quality of Christian books and materials has generally improved through the years. One factor is better writing. Increased competition for religious manuscripts and more sophisticated graphics and printing have also improved quality.

Three national associations coordinate the work of Christian religious publishing. The Christian Booksellers Association (Colorado Springs), established in 1950, is an association of religious bookstores and distributors. Thousands attend the annual convention that features new products from the publishers and offers awards for noteworthy publishing efforts. The second association is the Protestant Church Owned Publishers Association (St. Charles, Mo.), smaller than CBA, but equally valuable in coordinating the work of the publishers associated with it. The third organization is the Evangelical Christian Publishers Association (Tempe, Ariz.). Each of these groups sponsors exhibits at the annual International Book Fair and other smaller book fairs throughout the world.

Religious publishing efforts are also present in areas other than the United States and Western Europe. Many materials and books published in the United States are translated and distributed in many countries. With the advent of desktop publishing and the use of computers, these materials can readily be produced for use by the Christian community outside North America.

The growth of Christian publishing has led to the compilation of a list of "best-sellers" in the religious market. Many of these books outsell books in the broader publishing market, largely, as recent news articles have pointed out, because these books, especially Christian fiction, present and reinforce values espoused by Christians.

Religious publishing extends beyond books, curriculum, and media. Religious periodicals are also important resources for Christian educators. Some publications are "official" publications for a denomination; others are "independent." Some are written at a popular level, while others are scholarly in nature. Some deal with biblical and theological issues; others are "how-to" helps for ministry.

Three organizations promote and coordinate these journals. The Associated Church Press (Ada, Mich.), Evangelical Press Association (Earlysville, Va.), and Catholic Press Association (Phoenix, Ariz.) represent many of the Christian periodicals and newspapers published in the United States. Not all publications belong to an association.

All in all, religious publishing is doing well and reaching a widening market. Like all of the publishing industry, it is a changing business, with old companies disappearing and new ones emerging.

ELEANOR A. DANIEL

See also BIBLE TRANSLATIONS; CURRICULUM

Renaissance Education. The Renaissance was the reawakening of the ideas, values, and literature of the Greco-Roman world that had been suppressed by the traditionalism of the Middle Ages. Generally ascribed to the historical period of the fourteenth through sixteenth centuries, the Renaissance was the breaking away from the traditions of the church and ecclesiastical-centered culture toward a new worldview based on humanism and its human-centered philosophy and practices. Italy was the center of the Renaissance, just as it had been the center of philosophy and religion throughout the Middle Ages. Now, however, it was the "arts" and the rebirth of the sciences that influenced popular thinking rather than the teachings and sacraments of the Roman Catholic Church. The urban centers of Rome, Florence, Orleans, Naples, and Salerno were the primary cities where the spirit of the Renaissance flourished, especially in the universities, although Paris and London also made significant contributions. In many senses, the Renaissance was a cultural renewal of the mind (education), the body (arts), and the spirit (theology) of man. Notable persons in this Renaissance of culture included Thomas Aquinas (philosophy), Roger Bacon (science), Dante (literature), and Giotto (art).

As humanism flourished, God was increasingly placed in the background and forgotten in these times of individualism and prosperity. The feudal system of the Middle Ages was increasingly replaced with capitalism, and those not of noble birth found themselves for the first time with positions of power and authority, separate from the auspices of the church. The authority of the church was challenged as man's main purpose in glorifying God was replaced with the purpose of glorifying man and enjoying the fruits of his labors in the world. Thus arose the "Renaissance man," who enjoyed the arts, the sciences, and athletics with equal passion.

In the church, ancient literature and Scripture were rediscovered in the original languages of Hebrew and Greek, and studies in these languages came to supersede the traditional Latin and the Latin Vulgate. This Renaissance in the literature of the church would later lead to the Reformation of the church at the hands of Martin Luther. Three of Luther's Reformation principles—the authority of the Bible over the authority of the Roman Catholic Church, justification by faith in Christ alone, and the priesthood of all believers—were in part a result of his studying Scripture in the original languages. The prominence of the priesthood as the sole authoritative communicators and interpreters of God's truth was diminished as the Bible was translated into the German vernacular, and Luther expounded on the biblical mandate for the priesthood of all believers. Luther encouraged the education of the masses in fundamental reading skills so that children everywhere could learn to read the Scriptures for themselves and so come to know Jesus Christ as Lord and Savior. Towns and villages were encouraged to support these schooling efforts, and in the process, Christian education, like the priesthood, now was available for all believers.

Education also experienced a Renaissance as humanism influenced teachers, resulting in new concepts for schooling and the broadening of curriculums. Erasmus, for example, advocated the systematic training of teachers so that the pupil could be better educated. The harsh discipline of the student at the hands of erudite teachers was replaced with a tolerance of individual differences and greater respect for the learner. For Erasmus, man was fundamentally good in contrast to the Reformation teaching of the total depravity of man. The good life was attainable through education in what constituted the good life. Although strongly humanistic in his teaching, Erasmus did not diminish the quality of studies given his students: his core curriculum of the classics, the writings of the church fathers, and the Bible were pursued with precision and critical reflection.

MARK E. SIMPSON

Bibliography. K. O. Gangel and W. S. Benson (1983), *Christian Education: Its History and Philosophy;* M. J. Taylor, ed. (1960), *Religious Education: A Comprehensive Survey.*

See also DEWEY, JOHN; HUMANISM, CLASSICAL; HUMANISM, CHRISTIAN; PRIESTHOOD OF BELIEVERS; REFORMATION, THE

Renewal of Theological Education. Innovations in clergy education arising from an active openness to adapt or change training structures and strategies, more effectively to equip trainees for Christian ministry. Theological educators typically aspire toward excellence as scholars and teachers. Most seek to enhance their effectiveness in the classroom. Renewal of theological education elevates this aspiration and commitment to an institutional level.

There are firm biblical and theological grounds for adopting a mind-set toward renewal of theological education. As children of the kingdom in a world marred by sin, Christians are called to work for implementation of kingdom values in this age. Because educational structures reflect the sin-marred values of our cultures, we must search for training models which more effectively exhibit and cultivate kingdom values.

Not only our cultures, but also our persons bear the mark of sin. Through the redemptive power of the Word and the Spirit we experience sanctification in this age, yet the noetic and relational effects of sin persist. Because they persist, we constantly must resubmit our understandings and our relationships to the corrective scrutiny of Scripture. This necessarily includes the theoretical and relational dimensions of our ministry training programs. Until redemption is complete, we cannot be satisfied with intermediate programs and structures.

The history of clergy education in the West reflects a pattern of new beginnings, diminishing effectiveness, and an urgency for renewal. When Harvard University was founded in 1636, its purpose was to provide "a learned clergy" for the churches of the colonies. Other colleges followed but as university curricula diversified, ministry focus was lost.

Need for renewal led to the founding of Andover Seminary in 1808 and many other seminaries over the next few decades of the nineteenth century. Bible institutes, founded to equip lay ministers and missionaries, offered an attractive alternative for aspiring pastors. Beside promoting a conservative approach to Scripture, Bible institute curricula emphasized application of biblical truth in life and ministry. A century later, many again complain that North American seminary education fails to equip graduates for ministry leadership in the church.

Renewal also is an urgent agendum in "overseas theological education." As Western pioneer missionaries recognized a need to train leaders for the young churches planted in mission lands, they replicated the structures and curricula of the Bible schools and seminaries from which they graduated. Schools built by missionaries have produced thousands of graduates who minister faithfully, but leadership needs of the overseas church have not been well served. Johnstone (1993) reports that an inadequate supply of trained leaders—i.e., a failure of theological education—hobbles the vitality and expansion of the church in nearly every non-Western nation of the world at the dawn of the twenty-first century.

Although calls for renewal of theological education are often heard, sustained efforts toward renewal are few, isolated, and predominately non-Western. The most concentrated modern effort to reshape overseas theological education was launched in 1958 by the Theological Education Fund (TEF), which came under the World Council of Churches in 1961. In three "mandate periods" between 1958 and 1977, TEF channeled substantial resources into overseas theological schools. More than 400 Third World nationals received scholarships for graduate and postgraduate theological studies in the West. Since the scholars were directed to liberal theological schools, perhaps TEF's most enduring legacy is diffusion of Western liberal and postliberal theology among Latin American, African, and Asian churches.

Evangelical educators founded the International Council of Accrediting Agencies for Evangelical Theological Education (ICAA) in 1980. Three years later, ICAA adopted a "Manifesto on the Renewal of Evangelical Theological Education" which pledged to "introduce and reinforce" twelve critical aspects of theological education. The stirring rhetoric of the ICAA "Manifesto" has been grist for faculty discussions on six continents, but educators must tap their own creativity to discern how the commitments advocated can be implemented.

Theological education by extension (TEE) is the most widespread renewal movement to appear to date. In 1963 the faculty of a traditionally Western seminary in Guatemala faced the ineffectiveness of their training programs and determined to change. TEE emerged as an attempt to make ministry training accessible to functioning church leaders without disrupting their productive social, economic, and ministry relationships. This was achieved through self-instructional textbooks and frequent (often weekly) "seminars" local to the student, led by a "center leader" or "tutor."

TEE has brought significant benefit to churches and the theological schools that serve them. Although no hard statistics exist, many thousands of church leaders in Latin America, Africa, and Asia have received biblical, theological, and ministry instruction through TEE that they could not have obtained otherwise. Furthermore, theological educators in residential schools have been sensitized to educational issues and methods which challenge them who rethink their ministry training assumptions.

Other forms of nonformal education also have proven useful, although implementation typically is ad hoc and limited in scope. Pastors' conferences sometimes are employed as a medium for in-service training of untrained or under-trained clergy. Disciplining a Whole Nation (DAWN) in several nations, and Africa Ministries Network (AFMIN) in southern Africa, are two programs which make effective use of pastors' conferences for clergy education.

In North America, frustration with formal theological education has led some megachurches and churches in minority communities to launch church-based training programs. Initially intended to provide training for their own staff, church-based programs often expand to accommodate present and prospective staff from churches which share a common philosophy of ministry. In some cases these programs have built linkages to traditional seminaries or have sought academic recognition for their training offered.

Several avenues are open to theological educators who desire to promote renewal of theological education at their Bible school or seminary. Perhaps the most effective is to open channels of communication to the church or churches schools intend to serve. Listening must precede significant change. As lay church leaders and the pastors interpret the contexts in which they minister, faculty are more inclined and better able to adapt training programs.

An outcomes study can have a sobering effect on a theological faculty. It is easy to feel good about appreciative students and celebrating graduates, but a careful look at those same students five and ten years after graduation may evoke different emotions. When graduates leave the ministry or struggle for ministry effectiveness, doubt is cast on the appropriateness of training models and curricula. Educators must take responsibility for the effectiveness of their graduates.

Placing focus on the role of faculty as models also fosters a climate for renewal. In North American and some overseas seminaries, many faculty members are uncomfortable in evangelicalistic or pastoral roles. Despite the scholarship they offer, these teachers are ill-equipped to train pastors and missionaries. Teachers who regularly engage in the types of ministry for which they train, however, are models to their students both inside and outside the classroom.

When Bible school or seminary administrators and teachers are unfamiliar with adult education theory and methods, they may have difficulty challenging current models or envisioning alternatives. Faculty development workshops on adult education principles can provide information

and skills teachers need to see their task in new and more productive ways. Literature on the need for and means of renewal can be circulated to faculty and board members. Case studies of institutions that have implemented renewal values are especially suggestive.

Finally, renewal of theological education only can flourish in a climate which values ministry effectiveness and which encourages experimentation to that end. As long as training structures and methods cannot be questioned, renewal will not occur. Bible school and seminary principals, presidents, and academic deans hold the key to renewal of theological education in their institutions.

ROBERT W. FERRIS

Bibliography. "Excellence in Theological Education," *Evangelical Review of Theology* 19, no. 3 (1995); R. W. Ferris (1990), *Renewal in Theological Education: Strategies for Change;* M. C. Griffiths, *Vox Evangelica* 20, (1990): 7–19; P. Johnstone (1993), *Operation World: The Day-By-Day Guide to Praying for the World;* C. Lienemann-Perrin (1981), *Training for a Relevant Ministry: A Study of the Contribution of the Theological Education Fund.*

Repentance. Conscious rejection of a previous behavior and the desire to follow a new pattern. Addressing the Babylonian captives, the prophet Ezekiel delivered this message from God: "Repent! Turn away from all your offenses; then sin will not be your downfall. Rid yourselves of all the offenses you have committed, and get a new heart and a new spirit" (Ezek. 18:30–31).

The Scriptures record many incidents of human remorse in the face of divine judgment, but they also report moments when God himself repented of an action. In such instances, the idea of repentance does not include the human factors of humility and guilt. When God "repents," it is merely regret that human frailty has caused God to retract an act of generosity. When King Saul failed to follow God's orders to destroy the captured Amalekite livestock, God turned from Saul to David, saying, "I am grieved that I have made Saul king" (1 Sam. 15:11). Many scriptural references to repentance include information on how God responded. The Book of Joel describes a plague of locusts that ravaged Israel. Once the Israelites repented of their idolatrous behavior, God destroyed the locusts and restored the lost crops. "'Even now,' declares the LORD, 'return to me with all your heart, with fasting and weeping and mourning'" (Joel 2:12).

John the Baptist preached repentance. "Repent, for the kingdom of heaven is near" (Matt. 3:2). After confessing their sins, the people who came to John were baptized in the Jordan. Following his own baptism, Jesus went into Galilee and continued preaching the theme proclaimed by his imprisoned cousin. "Repent and believe the good news!" (Mark 1:15).

After his resurrection, Jesus appeared to the disciples and explained the prophecies concerning himself: "Repentance and forgiveness of sins will be preached in his name to all nations" (Luke 24:47). The Book of Acts records that Peter urged his listeners on the day of Pentecost to "Repent and be baptized . . . in the name of Jesus Christ for the forgiveness of your sins" (Acts 2:38).

In a letter to the Corinthian church, Paul spelled out the difference between simple remorse and the repentance that leads to salvation. "Godly sorrow brings repentance that leads to salvation and leaves no regret, but worldly sorrow brings death" (2 Cor. 7:10). Joel the prophet warned that God can spot someone who is only wallowing in the shallow remorse of ritual. "Rend your heart and not your garments" (Joel 2:13–14).

True repentance views sin through God's unwavering perspective and acknowledges that God's judgment is well deserved. Jeremiah described the agonizing grief of Ephraim: "After I strayed, I repented; after I came to understand, I beat my breast. I was ashamed and humiliated" (Jer. 31:19). The depth of repentance can best be measured by the resulting change in behavior. "Produce fruit in keeping with repentance," Jesus urged the Pharisees and Sadducees (Matt. 3:8).

Repentance must involve faith in Jesus Christ if it is to lead to salvation. The Book of Acts records Paul's words to the Ephesian elders: "I have declared to both Jews and Greeks that they must turn to God in repentance and have faith in our Lord Jesus." (Acts 20:21). Repentance can begin with a simple fear of consequences, but it must acknowledge guilt, see the necessity of forgiveness, and understand what sacrifice has made that forgiveness available.

Scripture is full of promises of forgiveness of a contrite heart. The parable of the Prodigal Son is one example. The celebration of the lost son's return is echoed in Christ's words, "There will be more rejoicing in heaven over one sinner who repents than over ninety-nine righteous persons who do not need to repent" (Luke 15:7). In Psalm 51, written after David had been confronted about his adultery with Bathsheba, he writes, "A broken and contrite heart, O God, you will not despise" (v. 17). At the dedication of the temple, David's son Solomon begged God to forgive Israel's sins. The king received this response: "If my people, who are called by my name, will humble themselves and pray and seek my face and turn from their wicked ways, then will I hear from heaven and will forgive their sin" (2 Chron. 7:14).

ROBERT J. CHOUN

Bibliography. E. F. Harrison, ed. (1960), *Baker's Dictionary of Theology;* A. Richardson, ed. (1969), *A Dictionary of Christian Theology;* C. Ryrie (1986), *Basic Theology;* D. L. Smith (1994), *With Willful Intent—A Theology of Sin.*

Replication. The essence of *replication* is "exact reproduction." Something is *replicated* when it is "reproduced just as it is first observed."

Neither *replication* nor *reproduced* is found in Scripture. The concept is certainly present, however. Paul affirmed that Timothy's faith was replicated from his mother and grandmother (2 Tim. 1:5). Paul urged Timothy to be involved in the ministry of replication when he told him to take the things he had learned and "these entrust to faithful men, who will be able to teach others also" (2 Tim. 2:2 NASB). The term *entrust*, from the Greek *paratithemi*, means "to put alongside of." It is used, however, in the sense of replicate and not merely "place in relation to." The King James Version translates it "commit."

The strongest illustration of replication is Jesus. He is "His only *begotten* Son" (John 3:16, see also Ps. 2:7; Acts 13:33; Heb. 1:5). The word *begotten* means to bear the "spiritual or moral likeness of." In Jesus' case he is the exact spiritual and moral replication of the Father.

Most Protestant evangelicals believe Christ's nature is to one degree or another replicated in us when we become Christians. Various faiths speak of this differently. Some believe Christ's nature, once given, becomes a permanent characteristic regardless of our attitudes or behavior. Others believe Christians are a conduit for the reflection of the divine nature and the reflection causes us to have Christ's nature replicated in us either instantly or over time as we become Christlike. Some teach the replication of Christ's nature occurs when we are sanctified.

ROY F. LYNN

Repression. In the psychodynamic branch of psychology, repression is the most basic defense mechanism. It involves the banishing of painful memories or feelings from the conscious mind. These feelings or memories are not actually forgotten but rather are submerged into the unconscious mind. They reappear indirectly in the form of other defense mechanisms, or sometimes as Freudian slips—slips of the tongue that reflect underlying unconscious thought (Meier et al., 1991). Some counselors assume that repressed memories can be recovered and worked through by means of psychoanalysis, a form of therapy emphasized by Sigmund Freud. However, the accuracy of such recalled memories is strongly debated, particularly in cases where alleged sexual abuse in childhood is involved (Benatar, 1998; Robbins, 1998).

A fairly extreme form of repression is illustrated by a child who suffers abuse at the hand of a parent, then as an adult finds it difficult to remember anything from the childhood years. While this kind of generalized amnesia is fairly rare, a more localized "forgetting"—such as the inability to recall an elementary teacher, or not recalling anything from an entire year of childhood—is more common. From the psychoanalytic frame of reference, the amnesia is most likely due to repressed memories and events associated with that time period. The mental discomfort that might result from recalling memories is avoided by repression.

Painful events associated with Christian education efforts may possibly cause repression. For example, extreme teasing received in a youth group activity may be repressed yet indirectly be expressed through critical remarks about youth activities by a church board member. He or she may vote against youth outings, ostensibly because they are "a waste of time," but actually the board member may be unconsciously avoiding the pain of his or her youth group experiences from long ago.

On the other hand, Christian education has the potential for helping those with repressed memories. Support groups for abused children and adults can provide a means of dealing with unpleasant memories within a caring, open environment, by discussing the past and receiving spiritual and emotional healing. It is imperative that Christian educators who lack a strong background in counseling know their personal limitations in this area and realize when referral of troubled people to a trained clinician is necessary.

DONALD E. RATCLIFF

Bibliography. M. Benatar (1998), *Taking Sides: Childhood and Society;* S. Freud (1938), *A General Introduction to Psychoanalysis;* T. Lidz (1968), *The Person;* P. Meier et al. (1991), *Introduction to Psychology and Counseling,* 2nd ed.; D. Ratcliff (1984), *Using Psychology in the Church;* S. Robbins (1998), *Taking Sides: Childhood and Society.*

Research Techniques. *See* Methodology (Teaching and Research).

Resources. Those items that are ready for use and can be drawn on to assist in the teaching and learning process. Resources may prove useful for the teacher and/or the student.

Resources would include but not be limited to filmstrips, transparencies, pictures, flannelgraph materials, posters, cassette players and tapes, CD players and CDs, VCRs and videos, TVs, overhead projectors, video data projectors, posters, games, maps, books, bulletin board supplies, computers, crayons, scissors, glue, craft materials, curriculum, and student workbooks. Such materials are often stored in individual teaching spaces, thus leading to duplication and unnecessary expense. Consolidating the resources into a resource center can provide ease in accessibility. The center will need a supervisor who collects, labels, displays, and circulates to teaching personnel a listing of available resources for teaching. Flexible times and checkout systems are vital.

In Christian education, human resources prove invaluable. The people in any congregation have skills, interests, and ministry aptitudes that can be called upon to enrich the teaching-learning environment. An annual survey of congregants and their willingness to make themselves available for the educational endeavor will yield cost-effective and ministry-intensive spiritual gift usage.

Buildings can be resources when used wisely and creatively to solve many ministry needs. Playgrounds, playing fields, and facilities of many descriptions can all be useful in the Christian educational process. Local libraries and community agencies are also rich sources of resource materials, knowledge, and persons.

CHERYL L. FAWCETT

Bibliography. R. J. Choun and M. S. Lawson, eds. (1993), *The Complete Handbook for Children's Ministry: How to Reach and Teach the Next Generation;* R. E. Clark, J. Brubaker, and R. B. Zuck, eds. (1986), *Childhood Education in the Church.*

See also FACILITY; MEDIA; PROGRAM

Restoration. *See* Recovery; Recovery Ministry.

Resurrection of Jesus Christ. The resurrection of Jesus Christ was the most significant event in history. Jesus himself offered it as the one sign he would give to confirm his authority concerning the things he said and did (John 2:18–22). The resurrection validates that his death had the power to save all who trust in him for forgiveness of their sins. It authenticates that Jesus Christ was the incarnation of the Son of God. The resurrection of Christ was proclaimed in every sermon recorded in the Book of Acts. The early Christians so marked the significance of the resurrection that they set aside Sunday, the first day of the week when Christ rose from the dead, as the day for their gathering together to worship. The apostle Paul wrote, "If Christ has not been raised, then our preaching is vain, your faith also is vain" (1 Cor. 15:14 NASB). It can also be said that without the resurrection of Christ, the entire work of the Christian educator is vain.

Critics of the Resurrection. Critics of Christianity have often concentrated their criticism on the resurrection. The Christian faith does not center on a set of mere moral principles. It does not give checklists or formulas for successful living. The Christian faith centers on the fact that man is fallen and in desperate need of repair. The death and resurrection of Jesus Christ as an historical event provides the means for the forgiveness of sins, reconciliation with God, and the beginning of the believer's pilgrimage toward the complete restoration of the image of Christ

(Rom. 8:28–29). Detractors attack the historic event of the resurrection in order to minimize the doctrines which are substantiated by it.

Attempts to explain away the resurrection began soon after the event took place. The Gospels record that the religious leaders paid the soldiers who had guarded the tomb of Jesus to say that while they were sleeping the disciples came and stole the body (Matt. 28:11–15). Of course sleeping soldiers could hardly be convincing, testifying to what occurred while they were fast asleep. Throughout the ages other suggestions have been attempted to explain away the empty tomb. G. D. Yarnold suggested that the body simply decayed over time through natural processes (*Risen Indeed*, 1959, 59). Three days after Christ's crucifixion, when the tomb was declared empty, hardly enough time had elapsed for natural processes to have eliminated the body. Kirsopp Lake explained that the women most likely went to the wrong burial place on that Sunday morning. They simply made a mistake and went to another tomb which happened to be empty (*The Historical Evidence for the Resurrection of Jesus Christ*, 1907, 250–53). It remains difficult to believe that the women who cared for Jesus would have mistaken something so important to them. It is equally difficult to believe that the disciples and others would have made the same mistake. This view is even more incredible since the Scriptures indicate that Jesus' body was not placed in a tomb in a cemetery but in the garden tomb of Joseph of Arimathea (Matt. 27:59–61; John 19:38–42). David Strauss suggested that Jesus never actually died on the cross, that he somehow survived the crucifixion, revived in the coolness of the tomb, and on the third day he was mistakenly believed to be resurrection (*The Life of Jesus for the People*, 1879, vol. I, 412). It is difficult to believe a man crucified and confirmed dead by a Roman soldier's spear thrust into his side could revive after three days without medical attention. It is even more difficult to believe that such a person, beaten, bruised, and bloody, could convince anyone of his triumphant resurrection from the dead. Joseph Klausner suggested that Joseph of Arimathea stole the body (*Jesus of Nazareth, His Life, Times and Teaching*, 1925, 357). It is hard to believe that Joseph had either the motive to steal the body or the strength to pull off the theft before the soldiers guarding the tomb. Many other views have been suggested. Each has various weaknesses. On the other hand, the New Testament narratives recount that over five hundred people were eyewitnesses to the resurrection of Jesus Christ (1 Cor. 15:3–8).

Significance of the Resurrection. Some neo-orthodox New Testament scholars, denying the resurrection as an historic event, still believe it has significance. Those like Rudolph Bultmann believe it had value in the subjective experience of the disciples. Marcus Borg says that the significance is mythological, not historical. The myth gives value by encouraging hope in the midst of the sufferings of life. Those who desire a hope beyond the wishful thinking of this position find greater encouragement in the credibility of the resurrection as an actual historical event. Hope is found in the fact that the resurrection confirms the message of Christ. His words are validated by his power to raise from the dead. It confirms his message of the forgiveness of sins. It also confirms his promises concerning eternal life. Paul wrote that: (1) Jesus was raised to justify, before God, those who believe in him (Rom. 4:25). (2) His resurrection makes it possible for believers to walk in newness of life (Rom. 6:4). (3) God, who raised Christ Jesus from the dead, will raise believers also (Rom. 8:11; 1 Cor. 6:14).

Importance of the Resurrection in Christian Education. The resurrection of Jesus Christ validates a supernaturalist approach to life. Paul said in his defense before Agrippa, "Why is it considered incredible among you people if God does raise the dead?" (Acts 26:8). The Christian educator should encourage others to think with Christian, that is supernatural, presuppositions. The naturalist cannot be as open-minded as the supernaturalist. The naturalist's presuppositions prejudice him toward all data before any investigation of the facts begins. While the supernaturalist may find natural explanations to events and circumstances in life, he or she is always open to exhibitions of divine intervention. The God of the resurrection will accomplish his purposes in the affairs of humankind. The resurrection itself is a confirmation of that fact.

The resurrection also stands as a teaching point to validate that the transcendent God is not apathetic about the circumstances of human life. The incarnation and the resurrection of Christ reveal God's proximity and his commitment to mend all that is broken about his creation. Furthermore if the resurrection confirms God's power to forgive sins, then the resurrection also stands as a rebuke against pretense. There is hope for the person who struggles in the Body of Christ. No one this side of heaven can claim perfection for himself. Consequently the need for Christ's resurrection power and hope is not casual, it is constant. In the midst of suffering or struggles believers may find comfort.

JERRY ROOT

Bibliography. L. Berkhof (1991), *Systematic Theology*; M. J. Boyd (1995), *Meeting Jesus Again for the First Time*; P. Carnley (1987), *The Structure of Resurrection Belief*; A. McGrath (1994), *Christian Theology: An Introduction*; P. Perkins (1984), *Resurrection: New Testament*

Witness and Contemporary Reflection; W. M. Smith (1945), *Therefore Stand: Christian Apologetics.*

Retreats. In the local church it is not difficult to find retreats being utilized as a vital part of the Christian education program. In addition to retreats where the youth take the church bus to a nearby camp for a weekend of fun, fellowship, and inspiration, it is quite common to have women's retreats, men's retreats, couples' retreats, single parent retreats, chorale retreats, and even church leadership retreats. As the benefits of these "time away" events have become evident to program planners, the number of groups holding retreats has grown and the focus has often become more specialized.

A critical question arises when one seeks to distinguish between a retreat and a conference, seminar, or any other short-term ministry. Although a retreat will have much in common with conferences and seminars, it is not the same.

Common elements would include things such as having a defined purpose, requiring adequate planning and preparation, and offering an opportunity for participants to be informed or challenged. However, the components that set a retreat apart are the setting, the role of the participants, and the opportunity for personal reflection and response.

Within the Christian church the retreat has been seen as a time away from the routine of life. It is a break, but not a vacation, for it has as its purpose a time for personal reflection and evaluation.

A retreat, therefore, requires a setting away from the noise and distractions of our technological society. This is why a camp or conference center can provide a retreat setting that cannot be found in a hotel or college campus. There is the need for participants to temporarily leave the distractions of their everyday lives and engage in prolonged periods of quiet and solitude.

Along with the setting, the role of the participants is unique, for at a retreat participants come together to form temporary communities. It is over a two- or three-day period that group members are asked to participate in the life of the retreat and thus develop a small community with shared experiences. It is through these shared experiences that communal trust and personal friendships often arise. These in turn become benefits of the retreat which cannot be programmed but need to be encouraged.

The third component, the opportunity for personal reflection and response, can only come about when there is an appropriate setting and the program makes provision for personal quiet time. In this sense, a retreat can lead the individual participant into an extended sabbath rest. Unfortunately, it is too often the case that retreat programs are so full of activity that the elements of quietness, reflection, and solitude are omitted;

participants return home tired instead of rested. Those who plan retreats may need to include some instruction to assist the participants in knowing how to be reflective and to listen.

It has long been acknowledged that quiet reflection in a setting away from the daily concerns of life can be very beneficial to one's spiritual growth. The role that retreats can play in a program of Christian education is often overlooked or underused. The benefits for the individual can be both personal and relational, and for the group of participants there can be an enhanced sense of community.

The variety of retreat settings and formats is often shaped by the traditions and locations of our churches. However, the function of the retreat is as old as the Master's word to his disciples to "come away . . . and rest a while" (Mark 6:31 NASB).

DOUGLAS BARCALOW

See also CHRISTIAN CAMPING INTERNATIONAL; OUTDOOR ACTIVITIES

Retrieval. Encoding is the beginning of the information-processing function and retrieval is the end result. Encoding allows information to be stored in the memory, allowing one to retrieve it at a later date. Encoding and retrieval involve a variety of techniques which are individual in nature. For example, one person may choose to encode a message by associating it with a prior experience. That way when the experience reoccurs, the item is retrieved. Others, especially students cramming for an exam the night before, may choose to encode the information using a variety of mnemonic devices. Once learned, the student then retrieves a long list of information simply by retrieving a smaller element of it.

MICHAEL J. ANTHONY

See also CHUNKING; INFORMATION PROCESSING; MEMORY; MNEMONIC DEVICES

Retroactive Inhibition. This term is also known as proactive interference. Retroactive inhibition is simply the forgetting of an earlier learned task produced by the effects of learning some new, similar task. Retroactive inhibition is most frequently found when memorizing lists of items. If students are asked to learn a new list of material that is somewhat similar to a previously learned list, the new learning will inhibit or interfere with the retention of the previously learned list. The term *retroactive* makes reference to the fact that the inhibition is affecting previously learned material, not the new material being currently learned.

An example of retroactive inhibition could be seen in Scripture memorization. During any give semester or quarter, a student may be expected to first memorize Galatians 5:22–23 and then later

Philippians 4:8. Because of the similarities of the concepts found in the two lists, if the student was ever asked to recall both sets of verses at the same time, the most recently memorized material in Philippians will probably cause the student to inaccurately recall the fruit of the Spirit in Galatians.

DALE L. MORT

See also PROACTIVE INHIBITION

Revelation. The church's theological claim that humankind's knowledge/encounter with God depends on God's initiative in disclosing himself to humanity. Revelation occurs whenever a particular event enables us to see the meaning of other events (Oden, 1987). Where these revelatory events occur, how revelation occurs, and our ability to accurately receive revelation are questions Christians have long debated.

A long tradition of theological thinking classifies God's revelatory acts as general or special revelation. *General revelation* refers to knowledge/encounter with God gained from sources accessible to all humans, regardless of their spiritual standing. Biblical warrants for general revelation are drawn from passages such as Psalm 19:1 ("The heavens declare the glory of God . . .") and Romans 1:20 ("For since the creation of the world God's invisible qualities—his eternal power and divine nature—have been clearly seen, being understood from what has been made").

Special revelation is often used in two different though related senses. First, special revelation sometimes refers to the limited scope of the disclosure. God discloses himself to one person or one group of people, but not to others. Second, special revelation describes extraordinary acts of disclosure: miracles, the disclosing word, and preeminently, the revelation that comes through Jesus Christ. These special revelatory acts stand behind the opening lines of Hebrews: "In the past God spoke to our forefathers through the prophets at many times and in various ways, but in these last days he has spoken to us by his Son. . . ."

While classifying revelation can be helpful, the line between general and special revelation should not be too sharply drawn since some distinctions traditionally made between the two are increasingly difficult to sustain. For example, some have held that general revelation is mediated and ambiguous, while special revelation is direct and clear. However, any disclosure of God is finally mediated: by the material world, our physical senses, and language. As Paul notes in 1 Corinthians 13:12 "Now I know in part; then I shall know fully. . . ."

One's theological perspective on revelation shapes both the theory and practice of Christian education. If God's revelation may be found in creation (general revelation) and in Christ (special revelation), then humans may seek truth in both realms. Humans inquire into creation through the natural and social sciences; humans learn of Christ through theological inquiry. Social science inquiry yields insights in human development, learning processes, relational dynamics, instructional theory, and social behavior. Theological inquiry yields insight into spiritual maturity, human nature, and the faith community. Some theorists examine Christian education through one stream of inquiry. Locke Bowman, for example, draws primarily on social science truths for guiding Christian education while Walter Brueggemann draws heavily on theological insights for guiding practice. Effective theory building in Christian education blends truth gained from both streams of inquiry.

One's understanding of revelation also shapes the practice of Christian education in three significant ways. First, educators will point learners toward the historical locations of God's self-disclosure, and most likely to those locales where the disclosure comes with particular clarity. Christian education may encourage study of God's revelation wherever found, but will likely emphasize the source of God's clearest self-disclosure.

Second, if the function of revelation is to illuminate, guide, and shed meaning on other events, Christian education must work to connect God's self-disclosure with the lives of learners. The events in which most people take interest are the events that comprise the story of their own lives. Christian educators can help learners find the story of their lives within God's story.

Third, if revelation is truly self-disclosure, Christian education must lead learners toward a personal encounter with God. In this encounter, learners face the living and active Word of God (Heb. 4:12).

Luke's account of the two disciples on the Emmaus road (Luke 24:13–35) provides an archetype for this threefold response to revelation. After the disciples describe their disappointment and confusion—"the things that have happened [here] in these days . . ." (v. 18)—Jesus gives them a history lesson, "beginning with Moses and all the Prophets" (v. 27a). He then connects the story of God's self-disclosure to their experience by explaining "to them what was said in all the Scriptures concerning himself" (v. 27b). Yet later, in the breaking of the bread, we learn that "their eyes were opened and they recognized him" (v. 31) and we note their inward response: "Were not our hearts burning within us while he . . . opened the Scriptures to us?" (v. 32).

Christian educators need to promote all three dimensions of revelation as essential for a full response to God. Emphasis on revelation as a past activity of God limits Christian education to a study of history. Emphasis on revelation as illuminating and guiding our lives limits Christian education to a study of morality. Emphasis on revelation as personal encounter privatizes Christian education to one's own experience, unchecked by the community of faith.

ROBERT DROVDAHL

Bibliography. W. J. Abraham (1982), *Divine Revelation and the Limits of Historical Criticism;* C. F. H. Henry (1958), *Revelation and the Bible;* T. C. Oden (1987), *The Living God.*

See also THEOLOGY OF EDUCATION

Revival. The term has Latin origins and literally means *to live again,* or *to arouse,* such as when smelling salts are used to revive someone who has passed out. The Bible speaks of God reviving his people spiritually. "Revive us, and we will call upon Thy name" (Ps. 80:18b NASB). "Wilt Thou not Thyself revive us again, That Thy people may rejoice in Thee?" (Ps. 85:6 NASB).

The term *revival* came into common usage in the early eighteenth century in order to describe what God was doing during the Great Awakening in America and Britain. In the colonies, spiritual lethargy prevailed in the churches until a spiritual awakening began to take place in New Jersey under the preaching of Theodore Frelinghuysen, a Dutch Reformed minister. Many developed a renewed sense of their sinful condition and need for deliverance while others were refreshed by a new appreciation for the grace of God in the gospel.

The Awakening soon spread to other parts of America as a cross-denominational phenomenon led by Jonathan Edwards, George Whitefield, John Wesley, and Samuel Davies. While their experiences were not uniform, spiritual growth was a common denominator. Isaac Watts, in his introduction to Jonathan Edwards's *A Narrative of Surprising Conversions,* wrote, "It pleased God . . . to display his free and sovereign mercy in the conversion of a great multitude of souls in a short space of time, turning them from a formal, cold and careless profession of Christianity, to the lively exercise of every Christian grace, and the powerful practice of our holy religion" (Edwards, 1991, 2).

While some view the Great Awakening as the first revival, similar times of spiritual renewal were experienced long before the eighteenth century. In the Bible, several examples of spiritual renewal occurred in the Book of Judges, under Hezekiah and Josiah, as well as at Pentecost in the New Testament. There were spiritual awakenings earlier in church history, such as the "conquering" of the Roman Empire and the Cluniac revival. Christians have generally understood the Reformation primarily as a spiritual revival rather than simply the religious manifestation of Enlightenment.

The contemporary understanding of revival was shaped by the Second Great Awakening of the early nineteenth century. It had several distinguishing characteristics from the first awakening. While Edwards spoke of the "surprising" work of God in revival, Charles Finney (1978), one of the leading revivalists of the second awakening, taught that a revival is the "result of the right use of the constituted means. . . . It consists entirely in the *right exercise* of the powers of nature" (4). He instituted his "New Measures" such as extended meetings and the anxious bench. Thus revivals are now scheduled since they describe the efforts expended as much as the results produced.

In the late nineteenth and early twentieth centuries famous revivalist preachers, such as Dwight L. Moody and Billy Sunday, began touring America resulting in many decisions for Christ. Billy Graham has carried on their tradition in the second half of the twentieth century. Other notable revivals include the Cane Ridge Revival, the Prayer Revival of 1858, and the Welsh Revival of 1906.

The common thread through all genuine revivals has been an emphasis on applying Scriptures to the lives of people both within and without the church. An urgent appeal to respond to the claims of the gospel has always characterized controversy. Unusual phenomena such as barking and swooning have taken place during revival meetings, discrediting them in the minds of many. Denominational splits and the rise of new ones have frequently characterized revivals.

An additional effect of revivals has been the creation of new educational endeavors. The large influx of new members into the churches caused by the revivals usually necessitated the training of more ministers, Christian educators, and missionaries. Thus, many colleges and seminaries such as Princeton, Brown, Dartmouth, and Moody Bible Institute trace their heritage to revivals or revivalisms. Similarly, new evangelical publishing firms and Sunday school boards were established in order to educate the new believers into the ways of the Christian faith and discipleship.

The success of a revival is found, not in how many people show up at a given meeting, nor how many followers a revival preacher can procure, nor even how many decisions can be obtained, but to what degree people's lives are changed as a result of the work of the Holy Spirit in their lives. While revivals have often started this process, it is the long process of discipleship and Christian education which brings it to fruitation.

DOUGLAS FALLS

Bibliography. L. W. Dorsett (1991), *Billy Sunday and the Redemption of Urban America;* J. Edwards (1991), *On Revival;* C. G. Finney (1978), *Revivals of Religion;* B. Hull (1998), *Revival That Reforms: Making It Last;* I. H. Murray (1994), *Revival & Revivalism: The Making and Marring of American Evangelicalism, 1750–1858;* H. S. Stout (1991), *The Divine Dramatist.*

See also GREAT AWAKENINGS; WESLEY, JOHN

Rewards. Reward is both a biblical concept and an important psychological reality. In common usage it is "that which is given in return for good or evil done or received, especially that which is in return for achievement or service" (Kellerman, 1977, 823). In biblical thought, the idea of reward is seen as a giving of felicity to the righteous, and as a warning of punishment upon the wicked. As used in psychology, reward usually is related to behaviorist theorists. In this context, it may be defined as the return for performance of a desired behavior, or positive reinforcement.

Biblical Rewards. The Bible seems to indicate that the Christian will be rewarded in heaven. Jesus said, "And, behold, I come quickly; and my *reward* is with me, to give every man according as his work shall be" (Rev. 22:12 KJV). This rewarding from God is a major motivator of faithfulness in the life of the Christian. Rewards are described as full (Ruth 2:12), sure (Prov. 11:18), great (Matt. 5:12), and open (Matt. 6:4, 6, 18). Apparently, all Christians will stand before the judgment seat of Christ (Rom. 14:10) to receive the results of their faithful work in Christ (2 Cor. 5:10). Richards asserts, "There is equitability in the moral universe. God is both a rewarder of good and a punisher of evil. The person who sows righteousness will surely reap a good reward" (1985, 531). These rewards are sometimes described as "crowns." There is the "crown of rejoicing" (1 Thess. 2:19), a "crown of righteousness" (2 Tim. 4:8), a "crown of glory" (1 Peter 5:4), and a "crown of life" (Rev. 2:10; James 1:12).

Psychological Rewards. Cognitive, humanistic, and social learning approaches to motivation would not utilize rewards as much as a behavioral theorist would. In typical behaviorist usage, reward speaks about a conditioner of response. Positive reinforcement would be a close synonym. Yount (1996) defines reinforcement as "any event that follows a behavior and increases the likelihood that the behavior will occur again, or any consequence that strengthens the behavior it follows" (165). Reward in this system of psychology could be defined as "an attractive object or event supplied as a consequence of a behavior" (Woolfolk, 1995, 333).

For the Christian educator, one certainly can see that the use of rewards (behavioral learning theory) does not necessarily bind them to a behaviorist viewpoint (Issler and Habermas, 1994, 209). We should be aware of the field of theory we are using, but keep consistent with the scriptural viewpoints.

GREGORY C. CARLSON

Bibliography. K. Issler and R. Habermas (1994), *How We Learn: A Christian Teacher's Guide to Educational Psychology;* D. F. Kellerman, ed. (1977), *The Lexicon Webster Dictionary,* vol. II; L. O. Richards (1985), *Expository Dictionary of Bible Words;* A. E. Woolfolk (1995), *Educational Psychology;* W. R. Yount (1996), *Created to Learn.*

Richards, Lawrence O. (1931–). Christian educator, teacher-lecturer, and author. He received a B.A. from the University of Michigan, a Th.M. from Dallas Theological Seminary, and a Ph.D. from Northwestern University in Evanston, Ill., through a joint program with Garrett Biblical Seminary. Richards, an ordained minister, taught as an assistant professor of theology for seven years in the Graduate School at Wheaton College in Wheaton, Illinois. He has also taught courses at Biola University, Princeton University, Regent College, Winnipeg Theological Seminary, and Bethany Nazarene.

Richards has developed his own line of Sunday school curriculum and has published over 120 books, including commentaries on every book of the Bible. Several of his books are in textbook format and have been used in various colleges and theological seminaries. Of particular note are *A Theology of Christian Education* (1988), *A Theology of Children's Ministry* (1983), and *A Theology of Church Leadership* (1980). All of these communicate his conviction that the way an educator does effective ministry must grow out of a theological understanding of that ministry and the persons to whom one is ministering. The need for a theological framework for ministry—those sets of beliefs and assumptions of both theology and the ministry target group—is foundational if Christian education is to be seen as a theological discipline.

Richards's theology of Christian education addresses the critical issues of the role of Scripture, the role of the teacher, and the role of relationships. His concern is with the tendency to limit educational thinking to the classroom and the methods employed there, rather than recognizing the need to consider the total life of the believer within the body of Christ. One of his key concerns is a more focused study of ecclesiology, which he views as the source of educational understanding. In his view, all educational ministries should be considered within the context of their function within the body and a recognition that the classroom is only part of the vision for Christian education. Christian education that is concerned only with the individual life without concern for the processes within the body that nurture corporate and individual growth in Christ is inadequate (*A Theology of Christian Education,* 16).

Another central idea for Richards is his belief that Christian education is a process rather than a product. This process deals with lifestyle issues affecting the whole person, not just knowledge and beliefs. If educators are to touch the total personality, then the context for teaching must take place outside of the classroom rather than solely during classtime. This basic belief led to an enthusiastic advocacy for informal and nonformal education which, he maintains, better fosters change and development in the total personality of students. He opposes a formal school approach to Christian education that depends exclusively on a subject-centered approach to nurture persons in the Christian faith and life. In fact, he feels that the church has seriously restricted itself by making too strong an investment in a formal schooling model. He believes that formal educational techniques are virtually useless for shaping faith in people because these approaches are unable to communicate life. "Formal education may be effective in dealing with symbols and concepts abstracted from life. But when change and development in the total personality are desired, non-formal education has all the advantages" (*A Theology of Christian Education*, 13). This has been labeled as a socialization/enculturation approach, where Christian life is more "caught than taught."

Richards has been criticized for his lack of regard for contextual factors and his insensitivity to denominational distinctives in renewal. He has also been criticized for his assumption that models and disciples who can live out the truths of Scripture are readily available in the local church (Pazmiño, 147). However, Richards does present an alternative paradigm for renewal in Christian education in the local church, with particular insight for use of nonformal education and use of socialization processes of Christian communities.

In 1985, Richards edited the *Expository Dictionary of Bible Words*. His purpose in undertaking such a work was his personal conviction regarding the significance of Scripture. The preface communicates his concern with allowing the Word of God to "reshape"a person's perspectives, relationships, choices, and actions. Richards's other varied works include *Death and the Caring Community* (1980), *Living in Touch with God* (1988), *Creative Bible Teaching* (1970), *Reshaping Evangelical Higher Education* (1972), *A Practical Theology of Spirituality* (1987), and *Remarriage: A Healing Gift from God* (1981). His material can be found in over a dozen languages.

Richards's influence on contemporary Christian education has been substantial. His textbooks are still used in Christian education classes, providing both theoretical and practical ideas for Christian educators.

NORMA S. HEDIN

Bibliography. R. W. Pazmiño (1997), *Foundational Issues in Christian Education*, 2nd ed.

See also ENCULTURATION; LESSON PLAN; THEOLOGY OF EDUCATION

Rogers, Carl (1902–87). American psychologist. Born in Oak Park, Ill., he was one of a large but noncommunicative family. His parents were fundamentalists and his mother insisted on separation from people of other faiths. Perhaps in a reaction to her intolerance, Rogers would maintain that people are not inherently evil, but good. Rogers attended the University of Wisconsin, where his initial intention was to study agriculture. His interests turned to theology and he chose to prepare for seminary and a life devoted to ministry. On a six-month trip to China as a student representative to a YMCA congress, Rogers fell away from his early religious training and took a more liberal view. After graduation and a short time at Union Theological Seminary, Rogers lost interest in theology and enrolled at Teachers College, Columbia University, to do postgraduate work in psychology.

It was at Columbia that Rogers was exposed to the ideas of John Dewey. Under Dewey's influence, Rogers felt free to rethink his Freudian training. He altered the Freudian therapist-centered approach to therapy in favor of a client-centered approach. After graduation from Columbia, Rogers worked for the Rochester, New York Society for the Prevention of Cruelty to Children. His work with the Society resulted in Rogers's first book, *Clinical Treatment of the Problem Child*. Moving to Ohio State University, Rogers taught psychology. It was there that he wrote *Counseling and Therapy*.

From Ohio State, Rogers moved to the University of Chicago, where he did research in psychotherapy and wrote *Client-Centered Therapy*. During a short-term return to the University of Wisconsin, Rogers taught psychology and psychiatry. In 1964 he was named resident fellow of the Western Behavioral Sciences Center in La Jolla, Cal. Rogers later worked at the Center for Studies of the Person, continuing his research in growth and learning. Rogers gradually moved away from individual counseling into group therapy and expanded his work to include education and family life. He authored *On Being a Person, Freedom to Learn, Carl Rogers on Encounter Groups, Carl Rogers on Personal Power*, and *A Way of Being*.

As a therapist, Rogers advocated client-centered therapy. He believed that people were controlled more by their own choices than by environment or unconscious motivations. Rogers believed that each person was his or her own architect. In client-centered therapy, the therapist leads the client to an understanding of his or her problems and experiences. The therapist assists by asking questions rather than by giving overt directions. The client sets the pace and direction of his or her own recovery. This approach is explained in *Client-Centered Therapy* and *Becoming a Person*.

Applying the same approach to education, Rogers maintained that the student is an explorer, while the teacher serves as a guide and encourager. In Rogers's humanistic view, the entire goal of education is self-actualization—the act of becoming an autonomous being. Each individual must discover and develop her or his full potential. Rogers' views are presented in *Freedom to Learn* and the follow-up *Freedom to Learn* in the 1980s.

In *Freedom*, Rogers affirms the human potential for learning. Learning will take place, however, only if the student can sense the relevance of the lesson to his or her own situation and needs. The best context for learning is where the environment is nonthreatening and the self-reliant student can actively participate in the learning process. Rogers promoted the involvement of the whole person—intellect and feelings—to maximize learning. Passive learners rarely bloom into creative thinkers.

In Rogers's ideal classroom, the teacher provides a wide variety of resources and processes for the learners to resolve a real problem. His emphasis is on what the teacher does *not* do. The teacher refrains from assigning reading, lecturing, evaluating, or grading. To Rogers, these practices guarantee that meaningful learning will be minimized. The teacher acts as a facilitator rather than an authoritarian. Without the traditional methods of assessment, it might be difficult to measure gains in such a classroom—and, in fact, Rogers's gains often defy measurement. The qualities of creativity, productivity, self-reliance, problem-solving ability, and self-motivation are the goals of learner-centered education. Teaching in the traditional mode is, according to Rogers, vastly overrated. To think that a lesson is learned simply because it is presented is a false assumption. Rogers advocates the facilitation of learning through a warm relationship between student and teacher. He promotes the positive influence of increased communication among students and among faculty members. Each teacher must be a real person to students. Each teacher must accept and value students and have trust in their potential to learn.

In Rogers's classroom, the most important lesson is learning how to learn. Due to our rapidly changing world the speed of new discoveries in science can render a lesson obsolete as soon as it is taught. Each day's events put history in a new perspective. Rogers's truly educated person adapts to change and answers challenges by relying on the ability to seek and obtain knowledge.

Although much of Rogers's educational research was done in the context of college- and graduate-level classrooms, his practices have relevance to a wide range of age levels and institutions. Learner-centered, discovery-oriented learning is common practice in classrooms across the country.

ROBERT J. CHOUN

Bibliography. D. Barlow (1985), *Educational Psychology;* D. G. Benner, ed. (1985), *Baker Encyclopedia of Psychology;* V. Cully and K. Brubaker, eds. (1990), *Harper's Encyclopedia of Religious Education;* R. I. Evans (1975), *Carl Rogers: The Man and His Ideas;* C. R. Rogers (1989), *A Carl Rogers Reader.*

See also DEWEY, JOHN; FREUD, SIGMUND; HIERARCHY OF NEEDS; HUMANISM, CLASSICAL; NOUTHETIC COUNSELING; PSYCHOLOGY OF RELIGION

Role. Role theory stems from social psychology's effort to explain the complex interaction between the individual and society. It assumes a social system creates and maintains roles that enable the system to operate effectively (a structural functionalist theory). It also assumes that our interaction with others (symbolic interactionalist theory) define the self.

Churches are social systems. Christian educators must recognize both formal expectations (a duty identified in the position description) and informal expectations (a duty because the previous person did that job). Success requires fulfilling both formal and informal role expectations.

Healthy role relations exist when: (1) role expectations are known by all parties; (2) all members of the social system agree on the expectations; and (3) the demands of the role are congruous with the abilities of the actor. In Christian education, healthy role performance also requires that Christian educators sustain continuity between the role and their inner life. While role theory allows for performing a role, the Christian educator must guard against pretending in a role.

ROBERT DROVDAHL

Bibliography. B. J. Biddle (1979), *Role Theory: Expectations, Identities, and Behaviors;* G. H. Mead (1934), *Mind, Self, and Society.*

Role Confusion. Erik Erikson's theory of the development of the personality states that the ego, like the body, goes through a sequence of stages. He describes each of those stages in terms of its outstanding negative and positive characteristics. For instance, the stage labeled "identity vs. role confusion" comes during the teenage years. At that time, the consistency of an individual's identity is challenged by new experiences that can lead to role confusion. Primary among these new experiences are sexual experiences and career decisions. Erikson's descriptions of the previous childhood stages suggest that children need to develop independence, self-confidence, and initiative in order to be grounded in an identity that will see them through the teenage years.

Erikson's description of the positive trait "identity" defines it as a feeling of psychosocial well-being, a sense of being comfortable with your own body, possessing a set of personal goals, and an awareness of being accepted. The opposite is the negative trait he terms "role confusion." The teenager who asks himself, "Who am I? What are my values? What am I going to do with my life?" is going through a normal stage experienced by every adult, but the individual who cannot resolve these questions suffers a loss of identity and experiences role confusion. These questions are more challenging today than every before. Traditional sex roles are changing, and an ever-expanding world of career choices can cause anxiety and bewilderment.

An individual's inability to resolve role confusion can lead to defiant behavior and the development of "negative identity." At this point, the range of alternatives available to a young person may become more detrimental than advantageous. Increasing numbers of teens are engaging in unmarried sex. The need to affirm sexual identity, establish independence, and impress peers may override the individual's moral sense that the activity is wrong. These years are also the time to realistically reevaluate childhood career fantasies and begin to make plans for a vocation.

Teachers of this age group should be aware that it is a time of reevaluation and a struggle for independence from authority. Cliques will be formed by boys and girls looking for shared identity. Individuals this age will learn best when they have the freedom to choose from a range of lesson-direction activities and have opportunities to express their own ideas. Because teens tend to use peers and adults as resources for different types of information and advice, churches can minister by training mature individuals of both age groups in counseling skills. Churches can also minister to youth by offering parents training in how best to present sex education in a Christian context.

ROBERT J. CHOUN

Bibliography. R. F. Biehler (1976), *Child Development—An Introduction;* E. H. Erikson (1968), *Identity: Youth and Crises;* M. S. Smart and R. C. Smart (1977), *Children—Development and Relationships.*

Role Play. Type of simulated learning that focuses on interpersonal learning. Similar to improvisation in theater, the actors in a role play perform a role without a script. Role-playing aims at three significant learning outcomes: (1) practicing interpersonal skills; (2) developing empathy through perspective taking; and (3) exploring the affective dimension of interpersonal relations.

Since role players follow no script, effective role plays require two conditions for the actors. First, the actors need a rudimentary appreciation for the demands, motives, and emotions present in the assigned role. If the actors cannot identify with the characters played, they cannot create a realistic role performance. Second, the actors must possess sufficient information to launch and sustain the role play. Minimally this includes: (1) the characters and situations they play (e.g., as the parent of a 16-year-old, you serve on the interview team for a youth pastor candidate); (2) the significant emotions and attitudes present (your child no longer attends so you hope a new youth pastor will reconnect your child); and (3) the task assigned (in the interview ask about the person's strategy to reach marginal youth). If the role play involves several people the characters, situation, moods, and tasks may be printed out and distributed to players.

When introducing role play, actors will need some time to settle into their roles. Once the role play begins let the action and dialogue unfold naturally. The play's length will be determined by the number of participants, their ability to sustain their roles, and the complexity of the task.

Debriefing a role play follows the same pattern used for debriefing any simulation. Begin by asking participants to describe what happened. After careful observation of interactions, the facilitator next guides participants to the affective level, exploring feelings and motives present. Finally, the facilitator guides discussion toward learning which might transfer to actual interpersonal situations.

ROBERT DROVDAHL

Bibliography. M. Van Ments (1994), *The Effective Use of Role-Play: A Handbook for Teachers and Trainers.*

Role Reversal. Social thought process that describes an advanced cognitive ability to vicariously "become" a significant other person or another part of the self. In Christian education, role reversal is often utilized in the teaching methodology of roleplay. The educational and therapeutic purposes of role reversal are many: (1) to allow the participant to understand and experience the thoughts and feelings of others, (2) to provide a basis for awareness of the consequences of behaviors without the actual experience, (3) to facilitate the evaluation of the content of relationships, (4) to demonstrate alternative actions or reactions to specific situations, and (5) to explore emotions from a new or difficult experience within a safe, protected environment.

Role reversal is made possible by the development of formal operational thought as described in Jean Piaget's cognitive structural theory. As a person's thought processes develop beyond the naïve realism in which only personal concrete experience may be perceived as reality, a sophistication of thought allows the imagined thoughts and actions of others to have validity. Further, a growing social awareness which accompanies the developing thought processes decreases the cognitive egocentrism (i.e., self as the only valid perceiver) and provides an expanded frame of social cognition which includes both one's immediate environment (home, friends, community) and the world beyond one's experience (intergenerational, regional, and global cultures). This ability to assume another person's perspective and understanding his or her feelings is called social perspectivism.

Robert Selman describes this maturing social perspectivism as mutual perspective taking, where one realizes that both self and others can view each other mutually and simultaneously as subjects. One can step outside a two-person dyad and view the interaction from a third-person perspective. A higher level of social cognition realizes that mutual perspective taking does not always lead to specific understanding and yet presses for the necessity of more general social ways of thinking and acting which allows the opportunity of role reversal within contexts that the person has never directly experienced.

Educationally, effective role play encourages active participation in the learning process, stimulates inductive thought, and enhances application to real life situations. It also provides opportunities for students to identify with others and gain insights into their thoughts and behaviors. This methodology is particularly appropriate in cross-cultural education through the use of simple impromptu drama as well as complex instructional simulations.

EDWIN ROBINSON

Bibliography. M. Lefevre (1996), *Creative Teaching Methods: Be an Effective Christian Teacher;* J. Piaget (1954), *The Construction of Reality in the Child;* R. L. Selman (1980), *The Growth of Interpersonal Understanding.*

Roman Catholic Education. Catholic education in America attempted to do several crucial things for the Catholic populace. Like other minorities, Roman Catholics found themselves resented and rejected, so a school system would be one way to ensure perpetuation of the faith. The Catholic faith required, at least then, rigid obedience to church authority. The school served as a vehicle for preserving this tradition.

The Roman Catholic school system represents the largest parochial, church-supported elementary system in the world. In the early nineteenth century pastors were ordered to open schools in the New World. In most states this was illegal except among the German settlements in Pennsylvania and Maryland. For many Protestant parishes, the Sunday school provided the religious education beyond that given in the home. However, among German Lutherans separate parochial schools were demanded.

Notre Dame University history professor Jay P. Dolan (1992) states that "the school became an essential part of the church's evangelization program. The shift from the primacy of informal re-

ligious education to formal religious instruction, from family to school, was critical to the development of a Catholic school system" (276).

Dolan contends further "that the Catholic commitment to parochial schools got stronger just as the public school commitment to religion weakened. The walls separating church and state in the area of education had steadily risen in the late nineteenth century; this development canceled out any attempt at compromise between Catholics and a state-supported system of education" (276).

Roman Catholic lay people and clergy alike rejected schools based on a Protestant ideology that was growing more pluralistic even then. What Horace Mann and Henry Barnard initiated and advocated drove the Catholics away from the public schools.

In summary, four elements caused Catholics to establish a separate school system in the nineteenth century:

1. Catholic lay people put a primary value on the need for religious instruction;
2. The development of the ideology of the common-school system with its pluralistic tendencies;
3. The commitment to perpetuate the Catholic faith with their children;
4. The availability of the large pool of Roman Catholic religious—the sisters—to staff the schools. (Dolan, 1992, 276–77)

That is why the pastors were ordered to open schools in the New World. The Germans promoted additional reasons as they desired to retain their language and culture. Of course the Irish did not see the language factor as a vital reason—their issue was the matter of doctrine.

In the 1830s Roman Catholic families were of the opinion that they, the families, could give a proper religious education to their children. By the 1840s church leaders were ambivalent and would accept a good nonsectarian public school. The terms *heretical* and *infidel* were being used by Catholics of the Protestant emphases of the public schools. An evenhanded public school view of the Christian faith was no longer seen as a possibility for the Catholic population. State-supported public education had become a given (Dolan, 1992, 276).

This stance brought much unfavorability to Roman Catholics from the Protestants and in the 1850s and 1860s "Catholic pastors were now beginning to deny the sacraments to parents who refused to send their children to the Catholic school." Yet, there was never a total commitment to the parochial system in that century. The people's support was "very selective" (Dolan, 1992, 269).

With the twentieth century the quality of elementary and secondary education in Catholic schools was on the rise. Teachers' colleges such as Catholic University in Washington, D.C., Creighton University, and DePaul University brought certification and standardization to the system. The host church pastors often in effect were the superintendent of schools. These Catholic leaders became more powerful with the years.

After 1945 a growing number of Catholic leaders favored federal aid to education, provided it did not entail federal control. Government contracts to train army and navy personnel enabled many Catholic colleges and universities to survive the war years, and more Catholic educators realized that acceptance of federal funds did not lessen the autonomy of their institutions (Dolan, 1992, 283). Following those war years Catholic leaders were aggressively seeking financial assistance from the government.

It is the judgment of Leahy, a leading Catholic thinker and educational strategist, that "Catholic higher education generally remains undistinguished in American intellectual culture, despite nearly four decades of effort and expenditure of millions of dollars . . . . Only a few Catholic higher educational institutions exceeded the improvement in American higher education and advanced significantly in academic reputation" (Dolan, 1992, 135, 146).

Finances for these schools remain a problem. It seems that a biblical education of tithing and giving has never been done on an extensive basis. However, very wealthy people have undergirded their graduate schools and seminaries. Other major problems in the twentieth century were the rapid decline of men taking the vows of the priesthood and the dwindling number of women religious educators to teach in their school system. The twenty-first century may bring the demise of this powerful system or the public school may be weakened to the point that the American people may be forced to financially support the Catholic schools so that more children may receive a better education. It has been and continues to be a powerful education movement.

WARREN S. BENSON

Bibliography. M. C. Boys (1989), *Educating in Faith: Maps and Visions;* J. P. Dolan (1992), *The American Catholic Experience: A History From Colonial Times to the Present;* J. M. O'Keefe (1997), *Catholic Education at the Turn of the Century.*

Roman Education. According to tradition, Rome was founded in 753 B.C. on Palatine Hill, one of the seven hills surrounding that region. While much of the early history of the Italic people remains ambiguous, it is known that by the fourth century B.C., the unpretentious and agrarian Romans had determined that the primary goal of education should be character develop-ment. These simple, hardworking people idolized the character traits of filial duty, honesty, courage, integrity, and dignity. By the second century B.C., a pedagogy was developed that would create a citizenry capable of serving the gods, the state, and the family. It was believed that by serving these institutions, one could achieve the highest good. Two prominent features of Roman education emerged from this pedagogy; first, it was an education based on tradition, and second, it was an education managed by the family. The Romans maintained that tradition-based, family oriented education was the way to virtue and character.

Educational Stages. The history of Roman education, from the founding of the city in 753 B.C. to the closing of Greek schools by Justinian in A.D. 529, falls into four developmental periods (Reed and Prevost, 1993; Mulhem, 1959; Smith, 1955). These educational movements are classified as the *Native Roman Period* (700 B.C.–250 B.C.), the *Transition Period* (250 B.C.–55 B.C.), the *Hellenized Roman Period* (55 B.C.–A.D. 200), and the *Period of Decline* (A.D. 200–529).

The Native Roman Period began when the Etruscans, an enigmatic people who migrated to the region from Asia Minor about 900 B.C. and who disappeared at the beginning of the fifth century B.C., introduced to the Italic peoples their alphabet, which, over time, was modified to meet the needs of the Latin language. The Native Roman Period ended when the educational practices and ideals of the Greeks were introduced to Rome. Since the Romans lacked creative ingenuity and innovative imagination, they contributed very little to the educational ideals and practices of the ancient world. However, they excelled in taking the theoretical concepts of other people and applying them to the building of roads, bridges, houses, and temples. Romans' genius for modification and application was far greater than any gift for originality and creativity,

The Transition Phase of education was launched when Greek culture was introduced into Roman life. Two factors precipitated this movement. First, the Romans began a series of military conquests that ultimately gave them control of the Mediterranean world. Conquest transformed Rome as thousands of Hellenized captives were brought into the city. Many of these slaves, who had been educated according to Greek ideals, took positions as teachers in the households of the wealthy. One of the most notable among the captives was Livius Andronicus who, in 250 B.C., translated Homer's *Odyssey* into Latin. This event was the second contributing factor in the transition of Rome from a provincial town to a cosmopolitan city. This translation, which served as a primary textbook for several centuries, was so well received by the Romans that translations of additional Greek literature soon followed.

The Hellenized Roman Period began in 55 B.C. when Cicero, a Roman who advocated Greek pedagogy, wrote *De Oratore* (On the Education of an Orator). This work marked the beginning of a period in which Greek culture, practices, and educational ideals were widely accepted throughout Rome. This period lasted until approximately A.D. 200 when, in a Period of Decline, imperial edicts killed freedom of speech and the state established a monopoly over the schools. Roman higher education came to an end in A.D. 529 when Emperor Justinian closed the schools of philosophy and law in Athens and all schools of higher learning in Rome except the law schools.

Educational Models. The earliest educational model adopted by the Romans was that of the Etruscans. In addition to giving the Romans their alphabet and a great number of words, these early inhabitants excelled in the areas of building, engineering, mining, farming, and commerce. This utilitarian model of education suited the unpretentious Romans, who appreciated a practical, simple lifestyle.

The Etruscan dynasty was expelled from Rome in 509 B.C. as a result of a revolt led by patrician Roman families. An outcome of this struggle was a growing democracy which, in 450 B.C., resulted in the publication of the *Laws of the Twelve Tables.* This document expressed the civic responsibilities and outlined the acceptable religious beliefs of the Roman citizenry and was the only major literary work produced by the Romans in five hundred years. For the next two centuries this code remained virtually the sole text for the intellectual basis of Roman life. Since there were no formal schools in Rome at this time, parents taught the contents of this document to their children, who memorized it by chanting and singing select passages.

A great change occurred in the character of Roman education about 250 B.C. when, through territorial expansion and commercial growth, the Romans came in contact with Greek colonies in Sicily and southern Italy. Roman travelers and officials found it advantageous to learn the Greek language and customs. When Greek slaves began working in Roman households as servants and teachers, they introduced a culture and philosophy that was at least two centuries ahead of where the Romans were at that time. Educational ideals and practices became more cosmopolitan as Greek influence proliferated throughout the Roman Republic.

Educational Institutions. During the Native Roman Period (700–250 B.C.), the primary force in education was the family. The goal of education during this time was to shape young people to the community ideals, which consisted of a reverence for the gods, the laws, and the family. The intellectual training within the home did not usually advance beyond basic reading and writing and the earliest stages of arithmetic.

One of the most fundamental principles of Roman education was learning by doing. At the age of 7, boys were often trained in their fathers' occupations by acting as their apprentices. They became acquainted with government as they accompanied their fathers about the city. They familiarized themselves with religion by participating in the many cultic ceremonies that were practiced at home, in the fields, and in the temples. At age 16 the boy was presented with a *toga virilis,* or the attire of a male citizen, and sent to an army camp for three years of active military service, which completed his education. The Roman ideal of family education was never allowed to be put on an impractical or aesthetic level but was confined to the practical and functional levels.

During the Transition and Hellenized Periods (250 B.C.–A.D. 200) education became more formal and structured as Greek culture influenced Roman thinking. It was during these educational movements that Latin scholars modified, codified, and systematized the liberal arts of Greece. It was generally understood among the intellectuals that the liberally educated Roman should be knowledgeable in the disciplines of grammar, rhetoric, logic, arithmetic, geometry, astronomy, music, architecture, and medicine. Eventually, Greek pedagogy became the model for Roman education.

The Hellenization of the Roman Republic created three levels of schools. The elementary school, or *ludus* (which means "play'" or "sport"), was for children ages 7 to 12. This school was designed primarily to teach reading, writing, and arithmetic. Children were given a stylus and wax tablet for writing and an abacus for counting. Such schools were staffed with *litteratores* ("teachers of letters") and often convened in the streets, marketplaces, or porches of the city. The *litteratores* were usually individuals without academic or scholarly qualifications. Classes started before sunrise and sometimes lasted until dark. The major educational methods employed were memorization, drill, and harsh discipline.

The secondary school, or *grammaticus,* was for youths ages 12 to 16. Studies consisted of Latin and Greek grammar, literature, history, philosophy, science, mythology, and religion. The educational ideals and practices expressed by the Romans in these schools were similar to those advocated by the Greeks. However, unlike their counterparts in elementary schools, grammar school teachers were required to be skilled and knowledgeable in the liberal arts.

Roman higher education, evidenced in the rhetorical school, was reserved primarily for children of the Roman elite, 16 to 18 years of age. The school was modeled after the rhetorical schools of Athens whose goal was to train public speakers. The art of rhetoric was recognized as a useful accomplishment for a rising politician. In fact, rhetorical and oratorical skills were considered prerequisites to a successful public life. Eventually, the training of the orator, or *rhetor*, became the supreme aim and content of all higher education. Students were trained in public speaking, politics, and public service. They studied logic, debate, ethics, oratory, grammar, and literature, It was believed that encyclopedic knowledge was essential for success in oratory.

DAN K. BALL

Bibliography. C. Atkinson and E. T. Maleska (1965), *The Story of Education;* R. F. Butts (1973), *The Education of the West: A Formative Chapter in the History of Civilization;* F. Eby and C. F. Arrowood (1940), *The History and Philosophy of Education Ancient and Medieval;* K. O. Gangel and W. S. Benson (1983), *Christian Education: Its History and Philosophy;* J. Mulhern (1959), *A History of Education: A Social Interpretation;* J. E. Reed and R. Prevost (1993), *A History of Christian Education;* W. Smith (1955), *Ancient Education.*

Romanticism. Literary, artistic, and philosophical movement originating in the late eighteenth century. It may also be seen as an underpinning worldview for such educational theories as progressivism, humanism, and reconstructionism. Romanticism places an emphasis on the innate goodness of human beings, the valuing of emotion and imagination over reason, and the "natural" inclination of people to produce good when not corrupted by social institutions. Romanticism may be characterized as a reaction to classical rationalism, or the accentuation of reason over intuition. Today, romanticism can also have a broader meaning of "freedom from formalities and conventions, its pursuit of the truths of feeling and imagination, its inwardness and subjectivity" (Cranston, 1983, 138).

History. Jean-Jacques Rousseau may be called the first romanticist philosopher. The publishing of his *La nouvelle Heloise,* which might be considered the original romantic novel, initiated the movement that came to be called Romanticism. Rousseau perhaps reacted to what has been called Classicism, which is considered the opposite of Romanticism. Classicists usually derived their models from the ancient Greeks and Romans and held that knowledge was absolute. Rousseau proposed that "the self" was the standard, and strongly opposed all influences that diminished the development of the "noble savage" within. In summary, Romanticism holds to the central idea of liberty, freedom, emotion, and imagination as opposed to the classical favoring of rationality, restraint, the use of strict forms, and civilization.

Other early romantic philosophers include Diderot, a contemporary of Rousseau; Johann Gott-

fried Herder, Johann Gottlieb Fichte, August Wilhelm and Friedrich Schlegel, Germans; French Germaine de Stael, known as the "mistress of the age"; Benjamin Constant, Vicomte de Chateaubriand, novelists, and Victor Hugo, poet; Ugo Foscolo, Ludovico di Breme, and Alessandro Manzoni, Italians; and a host of English literarists, including Samuel Taylor Coleridge, William Wordsworth, Percy Bysshe Shelly, John Keats, and Lord George Gordon Byron. Mostly developed via a close association, at least with the writings of the others, these persons developed a varied philosophical movement. In the twentieth century, prominent humanists and a variety of critics have spread to such diverse areas as Russia, Australia, and America.

Tenets. Metaphysics. Truth, for the romantic, is an inward thing. Therefore, romantic ideas could be said to be akin to Existentialism. However, the romantic had a much simpler (and coherent, perhaps less individualized) view of what truth might be. Reality, for the romantic, is the common state which all will attain if environmental factors are conducive to such. To be finding good in the world through a natural journey would seem to be how a romantic would describe truth. Truth also had the elements of discovery and change to heighten the curiosity of a person. Experience rather than reason is the basis of knowing truth.

Goals. The goals of the romantic are to acquire the freedom of soul and nature that would put persons in their most noble state. In other words, the goals of romantic education are to find meaning in the life of the child. It is in the child that natural curiosity and discovery dwell. The children therefore should be enabled to solve their problems and fulfill their desires. "The solution to the Romantic problem lies not in attempting the impossible, not in trying to stabilize the Self, but in continuous self-transformation, in continuously transcending tragedy, and comedy, and good, and evil" (Peckham, 1965, 351). The chief goal of an education is to provide a child the opportunity to discover and grow naturally, freeing him or her from society's corrupt influence.

Role of the Teacher. A teacher, according to a romantic educator, should be a facilitator, not a dispenser of information. "The teacher's role is that of advisor, guide, and fellow traveler, rather than that of authoritarian and classroom director" (Knight, 1989, 95). Teachers possess greater experience and knowledge. They therefore become advisors and guides to their students.

Nature of the Student. The nature of the pupil is considered active rather than passive, and good as opposed to evil. This then gives rise to the concept that a person should best be educated by being unhindered in that learning. Pestalozzi followed a romantic idea that "evil originates in a distorted social environment rather than in human nature"

(Gangel, 1983, 198). The "noble savage" of Rousseau best capsulizes the image or nature of people for the romanticist. The surroundings then become the deterrent to education. "Let us lay down as an incontrovertible rule that the first impulses of nature are always right; there is no original sin in the human heart; the how and why of the entrance of every vice can be traced" (Rousseau, 1953, 63).

Process of Education. To involve oneself in education, a process of natural play and discovery should take place. That is why one could see Romanticism as the precursor to Dewey's progressivism. "Dewey had based his philosophy of education upon the idea that playful, imaginative participation in activities was the way in which children could best be stimulated to learn" (Wheeler, 1993, 208). So the entire endeavor of education could be viewed more as art than as science. As such, education should focus on solving problems more than on teaching a specific content or subject. Rousseau outlined five naturally occurring stages: infancy, childhood, early adolescence, late adolescence, and young adulthood. "The stages of childhood development should determine educational content and method" (Reed, 1993, 242).

Evaluation. One evaluates the outcome of education for the romanticist by measuring against the concept of naturalism. Is there a natural curiosity and desire to learn? Is the student unhindered in their development? These questions focus the nature of romantic evaluation.

Present Day. The current educational landscape has certainly been influenced by romantic ideas. Dewey's educational progressivism, the present deschooling movement, the reconstructionist, and the nonbiblical humanist could all derive their roots in Romanticism. As such, we do well to study the writers listed above and observe our own culture to guard and to guide in relation to their thinking.

GREGORY C. CARLSON

Bibliography. M. Cranston (1983), *The Romantic Movement;* K. O. Gangel and W. S. Benson (1983), *Christian Education: Its History and Philosophy;* G. Knight (1989), *Philosophy and Education: An Introduction in Christian Perspective;* M. Peckham, ed. (1965), *Romanticism: The Culture of the Nineteenth Century;* J. E. Reed and R. Prevost (1993), *A History of Christian Education;* J.-J. Rousseau (1953), *Emile: French Thought in the Eighteenth Century;* K. Wheeler (1993), *Romanticism, Pragmatism and Deconstruction.*

See also DEWEY, JOHN; HUMANISM, CLASSICAL; PESTALOZZI, JOHANN HEINRICH; ROUSSEAU, JEAN-JACQUES

Rosh Hashanah. Jewish New Year, the autumn festival celebrated on the first and second days of the month of Tishri.

For Judaism, the New Year begins the "Days of Awe," the penitential season that culminates in Yom Kippur, the Day of Atonement. Traditionally, this festival commemorated the creation of the world, but the ritual that included as many as one hundred blasts on a ram's horn (*shofar*) also called the participants to a solemn period of self-examination and repentance.

In the rabbinical literature, Rosh Hashanah is called a Day of Judgment (*Yom Ha-Din*) and a Day of Remembrance (*Yom Ha-Zikkaron*). On that day all humankind was seen as passing by the great judgment throne. Each individual was to recount his or her actions of the past year and to seek mercy for the year to come. On this day, too, God as King "remembers" the deeds of his subjects long forgotten through the year.

In the Bible, the term *Rosh Hashanah* occurs only in a date formula in Ezekiel 40:1, where it refers to the beginning of the year and not to the festival. Scholars disagree as to the precise date alluded to in this passage because two calendars were used in ancient Israel: the cultic sequence beginning in the month of Nisan (March/April), and the agricultural cycle starting in the month of Tishri (September/October).

Exodus 12:2 specifies that in commemoration of Israel's deliverance from Egypt the Passover month (Nisan) was to be the first month of the year for the Israelites. However, some evidence does suggest that at different periods of time and in different locations an autumnal New Year was celebrated. As noted above, later Judaism came to observe the fall Tishri date as the New Year.

Although not specifically called Rosh Hashanah, this autumn festival is described in the Bible as a "holy convocation," a "memorial proclaimed with the blast of horns," and "a day of blowing the horn" (Lev. 23:23–25; Num. 29:1–6; cf. Ps. 81:3–4). The same festival may have been observed when Ezra read the book of the Law before the people (Neh. 8:1–8).

STEPHEN J. ANDREWS

Bibliography. D. I. Block (1986), *The International Standard Bible Encyclopedia,* 3:529–32; L. Jacobs (1971), *Encyclopaedia Judaica,* 14:305–10; J. C. Vanderkam (1992), *The Anchor Bible Dictionary* 1:814–20.

See also HEBREW EDUCATION THROUGH FEASTS AND FESTIVALS; JEWISH EDUCATION; RABBI AS EDUCATOR

Rousseau, Jean-Jacques (1712–78). Philosopher and social critic. Born in Geneva of Swiss-French descent, Rousseau was frequently given to bouts of emotional instability. The loss of his mother while she was giving birth to him and the abandonment by his father when he was ten no doubt were precipitating factors. He was raised by an aunt, who was a staunch Calvinist, and left home at the age of sixteen. He spent several years wandering from place to place, at last finding a protector in Madame de Warens at Chambery. Under her influence he converted to Catholicism and briefly served as a tutor at Lyon.

His musical interests led him to settle in Paris in 1742, where he composed an opera entitled *Le Devin du Village* (1752), which was performed before Louis XV. Despite his involvement with the arts, he published his first writing, *Discourse on the Arts and Sciences* (1750), which decried them as egotistical expressions devoid of addressing human needs.

In 1754 he reconverted to Protestantism. One of the most influential social and philosophic voices of the Enlightenment and the French Revolution, Rousseau is frequently referred to as the "father of naturalism," believing that society had perverted the natural instincts of man. Left to himself, he contended, man lived harmoniously with nature and free from selfishness, want, possessiveness, or jealousy. In stressing man's inner life of feeling and sentiment, he differed sharply with Diderot.

His opposition to science and art as paths to progress demarcated him from other Enlightenment voices and placed him in the camp of the romanticists. Following Comenius and other educational theorists, Rousseau believed that learning should be built on recognized stages of human growth and development: infancy (birth to age 5), childhood (ages 5–12), boyhood (ages 12–15), adolescence (ages 15–18), and the final stage (ages 18–20). But he departed sharply from the "faith in reason" requisite of the other philosophes, emphasizing instead the "inner life" as a source of truth. He stressed that knowledge was obtained through human instincts ("naturalism") rather than through books or formal schooling, which often interfered with and impeded the natural learning process. In essence, for Rousseau, the best education was virtually the absence of education.

His most famous work, *Emile,* written as a novel, illustrated his philosophy of education. In it he attacked the doctrine of child depravity and the existence of social institutions, such as the church and the school, believing they "imprisoned" and constrained the development of natural interests and inclinations. To Rousseau humankind was basically good and, if allowed to develop properly, this natural goodness could be shielded from the many corrupting influences of society. "Man is born free," he wrote, "but everywhere he is in chains!" That same year (1762), he also published *The Social Contract,* the statement of his political philosophy and his twofold remedy for a corrupt society. First, politics and morality should never be separated. When a state fails to act in a moral fashion, then it ceases to function as a state and no longer exerts genuine authority over the individual. Second, individual freedom must be maintained, for that is what the state has been created to preserve.

Rousseau further held that social class distinctions based on wealth, property, and prestige created artificial barriers between people, producing social and educational inequities and corruption. He opposed the right of the individual to privately own property. As his politics gained notoriety, Rousseau's temperamental and emotional outbursts became more frequent. He moved to England in 1766 at the invitation of the Scottish philosopher David Hume. Even there he was unable to discuss in a civil manner differences with other spokesmen of the Enlightenment, resulting in his falling out with Hume and his return to France. He was often shunned, and in his later years became progressively withdrawn. Retreating into a shell of paranoia, he spent the final decade of his life penning his *Confessions,* a melancholic autobiographical work of deep introspection. In its preface he wrote, "I have begun on a work which is without precedent, whose accomplishment will have no imitator. I propose to set before my fellow-mortals a man in all the truth of nature, and this man shall be myself." He died in Paris. The impact of Rousseau's educational philosophy began immediately with thinkers like Immanuel Kant and extends to the "content-neutral" and "natural development" forms of twentieth-century education espoused by John Dewey and others.

DAVID GOUGH

Bibliography. H. Bloom, ed. (1988), *Jean-Jacques Rousseau (Modern Critical Views);* L. G. Crocker (1968–73), *Jean-Jacques Rousseau: A New Interpretive Analysis of His Life and Works,* 2 vols.

See also DEWEY, JOHN; ENLIGHTENMENT; HUMANISM, CLASSICAL; HUME, DAVID; KANT, IMMANUEL; LIBERAL ARTS; PESTALOZZI, JOHANN HEINRICH; ROMANTICISM

R-S Bonds. In the 1930s and 1940s, B. F. Skinner departed from the behavioral mainstream of the S-R bonds. Skinner's conceptual innovation was to reformulate the idea of the reflex. In classical conditioning, for example, the organism is passively reactive, but in instrumental conditioning the response has an effect on, and in that sense operates on the environment. This led Skinner to propose the term *operant conditioning* to denote the activity of conditioning.

Organisms act, or operate, upon their environment. These operants are selected by their consequences through processes such as reinforcement, punishment, and extinction. In operant conditioning, a change in behavior is produced by a contingency between the subject's responding and a stimulus event. Typically, some arbitrary response (R) is consistently followed by some motivationally significant event (SR); for example, the exhibition of a cheerful disposition is often followed by greater feedback of interpersonal cheer in return. Unlike classical conditioning, the stimulus event is called the reinforcer because it follows the activity of the subject and increases the probability of the recurrence of the initiating response.

In teaching, operant conditioning has inspired the development of programs of mechanical instruction. Teaching machines ask questions, display alternative answers, allow review and additional choices, and reinforce the student when a correct response is made. Apart from this programmed instruction of teaching machines, reinforcement is also used as a popular method of treatment known as behavior modification and contingency management. In such cases, undesirable behavior is extinguished by the establishment of a reward, or reinforcement schedule, in favor of a more desirable activity.

STEVEN PATTY

See also ASSOCIATION/CONNECTIONIST THEORIES; BEHAVIORISM, THEORIES OF; OPERANT CONDITIONING; SKINNER, BURRHUS FREDERIC

Ss

Sacrament. *See* Communion.

Sacraments. *See* Liturgy.

Salvation. Deliverance from sin—past (Rom. 5:1, 8:1); present (1 Cor. 1:18; Phil. 2:12, 13); and future (Rom. 13:11, 8:30). It restores a relationship with God through his Son Jesus Christ. All people have sinned (Rom. 3:23), and all sin is contrary to the will and purposes of God. Sin alienates people from a holy God. People have no ability to manufacture salvation. Because he is righteous, God cannot tolerate sin; he has judged sin and imposed the death penalty. But Jesus—through his birth, life, ministry, suffering, death on the cross, and resurrection—has made salvation possible.

People can be saved from the penalty of sin (justification), the power of sin (sanctification), and ultimately the presence of sin (glorification). To be saved is to be delivered from bondage, brought into freedom, rescued from death, given a new lease on life. That which is reclaimed by God's saving action is life—abundant life, eternal life, life in the Spirit (John 5, 6; Rom. 8:1–10; 1 John 5) (Oden, 1992, 80).

Views of salvation vary along several dimensions (Erickson, 1985, 888–91): (1) time—a single occurrence at the beginning of the Christian life, a process continuing throughout the Christian life, or a future event; (2) the nature and locus of the need, that is, a vertical relationship between persons and God, or horizontal relationships, between persons or society as a whole; (3) the medium of salvation—how salvation is obtained, as in sacramentally or by moral action or by faith; (4) the direction of movement in salvation, that is, saving individuals first and through them transforming society, or changing individuals by first altering the structures of society; (5) the extent of salvation—who and how many will be saved?; (6) the objects of salvation—only individuals versus the entire cosmos. Primarily, however, the concern of the study of salvation is the clarification of the steps along the way, problems associated with these steps, and the grace that enables each step (Oden, 1992, 81).

The sequence of salvation (*ordo salutis*) in one theological system includes effectual calling, conversion, regeneration, union with Christ, justification, adoption, sanctification, perseverance, and glorification. Another system assumes prevenient grace, convincing grace and repentance, justification by faith, and sanctification. Differences in understanding hinge to a large extent on one's understanding of the prior electing work of God and the role of human choice. Both insist on the total inability of persons to do anything to save themselves due to the effect of original sin. Both assert the necessity of the life, death, and resurrection of Jesus as the foundation for salvation. The former system assumes, however, that only those whom God elected to be saved will be saved; the latter system asserts that all those who choose to respond to God's gracious invitation to relationship with him will be saved.

The Human Condition. The Bible records the story of God's activity to reverse the effects of Adam and Eve's disobedience in the Garden of Eden. God endowed the first man and woman with the capacity to choose, since he wanted a freely chosen relationship with the crown jewels of his creation. Within an environment of earthly bliss, Adam and Eve were assigned management responsibility over all other created beings. God restricted this first couple only from eating from the tree of the knowledge of good and evil (Gen. 2:16, 17).

Adam and Eve were seduced by the provocative idea of being like God, that is, of knowing good and evil (Gen. 3:4). In pride they ate the forbidden fruit and set their wills against God (Augustine, Oden). With that one act of willful disobedience, the entire human race was thrust under the guilt of sin and became subject to God's judgment. From this point on, human nature was bent on rebellion, for all have sinned and fall short of the glory of God (Rom. 3:23). All of us have become like one who is unclean, and

612

all our righteous acts are like filthy rags (Isa. 64:6). Adam and Eve disobeyed God, pridefully assuming they were wise enough to choose over God's command. Sin has subsequently infected every person without exception. Just as Adam and Eve were banished from the Garden of Eden because of sin, so also all their heirs must face the ultimate penalty for sin, for the wages of sin is death (Rom. 6:23).

Not only are all people guilty of sin, but they are also bereft of the possibility of doing good apart from God. Everyone has turned away, they have together become corrupt; there is no one who does good, not even one (Ps. 53:3; cf. Rom. 3:10–12). For Calvinists, total depravity refers to the radical and thoroughgoing nature of human sin. It renders individuals unable to respond to any offer of grace (Erickson, 1985, 905, 915). John Wesley, too, believed that persons in the natural state are void of all good, wholly fallen, and totally corrupted (Collins, 1989, 22). In their sinful state, all people are condemned to an eternity separated from God and subject to endless, profound suffering.

The Divine Initiative. If people are bereft of any ability to save themselves, then God must necessarily take the initiative to restore relationship with his created beings. Consequently, God sent Jesus, his Word of invitation to start life anew, wrapped in humanity. Jesus' life pictures what God does for all people. He walked through life. He convinced people of their sinfulness. He graciously comes to us before we ask. He speaks as God's convincing grace. Sent by God, Jesus, his only Son, was born of a virgin and lived among humankind without sin. By virtue of his sinless life, Jesus alone was worthy to bear the weight of God's judgment upon sin, death by crucifixion. Jesus' death on the cross became a substitutional offering of Christ's goodness for our sin (Oden, 1992, 123; Rom. 3:21–15; 2 Cor. 5:21).

But who may be saved? Calvinists speak of God's saving work in terms of the following descriptors: Total depravity, Unconditional predestination, Limited atonement, Irresistible grace, and Perseverance of the saints (TULIP). God has elected certain individuals to be saved. In fact, God not only elects to save some, but he also elects to condemn others. But we have no cause for complaint. This is not unfair because we are so graced to be saved (Augustine). Before time began, God chose those who were to be saved. In time God enacted the way of salvation through his Son which is given irresistibly to those who are chosen. God's grace is so winsome it cannot be refused. It is not for the whole world, however. Those who have been chosen and given salvation will persevere to the end because they are eternally held by God. This position maintains a very high view of God, who is holy and hates sin, and a low view of humanity, including a low view of human will.

In the Calvinist perspective, God saves only those whom he has elected. We may distinguish between general election and special election. The latter refers to God's selection of certain individuals to receive his special favor (Eph. 1:4–5; John 15:16). God has sovereignly chosen some from all eternity and because they have been chosen they will have faith to believe. As Augustine said, "Let us, then, understand the calling whereby they become elected—not those who are elected because they have believed, but who are elected that they might believe."

Wesleyan-Arminians, on the other hand, believe that God has graciously bestowed grace on all persons, which then enables them to respond to the divine invitation. Human choice becomes decisive in salvation. Both agree, however, that salvation comes "by grace . . . through faith—and this not from yourselves, it is the gift of God—not by works, so that no one can boast" (Eph. 2:8, 9).

Wesleyans believe God hates sin because of what it does to his children. Prevenient grace is available to everyone, and is active in humanity even before people know about it. It is the source of all that is good in humans, that which enables humans to choose toward God. It is lavishly and liberally given without any necessity of the human participating. Convincing grace is that which persuades persons of their lostness and of their need of God. It encourages sinful people to turn to God. It is the voice of God specifically to the individual. Wesley taught that there are good works which precede justification but that they are not the basis of salvation (Collins, 1989, 41). They have no merit, and individuals cannot work out a way to heaven. Faith is the only condition of justification (Collins, 1989, 42), both necessary and sufficient to justify the believer.

The Human Response. As Jesus lived and walked among people, his invitation was twofold: repent and follow me. The word *repentance* comes from the Greek word *metanoia*, meaning a change of mind. Jesus was saying, Give up your old way of being and trust me instead. He called people to repent at every level, both corporate and personal.

At the point of this turnaround encounter with Jesus, Lord and Savior, God justifies the individual. Sometimes described by the phrase "just-as-if-I-had-never-sinned," justification is a legal transaction in which God declares repentant sinners to be righteous on the basis of Christ's death on the cross. When God looks at the justified individual, he no longer sees a sinner wearing sin-stained garments, but instead sees a redeemed child dressed in the righteousness of his Son Jesus.

It is as if the liabilities of the sinner have been merged with the assets of the Savior and all debts liquidated. God gives justification. As a gift it cannot be earned by human merit (Rom. 6:23; Eph. 2:8–9). Justifying faith's object is Christ; it is a disposition of the heart, and it acknowledges the necessity and merit of his death and the power of his resurrection. It is an assent to the whole gospel (Collins, 1989, 47).

Not only is the new child of God justified in a legal sense, but peace is established between God and the believer. Jesus paid the penalty for sin by his death on the cross. God accepted his death as the substitute for debt owed by sinners. Consequently, the enmity that existed between God and his human creation was annulled on the basis of Christ's substitionary death on the cross. Christ and believing Christians are as one with a holy God (atonement). The sinner has been born again or converted and begun a new life in the Spirit of Christ (regeneration).

Life in the Spirit. Sanctification is a continuation of regeneration whereby individuals are set apart to live holy lives in obedience to the will of God and to become like God. Sanctification, like justification, is the work of God carried out in the believer by God's Spirit. It involves separation from sin, dedication to God, and living a life that is morally good and spiritually worthy. God desires the believer to be totally sanctified: "May God himself, the God of peace, sanctify you through and through. May your whole spirit, soul and body be kept blameless at the coming of our Lord Jesus Christ" (1 Thess. 5:23).

Justification occurs instantly but sanctification takes place over a lifetime. While one either is or is not justified, one may experience degrees of sanctification. God declares sinners to be justified (objective); in sanctification the Spirit works to transform the character and condition of the person (subjective) (Erickson, 1985, 969).

Love is the motivation and goal of sanctification; being perfected in love is living in such relationship with God that one no longer desires to sin. For some this growth in love is a result of consistent, day-by-day obedience to the known will of God. For others, it begins with an experience brought about by acute consciousness of one's inability to live up to the demands of a holy God followed by an encounter with the love of God that is so transforming that the whole person submits to God. The Spirit of God is given complete reign at that point. While present at conversion, the Holy Spirit comes at distinctive points along the journey to fill and indwell and empower the believer for holy living. Life in the Spirit is more than obedience, as foundational as that is. The Spirit works with the human will to empower it to choose to live godly and uprightly.

LESLIE A. ANDREWS

Bibliography. K. J. Collins (1989), *Wesley on Salvation: A Study in the Standard Sermons;* M. J. Erickson (1985), *Christian Theology;* T. C. Oden (1992), *Systematic Theology.*

Salvation Army. The religious movement known as The Salvation Army was commenced in 1865 by William Booth and his wife, Catherine (Mumford), often described as "the Founder" and "the Army Mother," respectively. Moved with compassion for the multitudes outside the influence of organized religion in the mid–nineteenth century in London, England, William Booth set himself to discover how to reach the masses with the gospel. William was, at the time, a young Methodist evangelist, deeply moved by the needs of the poor in the East End of London. Street meetings became an essential element of the early days of the then-named Christian Mission. Men and women from the depths of despair found hope in the message proclaimed to the "whosoever." The Good News of the gospel became personal good news and hope was born where life previously seemed hopeless.

William Booth was born on April 10, 1829, at Nottingham and served as the leader of the Salvation Army until his death on August 20, 1912. William wrote *In Darkest England and the Way Out,* which became the blueprint for all of the subsequent social ministry of this organization. Catherine Booth was born on January 17, 1829, at Ashbourne. Catherine authored such works as *Female Ministry and Aggressive Christianity* before her death on October 4, 1890.

Early in the ministry of William and Catherine Booth the philosophy of work therapy in rehabilitation was actualized as new converts were given work and a purpose. The quasi-military command structure aided in the rapid growth of the Salvation Army in the early days. Men and women responded to the demands placed upon them by the leadership. Based on scriptural injunctions to Christian lifestyle, the Salvation Army set out a strict code of behavior for those who would be soldiers (members) of the Salvation Army (so named in 1878). Trust and confidence were placed in the new followers and expectations were often met.

The quasi-military structure born in its days carries on into the present day. The General, located at International Headquarters in London, England, gives leadership to the worldwide ministry. Zonal Departments are overseen by leaders chosen by the General who keep him or her informed as to the work in their region. Full-time commissioned officers serve as the ordained clergy with all the rights and privileges of any minister of religion. Soldiers are the members of the various congregations and adherents are people who look to the Salvation Army as their church home but who have not chosen to be enrolled as soldiers. To be a soldier involves promises of abstaining from alcohol, all harmful drugs, and tobacco. Soldiers sign The Articles of War as a part of their enrollment as members of this church. Only soldiers and officers are allowed to wear the uniform which marks members of this organization out to the public.

The Salvation Army is an international movement serving in 103 countries as an integral part of the evangelical universal Christian church. The message of the Salvation Army is based on the Bible. Its ministry is motivated by love for God and its mission is to preach the gospel of Jesus Christ and meet human needs in his name without discrimination. The Army's eleven-point doctrine follows the mainstream of Christian belief emphasizing God's saving grace. The message and mission of the Salvation Army has not changed though the means of ministering to people has altered with the various needs through the years of its existence. Simply stated, it is to feed the hungry, cloth the naked, provide shelter to the homeless, give a cup of water to the thirsty, and visit the prisoner following Christ's example. The nature and complexity of disasters that affect people may change but the humanitarian need to care continues. The Salvation Army strives to walk alongside people during their personal crises, and provide them with the Christian confidence of hope.

The Salvation Army therefore runs homes for rehabilitation to bring hope where no hope has been. It provides shelter and food for the needy and is in attendance to aid at all natural disasters. Not only is clothing and food distributed but counselors are available to aid victims. The diversity of ministries offered by the Salvation Army worldwide is determined by the human need of any given area. When William Booth saw people in need he pleaded with his followers to "Do Something."

The motto of the Salvation Army is clearly stated: "With heart to God and hand to man."

ELAINE BECKER

Bibliography. K. Thompson (1996), *The Salvation Army Year Book.*

Schema. *Schema* (singular) and *schemata* (plural) are terms Piaget used to describe the cognitive structures individuals use to understand their experiences. These structures are abstract, organized patterns of thought or behavior. These patterns are created through interaction with the environment. Schemata help a person learn in two ways. (1) They provide structure into which new information can be fitted. (2) They also relate new information to long-term memory, helping the learner to know what to expect from incoming information (Dembo, 1994). Schemata change constantly as the individual grows and matures. The changes in schemata are most clearly seen in Piaget's stages of cognitive devel-

opment: sensorimotor, preoperational, concrete operational, and formal operational. In each stage the learner relates to information in ever maturing ways. The process of schemata growth and change is called adaptation. Adaptation consists of two related parts: *assimilation* and *accommodation.* Assimilation is how one interprets experience to fit into what one knows. Accommodation is adjusting schemata to fit one's experiences. To mature appropriately, one must keep these processes in balance. Adaptation is necessary when new knowledge does not fit into prior knowledge (Yount, 1996).

Today the more popular term "scheme" is often used to describe the same concepts. In fact, Campbell (1977) asserted that even Piaget used his original schema and schemata interchangeably and used various definitions throughout his writings.

WALTER H. NORVELL

Bibliography. S. F. Campbell, ed. (1997), *Piaget Sampler: An Introduction to Jean Piaget Through His Own Words;* M. H. Dembo (1994), *Applying Educational Psychology;* W. R. Yount (1996), *Created to Learn.*

Schizophrenia. *See* Identity Diffusion.

Scholasticism. Approach to understanding and blending the study of theology with philosophy that reached its zenith between the ninth and fourteenth centuries. In its early stages of development, each scholastic teacher considered himself a Christian educator (Reed and Prevost, 1993). However, in reality few scholastic instructors cared enough about the practical application of philosophic thought to be of much value to the church or even society at large. As the university developed during this historic period, the leader of the university was knows as a *scholasticus.* It is from this title that we draw the term *Scholasticism.*

By the middle of the thirteenth century the seven liberal arts were at the forefront of education. These disciplines were divided into the trivium (dialectic, rhetoric, and grammar) and the quadrivium (arithmetic, geometry, astronomy, and music). The scholastics were not content with these subjects and wanted the study of philosophy to receive greater importance. They felt that philosophy presented a more synthetic approach to understanding the entire scientific field. Following the example first established by Aristotle (384–322 B.C.) philosophy was subdivided into two classifications: the theoretical (physics, mathematics, and metaphysics) and the practical (logic, ethics, and esthetics). Scholasticism considered the study of theology to be the queen of sciences whose light contributed to the brilliance of all other fields of knowledge (Mayer, 1966).

Thomas Aquinas (1225–1274) is one of Scholasticism's greatest contributors. His book *Summa Theologica* sought to explain Christian theology through the lens of Aristotelian metaphysics and epistemology. Scholastic thought held that faith and reason were both to be highly esteemed and that one could not contradict the other. To Aquinas, reason constituted a philosophical base while faith provided for a theological foundation. Although both provided a source of knowledge, faith was to be viewed as superior to reason. Seen in this way, reason could support what a person had come to know through faith but reason could not overrule what one held to in belief. Given this priority, it is not surprising that the Catholic Church supported much of this methodology for instruction (Reed and Prevost, 1993).

This biblical epistemology was not to last. The divorce between faith and reason gave way to an emphasis upon the latter. Reason was seen as a superior source of knowledge. Those who believed in the supremacy of faith were viewed as almost unintelligent. The dichotomy that later developed sought to denigrate the study of theology and the value of holding to a biblical worldview.

Toward the end of the fourteenth century scholastic thought held that matters of the supernatural, which required faith to believe, should be given over to the church since one could not arrive at a knowledge of such views based upon reason. The miracles taught in Scripture were simply not reasonable to believe since they defied the laws of science. No church doctrine, after all, could be demonstrated by reason. Scholasticism came to overemphasize human reason. A great deal of energy was spent debating the theories of metaphysics and ontology with little, if any, practical benefit (Eavey, 1964). Though beneficial as a means of organizing and systematizing knowledge, Scholasticism had a detrimental effect upon Christian education during the period of medieval education.

MICHAEL J. ANTHONY

Bibliography. C. B. Eavy (1964), *History of Christian Education;* E. F. Frost (1966), *Historical and Philosophical Foundations of Western Education;* K. O. Gangel and W. S. Benson (1983), *Christian Education: Its History and Philosophy;* M. Mayer (1966), *A History of Educational Thought;* J. E. Reed and R. Prevost (1993), *A History of Christian Education;* A. E. Sanner and A. F. Harper (1978), *Exploring Christian Education.*

See also AQUINAS, THOMAS; ARISTOTLE; MEDIEVAL EDUCATION

Scope. Term used in curriculum design that attempts to answer the question, "What shall we study?" Content is the term used to describe what is in fact dealt with. Scope is a broader term. Colson defines scope as "all that is appropriate to be dealt with in the curriculum" (Colson and Rigdon,

1981, 46). The Bible is the basis for the scope of the curriculum in Christian education, but it also entails all of human experience as well.

The mission or purpose statement of the school or ministry helps to determine what is appropriate for its curriculum. For example, the educational ministry of the church might conclude from its mission statement that car repair is not an appropriate subject for Sunday school. A public school might conclude that a study of evangelical theologies is not appropriate, based on its purpose statement. Determining what the curriculum should include or not include is the purpose of scope.

The Cooperative Curriculum Project defined the scope of Christian education as "the whole field of relationships in light of the gospel" (Colson, 1981, 47). Four relationships were initially identified: humanity's relationship to God; humanity's relationship to one another; humanity's relationship to nature; and humanity's relationship to history. While a public school might study several of these relationships, it is the study of these relationships *in light of the gospel* which distinguishes the public school's curriculum from the church's curriculum. A public school curriculum might explore humanity's relationship with one another in a psychology or anthropology course. A Christian school might also explore those same relationships. However, for a Christian school its biblical theology becomes the filter that interprets those relationships.

Since scope is a rather theoretical concept, curriculum designers often choose to organize scope into curriculum areas. The scope of seminaries may be organized around such studies as: Old Testament, New Testament, Evangelism, Preaching, or Christian Education. A college might divide its curriculum into departments of study such as Psychology, English, Mathematics, or Chemistry. In the church school, scope can be organized around curriculum areas such as: Bible, Christian Doctrine, Discipleship, Christian History, Ethics, or Missions education. Scope can also be organized around themes in the Bible such as Life and its Setting, Revelation, Sonship, Vocation, or the Church.

Age-level scope defines what is appropriate for a particular age group to study. For example, at what age do you introduce the abstract concept of the Trinity? Curriculum designers and writers consider the cognitive abilities and development of an age group in determining which subjects are appropriate to be studied.

DARYL ELDRIDGE

Bibliography. H. P. Colson and R. M. Rigdon (1981), *Understanding Your Church's Curriculum;* L. Ford (1991), *A Curriculum Design Manual for Theological Education;* R. Tyler (1949), *Basic Principles Curriculum and Instruction.*

See also CONTENT; INTEGRATION OF THEOLOGY AND EDUCATIONAL PHILOSOPHY; SEQUENCE

Scripture as Truth and Authority. One important issue facing Protestantism from the late nineteenth through the twentieth centuries concerned the nature of the Bible. The historic consensus that the Bible was true and authoritative in all that it taught was questioned. Those who opposed the traditional view judged the Bible to be simply a human book that should be treated like other ancient literature. The evangelical wing of Protestantism argued vigorously for the plenary verbal inspiration of the Bible—that every word of the Bible as originally given was inspired by God, and therefore, was without error.

The controversy over Scripture caused less furor in Roman Catholic circles. The Roman Church teaches that the Bible is the Word of God but it needs to be interpreted. The only reliable interpreter of the Bible is the church. Although modern critical scholarship strongly influenced the Roman Catholic Church, the traditional point of view plays an important role in church doctrine.

Within Protestantism three distinct approaches to the nature and authority of the Bible developed. Liberalism recognizes the Bible as a special piece of ancient literature that Christians treasure, respect, and study. It contains truths central to the Christian faith. Liberal scholars treat the Bible, its authority, and trustworthiness as an ancient document and evaluate it using the tools of critical scholarship.

Neoorthodoxy recognizes the Bible as a special book through which God continues to speak. They believe that the words of the Bible bear witness to the Word of God. The Holy Spirit enables a person to recognize the Word of God as one experiences a sense of transcendence in either the reading or preaching of the Bible.

The Chicago Statement on Inerrancy adopted in 1978 by the International Council on Biblical Inerrancy summarized the evangelical position on the authority and truthfulness of the Bible. It states: "Holy Scripture, being God's own word, written by men prepared and superintended by His Spirit, is of infallible divine authority in all matters upon which it touches: it is to be believed, as God's instruction, in all that it affirms; obeyed as God's command, in all that it requires; embraced, as God's pledge, in all that it promises" (Geisler, 1979, 494).

Evangelicalism takes the Bible as being the Word of God. God controlled the writers so they wrote the words God intended for them to record. Because the words were from God, they were without error and true and authoritative for belief and practice.

Evangelicals do not contend that God dictated the Bible. They recognize that the words of the Bible are also the words of human beings. The evangelical position acknowledges that the human authors of the Bible were sinful and fallible. Nevertheless, they believe the Bible remains the Word of God.

Evangelicals base their view of the Bible on the same foundation as any other Christian doctrine. They look to the Bible to see what it teaches about itself. Some accuse evangelicals of circular reasoning when they use the Bible to prove its own infallibility. However, all arguments about ultimate authority are circular in nature. If the Bible is the final authority for Christian doctrine, then it must be the final arbiter of controversies about its nature. To use any other criterion would mean that the Bible was not the final authority on all Christian doctrines.

The Bible's view of its own origin consistently teaches that God is the source of the words as well as the ideas. The most pointed example of this is found in the description of how the Lord wrote the Ten Commandments on the tablets of stone (Exod. 34:1). The Old Testament frequently claims to be the word of the Lord with phrases like "Thus says the Lord" (Isa. 31:4; Jer. 13:1). In addition, Deuteronomy 18:18–20 requires the people to obey the words of the prophet because they are the words of God.

The New Testament views the Old Testament as the Word of God. The Lord Jesus quoted the Old Testament as words that came from God. In his controversy with the Jews, recorded in John 10:31–39, Jesus quoted from Psalm 82. He confirmed his argument by claiming "the Scripture cannot be broken." "Scripture" refers to the Old Testament.

The apostles reasoned similarly. Paul says "All Scripture is inspired by God and profitable for teaching, for reproof, for correction, for training in righteousness; that the man of God may be adequate, equipped for every good work" (2 Tim. 3:16, 17 NASB). The word *inspired* means "breathed out by God." Peter contended "no prophecy was ever made by an act of human will, but men moved by the Holy Spirit spoke from God" (2 Peter 1:21 NASB). The New Testament treats each word as coming from God. For example, Paul, in Galatians 3:16, supports an argument by referring to the singular rather than the plural in his quotation from Genesis 13:15 and 17:8.

The New Testament claims the same authority for itself that it attributes to the Old Testament. Peter speaks of the words of Paul as hard to understand, but he claims that they are Scripture just like the Old Testament (2 Peter 3:16). In 1 Timothy 5:18 Paul quotes from Deuteronomy 25:4 and from Luke 10:7 and calls both passages Scripture, indicating that they are equally breathed out by God.

All of these arguments make sense to the Christian because the Holy Spirit uses the words of the

Bible to convince the Christian that they are the Word of God and therefore authoritative. The Holy Spirit does not give new or different testimony, but convinces on the basis of the teaching of the words themselves that they are what they claim to be. This description of the internal testimony of the Spirit differs from the one offered by those who hold to the neoorthodox approach to the Bible.

The historic Protestant position maintains that all the words of the Bible come from God, "who cannot lie " (Titus 1:2 NASB), hence they are trustworthy. The veracity of the Bible depends upon the truthfulness of its ultimate author, God himself.

All the arguments for the origin and trustworthiness of the Bible refer to the original texts. We no longer have any of these manuscripts. Some argue that the evangelical position of plenary verbal inspiration is interesting but insignificant without the originals. However, the church has carefully preserved ancient manuscripts and there is an overwhelming correspondence among them. No major doctrines of the Christian faith are called into question because of differences in manuscripts. The study of textual criticism provides means to evaluate manuscripts and see which most closely parallels the originals. Christians have ample reason to trust the text of the Bible.

The Bible consists of many pieces of literature coming from different eras. Determining the canon (a list of books that constitute the Bible) grows out of one's doctrine of Scripture. If the Bible consists of the words that God intended to preserve for his people, and the Holy Spirit enables believers to recognize this fact, it is no surprise that the Spirit enables them to recognize which books have divine origin. Historically Protestants have accepted the Old Testament available in the days the Lord Jesus lived on the earth. The New Testament canon was forged in the early church. Christians can be sure of the canon of Scripture because the Holy Spirit enables them to recognize its inherent authority.

Other arguments proffered for the uniqueness of the Scriptures include the wonder of the style, the consistent teaching of the doctrines of the Christian religion, and the great story of salvation. None of these by themselves provides sufficient reason to hold to the inerrant authority of the Bible, but they do provide corroboratory evidence of the uniqueness of the written Word of God.

Because of God's authorship the Bible is not only inerrant but also useful for the Christian educator. Second Timothy 3:16 clearly teaches that one of the consequences of divine authorship of the Bible is its usefulness for those seeking to live the Christian life.

Theologians characterize the Bible as clear, necessary, and sufficient. The clarity of Scripture means that all who earnestly seek to understand and obey it will be able to do so. It does not follow that everyone will understand every line of the Bible or that no one will ever be confused by the Bible. The overall message of Scripture can be grasped by anyone who diligently and humbly seeks to understand it.

The necessity of the Bible flows from the fact that without it one would never discover the good news of Christ's work. The revelation of God in nature shows "His eternal power and divine nature" (Rom. 1:20), but only in the Bible can one find God's remedy for sin, what we are to believe about God's character and nature, and what duties God requires of us. When God caused his word to be written and preserved, he made it possible for people to have access to his way. The Bible as a written document is necessary for the Christian.

The sufficiency of Scripture means that it contains all that one needs to know to be a true follower of God. There is nothing that God intended for his people to know that is left out of the Bible. It is the final and complete rule for faith and practice. The Christian does not need to add to it.

Christian educators will find the doctrine of the authority and truthfulness of the Bible to be important in their ministries. Because the Bible provides a trustworthy record of what God wants his followers to know and believe, they will be able to instruct the people of God with confidence.

DAVID A. CURRY

Bibliography. D. G. Bloesch (1994), *Holy Scripture: Revelation, Inspiration and Interpretation;* N. L. Geisler, ed. (1979) *Inerrancy;* W. Grudem (1994), *Systematic Theology: An Introduction to Biblical Doctrine;* J. I. Packer (1958), *Fundamentalism and the Word of God;* J. B. Rogers and D. K. McKim (1979), *The Authority and Interpretation of the Bible: An Historical Approach;* N. B. Stonehouse and P. Wooley, eds. (1953), *The Infallible Word;* B. B. Warfield (1948), *The Inspiration and Authority of the Bible.*

See also BIBLE TRANSLATIONS; NEOORTHODOXY; INERRANCY OF SCRIPTURE

Scripture Memory. Memorizing Bible verses has long been a valued practice in evangelical Christian education. The Old Testament Scriptures held a prominent place in the Jewish community with its emphasis on knowledge and obedience to the Torah. In the early church there are indications that the practice of memorizing Scripture was a part of training new converts. During the Reformation, both Luther and Calvin placed great emphasis on memorizing Bible passages.

With the rise of the American Sunday School Union in the nineteenth century, renewed focus was placed on memorizing Scripture. The curriculum was content-centered with an emphasis on mastery of the Bible content. During the twentieth century there appears to have been a gradual decline in the practice of adults memorizing Bible verses as a part of Christian education in the church. One exception was the parachurch organizations. These organizations were primarily introducing young adults to the Christian faith and embraced Scripture memory as an important discipline in Christian practice.

The motivation for memorizing Bible verses may be tied to two characteristics of evangelical Christian education. First, evangelicals have largely embraced a transmissive model of Christian education. This model holds to the idea that transmission of the unique Christian message will ensure the desired cognitive, affective, and overt behaviors of learners. Further, evangelicals believe the Bible is the authoritative Word of God and is the indispensable sourcebook of Christian faith and practice.

While it can contribute to the spiritual formation of Christians and become a rich part of one's spiritual life, the practice of Scripture memory can also fall prey to several destructive educational practices and underlying assumptions. First, there is the danger of relating the memorization of Scripture directly to the far more complex process of spiritual maturation. Western cultures have often equated the accumulation of knowledge with resultant behavior change. This can lead to embracing a simplistic causal relationship between the memorization of Scripture and expected behavior change. In contrast, the reality of spiritual transformation is a complex and supernatural process not easily controlled by the accumulation of Bible knowledge.

A second danger is to embrace characteristics of a schooling approach to education for training in Scripture memory. This can include utilizing competition as a primary motivation, where one child is pitted against another and the goal is to "win" by memorizing the most Bible verses. A Sunday school teacher's question, "Who can be the first to recite all this week's Bible verses without a mistake?" creates a competitive environment where the practice of Scripture memory may become tied to a cultural value largely antithetical to the gospel. Another danger is to place greater emphasis on accurate recall of the Bible verses than on a deepening understanding of the meaning of the passage. The educational task of training for accurate recall can be much easier to achieve than is the task of nurturing comprehension and life integration. In the practice of training one to memorize, knowledge can become an end in itself, rather than merely one bridge toward a more meaningful relationship with Christ. Performance can also be tied to memorization, leaving children with the hidden message that Bible memory is more about performing for others in special events. Finally, little awareness of the learning differences of students for memorizing facts may enter the practice of Scripture memory. Some people can more easily memorize than others can, while another may be more gifted in understanding and describing concepts.

Scripture memory is best practiced in a holistic context. First, there is the holistic balance of memory and life integration of meaning. Second, the practice of Scripture memory builds the holistic experience of the faith community when leaders, adults, parents, and children are sharing together. Sharing memorized Scripture together can make a significant contribution to times of worship or during times of prayer, as expressions of joy and thankfulness for who God is and what he has done. In this way memorizing Scripture becomes a central part of the life of faith for the whole church, not just by a few children in Sunday school. In this way the discipline of Scripture memory can contribute to one's spiritual formation.

MERILYN J. MACLEOD

Bibliography. H. W. Burgess (1996), *Models of Religious Education: Theory and Practice in Historical and Contemporary Perspective;* M. L. Roloff (1987), *Education for Christian Living: Strategies for Nurture Based on Biblical and Historical Foundations;* M. J. Taylor, ed. (1960), *Religious Education: A Comprehensive Survey.*

Sect. *See* Cult.

Seeker Services. Worship services planned specifically to attract non-Christians. Popularized in the 1980s and 1990s, seeker churches devised methods for reaching unchurched people, drawing them into a local church body and introducing them to the saving knowledge of Jesus Christ.

During the Protestant Reformation, Martin Luther rejected many of the common church structures in order to introduce pagans to Christ, even writing Christian lyrics to their drinking songs. In our modern day, seeker churches developed out of the church growth movement of the 1970s and early 1980s, as congregations looked for new ways to attract an increasingly secularized populace. Led by Willow Creek Community Church of Illinois, seeker services grew rapidly in the United States, particularly among charismatic denominations.

There are two forms of seeker services. The Seeker Centered service has a major emphasis in contemporary worship whereas the Seeker Sensitive service is more of a blend between contemporary worship and traditional forms of worship expression. The former is far more difficult to conduct as it requires a radical shift in ministry philosophy. The latter approach is far more common in established churches across North America today.

Nearly every seeker service tries to provide a warm and friendly atmosphere that appeals to those unfamiliar with common church structures. The use of small groups to better assimilate new worshipers is almost universal in seeker churches, and the leadership has often thought through issues of modern convenience (child care, scheduling, etc.) that escape many mainline churches. Most seeker services eschew hymnbooks and organs in favor of keyboards, guitars, and drums, relying on upbeat modern worship choruses that focus more on singing to God than singing about him. Drama and the use of multimedia are commonly used to convey a message, rather than relying on a lengthy sermon. The teaching time is often short, offering an introduction to the things of God rather than an in-depth study. The purpose of the service is to introduce the character of God and offer healing and acceptance to those who have not yet met the Lord.

JERRY CHIP MACGREGOR

Bibliography. L. and B. Hybels (1995), *Rediscovering Church: The Story and Vision of Willow Creek Community Church;* C. Smith, ed., *Worship and Music Ministry.*

See also BABY BOOM GENERATION; BUILDER GENERATION; CHURCH GROWTH; GENERATIONAL IMPACT; MILLENIAL GENERATION; WORSHIP

Self-Actualization. Process of becoming all that one can become. A. H. Maslow identifies it as the highest level on his hierarchy of needs. Maslow first presented the hierarchy of needs in "Theory of Human Motivation" that appeared in *Psychological Review* in 1943 (Lowry, 1973). The term *self-actualization* was first used by Kurt Goldstein to refer to the tendency to become actualized in what one is potentially (Maslow, 1943).

A description of self-actualization would include use of talents, capacities, and potentiality that allows the individual to develop to the full statue of which one is capable (Maslow, 1970). It refers to the highest level of human growth where one has reached one's fullest potential (Brockett and Hiemstra, 1991).

As lower level needs are satisfied new needs will emerge that hunger to be met. The emergence of higher level needs rest on prior satisfaction of physiological, safety, love, and esteem needs (Maslow, 1943).

Much of Maslow's work placed self-actualization as the highest of the seven levels of need. The difficulty with studying self-actualized people is that so few can be considered to have achieved this level. His later work included an eighth level called transcendence (Hamachek, 1990).

Self-actualizers have a great deal of self-understanding and insight. They are creative and are not afraid to deal with unstructured situations or march to the beat of a different drummer. These individuals are consistently working toward higher levels and are able to utilize resources to their greatest potential (Brockett and Hiemstra, 1991).

Maslow conducted research in an attempt to identify characteristics of self-actualized individuals, which need to be followed with more studies. The following characteristics were identified: perception of reality, acceptance, spontaneity, problem centering, solitude, autonomy, fresh appreciation, peak experiences, human kinship, humility and respect, interpersonal relationships, ethics, means and ends, humor, creativity, resistance to enculturation, imperfections, values, and resolution of dichotomies (Maslow, 1970).

GARY WALLER

Bibliography. R. G. Brockett and R. Hiemstra (1991), *Self-Direction in Adult Learning;* D. Hamachek (1990), *Psychology in Teaching, Learning, and Growth;* R. J. Lowry, ed. (1973), *Dominance, Self-Esteem, Self-Actualization: Germinal Papers of A. H. Maslow;* A. H. Maslow (1973), *Dominance, Self-esteem, Self-actualization: Germinal Papers of A. H. Maslow* pp. 153–73; idem (1970), *Motivation and Personality.*

See also MASLOW, ABRAHAM HAROLD

Self-Centered. *See* Egocentrism.

Self-Concept. Total view of one's self as an object. It includes several dimensions, such as self-worth, self-esteem, self-cognition, self-confidence, body image, and self-evaluation. Body image, academic performance, and athletic performance are often included in constructs of the self-concept.

The concept of the multidimensional self began with the I-Me view of William James (1890). James saw the self as consisting of "I," or the self as the knower, and "Me," or the self as being known. He divided the self into three major components: (1) the *material self,* which includes all aspects of the "material," as in our clothing choices, our family, and our personal property; (2) the *social self,* which includes the recognition one gets from his mates or friends; and (3) the *spiritual self,* which is the inner or subjective being of a person, encompassing one's ability to think about one's self as a thinker.

Until recently, most research into the self used global measures to look at self-esteem. However, the terms *self-esteem* and *self-concept* were often used interchangeably. In more recent years researchers have been exploring multidimensionality in self-concept.

Several researchers have developed models of the self-concept, most notably R. J. Shavelson and S. Epstein. Shavelson's work has demonstrated the importance of one's environment in shaping the self-concept, particularly the evaluations of significant others (Marsh, Byrne, and Shavelson, 1992; Marsh and Shavelson, 1985; Shavelson, Hubner, and Stanton, 1976). Shavelson and his colleagues developed various features of self-concept, showing hierarchical, multifaceted constructs of the self. Epstein (1973, 1975) saw the self-concept as a highly organized, differentiated, and integrated system, ranging from lower to higher order, which helped to identify one's perception of reality. Studies have supported both of their theories.

Understanding how the self-concept develops is important for Christian educators so that they may assist the believer in understanding one's position in Christ, fulfilling one's complete potential as a Christian. Though humanity is united to Adam in sin (Rom. 5:12–21), through Christ believers are given worth and responsibility in life. A biblical self-concept must first begin with an understanding of who we are without Christ, what he has done on our behalf, and who we are in Christ. Our self-concept must begin with an understanding of who we are in Christ. Our self-concept begins and our self-worth comes to us because God has valued us first as created beings (Gen. 1:31), and again as restored members of his family through the redemptive work of Christ (John 1:12). God has bestowed upon us through the Holy Spirit talents and abilities that we must use with confidence for the purpose of building up others (1 Cor. 12, 14; Eph. 4). By understanding how people develop their concept of their self, we can better develop curriculums and environments that support healthy self-concept in Christ.

JAMES W. MOHLER

Bibliography. N. T. Anderson (1990), *Victory Over the Darkness;* B. A. Bracken and K. K. Howell, *Journal of Psychoeducational Assessment* 9, no. 4 (1991): 319–28; S. Epstein, *American Psychologist* 28 (1973): 404–16; idem, *Journal for the Theory of Social Behavior* 15 (1985): 283–310; J. Harvill, *Discipleship Journal* 7, no. 39 (1987): 38–40; J. Hattie (1992), *Self-Concept;* A. A. Hoekema (1986), *Created in God's Image;* W. James (1890), *Great Books of the Western World,* vol. 53; H. W. Marsh, B. M. Byrne, and R. J. Shavelson (1992), *The Self: Definitional and Methodological Issues,* pp. 137–71; H. W. Marsh and R. J. Shavelson, *Journal of Personality and Social Psychology* 45, no. 1 (1985): 173–87; R. J. Shavelson, J. J. Hubner, and G. C. Stanton, *Review of Educational Research* 46 (1976): 407–41; R. C. Wylie (1989), *Measures of Self-Concept.*

Self-Disclosure. Revelation of one's thoughts, feelings, and experiences. This is typically done through a verbal medium (direct self-disclosure); however, a person's nonverbal communication such as body language, apparel, and tone of voice also contributes to self-disclosure (indirect self-disclosure). Effective self-disclosure holds the potential for increasing intimacy in communication and moving beyond superficial relationships to relationships of depth.

Self-disclosure can empower the active listening process. Appropriate self-disclosure by the lis-

tener encourages the speaker to share more deeply and intimately. The active listener performs a role-modeling function by demonstrating how to communicate in this fashion. Self-disclosure can foster trust and compassion when used judiciously.

Misuse of self-disclosure can have a negative impact on communication. When a person discloses only personal strengths and successes, others may feel distanced or inadequate in comparison. Self-disclosure that is heavily weighted with personal weaknesses or failings can have equally negative results. Another trap in self-disclosure is feeling the need to reveal a personal anecdote in response to every situation.

Awareness of cultural differences is helpful when assessing the appropriate use of self-disclosure. A person who offers limited self-disclosure can be viewed in a variety of ways, from being professional in one setting to being secretive and untrustworthy in another context.

The opposite of self-disclosure is self-concealment. This lack of transparency occurs when an individual relates to others through a facade. Common roadblocks to self-disclosure include fear of intimacy, shame, lack of trust, unwillingness to risk, and the potential of rejection. Self-concealment can require a great deal of energy and may result in loneliness and depression. Stress increases as the individual strives to maintain the image projected to others. Self-concealment distances the individual from other people and destroys community.

Self-disclosure in personal relationships focuses on the communication process between speaker and listener. John Powell's classic, *Why Am I Afraid To Tell You Who I Am?,* delineates five levels of communication (Powell, 1969, 54–62).

Level Five: Cliché Conversation—"safe talk" with no personal self-disclosure (i.e., "How are you?" "What did you think of that game last night?").

Level Four: Reporting the Facts about Others—describing the events of the day and what others said or did with no personal response.

Level Three: My Ideas and Judgments—self-disclosure in communication begins at this level. People share their ideas and decisions, and may retreat if rejection is hinted.

Level Two: My Feelings and Emotions—self-disclosure increases as the person shares feelings on an emotional level.

Level One: Complete Emotional and Personal Truthful Communication—self-disclosure in which there is absolute openness and honesty, a risky type of communication due to the possibility of rejection, but necessary for intimacy to grow.

Self-disclosure in group settings is an integral component of small group functioning. Healthy self-disclosure contributes to the building of community within groups. Groups will often develop contracts regarding the amount of self-disclosure that is expected from the members. Groups vary in terms of the amount of self-disclosure considered desirable. The following groups typically found within the church are ranked from lowest levels of self-disclosure to highest levels:

1. Business meetings—church boards, teachers in-service gatherings;
2. Discussion groups—book clubs, Bible study groups;
3. Small groups—growth groups, home Bible study fellowships, premarital or marital enrichment groups;
4. Support groups—divorce recovery groups, drug and alcohol recovery groups, grief groups;
5. Therapeutic groups—under the guidance of a trained counselor/therapist located within the church context.

Self-disclosure in professional relationships raises issues of professional identity and integrity. People in positions of leadership must examine their approach to self-disclosure. The following suggestions are adapted from *The Skilled Helper* (179–80), and are translated into the church leadership context:

- Make sure that your disclosures are appropriate. Self-disclosure that is exhibitionist or engaged in for effect is obviously inappropriate.
- Timing in the self-disclosure process is critical. Too much shared too soon can create barriers. But at the same time restricting self-disclosure may thwart the development of the relationship between church professional and parishioner.
- Keep self-disclosures selective and focused. Don't detract from the professional relationship with rambling stories about yourself. Remember that your role is to assist the growth and development of the parishioner.
- Remain flexible. Adapt self-disclosures to different situations. While a certain level of self-disclosure may be appropriate in one setting with one group of people, the same level of self-disclosure may be totally inappropriate with another group of people in a different context.

DENISE MUIR KJESBO

Bibliography. J. Powell (1969), *Why Am I Afraid To Tell You Who I Am?*; J. Egan (1994), *The Skilled Helper: A Problem-Management Approach to Helping*; M. Westra (1996), *Active Communication*.

Self-Evaluation. *See* Critical Reflection.

Self-Governing. *See* Autonomy.

Self-Help. *See* Adult Children of Alcoholics.

Self-Indulgence. *See* Egocentriscm.

Self-Questioning. Learning strategy that utilizes questions about material to be learned in an attempt to increase comprehension. As a strategy self-questioning allows the learner to check on how well one is comprehending what is being studied. With adequate training for generating one's questions, normally better comprehension will result.

As a method of learning one will find this approach effective for written and oral presented material. Asking and answering questions, especially high-level questions, during learning experiences can facilitate comprehension by directing the student in activities that focus attention, organizes the material, and integrates the information with existing knowledge (Palincsar, 1984).

Wittrock suggests that generative learning and study strategies, where students interact with the material to generate unique learning, is the most conducive to learning.

In Wittrock's generative model of learning, students will comprehend new material best when they use prior knowledge and experience to reconstruct the information in a new and meaningful way. The concept is to build a relationship between new information and their own knowledge and experience (Wittrock, 1990).

Reformulating given information or generating new information based on what is provided will allow the student to build cognitive structures connecting the new ideas together and linking them to what the student already knows. Creating such structures in long-term memory facilitates understanding of the new material and makes it easier to remember (Brown, 1986).

Two generative learning strategies commonly used with written material are *self-questioning*, where a set of question and answers are used, and *summarizing*, which results in a summation. Previous research has revealed self-questioning and summarizing are both effective strategies for encoding and comprehending material from a written format (King, 1992).

Based on the level of questions, either general or specific, the student's learning will be influenced, resulting in greater comprehension of material or skills to be learned. With increased understanding a student should have greater memory or recall of the material presented either in written or oral form.

Research conducted by King studied the effects on learning of lecture notes by self-questioning, summarizing, and note review. Students utilizing self-questioning and summarizing comprehended more on immediate testing than students that reviewed notes. However, when testing occurred after one week only self-questioning appeared to be superior (King, 1992).

The more information is processed the greater the retention over time. Summarizing strategy makes internal connections with the lecture ideas while self-questioning promotes internal and external connections. Questions and answers guide students to connect ideas from lectures in specific ways that prompt students to elaborate on the material by going beyond what was in the lecture. Many of the questions will require students to generate inferences, draw conclusions, and make evaluations. Such strategy results in information encoding making it more meaningful (King, 1992).

GARY WALLER

Bibliography. A. L. Brown and J. C. Campione, *American Psychologist* 41 (1986): 1059–68; A. King, *American Educational Research Journal* (Summer 1992): 303–23; A. S. Palincsar and A. L. Brown, *Cognition and Instruction* 1 (1984): 117–75; M. C. Wittrock, *Educational Psychologist* 24 (1990): 345–76.

Seminar. Collective learning takes many forms. A seminar describes one particular form of learning together. The significant features of this form of group learning emerge from a study of the term's linguistic and historic roots.

Seminar's linguistic roots come from the Latin term, *seminarium*, which means "pertaining to a seed." The image seems to accent the idea of beginnings. The historical roots of seminar rest in German universities, where small groups of scholars gathered for advanced study in a chosen subject area. George Ticknor, the first American engaged in advanced scholarship in Germany, provided the bridge for seminars to enter the American educational enterprise. After studying in Germany in 1815, he assumed a professorship at Harvard College in 1819. Frustrated with educational methods that relied heavily on recitation, Ticknor agitated for reform. Finally in 1831 Harvard established an advanced *seminar* for studying the classics (Rudolph, 1963).

If we take our clues from these historical and linguistic roots, we can identify key features to a seminar:

1. A small number of learners;
2. Equal contribution of participants to the seminar's content;
3. Highly focused content to learners' work;
4. Emphasis on sharing new information and ideas;
5. Learning both brought and taken by participants; and
6. Emphasis on advanced learning in a field.

Often enough, a seminar may only mean a small class. Because Christian education tends to aim for a general audience and prefers inclusive events, seminars do not occupy a large place in the local church's educational programs. They do play a larger role in advanced forms of Christian education, particularly in training specialists in various subject areas.

ROBERT DROVDAHL

Bibliography. F. Rudolph (1963), *The American College and University.*

Seminary. *See* Higher Education, Christian.

Senior Pastor. The title *senior pastor* combines the designation for *older* with the Latin word for *shepherd.* The term evolved to describe the experienced clergyman who worked in association with one or more younger colleagues. The senior pastor was traditionally not only older but held much more authority because of his years of service to the congregation. Younger clergy were considered trainees getting the experience they would need to someday pastor a church of their own.

Today, the term *senior pastor* indicates a multiple-staff situation. It is not a guarantee of age, authority, or years of service. Management expert Marvin Judy (1969) described the role as "executive minister" (92). Harold Westing (1985) called the position "first among equals" (25).

Some senior pastors view their roles in the traditional mold of an autocratic leader assisted by mere helpers. In contrast, the team leader's style is to consider fellow staff members as coworkers. The team leader's job is to nurture an atmosphere of creativity and cooperation as communicator, motivator, enabler, equipper, delegator, and administrator.

Management and church growth expert Lyle Schaller (1980) identifies the role of the senior pastor as "tribal chief, number one medicine man and chief administrative officer of the congregation" (106). As tribal chief, the pastor establishes relationships with church members and offers guidance. As medicine man the pastor officiates at ceremonies and provides pastoral care. As chief administrative officer, the senior pastor organizes and administrates the church and its staff.

To alleviate some of the burden of the senior pastor, churches may hire a business administrator to handle the business functions of the church and free the rest of the pastoral staff to devote themselves to other ministries. This is one way to answer the problem of talented preachers who build small churches into large ones that outstrip their own administrative abilities.

As a church grows and its organizational chart becomes more complex, the senior pastor is faced with the task of delegating duties. Autocratic leaders will respond by micromanaging every detail of church administration. Team leaders will respond by seeking out associates whose strengths are different from their own, delegating authority, and giving associates the freedom to do their jobs well. As members of the congregation begin to polarize into small groups identified with certain neighborhoods, needs, or age groups, there will be a need for the senior pastor to maintain the unity of the congregation.

Unfortunately, jealousy and rivalry can disrupt a multiple staff situation. Senior pastors may resent colleagues who shine in areas where they are weak. They may even find themselves maneuvering for space beside associates whose gifts mirror their own. Paul's letter to the Corinthians addressed this problem, saying, "there should be no division in the body, but . . . its parts should have equal concern for each other" (1 Cor. 12:25).

When the senior pastor of a small church leaves, church leadership is usually so spread out among the laity that the departure does not cause a major disruption. Another factor in the stability of the small church under these circumstances is the likelihood that at least one remaining staff member is a generalist, rather than a specialist, and can step into many of the duties of the senior pastor. In a large church, the majority of the staff will be specialists devoted to a specific ministry rather than generalists training for the senior pastor role. The departure of the key administrative person in this situation can be cataclysmic.

With regard to the educational ministry, the senior pastor usually has little time for involvement. As a generalist rather than a specialist, the senior pastor probably has limited training or experience in this area. In many cases, the first additional staff member will be an educational specialist hired to step into the leadership gap.

The senior pastor's participation may be limited to teaching an adult Sunday school or a midweek study group. A traditional Sunday morning schedule keeps the pastor occupied with other responsibilities during the peak hours of the educational ministry. As a result, the senior pastor may tend to lose touch with all but the adult level of the educational program. This situation can cause problems for the educational specialist as well. Hard at work supervising the Sunday morning programs while most adults attend worship or an adult class, the specialist may not even be recognizable to most church members. If the educational program provides age level worship services for children and youth, many of them will not know the senior pastor.

Because their paths rarely cross, the senior pastor and the educational specialist must make a special effort to work together and ensure that the church's ministries remain unified in mission and doctrinal position. The senior pastor must make a consistent effort to promote the programs and needs of the educational ministry. High visibility and status places the senior pastor in a good po-

sition to recruit workers, acknowledge volunteers, and solicit funding. By acknowledging from the pulpit the importance of the educational program, the senior pastor can significantly increase prayer, financial support, and participation.

ROBERT J. CHOUN

Bibliography. K. O. Gangel (1990), *Feeding and Leading;* K. O. Gangel and J. C. Wilhoit (1995), *The Christian Educator's Handbook of Spiritual Formation;* M. T. Judy (1969), *The Multiple Staff Ministry;* L. Schaller (1980), *The Multiple Staff and the Larger Church;* H. J. Westing (1985), *Multiple Church Staff Handbook.*

See also ASSOCIATE PASTOR; ELDER; MINISTER; ORGANIZATIONAL CHART

Sensory Registers. In information processing, sensory registers (sometimes abbreviated SRs) serve as the first stage in the metacognitive process. Sensory registers are the sensory organs or receptors (eyes, ears, skin, taste buds, and olfaction) by which persons experience and perceive the environment (world). Each person is bombarded with scores, even hundreds of stimuli, often in a simultaneous fashion. No one can attend all stimuli at all times. Therefore, as stimuli are experienced, the sensory registers act as a buffer, helping the person sort the incoming information. Only a tiny portion of those stimuli are given attention, being held there for only a fraction of a second. Without attention (called selective focusing), the information is lost. If the individual attends to a stimulus, the sensory registers move that information to the short-term (working) memory where it is again evaluated. Again, the information is lost unless more attention is given to it. Further selective focusing moves it to long-term (storage) memory (Biehler and Snowman, 1993; Yount, 1996). Dembo (1994) refers to the sensory registers as short-term sensory storage (STSS).

WALTER H. NORVELL

Bibliography. R. F. Biehler and J. Snowman (1993), *Psychology Applied to Teaching;* M. H. Dembo (1994), *Applying Educational Psychology;* W. R. Yount (1996), *Created to Learn.*

Separation. *See* Divorce.

Sequence. Characteristic of the curriculum plan that arranges learning experiences in the best order for learning to occur (Colson, 1981, 51). If scope is the "what of curriculum," that sequence is the "when of curriculum" (Wulf and Shave, 1984, 71). Sequencing refers to the arrangement of lessons, content, learning activities, and processes in the curriculum plan.

Smith, Stanley, and Shores (1957) identified four major principles in the curriculum: simple to complex, prerequisite learning, whole to part learning, and chronological learning (Smith, 1957).

The *principle of simple to complex* contends that learning is fostered when the presentation begins with easy, concrete ideas and moves to more difficult, often abstract content. The *principle of prerequisite learning* asserts that a base of learning is required before higher levels of understanding are attained. Prerequisite learning works on the assumption that bits of learning are assimilated until the whole is learned. The *principle of whole to part* suggests that the content or experience is presented as an overview and is then broken down into smaller pieces. *Chronological learning* sequences content and experiences according to the time frame in which they occurred.

Effective curriculum designers examine the objectives for curriculum, the abilities of the learners, and the nature of the content, experience, or skills to determine what will be the best approach to sequence the learning experience for optimal results.

DARYL ELDRIDGE

Bibliography. H. P. Colson and R. M. Rigdon (1981), *Understanding Your Church's Curriculum;* B. O. Smith, W. O. Stanley, and H. J. Shores (1957), *Fundamentals of Curriculum Design;* H. M. Wulf and B. Schave (1984), *Curriculum Design.*

See also CURRICULUM; SCOPE

Sermon. *See* Preaching.

Sermon, Children's. Proclamation of biblical faith designed for the understanding level of children. The children's sermon may refer to the major presentation in children's worship or to a specific time designed for children in the congregational worship time.

A good children's sermon demonstrates the following characteristics:

1. Based on scriptural foundation. Like any sermon, it is a declaration of God's truth.
2. Develops the theme of the worship service. It likely sets the theme for the worship in a children's church program. As an element in the congregational worship experience, it should develop the theme of the service.
3. Remains relatively brief. Children have a limited attention span, shorter on the average than that of adults. Therefore, the children's sermon may have only one main point.
4. Contains visuals and illustrations. Visualization could include pictures, puppets, books, objects, and the like. Experiences and stories contribute to the goal of making the concepts and the main point of the sermon more understandable.

5. Communicated in children's language. Vocabulary and experiences are chosen carefully to be at the understanding level of the children.

Many churches conduct a separate children's church program. The most effective children's church programs are planned to help children to worship on their own level. The worship may include all of the elements included in the adult worship service, but with music and Scripture chosen to relate to the age level for which it is planned. The children's sermon is an important element in the worship. Older children may want to utilize note sheets to follow the development of the sermon.

Other churches choose not to separate children from the larger church body during worship. They believe that children and adults both need intergenerational worship experiences. They often include a brief children's sermon in the worship service. Children are invited to come to a designated place in the worship center to participate in the children's sermon led by the pastor or another staff member.

The topic of children in worship has been widely discussed in recent years. Some insist that children's church is essential if the church is to have a viable outreach to families. But others have raised the question of how values and faith can be taught effectively if children are isolated from adults in the congregation. Some congregational leaders have concluded that there is value in both approaches and therefore offer a children's church program perhaps three Sundays out of four, with children involved in the congregational worship the remaining one-fourth of the time.

ELEANOR A. DANIEL

Bibliography. P. M. Adams (1994), *The Sermon for Children;* S. C. Juengst (1994), *Sharing Faith with Children: Rethinking the Children's Sermon;* G. W. Prichard (1992), *Offering the Gospel to Children.*

Servant. The contrast could not be more sharply drawn than from Jesus' own response to James and John in Mark 10:42–43: ". . . those who are regarded as rulers of the Gentiles lord it over them. . . . Not so with you. Instead, whoever wants to become great among you must be your servant." In this confrontation engendered by James and John's desire for a place of prominence in God's kingdom, Jesus makes it abundantly clear that leadership among his followers requires a new and radically different way of leadership. The community of faith still requires leadership (see Heb. 13:7), but it must be exercised through serving. In Christian education, this new way of leadership typically is termed *servant-leadership.* Jesus' teaching and life outline three main contours of servanthood.

First, a servant must be willing to go beyond the call of duty. In Luke 17:4–10, Jesus suggests a servant/slave cannot be focused on duties, fairness, or expected rewards. In the parable, a hard day's work in the field does not entitle the slave to a comfortable dinner. Rather, the slave must prepare the master's dinner and not even expect thanks. The doxology in Philippians 2:6–11 exalts Jesus because he "did not regard equality with God something to be grasped, but made himself nothing, taking the very nature of a servant." In Christian education leading in a servant manner might be described as going the extra mile and not expecting thanks for it.

Second, a servant's position attracts little attention. Correspondingly, a servant should not seek attention. In Matthew 23, Jesus condemns the leaders who do everything "for men to see" (v. 5). Their attention-seeking behavior includes outward displays of religious fervor (v. 5), special privileges (v. 6), and status symbols (v. 7). The attention sought seems willingly granted by the followers in this passage and we should expect no different today. Servant-leaders must guard against others' desire and their own desire to be "really important people."

The antidote for this temptation is humility. C. S. Lewis describes the truly humble person as one who takes "a real interest in what *you* said to *him*. . . . He will not be thinking about humility: he will not be thinking about himself at all" (Lewis, 1943, 114).

Third, a servant looks out for the master's interests. When Paul encourages the Philippian church toward unity, he advises them to "look not only to your own interests, but also to the interests of others" (2:4). Paul derives this principle from Jesus, who gave up his interests and "made himself nothing, taking the very nature of a servant" (2:7).

Servant theology used in isolation can lead to distorted attitudes and actions in the teaching office. The servant-leader is worthy of honor and compensation (1 Tim. 5:17–18) and may still exercise authority (Heb. 13:17). Servant-leaders exercise authority with kindness, patience, and gentleness. (2 Tim. 2:24–25).

ROBERT DROVDAHL

Bibliography. C. S. Lewis (1943), *Mere Christianity.*

See also ADMINISTRATION; DEACON; LEADERSHIP; LEADERSHIP PRINCIPLES; MANAGEMENT

Servant Leader. Although the position of "servant" is not among the church leadership roles listed in Paul's letter to the Ephesians (4:11), it is the leadership model exemplified by Jesus. In the thirteenth chapter of his Gospel, John reported that Jesus washed the feet of his disciples. Luke's account of the same evening includes Christ's ad-

monition of his squabbling followers: "The greatest among you should be like the youngest, and the one who rules like the one who serves" (Luke 22:26).

Peter expounded on the theme of servant leadership in one of his letters. Writing to his fellow elders, Peter encouraged them to be "shepherds of God's flock . . . serving as overseers–not because you must, but because you are willing . . . not greedy for money, but eager to serve; not lording it over those entrusted to you, but being examples to the flock" (1 Peter 5:1–3). Paul specifically warned young Timothy against the misconception "that godliness is a means to financial gain" (1 Tim. 6:5).

When James and John created disharmony among the disciples by asking for positions of special status, Jesus responded by stating that his followers had to adopt a radical new view of greatness. Don't be like the rulers of the Gentiles, he advised, "[who] lord it over them, and . . . exercise authority over them. . . . Instead, whoever wants to become great among you must be your servant, and whoever wants to be first must be slave of all" (Mark 10:42).

The Old Testament records what can happen when leaders refuse to be servants. Rehoboam, whose father had ruled Israel with a heavy hand, went to the elders at the beginning of his reign for some counsel on leading the nation. They advised the new ruler to be the servant of his people. Rehoboam ignored the words of the elders and listened instead to companions who urged a policy of harsh authoritarianism. As a result, the king's reign was plagued by internal division.

In the New Testament Jesus warned against the pride of the Pharisees, who wanted places of honor but balked at service (Mark 23:1–12). Jesus' own leadership style was the personification of the servant role. It stands as an example to his church regarding our interpersonal relations as well.

These biblical leadership principles—concern for others, willingness to serve, noble motivations, and a sense of humility—are valued not only in church leadership but also in the corporate world. Many secular leadership gurus advocate a management style that succeeds by making others successful. Managers are advised to affirm workers and to provide them with opportunities for growth and development. Managers are urged to make themselves available, share information, and create an atmosphere of teamwork. Workers will then be motivated to participate in the decision-making process, develop their own creativity, and use more self-direction. The servant leader must abandon what leadership trainer Hans Finzel (1994) termed "top-down autocratic arrogance" (22).

Finzel's "top-down" terminology refers to the traditional pyramid model in which the workers serve and support top management. The servant leader model tips over the pyramid until it balances on its apex, making the "top" executives support the workers.

One of the factors that distinguish Christian organizations is the high degree of volunteerism. Management experts Engstrom and Dayton (1976) maintain that this distinctive makes the local church "one of the most complicated and sophisticated kinds of organizations in the world" (16). Workers who donate their own time and talent are likely to expect a similar measure of commitment from their leaders. Volunteers who are not provided with encouragement, support, and motivation are candidates for burnout. To answer this need, the servant leader must build relationships with the members of the team. Relationships nurture cooperation, and cooperation boosts participation. Servant leaders understand that commitment to the work of Christ means a commitment to the body of Christ. The servant leader directs his team toward shared goals, but does it without manipulation or exploitation.

ROBERT J. CHOUN

Bibliography. T. Engstrom and E. R. Dayton (1976), *The Art of Management for Christian Leaders;* H. Finzel (1994), *The Top Ten Mistakes Leaders Make;* K. O. Gangel (1974), *Competent to Lead;* D. Hocking (1991), *The Seven Laws of Christian Leadership;* M. Rush (1983), *Management: A Biblical Perspective.*

See also DEACON; DEACONESS; LEADERSHIP; MINISTER

Service Project. Activity that involves making a contribution to the church or community at large by helping with an identified area of need. If the aims of Christian education include having a profound impact on the church, reaching out to fallen humankind, and becoming a responsible Christian citizen in society and the world (LaBar, 1964), then service opportunities are an integral part of a well-balanced program for children, youth, and adults. A service project can be used both as a method of learning and as a means of expressing what one has learned on a cognitive level. Social science research indicates that people are more likely to behave their way into thinking than to think their way into behaving (McNabb and Mabry, 1990). In other words, as people are given opportunities to act out positive values and see the results and the benefits of those actions through various projects and activities, they are more likely to adopt those values as their own. Service projects are a means of encouraging positive, Christlike, other-centered actions that allow participants to practice living out their faith. This can facilitate a deeper knowledge and understanding of what it means to be a

Christian as well as promote a positive attitude toward Christian service.

Service projects may be most effective as a learning tool when participants have explored biblical models for service, incorporated prayer as a means of personal preparation, and received any specialized training that may be necessary for the service to be performed. They should not be approached as activity for activity's sake, social opportunities, or as a means to receive status within the group. Careful modeling of Christlike servanthood on the part of the leader is important.

There are numerous types of possible service projects (for some helpful suggestions, see Crandall, 1978; and LeFever, 1978). Projects may focus on ministering to the church, ministering to the local community, ministering in another region or foreign country, or ministering in special circumstances (such as providing relief to victims of a tragedy or natural disaster). A project may focus on meeting a physical need, such as cleaning up a neighborhood park, taking food to needy families during holidays, raking leaves for the elderly, painting the church, raising money for a missionary project, or serving at a soup kitchen. Or it may focus on an emotional need, such as cheering up seniors in a nursing home, offering companionship to homebound handicapped citizens, providing "latchkey" children with a place to go after school, or writing encouraging letters to missionaries overseas. Service projects may be short-term (a one-time activity) or long-term (an ongoing program that meets a particular need) and may be short in duration (a Saturday afternoon project) or lengthy (a three week mission trip to another country).

JANA SUNDENE

Bibliography. R. Crandall (1978), *Youth Education in the Church,* pp. 334–48; L. LaBar (1964), *An Introduction to Evangelical Education,* p. 93; M. LeFever (1978), *Youth Education in the Church,* pp. 406–21; B. McNabb and S. Marby (1990), *Teaching the Bible Creatively.*

Seventh-Day Adventist Education. Seventh-Day Adventism developed out of the widespread interchurch interest in the premillennial second coming of Christ in the 1840s that centered around the work of William Miller, a Baptist preacher. The denomination was organized between 1861 and 1863. As of the beginning of 1997, the worldwide church had a membership of 9,296,127.

Nonschooling Forms of Education. Adventist educational endeavors have developed around four foci. The first is the denomination's publishing work, which began with the publication of *Present Truth* in 1849. That periodical was soon followed by one in 1852 specifically directed at young people. *The Youth's Instructor* aimed at warning young Adventists against the perils of the world and at teaching them basic Christian concepts from the Adventist perspective. As of the beginning of 1997, the denomination had some 55 publishing houses operating in 238 languages. Much of the output is evangelistically educational while other products are aimed specifically at youth, including a very substantial investment in Christian textbooks.

A second focus of Adventist education centers in the church. The denomination formed its first Sabbath School in 1852 in connection with the beginning of *The Youth's Instructor*. At the beginning of 1997, there were 88,993 Sabbath Schools with 10,943,674 members. In addition, many congregations sponsor Adventist Youth Societies and Pathfinder Clubs (similar to scouting programs). Youth camps also became important in the twentieth century.

A third focus of Adventist education is found in home and family life education. From its very beginning the denomination has seen the home as the primary educational institution, but it was not until the end of the second half of the twentieth century that this crucial area began to be developed systematically. Since 1975 this work has been coordinated by the Family Ministries Department of the denomination's General Conference.

The fourth focus of Adventist education is that of schooling. At the beginning of 1997, the denomination operated 5,478 schools worldwide. In the United States there were 941 elementary schools with 47,773 students, 96 secondary schools with 13,361 students, and 8 colleges and 6 universities with 19,987 students. These schools were part of a worldwide system comprised of 4,416 elementary schools, 940 secondary schools, and 87 colleges and universities, with a total student population of 914,787.

Yet Adventists were not always supporters of formal education. Some early believers held that it was wrong to send children to school since the Lord was to return soon and they would have no chance to use their hardearned knowledge. Schooling from that perspective was seen as a denial of the faith.

But there was another view on the topic. James and Ellen White, two of the founders of the denomination, believed that "a well-disciplined and informed mind can best receive and cherish the sublime truths of the Second Advent."

The pro-schooling Adventists founded several elementary schools in the 1850s and early 1860s, but none of them lasted more than two or three years. The real beginning of Adventist schooling goes back to 1867, when a recent convert by the name of Goodloe Harper Bell founded an elementary/secondary school at denominational headquarters in Battle Creek, Michigan. By 1874 Bell's school had become Battle Creek College, with the primary mission of training church workers.

Unfortunately, the earliest attempts at Adventist education turned out to have more of a classical emphasis than they did a distinctive Christian/Adventist focus. That would change in the 1890s in the wake of a Christocentric revival in the denomination's theology.

The 1890s saw what might be considered the "baptism" of Adventist education through revolutionary curricular innovations stimulated by Ellen White at the Avondale School for Christian Workers in Australia. In addition to other reforms, the Bible now came to the center in place of the classics. The Avondale reform rapidly spread to the United States, where the reform element among the leadership led out in the transformation of Adventist education at the collegiate level and among the developing secondary schools.

Another major dynamic of the 1890s was the beginning of the Adventist elementary movement. The number of schools skyrocketed from 18 in 1895 to 220 in 1900, 417 in 1905, and 594 in 1910. By that time the Adventist schooling system was in place.

The twentieth century built upon the foundation of the nineteenth. The early decades of the century were spent refining curricula and professionalizing the teaching force. From the 1920s through the 1940s the denomination struggled with the issue of accreditation, which it eventually opted for. By the 1960s the Adventist educational system had reached a level of maturity that allowed it to develop universities in the United States that by the early 1970s would be offering Ed.D.s and Ph.D.s in such areas as education and religious studies. The late 1980s and the 1990s saw the Adventist university movement go worldwide, with some institutions granting their own doctorates in areas that a few decades ago were thought of as somewhat primitive "mission fields."

Adventist educational philosophy centers on education as being redemptive. Other aspects of that philosophy highlight the primacy of the Bible as the integrative focal point of the curriculum; the education of the whole person, including the physical, mental, spiritual, and social aspects; the necessity of balancing the practical with the theoretical; and the importance of the role model of both teachers and parents. The ultimate aim of education is seen as Christian service.

GEORGE R. KNIGHT

Bibliography. M. Hogden, ed. (1978), *School Bells and Gospel Trumpets: A Documentary History of Seventh-Day Adventist Education in North America*; G. R. Knight, ed. (1983), *Early Adventist Educators*; G. R Knight (1984), *Religious Schooling in America*, pp. 85–109; D. F. Neufield, ed. (1996), *Seventh-Day Adventist Encyclopedia; Review and Herald*; E. White (1903), *Education*; idem (1923), *Fundamentals of Christian Education*.

Sex Education. Sex education in the United States emerged in response to the government's concern about excess population. The Commission on Population Growth and the American Future was established in 1970 to address population growth among poor, minority women. Following two years of study, this federal commission recommended that schools assume the responsibility of teaching family planning, population control, and sexuality education, which was to be financed by the Department of Health Services.

The question of whether sex education increased sexual activity was of major concern. Between 1970 and 1988, the number of sexually active white adolescents increased from 2.2 million to 3.7 million while sexual activity rates among African American adolescents increased from 0.6 million to 0.8 million. A 1986 poll by Louis Harris and Associates found that 46 percent of sexually active teens had received comprehensive sex education—sex education that covers the basics such as menstruation, human reproduction, and sexually transmitted diseases including HIV/AIDS, in addition to providing information on contraception, birth control, abortion, masturbation, and homosexuality. Nineteen percent of sexually active teens had received limited sex education, and 34 percent of sexually active teens had received no sex education. Research indicates that adolescent women 15 to 18 years old who had taken a course in sex education are more likely to initiate sexual activity; contraceptive education is significantly related to first incidence of coitus among early adolescents.

After two decades of sex education, over a million sexually active teenage girls become pregnant annually. The United States has the highest teen pregnancy rate in the world—96 pregnancies per 1,000 women age 15 to 19—a rate double that of England's, triple that of Sweden's, and seven times higher than that in the Netherlands. According to the Centers for Disease Control, the United States also has the highest abortion rate.

The National Association of School Psychologists, the American Medical Association, the National School Boards Association, and the Society for Adolescent Medicine support comprehensive sex education. The national workshop of Comprehensive School Education Programs, which convened in 1992, developed a plan to mandate comprehensive sex education in all schools and in all grades by the year 2000. The plan also includes the goal of establishing school-based clinics (SBCs), also called school-based health centers (SBHCs), in every school at every grade level. SBHCs and SBCs are family planning clinics located on school grounds. School-linked clinics (SLCs) are not actually on school grounds but are located near the campus. SBCs, SBHCs, or SLCs operate as independent agencies; they are neither monitored by nor subject to school district guidelines for medical services. However, clinic nurses work in cooperation with sex education classes and may teach the class or make special presentations. Students are invited to visit the family-planning clinics, and some schools offer prizes and incentives, such as pizza parties, school dances, and free tickets to sports events for those students who register.

To allay parental concerns, clinics minimize their reproductive health services and promote themselves as multiservice health units. Physical examinations and treatment of minor illnesses such as colds, ear infections, or sports injuries are stressed. Whatever the reason for the initial visit, however, students are given psychosocial evaluations and questioned about their sexual activity. Contraceptives and birth control are recommended.

Concern over the HIV/AIDS epidemic has prompted many school districts to provide students with sex education, condom availability, and family planning clinic services. Courses in comprehensive sex education usually precede clinic introduction. To minimize community objection to these clinics, family planning services are not advertised or promoted. Clinic staff are advised not to dispense contraceptives until the second year of operation, after the controversy over opening the clinic has subsided.

An evaluation of four SBCs in California demonstrated that school availability of contraceptives as an important convenience factor had no positive effect on whether students consistently used contraceptives. Research indicates that condom availability may contribute to sexually permissive attitudes among teenage males, who feel that because condoms are available in their school, sexual intercourse is expected and accepted. Where there are family planning clinics in communities, there is an increase of 120 pregnancies per 1,000 among 15 to 19 year olds. In high schools with family planning clinics, nearly twice as many females transition from virgin to nonvirgin status than in high schools without clinics. Studies also find high rates of partner switching and increased rates of sexually transmitted diseases among sexually active students in SBC schools.

Research indicates that parents favor abstinence education and reject comprehensive sex education. Teaching abstinence and resistance skills is an effective intervention which gives students the social skills they need to delay early coitus. A National Adolescent Student Health Survey of 11,000 eighth and tenth graders demonstrated that abstinence was acceptable to 94 percent of adolescent females; 76 percent of adolescent males believed that "saying no" to premarital sexual intercourse was acceptable. In comprehensive sex education classes, abstinence may also be taught, but the Sex Information and Education Council of the United States (SIECUS) considers curricula that emphasizes abstinence and monogamous heterosexual marriage to be inadequate.

Best Friends, an abstinence education program that began in Washington, D.C., utilizes peer support as the means to control unwanted teenage pregnancies. With exceptionally low pregnancy rates, this program has been extremely successful and may serve as a model for schools, churches, and religious organizations.

Teaching abstinence should be a major component in every Christian education program or ministry. Research demonstrates that religiosity as measured by church attendance one or more times a week reduces the odds of first coitus at all ages. The biblical basis that sex is God's idea, beginning with Adam and Eve, and that everything God created is good, forms the framework for a positive approach to abstinence education. While sex education teaches how to have "safer sex," abstinence education stresses making healthy decisions essential in every aspect of life, not just in delay of premarital sexual intercourse. For example, research indicates that the fewer number of nights per week that seniors go out, coupled with their plans for college, is an additional predictor of delay of premarital sexual intercourse and is an important emphasis in abstinence education. Teenagers' future orientation, educational goals, and the presence of both parents in the home are additional contributing factors that reduce the risk of early coitus.

Christian chastity programs, where teens en masse take vows of abstinence, capitalize upon positive peer pressure. Equipping students who attend public schools as "peer models" so that they are articulate in classroom debates or in lunchroom discussions is another way that Christian education can meet the need of its teenagers. Peer models may also be trained to teach resistance skills to their friends and classmates. Those who successfully complete such training and remain abstinent might earn college scholarships to be awarded by the churches they attend. Also, church clubs, rites of passage or manhood training ministries, discipleship groups, camps, choirs, and youth groups should intentionally incorporate abstinence education into their curricula.

LaVerne A. Tolbert

Bibliography. N. Bearss, J. S. Santelli, and P. Papa, *Journal of Adolescent Health* 17 (1985): 178–83; P. L. Beilnsom, E. S. Miola, and M. Farmer, *American Journal of Public Health* 85 (1995): 309–11; J. O. G. Billy, K. L. Brewster, and W. R. Grady, *Journal of Marriage and the Family* 56 (1994): 387–404; D. Brindis, S. Starbuck Morales, A. L. Wolfe, and V. McCarter, *Family Planning Perspectives* 26 (1994): 160–64; Center for Population Options (1993), *Designing and Implementing School-Based and School-Linked Health Centers: vol. 2, A Guide to School-Based and School-Linked Health Centers;* D. de Mauro, *SIECUS Report* 18 (1989–90): 1–9; J. Drufoos, *Family Planning Perspectives* 17 (1985):

70–75; J. Hayden, *Journal of American College Health* 42 (1993): 133–36; D. Kirby, C. Waszak, and J. Ziegler, *Family Planning Perspectives* 23 (1991): 6–16; B. C. Miller and K. A. Moore, *Journal of Marriage and the Family* 52 (1990): 1025–44; J. A. Olsen and S. E. Weed, *Family Perspective* 20 (1987): 153–95; E. W. Paul and H. F. Pipel, *Family Planning Perspectives* 11 (1979): 297–301; U.S. Department of Health and Human Services (1991), ERIC Document Reproduction Service No. ED-359-189; Sex Information and Education Council of the United States (1992), *Future Directions: HIV/AIDS Education in the Nation's Schools;* L. Tolbert (1998), *Condom Availability Programs, School-Based Clinics, and Sexual Permissiveness among Inner-City African American Students,* unpublished manuscript; C. Warren (1987), *Improving Students' Access to Health Care: School-Based Health Clinics.*

See also ABSTINENCE; ACQUIRED IMMUNODEFICIENCY SYNDROME; TRUE LOVE WAITS

Sexuality, Adolescent. Adolescence begins with the onset of puberty. *Puberty* is the stage in development where the human body becomes capable of reproduction. This physiological development begins when the pituitary gland, ovaries in the female, and testicles in the male begin to secrete large quantities of sex hormones known as *gonadotropins.* These hormones are responsible for healthy physiological and sexological maturation, as well as controlling sexual drive or desire. In addition to this hormonal activity, social, psychological, and nutritional factors also influence the onset of puberty. Females usually begin this stage as early as 8 or 9 years of age, or as late as age 12 or 13. Males may start their sexual development as early as age 9 or 10 and as late as age 13 or 14.

The physiological changes in adolescence are commonly categorized as *primary* and *secondary sex characteristics. Secondary sex characteristics* develop first. These are characteristics that give the adolescent the look of an adult and define the look of gender. Increased skeletal and muscle growth, defined body shape, growth of pubic and body or axillary hair, and changes in voice pitch are secondary characteristics. *Primary sex characteristics* follow and are labeled *primary* because these changes occur in genitalia and reproductive organs. In females, breast development, increased size and pigment change of the vulva, and the onset of the menstrual cycle mark primary sexual development. Females experience first menstruation, which is known as *menarche.* In males, the penis and testicle increase in size, the scrotum darkens, and the male body produces sperm and semen. Adolescent males may experience frequent spontaneous erections, increased sensitivity to sexual stimuli, and ejaculation through nocturnal emissions, or "wet dreams," and masturbation.

During adolescence, the individual experiences strong sexual desires. These are normal and can often be confused as lust. These desires ultimately lead to mate selection. In Western culture adolescents date as part of developing their sexual identity. Sexual behavior is often discussed in an attempt to define acceptable boundaries for physical touch. Kissing, holding, caressing, and other forms of affection become part of acceptable sexual behavior. Adolescents can and often do experience other sexual behaviors from mutual fondling (petting) to sexual intercourse. Issues of virginity are fundamental during this age stage because of the adolescent's ability and desire to be sexually active. The teaching and internalizing of sexual morals and values are critical to adolescence. Adolescents formulate their sexual morals and values from parental and family modeling, peers, media, school sex education programs, and the church. In past decades the church and family have taken a passive role about sexuality. This silence has perpetuated a negative value of sexuality. Christian educators and parents are now becoming more aggressive in teaching God's design for sexuality, reclaiming ground in an adolescent's moral development that once had been lost.

Adolescent sexuality also involves *gender identity development*. This is the formation of concepts, roles, and characteristics that an individual embraces in regard to masculinity or femininity. Often referred to as *psychosexual development*, gender identity development is shaped by parental influence, peer influence, religious convictions, significant role models, and the media. *Gender identity* is the adolescent's personal sense of being male or female. *Gender roles* are the behaviors that an adolescent adopts based on perception of the cultural expectations for men and women within various social contexts. Certain behaviors may be shunned as gender inappropriate. Adolescents also learn that there may be a blending of masculine and feminine attributes such as men showing their emotions and women pursuing assertive and direct leadership positions. This blending of gender attributes and roles is known as *androgyny*.

Sexual issues commonly faced by adolescents include body consciousness; defining normal sexual development and desires; masturbation; dating; boundaries on sexual activity; use and knowledge of contraceptives; sexually transmitted disease; teen pregnancy and abortion; sexual orientation; sexual deviant behaviors; sexual abuse; and virginity.

STEVEN GERALI

Bibliography. C. Byer and L. Shainberg (1994), *Dimensions of Human Sexuality;* K. McCoy and C. Wibblelsman (1978), *The Teenage Body Book;* K. Olsen (1984), *Counseling Teenagers: The Complete Guide to Understanding and Helping Adolescents;* R. Rothenberg, ed. (1959), *The New Medical Encyclopedia for Home Use;* G. Zgourides (1996), *Human Sexuality: Contemporary Perspectives.*

Sexuality, Child. *Physical Development.* Children are sexual beings from the moment of conception, when chromosomes determine the sex of the yet unborn baby. By the sixth week in the womb the child displays distinct sexual characteristics. The baby's brain, meanwhile, is being set to direct and regulate the hormones crucial to normal sexual development. As infants, children naturally explore their own bodies and discover sexual physical pleasure. By the age of 2 or 3, toddlers recognize gender differences and are aware of their own sexual identity. Preschoolers will engage in some form of sex-related play, usually out of simple curiosity. By puberty, individuals have become interested in the opposite sex and are becoming capable of sexual intercourse and reproduction. Puberty happens anytime between the ages of 8 and 13. Girls typically reach puberty at 12 years of age, at least two years ahead of boys.

Sexuality and Psychology. Freud regarded sex as the basic motivation behind most human behavior. Psychologists like Jung modified Freud's view to say sex dictates only some behavior. Educator and psychologist Carl Rogers further demoted the influence of sex on behavior by declaring that its impact lay in its relation to self-identification and self-esteem. Many behaviors once thought to be gender-related have been proven to originate in cultural influence and parental expectations.

Sex Education/Christian Education. The Old Testament promoted sex within marriage as a divine gift. God was the creator of sexual differences, and encouraged the sexual union of Adam and Eve before the advent of sin. What is the role of Christian education in regard to a child's sex education?

Religious education and sex education are naturally integrated. Sex education taught without the context of the biblical values system leaves out the absolutes of right and wrong as set down by God.

God's design for religious instruction (Deut. 6:6) dictates that his commands be taught in a natural manner, connected to the teachable moments of everyday activities. Applied to sex education, this teaching method means that parents should be prepared to answer questions in an open, honest manner and should model the attitudes and behaviors desired in their children. The school and the church are to be resources, offering help in the form of parent training and perhaps parent/child seminars.

The Role of the Parents. The most important job of the parent in childhood sex education is to provide a role model for gender identification. A nurturing father, for example, will probably raise a nurturing son. As their children begin to ask questions about body parts and reproduction, parents should be prepared with age-appropriate, correct answers. Because of their exposure to unbiblical examples of sexual behavior outside the home and in the media, children need the example of a husband and wife who share a healthy relationship. Parents should feel comfortable with displays of physical affection in front of their children, while reserving behavior that requires privacy for times they can be alone. Children can understand that sexual intimacy between their parents is behind closed doors for the sake of privacy and not out of a sense of shame.

Parents can help children develop a healthy awareness of their own bodies by designating certain body parts "private" rather than dirty or shameful. If children persist in sex-related play that invades the privacy of other children, parents should step in without overreacting.

By building the self-esteem of their children, especially daughters, parents can help them avoid sexual activity for the sake of popularity. Children who receive appropriate physical affection from parents are less likely to seek it in inappropriate ways.

With the age of puberty steadily dropping, wise parents will prepare their children for the body changes that can come as early as 8 years of age. Children should also be cautioned about forms of sexual exploitation and inappropriate touches that can come even from family members. Children need parents who are willing to communicate honestly and openly about sexuality. Parents need religious educators who will help them explain the facts of life in the context of biblical truth.

ROBERT J. CHOUN

Bibliography. D. G. Benner, ed. (1985), *Baker Encyclopedia of Psychology*; R. E. Clark, J. Brubaker, and R. B. Zuck, eds. (1975, 1986), *Childhood Education in the Church*; I. V. and K. B. Cully, eds. (1990), *Harper's Encyclopedia of Religious Education*; D. Elkind (1981), *The Hurried Child*; Maxine Hancock, and K. B. Mains (1987), *Child Sexual Abuse: A Hope for Healing*; J. Kesler, R. Beers, and L. Neff, (1986), *Parents and Children*; G. H. Ketterman (1981), *How to Teach Your Child about Sex*; M. S. and R. C. Smart (1977), *Children: Development and Relationships*.

Sexually Transmitted Disease. *See* Acquired Immunodeficiency Syndrome.

Shared Goverance. *See* Democratic Approach to Groups.

Short-Term Missions. Christian service done crossculturally, either overseas or at home, for periods lasting between one week and two years.

Within the history of modern missions, short-term missions is a recent but exploding phenomenon. In the first two hundred years of the modern missionary movement, missionary service was a lifetime career commitment. This was due in part to the travel, expense, and health risks involved. In the early part of the twentieth century, mainline denominations began using short-term people, mainly teachers, in overseas missionary work. But it was not until the middle of the century that mission boards began to actively recruit short-term volunteers to supplement the work of career missionaries. Today, almost half of all missionaries in the world are short-term personnel. There are over three hundred organizations that sponsor short-term missions endeavors. The largest, Youth with a Mission (YWAM), has over twenty thousand short-term volunteers every year. Short-term personnel range from junior high school students to retirees, although most are college age. They perform a wide variety of missionary services, from building houses to street evangelism to modular teaching to heart surgery.

The purpose of short-term missions projects is evangelism and service. A byproduct of the experience is strengthening spiritual relationships among the short-term team members and building relationships with missionaries and nationals.

While the value of short-term missions is debated among mission organizations, missionaries, and churches, two things seem clear. People with short-term missions experience are valuable members of the church and are often candidates for career missions experience. For them, the value of short-term experience is the ensuing vision for missions and identification with the missions experience. In short, they become informed senders in the church. Statistics vary, but many short-term missionaries become career missionaries. "Testing the waters" is a common objective, particularly for college-age students who do short-term missions assignments. They often use the assignment to overcome cross-cultural apprehensions and to try out the missions career field without the pressure of a long-term commitment.

Anthony's book, *The Short-Term Missions Boom: A Guide to International and Domestic Involvement* (1994), discusses some keys to a successful short-term missions experience. They include selecting a sponsoring agency that is equipped to serve the church and group being sent, maintaining a balance between work and service projects, paying attention to the selection process in putting together a short-term team, and using pretrip training of leaders and volunteers to educate and prepare for the experience.

Missiologist J. H. Kane (1978) suggests several disadvantages of the short-term missionary experience. Short-term missionaries lack experience, an understanding of the culture, and an ability to communicate in the language of the people. The high cost of the trip, possible relationship problems with veteran missionaries, and a lack of continuity in the missionary program of the host country are other possible problems. To this list must be added the burden and added responsibilities that the career missionary assumes in hosting the short-termer.

PHILIP BUSTRUM

Bibliography. M. Anthony, ed. (1994), *The Short-Term Missions Boom: A Guide to International and Domestic Involvement;* T. Gibson, S. Hawthorne, R. Krekel, and K. Moy (1992), *Stepping Out: A Guide to Short Term Missions;* J. H. Kane (1978), *A Concise History of the Christian World Mission: A Panoramic View of Missions from Pentecost to the Present.*

Significance. *See* Meaningfulness.

Signs and Wonders. Activities, events, or actions that reveal the character, glory, and miraculous power of God. Signs and wonders in Scripture are evidence of the authority of God. The miracles found in the Bible always take place with a particular purpose in mind. John MacArthur indicates that there are elements in the miracles that help us understand why they take place. (1) Miracles introduced a new era of revelation. Examples of this would be Moses and the New Testament apostolic era. (2) Miracles authenticated the messengers of revelation. This is found in the life of Elijah and especially the ministry of Jesus. (3) Miracles called the attention of those listening to hear the new revelation. Again, Moses, Elijah, and Jesus are examples of this principle (75–76).

In recent years a controversy has erupted over what has been referred to as the signs and wonders movement. Proponents of this movement argue that miracles did not cease with the apostolic age but have been in continuous existence throughout history. They point out that the Great Commission involves a promise of power that can be appropriated in the lives of believers. These promises are found in the following Scripture verses: (1) Matthew 28:18, "All authority in heaven and on earth has been given to me"; (2) Mark 16:17, "And these signs will accompany those who believe"; and (3) Acts 1:8, "But you will receive power when the Holy Spirit comes on you."

Advocates of the signs and wonders movement see miracles as evidence that the kingdom of God is at hand both from a biblical and contemporary perspective. They emphasize that miracles should play an important part in the day-by-day activities of believers and should be at the heart of a church's approach to evangelism and ministry. People are attracted to God because of a power encounter, where the power of God overcomes the dominion of Satan. Also, they stress that the main reason believers do not experience miracles is that they are not open to the experience.

Christians who oppose the signs and wonders movement argue that nowhere in the Bible are Christians commanded to seek the miraculous.

Also, in some instances there has been more of an emphasis on spiritual gifts than on the giver of the gifts. Because of an overemphasis on seeking the miraculous, some believers have minimized the importance of the Christian disciplines and the fruit of the Spirit. There are mature Christians on both sides of this controversy and it will probably be an issue addressed by Christians for many years to come.

J. GREGORY LAWSON

Bibliography. J. MacArthur (1978), *The Charismatics;* C. Wagner, ed. (1983), *Signs and Wonders Today.*

Simulation. Simulations foster dynamic, problem-centered learning by creating an artificial learning environment parallel to a real one. A simulation's power resides in its ability to re-create crucial elements of the real learning situation. This artificially created and controlled environment calls forth the knowledge, emotions, and skills necessary for effective performance in the "real world." Virtual reality activities represent the most sophisticated forms of simulations, but any learning activity that seeks to re-create a real-world environment qualifies as a simulation. Using a mannequin to teach CPR involves simulation. Role-playing interactions in a social system involve simulation. The goal is to duplicate the critical features of a real-world situation that allow for experiential learning. Learners experience simulated consequences of learning (or failing to learn). Simulations were practiced long before they were named. The term was first applied to flight training devices used in World War II. Today role-playing, games, and computer simulations are types of simulations widely used in a variety of educational settings.

Leading a simulation requires effectively managing the materials (preparation), the activity, and the educational objectives. A competent facilitator gathers all the materials needed for the simulation, makes the necessary space arrangements, and visualizes how the simulation will unfold. During the simulation, a competent facilitator communicates directions clearly, keeps the simulation flowing naturally, and observes and listens carefully. A competent facilitator manages the educational objectives by identifying clearly the purposes of the simulation, knowing the motivations and interests of participants, and adjusting the simulation to get the best match between participants' needs and the simulation's purpose.

Since a simulation aims at transfer of learning, debriefing the activity is critical to its success. Debriefing includes three foci for discussion. First, participants should describe "what happened." Careful observation by the leader or assigned observers will strengthen this descriptive task. Next, debriefing moves to the interior level;

participants' feelings, motives, purposes, and meanings experienced in response to the activity. Last, debriefing then shifts to learning that corresponds and transfers to the real environment.

ROBERT DROVDAHL

Bibliography. W. Heitzmann (1983), *Educational Games and Simulations;* K. Jones (1995), *Simulations: A Handbook for Teachers and Trainers.*

Sin. The obvious need for the study of sin is simply the seriousness of the subject. The destructive force of sin represents the antithesis of a Creator God. Sin impacts the entirety of creation, including humankind. Only the redemptive initiative of God to countermand the impact of sin can neutralize and one day eliminate the results of the pervasive nature of sin.

Wayne Grudem (1994) defines sin as any failure to conform to the moral law of God in act, attitude, or nature. While such a definition synthesizes a biblical-historical baseline, different views of sin call for our critical investigation because they do influence people directly and indirectly. For example, the existentialism of Kierkegaard yields a perspective of sin that has more tension, anxiety, or victimization than personal accountability. Other definitions suggest sin is merely an illusion that can be resolved with the proper cognitive adjustment. Using Marxist social analysis, ethno-theologians globally have defined sin in terms of social conditions that result in systemic injustice and oppression. The removal of such evil structures/conditions extracts sin and its influence, liberating humanity from the domination of sin. Dualistic views of sin, both ancient and modern, reduce sin to some amoral trivia. This perspective is seen in a variety of Asian religions and their New Age offshoots. Ancient Near Eastern religions have always posited a struggle between preexistent and vying gods of good and evil whose struggle causes sin in human existence. Certain modern theologies see "god" as an evolving entity. Such blending of physics and Eastern mysticism is represented in process theology's view of sin.

Various traditions within evangelical Christianity place emphases on different aspects of sin moving on a continuum from sin as the infringement of a moral code toward sin as the breaking of convenantal relationship. Biblical faith must acknowledge the legal dimensions of sin, recognizing that the righteous requirements of the law need to be satisfied. Biblical faith must also perceive sin as including the destruction of a personal relationship between God and humankind, where the need is not only a payment of debt, but reconciliation between Creator and created.

Orginal Sin. Where/what is the origin of sin? Construction of a theological response to such a complex question must consider a variety of sources. Jewish ideas on original sin would include several themes: (1) a struggle between good and evil (Gen. 6:5; 8:21); (2) angels whose task it was to oversee humanity, but sinned with human females, (Gen. 6:1–4); (3) ideas on original sin similar to Christian ideas of connection to the sin of the first created human.

The theory of natural and genetic transmission holds that like spiritual traits, corrupt traits can be transmitted as well. However, such theories never discuss guilt nor do they explain how Christ could have a human nature free from sin.

The theory of mediate imputation posits that God charged guilt to Adam's descendants. As a natural consequence, all who descend from Adam receive his guilt nature. Before they commit any actual personal sin, God judges people guilty for simply possessing this corrupted nature.

The realism theory holds the essence of all people was personally in Adam and that we all actually participated corporately in his sin. A closely related perspective is the federalist theory, which holds that corruption and guilt come upon humans because Adam was the head of the race in a federal/representative sense as he sinned. The theory usually distinguishes between inherited sin (corruption) and imputed sin (guilt) from Adam. All people in a guilty state are liable to hell, but persons have not inherited sin and thus are not sinful until they actually commit sin.

Regardless of a variety of theories, Genesis 3 makes evident that the fall of Adam and Eve in Eden is an historical event and must be a central point for any discussion about "original sin." This biblical account makes evident that God does not author sin. Sin is implicit in the disobedience of humankind to a specific direction by God. Adam and Eve had an immediate awareness of the gravity of their rebellious activity, which led to a penalty of death inflicted on the human race who descend from Adam and Eve (Gen. 4–6).

The Extent of Sin. Sin is real and personal. Sin is not only isolated actions, it is also a reality within a human being. Sin as nature serves as the source of sinful action and sin's universality is testified to throughout Scripture. The psalms bear witness to the Old Testament's understanding of sin's universality (14:3; 143:2). Paul makes quite clear in his forensic argument in Romans 1–3 that ultimately all have sinned (Rom. 3:23). John's writings are very clear about humanity not deceiving themselves into believing that they have avoided the impact of sin (1 John 1:8–10).

The extent of sin's influence has ontological reality as well (Eph. 2:3). The New Testament uses a variety of locations to speak of the extent of the sin nature. The "flesh" is viewed as the seat of destructive desire (Eph. 2:3; 1 Peter 4:2). The heart can also be the source of wrong desires (Rom. 1:24). The mind can be evil in its impact (Eph.

4:17; 1 Tim. 6:5). The indwelling of sin in a person can produce a whole plethora of unholy desires (Rom. 1:24; 7:8; Titus 2:12). Sin is like a cancer that grows and enslaves a person. Paul describes the downward slope of human beings, who move from willful rejection of God to complete submission to the destructiveness of ontological sin that is expressed tangibly (Rom. 1:18–32).

The extent of sin must also be considered beyond the obvious and tragic devastation resulting from personal sin. The Bible clearly condemns sin (evil) which is expressed through systemic means. The Old Testament prophets condemned drunkenness and structural evil in the same prophetic utterances (Isa. 5:8–11, 22–23). God's displeasure at sin expressed through societal structures is clearly seen in Amos 5:10–15. God forcefully speaks against wicked individuals and the laws they use for their own sinful advantage (Ps. 94:20–23).

Institutionalized sin can also be so subtle that individuals may unwittingly be a part of its cancerous influences with very little realization of what is occurring. Amos 4:1–2 speaks of society elites who enjoyed their comforts with little realization of how their position was achieved or maintained. The group may have had minimal contact with the poverty-stricken, but God obviously sees their position as an affront to his holy character and judges them accordingly.

Contemporary Christianity tends to have a propensity toward focusing on personal sin to the exclusion of systemic evil or vice versa. The Bible speaks about God's concern for both societal evil and personally expressed idolatry as exemplified in his punishment of both Israel and Judah for their disobedience personally and injustice systemically.

The Impact of Sin. The extent of sin begins to unfold the impact that sin will have on people. The result of sin is always destructive. Depravity is a word usually associated with a discussion of the impact of sin, with "total depravity" the term defining its breadth. Total depravity does not mean that a person is devoid of any virtuous qualities. The Gospel writers do chronicle the fact that people can innately have pleasing qualities (Mark 10:21; Matt. 23:23). However, total depravity means that every human being is destitute of the love toward God which is required by the Law and simply has a natural preference for living life by a personal set of rules (2 Tim. 3:2–4; Eph. 2:1–8).

What most fail to recognize is that sin also impacts God. Scriptures speaks of God's hatred of sin (Ps. 11:5), his lament over the lost (Matt. 23:27), his patience toward sinners (Exod. 34:6), and his ultimate response in Christ to remedy sin (Mark 10:45). The impact of sin is clearly seen in the structures of societies as social systems are perverted by sin. This is seen socially (James 2:9), economically (James 5:1–4), and physically (James 5:14). The natural world suffers from the impact of sin, which is seen in decaying health and polluted environment (Rom. 8). The complexity of sin's impact is seen broadly in humanity. Sin can actually produce temporary happiness (Ps. 10:1–11), but ultimately this same sin spawns a self-delusion (Isa. 5:20) that leads to deep futility in life (Eccles. 1:2). Sin overtakes a human being in a demanding reliance on wicked rebellion which can take the form of challenging God (1 Cor. 10:9) or of hostility toward God that leads to God's wrath. Death is thus sin's final result. Physical death is a penalty for sin (Matt. 10:28). Spiritual death is the ultimate experience in the soul's alienation from God (Eph 2:1–6; 1 John 5:12). Such far-reaching punishment of sin by God is primarily because God's righteousness demands it. In the cross is a clear demonstration of the reason God punishes sin. To not punish sin would reveal a God who is not righteous and the nonexistence of any ultimate justice in the universe. Sin that is punished demonstrates a God who is a righteous and faithful God over all and reveals that justice is being done in the universe.

BYRON D. KLAUS

Bibliography. L. Berkhof (1949), *Systematic Theology;* D. Bloesch (1982), *Essentials of Evangelical Theology;* M. Erickson (1984) *Christian Theology;* W. Grudem (1994), *Systematic Theology;* S. Horton (1994), *Systematic Theology: Pentecostal Perspectives;* C. Ryrie (1989), *Basic Theology;* H. Theissen (1949), *Lectures in Systematic Theology;* J. R. Williams (1988), *Renewal Theology: God, The World and Redemption.*

Single Adults. The most diverse and growing group in America during the second half of the twentieth century was single adults. Some estimates state that of the American population age 15 and above, approximately 50 percent are now single. One of the greatest fields of evangelism in the 1990s has been the single adult ministry. Single people living alone are the fastest growing of all households in the United States—one in four households in 1995 contained just one person. According to the U.S. Census Bureau, single-person households will continue to grow faster than all households. Predictions for the year 2010 are that nonfamily households—people living alone or with a nonrelative—and single-parent families will be the fastest growing households.

If the never-married population continues to grow, the United States could become a nation with more unmarrieds than marrieds. In 1995, 43,900,000 were never married compared to 21,400,000 in 1970. According to the 1995 United States Census Bureau figures there were 74,935,000 singles—34,277,000 men, 40,658,000 women.

There has been a marked change in the public opinion of Americans toward singles. In the early portion of the twentieth century singles were old maids and spinsters. As divorce became common in the 1960s, some positives of being single began to be noted. By the late 1960s swinging singles became attractive to many adults. As the twentieth century closes, singles are becoming a dominant force in the American culture.

General Facts Concerning Singles. All singles have some basic needs in common. They need relationships and most seek to fulfill that need. An active social life is characteristic of most singles, with those not engaging in relationships normally being ill-fitted to and disgruntled with society and life in general. All singles have spiritual needs as well—to know the Lord and to grow in their walk with him. Healthy adults also seek to develop their intellect and appreciate a mental challenge. God has made us emotional beings and singles have hurts, longings, and desires that need to be met.

In our present culture, singles frequent clubs, bars, and restaurants seeking to develop meaningful, personal relationships. Age and circumstances determine many of their personal concerns. Young singles often tend to lack commitment, put off marriage to attend college or get established in a career, and view independence as attractive.

Often single parents feel there is no hope for them and many become lonely and bitter either from never having a spouse or experiencing the loss of spouse through divorce or death. Single parents are a significant growing segment of the American population.

A growing number of singles practice cohabitation in our present culture, but this has caused added frustration and stress. It remains difficult to establish a relationship without a strong commitment to marriage. The divorce rate of those who have cohabitated is also much higher than those who have not.

Singles in America have some basic characteristics. Entering the twenty-first century, the average income for the single is $20,000 or less with the main occupation being in the professional areas. At least 50 percent of all singles work nine hours or more a day. Most of them live in rented housing. The answers given for being single range from schooling or military obligations (17 percent), to personal choice (38 percent), to circumstances (45 percent).

Advantages of the single life involve mobility and freedom, ample time for personal interests, time for an active social life, and personal privacy. Disadvantages include loneliness, restrictions on sex life, the tendency to be self-centered, and financial insecurity. Fears include being abandoned by family and friends, messing up one's life, not advancing in life, and losing one's health.

Theology of Singleness. An understanding of God's perspective on singles provides a foundation for ministry to singles within the church. Generally, there are five categories of singles. For some, being single is a matter of choice. Matthew 19 indicates that some are eunuchs (single) by the act of another man, some by God, and others by their personal choice. Some make the choice to be single. Some never marry due to circumstances such as schooling, finances, no one asks, or a refusal to a proposal. Comprising a third category are those single by divorce (divorce has increased 700 percent in America during the twentieth century). A fourth is the result of separation between married couples. A final condition is the death of the spouse. Widows spend an average of eighteen years as a widow and eight out of ten women are widowed. One of the greatest stresses of life is when someone has singleness thrust upon her or him by death or divorce.

Jeremiah was asked by God to remain single throughout his ministry (chap. 16). Other famous singles of the Old Testament include Joseph, Elijah, Elisha, and Daniel. In the New Testament it appears that Mary, Martha, Dorcas, and Paul were singles. Lois and Eunice may have served as single parents for at least part of Timothy's life. The New Testament teaches that celibacy is a gift from God (Matt. 19; 1 Cor. 7), and clearly has some spiritual benefits, such as serving God with singleness of being and without distraction.

Singleness is an acceptable minority opportunity in the plan of God (Gen. 2:18). Marriage is the rule, being single the exception. Matthew 19:3–12 and 1 Corinthians 7 present singleness in positive ways: less stress in this present world; fewer complications with which to deal; more time to spend on spiritual matters; and fewer distractions in one's relationship to God. It should be considered a gift from God as to whether one is married or single (1 Cor. 7:6–9).

Adult Groups. *Ages 18–24. Concerns.* The challenge of separating from his birth family, establishing her own identity and role as an adult, and developing a new home are major concerns. For most, there is a gradual reduction of dependence on their parents. During this stage they seek answers to the questions "Who am I?", "What am I going to do with my life?", and "Where do I fit in?"

Features. Leaving home and living autonomously are normal expectations of young adults. The forming of adult relationships for many has as much impact as the choice of college major and career.

Adjustments. Many young adults have a difficult time being in a family and moving out of it in order to establish their own living arrangement. Young adults often are slow in learning to be independent especially when compared to those in the earlier part of the twentieth century. The number of choices and the moral relativism of today make it difficult for young adults to forge their own belief system and values. Difficult also are time management and living on a limited income.

Ages 25–39. Concerns. Most singles in this stage of life are established in their occupations and have accepted singleness. However, some are longing for the intimacy of marriage while others are adapting to divorce and single parenthood. Some have money and security, but grapple with meaningful relationships, finding a mentor, or seeking answers to life's deeper meanings.

Features. Today's adult can expect approximately five career changes, and this is likely to occur at least once during these years. While most singles live in rented facilities, many in this stage will purchase a home. Many also will adjust to their first marriage while others will join the ranks of singleness as a result of divorce.

Adjustments. Genuineness, following a dream, and building for the future become essentials to a well-adjusted life. Questions to be answered are, "What is life all about?" and "What do I want out of life?"

Ages 40–55. Concerns. Adjustment to midlife and its resulting crisis are common to many. Although many are established and accustomed to singleness, there is still a struggle with loneliness. Tiredness enters the picture as physical endurance begins to wane. There are health concerns, adjustment to body changes, and the pressure of caring for aging parents. The biological clock for bearing children is winding down for women, and for those who have longed for marriage and children this can be a time of deep depression.

Features. Realizing that the time in which to accomplish their dreams and goals is getting shorter, people at this stage reevaluate previously determined ambitions. For some, it is a time of divorce and remarriage. Many go through the difficulty of seeing parents age and die. A rewarding aspect for some is the privilege of becoming a mentor and seeing fruit beyond one's own personal life.

Adjustments. Some join the ranks of singles because of death or midlife divorce of a spouse. Single parents face the "empty nest."

Midlife single men are among the most demanding singles. They are set in a particular lifestyle and are known as confirmed singles. Midlife single men sometimes struggle to the point of suicide. Because they tend to be less conventional and compliant, impacted by a strong desire for independence, negativism, and selfishness, some fall into deep depression or a criminal lifestyle.

Women singles in midlife tend to be happier than many married women. They are reliable workers and while goals may be shifting they are often motivated, self-controlled, and enjoying their personal freedom. Middle-aged single females are among the healthiest segment of society. They experience fewer incidents of mental and physical illness.

Ages 55 and Above. Concerns. For many it is a time of loneliness due to the loss of a mate, which has suddenly made them a single. They are concerned about their own health and tend to reassess finances to ascertain what type of retirement they will have. Some have goals to yet achieve, while others take time for deepening relationships.

Features. Many face singleness for the first time as they experience widowhood. Others who have been single face the challenge of remarriage. New opportunities are often abundant, but the deaths of friends and loved ones are likely.

Adjustments. Passive mastery is achieved by many as they enter a stage of introspection about life and are more contemplative. There is continuous adjustment to the aging process, living on a fixed income, and being a steward of the golden years.

The Church's Response to Singles. Many churches simply allow singles to blend into the congregation. Often church leadership feels that one class fits all adults. Unfortunately, other churches ignore singles completely. Today, churches are beginning to sense the need to shift the emphasis toward developing ministries for singles.

Many churches struggle over finding the best ways to reach this growing segment of our population. Most singles feel too young or too old for the traditional college and career Sunday school class. Many singles feel lonely and neglected in the church due to a public platform and program emphasis on marriage and the family.

Churches with strong ministries to singles have utilized successfully several means: small groups (one of the most effective), retreats and special events specifically for singles, resources (books, seminars, and counseling), and meaningful ministry opportunities of service.

An effective church ministry to singles involves a teaching ministry which may meet in a non-traditional place like a restaurant or private home, home Bible studies during the week, seminars dealing with special topics of interest to singles, with retreats specifically for singles. A counseling ministry provides personal counseling and group instruction with seminars. Outreach and service opportunities include ministering in inner-city areas and adopting a family, planning and going on foreign mission short-term trips, visiting rest homes and hospitals. Evangelism is another area of ministry involving group activities and recreation, home Bible studies, and visitation. Evangelism incorporates group activities, recreation, and home Bible studies. Whatever is offered, the concept of community is significant to singles for group ownership and involvement.

TERRY PRICE

Bibliography. G. Barna (1987), *Single Adults in America;* R. Barnes (1992), *Single Parenting;* D. Fager-strom (1991), *Baker Handbook of Single Adult Ministry;* T. Hershey (1986), *Young Adult Ministry;* J. Jones, ed. (1991), *Growing Your Single Adult Ministry;* C. Koons and M. Anthony (1991), *Single Adult Passages;* K. Welch (1987), *Successful Single Ministry.*

Single-Parenting. The formation of a single-parent family is often the result of the traumatic events of divorce, death of a spouse, separation (whether through the military, prison, or abuse), and unwed teenage mothers unwilling to give up their children for adoption. The child in any of these situations is oftentimes left in the care of one parent, typically the mother.

The parent that must raise a child alone faces a number of problems: maintaining discipline, lower income while needing to provide food, clothing, and shelter; lack of emotional support and physical assistance in managing the home; and a limited sense of power and control.

There may be other, sometimes hidden, problems for the single parent, such as the relationship with the absent parent, if there is one. The presence of a stepparent or live-in companion may constitute problems of a different sort. Children from this liaison may be seen as competition. Another problem these stepchildren may create is a lack of money to support the children from the first family. There simply may not be enough money to support two families. As a result, many fathers have not been paying child support for their first family. This has earned these fathers the uncomplimentary name of "Deadbeat Dads." Sometimes the presence of a second family may force the fathers to lose contact with the children from their first marriages. Those children may become rebellious or resentful of their fathers. These are just some of the problems that may cause stress on the parent who is responsible for the child rearing and for the child (or children).

Frequently with a bitter divorce, either parent may try to manipulate their children into being unwilling messengers to the opposite parent, or worse, require the children to spy on the parent and his or her family, reporting what they saw or did. This is stressful for the child, especially when reports reach the one who was spied on. Retribution for the "tattletale" may result.

The single parent family may feel diminished social support and involvement from various sources. It may inadvertently have an effect on the children, for they may feel some discrimination from their peers and teachers in school. For the parent, it may come from the community, co-workers, or social situations, including the parents and teachers at the child's school.

Frequently young children become occupants of day care centers while the single parent works.

More and more single fathers as well as mothers need the services of day care centers while they are at work. When the children no longer need day care, they are in school. Thus, these children grow up removed from parental supervision or care.

When the child of a single parent is out of school for the day (or holidays) and there is no child care available, the child becomes a "latch-key kid," meaning the child may wear a house key attached to a chain or cord around his or her neck. Thus, after school, when the child gets home he or she can let himself in to an empty house. There may or may not be rules. But since there is no supervision of the child (or children), anything can, and often does, happen.

Anger and frustration, loneliness and fear, lack of love, or a satisfactory sexual relationship and fulfillment often fill the life of the single parent. When stress overtakes the parent, who may be wearing too many hats, he or she may begin to abuse the children. It is too easy to take out pain and frustration on those nearby, as well as the most vulnerable who cannot fight back (Gelles, 1995, 449).

Cross-cultural research indicates that the single-parent family is not unique to America. Other countries find they are also struggling to resolve the problems of single parents (Gelles, 1995, 395).

In spite of the dismal picture which emerges from so many disheartening facts, there is help and relief for those who find themselves in these circumstances. Help frequently comes from relief agencies in the community. Unfortunately, the church is often slow to supply help.

The first line of assistance usually comes in the form of welfare. During the Great Depression, the welfare system was created to assist those in hopeless poverty to keep them from starving and being homeless. A meager stipend was doled out to the many unfortunate individuals who, without the assistance, would have perished while living in the "Land of Plenty." That system is still in place.

Welfare has created a subculture of poor, or "welfare families." It has been the safety net for millions, while millions more have openly abused the system. Some have been in the system so long that the third and fourth generations of welfare families have found it to be a way of life. Money comes in while no one works for it. It has been a drain on the pocketbook of American taxpayers, and many resent what appears to be a lazy segment of the population with a bad attitude. It has also become an international embarrassment.

Something had to be done. Much of the literature on family structure and family life makes suggestions on how to reform the system. In 1997, Congress finally passed a welfare reform bill that limited the financial support that many on the dole had come to expect as their "right." In addition, some states put requirements on those receiving welfare by expecting them to seek employment or their assistance would be reduced, even withdrawn. Some claim it has created enormous hardships for those unfortunates who are not able to work. Others believe it will be the salvation of individuals who can finally hold their heads up in public, by forcing them to get jobs and, with that, self-esteem.

In 1990, the percentage of employed single parents with children under the age of 18 was 25 percent of the population (Gelles, 1995, 119) . The vast majority of those in poverty in America at the end of the twentieth century in the wealthiest country in the world are women with children. Two out of three poor adults are women. According to the statistics from the U.S. Census Bureau, the economic status of families headed by women is declining, as they are the first to fall into poverty (Bender and Leone, 1992, 119).

Besides welfare, other help is available. There are job training programs, some sponsored by the Welfare Department, others in community colleges and employment development departments. Day care centers, while not adequate, at least may be available to the single parent who needs them while trying to find employment or while working. In fact, one of the greatest needs for the employed single parent is day care for young children.

Many churches across the United States have provided day care centers for the children of working singles. However, many more churches need to investigate the demographics of their community in order to learn how they can meet this need. Churches seem reluctant to open their doors for child care for various reasons. Day care can provide ministry to parents and, if run efficiently, can pay for itself.

Another need some communities are beginning to provide is after-school child care. Tutoring, recreation, homework assistance, and activities such as arts, crafts, and music lessons are offered. The children benefit greatly and the parents are relieved and grateful for the loving assistance to their childrearing duties.

Parents without Partners is an organization that provides social activities for the single parent, as well as family gatherings. Churches can reach out to single parents as well—not just members of their congregation, but also open to single parents in the community.

Sensitivity to the single-parent families in the church is a growing need as more and more adults find themselves in this situation. To ignore it and hope that the problem of divorced adults raising children alone will vanish is to hide one's head in the sand. The problem is not going away, as shown in the statistics; it is, in fact, growing.

Instead of having "mother-daughter" luncheons or "father-son" outings, the church should make it a time when the single parent can be included with either son or daughter.

From the available research on the family, it appears that there will have to be a rethinking of the definition of "family." This "rethinking" will have to be done in the church education ministry as well as in relief agencies. There are some unconventional forms of family today. Among those are single adults adopting a child. Another unusual and unconventional family form is the single grandparent raising one or more grandchildren due to the death, imprisonment, or the inability of an offspring to raise the child because of substance abuse, financial problems, or abandonment of the child.

The incidence of premarital births continues to escalate. In the decade from 1980 (with the birth rate at 18.4 percent) to 1990 (when the birth rate had increased to 27 percent) the increase was a significant 28 percent, over one-quarter of the unmarried population bearing a child. Many, if not most, of these mothers are teens, who struggle either to raise the child alone or with help from their family. Few of them marry the father of their child, and fewer yet receive any financial assistance from the father.

Day care or after-school child care remain two of the most useful ministries a church can offer a single parent. The church can minister to the adult who is the single parent by including the parent in social activities, or minister to the single-parent family by including them in family activities. It may take effort on the part of the church to communicate to the single parent that there is genuine interest in being of assistance when in the past it has not been available. Rewards are many for all involved. While single parents and their children need to develop relationships outside the home, there is less time for it than ever before (Bender and Leone, 1992, 19). But single-parent families need it more.

According to a 1991 national survey of singles, over 15 million children from birth to age 17 live in a single-parent family. However, "when considering the needs of these children and their families, a program or service targeted primarily at preschool age children might reach less than one-third of those children actually in one-parent homes" (Koons and Anthony, 1991, 167). The education ministry of the church must respond to the older children and parents also.

There is pain, frustration, loneliness, and fear behind every statistic quoted. This provides a great opportunity for the church to do what Jesus said when he told his disciples, "I was hungry, . . . I was thirsty, . . . I was a stranger, . . . naked, . . . I was sick, . . . I was in prison. . . . Then the righteous will answer Him, saying, 'Lord, when did we see You hungry, . . . or thirsty, . . . or a stranger, . . . or naked, . . . sick, or in prison . . . ?' And the King will answer and say to them, 'Truly I say to you, to the extent that you did it to one of these brothers [sisters, families] of Mine, even the least of them, you did it to Me'" (Matt. 25:36–40 NASB).

The great challenge for the American church is to obey each of these exhortations—and to do it in the name of Jesus as he would desire. It may mean we are to provide for the least of the people, remembering that among those are single parents trying to make ends meet and care for their offspring alone.

PATRICIA A. CHAPMAN

Bibliography. G. Barna (1980), *The Frog in the Kettle;* idem (1987), *Single Adults in America;* D. L. Bender and B. Leone (1992), *The Family in America: Opposing Viewpoints;* D. Elkind (1984), *All Grown Up and No Place to Go;* R. J. Gelles (1995), *Contemporary Families: A Sociological View;* D. L. Fagerstrom, ed. (1988), *Singles Ministry Handbook;* J. W. Fowler (1978), *Stages of Faith;* D. C. Kimmel (1980), *Adulthood and Aging;* C. Koons and M. Anthony (1991), *Single Adult Passages;* P. H. Miller (1983), *Theories of Developmental Psychology;* B. Okun (1984), *Working with Adults: Individual, Family, and Career Development;* R. Peterson and A. Palmer (1988), *When It Hurts to Be Single;* K. S. Welsh, ed. (1987), *Successful Single Adult Ministry.*

See also BLENDED FAMILIES; LATCHKEY CHILDREN

Situational Leadership. The serious study of leadership began in the 1800s, motivated in part by the desire to discover "the ideal man." This early research focused on identifying the traits characteristic of proven leaders. Because it was assumed that exceptional leaders were born with certain character qualities (or personality traits), it seemed reasonable that an organization could save time and money by identifying people with the appropriate traits and then promoting them into positions of leadership. Since there are a countless number of identified traits, however, this method of leadership development was abandoned.

In more recent years a broader and more flexible approach to understanding leadership has come to the forefront of discussion. This approach recognizes that leadership should not be so narrowly defined. That is, a leader may be effective in one location and under certain favorable circumstances, but may be ineffective in a different set of circumstances. The circumstance, or situation, therefore, has much to do with the conception of what makes a leader truly gifted. It is now generally agreed that flexibility is the key to effectiveness as a leader.

There are many external conditions that can have a profound impact on the leader's ability to lead. Likewise, there are internal organizational factors that can influence leadership performance as well. One cannot ignore either of these realities.

Perhaps an example will show the dynamic relationship that should exist in the application of one's leadership style. A new executive director has been called to administrate a nonprofit organization. The organization is under a high degree of stress because the previous director lost trust with the board of directors for not regulating the flow of financial resources. When the new executive director comes in, he or she will probably need to keep a tight rein on the cash flow by setting up a system of financial accountability. This can be accomplished by developing a check requisition procedure, weekly cash expenditure notices, monthly finance review meetings, and so on. This may appear to be quite autocratic to those in the organization. Given the mandate from the board to make some changes, however, it is expedient that this style of leadership be implemented.

Over time, the executive director builds trust with both the governing board and the employees. As a result of this increased level of trust, the stringent controls may be relaxed. The weekly accountability reports may become monthly or perhaps even quarterly. The executive director may implement some of the recommendations of his employees. Acting in this democratic fashion, continued trust is established. Over several years, this democratic style of leadership may evolve into what may be perceived as a laissez-faire style because the executive director no longer requires as stringent a reporting system since everyone has agreed to the new procedures and is highly supportive of the changes that have been made.

Acting in this manner, the executive director has modified his leadership style according to the situation. This is a simplistic description of a process of leadership but it helps to illustrate that the issue may not be a matter of a right or wrong style of leadership but rather one of acknowledging what is most appropriate given a certain set of external and/or internal environmental conditions—conditions that change over time as well.

MICHAEL J. ANTHONY

Bibliography. M. J. Anthony (1993), *The Effective Church Board: A Handbook for Mentoring and Training Servant Leaders; Stogdill's Handbook of Leadership* (1981).

Skinner, Burrhus Frederic (1904–90). American psychologist best known for his research into the learning process. As an undergraduate student at Hamilton College, Skinner became interested in the research of Russian physiologist Ivan Pavlov, famous for exploring the reflexive reactions of animals. Skinner did his doctoral studies at Harvard University, taking Pavlov's model and studying animal learning and the functions of the human central nervous system. Whereas Pavlov used classic conditioning to develop a conditioned response in his dogs, Skinner's research suggested that learning is a habit, and that humans would learn best in a controlled environment. Influenced by the writings of behavioral psychologist John B. Watson, Skinner began exploring how humans respond to rewards and punishments, and how they can best be trained to learn new things and change.

Operant Conditioning and Stimulus Response. Skinner conducted experiments using operant conditioning, in which the subject operates on the environment to produce some effect. For example, he trained rats to walk through mazes and press buttons to get their food. Rather than leaving the results of such experiments to trial and error, Skinner noted the experiments revealed an animal's ability to learn skills sequentially, and suggested that humans learn the same way. He theorized that we form complicated behavior patterns developmentally, building complex behaviors on simple behaviors learned earlier in life. Therefore learning, according to Skinner, was basically the forming of new habits. When people learn, they connect a new action with a new result. Skinner referred to this as *stimulus-response*, in which the subject responds to some sort of change instigated by the researcher. The subject develops a connection between a stimulus and a response that did not exist previously, adding to a knowledge base. As the process is repeated, the subject develops a habit.

Skinner also noticed that most people, when faced with a problem, will go through their old habits to try and solve it. If they are unable to solve the problem using old information and habits, they will move toward trying some sort of new behavior in a trial-and-error system. That led to Skinner's argument that if we can develop the habits of people by designing a good training program, we not only help people learn better, but help develop better people.

Behavior Modification. This focus on training people by shaping their behavioral choices became known as *behavior modification*, and is one of the core theories of developmental psychology. While others studied heredity and psychoanalysis as the basis of human development, Skinner argued that children basically learn through interaction with adults and their environment. These interactions regularly result in either a reward or a punishment of some kind. Behaviors that are rewarded are continued, while behaviors that are punished are extinguished. Most children, according to Skinner, are motivated by reward and can learn new things quickly if they know they will be immediately rewarded for their new knowledge. The task of a teacher, therefore, is to arrange the student's environment in such a way that it provides suitable and effective reinforcements for desired behavior.

Skinner believed so strongly in the ability of behavior modification to shape people that, while a faculty member at the University of Minnesota, he designed a "baby box"—a controlled environment for maximizing a child's learning—then proceeded to place his daughter Deborah in it for almost two years. He hoped to show that by relying on rewards and punishments, a training environment could significantly alter not only the learning but the character of the individual. To that end, he wrote *Walden Two*, in which he described his ideas for a perfect society based entirely upon the principles of learning he espoused. Later in life he authored his magnum opus, *Beyond Freedom and Dignity*, in which he argued that if humankind gives up its old notions of freedom, we can train better people. In essence Skinner called for a restriction on individual freedoms that hinder the development of an ideal world.

His belief that we can help shape the character of individuals by reshaping their environments is something every parent understands instinctively, for all children respond to the guidance offered by rewards and punishments. But taken to its logical conclusion, Skinner's argument is that we can create supermen, whose behavior is modified in such a way that the subject would be trained to only respond in a desired way. That is both anti-biblical and scary. Human beings are lost in sin, and no amount of moral training will break them of the habit, so Skinner's argument ultimately falls apart. There is also a danger, for if the teacher in charge of creating the environment is evil, the environment they create must also be evil.

Programmed Instruction. Through several of his books, particularly *The Technology of Teaching*, Skinner helped reshape the method of teaching in America. His perspective that students learn best by working in small steps that gradually increase in difficulty caused many teachers, and most textbook writers, to rethink their strategies. He was a leading supporter of programmed instruction, in which principles of learning observed in a laboratory were applied to classroom instruction.

In 1948 Skinner moved to the psychology department at Harvard University, where he proposed the development of a "teaching machine"— a device that presents instructional material to students in the best possible manner, then requires their response. Immediately after the response, the machine tells whether the answer was right or wrong, then presents additional material. In programmed instruction, students work through the material in order, although at their own pace. The early parts of the information offer much help to the learner, with assistance decreasing as the student grasps the fundamentals and moves on to more difficult tasks. A constant exchange between the student and the machine occurs, so that rather than simply presenting a volume of information, the machine makes sure the student understands the information before moving ahead. Unlike a television set, a teaching machine demands active participation from the student. Test-taking machines had been around since the 1920s, but it was Skinner who investigated the learning process and found that people learn difficult material faster and better if they receive immediate knowledge of results. His early development of both linear and branching programs used in teaching machines led directly to the development of computer assisted instruction. Critics argue that such reliance on technology neglects the importance of personal relationships between teachers and students.

JERRY CHIP MACGREGOR

Bibliography. R. Nye (1979), *What Is B. F. Skinner Really Saying?*; B. F. Skinner (1976), *Particulars of My Life;* idem (1979), *The Shaping of a Behaviorist;* idem (1983), *A Matter of Consequences.*

See also ASSOCIATION/CONNECTIONIST THEORIES; BEHAVIOR MODIFICATION; BEHAVIORISM, THEORIES OF; CLASSICAL CONDITIONING; COMPUTER-ASSISTED INSTRUCTION (CAI); LEARNING THEORIES; OPERANT CONDITIONING

Small Church Ministry. There is not a consensus about what constitutes a small church. Some church growth consultants consider churches with a worship attendance of 150 or less to be small. According to Lyle Schaller, a church is small when it is between 55 and 113 people, which is the median church attendance in America. Small churches usually have only one employee, the pastor. The smaller the church, the greater the likelihood the pastor is a part-time employee. As a church gets closer to between 125 and 150 in attendance, one or more part-time employees will be added.

There are a number of reasons why a church is small. It may be because it is a new church or located in an area with dramatically changing demographics. A church may be small because it is situated in an isolated rural area with slim prospects for growth, or it may be an old church that has been gradually dying. In any case, small churches play an integral role in the life of those who attend.

Leaders of the program of Christian education in the small church face the challenge of meeting many of the same needs of larger churches but with fewer resources. To be effective in ministry, the small church should carefully consider five critical areas of Christian education ministry.

Leadership Structure. In small churches, laypeople shoulder the major responsibilities for educational ministries. While the pastor should be involved, especially at the policy and planning level, laypeople must do the actual hands-on ministry.

In many small churches, the administrative duties of Christian education fall to a Christian education board or committee. This board is made up of the pastor and representatives from the major educational ministries in the church, such as the Sunday school, club program for children, youth ministry, and so on. The Christian education board will seek to answer these questions:

1. *What is the overall philosophy of Christian education of the church?*
2. *What educational ministries are needed and wanted?* A needs survey of the congregation will help answer this question.
3. *How should educational needs/wants be prioritized?* Of necessity, the small church cannot do everything a large church may be able to do, much less do everything well. Thus, the small church leadership must invest carefully in the educational areas that will yield the greatest return.
4. *What current programs should be continued and what new programs should be added?*
5. *What are basic policies and procedures of selecting ministry leaders?*
6. *How will age groups be divided or combined?*
7. *How will educational ministry efforts be coordinated?*
8. *What criteria will be used to help the board determine if the overall educational ministry is effective?*

Ministry Goals. What are the goals for the educational ministries that the small church has decided should be done? Individuals involved in each specific educational ministry should be given input into the development and implementation of ministry goals.

Recruiting/Training of Teachers and Workers. The Christian education board should develop simple manuals for each educational ministry in the church. Such a manual would include a basic description of the ministry, goals of the ministry, job descriptions for each position, resources available to the ministry, and criteria used to evaluate the ministry on a regular basis.

The Christian education board should decide the qualifications for teachers and workers and then design a training program to help equip those people for service. The small church should carefully investigate training opportunities that may be available at a local Bible college, Christian college, seminary, or Christian education convention. Small churches should also avail themselves of the many training resources in print as well as audio and videotapes from both denominational and independent publishers.

Budget. The small church will usually have limited financial resources to invest in Christian education. One of the ways to stretch limited dollars is to carefully file and recycle all curriculum materials.

Facilities. In most small churches space is at a premium and often dictates the educational ministries that can be attempted. Creativity must be exercised. Partitions may be made or purchased to divide larger areas into small ones. Usable space adjacent to the church building should be investigated such as an apartment complex with a meeting room, a nearby office building with a conference room, the home of a member who lives close by, or a public school building. Flexible scheduling should be carefully considered, such as a Sunday school program that meets on Sunday evening or Wednesday evening.

The fact that a church is small numerically does not mean it is unimportant. A small church can have a dynamic ministry of Christian education as a church's resources of people are properly trained and focused.

JONATHAN N. THIGPEN

Bibliography. C. C. Brown (1982), *Developing Christian Education in the Smaller Church;* N. T. Foltz, ed. (1990), *Religious Education in the Small Membership Church;* D. L. Griggs and J. M. Walther (1988), *Christian Education in the Small Church;* L. E. Schaller (1993), *44 Steps Up off the Plateau.*

Small Group, Youth. Interactive gathering of approximately three to twelve students that is intentional in purpose and relational in context. Small groups for youth often have a leader who is an adult or an older peer. The small group context is a valuable asset to the education of Christian youth in many ways. It provides a context for relational intimacy that may be absent in home or community, an opportunity for students to understand and practice the interconnectedness of the Body of Christ, a forum where youth can begin to integrate beliefs and scriptural truth with their worlds, and a means of being mentored, discipled, and held accountable. Small groups are particularly appropriate for adolescents because they provide a place where they can begin to wrestle with identity issues—for it is in the presence of others who complement each other in making up the body of Christ that the most accurate picture of individual identity can be discovered (Gorman, 1993, 19).

Youth ministries and Christian education programs have used many types of small groups to meet their educational and ministry goals. There are discipleship groups, which have as their primary focus growing into the likeness of Christ through Bible study, accountability, and prayer. There are also discussion groups, which focus on getting students to talk about various issues and

may be used as an adjunct to other programming. Evangelistic small groups which are apologetic in nature provide an opportunity for non-Christian teens to explore their questions about the Christian faith. Peer counseling groups and special support groups are groups that allow for special care and healing. Finally, leadership groups focus on developing leadership qualities in students necessary to share their faith and serve their peers (Sundene, 1997, 654). Small groups may be short term in nature (such as a small group formed for the length of a summer retreat) or long term (such as a discipleship group led by an adult leader which may last a year or years in length).

Important elements of the most common type of small group for youth, the discipleship or Bible study group, have been identified as: quality biblical content, development of community among group members, the opportunity for active, self-discovered learning, an emphasis on application and progressive life change, and the eventual ability for outward impact (Hove, 1995, 18–21). Other elements that must be considered when forming small groups for adolescents are age and gender. It is important to weigh differing developmental levels and abilities in students when determining the ages to be represented in a small group. Placing students in same-gender groups may enhance safety in disclosure and facilitate less distracted learning, especially in early adolescence. Mixed gender groups assist students in developing healthy relationships with the opposite gender.

JANA SUNDENE

Bibliography. J. Gorman (1993), *Community That Is Christian: A Handbook on Small Groups;* R. Hove (1995), *Leading a Small Group: The Ultimate Road Trip;* J. Sundene (1997), *Reaching a Generation for Christ,* pp. 651–69.

Small Group Deviant. Group member who is viewed by other members as being substantially different from the others in some significant manner. Two common examples of deviants are group members who do not actively participate in group activities or discussions, and those who tend to disagree or express incompatible views about issues (Brilhart and Galanes, 1995, 259). Generally, members try to encourage deviants to conform to the thinking of the group through four stages of pressure: reason, seduction, coercion, and isolation (Tubbs, 1995, 159).

While deviants are often viewed as being contrary or abnormal, and tend to make the group feel uncomfortable, they do play a potentially valuable role in the small group in at least three ways. First, deviants can account for a considerable portion of group interaction, as their disagreements or challenges encourage other group members to critically think through and reflect on their own positions. Second, deviant opinions and ideas, when expressed in an articulate and sensitive manner, can help a small group make better decisions. Third, deviants contribute through creativity. Creativity, by its very definition, is deviance, and creative minds are often needed to solve problems or introduce new and better ways of doing things (Brilhart and Galanes, 1995, 260; Griffin, 1982, 191–93). Deviants can be detrimental to the functioning and ongoing development of a group when they withdraw or intentionally block group goals for self-centered reasons.

HARLEY ATKINSON

Bibliography. J. Brilhart and G. Galanes (1995), *Effective Group Discussion;* E. Griffin (1982), *Getting Together;* S. Tubbs (1995), *A Systems Approach to Small Group Interaction.*

See also SMALL GROUPS

Small Groups. In 1982 the Lilly Foundation first reported that more people participate in some form of religious small group than attend Sunday school. Since that time the numbers of people in small groups have continued to expand.

Foundation and Size. It is likely that the small group is a generic form of human community. Icenogle (1994) suggests that the small group is a transcultural, transgenerational, and transcendent reality. God as Being exists in community. It is a natural demonstration of God's communal image for humanity to gather as a small group.

Bonhoeffer wisely emphasized that a small group experience is an expression of our common "life together." Our relationships with God through Jesus Christ and with one another are so closely interwoven and linked together it is difficult to separate the two theologically. Because of this, every believer is responsible to promote and practice genuine fellowship, and is corporately accountable to exhibit deep, caring concern for each other. We are interdependent on one another for personal spiritual growth and are to serve humanity in love. Increased recognition of these theological underpinnings has formed the bedrock upon which the small group movement has burgeoned in the past fifty years.

There is currently no uniform size for a small group. Most authors prefer to limit the amount from three to twelve, or from three to twenty (Hestenes and Gorman, 1993; Griffin, 1982). Nonreligious small groups allow for between two and thirty participants.

The distinctive characteristics of a small group may be more important than the specific size. A small group includes a face-to-face gathering of people to share in and to act for the betterment of one another and the broader good of others.

As such, the small group forms the primary vehicle for Christian ministry in a hostile world.

History. The use of small groups for religious growth and development, and for ministry is not a phenomenon unique to this era. Church antiquity is replete with vivid examples of small conclave care-support systems that emphasized interpersonal relationships, growth, and service. Baptists, Moravian Brethren, Methodists, Quakers, Lutherans, Benedictines, Teresa of Avila, the desert fathers of the second and third centuries, and many others all used small groups for spiritual growth, direction, and service.

Over the past fifty years outstanding leaders have included Sam Shoemaker (Faith at Work), Elton Trueblood (Yokefellows), Dawson Trotman (Navigators), Keith Miller (Laity Lodge), Bruce Larson and Wally Howard (Faith At Work), Lyman Coleman (Serendipity), Father Barry (The Franciscan Center), and Ken Haugk (Stephen Ministry). Notable special interest groups have been Parent Effectiveness Training, Marriage Encounter/Enrichment, Cursillo, Singles, Grief and Divorce Recovery, and the "Twelve Step" Programs.

Today every church has multiple types of groups. In some instances they are mainlined into the basic structure of the church. In other places they are optional add-ons for interested people.

Types of Groups. Many types of small groups are currently in vogue in the church. A representative sample includes the follwing:

1. *House Church Model.* Is a significant standard in many foreign countries. Its numbers have been increasing in North America. It attempts to embody all aspects of a New Testament church in a small group meeting in homes rather than in a church building. House churches may be single or federated together across a given area. Very useful in countries where direct proclamation of the gospel is prohibited.

2. *Evangelistic Group Model.* Attempts to be evangelistic in the group meeting(s), or to train group members in effective sharing of the gospel outside the group.

3. *Nurture Model.* Aims to provide a wide range of spiritual growth opportunities to believers. Multiple types are best in order to meet the variety of spiritual needs and commitment levels represented in a parish.

   a. *Level 101—Integrated Group.* Links the teaching on Sunday (either worship service or Sunday school class) to a small group during the week for application and support.

   b. *Level 201—Bible Study Group.* Focus ranges from understanding the content of the Bible, doctrine, or topic to engaging the Word for life application. May be inductive or deductive.

   c. *Level 301—Support-Growth Groups.* Targets members who are open to further commitment. Typical activities may include times of personal sharing, Bible study, prayer, and mutual support. May range from little to mild accountability through group covenant.

d. *Level 401—Discipleship/Spiritual Formation Group.* For highly committed people desirous of growing deeper in Christ. A closed group after covenant signing. Features intentional practice of select disciplines to enhance personal spiritual formation. Best when done for a designated time period with possibility of renewal. These may include spiritual gift training. Moderate to strong group accountability.

4. *Pastoral Care/Shepherd Group Model.* For church members or constituents. To provide care and general shepherding of the people. Often involves love and care for one another, experiencing fellowship, and encouragement/affirmation of group members. May provide a social mixer occasionally or address issues of concern associated with normative life cycle events.

5. *Ministry Group Model.* Primary aim is to provide service to others.

a. *Recovery Groups.* Targets people who are hurting. Provides mutual support or assistance to people having significant difficulties in their lives. Ground rules are carefully spelled out (may include termination date). Many use the "Twelve-Step" approach. Three areas dominate: abuse, addictions, or adult life crisis. Someone with life experience in the issue often makes the best leader.

b. *Advocacy Group.* To undertake a cause and champion its outcome to the church and/or community.

c. *Leadership Training Group.* This type targets the 27 percent of the population having leadership abilities and gifts. It aims to motivate, equip, and encourage individuals to manage boards, committees, or coordinating teams in an efficient and Christlike manner.

d. *Service/Task Force Group.* To cooperatively accomplish a designated ministry or service. May be short-term (elective or single event) or ongoing (regular and routine).

It is important that leadership provide a "community/care" dimension to each ministry team as 50 percent of those serving in a task group will not join a traditional fellowship cell.

Many small groups defy the above delineations. For example "Cell Groups," patterned after Cho or Neighbors, often try to be evangelistic and nurturing at the same time. Such hybriding has worked in some locations, but not in all. It is generally better to be specific about the group's purpose.

From the beginning humanity has struggled with maintaining integrity of community with God and with one another. Small groups, while not a panacea for the church, hold great potential to provide a focused demonstration of God's reconciling movement through Jesus Christ.

JAMES A. DAVIES

Bibliography. J. Gorman (1992), *Community That Is Christian;* E. Griffin (1982), *Getting Together;* R. Hestenes (1983), *Using the Bible in Groups;* G. W. Icenogle (1994), *Biblical Foundations for Small Group Ministry;* N. McBride (1995), *How to Build a Small Groups Ministry.*

See also RECOVERY MINISTRIES

Small Groups and Children. Small groups in the traditional sense of the term are not typically used with children. The reasons for this are developmentally based. Often small group materials are dependent on a discussion format. Active learning methods are used more frequently than discussion methods with children. In addition, small groups encourage self-disclosure and children are not likely to be able to engage in this process due to their social, cognitive, and emotional developmental stage.

If an understanding of small groups is broadened, then children's Sunday school and other traditional programming which organizes children in groups of eight to twelve could be considered an effective, age-level, appropriate use of small groups with children. Some curriculum materials encourage children to move into small groups briefly for reflection, discussion, or accomplishment of an assignment.

Another effective use of groups with children is the support group. Groups facilitated by a professional counselor have been effectively used to aid children in crises such as divorce or grieving the loss of a loved one. These groups are similar to support groups formed for youth and adults, but may use play therapy or other age-level appropriate counseling techniques.

A final type of small group present in children's ministry is the discipleship group. These are baptismal classes for children in churches which practice believer's baptism. Other discipleship groups encourage upper elementary children to begin to read their Bibles, journal, and pray. These groups may have a certain level of accountability present which is focused on encouraging children to be consistent and to live out the commitments they have made in their spiritual journey.

DENISE MUIR KJESBO

Smart, James D. (1906–82). Canadian pastor, theologian, lecturer in Christian education, and author. From 1944 to 1950, he was chief architect and first editor in chief of *The Christian Faith and Life Curriculum: A Program for Church and Home,* a curriculum development project for the Board of Christian Education of the Presbyterian Church (USA). After his involvement in the curriculum project, he returned to the pastorate in Toronto, where he also taught Christian education at Knox College. After serving his Toronto parish for a number of years, he taught biblical interpretation at Union Theological Seminary, New York.

Smart's involvement with curriculum forced him to think through the theological foundations of the church's educational program and eventually he penned his thoughts in a highly influential book *The Teaching Ministry of the Church* (1954). While writing from a Presbyterian perspective, Smart was relatively conservative and the book jolted the liberal church considerably. He accused the religious education movement of the first half of the twentieth century of being much happier to have its roots in secular education than in church tradition. Christian education literature was marked by the absence of any serious theological investigation. Consequently, he asserted, schools for training education directors were strong in educational subjects but weak in subject matter related to Bible and theology. Training programs for church school teachers were effective in answering questions of methodology but vague and ineffective when dealing with theological issues related to the gospel or to the church.

Smart argued for a recovery of the unity between Christian education and theology. As such, he insisted that on one hand Christian education be given a rightful position in the total structure of theology, and on the other hand that Christian educators return to an emphasis on theology and biblical content in the work of church education. Among his prescriptions for a revitalization of church education were: (1) a serious emphasis on Christian education beyond childhood; (2) a centrality of the Scriptures in curriculum; (3) a reconsideration of the place of Christian education in theological disciplines as well as the stature of theological disciplines in schools of education; and (4) an aim for education that regains its evangelizing power.

He was the author of numerous scholarly and popular works and his writings significantly impacted a generation of pastors, Christian educators, theologians, and seminary students who otherwise viewed Christian education as a discipline with little future. Other books by Smart include *What a Man Can Believe* (1943), *The Recovery of Humanity* (1953), *The Rebirth of Ministry* (1960), *The Interpretation of Scripture* (1961), and *The Creed in Christian Teaching* (1962).

HARLEY ATKINSON

Bibliography. K. Cully (1965), *The Search for a Christian Education—Since 1940;* S. Little (1961), *The Role of the Bible in Contemporary Christian Education;* J. Smart (1954), *The Teaching Ministry of the Church.*

See also THEOLOGY OF EDUCATION

Smith, H. Shelton (1893–1987). American professor of religious thought. Born in McLeansville, North Carolina, he pursued an undergraduate degree at Elon College and graduated in 1917. While a student at the college, he was ordained in the First Congregational Christian Church in Durham. Following service in World War I, Smith completed a B.D. degree and a Ph.D. degree from Yale University in 1923. During those years Smith was greatly influenced by John Dewey and George Albert Coe. Upon graduation, Smith became director of the International Council for Religious Education. He left that position in 1928 to join the faculty at Columbia University and then went to Yale in 1929. In 1931 he went to Duke to develop a program in religious education. Along with religious education, he taught Christian ethics and American religious thought. In 1945 he assumed the position of James B. Duke Professor of American Religious Thought. He never again returned to religious education. Rather, he established the Ph.D. program in religion at Duke and continued to direct that program until his retirement in 1962.

In the 1930s Smith wrestled with the issues that emerged from the liberal theological position. He had espoused that position during his studies at Yale and in his long association with the International Council on Religious Education and his other teaching positions. However, after careful reflection he came to the conclusion that he would either have to turn away from Christianity and adopt the philosophy of Dewey or reject the church.

In 1940, Harrison Elliott, professor of religious education at Union Seminary in New York, published a book, *Can Religious Education Be Christian?* Elliott proposed that one did not have to adopt the theology of Barth and Brunner. Rather, given his definition of a Christian, it would be possible to remain a Christian. Smith had read a prepublication copy of the manuscript.

The publication of *Faith and Nurture* in 1941 forced theorists and practitioners alike to rethink the theological underpinnings of Christian education. It signaled a departure from the dominant liberal perspective in religious education programs in colleges and seminaries. While Smith left the construction of a new theology to those who followed him, his writing stimulated new directions for the field. Instead of religious education based on the speculations of Dewey and Coe, the new approach demanded a firm theological foundation.

The writing of H. Shelton Smith marked a major change in the thinking of religious educators. Smith never returned to follow up the issues raised by the publication of his study. While his book *Faith and Nurture* made an important contribution, many conservative Christian educators have wished that he would have gone much further.

EDWARD A. BUCHANAN

See also COE, GEORGE A.; DEWEY, JOHN; THEOLOGY OF EDUCATION

Social Cognitive Theory. Bandura's (1977) social cognitive theory posits that societal norms may be appropriated. Through the cognitive, behavioral, and environmental process called observational learning, appropriate or inappropriate social behavior is learned.

Observational learning is conveyed through modeling (Bandura, 1977). The learner must "(1) observe the model's behavior, (2) retain what has been observed, and (3) have the skills needed to reproduce the model's behavior, but must also (4) perceive the consequences of the model's actions as desirable or reinforcing" (Wren, 1991, 58). Retainment of the model's behavior is achieved through the process of encoding, along with the mental ability to think hypothetically (Wren, 1991).

By observing consequences such as reward and punishment, behavior is reinforced, and this reinforcement provides information and motivation which, in turn, strengthens the behavior. The rewards or punishments which are observed by the learner serve as social cues which inhibit or disinhibit the behavior (Bandura, 1977).

Models can be influential in altering behavior as they provide the learner with social cues or social prompts. The more status a model has, the more his or her cuing function is enhanced (Bandura, 1977, 1986).

A model who demonstrates desired activities over and over, who instructs observers to follow the behavior, who prompts them verbally and physically when they fail, and who then rewards them when they succeed, will eventually evoke matching performances (Bandura, 1986, 69). Pastors, ministers, leaders, parents, teachers, and peers are examples of those who serve as models.

Modeling is useful in many important arenas. For example, for children in the home and school who are learning appropriate sex-role information, modeling is a major conveyer of information. "Social cognitive theory posits that, through cognitive processing of direct and vicarious experiences, children come to know their gender identity, gain substantial knowledge of sex roles, and extract rules as to what types of behavior are considered appropriate for their own sex" (Bandura, 1986, 97).

Modeled gender roles alone do not prompt individuals to adopt what has been modeled. "Both the valuation of certain attributes and roles and the eagerness to adopt them are strongly influenced by the value society places on them" (Bandura, 1986, 97). Since children are largely influ-

enced by the beliefs and attitudes of their teachers who may be perceived as representatives of society, it is important that values conveyed in the classroom are in keeping with standards which have been set in the home.

Adolescents also learn through modeling. Through the community—school, church, and neighborhood—modeling provides a sense of values that the adolescent uses as part of his or her decision making process. Again, the school-setting is vital in communicating acceptable behavior. Media is particularly influential. Teenagers determine their life goals largely by the influence of role models.

Peer influence is based on the approach that peer pressure is a major factor in abusive or risk-taking behaviors among adolescents. Teaching teens refusal and coping skills are effective interventions. Social inoculation programs which teach how to be abstinent, for example, are successful in reducing teenage pregnancy as they have been in reducing other risk-taking behaviors such as smoking (Rotheram-Borus, Mahler, and Rosario, 1995). "Behavior that violates prevailing social norms brings social censure or other punishing consequences, whereas behavior that fulfills socially valued norms is approved and rewarded" (Bandura, 1992, 108). Personal change "occurs within a network of social influences. Depending on their nature, social influences can aid, retard, or undermine efforts at personal change" (Bandura, 1992, 108). In areas involving responsible behavior, an environment conducive to social cognitivism includes peer support, leaders who demonstrate effective coping skills, and a system of rewards as reinforcement (Rotheram-Borus et al., 1995).

In the church setting, positive peer pressure is very effective with youth programs stressing Christian values. Discipleship or small groups which focus on accountability help youth identify aspects of their lifestyle which are contrary to biblical principles and are hence, unacceptable to their peers. Sharing honestly, keeping journals, and working with team or youth leaders who demonstrate their commitment by giving the gift of time are examples of ways to reinforce godly behavior.

LaVERNE A. TOLBERT

Bibliography. A. Bandura (1977), *Social Learning Theory;* idem (1986), *Social Foundations of Thought and Action;* M. J. Rotheram-Borus, K. A. Mahler, and M. Rosario, *AIDS Education and Prevention* 7 (1995): 320–36; T. E. Wren (1991), *Caring about Morality.*

See also OBSERVATIONAL LEARNING

Social Darwinism. Social philosophy articulated in the later nineteenth and early twentieth centuries which extended principles of biological evolution to that of social development. Social selection is believed to operate in the same manner as that of natural selection in nature, during which the unfit are eliminated. The fundamental principle of Social Darwinism then is that only the strongest should survive. This belief is used as an argument for laissez-faire capitalism including limiting interventions by government and abstaining from relief for the poor and the weak. Individualism, individual rights, self-interest, and sharp competition are legitimized. Social Darwinism stands in contrast to socialism.

There is less connection between Charles Darwin (1809–82) and "Social Darwinism" than the name of this theory would imply. In 1852 (seven years before Darwin's *Origin of the Species*) the British social philosopher Herbert Spencer (1820–1903) compared the development of societies to that of organisms. It was he who used the term "survival of the fittest" while Darwin employed the more subtle and complex idea of "natural selection." Darwin actually expounded social and moral conclusions quite opposite to the those of Social Darwinism (Heyer, 1982, 18). John Dewey would more naturally embrace Darwin's position rather than that of Spencer. To Dewey, people live in a social as well as a purely physical environment. Group life tends to promote the desire for survival by providing security. Dewey rejected Spencer's attempt to apply competitive ethics to society (Gutek, 1974, 111–12). Spencer was popular in the United States and other sociologists such as the Americans William Graham Sumner (1840–1910) and Lester F. Ward (1841–1913) developed variations of Social Darwinism.

Sumner (1963) argued that there were two realms of survival. First, humans contend with nature for the provision of our needs ("the struggle for existence"). But because nature does not usually provide enough for all, people then have to contend with each other for the limited resources "the competition of life" (37). Some of the competition would be within the group, but inevitable and necessarily there would be war among groups. Social Darwinism has been used as a legitimating ideology for state sponsored mass murder by the Nazis and others in the twentieth century (Rubenstein, 1983, 85).

Social Darwinism provides a valid description of the human condition to some extent. But its prescriptions are in contrast to the kingdom of God at nearly every point. In the Sermon on the Mount (Matt. 5–7). Jesus extolled the merciful, recognized the almsgiver, warned the contentious and greedy, and taught that God was not limited in ability to provide through various means the necessities for all. Social Darwinism fails to take into account the providence of God and the biblical mandate to love our neighbors as ourselves.

PAUL BRAMER

Bibliography. P. Heyer (1982), *Nature, Human Nature, and Society;* G. L. Gutek (1974), *Philosophical Alternatives in Education;* W. G. Sumner (1963), *Social Darwinism: Selected Essays;* R. R. L. Rubenstein (1983), *The Age of Triage.*

Social Gospel. Term growing out of tensions that developed in the mid–1800s and early 1900s regarding the mission of the church. Seeing the injustice that had taken place in many communities across America, the church felt an urgent need to minister to those who were oppressed, poor, homeless, and destitute. This attitude, together with a desire to win the lost to Christ, contributed to a dilemma. Which need was most important, spiritual or physical?

Some felt that the best approach was simply to evangelize the lost and leave other less important matters to community relief agencies. Others, pointing to biblical references such as Matthew 25:31–46 and James 1:27, believed the church had a moral and ethical obligation to do more than simply preach to the lost. One such individual was a Congregational minister by the name of Washington Gladden (1836–1918), who developed a reputation for defending the rights of the working-class poor. He encouraged them to form labor unions at a time in American history when there was significant strife between capitalistic ideology and labor interests. For this, he became known as the "Father of the Social Gospel."

Social gospel theology led inspired churches to begin programs to feed the homeless, clothe the poor, visit prisoners, educate the disadvantaged, and many other noble causes. However, when the focus of their causes became their main purpose and evangelism was seldom if ever presented, then the church program was said to have fallen victim to a social gospel approach to ministry.

There is a balance to be found in both concerns. Indeed, the church is obviously called to evangelize the lost but it is also called to be the incarnational character of Christ to a lost and needy world. Jesus' own example of meeting the needs of those around him in a holistic manner should be ours as well.

MICHAEL J. ANTHONY

Bibliography. L. F. Cross and E. A. Livingston (1997), *The Oxford Dictionary of the Christian Church;* E. L. Towns (1995), *Evangelism and Church Growth.*

Socialization of the Child. Process of teaching and enforcing group norms and values to new group members. According to social cognitive theory, social behavior, learned through the cognitive, behavioral, and environmental process called observational learning, is conveyed through modeling. Children imitate adults who model behaviors, perform tasks, and express attitudes and values. By observing consequences such as reward and punishment, which inhibit or disinhibit, behavior is reinforced. The judgments of parents, teachers, and peers can be influential in altering behavior through the provision of social cues or social prompts. The more status a model has, the more his or her cueing function is enhanced.

The home, school, and religious institution are environments where socialization of the child occurs. In the home parents are the child's primary role models, shaping the child's values and establishing boundaries for those behaviors which are acceptable or unacceptable. Children come to know their gender identity and gain substantial knowledge of sex roles through parental modeling and valuation.

The teacher is the child's next role model. As an authority figure, the teacher imparts new information, guidelines, and standards, hopefully reinforcing what has been learned in the home. Cooperation, honesty, acceptance of differences, fair play, and learning for intrinsic rewards are examples of "lessons" that are as important as reading, 'riting, and 'rithmetic. These lessons cannot be learned in isolation. The presence and involvement of others provide the child with social cues and appropriate reinforcement. The importance of the school as a social learning environment is underscored because the school also provides the context of moral standards, situational ethics, and values. As the child enters adolescence, the school becomes an extension of the peer group to form the peer environment.

The church or religious institution contributes to the spiritual and psychoeducational development of the child. Within this institution, the child is again provided with role models in the teachers and peer models in the students. The collective partnership of the home, school/community, and church is vital to the child's socialization process.

Activities that contribute to the socialization of the child are sports or athletics, youth groups, clubs, gender-specific groups such as Boy Scouts and Girl Scouts, drill team, choirs, and specialized groups such as drama, music, dance, or scholastic clubs. Learning the value of caring for others through such tasks as volunteering or baby-sitting are also important in the socialization process.

LaVerne A. Tolbert

Bibliography. B. M. and P. R. Newman (1991), *Development Through Life: A Psychosocial Approach.*

Socialization of Youth. The process of socialization, when considered in the context of adolescent development, speaks of how one's values, attitudes, beliefs, and behaviors are shaped through the shared experiences of a teenager's life community. While socialization is not limited to any particular age group, the heightened social awareness of teens makes this a particularly powerful element in their overall formation process.

Social contexts shape everyone, and the junior high and senior high school years contribute richly to this process. Each person's personal sociodevelopmental tools are dramatically initiated during the adolescent years. While youth workers may project certain personal experiences as generally normal, they may also hold to unwarranted assumptions about the particular socialization each teen goes through. For example, not everyone has a first kiss during the adolescent years, feels intimidated by older students, or struggles with fitting in—as common as these experiences may be. The savvy youth minister will approach each social context in which he or she ministers as an ethnographic researcher, seeking to uncover the socialization particulars for the teens under his or her care. Important forces of influence (i.e., socialization) must be understood if a youth worker is to be effective in the transformational agenda assigned by the Lord Jesus Christ.

Persons who have worked in a variety of high school contexts will note that each school has its own culture. On the surface, there are distinctions between urban and suburban, small town and rural. Racial attitudes can be different. The sophistication of kids' experiences may also vary from school to school, as does the level of tolerance for persons who deviate from norms. Some schools have an enthusiastic unity. Fractured, dissimilar interest groups compose other schools.

It is largely because socialization is such a dynamic reality that some Christian educators have suggested that the church must do a better job at tapping into the formative power of this nonformal process (Richards, 1968; Westerhoff, 1976). Recognizing this educational strength has led others to evaluate anew the role of families in their youth ministry efforts (DeVries, 1994). Why is socialization so educationally substantive—and attractive—to Christian educators? The answer begins with an understanding of the ambitious nature of the goals of Christian education.

Because the church's mandate is not simply to instruct for understanding but to teach for obedience, it is useful to examine how educational experiences become transformational. When learning is truly *important to* and thoroughly *integrated with* a young person's present life circumstances, it will have a maximum impact. Teens move through a developmental transition during adolescence that has them shifting their highest conferred significance from their parents' opinions to those of their friends and peers. If the expectations of adults diminish in their importance during teen years, it is easy to understand why attending to socialization-as-shaping is critical for youth ministry effectiveness. When it is also understood that integration is easier if learning is connected to one's natural life patterns then it is easy to see why harnessing socialization for Christian formation among teens has a strategic ministry appeal.

What does youth ministry look like if socialization is a centralized strategy with adolescents? There is a disciplined effort on the part of adults to move into the world of their teens. These forays make possible a dynamic interaction that, when paired with the truth of Scripture, informs the ministry and curriculum employed. This heightened awareness helps youth ministers to create intentional faith-shaping communities among teens. Great effort is given to ensure that the youth ministry is socially safe for a teen's involvement. Peer leadership strategies are embraced. A climate of respect, love, and encouragement is developed.

How does a youth minister increase understanding of the socialization forces? A useful two-step process begins with determining the facts of teenage social life in a community. Where do kids hang out? When are they there? What do they do? Who spends time with whom? What are the various interest groups in the school and who are the chief influencers within each group? The wider and more varied the angles on this data collection, the better the opportunity to be accurate in assembling a larger picture of teen social activity. The second step is to try to learn what all the data mean to a variety of different teens. The goal of this step is to see the facts of the relevant social context through adolescent eyes, uncovering the meaning that the various social activities have for the teens in the community. This can be done through informed, observation-based questions, inviting teens to open up about their world. Many youth ministers find this a great agenda to pursue in individual or small group appointments.

Eventually these new insights about adolescent social life must be filtered through the mission, vision, and focus of one's particular youth ministry. When this is done, youth ministry practices have a chance to increase their relevance as they are influenced by the socialization patterns in the community. Such socially responsive youth ministries can soon enjoy an enhanced role in the socialization process of their young people, resulting in the creation of a healthy ministry effectiveness cycle.

DAVE RAHN

Bibliography. A. Campolo (1989), *Growing Up in America: A Sociology of Youth Ministry;* M. DeVries (1994), *Family-Based Youth Ministry;* R. R. Dunn and M. H. Senter III, eds. (1997), *Reaching a Generation for Christ;* L. O. Richards (1988), *Christian Education: Seeking to Become Like Jesus Christ;* J. Westford III (1976), *Will Our Children Have Faith?*

Social Psychology. *See* Identity Foreclosure.

Society. *See* Culture.

Sociology of Religion. Discipline encompassing the fields of both of its parent disciplines, the study of sociology and the study of religion. It studies the moral values and beliefs from a variety of religious and ethnic groups, as well as the contribution religion makes to society, and it reflects upon the sociological study of denominations and their membership.

The study of religion and sociology as interdisciplinary fields began in the late nineteenth century with the work of Auguste Comte (1798–1857), considered the founder of the discipline of sociology. He believed that the manner in which a person perceived the world was the basis of social organization. As the way in which one's view of the world changed from theological, with events explained in terms of the individual's relationship to the supernatural, to what he termed "positivistic," whereby one seeks answers in scientific and practical ways apart from the supernatural, so too, he believed, would the social order change.

Aside from early work by Karl Marx (1818–83), which reflected on class struggle and religion, two of the most influential theorists in the sociology of religion are Emile Durkheim (1858–1917) and Max Weber (1864–1920). Durkheim is best known for his *Elementary Forms of Religious Life,* in which he argues that the ideas of sacred and secular are fundamental to a society and that religion is the name given to these expressions of cohesion and order. He was primarily concerned with what religious belief does within a society. Weber claims that religious concepts and commitments have a formative effect on social structures. Contrasted with Durkheim, Weber was much more concerned about what happens to religion in the midst of social change. His most celebrated work appears in English as *The Protestant Ethic and the Spirit of Capitalism,* in which he observes an apparent connection between Protestantism and capitalism. A major contribution made by Weber was his systematic analysis of cultural traditions from the perspective of a sociologist.

Adding to the body of literature in this century, one would include authors such as Ernst Troeltsch, who considered the differences between church and sect and is known for his work *The Social Teaching of the Christian Churches,* Richard Niebuhr's *The Social Sources of Denominationalism,* and the American sociologist Peter Berger, whose work includes writings on religion and American cultural life.

The Christian educator who desires to reflect on the role of sociology within the framework of religion can find many examples for study in the lives of students, such as their cultural and religious values, racial and ethnic heritage, and societal demographics.

ELIZABETH A. LEAHY

Bibliography. R. Homan, comp. (1986), *The Sociology of Religion: A Bibliographical Survey;* B. Wilson (1981), *Religion in Sociological Perspective.*

Socratic Method. Socrates claimed not to know enough to teach, yet in the dialogues of Plato, he continually asks questions of his colleagues, seeking to apprehend concepts such as love, justice, and virtue. The Socratic method is teaching by asking questions. Along with the concept of universal definition, it has been considered Socrates's greatest contribution to humanity.

Socrates framed his own thoughts step by step and then looked for agreement from his companion in the dialogue. Though this person typically followed along, one of them, Meno, confessed to feeling bewitched by Socrates. His penetrating questions often exposed inconsistencies in their thinking. In fact, Socrates was executed for being an atheist and corrupting the youth of Athens who emulated him in cross-examination.

While any teaching method based upon questioning could be considered Socratic, modern applications of this ancient mode of teaching are the various forms of the small group discussion. Discussions range in format from completely undirected buzz groups or rap sessions to the seminar which has a specific topic and purpose. Discussions involve asking open-ended questions, questions that require more than a simple yes or no answer, from asking for an opinion or basic information to deeper questions of meaning and application. The latter can make seminars particularly powerful when dealing with issues and ideas.

The ability to ask thoughtful questions is an art that can lead to profound learning experiences. Asking questions forces students to think, to analyze in such a way that they reach conclusions for themselves rather than having them spoon fed. Articulating an answer requires a further learning process of sifting through thoughts, prioritizing, organizing, and synthesizing them into a coherent answer. The discussion leader then has the opportunity both to challenge and refine students' answers so that they are held with a greater degree of certainty.

The Socratic method corresponds with contemporary thought regarding the principles of andragogy. Andragogical theory views the learner as a resource possessing knowledge and life experience which enhance the learning situation when utilized. In small group discussions learners benefit from the insights of many rather than just the teacher.

Despite the popularity and strengths of the discussion format, it is not always the most appropriate method. Malcolm Knowles (1990), a leading proponent of andragogy, points out that when there is a lack of knowledge, experience, or motivation on the part of the learners, more "traditional" models are preferable. Nevertheless, when used appropriately, the Socratic method enables Christian educators to go beyond teaching at the surface level to plunge deeply into "the weightier provisions of the law: justice and mercy and faithfulness" (Matt. 23:23).

DOUGLAS FALLS

Bibliography. M. J. Adler, ed. (1984), *The Paideia Program: An Educational Syllabus*; M. Knowles (1990), *The Adult Learner: A Neglected Species*; K. Lee-Thorp (1998), *How to Ask Great Questions*; Plato (1872), *The Dialogues*, vols. 1–4.

Sodomite. *See* Homosexuality.

Solitary. *See* Loneliness; Single Adults.

Solitude. Act of drawing apart from the external world to a spiritual place where one meets God. It involves intentionally leaving the state of "being available" to the demands of the outside world and moving to a state of mind and heart in total surrender to and communion with God. It is not the same as the human desire for privacy or a time of quiet. It involves silence and active listening, with a heart listening to God. Solitude is not the same as loneliness. "Loneliness is inner emptiness. Solitude is inner fulfillment" (Foster, 1978, 84).

History contains numerous examples of men and women seeking solitude as a means of communion with God. Jesus maintained a regular, intentional moving into solitude for communion with God. As a result he lived an inward "heart solitude" that expressed itself outwardly in his unique ministry. In like manner, Christian educators must model and speak of this enriched personal aspect of Christian formation.

Solitude is a spiritual discipline to be taught. It requires a "leaving behind of one's many activities, concerns, plans and projects, opinions and convictions, and entering into the presence of our loving God, naked, vulnerable, open and receptive" (Nouwen, 1979, 27–28). Because of this vulnerability, many spiritual writers speak of encountering the "dark night of the soul" in solitude in which one comes face to face with one's true self, devoid of pretense and falseness (St. John of the Cross, 1964, 34). Solitude thus becomes the "furnace of transformation. It is the place of conversion where the old self dies and the new self is born" (Nouwen, 1981, 14–15). In this place of solitude "we come to know the Spirit who has already been given to us. The pains and struggles we encounter in our solitude thus become the way to hope, because our hope is not based on something that will happen after our sufferings are over, but on the real presence of God's healing spirit in the midst of these sufferings" (Nouwen, 1979, 43). "Settle yourself in solitude and you will come upon God in yourself" (Teresa of Avila).

Solitude paradoxically incorporates community. Dietrich Bonhoeffer best describes this integration: "Let him who cannot be alone beware of community. Let him who is not in community beware of being alone. One who wants fellowship without solitude plunges into the void of words and feelings, and one who seeks solitude without fellowship perishes in the abyss of vanity, self-infatuation, and despair" (1952, 77, 78). If one possesses inward solitude one will fear neither being alone nor being with others. In the midst of noise and confusion there is a settled, deep inner silence, a state of mind and heart allowing one to freely interact with the world and its clamor of demands, while providing a place of separateness where one's inner being is grounded in the presence of God. Foster counsels, "We must seek out the recreating stillness of solitude if we want to be with others meaningfully. We must seek the fellowship and accountability of others if we want to be alone safely" (Foster, 1978, 85).

The fruit of solitude is increased sensitivity and compassion for others. "In solitude we become compassionate people, deeply aware of our solidarity in brokenness with all of humanity and ready to reach out to anyone in need" (Nouwen, 1981, 20, 25).

DIANNE WHITING

Bibliography. J. Beumer (1997), *Henri Nouwen: A Restless Seeking for God;* D. Bonhoeffer (1952), *Life Together;* R. Foster (1978), *Celebration of Discipline;* H. Nouwen (1979), *Clowning in Rome: Reflections on Solitude, Celibacy, Prayer, and Contemplation;* idem (1981), *The Way of the Heart;* St. John of the Cross (1964), *The Collected Works of St. John of the Cross.*

See also LONELINESS; SINGLE ADULTS

Son City. Son City had its origins in 1972 at a youth program which began at South Park Church in Park Ridge, Ill. Although they originally focused on the development and edification of believers, Dave Holmbo and Bill Hybels wanted to begin targeting the friends of these churched youth who did not know Christ. They began to teach a series on evangelism and later created a weekly event targeted at unchurched kids. They held a second meeting during the week for believers.

After explaining this new strategy to the students, the youth group voiced their support. The plan was put in place and they kicked off a series with John Ankerberg teaching together with contemporary drama and music. Hybels continued the teaching and, over the next six months, the group experienced phenomenal success.

This Wednesday night outreach program became known as Son City while the believers' meeting was called Son Village. A singing group named Son Company provided much of the fine arts support. Week after week, series after series, the Son City service plainly but creatively presented the power of the gospel and the truth of Scripture with songs, drama, small groups, and relevant, life-changing messages. Students were coming to Christ and being connected to smaller groups for friendship, support, discipling, and care. Core believers were challenged to shepherd groups of newer students who had recently become Christians. Leaders emerged among the students, games and fun programs were designed to create a sense of joy and excitement, and young people were challenged to be intentional about their faith in Christ. Soon there were twice as many youth attending the church as adults! Little did they know at the time that this unique model of contemporary youth ministry would form the basis of the ministry philosophy for Willow Creek Community Church a few years later in 1975.

BILL DONAHUE

Sonlife Ministries. Presently headquartered in Elburn, Ill., seeks to train church leaders in the biblical method of ministry utilized by Jesus Christ. Begun in 1979 with a primary focus on youth ministries, Sonlife now is oriented toward targeting the entire ministry of the local church. They intentionally pursue the guiding objectives of their mission statement: to restore to the heart of the local church Great Commission passion. In essence, Sonlife Ministries is deeply committed to developing mature disciples of Jesus Christ as well as equipping church leaders and laypersons with the principles of discipleship as Jesus taught them.

Sonlife's founder and Executive Director, Dann Spader, wrote, "We passionately believe that without a strong Christology you end up with a distorted ecclesiology. As the modern church measures itself against the instruction of its founder we must return to a biblical balance in our disciplemaking."

Spader's personal passion for equipping church leaders began during his undergraduate years at Moody Bible Institute. It was there that he began an extensive study of how Jesus created a disciplemaking movement. After graduating from Moody in 1975, Spader served several stints in local churches as a youth pastor. But it was in the context of writing his Doctor of Ministry degree project at Trinity Evangelical Divinity School that he formulated the underlying principles and strategies that would guide Sonlife's ministry to local church leaders.

When Moody Bible Institute noted Spader's early efforts to create a movement to multiply disciples, they hired him to begin a ministry intentionally designed to train others. Ten years later, as the ministry grew, Spader left the auspices of Moody to set up Sonlife Ministries as an independent organization. Today Spader serves as a consultant to a wide variety of church denominations in the area of youth and church leadership. He has also authored numerous books and training manuals as well as produced several training videos.

Spader contends that Jesus' life modeled the three balanced priorities of making disciples:

- Introducing the lost to Christ;
- Establishing believers in their faith with a deepening knowledge of their Savior; and
- Assisting equipped workers to multiply this process.

This process of discipleship, Spader affirms, will produce individuals who are uniquely equipped to live the powerful life God's Son provided—the "Sonlife." Spader further argues that "this simple, biblical purpose becomes the evaluation standard for effectiveness. When any church is not essentially linked to the process of making disciples—we must make changes."

Annually, over 30,000 church leaders experience some aspect of Sonlife training. The ministry has grown into a complete series of training seminars designed to equip local church leadership. Such seminars are endorsed and supported by numerous church denominations. Presently Sonlife's leadership seminars are offered in over 200 venues in North America as well as internationally. There are international divisions of Sonlife currently in such diverse locations as Canada, Eastern Europe, Central America, and Australia. Sonlife has also produced a wide variety of training and support tools to facilitate their equipping process.

Currently, Sonlife Ministries offers a wide variety of training seminars such as the following two options:

Growing a Healthy Church Seminar—Training for church leaders in twelve essential components in Jesus' ministry designed to produce a balanced local church ministry. Through a seven-hour lecture and small group interaction format, participants learn how to implement Christ's philosophy of ministry in their own local church regardless of the church's size, tradition, or style of worship. A seventy-page manual is included. Sonlife also provides several other levels of advanced training in their Growing a Healthy Church seminar series.

Growing a Healthy Youth Ministry Strategy Seminar—An eight-hour overview of Christ's methodology for moving students through the process of becoming lifelong disciples. This seminar targets both volunteer and professional youth workers. Sonlife offers several other advanced seminars that supplement their training in youth ministry principles, including seminars that are designed specifically for student leaders.

SCOTT W. BENSON

Sorrow. *See* Grief; Recovery Ministry; Widows/Widowers.

Span of Control. Number of individuals a manager can reasonably and effectively supervise. The size of the span can have a profound impact on the organization and also on the relationships of those under the leader's control. It has been noted by previous studies that as the number of people (span) grows, the number of interactional relationships between members increases at an extremely rapid rate. This effect can contribute to increased levels of miscommunication and organizational frustration.

The recommended number of people that a leader should have reporting to him or her has been the subject of considerable debate among management researchers. Students of management have found that this number is usually four to eight subordinates at the upper levels of the organization and eight to fifteen at the lower levels.

The ideal number depends on a number of factors. The most critical issue is how much time the leader has available to spend in direct supervision of his or her subordinates. A narrow span (few subordinates) may allow for closer working relationships, better training, clearer communication, and increased levels of control. A wider span (larger numbers of subordinates) may allow for a broader range of options for delegating work responsibilities, more controlled rates of change within the organization, and a larger sphere of influence over the entire organization.

In a church context, the senior pastors may find that they are not able to balance the many demands placed on them in a rapidly growing church. The many hours required for sermon preparation conflict with the pastoral needs of counseling, visitation, staff relations, financial oversight, and a host of other important issues. These demands, in turn, can create a major source of pastoral anxiety. To alleviate this stress, many senior pastors have created a new role known as the *executive pastor*, which enfolds many of the managerial responsibilities of the senior pastor into this position. This action allows the senior pastor to reduce her or his span of control to a few selected individuals while delegating the larger responsibilities to this new associate.

MICHAEL J. ANTHONY

Bibliography. B. Bass (1981), *Stogdill's Handbook of Leadership;* H. Koontz and H. Weihrich (1990), *Essentials of Management.*

See also ADMINISTRATION; LEADERSHIP; MANAGEMENT; ORGANIZE

Spiraling. J. S. Bruner thought that children of different ages learned new materials on different levels. Therefore he suggested that teachers should present information on a subject in modes appropriate to the age of the learner. The young child learns in the *enactive mode*, perceiving the world as what can be acted on touched, tasted, manipulated, and so forth. Older children can deal with ideas through the use of pictures and other representations, a mode Bruner called the *iconic mode*. Still older children can deal with ideas represented by symbols like words and formulas, a mode Bruner called the *symbolic mode*. Realizing then, that nearly any subject could be taught to any age child as long as the material is age-appropriate, Bruner said that curriculum should spiral, touching a subject again and again as the learner matures in understanding increasing complex information (Biehler and Snowman, 1993). Bruner said, "A curriculum, as it develops, should revisit these basic ideas repeatedly, building upon them until the student has grasped the full formal apparatus that goes with them" (Bruner, 1960, 13). Math is taught in this spiraling manner. In religious education, preschoolers are taught the simple Bible thought, "God loves you." Older children can look at and talk about an artist's rendition of Jesus blessing the children. An adolescent learns to explain the meaning of the terms sacrifice, crucifixion, and redemption. Each learns about God's love in a spiral curriculum approach.

WALTER H. NORVELL

Bibliography. J. S. Bruner (1960), *The Process of Education;* R. F. Biehler and J. Snowman (1993), *Psychology Applied to Teaching,*

Spirit. *See* Demons.

Spiritual Body. *See* Church.

Spiritual Direction/Director. The aim of spiritual direction is to discern God's presence in one's life. That God is present and active always in our lives is a given. However, the problem is that we often find it difficult to notice, identify, or understand the activity of God in us. We also find it difficult to distinguish God's voice from other voices (e.g., the voices of culture, parents, needs and wants, aberrant desires, compulsions). We do not notice or understand what it is to which God is calling us. A spiritual director is a companion on the way with the gift of discernment, who assists us in the exploration of our inner, spiritual lives so as to enable us to respond to God in concrete ways.

Within the context of spiritual direction one seeks not only to nurture an awareness of God but also to develop those practices that keep one alert to and in touch with the presence of God (spiritual disciplines). This often involves learning new ways of prayer (e.g., daily prayers of examine) and Bible reading (e.g., *lectio divina*). In addition, spiritual direction involves seeking to discern the path God is calling one to take at various junctures in the spiritual pilgrimage when choices must be made.

Margaret Guenther calls spiritual direction "holy listening" in which a director brings presence, attentiveness, theological insight, and spiritual maturing into an encounter with a directee. In fact, as she and others assert, there is also a third party present in direction sessions: the Holy Spirit. The goal of the director is to assist the directee in discerning the gentle presence of the Spirit in his or her life.

Spiritual direction is not psychotherapy (though certain counseling skills such as active listening are used). Nor is it pastoral counseling in which the aim is to help "fix things" (though insight which leads to growth may emerge). It is not deep friendship where there is a mutuality. The director as a person vanishes into the background with all the attention on the directee (except in the case of what is called "spiritual friendship," in which two people take turns serving as directors for one another). It is not even "direction" in the sense of a mentor giving a novice information and advice about the spiritual life. Rather, spiritual direction is a kind of prayer encounter between two people. The aim of spiritual direction, in the end, is prayer in its broadest sense: to discern those prayers the Spirit is leading the directee to pray and to live out a life that is rooted in conscious awareness of God.

Spiritual direction has become deeply appealing to people these days because this is one relationship in which people are free to talk about God. Most people have few opportunities, if any, to explore the spiritual side of life openly and directly. Furthermore, this conversation about God is not philosophical or theoretical. It is deeply personal. Its aim is to grow one's relationship with God. That which moves people to enter into spiritual direction is the desire to know God better. Their hope is that the spiritual may more and more pervade their daily consciousness.

Spiritual direction can take place in groups as well as individually. In fact, given the increasing demand for spiritual directors, small group direction may become more and more common simply because there are not enough individual directors to go around (Dougherty, 1995). Generally a trained director guides such a small group. However, the group itself also plays an active role in the process.

The same challenges that confront individuals when it comes to discerning God's voice in their lives are present within Christian communities. What is God calling this community to do and be at this point in time? The process of discernment for a community is not dissimilar to discernment for individuals. However, the challenge is to draw in a variety of voices to this discernment process.

Charles Olsen and Danny Morris suggest ways in which communities can engage in such a process, including using an extended worship service as a means of discernment.

Spiritual direction has a long history in the church. It might even be argued that the roots of spiritual direction are found in the relationship between Jesus and the small group of men whom he called to be apostles or between Paul and the various individuals (such as Timothy) to whom he gave guidance. However, it was during the fourth to the sixth centuries when spiritual direction as we know it emerged. Following the Christianization of the Roman Empire in the fourth century, many Christians fled to the desert, being appalled at the rapid secularization of Christianity. Over time other Christians sought out these "desert fathers and mothers" for spiritual advice and the practice of spiritual direction was born. During the Reformation there was a reaction against spiritual direction and the view of spirituality it represented (which was thought to be works-based and not grace oriented). However, in the twentieth century many Protestants are rediscovering the power of spiritual direction.

While there is great benefit to the rediscovery of this ancient way of discernment, there is also danger. For one thing, spiritual direction may become trendy so that having a spiritual director is like having your own therapist: something that gives the impression of being particularly "holy" when, in fact, it simply allows us to dabble in the spiritual without the hard work of commitment and discipleship. Or the danger may be that spiritual direction is seen as "magical," an impression one might gain from popular portrayals of the process in a book like *Glittering Images* by Susan Howatch (New York: Knopf, 1987).

Key to this whole process is the spiritual director. A spiritual director is one who has traveled some distance in the Christian way and finds that he or she has the gift of discernment. While there are an increasing number of programs to train spiritual directors, this gift is discovered rather than taught. A spiritual director is one who finds people drawn to him or her for guidance. Furthermore, such guidance has the ring of truth to it that authenticates the gift.

The demand for spiritual directors should grow now that the Protestant world has rediscovered the gift of discernment. The challenge for Christian educators will be to explore ways to meet this felt-need. Some Christian education directors will want to obtain training and offer spiritual direction as part of their jobs. Of course, the number of people one director can see is limited so it will be necessary to explore other avenues by which direction can be offered. A good alternative which fits well with Protestant experience is to offer small group spiritual direction. Another alternative is to develop discernment groups following the Quaker model that will help individuals who seek to know God's mind related to specific issues (Farnham, 1991). Some churches will want to develop ways for the church as a whole to discern God's will, especially when major issues are concerned (Osborn and Morris, 1997).

RICHARD PEACE

Bibliography. W. A. Barry and William J. Connolly (1982), *The Practice of Spiritual Direction;* L. Bryne, ed. (1990), *Traditions of Spiritual Guidance;* R. M. Doughty (1995), *Group Spiritual Direction: Community for Discernment;* S. G. Farnham, J. P. Gill, R. T. McLean, and S. M. Ward (1991), *Listening Hearts: Discerning Call in Community;* M. Guenther (1992), *Holy Listening: The Art of Spiritual Direction;* D. E. Morris and C. M. Olsen (1997), *Discerning God's Will Together: A Spiritual Practice for the Church.*

Spiritual Disciplines. Exercises carried out on a regular basis by individuals or groups in order to make habitual certain actions and attitudes that open one up to God or express a way of life given over to God. For example, everyone acknowledges that prayer is a central activity in one's spiritual life. However, most people struggle to pray and when they do pray often lapse into certain rituals or forms of prayer. To approach prayer as a spiritual discipline is to build into one's life specific times for prayer; it is to explore and use new ways of prayer; and it is to learn to be conscious of an ongoing conversation with God in the midst of daily life. By means of this discipline, prayer moves from the periphery of life to its center.

In other words, the aim of the spiritual disciplines is to create space for God in our lives. They are a way to acknowledge our commitment to Jesus by seeking on a daily basis to make his Way our way. They are a way to respond to our hunger for God by opening up our lives to the world of Spirit in which we live but which we may not notice except on rare occasions.

It is important to remember, as Dallas Willard (1998) reminds us, that practicing spiritual disciplines is not a mark of exceptional piety; it is a sign of need. Had we mastered the skill in question we would not have to practice it; it would be habitual and part of our core personality. However, the disciplines are not ends in themselves; they are means to an end and that end is transformation into the image of Christ. The spiritual disciplines are not ways to earn God's favor; they are ways of putting us into a place where we are aware of God and open to God's power and presence.

There is no single list of all the spiritual disciplines. Different authors categorize the spiritual disciplines in different ways. For example, in *The Celebration of Discipline*, Richard Foster (1988) identifies twelve disciplines which he groups into three categories: the inward disciplines (meditation, prayer, fasting, and study); the outward disciplines (simplicity, solitude, submission, and service); and the corporate disciplines (confession, worship, guidance, and celebration). Foster's groundbreaking book is widely credited with sparking a renewal of interest in the spiritual disciplines on the part of evangelical Christians. Foster's mentor, Dallas Willard, divides the disciplines into two categories: the disciplines of abstinence (solitude, silence, fasting, chastity, secrecy, sacrifice) and the disciplines of engagement (study, worship, celebration, service, prayer, fellowship, confession, submission).

Marjorie Thompson (1995) and Simon Chan (1998) urge us to develop a "rule of life." "A rule of life is a pattern of spiritual disciplines that provides structure and direction for growth in holiness" (138). It is a way to develop a rhythm for daily life that keeps us in touch with the spiritual.

One of the key tasks of the Christian educator is to create various programs that enable individuals to learn and practice spiritual disciplines. The skills of the Christian life are not learned quickly (nor, in some cases, easily) so the challenge for the individual is to find sufficient time in which to engage in this learning process. Here is where small groups can be useful. While it is unlikely that most Christians will be able to live for extended periods of time in a monastic setting where such skills are traditionally acquired; it is possible for most people to schedule a weekly small group session that focuses on spiritual disciplines. The aim of such small group meetings is to explore various aspects of the discipline in question, to practice this skill during the group session, and to hold one another accountable for working on this skill during the week between small group sessions. Small groups have the added advantage of making the acquisition of such skills part of the community life together and not just an individual exercise. Richard Peace (1998) has designed small group materials to teach spiritual disciplines.

RICHARD PEACE

Bibliography. S. Chan (1998), *Spiritual Theology: A Systematic Study of the Christian Life*; R. J. Foster (1988), *Celebration of Discipline: The Path to Spiritual Growth*; R. Peace (1998), *Spiritual Journaling*, rev. ed.; *Spiritual Autobiography*, rev. ed.; *Contemplative Bible Reading*, rev. ed.; and *Meditative Prayer*; M. J. Thompson (1995), *Soul Feast: The Invitation to the Christian Spiritual Life*; D. Willard (1998), *The Spirit of the Disciplines: Understanding How God Changes Lives*.

Spiritual Gifts. There are four major New Testament references to spiritual gifts: Romans 12:6–8; 1 Corinthians 12:4–11, 27–31; Ephesians 4:11–16; 1 Peter 4:8–11. Based on the above Scriptures, we can make several observations.

1. Spiritual gifts are given by God through the Holy Spirit. The source is God; the resources are God's to give; the power to use the gifts comes from God; the purpose of the gifts is to build the church in love and unity. We are stewards of God's gifts to us. We are not given spiritual gifts to make us proud or superior or to make other people feel inferior.

2. God gives spiritual gifts according to his sovereign will. He chooses what gifts to give and to whom. God gives us spiritual gifts graciously; they are not earned nor are we entitled to them. Spiritual gifts are part of the showering of grace from God who in mercy called us to be his children. They are unearned, unmerited, and unconnected to our worthiness; they are connected only with the grace of God. We do not decide on our spiritual gifts; we recognize them in ourselves and in others. Gifts may be lifelong or temporary. God determines how long the gifts are to remain. Gifts are spiritual gifts only as they convey the grace of the Lord. The expectation is that each will use his or her spiritual gift(s) for the glory of God and for the upbuilding of the body of Christ so that the church can carry out its functions in this world.

3. There are diverse spiritual gifts. The reason for the differences is to provide various functions for believers to perform in the church and world. We need diversity in spiritual gifts in order for the church to function effectively. We cannot all be teachers or pastors. But the church needs all the gifts from the Holy Spirit. All the spiritual gifts are important. The body of Christ functions best when all parts fit together well and articulate together. One part is not more important than another even though one part may have a more prominent position in the body. All are vital. The Holy Spirit does not squander spiritual gifts nor does he give meaningless or frivolous gifts.

4. It may well be that the Spirit does not give just one isolated gift to an individual. Rather, he gives multiple, interconnected gifts in the measure that the Spirit determines. The result could be that one may have some measure of being a teacher plus a greater measure of encouragement and mercy. This sort of person would make a good counselor. Other believers could well have various measures of other gifts that qualify them for various responsibilities both in the church and in the world. In most cases, a person would need more than one gift in order to carry out one's calling.

5. We need to be wary. Some actions can appear to be a spiritual gift, but can actually be counterfeit. (See Matt. 7:21–23—prophecy, casting out demons, and miracles in Jesus' name do not automatically equate with spiritual gifts.) There are many validated instances of what Christians would call spiritual gifts being demonstrated by non-Christians. We must remember that outward manifestations of power are not associated only with God! Nor are spiritual gifts in themselves the sign of true spirituality. Spiritual

gifts are nothing compared to the fruit of the Holy Spirit. The Holy Spirit is more interested in our producing spiritual fruit than in our production of spiritual phenomena. It is unfortunate that the church has been buffeted with dissension over spiritual gifts. The Sovereign Lord gives what he wants and to whomever he desires. The task of the church is not to judge the validity of the gifts, but to affirm the Giver and the use of the gifts for the work of the ministry of Christ. What hubris allows members of the church to say what the Holy Spirit can and cannot do?

6. We are required to identify our spiritual gifts, develop those gifts, deploy them, and continue to enhance them. It is the task of Christian leaders to help other believers do this and to encourage others to do the same. Christian leaders help others to identify their spiritual gifts through various means. Some people have developed various "spiritual gifts inventories" that purport to help Christians pinpoint their spiritual gifts. These may be useful for some people. However, each of these inventories has a set of assumptions about the definitions of the various spiritual gifts in the New Testament that are not necessarily valid. Great caution should be exercised in using these inventories.

A better approach is for believers to ask themselves and their local fellowship some questions.

1. What needs exist in your environment—in your family, local church, city, world? Assumption: God will give someone, perhaps you, the spiritual gifts necessary to help meet these needs. Ask God what part you should take in helping to minister and serve.

2. What do you think the Holy Spirit is calling you to do? Assumption: The Holy Spirit has given each Christian at least one spiritual gift. He wants you to exercise your spiritual gifts for Christ in the church and world. You are open and sensitive to the leading of the Holy Spirit in your life. After you determine your gifts and the Spirit's direction in the use of the gifts, you will obey him.

3. Would you naturally choose what you think the Holy Spirit is telling you to do? Assumption: Usually the Holy Spirit will not lead us to do what we have no inclination to do, no liking to do, no skills, and no sensitivity about.

4. What natural talents, interests, abilities, or inclinations do you have already that God would normally use to begin with? Assumption: Usually the Lord starts with us where we are, not with trying to completely change our natural inclinations and interests. He starts with natural talents, natural interests that he gave us to begin with, and adds supernatural abilities as he wills.

5. What do you already do well? Assumption: What you do well already is probably an indication of some sort of gift from God. All that you are and have is from God. The Spirit may grant you additional gifts, but that is his decision, not yours. You start with what you know about yourself and develop from there.

6. What gifts do others in the body of Christ see in you? Assumption: The Holy Spirit does not work with us in isolation from the other members of the body of Christ. Others are given insight into our giftedness and we into theirs as means of checks and balances against our "old flesh" and the normal overuse of one gift. We need to help each other to be honest to God. So ask others what they think your spiritual gifts are.

7. What gifts do you seem to have? Decide this by prayer, asking God to make clear to you what your gifts are. Ask others what they think your spiritual gifts are.

8. Develop and deploy your spiritual gifts throughout your daily life: work, home, church, city, world.

The church is a charismatic, spiritually gifted community not dependent on one or two particular gifts or a few gifted people. All Christians should consider themselves as gifted by the Third Person of the Trinity! Having been gifted, we are to use those gifts for Christ and his rule in the church and the world.

JOHN M. DETTONI

See also CHURCH; COMMUNITY; MINISTRY; SIGNS AND WONDERS; TEACHING, GIFT OF

Spirituality. Spirituality is a term that is widely used today. However, it is one of those words that everyone knows (like *love*) but no one can define precisely because it carries such a wide range of meanings. For example, the word *spirituality* is used when discussing the discipline of prayer, the practice of voodoo in Haiti, the *Spiritual Exercise* of Ignatius of Loyola, the presence of angels, New Age organic gardening and holistic health care programs, appearances of the Virgin Mary, Zen meditation, as well as the books of M. Scott Peck (*The Road Less Traveled*), Teresa of Avila (*The Interior Castle*), Thomas Moore (*Care of the Soul*), and James Redfield (*The Celestine Prophesy*). In other words, once the word is invoked in conversation it is necessary to clarify just what it means to the person using it lest there be a fundamental misunderstanding.

Generally, however, when the word *spirituality* is used it has to do with experience related to transcendent reality. The emphasis is on *experience*. Experience is set over against ideas about God or religious communities that worship God. In fact, in the minds of many people today *spirituality* is distinguished from *religion*. *Religion* refers to doctrine and institutions, to the objective and external. *Spirituality* refers to individual practices and experiences, to the subjective and internal. Furthermore, spirituality is often seen as good whereas religion is some times seen as restrictive and, at times, in opposition to spirituality.

In this context it is well to be reminded of the wholistic vision of Friedrich von Hügel in *The Mystical Element of Religion*. He contends that the religious dimension in human beings is expressed in three ways: via the institutional (where our quest for the sacred is given shape, rendered visible, made concrete, and sustained over time), via the intellectual (by which we reflect critically on our search, convey our findings to others, and critique our experience), or via the mystical (which is the experiential dimension of the spiritual life) (Downey, 1997, 23–35).

Spirituality describes the quest for God. As such it involves the attitudes, actions, and beliefs associated with the human search to know and experience God (or supernatural reality in some form). Thus spirituality is all about prayer and the other spiritual disciplines; it is about spiritual direction and the other means afforded us within the religious communities to follow the way of spiritual pilgrims who have gone before us; it has to do with the devotional life and the life of worship whereby we acknowledge along with others in the community of faith the reality of God.

There is a second way in which the term *spirituality* is used. Spirituality is understood to be an innate characteristic of human beings. At our core, in the depths of our being, at the place where our true self exists we can and do meet God. Spirituality refers to the human capability for self-transcendence. We have been created by God in such a way that we have the capacity to know and experience God. To be engaged in a spiritual quest is to explore those means and methods that put one in touch with the depths of one's own being where one touches God.

In light of these general definitions of spirituality it is important to identify the distinctives of Christian spirituality. To talk of Christian spirituality is to talk of the Holy Spirit. In the New Testament, the words *spiritual* (*pneumatikos*) and *spirit* (*pneuma*) are the closest biblical terms to the word *spirituality*. When Paul uses the term *spiritual* he is describing that which is guided by the Holy Spirit. Paul sometimes contrasts a spiritual person to a natural person (1 Cor. 2:14–15). When he does this Paul "is not describing the spiritual dimension of the person, or the soul as an invisible and intangible reality, in contrast to the material dimension or the body of the person. Rather, he is distinguishing the person as a unified being who is moved by the presence and action of the Holy Spirit, in contradistinction to the person unaided by this gift" (Downey, 1997, 60). "Christian spirituality refers most fundamentally to living the Christian life in and through the presence and power of the Holy Spirit" (49). Sandra Schneiders defines Christian spirituality as "personal participation in the mystery of Christ begun in faith sealed by baptism into the death and resurrection of Jesus Christ, . . . nourished by sharing in the Lord's Supper, which the community celebrated regularly in memory of him who was truly present wherever his followers gathered (see Matt. 18:26), and . . . expressed by a simple life of universal love that bore witness to life in the Spirit and attracted others to faith (see Acts 4:32–35; 1 John 1; and elsewhere)" (McGinn and Meyendorff, 1987, 2).

The term *spirituality* is, in fact, relatively new. Even though the word *spiritualitas* can be traced back to the fifth century, it was not used much until the seventeenth century when it came to refer to the interior life and was used as a term of reproach, describing practices thought to be irrational, enthusiastic, and unorthodox. The sense of reproach was dropped in the eighteenth and nineteenth centuries when spirituality referred to the practices of the Christian life such as prayer or fasting. This "pursuit of perfection" was often understood to be a task reserved for a few monks, nuns, and priests and beyond the capability of the lay person. In fact, it was not until the mid–1960s that spirituality came to be widely used as a way of talking about religious practices as over against doctrine (Jones, Wainwright, and Yarnold, 1986, xxv). Today it is possible to talk about interest groups or causes in terms of spirituality (e.g., small group spirituality, marriage spirituality, and single life spirituality) or to distinguish between spiritualities organized around different theological interests such as Jesuit spirituality (which is "active"), Carmelite spirituality (which is contemplative) and Protestant spirituality (which is personal) (Chan, 1998, 15, 20).

The current interest in spirituality can be traced as much to social factors as to theological conversation. In the 1940s, the horrors of World War II brought a renewed interest in God (e.g., the writing of Thomas Merton). Then during the 1960s the first postdeterministic generation, the baby boomers, became fascinated with the reality of the spiritual and reasserted itself in a return to the Christian church. In the 1990s there was a widespread interest in spirituality along with a growing disinterest in religion (Wuthow, 1998).

It is important for the Christian education director to be aware of the deep yearning on the part of people today to know God. The search for the sacred has become central in many lives and is present in most lives. The church needs to respond in creative ways to this contemporary longing for God. Even as we do so we need also to be aware of the hesitation many have about religion (even while valuing spirituality). So the challenge for the Christian education director is to create learning environments in which people can explore the spiritual in ways to promote growth. This might involve small groups in which people learn about various spiritual disciplines while practicing them together. It might involve regular retreat programs where the focus is on silence and prayer and not activity and lecture. A book study group might explore the writings of mystics such as Julian of Norwich (*Revelations of Divine Love*), Thomas à Kempis (*The Imitation of Christ*), or Thomas R. Kelly (*A Testament of Devotion*). In addition, the Christian education director can assist other staff members in adding a focus on spirituality in their ministries. The choir, for example, could explore the teachings of Bernard of Clairvaux about divine love as they prepare to sing "Jesus, the Very Thought of Thee" or "Jesus, Thou Joy of Loving Hearts."

RICHARD PEACE

Bibliography. L. Bouyer, J. Leclercq, and F. Vendenbroucke (1982), *A History of Christian Spirituality* 3 vols.; S. Chan (1998), *Spirituality Theology: A Systematic Study of the Christian Life;* M. Downey (1997), *Understanding Christian Spirituality;* L. Dupré and D. E. Sailers, eds. (1991), *Christian Spirituality: Post-Reformation and Modern*, volume 18 of *World Spirituality: An Encyclopedic History of the Religious Quest;* C. Jones, G. Wainwright, and E. Yarnold, eds. (1986), *The Study of Spirituality;* B. McGinn and J. Meyendorff, eds. (1987), *Christian Spirituality: High Middle Ages and Reformation;* G. S. Wakefield, ed. (1983), *The Westminster Dictionary of Christian Spirituality;* R. Wuthow (1998), *After Heaven: Spirituality in America since the 1950's.*

Spiritual Maturity. Quality of being fully developed in spirit. For the Christian this development entails, more specifically, being conformed to the image of Christ. Christian spiritual maturity must be understood paradoxically; it is something we are, while being at the same time something we are not. It is a gift of grace given at our new birth, and yet we are called to grow into maturity through sanctification.

The language of sanctification has its scriptural roots in the Old Testament. In Leviticus 19:2 and 20:26, we are introduced to the call to sanctification. This is the call of holiness, to be set apart for God's use. This idea is utilized in 1 Peter 1:15, 16, where Christians are called to be holy, for God is holy. The Great Commandments of Matthew 22:37–39 state clearly the call and goal of Christian spiritual maturity: to love God with all our heart, soul, and mind, and to love our neighbor as ourselves. This quality of love is not something we have at new birth; it is something that must grow in us.

Paul's letters give us further insight into a scriptural understanding of spiritual maturity. It is clear from his writings that we are called to mature as Christians. Ephesians 4:11–16 is an important passage with regards to illustrating Paul's concern that we as Christians grow in our love of God. The goal to be attained is nothing less than the full stature of Christ. In Philippians 3 Paul again calls us to press on toward maturity. Clearly his usage of maturity here illustrates its twofold nature; maturity as both a gift and a goal. In Romans 12 we are called away from conformity to this world to transformation in Christ. Maturity for Paul has concrete implications for daily life. The maturing Christian loves others and shows preference for others over self. The maturing Christian exhibits an increasingly virtuous character. Galatians 5 speaks of the fruit of the Spirit as being love, joy, peace, patience, kindness, goodness, faithfulness, gentleness, and self-control. These are patterns of being which give evidence that the Holy Spirit is working in the life of the believer and are indications of maturation in the Christian life.

Maturity in the Christian life is characterized by several features. First, it manifests itself in cognitive, emotional, and behavioral change. To be maturing implies that we are growing in our love of God and neighbor through our intellect. Our minds must be renewed through study and good thought. The maturing believer also shows evidence of growth in the affective domain. Along with the fruit of the Spirit, the virtues of faith, hope, and love (1 Cor. 13:13) become more clearly exhibited in the maturing believer. Maturity also requires that one's emotions are becoming more disciplined. This does not imply a denial of emotions, but an awareness of one's emotions so that the destructive effects of negative emotions are minimized. Maturity implies that the believer's behavior is becoming more Christlike. The love of God and neighbor is exhibited in concrete and tangible ways. This typically entails a life which is less influenced by the things of the "world"—greed, lust, covetousness, and so forth—and more by a life of simplicity and peace.

Second, maturity in the Christian life is characterized by both personal and social holiness. A personal, private devotional life is essential to maturity. Maturity requires introspection, prayer, and meditation. A disciplined reading of Scripture is also considered essential to maturity in faith. Worship of God within the Christian community is central to our growth; we cannot grow in isolation. Practices of personal piety must also be accompanied by practices of social piety. The love of neighbor must manifest itself in concrete acts.

Third, maturity in the Christian life is understood developmentally. Paul speaks to this when he encourages Christians to no longer be infants, but to grow up. Maturity in faith is understood in relationship to our place in the human life-cycle. Certain ways in which it is appropriate for a child to speak of God would not be appropriate for an adult. This kind of maturity is not, however, something that develops in clearly defined intervals, but something that starts and stops based upon the contingencies of life.

The variety of Christian traditions brings complexity to our understanding of maturity. The Reformed tradition reminds us that our salvation is a gift of grace and to be careful not to be tempted into believing we can save ourselves. This tradition accentuates the importance of grace and tends to be less than optimistic about our ability to grow away from the constraints of sin. The Wesleyan/Methodist tradition reminds us of the need to be responsible for the grace freely given to us. John and Charles Wesley emphasized the need to grow in the love of God, or as they might say, to be perfected in love. This tradition emphasizes the need to actively practice personal and social holiness in order to mature. Both traditions are necessary to a complete understanding of maturity in the Christian life. The Reformed tradition keeps us centered on grace and the Wesleyan tradition reminds us to be responsible with that grace and to cooperate with the Holy Spirit as he works in our lives.

Beginning in the mid–1900s the social sciences became influential in defining spiritual maturity. Disciplines such as psychology began to contribute to our understanding of the nature of persons and therefore the direction of personal growth. Building on the work of Erik Erikson, Lewis Sherrill (1954) describes Christian growth as a life-long journey. Psychologist Gordon Allport (1957) writes of the characteristics of mature religion by drawing from the insights of humanistic models of psychology. More recently, developmental psychology has reminded us of the stages of growth toward maturity and the interrelationship of our cognitive, emotional, and physical growth with our spiritual growth. Most particularly, the work of James Fowler (1981) describes the trajectory of faith toward full participation with God. One of the dangers of incorporating the insights of psychology into our understanding of spiritual maturity is the possibility of importing non-Christian views of human nature into that understanding. Some popular psychological models assert that the goal of human maturity is self-actualization while the Christian view seeks to move beyond a preoccupation with the self. Some may also question the description of the mature stages of theories, such as James Fowler's, as to their theological claims. Nevertheless, our understanding of maturity in the Christian life has been helped greatly by these insights.

Currently there seems to be a desire to return to the insights of the early church to assist our understanding of spiritual maturity. Writers such as Richard Foster (1988) remind us of the rich heritage we have to draw on as a result of those who have gone before us.

Spiritual maturity means giving all I know of myself to all I know of God. This is a lifelong process of growing with God that is drawn forward by God's grace.

LES STEELE

Bibliography. G. Allport (1957), *The Individual and His Religion;* R. Foster (1988), *Celebration of Discipline;* J. Fowler (1981), *Stages of Faith: The Psychology of Human Development and the Quest for Meaning;* L. Sherrill (1954), *The Struggle of the Soul.*

Spiritual Retreat. Sustained period of quiet, uninterrupted time for one to be reflective and receptive in God's presence. The human heart has an intense desire to connect with God. While it is often difficult within the unrelenting activity of one's life to be quiet and ponder scriptural truths, a spiritual retreat offers a time to leave daily concerns, to connect with one's spiritual self, and to be attentive to the needs of one's soul. Many people seeking retreat time will identify a retreat center or a specific geographical place that offers an atmosphere conducive to this quiet reflection. "There must be [in a dynamic formational Christian life] a lived dialectic of contemplation and action, withdrawal and response, and this calls for actual physical places in which the contemplative dimensions of our lives can be nourished and strengthened" (Leech, 1989, 26).

The overall purpose of a spiritual retreat is to be transformed (in whatever manner God chooses). "In adult Christian education we need to give high priority to cultivating the experience of silence and solitude" in order to develop men and women of spiritual depth and insight (Leech, 1989, 28). One needs to avoid the temptation to "go on retreat" with a structured agenda to be accomplished. To be open to God's transformation requires a willingness to abide in God's presence in silence and solitude, relinquishing control to God in patient waiting. Withdrawing to a place of spiritual retreat offers a time for nourishing one's centered life in God, a time to encourage an interior and continual sense of God's presence which will then be a constant reality in everyday life.

DIANNE WHITING

Bibliography. K. Leech (1989), *Spirituality and Pastoral Care.*

Spiritual Warfare. The concept of spiritual warfare has been often misused and misunderstood. It is not merely a metaphor for the struggle between an abstract idea of good and evil any more than it can be limited to a designation for a special ministry of confronting demons. Spiritual warfare is the recognition that Satan is real, his forces are at work in our world, and Christians are under a biblical mandate to stand firm against the enemy (Eph. 6:10–20). It is neither optional nor limited to certain specialists, but is an integral part of living for Christ in this world.

In a Christian's response to Satan's activity, denial and fascination are equally dangerous. The hazards of these two extremes were definitively expressed a generation ago by C. S. Lewis in his book *Screwtape Letters*. Here he exhorts believers to guard against two extremes: first, to disbelieve in the reality of demonic existence, and second, to develop an excessive and unhealthy interest in them. In either case, the believer is put at a disadvantage and Satan's hosts receive the high ground in battle.

Among believers who recognize the reality of spiritual warfare there is disagreement on the particulars of when and how demonic powers are to be engaged. One point of debate is the extent to which it is possible for a demon to influence or possess a believer. Another area of disagreement concerns the existence, identification, and engagement of territorial demons (demonic spirits associated with certain geographic regions). This is the type of spiritual warfare identified by C. Peter Wagner as Strategic-Level Spiritual Warfare (1991) and includes the practice of spiritual mapping to identify demonic strongholds.

Spiritual warfare is often neglected because Christians underestimate the enemy. First Peter warns believers, "Your adversary, the devil, prowls about like a roaring lion, seeking someone to devour" (5:8 NASB) and 1 John declares that "the whole world lies in the power of the evil one" (5:19 NASB). Even more dangerous is for believers to underestimate the army to which we have been called. This is not because of the cumulative total of the strength of the soldiers, but rather a reflection of the power and might of our commander in chief, the Lord God Almighty. "Greater is He who is in you than he who is in the world" (1 John 4:4 NASB). Our enemy has already been dealt a mortal blow at Calvary: "When He had disarmed the rulers and authorities, He made a public display of them, having triumphed over them through Him" (Col. 2:15 NASB).

In the practical application of the principles of spiritual warfare as outlined in Ephesians 6:10–20 there exists much misunderstanding. The first concerns the nature of God's armor. The elements the armor depicts are not mere propositions we affirm nor are they merely representative of our position in Christ. They must be put on and taken up. This armoring for warfare is not optional, the verbs to *be strong in the Lord* (v. 10) and *put on* (v. 11) are imperatives, commands that must be obeyed. The components of the armor cannot be chosen piecemeal, it is the whole, the *full* armor we are commanded to put on (v. 11). This armor is only available through a close, consistent, ongoing walk with God and apart from it, we cannot successfully engage the enemy in spiritual warfare.

Another area of misunderstanding is the identity of the enemy. Christians too often see the enemy as the one who commits a heinous crime, the dealer in illicit substances who poisons our youth, the mocker who belittles our faith, the person in a position of authority who advocates acceptance and toleration of things God has declared as sin, or the terrorist who callously throws away lives to make a statement. None of these people are the enemy, although they give him (Satan) free rein in their lives. They are victims of the enemy, the very ones Christ died to redeem. God makes it very clear who the real enemy is: "For our struggle is not against flesh and blood, but against the rulers, against the powers, against the world forces of this darkness, against the spiritual forces of wickedness in the heavenly places" (v. 12).

A further area of misunderstanding is the nature of the weapons God assigns to us. The only part of the military metaphor that depicts an offensive weapon is the sword, which is characterized as both "of the Spirit" and "the word of God" (v. 17). The weapon is not of us and is not human in origin, it is God's. We must devote ourselves to the knowledge, appropriation, and application of the Word of God to every area of our life. Our principal weapon for engaging the enemy is prayer. Prayer is the ultimate weapon in spiritual warfare (vv. 18–20). The battle is won as believers exercise prayer.

A final area of misunderstanding is the objective of the warfare. It is not to win an engagement with the enemy for the sake of the conquest. An army's objective is never merely to destroy the army of the enemy; it is always to conquer the territory and overthrow the ruling authority. The army of God can never be satisfied with winning an engagement with the enemy. Our objective it is to overcome the enemy that we might win our world for Christ. Paul is very specific as to the content of the prayer he seeks from the Ephesian church, "that utterance may be given to me in the opening of my mouth, to make known with boldness the mystery of the gospel, for which I am an ambassador in chains; that in proclaiming it I might speak boldly, as I ought to speak" (vv. 19–20). Spiritual warfare is not only an appropriate metaphor for our calling as Christians, it is the reality of that calling. The enemy is real, the battle must be fought, but Scripture teaches that for the believer, the victory has already been assured.

DAVID BECK

Bibliography. C. Arnold (1997), *3 Crucial Questions about Spiritual Warfare;* M. Green (1981), *I Believe in Satan's Downfall;* C. H. Kraft (1992), *Behind Enemy*

Lines: An Advanced Guide to Spiritual Warfare; C. S. Lewis (1962), *The Screwtape Letters;* E. Murphy (1992), *The Handbook for Spiritual Warfare;* P. Wagner (1996), *Confronting the Powers: How the New Testament Church Experienced the Power of Strategic Level Spiritual Warfare;* idem (1991), *Warfare Prayer.*

Spurgeon, Charles Haddon (1834–92). Known as the "Prince of Preachers," Spurgeon is remembered principally as one of the greatest Baptist preachers of the nineteenth century. Descending from a long heritage of God-fearing preachers, Charles Haddon Spurgeon was born on June 19, 1834, in Essex, England. His grandfather was convicted and jailed for attending a nonconformist meeting. Charles Spurgeon was especially proud of his ancestors' convictions and would prove to be made from the very same Puritan stock (Gertz, 1970, 4).

Early Beginnings. His life however had its uncertain beginnings. At the age of eighteen months, Charles was transferred to live with his grandfather, Rev. James. He was mothered by a devoted Christian aunt in this home for five years. Apparently his parents were under serious financial stress and were unable to care for the eight of seventeen children who survived infancy. After Charles's sixth birthday he returned home to live with his parents. His mother made sure that he was liberally exposed to the Scriptures and a godly lifestyle (Gertz, 1970, 7).

Of all the fond memories of Charles's young and formative years stands out one of great value to both him and those who knew him. It was the tender and constant prayers of his mother on behalf of his life. Eliza, low in stature and plain, would tirelessly pray over her firstborn son, Charles, that he would become a mighty man for God. Spurgeon himself remembers, "I have not the powers of speech to set forth my valuation of the choice blessing which the Lord bestowed on me in making me the son of one who prayed for me and prayed with me" (Day, 1884, 39).

At the age of seven, Charles was sent to boarding school and had before long outridden the intelligence of his teachers. He had an insatiable thirst for books and literature. Especially fond of *Pilgrim's Progress* he was said to have read this book over one hundred times before his death. He also possessed a fertile mind for memorization. He would memorize sections of Scripture or hymns on a daily basis. This would prove to be an invaluable benefit for him in later years (Allen, n.d., 11).

Spurgeon's conversion took place in Colchester at the age of fifteen while under the ministry of a Primitive Methodist local preacher, and four months later he was baptized in the River Lark. Shortly after this, he moved to Cambridge to attend school and while there he joined the St. Andrew's Street Baptist Church where he would be exposed to his first preaching experiences. For three years he served here until his fame brought him to the attention of the New Park Baptist Church in south London. He accepted this call at the age of nineteen (Woodbridge, 1988, 336).

It wasn't long before Spurgeon's outspoken and direct manner created a profound impression. Within twelve months, this boy-preacher of unprecedented style had drawn crowds where even standing room could not be attained (Allen, n.d., 27). The necessity of finding a larger place to meet landed Spurgeon's congregation in the Surrey Gardens Music Hall. On October 19, 1856, the first night in the new building, over 10,000 were in attendance. The people were so packed in that when a false cry of "fire" was shouted, panic took the lives of seven individuals (Woodbridge, 1988, 336).

It was in 1861 that Spurgeon's congregation moved to its permanent residence in south London, "The Metropolitan Tabernacle" built especially to house the large crowds attracted by C. H. Spurgeon's preaching (Woodbridge, 1988, 334). The building was Grecian in style (because the New Testament was written in Greek) and had permanent seating for 3,600 and room for 2,000 more to squeeze in. During Spurgeon's ministry at this church 14,460 were baptized and added to the church (Woodbridge, 1998, 337).

Ministry Years. Of the many wondrous words that have been so eloquently spoken by Spurgeon, these help characterize him like no other. Consider these words given in his first address to his congregation at the Metropolitan Tabernacle, "I would propose that the subject of the ministry in this house, as long as this platform shall stand and as long as this house shall be frequented by worshipers, shall be the person of Jesus Christ. I am never ashamed to avow myself a Calvinist; I do not hesitate to take the name of Baptist; but if I am asked what is my creed, I reply, 'It is Jesus Christ.' My venerated predecessor, Dr. Gill, has left a body of divinity, admirable and excellent in its way; but the body of divinity to which I would pin and bind myself for ever, God helping, is not his system or any other human treatise; but Christ Jesus, who is the sum and substance of the Gospel, who is in Himself all Theology, the incarnation of every precious truth, the all-glorious personal embodiment of the way the truth and the life" (Spurgeon, 1978, 3).

In this quote one finds a wealth of understanding regarding this man's spirituality and piety. To him life was about Jesus Christ alone and making him known. He was an evangelist/preacher by heart and giftedness. His desire to seek and save the lost is evident in all of his passionate writings. It was deep within his emotional being that Christ was the source of all and was indeed the One honored in the success of his life.

Certainly Spurgeon was human as well. Although he was the best-known and most popular preacher of the nineteenth century, he is said to be egocentric, doctrinally rigid, sometimes bullheaded, uncooperative, and often appealing to an anti-intellectual constituency (Duke, 1989, 73). He was also criticized for remarking that he smoked a big black cigar "to the glory of God." Later his picture was beginning to appear on tobacco packets. He responded, "When I have found intense pain relieved, a weary brain soothed, and calm, refreshing sleep obtained by a cigar, I have felt grateful to God and have blessed his name." However, Spurgeon was known to criticize others, for example, for attending the theater (Fant, 1976, 4, 5).

Spurgeon's character was what impressed people even more than his eloquence and sermons. His personal character is noted by his deep faith in a sovereign God, earnestness, and perseverance at all costs. Once when interviewing a student for the college he asked what the lad had thought he'd do if he failed in ministry. The young man responded that he didn't think of failure. Spurgeon responded, "That is good. There is no failure except to the faithless, and to think of failure is nearly a betrayal" (Gertz, 1970, 29).

Common themes in Spurgeon's meditations on God and in his prayer life include the issues of social injustice, poverty, faith, and perseverance. It is evident when one looks at his writings and sermons that he was more concerned with the condition of life, the purity of the gospel preached, the fundamental truths and doctrines preserved than his prestigious preaching position itself. Consider these words of Spurgeon on faith in prayer: "Look at my orphanage. To keep it going entails an annual expenditure of about ten thousand pounds. Only one thousand four hundred pounds are provided pounds that come to me regularly in answer to prayer. I ask God for the cash and he sends it, without my advertising or writing begging letters or canvassing in any way. In every direction I am constantly witnessing the most unmistakable answers to prayer. My whole life is made up of them" (Houghton, 1892, 872).

When Spurgeon prayed, his prayers were simple and almost childlike in confidence. He lacked the usual stereotyped phraseology common in public prayers and it is said from those who heard him pray that he had "entered into the very throne room of grace." Because of this sincerity, the people loved him and realized the geniuses of his nature and mission.

Theological Orientation and Life Application. Spurgeon took the Bible in its most logical and literal sense. When at the age of sixteen he read that the Bible taught baptism by immersion, he immediately vowed himself a Baptist. Likewise, he took literally the claims of not being controlled by wine or given to excess of alcohol. His hardest blows seemed to be aimed directly at condemning alcohol, a stand which was not popular in his day (Fant, 1976, 6). He also used his platform and notoriety to plead for humane treatment seeing all as equal in the eyes of God. Spurgeon's hard stand on slavery severely cost him his popularity in the United States. He boldly spoke out against slavery with these words: "Slavery is the foulest blot that ever stained a national escutcheon, and may have to be washed out with blood. America is in many respects a glorious country, but it may be necessary to teach her some wholesome lessons at the point of the bayonet" (Carlile, 1933, 159–60).

At the age of twenty Spurgeon wrote this to an editor of a secular paper: "I am neither eloquent or learned, but the Head of the Church has given my sympathy with the masses, love to the poor, and the means of winning the attention of the ignorant and the unenlightened. . . . God has owned me to the most degraded and off-cast; let others serve their classes; these are mine and them I must keep" (Travis, 1992, 29). Charles Spurgeon once said, "The Christian man should always be the helper of everything which promotes the health and welfare of the people. If all other hands be fast closed, the hand of the Christian man should be always open to relieve human necessity." He took this literally from Jesus' admonition to "love your neighbor as yourself," and even the most saintliest of believers took some care of the physical body and needs (Travis, 1992, 35).

He was interested in multiplying his ministry through the training of young men for the pastorate. He founded Spurgeon's College (also known as Pastors' College) and began to publish *Lectures to His Students*. In these, a series of witty and incisive lectures, Spurgeon presents a comprehensive overview of the preacher and his work. In chapters such as "Attention" and "The Faculty of Impromptu Speech" Spurgeon tells his students how to gain the ears of the audience, and although radical for the nineteenth century, communication skills of our day have proved them to be accurate (Fant, 1976, 11).

His example of a church-based approach to training pastors has been widely respected and modeled by other pastors since his death (Towne, 1995, 373). The magazine *The Sword and the Trowel* was a monthly publication which began in 1865. This included his sermons which now house over sixty-three volumes of original work, the greatest of any individual alive or deceased.

Theologically grounded as a strict Calvinist, his ideas of predestination and foreknowledge certainly had an impact on his practical ministry. For Spurgeon, the needs of human suffering preceded strategies for "impersonal scalp-hunting" approaches of some evangelists. If one believes that God has already "chosen" the elect, then the issues of evangelism are directed toward merely communicating truth instead of the urgency of gaining the masses and creating methods to convert the lost.

When the Metropolitan Tabernacle was in need of $20,000 to open, Spurgeon left a note posted to the door letting everyone know of the need in order to open the new Tabernacle free of debt. In less than five months, Spurgeon left another note, this one stating the following: "We the undersigned . . . desire with overflowing hearts to make known and record the loving-kindness of our faithful God. We asked in faith, but our Lord has exceeded our desires, for not only was the whole sum given us, but far sooner than we had looked for it. Truly the Lord is good and worthy to be praised" (Ford, 1884, 43).

Our perspective has been broadened by seeing how God continues to use the humble things and people of this world to confound the wise. Humans might not have chosen a common lad from England with such poor beginnings to have had such a mighty impact on the entire world. His name is known and so is his message worldwide—the message of Jesus Christ. Certainly, he would have been viewed by human standards as too young, not formally trained in seminary or other schools, and without experience and expertise. Yet, God saw a man who hungered for Him and His Word and said, "Now there is a man I can use for my glory."

We must always remember the fact that it is not what we possess to do the work of God, but rather who we are in Christ and in His powers. The doors and avenues are wide open and nothing is impossible for us to accomplish if we are guided there by the very hand of God Himself. It is not our responsibility to prepare our strengths and procedures, but rather to simply prepare our heart.

MICHELLE D. ANTHONY

Bibliography. J. T. Allen (n.d.), *Life Story of C. H. Spurgeon*; J. C. Carlile (1933), *C. H. Spurgeon: An Interpretative Biography*; R. E. Day (1884), *The Shadow of the Broad Brim*; D. N. Duke (1989), *Evangelical Quarterly*, 1:71–80; C. E. Fant (1976), *20 Centuries of Great Preaching*, vol. VI; S. H. Ford (1884), *The Life and Labors of Charles H. Spurgeon*; G. S. Gertz (1970), *The Forty Year Ministry of Charles Haddon Spurgeon*; R. C. Houghton (1892), *Dictionary of Baptists in America*; C. H. Spurgeon (1878), *The Autobiography of Charles H. Spurgeon*; idem (1892), *C. H. Spurgeon Autobiography*, vol. 2: *The Full Harvest*; idem (1969), *The Pictorial Life of Charles Haddon Spurgeon*; E. Towne (1995), *Evangelism and Church Growth: A Practical Encyclopedia*; W. Travis (1992), *Urban Mission*, pp. 29–36; J. D. Woodbridge (1988), *Great Leaders of the Church*.

S-R Bonds. For the greater part of the twentieth century, social scientists have leaned heavily on the concept of contingency to explain the nature of growth and development of human beings. A contingency is a specified relationship between behavior and reinforcement. Apart from a change in behavior that can be explained by temporary states, maturation, or innate response tendencies, contingency has been the primary mode of explanation for learning until recent years.

Reinforcers have been defined in various ways by social scientists. Thorndike, for instance, considered reinforcement to be a state of satisfaction. C. Hull equated reinforcement with what he called drive reduction. B. F. Skinner proposed simply that an event is reinforcing if it increases the frequency of the behavior that is contingent upon the reinforcer. Thus, Skinner defined a reinforcement in terms of its influence on behavior.

An S-R bond, or stimulus-response bond, is the effect a stimulus exercises on the response of the organism. An S-R bond is the relationship of conditioning. For the behaviorist, human activity is best explained by the stimulus-response units that vary from the simple molecular level (e.g., an eyeblink from a flash of light) to the more complex activities of life (e.g., a shopping trip as a response to an empty refrigerator). Stimulus-response bonds that form chains of connecting events between environmental stimuli and deserved behavior are called habits by behaviorists.

The theory of classical conditioning that is popularly known through the work of I. Pavlov and his salivating dogs depends on the conditioning of the S-R bond to explain learning. Classical conditioning is a process of learning by which an *unconditioned stimulus* (UCS) that naturally produces an *unconditioned response* (UCR), like the presence of food naturally produces salivation in a dog, is paired with a *conditioned stimulus* (CS), like the ringing of a bell, to produce a *conditioned response* (CR). Salivation, then, becomes a learned response to a bell. Behaviorists describe much of the rudimentary elements of behavior in terms of classical conditioning.

STEVEN PATTY

See also BEHAVIORISM, THEORIES OF; CLASSICAL CONDITIONING; OPERANT CONDITIONING; SKINNER, BURRHUS FREDERIC

Stability. Being "fixed in position, stationary" with "firmness; permanence" (Morehead, 1981, 508). In education the term is usually applied to the lack of change in some human characteristic. The classic work in this area is *Stability and Change in Human Characteristics* by Benjamin S. Bloom (1964). He was able to show that certain characteristics stabilized at approximate ages and that environmental influence is at its maximum at particular times in the life of the person. For instance, human height increases at a rapid rate early in life and can be influenced by medical care, nutrition, exercise, and so on during that early period. At about age 20 height stabilizes and changes very little until late old age. Knowing stability points for physical characteristics, intelligence, achievement, attitudes, and personality variables can be helpful for educators.

Eugene S. Gibbs

Bibliography. B. S. Bloom (1964), *Stability and Change in Human Characteristics.*

Staff, Staffing. Personnel who are recruited, placed, and trained to carry out the function of the Christian education program. This term is used in two distinct ways in the church: professional ministry staff and volunteer staff.

Professional ministry staff. The professional staff person is defined as someone who, "(1) has mastered a theory or set of theories and (2) employs this theory in practice (3) for a meaningful compensation (i.e., a living wage)" (Ratcliff and Neff, 1993, 9). Referred to as pastor, associate pastor, Christian education director, and the like, this individual's responsibilities can include oversight for the whole ministry of the church (e.g., senior pastor), a specific age group division (e.g., children's ministry director, youth pastor, etc.), a target group (e.g., small group coordinator or recovery pastor), or a ministry focus group (e.g., worship or missions pastor). The professional staff members have responsibility for the overall ministry vision, goals, teaching, management, and personnel of their particular area. This includes the recruiting, training, and managing of professionals and volunteers who serve in their area.

Volunteer staff. The volunteer staff member (referred to as sponsor, small group leader, counselor, support staff, etc.) serves under or assists the professional staff in the responsibility for and functioning of the Christian education program. Volunteer staff fulfill two essential needs in ministry. First, they enable those who are leaders over them to delegate the responsibilities of the ministry to them in order to better manage and care for their ministry area. Second, they enable the fulfillment of proper student-teacher ratios (i.e., one teacher to five students in early childhood) in the various areas of the ministry. This provides the vehicle for a relationally focused ministry as students are cared for by volunteers in a smaller group context.

The recruiting, developing, and care for staff members fulfills biblical mandates for the use and development of one's spiritual gifts, personal abilities, and God-given calling (Eph. 4: 7–13; 1 Cor. 12:7–11). Those in leadership are also provided the opportunity to fulfill their calling to evangelize, develop disciples, and train leaders to assist in the spiritual care, teaching, and direction of the church (Matt. 28: 19–20; 2 Tim. 2:2).

Staffing specifically denotes the process of recruiting, placing, and training of personnel in Christian education. This is one of the most significant responsibilities for a Christian education professional because those who are recruited will contribute to the passion and direction of that ministry.

The activities involved in the staffing process include the identification of ministry needs, the development of appropriate job descriptions, recruitment, selection, and then subsequent training. One of the most important responsibilities of a professional staff member is the selection of those who will serve with him or her in the managerial function of leading the congregation.

Keith R. King

Bibliography. D. Ratcliff and B. J. Neff (1993), *The Complete Guide to Religious Education Volunteers.*

Stages of Life/Adulthood. In the twenty-first century, says the National Center for Education Statistics, the U.S. population will be dominated by persons in their middle years. There are several social changes regarding the learning habits of American adults: from linear to blended life plans, rising education attainment, credit learning, noncredit learning, changing career patterns, increased leisure, changing roles for women, and equal opportunity.

As a learning group, adults are quite different from children and youth. They bring to any learning environment a variable number of decades of experience. In any case, their readiness to learn is considerably higher than those other two basic stages of life, since they bring much greater self-direction and willingness to the learning situation. Motivation for adult education relates inseparably to what we might call "ownership"—adults must clearly understand that learning experiences relate and were not contrived just to keep educational machinery functioning.

Among the many educational axioms now being employed in andragogy (the art and science of teaching adults), two stand out. *Adults learn by their own initiative*—they are independent persons who come to a genuine unleashing of internal desire to learn; and *adults want to know the importance of learning any given subject.* Since learning serves as a means rather than an end, many resent learning situations which treat them like children.

McKenzie (1982) reminds us how recent the study of adults really is.

> Adulthood was "discovered" implicitly in the "discovery" of childhood. While many prominent persons in the history of philosophical thought wrote about children in broad terms, child psychology as a scientific specialization is less than

a century old. Correlative to the attention given to childhood in the latter part of the 19th century, the interest in adulthood, from a scientific standpoint as an issue for systematic inquiry, began with Adolph Quetelet in the middle of the 19th century. (46)

Within the broader built category, Ettoni picks up on Erikson's "eight ages of man." Half of them apply to the adult bracket beginning with the transitional age of identity vs. role confusion (older adolescence/younger adults); the age of intimacy vs. isolation (young adult); the age of generativity vs. stagnation (middle adulthood); and the age of ego integrity vs. despair (older adulthood) (Gangel and Wilhoit, 1993, 84–85).

KENNETH O. GANGEL

Bibliography. K. P. Cross (1981), *Adults as Learners;* K. O. Gangel and J. C. Wilhoit (1993), *The Christian Educator's Handbook on Adult Education;* M. S. Knowles (1970), *The Modern Practice of Adult Education;* L. McKenzie (1982), *The Religious Education of Adults;* C. M. Sell (1991), *Transitions through Adult Life.*

Standard. *See* Modeling.

Statistics. The parents of the child called statistics came from two very different families: the mother from government record keeping and the father from the laws of probability. The field of statistics gives attention to the orderly analysis of numbers.

The term specifically refers to three applications. First, when used with a plural verb, the term refers to numerical data (e.g., "The Sunday school statistics tell us that participation in Bible Study is increasing").

A second use involves the description of a sample. A sample is a subset of scores randomly drawn from a larger group, called a population. The mean (average of all scores, a measure of central tendency) and standard deviation (a measure of variability about the mean) of a population are called population parameters. The mean and standard deviation of a sample are called sample statistics.

The third use of the term, used with a singular verb, refers to a set of mathematical procedures that are used to analyze variables. A variable is an element that holds numerical values. People can be described by their weight, a variable. A particular person weighs 150 pounds. "150" is the value of this person's "weight." Statistics analyzes variables by mathematically manipulating their values. Two major types of analyses are "differences between groups" and "relationships between variables." These may be illustrated best by some examples.

A researcher compares the "religiosity" scores of selected missionaries with the U.S. average. The average score (mean) of the missionaries is computed. By dividing the difference between the national average (population mean m, pronounced "myu") and the missionary average by the variability of the missionaries' scores (standard deviation), a standard score (z) is calculated. A z-score greater than 1.96 would mean the difference is "significant," that is, greater than one would expect by chance. The calculated z-value in this study was more than 17!

A researcher wants to compare Bible-based counseling methods with humanistic counseling methods to see which is more effective in reducing anxiety. Two groups are randomly selected and assigned to the two treatments. At the end of twelve weeks, subjects are measured for anxiety. The independent samples t-test would be used to determine if the difference between the mean scores of the two groups is "significant."

The analysis of variance (ANOVA) procedure extends the t-test to three or more groups. Complexity of procedures increases as one adds independent variables (those controlled by the researcher, forming "factorial designs") and dependent variables (those measured by the researcher, forming "multivariate designs"): N-way analysis of variance, analysis of covariance, multivariate analysis of variance, and repeated measures analysis of variance, to name a few.

The second major type of statistical procedure focuses on measuring the relationship between variables. A researcher wants to know if regular Bible study is related to spiritual maturity in high school seniors. He or she uses a spiritual maturity inventory to obtain a score for each senior, and checks church attendance records to obtain an "attendance score" equal to the number of Sundays (out of the last 52) each senior was present. Applying the Pearson's R correlation coefficient, he or she finds that $R = +.70$. This single number condenses all the maturity and attendance scores to a single number which, being interpreted, means that there is a strong positive relationship between Bible study and spiritual maturity. Spearman's Rho and Kendall's Tau computes the relationship between two ordinal variables (ranks).

One can use linear regression to create a formula that measures how well one variable predicts another. Since a strong positive relationship exists between Bible study attendance and spiritual maturity, one could use linear regression to create a regression formula: enter the attendance and it will compute an estimated level of maturity.

Multiple regression extends linear regression to two or more predictor variables. One of our students computed a multiple regression formula in order to predict marital satisfaction among our seminary students. She analyzed over thirty variables, but only three proved significant negative factors, all related to "time." They were "number of months married," "hours wife works outside the home," and "hours the student husband serves a church." Grades, degree plans, schools, number of children, salary, and other variables dropped out of the picture of marital satisfaction. (The "longer married" gave up more to come to seminary than the "newly married," and found adjustment harder). Other, more advanced procedures, based on correlation and regression include discriminant analysis, canonical analysis, path analysis, and factor analysis.

Space does not allow more than this briefest excursion into the field of statistics, but why should we, as Christians, learn to use statistical procedures? I suggest three reasons: (1) The precision and objectivity of statistical analysis helps develop critical problem-solving skills in ministers, which enhances their service. (2) The language of statistical analysis, like Greek in the first century, opens the door of secular society to the gospel. Christians who are unable to do credible scientific research miss the opportunity to impact scientific literature with their Christian worldview. (3) While God cannot be put in a test tube, many areas of Christian ministry, including teaching, counseling, and leadership, are amenable to statistical analysis, and would greatly benefit from its application.

RICK YOUNT

See also MEASUREMENT AND CHRISTIAN EDUCATION

Stepfamilies. *See* Blended Families.

Stewardship. Management of resources in such a manner as to acknowledge that they are not your own but rather are entrusted to you for a temporary period of time.

The Old Testament concept of a steward was that of a man who was "over a house" as in the case of Eleazar of Damascus, who was under the employ of Abraham in this capacity (Gen. 15:2). Joseph assumed this role under Potiphar. Likewise, among the kings of Israel there are numerous examples of those who were employed as stewards (e.g., Ezek. 27:25; 1 Chron. 27:31; Isa. 22:15).

In the writings of the New Testament a steward was in a similar capacity as one who held the trust of the master to administrate his personal affairs (Matt. 20:8; Luke 8:3). In this role, the responsibilities of the steward may have included such things as the administration of personal finances, supervision of meals for the entire household, and oversight of the children's upbringing. In this expanded concept, it would also include that of guardian and curator, or manager.

Theologically speaking, stewardship is a concept that speaks of a Christian's responsibility as a superintendent of the things which God has given over to his or her oversight. A steward realizes that the things that he or she manages do not belong to them but rather to God. He or she has

simply been given the job of distributing them in a wise and expedient manner as an executor.

The New Testament reader is given a glimpse into God's perspective of stewardship in two parables (Luke 12:32–48; 16:1–13). These parables clearly teach that God expects his children to wisely and diligently administer his resources. Those who squander or waste God's provisions will be the recipient of his displeasure.

In a metaphorical sense, the term steward is used in the New Testament for pastors, teachers, elders, and bishops in churches (see 1 Cor. 4:1; Titus 1:7; 1 Peter 4:10).

MICHAEL J. ANTHONY

Bibliography. F. L. Cross and E. A. Livingstone (1997), *The Oxford Dictionary of the Christian Church;* J. D. Douglas (1975), *The New Bible Dictionary;* W. Duckat (1971), *Beggar to King;* W. E. Vine (1966), *An Expository Dictionary of New Testament Words.*

Story. *See* Parable.

Storytelling. From the dawn of time people have told stories that reveal facts about God and remind us of our history. The telling of stories has always been an important part of human communication, and is one of the characteristics that sets humankind apart from the rest of creation.

Children learn about their world through stories. A child's request to *Tell me a story!* is not merely a means of entertainment, but a method for understanding a complex world. Young people broaden their knowledge of the world by reading novels, and adults reflect on the human condition through hearing or reading stories. That is why great preachers from Jesus up to modern day tell stories to illustrate their points. Not just an ancient form of folk art, storytelling is a learning tool through which people of all ages hear and reflect on God's truth.

The History of Storytelling. Ancient people told stories about hunting and geography, including the facts of creation. Music and movement were probably an integral part of storytelling, and as people began to wonder about the greater world around them, they embroidered their stories with myth to explain natural phenomena. Within centuries after the flood, tales of superhuman people and their interaction with deity became popular. Storytellers became not just entertainers, but historians for an oral people. With the development of writing came recording of stories, and some of the most ancient writings are about humankind's search for God. When Moses, under the direct revelation of God, wrote the Pentateuch, humankind had a detailed record of God's involvement in this world. The Bible is largely the recorded story of God's plan for humanity, given to us so that we may have a reliable account and thus develop faith in him. We can trust the veracity of the Gospels because oral tradition demanded repetition in order to ensure details of the stories were accurate.

Storytelling evolved in the Middle Ages, as traveling musician-poets were welcomed into royal courts and marketplaces to share news, tell tales, and teach people a form of history. With the invention of moveable type in 1440, the reading of stories replaced the telling. The eighteenth century brought novels into the hands of everyday people, and in the nineteenth century writers began printing popular ancient folktales. The twentieth century saw an explosion of storytelling, with movies and television filling our lives with stories.

Forms of Stories. The Bible provides an abundance of rich stories, telling of real people encountering crises while seeking God. Each story offers not only history, but a lesson about God and ourselves. Believers can also rely on moral stories that reveal truth and cause us to reflect upon the Lord. A Christian teacher can use myths, legends, parables, fables, epic, folk tales, and literary tales. Fictitious stories should never be given the same weight as the accounts in Scripture, but all forms of stories may be useful in helping a listener understand a truth about God or life.

How to Tell a Story. Select a story that clearly reveals a principle. The characters and conflict must be clear, or the point of the story will be muted. Taking into account the intended audience will help you limit the length and complexity of the story. Small children enjoy stories about animals and other children, with visuals to aid the telling. Early schoolage children like longer stories, if the characters are few and the plot straightforward, while older children enjoy heroic, adventurous stories.

Learn the story thoroughly. Read it through several times, organizing the events and characters in your mind using an outline or key phrase. Practice telling the story out loud, to see how the characters sound. Poetry or literary tales should be memorized. The most important thing is to tell the story well. Words tell your story, so choose your words carefully, adding description to help your audience *see* the events unfold. Occasional movement implying action may assist the telling. Gestures may change according to the setting—a small classroom may not need much action, but speaking before a crowd in a sanctuary may require more physical movement to help everyone understand what is happening.

JERRY CHIP MACGREGOR

Bibliography. J. Maguire (1985), *Creative Storytelling: Choosing, Inventing and Sharing Tales for Children;* R. Sawyer (1942), *The Way of the Storyteller;* M. Shedlock (1951), *The Art of the Storyteller.*

See also METHODOLOGY; PARABLE

Storytelling, Children's. Stories appeal to people of all ages, but children especially enjoy listening to a good story. The best stories are true in the sense that they reveal life as it really is or as it should be.

Although there are many places to find good stories, the Bible is a distinguished source. Narrative is a dominant form in the Bible. In the beginning, there is the creation story. There are stories of kings, queens, prophets, priests, servant girls, fishermen, young and old, rich and poor, wise and foolish people. Then there are provocative parables that delight and inform. Generations of parents and educators have shared with their children the Bible stories they remember from their own childhood. Through the years a limited set of popular Bible stories has been established with regrettably many important stories being ignored. Storytellers are challenged to return to the biblical source and rediscover the wealth of stories there.

In selecting stories for children, consider the question, "With whom will the children identify in this story?" Letting this question guide the selection will impact the choice of story, the telling of the story, and the response to the story. For example, the well-known story of the infant Moses being hidden in a basket along the Nile River to protect him from the Pharaoh's edict to kill all Hebrew baby boys can be told from many points of view (Exod. 2:1–10). Since the younger children will likely identify with the infant Moses and the older children with his sister, Miriam, the story should be told to highlight the appropriate character's concerns.

Stories in the Bible are usually concise. The essential information is given. The language is full of imagery and rhythm but sparse. Events that took hours or days are recorded in a few sentences. The stories are in condensed form and can be expanded in the telling. As the story is told, relive the events that happened in that time and place. Pay attention to the details that the writer included because they are there for a reason. Explore the feelings of the characters. Imagine the sounds, smells, and sights. Consider the problem or situation that the characters are facing. How is the dilemma in the story like those the children might encounter today? Look for points of connection between the biblical events and the children's lives. Stories can be told with puppets, costumes, or props, but they are most powerful when the storyteller disappears and the hearers see the story come to life.

Stories can stand on their own without interpretation. Meaning is embedded in the story itself. However, stories can also stimulate reflection on the children's own feelings, conflicts, relationships, character, and commitments. Stories can console us by letting us know that we are not alone in our problems, expand our view of the world, arouse a longing to do what is good and right, and inspire us to action. Bible stories, in particular, can provide a grounding in what is "true, honorable, right, pure, lovely, and of good report" (Phil. 4:8).

BETH POSTERSKI

Bibliography. R. Grant and J. Reed (1990), *Telling Stories to Touch the Heart;* G. W. Pritchard (1992), *Offering the Gospel with Children;* W. R. White (1986), *Stories for Telling: A Treasury for Christian Storytellers.*

Strategic Planning. Long-range planning intended to affect every aspect of an organization. In strategic planning, the leaders of the organization seek to define the organization's most desirable future. They then describe their overall strategy to bring that future into being. Strategic planning is not concerned with details or short-term outcomes, but focuses on the next five to ten years and paints the picture with broad strokes.

In the professions of education and ministry, strategic planning is concerned with identifying goals and general strategies to reach those goals. Planners often start by denoting where the organization is at the present time; they state where they want to be at some point in the future; finally, they select a course to bring this future into being.

There are several reasons that explain why churches and Christian educators conduct strategic planning. One reason is that it draws all (or most) members of the organization into the planning process: this increases member loyalty to the organization and to the projected future; it also increases the likelihood of improving the quality of the plans the organization develops. Another reason to engage in strategic planning is that it increases each member's understanding of the organization, its strengths and limitations, and its opportunities and obstacles. Furthermore, since strategic planning represents a proactive stance, organizations that utilize it find themselves more likely to be fulfilling their mission.

The major steps in strategic planning are as follows: (1) Review the organization's mission statement. Make sure it accurately reflects the group's understanding of its reason for existence. (2) Identify the organization's strengths and limitations. (3) Examine the larger environment, the context in which the organization serves. (4) Brainstorm several possible futures for the organization, following the generally accepted procedures for brainstorming (all ideas are accepted; nothing is criticized or evaluated in any way; wild ideas are expected; practical considerations do not matter; the more ideas mentioned, the better; the quality of ideas is not important; there should be an accepting, cooperative atmosphere; all members should contribute ideas; all ideas should be recorded). (5) Systematically study all ideas generated in the brainstorming session, identifying the strengths and limitations of each one. (6) Identify the ideas that seem to represent a consensus of the group. (7) Use these ideas to write goals that state the desired future of the organization. State the goals in broad, general terms. (8) Identify general strategies to be used in reaching the goals, but stop short of writing detailed objectives and action plans; merely state overall strategies.

JOHN H. AUKERMAN

See also ADMINISTRATION; GOAL; MANAGEMENT; PLAN, PLANNING

Strategy. Strategies are very similar to policies, plans, and objectives. They are sometimes confused because all of these elements are in some way interrelated. Strategic planning is what guides an organization toward the successful accomplishment of its mission.

To be effective, strategic planning must take several elements into consideration. In a church context this would include the mission of the church and its values, the changing demographic condition of the community, the identification of internal resources (both human and material), as well as a realistic look at its strengths and weaknesses. Recognizing that no one church can possibly meet the needs of every individual within its community, some churches choose to focus their energies toward a specific target audience. This is a strategy.

For example, a church may have as its mission "To minister to broken families in the city of Smithdale." Since ministering to broken families is their mission, they will need to develop a strategic plan to accomplish their mission. This strategy may include a counseling program, educating their people through biblically based sermons on Sunday mornings, developing a support group program during midweek, and having age-level activities for children and youth. Evangelism will need to be an important dimension of their approach to ministry as well.

This strategy focuses their vision and forces them to make important decisions about opportunities that come along over time. Strategies give plans their meaning and help provide direction in the budgeting process. Staffing and physical resources should be guided by strategic planning as well.

MICHAEL J. ANTHONY

Bibliography. P. F. Drucker (1974), *Management: Tasks, Responsibilities, Practices;* H. Koontz and H. Weihrich (1990), *Essentials of Management;* J. A. Stoner (1978), *Management.*

Stratification. A concept associated with the Third Wave of psychology, developmentalism, and theorists Piaget, Kohlberg, Fowler, and others. This framework for understanding human behavior describes various strata or stages of growth. Stratification emphasizes the value of humans as thoughtfully and purposefully interactive with their environment.

Distinctive patterns of behavior and thought are empirically observed in various domains at each strata. Physical, cognitive, affective, social, moral decision making, and spiritual development have all been observed as progressing through sequential strata. Based on the conclusion that humans are more similar than dissimilar, each strata is a level of temporary destination that should be fully explored and experienced before the individual progresses to the next stage.

Environment can be instrumental in facilitating or slowing the development inherent in human genetic structure. Each strata is experienced in invariant and sequential patterns. Stages exist across cultures, genders, and eras of time though timing may be different within these variables.

CHERYL L. FAWCETT

Bibliography. P. G. Downs (1994), *Teaching for Spiritual Growth: An Introduction to Christian Education;* J. E. Loder (1976), *Foundations for Christian Education in an Era of Change,* p. 31.

See also AFFECTIVE DOMAIN; COGNITIVE DOMAIN; FOWLER, JAMES W., III; KOHLBERG, LAWRENCE; MORAL DEVELOPMENT; PIAGET, JEAN

Structure. Understanding the basic concepts or ideas of a subject is understanding that subject's structure. Jerome S. Bruner (1960) said, "Grasping the structure of a subject is understanding it in a way that permits many other things to be related to it meaningfully. To learn structure in short, is to learn how things are related" (7). For Bruner, the goal of teaching is to help learners grasp structure or relationships within and between information. Structure makes new learning possible and meaningful because learners have a sense of how new knowledge fits previous knowledge. Structure is likely to enable the learner to remember what he or she learns. Structure increases comprehension. The likelihood of the learner applying to life what he or she learned is enhanced. Critical thinking and problem-solving skills both require structure (Biehler and Snowman, 1993). Yount (1996) points out that learners will likely structure information if the appropriate mode (enactive, iconic, symbolic) is used, if the essential material is presented in small doses (economy), and if the new material is presented in a simple but powerful manner (power).

WALTER H. NORVELL

Bibliography. J. S. Bruner (1960), *The Process of Education;* R. F. Biehler and J. Snowman (1993), *Psychol-ogy Applied to Teaching;* W. R. Yount (1996), *Created to Learn.*

Subconscious. *See* Conscience.

Subcurriculum. *See* Curriculum, Hidden.

Submission. Humble or compliant behavior; humble or submissive deference in conduct or bearing. Submission plays a big role in the life of a Christian. When we look at the Old Testament, the idea of submission to God's laws and authority brings material blessing and prosperity. From Adam to the nation of Israel, this idea dominates. A good example is Abraham. He obeyed God even to the point of offering his son Isaac as a sacrifice. God blessed him for his submission to His will and made through his son Isaac the nation of Israel. The opposite of submission is rebellion, which always brought disaster, from the fall of Adam and Eve into sin to the deportation of the nation of Israel.

In the New Testament this idea is seen throughout the four Gospels in the life of Christ as he submitted to God's will because he knew the outcome was for God's glory and the salvation of humankind. Christ's prayer in the Garden of Gethsemane, "not My will, but Thine be done" (Luke 22:42b NASB), is a classic example of submission to God's will. Acts records God's blessing on a submissive church as they reach out to family, neighbors, and then cross-culturally to the Gentiles. It also records God's judgment on disobedience as seen in Acts 5 with Ananias and Sapphira.

Another idea of submission in the New Testament is 1 Peter 2:13 (NASB): "Submit yourselves for the Lord's sake to every human institution, whether to a king as the one in authority." The Christian is to be under the laws of the land. Usually these laws are for the good of the people and that is why we are admonished to be submissive to them. Submission should be voluntary and will impart a good conscience (Rom. 13:5). It will also give the Christian a good reputation. If human laws contradict God's laws as seen in the life of the apostles Peter and John (Acts 5:29) then God's law must come first.

Christians are to be submissive to the church leaders as seen in Hebrews 13:17a (NASB): "Obey your leaders, and submit to them." The leaders are looking out for the believers' good and are trying to prepare them for heaven. Submission to God's authority brings spiritual blessings more than material wealth as taught in the New Testament. Christians are to be submissive to each other as seen in Ephesians 5:21: "and be subject to one another in the fear of Christ." Submission is not always easy when making the right choice hurts in the present situation. It is impossible for the Christian to see the full outcome of choices and trust in an omnipotent God.

Submission in the home is seen in Ephesians 5:22, where wives are admonished to "be subject to your own husbands, as to the Lord." Children are also told to be submissive to their parents as seen in Ephesians 6:1–2. This is God's pattern of authority in the home to keep harmony.

A Christian must choose to be submissive on a daily basis. Choosing to respond to God will help us make the right choices. As Christians mature, they realize that God leads them in certain ways because he loves and cares more for them than any earthly friend. God has established authority for which the Christian is to be submissive. God is the utmost authority. Underneath him are the national, state, and local governments. Next in succession come the church, home, and lastly the individual. If submission is daily maintained in our lives, we can live a harmonious life before God and our fellow man.

BARBARA JEAN DEATON

Bibliography. *Discipleship Journal* 95 (1996); A. Hinthorn (1996), *Joyfully Following.*

Substance. *See* Content, Elements of.

Substance Abuse. *See* Drugs.

Suicide, Youth. Self-murder, the intentional taking of one's own life. Shocking figures indicate an annual increase in suicides, especially among adolescents. Suicide is often cited as the second leading cause of death in teenagers, surpassed only by automobile accidents. Since a number of automobile accidents are single-person events, there is reason to believe that these might often mask additional suicides.

Suicide is the ultimate cry for help. Reasons for suicide may seem illogical, but are nevertheless intense for adolescents. They include a desire to gain attention or manipulate someone close, sadness over failures, and attempts to be reunited with a deceased loved one. Other reasons include escape from problems that seem unsurmountable, to punish others or oneself, or to avoid being a burden. Modern extremist or cult groups have committed mass suicide to focus attention on their message. Suicide is often portrayed as heroic (the Jews at Masada, soldiers in battle who sacrifice themselves for comrades) or romantic (Romeo and Juliet) in literature and music.

Christian educators and parents should be sensitive to the signs of suicidal tendencies. Warning signs include talk about death and suicide, irrational outbursts, decline in performance, prolonged sadness or depression, giving away prized possessions, communication problems, drug and alcohol abuse, change in eating or sleeping habits, lack of alternatives to solve problems, and lack of hope. These are only signals and may not mean that a youth is on the verge of suicide, but each one should be taken seriously.

Suicide education through lectures, dialogues, discussion groups, and media is a logical first step in prevention. Educators and parents should also know basic steps in intervention with suicidal youth. (1) Treat suicide threats seriously. (2) Talk with the person directly about feelings and thoughts concerning suicide. (3) Find out about the method, means, and time of plans for suicide (the more specific and detailed, the greater the risk). (4) Express genuine interest and focus on hope. (5) Ask for a verbal contract that he or she will contact you or another designated person before acting on suicidal thoughts. Professional help is strongly suggested for those at risk of suicide.

WESLEY BLACK

Bibliography. B. Blackburn (1982), *What You Should Know about Suicide;* L. Parrot III (1993), *Helping the Struggling Adolescent.*

Sunday School. Agency that has served the church across North America in one form or another for more than two centuries as the primary arena in which the Bible is taught, particularly to children and youth. As we know it today, Sunday school had its beginnings in Gloucester, England, in 1780. A newspaper publisher named Robert Raikes began a school on Sundays for the children of Glouchester who were working the other six days in local factories spawned by the Industrial Revolution.

Sunday school was brought to America initially by the various devout religious groups who immigrated to this country from Europe and England and established Sunday schools in the colonies for the purposes of reinforcing religious and denominational teaching and dogma. Another wave of Sunday school emphasis was brought to North America by revivalist John Wesley and his followers.

More recently, Sunday school has been an agency of the church designed to teach the Bible to children, youth, and adults in local church ministries. The American Sunday school has been characterized by the following:

1. A largely volunteer superintending and teaching staff. Most Sunday school teachers and workers in local churches are volunteers who have careers or primary vocational interests in other fields and teach on Sunday without pay.

2. Being an agency strictly connected to the local church. Raikes and other initiators of the Sunday school idea did not have local church support or interest; however, in more modern times Sunday school has become strictly a local church agency. The local church sponsors it, manages it, and provides for its financial and facility needs.

3. Being an agency whose primary interest is in teaching children and young people. In many denominations, Sunday school is promoted to all ages and everyone "from the cradle to the grave" is encouraged to participate. Still, most of the emphasis in curriculum development, training support, and other resource materials is on the teaching of children and youth.

Traditionally, in North America Sunday school takes place for a period of time of not less than an hour and not more than ninety minutes just prior to the morning worship service in a typical church. Many current adults who participated in Sunday school as children remember Sunday school beginning mid-morning on Sunday followed by a church service which typically ended in time for lunch. That schedule of activities fit quite well with the predominately rural agrarian society of the late nineteenth century. However, churches in urban and suburban communities are increasingly finding that schedule to be less suited to the lifestyles and habits of modern city and suburb Christians. Thus, in recent years, many churches have greatly altered Sunday school or, in some cases, abandoned it completely in favor of other programs which better meet the needs and schedules of their members.

Sunday school has been promoted over the years by a number of societies and associations designed to encourage greater participation among American Christians. The American Sunday School Union (1824), the International Sunday School Association (1907), and the National Sunday School Association (1945), among other smaller or more regional associations, were founded for the purpose of promoting Sunday school and encouraging participation. Many of these associations held conventions at least annually for the purpose of encouraging and training volunteer leaders and teachers so that they could conduct their ministry more effectively.

Curricular needs emerged as Sunday school became more popular. In the early years of this century, leaders attempted to meet the curricular needs of all Sunday schools together in the form of the Uniform Sunday School Lesson. However, by 1930, for doctrinal, denominational, and logistical reasons, many churches had abandoned the Uniform Sunday School Lesson in favor of some other form of materials. Some noteworthy individuals such as David C. Cook, Clarence Benson, Victor Corey, and Henrietta Mears figured prominently in developing curriculum which reached across denominational lines for evangelical churches and their Sunday school ministries.

There have been times in the history of Sunday school when it appeared that it would be replaced by some other agency or means of teaching in the local church. The end of the twentieth century is such a time. Many significant churches in urban and suburban communities are seeking other programs, ministries, and ways to do the kind of teaching of the Bible that has in recent history been done in the Sunday school. On the other hand, there is evidence in some cities that Sunday school is being taken back to its roots in Gloucester, England, and once again being used as an agency of reaching out to underprivileged and needy children in the inner city. Robert Raikes would be deeply satisfied.

KEN GARLAND

Bibliography. J. Bayly (1978), *I Love to Tell the Story;* J. E. Reed and R. Prevost (1993), *A History of Christian Education;* E. Towns (1988), *154 Steps to Revitalize Your Sunday School;* W. R. Willis (1979), *Two Hundred Years and Still Counting.*

Sunday School, Early Origins. While the modern Sunday school movement bears little resemblance to the school established by its founder, Robert Raikes, in 1780, it continues to embody the creative passion of people committed to meeting the needs of others through Bible-based education and discipleship. Lessons learned throughout the history of the Sunday school can guide us as we design new approaches to meet people's needs through biblically based learning experiences.

Raikes's first Sunday school resembled more of an inner-city youth ministry than a typical Sunday school class today. Burdened by the growing problem on Sundays of poor children roaming the streets of Gloucester, England, Raikes established a simple school meeting in Mrs. Meredith's kitchen on Sooty Alley. Boys and girls ranging in age from 6 to 14, drawn from the lowest levels of society, were rounded up to attend school from ten a.m. until five p.m. on Sunday afternoon. In those early years, teachers were paid one shilling per day to teach the children reading and religion in order to reform their character and improve their lot in life. Using the Bible as the textbook, Raikes's approach was based on the integration of both social and spiritual needs. The results of his new Sunday schools were phenomenal. By the time of his death in 1811, over 400,000 pupils were in attendance in England alone. The movement soon spread to America, where it became one of the fastest growing evangelistic efforts in its history.

Several factors contributed to the success of the early Sunday school movement. First, it was primarily led by laypersons rather than clergy. In fact, in both England and America, it took years before the institutionalized church even encouraged the establishment of Sunday schools. Churches regarded the movement as a threat to their formal ministry of preaching and administrating the sacraments. This emphasis on lay leadership was one of the earliest and most widely spread movements to equip the laity for ministry since the Reformation. Second, the Sunday school movement in its growth years was characterized by a nonsectarian and interdenominational emphasis. By focusing on basic biblical teaching rather than denominational catechisms, the Sunday school movement was able to unify like-minded people from many denominations. This sparked a major evangelistic thrust in America in the mid-1800s. Third, the Sunday schools adapted to various social contexts to meet both educational and spiritual needs. While it began in England as a ministry exclusively to the poor, its purpose expanded in America to eventually include persons from all levels in society. Without minimizing their strong biblical base, Sunday schools in America expanded their educational emphasis to fill the educational vacuum before the establishment of public education. By 1859, the Sunday school movement had provided three-fifths of the libraries in America. Fourth, by securing the support of major benefactors and leaders in society, the Sunday school movement was able to gain national recognition and financial support. Throughout its history people such as Robert Raikes, William Fox, John Wesley, Dwight L. Moody, William R. Harper, and J. Edgar Hoover have helped to bring the Sunday school movement to the attention of the world.

The Sunday school movement continued to grow in America throughout the nineteenth century. While there were 8,268 Sunday schools in America in 1832, by 1875 the number had reached 65,000. It is estimated that by 1889 over ten million persons were enrolled. Yet, by the second decade of the twentieth century, Sunday school growth began to decline.

This decline can be attributed to several factors. The first was the influence of liberal theology. Horace Bushnell (1802–76) influenced this new liberalism within the Sunday school movement even though he did not associate with the movement during his lifetime. His belief that children should be brought up as Christians without the need for a conversion experience was contrary to the evangelistic emphasis of the Sunday schools of his day.

Yet his thinking seemed to resonate with the new religious leaders of the twentieth century. With the establishment of the Religious Education Association in 1903, liberal theology dominated the leadership circles of the Sunday school movement. Experience replaced the Bible as the basis of authority and social projects took the place of Bible study as the main activity in the Sunday schools. Conversion was replaced by natural processes of growth and development. Although this liberal agenda was initially held only by the leaders of the movement, it did not take long for it to influence the teachers and students.

The second factor leading to the decline of the Sunday school was the belief that education rather than Jesus Christ was what the world needed for its salvation. Based on the pragmatic educational ideas of John Dewey, the Religious Education Association began to integrate progressive education into the Sunday school. While some of these new approaches and methods were needed to make classes more student-centered, the emphasis on experience soon eliminated the need for the Bible in the curriculum. The Bible became just one of many sources to be used by students to help them to live in society. The supernatural was replaced by the secular.

The third factor related to the decline of the Sunday school in the first half of the twentieth century was the movement away from lay leadership to denominational and professional leadership. In an attempt to improve the educational standards of the Sunday school, the professional religious educator assumed more control over the program and curriculum. Trained at liberal seminaries or graduate schools, these new professionals took the leadership for the Sunday school away from laypersons. As the chasm between the mainline churches and the evangelicals widened, denominations took more and more responsibility for their own distinctive programs and curriculum. Ownership for the Sunday school moved farther away from the persons in the pew.

While Sunday school attendance declined in the mainline denominations during the first half of the twentieth century, there was a steady increase in many evangelical Sunday schools. In avoiding many of the pitfalls of liberalism and neoorthodoxy, evangelical Sunday schools have maintained their strong theological heritage to share with the world. Yet the world needs more than theological orthodoxy. The challenge faced today is similar to the challenge facing Robert Raikes. Although the needs in various cultures may differ, Christian education must design effective ways to help people to know God's Word and apply it in a way that affects how they live. This is the essence of the Sunday school movement. In Elmer Towns's (1993) survey of ten Sunday schools that dared to change in order to grow, he concludes that Sunday schools must do whatever it takes to adapt in order to reach people for Christ. This effort will require both the most effective educational strategies and a dependence on the supernatural power of the Holy Spirit revealed through God's Word.

GARY C. NEWTON

Bibliography. C. B. Eavey (1964), *History of Christian Education*; R. W. Lynn and E. Wright (1980), *The Big Little School*; J. E. Reed and R. Prevost (1993), *A History of Christian Education*; E. L. Towns (1993), *Ten Sunday Schools That Dared to Change*; W. R. Willis (1979), *200 Years—and Still Counting*.

Sunday School Movement. Most of the literature dealing with the history of Christian education traces the roots of the Sunday school movement to the city of Glouchester, England, in 1780 and a newspaper publisher named Robert Raikes. Raikes was concerned about the impoverished families and shiftless children of Gloucester who were laborers in the mills spawned by the Industrial Revolution in England and Europe. His answer to the needs he saw around him was Sunday school—a program developed by Raikes and his father to teach reading and ciphering to the children as well as instruct them in morals and manners. He chose the Bible as the primer for learning reading because he believed that in reading the Bible, his pupils would also learn much about morality (Willis, 1979).

Raikes's initial attempts at solving a major social ill in Glouchester may have never gotten started had it depended on the support of local churches. When he approached local pastors to seek permission to use their facilities for his schools, he was turned down almost unanimously by church leaders who were afraid his pupils would destroy their facilities. His idea was derisively known among church leaders as "Raikes Ragged School" (Bayly, 1978, 10) Furthermore, Sunday school may have remained a local phenomenon had it not been for the Methodist revivalist, John Wesley. After visiting one of Raikes's schools in Yorkshire, Wesley determined to promote Sunday school as part of what became the Methodist movement.

In 1785 William Fox, a Baptist businessman reared in a town near Gloucester, became concerned because so few adults in London could read the Bible. As a result of Fox's concern, a union of Baptist leaders met in August of that year and formed the first Sunday School Society whose purpose was to promote Sunday school throughout the British Dominions (Reed and Prevost, 1993). In 1803, the Sunday School Union was founded and became the first known organization to publish teaching books and a teacher's magazine.

In North America, the idea of Sunday school came to the colonies long before 1780. Sunday schools springing out of the Wesleyan Revival were founded in various communities in the colonies as early as 1737 (Savannah, Georgia). Unlike Raikes's experiments in Gloucester, these schools were decidedly religious and denominational. Also, unlike Raikes's schools, they were not open to all children but only to those already considered to be in the church fellowship. However, they did play a role in preparing the way for the Sunday school movement in the United States.

In 1824 the American Sunday School Union (ASSU) was founded out of efforts in Philadelphia to begin to plant Sunday schools in more rural and isolated areas of the continent. The first ASSU schools were founded in the Mississippi Valley and after mixed reviews early, the ASSU eventually participated significantly in the missionizing of the American West.

By 1832, there were more than 8,000 Sunday schools located in 27 states which were affiliated with the ASSU and by 1875 that number had grown to more than 65,000 Sunday schools in 36 states (Reed and Prevost, 1993). These schools featured teaching of reading using the Bible as primary curriculum and teachers who were almost exclusively untrained volunteers.

In the years following 1875, several developments marked the further advance of the Sunday school movement. The first known International Sunday School Convention was held in Baltimore in 1875 and by 1905, 11 more national and international conventions were held in various locations. The focus at these events was upon organization of the local schools and the provision of an experience based curriculum for pupils to study.

During this period, the focus shifted from teaching of basic reading and ciphering skills, which children were now receiving increasingly in public schools, to evangelism and outreach. Sunday school became the primary agency for reaching new children and families in local churches. An attempt at creating a nationally accepted uniform Sunday school lesson plan met with great disapproval and while the project continued well into the twentieth century, by 1930, most denominations had begun developing their own curriculum for use in Sunday schools (Willis, 1979).

In 1945 the National Sunday School Association was formed to promote and encourage participation in Sunday schools across America. The NSSA existed for twenty-five years before giving way to more regionally defined associations which were better able to develop programs to meet the needs of local and regional Sunday school workers.

Today, the Sunday school movement is a shell of its former self. Changes in culture, lifestyles, and participation habits of Christians have led to churches in many locations seeking other kinds of ministries that might better serve the needs in their congregations formerly met by Sunday school. The idea that the church has a responsibility to teach the Bible to its children, youth, and adults is still strongly believed by those in church leadership and many continue to search for agencies with which to do the task.

KEN GARLAND

Bibliography. J. Bayly (1978), *I Love to Tell the Story;* J. E. Reed and R. Prevost (1993), *A History of Christian Education;* W. R. Willis (1979), *Two Thousand Years and Still Counting.*

Superintendent. Primary leader, general administrator, and overseer of the entire Sunday school program. Too often the role of superintendent is rather narrowly defined as a minor detail manager of the operations of a Sunday school.

Superintendents function not just as managers but as a leaders who hold things together, help the staff determine and fulfill the purpose and vision of the Sunday school, steer the Sunday school in the right direction, provide leadership development for teachers and other staff, provide for the proper equipment, generally supervise the curriculum/curricula of the entire Sunday school, and help teachers and learners evaluate the learning that is supposed to have occurred in this educational program.

Superintendents need to raise the value of the Sunday school in the minds of their pastors, congregations, teachers, and learners. They should be the ones who champion the Sunday school to the official boards of their churches, to all teachers, and to actual and potential learners. They are the major communicators of the vision of what the Sunday school is and is attempting to be for their churches.

Superintendents need to be people of vision, unafraid to "color outside the lines," creative, encouragers, and evidencing the character of what they want their teachers to do and be. Superintendents need to be flexible, contemporary, constantly recruiting teachers, providing for teachers' continued development into effective teachers. Superintendents need to help their churches show appreciation to teachers and helpers.

Another primary responsibility for the superintendent is to help teachers and helpers become effective teachers and workers. This means spending time to determine those who are called to teach (not just those who "volunteer") and teacher/staff development, encouraging the teachers and staff to continue to learn how to be more effective teachers.

Superintendents need to demonstrate that they care for all the learners, regardless of ages, and for all the teachers and helpers. Superintendents are not caretakers but leaders who themselves are continually growing in their own understanding of what makes for effective teaching. They need to demonstrate their own Christian character, effectiveness as a leaders of teachers, and insights into all the age groups of the Sunday school.

JOHN M. DETTONI

See also CLERGY; LAITY; MINISTRY; SUNDAY SCHOOL; VOLUNTEER

Supervision. Administrative function that involves oversight of people as they perform tasks and activities related to the goals of an organization. Even though tasks are involved, supervision should be seen as primarily a people function. The driving force behind supervision must be a desire for improvement, not just correction. Since supervision is a part of the administrative process, it can occur at any time, whether planning, organizing, or evaluating is taking place.

Supervision is an essential element in a program of Christian education. It can take place at several different levels, such as when a pastor or minister of education supervises the personnel related to a particular component of the Christian education ministry. Routinely, supervision takes place through the volunteer leaders of a Sunday school program whenever a Sunday school superintendent supervises division, age group directors, or teachers.

If a supervisor is to be successful, he or she must also engage in self-evaluation. Kenneth Gangel suggests that the supervisor in the context of church ministry ask the following questions: (1) How many people are you losing? (2) What are the differences between the people who survive in your ministry and those who do not? (3) What is it costing you in terms of hours and dollars to replace workers each year? (4) Is there a pattern to the kinds of people who leave your church? (5) Could some of the losses have been retained with better supervisory processes? (6) Would transfer to another position rather than termination be an effective answer? (7) How many people are we keeping in ministry who really shouldn't be there? (8) What specific process do we follow when a person announces that he or she is leaving a certain kind of ministry? (9) What shrinkage has been due to deficiency on the part of the worker and how much due to the efficiency of the supervisor? (10) What program do we have for training supervisors? (306) After the supervisor engages in self-evaluation, the questions can be used with other supervisory personnel in the same organization.

J. GREGORY LAWSON

Bibliography. K. Gangel (1989), *Feeding and Leading.*

See also ADMINISTRATION; MANAGEMENT

Support Group. The term *support group* is used in two ways in the church. There is the common or general way. This represents how the average congregational member uses the expression. When conceived in this manner the term is associated with providing mutual support through love and care, experiencing fellowship, and promoting encouragement/affirmation to each group member. These groups use a wide variety of names—such as Bible study and prayer group, fellowship group, neighborhood cell, or flock. Typical activities include times of personal sharing, Bible study, prayer, and mutual support. A group covenant, if there is one, ranges from little to mild accountability.

Support groups are also used in a more clinical and technical sense. Found in the recovery group literature, these clusters provide service to individuals who have experienced abuse, addictions, or adult life crisis. The confessional motif emphasizing honesty before God and others serves as a foundation block for mutual support and assistance through the difficulty. Many units follow a twelve-step approach or some variation. Effective support groups carefully spell out their ground rules, and may include a termination date. Leaders need specific training and often come from the pool of people who have experienced victory over the difficulty in their own lives.

For the person in recovery, each day is filled with land mines of potential setbacks and relapses. To facilitate recovery and follow-up care Joseph White (1989) recommends each support group should: (1) provide frequent maintenance via a solid support system of encouraging peers; (2) recognize relapse warning signs, which may include being dishonest with one's self, justifying or rationalizing how one can resume codependency, expecting life to be perfect and becoming depressed or angry when it isn't, and denying that one has to worry about the difficulty anymore; and (3) incorporate a relationship with a primary resource person (counselor or mentor).

Morris's *The Complete Handbook for Recovery Ministry in the Church* (1993) provides fine guidelines on starting, organizing and maintaining Christ-centered support groups. The National Association of Christians in Recovery and Serendipity House are excellent sources of materials.

The true key to support groups—whether common or clinical—is the power of God expressed through love in a visible human community. Support groups provide hope and reconciliation. They become a microcosm and agent for God's continuing work of human transformation.

JAMES A. DAVIES

Bibliography. B. Morris (1993), *The Complete Handbook for Recovery Ministry in the Church;* J. White (1989), *Mutual Aid Groups and the Life Cycle.*

See also AUTHORITARIAN APPROACH TO GROUPS; RECOVERY; RECOVERY MINISTRY

Symbolism. Use of concrete examples to represent abstract concepts. Symbolism has a long history in Judeo-Christian education, almost out of necessity. How else could an invisible, spiritual, intangible Being communicate with humankind?

The Bible is replete with examples of visible, tangible, and concrete objects being invested with a symbolic meaning, to stand for or suggest something of God's truth. The tabernacle/temple of the Old Testament taught by symbolic means the holiness of God, the need for blood sacrifice, and so on. The Israelite feast and festival cycle signified the dependence of God's people on Jehovah. Prophets used graphic illustrations (for example, Amos's plumb line) to communicate

God's Word. Jesus employed parables to speak artfully about deep spiritual truths. He performed miracles which often became object lessons for his teaching. Metaphorical devices such as the apostle Paul's simile comparing the Christian life to a race are found throughout the Bible. Symbols such as the cross have been used throughout church history to inspire faith. So symbolism has been and is an integral part of teaching the Christian faith. Hence, it is not a question of whether to use symbolism as a tool within Christian education, but how and where.

For adults and many adolescents, symbolism and abstract generalizations are helpful tools for understanding biblical truths. Symbolism is useful in sermon illustrations, diagrams, allegories to access right-hemisphere human brain capabilities, complementing the rational, logical, linear, and sequential presentation of God's truth, so appropriate for left-hemisphere learning. In fact, some adults are more able to grasp God's truth through graphic contrasts or parables than through logical persuasion, analytical outlines, syllogisms, and the like.

A major issue confronting Christian educators is the appropriateness of the use of symbolism with children. It is not difficult to find children's curriculum featuring abstractions such as fruit of the Spirit (Gal. 5) or the Christian's armor (Eph. 6). Additionally, many so-called object lessons, *The Wordless Book*, and "Gospel Magic" rely on symbolism.

Nearly fifty years ago Mary and Lois LeBar questioned the effectiveness of using symbolism in children's education. They proposed instead teaching the Bible to children concretely with specific, literal, and immediate application to their lives (LeBar, 1952). About the same time, researcher Jean Piaget asserted that children are not ready to handle abstract and theoretical concepts until ages 11 to 14 (Piaget, 1954).

Modern brain research (Healy, 1990) corroborates Piaget's findings. The higher level thinking capacities required for effective understanding of symbolism are now known to be located in the frontal lobes of the human brain. Because these frontal lobes are only beginning to mature during late childhood, younger children are capable of thinking abstractly only in a very limited way. When there is a persistent use of symbolism in children's instruction, consequently, it is often ineffective and valueless.

DANIEL C. JESSEN

Bibliography. J. M. Healy (1990), *Endangered Minds: Why Our Children Don't Think;* idem (1994), *Your Child's Growing Mind: A Parent's Guide to Learning from Birth to Adolescence;* L. LeBar (1952), *Children in the Bible School;* J. Piaget (1954), *The Construction of Reality in the Child.*

See also LITURGY

Symposium. *See* Panel Discussion.

Synagogue. *See* Church; Hebrew Education Through Feasts and Festivals; Jewish Education.

Synagogue Schools. Soon after their return from exile in 538 B.C. the Jewish people realized the importance of maintaining their cultural and religious heritage. Being apart from their land and unable to worship in the manner in which they had been accustomed, Jewish leaders were concerned about the ability of the nation to survive without a strong educational system. This new approach to educating generations of young Jewish children would ensure a continuance of the Jewish people.

Since the synagogue system was already operating with success as a place of worship and adult instruction, Jewish leaders decided to use this facility as the basis for developing an educational system for children as well. Using the books of the Mosaic Law as a basis of curriculum, boys were required to memorize large portions of the Law. Content also included studies in mathematics and writing. Although voluntary at first, attendance became mandatory in A.D. 64, when it was ordered by Joshua ben Gamala, the high priest during the last days of the temple. Every community that had ten Jewish families was required to maintain such a school for their children. Schooling generally began at the age of 5.

In the fourth century B.C. Aramaic became the spoken language of the Jews, resulting in Hebrew becoming primarily a written language. The synagogue school was commissioned with the task of instructing boys in Hebrew so they would be able to read and study the Law. By age 10, these young boys were expected to be able to study the Mishnah, a textbook on the oral law. This included such topics as agricultural laws, marriage and divorce, laws related to the Jewish festivals and feasts, as well as civil and criminal laws. Those who excelled in their studies were sent to rabbinical school at the age of 15 for preparations of becoming a rabbi, or teacher of the Law.

It is no understatement to say that the preservation of the Jewish nation since the time of the exile is due to a large measure on the success of the synagogue school. Christians have much to learn from the value and importance placed on the instruction of children in the sacred Scrip-tures. Scripture memory was the focal content of the curriculum. What it meant to be a contributing member of Jewish society was the hidden agenda of each school. It would due well for our contemporary church leaders to see the Sunday school as a critical component of the preservation of our religious heritage as well.

MICHAEL J. ANTHONY

Bibliography. C. B. Eavey (1973), *History of Christian Education;* K. O. Gangel and W. S. Benson (1983), *Christian Education: Its History and Philosophy;* J. E. Reed and R. Prevost (1993), *A History of Christian Education.*

Synergy. Combined action of two or more distinct elements coming together for the common good. When this cooperative effort takes place, the end result is seen as making a greater contribution than the sum of the individual parts.

A synergistic approach is sometimes used in the development of Christian education theory or models of practice. For example, Michael Mack (1996) has advocated a strategy for integrating small groups and Sunday school. In Mack's model, Sunday school and small groups do not compete against each other but rather become the foundation for a full-service church where the small groups and Sunday school provide multiple entry points into the church. The end result of the combined approach is a local church that is much more effective in both discipleship and evangelism.

J. GREGORY LAWSON

Bibliography. M. Mack (1996), *The Synergy Church.*

See also SMALL GROUPS; SUNDAY SCHOOL

Syntality. This term was introduced by R. B. Cattell in 1966 and was described as being synonymous with the concept of national personality. Later research by Cattell has considered methods for making valid cross-cultural comparisons of syntality. The word has also been used as a registered trademark for the U-CANDU Learning Centers. In this context, syntality is an approach to accelerated learning accomplished by bringing together numerous learning techniques in a holistic approach to learning.

J. GREGORY LAWSON

Bibliography. R. B. Cattell, ed. (1988), *Handbook of Multivariate Experimental Psychology.*

Tt

Talented. *See* Exceptional Persons.

Target. *See* Goal.

Teachable Moments. Times when a person is particularly open to learning. When the individual is challenged and the environment supports learning, when the person is aware of needs, when the student's and teacher's goals are congruent, teachable moments occur. When there are times of crisis, when there is a sense of loss, or new opportunities are immanent, teachable moments occur. When personal needs are addressed or personal values are challenged, teachable moments occur. When the learner is faced with decisions about goals, priorities, choices of roles or responsibilities, or needed skills, teachable moments occur. When a person transitions in the life cycle, leaving the support of a current phase and taking steps to the new phase, teachable moments occur.

These optimal times for learning may include one person or a group and may involve formal or informal education. They often are culturally relevant, gender-sensitive, and developmentally appropriate, encouraging the learner to respond with his or her whole person.

The Holy Spirit is an important factor in teachable moments. The Spirit works through the Scriptures and biblical or theological understanding, through celebration or conviction, through circumstances, and through making God's presence felt. He designs and capitalizes on teachable moments!

JANET L. DALE

Bibliography. E. H. Erickson (1963), *Childhood and Society*; R. J. Havighurst (1982), *Handbook of Developmental Psychology*, pp. 49–65; D. J. Levinson, C. N. Darrow, E. B. Klein, M. H. Levinson, and B. McKee (1977), *Counseling Adults*, pp. 47–59; B. L. Neugarten (1977), *Counseling Adults*, pp. 34–45.

Teacher as Educator. The role of teacher/educator goes back to the founding of human society, when Adam taught his sons rudimentary agriculture. Thereafter, families and societies have passed important skills and information down through the generations.

Historically, the family and clan have been the locus of teaching values, attitudes, and survival skills, primarily assimilated by youth through the example of role models (see below). Parents and other recognized authority figures have also made sure that children receive any additional information necessary for cultural functioning. For example, in colonial New England towns, parents engaged a schoolmaster to teach their children to read the Bible. In addition, for centuries apprenticeship learning has been used effectively to teach skills and work habits. In brief, then, a "teacher/educator" is anyone who helps another person learn.

In today's world, the role of teacher/educator takes a variety of forms, both in and out of Christian education.

Teacher-as-Discloser. The conventional definition of teacher/educator connotes a person using classrooms, books, laboratories, and co-curricular teaching aids (visuals, computers, videotapes, etc.) to transmit information to students who are presumed to know little about the subject. This is usually the case in an institution such as a school or college, with lecture used as the primary method of instruction. Paulo Freire (1972) accurately characterized this approach as "banking"—students line up at the teller's window to have facts dispensed. The focus is on the teacher who exercises the important role of imparting information and perspective to learners. The goal of the teacher is to declare truth or, perhaps more popularly, to "cover the material." It is assumed that the student's role is to absorb the facts and be able to recall, perhaps even integrate, them in a test, often in written form. Some Sunday or church school teachers might perceive themselves to be in this category.

Certain settings and certain subject matters are appropriate for the disclosure approach to teaching. It is often regarded as an efficient means of instruction.

Teacher-as-Guide. The term *teacher/educator* is more infrequently used to describe a "guide of learners." Whether in a traditional school setting or in a nonformal program, the teacher/educator seeks to assist students through the learning process to its completion.

"Learning-by-doing," both in and out of the classroom, comprises a significant element of the learner-focused approach. A variety of teaching/learning strategies are also employed to capitalize on the varied learning styles of learners. Field trips, simulated and real-life experiences, drama, camping, other recreational activities, outside-of-class mentoring, apprenticeships, and the like are used by the learner-oriented teacher to aid the learners absorb such attitudes, values, and skills as *loyalty, cooperation,* and *conflict resolution.*

Within Christian education, effective Sunday school teachers, recreation/club leaders, youth sponsors, and camp counselors tend to be learner-sensitive in their teaching.

When students have participated in teacher-guided learning, their retention and ability to utilize the knowledge are often quite comprehensive.

Teacher-as-Model. Much human learning is derived from imitation. A person providing an example (or model), therefore, is serving as a teacher/educator, informally and perhaps unintentionally, as in the process by which parents socialize their offspring. According to Bandura (1971) and other social learning theorists, the model informs learners about values, attitudes, and skills simply by the way he or she performs tasks or experiences life. The learners observe and subsequently model their attitudes and behavior after the parent or other role model, often unconsciously.

The strong and lasting impact parents make on their children's values and attitudes testifies to the educational allure of modeling. Hence, the importance of helping Christian parents live biblical lifestyles consistently before their children. Likewise, the selection and preparation of Christian camp, recreation, and club personnel is very critical since their influence is so significant.

Teacher-as-Discloser/Guide/Model. This teacher/educator realizes that:

- disclosure, by itself, runs the risk of students failing to get beyond memorization and/or integration of data.
- guidance, standing alone, may produce skilled people who are lacking sufficient breath and depth of knowledge.
- modeling, per se, is often inadequate because implicit learnings, being ill-defined, may not be available to the learner for intelligent application.

The effective teacher/educator, then, attempts to combine these approaches in order to introduce learners to a total educational experience which can lead to in-depth mastery of what is to be learned.

Christian Teacher/Educator. Jesus instructed his disciples to teach others "to *observe* [or do] all things that I have commanded you" (Matt. 28:18–20 NKJV). Hence, Christian education that does not result in changed lives falls short of the mark. God's truth was never intended simply for intellectual contemplation or admiration; it was also intended to guide humankind to decide to love God and obey his commands. Christian education must motivate learners to integrate God's truth into their lives.

Planning for this kind of teaching begins with understanding the needs of the learners, then deciding how to lead them to lifestyle decisions. Christian education curriculum builds on behavioral objectives and all appropriate teaching/learning strategies are used to encourage the learners' understanding, competence, and desire to make life-application.

DANIEL C. JESSEN

Bibliography. A. Bandura (1971), *Social Learning Theory;* P. Downs (1994), *Teaching for Spiritual Growth;* P. Freire (1972), *Pedagogy of the Oppressed;* T. H. Groome (1980), *Christian Religious Education;* L. LeBar (1992), *Education That Is Christian;* R. Pazmiño (1992), *Principles and Practices of Christian Education;* L. O. Richards (1975), *A Theology of Christian Education.*

Teaching, Gift of. The spiritual gift of teaching is mentioned in several key New Testament passages listing spiritual gifts (Rom 12:7; 1 Cor. 12:29; Eph. 4:11). The gift of teaching had obvious prominence in the early church, thus underscoring the importance of the teaching ministry in the church today. The gift of teaching can be described as a supernatural, spiritually endowed ability to expound (explain and apply) the truth of God. This gift allows a person to show harmony and detail in the Bible that make its truths more readily and personally applicable. The teaching gift is also linked to the task of establishing the church and bringing to maturity a local community of believers who can discern and contribute their own gifts and in so doing build up the local body of believers (Eph. 4:11–13).

All members of a community of believers are ultimately taught by the Holy Sprit, and believers are responsible to edify one another through exhortation and instruction. However, the teaching gift is a special spiritual endowment that equips a person to function in a responsible manner for the maturing of believers. The teaching gift carries with it the implications that believers will mature in Christ as this gift is properly expressed. The Holy Spirit will teach Christians in the reception of truth, but gifts teachers to relate that truth in a digestible form.

The focus of the gift of teaching generally impacts the learners more than the teacher. Paul indicates that the goal of teaching God's Word is to impact dramatically the maturity of believers (Col. 1:28). Paul uses descriptions of this process, such as conformity to the image of Christ and attaining to the fullness of Christ (Eph. 4:13). While the gift of teaching may be expressed in a variety of settings, this critical function in the church requires tangible expressions of love if it is to be credible and effective (1 Cor. 12:1–3). The function of this gift is often seen in conjunction with the character qualities of spiritual leadership (1 Tim. 3:1–13). The emphasis of New Testament writers is always on the function of the gift of teaching. The idea of this gift focusing on the creation of an official office for a person is nowhere emphasized in the New Testament. The biblical emphasis is on people gifted to function in a strategic role of spearheading a strategic plan to bring to maturity a specific group of believers.

While teaching in the church does go on and must continue in a variety of situations, does everyone who is involved in the teaching ministry of the church have the gift of teaching? There is no doubt a linkage exists between natural propensities and spiritual gifting (including teaching) that is keyed to establishing the local church and maintaining its ongoing growth. Whether a ministry of teaching actually is a "gifted" ministry really finds its root in prayer, which is indicative of obedient reliance on the Spirit as the source for this ministry. There must also be concerted effort in study, developed from an ever-growing desire for in-depth study of God's Word. Motivation to be committed to the ongoing development of a teaching ministry is confirmed by ability and accompanied by blessing. As with all spiritual giftings, ongoing training and use of the gift is a reasonable response of human obedience to God's sovereign gifting. In addition, there must be cooperation with basic principles of learning and the developmental realities that can maximize the impact of the gift of teaching that the Holy Spirit has bestowed. Having the spiritual gift of teaching the Word of God need not be limited solely to the teaching of adults. The Holy Spirit is fully capable of gifting teachers for all age-level ministries in keeping with the function delineated in Ephesians 4:11–13. It is best to assume that the gift is not restricted to any one age level but rather refers to the process of instruction than the audience of it.

One of the most poignant personal examples in the New Testament of the importance of the gift and ministry of teaching is Paul's relationship with Timothy. False teachers are the scourge of this period and yet Paul wants to see truth passed on to future generations. The negative impact of these false teachers, if not countered with the Spirit-gifted teachers, is described in 1 Timothy 4:1. Paul believes the key is solid teaching to faithful believers who will in turn teach others (2 Tim. 2:2). Paul challenges Timothy to stir up the teaching gift God has sovereignly bestowed him with so as to counteract the negative impact of these false teachers. In 2 Timothy 1:13–14 Paul even goes so far as to link the sacred trust of the gospel with a protective stance that is to be demonstrated by an ongoing establishing of believers through the Spirit-empowered teaching ministry of the church. Paul also suggests that the gift can/should be fanned into flame when it is exercised or used. Contemporary expression of "fanning the flame" would include teaching others, observing other effective teachers, regular training on better principles, and having other teachers make helpful evaluations on your teaching.

BYRON D. KLAUS

Bibliography. M. Anthony, ed. (1992), *Foundations of Ministry: An Introduction to Christian Education for a New Generation;* R. Clark, L. Johnson, and A. Sloat, eds. (1991), *Christian Education: Foundations for the Future;* K. Gangel and H. Hendricks, eds. (1988), *The Christian Educator's Handbook on Teaching;* S. Horton, *What the Bible Says About the Holy Spirit.*

See also HOLY SPIRIT; SPIRITUAL GIFTS; TEACHINGS OF JESUS CHRIST

Teaching Environment. *See* Classroom Setting.

Teaching-Learning Process. Intentional, dynamic encounter between teachers and students, consisting of complex, multidimensional interactions, primarily to promote progress toward wholeness and maturity, often taking place within a group setting. Although God's nature and attributes are unchanging, humans come into this life as immature creatures who have been designed to change through supernatural transformation, human development, and human learning—and in this final aspect we have the most participation and influence. Essential to entering fully into the promise of abundant living is God's grace and our effort to learn. "Grace . . . is opposed to *earning,* not to *effort*" (Willard, 1997, 12). So we must learn to become wise, loving, forgiving, just, industrious, and skillful. Learning is necessary for human flourishing.

Although learning regularly takes place without any purposeful instruction—and at times without any awareness (e.g., acquiring our mother language as a child)—this article focuses on learning associated with teaching, distinctively, Christian teaching and learning.

Relationship Between Teaching and Learning. The relationship between teaching and learning is a complicated one. How one views this relationship has implications for educational research programs as well as teacher planning, since it delimits the role of the learner in the T-L process. Should it be comparable to coaching athletes, or machining a tool on a lathe? Is the relationship directly causal—so that a specific method always yields a specific result? Such a causal model is appropriate to the natural sciences investigating solely physical entities—of bombarding atoms and chemical reactions—but people are more than material objects. At the heart of the T-L process is a relationship among willing persons with a common purpose, that is, *a relationship of consensus*—a relationship among causal agents—implying some expression of free will.

As with any relationship involving persons, no specific action by one person ("teaching") can automatically guarantee a predetermined response by another person ("learning"). Each student is ultimately responsible for his or her own learning (Gowin, 1981). This explains why learning can occur without teaching (students learn on their own) and teaching can take place without learning (Mark 8:14–21).

Teachers intend to promote learning in students, and are often effective. Dewey (1933) suggested an analogy from retail sales. "There is the same exact equation between teaching and learning that there is between selling and buying" (36). Teachers engage in plans and activities to offer students opportunities for learning. Students expend their effort to learn, under the care of teachers, with the prospect of becoming, in some way, better persons. Although some learning may occur without willing students, human learning thrives best where human dignity and freedom are respected.

Yet, despite no direct causal relationship, teachers are not without any idea of how best to facilitate learning. Knowledge gleaned from research and reflective experience enables teachers to plan for instruction that will *likely* or *probably* facilitate student learning, given students who are willing and able (Shuell, 1996, Table 22–6). Teachers are accountable for faithfully carrying through with good intentions in their teaching, and for some measure of positive results in students. If a good number of students aren't "buying," we wonder if any legitimate "selling" is going on.

Is There Christian T-L Process? What is distinctive about the T-L process that is uniquely Christian? In many ways, as Lee (1996/1982) argues, teaching and learning about religious content within a religious setting is similar to teaching and learning about anything in any other place. To do it well, we must attend to the study and practice of these normal processes that are similar for believer and unbeliever alike. What offers the potential for a distinctively "Christian" T-L process is primarily the dynamic participation of a supernatural Being. When teachers and

learners are genuinely walking with the Spirit of God, the divine, transforming power that becomes available goes well beyond normal human capacities (Gal. 3:3; Eph. 3:16; 1 Cor. 12:29). Even studying the Word of God by itself cannot guarantee any *unique* effects—nonbelievers can make sense of much of the Bible—unless learners listen to the Spirit, who makes the Bible's words on a page become living and active in their hearts and minds (1 Cor. 2:10–16; Heb. 4:12). When participants are *filled*—not just indwelt—by the Spirit and are sustaining a dynamic supernatural relationship, then a distinctively Christian teaching and learning experience can unfold. In addition, the T-L process is carried out under the authority of God (Pazmino, 1994), and with God's commitment to supervise the process (Rom. 8:28; 1 Cor. 10:13), and ultimately to see the process to completion (Phil. 1:6; Eph. 4:11–16).

Goals of the T-L Process. Beyond its intrinsic worth, the T-L encounter has instrumental value. Each encounter has an end: the promotion of student learning. Ultimately, the task of Christian education revolves around sustaining believers' efforts, individually and corporately, to seek, love, and enjoy God with all of their being (Matt. 11:28–30; 22:37–38; 28:19–20; John 17:3) and to love others as themselves (Matt. 22:39–40). Maturity must lead to living abundantly. A car, computer, chair, or shopping mall fulfills its primary design when it functions properly. So, we fulfill God's purpose for us when we relate well with God and others, when we think and feel our faith deeply, when we engage in life's opportunities in a godly manner. As our Lord proclaimed, "I came that they may have life, and have it abundantly" (John 10:10 NRSV). The more we progress in maturity, the more we are able to experience abundant living.

Components of the T-L Process. Any T-L case or episode incorporates at least seven commonplaces: teacher, learner, subject matter, milieu or circumstances, purposes, activity, and result (Dillon, 1988). This framework can be used to analyze and diagnose what is happening. For example, consider a brief episode from Mark 13:1–4. The teacher is Jesus and his disciples are the learners. A few moments before, Jesus is sitting opposite the treasury in the temple area [circumstances], observing the donations offered by the multitudes. He makes a comment about the poor widow's sacrificial gift [activity], but no response is recorded for the disciples [results]. As the group leaves the temple area [circumstance], a disciple [learner] makes a statement to Jesus, praising the temple buildings themselves [subject matter]. In response, Jesus [teacher] announces provocatively that these buildings will all be destroyed [subject matter, activity]. No immediate comment is forthcoming from the disciples [results], but later, as they sit on the Mount of

Olives, opposite the temple, four disciples begin questioning Jesus "privately," wondering when this destruction will take place [result]. Jesus answers their inquiry [activity] as recorded in the rest of the chapter. Since we don't have Jesus' lesson plans, we can only infer what his purposes might have been that prompted such a provocative statement (v. 2), but the results imply his desire to teach about particulars of the future [subject matter].

Further questions can be asked about each commonplace as the analysis goes deeper into this T-L encounter. For instance, assuming all twelve disciples were with Jesus, note that only Peter, James, John, and Andrew pursued this private teaching session with Jesus. This initial review illustrates what kind of a tool the seven components can be for evaluating past T-L experiences or for planning future teaching opportunities (Habermas and Issler, 1992, chaps. 9–10).

Improving Practice. As mentioned, learners have a responsibility for their own learning. Since we have been created to learn, adopting a lifelong learning commitment and practice is fitting. As learners, we must become aware of conditions and channels that foster learning. These include association (operant and classical conditioning), example (observational learning), the cognitive channels that promote problem solving, and meaningful presentations (Issler and Habermas, 1994). Learners also develop preferences for learning and can gain insight from the various learning style theories that abound.

Teachers can support students in their learning quest by using teaching methods that promote learning and student motivation to learn. Methods may vary according to teaching purposes, learner need, interest, motivation, developmental level, and givens of the circumstance. Jesus' challenge in Luke 6:40—that a student becomes like the teacher—moves us beyond an exclusive emphasis on effective methods of teaching and learning to a focus also on the person and character of the teacher. Since loving God and others is central to our teaching purposes, teachers must embody a loving manner. Thus teachers must also pursue "virtuous" teaching—acquiring the habits, the virtues of the excellent teacher (Issler, 1996). The high calling and accountability for Christian teaching demands this pursuit of excellence (James 3:1).

KLAUS ISSLER

Bibliography. J. Dewey (1933), *How We Think;* J. T. Dillon (1988), *Questioning and Teaching: A Manual of Practice;* D. B. Gowin (1981), *Educating;* R. Habermas and K. Issler (1992), *Teaching for Reconciliation: Foundations and Practice of Christian Educational Ministry;* H. Hendricks (1987), *Teaching to Change Lives;* K. Issler (1996), *With an Eye on the Future: Development and Mission in the 21st Century. Essays in Honor of Ted Ward;* K. Issler and R. Habermas (1994), *How We Learn:*

A Christian Teacher's Guide to Educational Psychology; J. M. Lee (1973), *The Flow of Religious Instruction: A Social Science Approach;* idem (1996/1982), *Theological Perspectives on Christian Formation: A Reader on Theology and Christian Education;* R. R. Osmer (1990), *A Teachable Spirit: Recovering the Teaching Office in the Church;* R. W. Pazmiño (1994), *By What Authority Do We Teach? Sources for Empowering Christian Educators;* T. J. Shuell (1996), *Handbook of Educational Psychology;* D. Willard (1997), *Love Your God with All Your Mind;* W. R. Yount (1996), *Created to Learn: A Christian Teacher's Introduction to Educational Psychology.*

Teaching Methods. *See* Bible Study Methods.

Teaching Plan. *See* Curriculum; Lesson Plan.

Teaching Scripture to Children. God commanded that his Word be taught to children. Deuteronomy 6:6–9 (NASB) states, "And these words, which I am commanding you today, shall be on your heart; and you shall teach them diligently to your sons and shall talk of them when you sit in your house and when you walk by the way and when you lie down and when you rise up. And you shall bind them as a sign on your hand and they shall be as frontals on your forehead. And you shall write them on the doorposts of your house and on your gates." According to these verses, teaching was to be done by talking to children, by relating the truths to the activities of life, and also through using visual symbols. The use of the senses of hearing, moving, and seeing in this way is educationally referred to as using learning modalities. Children who learn best by hearing are referred to as *auditory learners*. Those who learn best through seeing are called *visual learners*. Children who prefer to move around are referred to as *tactile/kinesthetic learners* (tactile for the sense of touch and kinesthetic for need for large body movements). God intended that children be taught through all learning modalities.

All young children are tactile/kinesthetic learners. They learn best by moving and touching. Scripture is taught effectively to them by the use of active methods (interactive Bible stories, play acting, crafts, action songs, etc.). Some early elementary age children switch to a visual learning preference. These children learn best when they can see biblical truth illustrated (pictures, flannelgraph, videos, drama, objects, etc.). At about ages 10 to 12 some children's learning preferences switch to audio methods. They learn best by hearing biblical truths explained. Girls tend to prefer audio methods, while boys often prefer tactile/kinesthetic methods. Research varies on the percentage of children who prefer each learning modality. Teachers who use teaching methods in all learning modalities will be the most effective in teaching Scripture to a group of children.

Teaching Scripture to children implies more than giving them information. Scripture has not really been taught until children utilize the information. Children have learned biblical truth when they know it, understand it, and can put it into practice in their lives. To teach Scripture to children, teachers must know how children think, how they understand concepts, and which scriptural truths can be learned and practiced by children at different ages.

As children grow and develop physically, their ability to think and process biblical truth changes. Children are not miniature adults. They process information much differently than do adults. Jean Piaget (1896–1980), the Swiss researcher, studied children and described their cognitive development stages. Christian educators today use Piaget's four stages in selecting which biblical truths to teach children of various ages and in determining how best to communicate those truths.

During the first two years of life, Piaget found that children learn by responding to the world around them. They establish behavior patterns through their senses by interacting with that world. During this *sensorimotor stage*, children will learn about God by experiencing him through people who create a safe, loving environment for them. This is not the time to teach Bible content, but to help children explore their world and develop good behavior patterns.

During the second stage (approximately ages 2 to 7) children acquire language skills and are able to express their thinking in words. In this *preoperational stage* children think in specific details, but find it difficult to generalize and classify. They tend only to grasp one idea or one aspect of an object or truth. Therefore, applications must be specific and tangible, not generalized or expressed as principle. These children can be taught basic Bible stories, but teachers should emphasize only one simple truth from each story. This truth may be repeated many times in different ways during a class session. The children are able to focus on learning for only short periods of time, but they do enjoy and learn from repetition. These children can understand truths only from their own perspective. They will only apply truths that relate directly to their world. This egocentrism reflects the children's inability to see things from another person's perspective. Children can be taught that God loves them, but they will only want to love others if it is of benefit the them. They do not have the ability to understand how love affects another person.

From about ages 7 to 11 children enter the period of *concrete operations*. They think in very concrete, literal terms, but they have increased reasoning ability. This is an important transition because it is now possible for children to conceptualize scriptural truths. The conceptualization is, however, limited to particular situations and best explained by concrete examples. They have a growing ability to classify or group ideas into concepts. This ability to see relationships and categorize allows children to take truths and form them into useable principles. Although these children can classify, they need help in identifying what specific items should be grouped together. They can, for example, understand the concept of kindness, but they will need help in identifying the behavior that is kind.

Concept formation occurs when several related events, experiences, or ideas are logically connected together under one generalized idea. For example, the concept of honesty may be built around telling the truth, acting in truthful ways, not hiding truth, or not cheating. A teacher must help children relate these ideas and experiences to the concept of honesty. These children generally do not have the ability to form concepts without help. In the Scriptures there are many concepts that children can understand and practice if teachers help them make the appropriate relationships.

The growing ability to think logically and to understand time allows these children to think in new ways. They can define, compare, and contrast. They can solve problems and reason out cause and effect in life situations. They can understand time and learn from history. These new abilities are limited to concrete situations that children can see and experience and to literal interpretations of truth. But there are many truths from the Bible that these children can learn and practice in their lives. The use of concrete examples in teaching is very important in increasing understanding and application of the Scriptures.

Many children in the concrete learning period learn details readily. This is the best time for memorizing Scripture and lists of things such as the books of the Bible. These children can retain vast amounts of information. Teachers should be cautioned that verbalizing Scripture does not mean that it is understood or that it will be practiced. These children tend to verbalize knowledge that they do not understand and cannot apply to their lives.

After the age of 12 many children develop the ability to think abstractly through *formal operations*. These children think about the theoretical, the remote, and the future. They have greater abilities to classify and integrate truths and to do problem solving. They can look at truths learned in the past and give them new meaning by integrating them into new concepts. They are capable of understanding the symbolism found in the Scriptures as well as prophecies about the future. These children can understand most scriptural truths and should be helped to build a strong conceptual foundation that is practical for their lives. Although these children can understand most scriptural truths, they will only be interested in learning truths that relate to their lives. This is the time to introduce practical topical studies and to assist the children in finding what the Bible says about life-related issues. The children should be encouraged to do more hands-on Bible study.

A listing of many of the scriptural truths that can be taught to children at various ages from 2 years of age to 11 can be found in *Childhood Education in the Church, Revised and Expanded* (1986), edited by Robert E. Clark, Joanne Brubaker, and Roy B. Zuck (367–74).

EILEEN STARR

Bibliography. R. E. Clark, J. Brubaker, and R. B. Zuck, eds. (1986), *Childhood Education in the Church;* R. E. Clark, L. Johnson, and A. K. Sloat (1991), *Christian Education, Foundations for the Future;* P. Downs (1994), *Teaching for Spiritual Growth, An Introduction to Christian Education;* M. D. LeFever (1995), *Learning Styles, Reaching Everyone God Gave You to Teach.*

Teachings of Jesus Christ. Jesus of Nazareth came into this sinful, broken world as an incarnation of God's love and justice in order to transform all of creation into a new creation, a new world order within the reign of God. Who Jesus was as a person, fully divine and fully human, radically changed forever the reality—physical, emotional, intellectual, moral, social, spiritual—of human living, interacting, and growing. All of life is now lived within the new realm of God's presence. To say that Jesus is a teacher is to affirm that Jesus is doing away with the old creation, the old self, the old human society and is bringing new life for all God has made. In this sense Jesus' ministry of being God-with-us expresses and embodies the very essence of Christology and soteriology. God's redeeming, transforming presence in all of life, God's Word-become-flesh, calls us to leave behind our old selves and social patterns and enter into an eternal relationship that recreates everything we are, calls us to a discipleship of following the ways of God's new creation.

Jesus' ministry begins with the announcement that a new reality has come, a new day or aeon has begun: "The time is fulfilled, and the kingdom of God has come near" (Mark 1:15a NRSV). The fundamental message or truth that Jesus taught and incarnated was that God is initiating a new way of being personally present in human society and in all creation. The fullness of the Godhead is no longer to be understood as an otherworldly potentate who rules through Torah or all-encompassing principles for living and who metes out justice from on high, but is now a living, breathing, personal presence in the flesh who invites us into a heart-to-heart relationship. But this relationship of disciple to master begins in repentance and trusting God completely (Mark 1:15b), a radical reorienting of life from top to bottom. Instead of a world order centered in the power of Caesar who was to be revered and worshiped and followed as the ultimate authority and source of life in society, a God-centered pattern of existence now becomes normative. No more business as usual, no more status quo, no more of the old ways of relying on one's own human social and spiritual resources is possible in this new realm. Education in the new creation is not like traditional schooling, but is incarnational. It necessitates openness to God's Spirit being present with and breaking into human affairs to reveal, convict, encourage, and teach.

This inauguration of God into human history brought about a new social movement. Jesus' first and central ministry task was the formation of a cadre or network of associates who participated in this movement intended to transform first-century Palestine under Roman occupation and through it ultimately to the ends of the earth. The four Gospels are united in their depiction of the beginning of Jesus' work in the world as a calling or summoning of the disciples into relationship. This relationship was long-term, well-rounded, mutual, intimate, and touched all of life. Jesus' teaching first and foremost gathered together hurting, searching, marginal people into motley community. This is no utopian sect removed from everyday, ordinary living like at Qumran. No, new kingdom living completely revalues and refocuses daily experience in the totality of human cultural expression. In fact, human culture making becomes the expression of the divine image and the Spirit's presence, and thus all of life become a holy, sacred enterprise. In the new creation the participants in the Jesus movement join the new life redemptively in work and play, in family and friendships, in economics and politics, indeed, in everything. So disciple-making education is fundamentally relational for Jesus. Truth transforms most deeply when it occurs in a heart-to-heart communion.

The focus of this relational mode of instruction is personal spiritual formation. To be an intimate follower of Jesus, one must first of all relinquish control of life and let go of all competing, rival commitments. The first disciples left behind their vocational livelihoods such as fishing and tax collecting. They let go of family and friends as the central concerns of their lives. Discipleship in the new reign of God requires dying to oneself, taking up one's cross, and journeying with the countercultural Jesus. Only one master is possible in life, and all else is subordinated to this organizing center. When Jesus called people, he looked deeply, presciently into their inmost hearts. Jesus' new way touched deeply into each individual in unique ways. Some, like the rich young ruler, turned away because the cost was too high. Some are hungry for the healing and transformation Jesus offers. Those who persist as followers are characterized by the internal qualities described in the Beatitudes: those who know they are poor, who hunger and thirst for the right to prevail in the world, who mourn the brokenness within and all around, who strive for shalom within the entire human family. Jesus taught by living these qualities, by creating a place where people with hurts and longings and fears and brokenness can come and be themselves and fail and be forgiven. He formed a redemptive community of unconditional love that accepted people where they were in their journey, that entered into their pain and suffering, and that revealed one's own inner struggles. Jesus taught by being a companion with people in their quest for God, for wholeness, for justice. Jesus walked with these hungry, hurting, confused followers, no matter what they went through. He did not give up on them.

In addition to this broad process of spiritual formation, Jesus also taught through direct instruction. Jesus was a very creative teacher, but the major technique running throughout is dialogue. The Gospels preserve the genius of the master teacher as a person who asks probing questions, tells enigmatic parables, encounters Roman soldiers, tax collectors, religious leaders, widows, and blind men, engaging in life-changing discussion. Even as a lad of 12 Jesus spent time in debate with the religious leaders discussing the ways of God with humanity. For Jesus these personal, caring conversations were largely open-ended. Each person, each situation, required sensitivity. Jesus was person-centered as a teacher. Jesus discovered where people were and responded from the heart, rather than having predigested, canned lectures and rhetorical devices. Jesus, being so connected to God, and so focused on people as they are, could adapt creatively to any situation to bring the truth home to people.

In particular Jesus chose to become involved in his transformational ministry with persons who were outside the mainstream of society. He intentionally incorporated women, the diseased, disabled, non-Jews, the powerless, poor, children, the disenfranchised, and other social outcasts into the Jesus movement. It is also worth noting that much of Jesus' teaching was directed at the multitudes, the large peasant class in the Judean and Galilean countryside. Within this broad backdrop of landless, powerless peasants, the gospel writers recount episode after episode in which Jesus engages with the little ones of society. Jesus listens, responds, cries, and cares for the least of society (see especially Matt. 25). Jesus from the beginning states definitively that "the Spirit of the Lord is upon me, because he has anointed me to bring good news to the poor. He has sent me to proclaim release to the captives, and recovery of sight to the blind, to let the oppressed go free, to proclaim the year of the Lord's favor" (Luke 4:18–19). Jesus proclaims, teaches, and brings the good news of the reign of God to those left out in society.

Jesus spent a good deal of his teaching time challenging the thoughts of his disciples. For example, reading through the Book of Luke with an eye toward the questions Jesus asks will reveal a compelling argument for the Socratic method of instruction. It is as though Jesus never speaks without first interjecting a question into the discussion. In so doing he is trying to prime the cognitive pump with a stimulating thought. From there he either answers the question or leaves the listening with a thirst for self-instruction. It is a powerful lesson for modern-day Christian educators as well.

Jesus' educational ministry also involves equipping, empowering, and sending out his band of associates. The teaching-learning process was experience-based. On many occasions Jesus gave the disciples ministry tasks to do that were developmentally appropriate. In several instances Jesus sent them out in teams to practice ministry. For a little over three years this roving band was in full-time service of the sovereign God of the universe. They encountered firsthand healing, exorcism, miracles, death, children, and countless other real-life situations which stretched their ability to minister. They learned by doing, and by failing and not giving up. In this hands-on experiential learning they were empowered by the Holy Spirit. They were also supervised in their ministry by Jesus. They brought the hard cases to Jesus.

In this holistic, developmental process the key dynamic was an action-reflection model of learning. Days were filled with teachable moments for his disciples. Jesus went to where the people were. He hung out with the commoners in their natural environments, spending time with them. He talked with them about their daily experiences. He was very accessible to people as a wandering, charismatic teacher. Simply by being with people in the midst of their daily activities, in the streets, in their homes, sharing meals, around the docks, in the fields, and so forth, Jesus taught. He would often begin with probing questions, pregnant stories, enigmatic parables pointing to some aspect of experience. Also, people would often come to him with their concerns and questions. The activities and events of day-to-day living in a poor, menial, colonial situation were ample grist for life-changing interaction. With the Samaritan woman at the well (John 4), the action of drawing drinking water becomes an entry point into profound dialogue concerning religious, moral, and social inequities and problems. By naming these problematic realities, critical reflection on them can begin. Critical reflection delves into the causes, into the historical dimensions of each situation. It identifies what lies beneath the surface of the status quo. It goes on to imagine an alternative reality. It motivates and empowers people to envision a new way of living and to pursue boldly the new way.

Jesus also incarnated the new creation through challenging the principalities and powers that were allied against God's sovereign will. Many parts of the first century world were threatened by Jesus' transforming presence. They preferred to maintain the status quo and remain in power. Jesus deliberately confronted the earthly rulers and structures. This confrontation included accepted values and belief systems, social, economic, and political ideologies, and especially the religious establishment. For Jesus, discipleship and growth in the new way of God intrinsically involves a foundational commitment to God's justice on behalf of the poor and the powerless in society and the concomitant disestablishment of the ruling powers. Jesus often uses biting satire, polemical word pictures, barbed questions, symbolic actions, and other methods to awaken the apathetic, unnerve the self-righteous, and to denounce prophetically unjust practices incongruent with the reign of God. Jesus broke the mold of education in the first century. Although in some ways Jesus appeared like a Jewish rabbi or Greek philosopher instructing his pupils. But Jesus did not come to hand down accepted precepts, whether legal or philosophical. Jesus came with the authority of the reign of God. Jesus came to transform individuals and institutions and whole cultures. Jesus brought life, not abstract theories. Jesus touched people in their deepest hearts and souls.

VERNON L. BLACKWOOD

Bibliography. R. A. Culpepper (1975), *The Johannine School;* M. Hengel (1981), *The Charismatic Leader and His Followers;* R. Meye (1990), *Jesus and the Twelve;* P. Perkins (1990), *Jesus as Teacher;* M. Wilkins (1995), *Discipleship in the Ancient World and Matthew's Gospel;* idem (1992), *Following the Master—Discipleship in the Steps of Jesus;* R. B. Zuck (1995), *Teaching as Jesus Taught.*

Teachings of Paul. Paul, the apostle to the Gentiles, is the second most important human teacher identified in the New Testament. His teachings and the model of his teaching ministry is second only to that of the Master Teacher in Paul's life experience, the Lord Jesus Christ whom he encountered on the road to Damascus (Acts 9:1–19). Paul was a task theologian who spoke to the specific needs of various communities as they sought to live out the Christian faith. In his ministry he was fulfilling the commission of the resurrected Christ as recorded in Matthew 28:18–20 and Acts 1:8 with a particular commitment to share the gospel with the Gentiles. Paul serves as the key interpreter of the Christian gospel to the first-century world through his extensive writings and the per-

petuation of his theological perspectives by the early followers of "the Way" that was revealed in the Son of God. The teachings embodied in Paul's writings recount his pastoral response to the struggles of understanding and living the Christian faith in a hostile and religiously pluralistic world that involved conflict both within the church and the wider society. In many of his writings, Paul addressed Christians who were living in urban settings.

Paul's teachings were built upon his Jewish faith and his educational training under the tutelage of Gamaliel (Acts 5:34; 22:3) along with the influence of his family. Paul identified himself as an Israelite, of the tribe of Benjamin, and a Pharisee who sought to fulfill the law of God through a righteous and just life (Phil. 3:4–6). His radical conversion after encountering the resurrected Christ transformed his life and his initial relationship with the emerging Christian church. This relationship was understandably questioned because of his previous persecution of the followers of Jesus (Acts 8:1; 9:1–2). His transformation contributed to his hope that others would learn of Jesus and experience salvation in a similar way. The Book of Acts records the four missionary journeys of Paul and his companions in the teaching and preaching of what he identified as the glorious and joyous gospel of Jesus Christ of which the entire known world deserved to hear (Rom. 1:1–6; 1 Cor. 1:1–2; Gal. 1:1–5; Eph. 3:1–13; Titus 1:1–3). His teaching ministry extended beyond the confines of the Jewish nation and its scattered compatriots to include the Gentiles as co-citizens of a new humanity made possible in Jesus Christ (Gal. 2:11–21; 3:26–4:7; Eph. 2:11–22).

The teachings of the apostle Paul are embodied in the letters and epistles attributed to him in the New or Second Testament. A variety of theological themes are addressed in this corpus of literature that can be analyzed in relation to the inquiries directed to Paul and his response to particular first-century contexts. But like his Master Teacher's, Paul's teaching, although contextualized, had universal significance for the emergence and perpetuation of the Christian community and the faith that it embraced. One distinctive emphasis of Paul's teachings was an extensive exploration of the Christian faith in terms of true and right thinking about God, Jesus Christ, and the continued ministry of the Holy Spirit in the world. A second emphasis to complement the focus on Christian truth was how that truth issued in a transformed life for both individual persons and the Christian church, which is the corporate expression of Christ's body in the world (1 Cor. 12:1–31; Eph. 4:1–5:21). These two distinctives of Christian truth and Christian life were repeated themes in Paul's teachings. The Christian life for Paul was a life of faith, hope, and love that issued in joy, and an exploration of these Christian values was interwoven in the content of Paul's teaching. The life in Christ as Paul described it fulfilled the supreme ethic of love that Jesus himself modeled for his followers. Paul's own life and ministry (2 Cor. 4:7–5:10; 11:16–12:10) served as a living example of the suffering and joy the Christian life may hold for others.

In his letter to the Christians at Philippi, Paul identified a comprehensive curriculum for his teaching: "whatever is true, whatever is honorable, whatever is right, whatever is pure, whatever is lovely, whatever is of good repute, if there is any excellence and if anything worthy of praise, let your mind dwell on these things. The things you have learned and received and heard and seen in me, practice these things; and the God of peace shall be in you" (Phil. 4:8, 9 NASB). All that philosophers have sought throughout the ages in order to gain wisdom became the teaching agenda for Paul and for Christians in their thought and practice. All that Christians gain from their pursuit for truth and wisdom was to be passed onto others who in turn could teach (2 Tim. 2:2 NASB). Paul was clear about the source of this truth, for it is in Christ himself that "are hidden all the treasures of wisdom and knowledge" (Col. 2:3 NASB) and the task before Christians is "taking every thought captive to the obedience of Christ" (2 Cor. 10:5).

In relation to the emphasis upon the Christian life and it being a vehicle for teaching others, Paul's instructions to Timothy in 1 Timothy 4:11–12, 16 (NASB) are noteworthy: "Prescribe and teach these things. Let no one look down on your youthfulness, but rather in speech, conduct, love, faith and purity, show yourself an example of those who believe. . . . Pay close attention to yourself and to your teaching; persevere in these things; for as you do this you will insure salvation both for yourself and for those who hear you." Timothy was encouraged to consider not only his teaching or doctrine, but also his life, as it taught by example or imitation. The modeling of teachers like Paul (1 Cor. 11:1) set the terms for what content is embraced by those who are taught. A similar emphasis is found in Titus 2:1–15, where Paul outlined what Titus was to teach the various age groups with their distinct needs and responsibilities. Titus was advised both what to teach and how to teach. He was encouraged to teach various groups *to be* something with a definite emphasis upon character formation, the values that persons were embracing and living out. Paul indicated that good works and conduct flowed from sound doctrine and from a person's being in a right relationship with God and others. Titus was instructed by Paul to teach what is in accord with sound doctrine (2:1) and to exhort with all authority (2:15). Therefore Paul

emphasized a continuity with the apostolic educational tradition and an understanding of the basis for one's teaching authority.

Paul described teaching as one of the gifts bestowed upon the church by Christ through the Holy Spirit (Rom. 12:3–8; 1 Cor. 12:27–31; Eph. 4:7–13). Teaching was not only a Spirit-endowed and motivated gift, but teaching also required that the teacher be continually filled and guided by the Holy Spirit in the process of teaching (Eph. 4:29–32; 5:15–20). The spiritual dimensions of teaching were foundational in a Pauline perspective. One of the qualifications that Paul identified for leadership in the churches was that the person be apt or able to teach (1 Tim. 3:2; 2 Tim. 2:24). Paul described his own relationship with his Thessalonian disciples as one that included both maternal and paternal dimensions of care (1 Thess. 2:7–12). In verse 8, Paul observed that not only were ministers and teachers delighted to share the gospel of God, but their lives as well (also see 1 Tim. 4:16). The maternal dimension of teaching included care and nurture, while the paternal dimension included encouraging, comforting, and urging others to live lives worthy of God.

The content of Paul's teaching and that of the New Testament church is found in encapsulated form in the creedal summaries and hymns he cited (such as 1 Cor. 15:3–8; Phil. 2:5–11; 1 Tim. 3:16; 2 Tim. 2:11–13; Titus 3:4–7). A general pattern of Paul's teaching as reflected in the Book of Ephesians, but also in his other writings, was one that incorporates instruction, intercession, and exhortation (Stott, 1979, 146). In a more basic form, the pattern has been identified as first doctrinal and second ethical (Rom. 1–11 and 12–16; Gal. 1–4 and 5–6; Eph. 1–3 and 4–6; Col. 1–2 and 3–4) (Stott, 1964, 66). Instruction consisted of a focus upon the doctrinal content of the faith, upon what God has done. Intercession was prayer for those instructed, with a conscious dependence upon God and the work of the Holy Spirit. Intercession was one dimension of the spirituality of teaching that fostered a sense of wonder, awe, and reverence in communion with God. The third element of the pattern was exhortation, in which Paul specified what believers were to be and do in the light of the God's activities and revelation in Jesus Christ. The purposes of teaching this content for Paul included the edification and eventual glorification of the church in the areas of its unity and maturity (Eph. 4:7–16; Rom. 8; 1 Cor. 15) and the justification and sanctification of individual believers (Rom. 1–6; Eph. 2:8–10).

The theological themes of Paul's teachings can be summarized in relation to the three abiding Christian virtues of faith, hope, and love (1 Cor. 13:13). Christian faith was centered in Christ, in his person and his work that is a provision for the salvation of humanity. Christian hope was centered in the consummation of God's plan for all of creation (Col. 1:9–23) that awaits the second coming of Christ (1 Thess. 4:13–5:11; 2 Thess. 2:1–12; 1 Cor. 1:7; 15:35–57; Col. 3:4; Rom. 8:18–25). Christian love found expression in the church, the body of Christ, which was a new creation and model for a new humanity made possible in Christ. This love issued in an ethic of love that Christians extended to all (Gal. 6:10; Rom. 12:9–21; 1 Cor. 12:29–13:13; Col. 3:12–14; Eph. 5:25–33).

Robert W. Pazmiño

Bibliography. W. Barclay (1974), *Educational Ideals in the Ancient World;* D. L. Bartlett (1977), *Paul's Vision of the Teaching Church;* G. D. Fee (1996), *Paul, the Spirit, and the People of God;* J. P. Fitzpatrick (1990), *Paul: Saint of the Inner City;* K. Giles (1989), *Patterns of Ministry Among the First Christians;* L. E. Keck (1988), *Paul and His Letters;* R. N. Longnecker (1971), *The Ministry and Message of Paul;* idem (1975), *A History of Religious Educators;* W. A. Meeks (1983), *The First Urban Christians: The Social World of the Apostle Paul;* C. J. Roetzel (1991), *The Letters of Paul: Conversations in Context;* J. R. W. Stott (1964), *Basic Introduction to the New Testament;* idem (1979), *God's New Society: The Message of Ephesians;* D. Wenham (1995), *Paul: Follower of Jesus or Founder of Christianity?*

Teaching Tool. *See* Computer-Enhanced Learning.

Teaching Tools. *See* Bible Study Methods; Visual Methods.

Team. Term used in education, business, and increasingly in church-related ministry to refer to those who are on the same side, as in a *football team*. It also may describe a group which is organized to work together, as in a *team of administrators.* Katzenbach and Smith (1994) define a team as "a small number of people with complementary skills who are committed to a common purpose, performance goals, and an approach for which they hold themselves mutually accountable" (13). *Team* often means a group of people who are intentionally associated together to accomplish a task, gain insight, enhance fellowship, strengthen performance, share their collective expertise, or provide synergy. A team is a group of at least two people who join together to accomplish a common purpose or function. *Teamwork* is often viewed as synonymous with *team.* Sometimes called participative management, the team concept often relies on self-directedness and cross-functionality. *Team* is often used in combination with other nouns to define and clarify those concepts, such as team teaching, team management, team building, or team leadership.

Team Teaching. Team teaching is when two or more individuals assist each other and the class to create a learning environment where each is able to contribute. Team teachers work together to provide synergistic learning.

Team Management. Hughes et al. (1999) list eight helpful characteristics of effective teams (366–69). Teams have:

- a clear mission and high performance standards;
- taken stock of facilities, opportunities, outside resources, and equipment;
- assessed the technical skills needed to accomplish the task;
- secured the resources and skills needed;
- planned;
- organized;
- high levels of communication; and
- minimization of interpersonal conflicts.

Team Building. An important function of a leader or manager is to build the team. Reece and Brandt (1999) suggest consideration and structure as "team-building skills for leaders" (313–16). *Consideration* skills include recognizing accomplishments, providing for early and frequent success, taking a personal interest in each employee, establishing a climate of open communication, discovering individual employee's values. *Structure* skills include clearly defining goals, encouraging individual and team goal setting, providing specific feedback often, and dealing with poor performance.

Team Leadership. Kenneth Gangel (1997) summarized team leadership as "the exercise of one's spiritual gifts under the call of God to serve a certain group of people in achieving the goals God has given them toward the end of glorifying Christ" (12). Team leadership involves a mutuality, a building together on behalf of those one is leading. A team leader will typically demonstrate the following characteristics:

- Clarifying the system and group toward a common purpose.
- Mutually assessing the needs of the group and the individuals within it.
- Rallying followers to move toward goals.
- Organizing the efforts of the group for effectiveness and efficiency.
- Developing methods which work for the group.
- Encouraging ongoing evaluation for the group's cyclical life.

Gregory C. Carlson

Bibliography. J. R. Katzenbach and D. K. Smith (1993), *The Wisdom of Teams;* K. O. Gangel (1997), *Team Leadership in Christian Ministry;* B. L. Reece and R. Brandt (1999), *Effective Human Relations in Organizations;* P. Drucker (1992), *Harvard Business Review;*

R. L. Hughes, R. C. Ginnett, and G. J. Curphy (1999), *Leadership: Enhancing the Lessons of Experience*.

Team Teaching. Two or more people working together to teach a class session. It does *not* refer to two or more people taking turns teaching a class. It implies, instead, that two or more individuals form a team to plan and facilitate specific teaching sessions. All members of the team are involved in designing curriculum and making instructional decisions. All members of the team are involved in some aspect of leading each session.

Team teaching is a particularly useful approach for teaching children. Two or more teachers work together in the classroom. During each session, each teacher has specific responsibility for some part of the lesson development. For example, two teachers work together with a class of twelve preschool children, each teacher being responsible for development of a learning center. One will be storyteller while the other leads music. Both are responsible for a half-dozen children, following up absentees, remembering birthdays, and doing other contact work. Both are responsible for leading the six children for whom he or she is responsible in group activities and projects.

Team teaching is not limited to children, however. Some adult classes have effectively employed team teaching. Each team member is responsible for presentation/facilitation of some part of the Bible lesson and varied classroom responsibilities.

The advantage of team teaching is that more than one person is involved in planning the session. This usually allows for greater creativity, better insights into the Scripture, and more effective lesson presentation. The chief disadvantage is that teams must work together to plan the session—and that requires commitment to take the time to plan together.

Eleanor A. Daniel

Television and Teaching. The industrialized world has grown accustomed in the modern era to a steady diet of television viewing. In America, for instance, preschoolers between the ages of two and six watch, on average, over four hours of televised programming a day, seven days a week. Nielsen studies show that the television is on nearly eight hours a day in the typical American residence. Less than two percent of American homes are without televisions; a healthy majority own at least two.

This has had a distinct effect on the moral and intellectual development of today's society in general, and the church in particular. Moral dilemmas that come to virtual life through the television screen in the home today via televised news and other programming, whether age appropriate or not, are a virtual surety in most families today. Intellectually, television viewing has remarkable capacities to dispense information but has also shown itself capable of curbing attention spans, logical, sequential thinking, and creativity, imagination, problem-solving ability, communication, and social skills. For these reason some experts, like psychologist, author, and columnist John Rosemond, suggest no television viewing at all for preschoolers and limited use of home viewing thereafter.

Affectively, one of the most notable impacts of modern television programming is the ability to emotionally move viewers with a mixture of music and compelling message. This response to broadcasting can be used to tremendous effect as feelings constitute a gift from God. But it is also to be critically examined when it diminishes reason and circumvents the will as many critics suggest it can with extended use.

Even so, television, appropriately applied, can have substantial and positive educational impact. The term "substitute experience" has been applied to the vicarious experience of encountering historical and contemporary situations that, due to lack of proximity in time and place, would be otherwise impossible. Christian video resources in recent years have improved in quality and variety and brought such things as Bible animation, Christian drama, well-known speakers, and even musical concerts to audiences both large and small, remote and prominent. These are obviously good trends.

Christian educators need to learn how to disciple church members in the appropriate use of the television in the home, particularly considering current time involvement, and to nonetheless find ways to engage audiences and classrooms with a responsible utilization of audio-visual materials that bring to the church exciting opportunities for learning.

Matt Friedeman

Temple. *See* Church.

Teresa of Avila (1515–82). Spanish religious leader and mystic. She was universally admired for her legacy of love and of contemplation in action. At once a reformer, a mystic, and a humorist, she was a leading figure in restructuring the Carmelite order.

Born Teresa de Cepeda y Ahumada in Avila, Spain, she entered the Carmelite order in 1536. She vacillated spiritually for twenty years. When reading Augustine's *Confessions* she became convicted that even those called by God often fall and must rise and repent again. She called this her "second conversion." It proved to be a remarkable turning point in her life. Teresa entered this period with great trepidation, fearing that she would be led astray by the devil through her practice of contemplative prayer. But after being convinced that God's Spirit was behind it all, she began a period of intense prayer. Within a short time mystical experiences were sweeping her regularly.

In 1560 she felt commanded by God to form new Carmelite communities in which the original ardor of the tradition would be restored: rigorous fasting, many hours of daily prayer, modest clothing, silence, and solitude. She was an able manager and tireless worker. Despite opposition Teresa was able to establish seventeen convents and fourteen priories in her lifetime.

John of the Cross joined her reform movement, and together they forged a rare and lasting bond. Complete trust in John as her spiritual confessor, and a mutual goal of total renunciation of self to make room for God were hallmarks of their relationship.

The most important of her writings is *The Interior Castle* (1588), a descriptive treatise on the mystical journey of the soul to union with God. The castle is the soul where God takes his delight. It contains seven mansions. In the first three the beginner actively labors to cultivate the virtues of mental prayer, devotional reading, edifying conversations, and good works. The novice thus intentionally purges personal imperfections. The fourth mansion marks a transition from the purgative way to the illuminative way of proficients. Deepening recollection, quiet peace, and trusting are salient features of the fourth and fifth estates. The sixth mansion describes the transition from illumination to unification of love. Reflecting on personal suffering is a theme that recurs in the final movement. Throughout the work contemplative meditation balances with love. Other writings include *The Way of Perfection*, *The Life*, and *Foundations*.

Teresa is a classic example of one who combined a life of prayerful contemplation with intense action. She believed love was the essential feature of true mystical prayer. The flowering of love in every daily activity is the goal of spiritual life. Love and prayer were one and the same for the founder of the Discalced Carmelites, for love is the heart of prayer itself: "If you would progress a long way along this road, the important thing is not to think much, but to love much. Do then whatever arouses you to love" (1961, 86).

JAMES A. DAVIES

Bibliography. E. W. T. Dicken, *The Crucible of Love*; R. Fulop-Miller (1945), *The Saints That Moved the World*; Teresa of Avila (1961), *The Interior Castle*.

See also SPIRITUAL DIRECTION/DIRECTOR

Theological Education. In 1964, the Association of Theological Schools boasted ninety accredited Protestant seminaries. Of these ninety, seventy-two were mainline schools and eighteen were evangelical. At the end of the twentieth century, mainline Protestant schools numbered between eighty and ninety; evangelical schools numbered between fifty and sixty. While the number of mainline schools remained relatively stable, the number of evangelical (including Pentecostal) schools increased dramatically.

The growth of evangelical seminaries is usually attributed to three main sources: the decline of mainline churches; the growth of charismatic and Pentecostal churches; and the growth of parachurch movements. It is accurate to say that much of this growth is connected to strong religion-building impulses that have dramatically changed the complexion and nature of the church in North America during the twentieth century. In effect, there has been a restructuring of American religion. The American church of the eighteenth and nineteenth centuries is a story of the growth of denominationalism. Most likely the story of the twentieth-century church will include the demise of traditional denominationalism and the emergence of new allegiances. In the 1960s and 1970s, parachurch groups such as Young Life (YL), Youth for Christ (YFC), Campus Crusade for Christ (CCC), The Navigators (NAV) and InterVarsity Christian Fellowship (IVCF) plus the evangelical church mobilized thousands of students, some of whom availed themselves of a seminary education. Interdenominational and nondenominational seminaries have particularly benefited from a continuing influx of students from parachurch groups.

Long gone are the days when students went to the nearest seminary of their particular denomination. Many seminaries are now struggling to retain a weak constituency, or seeking to establish themselves as a unique place in the emerging constellation of institutions. On top of this, most seminaries must now offer a wider variety of degree programs to meet the changing needs of students and churches.

In a 1990 survey of twenty-six seminary presidents in North America, five major points of concern surfaced in answer to the question: "List some current tensions that concern you in theological education today" (Stewart, 1990). By far the most cited area was the tension between preparing students for academic pursuits versus preparing them for effective ministry. Other areas mentioned were professionalism versus spirituality, increasing numbers of older-age students, tensions between seminary objectives and church expectations, and increasing internationalization of student bodies.

From the left end of the theological spectrum there are those who demand rethinking and rebuilding programs in light of important shifts connected with the emergence of postmodern ways of thinking. This "crisis of sources" points to an increasing pluralism enveloping theological education. Theologies that previously thrived only marginally are competing for center positions, especially in mainline seminaries. "Feminist" theologies and "minority" theologies have become increasingly attractive to many.

From the other end of the spectrum, authors such as David Wells in his book *No Place for Truth* (1993) have issued a call for recentering theological education around historic and orthodox conceptions of truth and theology.

Perhaps more than any one, Edward Farley, professor of theology at Vanderbilt Divinity School, has stimulated discussion about fundamental issues regarding the "purpose," "focus," "center," and "integration" of theological education. Farley, in his 1983 book, *Theologia: The Fragmentation and Unity of Theological Education,* has offered a comprehensive and critical examination of underlying assumptions and paradigms upon which theological education has been built. Farley identified four models which have developed in the West, each of which reflects a particular period of history and a unique understanding of the purpose and function of theological education. The four models can be summarized as follows:

1. Theology as *habitus:* Theological education is the process of developing "life-wisdom." Focus is on a lifestyle of spirituality that is closely linked with cognitive apprehension of God's truth as revealed in revelation. Monastic models are classic examples of this type.
2. Theology as a *science:* Theology is the discipline of systematic inquiry and exposition, involving the ability to relate theology to other domains of knowledge. This is Farley's second stage—when theology becomes parallel to philosophy and other related disciplines.
3. Theology in the *university:* Theological study becomes the work of the department of theology, with specialized branches. Here, theology becomes a generic term for studies similar to the study of law, medicine, or liberal arts. This period saw the development of the classic fourfold *theological encyclopedia—* where theology is broken down into four areas of study: historical studies, biblical studies (including languages), systematic theology, and practical theology. This is the third and predominant model today, says Farley. (While most seminaries today are not connected to a university, most have patterned themselves according to this model.)
4. Theology in the *clerical paradigm:* As an attempt to unify the disparate clusters of theological study, this model is "professional" in its approach and specifically concerned with the inner-ecclesial needs of the Christian community. This is the fourth stage in Farley's scheme and finds expression in many mainline seminaries.

Most critics agree that the clerical paradigm aptly describes the curriculum of many seminaries. These same critics argue that the clerical paradigm spawns several undesirable results, two of which are prominent. One is the fragmentation and dispersion of the theological curriculum into a growing assortment of topics and themes. Farley writes, "Theology has long disappeared as the unity, subject matter, and end of clergy education and this disappearance is responsible more than anything for the problematic character of that education as a course of study" (1983, ix).

A second undesirable consequence is the emergence of an overly individualistic understanding of ministry. This manifests itself in some institutions as an undue concentration on ministry competencies and individual student development at the expense of more radical questions concerning truth, mission, and church.

Fragmentation of the theological curriculum, along with the individualization of ministry has produced a lack of cohesiveness and in some cases, reduced theological education to pragmatics and technology. It is understandable that new models are being put forth. There are *liberation and justice* models (Padilla, 1988), *spiritual formation* models (Oden, 1984), *action-reflection* models (Dykstra, 1991), *nonformal* models (Ward and Herzog, 1974), *contextualizing* models (Stackhouse, 1988), and *mission* models (Duraisingh, 1992).

Among the issues that surface most in recent literature, none seems as preeminent as the question, "How does theological education relate to the church?" There are those who argue that a new vision of theological education requires a renewed focus upon the centrality of the local church. Based on a recovery of the New Testament doctrine of the "priesthood of all believers," they advocate that theological education cannot be limited to the clerical elite, but is for all; the local church is the most appropriate context for theological education; theological education should be intimately related to discovery and development of spiritual gifts; and theological education should be available for persons at every socioeconomic level (Padilla, 1988). It is no accident that a number of church-based experiments are now under way with promising results.

Some churches that have a history of catechetical formation are beginning to develop new catechetical processes as a means to ministerial formation. Others are developing nonformal programs which generally do a better job of serving laypersons at the local church level.

Increasingly, seminaries are recognizing that the makeup of ecclesiastical structures has changed permanently. The traditional partnership between denomination and seminary must be revisioned if it is to be a vital one. More and more it appears there will be several layers of educational institutions that can serve the church at large. Such programs need to be structured around a thorough understanding of what it means to train and equip leaders for the church.

Some seminaries are bringing constituent churches together to enlist their help in charting new directions and implementing new plans. In some cities, intentionally created networks are being formed, with the goal of linking nonformal programs with formal seminary programs. Many seminaries are now making serious attempts to serve local churches by offering distance learning programs. Increasingly, churches, parachurch ministries, seminaries, and Bible colleges are finding ways to work together.

Talk about new paradigms, new models, and new structures raises important questions about the future of theological education. If the church is to communicate a compelling vision of what theological education should be, it will also need to think theologically about theological education. This is a rather self-conscious thing to do, but it needs to be done carefully and enthusiastically. Ultimately, the church (not our institutions of learning) will be responsible for articulating a vision for the future, as well as determining the role that theological education will play. With the passing of time, a closer partnership between *academia* and *ecclesia* should be the norm and not the exception.

STEVEN K. SANDVIG

Bibliography. C. Duraisingh, *International Review of Mission* 81, no. 231 (1992): 33–45; C. Dykstra (1991), *Shifting Boundaries: Contextual Approaches to the Structure of Theological Education*, pp. 35–66; E. Farley (1983), *Theologia: The Fragmentation and Unity of Theological Education*; T. C. Oden (1984), *Care of Souls in the Classic Tradition*; R. Padilla (1988), *New Alternatives in Theological Education*; B. C. Stewart, *ERT* 14, no. 1 (1990): 42–49; T. W. Ward and W. Herzog, eds. (1974), *Effective Learning in Non-formal Education: Program Studies in Non-formal Education*; D. F. Wells (1993), *No Place for Truth: Or Whatever Happened to Evangelical Theology?*

Theological Education by Extension. Theological Education by Extension, especially when the words are capitalized, refers to a specific innovation which had a beginning, a surge of popularity, and a significant long-term effect on the way that leadership education for the church is understood. Its origins are traceable to Presbyterian missionary-educators in Guatemala in the period from 1967 to 1970, when the Presbyterian seminary where they were assigned ran short of students. Ralph Winter and Jim Emery, followed somewhat later by Ross Kinsler and other Americans with a zeal for bringing biblically substantial and theologically worthy education to undereducated pastors, came to realize that a key problem was that the residential seminary had rather well served the needs in its immediate surroundings, but it had little prospect for reaching beyond these geographic limits. The problems of travel distance, bivocational responsibilities, cultural variation, and especially the problem of family responsibilities kept the residential model of education out-of-reach for older pastors, widely scattered rural pastors, and mature Christians who were not only serving churches but, at the same time, farming in order to provide for themselves and their families.

The first Theological Education by Extension was conducted by missionaries (and soon experienced national church pastors and leaders) who became part of a mobile task force moving on a schedule from location to location in order to bring educational opportunities to the learners.

The residential school approach to theological education is best attuned to younger persons who are in the "schooling years" of their lives, carry minimal financial burdens and few family responsibilities, and live close enough to the seminary or Bible college to be able to return to their homes and communities as necessary. The historical problems with the residential approach to the development of leadership for the church have arisen from the very fact that its presuppositions and procedures are drawn from the academic realm and are often in substantial contrast with the characteristics and needs of the church. Residential theological education is usually assessed in terms of information-retention, skills of intellectual argumentation, specialized narrowness, and in other such matters that are expected of the "schooled." The characteristics of personality, servant-leadership, compassionate ministry, and spiritual qualities which are commonly identified in the Bible's references to requirements for leadership in the church (e.g., 1 Tim 3) are not at the center of attention in ordinary approaches to schooling. Those who quickly adopted the general idea of Theological Education by Extension assumed that placement of the educational process closer to the experiences of ministry and pastoral life would have substantially more appropriate outcomes.

As expected in any locally popular innovation, the rise of TEE was widespread and enthusiastic, but before many years it began to wane. The peak of the *movement* occurred within ten years. Nevertheless, its influence persists thirty years and more later. Programs of theological education by extension are widespread. In India, for example, TEE is virtually the dominant mode of pastoral education. But the initial enthusiasm for TEE has generally waned for several distinct reasons.

First, the wisely chosen methodology in TEE called for three resources which were extremely rare. The instructional model called for students to read independently and in small self-led groups from materials carefully designed to provide an informational basis and preparation for weekly seminars (sometimes spaced across more time). This reading-plus-guided-discussion was to replace the time-honored lecturing-plus-note-taking of formal higher education. Herein lay the three problems.

1. Where were these appropriate teaching-learning materials? They had to be developed. Amazing responses by dedicated pastor-teachers and other writers emerged. But the demand was far greater, so all sorts of corners were trimmed to speed things up. A material that proved valuable in Zambia was translated for Brazil. A Peruvian material was lifted across formidable cultural barriers into Mexico, France, and India. What began as a reform movement fell back into the habits of the past. Education that promised to be based upon a more sensitive and relevant application of God's Word quickly degenerated into the old procedure of dumping information from one cultural form of Christianity into a contrasting cultural situation.

2. Even more serious was the lack of skilled discussion leaders. Hardly anyone in the movement counted on the difficulty of breaking the habit of teaching-as-telling. Almost anyone who has spent time in formal education is inclined to line people up and talk down to them for long periods of time, assuming that they either haven't read, haven't reasoned, or haven't understood what they have experienced in life. The TEE instructor-leaders were rarely any different, nor were any resources brought to bear to help retrain them into more effective models of seminar-style teaching.

3. Almost everyone underestimated the consuming power of threatened formal education institutions and their favorite ways of teaching. Some promoters of TEE presumed that the TEE model was inherently weak, and so they asserted that it could become "nearly as good as" the formal education programs. Such boldness not only irritated the older and well-entrenched hard core, but it overlooked the fact that TEE was intentionally different—aimed toward qualities that were based in different values, and not intended to be "as good as," given that its purposes were in some respects fundamentally *different from* formal theological education. The tendency to over-promise and to hide away these fundamental differences also produced another problem. In much of the educationally under-resourced parts of the world, the craving for education was then, and still is, all-consuming, but the *meaning* of education has been shaped by the colonial experience. Thus "education" of any sort has less to do with life-change as world view enlargement and spiritual transformation than with the economic advantages of coin-like degrees from "recognized" institutions and curricula.

The use of extension approaches to theological education, especially continuing education for ministry is, of course, much older than TEE. Especially since the period immediately after World War II, many theological schools have been emphasizing lifelong learning for ministers and educators. Such institutions are the modern rediscoverers of theological education by extension (small *t*, small *ee*). But the significance of TEE lies far deeper. First, it was one of the first instances of an innovation emerging from the missionary sector or the overseas churches finding its way into the patterns of education "back home." Second, the return to the experiential methods of Martin Luther, John Wesley, the Apostle Paul, Jesus, and others of the early nonformal education traditions stimulated an upsurge of general awareness that not all is as it should be in modern theological education. A slow-but-sure overhaul of the relationships of the academic and ecclesial relationships in the development of leadership is now underway. Third, it has stimulated the emergence of many new institutional and noninstitutional educational programs that reposition education *within* ministry, rather than as a formal rite-of-passage that *prepares for* ministry.

TED W. WARD

Bibliography. R. R. Covell and C. P. Wagner (1971), *An Extension Seminary Primer;* J. H. Emery (1976), *Extension Seminary;* R. D. Winter (1969), *Theological Education by Extension.*

Theology and Education. Both the Bible and theology require that education be carried out as a means of participation in God's redemptive activity in creation, as a means of advancing the kingdom of God. The church has been involved in education since its inception on the Day of Pentecost, in both informal and formal modes. For education to be truly *Christian*, it must be rooted soundly in biblical and theological imperatives. Educators must understand how to draw educational conclusions from theological premises.

The Bible places a strong emphasis on teaching as a means of bringing God's people to spiritual maturity. The Old Testament repeatedly stresses teaching as the means of helping Israel learn to live as God's people. For example, Deuteronomy 4:5–8 (NASB) reads, "See, I have taught you statutes and judgments just as the LORD my God commanded me, that you should do thus in the land where you are entering to possess it. So keep and do *them,* for that is your wisdom and your understanding in the sight of the peoples who will hear all these statutes and say, 'Surely this great nation is a wise and understanding people.' For what great nation is there that has a god so near to it as is the LORD our God whenever we call on Him? Or what great nation is there that has statutes and judgments as righteous as this whole law which I am setting before you today?"

Deuteronomy 6 places the context for teaching God's people in the home, with the mother and father as the primary teachers. The feasts and celebrations of Israel were also designed as means of instruction, both for the family and for the entire nation.

The Old Testament places special emphasis on the responsibility of the father to teach his sons (Exod. 10:2; 12:26; 13:8; Deut. 6:20ff.). Because of the clearly defined gender roles and restricted roles for women in that culture, it was the mother's responsibility to teach the girls. But it was also the responsibility of the mother to provide the moral education for the children and begin the foundations of their formal education (Prov. 1:8; 6:20).

Deuteronomy 31 provides guidance for teaching the nation God's word: "Then Moses commanded them, saying, 'At the end of *every* seven years, at the time of the year of remission of debts, at the Feast of Booths, when all Israel comes to appear before the LORD your God at the place which He will choose, you shall read this law in front of all Israel in their hearing. Assemble the people, the men and the women and children and the alien who is in your town, in order that they may hear and learn and fear the LORD your God, and be careful to observe all the words of this law. And their children, who have not known, will hear and learn to fear the LORD your God, as long as you live on the land which you are about to cross the Jordan to possess'" (vv. 10–13 NASB).

The passage calls for public reading of God's law and suggests a progression in learning from listening to learning to obeying all that God had commanded. The Hebrew understanding of learning always linked the cognitive (learning) with the volitional (doing). Learning was not complete until it was expressed by doing. The demonstration of learning in this passage is through a change in attitude ("fear God") and a change in action ("obey God"). The final outcome of learning was to be a holy lifestyle for the people of God.

The relation of teacher to student in the Old Testament was the relation of parent to child. Education was not to be impersonal or detached, but very personal and connected. It was in the context of relationship that instruction was to take place.

The New Testament continues the emphasis on teaching, again primarily in the context of relationships. While Jesus did teach the multitudes (Matt. 5–7) and in various local synagogues, his focus was the training of the Twelve. Mark records, "And He went up to the mountain and summoned those whom He Himself wanted, and they came to Him. And He appointed twelve, that they might be with Him, and that He might send

them out to preach, and to have authority to cast out the demons" (3:13–15 NASB). It was in the context of relationship that Jesus trained those he had called.

In the Sermon on the Mount the Lord again emphasizes the importance of living in obedience to God's commands, and teaching others to do the same (Matt. 5:19). Moreover, he was called "teacher" as an indication of one of the primary emphases of his public ministry.

The Great Commission is a call to teach, rooted in the lordship of Christ ("All authority is given to me . . ."). The command is to *make disciples*. The means of making disciples is *baptism* and *teaching*. Again, the goal of the instruction is obedience.

The ministry of the early church was, to a large extent, the ministry of evangelism and of education. The apostles proclaimed the gospel and then taught the people as a means of bringing them to maturity. We are told that after the great conversions on the Day of Pentecost that they ". . . devoted themselves to the apostles' teaching . . ." (Acts 2:42). Paul instructed Timothy, as a means of continuing the pattern of growth through education to ". . . entrust [the things learned from Paul] . . . to reliable people who will be qualified to teach others" (2 Tim. 2:2). Moreover, one of the primary qualities of elders (overseers) was that they should be "able to teach" (1 Tim. 3:2). In addition, Paul instructed Timothy, "Until I come, devote yourself to the public reading of Scripture, to preaching and to teaching" (1 Tim. 4:13).

The goal of the teaching of the church is the spiritual maturity of its members. The content of its education is to be God's revealed Word, presented as absolute Truth. Our Lord was uncompromising on this point, claiming, ". . . If you hold to my teaching, you are really my disciples. Then you will know the truth, and the truth will set you free" (John 8:31–32). His prayer for the church was, in part, "Sanctify them by the truth; your word is truth" (John 17:17). The content of the apostle Paul's ministry was Christ and his gospel. He explained, "We proclaim him, admonishing and teaching everyone with all wisdom, so that we may present everyone perfect in Christ" (Col. 1:28). His purpose ". . . [was] that they may be encouraged in heart and united in love, so that they may have the full riches of complete understanding, in order that they may know the mystery of God, namely, Christ, in whom are hidden all the treasures of wisdom and knowledge" (Col. 2:2–3).

Scripture places an emphasis on teaching as a means of bringing God's people to maturity, with the content being God's Word in its fullness. While modern forms of the educational structures, such as Sunday schools, youth groups, and adult Bible fellowships, are not mandated in Scripture, the imperative that the church must be a teaching institution is mandated. *How* the church structures its teaching ministry should be a matter of cultural preferences and styles. Paul adjusted his approach to the cultural norms of his day (1 Cor. 9:22). *That* the church must be focused on teaching as a means of making disciples is nonnegotiable. To fulfill its biblical mandate, the church must be, at its core, both a didactive and a doxological institution.

The church has always understood its role in society to be both prophetic and redemptive. In its prophetic ministry it proclaims the gospel and warns of the coming judgment of God upon all those who fail to heed the warnings and respond to God's grace. In its redemptive ministry, it seeks to bring the gospel to bear upon a broken and hurting world through acts of service. These acts of service may be direct acts, such as feeding the poor or healing the sick, or they may be prophylactic, as in educational interventions.

Education rooted in theological perspective is understood first to be a means of participation in God's redemptive work in the world. The story of the Bible is the story of God's redemptive activity in his creation. Redemptive history begins with the truth of God's creation, affirming that all that is comes from God, and that he has declared all of creation as "good." Humankind was given the mandate to ". . . fill the earth and subdue it. Rule over the fish of the sea and the birds of the air and over every living creature that moves on the ground" (Gen. 1:28).

Tied closely to the doctrine of creation is the doctrine of providence which affirms God's care for and continuing activity in his creation. Peter focuses on the Word of God as the means of creation and providence when he, referring back to Genesis 1, states, ". . . long ago by God's word the heavens existed and the earth was formed . . . and . . . by the same word the present heavens and earth are reserved for fire, being kept for the day of judgment . . ." (2 Peter 3:5–7).

Contained within created order are normative structures for how things *ought to be*. There is an orderliness to creation which is to be respected. While humankind has great latitude in our activities as stewards of creation and as image bearers for God, we do not have complete freedom. There are expectations regarding human behaviors and the structures of society and culture. Humankind is expected to be creative, artistic, thoughtful, energetic, and industrious, all as expressions of the *imago Dei* and as responsible stewards of God's creation. Therefore education that is *Christian* must value the arts, sciences, and humanities because each of these areas of inquiry and creative expression are valid aspects of God's created order.

The doctrine of creation also requires that education take seriously all aspects of God's created order, because creation itself is revelatory. Because "The heavens declare the glory of God; the

skies proclaim the work of his hands" (Ps. 19:1), it is both appropriate and required that Christians study and teach the natural sciences, as expressions of our responsibility to inquire into divine revelation. General revelation (creation) cannot be ignored by educators who are Christian. Moreover, inquiry into God's sixth day creation, humankind, is especially appropriate in that we bear God's image in our being. Therefore theology requires that education take seriously the social sciences precisely because they are inquiries into God's revelation of himself through humankind.

The story of the Bible does not end, however, with the story of creation. The reality of the fall of humankind must also be considered. The fall means that relationship with God, with others, with self, and with created order have all been broken or corrupted. As a result, humankind is now at enmity with God, with others, and with self. Sinfulness is all-pervasive, corrupting every aspect of the human person, so that we take that which is good and use it inappropriately, corrupting God's good gifts by our own sinfulness. Not only are humans polluted, but societies, institutions, and structures have all been influenced by our fallenness.

This theological understanding of the extent of and the influences of the fall requires that education must now become part of the solution rather than part of the problem. Human sinfulness causes us to create educational processes that are manipulative, competitive, and means of controlling others rather than means of liberation. Truth becomes an assault weapon, used to attack others and empower self, rather than the source of liberation envisioned by our Lord (John 8:32). Educational institutions become places of control and of ineffectiveness, rather than contexts of cooperation and learning for the common good.

If the paradigm of the fall becomes the theological framework for designing educational institutions and making curriculum decisions, an inadequate and unchristian form of education results. Reasoning only from a theology of sin causes educators to design highly controlled, teacher-dominated institutions, where the culture is one of suspicion and the processes of education are trivialized. If the only assumption is that the world is fallen and students are sinful, it then follows that the world must be avoided and the student must be controlled. The result is education which is neither liberating nor engaging with the broader culture.

The biblical story line does not end with the fall, but continues to proclaim the history of God's redemptive work in creation, restoring all that he has made back to its rightful condition and for its rightful purpose. Paul proclaims the extent of God's redemptive intention in Christ, explaining,

"For God was pleased to have all his fullness dwell in him, and through him to reconcile to himself all things, whether things on earth or things in heaven, by making peace through his blood, shed on the cross" (Col. 1:19–20). The redemption in Christ is *cosmic* in the sense that it restores the whole creation. "This fundamental confession has two distinct parts. The first is that redemption means *restoration*—that is, the return to the goodness of an originally unscathed creation and not merely the addition of something supracreational. The second is that this restoration affects the *whole* of creational life and not merely some limited area within it. Just as the effects of the fall were all-pervasive, so also the effects of redemption are all-pervasive. God's grace brings wholeness and restoration back to that which has been corrupted and shattered" (Wolters, 1985, 57).

A Christian perspective on education must be rooted in a theology of redemption, seeing the educational process as a means of participation with God in his redemptive activity. It is not a matter of adding to the work of the cross, but rather of participating with God in the establishment of his complete reign over all that he has made. The task of education becomes the returning of all of creation and all of human endeavors back to their rightful owner. Paul says, "We demolish arguments and every pretension that sets itself up against the knowledge of God, and we take captive every thought to make it obedient to Christ" (2 Cor. 10:5). The intellectual task of Christian education is the engagement of every field of study, to influence its use for the glory of God and the good of all of humankind. Every discipline should be examined as a means of engagement with the created order, and as a means of participating in its restoration to its proper use and function, all to the glory of God.

Because God's redemptive activity extends to all that he has made and has allowed humans to create, education must also extend to all aspects of creation and human endeavor. Rather than limited views of educational domains which only explore Bible and theology, a biblical theology requires that every domain can and should be studied and taught, so that redemption may be seen in all possible areas of study. It is incumbent upon us to include all areas of study in Christian institutions of learning.

Not only does theology dictate the scope of education, but it also speaks to educational structures and process. Because education is understood as a redemptive process it must avoid the romantic notions of education rooted only in creation theology, which fails to take sin seriously, and the controlling notions of education rooted in a theology of sin, which fails to consider God's redemptive grace in the world as he draws all that he has made back to himself. Education that is guided by a theology of redemption takes seri-

ously human sinfulness, but it also takes seriously the worth and dignity of all people, and the reality of God's grace being extended to all that he has made (Ps.145:8–9).

A redemptive process of education must be co-operative rather than competitive. The culture of a redemptive educational institution is one where people work together, striving for the common good rather than individual achievement. Individuals are respected and diversity is tolerated, only as it helps search for Truth. It is assumed that objective reality exists, and that it is at least partly knowable by limited and fallen human beings. The quest for Truth becomes the driving force of the educational task because it is understood that engagement with Truth brings liberation.

Because created order is valued, exploration into how God has created human beings to learn becomes a theological concern, rooted in the perspective that theories of teaching must be extrapolated from theories of learning. It is required of educators that they take students seriously, seeking to teach in ways that are developmentally and culturally appropriate to those whom God has entrusted to them. The educational task itself is sacred, because it concerns those who bear God's image, and is a means of participation in God's redemptive work in the world.

Theological integration and grounding of educational tasks is an ongoing task, achieved by beginning with a theological premise, such as "grace," or "mercy" or "justice," and then reasoning from it to a variety of educational concerns, asking how the theological premise might inform any given educational category. A constant conversation between theology and education becomes the goal, with theology providing the lens through which educational issues can be examined. Educational practice and structures worthy of the adjective *Christian* must be intentionally rooted in theological frameworks, and be guided by theological perspective.

PERRY G. DOWNS

Bibliography. A. M. Wolters (1985), *Creation Regained.*

Theology of Lay Leadership. The clue to the identity of the laity is provided by the term itself. The noun *laity* has its original source in the Greek word *laos* (people). Strictly speaking *laity* (*laikos*) does not appear in the Bible, but its meaning is clear: it pertains to the "laos," the people of God (Kraemer, 1958). Israel understood itself as *laos theou* (the people of God). Israel also understood herself as a chosen people of God with a covenant faith. God chose Israel not for privilege alone, but to be blessed to be blessings, to be a servant people. In this priestly service, all the people of Israel represent God to the world and the world to God. In Old Testament times the laity, *laos*, were composed of all people who belonged to Israel, to the people belonging (Swanson, 1994). This understanding of God's people passed from the Old Testament into the New Testament. In the New Testament, *laos* was not used to refer to the nation of Israel, but rather to the new Israel, the Christian community. Now, the circle of membership in the people of God is drawn from a new center, that of Jesus Christ, the Lord and Savior of the world.

In the New Testament as in the Old Testament, the priesthood and its responsibilities are assigned to the whole *laos,* the people of God. The people of God form the body of Christ, which is the church. "The essential aspects of the Church as the body which Christ creates to himself through the Holy Spirit are that the Church is missionary and ministerial" (Kraemer, 1958, 131). Kraemer (1958) asserts that the church is mission, rather than the church has missions, because "the Church is Mission implies that it is in all times and places the world-wide and local-near embrace of the world, in and to which it is sent" (132). The phrase "the Church is ministry" denotes a similar explanation. "It is a ministering to and in the world by the supremely necessary act: the proclaiming of Christ, the Truth, the Life, the Way, in word and deed" (137). The people of God do not have missions, but are mission, they do not have ministries, but are ministry. As a part of the Body of Christ, the people of God are all called priests and saints (Swanson, 1994). Hobbs (1990) states that "the Greek word for 'minister' is *diakonos* and is found sixteen times in the New Testament. It does not refer to a separate class of Christian but to the type of service to be performed by all believers in Christ. All Christians as slaves of Jesus Christ are to be involved in ministry" (57).

Different and Unique Functions. Young (1998) states that there are several false ideas that are erected upon a faulty, truncated understanding of the priesthood of all believers. First, everyone's opinion is equally correct. Second, the opinion of the majority is necessarily correct. Third, everyone in the church is the same. He adds that the priesthood of all believers in its simplest form means that the believer has been chosen and redeemed by God for a mission. The emphasis in being one of God's chosen priests is not one's status, but one's task. It means that every member ministers; however, this does not mean that every member does the same ministry.

Jesus Christ is head of the church. This means that each member is directly connected to the head. Members receive their signals and marching orders from the head. Members find that their functional role is often determined by the spiritual gifts assigned to them. The term *body* is by no means the only term applied to the church in the New Testament but is nevertheless the most important. Moore (1983) suggests that pas-

sages like Romans 12:6, 1 Corinthians 12, or Ephesians 4:11f. make plain that the comprehensive ministry of Christ continues in the diversity of functions and ministries performed by the individual members of the body. While the ministry is one, specific forms of ministry may emphasize special tasks, gifts, and skills, and the ordering of the offices of the ministry will affect this variety. One's function within the church is often predetermined by one's spiritual gifts. To those called to exercise special functions in the church, however, God gives suitable gifts for their various duties.

Steinbron (1997) shifts gears from being a passive recipient of the gift to an active participant. God provides the gifts and he determines each person's unique gift. God also gives with the expectation that people will use and develop them. It is our part to provide for the body as in Romans 12. We will need to provide time and skills. Steinbron explains this concept in simple sentences, "God's part and your part together make a whole. God is doing His part. When we do our part, His work gets done. God started the process by giving each of us gifts. Withholding our bodies, refusing to provide the time and failing to grow in skill stymies the process" (44).

The Historical Development of the Concept of Lay Leadership. Throughout church history numerous responses to the roles of laity and clergy have been developed. As the apostolic era ended, the community of the priesthood of all believers was gradually impacted through the organizational evolution of the church. "It passed from a rather non-structured, spirit-prompted, community-based fellowship of believers to an elaborate ecclesiology which institutionalized the ministry into an office and localized that ministry into the office of the clergy" (Crane, 1994).

The Early Church. When seeking reference to the popular term *laity* in the New Testament, the quest goes without resolution. The term *laity* (*laikos*) is not found in the New Testament nor is it found in the Septuagint (Crane, 1994). It is not until the end of the first century that the term is found in what might be considered the innocent beginning of a tradition which would end in a formal, institutionalized barrier between laity and clergy in our day.

The First Letter of Clement of Rome was a significant early church writing regarding the issue of laity (Eastwood, 1963). In that letter Clement addresses a Corinthian congregation experiencing a great deal of conflict. Evidently there were leaders who had served that church body faithfully but were at that time being expelled on faulty grounds. The conflict was so severe that it not only was a discouragement to those who were members of that church, but it was publicly known enough to have become an offense even to unbelievers. In Clement's attempt to restore order, he uses three analogies. The first employs the image of an army with soldiers who need to accept the authority of those who are placed over them, or their supervisors. Second, he emphasizes their need to practice mutual submission. Third, and of greatest importance, he refers to the Levitical hierarchy of the Old Testament. And paralleling his military model, he said there was a need to maintain rank within the church. The three Levitical roles described by Clement have specific functions or ministries and the layperson is bound by specific limitations (Crane, 1994). The three degrees of hierarchy stresses the importance of the layperson being submissive to their authority. Clement even uses Korah's rebellion as an example to warn of the consequences of disobedience to the authority.

It was Clement who introduced the term *lay* in the religious sense for the first time. Whether in Greek or in Latin, it was a long time before the term *lay* entered into current usage in religious language. Almost a century passed before it appeared a second time in Christian literature (Faiver, 1990). The term does not appear anywhere in the writing either of Justin Martyr or of Irenaeus, who were Christian authors from the second century. Justin never lays claim in his writings to any institutional recognition or to any ministry in an attempt to justify his authority. The name *Christian* was enough for Justin. It called for no particular function and no special distinction, responsibility, or ministry (Faiver, 1990). Borchert (1996) states that "this concept of being set apart for a function within the church's mission, became viewed in the second century as a sign of status as the church became identified with the bishop" (555).

The beginning of the third century was a turning point in the history of the believing people. The term *lay* suddenly came into use again. At the same time, the idea of *clergy* was formed and became used more extensively. At this time each church was a self-sufficient living organism that was able to create all the specific ministries that it found indispensable. There was only one exception to this principle of the autonomy of the local churches: the consecration of the bishop. Each bishop had to be consecrated by three existing bishops, and these were usually bishops of neighboring communities. Added to the consecration of the bishop, Christian communities almost everywhere were governed by a monarchical episcopate. This monarchical episcopate was strengthened by the principle of the apostolic succession. Finally and most important, there was what can be regarded from this time onward as a constant aspect of the Christian churches, namely, the distinction between *ordo* and *plebs*—in other words, a distinction between the clergy and the laity (Faiver, 1990). Faiver does not state clear reasons for this rapid change in Christian

communities; however, it is also true that there are many cases of times in history when events have speeded up and change has occurred quite abruptly. The *Apostolic Tradition* is a document containing the earliest rituals of ordination and in which a technical terminology was beginning to form. In this document, the distinction between clergy and "lay ministries" had already been made. It is stated that only the church's bishops, presbyters, and deacons were clergy and that the other functions were regarded as "lay ministries" (Faiver, 1990).

The Middle Ages. In the church of the Middle Ages, the laity was mostly satisfied to "supply and protect" the clergy. The laity did then what the clergy did not do. They hired the clergy to do its work for them. The laity participated in liturgical worship, but failed much of the time to grasp the ecclesiastical superiors. During this time the laity played an important part in the choosing of their bishop. The laity even heard confession. However, slowly, and inevitably, control passed from the laity to the clergy (Yorton, 1970). Borchert confirms Yorton by stating that in the Middle Ages with the establishment of a sacerdotal system of mediated grace, the laity became a submissive, docile part of the church with the priest holding authority over souls. The educational standards of the clergy began to rise somewhat, but the clergy regarded the laity as utterly different from themselves. Laymen were actually forbidden to hold offices as administrators or as ecclesiastical judges.

The Reformation. As the Middle Ages dawned there was stirring in the laity, which would eventually culminate in the Reformation. The Reformation, with its emphasis on vocation and the priesthood of the believers, proved to be a turning point in Western history. Its driving power was centered in the laity. The laity declared that the affairs of the church were also their responsibility, and they reacted against the sharp dichotomy between themselves and the clergy. The leaders of the Reformation were united on the fact that all Christians have the same standing before God, that every Christian is a priest, that each Christian has the office of sacrifice, and that every Christian has the duty to hand on the gospel he has received (Yorton, 1970).

The Modern Church. The radical reformers of the Anglo-Saxon free church tradition highlighted the equality of all believers and sought to present the church as a community of involved adult believers. Free churches became the forerunners in modern Western history of the democratic way of life, and lay theologians such as John Bunyan and John Milton exercised great influence (Borchert, 1996). In Europe most missionaries to the new movement emerged from the laity and performed ministerial duties on the field although they were unable to do so in their home churches. The youth movements of the nineteenth century such as the YMCA and the World Student Christian Fellowship also were a result of lay initiatives.

In East and West Germany, following the Second World War, a new lay renewal began with the initiation of evangelical academies and *Kirchentaen* that were designed to bring lay people and clergy together to deal with everyday problems, The World Council of Churches in 1954 also gave an impetus to the lay movement by adding a "Department of Laity" (Kraemer, 1958). In the twentieth century, the church in the United States has grown primarily as an institution located in a building. Clergy have increasingly become professional church workers, especially in the ministry of education. This increase was particularly marked in the Protestant churches between 1940 and 1970. With this increasing professionalization of leadership has come the tendency for the rest of the laity to hand over power to the leadership, lay and ordained (Page, 1993).

There is no mistaking the biblical imperative for lay leadership. The gifts of the Spirit of God were given for the purpose of lay involvement. The purpose of the clergy is to train the laity in the proper use of those gifts and to ensure their coordinated effort within the context of the local church. As each believer in Christ identifies his or her area of giftedness, receives instruction in the use of that gift, and then begins using the gift in the power provided by the Spirit of God, then and only then will the church fulfill her God-given responsibility to reach of world with the message of the gospel.

ESTHER YOU

Bibliography. I. Askola, *The Ecumenical Review* 45, no. 4 (1993): 388–91; D. A. Borchert, *Review and Expositor* 93, no. 4 (1996): 555–65; A. Faiver (1990), *The Emergence of the Laity in the Early Church*; J. L. Garlow (1981), *Partners in Ministry*; K. C. Haughk (1985), *The Christian Ministry*, pp. 5–8; H. H. Hobbs, (1990), *You Are Chosen*; W. Jacobsen, *Leadership Journal* 9, no. 3 (1988): 44–49; H. Kraemer (1958), *A Theology of the Laity*; B. Larson, *Leadership Journal* 10, 4:28–32; S. J. Menking (1984), *Helping Laity Help Others*; S. C. Neill and H. Weber, eds. (1963), *The Layman in Christian History*; R. A. Olson, *Religious Education* 84, no. 1 (1989): 606–19; P. N. Page (1993), *All God's People Are Ministers*; G. Peck and J. S. Hoffman, eds. (1984), *The Laity Ministry*; W. J. Rademacher (1991), *Lay Ministry: A Theological, Spiritual, and Pastoral Handbook*; K. Raiser, *The Ecumenical Review* 45, no. 4 (1993): 75–83; A. Rowthorn (1986), *The Liberation of the Laity*; N. Ritchie, *The Ecumenical Review* 45, no. 4 (1993): 385–87; M. J. Steinbron (1987), *Can the Pastor Do It Alone?*; idem (1997), *The Lay-Driven Church*; R. P. Stevens (1985), *Liberating the Laity*; L. Swanson (1984), *The Lay Ministry*; B. L. Yorton (1970), *The Recovery of the Potential of the Layman in the Church*.

Thomism. Philosophy and theology based on the thought of Thomas Aquinas. Aquinas was a Dominican priest, theologian, and philosopher (1225–74) whose greatest dogmatic work, *Summa Theologiae*, is a systematic explanation of theology and Christian philosophy based on Aristotelian metaphysics. Prior to him no such philosophical and theological synthesis can be found (Gilson, 1956, 7).

Thomism has been described as theistic realism (Gutek, 1974, 51). Aquinas's thought had a twofold focus which presented reality as having both material and spiritual dimensions. Influenced by the empirical philosophy of Aristotle, Aquinas placed great emphasis upon natural realism, yet, since he was chiefly a theologian, he gave primacy to the reality of the supernatural, and, specifically, to the revelation of Scripture as the source of divinely inspired truth. As such, Thomistic philosophy integrated philosophical elements within theological synthesis in order to provide integration of reason with faith. In doing this Aquinas sought to introduce "philosophy into theology without corrupting the essence of theology" (Gilson, 1956, 10).

The thought of Aquinas depicted a unified philosophical theology. Aquinas sought to hold in balance the contrasts between "nature and grace, reason and faith, determinism and freedom, the existence of the universe from eternity and its beginning in time, the soul as biological form and as spirit, and the role of the senses and of divine enlightenment in the acquisition of knowledge" (Gilby, 1967, 119).

Thomistic philosophy has been modified over the centuries. As theologians and philosophers engaged Aquinas's thought, they also exerted an influence upon Thomism, refining and sharpening it so that it continued to be persuasive as a philosophical system. They served to sharpen the distinctions between "essence and existence, matter and form, and substance and accident" (Gilby, 1967, 119). Within Scholasticism of the sixteenth to nineteenth centuries, Thomistic philosophy and theology continued to be the system which provided the foundation for understanding. Thomism was the beginning point for any theological and philosophical endeavor within the ecclesiastical schools. As a result, in 1879, Pope Leo XIII declared Thomism the recommended theology and philosophy of the Roman Catholic Church, and though Vatican II lessened this singular focus upon Thomism, it still remains a significant influence within Roman Catholic theology (Monti, 1990, 656, 657).

Thomism focuses on the elaboration of truth in conjunction with reason. Within Thomism faith and reason "can neither contradict each other nor ignore each other nor be confused with each other" (Gilson, 1956, 23). Reason cannot justify faith, nor transform it into reason. Faith cannot make reason more than it is so that it ceases to be itself. Rather, as both faith and reason maintain their unique essences they help each other. Therefore, both faith and reason are brought to the service of truth so that ". . . philosophy does not give up in any way its essential rationality, but it agrees to ordain its rationality towards a higher end" (Gilson, 1956, 23, 24). Each focuses upon that which is revealable so that truth is made known. Ultimately for Aquinas, human reason existed and was satisfied only as it sought to grasp hold of God. Likewise, God invited humanity to utilize reason to explore his essence and to intellectually engage the revelation of himself (cf. Gilson, 1956, 357).

Thomism has also influenced the practice of education, particularly Christian education, in defining the goal of education, in providing an understanding of the learner, and in presenting an epistemology. Thomism fosters a purpose for education which seeks the "perfection of the human being and the ultimate reunion of the soul with God" (Ozmon and Craver, 1990, 45). Because humanity is both spiritual and material, the learner, existing in place and time, seeks to engage in learning that contributes to spiritual, rational, moral, and social development. Since humanity is spiritual, the learner's priority must be upon spiritual formation. Yet, learners are also rational, so the cultivation of rationality is vital for the exercising of free choice. In being moral and social beings, learners also need "ethical, legal, political, and economic systems which contribute to . . . personal and social well being" as well as "communication and community" (Gutek, 1974, 54).

Thomistic epistemology focuses upon acquiring knowledge through the senses. The senses are a necessary condition of knowing. Yet, human beings have the further power to conceptualize from sensory data and to be involved in abstract speculation about reality, both material and spiritual. Therefore, Aquinas held that humanity's highest activity was rationality and the exercising of "intellectual and speculative power" (Gutek, 1974, 55). Further, knowledge through the senses could lead one to God. God can be known not just through faith, but also through reason as human beings engage the material world through their senses (Ozmon and Craver, 1990, 46).

It is this focus on rationality and intellectualism that is vital for moral education within Thomistic thought. Though reason does not necessarily promote the good, "only intelligent men and women can distinguish between moral right and wrong" (Gutek, 1974, 58). As human beings exercise freedom they "possess the ability to frame, to recognize, and to evaluate alternative courses of action" (Gutek, 1974, 58).

In this light Thomism elevates the role of critical thinking for effective education. It is thinking which is to be informed by both theological and natural or material understandings. It is thinking which is to be intellectually excellent. This has clear implications for Christian education in that learners are to engage in the development of not only their faith, but to develop their faith in conjunction with rationality. It is as Christians learn to integrate faith and reason, that they learn to think critically. As they are informed by both their understanding of the world and their biblical and theological perspectives, they are equipped to act and live their daily lives according to biblical teachings. In so doing, they will engage the world around them in order to reveal truth and to grow in the truth; a truth based in the reality of God who has created all things.

ROLAND G. KUHL

Bibliography. T. Gilby (1967), *The Encyclopedia of Philosophy,* vol. 7, pp. 119–21; E. Gilson (1956), *The Christian Philosophy of St. Thomas Aquinas;* G. L. Gutek (1974), *Philosophical Alternatives in Education;* R. McInerny (1990), *A First Glance at St. Thomas Aquinas;* J. Monti (1990), *Harper's Encyclopedia of Religious Education,* pp. 656–57; H. Ozmon and S. Craver (1990), *Philosophical Foundations of Education.*

See also PHILOSOPHY OF CHRISTIAN EDUCATION; PHILOSOPHY OF EDUCATION; PHILOSOPHY OF RELIGION

Thorndike, Edward (1874–1949). American educational psychologist. Born in Williamsburg, Mass., in 1895, he graduated from Wesleyan University and studied under the psychologist and philosopher William James at Harvard. Thorndike stayed on at Harvard to do postgraduate work before transferring to Columbia to earn a Ph.D. Aside from a short period of time at Western Reserve's department of education, the rest of Thorndike's career was spent at Columbia. While there, Thorndike applied the study of psychology to personnel problems in business, industry, and the military. By 1922, he was director of the university's division of psychology in the Institute of Educational Research.

The early 1900s have been categorized as the Child Study Era. During this time universities began to set up laboratory schools on campus in which to study children and their teachers. Various societies and professional journals were initiated to develop and share research. Government agencies were established to promote the study of children and their welfare. Child labor laws prevented the exploitation of underage workers.

At Columbia, Thorndike's work with animals had led him to an interest in human learning. He developed psychological tests and assessment tools for academic achievement, and wrote leading textbooks. Thorndike applied quantitative methods to the study of behavior and education. His major contribution to educational psychology was his work in the area of stimulus-response theory. Working with animals, sometimes in William James's basement, Thorndike observed how long it would take an animal to pull a string, open a trap door, and thereby escape from a box. The animal, usually a cat, would eventually learn the trick. Each time it was placed in the box it would require less time to escape. These experiments were the beginning of Thorndike's work in the stimulus-response bond.

Working from observations and scientific data, Thorndike developed three Laws of Learning. *The Law of Effect* stated that any response to a stimulus that resulted in an immediate reward would be reinforced and repeated. *The Law of Readiness* required that a learner be poised and ready to respond if learning was to be meaningful. *The Law of Exercise* declared that a stimulus-response bond practiced repeatedly would reinforce learning.

Thorndike was a prolific writer. One of his most important works is his doctoral thesis, *Animal Intelligence*. It was followed by the three-volume *Educational Psychology and Introduction to the Theory of Mental and Social Measurement*. Thorndike was a major figure of the Child Study Era and has become known as the dean of American educational philosophy. The Laws of Learning have had considerable impact on learning theory and contributed to the development of programmed learning, such as computers provide in today's classroom. Critics of the stimulus-response theory fault its lack of consideration for the learner's intelligence and purpose. Can the results of tests performed on animals be applied to humans? What about human social, emotional, and moral qualities? By taking Pavlov's views right into the classroom, Thorndike provided a preview of the work of B. F. Skinner. Skinner and the behaviorists maintained that learning comes from interactions with the environment rather than from the maturity that develops with age.

By testing Columbia extension students ranging in age from teens to senior adults, Thorndike discovered that the ability to learn increased until young adulthood and leveled off with only a slight decline in later years. This finding stimulated a great deal of subsequent interest in adult education. Thorndike also drew attention to the importance of the kindergarten and childhood health care. Thorndike's careful records of observations and use of scientific data ushered in a new appreciation for the science of detailed measurement within the context of educational research.

ROBERT J. CHOUN

Bibliography. D. G. Benner, ed. (1999), *Baker Encyclopedia of Psychology and Counseling*, 2d ed.; R. J. Corsini, ed. (1984), *Encyclopedia of Psychology*; D. L. Barlow (1985), *Educational Psychology*; E. L. Thorndike (1965), *Animal Intelligence; Experimental Studies*.

See also ASSOCIATION/CONNECTIONIST THEORIES; BEHAVIORISM, THEORIES OF; LAW OF EFFECT, LAW OF EXERCISE; LAW OF READINESS; SKINNER, BURRHUS FREDERIC; S-R BONDS

Torah. Transliterated Hebrew word usually translated "law," "teaching," or "instruction." The essential meaning of this noun is "teaching," whether it is the teaching a parent provides children or the instruction God provides for Israel.

Torah can refer to the teaching pertaining to rules concerning a specific issue, such as the laws related to sacrifice. It can just as easily refer to a collective set of laws.

When the definite article is prefixed to *torah*, it is usually used in reference to the "Law of Moses" (Josh. 8:31, 32; Mal. 4:4). The five Books of Moses, the Pentateuch, are often identified as the *torah*. However, it is more accurate to say that the *torah* is found within those books. Even in the Pentateuch, *torah* has various meanings. In Exodus 18:20, it refers to fair decisions. In Leviticus 6:9, it refers to specific actions involving sacrifice. In Exodus 12:4, it refers to the legal system.

After the death of Moses, Levitical priests became the custodians of the law. They were to teach the law to the people and follow its regulations. They were called "those who deal with the law" in Jeremiah 2:8. The priests were to assist the people in worship and sacrifice. It was the primary duty of the priests to teach the people how to maintain a proper relationship with God.

The family was the primary educational institution for the training of children in Old Testament times. Because of the patriarchal nature of family structure, it was the duty of every Jewish father to know the *torah* and teach it to his children. By teaching the *torah*, a father could impress on his children the importance of God's commandments and demonstrate proper relationship to God.

While the *torah* is a legal code, it came to represent much more. It is a way of life based on the covenant relationship between God and his people. The *torah* contains guidance and instruction in living. This broad way of defining the word communicates *torah* as divine instruction given through history, verse, and prophecy.

By the time of Jesus, most Jews thought of the *torah* as only a set of rules to follow. In fact, many more detailed and strict regulations were imposed in addition to the *torah* in the form of the Mishna and the Talmud. The Mishna was a collection of comments on the *torah*. Talmud was an oppressive collection of rabbinical laws. Taken in a purely legalistic way, the *torah* closes the dynamic window to a relationship with God that it was meant to open.

RONNIE J. JOHNSON

See also EDUCATION IN THE PENTATEUCH; JEWISH EDUCATION; JUDAISM

Total Quality Management. Management philosophy that seeks to enhance productivity and quality in organizations. This philosophy, and its attendant management practices, had become so common by the end of the 1980s that it was popularly known by the acronym TQM.

The philosophy and practice of TQM is credited to W. Edwards Deming. Assisted by statistician Walter A. Shewhart, Deming developed a set of management practices that enabled manufacturers to meet the U.S. military's tremendous needs for machines and material during World War II. The underlying ideas were to increase the quality of the product and the productivity of the factory.

In 1947, Deming went to Japan to assist in that country's rebuilding process following its devastation by the war. The Japanese quickly received his philosophy and management techniques, and as a result Japan's economic recovery has become one of history's most often repeated stories of business success.

In the 1980s, American corporations began adopting Deming's philosophy and statistical control methods in an effort to regain market share that had been lost to the Japanese in the previous three decades. By the early 1990s, many U.S. manufacturers had successfully recaptured some of their market share as a result of improving their productivity and the quality of their products.

JOHN H. AUKERMAN

See also ADMINISTRATION; EVALUATION; MANAGEMENT

TQM. *See* Competency-Based Education.

Transductive Reasoning. Jean Piaget observed a particular thought pattern in children in the preoperational cognitive development stage. In this stage a child might observe an event and reason that if A caused B, then B must also cause A. A comparison of transductive reasoning to inductive and deductive reasoning clarifies the concept. In deductive reasoning a generalization is applied to particular examples. In inductive reasoning specific examples allow the creation of a generalization. In transductive reasoning, the child's thought processes move from particular to particular without ever touching the generalization. Transductive reasoning is characterized as intuitive, freewheeling, and imaginative. Piaget used an experience from his own family to illustrate. He told how one day his daughter missed her afternoon nap. Later she declared that it could not possibly be afternoon since she had not napped. In this illustration, the girl had reasoned that her afternoon nap transformed morning into afternoon (Dembo, 1994).

WALTER H. NORVELL

Bibliography. M. H. Dembo (1994), *Applying Educational Psychology;* W. R. Yount (1996), *Created to Learn.*

Transfer. Process through which performance on one learning task affects another task either positively or negatively. Positive transfer is the ability of the student to apply learning in new situations, a process known as generalization, which is a major goal of Christian education. Positive transfer can be either *vertical,* making the student capable of more complex or difficult tasks, for example, moving from verbal association to concept learning to problem solving, or *horizontal,* allowing the student to apply a skill learned in one situation to a new but comparable situation. Negative transfer refers to the inhibiting of one learning task by another, a process known as interference, which may be either retroactive, that is, new information and skills interfering with the retention of old material, or proactive, that is, old information or skills interfering with the learning of new material. Negative transfer provides some explanation of why forgetting is such a difficult problem in the Christian education process. Positive transfer is best facilitated and negative transfer inhibited by ensuring that the material learned is meaningful rather than isolated, random facts and providing opportunity for student performance of the learning task in a variety of realistic situations and with feedback and positive and negative reinforcement.

JOHN R. YEATTS

Bibliography. J. S. Bruner (1977), *The Process of Education;* R. M. Gagne (1977), *The Conditions of Learning.*

See also INFORMATION PROCESSING

True Love Waits. Grassroots campaign originating with Southern Baptists in April 1993, True Love Waits is now an international campaign involving at least eighty other Christian entities. Its purpose is to challenge students to remain sexually abstinent until marriage. The campaign was initiated in response to the belief that many teenagers were committed to abstinence, yet hesitant to express their position due to society's predominant message promoting sexual permissiveness. The True Love Waits challenge is communicated by leaders to youth in churches, student organizations, health care groups, and on campuses. Those responding to the challenge of abstinence sign a covenant card which states, "Believing that true love waits, I make a commitment to God, myself, my family, my friends, my future mate, and my future children to be sexually abstinent from this day until the day I enter a biblical marriage relationship." Hundreds of thousands of students have signed these cards, often in public ceremonies. A gold ring symbolizing sexual purity is worn by some, as a reminder of their commitment to abstinence until marriage.

In July of 1994 a display of more than 210,000 cards on the National Mall in Washington, D.C., marked the first national celebration of True Love Waits. Since that time cards have been displayed at other sites on the national, state, and local levels, including a display at the International Date Line marking the new millennium.

Members of the House and Senate, the Surgeon General, and the office of the president were briefed on the True Love Waits message. The campaign has received national media coverage, has been mentioned in such magazines as *Rolling Stone* and *Playboy*, and appears as a history question in the "Trivial Pursuit-Genus III" board game.

Since True Love Waits began, the teenage birthrate declined for the first time in nearly two decades. Journalists and trends experts attributed the declines to a shift toward abstinence by teens. A study published in the *Journal of the American Medical Association* reported that teens who had taken a pledge to virginity were at a significantly lower risk of engaging in early sexual activity than those who had not taken a pledge. While it cannot be substantiated, these factors indicate that the True Love Waits Campaign has impacted the sexual behavior of students.

KAREN E. JONES

See also SEXUALITY; SEXUALITY, ADOLESCENT

Trustee. Individual belonging to a board that holds the legal responsibility for a Christian school, college, agency, or mission board that is organized for a not-for-profit purpose. Churches frequently have trustees to meet legal requirements, but policy decision is often directed by a general church board, a board of deacons, or a board of elders.

Most Christian organizations choose trustees carefully to maintain a balance on the board in terms of geographical representation, vocational skills, and spiritual sensitivity. Trustees are generally expected to be financial contributors to the organization. As a collective board, they represent the organization legally and officially. In many ways, trustees create and sustain the ethos of an organization.

A board of trustees provides general oversight for the organization. Its task is to set policy, then entrust day-by-day operation to an operating officer who handles daily decisions and staff management. Most boards meet on a regular basis to approve budgets, personnel decisions, and policy, and for future planning. Many boards organize to include an executive committee and working committees. The executive committee, composed of the chair and other trustees, provides counsel to the chief executive officer as needed. Working committees contribute to the vision and function of the organization, especially in financial and development areas.

ELEANOR A. DANIEL

See also CLERGY; DEACON; DEACONESS; NONPROFIT ORGANIZATIONS; SENIOR PASTOR

Twelve-Step Group. *See* Adult Children of Alcoholics; Recovery; Recovery Ministry.

Twelve-Step Program. Certain behaviors hold such an iron grip on their victims that even sincere Christians are driven to hopelessness because of addiction(s) to alcohol, illegal drugs, gambling, sexual gratification, and so on.

During the 1930s, an Episcopal priest, Sam Shoemaker, served as the inspiration for the establishment of Alcoholics Anonymous (AA), to help adults enslaved to addictive behavior find victory through dependence upon a "Higher Power." Today AA is a widespread, nonsectarian, theistically oriented recovery program, built upon the biblical principles of repentance, confession of wrongdoing, encouragement of others, restitution, compassion, and outreach. Similar so-called twelve-step programs have also been formed for sex addicts, compulsive gamblers, and so on. Related groups, such as Alanon for families of alcoholics, provide support for those having to live with an addict.

The foundation of the twelve-step program is interpersonal relationships growing out of frequent meetings (of addicts only), telephone dialogue, and mentoring. The program provides a caring community in which fellow strugglers experience authentic acceptance. Participants allow themselves to be loved and to care for others, addressing the core issues that have often fueled their addiction. Men especially are enabled by the anonymity factor—persons are only identified by their first names as they proceed through twelve recovery steps.

A closer conscious contact with one's "Higher Power" is fostered through prayer (both in the group and individually), meditation, and daily affirmation of one's absolute need for God's help to break the addiction. Addicts are encouraged to seek to make amends when appropriate for those they have hurt as a result of their addiction.

Many addicts have been helped to recover because they learn to depend upon God for spiritual strength. Thus humbled, they move into recovery with the knowledge that God cares for them and so do fellow-addicts. For many, this becomes a life-changing experience.

DANIEL C. JESSEN

Uu

Unification. *See* Cohesion in Groups.

Uniformity. *See* Homogeneity.

Uniform Lesson Series. Attempt to standardize both the content and caliber of Sunday school curriculum in the late nineteenth century. Opposite to the graded approach to Sunday school curriculum, the uniform series called for all classes of every age group represented in the Sunday school to study the same passage, differing only in application and depth of study. While the lesson series began as a curriculum for all ages, in 1924 its scope was reduced to include only the youth (intermediate, middle school age) and adult Sunday school departments. It was not until 1945 that it reencompassed its original scope, which included the children's classes. Hence, the uniformity in the lesson series was to be present on both the congregational level, in the classes themselves, and at the intercongregational level, standardizing the curriculum throughout the Sunday school movement.

The aims of the uniform series were simple: (1) provide an overview of the most significant portions of the Bible, and (2) focus on the passages considered most beneficial for moral and character development. The lessons of the uniform series were not complete lesson plans, since they lacked commentary, but rather were lesson briefs containing (1) title, (2) selection from the Bible, (3) topic for specific age group, (4) memory passage, and (5) home/family Bible readings.

Although standard for today's curriculum, the uniform lesson series' format was considered innovative for its era. The series as a curriculum utilized a six-year cycle, dividing the units into thirteen to fifteen weeks (quarters). The subject matter was typically thematic, not exegetical. The selection of biblical texts and passages was alternated quarterly between Old and New Testaments, or occasionally semiquarterly, depending on the subject matter.

The uniform lesson series was both Protestant and evangelical in character, emphasizing a return to the Bible as the center of the Sunday school's study. The uniform series since its inception was interdenominational and ecumenical, and hence it had the virtually insurmountable task of developing a Christian education curriculum that avoided theologically laden passages. The tension of being evangelical and biblical as well as interdenominational and ecumenical often proved to be a political more than educational matter. As previously mentioned, the series provided only lesson briefs, which promoted standardization, but also allowed denominations to theologically embellish the briefs.

Development of the Uniform Lesson Series. The rise of the Sunday school movement and standardization of public school curriculum created the impetus to standardize the Sunday school's curriculum. In this environment, the uniform lesson series developed from a local to a national and eventually to an international endeavor to standardize the Sunday school's curriculum, with each phase of its development representing a change in leadership.

The local endeavor was begun by John H. Vincent (Methodist), founder of *Chicago Sunday-School Teacher's Quarterly* in 1865. With better trained teachers in the Sunday school, the necessity of a more professional curriculum rose. In 1866, Vincent published a two-year lesson series on the life of Christ in the *Quarterly,* which was readily received by the Sunday schools in the Chicago area. Vincent later became the editor of the Berean Bible study series, a competitor to the uniform lesson series.

The local endeavor was expanded to the national level in 1867 by Edward Eggleston, Vincent's successor, who published the first national series of lessons in *National Sunday School Teacher,* noting the expansion from just the Chicago area Sunday schools. When the lesson series drew the attention of the National Sunday School convention, it was poised to enter the international arena. In 1872 B. F. Jacobs (Baptist layman), after two years of debate in previous conventions, convinced the National Sunday

School Convention meeting in Indianapolis to form a committee to explore and develop a uniform lesson series that could be used not only in the United States but also internationally. The convention agreed to appoint a ten-person committee (equally comprised of laity and clergymen) to explore this possibility.

The uniform lesson series is perpetuated by the same committee that had been originally established in 1872, with denominational representatives serving on it. While the committee has changed its name periodically, the current name is the Committee on the Uniform Series of the National Council of the Churches of Christ in the U.S.A.

Appraisal of the Uniform Lesson Series. The formation of a uniform series of Bible lessons was indeed an improvement to the condition of the Sunday school's curriculum. However, several concerns have been raised regarding its quality. First, the uniform series provides only a fragmented knowledge of the Bible due to its thematic and nonsequential arrangement. Although it does provide selections of significant passages from both the Old and New Testaments, it does *not* provide an overview of the Bible as a whole.

Second, as previously noted, the uniform lesson briefs lack any theological depth. However, the difficulty extends further due to the intentional selection of passages that are devoid of significant theological implications. Hence, even the attempt to embellish the lesson briefs theologically would be hindered by the lack of doctrinally laden biblical passages selected for the series.

Third, the educational approach of the uniform series is unmistakably content-centered rather than pupil-centered. The concern of the uniform series was the standardization of the lesson. This was to be expected since content-centered education was indeed the dominant approach to education in the late nineteenth century and developmental understandings of the student were somewhat absent.

Fourth, as with any attempt to standardize instruction there is a loss of flexibility and uniqueness in the curriculum. In this instance the reliance of Christian educators on the uniform lesson series does indeed remove to some degree the denominational or congregational influence over the curriculum.

JAMES RILEY ESTEP

Bibliography. C. B. Eavey (1964), *History of Christian Education;* C. M. Layman (1963), *Westminister Dictionary of Christian Education.*

See also CURRICULUM; LESSON PLAN; SUNDAY SCHOOL

Universal Ethical Principle. Conviction or belief that transcends the rules and mores of society and provides guidelines applicable to all people in all situations at all times. A universal ethical principle furnishes an understanding of the ultimate in moral attainment and is the end point by which less mature forms of thinking are judged. There may be exceptions to rules but there are no exceptions to principles.

Universal ethical principles do not prescribe specific behaviors but offer a guide for choosing among behaviors. They stand in sharp contrast to the relativist position that as people and societies change what is moral also changes. They are philosophical rather than scientific in that they evaluate beliefs and standards and provide the *ought* of human conduct rather than stating the facts or the *is* of human condition.

Principles may stem from divine law as revealed in Scripture, from natural law as recognized by all societies and implemented in courts of justice, or from reason as in a recognition of the rational and objective character of the moral order. They are forever in the mind of God, given to the human race by our being created in His image. Etched into our consciences, they bear witness to that which is true (Rom. 2:15). Examples in literature are Socrates' higher natural law, Immanuel Kant's categorical imperative, and Lawrence Kohlberg's concept of justice. As such, they are in opposition to Søren Kierkegaard's existential ethics, Schleiermacher's emphasis on intuitive religious feeling, and Joseph Fletcher's situation ethics. A universal ethical principle is normative rather than descriptive, objective rather than subjective, eternal rather than temporal.

Jesus stated that the universal ethical principle that superseded all others was love—love for "the Lord your God" and love for "your neighbor" (Matt. 22:37–40.) This was not a superficial love, but a love for God that consumed one's whole being, heart, soul, and mind, and a love for neighbor equal to the love for oneself.

BONNIDELL CLOUSE

University. The history of the present-day university system, with its colleges, faculties, degrees, and diverse collection of students, commences with the founding of the early European universities of Paris, Bologna, Oxford, and others. Despite the passage of over eight hundred years, the modern university still bears a marked resemblance to its medieval ancestors.

Without argument, much of the medieval university appears quaint to modern eyes. Students today no longer register their discontent with the locals by departing a university town en masse and starting the same university afresh in an entirely new location. Nor are individual professors required to pay a prescribed fine when they fail to keep their lectures within the prescribed time limits.

On the other hand, basic concepts that define the modern notion of a university find their origins in this early period. Terms such as *master* and *doctor* indicated, then as now, intellectual and scholastic achievement of the highest order. Further, because of the status of the universities granted by the pope or the state, these same degrees gradually acquired universal acceptance and recognition. A *doctor* in one university could, with some exceptions, expect to be accorded the same privileges at another institution. This element of standardization in addition to several other factors marked the university as a unique invention of twelfth- and thirteenth-century Europe.

Origins of the Medieval University. The most commonly cited ancestor of the medieval university is the cathedral school. Originally providing little more than basic education in the *trivium* of grammar, rhetoric, and logic (lower studies), some of the cathedral schools gradually fortified their curriculum. The *quadrivium* (higher studies) included the mathematical arts of arithmetic, geometry, music, and astronomy. Though under control of the local bishop, direct supervision of the cathedral schools was at times delegated to a *chancellor*.

At this point several factors began to converge. Cathedral schools with enhanced curriculum attracted additional students. Chancellors gradually acquired the authority to license teachers within their diocese. Eventually, to the chancellors of the most prominent cathedral schools, the pope granted the authority to issue a teaching license *ubique docendi*, entitling the bearer to teach anywhere in Christendom.

Students desirous of extending their education began seeking out the more popular teachers, often traveling great distances to achieve this end. Many such groups of international students gathered around the great Abelard, whose lectures some regard as the primal beginnings of the university in Paris.

The existence of cathedral schools, though significant, cannot completely explain the rise of the universities. Many universities developed independently of the cathedral schools. Other principal factors include the Crusades, whose dynamics brought the cultures of Islam and Christendom face to face and partially awakened Europe out of its long intellectual slumber. Concurrently, Europe was developing economically and politically, thus facilitating movements of individuals and ideas. Though the papacy reached its acme toward the end of the twelfth century in the person of Innocent III, it gradually began a decline of political influence in favor of the free city-states of Italy and the emerging unified kingdoms of France and England. Trade guilds also grew in their acquisition of political power, thus creating the unlikely mechanism whereby learners might eventually band together as guilds of students. Indeed, these guilds formed the first notion of the *universitas,* referring to the whole company of students in a certain location.

Conditions favoring the establishment of the first universities now unfolded at an ever-quickening pace. Educational, religious, and political leaders competed with one another for the affections of great teachers and their attendant retinue of hungry-hearted scholars. Centers of learning became medieval status symbols, especially as the advantages of education became fully realized. Rome discovered the pragmatic value of trained lawyers capably interpreting canon law. Southern European schools soon specialized in the disciplines of Law and Medicine. Northern Europe became intoxicated with the subtleties of philosophy and theology.

Though the pure love of learning contributed its share in the establishment of new universities, many of the other causes were less noble and more pragmatic. Ultimately, whether the reasons included papal prerogatives, local civic pride, eager students or compelling professors, a critical mass of twelfth-century social, political, economic, and religious conditions soon detonated. Europe witnessed the birth of a glittering new constellation and was bathed in the scholastic radiance of these fledgling universities.

Common Themes in the Medieval University. What did these new universities share, apart from a remarkably similar mode of birth? In contrast to modern institutions of higher learning, with their rigid departmentalization and wildly differing approaches to education, the medieval university enjoyed a universally accepted philosophic cohesiveness and worldview. Granted, this worldview merely reflected the prevailing theology of Christendom. Yet, Christian educators today find much to commend and emulate in the following seven evaluative propositions, distilled from regulations of the University of Paris circa 1215 (Rüegg, 1992, 32–33):

1. *God created an orderly universe, rational and accessible to human reason.* This proposition justified scientific and scholastic research in order to comprehend the rational order of God's handiwork.
2. *Humanity though perfectly created, fell into sin.* The proposition implied the limitations of human intellect, and the necessity of scholarly criticism, and provided ample reasons for collegial cooperation. The doctrine of the fall likewise led these early educators to project the ethical values of humility and reverence for God upon the image of the ideal scholar and scientist.
3. *Humanity, though fallen, still bears the* imago dei, *the image of God, and is to be accorded respect.* This proposition laid the foundation for academic freedom in research and teaching.

4. *God's nature is absolute, therefore the imperative of scientific truth is likewise absolute.* Christian educators hear the ancient cry of "all truth is God's truth" emanating from this statement. Medieval scholars founded basic norms of research and teaching here. For example, one's own assertions must be subject to valid rules of evidence, and that the nature of scholarly discussion is public and open.

5. *Scholarly and scientific knowledge is a gift of God and to be used for the public good.* Based upon this precept, the university had traditionally been less interested in research for the sake of monetary gain than in professions found outside of the ivy-covered walls.

6. *The principle of Reformatio counted an individual's scientific accomplishments as being part of an ongoing renewal and revision of previously established knowledge.* Current scientific inquiry stands on the shoulders of those who have gone before, thus the entire learning process is not one of *formation*, but of *re-formation*.

7. Finally, the proposition that *God created human beings in a state of fundamental equality* carried over into the medieval notions of scholar egalitarianism. Truth was not confined to any particular social strata or dependent upon like-mindedness in thought patterns. Whenever compelling new evidence could be presented, regardless of its source, true medieval scholars stood ready to amend their views. This solidarity among scholars contributed to the rise of science.

Later Developments. Blessed with extraordinary independence and a firm foundation for learning, medieval universities flourished for the first several centuries. The list of university towns included Oxford, Cambridge, London, Paris, Bologna, Toulouse, Naples, Prague, and Vienna, to name a few. Detailed regulations governed every aspect of university life and included rules for academic apparel, standards for issuance of degrees and licenses, behavior expectations for both professors and students, etc.

Though originally regarded as cutting edge international centers of science and learning, the universities gradually became more nationally oriented. By the sixteenth and seventeenth centuries, the standards of the academy had disintegrated to a point where it could no longer keep up with social change, and other nonuniversity organizations began to engage in scientific research.

New, autonomous, state-supported German and French universities emerged in the early nineteenth century and revived the concept of the university as a center of research. Unlike their medieval cousins, their disciplines were now bound together by philosophy rather than theology. Higher education was also reserved for the elite. German and French institutions provided a strong influence in the later development of contemporary American universities.

By contrast to the aristocratic Europeans, the Americans revived the proposition of egalitarianism, focusing on education for the masses. American higher education, though marked by a wide variety of programs and courses of study, is also hampered by an equally wide variety of competing philosophies and approaches to education. Modern Christian universities are now beginning to rediscover theology as a unifying and comprehensive approach to higher education. In doing so, they appeal both to Scripture for justification and to the medieval universities as worthy archetypes.

KENNETH V. BOTTON

Bibliography. L. J. Daly (1961), *The Medieval University;* C. B. Eavey (1964), *History of Christian Education;* K. O. Gangel and W. S. Benson (1983), *Christian Education: Its History and Philosophy;* C. H. Haskins (1957), *The Rise of the Universities;* A. S. Knowles (1977), *The International Encyclopedia of Higher Education;* W. Rüegg (1992), *A History of the University in Europe;* N. Schachner, (1962), *The Medieval Universities;* R. Ulich (1968), *A History of Religious Education.*

See also HIGHER EDUCATION, CHRISTIAN; MEDIEVAL EDUCATION

Upward Bound. Upward Bound was established through the Higher Education Act of 1965 (HEA Title IV). It was part of the legislation that became known as the War on Poverty. A federally funded program, it exists to help disadvantaged students discover the skills and motivation necessary for success in postsecondary education.

The target audience for the Upward Bound program is youth between the ages of 13 and 19. To qualify for the program, students must be from low-income homes (defined as less than 150 percent of poverty level) or be potential first-generation college students. (Two-thirds of all participants must meet both criteria.) Additional requirements include the completion of eight years of elementary education, plans to go to college, and recommendations from teachers and counselors.

Over 500 program sites serve 42,000 students annually in the Upward Bound program. Most programs are sponsored by institutions of higher education. All programs must provide instruction in math (through pre-calculus), laboratory science, foreign language, English, and composition. In addition, the programs typically offer assistance in study skills, academic counseling, tutorial services, financial aid, and career guidance. Other components of the programs will often include exposure to cultural events, field trips to various workplaces, and opportunities for wilderness trips.

Participants meet on a regular basis throughout the school year for instruction, counseling, mentoring, and support services. These activities are generally on weekends or after school. Another significant aspect of the Upward Bound program is the summer component. This is a residential program that lasts between five and eight weeks. Typically students will engage in academic classes, visit local business sites, and participate in intensive field trips. Government reports indicate a positive effect in the areas of reading achievement and educational expectations for participants in the Upward Bound program.

DOUGLAS BARCALOW

See also CHRISTIAN CAMPING INTERNATIONAL; OUTDOOR MINISTRIES

Urban Christian Education. Christian education in the modern urban world is about transformation. The urban environment is a vast, complicated web of diverse peoples interconnected in many ways who hunger for life in its fullness. These people come from every color, class, culture, lifestyle, belief system, and age group imaginable. They are participants in churches and other Christian institutions large and small, traditional and innovative, rich and poor. The reality of Christian education in the city touches on virtually the entire range of human experience. Christian education is rooted in and springs out of this incredible human tapestry. It will of necessity take many forms, be continuously flexible and open to change, and be responsive to the new works of God that break forth at any time on any day in any location. What holds urban Christian education together is its fundamental purpose of transforming hearts and lives and neighborhoods and institutions and cultures. A number of important principles of good practice for urban Christian education emerge from this integrating purpose.

1. Urban Christian education is context-dependent. Modern cities contain hundreds, even thousands, of unique social worlds intertwined in complex ways. In the city the political, economic, social, cultural, and religious dimensions of human society collide. Extremes of poverty and wealth, radical and conservative, old and young, sacred and secular, powerful and powerless coexist side by side. Social worlds vary in scale from small, intimate groups to large, impersonal institutions and systems. The urban natural environment physically tends to be densely populated, with many kinds of neighborhoods and buildings for living, working, servicing, administering, and manufacturing. Cities are also interdependent with their suburban and rural surrounding regions in that complicated networks of interchange mutually influence one another. Urban areas tend to be centers of innovation and social change and diversification within a society, and thus are rapidly changing, so that cities can be vibrant, dynamic, life-giving settings for a diverse spectrum of peoples. Many forms of injustice, marginalization, and discrimination can divide the multiplicity of urban dwellers and thus promote violence and crime.

Any church or parachurch group wanting to become a partner in transformation must first of all identify its context. Learning and growing are natural, integral dimensions of all of human life. Education that is Christian grows out of a particular people in a particular social situation. It links up with the resources and elements and people involved, rather than separating itself from the world. Its orientation is one of capacity building rather than need focused. Educators ideally should live among the people, identifying with them and becoming cosubjects with them in the process of transformation.

2. Christian education is holistic. It touches upon all of the lived experiences of people: work, play, housing, health care, transportation, relationships, and so on. Holism is about developing connection between realities that are separated or alienated in the city. Christian education seeks to foster connectedness between persons and God, among persons within the family of God, and between the family of God and its context. Christian education helps people see and experience God in new and lifechanging ways, It unites diverse people in a community of faith characterized by mutuality, servant love, creativity, and freedom. And it engages with the full range of neighbors, colleagues, and realities present in the social world.

3. The urban milieu requires that Christian education be participant-centered. God is at work in the hearts and lives of all of the people, and their gifts and resources and needs and visions comprise the grist for the process of teaching and learning. Instead of being a top-down imposition of truth and values, the process of teaching and learning is participatory in every way. Educational events and structures must build in the manifold contributions of whoever is involved. It must come to terms with the reality framework of the people, not the framework of another time or place or tradition. In so doing Christian education is empowering rather than disempowering.

4. The model of Christian education best suited to the city is an action-reflection or praxis model. The actions of life, the day-to-day lived realities, the colorful and vibrant and yet broken and unjust worlds of the city are the stuff of Christian education. Learning begins with experience. As the people of God come together they reconstruct the meaning of this experience by means of reflecting individually and dialoguing communally on their lives. As people name how God is present with them in their world they experience transformation and also become agents of trans-

formation of their urban context. Diverse people groups that are divided by race, class, ethnicity, gender, age, education, and the like, preserve unique elements of the image of God and have much to learn from one another through critical dialogue and joint action-reflection.

VERNON L. BLACKWOOD

Bibliography. P. Freire (1993), *Pedagogy of the City;* H. Huxhold, ed. (1968), *Christian Education and the Urban Parish;* D. Rogers, ed. (1989), *Urban Church Education.*

Urban Family. The urban family is immersed in a complex social environment that encompasses the entire breadth of human experience. To be a family in the city is to hear and see and smell very vividly every day the best and worst of humanity. The family is constantly evolving and being altered by being in the city, but not destroyed. The family functions as the primary place of belonging, nurture, and growth for most city dwellers. In the midst of both the stresses and strains and the rich treasures of urban life the family is an oasis of life where the joys and sorrows and struggles of making a way in the world are cared for. The urban family takes many forms, from single parents with children to two elderly siblings, from multigeneration immigrant clans to cohabiting partnerships. The structures, values, and lifestyles of urban families span a wide spectrum, and the love of God and the love of the people of God extend to them all. While family structures vary, the city intensifies family cohesion and importance for providing support and assistance. The urban family is a mechanism of survival, belonging, sharing life, working, recreation, socialization and learning, creativity, emotional support, brokering with the larger world, and much more.

A philosophy of family nurture contextualized in this urban world is the necessary starting point. To nurture family life in the city is to enter into the struggles and the experiences of real people who are both wounded and broken and yet alive and growing. The primary ingredient in building strong families in the city is acceptance and compassion for people whatever their situation. Unconditional love will create families of forgiveness and grace, tough love and accountability, freedom to explore and find oneself and change, caring for daily needs, and walking together through difficulties such as injustice, violence, loss of jobs, and death of loved ones. This love engages with people where they are and seeks wholeness, intimacy, and justice.

Christian education begins with and centers in the home. This is so because for both adults and children the family setting is where life begins, proceeds through the life cycle, and ends. But families cannot stand alone. The role of the church and other organizations is to support and enrich the family. It does this through nurturing individual transformation, resourcing the family system, and intermediating with the larger urban world. Educating Christianly in the home means fostering connections with God's presence in every aspect of life so that God's Spirit teaches, forms, and renews family members. The Old Testament Israelite family model created a covenantal ordering of each day, each week, each year, and the entire life span centered in the presence of Yahweh. Worship, dialogue, work, play, celebrations, rituals, language, meals, travel, and everything else incorporated and was punctuated by awareness of the Spirit of God. A holistic model for ministry with urban families consists of numerous components: cultivating God's presence, providing resources, parent education, counseling, retreats and camps, fighting injustice, health and nutrition education, basic education for adults and children, English as a Second Language training, computer instruction, a library with books, magazines, videos, CDs, and games, training in conflict management and peacemaking, Bible studies, mentoring of young people and of leaders, and whatever else persons and situations require to grow into wholeness.

VERNON L. BLACKWOOD

Bibliography. J. and J. Balswick (1989), *The Family: A Christian Perspective on the Contemporary Home;* R. Clapp (1993), *Families at the Crossroads;* C. Stack (1974), *All Our Kin.*

V v

Vacation Bible School (VBS). How does a church help children who have the summer off, have nothing to do, and need to learn more about the Bible? They develop VBS. These summer schools have provided intense biblical training and enriched the lives of millions of children throughout the world.

Most people trace VBS's history to the early summer schools of the First Church of Boston in 1866 or to Montreal, Quebec, and its summer school started in 1877. VBS probably became an official movement in the early twentieth century under the leadership of Robert G. Boville, executive secretary of the New York Baptist City Mission. Due to Boville's efforts, the National Committee on Daily Vacation Bible School was formed and included one hundred persons, involving teachers from over thirty colleges and representatives of many denominations. By 1912, 141 cities had individual churches or associations of churches enrolling more than 100,000 children in vacation Bible schools. Forty-five countries throughout the world participated in this new approach for ministering to children by 1941.

While the newly named International Association of Daily Vacation Bible School provided training, curricular guidance, and administrative assistance, each community or church uniquely designed its own school. Most VBS programs ran weekday mornings throughout the entire summer; others met all day and lasted for two to eight weeks. Similar to the history of the Sunday school, the attention focused upon the children, their needs, and how to best teach them the Bible. While each VBS developed its own curriculum, most included time for Bible study, hymns, Scripture memorization, crafts or handwork, and organized games. In addition, many VBS programs tried to encourage children to learn life skills and trades such as sewing and carpentry. Most VBS programs were a fun-filled time with excited, eager children learning the stories and heroes of the Bible.

Today, VBS continues as a ministry for churches to train children in the Bible, provide positive adult role models, and encourage children to live their lives following Christian principles. However, increased time pressures and demands, limited volunteer staff, the competition of year-round athletic leagues, and increased family travel have caused many churches to eliminate or reduce the length and scope of their VBS programs. Some churches now provide evening VBS and include adult programs such as computer training, financial planning, marriage and family training, and recreational or sports skills.

Excellent year-round ministries such as Christian Service Brigade, Pioneer Ministries, Awana, and similar weekly, school year ministries currently replace VBS in the programs of many churches. The increase of year-round schooling has also had an impact on the number of churches conducting VBS programs since fewer children have the summer free for such church-related activities.

Attempting to reach children not attending church, many churches provide neighborhood or backyard clubs that meet in neighborhood parks or homes of church members. These clubs follow the basic format of the historical VBS; however, they are much shorter in length and usually focus primarily upon biblical training, singing, crafts, and organized games.

G. CRAIG WILLIFORD

Bibliography. E. M. Butt (1957), *The Vacation Church School in Christian Education;* D. Freese (1977), *Vacation Bible School;* G. Getz (1962), *The VBS in the Local Church.*

See also AWANA CLUBS INTERNATIONAL; CHILD EVANGELISM FELLOWSHIP; CHILDHOOD CHRISTIAN EDUCATION; CHILDREN'S CHURCH; CHILDREN'S MINISTRY MODELS; CHRISTIAN SERVICE BRIGADE; PIONEER MINISTRIES

Values (Values-Based Education). Historically, one of the major functions of education has been the teaching of values held dear by a group or culture. Scripture highlights this educational concern throughout the Book of Proverbs, as illustrated by the passage, "Train up a child in the way he should go, and when he is old he will not turn from it" (22:6). Even though many people agree that the development of values is a legitimate and important purpose of education, there is considerable disagreement over how it is best brought about.

Traditional approaches to values-based education have emphasized a goal of passing on an already established body of moral principles or laws and promoting the student's acceptance of them. This was often done by direct instruction of the moral principles, telling or reading stories that reinforced them, and the example of teachers and heros who modeled them. Much of the educational efforts of ancient societies was directed toward the development of the ethical or moral individual and utilized these kinds of instructional methods. The common school movement of the early 1800s was characterized by this approach as well, utilizing Scripture readings and moral stories to pass on Protestant Christian values to American children (Tyack and Hansot, 1982).

The "character education" movement in the early twentieth century also reflected this traditional approach, combining reinforcement methods with instruction to encourage the development of certain habits, such as cleanliness and cooperation. Christian education of children and youth throughout the centuries has reflected this model as well—teaching specific virtues or values by precept with reinforcement by biblical story, exemplary models, past and present, and reinforcement through rewards. This "traditional" model has recently fallen into disfavor, denigrated as a "bag of virtues" approach with little impact on the learner. It has also been criticized for indoctrinating learners with culturally developed values when learners should be able to select and develop their own.

Alternative approaches have developed within the past century, reflecting changing philosophical foundations and perspectives. As traditional educational philosophies have given way to pragmatism, existentialism, and postmodern perspectives, and as secular humanistic assumptions regarding human nature have gained acceptance, the role of education in the transmission of values has been reconsidered. For many educators today, the role of education is to enable learners to develop and affirm their own sets of values, not "indoctrinate" them with a culturally accepted norm. In an era of sensitivity to multicultural education issues, a more relative stance of tolerance and private personal decision is advocated.

One example of this newer philosophical perspective is the values clarification movement of the 1960s–70s, which emphasized a democratic approach of freeing children to choose and create their own values (Raths, Harmin, and Simon, 1978). According to this model, the teacher's role is to present situations where students can reflect

on their own preferences and values, discuss them with fellow students, and clarify the values they want to accept and live by. These values are to be freely chosen from alternatives after thoughtful consideration of their consequences. Learners are to cherish and share their values with others, or to act upon their values and make them a life pattern (Raths et al., 1978, 28). According to this approach, there is no particular objective standard for value decisions. Learners need to personally assess the options and choose the values they will live by. Criticism of this approach has focused on the moral and individual relativism it reflects, the limited role of the teacher in the process, and potential negative outcomes for society if this approach is embraced. In this approach, all choices are valid if learners have worked through the choosing process and are willing to live authentically by their choices. There are no objective universal ethical principles to guide the development of values.

Another major contemporary approach, based on Piaget's theories of cognitive development and Kohlberg's stage theory of the development of moral reasoning, utilizes case studies as opportunities for students to explore moral dilemmas and to make choices regarding what is right to do and why. This approach, like values clarification, desires to avoid an indoctrination approach to transmitting values by encouraging reflective thinking by the students about their values and the reasoning behind them. Unlike values clarification, Kohlberg's model does assume some hierarchy of values culminating in universal ethical principles of justice, and affirms the importance of assisting students in developing higher stages of moral reasoning. The process of development involves group discussion of ethical dilemmas, enabling students to examine the adequacy of their reasoning and to be challenged to higher stages of reasoning that will more adequately address the dilemma. In this way, the teacher is an active guide, probing student responses and challenging them with issues that need to be resolved. Criticisms of this approach have focused on whether there are universal principles of justice and whether the discussion process actually assists in the development of moral behavior.

In recent years there has been a resurgence of more traditional approaches, seeking ways to teach specific beliefs and values and to help learners develop specific character traits or virtues. Newer approaches utilize teaching by precepts, stories, and models, but many also advocate the use of dialogue, reflection, active learning, and critical thinking to challenge students to personally "own" the values being taught (Thiessen, 1993; Bennett, 1993).

KEVIN E. LAWSON

Bibliography. W. J. Bennett, ed. (1993), *The Book of Virtues: A Treasury of Great Moral Stories;* K. M. Gow,

Yes, Virginia, There Is Right and Wrong; L. Raths, M. Harmin, and S. Simon (1978), *Values and Teaching: Working with Values in the Classroom;* E. J. Thiessen (1993), *Teaching for Commitment: Liberal Education, Indoctrination, and Christian Nurture;* D. Tyack and E. Hansot (1982), *Managers of Virtue: Public School Leadership in America, 1820–1980.*

See also CRITICAL THINKING; HUMANISM, CLASSICAL; HUMANISM, CHRISTIAN; LAWRENCE KOHLBERG; MORAL DILEMMA; MORAL EDUCATION; PIAGET, JEAN; REFLECTION; VALUES EDUCATION

Values Clarification. Method of defining an individual's values. Value clarification theory presumes that if an individual defines, clarifies, and internalizes personal and societal values then that individual's behavior will appropriately reflect the internalized values. Values clarification tends to be more concerned with the process of valuing than with the specific values internalized by the individual. According to Raths, Harmin, and Simon (1978), values are formed and clarified in three processes under sevenfold criteria. The first process involves *choice.* Three criteria govern choice: (1) choices must be made freely without coercion; (2) choices are made from many alternatives; and (3) the individual must thoughtfully consider the consequences of each alternative. The second process involves *prizing* or *cherishing* the choice. This embodies two criteria (1) the individual has a satisfaction over the choice made and (2) the individual publicly affirms his or her choice. The final process in values clarification is *action.* Two criteria mark this process: (1) the individual seeks to apply the choice to some specific action or behavior and (2) that individual begins to ingrain a pattern or lifestyle consistent with that choice.

The problem with a values clarification model for the Christian educator falls under the first criteria involving the individual's choices. While coercion is not acceptable, Scripture teaches the Christian educator to teach, model, handle accurately, and guide the individual to internalize biblical values (Deut. 6:5–9; Prov. 22:6; 2 Tim. 2:15; James 3:1). While a values clarification theorist would see this as more passive by creating a nonjudgmental, hands-off setting, the Christian educator sees involvement in the process as being more intentional and direct.

During adolescence an individual begins to internalize values. Prior to this time the child accepts values because of concrete operational thinking. When a child enters into a formal operational thought stage, that individual begins to question and challenge values so as to internalize those values. This process of internalizing or clarifying allows the individual to own those values as personal rather than those of their parents. Many parents and Christian educators find this process threatening and perceive it as a form of

rebellion. The threat is minimized if a strategy is employed to help the adolescent clarify values. Strategies should include asking *direct questions* and *raising value specific issues* for learners to wrestle through; *role modeling* behavior that corresponds with the verbal explanation of a value being modeled; *educating and informing* learners about the consequences and rewards of value-specific behaviors; being sensitive to and taking advantage of *teachable moments;* and, *rewarding* appropriate behavior, *disciplining* inappropriate behavior, and allowing adolescents to *suffer natural consequences* for their behaviors.

STEVEN GERALI

Bibliography. J. Fraenkel (1977), *How to Teach about Values: An Analytical Approach;* L. Raths, M. Harmin, and S. Simon (1978), *Values and Teaching.*

Values Education. Values are widely shared attitudes that influence the behavior of a society. While cultural variations abound, typical examples would include the preservation of human life, protection of children, and security of personal property. A primary goal of parents and teachers is the passing on of an intact values system to the next generation. Changes in society, however, trigger changes in values. Without an inflexible core of moral absolutes, a values system will be subject to review by each new generation. Much of the discussion of values involves the frustration of elders who complain that the young have no respect for traditional virtues. In some situations, objective reevaluation can reveal error. Before abolitionists revealed slavery as immoral, some considered the practice benign— even benevolent.

In a utilitarian society, values no longer considered productive are discontinued. Hedonists value whatever provides pleasure. Others give precedence to practices and attitudes that foster personal freedom. How are we to discern whether a behavior or attitude is worth preserving? What are the best ways to pass on our values to our children? These are the questions facing teachers and parents. In the 1960s, therapists and educators responded with a process of values clarification and education designed to help individuals formulate a personally relevant values system.

The Process of Values Education. The first step in values education involves the self-awareness of personal values and their clarification. "What do I consider important?" Once an individual has determined a system of values, he or she explores the principles on which they are based. "Why are these things important to me?" With a clear picture of what matters and why, the individual is motivated to put the values system into action. "What am I going to do about it?"

The concept that was at first only head knowledge nurtured an attitude that eventually propelled the learner to take action. Effective values education reaches the cognitive, affective, and behavioral levels of learning. An example of this process could be a person who hears about the needs of the homeless and decides to donate to the local shelter because community service is part of his or her values system.

The most influential teaching methods for values education apply concepts to everyday situations. Through the use of thought-provoking questions and careful observations, teachers can guide the conversation of learners in the course of common experiences so that the learners: (1) become more aware of their behavior, (2) examine their attitudes; and (3) modify their behavior. Drama methods such as role plays build empathy by helping learners experience the impact their own negative behavior can have on others. Stories told by teachers can illustrate abstract terms so that learners can better understand the application of unfamiliar concepts. Skilled discussion leaders can guide learners in the exploration of their attitudes and help them discover ways to act on their beliefs.

Research done with young learners affirms the value of the adult model in values education. A desirable behavior such as charitable giving is likely to become internalized and eventually part of a learner's own lifestyle if it is modeled and made completely voluntary. It is less likely to be reproduced in the learner if the behavior is simply described and enforced. Modeling has far greater impact than lecturing, but even the combined methods of modeling and lecturing have little effect if what the learner sees and hears are in opposition.

Values education benefits from consistency. If the values demonstrated by family, teachers, caregivers, and peers are similar, the input received by the learner is reviewed and reinforced. Mixed signals, however, will create the impression that values are relative to certain settings.

Correct discipline also has an effect on the learning of values. Rules must be clarified. Appropriate choices should be praised. Correction that is more punitive than educational leaves the impression that "wrong" is bad only if the wrongdoer is caught in the act. Instead of being linked to principles of morality, "right" seems to be whatever the individual can get away with. Discipline that teaches discernment and self-control results in internalized concepts of moral behavior. The ultimate goal of values education is an individual who behaves according to the prevailing value system but respects "right" and "wrong" as higher moral absolutes on which to base decisions.

Research and Scripture agree that the crucial time to instill values through modeling is early in the life of the learner. Moral lessons take on greater depth when the learner reaches the intellectual level at which he can distinguish intention from unintentional misbehavior. Behavior to gain praise gradually becomes behavior out of respect for the rules. An even higher level of thinking leads the learner to make decisions based on what is best for the group, rather than out of consideration of personal reward or punishment.

Christian Education and Values Systems. Thanks to the written Word of God, Christians have the distinct advantage of a solid base on which to build a curriculum for values education. In the Ten Commandments and the Golden Rule lie the moral absolutes needed to anchor a system and secure it against changing trends. Values education in a Christian context shares methodology with its secular counterpart, but revolves around a radically different center. The values clarification system developed by therapists in the 1960s assumed that a personal values system emerged from the person's collection of experiences rather than from an external source. Results were more often lists of personal preferences than moral choices. Instead of self-absorbed prioritizing of personal preferences, the Christian approach begins with the search for the will of God, the acknowledgment of his authority, and obedience to his commands. Instead of weighing attitudes and behaviors on the scales of pleasure, freedom, or usefulness, they are tested with Scripture.

Values clarification theory states that a value was not genuinely part of a personal system unless it was freely chosen and considered important enough to be acted upon. Motivation to moral action is the Christian's response to a loving God and a desire to glorify him.

ROBERT J. CHOUN

Bibliography. D. G. Benner (1985), *Baker Encyclopedia of Psychology;* R. E. Clark, J. Brubaker, and R. B. Zuck, eds. (1975), *Childhood Education in the Church;* B. Clouse (1993), *Teaching for Moral Growth;* I. V. Cully (1979), *Christian Child Development;* I. V. Cully and K. B. Cully, eds. (1990), *Harper's Encyclopedia of Religious Education;* K. M. Gow (1985), *Yes, Virginia, There Is a Right and Wrong;* M. S. and R. C. Smart (1977), *Children: Development and Relationships;* M. M. Wilcox (1979), *Developmental Journey.*

Vieth, Paul H. (1895–1978). American Christian educator. He attended Central Wesleyan College (A.B., 1917), Columbia University, and Yale University (B.D. 1924; Ph.D. 1928). From 1917 to 1920, he served as the field secretary for the Missouri Sunday School Association. He also served as their minister and director of religious education from 1922 to 1925. In addition, he served on the staff of the International Council of Religious Education for six years. He then moved to Yale University Divinity School in 1931. At Yale he was professor of religious education and director of field work (1931–63) and Horace Bushnell Professor of Christian Nurture (Reed and Prevost, 1993).

Vieth was a professional Christian educator in the local church for many years. Although he made numerous contributions to the field of religious education, clearly his greatest contributions were in character development, creative teaching in the church, and developing objectives in Christian education. Vieth felt that Christian education should be more than simply teaching biblical knowledge. Religious education was intended to touch the learner's whole life, leading her or him to purpose to do the will of God (Reed and Prevost, 1993).

In 1930 Vieth published two books arising out of his work as the executive director of the curriculum development arm of the International Council of Religious Education. One of those books, *Objectives in Religious Education and The Development of Curriculum of Religious Education*, dealt with the development of a well-rounded and cohesive church religious education curriculum through establishing comprehensive, clearly stated goals that reflect what the church means by "religious education." The objectives provided guidelines for twenty-five years for the International Lesson Committee of the Council and its constituent denominations. These guidelines also helped Christian educators and churches in general to rethink the intent of their educational ministries. The objectives reflected Vieth's concern for the affective dimension of Christian education, including not only the development of Christian character but also a "deep appreciation and love for the Bible" and "an acquaintance with and appreciation of religious culture as recorded in the fine arts." He edited *The International Journal of Religious Education* and three times was acting editor of *Religious Education* (1956–60, 1966–67, 1970) (Reed and Prevost, 1993, 344–45).

Vieth's writings are wide and varied, covering such topics as curriculum, objectives, administration, organization, worship, teaching, enlisting workers, training workers, record keeping, visual education, family and community in Christian education. He saw Christian education as "fundamentally the Christian community sharing its life with its members, young and older—its traditions, its experiences, its hopes, its faith, its mission. This means that every person in the Christian fellowship is at one and the same time a learner and a leader" (*The Church and Christian Education*, 193).

"Vieth served as a teacher, department principal, superintendent, director of Christian, and member of committees on Christian education in local churches throughout his career. His many books were both theoretical and practical and useful for practitioners" (Miller, 1990, 681).

NORMA S. HEDIN

Bibliography. R. C. Miller (1990), *Harper's Encyclopedia of Religious Education;* R. Prevost and J. Reed (1993), *A History of Christian Education.*

See also AFFECTIVE DOMAIN; CURRICULUM; RELIGIOUS EDUCATION ASSOCIATION; UNIFORM LESSON SERIES

Virtue. The concept of virtue is closely associated with the value of a person's character. If a person is marked by deeds of goodness, kindness, moral purity, courage, and the like, then the individual is said to be "virtuous."

When Christian authors discuss virtue they often refer to the classification first espoused by the church fathers Ambrose, Augustine, and Aquinas. Augustine defined virtue as "a good quality which one lives righteously, of which no one can make bad use, which God works in us without us" (Cessario, 1991, 53). There are four "cardinal virtues" and three "theological virtues." The cardinal virtues include prudence, temperance, fortitude, and justice. The theological virtues are faith, hope, and love (1 Cor. 13: 13). Kreeft (1986) compares and contrasts the seven deadly sins (vices) with the virtues which are proclaimed by Jesus as the Beatitudes. For example, the vice of pride is contrasted by the virtue of poverty; avarice versus mercy; envy versus mourning; wrath versus meekness; sloth versus hungering for righteousness; lust versus purity of heart; and gluttony versus bearing persecution (92).

Virtues are those character qualities that set a Christian apart from the world. Although it is possible for a non-Christian to be giving, the motivation may be insincere (e.g., self-serving or pride-based). However, the Christian is to be self-effacing and sacrificial not for what he or she may receive in return but simply because we are called to serve the needs of the poor (Mark 10:45; James 1:27). Christians are called to virtuous living because it is the example set for us by Christ himself. Paul tells us that when we have given our lives over to Christ's control we have become "new creatures" (1 Cor. 15:17) and as such, we are to demonstrate a new lifestyle, based upon the virtues of a disciplined life.

MICHAEL J. ANTHONY

Bibliography. O. P. Cessario (1991), *The Moral Virtues and Theological Ethics;* P. Kreeft (1986), *Back to Virtue;* E. A. Livingstone, ed. (1997), *The Dictionary of the Christian Church,* p. 287; M. G. Watkins and L. I. Watkins, eds. (1992), *The Complete Christian Dictionary for Home and School,* p. 769.

Vision. "A clear mental image of a preferable future imparted by God to His chosen servants . . . based upon an accurate understanding of God, self and circumstances" (Barna, 1992, 28). As such, vision develops out of a leader's or group's understanding of their God-given purpose, their particular ministry setting, and their available resources. It is a mental picture of how a group's purpose might and should be fulfilled in a concrete way in the future. This clear image of what God desires a group to accomplish serves as a catalyst to their evaluation of current conditions, resources, and ministry efforts, the development of priorities and plans for the future, and the expenditure of resources to help bring this future about. God-given vision for ministry is based on a knowledge of God's character and his purposes, and how they relate to the particular ministry organization's purpose, setting, and resources.

While a mission or purpose statement describes the general ministry objectives of a group, a vision statement is one that describes a more specific, concrete understanding of the envisioned end product of ministry efforts. While many educational ministries will have identical or similar mission or purpose statements, the vision statements of each will differ according to God's unique guidance in the particulars of their ministry setting. When a vision for ministry is clarified and communicated, it can motivate group members in their ministry efforts, help establish a healthy spirit of discontent with current ministry accomplishments, and create an organizational climate that is open to change.

KEVIN E. LAWSON

Bibliography. G. Barna (1992), *The Power of Vision: How You Can Capture and Apply God's Vision for Your Ministry;* A. Malphurs (1992), *Developing a Vision for Ministry in the 21st Century.*

Visual Aid. *See* Flannelgraph.

Visual Methods. Words, by themselves, often fail to communicate the fullness of biblical truth. But when a visual element is added to lectures, sermons, or other oral presentations, the likelihood for understanding increases. One input modality reinforces the other. For some people, the visual is a stronger modality than the oral. So it is essential in Christian teaching to use visual methods.

The Bible provides many examples of visual methods. The Levitical sacrificial system portrayed the necessity for blood sacrifice. The prophets employed object lessons in their teaching, as did Jesus. The resurrected Jesus showed the disciples his scarred hands and feet.

Today's visually based culture necessitates a more astute use of visual methods than a half century ago. Almost everyone is and has been influenced by the vast content available from television, video, and Internet Web sites. Furthermore, visual media have been shown to influence thought processes, even affecting the brain development of children. Hence, many people think mosaically, rather than linearly. Christian educators, therefore, are constrained not only to employ visual methods, but also to do so intentionally and skillfully.

The range of visual methods available is astounding. The Christian teacher needs to make selective use of pictures, charts, diagrams, maps, models, films, illustrations, videos, photographs, filmstrips, cartoons, banners, slides, and flannelgraphs. This is particularly the case in teaching children because they are lacking in life experience. Very few American/Canadian children, for example, have seen a walled city, so the story of the conquest of Jericho is meaningless without the use of some visual method(s). Visuals give children the necessary precepts upon which accurate biblical concepts can be built. Adults and youth also benefit greatly from instruction that includes judicious use of visual methods.

DANIEL C. JESSEN

Vittorino da Feltre (1378–1446). Vittorino da Feltre (originally named Vittore dei Ramboldini) was born in Feltre in 1378 and died in Mantua in 1446. He was an Italian educator who is regarded as one of the greatest Renaissance educators.

At age 18 he enrolled in the University of Padua, about 50 miles from his birthplace. For the next 25 years, he was associated with the university, earning his doctorate in 1411 and continuing there as an instructor. He was particularly gifted in the areas of Latin grammar and mathematics.

In 1423 Vittorino was invited to establish a school in Mantua. Gianfrancesco Gonzaga, Marquis of Mantua, wanted Vittorino to direct the education of his family. Having an aversion to court life, Vittorino agreed to come only if his school could be separated from the court and the political influences. Vittorino's school was called *La Giocosa* (House of Joy) and was established in a villa provided by Gonzaga.

Vittorino had studied and lectured on the writings of Plutarch, Quintilian, Plato, and Cicero, and incorporated educational ideas from them into his school. He built his curriculum around classical humanism, including the literature of Rome and Greece, mathematics, geometry, and music. He also believed that physical exercise was important and utilized organized games as well as hikes into the countryside.

As one responsible for the training of future rulers, Vittorino believed he could improve the lot of the common man by preparing leaders who could rule justly. However, besides future heads of state, Vittorino insisted the House of Joy include a large number of poor students who were selected to attend on the basis of their character and ability.

Besides being an outstanding humanist educator, Vittorino was also a devout Christian and sought to instill within his students an understanding of the Christian faith. In an era when re-

sent, he strove to provide, through admonition
and example, a spirit of reverence and devotion
to God and service to others. Vittorino believed
the relationship between student and teacher
should extend beyond the classroom. Therefore,
he ate with his students, joined them on their
outings, and if one needed special tutoring, he
would rise early to provide it.

Vittorino was a scholar who demanded quality
work from his students. He was also a caring
teacher who provided a pleasant place for students to engage in studies, recreation, and Christian community. He was honored by his contemporaries, has been recognized as a significant
Renaissance educator, and serves as a Christian
education model.

DOUGLAS BARCALOW

Bibliography. F. Eby and C. F. Arrowood (1940), *The
History and Philosophy of Education Ancient and Me-
dieval;* W. H. Woodward (1905), *Vittorino da Feltre and
Other Humanist Educators.*

See also HUMANISM, CLASSICAL; HUMANISM,
CHRISTIAN; LIBERAL ARTS; RENAISSANCE EDUCATION

Volunteer. From its inception, the church has
been an organization and organism that is led by
volunteers. Professional church leadership was
not a distinctive of the first-generation church,
although most churches today have at least one
paid or professional pastoral leader. Churches
rely on volunteer labor to accomplish most ministry activities. A volunteer is a person who
agrees to do a task knowing that he or she will be
donating their time and energy. It was reported
in the early 1990s that over one-fourth of all
adults volunteer time and effort sometime during
the week at their churches.

Evangelical churches find it easier to recruit
volunteers than mainline Protestant churches or
Roman Catholic churches. It has been further
discovered that modern churches find it easier to
recruit volunteers for specific tasks with a defined time frame for accomplishment (such as
serving on a task force, leading a fund-raising
drive, planning a social activity, leading a short-
term missions trip) as opposed to more open-
ended responsibilities (such as teaching a Sunday

school class every week, sponsoring a home fellowship, serving on a church board, etc.).

George Barna reports that modern Americans,
including Christians, have come to value time
more than they value money and that they will
often be more willing to donate money to hire
someone to accomplish a task rather than volunteer time to do the task themselves. Many further believe that hiring a trained professional to
do a task is better for the church in the long run
than having the task done by untrained amateur
volunteers.

In answer to the question: "Why should a
church recruit and train volunteers to serve?" Les
Christie (1992) offers the following reasons:

1. No leader in the church can do all the tasks
   of leadership alone.
2. Recruiting and training adult volunteers creates a variety of leadership mentors and models for church members to follow.
3. There is a biblical mandate for Christians to
   serve in the church in areas where they are
   gifted and talented to do so.
4. More people sharing the leadership load
   makes the burden of leadership lighter for all
   involved (13–21).

The three most significant tasks a ministry professional has to do with regard to volunteers are
recruiting new volunteers for ministry; training
and equipping volunteers to do the tasks for
which they are recruited; and retaining volunteers so that they continue to do their ministry
with enthusiasm and eagerness.

Since using one's spiritual gift(s) is a characteristic of spiritual maturity, volunteering to serve
in the local church is a natural response for
many Christians. It benefits both the individual
and the local body of Christ.

KEN GARLAND

Bibliography. G. Barna (1991), *What Americans Believe;* L. Christie (1992), *How to Recruit and Train Volunteer Workers;* D. W. Johnson (1978), *The Care and
Feeding of Volunteers;* M. Wilson (1983), *How to Mobilize Church Volunteers.*

Volunteerism. *See* Laity; Recruitment.

Walther League (Lutheran). Principal association of young adult societies within the congregations of the Lutheran Church-Missouri Synod for seventy-five years. The League was organized May 23, 1893, at Trinity Lutheran Church, Buffalo, N.Y., by representatives of young adult societies in twelve congregations of the Evangelical Lutheran Synodical Conference and named after C. F. W. Walther, a great pioneer of Confessional Lutheranism in America and an ardent voice for the development of Lutheran young people's societies. Divided into Junior (14–17 years) and Senior (18 and above) groups, the League focused its ministry to and through young people during their postconfirmation years of adolescence and young adulthood (mid–30s) with the intention that they remain steadfast in the true faith in the midst of a religiously pluralistic America. The League's stated purpose was to help young people grow as Christians through:

WORSHIP—building a stronger faith in the Triune God

EDUCATION—discovering the will of God for their daily life

SERVICE—responding to the needs of all men

RECREATION—keeping the joy of Christ in all activities

FELLOWSHIP—finding the power of belonging to others in Christ

(Peters, 1975, 836)

The League saw itself as a servant to the local church and confined itself to the presentation of a program and materials that would assist pastors and congregations in their spiritual ministry to young people.

Early in its history the League effected national, district, and zone structures to efficiently serve the ministry of the local societies. In 1920 Walter A. Maier became the League's first full-time executive secretary and in 1922 the national office located permanently in Chicago. In 1933 the League reorganized its structure into international, district, and (local) society levels and merged all program activities into two departments: Christian Knowledge and Christian Service.

The Department of Christian Knowledge divided into three tasks: Spiritual Training, with emphasis on Bible study and life application, especially in light of the dangers to a young person's faith presented by Darwinian evolutionary theory and the growing secularism of American society; Leadership Training to prepare (through camps, conferences, and institutes) spiritual leadership in the church; and Cultural Activities, with emphasis on music, literature, art, and oration as wholesome alternatives to the less edifying attractions of youth. To facilitate these activities, the League published such periodicals as *Bible Student, Walther League Messenger, Workers Quarterly,* and *The Cresset,* opened summer camps (Camp Arcadia being the best known), and established a churchwide leadership training program, Lutheran Service Volunteer Schools.

Christian Service included the areas of Missionary Endeavor, Recreation, Publicity, and Welfare. Well known among Lutherans was the Wheat Ridge Foundation (with its annual Christmas Seals campaign), a result of the League's humanitarian response at the turn of the century to tuberculosis, which especially threatened young people. The Foundation established and supported hospitals and sanitoria in the United States (Colorado) and several other countries. The League also encouraged its local societies (especially those in urban areas) to sponsor "Walther League Homes" to serve fellow Lutherans who were traveling or far away from home.

At its 1968 convention the League elected to reorganize itself as a youth-led, issue-oriented ministry. It officially dismantled its international organization with its network of districts, zones, and local societies, bringing to an end a seventy-five-year partnership with Lutheran congregations in young people's ministry. In 1977 the Walther League, as an organization, came to an end.

Robert D. Newton

Bibliography. T. Coates, *Walther League Messenger* (May 1945): 334–35; J. Pahl (1993), *Hopes and Dreams of All: The International Walther League and Lutheran Youth in American Culture, 1893–1993*; C. H. Peters (1975), *Lutheran Cyclopedia*, pp. 836–38; *Walther League Manual: A Basic Guide to the Work of the Local Society* (1935).

Watson, John B. (1878–1958). American behavioral psychologist. Watson received the first Ph.D. degree in psychology from the University of Chicago in 1903. He taught psychology in Chicago for five years before moving to Johns Hopkins University in Baltimore as full professor. He taught there until 1920, when his career suddenly ended. He entered the advertising business in New York City in 1921, where he worked until 1946.

Watson is often referred to as the father of behaviorism. In fact, it was Watson himself who coined the term "behaviorism." Watson insisted that psychology, as a scientific discipline, must focus on overt, measurable behaviors. He opposed the work of Wilhelm Wundt, who established a psychological laboratory in Leipzip, Germany, in 1879. Wundt sought to discover the inner workings, or "internal states," of human beings through the process of self-discovery and self-report, which he called introspection. Watson, however, believed that theorizing about thoughts, intentions, or other subjective experiences was unscientific. Watson sought to raise the field of psychology to the level of scientific verification enjoyed by physics or astronomy. Just as these sciences based their conclusions on the behavior of objects, so psychology should base its conclusions on the behavior of humans. Watson was greatly influenced by Ivan Pavlov's work and was the first to use it as the basis for learning theory. Watson discovered in Pavlov's S-R associations the basic element in human personality development to replace Wundt's internal states. He emphasized environment over heredity in shaping virtually all human learning and behavior.

Watson was an extremist. He made unsubstantiated claims in his writing and was ethically questionable in his research on young children. His best known experiment involved a young boy named Albert. Albert was given a small rat to handle. Then Watson made a loud noise by banging a metal bowl with a rod. The result was that Albert developed a fear of rats. Watson then showed this fear could be generalized to a rabbit, a dog, a sealskin coat, and, for a time, Santa Claus's beard.

Watson's contribution was demonstrating the role of conditioning in developing emotional responses such as fears, phobias, and prejudices. He believed that humans were born with a few reflexes and the emotional reactions of fear, love, and rage. All other behavior is established by building new S-R associations through conditioning. This development involved a "continuous, cumulative, and hierarchical process" marked by new and more complicated patterns of thought and behavior. While Watson never attempted to explain or identify the process, he laid the foundation for the later work of E. L. Thorndike, B. F. Skinner, and Albert Bandura. Watson's major contribution was explaining the development of fears, phobias, and prejudices as a result of building new S-R bonds through conditioning.

RICK YOUNT

Bibliography. M. H. Dembo (1994), *Applying Educational Psychology;* T. L. Good and J. E. Brophey (1990), *Educational Psychology: A Realistic Approach;* W. R. R. Yount (1996), *Created to Learn.*

See also ASSOCIATION/CONNECTIONIST THEORIES; BEHAVIORISM, THEORIES OF; SR BONDS; SKINNER, BURRHUS FREDERIC

Weekday Club. Weekly activity-centered program so named because it meets during the week in the afternoon or evening. A weekday club supplements the educational ministry of a local church by providing opportunities to nurture and evangelize children and youth other than on Sunday morning, often reaching out to persons in the neighborhood or community. Contact with parents becomes a leading "entry point" for their involvement in the church. Those who participate "join" as members, as if becoming part of a club.

More informal than the usual Sunday school class, these weekly gatherings emphasize fellowship, expression, activity, and achievement. They often include an incentive program that encourages participants to learn as they gain badges or rewards that result in advances in rank.

While many churches come up with their own unique program, most utilize curriculum and ideas from one or more of several organizations which have available material. Christian Service Brigade, Pioneer Clubs, Awana, Child Evangelism, and Bible Club Movement are the most common. Many churches sponsor Boy Scout or Girl Scout groups, which serve a similar purpose, but these usually do not seek to be evangelical. Some denominations offer their own curriculum such as Royal Ambassadors, Royal Rangers, and Missionettes. Most organizations sell an assortment of uniforms, badges, awards, and other paraphernalia to enhance the program.

There are numerous options available to suit a variety of needs. Programs geared to junior age children are the most common. Some material is gender specific, aimed to meet distinctive needs of boys or girls, while most is coed. Most programs utilize some combination of crafts, games, Bible lessons, stories, Scripture memory, interest areas, and/or skill development. A few are unique such as "Tree Climbers" (from Christian Service

Brigade) which seeks to build father-son relations for boys aged 6 and 7 and their dads.

These weekday club programs are often linked with a summer camp, which have been one of the most fruitful evangelistic tools in the twentieth century. The weekday club leaders are then able to follow up the decisions made at camp as campers return to local programs.

An effective way for smaller churches to provide a club experience is to work together with another congregation to make a positive contribution to the community and to reach out to young people and their families. In recent years, the "weekday club" experience has not been limited to children and youth. Various adult groups, senior citizens, and people with special needs (weight loss, addiction recovery, parents of teens, etc.) have had similar effectiveness in encouraging believers and reaching out to the nonchurched. Bringing people together in these types of short- or long-term fellowships has many options and applications.

The weekday club provides a great utilization of church facilities often dormant during the week. These clubs face increasing "competition" from community and school functions, but give the local church a tremendous opportunity to serve the needs of its constituents and potential ones.

RONALD H. RYND AND ELEANOR A. DANIEL

Bibliography. Awana Clubs International, 1 E. Bode Rd., Streamwood, IL 60103, 1–630–213–2000; Bible Club Movement, Inc., 237 Fairfield Ave., Upper Darby, PA 19082, 1–610–352–7177; Child Evangelism Fellowship, Box 348, Warrenton, MO 63358, 1–314–456–4321; Christian Service Brigade, Box 150, Wheaton, IL 60189, 1–800–815–5573; Pioneer Clubs, Box 788, Wheaton, IL 6189, 1–630–293–1600.

See also AWANA CLUBS INTERNATIONAL; CHILDREN'S MINISTRY, MODELS OF; CHRISTIAN SERVICE BRIGADE; PIONEER MINISTRIES

Wesley, John (1703–91). English religious leader. Educated at Oxford, as an ordained Anglican minister he assisted his minister father and taught Greek at the university. John and his brother, Charles, led a small religious society at Oxford they called the Holy Club. John Wesley was one of four members of the Holy Club commissioned to evangelize native Americans. He was sent to the Georgia colony in 1735. In the primitive setting of the colony, Wesley's Anglican liturgy seemed out of place. After a disastrous romance, Wesley sailed back to England.

While in Georgia, Wesley had come in contact with a community of Moravians. He became intrigued with the idea of a personal experience of God's saving grace. Back home in England, he met the Moravian leaders Peter Beohler and Nikolaus Zinzendorf. Wesley traveled to the Moravian community at Herrnhut, Germany, to study with Zinzendorf. While listening to a lecture on Martin Luther's defense of justification by faith, Wesley finally experienced the assurance he had been seeking.

Wesley's sermons now reflected his focus on justification by faith. One by one, Anglican pulpits were closed to him. Turned away by the church, Wesley took his message to the streets and fields of England. There he was enthusiastically received by the working class. Wesley became a leader in the revivalist movement throughout Great Britain.

The systematic Wesley organized his listeners into small, highly disciplined groups called classes. Each class of ten or twelve was headed by a lay leader charged with educational and pastoral duties. This system was necessary, Wesley believed, for the continued encouragement and education of the individual Christian. The classes, along with smaller "band meetings" of discipled believers, were organized into societies. "Select" societies were made up of lay preachers. Traveling preachers directly accountable to Wesley supervised the societies. Wesley's highly organized structure and innovative outreach program earned his group the name "Methodists."

Wesley believed that if children were not given religious instruction, the religious revival begun in his lifetime would not outlast a single generation. Education and religion were to be united in a mutually beneficial relationship. At a time when only one in fifty English people could read and write, Wesley saw the need for basic literacy integrated with religious instruction. To encourage reading, Wesley published hundreds of tracts, along with inexpensive editions of selected books. His emphasis on education was to be a major influence on the British school system.

Criticized by Anglican leaders, and years ahead of his friend Robert Raikes, Wesley and his followers pioneered the Sunday school. In Wesley's day, working-class children worked six days a week; Sunday was their only opportunity for any kind of schooling. In his schools, Wesley introduced organized classes, age-graded curriculum, and volunteer staff. Despite his enthusiasm for the Sunday school, Wesley considered it only supplemental to the religious instruction a child was to receive at home.

Best known of Wesley's schools was Kingswood, near Bristol. A full-time school, Kingswood's highly structured plan of curriculum and student life was designed to produce rational, scriptural Christians. Even before Wesley's death in 1791, American Methodists had established Cokesbury College on the Kingswood pattern. A hundred years later, over two hundred colleges, high schools, and seminaries had been established, many of them in remote areas.

In 1827 the Methodist Sunday School Union was created to promote Sunday schools and curriculum. Bishop John Vincent inspired the Chatauqua program for teacher training. Wesley's contributions to Christian education are numerous. Unlike some of the revivalists of his day, Wesley could see the need for a structure that would receive new believers and continue to guide their spiritual development. Recognizing the symbiosis of education and theology, Wesley founded schools that taught academics in the light of Scripture. A leader in the development of the Sunday school, Wesley called for a school in every Methodist church.

ROBERT J. CHOUN

Bibliography. I. V. and K. B. Cully, eds. (1990), *Harper's Encyclopedia of Religious Education;* M. L. Edwards (1953), *John Wesley and the Eighteenth Century;* W. S. Ethridge (1971), *Strange Fires: The True Story of John Wesley's Love Affair in Georgia;* K. O. Gangel and W. S. Benson (1983), *Christian Education: Its History and Philosophy;* J. E. Hakes, ed. (1964), *An Introduction to Evangelical Christian Education;* N. D. Hillis (1968), *Great Men as Prophets of a New Era;* H. H. Kroll (1954), *The Long Quest: The Story of John Wesley;* C. Ludwig and T. Bowers (1984), *Susanna Wesley: Mother of John and Charles;* F. J. McConnell (1939), *John Wesley;* J. Pudney (1978), *John Wesley and His World;* J. E. Reed and R. Prevost (1993), *A History of Christian Education;* E. Towns (1993), *Town's Sunday School Encyclopedia;* R. A. Tsanoff (1968), *Autobiographies of Ten Religious Leaders: Alternatives in Christian Experience;* W. Walker (1977), *Great Men of the Christian Church;* J. Wesley, *John Wesley's Journal.*

See also BIBLE COLLEGE MOVEMENT; COLONIAL EDUCATION; GREAT AWAKENINGS; RAIKES, ROBERT; SUNDAY SCHOOL

Westminster Catechism. *See* Catechism.

Wholistic Learning. Philosophy of education that emphasizes the importance of integrating various areas of life in the educational process. According to Holmes, a Christian worldview is characterized by a wholistic goal which strives to see every area of thought and life in an integrated fashion (Pazmiño, 1988, 76). Christian educators have realized that an effective means of developing a Christian worldview in learners is by implementing wholistic learning in the educational process. Practitioners advocating wholistic learning may approach it from one of three angles.

In the first, wholistic learning is contrasted with traditional education's focus on cognitive aspects of learning (verbalization, memorization, and reading) by acknowledging that learning which promotes spiritual maturity is not only cognitive/intellectual but also involves emotion and volition (Downs, 1994, 137). These are also referred to as rational, emotional, and behavioral, or as thinking, feeling, and doing (Yount, 1996, 253). Effective teaching engages learners by using a balance of all three areas of the human experience to encourage growth. Rational

or intellectual approaches to learning draw upon cognitive learning theory, discovery learning theory (Jerome Bruner), and information processing theory, which emphasize renewing the mind and promoting understanding. Emotional approaches draw upon humanistic learning theories that emphasize the attitudes and values of students. Behavioral approaches to learning are influenced by B. F. Skinner's operant conditioning theory and Albert Bandura's social learning theory, which stresses putting what is learned into practice.

A second possible emphasis in wholistic learning is to consider five interwoven aspects of the development of the human personality: physical (bodily growth), cognitive (thinking and knowing), emotional (feeling and valuing), social (relating to others and society), and moral (understanding right and wrong). Although each area may be identified separately, human beings are actually an integration of all these areas and it must be understood that each area influences and interacts with the others. Dirks (1991) suggests that each level of development in these areas has particular tasks and challenges that have the potential for prompting spiritual development. The whole person emphasis takes this into account and acknowledges that spiritual growth occurs as these other areas are interacted with in some way. An illustration attributed to Ted Ward uses the human hand. Each finger represents a different aspect of the human personality—the physical, cognitive, emotional, social, and moral—and the palm of the hand represents the spiritual essence or core of a person. The spiritual essence of a person is not seen as a *separate aspect* of the person, but each finger or aspect of the human personality is a means of touching a person's spiritual essence. Therefore Christian education must consider how to interact with and influence the spiritual essence to encourage spiritual growth by means of each aspect of the human personality. Downs's (1994) discussion of ministering to human beings as integrated wholes explains it this way: "We feed and clothe people, reason with them, love them, relate to them, and treat them justly, all as a means of ministering to them spiritually" (74–75). Because of this interconnectedness, it is essential that education involves all aspects of the human being.

A third emphasis one may encounter regarding wholistic learning is in connection with a wholistic learning environment. Issler and Habermas (1992) identify five factors to consider when creating a wholistic environment for teaching: physical factors, organizational factors, relational factors, cultural factors, and historical factors (145). Together, these five factors interact to either build bridges or create carriers to more effective learning.

JANA SUNDENE

Bibliography. D. Dirks (1991), *Christian Education: Foundations for the Future*, pp. 137–55; P. Downs (1994), *Teaching for Spiritual Growth;* K. Issler and R. Habermas (1992), *Teaching for Reconciliation: Foundations and Practice of Christian Educational Ministry;* R. Pazmiño (1988), *Foundational Issues in Christian Education: An Introduction in Evangelical Perspective;* W. Yount (1996), *Created to Learn.*

Widows/Widowers. Widow(er)hood is experienced by three out of four adults. By age 75, four out of five women will be widowed. Women are more likely to be widowed than men because of their greater longevity and the tendency of men to marry younger women. Christian educators' awareness of biblical perspectives about widows inform their responses to the needs of the bereaved.

Biblical References. Repeatedly, God commanded the nation of Israel to take care of widows (Exod. 22:22; Deut. 24:17; 26:12) and he threatened judgment when the widows were oppressed (Jer. 7:6; Zech. 7:8–14). In the New Testament Jesus demonstrated particular sensitivity to widows (Luke 7:11–15; 24:1–4). The early church cared for widows (Acts 6) and there was apparently an organization of widows who served in the church (1 Tim. 5:3–16). James (1:27) reflects God's concern for the defenseless when he defines "true" religion as care for the widows and orphans. While the legal and social position of widows is not as precarious in contemporary Western culture, these biblical perspectives continue to have instructive value.

Research about Widowhood and Bereavement. The death of a spouse is the most stress-inducing loss a person faces. There are heightened health risks and higher rates of depression, particularly in the first year of spousal bereavement (Stroebe and Stroebe, 1987). The mortality rate is higher for those who are widowed. Stress is exacerbated when there is diminished financial security and responsibility for children still in the home.

While the average time required to recover after spousal bereavement is two years (Stroebe, Stroebe, and Hansson, 1993), it is important to note that feelings of grief and loss can persist for many years. There are many similarities in the grieving process but there is some variance between groups. Younger widows tend to experience more severe initial symptoms of grief while older widows take more time to get over the loss (Sanders, 1981). Young widows tend to have a more severe reaction to the death of a spouse than young widowers, but within two to four years young widows return to adjustment levels that match their married counterparts (Parkes, 1988). Widowers are more likely than widows to remarry.

There is some evidence of the value of both public and private religious practices for those who have experienced spousal bereavement. In one study, the practice of mourning rituals and strong religious beliefs correlated negatively with both physical and psychosocial dysfunction after the death of a spouse. Frequency of attendance at worship services is the strongest predictor of level of positive affect in widows ages 60 to 89 (McGloshen and O'Bryant).

The Tasks of Grief. Stephen Shuchter (1988) describes several tasks of grief that address the multidimensional aspects of grief the widowed person experiences. These tasks can give direction to the educator who seeks to provide support and help for the bereaved.

First, the bereaved must deal with the feelings of grief and loss and find ways to cope with them as they surface. Second, health and other critical functions must be maintained. Third, a new relationship must be negotiated with the dead spouse. Fourth, the widow(er) must adapt to altered relationships. Fifth, a revitalized self-concept and stabilized worldview must emerge.

Educational Strategies and Programs. Because widow(er)s are often one of the "invisible" groups in the church community, educating the whole congregation about both widow(er)s' needs and biblical injunctions is important. Opportunities for relationships can diminish the social isolation widow(er)s experience. Perhaps the most helpful and well-received programs for widows are widow-to-widow programs (Silverman, 1986) which place a person who has been widowed for some time with a new widow for support. Some widow(er)s find help in support groups. Practical needs of the bereaved family need to be considered by churches and community not just in the initial weeks, but over extended time as the burden of finances, the home, and, for younger widow(er)s, parenting press in. For older widow(er)s opportunities for service can provide both relationship and a sense of significance.

FAYE CHECHOWICH

Bibliography. D. A. Lund, M. S. Caserta, and M. F. Dimond, *The Gerontologist* 26, no. 3 (1986); 314–20; T. McGloshen and O'Bryant, *Psychology of Women Quarterley* 12 no. 4 (1988): 365–73; C. Sanders, *Omega* 11, no. 3 (1981): 217–32; S. Shuchter (1988), *Dimensions of Grief Adjusting to the Death of a Spouse;* P. Silverman (1986), *Widow to Widow;* M. Stroebe, W. Stroebe, and R. Hansson (1993), *Handbook of Bereavement: Theory, Research and Intervention;* W. and M. Stroebe (1987), *Bereavement and Health: The Psychological and Physical Consequence of Partner Loss.*

Willow Creek Association. Accompanying the phenomenal growth and strength of the Willow Creek Community Church of South Barrington, Ill., has come the desire on the part of churches to build one like Willow Creek. That squares with the American way, that is, to duplicate successful ventures, whether it be in financial concerns or religious communities.

In June of 1999 the Willow Creek Association, a sister organization of the W.C.C., numbered over 2,200 churches around the world. The Association is constituted as an international network of churches that have a mission statement that reflects the attempt of Willow Creek Community Church "to turn irreligious people into fully devoted followers of Christ." Their promotional materials state that these churches are led by "forward thinking leaders who are building churches with a new emphasis: the presentation of the gospel in ways that penetrate secular culture and engage people who are far from Christ."

They courageously employ some of the local church philosophy of ministry pioneered by Bill Hybels and a large and faithful band of men and women at Willow Creek Community Church who have fashioned a seeker-sensitive approach to reaching people evangelistically.

In their own words these churches which are closely or loosely affiliated with the Willow Creek Association have in common a commitment to historic, biblical teachings of the Christian faith and vision for building biblically functioning communities that reach and disciple unchurched people—the vision Christ had as stated in the Great Commission and lived out in Acts 2. They believe the local church is more than just a place to go each week; it is the hope of the world.

Even Peter Jennings in an American Broadcasting Company (ABC) television special spoke of the Willow Creek Community Church as having started "something big and hundreds of churches all over the world want to be part of it." Having grown to become an international movement, Robert Buford of Leadership Network has said of them, "Willow Creek is the cue ball of the contemporary church movement. Their innovative approach has broken the mold. The impact of these innovations on the church around the world is incalculable."

W.C.A. International affiliates exist in Australia, New Zealand, the United Kingdom, Germany, and the Netherlands. In time they will hopefully develop self-sustaining ministries similar to WCA-United States. Published resources that serve as tools to help churches reach seekers and minister to Christians include books, small group curriculum, evangelism and spiritual gift training courses, videos, drama scripts, leadership training materials, and music.

Leadership conferences held at the church in South Barrington have enriched many churches beyond those that are officially members of the Willow Creek Association. For example, the Leadership Summit conference, held each August, has made a significant contribution to churches both internationally and in North America.

WARREN S. BENSON

Wisdom Literature. *See* Education in the Psalms and Proverbs.

Witchcraft. *See* Cults and Youth; Demons.

Women, Leadership Role of. Since the time that Eve offered Adam the forbidden fruit and Adam pointed the finger back at Eve, the question of appropriate roles for women in the church, home, and society has been debated. The focus of the following discussion will be on the role of women leaders in the context of ministry and the church.

Old and New Testament Examples. Both the Old and New Testaments provide examples of women who served in varying positions of official and unofficial leadership.

Old Testament. Sarah (Gen. 21:12) and Abigail (1 Sam. 25:1–35) are two women who exercised an unofficial leadership role at a specific time in the life of their family. The more official role of prophetess was filled by Miriam (Exod. 15:20–21), Huldah (2 Kings 22:14–20), Deborah (Judg. 4:4–5), Noadiah (Neh. 6:14), and several unnamed prophetesses (Isa. 8:3; Ezek. 13:17–24). Esther was an example of a reluctant but courageous civic leader in her role as a queen in the Persian empire (Esther 1–10).

New Testament. In the New Testament, prophetic leadership was exhibited in the words of praise proclaimed by Elizabeth and Mary, the mother of Jesus. Philip's four daughters prophesied (Acts 21:8–9). Dorcas (Acts 9:36–42) and Lydia (Acts 16:13–15) were unofficial, yet influential, leaders in their respective communities. Euodia and Syntyche are said to have labored with Paul in his ministry (Phil. 4:3). Priscilla, in partnership with her husband (Acts 18:26–28), is an example of a woman exercising her leadership gifts as a teacher and is called a "fellow worker" by Paul (Rom. 16:3). In addition, the passages on women as deacons indicate that women were serving in these official positions of the church (Rom. 16:1–2; 1 Tim. 3).

From these passages and others in the New Testament, it can be shown that women did hold significant leadership positions in the early church although the nature and scope of their leadership role are unclear. No gender distinctions are indicated in the assignment of spiritual gifts which include gifts of leadership and related areas (1 Cor. 12; Eph. 4). Women participated in public prayer services (Acts 12:12; 16:13; 1 Cor. 11:5), taught (Rom. 16; Titus 2:3–5), and prophesied with apostolic approval.

Two Paradigms. Two positions, placed at either end of a continuum, represent the primary perspectives on this issue. The traditionalist position, also referred to in some contexts as the hierarchical or complementarian view, restricts the role of women in leadership based on the principles of headship and submission as seen in the creation order (Gen. 1–3; Eph. 5:22–23). Strict interpretations of such passages as Galatians 3:26–28, 1 Corinthians 11:2–16, 1 Corinthians 14:34–35, and 1 Timothy 2:11–12 exclude women from participating in positions of authoritative preaching, teaching, or ruling over men. A modified viewpoint acknowledges that the head of woman is man and she may teach and exercise some types of authority if she is ultimately under a man. Complementarians stress that although men and women are equal in worth before God, they have been created to fulfill different roles in relation to each other and men have been charged by God with a leadership role distinct from that of women.

At the other end of the continuum are those who hold to an egalitarian position. Central to the egalitarian position is Galatians 3:26–28. This verse is interpreted to mean that oneness in Christ as male and female is not just for salvation but is to be a social reality as well with implications for both church and home. The related passages in 1 Corinthians 11, 14, and 1 Timothy 2 are seen as addressing specific cultural problems for the emerging church. Egalitarians defend the full equality of men and women as coleaders in ministry and believe that Scripture teaches that all offices of ministry are open to women.

Conclusion. Godly, evangelical scholars, devoted to sound exegesis, have studied key biblical passages and have arrived at different interpretations and applications. It is important for anyone concerned about this issue to review the passages of Scripture related to women in leadership, consider the evidence, and prayerfully make a decision.

SHELLY CUNNINGHAM

Bibliography. M. J. Anthony, ed. (1992), *Foundations of Ministry: An Introduction to Christian Education for a New Generation;* A. Mickelsen (1986), *Women, Authority and the Bible;* J. Piper and W. Grudem, eds. (1991), *Recovering Biblical Manhood and Womanhood: A Response to Evangelical Feminism;* A. Spencer (1985), *Beyond the Curse: Women Called to Ministry.*

See also EGALITARIAN; EGALITARIAN RELATIONSHIPS; FEMINISM; LEADERSHIP; TRADITIONAL ROLES; WOMEN, ORDINATION OF; WOMEN IN MINISTRY

Women, Ordination of. Although women have actively served in the local church since it was first created, the formalization of that service, as seen in the act of ordination, has been a more recent phenomena. Since ordination assumes a more authoritative designation it has become quite controversial in some denominational settings.

Ordination of women did not become popular until the late 1800s. Denominations that pioneered in this effort are the American Baptist Churches (1800), United Brethren in Christ (1889), and the African Methodist Episcopal Zion Church (1894). Women were ordained as elders in the churches of the Cumberland Presbyterian Church in the 1880s and 1890s. The larger Presbyterian Church in the U.S. in the North did not ordain women as ministers until 1955, and the Presbyterian Church in the U.S. in the South did not ordain women until 1964.

With limited opportunity for ordination, women served as leaders in the Protestant church movement, organizing their denominational groups, leading Bible studies and prayer, and building altar guilds, mutual aid societies, and missionary societies. They organized outside the church and focused on social issues such as temperance and abolition, and they demonstrated their power and success by their ability to raise money along with social consciousness.

Organizing within the church occurred in the context of women's groups such as the Women's Home and Foreign Missionary Society (A.M.E. Church), Colored Female Religious and Moral Society, Female Mite Society, the Female Religious Biography and Reading Societies, and the Women's Union Missionary Society of America. In addition to ministry within the church, many of these groups ran schools, hospitals, and orphanages.

Theological concerns about women as pastors encouraged many to leave the United States to serve in the mission field. Denominations were often more receptive to sending women to build churches and to establish schools abroad where their leadership and expertise would be accepted. Even in denominations that welcome ordination of women, such as the American Baptist Convention (ABC), a comparison of ordained men versus women demonstrates a discrepancy between theory and practice.

Culture, custom, and theology influence women's roles in the church. Where culture and custom rule, pulpit committees prefer to avoid controversy, possible threat to unity, and loss of membership by skirting the gender ordination issue. In the Southern Baptist Convention, which has no formal ruling on ordination of women, custom tends to rule, and more women are traditionally seen in positions such as mission outreach or Christian education rather than in ordained positions such as the pastorate.

Theologically, three viewpoints impact women's leadership roles and subsequent ordination. The traditionalist view holds that women should keep silent in the church and not exercise authority over men by teaching them (1 Cor. 14:34, 35). The male leadership view is a modified view which holds that the head of the woman is the man (1 Tim. 2:12–15). This allows women to teach under the authority of a man, who is the senior pastor, but the woman should not hold a position of authority. The equalitarian view defends the full equality of men and women in church leadership (Eph. 4:11–16). All offices of ministry are opened for women if they have been called by God and are so gifted by the Holy Spirit.

Each view provides a biblical rationale for its position. A defense of the equalitarian view explains the opposing views in this fashion. (1) An examination of the history and context of the Corinthians passage reveals that women were disturbing the church service by asking their husbands questions during the actual service. Such interruptions caused disorder. Paul writes to correct this practice by advising women to ask their husbands questions when they are at home as opposed to during church service. (2) The question of women in authority in the Timothy passage hinges upon the key word, "usurp" (KJV). Women preached a cult that because they gave birth, they were superior to men and therefore should have authority over men. Paul writes to correct such erroneous thinking. (3) In the Ephesians passage, when did "some" and "we" become men? The question of headship (Eph. 5:23) explains roles within marriage. Although Paul uses the church to describe a marriage, he does not use marriage to describe the church. The pastor is not the head of the church. Only Christ holds that position.

Regardless of the theological stance of a church or denomination, women seeking to be ordained face difficult, if not discouraging obstacles. Seeking to maintain the unity of the Spirit in the bond of peace, many women choose to serve the Lord faithfully without benefit of public affirmation through ordination.

LaVerne A. Tolbert

Bibliography. M. E. Howe (1982), *Women and Church Leadership;* V. M. McKenzie (1996), *Not without a Struggle.*

See also Clergy; Deaconess; Egalitarian; Egalitarian Relationships; Gender Roles; Ordination; Traditional Roles; Women in Ministry; Women, Leadership Role of

Women in Ministry. The phrase "women in ministry" raises a controversial issue for many. What ministry roles should be open to women? Some faith communities allow all ministry roles to be filled by those called by God and affirmed by the church, irrespective of gender. Other churches believe males must fill the clergy and lay leadership roles in the local church and at denominational levels, while still others not only bar women from leadership roles, but limit them to ministries of hospitality, ministry with children, and other women. How do sincere Christians advocate such different perspectives?

Some who speak out for women's rights view the Bible as one cause of the oppression of women and give no consideration to Scripture in their defense of women in ministry. But evangelical Christians, who acknowledge Scripture as their guide for faith and life, must take the Bible seriously in their belief formation. That commitment, however, has not led to a consensus among evangelicals on the issue of women in ministry. Two people who hold a high view of Scripture may approach biblical texts differently and come away with contrasting interpretations. The following is a thumbnail sketch of two divergent views on women in ministry, both held by many evangelicals who believe their position is biblical.

One group referred to as traditionalists or, as they prefer, complementarians, believes that the apostle Paul's statements in 1 Corinthians 11:3; 14:34–35, and 1 Timothy 2:11–12 are very clear. Women are under the headship of their husbands, are to be silent in church, and are not to teach or have authority over a man.

Genesis 2:20–22 states that God created woman because among the animals there was no helper suitable for Adam and that God took a rib from Adam to make woman. Based on this passage, complementarians believe that although women and men are both created in the image of God (Gen. 1:27), women are created to help men, not to lead and, since they were formed from man are to be submissive to him. After the fall, God told the woman that her desire would be for her husband and that he would rule over her (Gen. 3:16). Complementarians understand this statement to be God's *prescription* for the way men and women should relate to one another, the pattern of relationships that will work best.

Based on these biblical interpretations, complementarians believe that God has ordained distinct roles for each gender and it is not God's will for women to be ordained or to lead in the church. Biblical women in leadership positions and women in church history whose ministry of preaching and leadership bore spiritual fruit are viewed as exceptions allowed by the sovereign God, not as evidences of God's plan. The apostle Paul wrote, "There is neither Jew nor Greek, there is neither slave nor free man, there is neither male nor female; for you are all one in Christ Jesus" (Gal. 3:28 NASB). Complementarians explain that this verse refers only to a person's relationship with Christ, not to equality of roles and responsibilities in the home and church.

Another group of evangelicals, referred to as egalitarians, begin in Genesis 1 to search for a biblical perspective on women in ministry. Both male and female were created in the image of God, they note, and both were ordered to be fruitful and rule over the created world (Gen. 1:27–28). The Hebrew word used in Genesis 2 for "helper," appears an additional twenty times in the Old Testament, referring seventeen times to God as helper and in three cases to an army. The word *helper*, egalitarians conclude, does not carry a meaning of subordinate. The significance of the woman being created by God using the man's rib, they believe, is to make clear that male and female are of the same substance, suitable companions for one another. In the creation account egalitarians see no evidence of the subordination of woman to man, but, rather, total equality. Egalitarians understand God's words to Eve after the fall as a *description* of what would result from sin, that husbands would rule over wives.

Egalitarians pay special attention to Jesus' treatment of women. In a culture in which men were not to speak to women in public and did not believe women were worth teaching, Jesus' actions were radical. He initiated conversations with women, engaged them in theological discussions, affirmed them for taking the position of a disciple-learner, and even let them touch him. When the Samaritan woman became the first evangelist, Jesus did not reprimand her and after his resurrection appeared first to a woman, commanding her to proclaim the Good News of the resurrection. Egalitarians also believe that because Jesus came to save people from sin, those who respond in faith can be forgiven and released from the power of sin. That means men and women can again live the creation design of equality.

Moving on through the New Testament, egalitarians note Peter's proclamation on the Day of Pentecost: "In the last days, God says, that I will pour forth of My Spirit upon all mankind; and your sons and your daughters shall prophesy, . . . and upon My bondslaves, both men and women, I will in those days pour forth of My Spirit and they shall prophesy" (Acts 2:16–18). Egalitarians draw attention to the fact that Philip's four daughters prophesied (Acts 21:9), that Paul described what women should wear when they pray and prophesy in public (1 Corinthians 11:5), and that Paul referred to women fellow workers.

Against this backdrop, egalitarians seriously examine 1 Corinthians 11 and 14 and 1 Timothy 2. They believe one must understand the context of any statement to accurately interpret its meaning. In both 1 Corinthians and 1 Timothy Paul is writing to correct problems and abuses in worship practices and false teaching. The passages should therefore be interpreted in the light of what we can learn about the possible abuses, and principles drawn from our understanding of Paul's instructions should be applied in the church today. In these verses egalitarians see the message that neither women nor men should disrupt worship or teach falsehood.

Examining the meanings of words used in the original languages of Scripture is crucial for accurate interpretation. For example, the words translated "silence" in both 1 Corinthians 14:34 and 1 Timothy 2:11 are two different Greek words. In Corinthians Paul is saying, "stop talking." But the word in Timothy means an inner quietness. Paul actually encouraged the women of Ephesus to learn in inner quietness and submission to God's Word. Also, the word translated "authority" in 1 Timothy 2:12 appears only once in the New Testament here and is not the word Paul usually uses for authority. "To usurp authority" is a better translation of the Greek. Another concern for egalitarians is Jesus' teaching on authority. Jesus told his disciples they were to have nothing to do with lording it over others. They were called to serve as Jesus served. Neither men nor women should take authority by force in the church or lord it over others. But egalitarians encourage women and men to answer God's call to be servant leaders, proclaiming God's Word to a dying world.

Ever since biblical times, women have served in the ministry of the church. Scholars have identified a repeating cycle in church history. In times of awakening, when the church has been alive and growing rapidly, women have experienced greater freedom in ministry. Then, as the church becomes institutionalized and respectable, women's ministries are once again restricted. A careful study of history, however, reveals that dedicated women through the centuries heroically served their God, with or without the blessing and support of the church.

CATHERINE STONEHOUSE

Bibliography. B. and R. Clouse, eds. (1989), *Women in Ministry: Four Views;* R. T. France (1995), *Women in the Church's Ministry: A Test Case for Biblical Interpretation;* S. J. Grenz (1995), *Women in the Church: A Biblical Theology of Women in Ministry;* J. Piper and W. Grudem, eds. (1991), *Recovering Biblical Manhood and Womanhood: A Response to Evangelical Feminism;* B. T. Roberts (1891), *On Ordaining Women—Biblical and Historical Insights.*

See also DEACONESS

Women's Ministry. Women have made tremendous advances in society, business, and politics, not only in the United States, but in most developed countries in the world since the beginning of the twentieth century. Incredibly, the church at the end of the twentieth century is, in many cases, still a conspicuous holdout. When the *Mayflower* landed on the shores of the yet unexplored North American continent, the "Judaeo-Christian ethic was planted and nourished" (Kraft, 1992, 9). Women were able to take advantage of their newfound freedom and dignity in their adopted homeland.

Gradually, over the past three hundred years this freedom has slipped from the grasp of women. They have lost much of the freedom they experienced in those early years. In fact, it wasn't until early in this century, after years of struggle, that women in America were given the right men had exercised since the founding of this nation—the right to vote (1919).

For centuries, ministry by women to the church has been a significant part of their religious heritage. It was often taken for granted. In the societal upheaval in the United States of the 1960s and 1970s, an interest in ministry to women emerged in American churches. It was a period when seminaries training young men for ministry opened their doors to young women for ministry as well. They were exploring and experimenting with new ideas, new ways to meet the needs of various components of their congregations. It seemed an appropriate time to look at how to develop a ministry to women.

There is little in Scripture that endorses specialized ministry to women, children, youth, or men, or for that matter programs that would help abusers recover, or any of the numerous other ministries aimed at the contemporary congregation's needs.

The apostle Paul wrote instructions to Titus regarding the operation of the church. He included what should be expected of women and men as members of the church (Titus 2:1–5). Part of this passage (2:3–5) has been used as a guide for women's ministries (Berry, 1979, 38ff.).

This concept has mushroomed in recent years. Today, Bible colleges, Christian universities, and seminaries now include courses on women's ministries. Ministry to the women of the church is an accepted priority on the agenda of Christian education in the church.

The components of a women's ministry may include any of the following: Bible study, prayer ministry, fellowship, outreach, mission activity, support groups (or care groups), MOPS (Mothers of Preschoolers), widows, divorce recovery, little sister/big sister program, mother/daughter activities, counseling, personal development, deaconesses, retreats, and seminars.

Women's ministry in a church may include overlapping services. It creates opportunities for women of all ages and statuses to use their gifts and talents to uplift one another. This nurtures within each woman a desire to serve or help one another. Women are encouraged to reach out to meet a need as it arises in other women, to build women into fulfilled, responsible, active Christians who live out the concepts of Scripture in their everyday lives (Briscoe, 1995, 24ff).

A women's ministry should be a ministry of encouragement with older women encouraging the younger women (Titus 2:4) and of discipleship, which includes the unique combination of friendship, motherhood, and education and teaching, which is sharing or imparting information or skill to others (Titus 2:4–5; Acts 18:1–4).

Older women teaching, encouraging, and discipling younger women implies a stair-stepping ministry—the older to the younger (e.g., grandmothers to their daughters who are mothers, mothers to daughters, daughters to little sisters), not necessarily in the same family, but matching from among the women in the church. Informal or formal counseling often plays a role in a women's ministry in a church, especially if there are no women on the church staff.

It should be noted that the spiritual gifts are not given by gender: a list for men and a list for women. The Holy Spirit does not discriminate between genders in relation to gifts. They are given to all believers (1 Cor. 12:11–13). Let us not forget what the apostle Paul says is the greatest gift (1 Cor. 13:13): love.

Steps to begin a women's ministry in a church are as follows. (1) Contact interested women to pray about starting such a ministry. Motivated women come from activities already established in the church. These women coordinate the efforts into a more meaningful ministry to all the women of the church. (2) Determine the purpose or goals of a women's ministry in the church and develop a purpose statement (why it needs to be done) with either the pastoral staff or this group of interested women. (3) Ask this group of interested women to meet for a brainstorming session in order to start ideas flowing, using the stated purpose or goal of such a ministry. (4) Evaluate the ideas that result from the brainstorm session to see if they adequately reflect the needs of the women and the community in which the church resides. (5) Write out the positive and negative aspects and results of such a program. (6) Determine where finances will come from for such a ministry, and how it will be organized. (7) Develop a program plan. (8) Delegate responsibilities. (9) Prepare and publish the calendar of events for the year (Kraft, 1992, 24 ff).

Once these steps have been taken, plan a kickoff event around a theme that states concisely the objective for this ministry for this year. This should alert the women of the church and community that this ministry is vital to their spiritual growth. Set a date for the kickoff event, plan the program, and provide the calendar of activities/events with dates and times planned for the women in the coming year.

One of the basics of any women's ministry should be the element of Bible studies. These can be developed around focus groups—women with concerns that are common to them (e.g., widows, mothers of preschoolers, single moms, etc.).

Become aware of resources (other than financial) available to the women's ministries, such as other women or men who could teach, train, and counsel. Also consider the facilities for child care, space for the meetings, and other functional support available, such as the library, audiovisual technology, and the like.

Leaders must observe the program as it develops to critically evaluate every aspect of it. Watch for glitches that can hinder the spiritual growth of the participants, including communication to members of the opportunities regarding involvement and participation. Doing this will show the leadership what works and what doesn't, what to keep and what to cut out.

PATRICIA A. CHAPMAN

Bibliography. J. Berry (1979), *Growing, Sharing, Serving;* J. Briscoe, L. K. McIntyre, and B. Seversen (1995), *Designing Effective Women's Ministries;* V. Kraft (1992), *Women Centering Women.*

Wordless Book. Tool especially useful for teaching young children or others with limited or no reading ability. It is a book comprised entirely of pictures and designs intended to teach a concept or story. No words are printed in the book itself. Parents and teachers can readily construct these books for use with their children.

Because young children cannot read words, these books provide helpful resources for teaching narratives and concepts to them. The story develops as the child or the "reader" desires, taking form on the basis of the pictures and designs. Children enjoy "reading" these books because they can compose the story as they "read." It allows the reader, child or adult, to utilize creativity in developing the story.

Guidelines for these books are similar to those for any children's book. The artwork and pictures must be large and clear, accurately portraying the story or concept presented by the book. The story should convey the religious values and qualities that undergird the religious development of the child. Preschool children often like books with repetitive elements. It should also tell the story with power.

Several other criteria are important. Pictures should be tastefully and artistically done. Illustrations should also feature males and females in equal numbers. Professions should be pictured by function rather than gender. The books should foster a sense of wonder and awe.

ELEANOR A. DANIEL

See also CHILD EVANGELISM FELLOWSHIP; CHILDHOOD CHRISTIAN EDUCATION; CHILDREN'S CHURCH; EVANGELISM

Word of Life Fellowship. The purpose that fuels Word of Life activity is the evangelization and discipleship of youth through various means consistent with the Holy Scriptures to help build and strengthen the Church of Jesus Christ. The Schroon Lake, N.Y., headquarters serves as the hub for a wide spectrum of ministries, including summer camps, church-sponsored Bible clubs, Bible institutes, music/drama teams, short-term missions projects, and Bible curriculum materials. The "Word of Life" radio broadcast began in 1940, on a 500-watt station in Brooklyn. Now the program is carried on over one hundred stations.

This multifaceted organization was spawned in the late 1930s. Jack Wyrtzen invited three friends to join him for a Bible study in his home on Long Island, N.Y. The four young men pledged to win others for Christ, to furnish speakers for churches and rescue missions, and to distribute gospel literature. Before long twenty-one people were involved. Numbers mushroomed when the location changed to the nearby Republican headquarters. Members of the group started street meetings and rented a church building for Sunday night evangelistic rallies. In 1942, the band of dedicated Christians officially incorporated, becoming Word of Life Fellowship. Wyrtzen cited Philippians 2:16 as the keynote of the ministry: "Holding fast the word of life, so that in the day of Christ I may have cause to glory because I did not run in vain nor toil in vain" (NASB).

Prior to 1960, World of Life was known for staging large public rallies in major U.S. cities. Sites included Madison Square Garden, Yankee Stadium, Boston Garden, and the Philadelphia Convention Center. Jack Wyrtzen was recognized across the country as an evangelist to youth. Since then Word of Life has adapted by changing the forms intended to fulfill the organization's function. Replacing the public rallies are musical dramas and multimedia performances that reach over 160,000 people a year at over 170 sites throughout America. A timely example is *Born Again to a Living Hope,* the true story of two young people, presented in live drama, music, and video by a cast of 25. Jesus Christ rescued the teens from a life of drugs and promiscuity—before their lives were claimed by the AIDS virus.

Committed to grounding people in their local churches, Word of Life Clubs—over one thousand in the United States—affect over 22,000 youth each week. The clubs consist of Olympians (ages 6 to 11); Junior and Senior High (ages 12 to 17), plus College and Career Fellowship for young adults. Curriculum for these club meetings consists of a balanced spiritual diet of Bible doctrine, biblical insights on current issues facing youth, and training for personal evangelism/discipleship. Word of Life publishes age-graded "Quiet Time" diaries for all club participants. Area Word of Life missionaries assist over 750 local churches in their Christian education of young people.

In 1985, through a donation of 500 acres, Word of Life constructed the World Bible Conference and Resort Center in Hudson, Fla. The new site adds camping opportunities for hundreds of children, as well as Bible conferences for vacationers. The camps and conference centers in New York and Florida reach over ten thousand people every summer. Through a program called *Summer Training Corps*, more than four hundred young people age 16 and older staff the summer ministries. Both the New York and Florida sites offer the Word of Life Bible Institute, where high school graduates attend a series of three-day conferences scattered throughout the calendar year. Participants receive first-class instruction in Bible survey, Bible book studies, major doctrines, and current social trends. Each student in this two-year non-degree granting institute is also involved in a practical ministry, such as camp counseling, singing groups, open-air evangelism, or teaching children in a church.

Although the organization's purpose statement emphasizes ministry to youth, the two campus sites offer specialized conferences to meet distinctive needs of adult target groups. For instance, during winter months the Schroon Lake campus stages separate weekend events for men, women, singles, senior citizens, married couples, business executives, pastors, and law enforcement officers. While adults receive instruction and enjoy fellowship, Word of Life hosts a snow camp for the children.

Word of Life's mission to evangelize and disciple youth has expanded to thirty-seven countries, spanning six continents. By 1990, over three hundred full-time missionaries, both American and nationals, served overseas. The major thrust of overseas work remains evangelism through camping. The organization has launched the *Nehemiah Network* to facilitate church members' involvement in world missions. The Nehemiah Network connects individuals and churches with strategic needs and service opportunities around the globe. Areas of involvement include *hospitality* for missionaries on furlough; *short-term work projects* at overseas sites; *professional services;* and *provision of equipment* needed on the field. Members of the network include pastors, teachers, farmers, physicians, craftsmen—ordinary men and women who love Jesus Christ and care about reaching the world for him.

To support its varied ministries, Word of Life relies on a combination of financial gifts and program revenues. Wise management of resources is indicated by the low overhead costs. Only 10 percent of all expenditures go to administrative and support services. To obtain more information on this ambitious organization, write Word of Life Fellowship, P.O. Box 600, Schroon Lake, NY 12870.

TERRY POWELL

Workshop. Particular instructional format for group learning. A combination of four distinc-

tives differentiates the workshop from other instructional formats.

Problem/solution-driven. Workshops focus on specific, practical, and manageable problems and their solutions. "Sharing the Gospel with Children" would be a more typical workshop title than "Early Church History." Workshops may bring participants together to solve a onetime problem or learn skills to solve recurring problems. The outcome of workshop learning can often be expressed as "I learned *how to.*"

Action-oriented. It is a *work*shop and participants should be working. If the only one working is the instructor, it does not deserve the name *workshop.* Experiential learning activities are the primary tools: case studies, simulations, demonstrations, skill training and practice, and role play are typical strategies used in workshop formats.

Skill-focused. While knowledge and information are important elements of any workshop, they take a subordinate role to skill in the workshop format. A workshop's goal leans toward skills; participants solve a problem or learn skills to solve a problem. The skill learned may be verbal (telling stories), physical (tying knots), or cognitive (identifying figures of speech), but it can always be expressed as what skill the participant gains.

Problem-driven, action-oriented, and skill-focused are three primary characteristics of workshops. Typical secondary characteristics include a small number of participants, a short-term time framework, and intensive involvement.

Workshops are particularly important for training volunteers for educational ministry. Effective educational ministry requires a variety of skills: teaching skills, interpersonal skills, Bible study skills, and lesson planning skills. The workshop provides an ideal format "to equip the saints for the work of ministry" (Eph. 4:12 NRSV).

ROBERT DROVDAHL

Bibliography. P. A. Sharp (1993), *Sharing Your Good Ideas;* T. J. Sork (1984), *Designing and Implementing Effective Workshops.*

World Council of Christian Education. The nineteenth-century missionary expansion of Western Christianity around the world included an educational strategy built on the Sunday school model. From its beginnings in 1780 when Robert Raikes developed schools in Gloucester, England, to teach indigent children to read and write and learn morals and Christian ideals, the Sunday school spread to North America and gradually around the world. Focused on children, it enlisted persons committed to Christian nurture and evangelical Protestantism. One historian of the Sunday school called it "the incubator of conversion and the nursery of piety" (Knoff, 1979, xi).

The movement became organized around nondenominational Sunday School Associations in England and the United States, and in 1889 leaders chiefly from those two countries and Canada formed the World Sunday School Association (WSSA). The First Convention in London was followed by thirteen other such meetings and four "institutes." By 1947 its name combined the World Council of Christian Education (WCCE) and the World Sunday School Association. In 1971 it integrated with the World Council of Churches (WCC).

During its early years the WSSA embodied the optimism and confidence in organized Christian mission activity of English and American evangelicals. It saw itself as a great missionary agency for world evangelization, and like the broader missionary movement depended somewhat unwittingly on the economic and military power of North Atlantic nations. Its concerns for children and its hesitant commitments to social justice at home mirrored the general evangelical Protestant piety in the face of the problems resulting from growing industrialism and urbanization.

Basically a lay movement, the WSSA saw itself as an independent, self-constituting development related to but outside the denominations. In England and European countries which had established churches and education in the schools there was less enthusiasm for the Sunday school form of Christian education, so it grew more naturally alongside and as part of the "free churches," with zeal for "common Christianity" and cooperation in good works. Lay participants in the world meetings far outnumbered clergy. Of the 400 U.S. delegates sailing, with a full schedule of study and worship, to the 1889 London Convention, the American delegation included only 54 clergy. The Nairobi Assembly in 1967 included only 12.3 percent laypersons, and the majority were ordained staff in member churches and organizations, with their time and expenses paid by their denominational agencies.

Supported for most of its history by such wealthy persons as Lord Mackintosh, J. Arthur Rank, Dorothy Cadbury, and the Heinz family, the WCCE developed a wide variety of Christian education programs for its member organizations around the world. Curriculum programs and materials for children in Sunday schools, pictures for use in teaching (fifty million distributed by 1963!), audiovisuals, and helps in planning indigenous curricula and in strengthening teaching of Christian education in theological schools—all were major contributions to the education of the people of God around the world, especially children. Its partners in the newly formed churches realized that the patterns and styles of Christian education were imports from the United States, Canada and England, but they welcomed help in their efforts to raise their children and equip their youth and adults in the Christian faith.

As those earlier supporters were succeeded by less wealthy ones, and as denominational mission agencies increased their control through the International Missionary Council (IMC) and later in the WCC, the WCCE tried to adjust to the emerging, more structured ways of working together around the world. The different communions had many other educational investments, in higher and theological education, denominational youth and children's programs, and in lay and adult education. The WCCE moved into the larger ecumenical scene in the World Youth Assembly in 1939 and in 1950 with joint youth staff and activities with the World Council of Churches.

Financial support became increasingly difficult, as the WCCE found itself struggling to adjust to the newly competitive world of denominational funding, and as the IMC came into the World Council of Churches at its 1961 New Delhi Assembly. During its final two decades the WCCE drew on reserves in order to maintain its programs, and therefore became progressively weaker in the "dowry" it could bring into integration with the WCC.

During the 1960s WCCE staff, by then partially located in Geneva, was working more and more cooperatively with the WCC. The two organizations established a Joint Study Committee which brought to the WCC Assembly at Uppsala in 1968 a report and recommendation for moving toward integration of the two ecumenical organizations. There were some fears within the WCCE that the WCC, with its more hierarchical organization as a Council of Churches, would not be fully supportive of the WCCE's work with children. Within the WCC, some feared that bringing the older missionary agency focused on children might add pressures and diversions to the youth and laity and women's programs in its structures. Residual elements of both kinds of fears have persisted ever since.

In a conference center at Huampani, near Lima, Peru, the WCCE officially voted in 1971 to integrate with the WCC, and was allied with its new Office of Education. Since then gradually the WCCE's long tradition of Christian education for children has blended into the broader context of church educational work as the WCC has struggled to find the proper lodging and priorities for education in the totality of its ecumenical activities and structures. From its nineteenth-century origins in the evangelical missionary advance, the work and hopes of the WCCE now belong to the broader ecumenical movement, as understandings of mission and education keep changing into the twenty-first century.

Perhaps the longest lasting symbol of the contribution of the WCCE to world Christianity is what was often cited as the most widely known song in the world, "Jesus Loves Me."

WILLIAM B. KENNEDY

Bibliography. A. M. Boylan (1988), *Sunday School: The Formation of an American Institution;* W. B. Kennedy (1966), *The Shaping of Protestant Education: An Interpretation of the Sunday School and the Development of Protestant Educational Stragegy in the United States, 1789–1860;* G. E. Knoff (1979), *The World Sunday School Movement: The Story of a Broadening Mission;* R. W. Lynn and E. Wright (1971, 1980), *The Big Little School: 200 Years of the Sunday School.*

World Council of Churches. Founded in 1948, as a major development in the modern Ecumenical Movement, the World Council of Churches (WCC) has grown from its original 147 member churches to more than 330, in more than 100 countries. Representing a diversity of cultures and faith traditions through a half-century of massive global changes, it has built its support foundations and program partnerships in and through its member communions.

Each member church subscribes to the general belief that the Council is a fellowship of churches which confess the Lord Jesus Christ as God and Savior according to the Scriptures. Therefore, they seek to accomplish their common task which is to the glory of God in His triune state: Father, Son and Holy Spirit.

This broad based theological foundation gives moral authority to statements and actions which provide a common voice from its member bodies. These include most mainline Protestant churches in Europe and North America, the major Orthodox communions, churches in Africa, Asia, Australia, New Zealand, and Latin America. It has a cooperative relationship with the Roman Catholic Church and others. In 1961 it integrated with the International Missionary Council and in 1971 with the World Council of Christian Education, (WCCE). The stated purposes of WCC are: (1) To call the churches to the goal of visible unity in one faith and in one eucharistic fellowship expressed in worship and in common life in Christ, and to advance toward that unity in order that the world may believe. (2) To facilitate common witness of the churches in each place and in all places. (3) To support the churches in their worldwide missionary and evangelistic task. (4) To express the common concern of the churches in the service of human need, the breaking down of barriers between people, and the promotion of one human family in justice and peace.

Governed by an Assembly of delegates which meet approximately every seven years, and in between by an Assembly-elected Central Committee of more than a hundred, and a smaller Executive Committee, it works to bond the churches into networks around the world. With a staff of about a hundred professionals plus support personnel, the WCC develops communication and programs with and through the leaders, ecumenical staffs, and constituents of its member churches. Representative committees oversee the priorities and program developments approved by the Assemblies.

Its organizational structure has changed through the decades as new priorities emerged and as financial resources varied. For much of its life it was dominated by North Atlantic churches and their styles of work, but more recently the power of churches from elsewhere has been evident. Sensitivities to regional and local contexts and special problems, as well as to its global experiences, often lead the WCC to challenge particular members and world forces in ways that provoke criticisms from targeted groups within and without its membership. It reflects both the glories and the struggles of its member churches.

From its early days the WCC has had programs in education for mission and other kinds of educational work. In 1968 the Uppsala Assembly established the Office of Education, the subunit into which the WCCE was integrated. The WCC has helped its churches with the problems of adjusting from mission- and church-built schools to new government schools, with development education, and with preparation of curriculums for Sunday schools. In many "Third World" churches the WCC has supported and worked with theological education, and, with the World Student Christian Federation, in higher education. The Ecumenical Institute at Bossey trains younger church leaders and helps develop many of the Council's study conferences.

For further information contact World Council of Churches, P.O. Box 2100, 1211 Geneva 2, Switzerland; or the U.S. Office, 475 Riverside Drive, Room 915, New York, NY 10115–0050, 1-888-870–3340.

WILLIAM B. KENNEDY

Bibliography. A History of the Ecumenical Movement, 1517–1968 (1993); *Seeing Education Whole. Office of Education, World Council of Churches, Geneva,* (1971); Visser't Hooft (1973), *W.A. Memoirs;* H. R. Weber (1996), *A Laboratory for Ecumenical Life: The Story of Bossey 1946–1996.*

Worship. Act of expressing God's worthiness. Worship is one of the earliest recorded activities in Scripture. Cain and Abel were involved in bringing offerings to God as their expression of worship. The patriarchs expressed their individual worship of God by setting up physical reminders (pillars, altars, etc.) of God's blessings.

It would appear from a survey of the Old Testament that there was an evolution of thought and experience regarding worship. The tabernacle and the subsequent temple became the focal point of Hebrew worship. There the people gathered to offer sacrifices and offerings to God as an act of worship. There was little in this activity which represents worship as we know it today for there was no exposition of Scripture by the priest, no choirs leading the congregation in singing, not even public reading of Scripture. Worship was a ritual conducted in the context of the congregation.

In later years while in exile, the Jewish people established the synagogue to provide for the spiritual continuity of their faith. Here the rabbi led the congregation in worshipful expression as he read from the sacred scrolls, interpreted their meaning, and enjoined the people in public prayers. After their return and the subsequent rebuilding of the second temple, worship incorporated annual festivals and fasts, praises from the book of songs (Psalms), Sabbath observance, and more formal adherence to community involvement.

In the New Testament, worship is again seen in the activities of the Jerusalem temple. However, for members of the early church worship became personal as they suffered excommunication from corporate temple worship. Following the teachings of Jesus, who stated that worship was also an expression of one's individual relationship with God (John 4:20–24), worship would have its ultimate expression in personal spiritual formation.

As the church began to expand across Asia and Europe, worship again took on a corporate expression. As those with the spiritual gift of pastor began to organize and build the church, corporate worship became a focal point of church activity. Pastors led their congregations in singing, chants, public prayer, reading Scriptures, sermonizing the meaning of the Scriptures, and giving alms for the poor.

There are primarily four Greek words for worship. The first, *latreuo*, refers to the act of service or paying homage. Although it is sometimes translated "worship" in the New Testament, it is most often translated as "serve." In this sense, worship is seen as an act of service such as demonstrated by the prophetess Anna with her fasting and prayers at the temple (Luke 2:37).

The second Greek term, *proskuneo*, means "to do reverence" or "to make obeisance." It comes from the two words, *pros* (toward) and *kuneo* (kiss). Worship in this manner means the individual displays an attitude of reverence toward God. It is the most often used word for worship in the New Testament.

The third term, *sebomai*, means "to revere God" as one feels awe or devotion toward God. This word is translated four times in the New Testament as "devote" (see Acts 13:43, 40; 17:4, 17).

The fourth term used for worship in the new Testament is *eusebeo*, which means "to act piously toward God." This form of worship also demonstrates honor toward someone such as a parent or grandparent (1 Tim. 5:4).

With these definitions in mind it is important to note that there is no biblical prescription of worship. Instead, worship is seen as the direct acknowledgment or realization of who God is and how he deals with humankind. Worship flows out of our understanding of God's character and attributes. This attitude should be seen in both verbal expression (singing praises, prayer, etc.) and behavioral activities (deeds done as an acknowledgment of his character and nature).

Worship is a highly personal and dynamic expression of one's relationship with God. For this reason it is difficult to schedule or prescribe. It is far more than an intellectual activity although it may start with a cognitive awareness. True worship flows out of a heart which has been touched by the realization that God is gracious and merciful toward those who have repented of their sin, that God is tender with the brokenhearted, and that his kindness (as opposed to his wrath) motivates the sinner to repentance.

The act of corporate worship has been the source of contention in many churches across North America recently. Worship leaders who seek to dictate a form or style of worship as the "only right way" to worship God are guilty of misinterpretation of the scriptural teachings regarding worship. As demographic changes occur over time personal preferences toward worship in the church will likewise also change. Traditional forms of worship music such as singing church creeds or older hymns may be the preferred method of worship expression. Younger audiences may prefer more contemporary music to complement the singing of worship choruses. It is not that one expression is right and the other is wrong. One is simply more appropriate to a particular audience due to cultural, demographic, and sociological factors. Many churches have experienced a moderate degree of success by "blending" worship styles in the service. This approach seeks to have both hymns and choruses in the service. A good deal of care and forethought must be given to corporate worship as we continue to attempt to preserve the church's vitality and ability to impact the world for Christ.

MICHAEL J. ANTHONY

Bibliography. F. L. Cross and E. A. Livingston (1997), *The Oxford Dictionary of the Christian Church;* J. D. Douglas (1975), *The New Bible Dictionary;* E. L. Towns (1995), *Evangelism and Church Growth;* F. M. Segler (1967), *Christian Worship: Its Theology and Practice;* W. E. Vine (1966), *An Expository Dictionary of New Testament Words.*

Worship, Family. The adage "the family that prays together, stays together" is proven true as many families conduct a time for focus on the

Lord in the home. These parents engage in various activities of worship at home. Praying together with the children at meals and bedtime is a normal occurrence. For others it may be a daily or weekly time set apart to read the Word of God and have prayer. However, the vast majority of parents struggle in conducting any meaningful worship time as a family.

Deuteronomy 6 is often cited as the foundation for parents' responsibility to provide religious instruction and time for family worship and reflection (v. 7): "Impress them [God's commands] on your children. Talk about them when you sit at home and when you walk along the road, when you lie down and when you get up." The worship experience in the home is thus to be both formal and informal, planned and unplanned.

Children will grow in appreciation of God through family worship. A child can be taught to worship spontaneously as he or she experiences the world around him or her. The child can be guided by the parent to be in awe of what God is doing—from the gentle beauty of a flower to the scary roar of nighttime thunder.

Worship is a vital step in a child's faith development. "We will not hide them from their children; we will tell the next generation the praiseworthy deeds of the Lord, his power, and the wonders he has done. . . . Then they would put their trust in God" (Ps. 78:4, 7). As always, certain dangers and pitfalls exist. If family worship is boring or not geared to the needs of children, they could resent this time, or worse, cause them to not pursue their own spiritual development.

Many parents are choosing to take seriously the biblical admonition to be the spiritual leaders of their home and are reserving one night each week as "Family Night." This increasing trend among Christian homes across North America is having a profound impact on the transference of biblical values from one generation to another.

Family Night needs to be seen and designed around the interests of the youngest members of the family. After a dinner where the family shares about their daily happenings, the family enjoys an activity which involves all of the members of the family. Examples of such activities may include constructing a family collage, playing board games, making an album of photos from the last family vacation, baking cookies for a needy family in the neighborhood, etc. What you do is not as important as the process. What matters is that the family builds a sense of community and commitment together. After this activity a passage of Scripture is read, questions are asked to ensure understanding by all, and then the family sits in a circle, holds hands, and prays for one another.

Many resources exist which in combination with parents who portray the love of Christ and practice godly living as examples, will strengthen the home and produce future generations of those who put their trust in God. Visiting a Christian bookstore will reveal a host of contemporary resources to help make family worship an enjoyable event for all.

RONALD H. RYND

Bibliography. *Daylights*, Great Commission Association, 3611 Eisenhower, Ames, IA 50014; *Family Walk*, Walk Thru the Bible, Box 627, Mt. Morris, IL 61054, 1–800–763–5433; *Our Daily Bread*, RBC Ministries, 3000 Kraft Ave. SE, Grand Rapids, MI 49555.

Worship, Youth. Worship is focusing the attention of one's mind, emotions, will, and spirit on God. Worship is related to the Old English root words *weorth*, "worthy, worth," and *scipe*, "ship." Thus worship is declaring God's worth, his worthiness to be praised. It is the human response of adoration, praise, and supplication to the person and work of God.

Worship for youth can be categorized in three arenas: private worship, corporate worship, and family worship. Private worship emphasizes the personal relationship and responsibility of the believer. Private worship highlights the opportunity for prayer, quietness, solitude, and meditation. It affords the young believer a setting for personal confession, repentance, and supplication before God. It also provides the context for personal praise and thanksgiving.

Worship is most commonly associated with corporate worship, the gathered body of believers engaging in common worship. This context adds the horizontal relationship to the worship experience. This gives believers the opportunity to encourage and exhort one another during the acts of worship. The inherent dangers, of course, derive from the possibility of drawing more attention to the worshipers than to the One being worshiped. In today's congregations, with more and more emphasis on public performances, pageantry, and theatrical influences, this is a real danger to be avoided.

In youth ministry, corporate worship includes two dimensions—the entire church and the youth group. The entire church worshiping includes the young people as well as those of all ages. Adolescents need the models and guidance provided by those of other generations as they worship together. The church, in turn, needs the youthful idealism and compassion that can be provided by its teenage members. Youth, who once were only considered "the church of tomorrow," are also "the church of today."

A second dimension of corporate worship involves the youth group when they engage in worship apart from the entire congregation. Youth can and should be taught to lead and participate in worship. Youth group meetings, mission settings, camps, and retreats provide opportunities for young people to worship together. A danger to avoid is characterizing the youth group worship experience as only a "learning experience," not the real worship that takes place in "big church." Youth can and should engage in meaningful worship experiences in the context of youth group meetings.

A third arena of worship for youth is within the context of their homes. Deuteronomy 6:4–7 commands parents to teach their children the things of God as they go about their family routines. This includes family worship and is a different form of worship from those mentioned earlier. Family worship, while more relaxed and informal, should still be characterized by awe and reverence for God. Teenagers, parents, and younger siblings experience deeply personal, intimate, times of worship in the context of family devotional times.

Family worship normally does not include the same rituals and ceremonies of corporate worship (such as preaching, communion, baptism, and public commitments) but does involve more intimate moments of prayer, Scripture reading, discussion, music, repentance, and commitment. Teenagers can and should be included in the leadership of family worship experiences.

Youth worship is often pictured as "creative worship," with more emphasis on drama, visual elements, music, and unusual settings. For some adults, youth-led worship services can be times to anticipate or dread, depending on how receptive the congregants are or how "creative" the youth have been in the past. Youth can, with proper guidance and parameters, add new life and vitality to old routines and energize a church through creative and youthful approaches to worship.

Elements of worship include prayer; adoration and praise; exhortation, encouragement, and admonition; confession and repentance; expressions of response (singing, testimonies, speaking); and commitment. Worship is more than a checklist of these elements, however. True worship captures the will and commitment and leads to renewed service to the Lord. Worship that does not result in surrender and commitment to service is not true worship (Isa. 6:8–9).

These are all impacted by varying theological and denominational influences. Some faith communities will emphasize the sacramental and liturgical elements; others will emphasize preaching, exhortation, and evangelism; still others will focus on the charismatic moving of God's Spirit among his people. Among today's youth, there seems to be a renewed appreciation for the worship practices of others and a willingness to incorporate them across faith and denominational lines.

The field of Christian education often approaches worship with youth as a learning experience. Much time and energy is spent talking about worship and preparing youth for worship experiences. Youth group meetings are often described as worship times, when in reality they are learning sessions, wholesome Christian entertainment, and group process times. Christian educators should be careful to balance times of talking and teaching about worship (more cognitive) with times of authentic worship (involving personal involvement at the deepest human levels).

A final caution for Christian educators regarding youth in worship derives from the modern world's emphasis on high-tech, glitzy, theatrical performances. Youth are attracted to concerts, performances, multimedia productions, and staged productions. While elements of these can be included in youth worship experiences, leaders should be especially cautious to keep the focus on God and not on the production values of the "worship experience." Exodus 20:3 says, "You shall have no other gods before me." The danger facing youth leaders today is, rather than seeing God in worship, we see humans and their creations on center stage—programs, pageantry, singers, preachers, personalities, buildings, lights, and special effects. These too often fall into the category of "creative worship." Taken to extreme, these can replace authentic worship experiences for youth.

WESLEY BLACK

Bibliography. W. and S. Black (1985), *Discipleship in the Home;* A. C. Lovelace and W. C. Rice (1976), *Music and Worship in the Church;* D. Miller (1987), *Story and Context;* F. M. Segler (1996), *Understanding, Preparing for, and Practicing Christian Worship;* R. E. Webber (1996), *Worship Is a Verb.*

Worship and Children. Worship (from Anglo-Saxon *weorthscipe,* "worthship") means homage. For the Christian, worship is recognizing and responding to the worthiness of God to receive our devotion and praise.

The experience of worship is threaded through the Scriptures. Although the children's place in worship is not always explicitly noted, there are references to the role and image of children.

Jesus' admonition to "Let the children alone, and do not hinder them from coming to Me; for the kingdom of heaven belongs to such as these" (Matt. 19:14; Mark 10:14; Luke 18:16) challenges the too-common belief that true worship is really for adults. A child played a critical part in the miracle of the feeding of the multitudes by offering his lunch to Jesus (John 6:9). This incident illustrates that children were included in the crowds of people who gathered to hear Jesus teaching. They were very likely among the people who were "spreading their garments in the road" and "began to praise God joyfully with a loud voice" as Jesus made his triumphal entry into Jerusalem (Luke 19:36, 37; see also John 12:13 NASB).

When Jesus was asked about who was the greatest in the kingdom of heaven, he called a child to him (Matt. 18:3–5; Mark 10:14, 15). By this act, Jesus affirmed the place of children among his followers. The most important picture in the Scriptures of a child's place in the kingdom is the infant Jesus himself. The incarnation cautions us to never ignore the smallest child among us. Each child can be a reminder of the incarnation and of the qualities that Jesus expects in his followers (Sandell, 1991).

Worship is not limited to planned meetings of people in church or parachurch settings. The home is an important center for worship for Christian families. Deuteronomy 6 and 11 specifically instruct parents to share their commitment to and love for God with their children. Parents are encouraged to tell again and again the stories of God's greatness.

Children have been a part of the worshiping community from the beginning of the Christian church. The first Christians gathered regularly for worship in the Jerusalem temple and in the homes of believers. When whole households of people worshiping God are mentioned in the New Testament, children were no doubt included (Acts 20:20; Rom. 16:5).

For centuries children were expected to worship with their families. However, during the twentieth century, the place of children in the church was reexamined. Educational researchers began to study how children learn and concluded that it was important that they be taught in ways that were consistent with their age and experience. Christian educators began to wonder if children were present in the essentially adult worship service "in body but not necessarily in mind and spirit." The concern was that children were not understanding the Scripture reading, sermon, words of the hymns, and terminology in the prayers.

As public schools began to explore new teaching methods, the church considered ways to make worship more understandable and accessible to children. Some churches, especially larger ones, began to provide children's church, where a special worship time geared to children was offered usually at the same time as the adults were in their own worship service. An advantage of this for the adults was that they were able to concentrate on worship without the disruption of children. The disadvantage for the adults was that they lost the spontaneity, eagerness, motion, energy, and awareness that children can bring to the worship community.

Other churches decided that children would be better served by being included in an intergenerational worship experience. They emphasized that children are not just preparing to become worshipers but can actually enter into the experience of knowing, loving, and worshiping God (Cavalletti, 1982). Ng and Thomas (1981) have been especially strong proponents of including children as full participants in the worshiping community. They support this position by reminding us there are no age requirements in the body of Christ, that worship is a corporate act that should include children as well as adults, and that the church is bereft if some members of the body are excluded from participating in meaningful worship.

Whatever the context for children's worship, with the whole church community or in a distinct children's service, the intent is that they not only learn about God but experience and respond to God. The worship experiences that children have will positively or negatively color their later view of the church and their sense of identity as a part of the people of God.

BETH POSTERSKI

Bibliography. S. Cavalletti (1982), *The Religious Potential of the Child: The Description of an Experience with Children from Ages Three to Six;* D. Ng and V. Thomas (1981), *Children in the Worshipping Community;* E. J. Sandell (1991), *Including Children in Worship;* S. M. Stewart and J. W. Berryman (1989), *Young Children and Worship;* R. E. Webber (1994), *The Ministries of Christian Worship.*

Worship Service. The English word worship is derived from an Old English term *worthship,* which means "to ascribe worth." In a worship service, believers acknowledge God's great worth, rendering to him their honor and devotion. The Hebrew word literally means to *bow down* before God, acceding to his greatness and power.

Traditionally, the worship service has been understood as a great dialogue between God and human beings. First the congregation enters the sanctuary and is reminded of the holiness of God. In response, they bow down to him, confessing their sin, singing his praises, and exalting his name. Then God, in response to his people's obedience, speaks to them through his Word. The appropriate response to God's gracious teaching is one of joy and thankfulness, so that worship becomes not simply a gathering to reminisce but an encouragement toward obedience and service. A Christian should walk away from this dialogue changed, as Moses was changed after he interacted with God on Mount Sinai.

The History of Worship. In earliest times worship was not a formalized meeting—Adam and Eve simply *walked with God.* The sons of Adam were called to present a sacrifice before God, so there was always a sense of worship being a *giving up* toward God. Then Enosh began calling on the name of the Lord (Gen. 4:26), giving rise to the early form of worship as prayer and praise. Noah expressed his gratitude by building an altar and burning an offering before the Lord (Gen. 8:20), fixing worship in a particular place. The use of altars and memorial stones became common, and as Israel became a nation the development of rites and ceremonies brought symbolism and pattern to worship. The building of the temple gave God's true followers not only actions but a formal place in which to perform them.

Worship changed considerably with Christ's resurrection and the coming of the church. As the Christian church expanded, it included not only a place for believers to gather for prayer and praise, but presented an opportunity for service and evangelism. The form of worship may vary from one culture to another—as long as the Word and prayer are evident, the Holy Spirit may minister to the souls of men.

The Practice of Worship. Though the New Testament offers few details of early Christian worship services, there are few doubts regarding the essential elements. The first is prayer, whether done as intercession, recitation, exclamation, or blessing. Though modern services often neglect the role of public prayer, it is almost unthinkable to imagine a Christian service without some form of open communication with God. The second is praise, a confession of God's nature and works. Almost every prayer recorded in Scripture, from the Psalms to Revelation, contain some aspect of praise. The third is singing, closely related to the first two by relying upon reminders of the events and promises of God's Word. His people have always sung his praises, and Revelation reveals that the saints will be singing in heaven.

The fourth aspect of worship is the confession of sin and call for forgiveness, and the fifth is the confession of faith. Both acknowledge God's superiority, and both rely on his grace. The sixth is the reading of the Bible, in which God's very words are revealed to humankind, and the seventh is preaching, in which education and evangelism occur. The eighth and ninth are the two holy sacraments of the church: baptism, symbolizing one's entry into the family of God, and communion, symbolizing one's ongoing walk with him. The final aspect of worship is the collection, in which believers took care of one another through sharing their material blessing. (A case may also be made for occasional special services, such as the ordaining of leadership and the anointing of the sick.)

JERRY CHIP MACGREGOR

Bibliography. R. B. Allen and G. Borror (1982), *Worship: Rediscovering the Missing Jewel;* D. Hustad (1981), *Jubilate!;* R. P. Martin (1964), *Worship in the Early Church;* R. Webber (1982), *Worship Old and New.*

See also CHURCH; MUSIC; PROGRAM; SEEKER SERVICES; WORSHIP; WORSHIP AND CHILDREN

Wyckoff, DeWitte Campbell (1918–). D. Campbell Wyckoff has served as a leader in Christian education for much of the twentieth century. He has held leadership positions within the Religious Education Association and served as International Editor (1979–83) for the journal, *Reli-*

gious Education. In addition to the books and articles he has written, he is recognized for the contribution he has made in the development of bibliographical work in religious education.

Wyckoff began his studies at Columbia University's Teachers College in an experimental school called New College. His interests in religion and philosophy grew as a result of the influence of faculty, particularly Paul Limbert, who introduced him to the writing of Karl Barth. Limbert also introduced him personally to Reinhold Neibuhr, and during this time he discovered a richness in Christianity, in the Bible, and in the relationship of the church, faith, and culture, which greatly influenced his life from then on.

Wyckoff left New College and continued his undergraduate studies at New York University, completing a B.S. in 1939. He spent a year in Alpine, Tenn., as an intern with the Presbyterian Board of National Missions and then returned a year later to New York University to pursue a master's degree (A.M., 1942) and doctoral degree (Ph.D., 1949). In 1947 he joined the faculty of the Department of Religious Education (N.Y.U.). His first book, *The Task of Christian Education* (1955), describes the aim of Christian education as nurturing persons in the faith and drawing them into a deeper relationship with God.

In 1954 he accepted a position as the Thomas W. Synott Professor of Christian Education at Princeton Theological Seminary, an affiliation that was to last for nearly thirty years.

While at Princeton, Wyckoff wrote and taught on the role of method in Christian education. His writing during these years includes: *In One Spirit: Senior Highs and Missions* (1958), *The Gospel and Christian Education* (1959), *For Every Person* (1959), *Theory and Design of Christian Education Curriculum* (1961), *How to Evaluate Your Christian Education Program* (1962), *The Great Belonging* (1962), *The Church's Educational Ministry: A Curriculum Plan* (1965), *Learning Tasks in the Curriculum* (1965), *To Know God* (1972), and *Religious Education Ministry With Youth* (1981).

He retired from Princeton in 1983, having additionally served from 1961 to 1969 as the seminary's Director of Doctoral Studies, and from 1969 serving as the Director of the Summer School. He has written several additional books since his retirement: *Beautiful Upon the Mountains: A Handbook for Church Education in Appalachia* (coeditor, 1984), *Renewing the Sunday School and the CCD* (1986), and *Religious Education, 1960–1993: An Annotated Bibliography* (cocompiler, 1995).

ELIZABETH A. LEAHY

Bibliography. J. Reed and R. Prevost (1991), *A History of Christian Education;* D. C. Wyckoff (1982), *Modern Masters of Religious Education.*

Wycliffe. *See* Bible Translations.

Y2K Generation. *See* Millenial Generation.

Yom Kippur. Hebrew name of the Day of Atonement. The term *atonement* includes such biblical concepts as substitution, redemption, propitiation, and reconciliation. This annual Jewish fast day falls on the 10th day of the 7th month (Tishri), which corresponds roughly with our month of October. Biblical references that guide this day are drawn from Leviticus 16:23, 27–32 and Numbers 29:7–11. The Old Testament occurrence of this day is associated with the cleansing of the tabernacle, the high priest entering into the Holy of Holies, his subsequent sprinkling of the mercy seat with the blood of a sacrificial goat, and the scapegoat which is released into the wilderness.

In the New Testament the Day of Atonement was seen as an opportunity to reflect on the sacrificial offering of Christ on the cross to atone for the sins of the world. Jesus is seen as the great High Priest in the Book of Hebrews. The observance of the day declined as Christians grew in their theological understanding of the sufficiency of Christ's death on the cross.

In its contemporary setting, it is the last of the "Ten Days of Penitence," the first day being Rosh Hashanah (Jewish New Year's Day) and the last being Yom Kippur. This ten-day period is devoted to repentance, prayer, and fasting. Obviously, since the Jewish temple has been destroyed the sacrificial aspects of this feast are no longer observed. Jewish believers today celebrate this day by abstaining from food and attending services at their synagogue. On the evening of Yom Kippur, a ram's horn is blown to signal the beginning of the service for the congregation after which time the *Kol Nidre* (all vows) service is chanted. The congregation, recognizing their inability to keep God's laws, seeks God's forgiveness. It is an intensely meaningful service for Jews and represents one of the most sacred religious observances in the Jewish calendar.

MICHAEL J. ANTHONY

Bibliography. F. L. Cross and E. A. Livingstone (1997), *The Oxford Dictionary of the Christian Church;* J. D. Douglas (1962), *The New Bible Dictionary;* E. L. Towns (1995), *A Practical Encyclopedia of Evangelism and Church Growth.*

Young Life. Relational ministry of Christ-centered adults committed to reach adolescent youth with the Good News of Jesus Christ. Founded in 1941 by Jim Rayburn while in Dallas, Tex., the movement spread to 645 active areas in the United States in addition to Canadian ministries under a board based in Vancouver, B.C. By the end of 1997, the movement found homes in thirty-four other countries.

Following the conviction that the best way to reach young people is through genuine friendships, the movement focuses on four venues in which to develop authentic rapport.

Contact refers to the creative "hanging out" through which Christian adults find a comfortable way to enter the world of junior and senior high school youth. Close to 900 field staff and more than 9,000 volunteers take initiatives to "win the right to be heard" by as many as 450,000 adolescents annually. Often called "an incarnational witness" based on John 1:14, contact work dates back to Rayburn's ability to attract youth into healthy friendships which provided opportunities to discuss matters of a personal and spiritual nature.

Club is a place where adults and students meet. Initially clubs grow out of relationships staff or volunteers initiate with individuals and small clusters of students. Their function is twofold: to provide a weekly opportunity for relationships modeled after Jesus Christ to flower and grow, and to give adults a forum to address from a Christian perspective issues young people face. Humor and Christian insights blend in the club format. Many times young people sing and actively participate in the adult-led club meetings. There is no financial obligation on the part of students who are encouraged to bring friends to the meetings usually housed in homes and other locations off the school campus. The 1,500 high school and 350 junior high school clubs, sometimes called *proclamation units* because not all retain the original club format, mold the personality of the leaders and youth thy have befriended. During 1997, the average club attendance topped 85,000 each week.

Campaigners is an opportunity for young people who seek further understanding of the Christian faith and wish to walk in step with God. While this form of discipleship is perceived by some as a function of church ministry, Young Life leaders have a difficult time handing relationships associated with the spiritual nurturing process to church leaders who may not have earned their right to be heard in the lives of these same students. Consequently, a second weekly meeting, usually held on Sunday evenings, provides leaders with the opportunity to assist students to discuss and discover a personal walk with God through Jesus Christ. About 25,000 students are involved in Campaigner groups.

Camps complete the picture of the Young Life Ministry. Most of the eighteen camps, ranging in capacity from 426 people at Frontier to 30 at Pioneer Plunge, provide resort experiences with a powerful Christian witness. The others use stress camping to teach young people to get in touch with themselves and God. Attendance peaks in the summer when more than 32,000 students spend an unforgettable week at a Young Life camp. It is at camp that the vast majority of first time commitments to Jesus Christ are made in the Young Life movement.

With a 1997 annual budget in excess of $61 million, Young Life ranked among the largest not-for-profit organizations in America which focus their energies on serving youth. Nine percent of Young Life personnel are people of color. Twenty-five percent of the field staff are women.

American and international headquarters are in Colorado Springs, Colo. American Young Life is governed by a self-perpetuating National Board of corporate leaders. Denny Rydberg, the fifth president and the first one drawn from outside the movement, took over the leadership of Young Life in 1993, expanding both the camp ministries and the number of field staff. The National Service Center assist staff, volunteers, and local committees in 31 Regions across the United States and twelve frontiers which the movement considers to be under served. These include ministries in international schools, Hispanic, urban and rural communities in the United States. Canadian Young Life is led by Hal Merwood.

Young Life has made three major contributions to evangelical youth ministry: (1) From the outset, the movement has *focused on adult leaders as the missionaries* who must gain access to people in the youth culture as opposed to a peer ministry philosophy. The structure of the club program (adult led) and the sophistication of the training programs (including Young Life Institute) demonstrates the strategic role of adults in the movement. (2) Though all effective youth ministries have been relational, Young Life taught youth workers how to *touch a generation of relationship-starved youth one by one.* (3) Finally, leaders of Young Life demonstrated a *conversational style of public evangelistic communication* which broke with the preaching styles employed by traditional youth evangelists.

People formerly associated with Young Life have shaped relational ministries of many churches, publications, and organizations including the *fellowship* based in Washington D.C., which is best known for the prayer breakfast movement, including the Congressional Prayer Breakfast.

Mark H. Senter III

Bibliography. E. Cailliet (1963), *Young Life;* E. Campbell (1984), *Young Life's Malibu;* C. Merideth (1978), *It's a Sin to Bore a Kid;* J. Miller (1991), *Back to the Basics of Young Life;* J. Rayburn III (1984), *Dance Children Dance;* M. H. Senter III (1992), *The Coming Revolution in Youth Ministry.*

Youth and Missions. The principal responsibility of the Christian church throughout history has been to seek and save the lost through proclaiming the gospel of Jesus Christ. This evangelical command is found in Matthew 28:18–20, Luke 24:46–49, John 20:21, and Acts 1:8. The evangelistic advance of the church is the responsibility of all Christians, including the adolescent contingent.

Scripture affirms God's use of youth to fulfill his mission. At a time when youth maintained no societal status God introduced the world to Joseph, a 17-year-old who had a dream that thrust him into slavery, prison, power, and inevitably the salvation of God's people. Samuel heard the voice of God as a mere child. David defeated the Philistine as a young boy, and subsequently led God's people to victory.

The New Testament is no less infiltrated with youth. Mary was a teenager when she gave birth to the Son of God. Jesus went about his Father's business at age 12. Timothy led the Ephesian church in his youth. And, since most of the twelve disciples were probably under the age of 20, the Great Commission was in all likelihood given to a group of teenagers.

Throughout the growth of the contemporary church, youth have been used by God. Near the end of the nineteeneth century Dwight L. Moody challenged a group of teenagers to commit themselves to missions. As a result the Student Volunteer Movement carried the evangelical church well into the twentieth century, culminating in the deployment of thousands of missionaries. As the Student Volunteer Movement matured it became the catalyst for the YMCA and InterVarsity Christian Fellowship.

More recently the missionary efforts of adolescents have reached the ends of the earth. Youth with a Mission (YWAM) consistently dispatches young people around the globe and Operation Mobilization has used teenagers to penetrate the Muslim world through their *Logos* and *Doulos* ship ministries. In 1995, at the Global Consultation of World Evangelization in Seoul, South Korea, 80,000 Korean teenagers were commissioned to journey to every nation proclaiming the gospel.

Missiologist Paul Borthwick has suggested that youth who are involved in cross-cultural missions have the greatest opportunity for nurturing a vital spirituality, developing as leaders, and catching the vision for evangelism. Teenagers often return home from a mission trip with a new perspective on life, a deeper commitment to servanthood, and altered life goals.

Evangelism in the twentieth century was marked by a methodology which most often explains the gospel to teenagers and subsequently involves them in the work of the Christian life. In the twenty-first century mission challenges and experiences will change the evangelism paradigm. In contemporary American culture it is not difficult to assemble a missions team which includes a number of non-Christians interested in the humanitarian aspect of the mission. Pre-Christian students are involved in such efforts as feeding the hungry, building shelters for the homeless, clothing the poor, or visiting the imprisoned. In the midst of doing God's work they are introduced to the very person of Christ who has commissioned the work to be done.

MARK W. CANNISTER

Bibliography. M. J. Anthony (1994), *The Short-Term Missions Boom;* P. Borthwick (1988), *Youth and Missions: Expanding Your Students' Worldview;* R. Burns and N. Becchetti (1990), *The Complete Student Missions Handbook.*

Youth Culture. Unique language, artistic expressions, norms of behavior, relational values, and interpretative worldviews that characterize the experiences of adolescents in relationship to one another.

Youth culture, wherever it emerges, is rightly understood as a subculture. American youth culture and European youth culture, for instance, must be understood in relationship to their respective broader cultural contexts. Youth culture, however, has also become an increasingly global

subculture fueled by the advent of rapid advancement in global communication technologies. Teenagers in the Western Hemisphere, therefore, have a growing sense of shared culture with their peers in the East in spite of dramatic contrasts between their broader cultural heritages. It should be noted that global youth culture, because of its dependence upon accessible technology and expendable income to consume products (e.g., faddish clothing) and experiences (e.g., musical concerts, movies), is primarily a First World phenomenon. Global marketing strategies for youth culture products and experiences continue, however, to influence adolescents' sense of identity even in Third World contexts. Youth culture is, therefore, both a local and global phenomenon.

Youth culture emerges from the adolescent developmental process of identity formation. As adolescents seek to individuate, a bridge between childhood dependence on parents and the full responsibilities of adult independence must be built. That relational bridge consists of a world of peers who become the adolescent's most *immediate* source of feedback for the individuation process. Belonging to a particular peer group, and thereby finding one's "location" on the map of adolescent socialization in the school and community, becomes an important source for defining one's identity. Youth culture assists in the tasks of identifying with peers by setting standards for clothing styles, musical options, verbal cues (slang), and patterns of behavior. Youth culture, therefore, becomes an important resource for the process of an adolescent's quest to answer the question, "Who am I?"

The reality of youth culture is an important catalyst for youth-oriented Christian education ministries. Recognizing the significance of assisting adolescents in developing an identity that is grounded in Christ, churches and parachurch ministries attempt to reach and teach adolescents within their youth cultural experiences. Such ministries offer youth talks relevant to the relational and personal issues adolescents face, activities which are interesting and fun for adolescents looking for peer socialization, and mentoring relationships which provide guidance for navigating the passage from childhood to adulthood. The music, the discussions, the artistic expressions, and the styles of worship in such ministries have the look and feel of youth culture while maintaining the distinctive essence of the Christian faith. Without such experiences, adolescents often begin to question the relevance of Christ to the realities of their daily lives.

Highlighting the reality and powerful influence of youth culture in the practices of Christian education is John Detonni's proposal that youth ministry leaders must act as ethnographers. Dettoni (1993) describes the functions of such leaders as *describing* [its form], *analyzing* [how the various elements work together], *interpreting* [communicating its meaning to the youth themselves], and *predicting* [what will happen] in response to the unique elements of a specific youth cultural context. As ethnographers, youth leaders seek an accurate understanding of how adolescents in their own youth cultural experiences are making meaning of their faith in relationship to God, their peers, and their world. The importance of developing an informed perspective in response to youth culture is demonstrated by Richard Dunn (1977). He contends that understanding the world from an adolescent's cultural point of view: (1) bridges generational assumptions adults have about youth within their own culture; (2) bridges cultural assumptions adults have about youth in other cultures; (3) informs a holistic understanding of an individual youth's personal and spiritual development; (4) provides a framework for explaining adolescent choices and behaviors; (5) critiques the relevance of program strategies and instructional methodologies for a particular context; and (6) identifies tangible "touch points" where students can be spiritually served in a manner that is most personally meaningful to them.

Christian educators thus attempt to "exegete" a particular youth cultural context in order to create more effective ways to nurture adolescent spirituality within that environment. Inherent in the process is the realistic concern that adults, in their zeal to understand, may foreclose too quickly on their interpretation of the data. For instance, the music, slang, styles of dress, and body language dominant in a particular aspect of youth culture may be perceived by the adult as being evidence of rebellion. In fact, the expressions may be more of an indicator of attempts at individuation from adult culture rather than rebellion against adults themselves. On balance is the danger that adults take too lightly the significance of the impact of youth culture. Doing so results in adults being unavailable to guide students in their discernment of and response to the significant value-laden messages communicated in the various elements of youth culture. Failing to assist adolescents in navigating their spiritual journeys in the midst of often opposing youth cultural forces results in students who are inadequately equipped to complete the passage to adult Christian maturity.

Peer relationships, therefore, are not the only or even the most significant relationships an adolescent needs. Youth culture derives its power to shape attitudes and behaviors from the fact that adolescents look to peers as the most *immediate* influence in their lives. However, parents and significant other adult persons remain the most *important* influence for an adolescent. If parents and adults abdicate their meaningful roles in the lives of the youth in their sphere of influence, the adolescents become much more vulnerable to any unbiblical values in their immediate youth cultural context. Conversely, if parents provide nurture, guidance, support, prayer, and teaching, and are themselves models of authentic Christian maturity, adolescents can withstand the pressures of peers and fads. Christian adolescents increase in their degree of invulnerability to negative aspects of youth culture when they have secure, meaningful interpersonal relationships with both peers and significant adults. Effectively responding to youth culture, therefore, requires that adults respect its significance, understand its meanings, address its values with relevant biblical teachings, and engage its adolescent population with a desire to aid them in making sense of their faith in the midst of their highly significant peer socialization experiences. Central to this approach is the commitment to concentrate less on responding to the various expressions of youth culture and focusing one's ministry energies on responding to the individual adolescents who dwell within the relational walls of this potent subculture.

RICHARD R. DUNN

Bibliography. R. R. Dunn and M. H. Senter III (1997), *Reaching a Generation for Christ;* J. Dettoni (1993), *Introduction to Youth Ministry;* D. Elkind (1984), *All Grown Up and No Place to Go;* D. J. Hesselgrave and E. Rommen (1989), *Contextualization;* W. Mueller (1994), *Understanding Today's Youth Culture;* Q. Schultze et al. (1991), *Dancing in the Dark.*

Youth for Christ International. Global network of 65 national organizations whose common goal is to cooperate with the church in the evangelism and discipleship of young people. Operating with a total of 2,500 full-time staff and some 22,000 volunteers on a worldwide level, the organization registers a total of 120,000 commitments to Christ on an annual basis.

A principle of local and national autonomy governs the organization within its international fellowship. The General Assembly of Youth for Christ International provides a forum for mutual support and coordination among member nations. The international office is located in the Republic of Singapore. The Youth for Christ movement was born in the United States in the mid–1940s when leaders in different places had a common concern to evangelize young people who were not being reached by normal church channels. Youth evangelists using innovative methods began conducting mass rallies in more than a dozen cities, often under a common name, "Youth for Christ."

In order to handle the growing number of requests to start new rallies, Youth for Christ International was formally incorporated in July 1945 with Chicago pastor Torrey Johnson as the first president and evangelist Billy Graham as the first full-time worker. In the late 1940s and early 1950s, Youth for Christ evangelists and teams traveled widely and new rally centers sprang up in other cities around the world.

As some of the early leaders carried the gospel to different parts of the world, they acquired a new vision for specific concerns. As a result, new organizations were born, including World Vision International, Trans World Radio, Overseas Crusades, Far Eastern Gospel Crusade (now Send, Inc.), Greater Europe Mission, and the Billy Graham Evangelistic Association.

Youth for Christ's methodologies have diversified enormously over the years. The original idea of a youth rally adapted an older revival meeting format to the newly developing youth culture using culturally appropriate music and speaking styles, as well as the new technology of the radio and the grassroots involvement of local church groups. Later, talent contests and quizzing programs brought a higher degree of youth participation to these activities. The international trips of some of the teams that performed at the rallies were forerunners of the massive involvement of young people in short-term missions.

In the United States, the turbulent 1960s saw the curtailing of the rallies in many cities and the transition to a school club program called Campus Life. This program involves a topical, discussion-based presentation of the gospel with a strong emphasis on personal ministry. Although conceived as primarily an evangelistic program, the methodologies of the Campus Life ministry were widely adapted by the church for the purposes of the Christian education of youth. Many of these ideas were first disseminated through the publications of Youth Specialties, an organization begun in 1968 by former Youth for Christ staff members. Another innovation of this period was the development of the Youth Guidance ministry to delinquent youth. Although church youth groups tended to lose the original evangelistic fervor in their adaptation of the Campus Life model, they often had financial backing for full-time staff, an existing group of Christian youth, and a ready pool of volunteers that were less easily available to Youth for Christ. The advent of other parachurch youth organizations with a focus on evangelism has also tended to put a ceiling on the growth of Youth for Christ. One response to this changing context by Youth for Christ has been a stronger emphasis on partnership with local churches. Perhaps the most visible example of this trend is the Super Conference on Youth Evangelism held on a triennial basis in Washington, D.C., and Los Angeles. The objective of this conference, which saw some thirty thousand youth in combined attendance in 1997, is to train, inspire, and mobilize Christian youth to share their faith with their peers. Strategic cooperation with dozens of other youth organizations

and a focus on serving local church youth groups contribute to the success of the event. On an international level, the diversity of methods is almost unlimited. Some of the major ministry models are clubs, rallies, camps, social concern ministries, music, sports, television, radio, literature, and leadership training.

In 1994, the International General Assembly identified four new target groups for its ministry: preadolescents, youth in poor communities, displaced and immigrant youth, and youth from minority groups. In addition to its established programs, Youth for Christ is pioneering work in more than sixty new nations around the world and continues to be a source of innovation in youth ministry in many settings.

MARK A. DODRILL

Bibliography. J. Hefley (1970), *God Goes to High School;* T. M. Johnson and R. Cook (1944), *Reaching Youth for Christ;* M. Senter III (1992), *The Coming Revolution in Youth Ministry;* idem (1990), *The Youth for Christ Movement as an Educational Agency and Its Impact upon Protestant Churches.*

Youth Ministry. Youth ministry has been a relatively recent addition to the church's strategic mission response in the world. In suggesting that youth ministry has, in its purest forms, "always been relational, theological, and action oriented," Senter offers as early evidence the example of Dwight L. Moody beginning a Sunday school outreach to young boys in Chicago in 1859 (Dunn and Senter, 1997, 107). Senter also asserts that the first wave of youth ministry came to America as English-born innovations known as the Sunday school, Young Men's Christian Association (YMCA), and Young Women's Christian Association (YWCA) between 1824 and 1875. A second wave of youth ministry can be traced to the beginning of the Society for Christian Endeavor in 1881 and led to efforts to provide Christian growth activities for a church's own young people. The third wave, paving the way for the present state of youth ministry, was initiated with the birth of parachurch evangelistic agencies—Young Life (1941), Youth for Christ (1945), and Fellowship of Christian Athletes (1954)—which focused their strategies around public high schools (108).

By observing the number of specialized agencies and organizations in existence with the express purpose of supplying training and resources to youth ministry practitioners, it is natural to conclude that modern youth ministry is coming of age. A 1997 gathering of Youth Ministry Educators, populated largely by professors in the field, was attended by over seventy persons. Youth Specialties, begun in 1968, continues to enjoy record-breaking attendance at National Youth Worker's Convention; *Group* magazine's circulation and influence has increased dramatically since its beginning in 1974. The National Network of Youth Ministries—seeking to facilitate mission-driven cooperation between diverse church and parachurch organizations—sponsored a historic conference (Atlanta '95) where more than six thousand attendees gathered as a direct result of their lesser-known but strategic efforts with an annual gathering known as the Youth Ministry Executive Council.

As the field of youth ministry has grown more mature, it has been only recently that formal definitions have been proposed. Lamport has offered the following: "Youth Ministry is the purposive, determined, and persistent quest by both natural and supernatural means to expose, transmit, or otherwise share with adolescents God's message of good news, which is central to the Christian faith. Its ultimate end is to cultivate a life transformation of youth by the power of the Holy Spirit that they might be conformed to the revealed will of God as expressed in Scripture, and chiefly in the person of our Lord and Savior, Jesus Christ" (Lamport, 1996, 62). A combination of Senter's first three axioms of youth ministry can also be helpful in defining normative processes for youth ministry (Dunn and Senter, 1997). First, "youth ministry begins when a Christian adult finds a comfortable method of entering a student's world." Second, "youth ministry happens as long as a Christian adult is able to use his or her contact with a student to draw that student into a maturing relationship with God through Jesus Christ." The final relevant axiom, derived by logical extension from the first two is: "Youth ministry ceases to take place when the adult-student relationship is broken or no longer moves the student toward spiritual maturity."

A theology of youth ministry helps to identify much of what is similar and distinctive about youth ministry when compared to the other ministries of the church. Classic church doctrines about God, sin, humanity, salvation, and Scripture only need to be contextualized to adolescent levels of understanding to be useful in youth ministry. There are also more pointed theological emphases that contribute to a practical theology of youth ministry. These emphases come out of the experiences of youth ministry, and reflect some of the more urgent felt-needs concerns facing youth workers. How does the concept of a "youth church" both respond to and inform one's ecclesiology? What sort of biblical help is available to help frame theological responses to leisure, entertainment, materialism, sexuality, and competition? Games can meet psychosocial needs in teens, but is there any sense that youth ministry games may be enriched through clear theological reflection? A theology of youth ministry contributes a biblical foundation for answering the "why?" questions about youth ministry. Its scope and direction affirm both its connection to the larger body of Christ and its unique role in the Church.

A philosophy of youth ministry must be driven by a theology of youth ministry. Not every "why?" question about the practice of youth ministry is comprehensively answered through biblical exploration. For example, while theological truths about the *imago dei* and depravity inform ministry with all persons, much of what is needed for a specialized understanding of adolescents is derived from empirical sources of truth. Questions about how teens learn and grow in the faith, ultimate direction, short-term goals, and ministry assessment all are collected in a philosophy of ministry.

Youth ministry may be categorized by philosophy of ministry strategies. Relational-incarnational ministry is characterized by the centrality of adults who move into the world of adolescents in order to flesh out the love of God and build relational bridges across which that life-transforming love may be communicated. Young Life is one of the purest representations of this philosophy on the youth ministry horizon. Campus Life (YFC) may be considered relational-confrontational, stressing the importance of relationships in communicating the gospel, but accelerating the process of bringing a young person to a point of decision about the claims of Christ. Student Venture (Campus Crusade for Christ) condenses this time frame even more. Each of these organizations represents a place along the continuum in the family of evangelism-focused youth ministries that believe the high school campus is the best place to initiate contact with young people. These parachurch agencies have recently been joined by churches who want to move their locus of operation from centralized church programming to dispersed, high-school targeted communities in order to be more effective in evangelism. Willow Creek's Student Impact is a newer entry into this arena, seeking to create school-clustered clubs as socially safe gathering points for nonchurched teens. Numbers of Southern Baptists are doing the same. First Priority helps network Christian young people around their schools through teen-led campus/Bible clubs made possible by the Equal Access Act (1984). Specialized ministries targeted toward teen moms, urban gangs, and minorities are just a few of the parade of creative responses to the diverse adolescent population. Sonlife offers training that helps church-based youth workers learn a biblically informed way of balancing Great Commission priorities for youth ministry.

Each of these organizations, as well as local churches, is distinguished by the value they assign to the common pieces of a youth ministry philosophy. These values will be revealed as particular questions of strategy are explored. Is youth evangelism best done by inviting teens to good programming events or moving into their world? Through the training of students for peer evangelism or by paving the way for equipped adults to communicate the gospel? Should the youth ministry begin with an evangelism focus that leads to discipleship or a discipleship focus that leads to evangelism? What is the role of informal strategies and contexts as compared to formal methods and settings? Small groups versus large groups? Mission trips and ski trips? Are church connections a hindrance or help to evangelism? And how are new believers best assimilated into the church? These questions are but a few that help to bring a philosophy of youth ministry into sharper focus.

Youth ministry often progresses through predictable stages of strengths and weaknesses that can be readily observed in local contexts. A foundational set of skills for most persons moving into youth ministry cluster around relationship building. Novice youth ministers learn quickly—or, more likely, bring these skills to the job—how to initiate relationships with teens in their world, use shared experiences to build relationships, and employ local fast food joints for personal appointments. For youth groups of small to moderate size, these relational skills may be sufficient for the task that's expected of them.

Group meetings of less than forty students can be handled adequately by someone who has developed a solid relational infrastructure but does not possess great "up-front" gifts. However, as groups grow in size and influence, the youth minister will need to grow in programming skills, learning how to organize and implement well-executed, socially acceptable meetings for large groups on a weekly basis. Trips and big events require greater logistical planning as the number of teens who will be involved increases. For the youth minister who entered into the task with a vision of investing himself or herself in transformational relationships among adolescents, this programming stage can be quite frustrating. There is nothing particularly relational about some of the specialty programs designed to attract and involve the masses; the skills required are very different from those that may have been adequate to earlier successes.

Youth ministers who are effective at moving ministry through a relational phase and beyond the programming stage learn how to employ the critical leadership skills clustered around mobilizing and developing people for explosive ministry impact. These skills include vision-casting, volunteer recruitment, screening, training and supervision, community networking, and student leader development.

While there are clearly strengths from each stage of youth ministry that are brought into the next phase, the focus required for effectiveness in each phase is dramatically different. This reality, coupled with the ministry longevity necessary to grow in these diverse abilities, helps to explain why the proportion of youth ministries at any given time diminishes in pyramidal fashion as each of the three stages—relational, program, people development—ascend to the next.

DAVE RAHN

Bibliography. D. Borgman (1997), *When Kumbaya Is Not Enough: A Practical Theology for Youth Ministry;* B. Boshers (1997), *Student Ministry for the 21st Century;* A. Campolo (1989), *Growing Up in America: A Sociology of Youth Ministry;* M. DeVries (1994), *Family-Based Youth Ministry;* R. R. Dunn and M. H. Senter III, eds. (1997), *Reaching a Generation for Christ;* D. Fields (1998), *Purpose-Driven Youth Ministry;* M. A. Lamport, *Christian Education Journal* 16, no.3 (1996); D. Robbins (1990), *Youth Ministry Nuts and Bolts;* M. Senter III (1992), *The Coming Revolution in Youth Ministry;* D. Veerman (1988), *Youth Evangelism.*

Youth Ministry, Models of. Youth ministry is still a relatively new idea in the context of church ministry. Churches in the United States began to take specialized ministry to students who were neither children nor adults seriously sometime after the end of World War II. It is significant that initial ministries to youth were conducted by parachurch organizations such as Miracle Book Club, Young Life, Youth for Christ, and others, and that ministry to youth was not something most local churches considered important.

Early models of youth ministry were "club models" with actual club activities associated with local school campuses or connected to the youth community in some way other than through a local church. The club ministry model functioned with a person usually called a club director who had some kind of semiofficial reason to be on campus. He or she used on-campus time to connect with students and invite them to participate in club. Those who became club regulars began to ascend to leadership roles and were encouraged to bring friends to club as well. The club model usually contained some kind of rally function on a regular basis where students from various clubs could come together for encouragement and support.

When local churches began to take youth ministry seriously, most of their activities rotated around a weekly teaching time (usually Sunday school) and a weekly youth group meeting (usually on Sunday evening just before an evening worship service).

In recent years many youth ministry professionals have begun to take seriously the notion of there being several models for a youth ministry and that the selection of a model should relate directly to the mission statement of the church and its Christian education department. Mark Senter (1997) has identified several of these models.

1. *The Christian School Model.* Many youth leaders deal with a youth group in which a high

percentage of students attend private Christian junior high or high schools. They discover that many of these students are more closely associated with the school and its activities in their Christian lives than they are with the church youth group. The Christian school model, therefore, is designed to build young people into well-rounded Christian adults using the Christian school as a laboratory for the design.

2. *The Competition Model.* Some youth leaders build their youth ministry on the natural human inclination to be competitive. The competition model uses natural leaders from among the students to form teams for competition, discussion, learning, and articulation of issues related to faith.

3. *The Discipleship Model.* Many youth leaders build a youth ministry on a collection of small discipleship, caring, or accountability groups led by adult volunteers. The discipleship model is designed to train students to be God's people in an ungodly world. The focus is on Bible study, prayer, Scripture memorization, and defending the faith, all in a caring environment where students can share their lives with each other.

4. *The Ministry Model.* It is common for youth leaders to build a ministry around various service activities, mission trips, and personal evangelism. This model is designed to develop student ministry skills and to provide a context in which those skills can be exercised in a carefully planned exposure to human need, often in a cross-cultural environment. In this model it is important that the context be adult-led and provide various nurturing functions for the students who discover needs which their own abilities and skills will not be enough to satisfy.

5. *The Safe Place Model.* Some youth leaders conduct a youth ministry in a context which could be described as a modified "community center." In this model, activities and programs which meet needs of students in the community and surrounding areas are planned and carried out. The safe place model uses the facilities of the church in conjunction with loving Christian adult leaders to reach kids from the neighborhood and build spiritually accountable relationships with them.

Additionally, Duffy Robbins (1991) has identified three more models of youth ministry which he says are common today.

6. *The Hero Model.* This model is based upon the theory that we should build our youth programs around a central personality, some charismatic figure who is naturally attractive to teenagers. This model assumes that the relationships that students build with this personality will eventually transform into principles by which they choose to live their life because the role model did it and taught it.

7. *The Involvement Model.* The key word is *involvement.* The proponents of this model believe in creating as many possible ways for students to become involved in the ministry as is humanly possible to conduct. These involvements can be within the group (team leaders, A-V resource persons, music and worship leaders, greeters, officers, etc.) or outside the group being involved in meeting the needs of others with activities oriented toward outreach.

8. *The Relevancy Model.* Proponents of this model believe in being relevant to the students. Taken to an extreme, adult leaders using this model will dress, act, and talk in ways that they believe make them more relevant to students. Experience from as far back as the 1960s has shown us that most of these adults are seen more as silly than as relevant by students, but relevance to real and felt needs of students is important.

In summary, there are these popular models of ministry and many more. Knowledgeable youth leaders will select or construct models carefully based upon the needs of students, the mission statement and purpose of the church, and the capabilities, both real and potential, of the youth staff.

KEN GARLAND

Bibliography. D. Dunn and M. Senter (1997), *Reaching a Generation for Christ;* D. Robbins (1991), *Youth Ministry That Works.*

Youth Specialties (YS). Youth Specialties, from its beginning, has contributed to the advocacy of youth ministry, the professionalization of youth ministry and to the focus of being real, being honest, and telling the truth about oneself and the gospel. Youth Specialties most recently characterized its ministry as one of affirmation and encouragement, as well as providing materials and teaching. Still functioning as a prophetic gadfly to the evangelical church, YS prides itself on its refusal to promote or provide materials that reduce the gospel to a few unrealistic principles and promises. At the end of the twentieth century it is fair to say that the field of youth ministry has been significantly shaped by the 30 year efforts of the irreverent, authentic Christians who work for Youth Specialties.

Youth Specialties was founded in 1969 by Mike Yaconelli and Wayne Rice. These two seasoned youth workers began publishing ideas for churches that they had been using in their San Diego Youth for Christ/Campus Life ministry. Assembled and sold as they could be put together 200 at a time in a church basement, these IDEAS volumes evolved so that local church youth workers were paid for their contributions. The resulting product was a set of books that were fresh sources of creativity from a newly networked and diverse group of youth ministries. IDEAS volumes continue to be published as youth workers from around the world submitted their best youth ministry games, crowd-

Zz

Zinzendorf, Nicholas Ludwig von (1700–1760). Count Zinzendorf was part of the Pietist movement in Germany which emphasized personal devotion and emotional response in religious life. He has been called "the most influential German theologian between Luther and Schleiermacher," although he never formally studied theology.

In 1722, a group of Moravians asked Zinzendorf's permission to live on his land. He granted their request, and a small band crossed the border from Moravia to settle in a town they called Herrnhut. Influenced by their teachings, Zinzendorf chose to leave public life and spend his time working with the Moravians. He led them in daily Bible studies, helped them formulate the "Brotherly Agreement," which described the basic tenets of Christian behavior, and required them to sign a pledge to abide by these principles. Following this commitment, the Moravians experienced a powerful renewal, described as the "Moravian Pentecost."

Zinzendorf had chosen from an early age as his life motto, "I have one passion; it is Jesus, Jesus only." Flowing out of his passionate love for Christ came a disciplined life of prayer and a passion for the lost. He was determined to evangelize the world with a handful of saints, equipped only with a burning love for Jesus and the power of prayer. His leadership was pivotal in beginning the first organized Protestant mission work.

Zinzendorf's contributions in Christian education grew out of the educational processes he developed in the Moravian community. He believed in freedom in education, sensing that self-activity directed by the Holy Spirit in a religious environment was the best form of education. Shunning the intellectual emphasis of education, he educated children, adolescents, and adults in heart education. He divided the entire community into groups and attempted to identify the unique needs of each group. His two textbooks were the Bible and hymnbooks. He believed that exposition supported by hymn texts provided the best method for inculcating religious truth.

Zinzendorf's religious thought influenced Schleirmacher and John Wesley. He was also instrumental in the establishment of a Christian community still in existence today known as the Moravian Church in America.

NORMA S. HEDIN

Bibliography. G. W. Forell, trans. and ed. (1973), *Nine Public Lectures on Important Subjects in Religion;* A. Lewis (1962), *Zinzendorf the Ecumenical Pioneer;* H. Meyer (1928), *Child Nature and Nurture According to Nicolas Ludwig von Zinzendorf;* J. R. Weinlick (1956), *Count Zinzendorf.*

Zwingli, Ulrich (1484–1531). Reformation theologian. Born in Wildhaus, Switzerland, this Protestant theologian was instrumental in bringing the Reformation to his homeland in 1523. A contemporary of Martin Luther, Zwingli was educated in Catholicism and studied the classics in Vienna and Basel. In Basel he studied under Thomas Wyttenbach, who was the first person to challenge Zwingli regarding the abuses of the Catholic Church.

After his ordination to the priesthood, Zwingli served in Glarus from 1506 to 1516. While there he read Erasmus and was further influenced to oppose ecclesiastical abuses and devote himself to studying the Scripture. His own conversion happened gradually as he grew in his knowledge of the truth.

During his second pastorate in Einsiedeln from 1516 to 1518, Zwingli deepened in his knowledge of Scripture and the church fathers. He began to publicly attack the sale of indulgences and other church abuses and exhorted the people to worship Christ alone, not the Virgin Mary.

Zwingli next accepted a call to the Zurich Cathedral, serving in this prominent position until his death. He preached the Scriptures as the ultimate authority for life and the Christian faith. The civil government of the canton of Zurich ordered a public disputation between supporters and opponents of the Reformation on this issue. In preparation, Zwingli published his

Sixty-seven Conclusions. The council decided in favor of the Reformation.

It was not long before the Mass was gone, processions and pilgrimages ended, ministers took wives, and icons were abolished. In their place, the Reformation themes of justification by faith alone and the study of Scripture as the final authority were acknowledged and practiced.

In 1526 the government of Zurich, supported by Zwingli, persecuted and suppressed the Anabaptists, a radical separatist Reformation group. Next, they worked to suppress Catholicism. The papal forces retaliated by making war on Zurich in 1531. In the midst of battle on October 11, 1531, Zwingli fell and was executed.

SHELLY CUNNINGHAM

Bibliography. P. Schaff (1953), *The History of the Christian Church.*